Worlds of Fiction

Second Edition

Worlds of Fiction

Edited by

Roberta Rubenstein

American University, Washington D.C.

Charles R. Larson

American University, Washington D.C.

Prentice
Hall

Upper Saddle River, New Jersey 07458

Library of Congress Cataloging-in-Publication Data

Worlds of fiction/edited by Roberta Rubenstein, Charles R. Larson.—2nd ed.
   p. cm.
  ISBN 0-13-041639-8
    1. Short stories.   I. Rubenstein, Roberta.   II. Larson, Charles R.

PN6120.2.W665 2001
808.83'1—dc21   2001033834

Editor in chief: Leah Jewell
Senior acquisitions editor: Carrie Brandon
Editorial assistant: Thomas DeMarco
VP/Director of production and manufacturing: Barbara Kittle
Senior managing editor: Mary Rottino
Production editor: Kari Callaghan Mazzola
Project liaison: Randy Pettit
Marketing manager: Rachel Falk
Prepress and manufacturing manager: Nick Sklitsis
Prepress and manufacturing buyer: Sherry Lewis
Electronic page makeup: Kari Callaghan Mazzola and John P. Mazzola
Interior design: John P. Mazzola
Cover design: Robert Farrar-Wagner
Cover art: An untitled painting by Dr. Fuad Al-Futaih of Yemen

This book was set in 10/11 Goudy by Big Sky Composition
and was printed and bound by Courier Companies, Inc.
The cover was printed by Jaguar Graphics.

*Grateful acknowledgment is made to the copyright holders on pages 966–972,
which are hereby a continuation of this copyright page.*

© 2002, 1993 by Pearson Education, Inc.
Upper Saddle River, New Jersey 07458

Printed in the United States of America
10 9 8 7 6 5 4 3 2 1

ISBN 0-13-041639-8

Pearson Education LTD., London
Pearson Education Australia PTY, Limited, Sydney
Pearson Education Singapore, Pte. Ltd
Pearson Education North Asia Ltd, Hong Kong
Pearson Education Canada, Ltd., Toronto
Pearson Educación de Mexico, S.A. de C.V.
Pearson Education—Japan, Tokyo
Pearson Education Malaysia, Pte. Ltd
Pearson Education, Upper Saddle River, New Jersey

Contents

Geographical Contents

North America

Caribbean

Latin America

Europe

Africa

Middle East

Asia

Australia, New Zealand, South Pacific

Thematic Contents

Alienation

Allegory/Legend/Fable

The Artist

Death

Fantastic/Absurd

Gender

Humor/Comedy

Journey

Moral Dilemma

Nature/Environment

The Nature of Evil

Perspectives on Class

Racial or Cultural Dislocation/Conflict/Connection

Relationships: Parents and Children

Relationships: Men

Relationships: Women

Relationships: Women and Men

Youth/Initiation/Maturation

Preface

Until about two decades ago, most anthologies of short stories were comprised primarily of fiction by writers from North America and Europe; moreover, those stories were written predominantly by men of the majority culture. In the intervening years, scholars, teachers, editors, and readers have gained awareness of what has been missing in such selective collections: gender inclusiveness and cultural multiplicity. Editors of anthologies have begun to include more writing by women and writers of minority ethnic, if not geographical, origins.

The first edition of *Worlds of Fiction*, published in 1993, was conceived with the ambitious goal of extending the parameters of a short-fiction anthology to encompass fiction written by authors from areas of the world that are still only nominally (if at all) represented in most short-story anthologies—Africa, Asia, Latin America, and the Arabic world—as well as to include more ethnic minority voices from within the United States and more stories by women. This second edition reflects the same principles of selection. Moreover, in this new century and new millennium, we are more aware than ever of the need for increased cross-cultural awareness and understanding. Yet it is obviously impossible to achieve full geographical representativeness, even in an anthology of this size. Of the 113 stories included in this second edition of *Worlds of Fiction*, approximately one-third are by writers of major geographical areas outside of North America and Europe, while the rest are by North American and European writers. Twenty-five stories are new to this edition, including five by authors from countries or regions not previously represented: Cristina Peri Rossi, Uruguay; Véronique Tadjo, Ivory Coast; Haldun Taner, Turkey; Yvonne Vera, Zimbabwe; and Niaz Zaman, Bangladesh. This second edition also reflects an increase in the number of stories by women, including (in addition to the writers from South America, Africa, and South Asia named above) several modern classics—Kate Chopin's "The Story of an Hour," Virginia Woolf's "Kew Gardens," and Tillie Olsen's "I Stand Here Ironing"—as well as stories by Angela Carter, Jamaica Kincaid, Lorrie Moore, and Toni Morrison. To keep things interesting, we have substituted different stories by a cross-section of the classical writers whose fiction appeared in the previous edition, including Sherwood Anderson, Jorge Luis Borges, Italo Calvino, F. Scott Fitzgerald, Nadine Gordimer, Ernest Hemingway, Henry James, Franz Kafka, Doris Lessing, and Edith Wharton.

One change from the first edition is the omission from this second edition of novellas by Kate Chopin (*The Awakening*) and Mulk Raj Anand (*Untouchable*) to make space for more stories in a more compact volume. Students and teachers will find Chopin's novella readily available in a number of editions and Anand's in at least one. It is our hope that readers whose interest is stimulated by the stories by less-familiar writers anthologized here will seek out their other published works, including longer narratives. The headnotes include the titles of other works by each author to aid in this endeavor.

Realizing that students and teachers who are using *Worlds of Fiction* for the first time may feel somewhat uncertain about how to approach stories by unfamiliar writers from cultures and areas not frequently considered by most American readers, we continue to include in the headnote for each story biographical information as well as (where appropriate) suggestions for ways to understand a particular narrative within its cultural context. For a fuller discussion of reading with an enlarged cultural perspective—and for a fuller explanation of the guiding principles of this anthology—we urge you to read the Introduction that follows this Preface, which provides a close reading and interpretation of the story "Black Girl" by Senegalese writer Sembene Ousmane.

As in the first edition, the primary organization for this second edition is alphabetical by author's name, an arrangement that we believe is the most accessible for readers to locate (and also to discover) particular authors. We abide by traditional cultural usage concerning the alphabetical ordering of authors' names. For example, in Japan and China, a person's surname generally precedes his or her given name. Hence Mishima Yukio (a frequently anthologized Japanese author whose name is typically reversed, English style) still appears—although surname first—among the Ms, and Akutagawa Ryūnosuke appears among the As. Many Hispanic surnames are composed of both parents' family names; hence, García and Vargas are not the middle names of Gabriel García Márquez and Mario Vargas Llosa (respectively) but the first of two-part surnames and thus the ones used for correct reference to the authors as well as for alphabetization. Accordingly, Gabriel García Márquez appears among the Gs and Mario Vargas Llosa appears among the Vs.

In addition to the primary alphabetical Table of Contents, which includes a thumbnail description of each story, an alternative Geographical Table of Contents situates authors within their geographical contexts, and a Thematic Table of Contents features topical groupings of stories to stimulate comparative and cross-cultural thinking as well as ideas for writing. Questions are posed at the end of each story to guide readers in their consideration of major themes and ideas.

We hope that by offering an inviting mixture of recognizable and refreshingly unfamiliar authors and stories from around the world, this second edition of *Worlds of Fiction* will continue to stretch our readers' aesthetic imaginations as well as their global awareness and cross-cultural understanding.

We appreciate the advice of the following reviewers of this second edition: Dorothy G. Clark, Loyola Marymount University; Jacqueline Murphy, Rosemont

College; C. Jenise Williamson, Bowie State University; and Judith Brodhead, North Central College. We are also grateful for the support and assistance of Carrie Brandon, senior acquisitions editor at Prentice Hall, Kari Callaghan Mazzola of Big Sky Composition, and Mary Dalton-Hoffman.

Roberta Rubenstein
Charles R. Larson

Introduction

I

Although we think of the short story as a relatively recent literary form developed in the past 150 years, in a deeper sense stories are the oldest form of literature. People have always told stories. Long before narratives were shaped into written form, they were the stuff of imaginative communication, beginning with the proverbial, "It was a dark and stormy night," that a storyteller might have shared with a spellbound group around the campfire or next to the hearth. Recorded narratives are as old as the tales originally passed orally from one generation to the next in ancient Greece or medieval Arabia or modern Africa. All of us are creators of narrative: when we try to describe a particularly vivid dream to a friend, only to realize how much is lost in translation, or to invent an ingenious excuse for why a term paper deadline could not be met.

Granted, not all of these fictions qualify as short stories in the more controlled aesthetic sense. Yet the impulse to tell a story is one we can all recognize because we have participated in it. The writers who have found original ways to craft the common language of such narratives into art—to create verbal shapes for our own often shapeless inner stories as well as the stories of others whose lives we may enter for the first time—are the writers whom we read with the exhilaration of discovery and the reward of insight.

In reading many short stories written by authors from around the world in preparation for this anthology, we discovered how enormously large and rich and varied the reservoir of stories is in every language. For each story we ultimately selected for inclusion in this volume, literally dozens had to be excluded. Our choices were governed by several principles. First, we believe that an anthology of stories should reflect an even more inclusive international perspective than that encompassed by recent story anthologies. Traditionally (until the 1980s), short story collections were composed primarily of narratives from the United States, Great Britain, and Western Europe. Such collections tended to reinforce the sense of a given and limited "canon" of great writers and stories. In the past two decades, scholars, teachers, students, and book editors have challenged such assumptions, responding to the fact that what is included in a textbook or anthology also reveals what traditionally has been omitted: the voices of women and minorities, and other cultural perspectives besides the predominantly white, male, Western ones.

Concurrently, the canon of literary excellence has undergone reconceptualization. The view that literary traditions are static, objective, timeless judgments have given way to a view of literary canons composed of evolving choices based not only on aesthetic criteria but also on social and political realities that inevitably influence both how and what we read, both how and what is defined as the—or, more accurately—a "tradition." Bharati Mukherjee (who was born in India and now lives in the United States) expresses the challenge faced by immigrant writers representing a multicultural reality:

> My literary agenda begins by acknowledging that America has transformed *me*. It does not end until I show how I (and the hundreds of thousands like me) have transformed

America. . . . I have had to create an audience. I cannot rely on shorthand references to my community, my religion, my class, my region, or my old school ties. . . . My duty [as a writer] is to give voice to continents, but also to redefine the nature of *American* and what makes an American. In the process, work like mine and dozens like it will open up the canon of American literature. (*The Writer on Her Work: New Essays in New Territory*, edited by Janet Sternberg)

Inevitably and sometimes invisibly, the political complexion of the world has closed our eyes to the works of writers from certain areas. This politically induced blindness is compounded by several layers of artistic censorship. During most decades of the past century, a number of writers or would-be writers in countries within the (now dissolved) Communist bloc and in other areas of the world in which the freedoms of speech and artistic expression were severely restricted practiced self-censorship. No doubt speaking for many in his own and similar situations, the Russian writer Isaac Babel—a victim of severe political repression during the Stalinist era—described himself to the first Soviet Writers' Congress in 1934 as "a master of a new literary genre, the genre of silence." Moreover, limited access to the works of writers from these areas of the world has resulted in a corresponding limitation in the availability of translations into English. We want to acknowledge our indebtedness to the many fine translators who have given all of us access to stories originally written in other languages, rendering the universal language of the imagination into the English tongue.

Increasingly, the country of the mind, like the countries of the world, has opened to embrace larger, more interconnected, and sometimes more contradictory perspectives. As the novelist Virginia Woolf remarked in another context, we all observe the world from a necessarily limited point of view: "Either we are men, or we are women. Either we are cold, or we are sentimental. Either we are young, or growing old" (*Jacob's Room*). One might amend her observation to include distinctions other than polar ones that nonetheless acknowledge differences among us. Stories (and other forms of literature, of course) enable us to travel imaginatively outside those limiting boundaries—whether historical, political, cultural, or gendered—to enter experiences that originate not only in other times but also in other places and in people who seem quite different from ourselves. Through these passports into domains where previously we might not have been granted entrance, we may enlarge our understanding of the complex, multicultural world and, closer to home, of an increasingly culturally and ethnically diverse United States. As critic Paul Skenazy has phrased it, "Different ways of thinking don't just change the way we perceive the world; they recast what can and might be conceived of as the world."

Another principle of selection for this text has been our desire to include stories that provide variety across several different spectrums. Realizing that there is no way to achieve either true representativeness or comprehensiveness in an anthology that aspires to an international perspective, we have sought to include authors and stories that are "good," in our judgment, besides being fresh, accessible, and demonstrative of the enormous range of aesthetic, technical, and thematic possibilities within the form. We recognize that no anthology will please everyone ("What, you left out my favorite story by _____?!"). We also recognize that each of us reads and enjoys stories for a variety of reasons, both intellectual and emotional, public and private, ranging from the comforting rediscovery of the familiar to the startling discovery of the new or unfamiliar. Thus, the stories included here vary not only by nationality, culture, and gender of the author but by themes and subjects, plots and settings, styles and points of view, and length—ranging from a mere paragraph or a brief two pages (what the editors of one collection term "sudden fiction") to several longer stories and many in between.

We have included what we hope is an appealing mixture of well-known and new authors and stories: masterpieces by classic writers such as Nathaniel Hawthorne, Nikolai Gogol, and Edith Wharton, but also less-familiar stories by major writers such as Mark Twain, Anton Chekhov, Joseph Conrad, James Joyce, F. Scott Fitzgerald, and Katherine Anne Porter; more stories by women, by minority writers in the United States, by new writers, by writers from countries and cultures not typically included in short story anthologies. Of the 113 stories in this anthology, although approximately two-thirds are by North American and European authors, a number of those are represented by new or less familiar authors or by less frequently anthologized selections by well-known authors. The remaining third are drawn from the writers of other major geographical areas of the world: Latin America, Africa, Asia, the Middle East, and Australia, New Zealand, and the South Pacific. Again, some stories and writers will be familiar, but many more in the latter category will be unfamiliar. Accordingly, we have endeavored, in the headnote prefacing each story, to provide not only biographical information about the author but, where appropriate, comments that offer a cultural context for reading the story. The questions that follow each story are meant to provoke discussion, to initiate further thinking, and occasionally to suggest ideas and themes that can be fruitfully compared with those of other stories.

Having considered several different principles of organization for this volume, each of which had clear advantages and equally clear limitations, we ultimately chose the alphabetical organization in the hope that in this format readers would be able to locate authors most easily. A chronological organization works well for collections emphasizing the development of a tradition, particularly for national groupings of literature, but it is less useful across a number of cultures whose writers have entered the storytelling tradition at different points in time—whether or not they have been influenced by one another—and whose traditions are incompletely represented by a single story or two. To anchor each narrative in its appropriate historical moment, we have placed the date of publication at the end of each story. (Occasionally, when the original date of publication of a story originally written in another language cannot be established, we have given the date of publication in English translation.)

We considered organizing the volume by grouping authors by geographical points on the map (north, south, east, west, and "elsewhere" for works of fantasy and speculative fiction); however, we concluded that such an organization depended entirely—and misleadingly, for a volume claiming an international perspective—on where we drew the point of reference in relation to ourselves as North American readers. Alternatively, we have included two supplementary tables of contents. One identifies writers by major geographical areas, and the second groups stories by major themes or motifs, to permit readers to pursue interesting comparisons across times, nationalities, and cultures.

II

Even in these days of the global village, teachers may be reluctant to assign—and students to read—literary works by writers from non-Western cultures; we are all much more comfortable with what we know. Yet in yielding to the position of comfort, we deprive ourselves of insights into other ways of life, other perspectives on experience that may enrich our own. As the Native American writer Hyemeyohsts Storm wrote in the introduction to his unique novel about Plains Indian life and traditions, *Seven Arrows* (1972),

> If you and I were sitting in a circle of people on the prairie, and if I were then to place a painted drum or an eagle feather in the middle of this circle, each of us would perceive these objects differently. Our vision of them would vary according to our individual positions in the circle, each of which would be unique.
>
> Our personal perceptions of these objects would also depend upon much more than just the different positions from which we look upon them. For example, one or more of us might suffer from color blindness, or weak eyesight. Either of these two physical differences would influence our perceptions of these objects.
>
> There are levels upon levels of perspectives we must consider when we try to understand our individual perceptions of things, or when we try to relate our own perceptions to those of our brothers and sisters. Every single one of our previous experiences in life will affect in some way the mental perspective form which we see the world around us.

Storm emphasizes the uniqueness of our individual perceptions; he does not say that they are incorrect. Our angle of vision, as we observe the drum or the feather in the circle, shows each of us something slightly different, perhaps even radically different, depending on where we are standing, our physical attributes (including gender and race), and our previous experiences.

In one sense, these attributes and limitations are the same when we read what we consider to be familiar literature and when we read less familiar writing. Scholars have spent decades explicating Shakespeare's plays for modern readers, attempting to understand and convey what each word meant for the Elizabethan viewers of the bard's plays. An understanding of Puritanism is important for grasping the full meaning of many of Nathaniel Hawthorne's stories and novels; similarly, appreciation of the fiction of William Faulkner, the plays of Tennessee Williams, and the short stories of Flannery O'Connor is significantly enhanced by some awareness of life in the American South. On the other hand, these authors also *give us* perspectives on those times and places, so that the reader discovers something about Elizabethan England, Puritan New England, or the post-slavery South in the very act of reading those writers.

Thus, when we read and interpret (and understand) the literature of Western or American traditions, we do the same things that we do when we read literary works by writers from other cultural and national traditions: We invoke whatever we know and understand of culture, history, biography, sociology, anthropology, politics, economics, psychology, religion, gender, race, class, and our own experiences, to illuminate what we read. Of course, some elements may be unfamiliar and may require further information about cultural contexts in order to enhance our comprehension.

To demonstrate this process, let us consider the story "Black Girl" ("La Noire de . . .") by Senegalese writer and filmmaker Sembene Ousmane. Outwardly, Sembene's story takes the form of a journey—an almost universal narrative pattern because it invokes the human journey from birth to death that transcends cultural specifics. In this story, the central character, Diouana, takes a literal journey from Senegal, West Africa, to Antibes, France. The time is 1958 and Diouana leaves the country of her birth to rejoin her employers, the Pouchets, to continue working for them as a domestic who cares for their home and their children as she did when they resided in Dakar, Senegal. That is the literal journey of the story, but, as is often the case in fiction that employs a journey framework (for example, see Joseph Conrad's "Amy Foster," John Cheever's "The Swimmer," Dino Buzzati's "The Falling Girls," Naguib Mahfouz's "Half a Day," Es'kia Mphahlele's "Mrs. Plum," and a number of other stories included in this volume), the journey is figurative as well as literal: the transformation of Diouana's character as well as her body.

Chronologically, the story begins at its "end," with the discovery of Diouana's body in the bathtub. Western readers may consider the circumstances somewhat melodramatic or sensational: the arrival of the police, the body in the blanket, the blood on the steps. Even the reporters' perspective appears to support this response: "The suicide of a maid—even if she were black—didn't amount to a hill of beans." The final line in the story—the news item, "Homesick African Girl Cuts Throat in Antibes"—seems to underscore this attitude, reducing the incident to little more than a minor item buried in a back page of the newspaper. Yes, Diouana is another victim of racism, but her situation is pitiable, not necessarily tragic.

What, then, should the reader conclude is the central idea of "Black Girl"? Is it racism? Certainly, Diouana's situation with the Pouchets is one of increasing misery—distress that increases the longer she remains in France. Her employers treat her terribly: overworking her, demeaning her character and her differences from them. Even the children for whom she cares contribute to her victimization, referring to her in derogatory terms.

Certainly racism is an important issue in the story. If it is not the primary concern, then what is the theme? Lost ideals, changed perspectives, lost innocence? Indeed, these are also crucial elements of the story, accessible even to readers who lack knowledge of West African culture. Initially, Diouana is full of expectations for her journey to France: "She wanted to see it and make a triumphal return. This was where people got rich." So excited is Diouana by her anticipated move that she fails to heed the warnings of her compatriot, Tive Correa, who undertook a similar journey 20 years earlier. As the narrator informs us, "He had left, rich with youth, full of ambition, and come home a wreck. From having wanted everything he had returned with nothing but an excessive love for the bottle. For Diouana he predicted nothing but misfortune." Unfortunately, Diouana has already been seduced by the lure of money and the legitimate expectations of an improved lifestyle.

Thus far, what we have said about "Black Girl" depends very little on cultural elements that we are likely to misunderstand. We can sympathize with Diouana's lost dreams and with her situation once she arrives in France. But stated that way, these elements may seem almost too familiar; is "Black Girl" simply another story about prejudice or about the disillusionments of youth?

What we would like to suggest is that a central (and perhaps less immediately recognizable) theme of Sembene's story is *slavery*, a concept closely tied to the ideas already mentioned. The details that support such an interpretation are given near the beginning (in chronological time) of Diouana's story, while the girl is still in Dakar, fantasizing about her anticipated journey to France. One problem for Western readers is that, because the initial clues are tied to African history and geography, they may be overlooked. When Diouana, exhilarated, leans out her window and glances at the sea, watching "the birds flying high above in the immense expanse of blue," she is like any young girl imagining new possibilities for her life; additionally, it is easy to understand her desire for flight away from her dreary situation in Dakar as well as her eagerness to be on her way.

Yet in the next sentence, the narrator mentions the Island of Gorée, which Senegalese and other African readers would immediately recognize as an ominous symbol, particularly when juxtaposed with Diouana's earlier sense of freedom and flight. Historically, Gorée, an island approximately two miles off the coast of Senegal, was one of the major points of departure for the westbound slave trade in the eighteenth and nineteenth centuries. Hundreds of thousands of Africans are believed to have been shipped to the New World from Gorée. As a result of treacherous ocean currents, once Africans were transported to the slave pens on the island (where they were held until a vessel arrived to transport them to America), escape was virtually impossible. No one could swim against the perilous currents.

Ironically, the next sentence in Sembene's story, following the reference to Gorée, mentions Diouana's identity card, an aspect of contemporary indenture that distinguishes it from traditional slavery. Diouana regards her picture on the card, identifying it as "a gloomy one" or, in other words, an unflattering photograph; the word *gloomy* also suggests something darker and more fateful. The comment is the more suggestive because it follows the already disturbing reference to Gorée, hinting that Diouana is about to embark on a journey that may not be very different from that of the hundreds of thousands of Africans before her who departed (though involuntarily) from the Senegalese coast.

In 1958, two years before independence, Senegal was still a French colony. The reference to Algeria in the opening paragraph of the story is an allusion to the revolution in that country that would eventually lead to independence there as in other French and English colonies in Africa. (See Albert Camus's "The Guest," included in this volume, for another approach to the legacy of colonialism.) The reference thus invokes colonialism in general, of which the Pouchets are very much a part. The attitudes of Diouana's employers have been shaped by a sense of cultural and racial superiority; they believe that they can do whatever they please, essentially, with their African servants. The Pouchets' "Villa of Green Happiness" is an ironic name, because there is no happiness for Diouana at this villa. Green, a color suggesting life and growth, is also significant. On attaining independence, most African nations chose green as one of the colors for their countries' flags.

When the narrator describes the arrival of the police at the Pouchets' flat in Antibes, several important facts are introduced into the narrative. The first—the mention of April, the month when Diouana arrived in Antibes—is rather startling when we recall that the opening sentence of the story places the date of Diouana's death as June 23. Diouana has been driven to suicide in a brief three months.

The police ask Madame Pouchet a number of questions about their servant, the answers to which reveal more about the insensitivity of the French couple than about their employee. Madame does not know how old Diouana was. (Wasn't she interested enough to ask her?) Madame cannot imagine why Diouana would kill herself; after all, she ate the same food as the family and shared rooms with the children. (Why would Diouana prefer European food? Wouldn't she prefer to be treated as an adult and accorded privacy?) Madame reveals that Diouana did not have any friends of her own. In brief, her situation was almost identical to that of hundreds of thousands of slaves in the United States who were cut off from their families, from their traditional foods, from privacy, from communication even with other slaves because of mutually unintelligible African languages. The placement of this information concerning Diouana's situation in the Pouchets' home is particularly ironic because it comes before the scene describing Diouana's anticipated journey and before the reference to Gorée and the identity card.

The story then moves back in time to trace Diouana's voyage to France. (Significantly, Diouana travels by ship while the Pouchets travel by airplane.) Once in France, Diouana never sees "la belle France" of her imagination. The Pouchets frequently leave her with their four children, who quickly organize to persecute her. They refer to her color, stressing the fact that she is the *other*, different from them. Diouana repeatedly experiences the sensation of drowning. (We recall Diouana's ocean crossing. Some readers may be familiar with statistics on the number of slaves who took their lives into their own hands during the Middle Passage, jumping overboard rather than facing slavery in the New World.)

Overworked, patronized, humiliated, denied a moment to herself, and even unable to write or receive letters from home because she and her family are illiterate, Diouana finally informs us directly of her view of her situation: "'Sold, sold. Bought, bought. . . . They've bought me. For three thousand francs I do all this work. They lured me, tied me to them, and I'm stuck here like a slave.'" Economic exploitation: modern slavery. The situation in "Black Girl" intentionally echoes that of African slaves in the nineteenth century. As we read the remaining paragraphs of "Black Girl," including further details about Diouana's suicide, we cannot help but ask whether the investigators have drawn the wrong conclusion. The responsibility for Diouana's death rests with the Pouchets. Sembene's story is an indictment of the continuing practice of slavery—seen not from a European perspective but from an African one.

One final aspect of "Black Girl" remains to be considered: the matter of melodrama or sensationalism. Would an African reader consider Diouana's demise melodramatic? Here matters of cultural experience enter more directly into an understanding of the story and suggest rather different responses. In many traditional African societies, suicide is a taboo. Taking one's own life is tantamount to spilling blood on Mother Earth and polluting the community. Mother Earth may retaliate by punishing the entire community for such an act through drought, flood, or disease. However, Diouana has been cut off from her community, as the story repeatedly emphasizes. Nonetheless, in committing suicide she takes a drastic step by interrupting the cycles of life and procreation. According to animist belief, the link with the ancestors is vital; by breaking that link, Diouana will be cursed by her ancestors. Moreover, failing to participate in the cycle of procreation by producing children, she herself will leave no one who can worship her. Whether Diouana

herself is an animist or not is less important than the fact that many African readers will respond to her act as tragedy, not melodrama: Her suicide cuts her off forever from the sacred link with her people. (For a variation of this theme, read
"Sarzan" by Birago Diop, included in this volume.)

The logical question to ask is how valid is a Western reader's interpretation of
"Black Girl" without this piece of cultural information? Must we take a crash course
in each writer's culture before we can read his or her fiction? Although the more
we know, the better readers we can be, we can appreciate literature in various ways,
whatever our level of cultural or other information. Readers in other areas of the
world can comprehend the stories of Edgar Allan Poe or F. Scott Fitzgerald or Shirley
Jackson or Margaret Atwood without knowing much about life in North America.
We can read "Black Girl" and discover much of what we need to know in the story
itself. Joseph Conrad's story "Amy Foster" might be read together with Sembene's
"Black Girl" for its similar focus on the predicament of the *other*, or outsider: the
person from another culture or country (or class or race or linguistic group) whose
presence as a stranger in the community may produce occasions for connection as
well as for profound misunderstanding.

What we are suggesting is a combination of cultural humility (we should not, as
North American readers, presume that our perspective is the only one) and cultural
curiosity (the expectation that although we cannot get entirely outside of our own
reference points, we can become sensitive readers by maintaining an open ear so
that the initially unfamiliar may speak to us). We read to enjoy; we read to learn;
we read to escape. Most of us read fiction because we are also curious, and the information that we can gather from newspapers and magazines and works of non-
fiction does not satisfy a certain kind of curiosity. It does not provide us with the
sense of immediacy, with the depth of human character and emotion and possibility, even with the chaos or disorder of human experience, that imaginative literature does. We read fiction because we are thinking and feeling creatures, so
inquisitive that if we cannot have these glimpses into other people's lives and situations, we miss out on something vital for an understanding of our own lives.

III

The distinctive element of *Worlds of Fiction* is its international and multicultural
perspective, its conviction that the short story form and tradition, like the inherited literary canons that are in the process of revision and redefinition, may also be
inventively untraditional. As we have suggested in our close reading of "Black
Girl," reading habits are shaped by two paths that might be termed recognition of
the familiar, or "self," and acknowledgment of that which is unfamiliar, different,
foreign, or "other." We hope that the global and multicultural perspectives of this
volume will invite you, as readers and teachers, to discover that what you may previously have regarded as "foreign" or "other" is in fact not so different from yourself, or, at the very least, that it imaginatively enlarges your own point of view.

As the literary critic Leslie Fiedler has observed, "Literature never really changes
anything—it only makes you feel for a moment as though the world has changed."
He may be right; but the world itself has also literally changed, as events in just the

last two decades of the twentieth century in the former Soviet Union, Eastern Europe, and South Africa demonstrate. Although one might argue whether or not literature has had any part in such political transformations, in fact novelists and playwrights are in several instances also political leaders within their countries—both the acknowledged and "unacknowledged legislators of the world," as the poet Percy Bysshe Shelley phrased it. Paradoxically, encounters with good stories by authors who offer us a wide range of cultural perspectives remind us of the fundamental similarities we share as human beings. Through such diversity, we may become more attentive to the intersecting and overlapping worlds we simultaneously occupy: of cultural, social, and political spheres; of language; and of imaginative truth.

Chinua Achebe

(b. 1930)

Nigeria

The setting for Chinua Achebe's "Girls at War" couldn't cut closer to the edge. During the Nigerian Civil War (also referred to as the Biafran War, because the Ibos who seceded from Nigeria called their new nation Biafra), Chinua Achebe worked both within the secessionist territory and outside it to gain international recognition and support for the Biafran cause. Though the Nigerian Civil War is now regarded as little more than a footnote in West African history, during the years of the fighting (1967–1970) the eyes of the world were focused on Biafra as a test case for tribalism, imperialism, and the détente between the West and the Communist bloc. In large part, Biafra collapsed because few significant world powers recognized its sovereignty.

Today the Nigerian Civil War can be regarded as a turning point for many of the country's significant writers. In Chinua Achebe's case, the shift is obvious. Achebe's first novel, Things Fall Apart (1958), became the most widely read and admired piece of African writing of the twentieth century. A sequel, No Longer at Ease, was published in 1960, followed quickly by two other novels, Arrow of God in 1964 and A Man of the People in 1966. At the end of the war, Achebe published a volume of poems, Beware Soul Brother (1971), and a collection of short stories, Girls at War and Other Stories (1972), but the hiatus between his previous novel and his next one, Anthills of the Savannah (1987), lasted more than 20 years. However, one indisputable fact can be noted about Chinua Achebe during those two decades of novelistic silence: He became Africa's most deservedly beloved writer.

In Home and Exile (2000), a series of lectures Achebe delivered at Harvard in 1998, the writer made the following remark:

> Well, it is not true that my history is only in my heart; it is indeed there, but it is also in that dusty road in my town, and in every villager, living and dead, who has ever walked on it. It is in my country, too; in my continent and, yes, in the world. That dusty little road is my link to all the other destinations. To ask everybody to shut down their history, pack their bag, and buy a one-way ticket to Europe or America is just crazy, to my way of thinking. To suggest that the universal civilization is in place already is to be willfully blind to our present reality and, even worse, to trivialize the goal and hinder the materialization of a genuine universality in the future.

GIRLS AT WAR

The first time their paths crossed nothing happened. That was in the first heady days of warlike preparation when thousands of young men (and sometimes women too) were daily turned away from enlistment centres because far too many of them were coming forward burning with readiness to bear arms in defence of the exciting new nation.

The second time they met was at a check-point at Awka. Then the war had started and was slowly moving southwards from the distant northern sector. He was driving from Onitsha to Enugu and was in a hurry. Although intellectually he approved of thorough searches at road-blocks, emotionally he was always offended whenever he had to submit to them. He would probably not admit it but the feeling people got was that if you were put through a search then you could not really be one of the big people. Generally he got away without a search by pronouncing in his deep, authoritative voice: "Reginald Nwankwo, Ministry of Justice." That almost always did it. But sometimes either through ignorance or sheer cussedness the crowd at the odd checkpoint would refuse to be impressed. As happened now at Awka. Two constables carrying heavy Mark 4 rifles were watching distantly from the roadside, leaving the actual searching to local vigilantes.

"I am in a hurry," he said to the girl who now came up to his car. "My name is Reginald Nwankwo, Ministry of Justice."

"Good afternoon, sir. I want to see your boot."

"Oh Christ! What do you think is in the boot?"

"I don't know, sir."

He got out of the car in suppressed rage, stalked to the back, opened the boot and holding the lid up with his left hand he motioned with the right as if to say: After you!

"Are you satisfied?" he demanded.

"Yes, sir. Can I see your pigeon-hole?"

"Christ Almighty!"

"Sorry to delay you, sir. But you people gave us this job to do."

"Never mind. You are damn right. It's just that I happen to be in a hurry. But never mind. That's the glove-box. Nothing there as you can see."

"All right sir, close it." Then she opened the rear door and bent down to inspect under the seats. It was then he took the first real look at her, starting from behind. She was a beautiful girl in a breasty blue jersey, khaki jeans and canvas shoes with the new-style hair-plait which gave a girl a defiant look and which they called—for reasons of their own—"air force base"; and she looked vaguely familiar.

"I am all right, sir," she said at last meaning she was through with her task. "You don't recognize me?"

"No. Should I?"

"You gave me a lift to Enugu that time I left my school to go and join the militia."

"Ah, yes, you were the girl. I told you, didn't I, to go back to school because girls were not required in the militia. What happened?"

"They told me to go back to my school or join the Red Cross."

"You see I was right. So, what are you doing now?"

"Just patching up with Civil Defence."

"Well, good luck to you. Believe me you are a great girl."

That was the day he finally believed there might be something in this talk about revolution. He had seen plenty of girls and women marching and demonstrating before now. But somehow he had never been able to give it much thought. He didn't doubt that the girls and the women took themselves seriously, they obviously did. But so did the little kids who marched up and down the streets at the time drilling with sticks and wearing their mothers' soup bowls for steel helmets. The prime joke of the time among his friends was the contingent of girls from a local secondary school marching behind a banner: WE ARE IMPREGNABLE!

But after that encounter at the Awka check-point he simply could not sneer at the girls again, nor at the talk of revolution, for he had seen it in action in that young woman whose devotion had simply and without self-righteousness convicted him of gross levity. What were her words? We are doing the work you asked us to do. She wasn't going to make an exception even for one who once did her a favour. He was sure she would have searched her own father just as rigorously.

When their paths crossed a third time, at least eighteen months later, things had got very bad. Death and starvation having long chased out the headiness of the early days, now left in some places blank resignation, in others a rock-like, even suicidal, defiance. But surprisingly enough there were many at this time who had no other desire than to corner whatever good things were still going and to enjoy themselves to the limit. For such people a strange normalcy had returned to the world. All those nervous check-points disappeared. Girls became girls once more and boys boys. It was a tight, blockaded and desperate world but none the less a world—with some goodness and some badness and plenty of heroism which, however, happened most times far, far below the eye-level of the people in this story—in out-of-the-way refugee camps, in the damp tatters, in the hungry and barehanded courage of the first line of fire.

Reginald Nwankwo lived in Owerri then. But that day he had gone to Nkwerri in search of relief. He had got from Caritas in Owerri a few heads of stock-fish, some tinned meat, and the dreadful American stuff called Formula Two which he felt certain was some kind of animal feed. But he always had a vague suspicion that not being a Catholic put one at a disadvantage with Caritas. So he went now to see an old friend who ran the WCC depot at Nkwerri to get other items like rice, beans, and that excellent cereal commonly called *Gabon gari*.

He left Owerri at six in the morning so as to catch his friend at the depot where he was known never to linger beyond 8:30 for fear of air-raids. Nwankwo was very fortunate that day. The depot had received on the previous day large supplies of new stock as a result of an unusual number of plane landings a few nights earlier. As his driver loaded tins and bags and cartons into his car the starved crowds that perpetually hung around relief centres made crude, ungracious remarks like "War Can Continue!" meaning the WCC! Somebody else shouted "*Irevolu!*" and his friends replied "*shum!*" "*Irevolu!*" "*shum!*" "*Isofeli?*" "*shum!*" "*Isofeli?*" "*Mba!*"[1]

Nwankwo was deeply embarrassed not by the jeers of this scarecrow crowd of rags and floating ribs but by the independent accusation of their wasted bodies and sunken eyes. Indeed he would probably have felt much worse had they said nothing, simply looked on in silence, as his boot was loaded with milk and powdered egg and oats and tinned meat and stock-fish. By nature such singular good fortune in the midst of a general desolation was certain to embarrass him. But what could a man do? He had a wife and four children living in the remote village of Ogbu and completely dependent on what relief he could find and send them. He couldn't abandon them to kwashiokor. The best he could do—and did do as a matter of fact—was to make sure that whenever he got sizeable supplies like now he made over some of it to his driver, Johnson, with a wife and six, or was it seven?, children and a salary of ten pounds a month when

---

[1] "*Irevolu!*" "*shum!*" "*Isofeli?*" "*shum!*" "*Isofeli?*" "*Mba!*"   The first two words are a distortion of "revolution." Combined with "*Isofeli?*" ("Do you eat with them?") and "*Mba!*" ("No!"), the sequence implies that the speakers will have nothing to do with revolutionaries.

gari in the market was climbing to one pound per cigarette cup. In such a situation one could do nothing at all for crowds; at best one could try to be of some use to one's immediate neighbours. That was all.

On his way back to Owerri a very attractive girl by the roadside waved for a lift. He ordered the driver to stop. Scores of pedestrians, dusty and exhausted, some military, some civil, swooped down on the car from all directions.

"No, no, no," said Nwankwo firmly. "It's the young woman I stopped for. I have a bad tyre and can only take one person. Sorry."

"My son, please," cried one old woman in despair, gripping the door-handle.

"Old woman, you want to be killed?" shouted the driver as he pulled away, shaking her off. Nwankwo had already opened a book and sunk his eyes there. For at least a mile after that he did not even look at the girl until she finding, perhaps, the silence too heavy said:

"You've saved me today. Thank you."

"Not at all. Where are you going?"

"To Owerri. You don't recognize me?"

"Oh yes, of course. What a fool I am . . . You are . . ."

"Gladys."

"That's right, the militia girl. You've changed, Gladys. You were always beautiful of course, but now you are a beauty queen. What do you do these days?"

"I am in the Fuel Directorate."

"That's wonderful."

It was wonderful, he thought, but even more it was tragic. She wore a high-tinted wig and very expensive skirt and low-cut blouse. Her shoes, obviously from Gabon, must have cost a fortune. In short, thought Nwankwo, she had to be in the keep of some well-placed gentleman, one of those piling up money out of the war.

"I broke my rule today to give you a lift. I never give lifts these days."

"Why?"

"How many people can you carry? It is better not to try at all. Look at that old woman."

"I thought you would carry her."

He said nothing to that and after another spell of silence Gladys thought maybe he was offended and so added: "Thank you for breaking your rule for me." She was scanning his face, turned slightly away. He smiled, turned, and tapped her on the lap.

"What are you going to Owerri to do?"

"I am going to visit my girl-friend."

"Girl-friend? You sure?"

"Why not? . . . If you drop me at her house you can see her. Only I pray God she hasn't gone on weekend today; it will be serious."

"Why?"

"Because if she is not at home I will sleep on the road today."

"I pray to God that she is not at home."

"Why?"

"Because if she is not at home I will offer you bed and breakfast . . . What is that?" he asked the driver who had brought the car to an abrupt stop. There was no need for an answer. The small crowd ahead was looking upwards. The three scrambled out of the car and stumbled for the bush, necks twisted in a backward search of the sky. But the alarm was false. The sky was silent and clear except for two high-flying vultures. A humorist in the crowd called them Fighter and Bomber and everyone laughed in relief. The three climbed into their car again and continued their journey.

"It is much too early for raids," he said to Gladys, who had both her palms on her breast as though to still a thumping heart. "They rarely come before ten o'clock."

But she remained tongue-tied from her recent fright. Nwankwo saw an opportunity there and took it at once.

"Where does your friend live?"

"250 Douglas Road."

"Ah; that's the very centre of town—a terrible place. No bunkers, nothing. I won't advise you to go there before 6 P.M.; it's not safe. If you don't mind I will take you to my place where there is a good bunker and then as soon as it is safe, around six, I shall drive you to your friend. How's that?"

"It's all right," she said lifelessly. "I am so frightened of this thing. That's why I refused to work in Owerri. I don't even know who asked me to come out today."

"You'll be all right. We are used to it."

"But your family is not there with you?"

"No," he said. "Nobody has his family there. We like to say it is because of air-raids but I can assure you there is more to it. Owerri is real swinging now, and we live the life of gay bachelors."

"That is what I have heard."

"You will not just hear it; you will see it today. I shall take you to a real swinging party. A friend of mine, a Lieutenant-Colonel, is having a birthday party. He's hired the Sound Smashers to play. I'm sure you'll enjoy it."

He was immediately and thoroughly ashamed of himself. He hated the parties and frivolities to which his friends clung like drowning men. And to talk so approvingly of them because he wanted to take a girl home! And this particular girl too, who had once had such beautiful faith in the struggle and was betrayed (no doubt about it) by some man like him out for a good time. He shook his head sadly.

"What is it?" asked Gladys.

"Nothing. Just my thoughts."

They made the rest of the journey to Owerri practically in silence.

She made herself at home very quickly as if she was a regular girl-friend of his. She changed into a house dress and put away her auburn wig.

"That is a lovely hair-do. Why do you hide it with a wig?"

"Thank you," she said leaving his question unanswered for a while. Then she said: "Men are funny."

"Why do you say that?"

"You are now a beauty queen," she mimicked.

"Oh, that! I mean every word of it." He pulled her to him and kissed her. She neither refused nor yielded fully, which he liked for a start. Too many girls were simply too easy these days. War sickness, some called it.

He drove off a little later to look in at the office and she busied herself in the kitchen helping his boy with lunch. It must have been literally a look-in, for he was back within half an hour, rubbing his hands and saying he could not stay away too long from his beauty queen.

As they sat down to lunch she said: "You have nothing in your fridge."

"Like what?" he asked, half-offended.

"Like meat," she replied undaunted.

"Do you still eat meat?" he challenged.

"Who am I? But other big men like you eat."

"I don't know which big men you have in mind. But they are not like me. I don't make money trading with the enemy or selling relief or . . ."

"Augusta's boy-friend doesn't do that. He just gets foreign exchange."

"How does he get it? He swindles the government—that's how he gets foreign exchange, whoever he is. Who is Augusta, by the way?"

"My girl-friend."

"I see."

"She gave me three dollars last time which I changed to forty-five pounds. The man gave her fifty dollars."

"Well, my dear girl, I don't traffic in foreign exchange and I don't have meat in my fridge. We are fighting a war and I happen to know that some young boys at the front drink gari and water once in three days."

"It is true," she said simply. "Monkey de work, baboon de chop."

"It is not even that; it is worse," he said, his voice beginning to shake. "People are dying every day. As we talk now somebody is dying."

"It is true," she said again.

"Plane!" screamed his boy from the kitchen.

"My mother!" screamed Gladys. As they scuttled towards the bunker of palm stems and red earth, covering their heads with their hands and stopping slightly in their flight, the entire sky was exploding with the clamour of jets and the huge noise of home-made anti-aircraft rockets.

Inside the bunker she clung to him even after the plane had gone and the guns, late to start and also to end, had all died down again.

"It was only passing," he told her, his voice a little shaky. "It didn't drop anything. From its direction I should say it was going to the war front. Perhaps our people are pressing them. That's what they always do. Whenever our boys press them, they send an SOS to the Russians and Egyptians to bring the planes." He drew a long breath.

She said nothing, just clung to him. They could hear his boy telling the servant from the next house that there were two of them and one dived like this and the other dived like that.

"I see dem well well," said the other with equal excitement. "If no to say de ting de kill porson e for sweet for eye. To God."

"Imagine!" said Gladys, finding her voice at last. She had a way, he thought, of conveying with a few words or even a single word whole layers of meaning. Now it was at once her astonishment as well as reproof, tinged perhaps with grudging admiration for people who could be so lighthearted about these bringers of death.

"Don't be so scared," he said. She moved closer and he began to kiss her and squeeze her breasts. She yielded more and more and then fully. The bunker was dark and unswept and might harbour crawling things. He thought of bringing a mat from the main house but reluctantly decided against it. Another plane might pass and send a neighbour or simply a chance passer-by crashing into them. That would be only slightly better than a certain gentleman in another air-raid who was seen in broad daylight fleeing his bedroom for his bunker stark naked pursued by a woman in a similar state!

Just as Gladys had feared, her friend was not in town. It would seem her powerful boy-friend had wangled for her a flight to Libreville to shop. So her neighbours thought anyway.

"Great!" said Nwankwo as they drove away. "She will come back on an arms plane loaded with shoes, wigs, pants, bras, cosmetics and what have you, which she will then sell and make thousands of pounds. You girls are really at war, aren't you?"

She said nothing and he thought he had got through at last to her. Then suddenly she said, "That is what you men want us to do."

"Well," he said, "here is one man who doesn't want you to do that. Do you remember that girl in khaki jeans who searched me without mercy at the check-point?"

She began to laugh.

"That is the girl I want you to become again. Do you remember her? No wig. I don't even think she had any earrings . . ."

"Ah, na lie-o. I had ear-rings."

"All right. But you know what I mean."

"That time done pass. Now everybody want survival. They call it number six. You put your number six; I put my number six. Everything all right."

The Lieutenant-Colonel's party turned into something quite unexpected. But before it did things had been going well enough. There was goat-meat, some chicken and rice and plenty of home-made spirits. There was one fiery brand nicknamed "tracer" which indeed sent a flame down your gullet. The funny thing was looking at it in the bottle it had the innocent appearance of an orange drink. But the thing that caused the greatest stir was the bread—one little roll for each person! It was the size of a golf-ball and about the same consistency too! But it was real bread. The band was good too and there were many girls. And to improve matters even further two white Red Cross people soon arrived with a bottle of Courvoisier and a bottle of Scotch! The party gave them a standing ovation and then scrambled to get a drop. It soon turned out from his general behaviour, however, that one of the white men had probably drunk too much already. And the reason it would seem was that a pilot he knew well had been killed in a crash at the airport last night, flying in relief in awful weather.

Few people at the party had heard of the crash by then. So there was an immediate damping of the air. Some dancing couples went back to their seats and the band stopped. Then for some strange reason the drunken Red Cross man just exploded.

"Why should a man, a decent man, throw away his life. For nothing! Charley didn't need to die. Not for this stinking place. Yes, everything stinks here. Even these girls who come here all dolled up and smiling, what are they worth? Don't I know? A head of stock-fish, that's all, or one American dollar and they are ready to tumble into bed."

In the threatening silence following the explosion one of the young officers walked up to him and gave him three thundering slaps—right! left! right!—pulled him up from his seat and (there were things like tears in his eyes) shoved him outside. His friend, who had tried in vain to shut him up, followed him out and the silenced party heard them drive off. The officer who did the job returned dusting his palms.

"Fucking beast!" said he with an impressive coolness. And all the girls showed with their eyes that they rated him a man and a hero.

"Do you know him?" Gladys asked Nwankwo.

He didn't answer her. Instead he spoke generally to the party:

"The fellow was clearly drunk," he said.

"I don't care," said the officer. "It is when a man is drunk that he speaks what is on his mind."

"So you beat him for what was on his mind," said the host, "that is the spirit, Joe."

"Thank you, sir," said Joe, saluting.

"His name is Joe," Gladys and the girl on her left said in unison, turning to each other.

At the same time Nwankwo and a friend on the other side of him were saying quietly, very quietly, that although the man had been rude and offensive what he had said about the girls was unfortunately the bitter truth, only he was the wrong man to say it.

When the dancing resumed Captain Joe came to Gladys for a dance. She sprang to her feet even before the word was out of his mouth. Then she remembered immediately and turned round to take permission from Nwankwo. At the same time the Captain also turned to him and said, "Excuse me."

"Go ahead," said Nwankwo, looking somewhere between the two.

It was a long dance and he followed them with his eyes without appearing to do so. Occasionally a relief plane passed overhead and somebody immediately switched off the lights saying it might be the Intruder. But it was only an excuse to dance in the dark and make the girls giggle, for the sound of the Intruder was well known.

Gladys came back feeling very self-conscious and asked Nwankwo to dance with her. But he wouldn't. "Don't bother about me," he said, "I am enjoying myself perfectly sitting here and watching those of you who dance."

"Then let's go," she said, "If you won't dance."

"But I never dance, believe me. So please enjoy yourself."

She danced next with the Lieutenant-Colonel and again with Captain Joe, and then Nwankwo agreed to take her home.

"I am sorry I didn't dance," he said as they drove away. "But I swore never to dance as long as this war lasts."

She said nothing.

"When I think of somebody like that pilot who got killed last night. And he had no hand whatever in the quarrel. All his concern was to bring us food . . ."

"I hope that his friend is not like him," said Gladys.

"The man was just upset by his friend's death. But what I am saying is that with people like that getting killed and our own boys suffering and dying at the war fronts I don't see why we should sit around throwing parties and dancing."

"You took me there," said she in final revolt. "They are your friends. I don't know them before."

"Look, my dear, I am not blaming you. I am merely telling you why I personally refuse to dance. Anyway, let's change the subject . . . Do you still say you want to go back tomorrow? My driver can take you early enough on Monday morning for you to go to work. No? All right, just as you wish. You are the boss."

She gave him a shock by the readiness with which she followed him to bed and by her language.

"You want to shell?" she asked. And without waiting for an answer said, "Go ahead but don't pour in troops!"

He didn't want to pour in troops either and so it was all right. But she wanted visual assurance and so he showed her.

One of the ingenious economies taught by the war was that a rubber condom could be used over and over again. All you had to do was wash it out, dry it and shake a lot of talcum powder over it to prevent its sticking; and it was as good as new. It had to be the real British thing, though, not some of the cheap stuff they brought in from Lisbon which was about as strong as a dry cocoyam leaf in the harmattan.

He had his pleasure but wrote the girl off. He might just as well have slept with a prostitute, he thought. It was clear as daylight to him now that she was kept by some army officer. What a terrible transformation in the short period of less than two years! Wasn't it a miracle that she still had memories of the other life, that she even remembered her name? If the affair of the drunken Red Cross man should happen again now, he said to himself, he would stand up beside the fellow and tell the party that here was a man of truth. What a terrible fate to befall a whole generation! The mothers of tomorrow!

By morning he was feeling a little better and more generous in his judgments. Gladys, he thought, was just a mirror reflecting a society that had gone completely rotten and maggotty at the centre. The mirror itself was intact; a lot of smudge but no more. All that was needed was a clean duster. "I have a duty to her," he told himself, "the little girl that once revealed to me our situation. Now she is in danger, under some terrible influence."

He wanted to get to the bottom of this deadly influence. It was clearly not just her good-time girl-friend, Augusta, or whatever her name was. There must be some man at the centre of it, perhaps one of these heartless attack-traders who traffic in foreign currencies and make their hundreds of thousands by sending young men to hazard their lives bartering looted goods for cigarettes behind enemy lines, or one of those contractors who receive piles of money daily for food they never deliver to the army. Or perhaps some vulgar and cowardly army officer full of filthy barrack talk and fictitious stories of heroism. He decided he had to find out. Last night he had thought of sending his driver alone to take her home. But no, he must go and see for himself where she lived. Something was bound to reveal itself there. Something on which he could anchor his saving operation. As he prepared for the trip his feeling towards her softened with every passing minute. He assembled for her half of the food he had received at the relief centre the day before. Difficult as things were, he thought, a girl who had something to eat would be spared, not all, but some of the temptation. He would arrange with his friend at the WCC to deliver something to her every fortnight.

Tears came to Gladys's eyes when she saw the gifts. Nwankwo didn't have too much cash on him but he got together twenty pounds and handed it over to her.

"I don't have foreign exchange, and I know this won't go far at all, but . . ."

She just came and threw herself at him, sobbing. He kissed her lips and eyes and mumbled something about victims of circumstances, which went over her head. In deference to him, he thought with exultation, she had put away her high-tinted wig in her bag.

"I want you to promise me something," he said.

"What?"

"Never use that expression about shelling again."

She smiled with tears in her eyes. "You don't like it? That's what all the girls call it."

"Well, you are different from all the girls. Will you promise?"

"OK."

Naturally their departure had become a little delayed. And when they got into the car it refused to start. After poking around the engine the driver decided that the battery was flat. Nwankwo was aghast. He had that very week paid thirty-four pounds to change two of the cells and the mechanic who performed it had promised him six months' service. A new battery, which was then running at two hundred and fifty pounds was simply out of the question. The driver must have been careless with something, he thought.

"It must be because of last night," said the driver.

"What happened last night?" asked Nwankwo sharply, wondering what insolence was on the way. But none was intended.

"Because we use the headlight."

"Am I supposed not to use my light then? Go and get some people and try pushing it." He got out again with Gladys and returned to the house while the driver went over to neighbouring houses to seek the help of other servants.

After at least half an hour of pushing it up and down the street, and a lot of noisy advice from the pushers, the car finally spluttered to life shooting out enormous clouds of black smoke from the exhaust.

It was eight-thirty by his watch when they set out. A few miles away a disabled soldier waved for a lift.

"Stop!" screamed Nwankwo. The driver jammed his foot on the brakes and then turned his head towards his master in bewilderment.

"Don't you see the soldier waving? Reverse and pick him up!"

"Sorry, sir," said the driver. "I don't know Master want to pick him."

"If you don't know you should ask. Reverse back."

The soldier, a mere boy, in filthy khaki drenched in sweat lacked his right leg from the knee down. He seemed not only grateful that a car should stop for him but greatly surprised. He first handed in his crude wooden crutches which the driver arranged between the two front seats, then painfully he levered himself in.

"Thanks, sir," he said turning his neck to look at the back and completely out of breath.

"I am very grateful. Madame, thank you."

"The pleasure is ours," said Nwankwo. "Where did you get your wound?"

"At Azumini, sir. On tenth of January."

"Never mind. Everything will be all right. We are proud of you boys and will make sure you receive your due reward when it is all over."

"I pray God, sir."

They drove on in silence for the next half-hour or so. Then as the car sped down a slope towards a bridge somebody screamed—perhaps the driver, perhaps the soldier—"They have come!" The screech of the brakes merged into the scream and the shattering of the sky overhead. The doors flew open even before the car had come to a stop and they were fleeing blindly to the bush. Gladys was a little ahead of Nwankwo where they heard through the drowning tumult the soldier's voice crying: "Please come and open for me!" Vaguely he saw Gladys stop; he pushed past her shouting to her at the same time to come on. Then a high whistle descended like a spear through the chaos and exploded in a vast noise and motion that smashed up everything. A tree he had embraced flung him away through the bush. Then another terrible whistle starting high up and ending again in a monumental crash of the world; and then another, and Nwankwo heard no more.

He woke up to human noises and weeping and the smell and smoke of a charred world. He dragged himself up and staggered towards the source of the sounds.

From afar he saw his driver running towards him in tears and blood. He saw the remains of his car smoking and the entangled remains of the girl and the soldier. And he let out a piercing cry and fell down again.

[1972]

Questions

1. Because "Girls at War" is told from Reginald Nwankwo's point of view, the reader sees Gladys only through his eyes. What can be said about the validity of his perspective? Is Reginald any less an opportunist than Gladys?
2. Does the concluding scene in the story redeem Gladys?
3. What irony is implied by the story's title?
4. On numerous occasions, Achebe has described his role as an African writer as that of a teacher—informing, explaining, and, above all, educating his reader. "The role of the writer depends to some extent on the state of his society," he stated in an interview in *Transition* during the Biafran war. "In other words, if a society is ill he has a responsibility to point it out. If the society is healthy—I do not know of any one— his job is limited." How applicable are these remarks to "Girls at War"?

Ama Ata Aidoo
(b. 1942)
Ghana

Ama Ata Aidoo was born in Ghana in 1942. She received her B.A. from the University of Ghana in 1964, where she subsequently was a research fellow in the Institute of African Studies. She has taught at universities in the United States, where she has also lectured extensively. Her publications include two plays—The Dilemma of a Ghost (1965) and Anowa (1970). "Two Sisters" is from her short story collection, No Sweetness Here (1970). Ms. Aidoo has also published two novels, Our Sister Killjoy (1977) and Changes (1991).

In the past decade, Ama Ata Aidoo has taught at a number of American colleges and universities, including Smith and Mt. Holyoke, while continuing to publish numerous short stories in international publications. A number of these stories have been collected in The Girl Who Can and Other Stories (1999).

Writing about her compatriot Ayi Kwei Armah's The Beautyful Ones Are Not Yet Born (1968), Ms. Aidoo had this to say about Ghanaian women:

> [E]specially in the area of what exactly the African woman is, the assumption on the part of most Westerners [has been] that the poor African woman was a downtrodden wretch until the European missionary brought her Christianity, civilization, and emancipation. This may apply in certain areas of Africa, but certainly, for most Ghanaian women, the question of their emancipation is not really a problem to discuss since it has always been ensured by the system anyway. Nor is this an idealized view. It is there for anyone to see who is prepared to observe a society instead of imposing on it his own prejudices and syndromes.

TWO SISTERS

As she shakes out the typewriter cloak and covers the machine with it, the thought of the bus she has to hurry to catch goes through her like a pain. It is her luck, she thinks. Everything is just her luck. Why, if she had one of those graduates for a boyfriend, wouldn't he come and take her home every evening? And she knows that a girl does not herself have to be a graduate to get one of those boys. Certainly, Joe is dying to do exactly that—with his taxi. And he is as handsome as anything, and a good man, but you know . . . Besides there are cars and there are cars. As for the possibility of the other actually coming to fetch her—oh, well. She has to admit it will take some time before she can bring herself to make demands of that sort on *him*. She has also to admit that the temptation is extremely strong. Would it really be so dangerously indiscreet? Doesn't one government car look like another? The hugeness of it? Its shaded glass? The uniformed chauffeur? She can already see herself stepping out to greet the dead-with-envy glances of the other girls. To begin with, she will insist on a little discretion. The driver can drop her under the neem trees in the morning and pick her up from there in the evening . . . anyway, she will have to wait a little while for that and it is all her luck.

There are other ways, surely. One of these, for some reason, she has sworn to have nothing of. Her boss has a car and does not look bad. In fact the man is all right. But she keeps telling herself that she does not fancy having some old and dried-out housewife walking into the office one afternoon to tear her hair out and make a row. . . . Mm, so for the meantime, it is going to continue to be the municipal bus with its grimy seats, its common passengers and impudent conductors. . . . Jesus! She doesn't wish herself dead or anything as stupidly final as that. Oh no. She just wishes she could sleep deep and only wake up on the morning of her glory.

The new pair of black shoes are more realistic than their owner, though. As she walks down the corridor, they sing:

> Count, Mercy, count your blessings
> Count, Mercy, count your blessings
> Count, count, count your blessings.

They sing along the corridor, into the avenue, across the road and into the bus. And they resume their song along the gravel path, as she opens the front gate and crosses the cemented courtyard to the door.

"Sissie!" she called.

"*Hei* Mercy," and the door opened to show the face of Connie, big sister, six years or more older and now heavy with her second child. Mercy collapsed into the nearest chair.

"Welcome home. How was the office today?"

"Sister, don't ask. Look at my hands. My fingers are dead with typing. Oh God, I don't know what to do."

"Why, what is wrong?"

"You tell me what is right. Why should I be a typist?"

"What else would you be?"

"What a strange question. Is typing the only thing one can do in this world? You are a teacher, are you not?"

"But . . . but . . ."

"But what? Or you want me to know that if I had done better in the exams, I could have trained to be a teacher too, eh, sister? Or even a proper secretary?"

"Mercy, what is the matter? What have I done? What have I done? Why have you come home so angry?"

Mercy broke into tears.

"Oh I am sorry. I am sorry, Sissie. It's just that I am sick of everything. The office, living with you and your husband. I want a husband of my own, children. I want . . . I want . . ."

"But you are so beautiful."

"Thank you. But so are you."

"You are young and beautiful. As for marriage, it's you who are postponing it. Look at all these people who are running after you."

"Sissie, I don't like what you are doing. So stop it."

"Okay, okay, okay."

And there was a silence.

"Which of them could I marry? Joe is—mm, fine—but, but I just don't like him."

"You mean . . ."

"Oh, Sissie!"

"Little sister, you and I can be truthful with one another."

"Oh yes."

"What I would like to say is that I am not that old or wise. But still I could advise you a little. Joe drives someone's car now. Well, you never know. Lots of taxi drivers come to own their taxis, sometimes fleets of cars."

"Of course. But it's a pity you are married already. Or I could be a go-between for you and Joe!"

And the two of them burst out laughing. It was when she rose to go to the bedroom that Connie noticed the new shoes.

"*Ei*, those are beautiful shoes. Are they new?"

From the other room, Mercy's voice came interrupted by the motions of her body as she undressed and then dressed again. However, the uncertainty in it was due to something entirely different.

"Oh, I forgot to tell you about them. In fact, I was going to show them to you. I think it was on Tuesday I bought them. Or was it Wednesday? When I came home from the office, you and James had taken Akosua out. And later, I forgot all about them."

"I see. But they are very pretty. Were they expensive?"

"No, not really." This reply was too hurriedly said.

And she said only last week that she didn't have a penny on her. And I believed her because I know what they pay her is just not enough to last anyone through any month, even minus rent. . . . I have been thinking she manages very well. But these shoes. And she is not the type who would borrow money just to buy a pair of shoes, when she could have gone on wearing her old pairs until things get better. Oh I wish I knew what to do. I mean I am not her mother. And I wonder how James will see these problems.

"Sissie, you look worried."

"Hmm, when don't I? With the baby due in a couple of months and the government's new ruling on salaries and all. On top of everything, I have reliable information that James is running after a new girl."

Mercy laughed.

"Oh Sissie. You always get reliable information on these things."

"But yes. And I don't know why."

"Sissie, men are like that."

"They are selfish."

"No, it's just that women allow them to behave the way they do instead of seizing some freedom themselves."

"But I am sure that even if we were free to carry on in the same way, I wouldn't make use of it."

"But why not?"

"Because I love James. I love James and I am not interested in any other man." Her voice was full of tears. But Mercy was amused.

"O God. Now listen to that. It's women like you who keep all of us down."

"Well, I am sorry but it's how the good God created me."

"Mm. I am sure that I can love several men at the same time."

"Mercy!"

They burst out laughing again. And yet they are sad. But laughter is always best.

Mercy complained of hunger and so they went to the kitchen to heat up some food and eat. The two sisters alone. It is no use waiting for James. And this evening, a friend of Connie's has come to take out the baby girl, Akosua, and had threatened to keep her until her bedtime.

"Sissie, I am going to see a film." This from Mercy.

"Where?"

"The Globe."

"Are you going with Joe?"

"No."

"Are you going alone?"

"No."

Careful Connie.

"Whom are you going with?"

Careful Connie, please. Little sister's nostrils are widening dangerously. Look at the sudden creasing-up of her mouth and between her brows. Connie, a sister is a good thing. Even a younger sister. Especially when you have no mother or father.

"Mercy, whom are you going out with?"

"Well, I had food in my mouth! And I had to swallow it down before I could answer you, no?"

"I am sorry." How softly said.

"And anyway, do I have to tell you everything?"

"Oh no. It's just that I didn't think it was a question I should not have asked."

There was more silence. Then Mercy sucked her teeth with irritation and Connie cleared her throat with fear.

"I am going out with Mensar-Arthur."

As Connie asked the next question, she wondered if the words were leaving her lips. "Mensar-Arthur?"

"Yes."

"Which one?"

"*How many do you know?*"

Her fingers were too numb to pick up the food. She put the plate down. Something jumped in her chest and she wondered what it was. Perhaps it was the baby.

"Do you mean that member of Parliament?"

"Yes."

"But Mercy . . ."

Little sister only sits and chews her food.

"But Mercy . . ."

Chew, chew, chew.

"But Mercy . . ."

"What?"

She startled Connie.

"He is so old."

Chew, chew, chew.

"Perhaps, I mean, perhaps that really doesn't matter, does it? Not very much anyway. But they say he has so many wives and girl-friends."

Please little sister. I am not trying to interfere in your private life. You said yourself a little while ago that you wanted a man of your own. That man belongs to so many women already. . . .

That silence again. Then there was only Mercy's footsteps as she went to put her plate in the kitchen sink, running water as she washed her plate and her hands. She drank some water and coughed. Then as tears streamed down her sister's averted face, there was the sound of her footsteps as she left the kitchen. At the end of it all, she banged a door. Connie only said something like, "O Lord, O Lord," and continued sitting in the kitchen. She had hardly eaten anything at all. Very soon Mercy went to have a bath. Then Connie heard her getting ready to leave the house. The shoes. Then she was gone. She needn't have carried on like that, eh? Because Connie had not meant to probe or bring on a quarrel. What use is there in this old world for a sister, if you can't have a chat with her? What's more, things like this never happen to people like Mercy. Their parents were good Presbyterians. They feared God. Mama had not managed to give them all the rules of life before she died. But Connie knows that running around with an old and depraved public man would have been considered an abomination by the parents.

A big car with a super-smooth engine purred into the drive. It actually purrs: this huge machine from the white man's land. Indeed, its well-mannered protest as the tyres slid on to the gravel seemed like a lullaby compared to the loud thumping of the girl's stiletto shoes. When Mensar-Arthur saw Mercy, he stretched his arm and opened the door to the passenger seat. She sat down and the door closed with a civilized thud. The engine hummed into motion and the car sailed away.

After a distance of a mile or so from the house, the man started conversation.

"And how is my darling today?"

"I am well," and only the words did not imply tragedy.

"You look solemn today, why?"

She remained silent and still.

"My dear, what is the matter?"

"Nothing."

"Oh . . ." he cleared his throat again. "Eh, and how were the shoes?"

"Very nice. In fact, I am wearing them now. They pinch a little but then all new shoes are like that."

"And the handbag?"

"I like it very much too. . . . My sister noticed them. I mean the shoes." The tragedy was announced.

"Did she ask you where you got them from?"

"No."

He cleared his throat again.

"Where did we agree to go tonight?"

"The Globe, but I don't want to see a film."

"Is that so? Mm, I am glad because people always notice things."

"But they won't be too surprised."

"What are you saying, my dear?"

"Nothing."

"Okay, so what shall we do?"

"I don't know."

"Shall I drive to the Seaway?"

"Oh yes."

He drove to the Seaway. To a section of the beach they knew very well. She loves it here. This wide expanse of sand and the old sea. She has often wished she should do what she fancied: one thing she fancies. Which is to drive very near to the end of the sands until the tyres of the car touched the water. Of course it is a very foolish idea as he pointed out sharply to her the first time she thought aloud about it. It was in his occasional I-am-more-than-old-enough-to-be-your-father tone. There are always disadvantages. Things could be different. Like if one had a younger lover. Handsome, maybe not rich like this man here, but well-off, sufficiently well-off to be able to afford a sports car. A little something very much like those in the films driven by the white racing drivers. With tyres that can do everything . . . and they would drive exactly where the sea and the sand meet.

"We are here."

"Don't let's get out. Let's just sit inside and talk."

"Talk?"

"Yes."

"Okay. But what is it, my darling?"

"I have told my sister about you."

"Good God. Why?"

"But I had to. I couldn't keep it to myself any longer."

"Childish. It was not necessary at all. She is not your mother."

"No. But she is all I have. And she has been very good to me."

"Well, it was her duty."

"Then it is my duty to tell her about something like this. I may get into trouble."

"Don't be silly," he said, "I normally take good care of my girl-friends."

"I see," she said and for the first time in the one month since she agreed to be this man's lover, the tears which suddenly rose into her eyes were not forced.

"And you promised you wouldn't tell her." It was father's voice now.

"Don't be angry. After all, people talk so much, as you said a little while ago. She was bound to hear it one day."

"My darling, you are too wise. What did she say?"

"She was pained."

"Don't worry. Find out something she wants very much but cannot get in this country because of the import restrictions."

"I know for sure she wants an electric motor for her sewing machine."

"Is that all?"

"That's what I know of."

"Mm. I am going to London next week on some delegation, so if you bring me the details on the make of the machine, I shall get her the motor."

"Thank you."

"What else is worrying my Black Beauty?"

"Nothing."

"And by the way, let me know as soon as you want to leave your sister's place. I have got you one of the government estate houses."

"Oh . . . oh," she said, pleased, contented for the first time since this typically ghastly day had begun, at half-past six in the morning.

Dear little child came back from the playground with her toe bruised. Shall we just blow cold air from our mouth on it or put on a salve? Nothing matters really. Just see that she does not feel unattended. And the old sea roars on. This is a calm sea, generally. Too calm in fact, this Gulf of Guinea. The natives sacrifice to him on Tuesday and once a year celebrate him. They might save their chickens, their eggs and their yams. And as for the feast once a year, he doesn't pay much attention to it either. They are always celebrating one thing or another and they surely don't need him for an excuse to celebrate one day more. He has seen things happen along these beaches. Different things. Contradictory things. Or just repetitions of old patterns. He never interferes in their affairs. Why should he? Except in places like Keta where he eats houses away because they leave him no choice. Otherwise he never allows them to see his passions. People are worms, and even the God who created them is immensely bored with their antics. Here is a fifty-year-old "big man" who thinks he is somebody. And a twenty-three-year-old child who chooses a silly way to conquer unconquerable problems. Well, what did one expect of human beings? And so as those who settled on the back seat of the car to play with each other's bodies, he, the Gulf of Guinea, shut his eyes with boredom. It is right. He could sleep, no? He spread himself and moved further ashore. But the car was parked at a very safe distance and the rising tides could not wet its tyres.

James has come home late. But then he has been coming back late for the past few weeks. Connie is crying and he knows it as soon as he enters the bedroom. He hates tears, for like so many men, he knows it is one of the most potent weapons in women's bitchy and inexhaustible arsenal. She speaks first.

"James."

"Oh, are you still awake?" He always tries to deal with these nightly funeral parlour doings by pretending not to know what they are about.

"I couldn't sleep."

"What is wrong?"

"Nothing."

So he moves quickly and sits beside her.

"Connie, what is the matter? You have been crying again."

"You are very late again."

"Is that why you are crying? Or is there something else?"

"Yes."

"Yes to what?"

"James, where were you?"

"Connie, I have warned you about what I shall do if you don't stop examining me, as though I were your prisoner, every time I am a little late."

She sat up.

"A little late! It is nearly two o'clock."

"Anyway, you won't believe me if I told you the truth, so why do you want me to waste my breath?"

"Oh well." She lies down again and turns her face to the wall. He stands up but does not walk away. He looks down at her. So she remembers every night: they have agreed, after many arguments, that she should sleep like this. During her first pregnancy, he kept saying after the third month or so that the sight of her tummy the last thing before he slept always gave him nightmares. Now he regrets all this. The bed creaks as he throws himself down by her.

"James."

"Yes."

"There is something much more serious."

"You have heard about my newest affair?"

"Yes, but that is not what I am referring to."

"Jesus, is it possible that there is anything more important than that?"

And as they laugh they know that something has happened. One of those things which, with luck, will keep them together for some time to come.

"He teases me on top of everything."

"What else can one do to you but tease when you are in this state?"

"James! How profane!"

"It is your dirty mind which gave my statement its shocking meaning."

"Okay! But what shall I do?"

"About what?"

"Mercy. Listen, she is having an affair with Mensar-Arthur."

"Wonderful."

She sits up and he sits up.

"James, we must do something about it. It is very serious."

"Is that why you were crying?"

"Of course."

"Why shouldn't she?"

"But it is wrong. And she is ruining herself."

"Since every other girl she knows has ruined herself prosperously, why shouldn't she? Just forget for once that you are a teacher. Or at least, remember she is not your pupil."

"I don't like your answers."

"What would you like me to say? Every morning her friends who don't earn any more than she does wear new dresses, shoes, wigs and what-have-you to work. What would you have her do?"

"The fact that other girls do it does not mean that Mercy should do it too."

"You are being very silly. If I were Mercy, I am sure that's exactly what I would do. And you know I mean it too."

James is cruel. He is terrible and mean. Connie breaks into fresh tears and James comforts her. There is one point he must drive home though.

"In fact, encourage her. He may be able to intercede with the Ministry for you so that after the baby is born they will not transfer you from here for some time."

"James, you want me to use my sister!"

"She is using herself, remember."

"James, you are wicked."

"And maybe he would even agree to get us a new car from abroad. I shall pay for everything. That would be better than paying a fortune for that old thing I was thinking of buying. Think of that."

"You will ride in it alone."

"Well . . ."

That was a few months before the *coup*. Mensar-Arthur did go to London for a conference and bought something for all his wives and girl-friends, including Mercy. He even remembered the motor for Connie's machine. When Mercy took it to her she was quite confused. She had wanted this thing for a long time, and it would make everything so much easier, like the clothes for the new baby. And yet one side of her said that accepting it was a betrayal. Of what, she wasn't even sure. She and Mercy could never bring the whole business into the open and discuss it. And there was always James supporting Mercy, to Connie's bewilderment. She took the motor with thanks and sold even her right to dissent. In a short while, Mercy left the house to go and live in the estate house Mensar-Arthur had procured for her. Then, a couple of weeks later, the *coup*. Mercy left her new place before anyone could evict her. James never got his car. Connie's new baby was born. Of the three, the one who greeted the new order with undisguised relief was Connie. She is not really a demonstrative person but it was obvious from her eyes that she was happy. As far as she was concerned the old order as symbolized by Mensar-Arthur was a threat to her sister and therefore to her own peace of mind. With it gone, things could return to normal. Mercy would move back to the house, perhaps start to date someone more—ordinary let's say. Eventually, she would get married and then the nightmare of those past weeks would be forgotten. God being so good, he brought the *coup* early before the news of the affair could spread and brand her sister. . . .

The arrival of the new baby has magically waved away the difficulties between James and Connie. He is that kind of man, and she that kind of woman. Mercy has not been seen for many days. Connie is beginning to get worried. . . .

James heard the baby yelling—a familiar noise, by now—the moment he opened the front gate. He ran in, clutching to his chest the few things he had bought on his way home.

"We are in here."

"I certainly could hear you. If there is anything people of this country have, it is a big mouth."

"Don't I agree? But on the whole, we are well. He is eating normally and everything. You?"

"Nothing new. Same routine. More stories about the overthrown politicians."

"What do you mean, nothing new? Look at the excellent job the soldiers have done, cleaning up the country of all that dirt. I feel free already and I am dying to get out and enjoy it."

James laughed mirthlessly.

"All I know is that Mensar-Arthur is in jail. No use. And I am not getting my car. Rough deal."

"I never took you seriously on that car business."

"Honestly, if this were in the ancient days, I could brand you a witch. You don't want me, your husband, to prosper?"

"Not out of my sister's ruin."

"Ruin, ruin, ruin! Christ! See Connie, the funny thing is that I am sure you are the only person who thought it was a disaster to have a sister who was the girl-friend of a big man."

"Okay; now all is over, and don't let's quarrel."

"I bet the *coup* could have succeeded on your prayers alone."

And Connie wondered why he said that with so much bitterness. She wondered if . . .

"Has Mercy been here?"

"Not yet, later, maybe. Mm. I had hoped she would move back here and start all over again."

"I am not surprised she hasn't. In fact, if I were her, I wouldn't come back here either. Not to your nagging, no thank you, big sister."

And as the argument progressed, as always, each was forced into a more aggressive defensive stand.

"Well, just say what pleases you, I am very glad about the soldiers. Mercy is my only sister, brother; everything. I can't sit and see her life going wrong without feeling it. I am grateful to whatever forces there are which put a stop to that. What pains me now is that she should be so vague about where she is living at the moment. She makes mention of a girl-friend but I am not sure that I know her."

"If I were you, I would stop worrying because it seems Mercy can look after herself quite well."

"Hmm," was all she tried to say.

Who heard something like the sound of a car pulling into the drive? Ah, but the footsteps were unmistakably Mercy's. Are those shoes the old pair which were new a couple of months ago? Or are they the newest pair? And here she is herself, the pretty one. A gay Mercy.

"Hello, hello, my clan!" and she makes a lot of her nephew.

"Dow-dah-dee-day! And how is my dear young man today? My lord, grow up fast and come to take care of Auntie Mercy."

Both Connie and James cannot take their eyes off her. Connie says, "He says to Auntie Mercy he is fine."

Still they watch her, horrified, fascinated and wondering what it's all about. Because they both know it is about something.

"Listen people, I brought a friend to meet you. A man."

"Where is he?" from James.

"Bring him in," from Connie.

"You know, Sissie, you are a new mother. I thought I'd come and ask you if it's all right."

"Of course," say James and Connie, and for some reason they are both very nervous.

"He is Captain Ashley."

"Which one?"

"How many do you know?"

James still thinks it is impossible. "Eh . . . do you mean the officer who has been appointed the . . . the . . ."

"Yes."

"Wasn't there a picture in *The Crystal* over the week-end about his daughter's wedding? And another one of him with his wife and children and grandchildren?"

"Yes."

"And he is heading a commission to investigate something or other?"

"Yes."

Connie just sits there with her mouth open that wide. . . .

[1970]

Questions

1. Discuss "Two Sisters" in light of Ama Ata Aidoo's statement about Armah's *The Beautyful Ones Are Not Yet Born.*
2. What is Aidoo's picture of contemporary Ghana in this story? What does Aidoo admire in her culture? What does she criticize?
3. Is one sister's situation better than the other's?

Akutagawa Ryūnosuke
(1892–1927)
Japan

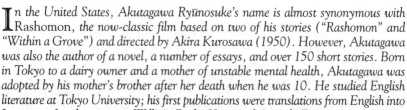

I n the United States, Akutagawa Ryūnosuke's name is almost synonymous with Rashomon, the now-classic film based on two of his stories ("Rashomon" and "Within a Grove") and directed by Akira Kurosawa (1950). However, Akutagawa was also the author of a novel, a number of essays, and over 150 short stories. Born in Tokyo to a dairy owner and a mother of unstable mental health, Akutagawa was adopted by his mother's brother after her death when he was 10. He studied English literature at Tokyo University; his first publications were translations from English into Japanese of such writers as William Butler Yeats and Anatole France.

Akutagawa's early fiction drew uniquely on elements of both Eastern and Western literary forms to produce a distinctly modern form of Japanese literature. Many of his early stories are interesting variations of traditional Japanese legends and tales; his later fiction is more autobiographical and ruminative. While he wrote fiction, Akutagawa also was a practicing journalist and foreign correspondent. During his assignment to China in the 1920s, his physical and mental health deteriorated and exacerbated his life-long obsession that he had inherited his mother's madness. He took his own life at the age of 35.

As Japanese scholar and translator James O'Brien observes of the story "Within a Grove," each character's testimony, rather than clarifying what actually happened, "further confuses the issue. In the end truth itself seems the principal victim. . . ."

WITHIN A GROVE

The Tale of the Woodcutter to the Magistrate

Yes, your honor, I'm the one who found the body. I was heading toward the far slope to cut cedar, just as I do every morning. He was in a grove beneath the mountain. Where exactly? Just a few furlongs in from the Yamashina Post Road.[1] It's an abandoned grove, only bamboo and some spindly cedars.

He was lying on his back in a silk hunting cloak and pleated cap. A blade had pierced his breast, and the bamboo leaves near his body were stained red. No, the blood had stopped flowing. A horsefly clung to the dried wound even as I approached.

---

[1]*Yamashina Post Road*   Yamashina occupied the southern part of Higashiyama, the "Eastern Mountain" area, of Heian-kyō. The Yamashina Post Road ran all the way to Azuma no Kuni, the eastern region of Honshū where Tokyo is now located. Posting stations were situated along the route. (Trans.)

A sword or anything? Not that I could see. There was a rope near one of the cedars, as well as a comb. But that's all. The grass and bamboo leaves around the corpse were trampled, so there must have been a struggle. A horse! A horse couldn't get in there. There's a trail, but it's beyond the next grove.

The Tale of the Itinerant Priest to the Magistrate

It must have been the dead man. I saw him yesterday about noon. I was going toward Yamashina from the barrier at Mount Ōsaka[2] when he passed in the opposite direction. The woman with him was on horseback, with a veil over her face. She wore a lilac cloak of some kind, but that's all I can say about her. The horse was a chestnut with a clipped mane. How large? I'm only a priest, I can hardly estimate the size of a horse. The man had . . . No, a sword. And a bow and arrows. I clearly remember a lacquered quiver with more than twenty arrows. They were primed, too.

I never imagined he would meet such a fate. Life in its brevity is well likened to a dewdrop. Or a flash of lightning even. I pity him more than I can say.

The Tale of the Arresting Officer to the Magistrate

The prisoner? There's no question about it. He's Tajōmaru, the notorious thief. He had fallen from his horse on the stone bridge at Awataguchi.[3] I arrested him as he lay there groaning. When was that? Yesterday about eight, as the night watch was getting underway. I recognized the indigo jacket he wore the day he eluded me. His sword was the same as then, too. It had a guarded hilt. As you can see, this time he carried a bow and arrows. They were the dead man's? There's no doubt about it, then. Tajōmaru killed him. And he took this leather-bound bow, lacquered quiver, and hawk-feather arrows, all seventeen of them. Yes, a chestnut with a clipped mane. Fate must have thrown him off. I found the horse just this side of the bridge, nibbling the roadside grass with its halter trailing along the ground.

Women were especially tempting to Tajōmaru—that's what all the thieves in the capital say. Perhaps you remember the woman and her attendant who went to the Toribe Temple[4] in the mountains last year? Apparently they were going to worship Binzura.[5] People say it was Tajōmaru who killed them. And if he killed the man who owned these weapons, imagine what he might do to the woman on the chestnut horse? Where could he have taken her? Would your honor look into this?

---

[2]*Mount Ōsaka*   A checkpoint in the mountain pass east of Heian-kyō. With its first syllable virtually a homonym for the verb, "to meet," the Barrier occasioned numerous tanka poems that played on the name. (Trans.)

[3]*Awataguchi*   Another district in the Higashiyama area of Heian-kyō. (Trans.)

[4]*Toribe Temple*   Located in Higashiyama near the crematorium for Heian-kyō. (Trans.)

[5]*Binzura*   A Buddhist disciple who remained in the world to save people rather than enter into Nirvana. In Japan, the sick would rub an image of Binzura in hopes of a cure. (Trans.)

The Tale of an Old Woman to the Magistrate

Yes, your honor, he was my daughter's husband. His name was Kanazawa no Takehiro, and he was twenty-six years old. He was a samurai,[6] but not from the capital. He was so gentle, no one should have been angry with him.

My daughter? Her name is Masago and she's nineteen. She's lively for a woman, but Takehiro was the only man in her entire life. She has a small oval face and dark complexion. There's a mole near the tip of her left eye, too.

Takehiro left yesterday for Wakasa,[7] along with my daughter. I don't know the specific reason, but his death must involve some sort of retribution. I'm resigned to that, yet I'm terribly worried about my daughter. Search the grasses and the brush even, but please find her. I'm an old woman, and that's my one wish. Come what may, I despise this Tajōmaru or whatever he's called. My son-in-law . . . and my daughter, too. . . . (She weeps, and her words trail off.)

Tajōmaru's Confession

I killed him, but not the woman. I don't know where she went, either. Look, don't be so impatient. I can't tell you what I don't know, regardless of how often you ask me. I'm not a coward. I won't conceal anything now.

It was slightly past noon yesterday when I encountered them. The breeze lifted the woman's veil. I saw her face, but only for a moment. Perhaps that's why she seemed a female Bodhisattva.[8] I wanted to have her, even if it meant killing the man.

Why kill him? Well, killing's not as difficult as you might think. And how else could I possess her? The sword at my waist would do the job. People like you use wealth and power rather than a sword. But you kill just the same. And you pretend to be doing good. Your victims don't shed their blood; they survive in fine health. You destroy them, anyway. Whose crime is worse, yours or mine? (He laughs sardonically.)

If only I could have her without killing him. . . . I would try my best, but I must find the right place. I decided to lure them from the Yamashina Post Road into the mountains.

It wasn't difficult. I spoke of an old mound on the farther slope. I had dug up many swords and mirrors there and hidden them away. I told him how I'd sell the whole lot at a bargain, if the right person came along. He listened more and more intently. And finally . . . Isn't greed a horrible thing? Soon they had turned their horse from the Yamashina Post Road and were heading into the mountains with me.

When we reached the grove, I said the treasure was buried within and urged them to enter. Driven by greed, the man could hardly object. The woman, however, said she would wait and remained on the horse. Her reluctance was not surprising, as the grove seemed quite dense. I had planned to separate them, anyway. Leaving the woman alone, the man and I went in.

---

[6]*samurai* A member of the military class in feudal Japan.
[7]*Wakasa* The western part of present-day Fukui Prefecture, facing the Sea of Japan. (Trans.)
[8]*Bodhisattva* A Bodhisattva is a Buddhist saint that remains in the world after attaining enlightenment in order to help others reach the same state. Strictly speaking, a Bodhisattva is of neither sex, save in popular religious belief. (Trans.)

For a while there was nothing but bamboo. After about fifty yards or so a cedar opening appeared, the perfect place to carry out my scheme. Even as we pushed through the thicket, I pointed to a row of spindly cedars among the scattered bamboo. Over there, I said, and immediately he rushed ahead. He was waiting when I came up from behind and pinned him to the ground. A sword-bearing samurai is always formidable, and he was no exception. I attacked too quickly for him, however. In a moment he was tied to the base of a cedar. The rope? Any thief knows the value of a rope. I might have to scale a wall at any moment, so I keep one on me. I stuffed the man's mouth with fallen bamboo leaves, so he couldn't cry out. After that he didn't give me any trouble.

Then I went back to the woman. I told her the man had suddenly become ill and she must attend him. Needless to say, she readily gave in. She removed her bonnet and allowed me to lead her into the grove by the hand. But when we reached the spot and she saw him tied to the cedar, she pulled a dagger from her cloak before I knew what was happening. Never have I met a woman so violent. Had I been careless, she would have stabbed me in the side. She slashed at me in desperation. If I had not dodged, she might have killed me. But I'm Tajōmaru. Somehow I knocked her dagger away without even drawing my sword. No matter how spirited, the woman had no chance without her weapon. I would have her in the end, without killing the man either.

Without killing him . . . I would manage without killing him. The woman lay weeping as I prepared to leave. Suddenly she seized my arm like one gone mad and uttered a breathless plea. One of us must be killed, either the husband or me. That's what I heard amid her weeping. She herself would choose death rather than have two men know of her shame. She would live with the one who survived.

I'll seem crueler here than you people. But none of you could see her face, especially her eyes. When I saw those flashing eyes, I wanted her for my wife. I wanted her, even if it meant being struck down by lightning. All I thought of was having her for good. Not out of lust, as you people might think. If that were all, I would have kicked her aside and left. And his blood would not have stained my sword. Ah, the expression on her face within that dim grove. I resolved to kill him before leaving.

I couldn't just murder him on the spot. So I undid the rope and ordered him to duel. (The rope lay forgotten by the cedar.) Turning white with anger, the man drew his great sword. Then he rushed me without a word. I needn't say how the duel turned out. On the twenty-third pass, my sword finally pierced his breast. The twenty-third—don't forget. I'm still astonished. No other man has lasted even twenty strokes. (He smiles contentedly.)

Once he fell, I put down my bloody sword to speak. I was going to tell her. . . . Imagine! She was gone. I searched among the cedar clumps, anxious to find out which way she had fled. But her footprint did not appear among the bamboo leaves. I listened carefully, but could hear nothing except the groans of a dying man.

Perhaps when the duel began, she had fled the grove in search of help. My own life might be at stake. Taking the man's sword as well as his bow and arrows, I immediately left the way I had come. The woman's horse was still outside, nibbling at the grass. To speak of what occurred after that would merely waste time. I did throw the sword away before entering the capital. That's all I have to confess. Just give me the worst sentence. I'm going to be hanged from an India tree anyway.

The Confession of a Woman Who Had Come to Kiyomizu Temple[9]

After he had attacked me, the man in the indigo jacket gazed at my husband and laughed contemptuously. My husband twisted this way and that, but the rope about his body merely tightened further. I would have rushed to his side, but the man kicked me to the ground. My husband's eyes flared. I cannot describe his look; the memory alone makes me shudder. He could not move his lips, but his look told all. There was cold contempt in it, more than anger and regret. That look hurt me more than getting kicked. I let out a cry, then fainted.

When I finally revived, the man in the indigo jacket had left. Only my husband remained, still bound to the cedar. Eventually I looked up from the bamboo leaves and gazed at him. He had not changed, except for the loathing that had crept into his expression of cold contempt. I can hardly name what I felt then. . . . Was it shame . . . regret . . . indignation . . . ? I struggled to my feet and went over to him.

"Husband, I am no longer yours. I've decided to die and be done with it. All I ask is that we die together. You have witnessed my shame and I cannot leave you behind."

He looked so disgusted I could hardly speak. Holding back my anguish, I looked for his sword. The thief had apparently taken it, along with the bow and arrows. Fortunately the dagger was still there, right at my feet. I picked it up.

"Give me your life," I exclaimed. "I shall attend you shortly."

When he heard these words, my husband finally moved his lips. I could hear no sound, as his mouth was crammed with leaves. All the same, I sensed his terrible message: "Go on, kill me!" Half in a dream, I drove the blade through his blue jacket and into his breast.

I must have fainted again. When I finally awoke, my husband had ceased breathing. He remained tied to the tree, his face lit beneath the bamboo and cedar by a ray of fading sunlight. Holding back my tears, I undid the rope from his corpse. And then? What happened next I don't have the strength to tell. Regardless of how I tried, I could not take my life. I stabbed at my throat and threw myself into a pond beneath the mountain. I tried everything, but could not die. I have survived, but I cannot take pride in that. Even the merciful Kannon probably abandons cowards like me. But what can I do? A thief has ravished me, and I have killed my husband. I really . . . I . . . (Suddenly she breaks down sobbing.)

The Tale of the Spirit as Told through a Medium

Once he had ravished my wife, the thief sat there consoling her. I remained tied to the cedar, unable to speak. All I could do was to keep winking at her, to warn against his lies. My wife sat disconsolate among the fallen leaves, gazing at her own knees. And yet, she seemed to hear him. I shuddered with jealousy as the thief adroitly talked of one thing and another. He said that her body was defiled and she could not rejoin her husband. Didn't she wish to be his instead? He had been violent only out of love for her. The thief boldly wooed her with such talk.

---

[9]*Kiyomizu Temple* A temple of the Hossō and Shin sects of Buddhism located in the Higashiyama foothills of Heian-kyō. Kannon, the Buddhist deity of mercy, is the principal object of veneration at the temple. (Trans.)

My wife seemed enchanted by his words. Never had she appeared so lovely. And what reply did she give the thief, even as I looked on? Take me with you, she pleaded, it doesn't matter where. Wandering in this limbo, I seethe with anger each time I remember.

If her crime had ended there, I wouldn't suffer so much. But that wasn't all. Won over by the thief, my wife was being led away by the hand when she suddenly turned pale and pointed at me. "So long as he lives, I cannot be yours"—that's what she said. Then she shrieked over and over: "Kill him!" Her words are like a howling storm even now. They threaten to cast me headlong into the darkness. The thief himself turned pale. He stared as my wife clung to his arm and repeated her shrill request. Then, so quickly I could not observe it, he kicked her down on the bamboo leaves. Folding his arms over his chest, he turned and asked, "What should I do with her? Shall I kill her? Or spare her? Just nod in reply. Kill her . . . ?"

For these words alone I wished to forgive the thief his crime. (Long silence again.)

As I hesitated, my wife cried out and rushed into the bamboo thicket. The thief sprang at her, but failed even to catch her sleeve. I watched as if in a dream.

After my wife had fled, the thief picked up my sword, along with my bow and arrows. He made a single cut in the rope that bound me all around. I remember him mumbling to himself as he disappeared into the thicket, "I'll be next. . . ."

Then quiet descended upon everything, except for the faint sound of weeping. I listened closely as I unwound the rope. Finally I realized this must be my own weeping.

At last I rose wearily from the foot of the cedar. Before me glistened the dagger which my wife had dropped. I picked it up and drove the blade into my breast. A blood lump rose to my mouth, but I did not feel any pain. My breast merely turned cold, and the surroundings fell even more silent. How quiet it seemed. Above the mountain grove not a single bird sang. The solitary sun merely floated beyond the tips of cedar and bamboo. Gradually the sun grew dim. And the cedar and bamboo faded. I lay wrapped in deep silence.

Then someone stole up close. I tried to see, but dusk had already fallen. A hand . . . someone's invisible hand gently removed the blade from my breast. In that moment the blood surged again into my mouth. Thereupon I subsided forever into this dark limbo. . . .

[1921]
Translated by
JAMES O'BRIEN

Questions

1. How does the multiple narrative structure contribute to the meaning of the story? Would a segment told from an omniscient perspective giving the "true" version of events enhance or detract from the effect of the conflicting testimonies?

2. Why does Tajōmaru, the robber, claim that he killed the husband? Why does the wife claim that she killed her husband? Why does the husband claim that he killed himself? Which testimony do you believe?

3. Does the presence of a supernatural element—the ghost of the dead husband testifying through a medium—detract from the otherwise realistic qualities of the story?

4. What is the "moral" of the story? What is its theme? How is the Japanese conception of honor central to the story?

Woody Allen

(b. 1935)
United States

W oody Allen is perhaps best known for the nearly 30 films he has written, directed, produced, and frequently starred in since his first screenplay, What's New, Pussycat? in 1964. As his scripts from Annie Hall to Zelig reveal, he is a master of ironic and romantic humor; he makes gentle fun of people's emotional longings and anxieties as he punctures their illusions about themselves. One biographer calls him the "auteur of angst." In addition to filmscripts, he has written and published three volumes of short fiction and sketches: Getting Even (1971), Without Feathers (1975), and Side Effects (1980), all of which demonstrate his versatile wit and cut-to-the-bone comic style. He is also a serious and highly regarded jazz musician who missed attending the Academy Awards ceremony during which his film Annie Hall was honored in order to play clarinet at his regular gig in Greenwich Village.

Allen was born in Brooklyn, New York, as Allen Stewart Konigsberg, the son of a waiter and jewelry engraver. His early life does not immediately reveal the direction his talent was to take. He dropped out of college twice (New York University and the City College of New York). Nonetheless, he eventually found his true talent in exposing, through his writing for film and in short fiction, the foibles and anxieties that we recognize in ourselves and thus cannot help but laugh at in his wonderfully self-deprecating characters. Expressing his aim for his life's work with characteristic humor, he said that he hoped to "forge in the smithy of my soul the uncreated conscience of my race. Then to see if they can be turned out in plastic."

"The Kugelmass Episode," originally published in The New Yorker in 1977, received an O. Henry Award as one of the best stories published that year.

THE KUGELMASS EPISODE

Kugelmass, a professor of humanities at City College, was unhappily married for the second time. Daphne Kugelmass was an oaf. He also had two dull sons by his first wife, Flo, and was up to his neck in alimony and child support.

"Did I know it would turn out so badly?" Kugelmass whined to his analyst one day. "Daphne had promised. Who suspected she'd let herself go and swell up like a beach ball? Plus she had a few bucks, which is not in itself a healthy reason to marry a person, but it doesn't hurt, with the kind of operating nut I have. You see my point?"

Kugelmass was bald and as hairy as a bear, but he had soul.

"I need to meet a new woman," he went on. "I need to have an affair. I may not look the part, but I'm a man who needs romance. I need softness, I need flirtation. I'm not getting younger, so before it's too late I want to make love in Venice, trade quips at "21,"[1] and exchange coy glances over red wine and candlelight. You see what I'm saying?"

Dr. Mandel shifted in his chair and said, "An affair will solve nothing. You're so unrealistic. Your problems run much deeper."

"And also this affair must be discreet," Kugelmass continued. "I can't afford a second divorce. Daphne would really sock it to me."

"Mr. Kugelmass—"

"But it can't be anyone at City College, because Daphne also works there. Not that anyone on the faculty at C.C.N.Y. is any great shakes, but some of those coeds . . ."

"Mr. Kugelmass—"

"Help me. I had a dream last night. I was skipping through a meadow holding a picnic basket and the basket was marked "Options." And then I saw there was a hole in the basket."

"Mr. Kugelmass, the worst thing you could do is act out. You must simply express your feelings here, and together we'll analyze them. You have been in treatment long enough to know there is no overnight cure. After all, I'm an analyst, not a magician."

"Then perhaps what I need is a magician," Kugelmass said, rising from his chair. And with that he terminated his therapy.

A couple of weeks later, while Kugelmass and Daphne were moping around in their apartment one night like two pieces of old furniture, the phone rang.

"I'll get it," Kugelmass said. "Hello."

"Kugelmass?" a voice said. "Kugelmass, this is Persky."

"Who?"

"Persky. Or should I say The Great Persky?"

"Pardon me?"

"I hear you're looking all over town for a magician to bring a little exotica into your life? Yes or no?"

"Sh-h-h," Kugelmass whispered. "Don't hang up. Where are you calling from, Persky?"

Early the following afternoon, Kugelmass climbed three flights of stairs in a broken-down apartment house in the Bushwick section of Brooklyn. Peering through the darkness of the hall, he found the door he was looking for and pressed the bell. I'm going to regret this, he thought to himself.

Seconds later, he was greeted by a short, thin, waxy-looking man.

"*You're* Persky the Great?" Kugelmass said.

"The Great Persky. You want a tea?"

"No, I want romance. I want music. I want love and beauty."

"But not tea, eh? Amazing. O.K., sit down."

Persky went to the back room, and Kugelmass heard the sounds of boxes and furniture being moved around. Persky reappeared, pushing before him a large object on squeaky roller-skate wheels. He removed some old silk handkerchiefs that were lying on its top and blew away a bit of dust. It was a cheap-looking Chinese cabinet, badly lacquered.

"Persky," Kugelmass said, "what's your scam?"

"Pay attention," Persky said. "This is some beautiful effect. I developed it for a Knights of Pythias date last year, but the booking fell through. Get into the cabinet."

"Why, so you can stick it full of swords or something?"

"You see any swords?"

---

[1]"*21*"   Famous New York City restaurant.

Kugelmass made a face and, grunting, climbed into the cabinet. He couldn't help noticing a couple of ugly rhinestones glued onto the raw plywood just in front of his face. "If this is a joke," he said.

"Some joke. Now, here's the point. If I throw any novel into this cabinet with you, shut the doors, and tap it three times, you will find yourself projected into that book."

Kugelmass made a grimace of disbelief.

"It's the emess,"[2] Persky said. "My hand to God. Not just a novel, either. A short story, a play, a poem. You can meet any of the women created by the world's best writers. Whoever you dreamed of. You could carry on all you like with a real winner. Then when you've had enough you give a yell, and I'll see you're back here in a split second."

"Persky, are you some kind of outpatient?"

"I'm telling you it's on the level," Persky said.

Kugelmass remained skeptical. "What are you telling me—that this cheesy homemade box can take me on a ride like you're describing?"

"For a double sawbuck."

Kugelmass reached for his wallet. "I'll believe this when I see it," he said.

Persky tucked the bills in his pants pocket and turned toward his bookcase. "So who do you want to meet? Sister Carrie? Hester Prynne? Ophelia? Maybe someone by Saul Bellow? Hey, what about Temple Drake?[3] Although for a man your age she'd be a workout."

"French, I want to have an affair with a French lover."

"Nana?"

"I don't want to have to pay for it."

"What about Natasha in 'War and Peace'?"

"I said French. I know! What about Emma Bovary?[4] That sounds to me perfect."

"You got it, Kugelmass. Give me a holler when you've had enough." Persky tossed in a paperback copy of Flaubert's novel.

"You sure this is safe?" Kugelmass asked as Persky began shutting the cabinet doors.

"Safe. Is anything safe in this crazy world?" Persky rapped three times on the cabinet and then flung open the doors.

Kugelmass was gone. At the same moment, he appeared in the bedroom of Charles and Emma Bovary's house at Yonville. Before him was a beautiful woman standing alone with her back turned to him as she folded some linen. I can't believe this, thought Kugelmass, staring at the doctor's ravishing wife. This is uncanny. I'm here. It's her.

Emma turned in surprise. "Goodness, you startled me," she said. "Who are you?" She spoke in the same fine English translation as the paperback.

It's simply devastating, he thought. Then, realizing that it was he whom she had addressed, he said, "Excuse me, I'm Sidney Kugelmass. I'm from City College. A professor of humanities. C.C.N.Y.? Uptown. I—oh, boy!"

---

[2]*emess* The truth.

[3]The women named in this conversation are famous female protagonists in literature: Carrie Meeber, *Sister Carrie* (1900) by Theodore Dreiser; Hester Prynne, *The Scarlet Letter* (1850) by Nathaniel Hawthorne; Ophelia, *Hamlet* (c. 1600) by William Shakespeare; Temple Drake, *Sanctuary* (1931) by William Faulkner.

[4]Nana, the female protagonist of *Nana* (1880), a novel by Emile Zola; Natasha, central female in *War and Peace* (1863–1871) by Leo Tolstoy. Emma Bovary is the protagonist of Gustave Flaubert's novel *Madame Bovary* (1865).

Emma Bovary smiled flirtatiously and said, "Would you like a drink? A glass of wine, perhaps?"

She is beautiful, Kugelmass thought. What a contrast with the troglodyte who shared his bed! He felt a sudden impulse to take this vision into his arms and tell her she was the kind of woman he had dreamed of all his life.

"Yes, some wine," he said hoarsely. "White. No, red. No, white. Make it white."

"Charles is out for the day," Emma said, her voice full of playful implication.

After the wine, they went for a stroll in the lovely French countryside. "I've always dreamed that some mysterious stranger would appear and rescue me from the monotony of this crass rural existence," Emma said, clasping his hand. They passed a small church. "I love what you have on," she murmured. "I've never seen anything like it around here. It's so . . . so modern."

"It's called a leisure suit," he said romantically. "It was marked down." Suddenly he kissed her. For the next hour they reclined under a tree and whispered together and told each other deeply meaningful things with their eyes. Then Kugelmass sat up. He had just remembered he had to meet Daphne at Bloomingdale's. "I must go," he told her. "But don't worry. I'll be back."

"I hope so," Emma said.

He embraced her passionately, and the two walked back to the house. He held Emma's face cupped in his palms, kissed her again, and yelled, "O.K., Persky! I got to be at Bloomingdale's by three-thirty."

There was an audible pop, and Kugelmass was back in Brooklyn.

"So? Did I lie?" Persky asked triumphantly.

"Look, Persky, I'm right now late to meet the ball and chain at Lexington Avenue, but when can I go again? Tomorrow?"

"My pleasure. Just bring a twenty. And don't mention this to anybody."

"Yeah. I'm going to call Rupert Murdoch."[5]

Kugelmass hailed a cab and sped off to the city. His heart danced on point. I am in love, he thought, I am the possessor of a wonderful secret. What he didn't realize was that at this very moment students in various classrooms across the country were saying to their teachers, "Who is this character on page 100? A bald Jew is kissing Madame Bovary?" A teacher in Sioux Falls, South Dakota, sighed and thought, Jesus, these kids, with their pot and acid. What goes through their minds!

Daphne Kugelmass was in the bathroom-accessories department at Bloomingdale's when Kugelmass arrived breathlessly. "Where've you been?" she snapped. "It's four-thirty."

"I got held up in traffic," Kugelmass said.

Kugelmass visited Persky the next day, and in a few minutes was again passed magically to Yonville. Emma couldn't hide her excitement at seeing him. The two spent hours together, laughing and talking about their different backgrounds. Before Kugelmass left, they made love. "My God, I'm doing it with Madame Bovary!" Kugelmass whispered to himself. "Me, who failed freshman English."

As the months passed, Kugelmass saw Persky many times and developed a close and passionate relationship with Emma Bovary. "Make sure and always get me into the book before page 120," Kugelmass said to the magician one day. "I always have to meet her before she hooks up with this Rodolphe character."

"Why?" Persky asked. "You can't beat his time?"

---

[5]*Rupert Murdoch*   Australian newspaper mogul who owns several American newspapers.

"Beat his time. He's landed gentry. Those guys have nothing better to do than flirt and ride horses. To me, he's one of those faces you see in the pages of *Women's Wear Daily.* With the Helmut Berger hairdo. But to her he's hot stuff."

"And her husband suspects nothing?"

"He's out of his depth. He's a lack-lustre little paramedic who's thrown in his lot with a jitterbug. He's ready to go to sleep by ten, and she's putting on her dancing shoes. Oh, well. . . . See you later."

And once again Kugelmass entered the cabinet and passed instantly to the Bovary estate at Yonville. "How you doing, cupcake?" he said to Emma.

"Oh, Kugelmass," Emma sighed. "What I have to put up with. Last night at dinner, Mr. Personality dropped off to sleep in the middle of the dessert course. I'm pouring my heart out about Maxim's[6] and the ballet, and out of the blue I hear snoring."

"It's O.K., darling, I'm here now," Kugelmass said, embracing her. I've earned this, he thought, smelling Emma's French perfume and burying his nose in her hair. I've suffered enough. I've paid enough analysts. I've searched till I'm weary. She's young and nubile, and I'm here a few pages after Léon and just before Rodolphe. By showing up during the correct chapters, I've got the situation knocked.

Emma, to be sure, was just as happy as Kugelmass. She had been starved for excitement, and his tales of Broadway night life, of fast cars and Hollywood and TV stars, enthralled the young French beauty.

"Tell me again about O. J. Simpson,"[7] she implored that evening, as she and Kugelmass strolled past Abbé Bournisien's church.

"What can I say? The man is great. He sets all kinds of rushing records. Such moves. They can't touch him."

"And the Academy Awards?" Emma said wistfully. "I'd give anything to win one."

"First you've got to be nominated."

"I know. You explained it. But I'm convinced I can act. Of course, I'd want to take a class or two. With Strasberg maybe. Then, if I had the right agent—"

"We'll see, we'll see. I'll speak to Persky."

That night, safely returned to Persky's flat, Kugelmass brought up the idea of having Emma visit him in the big city.

"Let me think about it," Persky said. "Maybe I could work it. Stranger things have happened." Of course, neither of them could think of one.

"Where the hell do you go all the time?" Daphne Kugelmass barked at her husband as he returned home late that evening. "You got a chippie stashed somewhere?"

"Yeah, sure, I'm just the type," Kugelmass said wearily. "I was with Leonard Popkin. We were discussing Socialist agriculture in Poland. You know Popkin. He's a freak on the subject."

"Well, you've been very odd lately," Daphne said. "Distant. Just don't forget about my father's birthday. On Saturday?"

"Oh, sure, sure," Kugelmass said, heading for the bathroom.

"My whole family will be there. We can see the twins. And Cousin Hamish. You should be more polite to Cousin Hamish—he likes you."

"Right, the twins," Kugelmass said, closing the bathroom door and shutting out the sound of his wife's voice. He leaned against it and took a deep breath. In a few hours,

---

[6]*Maxim's* Famous restaurant in Paris.

[7]*O. J. Simpson* An American professional football player when the story was published; more recently known as the key suspect—though legally acquitted—in his ex-wife's murder.

he told himself, he would be back in Yonville again, back with his beloved. And this time, if all went well, he would bring Emma back with him.

At three-fifteen the following afternoon, Persky worked his wizardry again. Kugelmass appeared before Emma, smiling and eager. The two spent a few hours at Yonville with Binet and then remounted the Bovary carriage. Following Persky's instructions, they held each other tightly, closed their eyes, and counted to ten. When they opened them, the carriage was just drawing up at the side door of the Plaza Hotel, where Kugelmass had optimistically reserved a suite earlier in the day.

"I love it! It's everything I dreamed it would be," Emma said as she whirled joyously around the bedroom, surveying the city from their window. "There's F. A. O. Schwartz.[8] And there's Central Park, and the Sherry is which one? Oh, there—I see. It's too divine."

On the bed there were boxes from Halston and Saint Laurent. Emma unwrapped a package and held up a pair of black velvet pants against her perfect body.

"The slacks suit is by Ralph Lauren," Kugelmass said. "You'll look like a million bucks in it. Come on, sugar, give us a kiss."

"I've never been so happy!" Emma squealed as she stood before the mirror. "Let's go out on the town. I want to see *Chorus Line* and the Guggenheim and this Jack Nicholson character you always talk about. Are any of his flicks showing?"

"I cannot get my mind around this," a Stanford professor said. "First a strange character named Kugelmass, and now she's gone from the book. Well, I guess the mark of a classic is that you can reread it a thousand times and always find something new."

The lovers passed a blissful weekend. Kugelmass had told Daphne he would be away at a symposium in Boston, and would return Monday. Savoring each moment, he and Emma went to the movies, had dinner in Chinatown, passed two hours at a discothèque, and went to bed with a TV movie. They slept till noon on Sunday, visited SoHo, and ogled celebrities at Elaine's. They had caviar and champagne in their suite on Sunday night and talked until dawn. That morning, in the cab taking them to Persky's apartment, Kugelmass thought, It was hectic, but worth it. I can't bring her here too often, but now and then it will be a charming contrast with Yonville.

At Persky's, Emma climbed into the cabinet, arranged her new boxes of clothes neatly around her, and kissed Kugelmass fondly. "My place next time," she said with a wink. Persky rapped three times on the cabinet. Nothing happened.

"Hmm," Persky said, scratching his head. He rapped again, but still no magic. "Something must be wrong," he mumbled.

"Persky, you're joking!" Kugelmass cried. "How can it not work?"

"Relax, relax. Are you still in the box, Emma?"

"Yes."

Persky rapped again—harder this time.

"I'm still here, Persky."

"I know, darling. Sit tight."

"Persky, we *have* to get her back," Kugelmass whispered. "I'm a married man, and I have a class in three hours. I'm not prepared for anything more than a cautious affair at this point."

"I can't understand it," Persky muttered. "It's such a reliable little trick."

---

[8]*F. A. O. Schwartz*   Famous New York toy store.

But he could do nothing. "It's going to take a little while," he said to Kugelmass. "I'm going to have to strip it down. I'll call you later."

Kugelmass bundled Emma into a cab and took her back to the Plaza. He barely made it to his class on time. He was on the phone all day, to Persky and to his mistress. The magician told him it might be several days before he got to the bottom of the trouble.

"How was the symposium?" Daphne asked him that night.

"Fine, fine," he said, lighting the filter end of a cigarette.

"What's wrong? You're as tense as a cat."

"Me? Ha, that's a laugh. I'm as calm as a summer night. I'm just going to take a walk." He eased out the door, hailed a cab, and flew to the Plaza.

"This is no good," Emma said. "Charles will miss me."

"Bear with me, sugar," Kugelmass said. He was pale and sweaty. He kissed her again, raced to the elevators, yelled at Persky over a pay phone in the Plaza lobby, and just made it home before midnight.

"According to Popkin, barley prices in Kraków have not been this stable since 1971," he said to Daphne, and smiled wanly as he climbed into bed.

The whole week went by like that. On Friday night, Kugelmass told Daphne there was another symposium he had to catch, this one in Syracuse. He hurried back to the Plaza, but the second weekend there was nothing like the first. "Get me back into the novel or marry me," Emma told Kugelmass. "Meanwhile, I want to get a job or go to class, because watching TV all day is the pits."

"Fine. We can use the money," Kugelmass said. "You consume twice your weight in room service."

"I met an Off Broadway producer in Central Park yesterday, and he said I might be right for a project he's doing," Emma said.

"Who is this clown?" Kugelmass asked.

"He's not a clown. He's sensitive and kind and cute. His name's Jeff Something-or-Other, and he's up for a Tony."

Later that afternoon, Kugelmass showed up at Persky's drunk.

"Relax," Persky told him. "You'll get a coronary."

"Relax. The man says relax. I've got a fictional character stashed in a hotel room, and I think my wife is having me tailed by a private shamus."[9]

"O.K., O.K. We know there's a problem." Persky crawled under the cabinet and started banging on something with a large wrench.

"I'm like a wild animal," Kugelmass went on. "I'm sneaking around town, and Emma and I have had it up to here with each other. Not to mention a hotel tab that reads like the defense budget."

"So what should I do? This is the world of magic," Persky said. "It's all nuance."

"Nuance, my foot. I'm pouring Dom Pérignon and black eggs into this little mouse, plus her wardrobe, plus she's enrolled at the Neighborhood Playhouse and suddenly needs professional photos. Also, Persky, Professor Fivish Kopkind, who teaches Comp Lit and who has always been jealous of me, has identified me as the sporadically appearing character in the Flaubert book. He's threatened to go to Daphne. I see ruin and alimony; jail. For adultery with Madame Bovary, my wife will reduce me to beggary."

---

[9]*shamus* Detective.

"What do you want me to say? I'm working on it night and day. As far as your personal anxiety goes, that I can't help you with. I'm a magician, not an analyst."

By Sunday afternoon, Emma had locked herself in the bathroom and refused to respond to Kugelmass's entreaties. Kugelmass stared out the window at the Wollman Rink and contemplated suicide. Too bad this is a low floor, he thought, or I'd do it right now. Maybe if I ran away to Europe and started life over . . . Maybe I could sell the *International Herald Tribune*, like those young girls used to.

The phone rang. Kugelmass lifted it to his ear mechanically.

"Bring her over," Persky said. "I think I got the bugs out of it."

Kugelmass's heart leaped. "You're serious?" he said. "You got it licked?"

"It was something in the transmission. Go figure."

"Persky, you're a genius. We'll be there in a minute. Less than a minute."

Again the lovers hurried to the magician's apartment, and again Emma Bovary climbed into the cabinet with her boxes. This time there was no kiss. Persky shut the doors, took a deep breath, and tapped the box three times. There was the reassuring popping noise, and when Persky peered inside, the box was empty. Madame Bovary was back in her novel. Kugelmass heaved a great sigh of relief and pumped the magician's hand.

"It's over," he said. "I learned my lesson. I'll never cheat again, I swear it." He pumped Persky's hand again and made a mental note to send him a necktie.

Three weeks later, at the end of a beautiful spring afternoon, Persky answered his doorbell. It was Kugelmass, with a sheepish expression on his face.

"O.K., Kugelmass," the magician said. "Where to this time?"

"It's just this once," Kugelmass said. "The weather is so lovely, and I'm not getting any younger. Listen, you've read *Portnoy's Complaint*? Remember The Monkey?"[10]

"The price is now twenty-five dollars, because the cost of living is up, but I'll start you off with one freebie, due to all the trouble I caused you."

"You're good people," Kugelmass said, combing his few remaining hairs as he climbed into the cabinet again. "This'll work all right?"

"I hope. But I haven't tried it much since all that unpleasantness."

"Sex and romance," Kugelmass said from inside the box. "What we go through for a pretty face."

Persky tossed in a copy of *Portnoy's Complaint* and rapped three times on the box. This time, instead of a popping noise there was a dull explosion, followed by a series of crackling noises and a shower of sparks. Persky leaped back, was seized by a heart attack, and dropped dead. The cabinet burst into flames, and eventually the entire house burned down.

Kugelmass, unaware of this catastrophe, had his own problems. He had not been thrust into *Portnoy's Complaint*, or into any other novel, for that matter. He had been projected into an old textbook, *Remedial Spanish*, and was running for his life over a barren, rocky terrain as the word *tener* ("to have")—a large and hairy irregular verb—raced after him on its spindly legs.

[1977]

---

[10]*The Monkey* A sexually uninhibited woman in Philip Roth's novel, *Portnoy's Complaint* (1969).

Questions

1. What makes this story funny? What particular details provoke laughter?
2. Why does Kugelmass choose a character from Flaubert's *Madame Bovary* as the object of his fantasies? Consider this observation about Emma Bovary as a way of answering the question:

   > [Emma] recalled the heroines of those books that she had read and the lyric legion of these adulterous women began to sing in her memory. . . . She became herself, as it were, an actual part of these lyrical imaginings; at long last as she saw herself among these lovers she had so envied, she fulfilled the love-dream of her youth. (*Madame Bovary*, Part 2, Chapter 9)

   How does Allen juxtapose the events of Flaubert's novel with contemporary elements to achieve humor?
3. What contemporary experiences and attitudes is Allen satirizing?
4. How do you understand the role of Persky?
5. How do you understand the ending of the story? Is Kugelmass's predicament resolved?

Isabel Allende
(b. 1942)
Chile

I sabel Allende was born in Peru into an upper-middle-class Chilean family; her father, a diplomat, and her mother were divorced when she was a child, and she had no further contact with her father. She grew up in the household of her mother's parents, experiencing a rather lonely childhood but one filled with interesting adults. Her grandfather was a complex man, capable of both violence and kindness; her grandmother was deeply interested in the occult. These influential figures later inspired Allende's first novel, The House of the Spirits (1982).

Allende's mother remarried (another diplomat) when Isabel was 15; the family lived in Bolivia, the Middle East, and Europe during Isabel's adolescence. Allende left school and returned to Chile at 16 to become a secretary for a United Nations organization. Her work with journalists led her to become a journalist herself, eventually developing her own television program as well as writing for a radical women's magazine and working on movie newsreels. By then married to an engineer and the mother of a son and a daughter, Allende began to write fiction, including several short stories for children.

"And then in 1973," as Allende phrases it, "the military coup changed everything, and I felt, as many Chileans did, that my life had been cut into pieces, and that I had to start over again." The assassination of Salvador Allende, the president of Chile and Isabel's uncle, made the political upheaval immediate and personal. Allende and her family relocated to Venezuela in 1975. Years later, after her grandparents had died, she began to write The House of the Spirits as a way to capture the memories of her grandparents and especially the important women of her family. The novel developed into a chronicle of several generations of the fictional Trueba family through whom Allende recreated a history of modern Chile. Her later fiction includes Of Love and Shadows (1986), Eva Luna (1988), The Stories of Eva Luna (1991), The Infinite Plan (1993), Aphrodite (1998), and Daughter of Fortune (1999). She has also published an autobiographical work based on the inexplicable death of her daughter, Paula (1995).

In her early fiction, Allende was a practitioner of "magical realism," the unique narrative focus created by Latin American writers; in her more recent fiction she has turned away from that form. About her writing, she has commented, "I have a feeling that I don't invent anything. That somehow I discover things that are in another dimension. That they are already there, and my job is to find them and bring them into the page." "And of Clay Are We Created" demonstrates Allende's insight into the relationship between the media and contemporary events: the problematic nature of "objective" reporting and the power of events to overtake their observers.

AND OF CLAY ARE WE CREATED

They discovered the girl's head protruding from the mudpit, eyes wide open, calling soundlessly. She had a First Communion name, Azucena. Lily. In that vast cemetery where the odor of death was already attracting vultures from far away, and where the weeping of orphans and wails of the injured filled the air, the little girl obstinately clinging to life became the symbol of the tragedy. The television cameras transmitted so often the unbearable image of the head budding like a black squash from the clay that there was no one who did not recognize her and know her name. And every time we saw her on the screen, right behind her was Rolf Carlé, who had gone there on assignment, never suspecting that he would find a fragment of his past, lost thirty years before.

First a subterranean sob rocked the cotton fields, curling them like waves of foam. Geologists had set up their seismographs weeks before and knew that the mountain had awakened again. For some time they had predicted that the heat of the eruption could detach the eternal ice from the slopes of the volcano, but no one heeded their warnings; they sounded like the tales of frightened old women. The towns in the valley went about their daily life, deaf to the moaning of the earth, until that fateful Wednesday night in November when a prolonged roar announced the end of the world, and walls of snow broke loose, rolling in an avalanche of clay, stones, and water that descended on the villages and buried them beneath unfathomable meters of telluric vomit. As soon as the survivors emerged from the paralysis of that first awful terror, they could see that houses, plazas, churches, white cotton plantations, dark coffee forests, cattle pastures—all had disappeared. Much later, after soldiers and volunteers had arrived to rescue the living and try to assess the magnitude of the cataclysm, it was calculated that beneath the mud lay more than twenty thousand human beings and an indefinite number of animals putrefying in a viscous soup. Forests and rivers had also been swept away, and there was nothing to be seen but an immense desert of mire.

When the station called before dawn, Rolf Carlé and I were together. I crawled out of bed, dazed with sleep, and went to prepare coffee while he hurriedly dressed. He stuffed his gear in the green canvas backpack he always carried, and we said goodbye, as we had so many times before. I had no presentiments. I sat in the kitchen, sipping my coffee and planning the long hours without him, sure that he would be back the next day.

He was one of the first to reach the scene, because while other reporters were fighting their way to the edges of that morass in jeeps, bicycles, or on foot, each getting there however he could, Rolf Carlé had the advantage of the television helicopter, which flew him over the avalanche. We watched on our screens the footage captured by his assistant's camera, in which he was up to his knees in muck, a microphone in his hand, in the midst of a bedlam of lost children, wounded survivors, corpses, and devastation. The story came to us in his calm voice. For years he had been a familiar figure in newscasts, reporting live at the scene of battles and catastrophes with awesome tenacity. Nothing could stop him, and I was always amazed at his equanimity in the face of danger and suffering; it seemed as if nothing could shake his fortitude or deter his curiosity. Fear seemed never to touch him, although he had confessed to me that he was not a courageous man, far from it. I believe that the lens of the camera had a strange effect on him; it was as if it transported him to a different time from which he could watch events without actually participating in them. When I knew him better, I came to realize that this fictive distance seemed to protect him from his own emotions.

Rolf Carlé was in on the story of Azucena from the beginning. He filmed the volunteers who discovered her, and the first persons who tried to reach her; his camera zoomed in on the girl, her dark face, her large desolate eyes, the plastered-down tangle of her hair. The mud was like quicksand around her, and anyone attempting to reach her was in danger of sinking. They threw a rope to her that she made no effort to grasp until they shouted to her to catch it; then she pulled a hand from the mire and tried to move, but immediately sank a little deeper. Rolf threw down his knapsack and the rest of his equipment and waded into the quagmire, commenting for his assistant's microphone that it was cold and that one could begin to smell the stench of corpses.

"What's your name?" he asked the girl, and she told him her flower name. "Don't move, Azucena," Rolf Carlé directed, and kept talking to her, without a thought for what he was saying, just to distract her, while slowly he worked his way forward in mud up to his waist. The air around him seemed as murky as the mud.

It was impossible to reach her from the approach he was attempting, so he retreated and circled around where there seemed to be firmer footing. When finally he was close enough, he took the rope and tied it beneath her arms, so they could pull her out. He smiled at her with that smile that crinkles his eyes and makes him look like a little boy; he told her that everything was fine, that he was here with her now, that soon they would have her out. He signaled the others to pull, but as soon as the cord tensed, the girl screamed. They tried again, and her shoulders and arms appeared, but they could move her no farther; she was trapped. Someone suggested that her legs might be caught in the collapsed walls of her house, but she said it was not just rubble, that she was also held by the bodies of her brothers and sisters clinging to her legs.

"Don't worry, we'll get you out of here," Rolf promised. Despite the quality of the transmission, I could hear his voice break, and I loved him more than ever. Azucena looked at him, but said nothing.

During those first hours Rolf Carlé exhausted all the resources of his ingenuity to rescue her. He struggled with poles and ropes, but every tug was an intolerable torture for the imprisoned girl. It occurred to him to use one of the poles as a lever but got no result and had to abandon the idea. He talked a couple of soldiers into working with him for a while, but they had to leave because so many other victims were calling for help. The girl could not move, she barely could breathe, but she did not seem desperate, as if an ancestral resignation allowed her to accept her fate. The reporter, on the other hand, was determined to snatch her from death. Someone brought him a tire, which he placed beneath her arms like a life buoy, and then laid a plank near the hole to hold his weight and allow him to stay closer to her. As it was impossible to remove the rubble blindly, he tried once or twice to dive toward her feet, but emerged frustrated, covered with mud, and spitting gravel. He concluded that he would have to have a pump to drain the water, and radioed a request for one, but received in return a message that there was no available transport and it could not be sent until the next morning.

"We can't wait that long!" Rolf Carlé shouted, but in the pandemonium no one stopped to commiserate. Many more hours would go by before he accepted that time had stagnated and reality had been irreparably distorted.

A military doctor came to examine the girl, and observed that her heart was functioning well and that if she did not get too cold she could survive the night.

"Hang on, Azucena, we'll have the pump tomorrow," Rolf Carlé tried to console her.

"Don't leave me alone," she begged.

"No, of course I won't leave you."

Someone brought him coffee, and he helped the girl drink it, sip by sip. The warm liquid revived her and she began telling him about her small life, about her family and her school, about how things were in that little bit of world before the volcano had erupted. She was thirteen, and she had never been outside her village. Rolf Carlé, buoyed by a premature optimism, was convinced that everything would end well: the pump would arrive, they would drain the water, move the rubble, and Azucena would be transported by helicopter to a hospital where she would recover rapidly and where he could visit her and bring her gifts. He thought, She's already too old for dolls, and I don't know what would please her; maybe a dress. I don't know much about women, he concluded, amused, reflecting that although he had known many women in his lifetime, none had taught him these details. To pass the hours he began to tell Azucena about his travels and adventures as a newshound, and when he exhausted his memory, he called upon imagination, inventing things he thought might entertain her. From time to time she dozed, but he kept talking in the darkness, to assure her that he was still there and to overcome the menace of uncertainty.

That was a long night.

Many miles away, I watched Rolf Carlé and the girl on a television screen. I could not bear the wait at home, so I went to National Television, where I often spent entire nights with Rolf editing programs. There, I was near his world, and I could at least get a feeling of what he lived through during those three decisive days. I called all the important people in the city, senators, commanders of the armed forces, the North American ambassador, and the president of National Petroleum, begging them for a pump to remove the silt, but obtained only vague promises. I began to ask for urgent help on radio and television, to see if there wasn't *someone* who could help us. Between calls I would run to the newsroom to monitor the satellite transmissions that periodically brought new details of the catastrophe. While reporters selected scenes with most impact for the news report, I searched for footage that featured Azucena's mudpit. The screen reduced the disaster to a single plane and accentuated the tremendous distance that separated me from Rolf Carlé; nonetheless, I was there with him. The child's every suffering hurt me as it did him; I felt his frustration, his impotence. Faced with the impossibility of communicating with him, the fantastic idea came to me that if I tried, I could reach him by force of mind and in that way give him encouragement. I concentrated until I was dizzy—a frenzied and futile activity. At times I would be overcome with compassion and burst out crying; at other times, I was so drained I felt as if I were staring through a telescope at the light of a star dead for a million years.

I watched that hell on the first morning broadcast, cadavers of people and animals awash in the current of new rivers formed overnight from the melted snow. Above the mud rose the tops of trees and the bell towers of a church where several people had taken refuge and were patiently awaiting rescue teams. Hundreds of soldiers and volunteers from the Civil Defense were clawing through rubble searching for survivors, while long rows of ragged specters awaited their turn for a cup of hot broth. Radio networks announced that their phones were jammed with calls from families offering shelter to orphaned children. Drinking water was in scarce supply, along with gasoline and food. Doctors, resigned to amputating arms and legs without anesthe-sia, pled that at least they be sent serum and painkillers and antibiotics; most of the roads, however, were impassable, and worse were the bureaucratic obstacles that stood in the way. To top it all, the clay contaminated by decomposing bodies threatened the living with an outbreak of epidemics.

Azucena was shivering inside the tire that held her above the surface. Immobili-ty and tension had greatly weakened her, but she was conscious and could still be heard when a microphone was held out to her. Her tone was humble, as if apologiz-ing for all the fuss. Rolf Carlé had a growth of beard, and dark circles beneath his eyes; he looked near exhaustion. Even from that enormous distance I could sense the qual-ity of his weariness, so different from the fatigue of other adventures. He had com-pletely forgotten the camera; he could not look at the girl through a lens any longer. The pictures we were receiving were not his assistant's but those of other reporters who had appropriated Azucena, bestowing on her the pathetic responsibility of em-bodying the horror of what had happened in that place. With the first light Rolf tried again to dislodge the obstacles that held the girl in her tomb, but he had only his hands to work with; he did not dare use a tool for fear of injuring her. He fed Azucena a cup of the cornmeal mush and bananas the Army was distributing, but she immediately vomited it up. A doctor stated that she had a fever, but added that there was little he could do: antibiotics were being reserved for cases of gangrene. A priest also passed by and blessed her, hanging a medal of the Virgin around her neck. By evening a gentle, persistent drizzle began to fall.

"The sky is weeping," Azucena murmured, and she, too, began to cry.

"Don't be afraid," Rolf begged. "You have to keep your strength up and be calm. Everything will be fine. I'm with you, and I'll get you out somehow."

Reporters returned to photograph Azucena and ask her the same questions, which she no longer tried to answer. In the meanwhile, more television and movie teams arrived with spools of cable, tapes, film, videos, precision lenses, recorders, sound consoles, lights, reflecting screens, auxiliary motors, cartons of supplies, electricians, sound technicians, and cameramen: Azucena's face was beamed to millions of screens around the world. And all the while Rolf Carlé kept pleading for a pump. The im-proved technical facilities bore results, and National Television began receiving sharp-er pictures and clearer sound; the distance seemed suddenly compressed, and I had the horrible sensation that Azucena and Rolf were by my side, separated from me by im-penetrable glass. I was able to follow events hour by hour; I knew everything my love did to wrest the girl from her prison and help her endure her suffering; I overheard fragments of what they said to one another and could guess the rest; I was present when she taught Rolf to pray, and when he distracted her with the stories I had told him in a thousand and one nights beneath the white mosquito netting of our bed.

When darkness came on the second day, Rolf tried to sing Azucena to sleep with old Austrian folk songs he had learned from his mother, but she was far beyond sleep. They spent most of the night talking, each in a stupor of exhaustion and hunger, and shaking with cold. That night, imperceptibly, the unyielding floodgates that had con-tained Rolf Carlé's past for so many years began to open, and the torrent of all that had lain hidden in the deepest and most secret layers of memory poured out, level-ing before it the obstacles that had blocked his consciousness for so long. He could not tell it all to Azucena; she perhaps did not know there was a world beyond the sea or time previous to her own; she was not capable of imagining Europe in the years of the war. So he could not tell her of defeat, nor of the afternoon the Russians had led them to the concentration camp to bury prisoners dead from starvation. Why should he describe to her how the naked bodies piled like a mountain of firewood resembled fragile china? How could he tell this dying child about ovens and gallows? Nor did he mention the night that he had seen his mother naked, shod in stiletto-heeled red boots, sobbing with humiliation. There was much he did not tell, but in those hours he relived for the first time all the things his mind had tried to erase. Azucena had surrendered her fear to him and so, without wishing it, had obliged Rolf to confront his own. There, beside that hellhole of mud, it was impossible for Rolf to flee from himself any longer, and the visceral terror he had lived as a boy suddenly invaded him. He reverted to the years when he was the age of Azucena, and younger, and, like her, found himself trapped in a pit without escape, buried in life, his head barely above ground; he saw before his eyes the boots and legs of his father, who had removed his belt and was whipping it in the air with the never-forgotten hiss of a viper coiled to strike. Sorrow flooded through him, intact and precise, as if it had lain always in his mind, waiting. He was once again in the armoire where his father locked him to punish him for imagined misbehavior, there where for eternal hours he had crouched with his eyes closed, not to see the darkness, with his hands over his ears, to shut out the beating of his heart, trembling, huddled like a cornered animal. Wandering in the mist of his memories he found his sister Katharina, a sweet, retarded child who spent her life hiding, with the hope that her father would forget the disgrace of her having been born. With Katharina, Rolf crawled beneath the dining room table, and with her hid there under the long white tablecloth, two children forever embraced, alert to footsteps and voices. Katharina's scent melded with his own sweat, with aromas of cooking, garlic, soup, freshly baked bread, and the unexpected odor of putrescent clay. His sister's hand in his, her frightened breathing, her silk hair against his cheek, the candid gaze of her eyes. Katharina . . . Katharina materialized before him, floating on the air like a flag, clothed in the white tablecloth, now a winding sheet, and at last he could weep for her death and for the guilt of having abandoned her. He understood then that all his exploits as a reporter, the feats that had won him such recognition and fame, were merely an attempt to keep his most ancient fears at bay, a stratagem for taking refuge behind a lens to test whether reality was more tolerable from that perspective. He took excessive risks as an exercise of courage, training by day to conquer the monsters that tormented him by night. But he had come face to face with the moment of truth; he could not continue to escape his past. He *was* Azucena; he was buried in the clayey mud; his terror was not the distant emotion of an almost forgotten childhood, it was a claw sunk in his throat. In the flush of his tears he saw his mother, dressed in black and clutching her imitation-crocodile pocketbook to her bosom, just as he had last seen her on the dock when she had come to put him on the boat to South America. She had not come to dry his tears, but to tell him to pick up a shovel: the war was over and now they must bury the dead.

"Don't cry. I don't hurt anymore. I'm fine," Azucena said when dawn came.

"I'm not crying for you," Rolf Carlé smiled. "I'm crying for myself. I hurt all over."

The third day in the valley of the cataclysm began with a pale light filtering through storm clouds. The President of the Republic visited the area in his tailored safari jacket to confirm that this was the worst catastrophe of the century; the country was in mourning; sister nations had offered aid; he had ordered a state of siege; the Armed Forces would be merciless, anyone caught stealing or committing other offenses would be shot on sight. He added that it was impossible to remove all the corpses or count the thousands who had disappeared; the entire valley would be declared holy ground, and bishops would come to celebrate a solemn mass for the souls of the victims. He went to the Army field tents to offer relief in the form of vague promises to crowds of the rescued, then to the improvised hospital to offer a word of encouragement to doctors and nurses worn down from so many hours of tribulations. Then he asked to be taken to see Azucena, the little girl the whole world had seen. He waved to her with a limp statesman's hand, and microphones recorded his emotional voice and paternal tone as he told her that her courage had served as an example to the nation. Rolf Carlé interrupted to ask for a pump, and the President assured him that he personally would attend to the matter. I caught a glimpse of Rolf for a few seconds kneeling beside the mudpit. On the evening news broadcast, he was still in the same position; and I, glued to the screen like a fortuneteller to her crystal ball, could tell that something fundamental had changed in him. I knew somehow that during the night his defenses had crumbled and he had given in to grief; finally he was vulnerable. The girl had touched a part of him that he himself had no access to, a part he had never shared with me. Rolf had wanted to console her, but it was Azucena who had given him consolation.

I recognized the precise moment at which Rolf gave up the fight and surrendered to the torture of watching the girl die. I was with them, three days and two nights, spying on them from the other side of life. I was there when she told him that in all her thirteen years no boy had ever loved her and that it was a pity to leave this world without knowing love. Rolf assured her that he loved her more than he could ever love anyone, more than he loved his mother, more than his sister, more than all the women who had slept in his arms, more than he loved me, his life companion, who would have given anything to be trapped in that well in her place, who would have exchanged her life for Azucena's, and I watched as he leaned down to kiss her poor forehead, consumed by a sweet, sad emotion he could not name. I felt how in that instant both were saved from despair, how they were freed from the clay, how they rose above the vultures and helicopters, how together they flew above the vast swamp of corruption and laments. How, finally, they were able to accept death. Rolf Carlé prayed in silence that she would die quickly, because such pain cannot be borne.

By then I had obtained a pump and was in touch with a general who had agreed to ship it the next morning on a military cargo plane. But on the night of that third day, beneath the unblinking focus of quartz lamps and the lens of a hundred cameras, Azucena gave up, her eyes locked with those of the friend who had sustained her to the end. Rolf Carlé removed the life buoy, closed her eyelids, held her to his chest for a few moments, and then let her go. She sank slowly, a flower in the mud.

You are back with me, but you are not the same man. I often accompany you to the station and we watch the videos of Azucena again; you study them intently, looking for something you could have done to save her, something you did not think of in time. Or maybe you study them to see yourself as if in a mirror, naked. Your cameras lie forgotten in a closet; you do not write or sing; you sit long hours before the window, staring at the mountains. Beside you, I wait for you to complete the voyage into yourself, for the old wounds to heal. I know that when you return from your nightmares, we shall again walk hand in hand, as before.

[1989]
Translated by
MARGARET SAYERS PEDEN

Questions

1. Who is the central character of this story: Azucena, Rolf Carlé, or the narrator? How is Rolf Carlé changed by his involvement with Azucena?

2. What does the story suggest about the relationship between human tragedy or catastrophe and media reportage? Does the presence of the journalist Rolf Carlé alter the situation in which Azucena is trapped? If so, how?

3. Why does Azucena die, despite the sustained human efforts and technological assistance enlisted on her behalf? What does the story suggest about the relationships between a developing country's response to a natural disaster, the international media's response to it, and the human costs?

Hanan Al-Shaykh

(b. 1945)

Lebanon/England

Hanan Al-Shaykh was raised in a traditional Shiite Moslem household in Lebanon. Beginning in 1963, she studied in Cairo at the American College for girls. After her return to Beirut four years later, she worked as a journalist and simultaneously began writing short stories and novels. Although her works have all originally been published in Lebanon, in Arabic, several have encountered censorship in other Islamic countries. Her works that have been translated into English include The Story of Zahra (1986), Women of Sand and Myrrh (1989), and Beirut Blues (1995), as well as a collection of short stories, I Sweep the Sun off Rooftops (1998).

Hanan Al-Shaykh has been described by one critic as a "reluctant feminist." In response to our query about "The Unseeing Eye," Hanan Al-Shaykh has written the following:

> I do not write only about Arab women and their place in society, and I cannot see myself being confined within such a narrow frame of reference. For me fiction has a power of its own, while to be a feminist is to have an ideological and political view of the world which may restrict the open, loosely-structured, imaginative qualities that I regard as positive features of my work.
>
> Fiction is the process by which a simple observation of human behaviour and emotions in certain surroundings can evolve into a story, an autonomous entity. I write because I am fascinated to see where the creation of such a story may lead me: I invent characters who behave and feel in certain ways, regardless of what I think of them, and eventually take over from me and dictate their own fate. I write in the hope that I may open people's eyes to certain situations, expose them to certain feelings and ways of thinking, sometimes in the context of extreme conditions like war and blatant oppression. At the same time I write to arouse some kind of response from those who feel the same way as [I do].
>
> I wrote "The Unseeing Eye" to show how people who are very close to one another take each other for granted. In particular, I was thinking about how men are sometimes not very curious about the women they share their lives with, while I cannot imagine a woman who has not observed her partner's features so closely that she knows them by heart, even if she is no longer interested in him.
>
> I also wanted to show how custom and habit interfere with and overshadow our lives, while we remain oblivious to their workings.

THE UNSEEING EYE

The old man stood there at a loss, his sunken eyes staring at the man seated behind the table. Raising his hand, he wiped the sweat from his forehead and heavily wrinkled face. He didn't use the traditional kerchief and headband though he could feel the sweat running down from his temples and neck, and he gave no reply to the man seated behind the table who went on asking him, "Why did you go in opening all the doors of the wards looking for your wife? Why didn't you come directly to Enquiries?" The old man kept silent. Why, though, was the man seated behind the table continuing to open one drawer after another? His eyes busy watching him, he said, "I came here the day before yesterday wanting the hospital and looking for the mother of my children."

The man seated behind the table muttered irritably, blaming himself for not having ever learnt how to ask the right questions, how to get a conversation going, and why it was that his questions, full of explanations, and sometimes of annoyance, weren't effective. He puffed at his cigarette as he enquired in exasperation, "What's your wife's name?" The old man at once replied, "Zeinab Mohamed." The man seated behind the table began flipping through the pages of the thick ledger; each time he turned over a page there was a loud noise that was heard by everyone sitting in the waiting-room. He went on flipping through the pages of his ledger, pursing his lips listlessly, then nervously, as he kept bringing the ledger close to his face until finally he said, "Your wife came in here the day before yesterday?" The old man in relief at once answered, "Yes, sir, when her heart came to a stop." Once again irritated, the man behind the table mumbled to himself, "Had her heart stopped she wouldn't be here, neither would you." With his eyes still on the ledger, he said, "She's in Ward 4, but it's not permitted for you to enter her ward because there are other women there." Yawning, he called to the nurse leaning against the wall. She came forward, in her hand a paper cup from which she was drinking. Motioning with his head to the man, he said, "Ward Number 4—Zeinab Mohamed." The nurse walked ahead, without raising her mouth from the cup. The old man asked himself how it was that this woman worked in a hospital that was crammed with men, even though she spoke Arabic. Having arrived at the ward, the nurse left him outside after telling him to wait; then, after a while, she came out and said to him, "There are two women called Zeinab Mohamed. One of them, though, has only one eye. Which one is your wife so that I can call her?"

The old man was thrown into confusion. One eye? How am I to know? He tried to recall what his wife Zeinab looked like, with her long gown and black headdress, the veil, and sometimes the black covering enveloping her face and sometimes removed and laying on her neck. He could picture her as she walked and sat, chewing a morsel and then taking it out of her mouth so as to place it in that of her first-born. Her children. One eye. How am I to know? He could picture her stretched out on the bed, her eyes closed. The old man was thrown into confusion and found himself saying, "When I call her she'll know my voice." The nurse doubted whether he was in fact visiting his wife; however, giving him another glance, she laughed at her suspicions and asked him, "How long have the two of you been married?" Again he was confused as he said, "Allah knows best— thirty, forty years. . . ."

[1989]
Translated by
DENYS JOHNSON-DAVIES

Questions

1. It can be argued that Islamic tradition has created the situation depicted in "The Unseeing Eye": Men have a lesser understanding of women than their counterparts have in the West. Do you think the author favors such an interpretation of her story?
2. Is the hospital setting crucial to our understanding of the story? Does it help to explain the husband's confusion?
3. Does the suggestion of distorted vision and understanding apply to anyone besides the husband?

Rudolfo A. Anaya

(b. 1937)

United States

Rudolfo A. Anaya grew up in New Mexico, where he attended the University of New Mexico and subsequently joined the faculty of the Department of English. He is the author of Bless Me, Ultima (1972), the classic novel of Chicano childhood. In this richly evocative story, a young boy named Tony comes to understand the delicate balance between good and evil. Guided in his education by the curandera (folkhealer) Ultima, Tony develops an understanding of the fusion in modern-day Chicano life between the Church (Catholicism) and the traditional mysteries of the past. In subsequent novels (Heart of Aztlan, 1978; Tortuga, 1979; The Legend of La Llorona, 1984; Albuquerque, 1992; and Jalamanta: A Message from the Desert, 1997), several detective novels set in the southwest, short stories, and essays, Anaya has established himself as one of the leading contemporary Chicano writers. He has received numerous honors for his work. In 1980, he was invited by presidential invitation to read from his work at the White House, during a National Salute to American Poets and Writers.

The following story—perhaps Anaya's major statement on his role as a writer— is best understood if we examine the old man's remarks at the end: ". . . a writer's job is to find and follow people like Justino. They're the source of life. . . . They may be illiterate, but they understand our descent into the pozo of hell, and they understand us because they're willing to share the adventure with us. You seek fame and notoriety and you're dead as a writer."

Rudolfo A. Anaya wrote the following introduction for Worlds of Fiction:

This story had an exciting and mysterious birth. In the summer of 1979 I set out for Cuernavaca with mi madre mexicana, Ana Rosinski. I was finished with my classes at the university and my wife was still teaching, so Ana and I went on ahead. To travel with a woman who escaped the Nazi occupation of Germany and who knew well the Mexican hustle is to travel in realms which lend themselves to story.

The events in the story are very much as I recall them. I began drinking beer in the train station in Juarez, but there is no train to Cuernavaca, so we gave up on a train and decided on the midnight flight to Mexico City. I began dreaming of B. Traven. In search of treasure, you see, but my treasure is the story I feel growing inside.

Coincidence piles on coincidence. The gardener at San Miquelito is new, and he is a storyteller. We trade stories and he becomes the gardener of the story. I don't know what I become in his story. My wife arrives, and Ana throws a small reception for us. To introduce the Chicano writer to the Cuernavaca writers. I am only thinking of B. Traven, and the treasure at the foot of Popo, the mysterious volcano one can see from Cuernavaca on a clear day.

From Traven, and my many observations, I understand the reality and poverty and the class system of Mexico. The revolution still barks at the door. From its people I understand love and joy and the magic of storytelling. I tried to incorporate both in the story, and to tell within the story the conception and gestation of a story. Stories like this allow me to get deep into the stream of magical realism. (Rudolfo A. Anaya, copyright 1992)

B. TRAVEN IS ALIVE AND WELL IN CUERNAVACA

I didn't go to Mexico to find B. Traven. Why should I? I have enough to do writing my own fiction, so I go to Mexico to write, not to search out writers. B. Traven? you ask. Don't you remember THE TREASURE OF THE SIERRA MADRE? A real classic. They made a movie from the novel. I remember seeing it when I was kid. It was set in Mexico, and it had all the elements of a real adventure story. B. Traven was an adventurous man, traveled all over the world, then disappeared into Mexico and cut himself off from society. He gave no interviews and allowed few photographs. While he lived he remained unapproachable, anonymous to his public, a writer shrouded in mystery.

He's dead now, or they say he's dead. I think he's alive and well. At any rate, he has become something of an institution in Mexico, a man honored for his work. The cantineros and taxi drivers in Mexico City know about him as well as the cantineros of Spain knew Hemingway, or they claim to. I never mention I'm a writer when I'm in a cantina, because inevitably some aficionado will ask, "Do you know the work of B. Traven?" And from some dusty niche will appear a yellowed, thumbworn novel by Traven. Thus if the cantinero knows his business, and they all do in Mexico, he is apt to say, "Did you know that B. Traven used to drink here?" If you show the slightest interest, he will follow with, "Sure, he used to sit right over here. In this corner. . . ." And if you don't leave right then you will wind up hearing many stories about the mysterious B. Traven while buying many drinks for the local patrons.

Everybody reads his novels, on the buses, on street corners; if you look closely you'll spot one of his titles. One turned up for me, and that's how this story started. I was sitting in the train station in Juárez, waiting for the train to Cuernavaca, which would be an exciting title for this story except that there is no train to Cuernavaca. I was drinking beer to kill time, the erotic and sensitive Mexican time which is so different from the clean-packaged, well-kept time of the Americanos. Time in Mexico can be cruel and punishing, but it is never indifferent. It permeates everything, it changes reality. Einstein would have loved Mexico because there time and space are one. I stare more often into empty space when I'm in Mexico. The past seems to infuse the present, and in the brown, wrinkled faces of the old people one sees the presence of the past. In Mexico I like to walk the narrow streets of the cities and the smaller pueblos, wandering aimlessly, feeling the sunlight which is so distinctively Mexican, listening to the voices which call in the streets, peering into the dark eyes which are so secretive and proud. The Mexican people guard a secret. But in the end, one is never really lost in Mexico. All streets lead to a good cantina. All good stories start in a cantina.

At the train station, after I let the kids who hustle the tourists know that I didn't want chewing gum or cigarettes, and I didn't want my shoes shined, and I didn't want a woman at the moment, I was left alone to drink my beer. Luke-cold Dos Equis. I don't remember how long I had been there or how many Dos Equis I had finished when I glanced at the seat next to me and saw a book which turned out to be a B. Traven novel, old and used and obviously much read, but a novel nevertheless. What's so strange about finding a B. Traven novel in the dingy little corner of a bar in the Juárez train station? Nothing, unless you know that in Mexico one never finds anything. It is a country that doesn't waste anything, everything is recycled. Chevrolets run with patched up Ford engines and Chrysler transmissions, buses are kept together, and kept running, with baling wire and home-made parts, yesterday's Traven novel is the pulp on which tomorrow's Fuentes story will appear. Time recycles in Mexico. Time returns to the past, and the Christian finds himself dreaming of ancient Aztec rituals. He who does not believe that Quetzalcoatl will return to save Mexico has little faith.

So the novel was the first clue. Later there was Justino. "Who is Justino?" you want to know. Justino was the jardinero who cared for the garden of my friend, the friend who had invited me to stay at his home in Cuernavaca while I continued to write. The day after I arrived I was sitting in the sun, letting the fatigue of the long journey ooze away, thinking nothing, when Justino appeared on the scene. He had finished cleaning the swimming pool and was taking his morning break, so he sat in the shade of the orange tree and introduced himself. Right away I could tell that he would rather be a movie actor or an adventurer, a real free spirit. But things didn't work out for him. He got married, children appeared, he took a couple of mistresses, more children appeared, so he had to work to support his family. "A man is like a rooster," he said after we talked awhile, "the more chickens he has the happier he is." Then he asked me what I was going to do about a woman while I was there, and I told him I hadn't thought that far ahead, that I would be happy if I could just get a damned story going. This puzzled Justino, and I think for a few days it worried him. So on Saturday night he took me out for a few drinks and we wound up in some of the bordellos of Cuernavaca in the company of some of the most beautiful women in the world. Justino knew them all. They loved him, and he loved them.

I learned something more of the nature of this jardinero a few nights later when the heat and an irritating mosquito wouldn't let me sleep. I heard music from a radio, so I put on my pants and walked out into the Cuernavacan night, an oppressive, warm night heavy with the sweet perfume of the dama de la noche bushes which lined the wall of my friend's villa. From time to time I heard a dog cry in the distance, and I remembered that in Mexico many people die of rabies. Perhaps that is why the walls of the wealthy are always so high and the locks always secure. Or maybe it was because of the occasional gunshots that explode in the night. The news media tell us that Mexico is the most stable country in Latin America and, with the recent oil finds, the bankers and the oil men want to keep it that way. I sense, and many know, that in the dark the revolution does not sleep. It is a spirit kept at bay by the high fences and the locked gates, yet it prowls the heart of every man. "Oil will create a new revolution," Justino had told me, "but it's going to be for our people. Mexicans are tired of building gas stations for the Gringos from Gringolandia." I understood what he meant: there is much hunger in the country.

I lit a cigarette and walked toward my friend's car, which was parked in the driveway near the swimming pool. I approached quietly and peered in. On the back seat with his legs propped on the front seat-back and smoking a cigar sat Justino. Two big, luscious women sat on either side of him running their fingers through his hair and whispering in his ears. The doors were open to allow a breeze. He looked content. Sitting there he was that famous artist on his way to an afternoon reception in Mexico City, or he was a movie star on his way to the premiere of his most recent movie. Or perhaps it was Sunday and he was taking a Sunday drive in the country, towards Tepoztlán. And why shouldn't his two friends accompany him? I had to smile. Unnoticed I backed away and returned to my room. So there was quite a bit more than met the eye to this short, dark Indian from Ocosingo.

In the morning I asked my friend, "What do you know about Justino?"

"Justino? You mean Vitorino."

"Is that his real name?"

"Sometimes he calls himself Trinidad."

"Maybe his name is Justino Vitorino Trinidad," I suggested.

"I don't know, don't care," my friend answered. "He told me he used to be a guide in the jungle. Who knows? The Mexican Indian has an incredible imagination. Really gifted people. He's a good jardinero, and that's what matters to me. It's difficult to get good jardineros, so I don't ask questions."

"Is he reliable?" I wondered aloud.

"As reliable as a ripe mango," my friend nodded.

I wondered how much he knew, so I pushed a little further. "And the radio at night?"

"Oh, that. I hope it doesn't bother you. Robberies and break-ins are increasing here in the colonia. Something we never used to have. Vitorino said that if he keeps the radio on low the sound keeps thieves away. A very good idea, don't you think?"

I nodded. A very good idea.

"And I sleep very soundly," my friend concluded, "so I never hear it."

The following night when I awakened and heard the soft sound of music from the radio and heard the splashing of water, I had only to look from my window to see Justino and his friends in the pool, swimming nude in the moonlight. They were joking and laughing softly as they splashed each other, being quiet so as not to awaken my friend, the patrón who slept so soundly. The women were beautiful. Brown skinned and glistened with water in the moonlight they reminded me of ancient Aztec maidens, swimming around Chac, their god of rain. They teased Justino, and he smiled as he floated on a rubber mattress in the middle of the pool, smoking his cigar, happy because they were happy. When he smiled the gold fleck of a filling glinted in the moonlight.

"¡Qué cabrón!" I laughed and closed my window.

Justino said a Mexican never lies. I believed him. If a Mexican says he will meet you at a certain time and place, he means he will meet you sometime at some place. Americans who retire in Mexico often complain of maids who swear they will come to work on a designated day, then don't show up. They did not lie, they knew they couldn't be at work, but they knew to tell the señora otherwise would make her sad or displease her, so they agree on a date so everyone would remain happy. What a beautiful aspect of character. It's a real virtue which Norteamericanos interpret as a fault in their character, because we are used to asserting ourselves on time and people. We feel secure and comfortable only when everything is neatly packaged in its proper time and place. We don't like the disorder of a free-flowing life.

Some day, I thought to myself, Justino will give a grand party in the sala of his patrón's home. His three wives, or his wife and two mistresses, and his dozens of children will be there. So will the women from the bordellos. He will preside over the feast, smoke his cigars, request his favorite beer-drinking songs from the mariachis, smile, tell stories and make sure everyone has a grand time. He will be dressed in a tuxedo, borrowed from the patrón's closet of course, and he will act gallant and show everyone that a man who has just come into sudden wealth should share it with his friends. And in the morning he will report to the patrón that something has to be done about the poor mice that are coming in out of the streets and eating everything in the house.

"I'll buy some poison," the patrón will suggest.

"No, no," Justino will shake his head, "a little music from the radio and a candle burning in the sala will do."

And he will be right.

I liked Justino. He was a rogue with class. We talked about the weather, the lateness of the rainy season, women, the role of oil in Mexican politics. Like other workers, he believed nothing was going to filter down to the campesinos. "We could all be real Mexican greasers with all that oil," he said, "but the politicians will keep it all."

"What about the United States?" I asked.

"Oh, I have traveled in the estados unidos to the north. It's a country that's going to the dogs in a worse way than Mexico. The thing I liked the most was your cornflakes."

"Cornflakes?"

"Sí. You can make really good cornflakes."

"And women?"

"Ah, you better keep your eyes open, my friend. Those gringas are going to change the world just like the Suecas changed Spain."

"For better or for worse?"

"Spain used to be a nice country," he winked.

We talked, we argued, we drifted from subject to subject. I learned from him. I had been there a week when he told the story which eventually led me to B. Traven. One day I was sitting under the orange tree reading the B. Traven novel I had found in the Juárez train station, keeping one eye on the ripe oranges which fell from time to time, my mind wandering as it worked to focus on a story so I could begin to write. After all, that's why I had come to Cuernavaca, to get some writing done, but nothing was coming, nothing. Justino wandered by and asked what I was reading and I replied it was an adventure story, a story of a man's search for the illusive pot of gold at the end of a make-believe rainbow. He nodded, thought awhile and gazed toward Popo, Popocatepetl, the towering volcano which lay to the south, shrouded in mist, waiting for the rains as we waited for the rains, sleeping, gazing at his female counterpart, Itza, who lay sleeping and guarding the valley of Cholula, there, where over four hundred years ago Cortés showed his wrath and executed thousands of Cholulans.

"I am going on an adventure," he finally said and paused. "I think you might like to go with me."

I said nothing, but I put my book down and listened.

"I have been thinking about it for a long time, and now is the time to go. You see, it's like this. I grew up on the hacienda of Don Francisco Jimenez, it's to the south, just a day's drive on the carretera. In my village nobody likes Don Francisco, they fear and hate him. He has killed many men and he has taken their fortunes and buried them. He is a very rich man, muy rico. Many men have tried to kill him, but Don Francisco is like the devil, he kills them first."

I listened as I always listen, because one never knows when a word or phrase or an idea will be the seed from which a story sprouts, but at first there was nothing interesting. It sounded like the typical patrón-peón story I had heard so many times before. A man, the patrón, keeps the workers enslaved, in serfdom, and because he wields so much power soon stories are told about him and he begins to acquire super-human powers. He acquires a mystique, just like the divine right of old. The patrón wields a mean machete, like old King Arthur swung Excaliber. He chops off heads of dissenters and sits on top of the bones and skulls pyramid, the king of the mountain, the top macho.

"One day I was sent to look for lost cattle," Justino continued. "I rode back into the hills where I had never been. At the foot of a hill, near a ravine, I saw something move in the bush. I dismounted and moved forward quietly. I was afraid it might be bandidos who steal cattle, and if they saw me they would kill me. When I came near the place I heard a strange sound. Somebody was crying. My back shivered, just like a dog when he sniffs the devil at night. I thought I was going to see witches, brujas who like to go to those deserted places to dance for the devil, or la Llorona."

"La Llorona," I said aloud. My interest grew. I had been hearing Llorona stories since I was a kid, and I was always ready for one more. La Llorona was that archetypal woman of ancient legends who murdered her children then, repentant and demented, she has spent the rest of eternity searching for them.

"Sí, la Llorona. You know that poor woman used to drink a lot. She played around with men, and when she had babies she got rid of them by throwing them into la barranca. One day she realized what she had done and went crazy. She started crying and pulling her hair and running up and down the side of cliffs of the river looking for her children. It's a very sad story."

A new version, I thought, and yes, a sad story. And what of the men who made love to the woman who became la Llorona, I wondered? Did they ever cry for their children? It doesn't seem fair to have only her suffer, only her crying and doing penance. Perhaps a man should run with her, and in our legends we would call him "El Mero Chingón," he who screwed up everything. Then maybe the tale of love and passion and the insanity it can bring will be complete. Yes, I think someday I will write that story.

"What did you see?" I asked Justino.

"Something worse than la Llorona," he whispered.

To the south a wind mourned and moved the clouds off Popo's crown. The bald, snow-covered mountain thrust its power into the blue Mexican sky. The light glowed like liquid gold around the god's head. Popo was a god, an ancient god. Somewhere at his feet Justino's story had taken place.

"I moved closer, and when I parted the bushes I saw Don Francisco. He was sitting on a rock, and he was crying. From time to time he looked at the ravine in front of him, the hole seemed to slant into the earth. That pozo is called el Pozo de Mendoza. I had heard stories about it before, but I had never seen it. I looked into the pozo, and you wouldn't believe what I saw."

He waited, so I asked, "What?"

"Money! Huge piles of gold and silver coins! Necklaces and bracelets and crowns of gold, all loaded with all kinds of precious stones! Jewels! Diamonds! All sparkling in the sunlight that entered the hole. More money than I have ever seen! A fortune, my friend, a fortune which is still there, just waiting for two adventurers like us to take it!"

"Us? But what about Don Francisco? It's his land, his fortune."

"Ah," Justino smiled, "that's the strange thing about this fortune. Don Francisco can't touch it, that's why he was crying. You see, I stayed there, and watched him closely. Every time he stood up and started to walk into the pozo the money disappeared. He stretched out his hand to grab the gold, and poof, it was gone! That's why he was crying! He murdered all those people and hid their wealth in the pozo, but now he can't touch it. He is cursed."

"El Pozo de Mendoza," he said aloud. Something began to click in my mind. I smelled a story.

"Who was Mendoza?" I asked.

"He was a very rich man. Don Francisco killed him in a quarrel they had over some cattle. But Mendoza must have put a curse on Don Francisco before he died, because now Don Francisco can't get to the money."

"So Mendoza's ghost haunts old Don Francisco," I nodded.

"Many ghosts haunt him," Justino answered. "He has killed many men."

"And the fortune, the money. . . ."

He looked at me and his eyes were dark and piercing. "It's still there. Waiting for us!"

"But it disappears as one approaches it, you said so yourself. Perhaps it's only an hallucination."

Justino shook his head. "No, it's real gold and silver, not hallucination money. It disappears for Don Francisco because the curse is on him, but the curse is not on us." He smiled. He knew he had drawn me into his plot. "We didn't steal the money, so it won't disappear for us. And you are not connected with the place. You are inno-cent. I've thought very carefully about it, and now is the time to go. I can lower you into the pozo with a rope, in a few hours we can bring out the entire fortune. All we need is a car. You can borrow the patrón's car, he is your friend. But he must not know where we're going. We can be there and back in one day, one night." He nod-ded as if to assure me, then he turned and looked at the sky. "It will not rain today. It will not rain for a week. Now is the time to go."

He winked and returned to watering the grass and flowers of the jardín, a wild Pan among the bougainvillea and the roses, a man possessed by a dream. The gold was not for him, he told me the next day, it was for his women, he would buy them all gifts, bright dresses, and he would take them on vacation to the United States, he would educate his children, send them to the best colleges. I listened and the germ of the story cluttered my thoughts as I sat beneath the orange tree in the mornings. I couldn't write, nothing was coming, but I knew that there were elements for a good story in Justino's tale. In dreams I saw the lonely hacienda to the south. I saw the pa-thetic, tormented figure of Don Francisco as he cried over the fortune he couldn't touch. I saw the ghosts of the men he had killed, the lonely women who mourned over them and cursed the evil Don Francisco. In one dream I saw a man I took to be B. Traven, a grey-haired distinguished looking gentleman who looked at me and nod-ded approvingly. "Yes, there's a story there, follow it, follow it. . . ."

In the meantime, other small and seemingly insignificant details came my way. During a luncheon at the home of my friend, a woman I did not know leaned toward me and asked me if I would like to meet the widow of B. Traven. The woman's hair was tinged orange, her complexion was ashen grey. I didn't know who she was or why she would mention B. Traven to me. How did she know Traven had come to haunt my thoughts? Was she a clue, which would help unravel the mystery? I didn't know, but I nodded. Yes, I would like to meet her. I had heard that Traven's widow, Rosa Elena, lived in Mexico City. But what would I ask her? What did I want to know? Would she know Traven's secret? Somehow he had learned that to keep his magic in-tact he had to keep away from the public. Like the fortune in the pozo, the magic feel for the story might disappear if unclean hands reached for it. I turned to look at the woman, but she was gone. I wandered to the terrace to finish my beer. Justino sat be-neath the orange tree. He yawned. I knew the literary talk bored him. He was eager to be on the way to el Pozo de Mendoza.

I was nervous, too, but I didn't know why. The tension for the story was there, but something was missing. Or perhaps it was just Justino's insistence that I decide whether I was going or not that drove me out of the house in the mornings. Time usually de-voted to writing found me in a small cafe in the center of town. From there I could watch the shops open, watch the people cross the zócalo, the main square. I drank lots of coffee, I smoked a lot, I daydreamed, I wondered about the significance of the pozo, the fortune, Justino, the story I wanted to write about B. Traven. In one of these moods I saw a friend from whom I hadn't heard in years. Suddenly he was there, trekking across the square, dressed like an old rabbi, moss and green algae for a beard, and followed by a troop of very dignified Lacandones, Mayan Indians from Chiapas.

"Victor," I gasped, unsure if he was real or a part of the shadows which the sun created as it flooded the square with its light.

"I have no time to talk," he said as he stopped to munch on my pan dulce and sip my coffee. "I only want you to know, for purposes of your story, that I was in a Lacandonian village last month, and a Hollywood film crew descended from the sky. They came in helicopters. They set up tents near the village, and big-bosomed, bikinied actresses emerged from them, tossed themselves on the cut trees which are the atrocity of the giant American lumber companies, and they cried while the director shot his film. Then they produced a grey-haired old man from one of the tents and took shots of him posing with the Indians. Herr Traven, the director called him."

He finished my coffee, nodded to his friends and they began to walk away.

"B. Traven?" I asked.

He turned. "No, an imposter, an actor. Be careful for imposters. Remember, even Traven used many disguises, many names!"

"Then he's alive and well?" I shouted. People around me turned to stare.

"His spirit is with us," were the last words I heard as they moved across the zócalo, a strange troop of near naked Lacandon Mayans and my friend the Guatemalan Jew, returning to the rain forest, returning to the primal, innocent land.

I slumped in my chair and looked at my empty cup. What did it mean? As their trees fall the Lacandones die. Betrayed as B. Traven was betrayed. Does each one of us also die as the trees fall in the dark depths of the Chiapas jungle? Far to the north, in Aztlán, it is the same where the earth is ripped open to expose and mine the yellow uranium. A few poets sing songs and stand in the way as the giant machines of the corporations rumble over the land and grind everything into dust. New holes are made in the earth, pozos full of curses, pozos with fortunes we cannot touch, should not touch. Oil, coal, uranium, from holes in the earth through which we suck the blood of the earth.

There were other incidents. A telephone call late one night, a voice with a German accent called my name, and when I answered the line went dead. A letter addressed to B. Traven came in the mail. It was dated March 26, 1969. My friend returned it to the post office. Justino grew more and more morose. He was under the orange tree and stared into space, my friend complained about the garden drying up. Justino looked at me and scowled. He did a little work then went back to daydreaming. Without the rains the garden withered. His heart was set on the adventure which lay at el pozo. Finally I said yes, dammit, why not, let's go, neither one of us is getting anything done here, and Justino, cheering like a child, ran to prepare for the trip. But when I asked my friend for the weekend loan of the car he reminded me that we were invited to a tertulia, an afternoon reception, at the home of Señora Ana R. Many writers and artists would be there. It was in my honor, so I could meet the literati of Cuernavaca. I had to tell Justino I couldn't go.

Now it was I who grew morose. The story growing within would not let me sleep. I awakened in the night and looked out the window, hoping to see Justino and women bathing in the pool, enjoying themselves. But all was quiet. No radio played. The still night was warm and heavy. From time to time gunshots sounded in the dark, dogs barked, and the presence of a Mexico which never sleeps closed in on me.

Saturday morning dawned with a strange overcast. Perhaps the rains will come, I thought. In the afternoon I reluctantly accompanied my friend to the reception. I had not seen Justino all day, but I saw him at the gate as we drove out. He looked tired, as if he, too, had not slept. He wore the white shirt and baggy pants of a campesino. His straw hat cast a shadow over his eyes. I wondered if he had decided to go to the pozo alone. He didn't speak as we drove through the gate, he only nodded. When I looked back I saw him standing by the gate, looking after the car, and I had a vague, uneasy feeling that I had lost an opportunity.

The afternoon gathering was a pleasant affair, attended by a number of affectionate artists, critics, and writers who enjoyed the refreshing drinks which quenched the thirst.

But my mood drove me away from the crowd. I wandered around the terrace and found a foyer surrounded by green plants, huge fronds and ferns and flowering bougainvillea. I pushed the green aside and entered a quiet, very private alcove. The light was dim, the air was cool, a perfect place for contemplation. At first I thought I was alone, then I saw the man sitting in one of the wicker chairs next to a small, wrought iron table. He was an elderly white-haired gentlemen. His face showed he had lived a full life, yet he was still very distinguished in his manner and posture. His eyes shone brightly.

"Perdón," I apologized and turned to leave. I did not want to intrude.

"No, no, please," he motioned to the empty chair, "I've been waiting for you." He spoke English with a slight German accent. Or perhaps it was Norwegian, I couldn't tell the difference. "I can't take the literary gossip. I prefer the quiet."

I nodded and sat. He smiled and I felt at ease. I took the cigar he offered and we lit up. He began to talk and I listened. He was a writer also, but I had the good manners not to ask his titles. He talked about the changing Mexico, the change the new oil would bring, the lateness of the rains and how they affected the people and the land, and he talked about how important a woman was in a writer's life. He wanted to know about me, about the Chicanos of Aztlán, about our work. It was the workers, he said, who would change society. The artist learned from the worker. I talked, and sometime during the conversation I told him the name of the friend with whom I was staying. He laughed and wanted to know if Vitorino was still working for him.

"Do you know Justino?" I asked.

"Oh, yes, I know that old guide. I met him many years ago, when I first came to Mexico," he answered. "Justino knows the campesino very well. He and I traveled many places together, he in search of adventure, I in search of stories."

I thought the coincidence strange, so I gathered the courage and asked, "Did he ever tell you the story of the fortune at el Pozo de Mendoza?"

"Tell me?" the old man smiled. "I went there."

"With Justino?"

"Yes, I went with him. What a rogue he was in those days, but a good man. If I remember correctly I even wrote a story based on that adventure. Not a very good story. Never came to anything. But we had a grand time. People like Justino are the writer's source. We met interesting people and saw fabulous places, enough to last me a lifetime. We were supposed to be gone for one day, but we were gone nearly three years. You see, I wasn't interested in the pots of gold he kept saying were just over the next hill, I went because there was a story to write."

"Yes, that's what interested me," I agreed.

"A writer has to follow a story if it leads him to hell itself. That's our curse. Ay, and each one of us knows our own private hell."

I nodded. I felt relieved. I sat back to smoke the cigar and sip from my drink. Somewhere to the west the sun bronzed the evening sky. On a clear afternoon, Popo's crown would glow like fire.

"Yes," the old man continued, "a writer's job is to find and follow people like Justino. They're the source of life. The ones you have to keep away from are the dilettantes like the ones in there." He motioned in the general direction of the noise of the party. "I stay with people like Justino. They may be illiterate, but they understand our descent into the pozo of hell, and they understand us because they're willing to share the adventure with us. You seek fame and notoriety and you're dead as a writer."

I sat upright. I understood now what the pozo meant, why Justino had come into my life to tell me the story. It was clear. I rose quickly and shook the old man's hand. I turned and parted the palm leaves of the alcove. There, across the way, in one of the streets that led out of the maze of the town towards the south, I saw Justino. He was walking in the direction of Popo, and he was followed by women and children, a rag-tail army of adventurers, all happy, all singing. He looked up to where I stood on the terrace, and he smiled as he waved. He paused to light the stub of a cigar. The women turned, and the children turned, and all waved to me. Then they continued their walk, south, towards the foot of the volcano. They were going to the Pozo de Mendoza, to the place where the story originated.

I wanted to run after them, to join them in the glorious light which bathed the Cuernavaca valley and the majestic snow-covered head of Popo. The light was everywhere, a magnetic element which flowed from the clouds. I waved as Justino and his followers disappeared in the light. Then I turned to say something to the old man, but he was gone. I was alone in the alcove. Somewhere in the background I heard the tinkling of glasses and the laughter which came from the party, but that was not for me. I left the terrace and crossed the lawn, found the gate and walked down the street. The sound of Mexico filled the air. I felt light and happy. I wandered aimlessly through the curving, narrow streets, then I quickened my pace because suddenly the story was overflowing and I needed to write. I needed to get to my quiet room and write the story about B. Traven being alive and well in Cuernavaca.

[1984]

Questions

1. What is the source of conflict in Anaya's story? Is it the same thing that connects the three parts of his narrative: the search for B. Traven, Justino's account of the gold, and the writer's search for material?

2. At the end of the story, we have a strong impression of Justino Vitorino Trinidad, the jardinero, but what do we know of the writer himself? How may the two characters be compared?

3. Is it B. Traven who appears at the conclusion of the story?

4. What does Anaya mean when he states, early in the narrative, "Time in Mexico can be cruel and punishing, but it is never indifferent. It permeates everything, it changes reality. Einstein would have loved Mexico because there time and space are one"? How does this statement expand our understanding of the story that follows?

Sherwood Anderson
(1876–1941)
United States

S herwood Anderson's voice is utterly distinctive in American literature. Growing up in the midwest—Camden, Ohio—he discovered that voice through listening and shaping the stories and narrative of small-town and rural life. His most highly regarded collection of stories, Winesburg, Ohio (1919), is a deeply sympathetic portrait of an entire community: simple people often caught in lives that they do not fully understand and are powerless to change. Many of Anderson's stories seem to hover around the unanswered question, "Why?"

Anderson came to fiction late, after working in a variety of trades from farm laborer and paint factory worker to advertising copywriter. Unhappy with the commercial life, he went to Chicago, where he found a group of like-minded friends, including Carl Sandburg and Theodore Dreiser, and began to write. Two novels and a volume of poetry preceded his discovery that the short story was his true form. Anderson described his struggle to capture a story in its appropriate form as a difficult gestation process:

> Having, from a conversation overhead or in some other way, got the tone of a tale I was like a woman who has just become impregnated. Something was growing inside me. At night when I lay in my bed I could feel the heels of the tale kicking against the walls of my body. Often as I lay thus every word of the tale came to me quite clearly but when I got out of bed to write it down the words would not come.

If it is not their form that distinguishes Anderson's stories, it is certainly their tone, a characteristic muted melancholy. In "Hands," as in most of his stories, Anderson conveys with unerring accuracy the errors of perception and failures of sympathy that produce despair.

HANDS

Upon the half decayed veranda of a small frame house that stood near the edge of a ravine near the town of Winesburg, Ohio, a fat little old man walked nervously up and down. Across a long field that had been seeded for clover but that had produced only a dense crop of yellow mustard weeds, he could see the public highway along which went a wagon filled with berry pickers returning from the fields. The berry pickers, youths and maidens, laughed and shouted boisterously. A boy clad in a blue shirt leaped from the wagon and attempted to drag after him one of the maidens, who screamed and protested shrilly. The feet of the boy in the road kicked up a cloud of dust that floated across the face of the departing sun. Over the long field came a thin girl-ish voice. "Oh, you Wing Biddlebaum, comb your hair, it's falling into your eyes," commanded the voice to the man, who was bald and whose nervous little hands fiddled about the bare white forehead as though arranging a mass of tangled locks.

Wing Biddlebaum, forever frightened and beset by a ghostly band of doubts, did not think of himself as in any way a part of the life of the town where he had lived for twenty years. Among all the people of Winesburg but one had come close to him. With George Willard, son of Tom Willard, the proprietor of the New Willard House, he had formed something like a friendship. George Willard was the reporter on the *Winesburg Eagle* and sometimes in the evenings he walked out along the highway to Wing Biddlebaum's house. Now as the old man walked up and down on the veranda, his hands moving nervously about, he was hoping that George Willard would come and spend the evening with him. After the wagon containing the berry pickers had passed, he went across the field through the tall mustard weeds and climbing a rail fence peered anxiously along the road to the town. For a moment he stood thus, rubbing his hands together and looking up and down the road, and then, fear overcoming him, ran back to walk again upon the porch on his own house.

In the presence of George Willard, Wing Biddlebaum, who for twenty years had been the town mystery, lost something of his timidity, and his shadowy personality, submerged in a sea of doubts, came forth to look at the world. With the young reporter at his side, he ventured in the light of day onto Main Street or strode up and down on the rickety front porch of his own house, talking excitedly. The voice that had been low and trembling became shrill and loud. The bent figure straightened. With a kind of wriggle, like a fish returned to the brook by the fisherman, Biddlebaum the silent began to talk, striving to put into words the ideas that had been accumulated by his mind during long years of silence.

Wing Biddlebaum talked much with his hands. The slender expressive fingers, forever active, forever striving to conceal themselves in his pockets or behind his back, came forth and became the piston rods of his machinery of expression.

The story of Wing Biddlebaum is a story of hands. Their restless activity, like unto the beating of the wings of an imprisoned bird, had given him his name. Some obscure poet of the town had thought of it. The hands alarmed their owner. He wanted to keep them hidden away and looked with amazement at the quiet inexpressive hands of other men who worked beside him in the fields, or passed, driving sleepy teams on country roads.

When he talked to George Willard, Wing Biddlebaum closed his fists and beat with them upon a table or on the walls of his house. The action made him more comfortable. If the desire to talk came to him when the two were walking in the fields, he sought out a stump or the top board of a fence and with his hands pounding busily talked with renewed ease.

The story of Wing Biddlebaum's hands is worth a book in itself. Sympathetically set forth it would tap many strange, beautiful qualities in obscure men. It is a job for a poet. In Winesburg the hands had attracted attention merely because of their activity. With them Wing Biddlebaum had picked as high as a hundred and forty quarts of strawberries in a day. They became his distinguishing feature, the source of his fame. Also they made more grotesque an already grotesque and elusive individuality. Winesburg was proud of the hands of Wing Biddlebaum in the same spirit in which it was proud of Banker White's new stone house and Wesley Moyer's bay stallion, Tony Tip, that had won the two-fifteen trot at the fall races in Cleveland.

As for George Willard, he had many times wanted to ask about the hands. At times an almost overwhelming curiosity had taken hold of him. He felt that there must be a reason for their strange activity and their inclination to keep hidden away and only a growing respect for Wing Biddlebaum kept him from blurting out the questions that were often in his mind.

Once he had been on the point of asking. The two were walking in the fields on a summer afternoon and had stopped to sit upon a grassy bank. All afternoon Wing Biddlebaum had talked as one inspired. By a fence he had stopped and beating like a giant woodpecker upon the top board had shouted at George Willard, condemning his tendency to be too much influenced by the people about him. "You are destroying yourself," he cried. "You have the inclination to be alone and to dream and you are afraid of dreams. You want to be like others in town here. You hear them talk and you try to imitate them."

On the grassy bank Wing Biddlebaum had tried again to drive his point home. His voice became soft and reminiscent, and with a sigh of contentment he launched into a long rambling talk, speaking as one lost in a dream.

Out of the dream Wing Biddlebaum made a picture for George Willard. In the picture men lived again in a kind of pastoral golden age. Across a green open country came clean-limbed young men, some afoot, some mounted upon horses. In crowds the young men came to gather about the feet of an old man who sat beneath a tree in a tiny garden and who talked to them.

Wing Biddlebaum became wholly inspired. For once he forgot the hands. Slowly they stole forth and lay upon George Willard's shoulders. Something new and bold came into the voice that talked. "You must try to forget all you have learned," said the old man. "You must begin to dream. From this time on you must shut your ears to the roaring of the voices."

Pausing in his speech, Wing Biddlebaum looked long and earnestly at George Willard. His eyes glowed. Again he raised the hands to caress the boy and then a look of horror swept over his face.

With a convulsive movement of his body, Wing Biddlebaum sprang to his feet and thrust his hands deep into his trousers pockets. Tears came to his eyes. "I must be getting along home. I can talk no more with you," he said nervously.

Without looking back, the old man had hurried down the hillside and across a meadow, leaving George Willard perplexed and frightened upon the grassy slope. With a shiver of dread the boy arose and went along the road toward town. "I'll not ask him about his hands," he thought, touched by the memory of the terror he had seen in the man's eyes. "There's something wrong, but I don't want to know what it is. His hands have something to do with his fear of me and of everyone."

And George Willard was right. Let us look briefly into the story of the hands. Perhaps our talking of them will arouse the poet who will tell the hidden wonder story of the influence for which the hands were but fluttering pennants of promise.

In his youth Wing Biddlebaum had been a school teacher in a town in Pennsylvania. He was not then known as Wing Biddlebaum, but went by the less euphonic name of Adolph Myers. As Adolph Myers he was much loved by the boys of his school.

Adolph Myers was meant by nature to be a teacher of youth. He was one of those rare, little-understood men who rule by a power so gentle that it passes as a lovable weakness. In their feeling for the boys under their charge such men are not unlike the finer sort of women in their love of men.

And yet that is but crudely stated. It needs the poet there. With the boys of his school, Adolph Myers had walked in the evening or had sat talking until dusk upon the schoolhouse steps lost in a kind of dream. Here and there went his hands, caressing the shoulders of the boys, playing about the tousled heads. As he talked his voice became soft and musical. There was a caress in that also. In a way the voice and the hands, the stroking of the shoulders and the touching of the hair were a part of the schoolmaster's effort to carry a dream into the young minds. By the caress that was in his fingers he expressed himself. He was one of those men in whom the force that creates life is diffused, not centralized. Under the caress of his hands doubt and disbelief went out of the minds of the boys and they began also to dream.

And then the tragedy. A half-witted boy of the school became enamored of the young master. In his bed at night he imagined unspeakable things and in the morning went forth to tell his dreams as facts. Strange, hideous accusations fell from his loose-hung lips. Through the Pennsylvania town went a shiver. Hidden, shadowy doubts that had been in men's minds concerning Adolph Myers were galvanized into beliefs.

The tragedy did not linger. Trembling lads were jerked out of bed and questioned. "He put his arms about me," said one. "His fingers were always playing in my hair," said another.

One afternoon a man of the town, Henry Bradford, who kept a saloon, came to the schoolhouse door. Calling Adolph Myers into the school yard he began to beat him with his fists. As his hard knuckles beat down into the frightened face of the schoolmaster, his wrath became more and more terrible. Screaming with dismay, the children ran here and there like disturbed insects. "I'll teach you to put your hands on my boy, you beast," roared the saloon keeper, who, tired of beating the master, had began to kick him about the yard.

Adolph Myers was driven from the Pennsylvania town in the night. With lanterns in their hands a dozen men came to the door of the house where he lived alone and commanded that he dress and come forth. It was raining and one of the men had a rope in his hands. They had intended to hang the schoolmaster, but something in his figure, so small, white, and pitiful, touched their hearts and they let him escape. As he ran away into the darkness they repented of their weakness and ran after him, swearing and throwing sticks and great balls of soft mud at the figure that screamed and ran faster and faster into the darkness.

For twenty years Adolph Myers had lived alone in Winesburg. He was but forty but looked sixty-five. The name of Biddlebaum he got from a box of goods seen at a freight station as he hurried through an eastern Ohio town. He had an aunt in Winesburg, a black-toothed old woman who raised chickens, and with her he lived until she died. He had been ill for a year after the experience in Pennsylvania, and after his recovery worked as a day laborer in the fields, going timidly about and striving to conceal his hands. Although he did not understand what had happened he felt that the hands must be to blame. Again and again the fathers of the boys had talked of the hands. "Keep your hands to yourself," the saloon keeper had roared, dancing with fury in the schoolhouse yard.

Upon the veranda of his house by the ravine, Wing Biddlebaum continued to walk up and down until the sun had disappeared and the road beyond the field was lost in the grey shadows. Going into his house he cut slices of bread and spread honey upon them. When the rumble of the evening train that took away the express cars loaded with the day's harvest of berries had passed and restored the silence of the summer night, he went again to walk upon the veranda. In the darkness he could not see the hands and they became quiet. Although he still hungered for the presence of the boy, who was the medium through which he expressed his love of man, the hunger became again a part of his loneliness and his waiting. Lighting a lamp, Wing Biddlebaum washed the few dishes soiled by his simple meal and, setting up a folding cot by the screen door that led to the porch, prepared to undress for the night. A few stray white bread crumbs lay on the cleanly washed floor by the table; putting the lamp upon a low stool he began to pick up the crumbs, carrying them to his mouth one by one with unbelievable rapidity. In the dense blotch of light beneath the table, the kneeling figure looked like a priest engaged in some service of his church. The nervous expressive fingers, flashing in and out of the light, might well have been mistaken for the fingers of the devotee going swiftly through decade after decade of his rosary.

[1919]

Questions

1. How does the first paragraph of the story establish the reader's expectations concerning Wing Biddlebaum?
2. Do you find Wing Biddlebaum to be a sympathetic character? If so, through what details does the narrator establish sympathy?
3. What is the significance of repeated references to dreams and to poets? What is suggested about Wing Biddlebaum through the narrator's use of such terms as *mystery*, *hunger*, and *waiting*?
4. The narrator asserts that "the story of Wing Biddlebaum is a story of hands." How is that claim illustrated in the story? What meaning is conveyed through the image of hands in the final sentence?

Margaret Atwood

(b. 1939)

Canada

Widely regarded as one of the most distinguished contemporary writers of Canada, Margaret Atwood is uniquely accomplished and equally at home with poetry and fiction. She has published more than a dozen volumes of poetry—several have been honored with Canada's prestigious Governor-General Award—as well as ten novels and four volumes of short stories to date. Her critical study of Canadian literature, Survival (1972), remains an important survey of themes and ideas in a national literary tradition that she helped to establish and identify. She is also artistically talented: She created the illustrations and cover designs for several volumes of her poetry.

Atwood was born in Ottawa, Ontario, one of three siblings; she spent her childhood in the "bush" (rural area) of northern Ontario and Quebec provinces, where her entomologist father conducted his research. Consequently, as she expressed it, "I did not have to go to school full time until I was in grade eight, and I think that was probably a good thing." During those years she wrote poetry, novels, stories, and plays. Subsequently, she attended the University of Toronto, publishing her first volume of poetry the year that she graduated (1962); she received her M.A. in Victorian literature at Harvard. For a time she taught English; since 1972 she has regarded herself as a professional writer. She lives with writer Graeme Gibson and their daughter Jess.

Because Atwood is so prolific in multiple genres it is difficult to generalize about her work. Several ideas and themes do recur, however, including explorations of the meaning of "survival," whether understood in political or personal terms; power and victimization; the significance of the past; the dualism or splitness of experience; and the problems of female selfhood. In novels such as The Edible Woman (1969), Surfacing (1972), and Lady Oracle (1976), Atwood explores the dilemmas of inwardly divided female protagonists who struggle to achieve wholeness and to resist the destructive influences of technological and commercial society. The Handmaid's Tale (1986) is a chilling dystopian novel of female reproductive oppression, while Cat's Eye (1988) focuses retrospectively on the dark side of childhood through the biography of a female painter. The Robber Bride (1993) features a truly evil and unforgettable female villain. Alias Grace (1996), based on a celebrated nineteenth-century Canadian crime, is told through the voice (among others) of the woman imprisoned for a murder she may or may not have committed years earlier; the truth remains elusive to the end. The Blind Assassin (2000) intertwines the story of an unsolved family mystery with other plot lines—a novel-within-a-novel scrambling levels of reality. Atwood's volumes of poetry range widely in subject, from The Journals of Susanna Moodie (1970), based on a historical Canadian pioneer woman, to the cryptic Two-Headed Poems (1980) and the intriguing prose poems of Good Bones and Simple Murders (1994).

Atwood is a master of sardonic, wry wit; at the same time her remarkable versatility with language is balanced by strong social commitment. She has described herself as a "pessimistic pantheist," meaning that "God is everywhere, but losing."

DANCING GIRLS

The first sign of the new man was the knock on the door. It was the landlady, knocking not at Ann's door, as she'd thought, but on the other door, the one east of the bathroom. Knock, knock, knock; then a pause, soft footsteps, the sound of unlocking. Ann, who had been reading a book on canals, put it down and lit herself a cigarette. It wasn't that she tried to overhear: in this house you couldn't help it.

"Hi!" Mrs. Nolan's voice loud, overly friendly. "I was wondering, my kids would love to see your native costume. You think you could put it on, like, and come down?"

A soft voice, unintelligible.

"Gee, that's great! We'd sure appreciate it!"

Closing and locking, Mrs. Nolan slip-slopping along the hall in, Ann knew, her mauve terry-cloth scuffies and flowered housecoat, down the stairs, hollering at her two boys. "You get into this room right now!" Her voice came up through Ann's hot air register as if the grate were a PA system. *It isn't those kids who want to see him*, she thought. *It's her.* She put out the cigarette, reserving the other half for later, and opened her book again. What costume? Which land, this time?

Unlocking, opening, soft feet down the hall. They sounded bare. Ann closed the book and opened her own door. A white robe, the back of a brown head, moving with a certain stealth or caution toward the stairs. Ann went into the bathroom and turned on the light. They would share it; the person in that room always shared her bathroom. She hoped he would be better than the man before, who always seemed to forget his razor and would knock on the door while Ann was having a bath. You wouldn't have to worry about getting raped or anything in this house though, that was one good thing. Mrs. Nolan was better than any burglar alarm, and she was always there.

That one had been from France, studying Cinema. Before him there had been a girl, from Turkey, studying Comparative Literature. Lelah, or that was how it was pronounced. Ann used to find her beautiful long auburn hairs in the washbasin fairly regularly; she'd run her thumb and index finger along them, enviously, before discarding them. She had to keep her own hair chopped off at ear level, as it was brittle and broke easily. Lelah also had a gold tooth, right at the front on the outside where it showed when she smiled. Curiously, Ann was envious of this tooth as well. It and the hair and the turquoise-studded earrings Lelah wore gave her a gypsy look, a wise look that Ann, with her beige eyebrows and delicate mouth, knew she would never be able to develop, no matter how wise she got. She herself went in for "classics," tailored skirts and Shetland sweaters; it was the only look she could carry off. But she and Lelah had been friends, smoking cigarettes in each other's room, commiserating with each other about the difficulties of their courses and the loudness of Mrs. Nolan's voice. So Ann was familiar with that room; she knew what it looked like inside and how much it cost. It was no luxury suite, certainly, and she wasn't surprised at the high rate of turnover. It had an even more direct pipeline to the sounds of the Nolan family than hers had. Lelah had left because she couldn't stand the noise.

The room was smaller and cheaper than her room, though painted the same depressing shade of green. Unlike hers, it did not have its own tiny refrigerator, sink and stove; you had to use the kitchen at the front of the house, which had been staked out much earlier by a small enclave of mathematicians, two men and one woman, from

Hong Kong. Whoever took that room either had to eat out all the time or run the gamut of their conversation, which even when not in Chinese was so rarefied as to be unintelligible. And you could never find any space in the refrigerator, it was always full of mushrooms. This from Lelah; Ann herself never had to deal with them since she could cook in her own room. She could see them, though, as she went in and out. At mealtimes they usually sat quietly at their kitchen table, discussing surds, she assumed. Ann suspected that what Lelah had really resented about them was not the mushrooms: they simply made her feel stupid.

Every morning, before she left for classes, Ann checked the bathroom for signs of the new man—hairs, cosmetics—but there was nothing. She hardly ever heard him; sometimes there was that soft, barefooted pacing, the click of his lock, but there were no radio noises, no coughs, no conversations. For the first couple of weeks, apart from that one glimpse of a tall, billowing figure, she didn't even see him. He didn't appear to use the kitchen, where the mathematicians continued their mysteries undisturbed; or if he did, he cooked while no one else was there. Ann would have forgotten about him completely if it hadn't been for Mrs. Nolan.

"He's real nice, not like some you get," she said to Ann in her piercing whisper. Although she shouted at her husband, when he was home, and especially at her children, she always whispered when she was talking to Ann, a hoarse, avid whisper, as if they shared disreputable secrets. Ann was standing in front of her door with the room key in her hand, her usual location during these confidences. Mrs. Nolan knew Ann's routine. It wasn't difficult for her to pretend to be cleaning the bathroom, to pop out and waylay Ann, Ajax and rag in hand, whenever she felt she had something to tell her. She was a short, barrel-shaped woman: the top of her head came only to Ann's nose, so she had to look up at Ann, which at these moments made her seem oddly childlike.

"He's from one of them Arabian countries. Though I thought they wore turbans, or not turbans, those white things, like. He just has this funny hat, sort of like the Shriners. He don't look much like an Arab to me. He's got these tattoo marks on his face. . . . But he's real nice."

Ann stood, her umbrella dripping onto the floor, waiting for Mrs. Nolan to finish. She never had to say anything much; it wasn't expected. "You think you could get me the rent on Wednesday?" Mrs. Nolan asked. Three days early; the real point of the conversation, probably. Still, as Mrs. Nolan had said back in September, she didn't have much of anyone to talk to. Her husband was away much of the time and her children escaped outdoors whenever they could. She never went out herself except to shop, and for Mass on Sundays.

"I'm glad it was you took the room," she'd said to Ann. "I can talk to you. You're not, like, foreign. Not like most of them. It was his idea, getting this big house to rent out. Not that he has to do the work or put up with them. You never know what they'll do."

Ann wanted to point out to her that she was indeed foreign, that she was just as foreign as any of the others, but she knew Mrs. Nolan would not understand. It would be like that fiasco in October. *Wear your native costumes.* She had responded to the invitation out of a sense of duty, as well as one of irony. Wait till they get a load of my native costume, she'd thought, contemplating snowshoes and a parka but actually putting on her good blue wool suit. There was only one thing *native costume* reminded her of: the cover picture on the Missionary Sunday School paper they'd once handed out, which showed children from all the countries of the world dancing in a circle around a smiling white-faced Jesus in a bedsheet. That, and the poem in the *Golden Windows Reader*:

Little Indian, Sioux or Cree,
Oh, don't you wish that you were me?

The awful thing, as she told Lelah later, was that she was the only one who'd gone. "She had all this food ready, and not a single other person was there. She was really upset, and I was so embarrassed for her. It was some Friends of Foreign Students thing, just for women: students and the wives of students. She obviously didn't think I was foreign enough, and she couldn't figure out why no one else came." Neither could Ann, who had stayed far too long and had eaten platefuls of crackers and cheese she didn't want in order to soothe her hostess' thwarted sense of hospitality. The woman, who had tastefully-streaked ash-blonde hair and a livingroom filled with polished and satiny traditional surfaces, had alternately urged her to eat and stared at the door, as if expecting a parade of foreigners in their native costumes to come trooping gratefully through it.

Lelah smiled, showing her wise tooth. "Don't they know any better than to throw those things at night?" she said. "Those men aren't going to let their wives go out by themselves at night. And the single ones are afraid to walk on the streets alone, I know I am."

"I'm not," Ann said, "as long as you stay on the main ones, where it's lighted."

"Then you're a fool," Lelah said. "Don't you know there was a girl murdered three blocks from here? Left her bathroom window unlocked. Some man climbed through the window and cut her throat."

"I always carry my umbrella," Ann said. Of course there were certain places where you just didn't go. Scollay Square, for instance, where the prostitutes hung out and you might get followed, or worse. She tried to explain to Lelah that she wasn't used to this, to any of this, that in Toronto you could walk all over the city, well, almost anywhere, and never have any trouble. She went on to say that no one here seemed to understand that she wasn't like them, she came from a different country, it wasn't the same; but Lelah was quickly bored by this. She had to get back to Tolstoy, she said, putting out her cigarette in her unfinished cup of instant coffee. (*Not strong enough for her, I suppose*, Ann thought.)

"You shouldn't worry," she said. "You're well off. At least your family doesn't almost disown you for doing what you want to do." Lelah's father kept writing her letters, urging her to return to Turkey, where the family had decided on the perfect husband for her. Lelah had stalled them for one year, and maybe she could stall them for one more, but that would be her limit. She couldn't possibly finish her thesis in that time.

Ann hadn't seen much of her since she'd moved out. You lost sight of people quickly here, in the ever-shifting population of hopeful and despairing transients.

No one wrote her letters urging her to come home, no one had picked out the perfect husband for her. On the contrary. She could imagine her mother's defeated look, the greying and sinking of her face, if she were suddenly to announce that she was going to quit school, trade in her ambitions for fate, and get married. Even her father wouldn't like it. *Finish what you start*, he'd say, *I didn't and look what happened to me*. The bungalow at the top of Avenue Road, beside a gas station, with the roar of the expressway always there, like the sea, and fumes blighting the Chinese elm hedge her mother had planted to conceal the pumps. Both her brothers had dropped out of high school; they weren't the good students Ann had been. One worked in a print shop now and had a wife; the other had drifted to Vancouver, and no one knew what he did. She remembered her first real boyfriend, beefy, easygoing Bill Decker, with his two-tone car that kept losing the muffler. They'd spent a lot of time parked on side streets, rubbing against each other through all those layers of clothes. But even in that sensual mist, the cocoon of breath and skin they'd spun around each other, those phone conversations that existed as a form of touch, she'd known this was not something she could get too involved in. He was probably flabby by now, settled. She'd had relationships with men since then, but she had treated them the same way. *Circumspect.*

Not that Mrs. Nolan's back room was any step up. Out one window there was a view of the funeral home next door; out the other was the yard, which the Nolan kids had scraped clean of grass and which was now a bog of half-frozen mud. Their dog, a mongrelized German Shepherd, was kept tied there, where the kids alternately hugged and tormented it. ("Jimmy! Donny! Now you leave that dog alone!" "Don't do that, he's filthy! Look at you!" Ann covering her ears, reading about underground malls.) She'd tried to fix the room up, she'd hung a Madras spread as a curtain in front of the cooking area, she'd put up several prints, Braque still-lifes of guitars and soothing Cubist fruit, and she was growing herbs on her windowsill; she needed surroundings that at least tried not to be ugly. But none of these things helped much. At night she wore earplugs. She hadn't known about the scarcity of good rooms, hadn't realized that the whole area was a student slum, that the rents would be so high, the available places so dismal. Next year would be different; she'd get here early and have the pick of the crop. Mrs. Nolan's was definitely a leftover. You could do much better for the money; you could even have a whole apartment, if you were willing to live in the real slum that spread in narrow streets of three-storey frame houses, fading mustard yellow and soot grey, nearer the river. Though Ann didn't think she was quite up to that. Something in one of the good old houses, on a quiet back street, with a little stained glass, would be more like it. Her friend Jetske had a place like that.

But she was doing what she wanted, no doubt of that. In high school she had planned to be an architect, but while finishing the preliminary courses at university she had realized that the buildings she wanted to design were either impossible— who could afford them?—or futile. They would be lost, smothered, ruined by all the other buildings jammed inharmoniously around them. This was why she had decided to go into Urban Design, and she had come here because this school was the best. Or rumoured to be the best. By the time she finished, she intended to be so well-qualified, so armoured with qualifications, that no one back home would dare turn her down for the job she coveted. She wanted to rearrange Toronto. Toronto would do for a start.

She wasn't yet too certain of the specific details. What she saw were spaces, beautiful green spaces, with water flowing through them, and trees. Not big golf-course lawns, though; something more winding, something with sudden turns, private niches, surprising vistas. And no formal flower beds. The houses, or whatever they were, set unobtrusively among the trees, the cars kept . . . where? And where would people shop, and who would live in these places? This was the problem: she could see the vistas, the trees and the streams or canals, quite clearly, but she could never visualize the people. Her green spaces were always empty.

She didn't see her next-door neighbour again until February. She was coming back from the small local supermarket where she bought the food for her cheap, carefully balanced meals. He was leaning in the doorway of what, at home, she would have called a vestibule, smoking a cigarette and staring out at the rain, through the glass panes at the side of the front door. He should have moved a little to give Ann room to put down her umbrella, but he didn't. He didn't even look at her. She squeezed in, shook her deflated umbrella and checked her mail box, which didn't have a key. There weren't usually any letters in it, and today was no exception. He was wearing a white shirt that was too big for him and some greenish trousers. His feet were not bare, in fact he was wearing a pair of prosaic brown shoes. He did have tattoo marks, though, or rather scars, a set of them running across each cheek. It was the first time she had seen him from the front. He seemed a little shorter than he had when she'd glimpsed him heading towards the stairs, but perhaps it was because he had no hat on. He was curved so listlessly against the doorframe, it was almost as if he had no bones.

There was nothing to see through the front of Mrs. Nolan's door except the traffic, sizzling by the way it did every day. He was depressed, it must be that. This weather would depress anyone. Ann sympathized with his loneliness, but she did not wish to become involved in it, implicated by it. She had enough trouble dealing with her own. She smiled at him, though since he wasn't looking at her this smile was lost. She went past him and up the stairs.

As she fumbled in her purse for her key, Mrs. Nolan stumped out of the bathroom. "You see him?" she whispered.

"Who?" Ann said.

"*Him.*" Mrs. Nolan jerked her thumb. "Standing down there, by the door. He does that a lot. He's bothered me, like. I don't have such good nerves."

"He's not doing anything," Ann said.

"That's what I mean," Mrs. Nolan whispered ominously. "He never does nothing. Far as I can tell, he never goes out much. All he does is borrow my vacuum cleaner."

"Your vacuum cleaner?" Ann said, startled into responding.

"That's what I said." Mrs. Nolan had a rubber plunger which she was fingering. "And there's more of them. They come in the other night, up to his room. Two more, with the same marks and everything, on their faces. It's like some kind of, like, a religion or something. And he never gave the vacuum cleaner back till the next day."

"Does he pay the rent?" Ann said, trying to switch the conversation to practical matters. Mrs. Nolan was letting her imagination get out of control.

"Regular," Mrs. Nolan said. "Except I don't like the way he comes down, so quiet like, right into my house. With Fred away so much."

"I wouldn't worry," Ann said in what she hoped was a soothing voice. "He seems perfectly nice."

"It's always that kind," Mrs. Nolan said.

Ann cooked her dinner, a chicken breast, some peas, a digestive biscuit. Then she washed her hair in the bathroom and put it up in rollers. She had to do that, to give it body. With her head encased in the plastic hood of her portable dryer she sat at her table, drinking instant coffee, smoking her usual half cigarette, and attempting to read a book about Roman aqueducts, from which she hoped to get some novel ideas for her current project. (An aqueduct, going right through the middle of the obligatory shopping centre? Would anyone care?) Her mind kept flicking, though, to the problem of the man next door. Ann did not often try to think about what it would be like to be a man. But this particular man . . . Who was he, and what was happening to him? He must be a student, everyone here was a student. And he would be intelligent, that went without saying. Probably on scholarship. Everyone here in the graduate school was on scholarship, except the real Americans, who sometimes weren't. Or rather, the women were, but some of the men were still avoiding the draft, though President Johnson had announced he was going to do away with all that. She herself would never have made it this far without scholarships; her parents could not have afforded it.

So he was here on scholarship, studying something practical, no doubt, nuclear physics or the construction of dams, and, like herself and the other foreigners, he was expected to go away again as soon as he'd learned what he'd come for. But he never went out of the house; he stood at the front door and watched the brutish flow of cars, the winter rain, while those back in his own country, the ones that had sent him, were confidently expecting him to return some day, crammed with knowledge, ready to solve their lives. . . . *He's lost his nerve*, Ann thought. *He'll fail.* It was too late in the year for him ever to catch up. Such failures, such paralyses, were fairly common here, especially among the foreigners. He was far from home, from the language he shared, the wearers of his native costume; he was in exile, he was drowning. What did he do, alone by himself in his room at night?

Ann switched her hair dryer to COOL and wrenched her mind back to aqueducts. She could see he was drowning but there was nothing she could do. Unless you were good at it you shouldn't even try, she was wise enough to know that. All you could do for the drowning was to make sure you were not one of them.

The aqueduct, now. It would be made of natural brick, an earthy red; it would have low arches, in the shade of which there would be ferns and, perhaps, some delphiniums, in varying tones of blue. She must learn more about plants. Before entering the shopping complex (trust him to assign a shopping complex; before that he had demanded a public housing project), it would flow through her green space, in which, she could now see, there were people walking. Children? *But not children like Mrs. Nolan's.* They would turn her grass to mud, they'd nail things to her trees, their mangy dogs would shit on her ferns, they'd throw bottles and pop cans into her aqueduct. . . . And Mrs. Nolan herself, and her Noah's Ark of seedy, brilliant foreigners, where would she put them? For the houses of the Mrs. Nolans of this world would have to go; that was one of the axioms of Urban Design. She could convert them to small offices, or single-floor apartments; some shrubs and hanging plants and a new coat of paint would do wonders. But she knew this was temporizing. Around her green space, she could see, there was now a high wire fence. Inside it were trees, flowers and grass, outside the dirty snow, the endless rain, the grunting cars and the half-frozen mud of Mrs. Nolan's drab backyard. That was what *exclusive* meant, it meant that some people were excluded. Her parents stood in the rain outside the fence, watching with dreary pride while she strolled about in the eternal sunlight. Their one success.

Stop it, she commanded herself. *They want me to be doing this.* She unwound her hair and brushed it out. Three hours from now, she knew, it would be limp as ever because of the damp.

The next day, she tried to raise her new theoretical problem with her friend Jetske. Jetske was in Urban Design, too. She was from Holland, and could remember running through the devastated streets as a child, begging small change, first from the Germans, later from American soldiers, who were always good for a chocolate bar or two.

"You learn how to take care of yourself," she'd said. "It didn't seem hard at the time, but when you are a child, nothing is that hard. We were all the same, nobody had anything." Because of this background, which was more exotic and cruel than anything Ann herself had experienced (what was a gas pump compared to the Nazis?), Ann respected her opinions. She liked her also because she was the only person she'd met here who seemed to know where Canada was. There were a lot of Canadian soldiers buried in Holland. This provided Ann with at least a shadowy identity, which she felt she needed. She didn't have a native costume, but at least she had some heroic dead bodies with which she was connected, however remotely.

"The trouble with what we're doing . . . ," she said to Jetske, as they walked towards the library under Ann's umbrella. "I mean, you can rebuild one part, but what do you do about the rest?"

"Of the city?" Jetske said.

"No," Ann said slowly. "I guess I mean of the world."

Jetske laughed. She had what Ann now thought of as Dutch teeth, even and white, with quite a lot of gum showing above them and below the lip. "I didn't know you were a socialist," she said. Her cheeks were pink and healthy, like a cheese ad.

"I'm not," Ann said. "But I thought we were supposed to be thinking in total patterns."

Jetske laughed again. "Did you know," she said, "that in some countries you have to get official permission to move from one town to another?"

Ann didn't like this idea at all. "It controls the population flow," Jetske said. "You can't really have Urban Design without that, you know."

"I think that's awful," Ann said.

"Of course you do," Jetske said, as close to bitterness as she ever got. "You've never had to do it. Over here you are soft in the belly, you think you can always have everything. You think there is freedom of choice. The whole world will come to it. You will see." She began teasing Ann again about her plastic headscarf. Jetske never wore anything on her head.

Ann designed her shopping complex, putting in a skylight and banks of indoor plants, leaving out the aqueduct. She got an A.

In the third week of March, Ann went with Jetske and some of the others to a Buckminster Fuller[1] lecture. Afterwards they all went to the pub on the corner of the Square for a couple of beers. Ann left with Jetske about eleven o'clock and walked a couple of blocks with her before Jetske turned off towards her lovely old house with the stained glass. Ann continued by herself, warily, keeping to the lighted streets. She carried her purse under her elbow and held her furled umbrella at the ready. For once it wasn't raining.

When she got back to the house and started to climb the stairs, it struck her that something was different. Upstairs, she knew. Absolutely, something was out of line. There was curious music coming from the room next door, a high flute rising over drums, thumping noises, the sound of voices. The man next door was throwing a party, it seemed. *Good for him*, Ann thought. He might as well do something. She settled down for an hour's reading.

---

[1]*Buckminster Fuller* American architect, designer, visionary, and philosopher (1895–1983) who designed the geodesic dome.

But the noises were getting louder. From the bathroom came the sound of retch-ing. There was going to be trouble. Ann checked her door to make sure it was locked, got out the bottle of sherry she kept in the cupboard next to the oven, and poured herself a drink. Then she turned out the light and sat with her back against the door, drinking her sherry in the faint blue light from the funeral home next door. There was no point in going to bed: even with her earplugs in, she could never sleep.

The music and thumpings got louder. After a while there was a banging on the floor, then some shouting, which came quite clearly through Ann's hot-air regis-ter. "I'm calling the police! You hear? I'm calling the police! You get them out of here and get out yourself!" The music switched off, the door opened, and there was a clattering down the stairs. Then more footsteps—Ann couldn't tell whether they were going up or down—and more shouting. The front door banged and the shouts continued on down the street. Ann undressed and put on her nightgown, still with-out turning on the light, and crept into the bathroom. The bathtub was full of vomit.

This time Mrs. Nolan didn't even wait for Ann to get back from classes. She waylaid her in the morning as she was coming out of her room. Mrs. Nolan was holding a can of Drano and had dark circles under her eyes. Somehow this made her look younger. *She's probably not much older than I am*, Ann thought. Until now she had considered her middle-aged.

"I guess you saw the mess in there," she whispered.

"Yes, I did," Ann said.

"I guess you heard all that last night." She paused.

"What happened?" Ann asked. In fact she really wanted to know.

"He had some dancing girls in there! Three dancing girls, and two other men, in that little room! I thought the ceiling was gonna come right down on our heads!"

"I did hear something like dancing," Ann said.

"Dancing! They were jumping, it sounded like they jumped right off the bed onto the floor. The plaster was coming off. Fred wasn't home, he's not home yet. I was afraid for the kids. Like, with those tattoos, who knows what they was working them-selves up to?" Her sibilant voice hinted of ritual murders, young Jimmy and runny-nosed Donny sacrificed to some obscure god.

"What did you do?" Ann asked.

"I called the police. Well, the dancing girls, as soon as they heard I was calling the police, they got out of here, I can tell you. Put on their coats and was down the stairs and out the door like nothing. You can bet they didn't want no trouble with the po-lice. But not the others, they don't seem to know what police means."

She paused again, and Ann asked, "Did they come?"

"Who?"

"The police."

"Well, you know around here it always takes the police a while to get there, un-less there's some right outside. I know that, it's not the first time I've had to call them. So who knows what they would've done in the meantime? I could hear them com-ing downstairs, like, so I just grabs the broom and I chased them out. I chased them all the way down the street."

Ann saw that she thought she had done something very brave, which meant that in fact she had. She really believed that the man next door and his friends were dangerous, that they were a threat to her children. She had chased them single-handedly, yelling with fear and defiance. But he had only been throwing a party.

"Heavens," she said weakly.

"You can say that again," said Mrs. Nolan. "I went in there this morning, to get his things and put them out front where he could get them without me having to see him. I don't have such good nerves, I didn't sleep at all, even after they was gone. Fred is just gonna have to stop driving nights, I can't take it. But you know? He didn't have no things in there. Not one. Just an old empty suitcase?"

"What about his native costume?" Ann said.

"He had it on," Mrs. Nolan said. "He just went running down the street in it, like some kind of a loony. And you know what else I found in there? In one corner, there was this pile of empty bottles. Liquor. He must've been drinking like a fish for months, and never threw out the bottles. And in another corner, there was this pile of burnt matches. He could've burnt the house down, throwing them on the floor like that. But the worst thing was, you know all the times he borrowed my vacuum cleaner?"

"Yes," Ann said.

"Well, he never threw away the dirt. There it all was, in the other corner of the room. He must've just emptied it out and left it there. I don't get it." Mrs. Nolan, by now, was puzzled rather than angry.

"Well," Ann said. "That certainly is strange."

"Strange?" Mrs. Nolan said. "I'll tell you it's strange. He always paid the rent though, right on time. Never a day late. Why would he put the dirt in a corner like that, when he could've put it out in a bag like everyone else? It's not like he didn't know. I told him real clear which were the garbage days, when he moved in."

Ann said she was going to be late for class if she didn't hurry. At the front door she tucked her hair under her plastic scarf. Today it was just a drizzle, not heavy enough for the umbrella. She started off, walking quickly along beside the double line of traffic.

She wondered where he had gone, chased down the street by Mrs. Nolan in her scuffies and flowered housecoat, shouting and flailing at him with a broom. She must have been at least as terrifying a spectacle to him as he was to her, and just as inexplicable. Why would this woman, this fat crazy woman, wish to burst in upon a scene of harmless hospitality, banging and raving? He and his friends could easily have overpowered her, but they would not even have thought about doing that. They would have been too frightened. What unspoken taboo had they violated? What would these cold, mad people do next?

Anyway, he did have some friends. They would take care of him, at least for the time being. Which was a relief, she guessed. But what she really felt was a childish regret that she had not seen the dancing girls. If she had known they were there, she might even have risked opening her door. She knew they were not real dancing girls, they were probably just some whores from Scollay Square. Mrs. Nolan had called them that as a euphemism, or perhaps because of an unconscious association with the word *Arabian*, the vaguely Arabian country. She never had found out what it was. Nevertheless, she wished she had seen them. Jetske would find all of this quite amusing, especially the image of her backed against the door, drinking sherry in the dark. It would have been better if she'd had the courage to look.

She began to think about her green space, as she often did during this walk. The green, perfect space of the future. She knew by now that it was canceled in advance, that it would never come into being, that it was already too late. Once she was qualified, she would return to plan tasteful mixes of residential units and shopping complexes, with a lot of underground malls and arcades to protect people from the snow. But she could allow herself to see it one last time.

The fence was gone now, and the green stretched out endlessly, fields and trees and flowing water, as far as she could see. In the distance, beneath the arches of the aqueduct, a herd of animals, deer or something, was grazing. (She must learn more about animals.) Groups of people were walking happily among the trees, holding hands, not just in twos but in threes, fours, fives. The man from next door was there, in his native costume, and the mathematicians, they were all in their native costumes. Beside the stream a man was playing the flute; and around him, in long flowered robes and mauve scuffies, their auburn hair floating around their healthy pink faces, smiling their Dutch smiles, the dancing girls were sedately dancing.

[1977]

Questions

1. How do Ann's and Mrs. Nolan's different assumptions about "foreigners" contribute to the story's central theme?
2. What is the basis of Mrs. Nolan's fear of the new foreign occupant of her boarding house? Through that fear, what do we learn about Mrs. Nolan?
3. How do Ann's fantasies of "urban design" contribute to the meaning of the story? How has her vision changed by the story's end?
4. What does this story suggest about cross-cultural understanding?

Isaac Babel
(1894–1941?)
Russia

I saac Emmanuilovich Babel, like many Russian writers before him, struggled with the difficult problem of freedom of artistic expression during a particularly oppressive period of Russian history. As a Jew, he was further threatened by the wave of pogroms (persecutions) sweeping Russia at the time. Although the Jews of Odessa—where Babel was born—were less oppressed than those elsewhere in Russia, when he was 10 years old he saw his family's shop looted and witnessed his father's humiliation by a Cossack officer.

As soon as he could, Babel left Odessa for Kiev and then St. Petersburg with the hope of becoming a writer. In St. Petersburg he met Maxim Gorki, a successful playwright, who encouraged Babel as a writer and who published his first two stories. In pursuit of adventure, Babel joined the Tsar's army and was stationed on the Romanian frontier and in Poland; his experiences during that time became the source for his most famous collection of stories, Red Cavalry (1926), in which he explores the cruelties of war along with the better qualities it may inspire in ordinary people. "My First Goose" first appeared in that collection. His other stories were collected in Tales of Odessa (1924), drawing on his formative years in Odessa, and Jewish Tales (1927).

As a result of the artistic repression in the Soviet Union during the Stalinist era, Babel published few stories after 1926. In 1934 he spoke to the first Writers' Congress, describing himself as "a master of a new literary genre, the genre of silence." In 1939 he was arrested, charged with espionage and illegal revolutionary activities, and sent to a Soviet concentration camp where he was tortured to confess to the false charges. He was convicted and shot, probably sometime in 1941; 14 years later, in a posthumous review of his case, Babel was cleared of all charges.

Like his predecessors, Turgenev and Chekhov, Babel is distinguished both for his poetic use of language and for his mastery of ironic detachment—a narrative strategy with political as well as aesthetic implications. From his perspective as a member of a persecuted religious minority, he also poignantly explored the circumstances of cultural marginality. Babel's nonjudgmental position obliges the reader to inquire into the moral issues that are compellingly explored in his stories.

MY FIRST GOOSE

Savistsky, Commander of the VI Division, rose when he saw me, and I wondered at the beauty of his giant's body. He rose, the purple of his riding breeches and the crimson of his little tilted cap and the decorations stuck on his chest cleaving the hut as a standard cleaves the sky. A smell of scent and the sickly sweet freshness of soap

emanated from him. His long legs were like girls sheathed to the neck in shining riding boots.

He smiled at me, struck his riding whip on the table, and drew toward him an
order that the Chief of Staff had just finished dictating. It was an order for Ivan Chesnokov to advance on Chugunov-Dobryvodka with the regiment entrusted to him, to
make contact with the enemy and destroy the same.

"For which destruction," the Commander began to write, smearing the whole
sheet, "I make this same Chesnokov entirely responsible, up to and including the
supreme penalty, and will if necessary strike him down on the spot; which you,
Chesnokov, who have been working with me at the front for some months now, cannot doubt."

The Commander signed the order with a flourish, tossed it to his orderlies and
turned upon me gray eyes that danced with merriment.

I handed him a paper with my appointment to the Staff of the Division.

"Put it down in the Order of the Day," said the Commander. "Put him down for
every satisfaction save the front one. Can you read and write?"

"Yes, I can read and write," I replied, envying the flower and iron of that youth-
fulness. "I graduated in law from St. Petersburg University."

"Oh, are you one of those grinds?" he laughed. "Specs on your nose, too! What a
nasty little object! They've sent you along without making any enquiries; and this is
a hot place for specs. Think you'll get on with us?"

"I'll get on all right," I answered, and went off to the village with the quartermaster to find a billet for the night.

The quartermaster carried my trunk on his shoulder. Before us stretched the village street. The dying sun, round and yellow as a pumpkin, was giving up its roseate
ghost to the skies.

We went up to a hut painted over with garlands. The quartermaster stopped, and
said suddenly, with a guilty smile:

"Nuisance with specs. Can't do anything to stop it, either. Not a life for the brainy
type here. But you go and mess up a lady, and a good lady too, and you'll have the boys
patting you on the back."

He hesitated, my little trunk on his shoulder; then he came quite close to me,
only to dart away again despairingly and run to the nearest yard. Cossacks were sitting there, shaving one another.

"Here, you soldiers," said the quartermaster, setting my little trunk down on the
ground. "Comrade Savitsky's orders are that you're to take this chap in your billets,
so no nonsense about it, because the chap's been through a lot in the learning line."

The quartermaster, purple in the face, left us without looking back. I raised my hand
to my cap and saluted the Cossacks. A lad with long straight flaxen hair and the
handsome face of the Ryazan Cossacks went over to my little trunk and tossed it out
at the gate. Then he turned his back on me and with remarkable skill emitted a series of shameful noises.

"To your guns—number double-zero!" an older Cossack shouted at him, and burst
out laughing. "Running fire!"

His guileless art exhausted, the lad made off. Then, crawling over the ground, I
began to gather together the manuscripts and tattered garments that had fallen out
of the trunk. I gathered them up and carried them to the other end of the yard. Near
the hut, on a brick stove, stood a cauldron in which pork was cooking. The steam

that rose from it was like the far-off smoke of home in the village, and it mingled hunger with desperate loneliness in my head. Then I covered my little broken trunk with hay, turning it into a pillow, and lay down on the ground to read in *Pravda* Lenin's speech at the Second Congress of the Comintern. The sun fell upon me from behind the toothed hillocks, the Cossacks trod on my feet, the lad made fun of me untiringly, the beloved lines came toward me along a thorny path and could not reach me. Then I put aside the paper and went out to the landlady, who was spinning on the porch.

"Landlady," I said, "I've got to eat."

The old woman raised to me the diffused whites of her purblind eyes and lowered them again.

"Comrade," she said, after a pause, "what with all this going on, I want to go and hang myself."

"Christ!" I muttered, and pushed the old woman in the chest with my fist. "You don't suppose I'm going to go into explanations with you, do you?"

And turning around I saw somebody's sword lying within reach. A severe-looking goose was waddling about the yard, inoffensively preening its feathers. I overtook it and pressed it to the ground. Its head cracked beneath my boot, cracked and emptied itself. The white neck lay stretched out in the dung, the wings twitched.

"Christ!" I said, digging into the goose with my sword. "Go and cook it for me, landlady."

Her blind eyes and glasses glistening, the old woman picked up the slaughtered bird, wrapped it in her apron, and started to bear it off toward the kitchen.

"Comrade," she said to me, after a while, "I want to go and hang myself." And she closed the door behind her.

The Cossacks in the yard were already sitting around their cauldron. They sat motionless, stiff as heathen priests at a sacrifice, and had not looked at the goose.

"The lad's all right," one of them said, winking and scooping up the cabbage soup with his spoon.

The Cossacks commenced their supper with all the elegance and restraint of peasants who respect one another. And I wiped the sword with sand, went out at the gate, and came in again, depressed. Already the moon hung above the yard like a cheap earring.

"Hey, you," suddenly said Surovkov, an older Cossack. "Sit down and feed with us till your goose is done."

He produced a spare spoon from his boot and handed it to me. We supped up the cabbage soup they had made, and ate the pork.

"What's in the newspaper?" asked the flaxen-haired lad, making room for me.

"Lenin writes in the paper," I said, pulling out *Pravda*. "Lenin writes that there's a shortage of everything."

And loudly, like a triumphant man hard of hearing, I read Lenin's speech out to the Cossacks.

Evening wrapped about me the quickening moisture of its twilight sheets; evening laid a mother's hand upon my burning forehead. I read on and rejoiced, spying out exultingly the secret curve of Lenin's straight line.

"Truth tickles everyone's nostrils," said Surovkov, when I had come to the end. "The question is, how's it to be pulled from the heap. But he goes and strikes at it straight off like a hen pecking at a grain!"

This remark about Lenin was made by Surovkov, platoon commander of the Staff Squadron; after which we lay down to sleep in the hayloft. We slept, all six of us, beneath a wooden roof that let in the stars, warming one another, our legs intermingled. I dreamed: and in my dreams saw women. But my heart, stained with bloodshed, grated and brimmed over.

[1925]
Translated by
WALTER MORISON

Questions

1. In what ways is the narrator different from the other Cossack soldiers of the story? How are those differences significant to what happens?
2. Why does the narrator kill the goose? Why is he accepted by the other Cossack soldiers afterwards?
3. What role does the old blind woman play in the story?
4. As the title suggests, one might call "My First Goose" a story of initiation. Into what is the narrator initiated? Does he change during the course of the story? If so, how?
5. How does the story's mixture of lyrical imagery and brutal actions affect you?

BarbaraNeely

(b. 1941)
United States

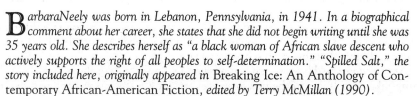

B arbaraNeely was born in Lebanon, Pennsylvania, in 1941. In a biographical comment about her career, she states that she did not begin writing until she was 35 years old. She describes herself as "a black woman of African slave descent who actively supports the right of all peoples to self-determination." "Spilled Salt," the story included here, originally appeared in Breaking Ice: An Anthology of Contemporary African-American Fiction, edited by Terry McMillan (1990).

In 1992, BarbaraNeely began publishing a series of detective novels, centering on a 40-year-old black domestic named Blanche White. The first volume, Blanche on the Lam, has been followed by three others: Blanche among the Talented Tenth (1994), Blanche Cleans Up (1998), and Blanche Passes Go (2000).

When asked to describe her own writing objectives, BarbaraNeely responded as follows:

> One of my major goals as a fiction writer is to explore the rich inner lives of people the larger society assumes have no inner life. . . . I am interested in how the world looks and feels to the people who make up the mud—the people who do menial jobs; who are chronically unemployed; the people whom the society discriminates against because they are too black, too old, the wrong kind of woman, conventionally unattractive, or in some other way different from the mainstream model—which is really most of us.

SPILLED SALT

"I'm home, Ma."

Myrna pressed down hard on the doorknob and stared blankly up into Kenny's large brown eyes and freckled face so much like her own he was nearly her twin. But he was taller than she remembered. Denser.

He'd written to say he was getting out. She hadn't answered his letter, hoping her lack of response would keep him away.

"You're here." She stepped back from the door, pretending not to see him reach out and try to touch her.

But a part of her had leaped to life at the sight of him. No matter what, she was glad he hadn't been maimed or murdered in prison. He at least looked whole and healthy of body. She hoped it was a sign that he was all right inside, too.

She tried to think of something to say as they stood staring at each other in the middle of the living room. A fly buzzed against the window screen in a desperate attempt to get out.

"Well, Ma, how've you—"

"I'll fix you something to eat," Myrna interrupted. "I know you must be starved for decent cooking." She rushed from the room as though a meal were already in the process of burning.

For a moment she was lost in her own kitchen. The table, with its dented metal legs, the green-and-white cotton curtains, and the badly battered coffeepot were all familiar-looking strangers. She took a deep breath and leaned against the back of a chair.

In the beginning she'd flinched from the very word. She couldn't even think it, let alone say it. Assault, attack, molest, anything but rape. Anyone but her son, her bright and funny boy, her high school graduate.

At the time, she'd been sure it was a frame-up on the part of the police. They did things like that. It was in the newspapers every day. Or the girl was trying to get revenge because he hadn't shown any interest in her. Kenny's confession put paid to all those speculations.

She'd have liked to believe that remorse had made him confess. But she knew better. He'd simply told the wrong lie. If he'd said he'd been with the girl but it hadn't been rape, he might have built a case that someone would have believed—although she didn't know how he could have explained away the wound on the neck where he'd held his knife against her throat to keep her docile. Instead, he'd claimed not to have offered her a ride home from the bar where she worked, never to have had her in his car. He'd convinced Myrna. So thoroughly convinced her that she'd fainted dead away when confronted with the semen, fiber, and hair evidence the police quickly collected from his car, and the word of the woman who reluctantly came forth to say she'd seen Kenny ushering Crystal Roberts into his car on the night Crystal was raped.

Only then had Kenny confessed. He'd said he'd been doing the girl a favor by offering her a ride home. In return, she'd teased and then refused him, he'd said. "I lost my head," he'd said.

"I can't sleep. I'm afraid to sleep." The girl had spoken in barely a whisper. The whole courtroom had seemed to tilt as everyone leaned toward her. "Every night he's there in my mind, making me go through it all over again, and again, and again."

Was she free now that Kenny had done his time? Or was she flinching from hands with short, square fingers, and crying when the first of September came near? Myrna moved around the kitchen like an old, old woman with bad feet.

After Kenny had confessed, Myrna spent days that ran into weeks rifling through memories of the past she shared with him, searching for some incident, some trait or series of events that would explain why he'd done such a thing. She's tried to rationalize his actions with circumstances: Kenny had seen his father beat her. They'd been poorer than dirt. And when Kenny had just turned six, she'd finally found the courage to leave Buddy to raise their son alone. What had she really known about raising a child? What harm might she have done out of ignorance, out of impatience and concentration on warding off the pains of her own life?

Still, she kept stumbling over the knowledge of other boys, from far worse circumstances, with mothers too tired and worried to do more than strike out at them. Yet those boys had managed to grow up and not do the kind of harm Kenny had done. The phrases "I lost my head," and "doing the girl a favor," reverberated through her brain, mocking her, making her groan out loud and startle people around her.

Myrna dragged herself around the room, turning eggs, bacon, milk, and margarine into a meal. In the beginning the why of Kenny's crime was like a tapeworm in her belly, consuming all her strength and sustenance, all her attention. In the first few months of his imprisonment she'd religiously paid a neighbor to drive her the long distance to the prison each visiting day. The visits were as much for her benefit as for his.

"But why?" she'd kept asking him, just as she'd asked him practically every day since he'd confessed.

He would only say that he knew he'd done wrong. As the weeks passed, silence became his only response—a silence that had remained intact despite questions like: "Would you have left that girl alone if I'd bought a shotgun and blown your daddy's brains out after the first time he hit me in front of you?" and, "Is there a special thrill you feel when you make a woman ashamed of her sex?" and, "Was this the first time? The second? The last?"

Perhaps silence was best, now, after so long. Anything could happen if she let those five-year-old questions come rolling out of her mouth. Kenny might begin to question her, might ask her what there was about her mothering that made him want to treat a woman like a piece of toilet paper. And what would she say to that?

It was illness that had finally put an end to her visits with him. She'd written the first letter—a note really—to say she was laid up with the flu. A hacking cough had lingered. She hadn't gotten her strength back for nearly two months. By that time their correspondence was established. Letters full of: How are you? I'm fine. . . . The weather is . . . The print shop is . . . The dress I made for Mrs. Rothstein was . . . were so much more manageable than those silence-laden visits. And she didn't have to worry about making eye contact with Kenny in a letter.

Now Myrna stood staring out the kitchen window while Kenny ate his bacon and eggs. The crisp everydayness of clothes flapping on the line surprised her. A leaf floated into her small cemented yard and landed on a potted pansy. Outside, nothing had changed; the world was still in spring.

"I can't go through this again," she mouthed soundlessly to the breeze.

"Come talk to me, Ma," her son called softly around a mouthful of food.

Myrna turned to look at him. He smiled an egg-flecked smile she couldn't return. She wanted to ask him what he would do now, whether he had a job lined up, whether he planned to stay long. But she was afraid of his answers, afraid of how she might respond if he said he had no job, no plans, no place to stay except with her and that he hadn't changed in any important way.

"I'm always gonna live with you, Mommy," he'd told her when he was a child, "Always." At the time, she'd wished it was true, that they could always be together, she and her sweet, chubby boy. Now the thought frightened her.

"Be right back," she mumbled, and scurried down the hall to the bathroom. She eased the lock over so that it made barely a sound.

"He's my son!" she hissed at the drawn woman in the mirror. Perspiration dotted her upper lip and glistened around her hair line.

"My son!" she repeated pleadingly. But the words were not as powerful as the memory of Crystal Roberts sitting in the courtroom, her shoulders hunched and her head hung down, as though she were the one who ought to be ashamed. Myrna wished him never born, before she flushed the toilet and unlocked the door.

In the kitchen Kenny had moved to take her place by the window. His dishes littered the table. He'd spilled the salt, and there were crumbs on the floor.

"It sure is good to look out the window and see something besides guard towers and cons." Kenny stretched, rubbed his belly, and turned to face her.

"It's good to see you, Ma." His eyes were soft and shiny.

Oh, Lord! Myrna moaned to herself. She turned her back to him and began carrying his dirty dishes to the sink: first the plate, then the cup, the knife, fork, and spoon, drawing out the chore.

"This place ain't got as much room as the old place," she told him while she made dishwater in the sink.

"It's fine, Ma, just fine."

Oh, Lord, Myrna prayed.

Kenny came to lean against the stove to her right. She dropped a knife and made the dishwater too cold.

"Seen Dad?"

"Where and why would I see *him?*" She tried to put ice in her voice. It trembled.

"Just thought you might know where he is." Kenny moved back to the window.

Myrna remembered the crippling shock of Buddy's fist in her groin and scoured Kenny's plate and cup with a piece of steel wool before rinsing them in scalding water.

"Maybe I'll hop a bus over to the old neighborhood. See some of the guys, how things have changed."

He paced the floor behind her. Myrna sensed his uneasiness and was startled by a wave of pleasure at his discomfort.

After he'd gone, she fixed herself a large gin and orange juice and carried it into the living room. She flicked on the TV and sat down to stare at it. After two minutes of frenetic, over-bright commercials, she got up and turned it off again. Outside, children screamed each other to the finish line of a footrace. She remembered that Kenny had always liked to run. So had she. But he'd had more childhood than she'd had. She'd been hired out as a mother's helper by the time she was twelve, and pregnant and married at sixteen. She didn't begrudge him his childhood fun. It just seemed so wasted now.

Tears slid down her face and salted her drink. Tears for the young Myrna who hadn't understood that she was raising a boy who needed special handling to keep him from becoming a man she didn't care to know. Tears for Kenny who was so twisted around inside that he could rape a woman. Myrna drained her gin; left Kenny a note reminding him to leave her door key on the kitchen table, and went to bed.

Of course, she was still awake when he came in. He bumped into the coffee table, ran water in the bathroom sink for a long time, then quiet. Myrna lay awake in the dark blue-gray night listening to the groan of the refrigerator, the hiss of the hot-water heater, and the rumble of large trucks on a distant street. *He* made no sound where he lay on the opened-sofa, surrounded by her sewing machine, dress dummy, marking tape, and pins.

When sleep finally came, it brought dreams of walking down brilliantly lit streets, hand in hand with a boy about twelve who looked, acted, and talked like Kenny but who she knew with certainty was not her son, at the same time she also knew he could be no one else.

She woke to a cacophony of church bells. It was late. Too late to make it to church service. She turned her head to look at the crucifix hanging by her bed and tried to pray, to summon up that feeling of near weightlessness that came over her in those moments when she was able to free her mind of all else and give herself over to prayer. Now nothing came but a dull ache in the back of her throat.

She had begun attending church regularly after she stopped visiting Kenny. His refusal to respond to her questions made it clear she'd have to seek answers elsewhere. She'd decided to talk to Father Giles. He'd been at St. Mark's, in their old neighborhood, before she and Kenny had moved there. He'd seen Kenny growing up. Perhaps he'd noticed something, understood something about the boy, about her, that would explain what she could not understand.

"It's God's will, my child—put it in His hands," he'd urged, awkwardly patting her arm and averting his eyes.

Myrna took his advice wholeheartedly. She became quite adept at quieting the questions boiling in her belly with, "His will," or "My cross to bear." Many nights she'd "Our Fathered" herself to sleep. Acceptance of Kenny's inexplicable act became a test God had given her. One she passed by visiting the sick, along with other women from the church; working on the neighborhood cleanup committee; avoiding all social contact with men. With sex. She put "widowed" on job applications and never mentioned a son to new people she met. Once she'd moved away from the silent accusation of their old apartment, prayer and good works became a protective shield separating her from the past.

Kenny's tap on her door startled her back to the present. She cleared her throat and straightened the covers before calling to him to come in.

A rich, aromatic steam rose from the coffee he'd brought her. The toast was just the right shade of brown, and she was sure that when she cracked the poached egg it would be cooked exactly to her liking. Not only was everything perfectly prepared, it was the first time she'd had breakfast in bed since he'd been arrested. Myrna couldn't hold back the tears or the flood of memories of many mornings, just so: him bending over her with a breakfast tray.

"You wait on people in the restaurant all day and sit up all night making other people's clothes. You need some waiting on, too."

Had he actually said that, this man as a boy? Could this man have been such a boy? Myrna nearly tilted the tray in her confusion.

"I need to brush my teeth." She averted her face and reached for her bathrobe.

But she couldn't avoid her eyes in the medicine cabinet mirror, eyes that reminded her that despite what Kenny had done, she hadn't stopped loving him. But her love didn't need his company. It thrived only on memories of him that were more than four years old. It was as much a love remembered as a living thing. But it was love, nonetheless. Myrna pressed her clenched fist against her lips and wondered if love was enough. She stayed in the bathroom until she heard him leave her bedroom and turn on the TV in the living room.

When he came back for the tray, she told him she had a sick headache and had decided to stay in bed. He was immediately sympathetic, fetching aspirin and a cool compress for her forehead, offering to massage her neck and temples, to lower the blinds and block out the bright morning sun. Myrna told him she wanted only to rest.

All afternoon she lay on her unmade bed, her eyes on the ceiling or idly roaming the room, her mind moving across the surface of her life, poking at old wounds, so amazingly raw after all these years. First there'd been Buddy. He'd laughed at her country ways and punched her around until he'd driven her and their child into the streets. But at least she was rid of him. Then there was his son. Her baby. He'd tricked a young woman into getting into his car where he proceeded to ruin a great portion of her life. Now he'd come back to spill salt in her kitchen.

I'm home, Ma, homema, homema. His words echoed in her inner ear and made her heart flutter. Her neighbors would want to know where he'd been all this time and why. Fear and disgust would creep into their faces and voices. Her nights would be full of listening. Waiting.

And she would have to live with the unblanketed reality that whatever anger and meanness her son held toward the world, he had chosen a woman to take it out on.

A woman.

Someone like me, she thought, like Great Aunt Faye, or Valerie, her eight-year-old niece; like Lucille, her oldest friend, or Dr. Ramsey, her dentist. A woman like all the women who'd helped feed, clothe, and care for Kenny; who'd tried their damndest to protect him from as much of the ugly and awful in life as they could; who taught him to ride a bike and cross the street. All women. From the day she'd left Buddy, not one man had done a damned thing for Kenny. Not one.

And he might do it again, she thought. The idea sent Myrna rolling back and forth across the bed as though she could actually escape her thoughts. She'd allowed herself to believe she was done with such thoughts. Once she accepted Kenny's crime as the will of God, she immediately saw that it wouldn't have made any difference how she'd raised him if this was God's unfathomable plan for him. It was a comforting idea, one that answered her question of why and how her much-loved son could be a rapist. One that answered the question of the degree of her responsibility for Kenny's crime by clearing her of all possible blame. One that allowed her to forgive him. Or so she'd thought.

Now she realized all her prayers, all her studied efforts to accept and forgive were like blankets thrown on a forest fire. All it took was the small breeze created by her opening the door to her only child to burn those blankets to cinders and release her rage—as wild and fierce as the day he'd confessed.

She closed her eyes and saw her outraged self dash wildly into the living room to scream imprecations in his face until her voice failed. Specks of froth gathered at the corners of her mouth. Her flying spit peppered his face. He cringed before her, his eyes full of shame as he tore at his own face and chest in self-loathing.

Yet, even as she fantasized, she knew Kenny could no more be creamed into contrition than Crystal or any woman could be bullied into willing sex. And what, in fact, was there for him to say or do that would satisfy her? The response she really wanted from him was not available: there was no way he could become the boy he'd been before that night four years ago.

No more than I can treat him as if he were that boy, she thought.

And the thought stilled her. She lay motionless, considering.

When she rose from her bed, she dragged her old green Samsonite suitcase out from the back of the closet. She moved with the easy, effortless grace of someone who knows what she is doing and feels good about it. Without even wiping off the dust, she plopped the suitcase on the bed. When she lifted the lid, the smell of leaving and good-bye flooded the room and quickened her pulse. For the first time in two days, her mouth moved in the direction of a smile.

She hurried from dresser drawer to closet, choosing her favorites: the black two-piece silk knit dress she'd bought on sale, her comfortable gray shoes, the lavender sweater she'd knitted as a birthday present to herself but had never worn, both her blue and her black slacks, the red crepe blouse she'd made to go with them, and the best of her underwear. She packed in a rush, as though her bus or train were even now pulling out of the station.

When she'd packed her clothes, Myrna looked around the room for other necessary items. She gathered up her comb and brush and the picture of her mother from the top of her bureau, then walked to the wall on the left side of her bed and lifted down the shiny metal and wooden crucifix that hung there. She ran her finger down the slim, muscular body. The Aryan plaster-of-Paris Christ seemed to writhe in bittersweet agony. Myrna stared at the crucifix for a few moments, then gently hung it back on the wall.

When she'd finished dressing, she sat down in the hard, straight-backed chair near the window to think through her plan. Kenny tapped at her door a number of times until she was able to convince him that she was best left alone and would be fine in the morning. When dark came, she waited for the silence of sleep, then quietly left her room. She set her suitcase by the front door, tiptoed by Kenny, where he slept on the sofa, and went into the kitchen. By the glow from the back alley streetlight, she wrote him a note and propped it against the sugar bowl:

Dear Kenny,

I'm sorry. I just can't be your mother right now. I will be back in one week. Please be gone. Much love, Myrna.

Kenny flinched and frowned in his sleep as the front door clicked shut.

[1990]

Questions

1. When Myrna says that a parent always loves a child, no matter what the circumstances, is she speaking truthfully or lying to herself?
2. Is Myrna the source of Kenny's anger? Is the rape his attempt to lash back at his mother?
3. Although Myrna leaves at the end of the story, are we to believe that she and her son will be reunited?
4. Although BarbaraNeely is an African-American writer, does "Spilled Salt" demand an ethnic interpretation, or is the situation it describes applicable to all women whose sons may become rapists?

Ann Beattie
(b. 1947)
United States

Ann Beattie was born in 1947 in Washington, D.C., where she attended American University. By the mid-seventies, when her stories were beginning to appear in The New Yorker and other magazines, she had already carved a niche for herself as spokesperson of the uptight generation. Critics have praised her attention to detail and her dialogue. Younger writers have tried to imitate her style but have been largely unsuccessful. Since the simultaneous publication of her first collection of short stories, Distortions, and her first novel, Chilly Scenes of Winter, in 1976, she has published a dozen other volumes, including Picturing Will (1989), a novel, and What Was Mine (1991), short stories. In 1998, many of her stories were brought together in Convergences: New and Selected Stories. The story included here is from The Burning House (1982).

In an interview with Bob Miner, describing her own work, Beattie said the following:

> My stories are a lot about chaos . . . and many of the simple flat statements that I bring together are usually non sequiturs or bordering on being non sequiturs—which reinforces the chaos. I write in those flat sentences because that's the way I think. I don't mean to do it as a technique. It might be just that I am incapable of breaking through to the complexities underlying all that sort of simple statement you find in my work.

THE BURNING HOUSE

Freddy Fox is in the kitchen with me. He has just washed and dried an avocado seed I don't want, and he is leaning against the wall, rolling a joint. In five minutes, I will not be able to count on him. However: he started late in the day, and he has already brought in wood for the fire, gone to the store down the road for matches, and set the table. "You mean you'd know this stuff was Limoges[1] even if you didn't turn the plate over?" he called from the dining room. He pretended to be about to throw one of the plates into the kitchen, like a Frisbee. Sam, the dog, believed him and shot up, kicking the rug out behind him and skidding forward before he realized his error; it was like the Road Runner tricking Wile E. Coyote into going over the cliff for the millionth time. His jowls sank in disappointment.

"I see there's a full moon," Freddy says. "There's just nothing that can hold a candle to nature. The moon and the stars, the tides and the sunshine—and we just don't stop for long enough to wonder at it all. We're so engrossed in ourselves." He takes a very long drag on the joint. "We stand and stir the sauce in the pot instead of going to the window and gazing at the moon."

---

[1]*Limoges*   Fine, expensive porcelain.

"You don't mean anything personal by that, I assume."

"I love the way you pour cream in a pan. I like to come up behind you and watch the sauce bubble."

"No, thank you," I say. "You're starting late in the day."

"My responsibilities have ended. You don't trust me to help with the cooking, and I've already brought in firewood and run an errand, and this very morning I exhausted myself by taking Mr. Sam jogging with me, down at Putnam Park. You're sure you won't?"

"No, thanks," I say. "Not now, anyway."

"I love it when you stand over the steam coming out of a pan and the hairs around your forehead curl into damp little curls."

My husband, Frank Wayne, is Freddy's half brother. Frank is an accountant. Freddy is closer to me than to Frank. Since Frank talks to Freddy more than he talks to me, however, and since Freddy is totally loyal, Freddy always knows more than I know. It pleases me that he does not know how to stir sauce; he will start talking, his mind will drift, and when next you look the sauce will be lumpy, or boiling away.

Freddy's criticism of Frank is only implied. "What a gracious gesture to entertain his friends on the weekend," he says.

"Male friends," I say.

"I didn't mean that you're the sort of lady who doesn't draw the line. I most certainly did not mean that," Freddy says. "I would even have been surprised if you had taken a toke of this deadly stuff while you were at the stove."

"O.K.," I say, and take the joint from him. Half of it is left when I take it. Half an inch is left after I've taken two drags and given it back.

"More surprised still if you'd shaken the ashes into the saucepan."

"You'd tell people I'd done it when they'd finished eating, and I'd be embarrassed. You can do it, though. I wouldn't be embarrassed if it was a story you told on yourself."

"You really understand me," Freddy says. "It's moon-madness, but I have to shake just this little bit in the sauce. I have to do it."

He does it.

Frank and Tucker are in the living room. Just a few minutes ago, Frank returned from getting Tucker at the train. Tucker loves to visit. To him, Fairfield County is as mysterious as Alaska. He brought with him from New York a crock of mustard, a jeroboam of champagne, cocktail napkins with a picture of a plane flying over a building on them, twenty egret feathers ("You cannot get them anymore—strictly, illegal," Tucker whispered to me), and, under his black cowboy hat with the rhinestone-studded chin strap, a toy frog that hopped when wound. Tucker owns a gallery in SoHo, and Frank keeps his books. Tucker is now stretched out in the living room, visiting with Frank, and Freddy and I are both listening.

". . . so everything I've been told indicates that he lives a purely Jekyll-and-Hyde existence. He's twenty years old, and I can see that since he's still living at home he might not want to flaunt his gayness. When he came into the gallery, he had his hair slicked back—just with water; I got close enough to sniff—and his mother was all but holding his hand. So fresh-scrubbed. The stories I'd heard. Anyway, when I called, his father started looking for the number where he could be reached in the Vineyard—very irritated, because I didn't know James, and if I'd just phoned James I could have found him in flash. He's talking to himself, looking for the number, and I say,

'Oh, did he go to visit friends or—' and his father interrupts and says, 'He was going to a gay pig roast. He's been gone since Monday.' *Just like that.*"

Freddy helps me carry the food out to the table. When we are all at the table, I mention the young artist Tucker was talking about. "Frank says his paintings are really incredible," I say to Tucker.

"Makes Estes look like an Abstract Expressionist," Tucker says. "I want that boy. I really want that boy."

"You'll get him," Frank says. "You get everybody you go after."

Tucker cuts a small piece of meat. He cuts it small so that he can talk while chewing. "Do I?" he says.

Freddy is smoking at the table, gazing dazedly at the moon centered in the window. "After dinner," he says, putting the back of his hand against his forehead when he sees that I am looking at him, "we must all go to the lighthouse."

"If only *you* painted," Tucker says, "I'd want you."

"You couldn't have me," Freddy snaps. He reconsiders. "That sounded halfhearted, didn't it? Anybody who wants me can have me. This is the only place I can be on Saturday night where somebody isn't hustling me."

"Wear looser pants," Frank says to Freddy.

"This is so much better than some bar that stinks of cigarette smoke and leather. Why do I do it?" Freddy says. "Seriously—do you think I'll ever stop?"

"Let's not be serious," Tucker says.

"I keep thinking of this table as a big boat, with dishes and glasses rocking on it," Freddy says.

He takes the bone from his plate and walks out to the kitchen, dripping sauce on the floor. He walks as though he's on the deck of a wave-tossed ship. "Mr. Sam!" he calls, and the dog springs up from the living-room floor, where he had been sleeping; his toenails on the bare wood floor sound like a wheel spinning in gravel. "You don't have to beg," Freddy says. "Jesus, Sammy—I'm just giving it to you."

"I hope there's a bone involved," Tucker says, rolling his eyes to Frank. He cuts another tiny piece of meat. "I hope your brother does understand why I couldn't keep him on. He was good at what he did, but he also might say just *anything* to a customer. You have to believe me that if I hadn't been extremely embarrassed more than once I never would have let him go."

"He should have finished school," Frank says, sopping up sauce on his bread. "He'll knock around a while longer, then get tired of it and settle down to something."

"You think I died out here?" Freddy calls. "You think I can't hear you?"

"I'm not saying anything I wouldn't say to your face," Frank says.

"I'll tell you what I wouldn't say to your face," Freddy says. "You've got a swell wife and kid and dog, and you're a snob, and you take it all for granted."

Frank puts down his fork, completely exasperated. He looks at me.

"He came to work once this stoned," Tucker says. "*Comprenez-vous?*"[2]

"You like me because you feel sorry for me," Freddy says.

He is sitting on the concrete bench outdoors, in the area that's a garden in the springtime. It is early April now—not quite spring. It's very foggy out. It rained while we were eating, and now it has turned mild. I'm leaning against a tree, across from him, glad it's so dark and misty that I can't look down and see the damage the mud is doing to my boots.

---

[2]*Comprenez-vous?"*   "Do you understand?" (French)

"Who's his girlfriend?" Freddy says.

"If I told you her name, you'd tell him I told you."

"Slow down. What?"

"I won't tell you, because you'll tell him that I know."

"He knows you know."

"I don't think so."

"How did you find out?"

"He talked about her. I kept hearing her name for months, and then we went to a party at Andy's, and she was there, and when I said something about her later he said, 'Natalie who?' It was much too casual. It gave the whole thing away."

He sighs. "I just did something very optimistic," he says. "I came out here with Mr. Sam and he dug up a rock and I put the avocado seed in the hole and packed dirt on top of it. Don't say it—I know: can't grow outside, we'll still have another snow, even if it grew, the next year's frost would kill it."

"He's embarrassed," I say. "When he's home, he avoids me. But it's rotten to avoid Mark, too. Six years old, and he calls up his friend Neal to hint that he wants to go over there. He doesn't do that when we're here alone."

Freddy picks up a stick and pokes around in the mud with it. "I'll bet Tucker's after that painter personally, not because he's the hottest thing since pancakes. That expression of his—it's always the same. Maybe Nixon really loved his mother, but with that expression who could believe him? It's a curse to have a face that won't express what you mean."

"Amy!" Tucker calls. "Telephone."

Freddy waves goodbye to me with the muddy stick. "'I am not a crook,'" Freddy says. "Jesus Christ."

Sam bounds halfway toward the house with me; then turns and goes back to Freddy. It's Marilyn, Neal's mother, on the phone.

"Hi," Marilyn says. "He's afraid to spend the night."

"Oh, no," I say. "He said he wouldn't be."

She lowers her voice. "We can try it out, but I think he'll start crying."

"I'll come get him."

"I can bring him home. You're having a dinner party, aren't you?"

I lowered my voice. "Some party. Tucker's here. J.D. never showed up."

"Well," she says. "I'm sure that what you cooked was good."

"It's so foggy out, Marilyn. I'll come get Mark."

"He can stay. I'll be a martyr," she says, and hangs up before I can object.

Freddy comes into the house, tracking in mud. Sam lies in the kitchen, waiting for his paws to be cleaned. "Come on," Freddy says, hitting his hand against his thigh, having no idea what Sam is doing. Sam gets up and runs after him. They go into the small downstairs bathroom together. Sam loves to watch people urinate. Sometimes he sings, to harmonize with the sound of the urine going into the water. There are footprints and pawprints everywhere. Tucker is shrieking with laughter in the living room. ". . . he says, he says to the other one 'Then, dearie, have you ever played *spin the bottle?*'" Frank's and Tucker's laughter drowns out the sound of Freddy peeing in the bathroom. I turn on the water in the kitchen sink, and it drowns out all the noise. I begin to scrape the dishes. Tucker is telling another story when I turn off the water: ". . . that it was Onassis in the Anvil,[3] and nothing would talk him out of it. They told

---

[3]*the Anvil* A raunchy gay bar in New York City.

him Onassis was dead, and he thought they were trying to make him think he was crazy. There was nothing to do but go along with him, but, God—he was trying to goad this poor old fag into fighting about Stavros Niarchos. You know—Onassis' *enemy*. He thought it was Onassis. In the *Anvil*." There is a sound of a glass breaking. Frank or Tucker puts "John Coltrane Live in Seattle" on the stereo and turns the volume down low. The bathroom door opens. Sam runs into the kitchen and begins to lap water from his dish. Freddy takes his little silver case and his rolling papers out of his shirt pocket. He puts a piece of paper on the kitchen table and is about to sprinkle grass on it, but realizes just in time that the paper has absorbed water from a puddle. He balls it up with his thumb, flicks it to the floor, puts a piece of rolling paper where the table's dry and shakes a line of grass down it. "You smoke this," he says to me. "I'll do the dishes."

"We'll both smoke it. I'll wash and you can wipe."

"I forgot to tell them I put ashes in the sauce," he says.

"I wouldn't interrupt."

"At least he pays Frank ten times what any other accountant for an art gallery would make," Freddy says.

Tucker is beating his hand on the arm of the sofa as he talks, stomping his feet. ". . . so he's trying to feel him out, to see if this old guy with the dyed hair knew *Maria Callas*. Jesus! And he's so out of it he's trying to think what opera singers are called, and instead of coming up with '*diva*' he comes up with '*duenna*.' At this point, Larry Betwell went up to him and tried to calm him down, and he breaks into song—some aria or something that Maria Callas was famous for. Larry told him he was going to lose his *teeth* if he didn't get it together, and . . ."

"He spends a lot of time in gay hangouts, for not being gay," Freddy says.

I scream and jump back from the sink, hitting the glass I'm rinsing against the faucet, shattering green glass everywhere.

"What?" Freddy says. "Jesus Christ, what is it?"

Too late, I realize what it must have been that I saw: J.D. in a goat mask, the puckered pink plastic lips against the window beside the kitchen sink.

"I'm sorry," J.D. says, coming through the door and nearly colliding with Frank, who has rushed into the kitchen. Tucker is right behind him.

"Ooh," Tucker says, feigning disappointment, "I thought Freddy smooched her."

"I'm sorry," J.D. says again. "I thought you'd know it was me."

The rain must have started again, because J.D. is soaking wet. He has turned the mask around so that the goat's head stares out from the back of his head. "I got lost," J.D. says. He has a farmhouse upstate. "I missed the turn. I went miles. I missed the whole dinner, didn't I?"

"What did you do wrong?" Frank asks.

"I didn't turn left onto 58. I don't know why I didn't realize my mistake, but I went *miles*. It was raining so hard I couldn't go over twenty-five miles an hour. Your driveway is all mud. You're going to have to push me out."

"There's some roast left over. And salad, if you want it," I say.

"Bring it in the living room," Frank says to J.D. Freddy is holding out a plate to him. J.D. reaches for the plate. Freddy pulls it back. J.D. reaches again, and Freddy is so stoned, that he isn't quick enough this time—J.D. grabs it.

"I thought you'd know it was me," J.D. says. "I apologize." He dishes salad onto the plate. "You'll be rid of me for six months, in the morning."

"Where does your plane leave from?" Freddy says.

"Kennedy."

"Come in here!" Tucker calls. "I've got a story for you about Perry Dwyer down at the Anvil last week, when he thought he saw Aristotle Onassis."

"Who's Perry Dwyer?" J.D. says.

"That is not the point of the story, dear man. And when you're in Cassis, I want you to look up an American painter over there. Will you? He doesn't have a phone. Anyway—I've been tracking him, and I know where he is now, and I am *very* interested, if you would stress that with him, to do a show in June that will be *only* him. He doesn't answer my letters."

"Your hand is cut," J.D. says to me.

"Forget it," I say. "Go ahead."

"I'm sorry," he says. "Did I make you do that?"

"Yes, you did."

"Don't keep your finger under the water. Put pressure on it to stop the bleeding."

He puts the plate on the table. Freddy is leaning against the counter, staring at the blood swirling in the sink, and smoking the joint all by himself. I can feel the little curls on my forehead that Freddy was talking about. They feel heavy on my skin. I hate to see my own blood. I'm sweating. I let J.D. do what he does; he turns off the water and wraps his hand around my second finger, squeezing. Water runs down our wrists.

Freddy jumps to answer the phone when it rings, as though a siren just went off behind him. He calls me to the phone, but J.D. steps in front of me, shakes his head no, and takes the dish towel and wraps it around my hand before he lets me go.

"Well," Marilyn says. "I had the best of intentions, but my battery's dead."

J.D. is standing behind me, with his hand on my shoulder.

"I'll be right over," I say. "He's not upset now, is he?"

"No, but he's dropped enough hints that he doesn't think he can make it through the night."

"O.K.," I say. "I'm sorry about all of this."

"Six years old," Marilyn says. "Wait till he grows up and gets that feeling."

I hang up.

"Let me see your hand," J.D. says.

"I don't want to look at it. Just go get me a Band-Aid, please."

He turns and goes upstairs. I unwrap the towel and look at it. It's pretty deep, but no glass is in my finger. I feel funny; the outlines of things are turning yellow. I sit in the chair by the phone. Sam comes and lies beside me, and I stare at his black-and-yellow tail, beating. I reach down with my good hand and pat him, breathing deeply in time with every second pat.

"*Rothko?*" Tucker says bitterly, in the living room. "Nothing is great that can appear on greeting cards. Wyeth is that way. Would 'Christina's World' look bad on a cocktail napkin? You know it wouldn't."

I jump as the phone rings again. "Hello?" I say, wedging the phone against my shoulder with my ear, wrapping the dish towel tighter around my hand.

"Tell them it's a crank call. Tell them anything," Johnny says. "I miss you. How's Saturday night at your house?"

"All right," I say. I catch my breath.

"Everything's all right here, too. Yes indeed. Roast rack of lamb. Friend of Nicole's who's going to Key West tomorrow had too much to drink and got depressed because he thought it was raining in Key West, and I said I'd go in my study and call the National Weather Service. Hello, Weather Service. How are you?"

J.D. comes down from upstairs with two Band-Aids and stands beside me, unwrapping one. I want to say to Johnny, "I'm cut. I'm bleeding. It's no joke."

It's all right to talk in front of J.D., but I don't know who else might overhear me. "I'd say they made the delivery about four this afternoon," I say.

"This is the church, this is the steeple. Open the door, and see all the people," Johnny says. "Take care of yourself. I'll hang up and find out if it's raining in Key West."

"Late in the afternoon," I say. "Everything is fine."

"Nothing is fine," Johnny says. "Take care of yourself."

He hangs up. I put the phone down, and realize that I'm still having trouble focusing, the sight of my cut finger made me so light-headed. I don't look at the finger again as J.D. undoes the towel and wraps the Band-Aids around my finger.

"What's going on in here?" Frank says, coming into the dining room.

"I cut my finger," I say. "It's O.K."

"You did?" he says. He looks woozy—a little drunk. "Who keeps calling?"

"Marilyn. Mark changed his mind about staying all night. She was going to bring him home, but her battery's dead. You'll have to get him. Or I will."

"Who called the second time?" he says.

"The oil company. They wanted to know if we got our delivery today."

He nods. "I'll go get him, if you want," he says. He lowers his voice. "Tucker's probably going to whirl himself into a tornado for an encore," he says, nodding toward the living room. "I'll take him with me."

"Do you want me to go get him?" J.D. says.

"I don't mind getting some air," Frank says. "Thanks, though. Why don't you go in the living room and eat your dinner?"

"You forgive me?" J.D. says.

"Sure," I say. "It wasn't your fault. Where did you get that mask?"

"I found it on top of a Goodwill box in Manchester. There was also a beautiful old birdcage—solid brass."

The phone rings again. I pick it up. "Wouldn't I love to be in Key West with you," Johnny says. He makes a sound as though he's kissing me and hangs up.

"Wrong number," I say.

Franks feels in his pants pocket for the car keys.

J.D. knows about Johnny. He introduced me, in the faculty lounge, where J.D. and I had gone to get a cup of coffee after I registered for classes. After being gone for nearly two years, J.D. still gets mail at the department—he said he had to stop by for the mail anyway, so he'd drive me to campus and point me toward the registrar's. J.D. taught English; now he does nothing. J.D. is glad that I've gone back to college to study art again, now that Mark is in school. I'm six credits away from an M.A. in art history. He wants me to think about myself, instead of thinking about Mark all the time. He talks as though I could roll Mark out on a string and let him fly off, high above me. J.D.'s wife and son died in a car crash. His son was Mark's age. "I wasn't prepared," J.D. said when we were driving over that day. He always says this when he talks about it. "How could you be prepared for such a thing?" I asked him. "I am now," he said. Then, realizing he was acting very hardboiled, made fun of himself. "Go on," he said, "punch me in the stomach. Hit me as hard as you can." We both knew he isn't prepared for anything. When he couldn't find a parking place that day, his hands were wrapped around the wheel so tightly that his knuckles turned white.

Johnny came in as we were drinking coffee. J.D. was looking at his junk mail—publishers wanting him to order anthologies, ways to get free dictionaries.

"You are so lucky to be out of it," Johnny said, by way of greeting. "What do you do when you've spent two weeks on 'Hamlet' and the student writes about Hamlet's good friend Horchow?"

He threw a blue book into J.D.'s lap. J.D. sailed it back.

"Johnny," he said, "this is Amy."

"Hi, Amy," Johnny said.

"You remember when Frank Wayne was in graduate school here? Amy's Frank's wife."

"Hi, Amy," Johnny said.

J.D. told me he knew it the instant Johnny walked into the room—he knew that second that he should introduce me as somebody's wife. He could have predicted it all from the way Johnny looked at me.

For a long time J.D. gloated that he had been prepared for what happened next— that Johnny and I were going to get together. It took me to disturb his pleasure in himself—me, crying hysterically on the phone last month, not knowing what to do, what move to make next.

"Don't do anything for a while. I guess that's my advice," J.D. said. "But you probably shouldn't listen to me. All I can do myself is run away, hide out. I'm not the learned professor. You know what I believe. I believe all that wicked fairy-tale crap: your heart will break, your house will burn."

Tonight, because he doesn't have a garage at his farm, J.D. has come to leave his car in the empty half of our two-car garage while he's in France. I look out the window and see his old Saab, glowing in the moonlight. J.D. has brought his favorite book, "A Vision,"[4] to read on the plane. He says his suitcase contains only a spare pair of jeans, cigarettes, and underwear. He is going to buy a leather jacket in France, at a store where he almost bought a leather jacket two years ago.

In our bedroom there are about twenty small glass prisms hung with fishing line from one of the exposed beams; they catch the morning light, and we stare at them like a cat eyeing catnip held above its head. Just now, it is 2 A.M. At six-thirty, they will be filled with dazzling color. At four or five, Mark will come into the bedroom and get in bed with us. Sam will wake up, stretch, and shake, and the tags on his collar will clink, and he will yawn and shake again and go downstairs, where J.D. is asleep in his sleeping bag and Tucker is asleep on the sofa, and get a drink of water from his dish. Mark has been coming into our bedroom for about a year. He gets onto the bed by climbing up on a footstool that horrified me when I first saw it—a gift from Frank's mother: a footstool that says "Today Is the First Day of the Rest of Your Life" in needlepoint. I kept it in a closet for years, but it occurred to me that it would help Mark get up into the bed, so he would not have to make a little leap and possibly skin his shin again. Now Mark does not disturb us when he comes into the bedroom, except that it bothers me that he has reverted to sucking his thumb. Sometimes he lies in bed with his cold feet against my leg. Sometimes, small as he is, he snores.

Somebody is playing a record downstairs. It's the Velvet Underground—Nico, in a dream or swoon, singing "Sunday Morning." I can barely hear the whispering and tinkling of the record. I can only follow it because I've heard it a hundred times.

---

[4] "A *Vision*" by William Butler Yeats, 1856–1939.

I am lying in bed, waiting for Frank to get out of the bathroom. My cut finger throbs. Things are going on in the house even though I have gone to bed; water runs, the record plays, Sam is still downstairs, so there must be some action.

I have known everybody in this house for years; and as time goes by I know them all less and less. J.D. was Frank's adviser in college. Frank was his best student, and they started to see each other outside of class. They played handball. J.D. and his family came to dinner. We went there. That summer—the summer Frank decided to go to graduate school in business instead of English—J.D.'s wife and son deserted him in a more horrible way, in that car crash. J.D. has quit his job. He has been to Las Vegas, to Colorado, New Orleans, Los Angeles, Paris twice; he tapes postcards to the walls of his living room. A lot of the time, on the weekends, he shows up at our house with his sleeping bag. Sometimes he brings a girl. Lately, not. Years ago, Tucker was in Frank's therapy group in New York and ended up hiring Frank to work as the accountant for his gallery. Tucker was in therapy at the time because he was obsessed with foreigners. Now he is also obsessed with homosexuals. Before the parties he does TM and yoga, and during the parties he does Seconals and isometrics. When I first met him, he was living for the summer in his sister's house in Vermont while she was in Europe, and he called us one night, in New York, in a real panic because there were wasps all over. They were "hatching," he said—big, sleepy wasps that were everywhere. We said we'd come; we drove all through the night to get to Brattleboro. It was true: there were wasps on the undersides of plates, in the plants, in the folds of curtains. Tucker was so upset that he was out behind the house, in the cold Vermont morning, wrapped like an Indian in a blanket, with only his pajamas on underneath. He was sitting in a lawn chair, hiding behind a bush, waiting for us to come.

And Freddy—"Reddy Fox," when Frank is feeling affectionate toward him. When we first met, I taught him to ice-skate and he taught me to waltz; in the summer, at Atlantic City, he'd go with me on a roller coaster that curved high over the waves. I was the one—not Frank—who would get out of bed in the middle of the night and meet him at an all-night deli and put my arm around his shoulders, the way he put his arm around my shoulders on the roller coaster, and talk quietly to him until he got over his latest anxiety attack. Now he tests me, and I retreat: this man he picked up, this man who picked him up, how it feels to have forgotten somebody's name when your hand is in the back pocket of his jeans and you're not even halfway to your apartment. Reddy Fox—admiring my new red silk blouse, stroking his fingertips down the front, and my eyes wide, because I could feel his fingers on my chest, even though I was holding the blouse in front of me on a hanger to be admired. All those moments, and all they meant was that I was fooled into thinking I knew these people because I knew the small things, the personal things.

Freddy will always be more stoned than I am, because he feels comfortable getting stoned with me and I'll always be reminded that he's more lost. Tucker knows he can come to the house and be the center of attention; he can tell all the stories he knows, and we'll never tell the story we know about him hiding in the bushes like a frightened dog. J.D. comes back from his trips with boxes full of postcards, and I look at all of them as though they're photographs taken by him, and I know, and he knows, that what he likes about them is their flatness—the unreality of them, the unreality of what he does.

Last summer, I read "The Metamorphosis" and said to J.D., "Why did Gregor Samsa wake up a cockroach?" His answer (which he would have toyed over with his students forever) was "Because that's what people expected of him."

They make the illogical logical. I don't do anything, because I'm waiting, I'm on hold (J.D.); I stay stoned because I know it's better to be out of it (Freddy); I love art because I myself am a work of art (Tucker).

Frank is harder to understand. One night a week or so ago, I thought we were really attuned to each other, communicating by telepathic waves, and as I lay in bed about to speak I realized that the vibrations really existed: they were him, snoring.

Now he's coming into the bedroom, and I'm trying again to think what to say. Or ask. Or do.

"Be glad you're not in Key West," he says. He climbs into bed.

I raise myself up on one elbow and stare at him.

"There's a hurricane about to hit," he says.

"What?" I say. "Where did you hear that?"

"When Reddy Fox and I were putting the dishes away. We had the radio on." He doubles up his pillow, pushes it under his neck. "Boom goes everything," he says. "Bam. Crash. Poof." He looks at me. "You look shocked." He closes his eyes. Then, after a minute or two, he murmurs, "Hurricanes upset you? I'll try to think of something nice."

He is quiet for so long that I think he has fallen asleep. Then he says, "Cars that run on water. A field of flowers, none alike. A shooting star that goes slow enough for you to watch. Your life to do over again." He has been whispering in my ear, and when he takes his mouth away I shiver. He slides lower in the bed for sleep. "I'll tell you something really amazing," he says. "Tucker told me he went into a travel agency on Park Avenue last week and asked the travel agent where he should go to pan for gold, and she told him."

"Where did she tell him to go?"

"I think somewhere in Peru. The banks of some river in Peru."

"Did you decide what you're going to do after Mark's birthday?" I say.

He doesn't answer me. I touch him on the side, finally.

"It's two o'clock in the morning. Let's talk about it another time."

"You picked the house, Frank. They're your friends downstairs. I used to be what you wanted me to be."

"They're your friends, too," he says. "Don't be paranoid."

"I want to know if you're staying or going."

He takes a deep breath, lets it out, and continues to lie very still.

"Everything you've done is commendable," he says. "You did the right thing to go back to school. You tried to do the right thing by finding yourself a normal friend like Marilyn. But your whole life you've made one mistake—you've surrounded yourself with me. Let me tell you something. All men—if they're crazy, like Tucker, if they're gay as the Queen of the May, like Freddy Fox, even if they're just six years old—I'm going to tell you something about them. Men think they're Spider-Man and Buck Rogers and Superman. You know what we all feel inside that you don't feel? That we're going to the stars."

He takes my hand. "I'm looking down on all of this from space," he whispers. "I'm already gone."

[1979]

Questions

1. Why does Amy put up with a house full of crazies? Why does she tolerate the situation around her?
2. How do you interpret the central metaphor of burning?
3. J.D. says to Amy, "'I believe all that wicked fairy-tale crap: your heart will break, your house will burn.'" Do you regard the story as an updated version of a traditional fairy tale?

Heinrich Böll

(1917–1985)

Germany

The fiction of Heinrich Böll, who has been described as the most popular of all German writers, has been translated into 45 languages; more than 20 million copies of his books have been sold worldwide. Böll was awarded the Nobel Prize for Literature in 1972. A prolific writer, he published novels, stories, plays, poetry, and essays that consistently reflect his blend of Christian ethics and social commitment. One of the few postwar German writers to take public positions on the social and political issues that had debilitated Germany, Böll was frequently identified by his German (and other) contemporaries as the moral conscience of his era. However, Böll repudiated this label, remarking that if writers, rather than public leaders, were the sole bearers of Germany's moral conscience, his country was doomed.

Böll's strong social commitment was forged by his own personal circumstances. Born in Cologne during the middle of World War I, the son of a wood sculptor and master furniture maker, he saw his family's economically comfortable life vanish precipitously during the Depression of 1930. Although during the early years of Hitler's reign his family tried to remain neutral, Böll was drafted into military service and sustained several serious injuries during his service in France, Poland, and the Crimea. His mother died during an air raid; Böll was taken prisoner by American troops in 1945.

Following his release at the end of the war, Böll returned to Cologne with his wife and young family and wrote while he remained involved with political issues, particularly as an advocate against war, militarism, and hypocrisy in all forms. His most widely praised novels, Group Portrait with a Lady (1973) and The Lost Honor of Katharina Blum (1975), demonstrate his consistent ideal: to conserve traditional human values while maintaining a healthy suspicion of power based on wealth, social position, or military force. Other highly regarded novels include The Clown (1963) and Safety Net (1975). In his Nobel Prize acceptance speech, Böll observed, "Art is always a good hiding-place, not for dynamite, but for intellectual explosives and social time bombs."

Böll's short stories that have been translated into English include Traveler, If You Come to Spa (1950), Eighteen Stories (1966), and The Stories of Heinrich Böll (1986). "The Laugher" (translated by Leila Vennewitz) effectively captures the poignant melancholy that characterizes Böll's bittersweet view of human experience.

THE LAUGHER

When someone asks me what business I am in, I am seized with embarrassment: I blush and stammer, I who am otherwise known as a man of poise. I envy people who can say: I am a bricklayer. I envy barbers, bookkeepers, and writers the simplicity of their avowal, for all these professions speak for themselves and need no lengthy explanation, while I am constrained to reply to such questions: I am a laugher. An admission of this kind demands another, since I have to answer the second question: "Is that how you make your living?" truthfully with "Yes." I actually do make a living at my laughing, and a good one too, for my laughing is—commercially speaking—much in demand. I am a good laugher, experienced, no one else laughs as well as I do, no one else has such command of the fine points of my art. For a long time, in order to avoid tiresome explanations, I called myself an actor, but my talents in the field of mime and elocution are so meager that I felt this designation to be too far from the truth: I love the truth, and the truth is: I am a laugher. I am neither a clown nor a comedian. I do not make people gay, I portray gaiety: I laugh like a Roman emperor, or like a sensitive schoolboy, I am as much at home in the laughter of the seventeenth century as in that of the nineteenth, and when occasion demands I laugh my way through the centuries, all classes of society, all categories of age: it is simply a skill which I have acquired, like the skill of being able to repair shoes. In my breast I harbor the laughter of America, the laughter of Africa, white, red, yellow laughter—and for the right fee I let it peal out in accordance with the director's requirements.

I have become indispensable; I laugh on records, I laugh on tape, and television directors treat me with respect. I laugh mournfully, moderately, hysterically; I laugh like a streetcar conductor or like an apprentice in the grocery business; laughter in the morning, laughter in the evening, nocturnal laughter, and the laughter of twilight. In short: wherever and however laughter is required—I do it.

It need hardly be pointed out that a profession of this kind is tiring, especially as I have also—this is my specialty—mastered the art of infectious laughter; this has also made me indispensable to third- and fourth-rate comedians, who are scared—and with good reason—that their audiences will miss their punch lines, so I spend most evenings in nightclubs as a kind of discreet claque, my job being to laugh infectiously during the weaker parts of the program. It has to be carefully timed: my hearty, boisterous laughter must not come too soon, but neither must it come too late, it must come just at the right spot: at the prearranged moment I burst out laughing, the whole audience roars with me, and the joke is saved.

But as for me, I drag myself exhausted to the checkroom, put on my overcoat, happy that I can go off duty at last. At home I usually find telegrams waiting for me: "Urgently require your laughter. Recording Tuesday," and a few hours later I am sitting in an overheated express train bemoaning my fate.

I need scarcely say that when I am off duty or on vacation I have little inclination to laugh: the cowhand is glad when he can forget the cow, the bricklayer when he can forget the mortar, and carpenters usually have doors at home which don't work or drawers which are hard to open. Confectioners like sour pickles, butchers like marzipan, and the baker prefers sausage to bread; bullfighters raise pigeons for a hobby, boxers turn pale when their children have nosebleeds: I find all this quite natural, for I never laugh off duty. I am a very solemn person, and people consider me—perhaps rightly so—a pessimist.

During the first years of our married life, my wife would often say to me: "Do laugh!" but since then she has come to realize that I cannot grant her this wish. I am happy when I am free to relax my tense face muscles, my frayed spirit, in profound solemnity. Indeed, even other people's laughter gets on my nerves, since it reminds me too much of my profession. So our marriage is a quiet, peaceful one, because my wife has also forgotten how to laugh: now and again I catch her smiling, and I smile too. We converse in low tones, for I detest the noise of the nightclubs, the noise that sometimes fills the recording studios. People who do not know me think I am taciturn. Perhaps I am, because I have to open my mouth so often to laugh.

I go through life with an impassive expression, from time to time permitting myself a gentle smile, and I often wonder whether I have ever laughed. I think not. My brothers and sisters have always known me for a serious boy.

So I laugh in many different ways, but my own laughter I have never heard.

[1966]

Translated by

LEILA VENNEWITZ

Questions

1. How would you characterize the narrator of the story? How can he be so successful in his profession and at the same time be incapable of genuine laughter?
2. What does the narrator mean when he says, "I do not make people gay, I portray gaiety"?
3. Is the story a satire? If so, what is Böll satirizing?
4. Does the story make you laugh? If so, what is the source of its humor? If not, what emotional response does it evoke in you?

Jorge Luis Borges
(1899–1986)
Argentina

W hen Latin American writers of the twentieth century are discussed, Jorge Luis Borges is likely to be mentioned first. His audience is truly international, as critics would also define the scope of his writing. A master storyteller, poet, essayist, and man of letters, Borges has had an enormous influence on contemporary Latin American writing. Some critics proclaim Borges to be the source of the boom in recent Latin American literature. Yet Borges's fame was slow to develop. The story he tells of himself is that when one of his early books was published, it sold only 37 copies. Borges was so humbled that he thought he should write each of the 37 people who purchased the book a personal letter of thanks.

Though born in Buenos Aires, Argentina, in 1899, Borges was educated primarily in Europe. His father was an educator, from whom he acquired an interest in intellectual puzzles. That fascination merged with an interest in several avant-garde literary currents in Europe in the early decades of the twentieth century. When he returned to Buenos Aires in 1921, he worked in the National Library, while simultaneously beginning his early experiments in writing. He confessed during his Paris Review interview that he enjoyed reading old encyclopedias, which may account for some of the obscure references in his short stories. Borges also liked to give his characters names from his own family, "to work in the names of [his] grandfathers, great-grandfathers, and so on. To give them a kind of, well, I won't say immortality, but that's one of the methods."

Borges's most popular books in the United States are collections of short stories: Fictions (1944) and Labyrinths (1972). In each of these works he employs the labyrinthian method, an elaborate physical maze that may in turn intellectually confuse the character (a detective, perhaps) at the center of the story. An anonymous reviewer in the Virginia Quarterly Review summed up his work as follows:

> Borges writes of skeptics overwhelmed by mystical event and of gangsters with the logic of Auguste Dupin. [His] remarkable stories which mix cabbalism with science fiction and the detective story deride, in their ironic reversals, the fictions of communication with others and make the communication of one with oneself the greater puzzle. In his stories, narratives, and prose pieces, Borges is among the leading writers of our time who are extending the boundaries of fiction into autobiography and essay.

THE SOUTH

The man who landed in Buenos Aires in 1871 bore the name of Johannes Dahlmann and he was a minister in the Evangelical Church. In 1939, one of his grandchildren, Juan Dahlmann, was secretary of a municipal library on Calle Córdoba, and he considered himself profoundly Argentinian. His maternal grandfather had been that Francisco Flores, of the Second Line-Infantry Division, who had died on the frontier of Buenos Aires, run through with a lance by Indians from Catriel; in the discord inherent between his two lines of descent, Juan Dahlmann (perhaps driven to it by his Germanic blood) chose the line represented by his romantic ancestor, his ancestor of the romantic death. An old sword, a leather frame containing the daguerreotype of a blank-faced man with a beard, the dash and grace of certain music, the familiar strophes of *Martín Fierro*, the passing years, boredom and solitude, all went to foster this voluntary, but never ostentatious nationalism. At the cost of numerous small privations, Dahlmann had managed to save the empty shell of a ranch in the South which had belonged to the Flores family; he continually recalled the image of the balsamic eucalyptus trees and the great rose-colored house which had once been crimson. His duties, perhaps even indolence, kept him in the city. Summer after summer he contented himself with the abstract idea of possession and with the certitude that his ranch was waiting for him on a precise site in the middle of the plain. Late in February, 1939, something happened to him.

Blind to all fault, destiny can be ruthless at one's slightest distraction. Dahlmann had succeeded in acquiring, on that very afternoon, an imperfect copy of Weil's edition of *The Thousand and One Nights*. Avid to examine this find, he did not wait for the elevator but hurried up the stairs. In the obscurity, something brushed by his forehead: a bat, a bird? On the face of the woman who opened the door to him he saw horror engraved, and the hand he wiped across his face came away red with blood. The edge of a recently painted door which someone had forgotten to close had caused this wound. Dahlmann was able to fall asleep, but from the moment he awoke at dawn the savor of all things was atrociously poignant. Fever wasted him and the pictures in *The Thousand and One Nights* served to illustrate night-mares. Friends and relatives paid him visits and, with exaggerated smiles, assured him that they thought he looked fine. Dahlmann listened to them with a kind of feeble stupor and he marveled at their not knowing that he was in hell. A week, eight days passed, and they were like eight centuries. One afternoon, the usual doctor appeared, accompanied by a new doctor, and they carried him off to a sanitarium on the Calle Ecuador, for it was necessary to X-ray him. Dahlmann, in the hackney coach which bore them away, thought that he would, at last, be able to sleep in a room different from his own. He felt happy and communicative. When he arrived at his destination, they undressed him, shaved his head, bound him with metal fastenings to a stretcher; they shone bright lights on him until he was blind and dizzy, auscultated him, and a masked man stuck a needle into his arm. He awoke with a feeling of nausea, covered with a bandage, in a cell with something of a well about it; in the days and nights which followed the operation he came to realize that he had merely been, up until then, in a suburb of hell. Ice in his mouth did not leave the least trace of freshness. During these days Dahlmann hated himself in minute detail: he hated his identity, his bodily necessities, his humiliation, the beard which bristled upon his face. He stoically endured the curative measures, which were painful, but when the surgeon told him he had been on the point of death from septicemia, Dahlmann dissolved in tears of self-pity for his fate. Physical wretchedness and the incessant anticipation of horrible nights had not allowed him time to think of anything so abstract as death. On another day, the surgeon told him he was healing and that, very soon, he would be able to go to his ranch for convalescence. Incredibly enough, the promised day arrived.

Reality favors symmetries and slight anachronisms: Dahlmann had arrived at the sanitarium in a hackney coach and now a hackney coach was to take him to the Constitución station. The first fresh tang of autumn, after the summer's oppressiveness, seemed like a symbol in nature of his rescue and release from fever and death. The city, at seven in the morning, had not lost that air of an old house lent it by the night; the streets seemed like long vestibules, the plazas were like patios. Dahlmann recognized the city with joy on the edge of vertigo: a second before his eyes registered the phenomena themselves, he recalled the corners, the billboards, the modest variety of Buenos Aires. In the yellow light of the new day, all things returned to him.

Every Argentine knows that the South begins at the other side of Rivadavia. Dahlmann was in the habit of saying that this was no mere convention, that whoever crosses this street enters a more ancient and sterner world. From inside the carriage he sought out, among the new buildings, the iron grill window, the brass knocker, the arched door, the entrance way, the intimate patio.

At the railroad station he noted that he still had thirty minutes. He quickly recalled that in a café on the Calle Brazil (a few dozen feet from Yrigoyen's house) there was an enormous cat which allowed itself to be caressed as if it were a disdainful divinity. He entered the café. There was the cat, asleep. He ordered a cup of coffee, slowly stirred the sugar, sipped it (this pleasure had been denied him in the clinic), and thought, as he smoothed the cat's black coat, that this contact was an illusion and that the two beings, man and cat, were as good as separated by a glass, for man lives in time, in succession, while the magical animal lives in the present, in the eternity of the instant.

Along the next to the last platform the train lay waiting. Dahlmann walked through the coaches until he found one almost empty. He arranged his baggage in the network rack. When the train started off, he took down his valise and extracted, after some hesitation, the first volume of *The Thousand and One Nights*. To travel with this book, which was so much a part of the history of his ill-fortune, was a kind of affirmation that his ill-fortune had been annulled; it was a joyous and secret defiance of the frustrated forces of evil.

Along both sides of the train the city dissipated into suburbs; this sight, and then a view of the gardens and villas, delayed the beginning of his reading. The truth was that Dahlmann read very little. The magnetized mountain and the genie who swore to kill his benefactor are—who would deny it?—marvelous, but not so much more than the morning itself and the mere fact of being. The joy of life distracted him from paying attention to Scheherezade and her superfluous miracles. Dahlmann closed his book and allowed himself to live.

Lunch—the bouillon served in shining metal bowls, as in the remote summers of childhood—was one more peaceful and rewarding delight.

Tomorrow I'll wake up at the ranch, he thought, and it was as if he was two men at a time: the man who traveled through the autumn day and across the geography of the fatherland, and the other one, locked up in a sanitarium and subject to methodical servitude. He saw unplastered brick houses, long and angled, timelessly watching the trains go by; he saw horsemen along the dirt roads; he saw gullies and lagoons and ranches; he saw great luminous clouds that resembled marble; and all these things were accidental, casual, like dreams of the plain. He also thought he recognized trees and crop fields; but he would not have been able to name them, for his actual knowledge of the countryside was quite inferior to his nostalgic and literary knowledge.

From time to time he slept, and his dreams were animated by the impetus of the train. The intolerable white sun of high noon had already become the yellow sun which precedes nightfall, and it would not be long before it would turn red. The rail-road car was now also different; it was not the same as the one which had quit the station siding at Constitución; the plain and the hours had transfigured it. Outside, the moving shadow of the railroad car stretched toward the horizon. The elemental earth was not perturbed either by settlements or other signs of humanity. The coun-try was vast but at the same time intimate and, in some measure, secret. The limit-less country sometimes contained only a solitary bull. The solitude was perfect, perhaps hostile, and it might have occurred to Dahlmann that he was traveling into the past and not merely south. He was distracted from these considerations by the railroad in-spector who, on reading his ticket, advised him that the train would not let him off at the regular station but at another: an earlier stop, one scarcely known to Dahlmann. (The man added an explanation which Dahlmann did not attempt to understand, and which he hardly heard, for the mechanism of events did not concern him.)

The train laboriously ground to a halt, practically in the middle of the plain. The station lay on the other side of the tracks; it was not much more than a siding and a shed. There was no means of conveyance to be seen, but the station chief supposed that the traveler might secure a vehicle from a general store and inn to be found some ten or twelve blocks away.

Dahlmann accepted the walk as a small adventure. The sun had already disap-peared from view, but a final splendor exalted the vivid and silent plain, before the night erased its color. Less to avoid fatigue than to draw out his enjoyment of these sights, Dahlmann walked slowly, breathing in the odor of clover with sumptuous joy.

The general store at one time had been painted a deep scarlet, but the years had tempered this violent color for its own good. Something in its poor architecture recalled a steel engraving, perhaps one from an old edition of *Paul et Virginie*. A number of horses were hitched up to the paling. Once inside, Dahlmann thought he recognized the shopkeeper. Then he realized that he had been deceived by the man's resemblance to one of the male nurses in the sanitarium. When the shopkeeper heard Dahlmann's request, he said he would have the shay made up. In order to add one more event to that day and to kill time, Dahlmann decided to eat at the general store.

Some country louts, to whom Dahlmann did not at first pay any attention, were eat-ing and drinking at one of the tables. On the floor, and hanging on to the bar, squat-ted an old man, immobile as an object. His years had reduced and polished him as water does a stone or the generations of men do a sentence. He was dark, dried up, diminutive, and seemed outside time, situated in eternity. Dahlmann noted with sat-isfaction the kerchief, the thick poncho, the long *chiripá*, and the colt boots, and told himself, as he recalled futile discussions with people from the Northern counties or from the province of Entre Rios, that gauchos like this no longer existed outside the South.

Dahlmann sat down next to the window. The darkness began overcoming the plain, but the odor and sound of the earth penetrated the iron bars of the window. The shop owner brought him sardines, followed by some roast meat. Dahlmann washed the meal down with several glasses of red wine. Idling, he relished the tart savor of the wine, and let his gaze, now grown somewhat drowsy, wander over the shop. A kerosene lamp hung from a beam. There were three customers at the other table: two of them appeared to be farm workers; the third man, whose features hint-ed at Chinese blood, was drinking with his hat on. Of a sudden Dahlmann felt some-thing brush lightly against his face. Next to the heavy glass of turbid wine, upon one of the stripes in the table cloth, lay a spit ball of breadcrumb. That was all: but some-one had thrown it there.

The men at the other table seemed totally cut off from him. Perplexed, Dahlmann decided that nothing had happened, and he opened the volume of *The Thousand and One Nights*, by way of suppressing reality. After a few moments another little ball landed on his table, and now the *peones* laughed outright. Dahlmann said to himself that he was not frightened, but he reasoned that it would be a major blunder if he, a convalescent, were to allow himself to be dragged by strangers into some chaotic quarrel. He determined to leave, and had already gotten to his feet when the owner came up and exhorted him in an alarmed voice:

"*Señor* Dahlmann, don't pay any attention to those lads; they're half high."

Dahlmann was not surprised to learn that the other man, now, knew his name. But he felt that these conciliatory words served only to aggravate the situation. Previous to this moment, the *peones*' provocation was directed against an unknown face, against no one in particular, almost against no one at all. Now it was an attack against him, against his name, and his neighbors knew it. Dahlmann pushed the owner aside, confronted the *peones*, and demanded to know what they wanted of him.

The tough with a Chinese look staggered heavily to his feet. Almost in Juan Dahlmann's face he shouted insults, as if he had been a long way off. His game was to exaggerate his drunkness, and this extravagance constituted a ferocious mockery. Between curses and obscenities, he threw a long knife into the air, followed it with his eyes, caught and juggled it, and challenged Dahlmann to a knife fight. The owner objected in a tremulous voice, pointing out that Dahlmann was unarmed. At this point, something unforeseeable occurred.

From a corner of the room, the old ecstatic gaucho—in whom Dahlmann saw a summary and cipher of the South (his South)—threw him a naked dagger, which landed at his feet. It was as if the South had resolved that Dahlmann should accept the duel. Dahlmann bent over to pick up the dagger, and felt two things. The first, that this almost instinctive act bound him to fight. The second, that the weapon, in his torpid hand, was no defense at all, but would merely serve to justify his murder. He had once played with a poniard, like all men, but his idea of fencing and knifeplay did not go further than the notion that all strokes should be directed upwards, with the cutting edge held inwards. *They would not have allowed such things to happen to me in the sanitarium,* he thought.

"Let's get on our way," said the other man.

They went out and if Dahlmann was without hope, he was also without fear. As he crossed the threshold, he felt that to die in a knife fight, under the open sky, and going forward to the attack, would have been a liberation, a joy, and a festive occasion, on the first night in the sanitarium, when they stuck him with the needle. He felt that if he had been able to choose, then, or to dream his death, this would have been the death he would have chosen or dreamt.

Firmly clutching his knife, which he perhaps would not know how to wield, Dahlmann went out into the plain.

[1956]
Translated by
ANTHONY KERRIGAN

Questions

1. Identify the significant stages of Dahlmann's journey.
2. What is the importance of the references to *The Thousand and One Nights*?
3. At what juncture in the story does realism give way to the fantastic?

Dino Buzzati

(1906–1972)

Italy

D ino Buzzati was a prolific writer in a variety of contexts. A lifelong journalist, he was editor and correspondent for the Corriere della Sera of Milan, one of Italy's largest daily newspapers and the first place of publication for many of his short stories. In addition to hundreds of stories, he wrote novels, poems, plays, librettos, and a children's book. He was also a painter. Buzzati is sometimes compared to Kafka and Borges for his genius in combining realism with fantasy to create what might be called fables for adults.

Buzzati's beginnings as a writer coincided with the Fascist period in Italy. His use of fantasy and allegory can be understood as an inventive narrative strategy for circumventing the censorship borne of political repression in Italy in the mid-twentieth century. Through a deliberately skewed perspective that makes use of allegory, satire, paradox, and the fusion of the unbelievable with the believable, Buzzati nonetheless wrote about the human condition and about distinctly credible human concerns, including fears of death, the unknown, and the unknowable. His best-known novels in English, Barnabo of the Mountains (1933) and The Tartar Steppe (1952), are, despite their enigmatic and surreal qualities, deeply concerned with real human problems, particularly the sense of futility in modern experience. As he phrased it, his fiction was about "things that do not exist, imagined by man for poetic ends." One of his commentators has described Buzzati's characteristic position as one of "melancholic compassion."

THE FALLING GIRL

Marta was nineteen. She looked out over the roof of the skyscraper, and seeing the city below shining in the dusk, she was overcome with dizziness.

The skyscraper was silver, supreme and fortunate in that most beautiful and pure evening, as here and there the wind stirred a few fine filaments of cloud against an absolutely incredible blue background. It was in fact the hour when the city is seized by inspiration and whoever is not blind is swept away by it. From that airy height the girl saw the streets and the masses of buildings writhing in the long spasm of sunset, and at the point where the white of the houses ended, the blue of the sea began. Seen from above, the sea looked as if it were rising. And since the veils of the night were advancing from the east, the city became a sweet abyss burning with pulsating lights. Within it were powerful men, and women who were even more powerful, furs and violins, cars glossy as onyx, the neon signs of nightclubs, the entrance halls of darkened mansions, fountains, diamonds, old silent gardens, parties, desires, affairs, and, above all, that consuming sorcery of the evening which provokes dreams of greatness and glory.

Seeing these things, Marta hopelessly leaned out over the railing and let herself go. She felt as if she were hovering in the air, but she was falling. Given the extraordinary height of the skyscraper, the streets and squares down at the bottom were very far away. Who knows how long it would take her to get there. Yet the girl was falling.

At that hour the terraces and balconies of the top floors were filled with rich and elegant people who were having cocktails and making silly conversation. They were scattered in crowds, and their talk muffled the music. Marta passed before them and several people looked out to watch her.

Flights of that kind (mostly by girls, in fact) were not rare in the skyscraper and they constituted an interesting diversion for the tenants; this was also the reason why the price of those apartments was very high.

The sun had not yet completely set and it did its best to illuminate Marta's simple clothing. She wore a modest, inexpensive spring dress bought off the rack. Yet the lyrical light of the sunset exalted it somewhat, making it chic.

From the millionaires' balconies, gallant hands were stretched out toward her, offering flowers and cocktails. "Miss, would you like a drink? . . . Gentle butterfly, why not stop a minute with us?"

She laughed, hovering, happy (but meanwhile she was falling): "No, thanks, friends. I can't. I'm in a hurry."

"Where are you headed?" they asked her.

"Ah, don't make me say," Marta answered, waving her hands in a friendly good-bye.

A young man, tall, dark, very distinguished, extended an arm to snatch her. She liked him. And yet Marta quickly defended herself: "How dare you, sir?" and she had time to give him a little tap on the nose.

The beautiful people, then, were interested in her and that filled her with satisfaction. She felt fascinating, stylish. On the flower-filled terraces, amid the bustle of waiters in white and the bursts of exotic songs, there was talk for a few minutes, perhaps less, of the young woman who was passing by (from top to bottom, on a vertical course). Some thought her pretty, others thought her so-so, everyone found her interesting.

"You have your entire life before you," they told her, "why are you in such a hurry? You still have time to rush around and busy yourself. Stop with us for a little while, it's only a modest little party among friends, really, you'll have a good time."

She made an attempt to answer but the force of gravity had already quickly carried her to the floor below, then two, three, four floors below; in fact, exactly as you gaily rush around when you are just nineteen years old.

Of course, the distance that separated her from the bottom, that is, from street level, was immense. It is true that she began falling just a little while ago, but the street always seemed very far away.

In the meantime, however, the sun had plunged into the sea; one could see it disappear, transformed into a shimmering reddish mushroom. As a result, it no longer emitted its vivifying rays to light up the girl's dress and make her a seductive comet. It was a good thing that the windows and terraces of the skyscraper were almost all illuminated and the bright reflections completely gilded her as she gradually passed by.

Now Marta no longer saw just groups of carefree people inside the apartments; at times there were even some businesses where the employees, in black or blue aprons, were sitting at desks in long rows. Several of them were young people as old as or older than she, and weary of the day by now, every once in a while they raised their eyes from their duties and from typewriters. In this way they too saw her, and a few ran to the windows. "Where are you going? Why so fast? Who are you?" they shouted to her. One could divine something akin to envy in their words.

"They're waiting for me down there," she answered. "I can't stop. Forgive me." And again she laughed, wavering on her headlong fall, but it wasn't like her previous laughter anymore. The night had craftily fallen and Marta started to feel cold.

Meanwhile, looking downward, she saw a bright halo of lights at the entrance of a building. Here long blacks cars were stopping (from the great distance they looked as small as ants), and men and women were getting out, anxious to go inside. She seemed to make out the sparkling of jewels in that swarm. Above the entrance flags were flying.

They were obviously giving a large party, exactly the kind that Marta dreamed of ever since she was a child. Heaven help her if she missed it. Down there opportunity was waiting for her, fate, romance, the true inauguration of her life. Would she arrive in time?

She spitefully noticed that another girl was falling about thirty meters above her. She was decidedly prettier than Marta and she wore a rather classy evening gown. For some unknown reason she came down much faster than Marta, so that in a few moments she passed by her and disappeared below, even though Marta was calling her. Without doubt she would get to the party before Marta; perhaps she had a plan all worked out to supplant her.

Then she realized that they weren't alone. Along the sides of the skyscraper many other young women were plunging downward, their faces taut with the excitement of the flight, their hands cheerfully waving as if to say: look at us, here we are, entertain us, is not the world ours?

It was a contest, then. And she only had a shabby little dress while those other girls were dressed smartly like high-fashion models and some even wrapped luxurious mink stoles tightly around their bare shoulders. So self-assured when she began the leap, Marta now felt a tremor growing inside her; perhaps it was just the cold; but it may have been fear too, the fear of having made an error without remedy.

It seemed to be late at night now. The windows were darkened one after another, the echoes of music became more rare, the offices were empty, young men no longer leaned out from the windowsills extending their hands. What time was it? At the entrance to the building down below—which in the meantime had grown larger, and one could now distinguish all the architectural details—the lights were still burning, but the bustle of cars had stopped. Every now and then, in fact, small groups of people came out of the main floor wearily drawing away. Then the lights of the entrance were also turned off.

Marta felt her heart tightening. Alas, she wouldn't reach the ball in time. Glancing upwards, she saw the pinnacle of the skyscraper in all its cruel power. It was almost completely dark. On the top floors a few windows here and there were still lit. And above the top the first glimmer of dawn was spreading.

In a dining recess on the twenty-eighth floor a man about forty years old was having his morning coffee and reading his newspaper while his wife tidied up the room. A clock on the sideboard indicated 8:45. A shadow suddenly passed before the window.

"Alberto!" the wife shouted. "Did you see that? A woman passed by."

"Who was it?" he said without raising his eyes from the newspaper.

"An old woman," the wife answered. "A decrepit old woman. She looked frightened."

"It's always like that," the man muttered. "At these low floors only falling old women pass by. You can see beautiful girls from the hundred-and-fiftieth floor up. Those apartments don't cost so much for nothing."

"At least down here there's the advantage," observed the wife, "that you can hear the thud when they touch the ground."

"This time not even that," he said, shaking his head, after he stood listening for a few minutes. Then he had another sip of coffee.

[1983—English translation]
Translated by
Lawrence Venuti

Questions

1. What different meanings of "falling" contribute to the story's effect and meaning?
2. How does time function in the story?
3. Why do only women "fall"? Why do only "old women" pass by the lower floors of the skyscraper?
4. What elements of society are being criticized or satirized in the story?
5. What is "The Falling Girl" really about? How do the improbable and fantastic qualities and the matter-of-fact tone of the story contribute to its meaning and effectiveness?

Italo Calvino
(1923–1985)
Italy

I talo Calvino is one of a group of twentieth-century writers—including Franz Kafka, Jorge Luis Borges, Gabriel García Márquez, and his near-contemporary Dino Buzzati—who have infused modern and contemporary fiction with fantasy, "magical realism," and the surreal. Like Buzzati, Calvino may have found the nonrealistic liberties of fantasy a useful narrative strategy for avoiding the restrictions of censorship and the political totalitarianism in the Italy of his youth. If realism was too close to the conventional world of social and political ideas that had failed, fantasy provided the opportunity to invent multiple alternative worlds.

In fact, Calvino used traditional forms to write uniquely nontraditional stories. In his own view, the traditional fable form offered a structure in which infinite variations and imaginative transformations could be created. As he phrased it in an essay, "The Lion's Marrow" (1955), "The mold of the most ancient fables, the child abandoned in the woods or the knight who must survive encounters with beasts and enchantments, remains the irreplaceable scheme of all human stories."

Calvino was born in Cuba of Italian parents, both of whom were tropical agronomists. He spent his childhood in Italy and, as a result of compulsory military service, saw action in World War II. He was active in the Italian Resistance; later he joined the Communist party but left it when Russia invaded Hungary. He was an editor at the Italian publishing firm Einaudi. As an intellectual, critic, and writer, Calvino was a major voice in recent Italian cultural history. His best-known novels, Cosmicomics (1968), Invisible Cities (1974), The Castle of Crossed Destinies (1976), and If on a Winter's Night a Traveler (1979) are not only imaginative adventures but frequently also explorations of the nature of fiction itself. In Invisible Cities, a young Marco Polo entertains an aged Kubla Khan with descriptions of his travels to places that exist in the past, present, and future.

Calvino's translator, William Weaver, describes the tales of Cosmicomics as "the outer space of Calvino's imagination." But Calvino's narratives are not simply entertaining, remote fantasies without links to human experience. Rather, even Qfwfq and the other tongue-trippingly-named time-traveling characters of Cosmicomics harbor decidedly human desires. As Calvino notes of his fiction, "If the reader looks, I think he will find plenty of moral and political ideas in my stories. I suffer from everyday life."

THE SPIRAL

For the majority of mollusks, the visible organic form has little importance in the life of the members of a species, since they cannot see one another and have, at most, only a vague perception of other individuals and of their surroundings. This does not prevent brightly colored stripings and forms which seem very beautiful to our eyes (as in many gastropod shells) from existing independently of any relationship to visibility.

I

Like me, when I was clinging to that rock, you mean?—*Qfwfq asked,*—With the waves rising and falling, and me there, still, flat, sucking what there was to suck and thinking about it all the time? If that's the time you want to know about, there isn't much I can tell you. Form? I didn't have any; that is, I didn't know I had one, or rather I didn't know you *could* have one. I grew more or less on all sides, at random; if this is what you call radial symmetry, I suppose I had radial symmetry, but to tell you the truth I never paid any attention to it. Why should I have grown more on one side than on the other? I had no eyes, no head, no part of the body that was different from any other part; now I try to persuade myself that the two holes I had were a mouth and an anus, and that I therefore already had my bilateral symmetry, just like the trilobites and the rest of you, but in my memory I really can't tell those holes apart, I passed stuff from whatever side I felt like, inside or outside was the same, differences and repugnances came along much later. Every now and then I was seized by fantasies, that's true; for example, the notion of scratching my armpit, or crossing my legs, or once even of growing a mustache. I use these words here with you, to make myself clear; then there were many details I couldn't foresee: I had some cells, one more or less the same as another, and they all did more or less the same job. But since I had no form I could feel all possible forms in myself, and all actions and expressions and possibilities of making noises, even rude ones. In short, there were no limitations to my thoughts, which weren't thoughts, after all, because I had no brain to think them; every cell on its own thought every thinkable thing all at once, not through images, since we had no images of any kind at our disposal, but simply in that indeterminate way of feeling oneself there, which did not prevent us from feeling ourselves equally there in some other way.

It was a rich and free and contented condition, my condition at that time, quite the contrary of what you might think. I was a bachelor (our system of reproduction in those days didn't require even temporary couplings), healthy, without too many ambitions. When you're young, all evolution lies before you, every road is open to you, and at the same time you can enjoy the fact of being there on the rock, flat mollusk-pulp, damp and happy. If you compare yourself with the limitations that came afterwards, if you think of how having one form excludes other forms, of the monotonous routine where you finally feel trapped, well, I don't mind saying life was beautiful in those days.

To be sure, I lived a bit withdrawn into myself, that's true, no comparison with our interrelated life nowadays; and I'll also admit that—partly because of my age and partly under the influence of my surroundings—I was what they call a narcissist to a slight extent; I mean I stayed there observing myself all the time, I saw all my good points and all my defects, and I liked myself for the former and for the latter; I had no terms of comparison, you must remember that, too.

But I wasn't so backward that I didn't know something else existed beyond me: the rock where I clung, obviously, and also the water that reached me with every wave, but other stuff, too, farther on: that is, the world. The water was a source of information, reliable and precise: it brought me edible substances which I absorbed through all my surface, and other inedible ones which still helped me form an idea of what there was around. The system worked like this: a wave would come, and I, still sticking to the rock, would raise myself up a little bit, imperceptibly—all I had to do was loosen the pressure slightly—and, splat, the water passed beneath me, full of substances and sensations and stimuli. You never knew how those stimuli were going to turn out, sometimes a tickling that made you die laughing, other times a shudder, a burning, an itch; so it was a constant seesaw of amusement and emotion. But you mustn't think I just lay there passively, dumbly accepting everything that came: after a while I had acquired some experience and I was quick to analyze what sort of stuff was arriving and to decide how I should behave, to make the best use of it or to avoid the more unpleasant consequences. It was all a kind of game of contractions, with each of the cells I had, or of relaxing at the right moment: and I could make my choices, reject, attract, even spit.

And so I learned that there were *the others*, the element surrounding me was filled with traces of them, *others* hostile and different from me or else disgustingly similar. No, now I'm giving you a disagreeable idea of my character, which is all wrong. Naturally, each of us went about on his own business, but the presence of the *others* reassured me, created an inhabited zone around me, freed me from the fear of being an alarming exception, which I would have been if the fact of existing had been my fate alone, a kind of exile.

So I knew that some of the *others* were female. The water transmitted a special vibration, a kind of brrrum brrrum brrrum, I remember when I became aware of it the first time, or rather, not the first, I remember when I became aware of being aware of it as a thing I had always known. At the discovery of these vibrations' existence, I was seized with a great curiosity, not so much to see them, or to be seen by them either— since, first, we hadn't any sight, and secondly, the sexes weren't yet differentiated, each individual was identical with every other individual and at looking at one or another I would have felt no more pleasure than in looking at myself—but a curiosity to know whether something would happen between me and them. A desperation filled me, a desire not to do anything special, which would have been out of place, knowing that there was nothing special to do, or nonspecial either, but to respond in some way to that vibration with a corresponding vibration, or rather, with a personal vibration of my own, because, sure enough, there was something there that wasn't exactly the same as the other, I mean now you might say it came from hormones, but for me it was very beautiful.

So then, one of them, shlup shlup shlup, emitted her eggs, and I, shlup shlup shlup, fertilized them: all down inside the sea, mingling in the water tepid from the sun; oh, I forgot to tell you, I could feel the sun, which warmed the sea and heated the rock.

One of them, I said. Because, among all those female messages that the sea slammed against me like an indistinct soup at first where everything was all right with me and I grubbed about paying no attention to what one was like or another, suddenly I understood what corresponded best to my tastes, tastes which I hadn't known before that moment, of course. In other words, I had fallen in love. What I mean is: I had begun to recognize, to isolate the signs of one of those from the others, in fact I waited for these signs I had begun to recognize, I sought them, responded to those signs I awaited with other signs I made myself, or rather it was I who aroused these signs from her, which I answered with other signs of my own, I mean I was in love with her and she with me, so what more could I want from life?

Now habits have changed, and it already seems inconceivable to you that one could love a female like that, without having spent any time with her. And yet, through that unmistakable part of her still in solution in the sea water, which the waves placed at my disposal, I received a quantity of information about her, more than you can imagine: not the superficial, generic information you get now, seeing and smelling and touching and hearing a voice, but essential information, which I could then develop at length in my imagination. I could think of her with minute precision, thinking not so much of how she was made, which would have been a banal and vulgar way of thinking of her, but of how from her present formlessness she would be transformed into one of the infinite possible forms, still remaining herself, however. I didn't imagine the forms that she might assume, but I imagined the special quality that, in taking them, she would give to those forms.

I knew her well, in other words. And I wasn't sure of her. Every now and then I was overcome with suspicion, anxiety, rage. I didn't let anything show, you know my character, but beneath that impassive mask passed suppositions I can't bring myself to confess even now. More than once I suspected she was unfaithful to me, that she sent messages not only to me but also to others; more than once I thought I had intercepted one, or that I had discovered a tone of insincerity in a message addressed to me. I was jealous, I can admit it now, not so much out of distrust of her as out of unsureness of myself: who could assure me that she had really understood who I was? Or that she had understood the fact that I was? This relationship achieved between us thanks to the sea water—a full, complete relationship, what more could I ask for?— was for me something, absolutely personal, between two unique and distinct individualities; but for her? Who could assure me that what she might find in me she hadn't also found in another, or in another two or three or ten or a hundred like me? Who could assure me that her abandon in our shared relations wasn't an indiscriminate abandon, slapdash, a kind of—who's next?—collective ecstasy?

The fact that these suspicions did not correspond to the truth was confirmed, for me, by the subtle, soft, private vibration, at times still trembling with modesty, in our correspondences; but what if, precisely out of shyness and inexperience, she didn't pay enough attention to my characteristics and others took advantage of this innocence to worm their way in? And what if she, a novice, believed it was still I and couldn't distinguish one from the other, and so our most intimate play was extended to a circle of strangers . . . ?

It was then that I began to secrete calcareous matter. I wanted to make something to mark my presence in an unmistakable fashion, something that would defend this individual presence of mine from the indiscriminate instability of all the rest. Now it's no use my piling up words, trying to explain the novelty of this intention I had; the first word I said is more than enough: *make*, I wanted to *make*, and considering the fact that I had never made anything or thought you could make anything, this in itself was a big event. So I began to make the first thing that occurred to me, and it was a shell. From the margin of that fleshy cloak on my body, using certain glands, I began to give off secretions which took on a curving shape all around, until I was covered with a hard and variegated shield, rough on the outside and smooth and shiny inside. Naturally, I had no way of controlling the form of what I was making: I just stayed there all huddled up, silent and sluggish, and I secreted. I went on even after the shell covered my whole body; I began another turn; in short, I was getting one of those shells all twisted into a spiral, which you, when you see them, think are so hard to make, but all you have to do is keep working and giving off the same matter without stopping, and they grow like that, one turn after the other.

Once it existed, this shell was also a necessary and indispensable place to stay inside of, a defense for my survival; it was a lucky thing I had made it, but while I was making it I had no idea of making it because I needed it; on the contrary, it was like when somebody lets out an exclamation he could perfectly well not make, and yet he

makes it, like "Ha" or "hmph!," that's how I made the shell: simply to express myself.
And in this self-expression I put all the thoughts I had about her, I released the anger
she made me feel, my amorous way of thinking about her, my determination to exist
for her, the desire for me to be me, and for her to be her, and the love for myself that
I put in my love for her—all the things that could be said only in that conch shell
wound into a spiral.

At regular intervals the calcareous matter I was secreting came out colored, so a
number of lovely stripes were formed running straight through the spirals, and this
shell was a thing different from me but also the truest part of me, the explanation of
who I was, my portrait translated into a rhythmic system of volumes and stripes and
colors and hard matter, and it was the portrait of her as she was, because at the same
time she was making herself a shell identical to mine and without knowing it I was
copying what she was doing and she without knowing it was copying what I was
doing, and all the others were copying all the others, so we would be back where we
had been before except for the fact that in saying these shells were the same I was a
bit hasty, because when you looked closer you discovered all sorts of little differences
that later on might become enormous.

So I can say that my shell made itself, without my taking any special pains to have
it come out one way rather than another, but this doesn't mean that I was absent-
minded during that time; I applied myself, instead, to that act of secreting, without
allowing myself a moment's distraction, never thinking of anything else, or rather:
thinking always of something else, since I didn't know how to think of the shell, just
as, for that matter, I didn't know how to think of anything else either, but I accompanied the effort of making the shell with the effort of thinking I was making something, that is anything: that is, I thought of all the things it would be possible to
make. So it wasn't even a monotonous task, because the effort of thinking which accompanied it spread toward countless types of thoughts which spread, each one, toward countless types of actions that might each serve to make countless things, and
making each of these things was implicit in making the shell grow, turn after turn . . .

II

*(And so now, after five hundred million years have gone by, I look around and, above the
rock, I see the railway embankment and the train passing along it with a party of Dutch girls
looking out of the window and, in the last compartment, a solitary traveler reading Herodotus
in a bilingual edition, and the train vanishes into the tunnel under the highway, where there is
a sign with the pyramids and the words "VISIT EGYPT," and a little ice-cream wagon tries to pass
a big truck laden with installments of Rh-Stijl, a periodical encyclopedia that comes out in paperback, but then it puts its brakes on because its visibility is blocked by a cloud of bees which
crosses the road coming from a row of hives in a field from which surely a queen bee is flying
away, drawing behind her a swarm in the direction opposite to the smoke of the train, which
has reappeared at the other end of the tunnel, so you can see hardly anything thanks to the
cloudy stream of bees and coal smoke, except a few yards farther up there is a peasant breaking the ground with his mattock and, unaware, he brings to light and reburies a fragment of a
Neolithic mattock similar to his own, in a garden that surrounds an astronomical observatory
with its telescopes aimed at the sky and on whose threshold the keeper's daughter sits reading
the horoscopes in a weekly whose cover displays the face of the star of Cleopatra: I see all this
and I feel no amazement because making the shell implied also making the honey in the wax
comb and the coal and the telescopes and the reign of Cleopatra and the films about Cleopatra*

and the pyramids and the design of the zodiac of the Chaldean astrologers and the wars and em-
pires Herodotus speaks of and the words written by Herodotus and the works written in all
languages including those of Spinoza in Dutch and the fourteen-line summary of Spinoza's life
and works in the installment of the encyclopedia in the truck passed by the ice-cream wagon,
and so I feel as if, in making the shell, I had also made the rest.

I look around, and whom am I looking for? She is still the one I seek; I've been in love for
five hundred million years, and if I see a Dutch girl on the sand with a beachboy wearing a gold
chain around his neck and showing her the swarm of bees to frighten her, there she is: I recog-
nize her from her inimitable way of raising one shoulder until it almost touches her cheek, I'm
almost sure, or rather I'd say absolutely sure if it weren't for a certain resemblance that I find
also in the daughter of the keeper of the observatory, and in the photograph of the actress made
up as Cleopatra, or perhaps in Cleopatra as she really was in person, for what part of the true
Cleopatra they say every representation of Cleopatra contains, or in the queen bee flying at the
head of the swarm with that forward impetuousness, or in the paper woman cut out and past-
ed on the plastic windshield of the little ice-cream wagon, wearing a bathing suit like the Dutch
girl on the beach now listening over a little transistor radio to the voice of a woman singing, the
same voice that the encyclopedia truck driver hears over his radio, and the same one I'm now
sure I've heard for five million years, it is surely she I hear singing and whose image I look for
all around, seeing only gulls volplaning on the surface of the sea where a school of anchovies
glistens and for a moment I am certain I recognize her in a female gull and a moment later I
suspect that instead she's an anchovy, though she might just as well be any queen or slave-girl
named by Herodotus or only hinted at in the pages of the volume left to mark the seat of the
reader who has stepped into the corridor of the train to strike up a conversation with the party
of Dutch tourists; I might say I am in love with each of those girls and at the same time I am
sure of being in love always with her alone.

And the more I torment myself with love for each of them, the less I can bring myself to say
to them: "Here I am!," afraid of being mistaken and even more afraid that she is mistaken, tak-
ing me for somebody else, for somebody who, for all she knows of me, might easily take my place,
for example the beachboy with the gold chain, or the director of the observatory, or a gull, or a
male anchovy, or the reader of Herodotus, or Herodotus himself, or the vendor of ice cream,
who has come down to the beach along a dusty road among the prickly pears and is now sur-
rounded by the Dutch girls in their bathing suits, or Spinoza, or the truck driver who is trans-
porting the life and works of Spinoza summarized and repeated two thousand times, or one of
the drones dying at the bottom of the hive after having fulfilled his role in the continuation of
the species.)

III

. . . Which doesn't mean that the shell wasn't, first and foremost, a shell, with its particular form, which couldn't be any different because it was the very form I had given
it, the only one I could or would give it. Since the shell had a form, the form of the
world was also changed, in the sense that now it included the form of the world as it
had been without a shell plus the form of the shell.

And that had great consequences: because the waving vibrations of light, striking
bodies, produce particular effects from them, color first of all, namely, that matter I
used to make stripes with which vibrated in a different way from the rest; but there
was also the fact that a volume enters into a special relationship of volumes with
other volumes, all phenomena I couldn't be aware of, though they existed.

The shell in this way was able to create visual images of shells, which are things
very similar—as far as we know—to the shell itself, except that the shell is here,
whereas the images of it are formed elsewhere, possibly on a retina. An image

therefore presupposes a retina, which in turn presupposes a complex system stemming from an encephalon. So, in producing the shell, I also produced its image—not one, of course, but many, because with one shell you can make as many shell-images as you want—but only potential images because to form an image you need all the requisites I mentioned before: an encephalon with its optic ganglia, and an optic nerve to carry the vibrations from outside to inside, and this optic nerve at the other extremity, ends in something made purposely to see what there is outside, namely the eye. Now it's ridiculous to think that, having an encephalon, one would simply drop a nerve like a fishing line cast into the darkness; until the eyes crop up, one can't know whether there is something to be seen outside or not. For myself, I had none of this equipment, so I was the least authorized to speak of it; however, I had conceived an idea of my own, namely that the thing was to form some visual images, and the eyes would come later in consequence. So I concentrated on making the part of me that was outside (and even the interior part of me that conditioned the exterior) give rise to an image, or rather to what would later be called a lovely image (when compared to other images considered less lovely, or rather ugly, or simply revoltingly hideous).

When a body succeeds in emitting or in reflecting luminous vibrations in a distinct and recognizable order—I thought—what does it do with these vibrations? Put them in its pocket? No, it releases them on the first passer-by. And how will the latter behave in the face of vibrations he can't utilize and which, taken in this way, might even be annoying? Hide his head in a hole? No, he'll thrust it out in that direction until the point most exposed to the optic vibrations becomes sensitized and develops the mechanism for exploiting them in the form of images. In short, I conceived of the eye-encephalon link as a kind of tunnel dug from the outside by the force of what was ready to become image, rather than from within by the intention of picking up any old image.

And I wasn't mistaken: even today I'm sure that the project—in its overall aspect— was right. But my error lay in thinking that sight would also come to us, that is to me and to her. I elaborated a harmonious, colored image of myself to enter her visual receptivity, to occupy its center, to settle there, so that she could utilize me constantly, in dreaming and in memory, with thought as well as with sight. And I felt at the same time she was radiating an image of herself so perfect that it would impose itself on my foggy, backward senses, developing in me an interior visual field where it would blaze forth definitely.

So our efforts led us to become those perfect objects of a sense whose nature nobody quite knew yet, and which later became perfect precisely through the perfection of its object, which was, in fact, us. I'm talking about sight, the eyes; only I had failed to foresee one thing: the eyes that finally opened to see us didn't belong to us but to others.

Shapeless, colorless beings, sacks of guts stuck together carelessly, peopled the world all around us, without giving the slightest thought to what they should make of themselves, to how to express themselves and identify themselves in a stable, complete form, such as to enrich the visual possibilities of whoever saw them. They came and went, sank a while, then emerged, in that space between air and water and rock, wandering about absently; and we in the meanwhile, she and I and all those intent on squeezing out a form of ourselves, were there slaving away at our dark task. Thanks to us, that badly defined space became a visual field; and who reaped the benefit? These intruders, who had never before given a thought to the possibility of eyesight (ugly as they were, they wouldn't have gained a thing by seeing one another), these creatures who had always turned a deaf ear to the vocation of form. While we were bent over, doing the hardest part of the job, that is, creating something to be seen, they were quietly taking on the easiest part: adapting their lazy, embryonic receptive organs to what there was to receive; our images. And they needn't try telling me now that their job was toilsome too: from that gluey mess that filled their heads anything could have come out, and a photosensitive mechanism doesn't take all that much trouble to put together. But when it comes to perfecting it, that's another story! How can you, if you don't have visible objects to see, gaudy ones even, the kind that impose themselves on the eyesight? To sum it up in a few words: they developed eyes at our expense.

So sight, *our* sight, which we were obscurely waiting for, was the sight that the others had of us. In one way or another, the great revolution had taken place: all of a sudden, around us, eyes were opening, and corneas and irises and pupils: the swollen, colorless eye of polyps and cuttlefish, the dazed and gelatinous eyes of bream and mullet, the protruding and peduncled eyes of crayfish and lobsters, the bulging and faceted eyes of flies and ants. A seal now comes forward, black and shiny, winking little eyes like pinheads. A snail extends ball-like eyes at the end of long antennae. The inexpressive eyes of the gull examine the surface of the water. Beyond a glass mask the frowning eyes of an underwater fisherman explore the depths. Through the lens of a spyglass a sea captain's eyes and the eyes of a woman bathing converge on my shell, then look at each other, forgetting me. Framed by far-sighted lenses I feel on me the far-sighted eyes of a zoologist, trying to frame me in the eye of a Rolleiflex. At that moment a school of tiny anchovies, barely born, passes before me, so tiny that in each little white fish it seems there is room only for the eye's black dot, and it is a kind of eye-dust that crosses the sea.

All these eyes were mine. I had made them possible; I had had the active part; I furnished them the raw material, the image. With eyes had come all the rest, so everything that the others, having eyes, had become, their every form and function, and the quantity of things that, thanks to eyes, they had managed to do, in their every form and function, came from what I had done. Of course, they were not just casually implicit in my being there, in my having relations with others, male and female, et cetera, in my setting out to make a shell, et cetera. In other words, I had foreseen absolutely everything.

And at the bottom of each of those eyes I lived, or rather another me lived, one of the images of me, and it encountered the image of her, the most faithful image of her, in that beyond which opens, past the semiliquid sphere of the irises, in the darkness of the pupils, the mirrored hall of the retinas, in our true element which extends without shores, without boundaries.

[1965]
Translated by
WILLIAM WEAVER

Questions

1. How is the narrator "characterized"? What are his unique qualities?
2. What effect does Calvino create by making the narrator a creature with—initially— "no form" but with the capacities of consciousness, self-reflection, and imagination?
3. What event catalyzes change in the narrator? What kinds of changes result?
4. What is the "great revolution"? What does it mean for the narrator?

Albert Camus

(1913–1960)

Algeria/France

O ne of the most famous French existentialists, Albert Camus was born in Mondovi, Algeria, in 1913 and died in an automobile accident near Paris in 1960. In addition to writing numerous essays and dramas, Camus published four works of fiction before his untimely death: The Stranger (1942); The Plague (1948); The Fall (1956); and a volume of short stories, Exile and the Kingdom (1957). "The Guest," which is from the latter volume, relies directly on the author's Algerian heritage. Albert Camus was awarded the Nobel Prize for Literature in 1957. In his acceptance speech for the award, he described himself as an "Algerian Frenchman."

The "wartime" referred to early in "The Guest" is the French/Algerian war, which lasted from 1954 to 1962. Camus wrote numerous essays about the relationship of the two countries, historically bound to one another by what he called inevitable solidarity. Although the Algerian struggle was bloody, he often spoke of the "community of hope" that would reconcile the two countries' differences. In his "Appeal for a Civilian Truce" (1956), he wrote the following:

> On this soil there are a million Frenchmen who have been here for a century, millions of Moslems, either Arabs or Berbers, who have been here for centuries, and several vigorous religious communities. Those men must live together at the crossroads where history put them. They can do so if they will take a few steps toward each other in an open confrontation. Then our differences ought to help us instead of dividing us. As for me, here as in every domain, I believe only in differences and not in uniformity. First of all, because differences are the roots without which the tree of liberty, the sap of creation and of civilization, dries up.

On the artist's role, Camus wrote the following:

> The aim of art, the aim of a life can only be to increase the sum of freedom and responsibility to be found in every man and in the world. It cannot, under any circumstances, be to reduce or suppress that freedom, even temporarily. There are works of art that tend to make man conform and to convert him to some external rule. Others tend to subject him to whatever is worst in him, to terror or hatred. Such works are valueless to me. No great work has ever been based on hatred or contempt. On the contrary, there is not a single true work of art that has not in the end added to the inner freedom of each person who has known and loved it. ("The Wager of Our Generation," 1957)

THE GUEST

The schoolmaster was watching the two men climb toward him. One was on horseback, the other on foot. They had not yet tackled the abrupt rise leading to the schoolhouse built on the hillside. They were toiling onward, making slow progress in the snow, among the stones, on the vast expanse of the high, deserted plateau. From time to time the horse stumbled. Without hearing anything yet, he could see the breath issuing from the horse's nostrils. One of the men, at least, knew the region. They were following the trail although it had disappeared days ago under a layer of dirty white snow. The schoolmaster calculated that it would take them half an hour to get onto the hill. It was cold; he went back into the school to get a sweater.

He crossed the empty, frigid classroom. On the blackboard the four rivers of France, drawn with four different colored chalks, had been flowing toward their estuaries for the past three days. Snow had suddenly fallen in mid-October after eight months of drought without he transition of rain, and the twenty pupils, more or less, who lived in the villages scattered over the plateau had stopped coming. With fair weather they would return. Daru now heated only the single room that was his lodging, adjoining the classroom and giving also onto the plateau to the east. Like the class windows, his window looked to the south too. On that side the school was a few kilometers from the point where the plateau began to slope toward the south. In clear weather could be seen the purple mass of the mountain range where the gap opened onto the desert.

Somewhat warmed, Daru returned to the window from which he had first seen the two men. They were no longer visible. Hence they must have tackled the rise. The sky was not so dark, for the snow had stopped falling during the night. The morning had opened with a dirty light which had scarcely become brighter as the ceiling of clouds lifted. At two in the afternoon it seemed as if the day were merely beginning. But still this was better than those three days when the thick snow was falling amidst unbroken darkness with little gusts of wind that rattled the double door of the classroom. Then Daru had spent long hours in his room, leaving it only to go to the shed and feed the chickens or get some coal. Fortunately the delivery truck from Tadjid, the nearest village to the north, had brought his supplies two days before the blizzard. It would return in forty-eight hours.

Besides, he had enough to resist a siege, for the little room was cluttered with bags of wheat that the administration left as a stock to distribute to those of his pupils whose families had suffered from the drought. Actually, they had all been victims because they were all poor. Every day Daru would distribute a ration to the children. They had missed it, he knew, during these bad days. Possibly one of the fathers or big brothers would come this afternoon and he could supply them with grain. It was just a matter of carrying them over to the next harvest. Now shiploads of wheat were arriving from France and the worst was over. But it would be hard to forget that poverty, that army of ragged ghosts wandering in the sunlight, the plateaus burned to a cinder month after month, the earth shriveled up little by little, literally scorched, every stone bursting into dust under one's foot. The sheep had died then by thousands and even a few men, here and there, sometimes without anyone's knowing.

In contrast with such poverty, he who lived almost like a monk in his remote schoolhouse, nonetheless satisfied with the little he had and with the rough life, had felt like a lord with his whitewashed walls, his narrow couch, his unpainted shelves, his well, and his weekly provision of water and food. And suddenly this snow, without warning, without the foretaste of rain. This is the way the region was, cruel to live in, even without men—who didn't help matters either. But Daru had been born here. Everywhere else, he felt exiled.

He stepped out onto the terrace in front of the schoolhouse. The two men were now halfway up the slope. He recognized the horseman as Balducci, the old gendarme[1] he had known for a long time. Balducci was holding on the end of a rope an Arab who was walking behind him with hands bound and head lowered. The gendarme waved a greeting to which Daru did not reply, lost as he was in contemplation of the Arab dressed in a faded blue jellaba,[2] his feet in sandals but covered with socks of heavy raw wool, his head surmounted by a narrow, short chèche.[3] They were approaching. Balducci was holding back his horse in order not to hurt the Arab, and the group was advancing slowly.

Within earshot, Balducci shouted: "One hour to do the three kilometers from El Ameur!" Daru did not answer. Short and square in his thick sweater, he watched them climb. Not once had the Arab raised his head. "Hello," said Daru when they got up onto the terrace. "Come in and warm up." Balducci painfully got down from his horse without letting go the rope. From under his bristling mustache he smiled at the schoolmaster. His little dark eyes, deep-set under a tanned forehead, and his mouth surrounded with wrinkles made him look attentive and studious. Daru took the bridle, led the horse to the shed, and came back to the two men, who were now waiting for him in the school. He led them into his room. "I am going to heat up the classroom," he said. "We'll be more comfortable there." When he entered the room again, Balducci was on the couch. He had undone the rope tying him to the Arab, who had squatted near the stove. His hands still bound, the chèche pushed back on his head, he was looking toward the window. At first Daru noticed only his huge lips, fat, smooth, almost Negroid; yet his nose was straight, his eyes were dark and full of fever. The chèche revealed an obstinate forehead and, under the weathered skin now rather discolored by the cold, the whole face had a restless and rebellious look that struck Daru when the Arab, turning his face toward him, looked him straight in the eyes. "Go into the other room," said the schoolmaster, "and I'll make you some mint tea." "Thanks," Balducci said. "What a chore! How I long for retirement." And addressing his prisoner in Arabic: "Come on, you." The Arab got up and slowly, holding his bound wrists in front of him, went into the classroom.

With the tea, Daru brought a chair. But Balducci was already enthroned on the nearest pupil's desk and the Arab had squatted against the teacher's platform facing the stove, which stood between the desk and the window. When he held out the glass of tea to the prisoner, Daru hesitated at the sight of his bound hands. "He might perhaps be untied." "Sure," said Balducci. "That was for the trip." He started to get to his feet. But Daru, setting the glass on the floor, had knelt beside the Arab. Without saying anything, the Arab watched him with his feverish eyes. Once his hands were free, he rubbed his swollen wrists against each other, took the glass of tea, and sucked up the burning liquid in swift little sips.

"Good," said Daru. "And where are you headed?"

Balducci withdrew his mustache from the tea. "Here, son."

"Odd pupils! And you're spending the night?"

"No, I'm going back to El Ameur. And you will deliver this fellow to Tinguit. He is expected at police headquarters."

---

[1]*gendarme*   French: armed policeman; constable.
[2]*jellaba*   Traditional dress, like a flowing robe.
[3]*chèche*   French: scarf.

Balducci was looking at Daru with a friendly little smile.

"What's this story?" asked the schoolmaster. "Are you pulling my leg?"

"No, son. Those are the orders."

"The orders? I'm not. . . ." Daru hesitated, not wanting to hurt the old Corsican. "I mean, that's not my job."

"What! What's the meaning of that? In wartime people do all kinds of jobs."[4]

"Then I'll wait for the declaration of war!"

Balducci nodded.

"O.K. But the orders exist and they concern you too. Things are brewing, it appears. There is talk of a forthcoming revolt. We are mobilized, in a way."

Daru still had his obstinate look.

"Listen, son," Balducci said. "I like you and you must understand. There's only a dozen of us at El Ameur to patrol throughout the whole territory of a small department and I must get back in a hurry. I was told to hand this guy over to you and return without delay. He couldn't be kept there. His village was beginning to stir; they wanted to take him back. You must take him to Tinguit tomorrow before the day is over. Twenty kilometers shouldn't faze a husky fellow like you. After that, all will be over. You'll come back to your pupils and your comfortable life."

Behind the wall the horse could be heard snorting and pawing the earth. Daru was looking out the window. Decidedly, the weather was clearing and the light was increasing over the snowy plateau. When all the snow was melted, the sun would take over again and once more would burn the fields of stone. For days, still, the unchanging sky would shed its dry light on the solitary expanse where nothing had any connection with man.

"After all," he said, turning around toward Balducci, "what did he do?" And before the gendarme had opened his mouth, he asked: "Does he speak French?"

"No, not a word. We had been looking for him for a month, but they were hiding him. He killed his cousin."

"Is he against us?"

"I don't think so. But you can never be sure."

"Why did he kill?"

"A family squabble, I think. One owed the other grain, it seems. It's not at all clear. In short, he killed his cousin with a billhook. You know, like a sheep, *kreezk!*"

Balducci made the gesture of drawing a blade across his throat and the Arab, his attention attracted, watched him with a sort of anxiety. Daru felt a sudden wrath against the man, against all men with their rotten spite, their tireless hates, their blood lust.

But the kettle was singing on the stove. He served Balducci more tea, hesitated, then served the Arab again, who, a second time, drank avidly. His raised arms made the jellaba fall open and the schoolmaster saw his thin, muscular chest.

"Thanks, kid," Balducci said. "And now, I'm off."

He got up and went toward the Arab, taking a small rope from his pocket.

"What are you doing?" Daru asked dryly.

Balducci, disconcerted, showed him the rope.

"Don't bother."

The old gendarme hesitated. "It's up to you. Of course, you are armed?"

---

[4]A reference to the French/Algerian war, which began in 1954.

"I have my shotgun."

"Where?"

"In the trunk."

"You ought to have it near your bed."

"Why? I have nothing to fear."

"You're crazy, son. If there's an uprising, no one is safe, we're all in the same boat."

"I'll defend myself. I'll have time to see them coming."

Balducci began to laugh, then suddenly the mustache covered the white teeth.

"You'll have time? O.K. That's just what I was saying. You have always been a little cracked. That's why I like you, my son was like that."

At the same time he took out his revolver and put it on the desk.

"Keep it; I don't need two weapons from here to El Ameur."

The revolver shone against the black paint of the table. When the gendarme turned toward him, the schoolmaster caught the smell of leather and horseflesh.

"Listen, Balducci," Daru said suddenly, "every bit of this disgusts me, and first of all your fellow here. But I won't hand him over. Fight, yes, if I have to. But not that."

The old gendarme stood in front of him and looked at him severely.

"You're being a fool," he said slowly. "I don't like it either. You don't get used to putting a rope on a man even after years of it, and you're even ashamed—yes, ashamed. But you can't let them have their way."

"I won't hand him over," Daru said again.

"It's an order, son, and I repeat it."

"That's right. Repeat to them what I've said to you: I won't hand him over."

Balducci made a visible effort to reflect. He looked at the Arab and at Daru. At last he decided.

"No, I won't tell them anything. If you want to drop us, go ahead; I'll not denounce you. I have an order to deliver the prisoner and I'm doing so. And now you'll just sign this paper for me."

"There's no need. I'll not deny that you left him with me."

"Don't be mean with me. I know you'll tell the truth. You're from hereabouts and you are a man. But you must sign, that's the rule."

Daru opened his drawer, took out a little square bottle of purple ink, the red wooden penholder with the "sergeant-major" pen he used for making models of penmanship, and signed. The gendarme carefully folded the paper and put it into his wallet. Then he moved toward the door.

"I'll see you off," Daru said.

"No," said Balducci. "There's no use being polite. You insulted me."

He looked at the Arab, motionless in the same spot, sniffed peevishly, and turned away toward the door. "Good-by, son," he said. The door shut behind him. Balducci appeared suddenly outside the window and then disappeared. His footsteps were muffled by the snow. The horse stirred on the other side of the wall and several chickens fluttered in fright. A moment later Balducci reappeared outside the window leading the horse by the bridle. He walked toward the little rise without turning around and disappeared from sight with the horse following him. A big stone could be heard bouncing down. Daru walked back toward the prisoner, who, without stirring, never took his eyes off him.

"Wait," the schoolmaster said in Arabic and went toward the bedroom. As he was going through the door, he had a second thought, went to the desk, took the revolver, and stuck it in his pocket. Then, without looking back, he went into his room.

For some time he lay on his couch watching the sky gradually close over, listening to the silence. It was this silence that had seemed painful to him during the first days here, after the war. He had requested a post in the little town at the base of the foothills separating the upper plateaus from the desert. There, rocky walls, green and black to the north, pink and lavender to the south, marked the frontier of eternal summer. He had been named to a post farther north, on the plateau itself. In the beginning, the solitude and the silence had been hard for him on these wastelands peopled only by stones. Occasionally, furrows suggested cultivation, but they had been dug to uncover a certain kind of stone good for building. The only plowing here was to harvest rocks. Elsewhere a thin layer of soil accumulated in the hollows would be scraped out to enrich paltry village gardens. This is the way it was: bare rock covered three quarters of the region. Towns sprang up, flourished, then disappeared; men came by, loved one another or fought bitterly, then died. No one in this desert, neither he nor his guest, mattered. And yet, outside this desert neither of them, Daru knew, could have really lived.

When he got up, no noise came from the classroom. He was amazed at the unmixed joy he derived from the mere thought that the Arab might have fled and that he would be alone with no decision to make. But the prisoner was there. He had merely stretched out between the stove and the desk. With eyes open, he was staring at the ceiling. In that position, his thick lips were particularly noticeable, giving him a pouting look. "Come," said Daru. The Arab got up and followed him. In the bedroom, the schoolmaster pointed to a chair near the table under the window. The Arab sat down without taking his eyes off Daru.

"Are you hungry?"

"Yes," the prisoner said.

Daru set the table for two. He took flour and oil, shaped a cake in a frying-pan, and lighted the little stove that functioned on bottled gas. While the cake was cooking, he went out to the shed to get cheese, eggs, dates, and condensed milk. When the cake was done he set it on the window sill to cool, heated some condensed milk diluted with water, and beat up the eggs into an omelette. In one of his motions he knocked against the revolver stuck in his right pocket. He set the bowl down, went into the classroom, and put the revolver in his desk drawer. When he came back to the room, night was falling. He put on the light and served the Arab. "Eat," he said. The Arab took a piece of cake, lifted it eagerly to his mouth, and stopped short.

"And you?" he asked.

"After you. I'll eat too."

The thick lips opened slightly. The Arab hesitated, then bit into the cake determinedly.

The meal over, the Arab looked at the schoolmaster. "Are you the judge?"

"No, I'm simply keeping you until tomorrow."

"Why do you eat with me?"

"I'm hungry."

The Arab fell silent. Daru got up and went out. He brought back a folding bed from the shed, set it up between the table and the stove, perpendicular to his own bed. From the large suitcase which, upright in a corner, served as a shelf for papers, he took two blankets and arranged them on the camp bed. Then he stopped, felt useless, and sat down on his bed. There was nothing more to do or to get ready. He had to look at this man. He looked at him, therefore, trying to imagine his face bursting with rage. He couldn't do so. He could see nothing but the dark yet shining eyes and the animal mouth.

"Why did you kill him?" he asked in a voice whose hostile tone surprised him.

The Arab looked away.

"He ran away. I ran after him."

He raised his eyes to Daru again and they were full of a sort of woeful interrogation. "Now what will they do to me?"

"Are you afraid?"

He stiffened, turning his eyes away.

"Are you sorry?"

The Arab stared at him openmouthed. Obviously he did not understand. Daru's annoyance was growing. At the same time he felt awkward and self-conscious with his big body wedged between the two beds.

"Lie down there," he said impatiently. "That's your bed."

The Arab didn't move. He called to Daru:

"Tell me!"

The schoolmaster looked at him.

"Is the gendarme coming back tomorrow?"

"I don't know."

"Are you coming with us?"

"I don't know. Why?"

The prisoner got up and stretched out on top of the blankets, his feet toward the window. The light from the electric bulb shone straight into his eyes and he closed them at once.

"Why?" Daru repeated, standing beside the bed.

The Arab opened his eyes under the blinding light and looked at him, trying not to blink.

"Come with us," he said.

In the middle of the night, Daru was still not asleep. He had gone to bed after undressing completely; he generally slept naked. But when he suddenly realized that he had nothing on, he hesitated. He felt vulnerable and the temptation came to him to put his clothes back on. Then he shrugged his shoulders; after all, he wasn't a child and, if need be, he could break his adversary in two. From his bed he could observe him, lying on his back, still motionless with his eyes closed under the harsh light. When Daru turned out the light, the darkness seemed to coagulate all of a sudden. Little by little, the night came back to life in the window where the starless sky was stirring gently. The schoolmaster soon made out the body lying at this feet. The Arab still did not move, but his eyes seemed open. A faint wind was prowling around the schoolhouse. Perhaps it would drive away the clouds and the sun would reappear.

During the night the wind increased. The hens fluttered a little and then were silent. The Arab turned over on his side with his back to Daru, who thought he heard him moan. Then he listened for his guest's breathing to become heavier and more regular. He listened to that breath so close to him and mused without being able to go to sleep. In this room where he had been sleeping alone for a year, this presence bothered him. But it bothered him also by imposing on him a sort of brotherhood he knew well but refused to accept in the present circumstances. Men who share the same rooms, soldiers or prisoners, develop a strange alliance as if, having cast off their armor with their clothing, they fraternized every evening, over and above their differences, in the ancient community of dream and fatigue. But Daru shook himself, he didn't like such musings, and it was essential to sleep.

A little later, however, when the Arab stirred slightly, the schoolmaster was still not asleep. When the prisoner made a second move, he stiffened, on the alert. The Arab was lifting himself slowly on his arms with almost the motion of a sleepwalker. Seated upright in bed, he waited motionless without turning his head toward Daru, as if he were listening attentively. Daru did not stir; it had just occurred to him that the revolver was still in the drawer of his desk. It was better to act at once. Yet he continued to observe the prisoner, who, with the same slithery motion, put his feet on the ground, waited again, then began to stand up slowly. Daru was about to call out to him when the Arab began to walk, in a quite natural but extraordinarily silent way. He was heading toward the door at the end of the room that opened into the shed. He lifted the latch with precaution and went out, pushing the door behind him but without shutting it. Daru had not stirred. "He is running away," he merely thought. "Good riddance!" Yet he listened attentively. The hens were not fluttering; the guest must be on the plateau. A faint sound of water reached him, and he didn't know what it was until the Arab again stood framed in the doorway, closed the door carefully, and came back to bed without a sound. Then Daru turned his back on him and fell asleep. Still later he seemed, from the depths of his sleep, to hear furtive steps around the schoolhouse. "I'm dreaming! I'm dreaming!" he repeated to himself. And he went on sleeping.

When he awoke, the sky was clear; the loose window let in a cold, pure air. The Arab was asleep, hunched up under the blankets now, his mouth open, utterly relaxed. But when Daru shook him, he started dreadfully, staring at Daru with wild eyes as if he had never seen him and such a frightened expression that the schoolmaster stepped back. "Don't be afraid. It's me. You must eat." The Arab nodded his head and said yes. Calm had returned to his face, but his expression was vacant and listless.

The coffee was ready. They drank it seated together on the folding bed as they munched their pieces of the cake. Then Daru led the Arab under the shed and showed him the faucet where he washed. He went back into the room, folded the blankets and the bed, made his own bed and put the room in order. Then he went through the classroom and out onto the terrace. The sun was already rising in the blue sky; a soft, bright light was bathing the deserted plateau. On the ridge the snow as melting in spots. The stones were about to reappear. Crouched on the edge of the plateau, the schoolmaster looked at the deserted expanse. He thought of Balducci. He had hurt him, for he had sent him off in a way as if he didn't want to be associated with him. He could still hear the gendarme's farewell and, without knowing why, he felt strangely empty and vulnerable. At that moment, from the other side of the schoolhouse, the prisoner coughed. Daru listened to him almost despite himself and then, furious, threw a pebble that whistled through the air before sinking into the snow. That man's stupid crime revolted him, but to hand him over was contrary to honor. Merely thinking of it made him smart with humiliation. And he cursed at one and the same time his own people who had sent him this Arab and the Arab too who had dared to kill and not managed to get away. Daru got up, walked in a circle on the terrace, waited motionless, and then went back into the schoolhouse.

The Arab, leaning over the cement floor of the shed, was washing his teeth with two fingers. Daru looked at him and said: "Come." He went back into the room ahead of the prisoner. He slipped a hunting jacket on over his sweater and put on walking shoes. Standing, he waited until the Arab had put on his *chèche* and sandals. They went into the classroom and the schoolmaster pointed to the exit, saying: "Go ahead."

The fellow didn't budge. "I'm coming," said Daru. The Arab went out. Daru went back into the room and made a package of pieces of zwieback, dates, and sugar. In the classroom, before going out, he hesitated a second in front of his desk, then crossed the threshold and locked the door. "That's the way," he said. He started toward the east, followed by the prisoner. But, a short distance from the schoolhouse, he thought he heard a slight sound behind them. He retraced his steps and examined the surroundings of the house; there was no one there. The Arab watched him without seeming to understand. "Come on," said Daru.

They walked for an hour and rested beside a sharp peak of limestone. The snow was melting faster and faster and the sun was drinking up the puddles at once, rapidly cleaning the plateau, which gradually dried and vibrated like the air itself. When they resumed walking, the ground rang under their feet. From time to time a bird rent the space in front of them with a joyful cry. Daru breathed in deeply the fresh morning light. He felt a sort of rapture before the vast familiar expanse, now almost entirely yellow under its dome of blue sky. They walked an hour more, descending toward the south. They reached a level height made up of crumbly rocks. From there on, the plateau sloped down, eastward, toward a low plain where there were a few spindly trees and, to the south, toward outcroppings of rock that gave the landscape a chaotic look.

Daru surveyed the two directions. There was nothing but the sky on the horizon. Not a man could be seen. He turned toward the Arab, who was looking at him blankly. Daru held out the package to him. "Take it," he said. "There are dates, bread, and sugar. You can hold out for two days. Here are a thousand francs too." The Arab took the package and the money but kept his full hands at chest level as if he didn't know what to do with what was given him. "Now look," the schoolmaster said as he pointed in the direction of the east, "there's the way to Tinguit. You have a two-hour walk. At Tinguit you'll find the administration and the police. They are expecting you." The Arab looked toward the east, still holding the package and the money against his chest. Daru took his elbow and turned him rather roughly toward the south. At the foot of the height on which they stood could be seen a faint path. "That's the trail across the plateau. In a day's walk from here you'll find pasturelands and the first nomads. They'll take you in and shelter you according to their law." The Arab had now turned toward Daru and a sort of panic was visible in his expression. "Listen," he said. Daru shook his head: "No, be quiet. Now I'm leaving you." He turned his back on him, took two long steps in the direction of the school, looked hesitantly at the motionless Arab, and started off again. For a few minutes he heard nothing but his own step resounding on the cold ground and did not turn his head. A moment later, however, he turned around. The Arab was still there on the edge of the hill, his arms hanging now, and he was looking at the schoolmaster. Daru felt something rise in his throat. But he swore with impatience, waved vaguely, and started off again. He had already gone some distance when he again stopped and looked. There was no longer anyone on the hill.

Daru hesitated. The sun was now rather high in the sky and was beginning to beat down on his head. The schoolmaster retraced his steps, at first somewhat uncertainly, then with decision. When he reached the little hill, he was bathed in sweat. He climbed it as fast as he could and stopped, out of breath, at the top. The rock-fields to the south stood out sharply against the blue sky, but on the plain to the east a steamy heat was already rising. And in that slight haze, Daru, with heavy heart, made out the Arab walking slowly on the road to prison.

A little later, standing before the window of the classroom, the schoolmaster was watching the clear light bathing the whole surface of the plateau, but he hardly saw it. Behind him on the blackboard, among the winding French rivers, sprawled the clumsily chalked-up words he had just read: "You handed over our brother. You will pay for this." Daru looked at the sky, the plateau, and, beyond, the invisible lands stretching all the way to the sea. In this vast landscape he had loved so much, he was alone.

[1957]
Translated by
JUSTIN O'BRIEN

Questions

1. What are the differing attitudes that Daru and Balducci demonstrate toward the Arab? Why?

2. By attempting to remain uninvolved, has Daru created a trap for himself; or, has his desire from the beginning been to act, to become involved in some elemental way?

3. Camus's story posits the centuries-old unspoken rule of hospitality: a guest (especially one with whom one has shared food) is safe—never to be harmed. Does Daru deviate from this belief in any manner?

4. Why does the Arab decide to walk on the road toward the prison at the end of the story? In explaining your answer, you might consider the Arab's earlier response to Daru's question about the murder: "'Are you sorry?'"

5. What is the theme of the story?

Angela Carter

(1940–1992)

England

Although the term magical realism *is most often associated with Latin American writers like Gabriel García Márquez, Angela Carter's fiction is filled with fantastic events and characters. She enjoyed pushing the boundaries of fiction, so seamlessly blending dream, illusion, and elements of Gothic and the fantastic with credible events that readers find themselves pondering what "real" means. The protagonist of* Nights at the Circus *(1984) is a Cockney trapeze artist at the end of the nineteenth century who dazzles her audiences as she literally flies through the air on her own wings—or, as the narrative playfully teases us, does she really have wings? Indeed, in five novels and several collections of short stories, Carter is a kind of literary high-wire artist herself, taking narrative risks without a safety net in order to surprise, delight, and disturb her readers. Among her preoccupations is the nature of sexuality, often explored through her characters' sexual fantasies and desires, as in* The Magic Toyshop *(1967) and* The Infernal Desire Machines of Doctor Hoffman *(1972). In* The Passion of New Eve *(1977), Carter examines the social construction of gender roles and of attitudes toward sexuality itself through the experiences of a male character who (involuntarily) changes sex midway through the narrative.*

In the stories collected in The Bloody Chamber, *Carter revises and plays with traditional fairy tales like "Beauty and the Beast" and "Little Red Riding Hood," investing them with contemporary—and adult—preoccupations: love and loyalty, sexuality and desire, ambition and aggression. In the afterword to* Fireworks: Nine Profane Pieces *(1974), she explained that her stories draw on the tradition of Poe and Hoffman—"Gothic tales, cruel tales, tales of wonder, tales of terror, fabulous narratives that deal directly with the imagery of the unconscious—mirrors; the externalized self; forsaken castles; forbidden sexual objects. Formally the tale differs from the short story in that it makes few pretences at the imitation of life." Elsewhere, she commented, "I am all for putting new wine in old bottles, especially if the pressure of the new wine makes the old bottles explode."*

Salman Rushdie, *mourning Carter's premature death in* The New York Times, *calls her English literature's "high sorceress, its benevolent witch queen, a burlesque artist of genius and antic grace."*

THE COURTSHIP OF MR. LYON

Outside her kitchen window, the hedgerow glistened as if the snow possessed a light of its own; when the sky darkened towards evening, an unearthly, reflected pallor remained behind upon the winter's landscape, while still the soft flakes floated down. This lovely girl, whose skin possesses that same, inner light so you would have thought she, too, was made all of snow, pauses in her chores in the mean kitchen to look out at the country road. Nothing has passed that way all day; the road is white and un-marked as a spilled bolt of bridal satin.

Father said he would be home before nightfall.

The snow brought down all the telephone wires; he couldn't have called, even with the best of news.

The roads are bad. I hope he'll be safe.

But the old car stuck fast in a rut, wouldn't budge an inch; the engine whirred, coughed and died and he was far from home. Ruined, once; then ruined again, as he had learnt from his lawyers that very morning; at the conclusion of the lengthy, slow attempt to restore his fortunes, he had turned out his pockets to find the cash for petrol to take him home. And not even enough money left over to buy his Beauty, his girl-child, his pet, the one white rose she said she wanted; the only gift she want-ed, no matter how the case went, how rich he might once again be. She had asked for so little and he had not been able to give it to her. He cursed the useless car, the last straw that broke his spirit; then, nothing for it but to fasten his old sheepskin coat around him, abandon the heap of metal and set off down the snow-filled lane to look for help.

Behind wrought-iron gates, a short, snowy drive performed a reticent flourish be-fore a miniature, perfect Palladian house that seemed to hide itself shyly behind snow-laden skirts of an antique cypress. It was almost night; that house, with its sweet, retiring, melancholy grace, would have seemed deserted but for a light that flickered in an upstairs window, so vague it might have been the reflection of a star, if any stars could have penetrated the snow that whirled yet more thickly. Chilled through, he pressed the latch of the gate and saw, with a pang, how, on the withered ghost of a tangle of thorns, there clung, still, the faded rag of a white rose.

The gate clanged loudly shut behind him; too loudly. For an instant, that rever-berating clang seemed final, emphatic, ominous as if the gate, now closed, barred all within it from the world outside the walled, wintry garden. And, from a distance, though from what distance he could not tell, he heard the most singular sound in the world: a great roaring, as of a beast of prey.

In too much need to allow himself to be intimidated, he squared up to the ma-hogany door. This door was equipped with a knocker in the shape of a lion's head, with a ring through the nose; as he raised his hand towards it, it came to him this lion's head was not, as he had thought at first, made of brass, but, instead, of gold. Before, however, he could announce his presence, the door swung silently inward on well-oiled hinges and he saw a white hall where the candles of a great chandelier cast their benign light upon so many, many flowers in great, free-standing jars of crystal that it seemed the whole of spring drew him into its warmth with a profound intake of perfumed breath. Yet there was no living person in the hall.

The door behind him closed as silently as it had opened, yet, this time, he felt no fear although he knew by the pervasive atmosphere of a suspension of reality that he had entered a place of privilege where all the laws of the world he knew need not necessarily apply, for the very rich are often very eccentric and the house was plain-ly that of an exceedingly wealthy man. As it was, when nobody came to help him with his coat, he took it off himself. At that, the crystals of the chandelier tinkled a little, as if emitting a pleased chuckle, and the door of a cloakroom opened of its own accord. There were, however, no clothes at all in this cloakroom, not even the statutory country-garden mackintosh to greet his own squirearchal sheepskin, but, when he emerged again into the hall, he found a greeting waiting for him at last—there was, of all things, a liver and white King Charles spaniel crouched with head intelligently cocked, on the kelim runner. It gave him further, comforting proof of his unseen host's wealth and eccentricity to see the dog wore, in place of a collar, a diamond necklace.

The dog sprang to its feet in welcome and busily shepherded him (how amusing!) to a snug little leather-panelled study on the first floor, where a low table was drawn up to a roaring log fire. On the table, a silver tray; round the neck of the whisky decanter, a silver tag with the legend: *Drink me*, while the cover of the silver dish was engraved with the exhortation: *Eat me*, in a flowing hand. This dish contained sandwiches of thick-cut roast beef, still bloody. He drank the one with soda and ate the other with some excellent mustard thoughtfully provided in a stoneware pot, and, when the spaniel saw to it he had served himself, she trotted off about her own business.

All that remained to make Beauty's father entirely comfortable was to find, in a curtained recess, not only a telephone but the card of a garage that advertised a twenty-four-hour rescue service; a couple of calls later and he had confirmed, thank God that there was no serious trouble, only the car's age and the cold weather . . . could he pick it up from the village in an hour? And directions to the village, but half a mile away, were supplied, in a new tone of deference, as soon as he described the house from where he was calling.

And he was disconcerted but, in his impecunious circumstances, relieved to hear the bill would go on his hospitable if absent host's account; no question, assured the mechanic. It was the master's custom.

Time for another whisky as he tried, unsuccessfully, to call Beauty and tell her he would be late; but the lines were still down, although, miraculously, the storm had cleared as the moon rose and now a glance between the velvet curtains revealed a landscape as of ivory with an inlay of silver. Then the spaniel appeared again, with his hat in her careful mouth, prettily wagging her tail, as if to tell him it was time to be gone, that this magical hospitality was over.

As the door swung to behind him, he saw the lion's eyes were made of agate.

Great wreaths of snow now precariously curded the rose trees and, when he brushed against a stem on his way to the gate, a chill armful softly thudded to the ground to reveal, as if miraculously preserved beneath it, one last, single, perfect rose that might have been the last rose left living in all the white winter, and of so intense and delicate a fragrance it seemed to ring like a dulcimer on the frozen air.

How could his host, so mysterious, so kind, deny Beauty her present?

Not now distant but close to hand, close as the mahogany front door, rose a mighty, furious roaring; the garden seemed to hold its breath in apprehension. But still, because he loved his daughter, Beauty's father stole the rose.

At that, every window of the house blazed with furious light and a fugal baying, as if a pride of lions, introduced his host.

There is always a dignity about great bulk, an assertiveness, a quality of being more *there* than most of us are. The being who now confronted Beauty's father seemed to him, in his confusion, vaster than the house he owned, ponderous yet swift, and the moonlight glittered on his great, mazy head of hair, on the eyes green as agate, on the golden hairs of the great paws that grasped his shoulders so that their claws pierced the sheepskin as he shook him like an angry child shakes a doll.

This leonine apparition shook Beauty's father until his teeth rattled and then dropped him sprawling on his knees while the spaniel, darting from the open door, danced round them, yapping distractedly, like a lady at whose dinner party blows have been exchanged.

"My good fellow—" stammered Beauty's father; but the only response was a renewed roar.

"Good fellow? I am no good fellow! I am the Beast, and you must call me Beast, while I call you, Thief!"

"Forgive me for robbing your garden, Beast!"

Head of a lion; mane and mighty paws of a lion; he reared on his hind legs like an angry lion yet wore a smoking jacket of dull red brocade and was the owner of that lovely house and the low hills that cupped it.

"It was for my daughter," said Beauty's father. "All she wanted, in the whole world, was one white, perfect rose."

The Beast rudely snatched the photograph her father drew from his wallet and inspected it, first brusquely, then with a strange kind of wonder, almost the dawning of surmise. The camera had captured a certain look she had, sometimes, of absolute sweetness and absolute gravity, as if her eyes might pierce appearances and see your soul. When he handed the picture back, the Beast took good care not to scratch the surface with his claws.

"Take her her rose, then, but bring her to dinner," he growled; and what else was there to be done?

Although her father had told her of the nature of the one who waited for her, she could not control an instinctual shudder of fear when she saw him, for a lion is a lion and a man is a man and, though lions are more beautiful by far than we are, yet they belong to a different order of beauty and, besides, they have no respect for us: why should they? Yet wild things have a far more rational fear of us than is ours of them, and some kind of sadness in his agate eyes, that looked almost blind, as if sick of sight, moved her heart.

He sat, impassive as a figurehead, at the top of the table; the dining room was Queen Anne, tapestried, a gem. Apart from an aromatic soup kept hot over a spirit lamp, the food, though exquisite, was cold—a cold bird, a cold soufflé, cheese. He asked her father to serve them from a buffet and, himself, ate nothing. He grudgingly admitted what she had already guessed, that he disliked the presence of servants because, she thought, a constant human presence would remind him too bitterly of his otherness, but the spaniel sat at his feet throughout the meal, jumping up from time to time to see that everything was in order.

How strange he was. She found his bewildering difference from herself almost intolerable; its presence choked her. There seemed a heavy, soundless pressure upon her in his house, as if it lay under water, and when she saw the great paws lying on the arm of his chair, she thought: they are the death of any tender herbivore. And such a one she felt herself to be, Miss Lamb, spotless, sacrificial.

Yet she stayed, and smiled, because her father wanted her to do so; and when the Beast told her how he would aid her father's appeal against the judgement, she smiled with both her mouth and her eyes. But when, as they sipped their brandy, the Beast, in the diffuse, rumbling purr with which he conversed, suggested, with a hint of shyness, of fear of refusal, that she should stay here, with him, in comfort, while her father returned to London to take up the legal cudgels again, she forced a smile. For she knew with a pang of dread, as soon as he spoke, that it would be so and her visit to the Beast must be, on some magically reciprocal scale, the price of her father's good fortune.

Do not think she had no will of her own; only, she was possessed by a sense of obligation to an unusual degree and, besides, she would gladly have gone to the ends of the earth for her father, whom she loved dearly.

Her bedroom contained a marvellous glass bed; she had a bathroom, with towels thick as fleece and vials of suave unguents; and a little parlour of her own, the walls of which were covered with an antique paper of birds of paradise and Chinamen, where there were precious books and pictures and the flowers grown by invisible gardeners in the Beast's hothouses. Next morning, her father kissed her and drove away with a renewed hope about him that made her glad, but, all the same, she longed for the shabby home of their poverty. The unaccustomed luxury about her she found poignant, because it gave no pleasure to its possessor and himself she did not see all day as if, curious reversal, she frightened him, although the spaniel came and sat with her, to keep her company. Today, the spaniel wore a neat choker of turquoises.

Who prepared her meals? Loneliness of the Beast; all the time she stayed there, she saw no evidence of another human presence but the trays of food had arrived on a dumb waiter inside the mahogany cupboard in her parlour. Dinner was eggs Benedict and grilled veal; she ate it as she browsed in a book she had found in the rosewood revolving bookcase, a collection of courtly and elegant French fairy tales about white cats who were transformed princesses and fairies who were birds. Then she pulled a sprig of muscat grapes from a fat bunch for her dessert and found herself yawning; she discovered she was bored. At that, the spaniel took hold of her skirt with its velvet mouth and gave a firm but gentle tug. She allowed the dog to trot before her to the study in which her father had been entertained and there, to her well-disguised dismay, she found her host, seated beside the fire with a tray of coffee at his elbow from which she must pour.

The voice that seemed to issue from a cave full of echoes, his dark, soft rumbling growl; after her day of pastel-coloured idleness, how could she converse with the possessor of a voice that seemed an instrument created to inspire the terror that the chords of great organs bring? Fascinated, almost awed, she watched the firelight play on the gold fringes of his mane; he was irradiated, as if with a kind of halo, and she thought of the first great beast of the Apocalypse, the winged lion with his paw upon the Gospel, Saint Mark. Small talk turned to dust in her mouth; small talk had never, at the best of times, been Beauty's forte, and she had little practice at it.

But he, hesitantly, as if he himself were in awe of a young girl who looked as if she had been carved out of a single pearl, asked after her father's law case; and her dead mother; and how they, who had been so rich, had come to be so poor. He forced himself to master his shyness, which was that of a wild creature, and so, she contrived to master her own—to such effect that soon she was chattering away to him as if she had known him all her life. When the little cupid in the gilt clock on the mantelpiece struck its miniature tambourine, she was astonished to discover it did so twelve times.

"So late! You will want to sleep," he said.

At that, they both fell silent, as if these strange companions were suddenly overcome with embarrassment to find themselves together, alone, in that room in the depths of winter's night. As she was about to rise, he flung himself at her feet and buried his head in her lap. She stayed stock-still, transfixed; she felt his hot breath on her fingers, the stiff bristles of his muzzle grazing her skin, the rough lapping of his tongue and then, with a flood of compassion, understood: all he is doing is kissing my hands.

He drew back his head and gazed at her with his green, inscrutable eyes, in which she saw her face repeated twice, as small as if it were in bud. Then, without another word, he sprang from the room and she saw, with an indescribable shock, he went on all fours.

Next day, all day, the hills on which the snow still settled echoed with the Beast's rumbling roar: has master gone a-hunting? Beauty asked the spaniel. But the spaniel growled, almost bad-temperedly, as if to say, that she would not have answered, even if she could have.

Beauty would pass the day in her suite reading or, perhaps, doing a little embroidery; a box of coloured silks and a frame had been provided for her. Or, well wrapped up, she wandered in the walled garden, among the leafless roses, with the spaniel at her heels, and did a little raking and rearranging. An idle, restful time; a holiday. The enchantment of that bright, sad pretty place enveloped her and she found that, against all her expectations, she was happy there. She no longer felt the slightest apprehension at her nightly interviews with the Beast. All the natural laws of the world were held in suspension, here, where an army of invisibles tenderly waited on her, and she would talk with the lion, under the patient chaperonage of the brown-eyed dog, on the nature of the moon and its borrowed light, about the stars and the substances of which they were made, about the variable transformations of the weather. Yet still his strangeness made her shiver; and when he helplessly fell before her to kiss her hand, as he did every night when they parted, she would retreat nervously into her skin, flinching at his touch.

The telephoned shrilled; for her. Her father. Such news!

The Beast sunk his great head on to his paws. You will come back to me? It will be lonely here, without you.

She was moved almost to tears that he should care for her so. It was in her heart to drop a kiss upon his shaggy mane but, though she stretched out her hand towards him, she could not bring herself to touch him of her own free will, he was so different from herself. But, yes, she said; I will come back. Soon, before the winter is over. Then the taxi came and took her away.

You are never at the mercy of the elements in London, where the huddled warmth of humanity melts the snow before it has time to settle; and her father was as good as rich again, since his hirsute friend's lawyers had the business so well in hand that his credit brought them nothing but the best. A resplendent hotel; the opera, theatres; a whole new wardrobe for his darling, so she could step out on his arm to parties, to receptions, to restaurants, and life was as she had never known it, for her father had ruined himself before her birth killed her mother.

Although the Beast was the source of his new-found prosperity and they talked of him often, now that they were so far away from the timeless spell of his house it seemed to possess the radiant and finite quality of dream and the Beast himself, so monstrous, so benign, some kind of spirit of good fortune who had smiled on them and let them go. She sent him flowers, white roses in return for the ones he had given her; and when she left the florist, she experienced a sudden sense of perfect freedom, as if she had just escaped from an unknown danger, had been grazed by the possibility of some change but, finally, left intact. Yet, with this exhilaration, a desolating emptiness. But her father was waiting for her at the hotel; they had planned a delicious expedition to buy her furs and she was as eager for the treat as any girl might be.

Since the flowers in the shop were the same all the year round, nothing in the window could tell her that winter had almost gone.

Returning late from supper after the theatre, she took off her earrings in front of the mirror; Beauty. She smiled at herself with satisfaction. She was learning, at the end of her adolescence, how to be a spoiled child and that pearly skin of hers was plumping out, a little, with high living and compliments. A certain inwardness was beginning to transform the lines around her mouth, those signatures of the personality, and her sweetness and her gravity could sometimes turn a mite petulant when things went not quite as she wanted them to go. You could not have said that her freshness was fading but she smiled at herself in mirrors a little too often, these days, and the face that smiled back was not quite the one she had seen contained in the Beast's agate eyes. Her face was acquiring, instead of beauty, a lacquer of the invincible prettiness that characterises certain pampered, exquisite, expensive cats.

The soft wind of spring breathed in from the nearby park through the open window; she did not know why it made her want to cry.

There was a sudden urgent, scrambling sound, as of claws, at her door.

Her trance before the mirror broke; all at once, she remembered everything perfectly. Spring was here and she had broken her promise. Now the Beast himself had come in pursuit of her! First, she was frightened of his anger; then, mysteriously joyful, she ran to open the door. But it was his liver and white spotted spaniel who hurled herself into the girl's arms in a flurry of little barks and gruff murmurings, of whimpering and relief.

Yet where was the well-brushed, jewelled dog who had sat beside her embroidery frame in the parlour with birds of paradise nodding on the walls? This one's fringed ears were matted with mud, her coat was dusty and snarled, she was thin as a dog that has walked a long way and, if she had not been a dog, she would have been in tears.

After that first, rapturous greeting, she did not wait for Beauty to order her food and water; she seized the chiffon hem of her evening dress, whimpered and tugged. Threw back her head, howled, then tugged and whimpered again.

There was a slow, late train that would take her to the station where she had left for London three months ago. Beauty scribbled a note for her father, threw a coat round her shoulders. Quickly, quickly, urged the spaniel soundlessly; and Beauty knew the Beast was dying.

In the thick dark before dawn, the station master roused a sleepy driver for her. Fast as you can.

It seemed December still possessed his garden. The ground was hard as iron, the skirts of the dark cypress moved on the chill wind with a mournful rustle and there were no green shoots on the roses as if, this year, they would not bloom. And not one light in any of the windows, only, in the topmost attic, the faintest smear of radiance on a pane. The thin ghost of a light on the verge of extinction.

The spaniel had slept a little, in her arms, for the poor thing was exhausted. But now her grieving agitation fed Beauty's urgency and, as the girl pushed open the front door, she saw, with a thrust of conscience, how the golden door knocker was thickly muffled in black crêpe.

The door did not open silently, as before, but with a doleful groaning of the hinges and, this time, on to perfect darkness. Beauty clicked her gold cigarette lighter; the tapers in the chandelier had drowned in their own wax and the prisms were wreathed with dreadful arabesques of cobwebs. The flowers in the glass jars were dead, as if nobody had had the heart to replace them after she was gone. Dust, everywhere; and it was cold. There was an air of exhaustion, of despair in the house and, worse, a kind of physical disillusion, as if its glamour had been sustained by a cheap conjuring trick and now the conjurer, having failed to pull the crowds, had departed to try his luck elsewhere.

Beauty found a candle to light her way and followed the faithful spaniel up the staircase, past the study, past her suite, through a house echoing with desertion up a little back staircase dedicated to mice and spiders, stumbling, ripping the hem of her dress in her haste.

What a modest bedroom! An attic, with a sloping roof, they might have given the chambermaid if the Beast had employed staff. A night light on the mantel-piece, no curtains at the windows, no carpet on the floor and a narrow, iron bed-stead on which he lay, sadly diminished, his bulk scarcely disturbing the faded patchwork quilt, his mane a greyish rat's nest and his eyes closed. On the stick-backed chair where his clothes had been thrown, the roses she had sent him were thrust into the jug from the washstand but they were all dead.

The spaniel jumped up on the bed and burrowed her way under the scanty cov-ers, softly keening.

"Oh, Beast," said Beauty. "I have come home."

His eyelids flickered. How was it she had never noticed before that his agate eyes were equipped with lids, like those of a man? Was it because she had only looked at her own face, reflected there?

"I'm dying, Beauty," he said in a cracked whisper of his former purr. "Since you left me, I have been sick. I could not go hunting, I found I had not the stomach to kill the gentle beasts, I could not eat. I am sick and I must die; but I shall die happy because you have come to say goodbye to me."

She flung herself upon him, so that the iron bedstead groaned, and covered his poor paws with her kisses.

"Don't die, Beast! If you'll have me, I'll never leave you."

When her lips touched the meat-hook claws, they drew back into their pads and she saw how he had always kept his fists clenched, but now, painfully, tenta-tively, at last began to stretch his fingers. Her tears fell on his face like snow and, under their soft transformation, the bones showed through the pelt, the flesh through the wide, tawny brow. And then it was no longer a lion in her arms but a man, a man with an unkempt mane of hair and, how strange, a broken nose, such as the noses of retired boxers, that gave him a distant, heroic resemblance to the handsomest of all the beasts.

"Do you know," said Mr. Lyon, "I think I might be able to manage a little break-fast today, Beauty, if you would eat something with me."

Mr. and Mrs. Lyon walk in the garden; the old spaniel drowses on the grass, in a drift of fallen petals.

[1979]

Questions

1. In what specific ways does Carter's revision of "Beauty and the Beast" depart from the original tale?
2. How is Beauty characterized? How is the Beast characterized? Which character or characters change? In what sense?
3. What is the conflict in the story? How is it resolved?
4. What human truths does the story convey through its blending of fairy tale and realistic elements?

Raymond Carver

(1938–1989)
United States

C ritics often state that Raymond Carver's life reads as if it were one of his own stories. He grew up in a logging town in Oregon, married before he was 20, sporadically acquired an education, and (at least early in his adult life) held a series of low-paying jobs. Bruce Weber, in the New York Times Magazine, described these positions as follows: "He picked tulips, pumped gas, swept hospital corridors, swabbed toilets, managed an apartment complex." Carver's fictive world of the working class grew out of his own life experiences. By the end of his short writing career, however, his collections of short stories had been nominated for the National Book Award, the National Book Critics Circle Award, and the Pulitzer Prize; and he had held several prestigious grants, including a Guggenheim fellowship, a National Endowment for the Arts Award in fiction, and the Mildred and Harold Strauss Living Award from the American Academy and Institute of Arts and Letters. Carver is equally revered for his poetry and fiction, especially for his two short story collections: Will You Please Be Quiet, Please? (1976) and Cathedral (1984).

In a foreward he wrote to John Gardner's On Becoming a Novelist (1953), Carver described his own education:

> I put a very high premium on education then—much higher in those days than now, I'm sure, but that's because I'm older and have an education. Understand that nobody in my family had ever gone to college or for that matter had got beyond the mandatory eighth grade in high school. I didn't know anything, but I knew I didn't know anything.

Carver made the following remark about the creative writing course he took from John Gardner at Ohio State:

> It was his conviction that if the words in the story were blurred because of the author's insensitivity, carelessness, or sentimentality, then the story suffered a tremendous handicap. But there was something even worse and something that must be avoided at all costs: If the words and sentiments were dishonest, the author was faking it, writing about things he didn't care about or believe in, then nobody could ever care anything about it.

WHERE I'M CALLING FROM

J. P. and I are on the front porch at Frank Martin's drying-out facility. Like the rest of us at Frank Martin's, J. P. is first and foremost a drunk. But he's also a chimney sweep. It's his first time here, and he's scared. I've been here once before. What's to say? I'm back. J. P.'s real name is Joe Penny, but he says I should call him J. P. He's about thirty years old. Younger than I am. Not much younger, but a little. He's telling me how he decided to go into his line of work, and he wants to use his hands when he talks. But his hands tremble. I mean, they won't keep still. "This has never happened to me before," he says. He means the trembling. I tell him I sympathize. I tell him the shakes will idle down. And they will. But it takes time.

We've only been in here a couple of days. We're not out of the woods yet. J. P. has these shakes, and every so often a nerve—maybe it isn't a nerve, but it's something—begins to jerk in my shoulder. Sometimes it's at the side of my neck. When this happens, my mouth dries up. It's an effort just to swallow then. I know something's about to happen and I want to head it off. I want to hide from it, that's what I want to do. Just close my eyes and let it pass by, let it take the next man. J. P. can wait a minute.

I saw a seizure yesterday morning. A guy they call Tiny. A big fat guy, an electrician from Santa Rosa. They said he'd been in here for nearly two weeks and that he was over the hump. He was going home in a day or two and would spend New Year's Eve with his wife in front of the TV. On New Year's Eve, Tiny planned to drink hot chocolate and eat cookies. Yesterday morning he seemed just fine when he came down for breakfast. He was letting out with quacking noises, showing some guy how he called ducks right down onto his head. "Blam. Blam," said Tiny, picking off a couple. Tiny's hair was damp and was slicked back along the sides of his head. He'd just come out of the shower. He'd also nicked himself on the chin with his razor. But so what? Just about everybody at Frank Martin's has nicks on his face. It's something that happens. Tiny edged in at the head of the table and began telling about something that had happened on one of his drinking bouts. People at the table laughed and shook their heads as they shoveled up their eggs. Tiny would say something, grin, then look around the table for a sign of recognition. We'd all done things just as bad and crazy, so, sure, that's why we laughed. Tiny had scrambled eggs on his plate, and some biscuits and honey. I was at the table, but I wasn't hungry. I had some coffee in front of me. Suddenly, Tiny wasn't there anymore. He'd gone over in his chair with a big clatter. He was on his back on the floor with his eyes closed, his heels drumming the linoleum. People hollered for Frank Martin. But he was right there. A couple of guys got down on the floor beside Tiny. One of the guys put his fingers inside Tiny's mouth and tried to hold his tongue. Frank Martin yelled, "Everybody stand back!" Then I noticed that the bunch of us were leaning over Tiny, just looking at him, not able to take our eyes off him. "Give him air!" Frank Martin said. Then he ran into the office and called the ambulance.

Tiny is on board again today. Talk about bouncing back. This morning Frank Martin drove the station wagon to the hospital to get him. Tiny got back too late for his eggs, but he took some coffee into the dining room and sat down at the table anyway. Somebody in the kitchen made toast for him, but Tiny didn't eat it. He just sat with his coffee and looked into his cup. Every now and then he moved his cup back and forth in front of him.

I'd like to ask him if he had any signal just before it happened. I'd like to know if he felt his ticker skip a beat, or else begin to race. Did his eyelid twitch? But I'm not about to say anything. He doesn't look like he's hot to talk about it, anyway. But what happened to Tiny is something I won't ever forget. Old Tiny flat on the floor, kicking his heels. So every time this little flitter starts up anywhere, I draw some breath and wait to find myself on my back, looking up, somebody's fingers in my mouth.

In his chair on the front porch, J. P. keeps his hands in his lap. I smoke cigarettes and use an old coal bucket for an ashtray. I listen to J. P. ramble on. It's eleven o'clock in the morning—an hour and a half until lunch. Neither one of us is hungry. But just the same we look forward to going inside and sitting down at the table. Maybe we'll get hungry.

What's J. P. talking about, anyway? He's saying how when he was twelve years old he fell into a well in the vicinity of the farm he grew up on. It was a dry well, lucky for him. "Or unlucky," he says, looking around him and shaking his head. He says how late that afternoon, after he'd been located, his dad hauled him out with a rope. J. P. had wet his pants down there. He's suffered all kinds of terror in that well, hollering for help, waiting, and then hollering some more. He hollered himself hoarse before it was over. But he told me that being at the bottom of that well had made a lasting impression. He'd sat there and looked up at the well mouth. Way up at the top, he could see a circle of blue sky. Every once in a while a white cloud passed over. A flock of birds flew across, and it seemed to J. P. their wingbeats set up this odd commotion. He heard other things. He heard tiny rustlings above him in the well, which made him wonder if things might fall down into his hair. He was thinking of insects. He heard wind blow over the well mouth, and that sound made an impression on him, too. In short, everything about his life was different for him at the bottom of that well. But nothing fell on him and nothing closed off that little circle of blue. Then his dad came along with the rope, and it wasn't long before J. P. was back in the world he'd always lived in.

"Keep talking, J. P. Then what?" I say.

When he was eighteen or nineteen years old and out of high school and had nothing whatsoever he wanted to do with his life, he went across town one afternoon to visit a friend. This friend lived in a house with a fireplace. J. P. and his friend sat around drinking beer and batting the breeze. They played some records. Then the doorbell rings. The friend goes to the door. This young woman chimney sweep is there with her cleaning things. She's wearing a top hat, the sight of which knocked J. P. for a loop. She tells J. P.'s friend that she has an appointment to clean the fireplace. The friend lets her in and bows. The young woman doesn't pay him any mind. She spreads a blanket on the hearth and lays out her gear. She's wearing these black pants, black shirt, black shoes and socks. Of course, by now she's taken her hat off. J. P. says it nearly drove him nuts to look at her. She does the work, she cleans the chimney, while J. P. and his friend play records and drink beer. But they watch her and they watch what she does. Now and then J. P. and his friend look at each other and grin, or else they wink. They raise their eyebrows when the upper half of the young woman disappears into the chimney. She was all-right-looking, too, J. P. said.

When she'd finished her work, she rolled her things up in the blanket. From J. P.'s friend, she took a check that had been made out to her by his parents. And then she asks the friend if he wants to kiss her. "It's supposed to bring good luck," she says. That does it for J. P. The friend rolls his eyes. He clowns some more. Then, probably blushing, he kisses her on the cheek. At this minute, J. P. made his mind up about something. He put his beer down. He got up from the sofa. He went over to the young woman as she was starting to go out the door.

"Me, too?" J. P. said to her.

She swept her eyes over him. J. P. says he could feel his heart knocking. The young woman's name, it turns out, was Roxy.

"Sure," Roxy says. "Why not? I've got some extra kisses." And she kissed him a good one right on the lips and then turned to go.

Like that, quick as a wink, J. P. followed her onto the porch. He held the porch screen door for her. He went down the steps with her and out to the drive, where she'd parked her panel truck. It was something that was out of his hands. Nothing else in the world counted for anything. He knew he'd met somebody who could set his legs atremble. He could feel her kiss still burning on his lips, etc. J. P. couldn't begin to sort anything out. He was filled with sensations that were carrying him every which way.

He opened the rear door of the panel truck for her. He helped her store her things inside. "Thanks," she told him. Then he blurted it out—that he'd like to see her again. Would she go to a movie with him sometime? He'd realized, too, what he wanted to do with his life. He wanted to do what she did. He wanted to be a chimney sweep. But he didn't tell her that then.

J. P. says she put her hands on her hips and looked him over. Then she found a business card in the front seat of her truck. She gave it to him. She said, "Call this number after ten tonight. We can talk. I have to go now." She put the top hat on and then took it off. She looked at J. P. once more. She must have liked what she saw, because this time she grinned. He told her there was a smudge near her mouth. Then she got into her truck, tooted the horn, and drove away.

"Then what?" I say. "Don't stop now, J. P."

I was interested. But I would have listened if he'd been going on about how one day he'd decided to start pitching horseshoes.

It rained last night. The clouds are banked up against the hills across the valley. J. P. clears his throat and looks at the hills and the clouds. He pulls his chin. Then he goes on with what he was saying.

Roxy starts going out with him on dates. And little by little he talks her into letting him go along on jobs with her. But Roxy's in business with her father and brother and they've got just the right amount of work. They don't need anybody else. Besides, who was this guy J. P.? J. P. what? Watch out, they warned her.

So she and J. P. saw some movies together. They went to a few dances. But mainly the courtship revolved around their cleaning chimneys together. Before you know it, J. P. says, they're talking about tying the knot. And after a while they do it, they get married. J. P.'s new father-in-law takes him in as a full partner. In a year or so, Roxy has a kid. She's quit being a chimney sweep. At any rate, she's quit doing the work. Pretty soon she has another kid. J. P.'s in his mid-twenties by now. He's buying a house. He says he was happy with his life. "I was happy with the way things were going," he says. "I had everything I wanted. I had a wife and kids I loved, and I was doing what I wanted to do with my life." But for some reason—who knows why we do what we do?—his drinking picks up. For a long time he drinks beer and beer only. Any kind of beer—it didn't matter. He says he could drink beer twenty-four hours a day. He'd drink beer at night while he watched TV. Sure, once in a while he drank hard stuff. But that was only if they went out on the town, which was not often, or else when they had company over. Then a time comes, he doesn't know why, when he makes the switch from beer to gin-and-tonic. And he'd have more gin-and-tonic after dinner, sitting in front of the TV. There was always a glass of gin-and-tonic in his hand. He says he actually liked the taste of it. He began stopping off after work for drinks before he went home to have more drinks. Then he began missing some dinners. He just wouldn't show up. Or else he'd show up, but he wouldn't want anything to eat. He'd filled up on snacks at the bar. Sometimes he'd walk in the door and for no good reason throw his lunch pail across the living room. When Roxy yelled at him, he'd turn around and go out again. He moved his drinking time up to early afternoon, while he was still supposed to be working. He tells me that he was starting off the morning with a couple of drinks. He'd have a belt of the stuff before he brushed his teeth. Then he'd have his coffee. He'd go to work with a thermos bottle of vodka in his lunch pail.

J. P. quits talking. He just clams up. What's going on? I'm listening. It's helping me relax, for one thing. It's taking me away from my own situation. After a minute, I say, "What the hell? Go on, J. P." He's pulling his chin. But pretty soon he starts talking again.

J. P. and Roxy are having some real fights now. I mean *fights*. J. P. says that one time she hit him in the face with her fist and broke his noise. "Look at this," he says. "Right here." He shows me a line across the bridge of his nose. "That's a broken nose." He returned the favor. He dislocated her shoulder for her. Another time he split her lip. They beat on each other in front of the kids. Things got out of hand. But he kept on drinking. He couldn't stop. And nothing could make him stop. Not even with Roxy's dad and her brother threatening to beat the hell out of him. They told Roxy she should take the kids and clear out. But Roxy said it was her problem. She got herself into it, and she'd solve it.

Now J. P. gets real quiet again. He hunches his shoulders and pulls down in his chair. He watches a car driving down the road between this place and the hills.

I say, "I want to hear the rest of his, J. P. You better keep talking."

"I just don't know," he says. He shrugs.

"It's all right," I say. And I mean it's okay for him to tell it. "Go on, J. P."

One way she tried to fix things, J. P. says, was by finding a boyfriend. J. P. would like to know how she found the time with the house and kids.

I look at him and I'm surprised. He's a grown man. "If you want to do that," I say, "You find the time. You make the time."

J. P. shakes his head. "I guess so," he says.

Anyway, he found out about it—about Roxy's boyfriend—and he went wild. He manages to get Roxy's wedding ring off her finger. And when he does, he cuts it into several pieces with a pair of wire-cutters. Good, solid fun. They'd already gone a couple of rounds on this occasion. On his way to work the next morning, he gets arrested on a drunk charge. He loses his driver's license. He can't drive the truck to work anymore. Just as well, he says. He'd already fallen off a roof the week before and broken his thumb. It was just a matter of time until he broke his neck, he says.

He was here at Frank Martin's to dry out and to figure how to get his life back on track. But he wasn't here against his will, any more than I was. We weren't locked up. We could leave any time we wanted. But a minimum stay of a week was recommended, and two weeks or a month was, as they put it, "strongly advised."

As I said, this is my second time at Frank Martin's. When I was trying to sign a check to pay in advance for a week's stay, Frank Martin said, "The holidays are always bad. Maybe you should think of sticking around a little longer this time? Think in terms of a couple of weeks. Can you do a couple of weeks? Think about it, anyway. You don't have to decide anything right now," he said. He held his thumb on the check and I signed my name. Then I walked my girlfriend to the front door and said goodbye. "Goodbye," she said, and she lurched into the doorjamb and then onto the porch. It's late afternoon. It's raining. I go from the door to the window. I move the curtain and watch her drive away. She's in my car. She's drunk. But I'm drunk, too, and there's nothing I can do. I make it to a big chair that's close to the radiator, and I sit down. Some guys look up from their TV. Then they shift back to what they were watching. I just sit there. Now and then I look up at something that's happening on the screen.

Later that afternoon the front door banged open and J. P. was brought in between these two big guys—his father-in-law and brother-in-law, I found out afterward. They steered J. P. across the room. The old guy signed him in and gave Frank Martin a check. Then these two guys helped J. P. upstairs. I guess they put him to bed. Pretty soon the old guy and the other guy came downstairs and headed for the front door. They couldn't seem to get out of this place fast enough. It was like they couldn't wait to wash their hands of all this. I didn't blame them. Hell, no. I don't know how I'd act if I was in their shoes.

A day and a half later J. P. and I meet up on the front porch. We shake hands and comment on the weather. J. P. has a case of the shakes. We sit down and prop our feet up on the railing. We lean back in our chairs like we're just out there taking our ease, like we might be getting ready to talk about our bird dogs. That's when J. P. gets going with his story.

It's cold out, but not too cold. It's a little overcast. Frank Martin comes outside to finish his cigar. He has on a sweater buttoned all the way up. Frank Martin is short and heavy-set. He has curly gray hair and a small head. His head is too small for the rest of his body. Frank Martin puts the cigar in his mouth and stands with his arms crossed over his chest. He works that cigar in his mouth and looks across the valley. He stands there like a prizefighter, like somebody who knows the score.

J. P. gets quiet again. I mean, he's hardly breathing. I toss my cigarette into the coal bucket and look hard at J. P., who scoots farther down in his chair. J. P. pulls up his collar. What the hell's going on? I wonder. Frank Martin uncrosses his arms and takes a puff on the cigar. He lets the smoke carry out of his mouth. Then he raises his chin toward the hills and says, "Jack London used to have a big place on the other side of this valley. Right over there behind that green hill you're looking at. But alcohol killed him. Let that be a lesson to you. He was a better man than any of us. But he couldn't handle the stuff, either." Frank Martin looks at what's left of his cigar. It's gone out. He tosses it into the bucket. "You guys want to read something while you're here, read that book of his, *The Call of the Wild*. You know the one I'm talking about? We have it inside if you want to read something. It's about this animal that's half dog and half wolf. End of sermon," he says, and then hitches his pants up and tugs his sweater down. "I'm going inside," he says. "See you at lunch."

"I feel like a bug when he's around," J. P. says. "He makes me feel like a bug." J. P. shakes his head. Then he says, "Jack London. What a name! I wish I had me a name like that. Instead of the name I got."

My wife brought me up here the first time. That's when we were still together, trying to make things work out. She brought me here and she stayed around for an hour or two, talking to Frank Martin in private. Then she left. The next morning Frank Martin got me aside and said, "We can help you. If you want help and want to listen to what we say." But I didn't know if they could help me or not. Part of me wanted help. But there was another part.

This time around, it was my girlfriend who drove me here. She was driving my car. She drove us through a rainstorm. We drank champagne all the way. We were both drunk when she pulled up in the drive. She intended to drop me off, turn around, and drive home again. She had things to do. One thing she had to do was to go to work the next day. She was a secretary. She had an okay job with this electronic-parts firm. She also had this mouthy teenaged son. I wanted her to get a room in town, spend the night, and then drive home. I don't know if she got the room or not. I haven't heard from her since she led me up the front steps the other day and walked me into Frank Martin's office and said, "Guess who's here."

But I wasn't mad at her. In the first place, she didn't have any idea what she was letting herself in for when she said I could stay with her after my wife asked me to leave. I felt sorry for her. The reason I felt sorry for her was that on the day before Christmas her Pap smear came back, and the news was not cheery. She'd have to go back to the doctor, and real soon. That kind of news was reason enough for both of us to start drinking. So what we did was get ourselves good and drunk. And on Christmas Day we were still drunk. We had to go out to a restaurant to eat, because she didn't feel like cooking. The two of us and her mouthy teenaged son opened some presents, and then we went to this steakhouse near her apartment. I wasn't hungry. I had some soup and a hot roll. I drank a bottle of wine with the soup. She drank some wine, too. Then we started in on Bloody Marys. For the next couple of days, I didn't eat anything except salted nuts. But I drank a lot of bourbon. Then I said to her, "Sugar, I think I'd better pack up. I better go back to Frank Martin's."

She tried to explain to her son that she was going to be gone for a while and he'd have to get his own food. But right as we were going out the door, this mouthy kid screamed at us. He screamed, "The hell with you! I hope you never come back. I hope you kill yourselves!" Imagine this kid!

Before we left town, I had her stop at the package store, where I bought us the champagne. We stopped someplace else for plastic glasses. Then we picked up a bucket of fried chicken. We set out for Frank Martin's in this rainstorm, drinking and listening to music. She drove. I looked after the radio and poured. We tried to make a little party of it. But we were sad, too. There was that fried chicken, but we didn't eat any.

I guess she got home okay. I think I would have heard something if she didn't. But she hasn't called me, and I haven't called her. Maybe she's had some news about herself by now. Then again, maybe she hasn't heard anything. Maybe it was all a mistake. Maybe it was somebody else's smear. But she has my car, and I have things at her house. I know we'll be seeing each other again.

They clang an old farm bell here to call you for mealtime. J. P. and I get out of our chairs and we go inside. It's starting to get too cold on the porch, anyway. We can see our breath drifting out from us as we talk.

New Year's Eve morning I try to call my wife. There's no answer. It's okay. But even if it wasn't okay, what am I supposed to do? The last time we talked on the phone, a couple of weeks ago, we screamed at each other. I hung a few names on her. "Wet brain!" she said, and put the phone back where it belonged.

But I wanted to talk to her now. Something had to be done about my stuff. I still had things at her house, too.

One of the guys here is a guy who travels. He goes to Europe and places. That's what he says, anyway. Business, he says. He also says he has his drinking under control and he doesn't have any idea why he's here at Frank Martin's. But he doesn't remember getting here. He laughs about it, about his not remembering. "Anyone can have a blackout," he says. "That doesn't prove a thing." He's not a drunk—he tells us this and we listen. "That's a serious charge to make," he says. "That kind of talk can ruin a good man's prospects." He says that if he'd only stick to whiskey and water, no ice, he'd never have these blackouts. It's the ice they put into your drink that does it. "Who do you know in Egypt?" he asks me. "I can use a few names over there."

For New Year's Eve dinner Frank Martin serves steak and baked potato. My appetite's coming back. I clean up everything on my plate and I could eat more. I look over at Tiny's plate. Hell, he's hardly touched a thing. His steak is just sitting there. Tiny is not the same old Tiny. The poor bastard had planned to be at home tonight. He'd planned to be in his robe and slippers in front of the TV, holding hands with his wife. Now he's afraid to leave. I can understand. One seizure means you're ready for another. Tiny hasn't told any more nutty stories on himself since it happened. He's stayed quiet and kept to himself. I ask him if I can have his steak, and he pushes his plate over to me.

Some of us are still up, sitting around the TV, watching Times Square, when Frank Martin comes in to show us his cake. He brings it around and shows it to each of us. I know he didn't make it. It's just a bakery cake. But it's still a cake. It's a big white cake. Across the top there's writing in pink letters. The writing says, HAPPY NEW YEAR— ONE DAY AT A TIME.

"I don't want any stupid cake," says the guy who goes to Europe and places. "Where's the champagne?" he says, and laughs.

We all go into the dining room. Frank Martin cuts the cake. I sit next to J. P. J. P. eats two pieces and drinks a Coke. I eat a piece and wrap another piece in a napkin, thinking of later.

J. P. lights a cigarette—his hands are steady now—and he tells me his wife is coming in the morning, the first day of the new year.

"That's great," I say. I nod. I lick the frosting off my finger. "That's good news, J. P."

"I'll introduce you," he says.

"I look forward to it," I say.

We say goodnight. We say Happy New Year. I use a napkin on my fingers. We shake hands.

I go to the phone, put in a dime, and call my wife collect. But nobody answers this time, either. I think about calling my girlfriend, and I'm dialing her number when I realize I really don't want to talk to her. She's probably at home watching the same thing on TV that I've been watching. Anyway, I don't want to talk to her. I hope she's okay. But if she has something wrong with her, I don't want to know about it.

After breakfast, J. P. and I take coffee out to the porch. The sky is clear, but it's cold enough for sweaters and jackets.

"She asked me if she should bring the kids," J. P. says. "I told her she should keep the kids at home. Can you imagine? My God, I don't want my kids up here."

We use the coal bucket for an ashtray. We look across the valley to where Jack London used to live. We're drinking more coffee when this car turns off the road and comes down the drive.

"That's her!" J. P. says. He puts his cup next to his chair. He gets up and goes down the steps.

I see this woman stop the car and set the brake. I see J. P. open the door. I watch her get out, and I see them hug each other. I look away. Then I look back. J. P. takes her by the arm and they come up the stairs. This woman broke a man's nose once. She has had two kids, and much trouble, but she loves this man who has her by the arm. I get up from the chair.

"This is my friend," J. P. says to his wife. "Hey, this is Roxy."

Roxy takes my hand. She's a tall, good-looking woman in a knit cap. She has on a coat, a heavy sweater, and slacks. I recall what J. P. told me about the boyfriend and the wire-cutters. I don't see any wedding ring. That's in pieces somewhere, I guess. Her hands are broad and the fingers have these big knuckles. This is a woman who can make fists if she has to.

"I've heard about you," I say. "J. P. told me how you got acquainted. Something about a chimney, J. P. said."

"Yes, a chimney," she says. "There's probably a lot else he didn't tell you," she says. "I bet he didn't tell you everything," she says, and laughs. Then—she can't wait any longer—she slips her arm around J. P. and kisses him on the cheek. They start to move to the door. "Nice meeting you," she says. "Hey, did he tell you he's the best sweep in the business?"

"Come on now, Roxy," J. P. says. He has his hand on the doorknob.

"He told me he learned everything he knew from you," I say.

"Well, that much is sure true," she says. She laughs again. But it's like she's thinking about something else. J. P. turns the doorknob. Roxy lays her hand over his. "Joe, can't we go into town for lunch? Can't I take you someplace?"

J. P. clears his throat. He says, "It hasn't been a week yet." He takes his hand off the doorknob and brings his fingers to his chin. "I think they'd like it if I didn't leave the place for a little while yet. We can have some coffee here," he says.

"That's fine," she says. Her eyes work over to me again. "I'm glad Joe's made a friend. Nice to meet you," she says.

They start to go inside. I know it's a dumb thing to do, but I do it anyway. "Roxy," I say. And they stop in the doorway and look at me. "I need some luck," I say. "No kidding. I could do with a kiss myself."

J. P. looks down. He's still holding the knob, even though the door is open. He turns the knob back and forth. But I keep looking at her. Roxy grins. "I'm not a sweep anymore," she says. "Not for years. Didn't Joe tell you that? But, sure, I'll kiss you, sure."

She moves over. She takes me by the shoulders—I'm a big man—and she plants this kiss on my lips. "How's that?" she says.

"That's fine," I say.

"Nothing to it," she says. She's still holding me by the shoulders. She's looking me right in the eyes. "Good luck," she says, and then she lets go of me.

"See you later, pal," J. P. says. He opens the door all the way, and they go in.

I sit down on the front steps and light a cigarette. I watch what my hand does, then I blow out the match. I've got the shakes. I started out with them this morning. This morning I wanted something to drink. It's depressing, but I didn't say anything about it to J. P. I try to put my mind on something else.

I'm thinking about chimney sweeps—all that stuff I heard from J. P.—when for some reason I start to think about a house my wife and I once lived in. That house didn't have a chimney, so I don't know what makes me remember it now. But I remember the house and how we'd only been in there a few weeks when I heard a noise outside one morning. It was Sunday morning and it was still dark in the bedroom. But there was this pale light coming in from the bedroom window. I listened. I could hear something scrape against the side of the house. I jumped out of bed and went to look.

"My God!" my wife says, sitting up in bed and shaking the hair away from her face. Then she starts to laugh. "It's Mr. Venturini," she says. "I forgot to tell you. He said he was coming to paint the house today. Early. Before it gets too hot. I forgot all about it," she says, and laughs. "Come on back to bed, honey. It's just him."

"In a minute," I say.

I push the curtain away from the window. Outside, this old guy in white coveralls is standing next to his ladder. The sun is just starting to break above the mountains. The old guy and I look each other over. It's the landlord, all right—this old guy in coveralls. But his coveralls are too big for him. He needs a shave, too. And he's wearing this baseball cap to cover his bald head. Goddamn it, I think, if he isn't a weird old fellow. And a wave of happiness comes over me that I'm not him—that I'm me and that I'm inside this bedroom with my wife.

He jerks his thumb toward the sun. He pretends to wipe his forehead. He's letting me know he doesn't have all that much time. The old fart breaks into a grin. It's then I realize I'm naked. I look down at myself. I look at him again and shrug. What did he expect?

My wife laughs. "Come *on*," she says. "Get back in this bed. Right now. This minute. Come on back to bed."

I let go of the curtain. But I keep standing there at the window. I can see the old fellow nod to himself like he's saying, "Go on, sonny, go back to bed. I understand." He tugs on the bill of his cap. Then he sets about his business. He picks up his bucket. He starts climbing the ladder.

I lean back into the step behind me now and cross one leg over the other. Maybe later this afternoon I'll try calling my wife again. And then I'll call to see what's happening with my girlfriend. But I don't want to get her mouthy kid on the line. If I do call, I hope he'll be out somewhere doing whatever he does when he's not around the house. I try to remember if I ever read any Jack London books. I can't remember. But there was a story of his I read in high school. "To Build a Fire," it was called. This guy in the Yukon is freezing. Imagine it—he's actually going to freeze to death if he can't get a fire going. With a fire, he can dry his socks and things and warm himself.

He gets his fire going, but then something happens to it. A branchful of snow drops on it. It goes out. Meanwhile, it's getting colder. Night is coming on.

I bring some change out of my pocket. I'll try my wife first. If she answers, I'll wish her a Happy New Year. But that's it. I won't bring up business. I won't raise my voice. Not even if she starts something. She'll ask me where I'm calling from, and I'll have to tell her. I won't say anything about New Year's resolutions. There's no way to make a joke out of this. After I talk to her, I'll call my girlfriend. Maybe I'll call her first. I'll just have to hope I don't get her kid on the line. "Hello, sugar," I'll say when she answers. "It's me."

[1983]

Questions

1. Is Carver's story guilty of the sentimentality John Gardner warned him about?
2. What is the theme of Carver's story?
3. Of what importance are the several references to Jack London and his work?
4. Why is so much space devoted to J. P.'s story?

John Cheever
(1912–1982)
United States

By the time of his death in 1982, John Cheever had not only earned the title of master storyteller but also created such a timeless milieu for his characters that critics commonly referred to it as Cheever Country. Broadly defined as the suburban communities in Connecticut north of New York City, the upper middle class, and sometimes even the rich, Cheever Country is typified by characters who appear to have reached a stage of complacency in their lives. They are bored with their jobs, their spouses, their friends, and above all with their comfortable life-styles. Their lives bear enough of a similarity to the characters in the works of Anton Chekhov that John Leonard once called Cheever "the Chekhov of the suburbs."

Cheever began publishing when he was 17, when The New Republic accepted his first story. Shortly thereafter, his stories appeared in The New Yorker, where they were published with such frequency that they helped define the kind of fiction often associated with the magazine. His first collection of stories, The Way Some People Live, was published in 1942. By the time he won the Pulitzer Prize for The Stories of John Cheever in 1978, Cheever had published 10 volumes of stories and four novels: The Wapshot Chronicle (1957), The Wapshot Scandal (1964), Bullet Park (1969), and Falconer (1977). One final novel appeared during the year of his death: Oh, What a Paradise It Seems (1982).

Cheever's accomplishment as a writer of short stories is best summed up by another writer, John Gardner, who said: "Cheever is one of the few living novelists who might qualify as true artists." Responding to his own question of who reads short stories, Cheever (in "Why I Write Short Stories" [1978]) gave the following reply:

> I like to think that they are read by men and women in the dentist's office, waiting to be called to the chair; they are read on transcontinental plane trips instead of watching a banal and vulgar film spin out the time between our coasts; they are read by discerning and well-informed men and women who seem to feel that narrative fiction can contribute to our understanding of one another and the sometimes bewildering world around us.

THE SWIMMER

It was one of those midsummer Sundays when everyone sits around saying, "I *drank* too much last night." You might have heard it whispered by the parishioners leaving church, heard it from the lips of the priest himself, struggling with his cassock in the *vestiarium*, heard it from the golf links and the tennis courts, heard it from the wildlife preserve where the leader of the Audubon group was suffering from a terrible hangover. "I *drank* too much," said Donald Westerhazy. "We all *drank* too much," said Lucinda Merrill. "It must have been the wine," said Helen Westerhazy. "I *drank* too much of that claret."

This was the edge of the Westerhazy's pool. The pool, fed by an artesian well with a high iron content, was a pale shade of green. It was a fine day. In the west there was a massive stand of cumulus cloud so like a city seen from a distance—from the bow of an approaching ship—that it might have had a name. Lisbon. Hackensack. The sun was hot. Neddy Merrill sat by the green water, one hand in it, one around a glass of gin. He was a slender man—he seemed to have the especial slenderness of youth— and while he was far from young he had slid down his banister that morning and given the bronze backside of Aphrodite on the hall table a smack, as he jogged to- ward the smell of coffee in his dining room. He might have been compared to a sum- mer's day,[1] particularly the last hours of one, and while he lacked a tennis racket or a sail bag the impression was definitely one of youth, sport, and clement weather. He had been swimming and now he was breathing deeply, stertorously as if he could gulp into his lungs the components of that moment, the heat of the sun, the intenseness of his pleasure. It all seemed to flow into his chest. His own house stood in Bullet Park, eight miles to the south, where his four beautiful daughters would have had their lunch and might be playing tennis. Then it occurred to him that by taking a dogleg to the southwest he could reach his home by water.

His life was not confining and the delight he took in this observation could not be explained by its suggestion of escape. He seemed to see, with a cartographer's eye, that string of swimming pools, that quasi-subterranean stream that curved across the country. He had made a discovery, a contribution to modern geography; he would name the stream Lucinda after his wife. He was not a practical joker nor was he a fool but he was determinedly original and had a vague and modest idea of himself as a leg- endary figure. The day was beautiful and it seemed to him that a long swim might en- large and celebrate its beauty.

He took off a sweater that was hung over his shoulders and dove in. He had an in- explicable contempt for men who did not hurl themselves into pools. He swam a choppy crawl, breathing either with every stroke or every fourth stroke and count- ing somewhere well in the back of his mind the one-two one-two of a flutter kick. It was not a serviceable stroke for long distances but the domestication of swimming had saddled the sport with some customs and in his part of the world a crawl was cus- tomary. To be embraced and sustained by the light green water was less a pleasure, it seemed, than the resumption of a natural condition, and he would have liked to swim without trunks, but this was not possible, considering his project. He hoisted himself up on the far curb—he never used the ladder—and started across the lawn. When Lu- cinda asked where he was going he said he was going to swim home.

The only maps and charts he had to go by were remembered or imaginary but these were clear enough. First there were the Grahams, the Hammers, the Lears, the Howlands, and the Crosscups. He would cross Ditmar Street to the Bunkers and come, after a short portage, to the Levys, the Welchers, and the public pool in Lan- caster. Then there were the Hallorans, the Sachses, the Biswangers, Shirley Adams, the Gilmartins, and the Clydes. The day was lovely, and that he lived in a world so generously supplied with water seemed like a clemency, a beneficence. His heart was

---

[1] *compared to a summer's day*   A reference to Shakespeare's Sonnet 18.

high and he ran across the grass. Making his way home by an uncommon route gave him the feeling that he was a pilgrim, an explorer, a man with a destiny, and he knew that he would find friends all along the way; friends would line the banks of the Lucinda River.

He went through a hedge that separated the Westerhazys' land from the Grahams', walked under some flowering apple trees, passed the shed that housed their pump and filter, and came out at the Grahams' pool. "Why, Neddy," Mrs. Graham said, "what a marvelous surprise. I've been trying to get you on the phone all morning. Here, let me get you a drink." He saw then, like any explorer, that the hospitable customs and traditions of the natives would have to be handled with diplomacy if he was ever going to reach his destination. He did not want to mystify or seem rude to the Grahams nor did he have the time to linger there. He swam the length of their pool and joined them in the sun and was rescued, a few minutes later, by the arrival of two carloads of friends from Connecticut. During the uproarious reunions he was able to slip away. He went down by the front of the Grahams' house, stepped over a thorny hedge, and crossed a vacant lot to the Hammers'. Mrs. Hammer, looking up from her roses, saw him swim by although she wasn't quite sure who it was. The Lears heard him splashing past the open windows of their living room. The Howlands and the Crosscups were away. After leaving the Howlands' he crossed Ditmar Street and started for the Bunkers', where he could hear, even at that distance, the noise of a party.

The water refracted the sound of voices and laughter and seemed to suspend it in midair. The Bunkers' pool was on a rise and he climbed some stairs to a terrace where twenty-five or thirty men and women were drinking. The only person in the water was Rusty Towers, who floated there on a rubber raft. Oh, how bonny and lush were the banks of the Lucinda River! Prosperous men and women gathered by the sapphire-colored waters while caterer's men in white coats passed them cold gin. Overhead a red de Haviland trainer was circling around and around and around in the sky with something like the glee of a child in a swing. Ned felt a passing affection for the scene, a tenderness for the gathering, as if it was something he might touch. In the distance he heard thunder. As soon as Enid Bunker saw him she began to scream: "Oh, look who's here! What a marvelous surprise! When Lucinda said you couldn't come I thought I'd *die*." She made her way to him through the crowd, and when they had finished kissing she led him to the bar, a progress that was slowed by the fact that he stopped to kiss eight or ten other women and shake the hands of as many men. A smiling bartender he had seen at a hundred parties gave him a gin and tonic and he stood by the bar for a moment, anxious not to get stuck in any conversation that would delay this voyage. When he seemed about to be surrounded he dove in and swam close to the side to avoid colliding with Rusty's raft. At the far end of the pool he bypassed the Tomlinsons with a broad smile and jogged up the garden path. The gravel cut his feet but this was only unpleasantness. The party was confined to the pool, and as he went toward the house he heard the brilliant, watery sound of voices fade, heard the noise of a radio from the Bunkers' kitchen, where someone was listening to a ball game. Sunday afternoon. He made his way through the parked cars and down the grassy border of their driveway to Alewives Lane. He did not want to be seen on the road in his bathing trunks but there was no traffic and he made the short distance to the Levys' driveway, marked with a PRIVATE PROPERTY sign and a green tube for *The New York Times*. All the doors and windows of the big house were open but there were no signs of life; not even a dog barked. He went around the side of the house to the pool and saw that the Levys had only recently left. Glasses and bottles and dishes of nuts were on a table at the deep end, where there was a bath-house or gazebo, hung with Japanese lanterns. After swimming the pool he got himself a glass and poured a drink. It was his fourth or fifth drink and he had swum nearly half the length of the Lucinda River. He felt tired, clean, and pleased at that moment to be alone; pleased with everything.

It would storm. The stand of cumulus cloud—that city—had risen and darkened, and while he sat there he heard the percussiveness of thunder again. The de Haviland trainer was still circling overhead and it seemed to Ned that he could almost hear the pilot laugh with pleasure in the afternoon; but when there was another peal of thunder he took off for home. A train whistle blew and he wondered what time it had gotten to be. Four? Five? He thought of the provincial station at that hour, where a waiter, his tuxedo concealed by a raincoat, a dwarf with some flowers wrapped in newspaper, and a woman who had been crying would be waiting for the local. It was suddenly growing dark; it was that moment when the pin-headed birds seemed to organize their song into some acute and knowledgeable recognition of the storm's approach. Then there was a fine noise of rushing water from the crown of an oak at his back, as if a spigot there had been turned. Then the noise of fountains came from the crowns of all the tall trees. Why did he love storms, what was the meaning of his excitement when the door sprang open and the rain wind fled rudely up the stairs, why had the simple task of shutting the windows of an old house seemed fitting and urgent, why did the first watery notes of a storm wind have for him the unmistakable sound of good news, cheer, glad tidings? Then there was an explosion, a smell of cordite, and rain lashed the Japanese lanterns that Mrs. Levy had bought in Kyoto the year before last, or was it the year before that?

He stayed in the Levy's gazebo until the storm had passed. The rain had cooled the air and he shivered. The force of the wind had stripped a maple of its red and yellow leaves and scattered them over the grass and the water. Since it was midsummer the tree must be blighted, and yet he felt a peculiar sadness at this sign of autumn. He braced his shoulders, emptied his glass, and started for the Welchers' pool. This meant crossing the Lindleys' riding ring and he was surprised to find it overgrown with grass and all the jumps dismantled. He wondered if the Lindleys had sold their horses or gone away for the summer and put them out to board. He seemed to remember having heard something about the Lindleys and their horses but the memory was unclear. On he went, barefoot through the wet grass, to the Welchers', where he found their pool was dry.

This breach in his chain of water disappointed him absurdly, and he felt like some explorer who seeks a torrential headwater and finds a dead stream. He was disappointed and mystified. It was common enough to go away for the summer but no one ever drained his pool. The Welchers had definitely gone away. The pool furniture was folded, stacked, and covered with a tarpaulin. The bathhouse was locked. All the windows of the house were shut, and when he went around to the driveway in front he saw a FOR SALE sign nailed to a tree. When had he last heard from the Welchers—when, that is, had he and Lucinda last regretted an invitation to dine with them? It seemed only a week or so ago. Was his memory failing or had he so disciplined it in the repression of unpleasant facts that he had damaged his sense of the truth? Then in the distance he heard the sound of a tennis game. This cheered him, cleared away all his apprehensions and let him regard the overcast sky and the cold air with indifference. This was the day that Neddy Merrill swam across the country. That was the day! He started off then for his most difficult portage.

Had you gone for a Sunday afternoon ride that day you might have seen him, close to naked, standing on the shoulders of Route 424, waiting for a chance to cross. You might have wondered if he was the victim of foul play, had his car broken down, or was he merely a fool. Standing barefoot in the deposits of the highway—beer cans, rags, and blowout patches—exposed to all kinds of ridicule, he seemed pitiful. He had known when he started that this was a part of his journey—it had been on his maps—but confronted with the lines of traffic, worming through the summery light, he found himself unprepared. He was laughed at, jeered at, a beer can was thrown at him, and he had no dignity or humor to bring to the situation. He could have gone back, back to the Westerhazys', where Lucinda would still be sitting in the sun. He had signed nothing, vowed nothing, pledged nothing, not even to himself. Why, believing as he did, that all human obduracy was susceptible to common sense, was he unable to turn back? Why was he determined to complete his journey even if it meant putting his life in danger? At what point had this prank, this joke, this piece of horseplay become serious? He could not go back, he could not even recall with any clearness the green water at the Westerhazys', the sense of inhaling the day's components, the friendly and relaxed voices saying that they had *drunk* too much. In the space of an hour, more or less, he had covered a distance that made his return impossible.

An old man, tooling down the highway at fifteen miles an hour, let him get to the middle of the road, where there was a grass divider. Here he was exposed to the ridicule of the northbound traffic, but after ten or fifteen minutes he was able to cross. From here he had only a short walk to the Recreation Center at the edge of the village of Lancaster, where there were some handball courts and a public pool.

The effect of the water on voices, the illusion of brilliance and suspense, was the same here as it had been at the Bunkers' but the sounds here were louder, harsher, and more shrill, and as soon as he entered the crowded enclosure he was confronted with regimentation. "ALL SWIMMERS MUST TAKE A SHOWER BEFORE USING THE POOL. ALL SWIMMERS MUST USE THE FOOTBATH. ALL SWIMMERS MUST WEAR THEIR IDENTIFICATION DISKS." He took a shower, washed his feet in a cloudy and bitter solution, and made his way to the edge of the water. It stank of chlorine and looked to him like a sink. A pair of lifeguards in a pair of towers blew police whistles at what seemed to be regular intervals and abused the swimmers through a public address system. Neddy remembered the sapphire water at the Bunkers' with longing and thought that he might contaminate himself—damage his own prosperousness and charm—by swimming in this murk, but he reminded himself that he was an explorer, a pilgrim, and that this was merely a stagnant bend in the Lucinda River. He dove, scowling with distaste, into the chlorine and had to swim with his head above water to avoid collisions, but even so he was bumped into, splashed, and jostled. When he got to the shallow end both lifeguards were shouting at him: "Hey, you, you without the identification disk, get outa the water." He did, but they had no way of pursuing him and he went through the reek of suntan oil and chlorine out through the hurricane fence and passed the handball courts. By crossing the road he entered the wooded part of the Halloran estate. The woods were not cleared and the footing was treacherous and difficult until he reached the lawn and the clipped beech hedge that encircled their pool.

The Hallorans were friends, an elderly couple of enormous wealth who seemed to bask in the suspicion that they might be Communists. They were zealous reformers but they were not Communists, and yet when they were accused, as they sometimes were, of subversion, it seemed to gratify and excite them. Their beech hedge was yellow and he guessed this had been blighted like the Levys' maple. He called hullo, hullo, to warn the Hallorans of his approach, to palliate his invasion of their privacy. The Hallorans, for reasons that had never been explained to him, did not wear bathing suits. No explanations were in order, really. Their nakedness was a detail in their uncompromising zeal for reform and he stepped politely out of his trunks before he went through the opening in the hedge.

Mrs. Halloran, a stout woman with white hair and a serene face, was reading the *Times*. Mr. Halloran was taking beech leaves out of the water with a scoop. They seemed not surprised or displeased to see him. Their pool was perhaps the oldest in the country, a fieldstone rectangle, fed by a brook. It had no filter or pump and its waters were the opaque gold of the stream.

"I'm swimming across the county," Ned said.

"Why, I didn't know one could," exclaimed Mrs. Halloran.

"Well, I've made it from the Westerhazys'," Ned said. "That must be about four miles."

He left his trunks at the deep end, walked to the shallow end, and swam this stretch. As he was pulling himself out of the water he heard Mrs. Halloran say, "We've been *terribly* sorry to hear about all your misfortunes, Neddy."

"My misfortunes?" Ned asked. "I don't know what you mean."

"Why we hard that you'd sold the house and that your poor children. . . ."

"I don't recall having sold the house," Ned said, "and the girls are at home."

"Yes," Mrs. Halloran sighed. "Yes. . . ." Her voice filled the air with an unseasonable melancholy and Ned spoke briskly. "Thank you for the swim."

"Well, have a nice trip," said Mrs. Halloran.

Beyond the hedge he pulled on his trunks and fastened them. They were loose and he wondered if, during the space of an afternoon, he could have lost some weight. He was cold and he was tired and the naked Hallorans and their dark water had depressed him. The swim was too much for his strength but how could he have guessed this, sliding down the banister that morning and sitting in the Westerhazys' sun? His arms were lame. His legs felt rubbery and ached at the joints. The worst of it was the cold in his bones and the feeling that he might never be warm again. Leaves were falling down around him and he smelled wood smoke on the wind. Who would be burning wood at this time of the year?

He needed a drink. Whiskey would warm him, pick him up, carry him through the last of his journey, refresh his feeling that it was original and valorous to swim across the county. Channel swimmers took brandy. He needed a stimulant. He crossed the lawn in front of the Hallorans' house and went down a little path to where they had built a house for their only daughter, Helen, and her husband, Eric Sachs. The Sachses' pool was small and he found Helen and her husband there.

"Oh, *Neddy*," Helen said. "Did you lunch at Mother's?"

"Not *really*," Ned said. "I *did* stop to see your parents." This seemed to be explanation enough. "I'm terribly sorry to break in on you like this but I've taken a chill and I wonder if you'd give me a drink."

"Why, I'd *love* to," Helen said, "but there hasn't been anything in this house to drink since Eric's operation. That was three years ago."

Was he losing his memory, had his gift for concealing painful facts let him forget that he had sold his house, that his children were in trouble, and that his friend had been ill? His eyes slipped from Eric's face to his abdomen, where he saw three pale, sutured scars, two of them at least a foot long. Gone was his navel, and what, Neddy

thought, would the roving hand, bed-checking one's gifts at 3 A.M., make of a belly
with no navel, no link to birth, this breach in the succession?

"I'm sure you can get a drink at the Biswangers'," Helen said. "They're having an
enormous do. You can hear it from here. Listen!"

She raised her head and from across the road, the lawns, the gardens, the woods,
the fields, he heard again the brilliant noise of voices over water. "Well, I'll get wet,"
he said, still feeling that he had no freedom of choice about his means of travel. He
dove into the Sachses' cold water, and gasping, close to drowning, made his way from
one end of the pool to the other. "Lucinda and I want *terribly* to see you," he said
over his shoulder, his face set toward the Biswangers'. "We're sorry it's been so long
and we'll call you *very* soon."

He crossed some fields to the Biswangers' and the sounds of revelry there. They
would be honored to give him a drink, they would be happy to give him a drink. The
Biswangers invited him and Lucinda for dinner four times a year, six weeks in advance.
They were always rebuffed and yet they continued to send out their invitations, unwilling to comprehend the rigid and undemocratic realities of their society. They were
the sort of people who discussed the price of things at cocktails, exchanged market tips
during dinner, and after dinner told dirty stories to mixed company. They did not belong to Neddy's set—they were not even on Lucinda's Christmas card list. He went toward the their pool with feelings of indifference, charity, and some unease, since it
seemed to be getting dark and these were the longest days of the year. The party when
he joined it was noisy and large. Grace Biswanger was the kind of hostess who asked
the optometrist, the veterinarian, the real-estate dealer, and the dentist. No one was
swimming and the twilight, reflected on the water of the pool, had a wintry gleam.
There was a bar and he started for this. When Grace Biswanger saw him she came toward him, not affectionately as he had every right to expect, but bellicosely.

"Why, this party has everything," she said loudly, "including a gate crasher."

She could not deal him a social blow—there was no question about this and he
did not flinch. "As a gate crasher," he asked politely, "do I rate a drink?"

"Suit yourself," she said. "You don't seem to pay much attention to invitations."

She turned her back on him and joined some guests, and he went to the bar and
ordered a whiskey. The bartender served him but he served him rudely. His was a
world in which the caterer's men kept the social score, and to be rebuffed by a part-
time barkeep meant that he had suffered some loss of social esteem. Or perhaps the
man was new and uninformed. Then he heard Grace at his back say: "They went for
broke overnight—nothing but income—and he showed up drunk one Sunday and
asked us to loan him five thousand dollars. . . ." She was always talking about money.
It was worse than eating your peas off a knife. He dove into the pool, swam its length,
and went away.

The next pool on his list, the last but two, belonged to his old mistress, Shirley
Adams. If he had suffered any injuries at the Biswangers' they would be cured here.
Love—sexual roughhouse in fact—was the supreme elixir, the pain killer, the brightly colored pill that would put the spring back into his step, the joy of life in his heart.
They had had an affair last week, last month, last year. He couldn't remember. It was
he who had broken it off, his was the upper hand, and he stepped through the gate
of the wall that surrounded her pool with nothing so considered as self-confidence.
It seemed in a way to be his pool, as the lover, particularly the illicit lover, enjoys the
possessions of his mistress with an authority unknown to holy matrimony. She was

there, her hair the color of brass, but her figure, at the edge of the lighted, cerulean water, excited in him no profound memories. It had been, he thought, a lighthearted affair, although she had wept when he broke it off. She seemed confused to see him and he wondered if she was still wounded. Would she, God forbid, weep again?

"What do you want?" she asked.

"I'm swimming across the county."

"Good Christ. Will you ever grow up?"

"What's the matter?"

"If you've come here for money," she said, "I won't give you another cent."

"You could give me a drink."

"I could but I won't. I'm not alone."

"Well, I'm on my way."

He dove in and swam the pool, but when he tried to haul himself up onto the curb he found that the strength in his arms and shoulders had gone, and he paddled to the ladder and climbed out. Looking over his shoulder he saw, in the lighted bathhouse, a young man. Going out onto the dark lawn he smelled chrysanthemums or marigolds—some stubborn autumnal fragrance—on the night air, strong as gas. Looking overhead he saw that the stars had come out, but why should he seem to see Andromeda, Cepheus, and Cassiopeia? What had become of the constellations of midsummer? He began to cry.

It was probably the first time in his adult life that he had ever cried, certainly the first time in his life that he had ever felt so miserable, cold, tired, and bewildered. He could not understand the rudeness of the caterer's barkeep or the rudeness of a mistress who had come to him on her knees and showered his trousers with tears. He had swum too long, he had been immersed too long, and his nose and his throat were sore from the water. What he needed then was drink, some company, and some clean, dry clothes, and while he could have cut directly across the road to his home he went on to the Gilmartins' pool. Here, for the first time in his life, he did not dive but went down the steps into the icy water and swam a hobbled sidestroke that he might have learned as a youth. He staggered with fatigue on his way to the Clydes' and paddled the length of their pool, stopping again and again with his hand on the curb to rest. He climbed up the ladder and wondered if he had the strength to get home. He had done what he wanted, he had swum the county, but he was so stupefied with exhaustion that his triumph seemed vague. Stooped, holding on to the gateposts for support, he turned up the driveway of his own house.

The place was dark. Was it so late that they had all gone to bed? Had Lucinda stayed at the Westerhazys' for supper? Had the girls joined her there or gone someplace else? Hadn't they agreed, as they usually did on Sunday, to regret all their invitations and stay at home? He tried the garage doors to see what cars were in but the doors were locked and rust came off the handles onto his hands. Going toward the house, he saw the force of the thunderstorm had knocked one of the rain gutters loose. It hung down over the front door like an umbrella rib, but it could be fixed in the morning. The house was locked, and he thought that the stupid cook or the stupid maid must have locked the place up until he remembered that it had been some time since they had employed a maid or a cook. He shouted, pounded on the door, tried to force it with his shoulder, and then, looking in at the windows, saw that the place was empty.

[1964]

Questions

1. To what extent is Neddy Merrill's "journey" a heroic one, comparable to that of the protagonists in classical epics and sagas? What are the specific stages of his journey? What are the obstacles he must overcome?
2. What social commentary is implicit in "The Swimmer"?
3. Does the swimming metaphor in Cheever's story bear any similarity to the one in Graham Swift's "Learning to Swim"?

Anton Chekhov

(1860–1904)

Russia

Anton Chekhov's enduring contribution to literature is based on both a body of dramatic works that revolutionized modern drama and an equally distinctive body of short fiction. As the grandson of a serf who bought his own freedom, and the son of an impoverished grocer, Chekhov was raised in humble circumstances in Taganrog, Russia. He began to write short fiction and humorous sketches to support his family while studying medicine at the University of Moscow. Although he practiced medicine, he soon determined that his real love was literature. He wrote prolifically, publishing nearly 800 short stories as well as 18 plays, many of which are justifiably termed classics: The Cherry Orchard, Three Sisters, Uncle Vanya, and The Seagull. Shortly after Chekhov's plays were translated into English in the early twentieth century, it was not unusual for half a dozen of them to be staged simultaneously in London theatres.

Chekhov was a true innovator in both forms in which he wrote. Less concerned about "plot" in the traditional sense, he focused on the nuances of feeling and circumstance to explore a broad palette of human emotions from pathos and loss to humor and absurdity; because he saw life as fundamentally plotless he chose to mirror that plotlessness rather than to impose a false shape on the experiences he explored. His view of social injustice is set against an indifferent universe—a moral perspective that exposed his distance from, if not disillusionment concerning, religious certainties. His fiction and drama are sometimes said to be written in a minor key because they often conclude without traditional resolutions. This modern sensibility, with its implications for literary form and meaning, was deeply influential for twentieth century writers in both fiction and drama. The modernist Virginia Woolf (whose own experiments in fiction owe a debt to Chekhov) wrote the following in her essay "The Russian Point of View":

> [Chekhov's stories] are inconclusive, we say, and proceed to frame a criticism based upon the assumption that stories ought to conclude in a way that we recognize. . . . [W]here the tune is unfamiliar and the end a note of interrogation or merely the information that they went on talking, . . . we need a very daring and alert sense of literature to make us hear the tune, and in particular those last notes which complete the harmony.

In Chekhov's view the function of literature was not to "solve problems" but to present those problems honestly to the reader. Chekhov wrote the following to another writer, Alexander Tikhonov:

> All I wanted was to say honestly to people: "Have a look at yourselves and see how bad and dreary your lives are!" The important thing is that people should realize that, for when they do, they will most certainly create another and better life for themselves.

In fact, Chekhov was a kind of doctor of spiritual ills; he diagnosed them, but he offered no cure.

Ironically, Chekhov contracted tuberculosis at the age of 29 and suffered poor health for much of his life. Although he was married to the Moscow Art Theatre's leading actress, Olga Knipper, the couple spent little time together because his poor health forced him to live in a warmer climate while she performed in Moscow. When he died at the age of 44, his body was transferred in a train car refrigerated for the shipment of oysters—an absurd circumstance that Chekhov might well have invented for one of his own stories.

THE KISS

At eight o'clock on the evening of the twentieth of May all the six batteries of the N____ Reserve Artillery Brigade halted for the night in the village of Mestechki on their way to camp. At the height of the general commotion, while some officers were busily occupied around the guns, and others, gathered together in the square near the church enclosure, were receiving the reports of the quartermasters, a man in civilian dress, riding a queer horse, came into sight round the church. The little dun-colored horse with a fine neck and a short tail came, moving not straight forward, but as it were sideways, with a sort of dance step, as though it were being lashed about the legs. When he reached the officers the man on the horse took off his hat and said:

"His Excellency Lieutenant-General von Rabbeck, a local landowner, invites the officers to have tea with him this minute. . . ."

The horse bowed, danced, and retired sideways; the rider raised his hat once more and in an instant disappeared with his strange horse behind the church.

"What the devil does it mean?" grumbled some of the officers, dispersing to their quarters. "One is sleepy, and here this von Rabbeck with his tea! We know what tea means."

The officers of all the six batteries remembered vividly an incident of the previous year, when during maneuvers they, together with the officers of a Cossack regiment, were in the same way invited to tea by a count who had an estate in the neighborhood and was a retired army officer; the hospitable and genial count made much of them, dined and wined them, refused to let them go to their quarters in the village, and made them stay the night. All that, of course, was very nice—nothing better could be desired, but the worst of it was, the old army officer was so carried away by the pleasure of the young men's company that till sunrise he was telling the officers anecdotes of his glorious past, taking them over the house, showing them expensive pictures, old engravings, rare guns, reading them autograph letters from great people, while the weary and exhausted officers looked and listened, longing for their beds and yawning in their sleeves; when at last their host let them go, it was too late for sleep.

Might not this von Rabbeck be just such another? Whether he were or not, there was no help for it. The officers changed their uniforms, brushed themselves, and went all together in search of the gentleman's house. In the square by the church they were told they could get to his Excellency's by the lower road—going down behind the church to the river, walking along the bank to the garden, and there the alleys would take them to the house; or by the upper way—straight from the church by the road which, half a mile from the village, led right up to his Excellency's barns. The officers decided to go by the upper road.

"Which von Rabbeck is it?" they wondered on the way. "Surely not the one who was in command of the N_____ cavalry division at Plevna?"

"No, that was not von Rabbeck, but simply Rabbe and no 'von.'"

"What lovely weather!"

At the first of the barns the road divided in two: one branch went straight on and vanished in the evening darkness, the other led to the owner's house on the right. The officers turned to the right and began to speak more softly. . . . On both sides of the road stretched stone barns with red roofs, heavy and sullen-looking, very much like barracks in a district town. Ahead of them gleamed the windows of the manor house.

"A good omen, gentlemen," said one of the officers. "Our setter leads the way; no doubt he scents game ahead of us! . . ."

Lieutenant Lobytko, who was walking in front, a tall and stalwart fellow, though entirely without mustache (he was over twenty-five, yet for some reason there was no sign of hair on his round, well-fed face), renowned in the brigade for his peculiar ability to divine the presence of women at a distance, turned round and said:

"Yes, there must be women here; I feel that by instinct."

On the threshold the officers were met by von Rabbeck himself, a comely looking man of sixty in civilian dress. Shaking hands with his guests, he said that he was very glad and happy to see them, but begged them earnestly for God's sake to excuse him for not asking them to stay the night; two sisters with their children, his brothers, and some neighbors, had come on a visit to him, so that he had not one spare room left.

The General shook hands with everyone, made his apologies, and smiled, but it was evident by his face that he was by no means so delighted as last year's count, and that he had invited the officers simply because, in his opinion, it was a social obligation. And the officers themselves, as they walked up the softly carpeted stairs, as they listened to him, felt that they had been invited to his house simply because it would have been awkward not to invite them; and at the sight of the footmen, who hastened to light the lamps at the entrance below and in the anteroom above, they began to feel as though they had brought uneasiness and discomfort into the house with them. In a house in which two sisters and their children, brothers, and neighbors were gathered together, probably on account of some family festivity or event, how could the presence of nineteen unknown officers possibly be welcome?

Upstairs at the entrance to the drawing room the officers were met by a tall, graceful old lady with black eyebrows and a long face, very much like the Empress Eugénie. Smiling graciously and majestically, she said she was glad and happy to see her guests, and apologized that her husband and she were on this occasion unable to invite *messieurs les officiers*[1] to stay the night. From her beautiful majestic smile, which instantly vanished from her face every time she turned away from her guests, it was evident that she had seen numbers of officers in her day, that she was in no humor for them now, and if she invited them to her house and apologized for not doing more, it was only because her breeding and position in society required it of her.

---

[1]*messieurs les officiers* French: the honorable officers.

When the officers went into the big dining-room, there were about a dozen people, men and ladies, young and old, sitting at tea at the end of a long table. A group of men wrapped in a haze of cigar smoke was dimly visible behind their chairs; in the midst of them stood a lanky young man with red whiskers, talking loudly in English, with a burr. Through a door beyond the group could be seen a light room with pale blue furniture.

"Gentlemen, there are so many of you that it is impossible to introduce you all!" said the General in a loud voice, trying to sound very gay. "Make each other's acquaintance, gentlemen, without any ceremony!"

The officers—some with very serious and even stern faces, others with forced smiles, and all feeling extremely awkward—somehow made their bows and sat down to tea.

The most ill at ease of them all was Ryabovich—a short, somewhat stooped officer in spectacles, with whiskers like a lynx's. While some of his comrades assumed a serious expression, while others wore forced smiles, his face, his lynx-like whiskers, and spectacles seemed to say, "I am the shyest, most modest, and most undistinguished officer in the whole brigade!" At first, on going into the room and later, sitting down at table, he could not fix his attention on any one face or object. The faces, the dresses, the cut-glass decanters of brandy, the steam from the glasses, the molded cornices—all blended in one general impression that inspired in Ryabovich alarm and a desire to hide his head. Like a lecturer making his first appearance before the public, he saw everything that was before his eyes, but apparently only had a dim understanding of it (among physiologists this condition, when the subject sees but does not understand, is called "mental blindness"). After a little while, growing accustomed to his surroundings, Ryabovich regained his sight and began to observe. As a shy man, unused to society, what struck him first was that in which he had always been deficient—namely, the extraordinary boldness of his new acquaintances. Von Rabbeck, his wife, two elderly ladies, a young lady in a lilac dress, and the young man with the red whiskers, who was, it appeared, a younger son of von Rabbeck, very cleverly, as though they had rehearsed it beforehand, took seats among the officers, and at once got up a heated discussion in which the visitors could not help taking part. The lilac young lady hotly asserted that the artillery had a much better time than the cavalry and the infantry, while von Rabbeck and the elderly ladies maintained the opposite. A brisk interchange followed. Ryabovich looked at the lilac young lady who argued so hotly about what was unfamiliar and utterly uninteresting to her, and watched artificial smiles come and go on her face.

Von Rabbeck and his family skillfully drew the officers into the discussion, and meanwhile kept a sharp eye on their glasses and mouths, to see whether all of them were drinking, whether all had enough sugar, why someone was not eating cakes or not drinking brandy. And the longer Ryabovich watched and listened, the more he was attracted by this insincere but splendidly disciplined family.

After tea the officers went into the drawing-room. Lieutenant Lobytko's instinct had not deceived him. There were a great many girls and young married ladies. The "setter" lieutenant was soon standing by a very young blonde in a black dress, and, bending over her jauntily, as though leaning on an unseen sword, smiled and twitched his shoulders coquettishly. He probably talked very interesting nonsense, for the blonde looked at his well-fed face condescendingly and asked indifferently, "Really?" And from that indifferent "Really?" the "setter," had he been intelligent, might have concluded that she would never call him to heel.

The piano struck up; the melancholy strains of a waltz floated out of the wide open windows, and everyone, for some reason, remembered that it was spring, a May evening. Everyone was conscious of the fragrance of roses, of lilac, and of the young leaves of the poplar. Ryabovich, who felt the brandy he had drunk, under the influence of the music stole a glance towards the window, smiled, and began watching the movements of the women, and it seemed to him that the smell of roses, of poplars, and lilac came not from the garden, but from the ladies' faces and dresses.

Von Rabbeck's son invited a scraggy-looking young lady to dance and waltzed round the room twice with her. Lobytko, gliding over the parquet floor, flew up to the lilac young lady and whirled her away. Dancing began. . . . Ryabovich stood near the door among those who were not dancing and looked on. He had never once danced in his whole life, and he had never once in his life put his arm round the waist of a respectable woman. He was highly delighted that a man should in the sight of all take a girl he did not know round the waist and offer her his shoulder to put her hand on, but he could not imagine himself in the position of such a man. There were times when he envied the boldness and swagger of his companions and was inwardly wretched; the knowledge that he was timid, round-shouldered, and uninteresting, that he had a long waist and lynx-like whiskers deeply mortified him, but with years he had grown used to this feeling, and now, looking at his comrades dancing or loudly talking, he no longer envied them, but only felt touched and mournful.

When the quadrille began, young von Rabbeck came up to those who were not dancing and invited two officers to have a game at billiards. The officers accepted and went with him out of the drawing room. Ryabovich, having nothing to do and wishing to take at least some part in the general movement, slouched after them. From the big drawing room they went into the little drawing room, then into a narrow corridor with a glass roof, and thence into a room in which on their entrance three sleepy-looking footmen jumped up quickly from couches. At last, after passing through a long succession of rooms, young von Rabbeck and the officers came into a small room where there was a billiard table. They began to play.

Ryabovich, who had never played any game but cards, stood near the billiard table and looked indifferently at the players, while they in unbuttoned coats, with cues in their hands, stepped about, made puns, and kept shouting out unintelligible words.

The players took no notice of him, and only now and then one of them, shoving him with his elbow or accidentally touching him with his cue, would turn round and say "*Pardon!*" Before the first game was over he was weary of it, and began to feel that he was not wanted and in the way. . . . He felt disposed to return to the drawing-room and he went out.

On his way back he met with a little adventure. When he had gone half-way he noticed that he had taken a wrong turning. He distinctly remembered that he ought to meet three sleepy footmen on his way, but he had passed five or six rooms, and those sleepy figures seemed to have been swallowed up by the earth. Noticing his mistake, he walked back a little way and turned to the right; he found himself in a little room which was in semidarkness and which he had not seen on his way to the billiard room. After standing there a little while, he resolutely opened the first door that met his eyes and walked into an absolutely dark room. Straight ahead could be seen the crack in the doorway through which came a gleam of vivid light; from the other side of the door came the muffled sound of a melancholy mazurka. Here, too, as in the drawing-room, the windows were wide open and there was a smell of poplars, lilac, and roses. . . .

Ryabovich stood still in hesitation. . . . At that moment, to his surprise, he heard hurried footsteps and the rustling of a dress, a breathless feminine voice whispered "At last!" and two soft, fragrant, unmistakably feminine arms were clasped about his neck; a warm cheek was pressed against his, and simultaneously there was the sound of a kiss. But at once the bestower of the kiss uttered a faint shriek and sprang away from him, as it seemed to Ryabovich, with disgust. He, too, almost shrieked and rushed towards the gleam of light at the door. . . .

When he returned to the drawing-room his heart was palpitating and his hands were trembling so noticeably that he made haste to hide them behind his back. At first he was tormented by shame and dread that the whole drawing-room knew that he had just been kissed and embraced by a woman. He shrank into himself and looked uneasily about him, but as he became convinced that people were dancing and talking as calmly as ever, he gave himself up entirely to the new sensation which he had never experienced before in his life. Something strange was happening to him. . . . His neck, round which soft, fragrant arms had so lately been clasped, seemed to him to be anointed with oil; on his left cheek near his mustache where the unknown had kissed him there was a faint chilly tingling sensation as from peppermint drops, and the more he rubbed the place the more distinct was the chilly sensation; all of him, from head to foot, was full of a strange new feeling which grew stronger and stronger. . . . He wanted to dance, to talk, to run into the garden, to laugh aloud. . . . He quite forgot that he was round-shouldered and uninteresting, that he had lynx-like whiskers and an "undistinguished appearance" (that was how his appearance had been described by some ladies whose conversation he had accidentally overheard). When von Rabbeck's wife happened to pass by him, he gave her such a broad and friendly smile that she stood still and looked at him inquiringly.

"I like your house immensely!" he said, setting his spectacles straight.

The General's wife smiled and said that the house had belonged to her father; then she asked whether his parents were living, whether he had long been in the army, why he was so thin, and so on. . . . After receiving answers to her questions, she went on, and after his conversation with her his smiles were more friendly than ever, and he thought he was surrounded by splendid people. . . .

At supper Ryabovich ate mechanically everything offered him, drank, and without listening to anything, tried to understand what had just happened to him. . . . The adventure was of a mysterious and romantic character, but it was not difficult to explain it. No doubt some girl or young married lady had arranged a tryst with some man in the dark room; had waited a long time, and being nervous and excited had taken Ryabovich for her hero; this was the more probable as Ryabovich had stood still hesitating in the dark room, so that he, too, had looked like a person waiting for something. . . . This was how Ryabovich explained to himself the kiss he had received.

"And who is she?" he wondered, looking round at the women's faces. "She must be young, for elderly ladies don't arrange rendezvous. That she was a lady, one could tell by the rustle of her dress her perfume, her voice. . . ."

His eyes rested on the lilac young lady, and he thought her very attractive; she had beautiful shoulders and arms, a clever face, and a delightful voice. Ryabovich, looking at her, hoped that she and no one else was his unknown. . . . But she laughed somehow artificially and wrinkled up her long nose, which seemed to him to make her look old. Then he turned his eyes upon the blonde in a black dress. She was younger, simpler, and more genuine, had a charming brow, and drank very daintily out of her wineglass. Ryabovich now hoped that it was she. But soon he began to think her face flat, and fixed his eyes upon the one next her.

"It's difficult to guess," he thought, musing. "If one were to take only the shoulders and arms of the lilac girl, add the brow of the blonde and the eyes of the one on the left of Lobytko, then . . ."

He made a combination of these things in his mind and so formed the image of the girl who had kissed him, the image that he desired but could not find at the table. . . .

After supper, replete and exhilarated, the officers began to take leave and say thank you. Van Rabbeck and his wife began again apologizing that they could not ask them to stay the night.

"Very, very glad to have met you, gentlemen," said von Rabbeck, and this time sincerely (probably because people are far more sincere and good-humored at speeding their parting guests than on meeting them). "Delighted. Come again on your way back! Don't stand on ceremony! Where are you going? Do you want to go by the upper way? No, go across the garden; it's nearer by the lower road."

The officers went out into the garden. After the bright light and the noise the garden seemed very dark and quiet. They walked in silence all the way to the gate. They were a little drunk, in good spirits, and contented, but the darkness and silence made them thoughtful for a minute. Probably the same idea occurred to each one of them as to Ryabovich: would there ever come a time for them when, like von Rabbeck, they would have a large house, a family, a garden—when they, too, would be able to welcome people, even though insincerely, feed them, make them drunk and contented?

Going out of the garden gate, they all began talking at once and laughing loudly about nothing. They were walking now along the little path that led down to the river and then ran along the water's edge, winding round the bushes on the bank, the gulleys, and the willows that overhung the water. The bank and the path were scarcely visible, and the other bank was entirely plunged in darkness. Stars were reflected here and there in the dark water; they quivered and were broken up—and from that alone it could be seen that the river was flowing rapidly. It was still. Drowsy sandpipers cried plaintively on the farther bank, and in one of the bushes on the hither side a nightingale was trilling loudly, taking no notice of the crowd of officers. The officers stood round the bush, touched it, but the nightingale went on singing.

"What a fellow!" they exclaimed approvingly. "We stand beside him and he takes not a bit of notice! What a rascal!"

At the end of the way the path went uphill, and, skirting the church enclosure, led into the road. Here the officers, tired with walking uphill, sat down and lighted their cigarettes. On the farther bank of the river a murky red fire came into sight, and having nothing better to do, they spent a long time in discussing whether it was a camp fire or a light in a window, or something else. . . . Ryabovich, too, looked at the light, and he fancied that the light looked and winked at him, as though it knew about the kiss.

On reaching his quarters, Ryabovich undressed as quickly as possible and got into bed. Lobytko and Lieutenant Merzlyakov—a peaceable, silent fellow, who was considered in his own circle a highly educated officer, and was always, whenever it was possible, reading *The Messenger of Europe*, which he carried about with him everywhere—were quartered in the same cottage with Ryabovich. Lobytko undressed, walked up and down the room for a long while with the air of a man who has not been satisfied, and sent his orderly for beer. Merzlyakov got into bed, put a candle by his pillow and plunged into *The Messenger of Europe*.

"Who was she?" Ryabovich wondered, looking at the sooty ceiling.

His neck still felt as though he had been anointed with oil, and there was still the chilly sensation near his mouth as though from peppermint drops. The shoulders and arms of the young lady in lilac, the brow and the candid eyes of the blonde in black, waists, dresses, and brooches, floated through his imagination. He tried to fix his attention on these images, but they danced about, broke up and flickered. When these images vanished altogether from the broad dark background which everyone sees when he closes his eyes, he began to hear hurried footsteps, the rustle of skirts, the sound of a kiss—and an intense baseless joy took possession of him. . . . Abandoning himself to this joy, he heard the orderly return and announce that there was no beer. Lobytko was terribly indignant, and began pacing up and down the room again.

"Well, isn't he an idiot?" he kept saying, stopping first before Ryabovich and then before Merzlyakov. "What a food and a blockhead a man must be not to get hold of any beer! Eh? Isn't he a blackguard?"

"Of course you can't get beer here," said Merzlyakov, not removing his eyes from *The Messenger of Europe*.

"Oh! Is that your opinion?" Lobytko persisted. "Lord have mercy upon us, if you dropped me on the moon I'd find you beer and women directly! I'll go and find some at once. . . . You may call me a rascal if I don't!"

He spent a long time in dressing and pulling on his high boots, then finished smoking his cigarette in silence and went out.

"Rabbeck, Grabbeck, Labbeck," he muttered, stopping in the outer room. "I don't care to go alone, damn it all! Ryabovich, wouldn't you like to go for a walk? Eh?"

Receiving no answer, he returned, slowly undressed, and got into bed. Merzlyakov sighed, put *The Messenger of Europe* away, and extinguished the light.

"H'm! . . ." muttered Lobytko, lighting a cigarette in the dark.

Ryabovich pulled the bedclothes over his head, curled himself up in bed, and tried to gather together the flashing images in his mind and to combine them into a whole. But nothing came of it. He soon fell asleep, and his last thought was that someone had caressed him and made him happy—that something extraordinary, foolish, but joyful and delightful, had come into his life. The thought did not leave him even in his sleep.

When he woke up the sensations of oil on his neck and the chill of peppermint about his lips had gone, but joy flooded his heart just as the day before. He looked enthusiastically at the window-frames, gilded by the light of the rising sun, and listened to the movement of the passers-by in the street. People were talking loudly close to the window. Lebedetzky, the commander of Ryabovich's battery, who had only just overtaken the brigade, was talking to his sergeant at the top of his voice, having lost the habit of speaking in ordinary tones.

"What else?" shouted the commander.

"When they were shoeing the horses yesterday, your Honor, they injured Pigeon's hoof with a nail. The vet put on clay and vinegar; they are leading him apart now. Also, your Honor, Artemyev got drunk yesterday, and the lieutenant ordered him to be put in the limber of a spare gun-carriage."

The sergeant reported that Karpov had forgotten the new cords for the trumpets and the pegs for the tents, and that their Honors the officers had spent the previous evening visiting General von Rabbeck. In the middle of this conversation the red-bearded face of Lebedetzky appeared in the window. He screwed up his short-sighted eyes, looking at the sleepy faces of the officers, and greeted them.

"Is everything all right?" he asked.

"One of the horses has a sore neck from the new collar," answered Lobytko yawning.

The commander sighed, thought a moment, and said in a loud voice:

"I am thinking of going to see Alexandra Yevgrafovna. I must call on her. Well, good-by. I shall catch up with you in the evening."

A quarter of an hour later the brigade set off on its way. When it was moving along the road past the barns, Ryabovich looked at the house on the right. The blinds were down in all the windows. Evidently the household was still asleep. The one who had kissed Ryabovich the day before was asleep too. He tried to imagine her asleep. The wide-open window of the bedroom, the green branches peeping in, the morning freshness, the scent of the poplars, lilac, and roses, the bed, a chair, and on it the skirts that had rustled the day before, the little slippers, the little watch on the table—all this he pictured to himself clearly and distinctly, but the features of the face, the sweet sleepy smile, just what was characteristic and important, slipped through his imagination like quicksilver through the fingers. When he had ridden a third of a mile, he looked back: the yellow church, the house, and the river, were all bathed in light; the river with its bright green banks, with the blue sky reflected in it and glints of silver in the sunshine here and there, was very beautiful. Ryabovich gazed for the last time at Mestechki, and he felt as sad as though he were parting with something very near and dear to him.

And before him on the road were none but long familiar, uninteresting scenes. . . . To right and to left, fields of young rye and buckwheat with rooks hopping about in them; if one looked ahead, one saw dust and the backs of men's heads; if one looked back, one saw the same dust and faces. . . . Foremost of all marched four men with sabers—this was the vanguard. Next came the singers, and behind them the trumpeters on horseback. The vanguard and the singers, like torch-bearers in a funeral procession, often forgot to keep the regulation distance and pushed a long way ahead. . . . Ryabovich was with the first cannon of the fifth battery. He could see all the four batteries moving in front of him. To a civilian the long tedious procession which is a brigade on the move seems an intricate and unintelligible muddle; one cannot understand why there are so many people round one cannon, and why it is drawn by so many horses in such a strange network of harness, as though it really were so terrible and heavy. To Ryabovich it was all perfectly comprehensible and therefore uninteresting. He had known for ever so long why at the head of each battery beside the officer there rode a stalwart noncom, called bombardier; immediately behind him could be seen the horsemen of the first and then of the middle units. Ryabovich knew that of the horses on which they rode, those on the left were called one name, while those on the right were called another—it was all extremely uninteresting. Behind the horsemen came two shaft-horses. On one of them sat a rider still covered with the dust of yesterday and with a clumsy and funny-looking wooden guard on his right leg. Ryabovich knew the object of this guard, and did not think it funny. All the riders waved their whips mechanically and shouted from time to time. The cannon itself was not presentable. On the limber lay sacks of oats covered with a tarpaulin, and the cannon itself was hung all over with kettles, soldiers' knapsacks, bags, and looked like some small harmless animal surrounded for some unknown reason by men and horses. To the leeward of it marched six men, the gunners, swinging their arms. After the cannon there came again more bombardiers, riders, shaft-horses, and behind them another cannon, as unpresentable and unimpressive as the first. After the second came a third, a fourth; near the fourth there was an officer, and so on. There were six batteries in all in the brigade, and four cannon in each battery. The procession covered a third of a mile; it ended in a string of wagons near which an extremely appealing creature—the ass, Magar, brought by a battery commander from Turkey—paced pensively, his long-eared head drooping.

Ryabovich looked indifferently ahead and behind him, at the backs of heads and at faces; at any other time he would have been half asleep, but now he was entirely absorbed in his new agreeable thoughts. At first when the brigade was setting off on the march he tried to persuade himself that the incident of the kiss could only be interesting as a mysterious little adventure, that it was in reality trivial, and to think of it seriously, to say the least, was stupid; but now he bade farewell to logic and gave himself up to dreams. . . . At one moment he imagined himself in von Rabbeck's drawing-room beside a girl who was like the young lady in lilac and the blonde in black; then he would close his eyes and see himself with another, entirely unknown girl, whose features were very vague. In his imagination he talked, caressed her, leaned over her shoulder, pictured war, separation, then meeting again, supper with his wife, children. . . .

"Brakes on!" The word of command rang out every time they went downhill.

He, too, shouted "Brakes on!" and was afraid this shout would disturb his reverie and bring him back to reality. . . .

As they passed by some landowner's estate Ryabovich looked over the fence into the garden. A long avenue, straight as a ruler, strewn with yellow sand and bordered with young birch-trees, met his eyes. . . . With the eagerness of a man who indulges in daydreaming, he pictured to himself little feminine feet tripping along yellow sand, and quite unexpectedly had a clear vision in his imagination of her who had kissed him and whom he had succeeded in picturing to himself the evening before at supper. This image remained in his brain and did not desert him again.

At midday there was a shout in the rear near the string of wagons:

"Attention! Eyes to the left! Officers!"

The general of the brigade drove by in a carriage drawn by a pair of white horses. He stopped near the second battery, and shouted something which no one understood. Several officers, among them Ryabovich, galloped up to him.

"Well? How goes it?" asked the general, blinking his red eyes. "Are there any sick?"

Receiving an answer, the general, a little skinny man, chewed, thought for a moment and said, addressing one of the officers:

"One of your drivers of the third cannon has taken off his leg-guard and hung it on the fore part of the cannon, the rascal. Reprimand him."

He raised his eyes to Ryabovich and went on:

"It seems to me your breeching is too long."

Making a few other tedious remarks, the general looked at Lobytko and grinned.

"You look very melancholy today, Lieutenant Lobytko," he said. "Are you pining for Madame Lopuhova? Eh? Gentlemen, he is pining for Madame Lopuhova."

Madame Lopuhova was a very stout and very tall lady long past forty. The general, who had a predilection for large women, whatever their ages, suspected a similar taste in his officers. The officers smiled respectfully. The general, delighted at having said something very amusing and biting, laughed loudly, touched his coachman's back, and saluted. The carriage rolled on. . . .

"All I am dreaming about now which seems to me so impossible and unearthly is really quite an ordinary thing," thought Ryabovich, looking at the clouds of dust racing after the general's carriage. "It's all very ordinary, and everyone goes through it. . . . That general, for instance, was in love at one time; now he is married and has children. Captain Wachter, too, is married and loved, though the nape of his neck is very red and ugly and he has no waist. . . . Salmanov is coarse and too much of a Tartar, but he had a love affair that has ended in marriage. . . . I am the same as everyone else, and I, too, shall have the same experience as everyone else, sooner or later. . . ."

And the thought that he was an ordinary person and that his life was ordinary delighted him and gave him courage. He pictured *her* and his happiness boldly, just as he liked. . . .

When the brigade reached their halting-place in the evening, and the officers were resting in their tents, Ryabovich, Merzlyakov, and Lobytko were sitting round a chest having supper. Merzlyakov ate without haste and, as he munched deliberately, read *The Messenger of Europe*, which he held on his knees. Lobytko talked incessantly and kept filling up his glass with beer, and Ryabovich, whose head was confused from dreaming all day long, drank and said nothing. After three glasses he got a little drunk, felt weak, and had an irresistible desire to relate his new sensations to his comrades.

"A strange thing happened to me at those von Rabbecks'," he began, trying to impart an indifferent and ironical tone to his voice. "You know I went into the billiard-room. . . ."

He began describing very minutely the incident of the kiss, and a moment later relapsed into silence. . . . In the course of that moment he had told everything, and it surprised him dreadfully to find how short a time it took him to tell it. He had imagined that he could have been telling the story of the kiss till next morning. Listening to him, Lobytko, who was a great liar and consequently believed no one, looked at him skeptically and laughed. Merzlyakov twitched his eyebrows and, without removing his eyes from *The Messenger of Europe*, said:

"That's an odd thing! How strange! . . . throws herself on a man's neck, without addressing him by name. . . . She must have been some sort of lunatic."

"Yes, she must," Ryabovich agreed.

"A similar thing once happened to me," said Lobytko, assuming a scared expression. "I was going last year to Kovno. . . . I took a second-class ticket. The train was crammed, and it was impossible to sleep. I gave the guard half a ruble; he took my luggage and led me to another compartment. . . . I lay down and covered myself with a blanket. . . . It was dark, you understand. Suddenly I felt someone touch me on the shoulder and breathe in my face. I made a movement with my hand and felt somebody's elbow. . . . I opened my eyes and only imagine—a woman. Black eyes, lips red as a prime salmon, nostrils breathing passionately—a bosom like a buffer. . . ."

"Excuse me," Merzlyakov interrupted calmly, "I understand about the bosom, but how could you see the lips if it was dark?"

Lobytko began trying to put himself right and laughing at Merzlyakov's being so dull-witted. It made Ryabovich wince. He walked away from the chest, got into bed, and vowed never to confide again.

Camp life began. . . . The days flowed by, one very much like another. All those days Ryabovich felt, thought, and behaved as though he were in love. Every morning when his orderly handed him what he needed for washing, and he sluiced his head with cold water, he recalled that there was something warm and delightful in his life.

In the evenings when his comrades began talking of love and women, he would listen, and draw up closer; and he wore the expression of a soldier listening to the description of a battle in which he has taken part. And on the evenings when the officers, out on a spree with the setter Lobytko at their head, made Don-Juanesque raids on the neighboring "suburb," and Ryabovich took part in such excursions, he always was sad, felt profoundly guilty, and inwardly begged *her* forgiveness. . . . In hours of leisure or on sleepless nights when he felt moved to recall his childhood, his father and mother—everything near and dear, in fact, he invariably thought of Mestechki, the queer horse, von Rabbeck, his wife who resembled Empress Eugénie, the dark room, the light in the crack of the door. . . .

On the thirty-first of August he was returning from the camp, not with the whole brigade, but with only two batteries. He was dreamy and excited all the way, as though he were going home. He had an intense longing to see again the queer horse, the church, the insincere family of the von Rabbecks, the dark room. The "inner voice," which so often deceives lovers, whispered to him for some reason that he would surely see her. . . . And he was tortured by the questions: How would he meet her? What would he talk to her about? Had she forgotten the kiss? If the worst came to the worst, he thought, even if he did not meet her, it would be a pleasure to him merely to go through the dark room and recall the past. . . .

Towards evening there appeared on the horizon the familiar church and white barns. Ryabovich's heart raced. . . . He did not hear the officer who was riding beside him and saying something to him, he forgot everything, and looked eagerly at the river shining in the distance, at the roof of the house, at the dovecote round which the pigeons were circling in the light of the setting sun.

When they reached the church and were listening to the quartermaster, he expected every second that a man on horseback would come round the church enclosure and invite the officers to tea, but . . . the quartermaster ended his report, the officers dismounted and strolled off to the village, and the man on horseback did not appear.

"Von Rabbeck will hear at once from the peasants that we have come and will send for us," thought Ryabovich, as he went into the peasant cottage, unable to understand why a comrade was lighting a candle and why the orderlies were hastening to get the samovars going.

A crushing uneasiness took possession of him. He lay down, then got up and looked out of the window to see whether the messenger were coming. But there was no sign of him.

He lay down again, but half an hour later he got up and, unable to restrain his uneasiness, went into the street and strode towards the church. It was dark and deserted in the square near the church enclosure. Three soldiers were standing silent in a row where the road began to go down-hill. Seeing Ryabovich, they roused themselves and saluted. He returned the salute and began to go down the familiar path.

On the farther bank of the river the whole sky was flooded with crimson: the moon was rising; two peasant women, talking loudly, were pulling cabbage leaves in the kitchen garden; beyond the kitchen garden there were some cottages that formed a dark mass. . . . Everything on the near side of the river was just as it had been in May; the path, the bushes, the willows overhanging the water . . . but there was no sound of the brave nightingale and no scent of poplar and young grass.

Reaching the garden, Ryabovich looked in at the gate. The garden was dark and still. . . . He could see nothing but the white stems of the nearest birch-trees and a little bit of the avenue; all the rest melted together into a dark mass. Ryabovich looked and listened eagerly, but after waiting for a quarter of an hour without hearing a sound or catching a glimpse of a light, he trudged back. . . .

He went down to the river. The General's bathing cabin and the bath-sheets on the rail of the little bridge showed white before him. . . . He walked up on the bridge, stood a little, and quite unnecessarily touched a sheet. It felt rough and cold. He looked down at the water. . . . The river ran rapidly and with a faintly audible gurgle round the piles of the bathing cabin. The red moon was reflected near the left bank; little ripples ran over the reflection, stretching it out, breaking it into bits, and seemed trying to carry it away. . . .

"How stupid, how stupid!" thought Ryabovich, looking at the running water. "How unintelligent it all is!"

Now that he expected nothing, the incident of the kiss, his impatience, his vague hopes and disappointment, presented themselves to him in a clear light. It no longer seemed to him strange that the General's messenger never came and that he would never see the girl who had accidentally kissed him instead of someone else; on the contrary, it would have been strange if he had seen her. . . .

The water was running, he knew not where or why, just as it did in May. At that time it had flowed into a great river, from the great river into the sea; then it had risen in vapor, turned into rain, and perhaps the very same water was running now before Ryabovich's eyes again. . . . What for? Why?

And the whole world, the whole of life, seemed to Ryabovich an unintelligible, aimless jest. . . . And turning his eyes from the water and looking at the sky, he remembered again how Fate in the person of an unknown woman had by chance caressed him, he recalled his summer dreams and fancies, and his life struck him as extraordinarily meager, poverty-stricken, and drab. . . .

When he had returned to the cottage he did not find a single comrade. The orderly informed him that they had all gone to "General Fontryabkin, who had sent a messenger on horseback to invite them. . . ."

For an instant there was a flash of joy in Ryabovich's heart, but he quenched it at once, got into bed, and in his wrath with his fate, as though to spite it, did not go the General's.

[1887]
Translated by
CONSTANCE GARNETT

Questions

1. How does the kiss transform Ryabovich?
2. Why do the other officers respond the way they do to Ryabovich's story?
3. How would you describe the tone of the story? Is Chekhov's presentation of Ryabovich sympathetic or mocking?
4. How does the ending contribute to your understanding of Ryabovich and to the story's theme?
5. What does the story suggest about romance? About self-deception?

Kate Chopin
(1851–1904)
United States

Born Katherine O'Flaherty, Kate Chopin was the daughter of an Irish immigrant father and a French Creole mother. Raised in St. Louis, she lost her father, mother, and brother during her childhood and youth. At the age of twenty she married a French Creole cotton broker, Oscar Chopin, and settled in New Orleans, bearing six children in nine years while also attending to the social obligations required by her role as a successful businessman's wife. When the business failed, the Chopins moved to central Louisiana, where they managed a large plantation until Oscar died of swamp fever in 1882; at the age of 32, Kate Chopin found herself a widow with six children and limited financial resources. She returned with her children to St. Louis and began to write poetry and fiction, publishing her work in journals such as Harper's Bazaar and Century. In a relatively short ten years, she published an astonishing 95 short stories, 2 novels, a play, a number of poems, and several essays of literary criticism.

For years, Chopin's classification as a "regional writer" obscured the power of her best fiction, which exposed with probing insight the conflicting cultural and social values of her milieu, not only between people of different ethnic backgrounds and classes in the Creole South of Louisiana, but also between men and women. A number of her stories, exploring such sensitive and even—for her time—taboo themes as divorce, alcoholism, and female desire, shocked the sensibilities of her contemporaries. In her best-known novel, The Awakening (1899), the central character, Edna Pontellier, leaves her husband and children to pursue her independent desires and to claim her own selfhood. Many reviewers found Edna's behavior scandalous and Chopin's unwillingness to offer any moral judgment of her character even more shocking. One contemporary reviewer of the novel flatly stated, "It is not a healthy book."

Chopin's stories and novels often address the conflict between social custom and individual freedom as well as the gap between the inner and the outer life. "The Story of an Hour," despite its brevity, powerfully expresses these concerns.

THE STORY OF AN HOUR

Knowing that Mrs. Mallard was afflicted with a heart trouble, great care was taken to break to her as gently as possible the news of her husband's death.

It was her sister Josephine who told her, in broken sentences; veiled hints that revealed in half concealing. Her husband's friend Richards was there, too, near her. It was he who had been in the newspaper office when intelligence of the railroad disaster was received, with Brently Mallard's name leading the list of "killed." He had only taken the time to assure himself of its truth by a second telegram, and had hastened to forestall any less careful, less tender friend in bearing the sad message.

She did not hear the story as many women have heard the same, with a paralyzed inability to accept its significance. She wept at once, with sudden, wild abandonment, in her sister's arms. When the storm of grief had spent itself she went away to her room alone. She would have no one follow her.

There stood, facing the open window, a comfortable, roomy armchair. Into this she sank, pressed down by a physical exhaustion that haunted her body and seemed to reach into her soul.

She could see in the open square before her house the tops of trees that were all aquiver with the new spring life. The delicious breath of rain was in the air. In the street below a peddler was crying his wares. The notes of a distant song which some one was singing reached her faintly, and countless sparrows were twittering in the eaves.

There were patches of blue sky showing here and there through the clouds that had met and piled one above the other in the west facing her window.

She sat with her head thrown back upon the cushion of the chair, quite motionless, except when a sob came up into her throat and shook her, as a child who has cried itself to sleep continues to sob in its dreams.

She was young, with a fair, calm face, whose lines bespoke repression and even a certain strength. But now there was a dull stare in her eyes, whose gaze was fixed away off yonder on one of those patches of blue sky. It was not a glance of reflection, but rather indicated a suspension of intelligent thought.

There was something coming to her and she was waiting for it, fearfully. What was it? She did not know; it was too subtle and elusive to name. But she felt it, creeping out of the sky, reaching toward her through the sounds, the scents, the color that filled the air.

Now her bosom rose and fell tumultuously. She was beginning to recognize this thing that was approaching to possess her, and she was striving to beat it back with her will—as powerless as her two white slender hands would have been.

When she abandoned herself a little whispered word escaped her slightly parted lips. She said it over and over under her breath: "free, free, free!" The vacant stare and the look of terror that had followed it went from her eyes. They stayed keen and bright. Her pulses beat fast, and the coursing blood warmed and relaxed every inch of her body.

She did not stop to ask if it were or were not a monstrous joy that held her. A clear and exalted perception enabled her to dismiss the suggestion as trivial.

She knew that she would weep again when she saw the kind, tender hands folded in death; the face that had never looked save with love upon her, fixed and gray and dead. But she saw beyond that bitter moment a long procession of years to come that would belong to her absolutely. And she opened and spread her arms out to them in welcome.

There would be no one to live for her during those coming years; she would live for herself. There would be no powerful will bending hers in that blind persistence with which men and women believe they have a right to impose a private will upon a fellow-creature. A kind intention or a cruel intention made the act seem no less a crime as she looked upon it in that brief moment of illumination.

And yet she had loved him—sometimes. Often she had not. What did it matter! What could love, the unsolved mystery, count for in face of this possession of self-assertion which she suddenly recognized as the strongest impulse of her being!

"Free! Body and soul free!" she kept whispering.

Josephine was kneeling before the closed door with her lips to the keyhole, imploring for admission. "Louise, open the door! I beg; open the door—you will make yourself ill. What are you doing, Louise? For heaven's sake open the door."

"Go away. I am not making myself ill." No; she was drinking in a very elixir of life through that open window.

Her fancy was running riot along those days ahead of her. Spring days, and summer days, and all sorts of days that would be her own. She breathed a quick prayer that life might be long. It was only yesterday she had thought with a shudder that life might be long.

She arose at length and opened the door to her sister's importunities. There was a feverish triumph in her eyes, and she carried herself unwittingly like a goddess of Victory. She clasped her sister's waist, and together they descended the stairs. Richards stood waiting for them at the bottom.

Some one was opening the front door with a latchkey. It was Brently Mallard who entered, a little travel-stained, composedly carrying his grip-sack and umbrella. He had been far from the scene of accident, and did not even know there had been one. He stood amazed at Josephine's piercing cry; at Richards' quick motion to screen him from the view of his wife.

But Richards was too late.

When the doctors came they said she had died of heart disease—of joy that kills.

[1894]

Questions

1. What is the conflict in the story? What is the story really about?

2. How does Chopin prepare the reader for the story's ending?

3. How does Chopin's style—particularly imagery and repetition—shape the story?

4. What is "the joy that kills"? Of what does Mrs. Mallard die?

Gabrielle-Sidonie Colette
(1873–1954)
France

G abrielle-Sidonie Colette lived à colorful and occasionally (for her time) even scandalous life that also inspired and fed her fiction. Born and raised in the Burgundy countryside, she experienced a happy childhood, which became the subject and setting for the reminiscences of childhood captured in her early "Claudine" novels. She married young, in a match arranged by her parents as a result of their failing financial solvency. Henry Gauthier-Villars, a music critic and journalist who was significantly older than Colette and rarely faithful to her, prompted her to write about her childhood and not to be shy of adding "spicy details." Her first novel, Claudine at School, was published in 1900 under Gauthier-Villars's pen name, "Willy." Gauthier-Villars then virtually compelled Colette to write three more "Claudine" novels, all somewhat titillating and all published under his pen name. Gauthier-Villars's philandering ultimately led the unhappy Colette to leave the marriage, after which she supported herself as a dancer and mime on the music hall stage.

Besides being married three times, Colette also had several lesbian relationships as well as a brief liaison with the son of her second husband. Many of her stories and novels frankly explore through the themes of love and sexuality the experiences she discovered through her own bisexuality. Drawing on what she called "mental androgyny," she expressed the tension between the masculine and feminine qualities that she felt were present in all human beings.

Colette's early fiction, particularly the "Claudine" novels, brought to life delicate renderings of nature and an unerring evocation of childhood. She is also justly admired for her exceptional psychological insight into female experience and relationships, including the conflict for a woman between self-discovery and career (The Vagabond, 1911), as well as the spectrum of emotional possibilities encompassed in the idea of love (Mitsou, ou Comment l'esprit vient aux filles, translated as Mitsou, or How Girls Grow Wise, 1919; Cheri, 1920; and Gigi, 1944; among others). Also among her fictional subjects are her adored and idealized mother, "the most important person in all my life," whom she fictionalized as "Sido," and her daughter, born when Colette was 40 and fictionalized as "Bel-Gazou." Her characters Mitsou (a music hall artist), Claudine, Cheri, and Gigi are among Colette's other enduring creations, many of whom are drawn directly from the author's own unconventional life. As Elaine Marks phrases it, Colette was her own "greatest fictional character."

The author of more than 50 books, including novels and collections of stories, Colette was much loved and honored by her country. At her death, she was the first French woman writer ever to be honored by a state funeral.

THE SEAMSTRESS

"Do you mean to say your daughter is *nine years old*," said a friend, "and she doesn't know how to sew? She really must learn to sew. In bad weather sewing is a better occupation for a child of that age than reading storybooks."

"Nine years old? And she can't sew?" said another friend. "When she was eight, my daughter embroidered this tray cloth for me, look at it. . . . Oh, I don't say it's fine needlework, but it's nicely done all the same. Nowadays my daughter cuts out her own underclothes. I can't bear anyone in my house to mend holes with pins!"

I meekly poured all this domestic wisdom over Bel-Gazou.

"You're nine years old and you don't know how to sew? You really must learn to sew. . . ."

Flouting truth, I even added: "When I was eight years old, I remember I embroidered a tray cloth . . . Oh, it wasn't fine needlework, I dare say. . . . And then, in bad weather . . ."

She has therefore learned to sew. And although—with one bare sunburned leg tucked beneath her, and her body at ease in its bathing suit—she looks more like a fisherboy mending a net than an industrious little girl, she seems to experience no boyish repugnance. Her hands, stained the color of tobacco juice by sun and sea, hem in a way that seems against nature; their version of the simple running stitch resembles the zigzag dotted lines of a road map, but she buttonholes and scallops with elegance and is severely critical of the embroidery of others.

She sews and kindly keeps me company if rain blurs the horizon of the sea. She also sews during the torrid hour when the spindle bushes gather their circles of shadow directly under them. Moreover, it sometimes happens that a quarter of an hour before dinner, black in her white dress—"Bel-Gazou! your hands and frock are clean, and don't forget it!"—she sits solemnly down with a square of material between her fingers. Then my friends applaud: "Just look at her! Isn't she good? That's right! Your mother must be pleased!"

Her mother says nothing—great joys must be controlled. But ought one to feign them? I shall speak the truth: I don't much like my daughter sewing.

When she reads, she returns all bewildered and with flaming cheeks, from the island where the chest full of precious stones is hidden, from the dismal castle where a fair-haired orphan child is persecuted. She is soaking up a tested and time-honored poison, whose effects have long been familiar. If she draws, or colors pictures, a semi-articulate song issues from her, unceasing as the hum of bees around the privet. It is the same as the buzzing of flies as they work, the slow waltz of the house painter, the refrain of the spinner at her wheel. But Bel-Gazou is silent when she sews, silent for hours on end, with her mouth firmly closed, concealing her large, new-cut incisors that bite into the moist heart of a fruit like little saw-edged blades. She is silent, and she—why not write down the word that frightens me—she is thinking.

A new evil? A torment that I had not foreseen? Sitting in a grassy dell, or half buried in hot sand and gazing out to sea, she is thinking, as well I know. She thinks rapidly when she is listening, with a well-bred pretense of discretion, to remarks imprudently exchanged above her head. But it would seem that with this needleplay she has discovered the perfect means of adventuring, stitch by stitch, point by point, along a road of risks and temptations. Silence . . . the hand armed with the steel dart moves back and forth. Nothing will stop the unchecked little explorer. At what moment must I utter the "Halt!" that will brutally arrest her in full flight? Oh, for those young embroiderers of bygone days, sitting on a hard little stool in the shelter of their mother's ample skirts! Maternal authority kept them there for years and years, never rising except to change the skein of silk, or to elope with a stranger. Think of Philomène de Watteville and her canvas, on which she embroidered the loss and the despair of Albert Savarus. . . .[1]

"What are you thinking about, Bel-Gazou?"

"Nothing, Mother. I'm counting my stitches."

Silence. The needle pierces the material. A coarse trail of chain stitch follows very unevenly in its wake. Silence . . .

"Mother?"

"Darling?"

"Is it only when people are married that a man can put his arm around a lady's waist?"

"Yes . . . No . . . It depends. If they are very good friends and have known each other a long time, you understand. . . . As I said before: it depends. Why do you want to know?"

"For no particular reason, Mother."

Two stitches, ten misshapen chain stitches.

"Mother? Is Madame X married?"

"She has been. She is divorced."

"I see. And Monsieur F., is he married?"

"Why, of course he is; you know that."

"Oh! Yes . . . Then it's all right if one of the two is married?"

"What is all right?"

"To depend."

"One doesn't say: 'to depend.'"

"But you said just now that it depended."

"But what has it got to do with you? Is it any concern of yours?"

"No, Mother."

I let it drop. I feel inadequate, self-conscious, displeased with myself. I should have answered differently and I could not think what to say.

Bel-Gazou also drops the subject; she sews. But she pays little attention to her sewing, overlaying it with pictures, associations of names and people, all the results of patient observation. A little later will come other curiosities, other questions, and especially other silences. Would to God that Bel-Gazou were the bewildered and simple child who questions crudely, open-eyed! But she is too near the truth, and too natural not to know, as a birthright, that all nature hesitates before that most majestic and most disturbing of instincts, and that it is wise to tremble, to be silent, and to lie when one draws near to it.

Translated by
Una Vicenzo Troubridge
and Enid McLeod

---

[1]*Albert Savarus* The central character of a novel of that name by Honoré de Balzac (1799–1850); *Philomène de Watteville* is a female character in the novel.

Questions

1. Why does the mother encourage her daughter to learn to sew when she does not really like the idea?
2. How is Bel-Gazou initially described? How does she change? Why does the mother believe that these changes are related to her daughter's learning to sew?
3. The mother and daughter are revealed both through the mother's perspective and through a dialogue between them. How do these perspectives complement each other and convey different kinds of information about the two characters?

Joseph Conrad

(1857–1924)

Poland/England

It is an irony that Conrad would have enjoyed: that a writer who did not even learn English until he was 21 would become one of its literary masters, a giant of twentieth-century literature and one of its first modern writers. Born Josef Teodor Konrad Nalecz Korzeniowski, Conrad was the only child of a Polish-Ukrainian farmer who left his wife and small son to join a radical political party in Warsaw. Eventually both parents were arrested for political treason and sent into exile in Siberia when Conrad was five years old. From the effects of cold and deprivation, Conrad's mother died when he was seven; in 1867 the Russian government commuted his father's exile, and father and son returned to Poland, where Conrad's father died when Conrad was 12.

Having learned about adventure less from his family's painful exile than through his avid reading as a youth, Conrad ran away from his uncle/guardian when he was 16, joining a ship in Marseilles. For eight years he lived a sailor's life, moving through the ranks to become captain of a ship. In 1878 he joined an English ship, although the only English he knew he had learned at sea; later he refined his knowledge of the language through reading Shakespeare, the Bible, and the London newspaper. His adopted language eventually became the only one in which he felt he could express himself as a writer; as he observed in a letter to a friend in 1918, "I began to think in English long before I mastered, I won't say the style (I haven't done that yet), but the mere uttered speech. . . . If I had not known English I wouldn't have written a line for print, in my life."

Although Conrad resigned from his captaincy and apparently gave up life on the seas in 1895, he returned to it several more times, including one journey to the Congo that became the source for his classic novella of corrupted colonialism, Heart of Darkness (1902). In many of his more than 20 novels and numerous short stories, Conrad incorporated his vision of the sea as a mysterious element—a psychological as well as physical landscape in which an individual's assumptions, values, and deepest soul were ultimately tested. A moralist during an uncertain time (the turn of the century), Conrad placed his characters in circumstances of isolation and loneliness in which they were challenged to act decisively and in which those actions revealed their true moral compass as well as the ambiguity of human truth.

Exploring those themes in such novels as Lord Jim (1900), Heart of Darkness (1902), "The Secret Sharer" (1912), Chance (1914), Victory (1915), and other novels and stories, Conrad probed with unexcelled psychological accuracy that unconscious dimension of the self that exists beneath the social arrangements that frame most human actions. As critic David Daiches has observed, Conrad's greatest novels "are all concerned, directly or obliquely, with situations to which public codes—any public codes—are inapplicable, situations which yield a dark and disturbing insight which cannot be related to any of the beliefs which make human societies possible."

Rarely anthologized, the story "Amy Foster" (1903) is especially interesting because it not only embodies a number of Conrad's preoccupations but also draws on his personal experience as an exile from another country and language: his profound awareness of the chasms in communication that expose the irreducible loneliness at the heart of the human condition. In An Outcast of the Islands (1896), Conrad described "the tremendous fact of our isolation, of the loneliness impenetrable and transparent, elusive and everlasting; of the indestructible loneliness that surrounds, envelops, clothes every human soul from the cradle to the grave, and, perhaps, beyond."

AMY FOSTER

Kennedy is a country doctor, and lives in Colebrook, on the shores of Eastbay. The high ground rising abruptly behind the red roofs of the little town crowds the quaint High Street against the wall which defends it from the sea. Beyond the sea-wall there curves for miles in a vast and regular sweep the barren beach of shingle, with the village of Brenzett standing out darkly across the water, a spire in a clump of trees; and still further out the perpendicular column of a lighthouse, looking in the distance no bigger than a lead pencil, marks the vanishing-point of the land. The country at the back of Brenzett is low and flat, but the bay is fairly well sheltered from the seas, and occasionally a big ship, windbound or through stress of weather, makes use of the anchoring ground a mile and a half due north from you as you stand at the back door of the "Ship Inn" in Brenzett. A dilapidated windmill near by lifting its shattered arms from a mound no loftier than a rubbish heap, and a Martello tower squatting at the water's edge half a mile to the south of the Coastguard cottages, are familiar to the skippers of small craft. These are the official seamarks for the patch of trustworthy bottom represented on the Admiralty charts by an irregular oval of dots enclosing several figures six, with a tiny anchor engraved among them, and the legend "mud and shells" over all.

The brow of the upland overtops the square tower of the Colebrook Church. The slope is green and looped by a white road. Ascending along this road, you open a valley broad and shallow, a wide green trough of pastures and hedges merging inland into a vista of purple tints and flowing lines closing the view.

In this valley down to Brenzett and Colebrook and up to Darnford, the market town fourteen miles away, lies the practice of my friend Kennedy. He had begun life as surgeon in the Navy, and afterwards had been the companion of a famous traveller, in the days when there were continents with unexplored interiors. His papers on the fauna and flora made him known to scientific societies. And now he had come to a country practice—from choice. The penetrating power of his mind, acting like a corrosive fluid, had destroyed his ambition, I fancy. His intelligence is of a scientific order, of an investigating habit, and of that unappeasable curiosity which believes that there is a particle of a general truth in every mystery.

A good many years ago now, on my return from abroad, he invited me to stay with him. I came readily enough, and as he could not neglect his patients to keep me company, he took me on his rounds—thirty miles or so of an afternoon, sometimes. I waited for him on the roads; the horse reached after the leafy twigs, and, sitting high in the dogcart, I could hear Kennedy's laugh through the half-open door left open of some cottage. He had a big, hearty laugh that would have fitted a man twice his size, a brisk manner, a bronzed face, and a pair of grey, profoundly attentive eyes. He had the talent of making people talk to him freely, and an inexhaustible patience in listening to their tales.

One day, as we trotted out of a large village into a shady bit of road, I saw on our left hand a low, black cottage, with diamond panes in the windows, a creeper on the end wall, a roof of shingle, and some roses climbing on the rickety trellis-work of the tiny porch. Kennedy pulled up to a walk. A woman, in full sunlight, was throwing a dripping blanket over a line stretched between two old apple-trees. And as the bobtailed, long-necked chestnut, trying to get his head, jerked the left hand, covered by a thick dogskin glove, the doctor raised his voice over the hedge: "How's your child, Amy?"

I had the time to see her dull face, red, not with a mantling blush, but as if her flat cheeks had been vigorously slapped, and to take in the squat figure, the scanty, dusty brown hair drawn into a tight knot at the back of the head. She looked quite young. With a distinct catch in her breath, her voice sounded low and timid.

"He's well, thank you."

We trotted again. "A young patient of yours," I said; and the doctor, flicking the chestnut absently, muttered, "Her husband used to be."

"She seems a dull creature," I remarked listlessly.

"Precisely," said Kennedy. "She is very passive. It's enough to look at the red hands hanging at the end of those short arms, at those slow, prominent brown eyes, to know the inertness of her mind—an inertness that one would think made it everlastingly safe from all the surprises of imagination. And yet which of us is safe? At any rate, such as you see her, she had enough imagination to fall in love. She's the daughter of one Isaac Foster, who from a small farmer has sunk into a shepherd; the beginning of his misfortunes dating from his runaway marriage with the cook of his widowed father— a well-to-do, apoplectic grazier, who passionately struck his name off his will, and had been heard to utter threats against his life. But this old affair, scandalous enough to serve as a motive for a Greek tragedy, arose from the similarity of their characters. There are other tragedies, less scandalous and of a subtler poignancy, arising from irreconcilable differences and from that fear of the Incomprehensible that hangs over all our heads—over all our heads. . . ."

The tired chestnut dropped into a walk; and the rim of the sun, all red in a speckless sky, touched familiarly the smooth top of a ploughed rise near the road as I had seen it times innumerable touch the distant horizon of the sea. The uniform brownness of the harrowed field glowed with a rosy tinge, as though the powdered clods had sweated out in minute pearls of blood the toil of uncounted ploughmen. From the edge of a copse a waggon with two horses was rolling gently along the ridge. Raised above our heads upon the sky-line, it loomed up against the red sun, triumphantly big, enormous, like a chariot of giants drawn by two slow-stepping steeds of legendary proportions. And the clumsy figure of the man plodding at the head of the leading horse projected itself on the background of the Infinite with a heroic uncouthness. The end of his carter's whip quivered high up in the blue. Kennedy discoursed.

"She's the eldest of a large family. At the age of fifteen they put her out to service at the New Barns Farm. I attended Mrs. Smith, the tenant's wife, and saw that girl there for the first time. Mrs. Smith, a genteel person with a sharp nose, made her put on a black dress every afternoon. I don't know what induced me to notice her at all. There are faces that call your attention by a curious want of definiteness in their whole aspect, as, walking in a mist, you peer attentively at a vague shape which, after all, may be nothing more curious or strange than a signpost. The only peculiarity I perceived in her was a slight hesitation in her utterance, a sort of preliminary stammer which passes away with the first word. When sharply spoken to, she was apt to lose her head at once; but her heart was of the kindest. She had never been heard to express a dislike for a single human being, and she was tender to every living creature. She was devoted to Mrs. Smith, to Mr. Smith, to their dogs, cats, canaries; and as to Mrs. Smith's grey parrot, its peculiarities exercised upon her a positive fascination. Nevertheless, when that outlandish bird, attacked by the cat, shrieked for help in human accents, she ran out into the yard stopping her ears, and did not prevent the crime. For Mrs. Smith this was another evidence of her stupidity; on the other hand, her want of charm, in view of Smith's well-known frivolousness, was a great recommendation. Her short-sighted eyes would swim with pity for a poor mouse in a trap, and she had been seen once by some boys on her knees in the wet grass helping a toad in difficulties. If it's true, as some German fellow has said, that without phosphorus there is no thought, it is still more true that there is no kindness of heart without a certain amount of imagination. She had some. She had even more than is necessary to understand suffering and to be moved by pity. She fell in love under circumstances that leave no room for doubt in the matter; for you need imagination to form a notion of beauty at all, and still more to discover your ideal in an unfamiliar shape.

"How this aptitude came to her, what it did feed upon, is an inscrutable mystery. She was born in the village, and had never been further away from it than Colebrook or perhaps Darnford. She lived for four years with the Smiths. New Barns is an isolated farmhouse a mile away from the road, and she was content to look day after day at the same fields, hollows, rises; at the trees and the hedgerows; at the faces of the four men about the farm, always the same—day after day, month after month, year after year. She never showed a desire for conversation, and, as it seemed to me, she did not know how to smile. Sometimes of a fine Sunday afternoon she would put on her best dress, a pair of stout boots, a large grey hat trimmed with a black feather (I've seen her in that finery), seize an absurdly slender parasol, climb over two stiles, tramp over three fields and along two hundred yards of road—never further. There stood Foster's cottage. She would help her mother to give their tea to the younger children, wash up the crockery, kiss the little ones, and go back to the farm. That was all. All the rest, all the change, all the relaxation. She never seemed to wish for anything more. And then she fell in love. She fell in love silently, obstinately—perhaps helplessly. It came slowly, but when it came it worked like a powerful spell; it was love as the Ancients understood it: an irresistible and fateful impulse—a possession! Yes, it was in her to become haunted and possessed by a face, by a presence, fatally, as though she had been a pagan worshipper of form under a joyous sky—and to be awakened at last from that mysterious forgetfulness of self, from that enchantment, from that transport, by a fear resembling the unaccountable terror of a brute. . . ."

With the sun hanging low on its western limit, the expanse of the grass-lands framed in the counter-scraps of the rising ground took on a gorgeous and sombre aspect. A sense of penetrating sadness, like that inspired by a grave strain of music, disengaged itself from the silence of the fields. The men we met walked past slow, unsmiling, with downcast eyes, as if the melancholy of an over-burdened earth had weighted their feet, bowed their shoulders, borne down their glances.

"Yes," said the doctor to my remark, "one would think the earth is under a curse, since of all her children these that cling to her the closest are uncouth in body and as leaden of gait as if their very hearts were loaded with chains. But here on this same road you might have seen amongst these heavy men a being lithe, supple, and long-limbed, straight like a pine with something striving upwards in his appearance as though the heart within him had been buoyant. Perhaps it was only the force of the contrast, but when he was passing one of these villagers here, the soles of his feet did not seem to me to touch the dust of the road. He vaulted over the stiles, paced these slopes with a long elastic stride that made him noticeable at a great distance, and had lustrous black eyes. He was so different from the mankind around that, with his freedom of movement, his soft—a little startled, glance, his olive complexion and graceful bearing, his humanity suggested to me the nature of a woodland creature. He came from there."

The doctor pointed with his whip, and from the summit of the descent seen over the rolling tops of the trees in a park by the side of the road, appeared the level sea far below us, like the floor of an immense edifice inlaid with bands of dark ripple, with still trails of glitter, ending in a belt of glassy water at the foot of the sky. The light blur of smoke, from an invisible steamer, faded on the great clearness of the horizon like the mist of a breath on a mirror; and, inshore, the white sails of a coaster, with the appearance of disentangling themselves slowly from under the branches, floated clear of the foliage of the trees.

"Shipwrecked in the bay?" I said.

"Yes; he was a castaway. A poor emigrant from Central Europe bound to America and washed ashore here in a storm. And for him, who knew nothing of the earth, England was an undiscovered country. It was some time before he learned its name; and for all I know he might have expected to find wild beasts or wild men here, when, crawling in the dark over the sea-wall, he rolled down the other side into a dyke, where it was another miracle he didn't get drowned. But he struggled instinctively like an animal under a net, and this blind struggle threw him out into a field. He must have been, indeed, of a tougher fibre than he looked to withstand without expiring such buffetings, the violence of his exertions, and so much fear. Later on, in his broken English that resembled curiously the speech of a young child, he told me himself that he put his trust in God, believing he was no longer in this world. And truly—he would add—how was he to know? He fought his way against the rain and the gale on all fours, and crawled at last among some sheep huddled close under the lee of a hedge. They ran off in all directions, bleating in the darkness, and he welcomed the first familiar sound he heard on these shores. It must have been two in the morning then. And this is all we know of the manner of his landing, though he did not arrive unattended by any means. Only his grisly company did not begin to come ashore till much later in the day. . . ."

The doctor gathered the reins, clicked his tongue; we trotted down the hill. Then turning, almost directly, a sharp corner into the High Street, we rattled over the stones and were home.

Late in the evening Kennedy, breaking a spell of moodiness that had come over him, returned to the story. Smoking his pipe, he paced the long room from end to end. A reading-lamp concentrated all its light upon the papers on his desk; and, sitting by the open window, I saw, after the windless, scorching day, the frigid splendour of a hazy sea lying motionless under the moon. Not a whisper, not a splash, not a stir of the shingle, not a footstep, not a sigh came up from the earth below—never a sign of life but the scent of climbing jasmine; and Kennedy's voice, speaking behind me, passed through the wide casement, to vanish outside in a chill and sumptuous stillness.

". . . The relations of shipwrecks in the olden time tell us of much suffering. Often the castaways were only saved from drowning to die miserably from starvation on a barren coast; others suffered violent death or else slavery, passing through years of precarious existence with people to whom their strangeness was an object of suspicion, dislike or fear. We read about these things, and they are very pitiful. It is indeed hard upon a man to find himself a lost stranger, helpless, incomprehensible, and of a mysterious origin, in some obscure corner of the earth. Yet amongst all the adventurers shipwrecked in all the wild parts of the world there is not one, it seems to me, that ever had to suffer a fate so simply tragic as the man I am speaking of, the most innocent of adventurers cast out by the sea in the bight of this bay, almost within sight from this very window.

"He did not know the name of his ship. Indeed, in the course of time we discovered he did not even know that ships had names—'like Christian people'; and when, one day, from the top of the Talfourd Hill, he beheld the sea lying open to his view, his eyes roamed afar, lost in an air of wild surprise, as though he had never seen such a sight before. And probably he had not. As far as I could make out, he had been hustled together with many others on board an emigrant-ship lying at the mouth of the Elbe, too bewildered to take note of his surroundings, too weary to see anything, too anxious to care. They were driven below into the 'tweendeck and battened down from the very start. It was a low timber dwelling—he would say—with wooden beams overhead, like the houses in his country, but you went into it down a ladder. It was very large, very cold, damp and sombre, with places in the manner of wooden boxes where people had to sleep, one above another, and it kept on rocking all ways at once all the time. He crept into one of these boxes and laid down there in the clothes in which he had left his home many days before, keeping his bundle and his stick by his side. People groaned, children cried, water dripped, the lights went out, the walls of the place creaked, and everything was being shaken so that in one's little box one dared not lift one's head. He had lost touch with his only companion (a young man from the same valley, he said), and all the time a great noise of wind went on outside and heavy blows fell—boom! boom! An awful sickness overcame him, even to the point of making him neglect his prayers. Besides, one could not tell whether it was morning or evening. It seemed always to be night in that place.

"Before that he had been travelling a long, long time on the iron track. He looked out of the window, which had a wonderfully clear glass on it, and the trees, the houses, the fields, and the long roads seemed to fly round and round about him till his head swam. He gave me to understand that he had on his passage beheld uncounted multitudes of people—whole nations—all dressed in such clothes as the rich wear. Once he was made to get out of the carriage, and slept through a night on a bench in a house of bricks with his bundle under his head; and once for many hours he had to sit on a floor of flat stones dozing, with his knees up and with his bundle between his feet. There was a roof over him, which seemed made of glass, and was so high that the tallest mountain-pine he had ever seen would have had room to grow under it. Steam-machines rolled in at one end and out at the other. People swarmed more than you can see on a feast-day round the miraculous Holy Image in the yard of the Carmelite Convent down in the plains where, before he left his home, he drove his mother in a wooden cart—a pious old woman who wanted to offer prayers and make a vow for his safety. He could not give me an idea of how large and lofty and full of noise and smoke and gloom, and clang of iron, the place was, but some one had told him it was called Berlin. Then they rang a bell, and another steam-machine came in, and again he was taken on and on through a land that wearied his eyes by its flatness without a single bit of a hill to be seen anywhere. One more night he spent shut up in a building like a good stable with a litter of straw on the floor, guarding his bundle amongst a lot of men, of whom not one could understand a single word he said. In the morning they were all led down to the stony shores of an extremely broad muddy river, flowing not between hills but between houses that seemed immense. There was a steam-machine that went on the water, and they all stood upon it packed tight, only now there were with them many women and children who made much noise. A cold rain fell, the wind blew in his face; he was wet through, and his teeth chattered. He and the young man from the same valley took each other by the hand.

"They thought they were being taken to America straight away, but suddenly the steam-machine bumped against the side of a thing like a house on the water. The walls were smooth and black, and there uprose, growing from the roof as it were, bare trees in the shape of crosses, extremely high. That's how it appeared to him then, for he had never seen a ship before. This was the ship that was going to swim all the way to America. Voices shouted, everything swayed; there was a ladder dipping up and down. He went up on his hands and knees in mortal fear of falling into the water below, which made a great splashing. He got separated from his companion, and when he descended into the bottom of that ship his heart seemed to melt suddenly within him.

"It was then also, as he told me, that he lost contact for good and all with one of those three men who the summer before had been going about through all the little towns in the foothills of his country. They would arrive on market days driving in a peasant's cart, and would set up an office in an inn or some other Jew's house. There were three of them, of whom one with a long beard looked venerable; and they had red cloth collars round their necks and gold lace on their sleeves like Government officials. They sat proudly behind a long table; and in the next room, so that the common people shouldn't hear, they kept a cunning telegraph machine, through which they could talk to the Emperor of America. The fathers hung about the door, but the young men of the mountains would crowd up to the table asking many questions, for there was work to be got all the year round at three dollars a day in America, and no military service to do.

"But the American Kaiser would not take everybody. Oh, no! He himself had a great difficulty in getting accepted, and the venerable man in uniform had to go out of the room several times to work the telegraph on his behalf. The American Kaiser engaged him at last at three dollars, he being young and strong. However, many able young men backed out, afraid of the great distance; besides, those only who had some money could be taken. There were some who sold their huts and their land because it cost a lot of money to get to America; but then, once there, you had three dollars a day, and if you were clever you could find places where true gold could be picked up on the ground. His father's house was getting over full. Two of his brothers were married and had children. He promised to send money home from America by post twice a year. His father sold an old cow, a pair of piebald mountain ponies of his own raising, and a cleared plot of fair pasture land on the sunny slope of a pine-clad pass to a Jew inn-keeper in order to pay the people of the ship that took men to America to get rich in a short time.

"He must have been a real adventurer at heart, for how many of the greatest enterprises in the conquest of the earth had for their beginning just such a bargaining away of the paternal cow for the mirage or true gold far away! I have been telling you more or less in my own words what I learned fragmentarily in the course of two or three years, during which I seldom missed an opportunity of a friendly chat with him. He told me this story of his adventure with many flashes of white teeth and lively glances of black eyes, at first in a sort of anxious baby-talk, then, as he acquired the language, with great fluency, but always with that singing, soft, and at the same time vibrating intonation that instilled a strangely penetrating power into the sound of the most familiar English words, as if they had been the words of an unearthly language. And he always would come to an end, with many emphatic shakes of his head, upon that awful sensation of his heart melting within him directly he set foot on board that ship. Afterwards there seemed to come for him a period of blank ignorance, at any rate as to facts. No doubt he must have been abominably sea-sick and abominably unhappy—this soft and passionate adventurer, taken thus out of his knowledge, and feeling bitterly as he lay in his emigrant bunk his utter loneliness; for his was a highly sensitive nature. The next thing we know of him for certain is that he had been hiding in Hammond's pig-pound by the side of the road to Norton six miles, as the crow flies, from the sea. Of these experiences he was unwilling to speak: they seemed to have seared into his soul a sombre sort of wonder and indignation. Through the rumours of the country-side, which lasted for a good many days after his arrival, we know that the fishermen of West Colebrook had been disturbed and startled by heavy knocks against the walls of weatherboard cottages, and by a voice crying piercingly strange words in the night. Several of them turned out even, but, no doubt, he had fled in sudden alarm at their rough angry tones hailing each other in the darkness. A sort of frenzy must have helped him up the steep Norton hill. It was he, no doubt, who early the following morning had been seen lying (in a swoon, I should say) on the roadside grass by the Brenzett carrier, who actually got down to have a nearer look, but drew back, intimidated by the perfect immobility, and by something queer in the aspect of that tramp, sleeping so still under the showers. As the day advanced, some children came dashing into school at Norton in such a fright that the schoolmistress went out and spoke indignantly to a 'horrid-looking man' on the road. He edged away, hanging his head, for a few steps, and then suddenly ran off with extraordinary fleetness. The driver of Mr. Bradley's milk-cart made no secret of it that he had lashed with his whip at a hairy sort of gipsy fellow who, jumping up at a turn of the road by the Vents, made a snatch at the pony's bridle. And he caught him a good one too, right over the face, he said, that made him drop down in the mud a jolly sight quicker than he had jumped up; but it was a good half-a-mile before he could stop the pony. Maybe that in his desperate endeavours to get help, and in his need to get in touch with some one, the poor devil had tried to stop the cart. Also three boys confessed afterwards to throwing stones at a funny tramp, knocking about all wet and muddy, and, it seemed, very drunk, in the narrow deep lane by the limekilns. All this was the talk of three villages for days; but we have Mrs. Finn's (the wife of Smith's waggoner) unimpeachable testimony that she saw him get over the low wall of Hammond's pig-pound and lurch straight at her, babbling aloud in a voice that was enough to make one die of fright. Having the baby with her in a perambulator, Mrs. Finn called out to him to go away, and as he persisted in coming nearer, she hit him courageously with her umbrella over the head and, without once looking back, ran like the wind with the perambulator as far as the first house in the village. She stopped then, out of breath, and spoke to old Lewis, hammering there at a heap of stones; and the old chap, taking off his immense black wire goggles, got up on his shaky legs to look where she pointed. Together they followed with their eyes the figure of the man running over a field; they saw him fall down, pick himself up, and run on again, staggering and waving his long arms above his head, in the direction of the New Barns Farm. From that moment he is plainly in the toils of his obscure and touching destiny. There is no doubt after this of what happened to him. All is certain now: Mrs. Smith's intense terror; Amy Foster's stolid conviction held against the other's nervous attack, that the man 'meant no harm'; Smith's exasperation (on his return from Darnford Market) at finding the dog barking himself into a fit, the back-door locked, his wife in hysterics; and all for an unfortunate dirty tramp, supposed to be even then lurking in his stackyard. Was he? He would teach him to frighten women.

"Smith is notoriously hot-tempered, but the sight of some nondescript and miry creature sitting crosslegged amongst a lot of loose straw, and swinging itself to and fro like a bear in a cage, made him pause. Then this tramp stood up silently before him, one mass of mud and filth from head to foot. Smith, alone amongst his stacks with this apparition, in the stormy twilight ringing with the infuriated barking of the dog, felt the dread of an inexplicable strangeness. But when that being, parting with his black hands the long matted locks that hung before his face, as you part the two halves of a curtain, looked out at him with glistening, wild, black-and-white eyes, the weirdness of this silent encounter fairly staggered him. He has admitted since (for the story has been a legitimate subject of conversation about here for years) that he made more than one step backwards. Then a sudden burst of rapid, senseless speech persuaded him at once that he had to do with an escaped lunatic. In fact, that impression never wore off completely. Smith has not in his heart given up his secret conviction of the man's essential insanity to this very day.

"As the creature approached him, jabbering in a most discomposing manner, Smith (unaware that he was being addressed as 'gracious lord,' and adjured in God's name to afford food and shelter) kept on speaking firmly but gently to it, and retreating all the time into the other yard. At last, watching his chance, by a sudden change he bundled him headlong into the wood-lodge, and instantly shot the bolt.[1] Thereupon he wiped his brow, though the day was cold. He had done his duty to the community by shutting up a wandering and probably dangerous maniac. Smith isn't a hard man at all, but he had room in his brain only for that one idea of lunacy. He was not imaginative enough to ask himself whether the man might not be perishing with cold and hunger. Meantime, at first, the maniac made a great deal of noise in the lodge. Mrs. Smith was screaming upstairs, where she had locked herself in her bedroom; but Amy Foster sobbed piteously at the kitchen door, wringing her hands and muttering, 'Don't! don't!" I daresay Smith had a rough time of it that evening with one noise and another, and this insane, disturbing voice crying obstinately through the door only added to his irritation. He couldn't possibly have connected this troublesome lunatic with the sinking of a ship in Eastbay, of which there had been a rumour in the Darnford marketplace. And I daresay the man inside had been very near to insanity on that night. Before his excitement collapsed and he became unconscious he was throwing himself violently about in the dark, rolling on some dirty sacks, and biting his fists with rage, cold, hunger, amazement, and despair.

"He was a mountaineer of the eastern range of the Carpathians, and the vessel sunk the night before in Eastbay was the Hamburg emigrant-ship *Herzogin Sophia-Dorothea*, of appalling memory.

---

[1]*shot the bolt*   Locked the door.

"A few months later we could read in the papers the accounts of the bogus 'Emigration Agencies' among the Sclavonian peasantry in the more remote provinces of Austria. The object of these scoundrels was to get hold of the poor ignorant people's homesteads, and they were in league with the local usurers. They exported their victims through Hamburg mostly. As to the ship, I had watched her out of this very window, reaching close-hauled under short canvas into the bay on a dark, threatening afternoon. She came to an anchor, correctly by the chart, off the Brenzett Coastguard station. I remember before the night fell looking out again at the outlines of her spars and rigging that stood out dark and pointed on a background of ragged, slaty clouds like another and a slighter spire to the left of the Brenzett church-tower. In the evening the wind rose. At midnight I could hear in my bed the terrific gusts and the sounds of a driving deluge.

"About that time the Coastguardmen thought they saw the lights of a steamer over the anchoring-ground. In a moment they vanished; but it is clear that another vessel of some sort had tried for shelter in the bay on that awful, blind night, had rammed the German ship amidships (a breach—as one of the divers told me afterwards—'that you could sail a Thames barge through'), and then had gone out either scathless or damaged, who shall say; but had gone out, unknown, unseen, and fatal, to perish mysteriously at sea. Of her nothing ever came to light, and yet the hue and cry that was raised all over the world would have found her out if she had been in existence anywhere on the face of the waters.

"A completeness without a clue, and a stealthy silence as of a neatly executed crime, characterise this murderous disaster, which, as you may remember, had its gruesome celebrity. The wind would have prevented the loudest outcries from reaching the shore; there had been evidently no time for signals of distress. It was death without any sort of fuss. The Hamburg ship, filling all at once, capsized as she sank, and at daylight there was not even the end of a spar to be seen above water. She was missed, of course, and at first the Coastguardmen surmised that she had either dragged her anchor or parted her cable some time during the night, and had been blown out to sea. Then, after the tide turned, the wreck must have shifted a little and released some of the bodies, because a child—a little fair-haired child in a red frock—came ashore abreast of the Martello tower. By the afternoon you could see along three miles of beach dark figures with bare legs dashing in and out of the tumbling foam, and rough-looking men, women with hard faces, children, mostly fair-haired, were being carried, stiff and dripping, on stretchers, on wattles, on ladders, in a long procession past the door of the 'Ship Inn,' to be laid out in a row under the north wall of the Brenzett Church.

"Officially, the body of the little girl in the red frock is the first thing that came ashore from that ship. But I have patients amongst the seafaring population of West Colebrook, and, unofficially, I am informed that very early that morning two brothers, who went down to look after their cobble hauled up on the beach, found, a good way from Brenzett, an ordinary ship's hencoop lying high and dry on the shore, with eleven drowned ducks inside. Their families ate the birds, and the hencoop was split into firewood with a hatchet. It is possible that a man (supposing he happened to be on deck at the time of the accident) might have floated ashore on that hencoop. He might. I admit it is improbable, but there was the man—and for days, nay, for weeks—it didn't enter our heads that we had amongst us the only living soul that had escaped from that disaster. The man himself, even when he learned to speak intelligibly, could tell us very little. He remembered he had felt better (after the ship had anchored, I suppose), and that the darkness, the wind, and the rain took his breath away. This looks as if he had been on deck some time during that night. But we mustn't forget he had been taken out of his knowledge, that he had been sea-sick and battened down below for four days, that he had no general notion of a ship or of the sea, and therefore could have no definite idea of what was happening to him. The rain, the wind, the darkness he knew; he understood the bleating of the sheep, and he remembered the pain of his wretchedness and misery, his heartbroken astonishment that it was neither seen nor understood, his dismay at finding all the men angry and all the women fierce. He had approached them as a beggar, it is true, he said; but in his country, even if they gave nothing, they spoke gently to beggars. The children in his country were not taught to throw stones at those who asked for compassion. Smith's strategy overcame him completely. The wood-lodge presented the horrible aspect of a dungeon. What would be done to him next? . . . No wonder that Amy Foster appeared to his eyes with the aureole of an angel of light. The girl had not been able to sleep for thinking of the poor man, and in the morning, before the Smiths were up, she slipped out across the back yard. Holding the door of the wood-lodge ajar, she looked in and extended to him half a loaf of white bread—'such bread as the rich eat in my country,' he used to say.

"At this he got up slowly from amongst all sorts of rubbish, stiff, hungry, trembling, miserable, and doubtful. 'Can you eat this?' she asked in her soft and timid voice. He must have taken her for a 'gracious lady.' He devoured ferociously, and tears were falling on the crust. Suddenly he dropped the bread, seized her wrist, and imprinted a kiss on her hand. She was not frightened. Through his forlorn condition she had observed that he was good-looking. She shut the door and walked back slowly to the kitchen. Much later on, she told Mrs. Smith, who shuddered at the bare idea of being touched by that creature.

"Through this act of impulsive pity he was brought back again within the pale of human relations with his new surroundings. He never forgot it—never.

"That very same morning old Mr. Swaffer (Smith's nearest neighbour) came over to give his advice, and ended by carrying him off. He stood, unsteady on his legs, meek, and caked over in half-dried mud, while the two men talked around him in an incomprehensible tongue. Mrs. Smith had refused to come downstairs till the madman was off the premises; Amy Foster, far from within the dark kitchen, watched through the open back door; and he obeyed the signs that were made to him to the best of his ability. But Smith was full of mistrust. 'Mind, sir! It may be all his cunning,' he cried repeatedly in a tone of warning. When Mr. Swaffer started the mare, the deplorable being sitting humbly by his side, through weakness, nearly fell out over the back of the high two-wheeled cart. Swaffer took him straight home. And it is then that I come upon the scene.

"I was called in by the simple process of the old man beckoning to me with his forefinger over the gate of his house as I happened to be driving past. I got down, of course.

"'I've got something here,' he mumbled, leading the way to an outhouse at a little distance from his other farm-buildings.

"It was there that I saw him first, in a long low room taken upon the space of that sort of coachhouse. It was bare and whitewashed, with a small square aperture glazed with one cracked, dusty pane at its further end. He was lying on his back upon a straw pallet; they had given him a couple of horse-blankets, and he seemed to have spent the remainder of his strength in the exertion of cleaning himself. He was almost speechless; his quick breathing under the blankets pulled up to his chin, his glittering, restless black eyes reminded me of a wild bird caught in a snare. While I was examining him, old Swaffer stood silently by the door, passing the tips of his fingers along his shaven upper lip. I gave some directions, promised to send a bottle of medicine, and naturally made some inquiries.

"'Smith caught him in the stackyard at New Barns,' said the old chap in his deliberate, unmoved manner, and as if the other had been indeed a sort of wild animal. 'That's how I came by him. Quite a curiosity, isn't he? Now tell me, doctor—you've been all over the world—don't you think that's a bit of a Hindoo[2] we've got hold of here.'

"I was greatly surprised. His long black hair scattered over the straw bolster contrasted with the olive pallor of his face. It occurred to me he might be a Basque. It didn't necessarily follow that he should understand Spanish; but I tried him with the few words I know, and also with some French. The whispered sounds I caught by bending my ear to his lips puzzled me utterly. That afternoon the young ladies from the Rectory (one of them read Goethe with a dictionary, and the other had struggled with Dante for years), coming to see Miss Swaffer, tried their German and Italian on him from the doorway. They retreated, just the least bit scared by the flood of passionate speech which, turning on his pallet, he let out at them. They admitted that the sound was pleasant, soft, musical—but, in conjunction with his looks perhaps, it was startling—so excitable, so utterly unlike anything one had ever heard. The village boys climbed up the bank to have a peep through the little square aperture. Everybody was wondering what Mr. Swaffer would do with him.

"He simply kept him.

"Swaffer would be called eccentric were he not so much respected. They will tell you that Mr. Swaffer sits up as late as ten o'clock at night to read books, and they will tell you also that he can write a cheque for two hundred pounds without thinking twice about it. He himself would tell you that the Swaffers had owned land between this and Darnford for these three hundred years. He must be eighty-five to-day, but he does not look a bit older than when I first came here. He is a great breeder of sheep, and deals extensively in cattle. He attends market days for miles around in every sort of weather, and drives sitting bowed low over the reins, his lank grey hair curling over the collar of his warm coat, and with a green plaid rug round his legs. The calmness of advanced age gives solemnity to his manner. He is clean-shaved; his lips are thin and sensitive; something rigid and monachal in the set of his features lends a certain elevation to the character of his face. He has been known to drive miles in the rain to see a new kind of rose in somebody's garden, or a monstrous cabbage grown by a cottager. He loves to hear tell of or to be shown something that he calls 'outlandish.' Perhaps it was just that outlandishness of the man which influenced old Swaffer. Perhaps it was only an inexplicable caprice. All I know is that at the end of three weeks I caught sight of Smith's lunatic digging in Swaffer's kitchen garden. They had found out he could use a spade. He dug barefooted.

"His black hair flowed over his shoulders. I suppose it was Swaffer who had given him the striped old cotton shirt; but he wore still the national brown cloth trousers (in which he had been washed ashore) fitting to the leg almost like tights; was belted with a broad leather belt studded with little brass discs; and had never yet ventured

---

[2]*Hindoo*   Hindu (Indian).

into the village. The land he looked upon seemed to him kept neatly, like the grounds round a landowner's house; the size of the cart-horses struck him with astonishment; the roads resembled garden walks, and the aspect of the people, especially on Sundays, spoke of opulence. He wondered what made them so hardhearted and their children so bold. He got his food at the back door, carried it in both hands carefully to his outhouse, and, sitting alone on his pallet, would make the sign of the cross before he began. Beside the same pallet, kneeling in the early darkness of the short days, he recited aloud the Lord's Prayer before he slept. Whenever he saw old Swaffer he would bow with veneration from the waist, and stand erect while the old man, with his fingers over his upper lip, surveyed him silently. He bowed also to Miss Swaffer, who kept house frugally for her father—a broad-shouldered, a big-boned woman of forty-five, with the pocket of her dress full of keys, and a grey, steady eye. She was Church—as people said (while her father was one of the trustees of the Baptist Chapel[3])—and wore a little steel cross at her waist. She dressed severely in black, in memory of one of the innumerable Bradleys of the neighbourhood, to whom she had been engaged some twenty-five years ago—a young farmer who broke his neck out hunting on the eve of the wedding day. She had the unmoved countenance of the deaf, spoke very seldom, and her lips, thin like her father's, astonished one sometimes by a mysteriously ironic curl.

"These were the people to whom he owed allegiance, and an overwhelming loneliness seemed to fall from the leaden sky of that winter without sunshine. All the faces were sad. He could talk to no one, and had no hope of ever understanding anybody. It was as if these had been the faces of people from the other world—dead people— he used to tell me years afterwards. Upon my word, I wonder he did not go mad. He didn't know where he was. Somewhere very far from his mountains—somewhere over the water. Was this America, he wondered?

"If it hadn't been for the steel cross at Miss Swaffer's belt he would not, he confessed, have known whether he was in a Christian country at all. He used to cast stealthy glances at it, and feel comforted. There was nothing here the same as in his country! The earth and the water were different; there were no images of the Redeemer by the roadside. The very grass was different, and the trees. All the trees but the three old Norway pines on the bit of lawn before Swaffer's house, and these reminded him of his country. He had been detected once, after dusk, with his forehead against the trunk of one of them, sobbing, and talking to himself. They had been like brothers to him at that time, he affirmed. Everything else was strange. Conceive you the kind of an existence overshadowed, oppressed, by the everyday material appearances, as if by the visions of a nightmare. At night, when he could not sleep, he kept on thinking of the girl who gave him the first piece of bread he had eaten in this foreign land. She had been neither fierce nor angry, nor frightened. Her face he remembered as the only comprehensible face amongst all these faces that were as closed, as mysterious, and as mute as the faces of the dead who are possessed of a knowledge beyond the comprehension of the living. I wonder whether the memory of her compassion prevented him from cutting his throat. But there! I supposed I am an old sentimentalist, and forget the instinctive love of life which it takes all the strength of an uncommon despair to overcome.

---

[3]*Church* and *Chapel*   In Great Britain *Church* refers to the official Episcopal Church of England; *Chapel* refers to places of worship for those who are not members of the established Church or, broadly, to the practitioners of such worship.

"He did the work which was given him with an intelligence which surprised old Swaffer. By-and-by it was discovered that he could help at the ploughing, could milk the cows, feed the bullocks in the cattle-yard, and was of some use with the sheep. He began to pick up words, too, very fast; and suddenly, one fine morning in spring, he rescued from an untimely death a grand-child of old Swaffer.

"Swaffer's younger daughter is married to Willcox, a solicitor and the Town Clerk of Colebrook. Regularly twice a year they come to stay with the old man for a few days. Their only child, a little girl not three years old at the time, ran out of the house alone in her little white pinafore, and, toddling across the grass of a terraced garden, pitched herself over a low wall head first into the horse-pond in the yard below.

"Our man was out with the waggoner and the plough in the field nearest to the house, and as he was leading the team round to begin a fresh furrow, he saw, through the gap of the gate, what for anybody else would have been a mere flutter of something white. But he had straight-glancing, quick, far-reaching eyes, that only seemed to flinch and lose their amazing power before the immensity of the sea. He was barefooted, and looking as outlandish as the heart of Swaffer could desire. Leaving the horses on the turn, to the inexpressible disgust of the waggoner he bounded off, going over the ploughed ground in long leaps, and suddenly appeared before the mother, thrust the child into her arms, and strode away.

"The pond was not very deep; but still, if he had not had such good eyes, the child would have perished—miserably suffocated in the foot or so of sticky mud at the bottom. Old Swaffer walked out slowly into the field, waited till the plough came over to his side, had a good look at him, and without saying a word went back to the house. But from that time they laid out his meals on the kitchen table; and at first, Miss Swaffer, all in black and with an inscrutable face, would come and stand in the doorway of the living-room to see him make a big sign of the cross before he fell to. I believe that from that day, too, Swaffer began to pay him regular wages.

"I can't follow step by step his development. He cut his hair short, was seen in the village and along the road going to and fro to his work like any other man. Children ceased to shout after him. He became aware of social differences, but remained for a long time surprised at the bare poverty of the churches among so much wealth. He couldn't understand either why they were kept shut up on week days. There was nothing to steal in them. Was it to keep people from praying too often? The rectory took much notice of him about that time, and I believe the young ladies attempted to prepare the ground for his conversion. They could not, however, break him of his habit of crossing himself, but he went so far as to take off the string with a couple of brass medals the size of a sixpence, a tiny metal cross, and a square sort of scapulary which he wore round his neck. He hung them on the wall by the side of his bed, and he was still to be heard every evening reciting the Lord's Prayer, in incomprehensible words and in a slow, fervent tone, as he had heard his old father do at the head of all the kneeling family, big and little, on every evening of his life. And though he wore corduroys at work, and a slop-made pepper-and-salt suit on Sundays, strangers would turn round to look after him on the road. His foreignness had a peculiar and indelible stamp. At last people became used to seeing him. But they never became used to him. His rapid, skimming walk; his swarthy complexion; his hat cocked on the left ear; his habit, on warm evenings, of wearing his coat over one shoulder, like a hussar's dolman; his manner of leaping over the stiles, not as a feat of agility, but in the ordinary course of progression—all these peculiarities were, as one may say, so many causes of scorn and offence to the inhabitants of the village. *They* wouldn't in their dinner hour lie flat on their backs on the grass to stare at the sky. Neither did they go about the fields screaming dismal tunes. Many times have I heard his high-pitched voice from behind the ridge of some sloping sheep-walk, a voice light and soaring, like a lark's, but with a melancholy human note, over our fields that hear only the song of birds. And I should be startled myself. Ah! He was different: innocent of heart, and full of good will, which nobody wanted, this castaway, that, like a man transplanted into another planet, was separated by an immense space from his past and by an immense ignorance from his future. His quick, fervent utterance positively shocked everybody. 'An excitable devil,' they called him. One evening, in the taproom of the Coach and Horses (having drunk some whisky), he upset them all by singing a love song of his country. They hooted him down, and he was pained; but Preble, the lame wheelwright, and Vincent, the fat blacksmith, and the other notables too, wanted to drink their evening beer in peace. On another occasion he tried to show them how to dance. The dust rose in clouds from the sanded floor; he leaped straight up amongst the deal tables, struck his heels together, squatted on one heel in front of old Preble, shooting out the other leg, uttered wild and exulting cries, jumped up to whirl on one foot, snapping his fingers above his head—and a strange carter who was having a drink in there began to swear, and cleared out with his half-pint in his hand into the bar. But when suddenly he sprang upon a table and continued to dance among the glasses, the landlord interfered. He didn't want any 'acrobat tricks in the taproom.' They laid their hands on him. Having had a glass or two, Mr. Swaffer's foreigner tried to expostulate: was ejected forcibly: got a black eye.

"I believe he felt the hostility of his human surroundings. But he was tough—tough in spirit, too, as well as in body. Only the memory of the sea frightened him, with that vague terror that is left by a bad dream. His home was far away; and he did not want now to go to America. I had often explained to him that there is no place on earth where true gold can be found lying ready and to be got for the trouble of the picking up. How then, he asked, could he ever return home with empty hands when there had been sold a cow, two ponies, and a bit of land to pay for his going? His eyes would fill with tears, and, averting them from the immense shimmer of the sea, he would throw himself face down on the grass. But sometimes, cocking his hat with a little conquering air, he would defy my wisdom. He had found his bit of true gold. That was Amy Foster's heart; which was 'a golden heart, and soft to people's misery,' he would say in the accents of overwhelming conviction.

"He was called Yanko. He had explained that this meant little John; but as he would also repeat very often that he was a mountaineer (some word sounding in the dialect of his country like Goorall) he got it for his surname. And this is the only trace of him that the succeeding ages may find in the marriage register of the parish. There it stands—Yanko Goorall—in the rector's handwriting. The crooked cross made by the castaway, a cross whose tracing no doubt seemed to him the most solemn part of the whole ceremony, is all that remains now to perpetuate the memory of his name.

"His courtship had lasted some time—ever since he got his precarious footing in the community. It began by his buying for Amy Foster a green satin ribbon in Darnford. This was what you did in his country. You bought a ribbon at a Jew's stall on a fair-day. I don't suppose the girl knew what to do with it, but he seemed to think that his honourable intentions could not be mistaken.

"It was only when he declared his purpose to get married that I fully understood how, for a hundred futile and inappreciable reasons, how—shall I say odious?—he was to all the countryside. Every old woman in the village was up in arms. Smith, coming upon him near the farm, promised to break his head for him if he found him about again. But he twisted his little black moustache with such a bellicose air and rolled such big, black fierce eyes at Smith that this promise came to nothing. Smith, however, told the girl that she must be mad to take up with a man who was surely wrong in his head. All the same, when she heard him in the gloaming whistle from beyond the orchard a couple of bars of a weird and mournful tune, she would drop whatever she had in her hand—she would leave Mrs. Smith in the middle of a sentence—and she would run out to his call. Mrs. Smith called her a shameless hussy. She answered nothing. She said nothing at all to anybody, and went on her way as if she had been deaf. She and I alone in all the land, I fancy, could see his very real beauty. He was very good-looking, and most graceful in his bearing, with that something wild as of a woodland creature in his aspect. Her mother moaned over her dismally whenever the girl came to see her on her day out. The father was surly, but pretended not to know; and Mrs. Finn once told her plainly that 'this man, my dear, will do you some harm some day yet.' And so it went on. They could be seen on the roads, she tramping stolidly in her finery—grey dress, black feather, stout boots, prominent white cotton gloves that caught your eye a hundred yards away; and he, his coat slung picturesquely over one shoulder, pacing by her side, gallant of bearing and casting tender glances upon the girl with the golden heart. I wonder whether he saw how plain she was. Perhaps among types so different from what he had ever seen, he had not the power to judge; or perhaps he was seduced by the divine quality of her pity.

"Yanko was in great trouble meantime. In his country you get an old man for an ambassador in marriage affairs. He did not know how to proceed. However, one day in the midst of sheep in a field (he was now Swaffer's under-shepherd with Foster) he took off his hat to the father and declared himself humbly. 'I daresay she's fool enough to marry you,' was all Foster said. 'And then,' he used to relate, 'he puts his hat on his head, looks black at me as if he wanted to cut my throat, whistles the dog, and off he goes, leaving me to do the work.' The Fosters, of course, didn't like to lose the wages the girl earned: Amy used to give all her money to her mother. But there was in Foster a very genuine aversion to that match. He contended that the fellow was very good with sheep, but was not fit for any girl to marry. For one thing, he used to go along the hedges muttering to himself like a dam' fool; and then, these foreigners behave very queerly to women sometimes. And perhaps he would want to carry her off somewhere—or run off himself. It was not safe. He preached it to his daughter that the fellow might ill-use her in some way. She made no answer. It was, they said in the village, as if the man had done something to her. People discussed the matter. It was quite an excitement, and the two went on 'walking out' together in the face of opposition. Then something unexpected happened.

"I don't know whether old Swaffer ever understood how much he was regarded in the light of a father by his foreign retainer. Anyway the relation was curiously feudal. So when Yanko asked formally for an interview—'and the Miss too' (he called the severe, deaf Miss Swaffer simply Miss)—it was to obtain their permission to marry. Swaffer heard him unmoved, dismissed him by a nod, and then shouted the intelligence into Miss Swaffer's best ear. She showed no surprise, and only remarked grimly, in a veiled blank voice, 'He certainly won't get any other girl to marry him.'

"It is Miss Swaffer who has all the credit of the munificence: but in a very few days it came out that Mr. Swaffer had presented Yanko with a cottage (the cottage you've seen this morning) and something like an acre of ground—had made it over to him in absolute property. Willcox expedited the deed, and I remember him telling me he had a great pleasure in making it ready. It recited: 'In consideration of saving the life of my beloved grandchild, Bertha Willcox.'

"Of course, after that no power on earth could prevent them from getting married.

"Her infatuation endured. People saw her going out to meet him in the evening. She stared with unblinking, fascinated eyes up the road where he was expected to appear, walking freely, with a swing from the hip, and humming one of the love-tunes of his country. When the boy was born, he got elevated at the 'Coach and Horses,' essayed again a song and a dance, and was again ejected. People expressed their commiseration for a woman married to that Jack-in-the-box. He didn't care. There was a man now (he told me boastfully) to whom he could sing and talk in the language of his country, and show how to dance by-and-by.

"But I don't know. To me he appeared to have grown less springy of step, heavier in body, less keen of eye. Imagination, no doubt; but it seems to me now as if the net of fate had been drawn closer round him already.

"One day I met him on the footpath over the Talfourd Hill. He told me that 'women were funny.' I had heard already of domestic differences. People were saying that Amy Foster was beginning to find out what sort of man she had married. He looked upon the sea with indifferent, unseeing eyes. His wife had snatched the child out of his arms one day as he sat on the doorstep crooning to it a song such as the mothers sing to babies in his mountains. She seemed to think he was doing it some harm. Women are funny. And she had objected to him praying aloud in the evening. Why? He expected the boy to repeat the prayer aloud after him by-and-by, as he used to do after his old father when he was a child—in his own country. And I discovered he longed for their boy to grow up so that he could have a man to talk with in that language that to our ears sounded so disturbing, so passionate, and so bizarre. Why his wife should dislike the idea he couldn't tell. But that would pass, he said. And tilting his head knowingly, he tapped his breastbone to indicate that she had a good heart: not hard, not fierce, open to compassion, charitable to the poor!

"I walked away thoughtfully; I wondered whether his difference, his strangeness, were not penetrating with repulsion that dull nature they had begun by irresistibly attracting. I wondered. . . ."

The Doctor came to the window and looked out at the frigid splendour of the sea, immense in the haze, as if enclosing all the earth with all the hearts lost among the passions of love and fear.

"Physiologically, now," he said, turning away abruptly, "it was possible. It was possible."

He remained silent. Then went on—

"At all events, the next time I saw him he was ill—lung trouble. He was tough, but I daresay he was not acclimatised as well as I had supposed. It was a bad winter; and, of course, these mountaineers do get fits of home sickness; and a state of depression would make him vulnerable. He was lying half dressed on a couch downstairs.

"A table covered with a dark oilcloth took up all the middle of the little room. There was a wicker cradle on the floor, a kettle spouting steam on the hob, and some child's linen lay drying on the fender. The room was warm, but the door opens right into the garden, as you noticed perhaps.

"He was very feverish, and kept on muttering to himself. She sat on a chair and looked at him fixedly across the table with her brown, blurred eyes. 'Why don't you have him upstairs?' I asked. With a start and a confused stammer she said, 'Oh, ah! I couldn't sit with him upstairs, Sir.'

"I gave her certain directions; and going outside, I said again that he ought to be in bed upstairs. She wrung her hands. 'I couldn't. I couldn't. He keeps on saying something—I don't know what.' With the memory of all the talk against the man that had been dinned into her ears, I looked at her narrowly. I looked into her short-sighted eyes, at her dumb eyes that once in her life had seen an enticing shape, but seemed, staring at me, to see nothing at all now. But I saw she was uneasy.

"'What's the matter with him?' she asked in a sort of vacant trepidation. 'He doesn't look very ill. I never did see anybody look like this before. . . .'

"'Do you think,' I asked indignantly, 'he is shamming?'

"'I can't help it, sir,' she said stolidly. And suddenly she clapped her hands and looked right and left. 'And there's the baby. I am so frightened. He wanted me just now to give him the baby. I can't understand what he says to it.'

"'Can't you ask a neighbour to come in tonight?' I asked.

"'Please, sir, nobody seems to care to come,' she muttered, dully resigned all at once.

"I impressed upon her the necessity of the greatest care, and then had to go. There was a good deal of sickness that winter. 'Oh, I hope he won't talk!' she exclaimed softly just as I was going away.

"I don't know how it is I did not see—but I didn't. And yet, turning in my trap, I saw her lingering before the door, very still, and as if meditating a flight up the miry road.

"Towards the night his fever increased.

"He tossed, moaned, and now and then muttered a complaint. And she sat with the table between her and the couch, watching every movement and every sound, with the terror, the unreasonable terror, of that man she could not understand creeping over her. She had drawn the wicker cradle close to her feet. There was nothing in her now but the maternal instinct and that unaccountable fear.

"Suddenly coming to himself, parched, he demanded a drink of water. She did not move. She had not understood, though he may have thought he was speaking in English. He waited, looking at her, burning with fever, amazed at her silence and immobility, and then he shouted impatiently, 'Water! Give me water!'

"She jumped to her feet, snatched up the child, and stood still. He spoke to her, and his passionate remonstrances only increased her fear of that strange man. I believe he spoke to her for a long time, entreating, wondering, pleading, ordering, I suppose. She says she bore it as long as she could. And then a gust of rage came over him.

"He sat up and called out terribly one word—some word. Then he got up as though he hadn't been ill at all, she says. And as in fevered dismay, indignation, and wonder he tried to get to her round the table, she simply opened the door and ran out with the child in her arms. She heard him call twice after her down the road in a terrible voice—and fled. . . . Ah! but you should have seen stirring behind the dull, blurred glance of those eyes the spectre of the fear which had hunted her on that night three miles and a half to the door of Foster's cottage! I did the next day.

"And it was I who found him lying face down and his body in a puddle, just outside the little wicket-gate.

"I had been called out that night to an urgent case in the village, and on my way home at day-break passed by the cottage. The door stood open. My man helped me to carry him in. We laid him on the couch. The lamp smoked, the fire was out, the chill of the stormy night oozed from the cheerless yellow paper on the wall. 'Amy!' I called aloud, and my voice seemed to lose itself in the emptiness of this tiny house as if I had cried in a desert. He opened his eyes. 'Gone!' he said distinctly. 'I had only asked for water—only for a little water. . . .

"He was muddy. I covered him up and stood waiting in silence, catching a painfully gasped word now and then. They were no longer in his own language. The fever had left him, taking with it the heat of life. And with his panting breast and lustrous eyes he reminded me again of a wild creature under the net; of a bird caught in a snare. She had left him. She had left him—sick—helpless—thirsty. The spear of the hunter had entered his very soul. 'Why?' he cried in the penetrating and indignant voice of a man calling to a responsible Maker. A gust of wind and a swish of rain answered.

"And as I turned away to shut the door he pronounced the word 'Merciful!' and expired.

"Eventually I certified heart-failure as the immediate cause of death. His heart must have indeed failed him, or else he might have stood this night of storm and exposure, too. I closed his eyes and drove away. Not very far from the cottage I met Foster walking sturdily between the dripping hedges with his collie at his heels.

"Do you know where your daughter is?' I asked.

"'Don't I!' he cried. 'I am going to talk to him a bit. Frightening a poor woman like this.'

"'He won't frighten her any more,' I said. 'He is dead.'

"He struck with his stick at the mud.

"'And there's the child.'

"Then, after thinking deeply for a while—

"'I don't know that it isn't for the best.'

"That's what he said. And she says nothing at all now. Not a word of him. Never. Is his image as utterly gone from her mind as his lithe and striding figure, his carolling voice are gone from our fields? He is no longer before her eyes to excite her imagination into a passion of love or fear; and his memory seems to have vanished from her dull brain as a shadow passes away upon a white screen. She lives in the cottage and works for Miss Swaffer. She is Amy Foster for everybody, and the child is 'Amy Foster's boy.' She calls him Johnny—which means Little John.

"It is impossible to say whether this name recalls anything to her. Does she ever think of the past? I have seen her hanging over the boy's cot in a very passion of maternal tenderness. The little fellow was lying on his back, a little frightened at me, but very still, with his big black eyes, with his fluttered air of a bird in a snare. And looking at him I seemed to see again the other one—the father, cast out mysteriously by the sea to perish in the supreme disaster of loneliness and despair."

[1903]

Questions

1. Why does the narrator refer several times to the villagers' lack of imagination? How does this lack affect their response to the foreigner? Why do their suspicions persist long after Yanko settles into village life?

2. What is Amy Foster's role in Yanko's initial survival after the shipwreck and in his eventual death? What accounts for the difference in her responses to him in his moments of extremity?

3. What does the story suggest about the nature and limitations of communication, especially across cultural and linguistic barriers? What does it suggest about people's perceptions of and reaction to foreigners?

4. Compare this story, and the dilemmas inherent in cross-cultural communication and understanding, with R. K. Narayan's "A Horse and Two Goats," Sembene Ousmane's "Black Girl," and Margaret Atwood's "Dancing Girls."

Birago Diop
(1906–1989)
Senegal

Birago Diop was born in Senegal, where he received part of his education at the Lycée Faidherbe in St. Louis. He furthered his studies in France, at the University of Toulouse, becoming a veterinary surgeon. We mention this fact because the narrator of "Sarzan" identifies himself as a veterinarian who has been in Europe yet who clearly has managed to reconcile his traditional African background with Western culture in a way that Sarzan has not. "Sarzan," thus, posits an interesting dilemma: The story is told by someone who has presumably undergone many of the same cultural conflicts as the main character yet has apparently resolved them. One must ask, then, how relevant is the narrator's point of view to the story he tells? An appreciation for "Sarzan" is equally dependent on an understanding of animism—the belief in the power that one's ancestors have over the living. As you read the story, pay particular attention to the poems that Sarzan recites, his so-called babbling.

Often considered one of the founders of négritude, Diop published numerous volumes of poetry and short stories during his life. Besides his career as a veterinary surgeon, he held a number of positions as a civil servant, including Ambassador to Tunisia in the early 1960s. "Sarzan" is from Les Contes d'Amadou Koumba (1947).

SARZAN

It was hard to distinguish the piles of ruins from the termite mounds, and only an ostrich shell, cracked and yellowed by the weather, still indicated at the tip of a tall column what once had been the *mirab* of the mosque El Hadj Omar's[1] warriors had built. The Toucouleur conqueror had shorn the hair and shaved the heads of the forbears of those who are now the village elders. He had decapitated those who would not submit to Koranic law. Once again, the village elders wear their hair in braids. The sacred woods long ago burnt by the fanatic Talibés have long since grown tall again, and still harbour the cult objects, pots whitened from the boiling of millet or browned by the clotted blood of sacrificed chickens and dogs.

Like grain felled at random beneath the flail, or ripe fruits that drop from branches filled with sap, whole families left Dougouba to form new villages, Dougoubanis. Some of the young people would go off to work in Segou, in Bamako, in Kayes, or Dakar; others went to work the Senegalese groundnut fields, returning when the harvest was in and the product had been shipped. All knew the root of their lives was still in Dougouba, which had long ago erased all traces of the Islamic hordes and returned to the teachings of the ancestors.

---

[1] *El Hadj Omar*   Islamic conqueror of much of upper Senegal who died in 1864.

One son of Dougouba had ventured farther and for a longer time than any of the others: Thiemokho Keita.

From Dougouba he went to the local capital, from there to Kati, from Kati to Dakar, from Dakar to Casablanca, from Casablanca to Frejus, and then to Damascus. Leaving the Sudan to be a soldier, Thiemokho Keita had been trained in Senegal, fought in Morocco, stood guard in France, and patrolled in Lebanon. He returned to Dougouba a sergeant, catching a lift in my medical caravan.

I had been making my veterinarian's rounds in the heart of the Sudan when I met Sergeant Keita in a local administrator's office. He had just been discharged from the service and wanted to enlist in the local police, or to be taken on as an interpreter.

"No," the local commandant told him. "You can do more for the administration by returning to your village. You who have travelled so much and seen so much, you can teach the others something about how white men live. You'll 'civilize' them a bit. Say there, Doctor," he continued, turning to me, "since you're going in that direction, won't you take Keita with you? It will spare him the wear and tear of the road and save him some time. It's fifteen years he's been gone."

So we set out. The driver, the sergeant and I occupied the front seat of the little truck, while behind, the cooks, medical aides, driver's helper and civil guard were crowded together among the field kitchen, the camp bed and the cases of serum and vaccine. The sergeant told me about his life as a soldier, then as a noncommissioned officer. I heard about the Riff Wars from the viewpoint of a Sudanese rifleman; he talked about Marseille, Toulon, Frejus, Beirut. He seemed no longer to see the road in front of us. Rough as a corrugated tin room, it was paved with logs covered with a layer of clay, disintegrating into dust now because of the torrid heat and the extreme dryness. It was an unctuous oily dust that stuck to our faces like a yellow mask, making our teeth gritty and screening from our view the chattering baboons and frightened does that leaped about in our wake. Through the choking haze, Keita seemed to see once more the minarets of Fez, the teeming crowds of Marseille, the great tall buildings of France, the blue sea.

By noon we reached the town of Madougou, where the road ended. To reach Dougouba by nightfall, we took horses and bearers.

"When you come back this way again," Keita said, "you'll go all the way to Dougouba by car. Tomorrow I'm going to get started on a road."

The muffled rolling of a tom-tom announced that we were nearing the village. A grey mass of huts appeared, topped by the darker grey of three palm trees against a paler grey sky. The rumbling was accompanied now by the sharp sound of three notes on a flute. We were in Dougouba. I got down first and asked for the village chief.

"*Dougou-tigui*,[2] here is your son, the Sergeant Keita."

Thiemokho Keita jumped down from his horse. As if the sound of his shoes on the ground had been a signal, the drumming stopped and the flute was silent. The aged chief took Keita's two hands while other old men examined his arms, his shoulders, his decorations. Some old women ran up and began fingering the puttees at his knees. Tears shone on the dark faces, settling in the wrinkles that crossed their ritual scars. Everyone was saying:

"Keita, Keita, Keita!"

---

[2]*Dougou-tigui* Honorific title.

"Those," the old man quavered at last, "those who brought your steps back to our village on this day are generous and good."

It was in fact a day unlike other days in Dougouba. It was the day of the Kotéba, the day of the Testing.

The drum resumed its rumbling, pierced by the sharp whistles of the flute. Inside the circle of women, children, and grown men, bare-chested youngsters, each carrying a long branch of balazan wood, stripped clean and supple as a whip, were turning about to the rhythm of the tom-tom. In the centre of this moving circle, crouching with his knees and elbows on the ground, the flute player gave forth three notes, always the same. Above him a young man would come to stand, legs apart, arms spread in the shape of a cross, while the others, passing close to him, let their whips whistle. The blows fell on his chest, leaving a stripe wide as a thumb, sometimes breaking the skin. The sharp voice of the flute would go a note higher, the tom-tom would grow softer, as the whips whistled and the blood ran. Firelight gleamed on the black-brown body and light from the embers leaped to the tops of the palm trees, softly creaking in the evening wind. Kotéba! the test of endurance, the testing for insensibility to pain. The child who cries when he hurts himself is only a child; the child who cries when he is hurt will not make a man.

Kotéba! to offer one's back, receive the blow, turn around and give it back to someone else. Kotéba!

"This, these are still the ways of savages!"

I turned round, it was Sergeant Keita who had come to join me by the drum.

The ways of savages? This testing, which among other things produced men who were hard and tough! What was it that had enabled the forbears of these youngsters to march with enormous burdens on their heads for whole days without stopping? What had made Thiemokho Keita himself, and others like him, able to fight valiantly beneath skies where the sun itself is very often sickly, to labour with heavy packs on their backs, enduring cold, thirst, and hunger?

The ways of savages? Perhaps. But I was thinking that elsewhere, where I came from, we had left these initiations behind. For our adolescents there was no longer a 'house of men' where the body, the mind and the character were tempered; where the ancient *passines*, the riddles and conundrums, were learned by dint of beatings on the bent back and the held-out fingers, and where the *kassaks*, the age-old memory training songs whose words and wisdom descend to us from the dark nights, were assured their place in our heads by the heat of live coals that burned the palms of our hands. I was thinking that as far as I could see we had still gained nothing, that perhaps we had left these old ways behind without having caught up with the new ones.

The tom-tom murmured on, sustaining the piercing voice of the flute. The fires died and were born again. I went to the hut that had been prepared for me. Inside, mixed with the thick smell of *banco*—the dried clay kneaded with broken rotten straw that made the hut rainproof—a subtler odour hung, the fragrance of the dead, whose number, three, was indicated by animal horns fixed to the wall at the level of a man's height. For, in Dougouba, the cemetery too had disappeared, and the dead continued to live with the living. They were buried in the huts.

The sun was already warm when I took my leave, but Dougouba was still asleep: drunk, both from fatigue and from the millet beer that had circulated in calabashes from hand to mouth and mouth to hand the whole night long.

"Good bye," said Keita. "The next time you come there will be a road, I promise you."

The work in other sectors and localities kept me from returning to Dougouba until the following year.

It was late in the afternoon after a hard journey. The air seemed a thick mass, hot and sticky, that we pushed our way through with great effort.

Sergeant Keita had kept his word; the road went all the way to Dougouba. As in all the villages at the sound of the car a swarm of naked children appeared at the end of the road, their little bodies grey-white with dust, and on their heels came the reddish-brown dogs with cropped ears and bony flanks. In the midst of the children a man was gesticulating, waving a cow's tail attached to his right wrist. When the car stopped, I saw it was the sergeant, Thiemokho Keita. He wore a faded fatigue jacket, without buttons or stripes. Underneath were a *boubou* and pants made of strips of khaki-coloured cotton, like the ones worn by the village elders. His pants stopped above the knee and were held together with pieces of string. His puttees were in rags. He was barefoot but wore a *képi*[3] on his head.

"Keita!"

The children scattered like a volley of sparrows, chirping:

"Ayi! Ayi!" (No! No!)

Theimokho Keita did not take my hand. He looked at me, but seemed not to see me. His gaze was so distant that I couldn't help turning around to see what his eyes were fixed upon through mine. Suddenly, agitating his cowtail, he began to cry out in a hoarse voice:

> *Listen to things*
> *More often than beings*
> *Hear the voice of fire*
> *Hear the voice of water*
> *Listen in the wind to*
> *the sighs of the bush*
> *This is the ancestors breathing.*

"He's mad," said my driver, whom I silenced with a gesture. The sergeant was still chanting, in a strange, sing-song voice:

> *Those who are dead are not ever gone*
> *They are in the darkness that grows lighter*
> *And in the darkness that grows darker*
> *The dead are not down in the earth*
> *They are in the trembling of the trees*
> *In the moaning of the woods*
> *In the water that runs*
> *In the water that sleeps*
> *They are in the hut, they are in the crowd.*
>
> > *The dead are not dead.*
> > *Listen to things*

---

[3]*képi* French: military cap.

More often than beings
Hear the voice of fire
Hear the voice of water
Listen in the wind
To the bush that is sighing
This is the breathing of ancestors
Who have not gone away
Who are not under earth
Who are not really dead.

Those who are dead are not ever gone
They are in a woman's breast
In a child's wailing
and the log burning
in the moaning rock and
in the weeping grasses
in the forest in the home
The dead are not dead.

Hear the fire speak
Hear the water speak
Listen in the wind to
the bush that is sobbing
This is the ancestors breathing.

Each day they renew ancient bonds
Ancient bonds that hold fast
Binding our lot to their law
To the will of the spirits stronger than we are
Whose covenant binds us to life
Whose authority binds to their will
The will of the spirits that move
In the bed of the river, on the banks of the river
The breathing of ancestors
Wailing in the rocks and weeping in the grasses.

Spirits inhabit
the darkness that lightens, the darkness that darkens
the quivering tree, the murmuring wood
the running and the sleeping waters
Spirits much stronger than we are
The breathing of the dead who are not really dead
Of the dead who are not really gone
Of the dead now no more in the earth.
Listen to things
More often than beings. . . .

The children returned, circling round the old chief and the village elders. After the greetings, I asked what had happened to Sergeant Keita.

"Ayi! Ayi! said the old men. "Ayi! Ayi!" echoed the children.

"No, not Keita!" said the old father, "Sarzan,[4] just Sarzan. We must not rouse the anger of the departed. Sarzan is no longer a Keita. The Dead and the Spirits have punished him for his offences."

It had begun the day after his arrival, the very day of my departure from Dougouba.

Sergeant Keita had wanted to keep his father from sacrificing a white chicken to thank the ancestors for having brought him home safe and sound. Keita declared that if he had come home it was quite simply that he had had to, and that the ancestors had had nothing to do with it.

"Leave the dead be," he had said. "They can no longer do anything for the living." The old chief had paid no attention and the chicken had been sacrificed.

When it was time to work the fields, Thiemokho had called it useless and even stupid to kill black chickens and pour their blood into a corner of the fields. The work, he said, was enough. Rain would fall if it was going to. The millet, corn, groundnuts, yams and beans would grow all by themselves, and would grow better if the villagers would use the ploughs the local administrator had sent him. Keita cut down and burned the branches of Dassiri, the sacred tree, protector of the village and the cultivated fields, at whose foot the dogs were sacrificed.

On the day when the little boys were to be circumcised and the little girls excised,[5] Sergeant Keita had leaped upon their teacher, the Gangourang, who was dancing and chanting. He tore off the porcupine quills the Gangourang wore upon his head, and the netting that hid his body. From the head of Mama Djombo, the venerable grandfather who taught the young girls, Keita had ripped the cone-shaped yellow headdress topped with gri-gri charms and ribbons. All this he called "the ways of savages." And yet he had been to Nice, and seen the carnival with the funny and frightening masks. The Whites, the Toubabs, it is true, wore masks for fun and not in order to teach their children the wisdom of the ancients.

Sergeant Keita had unhooked the little bag hanging in his hut which held the Nyanaboli, the Keita family spirit, and had thrown it into the yard, where the skinny dogs nearly won it from the children before the chief could get there.

One morning he had gone into the sacred wood and broken the pots of boiled millet and sour milk. He had pushed over the little statues and pulled up the forked stakes tipped with hardened blood and chicken feathers. "The ways of savages," he called them. The sergeant, however, had been in churches. He had seen little statues there of saints and the Holy Virgins that people burned candles to. These statues, it is true, were covered with gilt and painted in bright colours—blues, reds and yellows. Certainly they were more beautiful than the blackened pygmies with long arms and short legs carved of cailcedrat or ebony that inhabited the sacred forest.

"You'll civilize them a bit," the local administrator had said. Sergeant Thiemokho Keita was going to "civilize" his people. It was necessary to break with tradition, do away with the beliefs upon which the village life, the existence of the families, the people's behaviour had always rested. Superstition had to be eradicated. The ways of savages. Ways of savages, the hard treatment inflicted on the young initiates at circumcision to open their minds, form their character and teach them that nowhere, at any moment of their lives, can they, will they ever be alone. A way of savages, the

---

[4]*Sarzan*   A Senegalese pronunciation of *sergeant*, the French for sergeant (Trans.).
[5]*excised*   Female circumcision.

Kotéba, which forges real men on whom pain can hold no sway. The ways of savages, the sacrifices, the blood offered to the ancestors and the earth . . . the boiling of millet and curdled milk poured out to the wandering spirits and the protective genies . . . the ways of savages.

All this Sergeant Keita proclaimed to the young and old of the village, standing in the shade of the palaver-tree.

It was nearly sunset when Thiemokho Keita went out of his mind. He was leaning against the palaver-tree, talking, talking, talking, against the medicine man who had sacrificed some dogs that very morning, against the old who didn't want to hear him, against the young who still listened to the old. He was still speaking, when suddenly he felt something like a prick on his left shoulder. He turned his head. When he looked at his listeners again, his eyes were no longer the same. A white, foamy spittle appeared at the corners of his mouth. He spoke, but it was no longer the same words that emerged from his lips. The spirits had taken his mind, and now they cried out their fear:

Black night! Black night!

He called at nightfall, and the women and children trembled in their huts:

Black night! Black night!

he cried at daybreak:

Black night! Black night!

he howled at high noon. Night and day the spirits and the genies and the ancestors made him speak, cry out and chant. . . .

It was only at dawn that I was able to doze off in the hut where the dead lived. All night I had heard Sergeant Keita coming and going, howling, weeping, and singing:

Trumpeting elephants hoot
In the darkening wood
Above the cursèd drums,
Black night, black night!

Milk sours in the calabash
Gruel hardens in the jar
And fear stalks in the hut,
Black night, black night!

The torches throw
Bodiless flames
In the air
And then, quietly, glarelessly
Smoke,
Black night, black night!

Restless spirits
Meander and moan
Muttering lost words,
Words that strike fear,
Black night, black night!

From the chickens' chilled bodies
Or the warm moving corpse
Not a drop of blood runs
Neither black blood nor red,
Black night, black night!
Trumpeting elephants hoot
Above the cursèd drums,
Black night, black night!

Orphaned, the river calls out
In fear for the people
Endlessly, fruitlessly wandering
Far from its desolate banks,
Black night, black night!

And in the savannah, forlorn
Deserted by ancestors' spirits
The trumpeting elephants hoot
Above the cursèd drums,
Black night, black night!

Sap freezes in the anxious trees
In trunks and leaves
That no longer can pray
To the ancestor haunting their feet,
Black night, black night!

Fear lurks in the hut
In the smoking torch
In the orphaned river
In the weary, soulless forest
In the anxious, faded trees

Trumpeting elephants hoot
In the darkening woods
Above the cursèd drums,
Black night, black night!

No one dared call him by his name any more for the spirits and the ancestors had made another man of him. Thiemokho Keita was gone for the villagers. Only "Sarzan" was left, Sarzan-the-Mad.

[1947]
Translated by
ELLEN CONROY KENNEDY

Questions

1. How important is the reference to Islam at the beginning of the story? In what way does it anticipate certain aspects of Sarzan's situation?
2. Can the dead drive living people insane?
3. Is the title of the story, the main character's nickname, intended to be ironic?

José Donoso

(1924–1996)
Chile

J osé Donoso was born in Santiago, Chile, in 1924. His higher education was pursued both in Chile and in the United States. Three of his early translated novels received widespread attention in the United States: Coronation (1965), Hell Has No Limits (1966), and The Obscene Bird of Night (1973). Other works have followed, including The Boom in Spanish American Literature (1971). In that work, Donoso wrote the following:

> In any case, maybe it is worthwhile to begin by pointing out that on the simplest level and prior to possible, and possibly accurate, historical and cultural explanations, there exists the fortuitous circumstance that on the same continent, in twenty-one republics where more or less recognizable varieties of Spanish are written, and during a period of a very few years, there appeared both the brilliant first novels by authors who matured very or relatively early—Vargas Llosa and Carlos Fuentes, for example—and the major novels by older, prestigious authors—Ernesto Sábato, Onetti, Cortázar—which thus produced a spectacular conjunction. In a period of scarcely six years, between 1962 and 1968, I read The Death of Artemio Cruz, The Time of the Hero, The Green House, The Shipyard, Paradiso, Hopscotch, Sobre héroes y tumbas (About Heroes and Tombs), One Hundred Years of Solitude, and other novels all recently published at that time. Suddenly, there burst into view about a dozen novels, noteworthy at the very least and populating a previously uninhabited space.

Donoso concludes his work by saying, "The Boom has been a game; perhaps more precisely, a cultural broth that nourished the tired form of the novel in Latin America for a decade."

Besides being a prolific writer, Donoso—in different stages of his life—worked as a reporter, an English teacher, and a sheep farmer. He received his country's highest literary award: the Chilean National Literature Prize in 1990.

In her notes to "Paseo" in Contemporary Latin American Short Stories, Pat McNees notes a ubiquitous theme in Donoso's writing: "[I]n everyone exists the possibility of being both beautiful and monstrous." As you read the story, consider the appropriateness of this theme to Aunt Mathilda's situation.

PASEO

I

This happened when I was very young, when my father and Aunt Mathilda, his maiden sister, and my uncles Gustav and Armand were still living. Now they are all dead. Or I should say, I prefer to think they are all dead: it is too late now for the questions they did not ask when the moment was right, because events seemed to freeze all of them into silence. Later they were able to construct a wall of forgetfulness or indifference to shut out everything, so that they would not have to harass themselves with impotent conjecture. But then, it may not have been that way at all. My imagination and my memory may be deceiving me. After all, I was only a child then, with whom they did not have to share the anguish of their inquiries, if they made any, nor the result of their discussions.

What was I to think? At times I used to hear them closeted in the library, speaking softly, slowly, as was their custom. But the massive door screened the meaning of their words, permitting me to hear only the grave and measured counterpoint of their voices. What was it they were saying? I used to hope that, inside there, abandoning the coldness which isolated each of them, they were at last speaking of what was truly important. But I had so little faith in this that, while I hung around the walls of the vestibule near the library door, my mind became filled with the certainty that they had chosen to forget, that they were meeting only to discuss, as always, some case in jurisprudence relating to their speciality in maritime law. Now I think that perhaps they were right in wanting to blot out everything. For why should one live with the terror of having to acknowledge that the streets of a city can swallow up a human being, leaving him without life and without death, suspended as it were, in a dimension more dangerous than any dimension with a name?

One day, months after, I came upon my father watching the street from the balcony of the drawing-room on the second floor. The sky was close, dense, and the humid air weighed down the large, limp leaves of the ailanthus trees. I drew near my father, eager for an answer that would contain some explanation:

"What are you doing here, Papa?" I murmured.

When he answered, something closed over the despair on his face, like the blow of a shutter closing on a shameful scene.

"Don't you see? I'm smoking . . ." he replied.

And he lit a cigarette.

It wasn't true. I knew why he was peering up and down the street, his eyes darkened, lifting his hand from time to time to stroke his smooth chestnut whiskers: it was in hope of seeing them reappear, returning under the trees of the sidewalk, the white bitch trotting at heel.

Little by little I began to realize that not only my father but all of them, hiding from one another and without confessing even to themselves what they were doing, haunted the windows of the house. If someone happened to look up from the sidewalk he would surely have seen the shadow of one or another of them posted beside a curtain, or faces aged with grief spying out from behind the window panes.

In those days the street was paved with quebracho wood, and under the ailanthus trees a clangorous streetcar used to pass from time to time. The last time I was there neither the wooden pavements nor the streetcars existed any longer. But our house was still standing, narrow and vertical like a little book pressed between the bulky volumes of new buildings, with shops on the ground level and a crude sign advertising knitted undershirts covering the balconies of the second floor.

When we lived there all the houses were tall and slender like our own. The block was always happy with the games of children playing in the patches of sunshine on the sidewalks, and with the gossip of the servant girls on their way back from shopping. But our house was not happy. I say it that way, "it was not happy" instead of "it was sad," because that is exactly what I mean to say. The word "sad" would be wrong because it has too definite a connotation, a weight and a dimension of its own. What took place in our house was exactly the opposite: an absence, a lack, which because it was unacknowledged was irremediable, something that if it weighed, weighed by not existing.

My mother died when I was only four years old, so the presence of a woman was deemed necessary for my care. As Aunt Mathilda was the only woman in the family and she lived with my uncles Armand and Gustav, the three of them came to live at our house, which was spacious and empty.

Aunt Mathilda discharged her duties towards me with that propriety which was characteristic of everything she did. I did not doubt that she loved me, but I could never feel it as a palpable experience uniting us. There was something rigid in her affections, as there was in those of the men of the family. With them, love existed confined inside each individual, never breaking its boundaries to express itself and bring them together. For them to show affection was to discharge their duties to each other perfectly, and above all not to inconvenience, never to inconvenience. Perhaps to express love in any other way was unnecessary for them now, since they had so long a history together, had shared so long a past. Perhaps the tenderness they felt in the past had been expressed to the point of satiation and found itself stylized now in the form of certain actions, useful symbols which did not require further elucidation. Respect was the only form of contact left between those four isolated individuals who walked the corridors of the house which, like a book, showed only its narrow spine to the street.

I, naturally, had no history in common with Aunt Mathilda. How could I, if I was no more than a child then, who could not understand the gloomy motivations of his elders? I wished that their confined feeling might overflow and express itself in a fit of rage, for example, or with some bit of foolery. But she could not guess this desire of mine because her attention was not focused on me: I was a person peripheral to her life, never central. And I was not central because the entire center of her being was filled up with my father and my uncles. Aunt Mathilda was born the only woman, an ugly woman moreover, in a family of handsome men, and on realizing that for her marriage was unlikely, she dedicated herself to looking out for the comfort of those three men, by keeping house for them, by taking care of their clothes and providing their favorite dishes. She did these things without the least servility, proud of her role because she did not question her brothers' excellence. Furthermore, like all women, she possessed in the highest degree the faith that physical well-being is, if not principal, certainly primary, and that to be neither hungry nor cold nor uncomfortable is the basis for whatever else is good. Not that these defects caused her grief, but rather they made her impatient, and when she saw affliction about her she took immediate steps to remedy what, without doubt, were errors in a world that should be, that had to be, perfect. On another plane, she was intolerant of shirts which were not stupendously well-ironed, of meat that was not of the finest quality, of the humidity that owing to someone's carelessness had crept into the cigar-box.

After dinner, following what must have been an ancient ritual in the family, Aunt Mathilda went upstairs to the bedrooms, and in each of her brothers' rooms she prepared the beds for sleeping, parting the sheets with her bony hands. She spread a shawl at the foot of the bed for that one, who was subject to chills, and placed a feather pillow at the head of this one, for he usually read before going to sleep. Then, leaving the lamps lighted beside those enormous beds, she came downstairs to the billiard room to join the men for coffee and for a few rounds, before, as if bewitched by

her, they retired to fill the empty effigies of the pajamas she had arranged so carefully upon the white, half-opened sheets.

But Aunt Mathilda never opened my bed. Each night, when I went up to my
room, my heart thumped in the hope of finding my bed opened with the recognizable
dexterity of her hands. But I had to adjust myself to the less pure style of the servant
girl who was charged with doing it. Aunt Mathilda never granted me that mark of importance because I was not her brother. And not to be "one of my brothers" seemed
to her a misfortune of which many people were victims, almost all in fact, including
me, who after all was only the son of one of them.

Sometimes Aunt Mathilda asked me to visit her in her room where she sat sewing
by the tall window, and she would talk to me. I listened attentively. She spoke to me
about her brothers' integrity as lawyers in the intricate field of maritime law, and she
extended to me her enthusiasm for their wealth and reputation, which I would carry
forward. She described the embargo on a shipment of oranges, told of certain damages caused by miserable tugboats manned by drunkards, of the disastrous effects
that arose from the demurrage of a ship sailing under an exotic flag. But when she
talked to me of ships her words did not evoke the hoarse sound of ships' sirens that
I heard in the distance on summer nights when, kept awake by the heat, I climbed
to the attic, and from an open window watched the far-off floating lights, and those
blocks of darkness surrounding the city that lay forever out of reach for me because
my life was, and would ever be, ordered perfectly. I realize now that Aunt Mathilda
did not hint at this magic because she did not know of it. It had no place in her life,
as it had no place in the life of anyone destined to die with dignity in order afterwards to be installed in a comfortable heaven, a heaven identical to our house. Mute,
I listened to her words, my gaze fastened on the white thread that, as she stretched
it against her black blouse, seemed to capture all of the light from the window. I exulted at the world of security that her words projected for me, that magnificent
straight road which leads to a death that is not dreaded since it is exactly like this
life, without anything fortuitous or unexpected. Because death was not terrible.
Death was the final incision, clean and definitive, nothing more. Hell existed, of
course, but not for us. It was rather for chastising the other inhabitants of the city
and those anonymous seamen who caused the damages that, when the cases were
concluded, filled the family coffers.

Aunt Mathilda was so removed from the idea of fear that, since I now know that
love and fear go hand in hand, I am tempted to think that in those days she did not
love anyone. But I may be mistaken. In her rigid way she may have been attached to
her brothers by a kind of love. At night, after supper, they gathered in the billiard room
for a few games. I used to go in with them. Standing outside that circle of imprisoned affections, I watched for a sign that would show me the ties between them did
exist, and did, in fact, bind. It is strange that my memory does not bring back anything but shades of indeterminate grays in remembering the house, but when I evoke
that hour, the strident green of the table, the red and white of the balls and the little cube of blue chalk become inflamed in my memory, illumined by the low lamp
whose shade banished everything else into dusk. In one of the family's many rituals,
the voice of Aunt Mathilda rescued each of the brothers by turn from the darkness,
so that they might make their plays.

"No, Gustav . . ."

And when he leaned over the green table, cue in hand, Uncle Gustav's face was
lit up, brittle as paper, its nobility contradicted by his eyes, which were too small and

spaced too close together. Finished playing, he returned to the shadow, where he lit a cigar whose smoke rose lazily until it was dissolved in the gloom of the ceiling. Then his sister said:

"All right, Armand . . ."

And the soft, timid face of Uncle Armand, with his large, sky-blue eyes concealed by gold-rimmed glasses, bent down underneath the light. His game was generally bad because he was "the baby" as Aunt Mathilda sometimes referred to him. After the comments aroused by his play he took refuge behind his newspaper and Aunt Mathilda said:

"Pedro, your turn . . ."

I held my breath when I saw him lean over to play, held it even more tightly when I saw him succumb to his sister's command. I prayed, as he got up, that he would rebel against the order established by his sister's voice. I could not see that this order was in itself a kind of rebellion, constructed by them as a protection against chaos, so that they might not be touched by what can be neither explained nor resolved. My father, then, leaned over the green cloth, his practiced eye gauging the exact distance and positions of the billiards. He made his play, and making it, he exhaled in such a way that his moustache stirred about his half-opened mouth. Then he handed me his cue so I might chalk it with the blue cube. With this minimal role that he assigned to me, he let me touch the circle that united him with the others, without letting me take part in it more than tangentially.

Now it was Aunt Mathilda's turn. She was the best player. When I saw her face, composed as if from the defects of her brothers' faces, coming out of the shadow, I knew that she was going to win. And yet . . . had I not seen her small eyes light up that face so like a brutally clenched fist, when by chance one of them succeeded in beating her? That spark appeared because, although she might have wished it, she would never have permitted herself to let any of them win. That would be to introduce the mysterious element of love into a game that ought not to include it, because affection should remain in its place, without trespassing on the strict reality of a carom shot.

II

I never did like dogs. One may have frightened me when I was very young, I don't know, but they have always displeased me. As there were no dogs at home and I went out very little, few occasions presented themselves to make me uncomfortable. For my aunt and uncles and for my father, dogs, like all the rest of the animal kingdom, did not exist. Cows, of course, supplied the cream for the dessert that was served in a silver dish on Sundays. Then there were the birds that chirped quite agreeably at twilight in the branches of the elm tree, the only inhabitant of the small garden at the rear of the house. But animals for them existed only in the proportion in which they contributed to the pleasure of human beings. Which is to say that dogs, lazy as city dogs are, could not even dent their imagination with a possibility of their existence.

Sometimes, on Sunday, Aunt Mathilda and I used to go to mass early to take communion. It was rare that I succeeded in concentrating on the sacrament, because the idea that she was watching me without looking generally occupied the first plane of my conscious mind. Even when her eyes were directed to the altar, or her head bowed before the Blessed Sacrament, my every movement drew her attention to it. And on leaving the church she told me with sly reproach that it was without doubt a flea trapped in the pews that prevented me from meditating, as she had suggested, that death is the good foreseen end, and from praying that it might not be painful, since that was the purpose of masses, novenas and communions.

This was such a morning. A fine drizzle was threatening to turn into a storm, and the quebracho pavements extended their shiny fans, notched with streetcar rails, from sidewalk to sidewalk. As I was cold and in a hurry to get home I stepped up the pace beside Aunt Mathilda, who was holding her black mushroom of an umbrella above our heads. There were not many people in the street since it was so early. A dark-complexioned gentleman saluted us without lifting his hat, because of the rain. My aunt was in the process of telling me how surprised she was that someone of mixed blood had bowed to her with so little show of attention, when suddenly, near where we were walking, a streetcar applied its brakes with a screech, making her interrupt her monologue. The conductor looked out through his window:

"Stupid dog!" he shouted.

We stopped to watch.

A small white bitch escaped from between the wheels of the streetcar and, limping painfully, with her tail between her legs, took refuge in a doorway as the streetcar moved on again.

"These dogs," protested Aunt Mathilda. "It's beyond me how they are allowed to go around like that."

Continuing our way we passed by the bitch huddled in the corner of a doorway. It was small and white, with legs which were too short for its size and an ugly pointed snout that proclaimed an entire genealogy of misalliances: the sum of unevenly matched breeds which for generations had been scouring the city, searching for food in the garbage cans and among the refuse of the port. She was drenched, weak, trembling with cold or fever. When we passed in front of her I noticed that my aunt looked at the bitch, and the bitch's eyes returned her gaze.

We continued on our way home. Several steps further I was on the point of forgetting the dog when my aunt surprised me by abruptly turning around and crying out:

"Psst! Go away . . .!"

She had turned in such absolute certainty of finding the bitch following us that I trembled with the mute question which arose from my surprise: How did she know? She couldn't have heard her, since she was following us at an appreciable distance. But she did not doubt it. Perhaps the look that had passed between them of which I saw only the mechanics—the bitch's head raised slightly toward Aunt Mathilda, Aunt Mathilda's slightly inclined toward the bitch—contained some secret commitment? I do not know. In any case, turning to drive away the dog, her peremptory "psst" had the sound of something like a last effort to repel an encroaching destiny. It is possible that I am saying all this in the light of things that happened later, that my imagination is embellishing with significance what was only trivial. However, I can say with certainty that in that moment I felt a strangeness, almost a fear of my aunt's sudden loss of dignity in condescending to turn around and confer rank on a sick and filthy bitch.

We arrived home. We went up the stairs and the bitch stayed down below, looking up at us from the torrential rain that had just been unleashed. We went inside, and the delectable process of breakfast following communion removed the white bitch from my mind. I have never felt our house so protective as that morning, never rejoiced so much in the security derived from those old walls that marked off my world.

In one of my wanderings in and out of the empty sitting-rooms, I pulled back the curtain of a window to see if the rain promised to let up. The storm continued. And, sitting at the foot of the stairs still scrutinizing the house, I saw the white bitch. I dropped the curtain so that I might not see her there, soaked through and looking like one spellbound. Then, from the dark outer rim of the room, Aunt Mathilda's low voice surprised me. Bent over to strike a match to the kindling wood already arranged in the fireplace, she asked:

"Is it still there?"

"What?"

I knew what.

"The white bitch . . ."

I answered yes, that it was.

III

It must have been the last storm of the winter, because I remember quite clearly that the following days opened up and the nights began to grow warmer.

The white bitch stayed posted on our doorstep scrutinizing our windows. In the mornings, when I left for school, I tried to shoo her away, but barely had I boarded the bus when I would see her reappear around the corner or from behind the mailbox. The servant girls also tried to frighten her away, but their attempts were as fruitless as mine, because the bitch never failed to return.

Once, we were all saying good-night at the foot of the stairs before going up to bed. Uncle Gustav had just turned off the lights, all except the one on the stairway, so that the large space of the vestibule had become peopled with the shadowy bodies of furniture. Aunt Mathilda, who was entreating Uncle Armand to open the window of his room so a little air could come in, suddenly stopped speaking, leaving her sentence unfinished, and the movements of all of us, who had started to go up, halted.

"What is the matter?" asked Father, stepping down one stair.

"Go on up," murmured Aunt Mathilda, turning around and gazing into the shadow of the vestibule.

But we did not go up.

The silence of the room was filled with the secret voice of each object: a grain of dirt trickling down between the wallpaper and the wall, the creaking of polished woods, the quivering of some loose crystal. Someone, in addition to ourselves, was where we were. A small white form came out of the darkness near the service door. The bitch crossed the vestibule, limping slowly in the direction of Aunt Mathilda, and without even looking at her, threw herself down at her feet.

It was as though the immobility of the dog enabled us to move again. My father came down two stairs. Uncle Gustav turned on the light. Uncle Armand went upstairs and shut himself in his room.

"What is this?" asked my father.

Aunt Mathilda remained still.

"How could she have come in?" she asked aloud.

Her question seemed to acknowledge the heroism implicit in having either jumped walls in that lamentable condition, or come into the basement through a broken pane of glass, or fooled the servants' vigilance by creeping through a casually opened door.

"Mathilda, call one of the girls to take her away," said my father, and went upstairs followed by Uncle Gustav.

We were left alone looking at the bitch. She called a servant, telling the girl to give her something to eat and the next day to call a veterinarian.

"Is she going to stay in the house?" I asked.

"How can she walk in the street like that?" murmured Aunt Mathilda. "She has to get better so we can throw her out. And she'd better get well soon because I don't want animals in the house."

Then she added:

"Go upstairs to bed."

She followed the girl who was carrying the dog out.

I sensed that ancient drive of Aunt Mathilda's to have everything go well about her, that energy and dexterity which made her sovereign of immediate things. Is it possible that she was so secure within her limitations, that for her the only necessity was to overcome imperfections, errors not of intention or motive, but of condition? If so, the white bitch was going to get well. She would see to it because the animal had entered the radius of her power. The veterinarian would bandage the broken leg under her watchful eye, and protected by rubber gloves and an apron, she herself would take charge of cleaning the bitch's pustules with disinfectant that would make her howl. But Aunt Mathilda would remain deaf to those howls, sure that whatever she was doing was for the best.

And so it was. The bitch stayed in the house. Not that I saw her, but I could feel the presence of any stranger there, even though confined to the lower reaches of the basement. Once or twice I saw Aunt Mathilda with the rubber gloves on her hands, carrying a vial full of red liquid. I found a plate with scraps of food in a passage of the basement where I went to look for the bicycle I had just been given. Weakly, buffered by walls and floors, at times the suspicion of a bark reached my ears.

One afternoon I went down to the kitchen. The bitch came in, painted like a clown with red disinfectant. The servants threw her out without paying her any mind. But I saw that she was not hobbling any longer, that her tail, limp before, was curled up like a feather, leaving her shameless bottom in plain view.

That afternoon I asked Aunt Mathilda:

"When are you going to throw her out?"

"Who?" she asked.

She knew perfectly well.

"The white bitch."

"She's not well yet," she replied.

Later I thought of insisting, of telling her that surely there was nothing now to prevent her from climbing the garbage cans in search of food. I didn't do it because I believe it was the same night that Aunt Mathilda, after losing the first round of billiards, decided that she did not feel like playing another. Her brothers went on playing, and she, ensconced in the leather sofa, made a mistake in calling their names. There was a moment of confusion. Then the thread of order was quickly picked up again by the men, who knew how to ignore an accident if it was not favorable to them. But I had already seen.

It was as if Aunt Mathilda were not there at all. She was breathing at my side as she always did. The deep, silencing carpet yielded under her feet as usual and her tranquilly crossed hands weighed on her skirt. How is it possible to feel with the certainty I felt then the absence of a person whose heart is somewhere else? The following nights were equally troubled by the invisible slur of her absence. She seemed to have lost all interest in the game, and left off calling her brothers by their names. They appeared not to notice it. But they must have, because their games became shorter and I noticed an infinitesimal increase in the deference with which they treated her.

One night, as we were going out of the dining-room, the bitch appeared in the doorway and joined the family group. The men paused before they went into the library so that their sister might lead the way to the billiard room, followed this time by the white bitch. They made no comment, as if they had not seen her, beginning their game as they did every night.

The bitch sat down at Aunt Mathilda's feet. She was very quiet. Her lively eyes examined the room and followed the players' strategies as if all of that amused her greatly. She was fat now and had a shiny coat. Her whole body, from her quivering snout to her tail ready to waggle, was full of an abundant capacity for fun. How long had she stayed in the house? A month? Perhaps more. But in that month Aunt Mathilda had forced her to get well, caring for her not with displays of affection, but with those hands of hers which could not refrain from mending what was broken. The leg was well. She had disinfected, fed and bathed her, and now the white bitch was whole.

In one of his plays Uncle Armand let the cube of blue chalk fall to the floor. Immediately, obeying an instinct that seemed to surge up from her picaresque past, the bitch ran towards the chalk and snatched it with her mouth away from Uncle Armand, who had bent over to pick it up. Then followed something surprising: Aunt Mathilda, as if suddenly unwound, burst into a peal of laughter that agitated her whole body. We remained frozen. On hearing her laugh, the bitch dropped the chalk, ran towards her with her tail waggling aloft, and jumped up onto her lap. Aunt Mathilda's laugh relented, but Uncle Armand left the room. Uncle Gustav and my father went on with the game: now it was more important than ever not to see, not to see anything at all, not to comment, not to consider oneself alluded to by these events.

I did not find Aunt Mathilda's laugh amusing, because I may have felt the dark thing that had stirred it up. The bitch grew calm sitting on her lap. The cracking noises of the balls when they hit seemed to conduct Aunt Mathilda's hand first from its place on the edge of the sofa, to her skirt, and then to the curved back of the sleeping animal. On seeing that expressionless hand reposing there, I noticed that the tension which had kept my aunt's features clenched before, relented, and that a certain peace was now softening her face. I could not resist. I drew closer to her on the sofa, as if to a newly kindled fire. I hoped that she would reach out to me with a look or include me with a smile. But she did not.

IV

When I arrived from school in the afternoon, I used to go directly to the back of the house and, mounting my bicycle, take turn after turn around the narrow garden, circling the pair of cast-iron benches and the elm tree. Behind the wall, the chestnut trees were beginning to display their light spring down, but the seasons did not interest me for I had too many serious things to think about. And since I knew that no one came down into the garden until the suffocation of midsummer made it imperative, it seemed to be the best place for mediating about what was going on inside the house.

One might have said that nothing was going on. But how could I remain calm in the face of the entwining relationship which had sprung up between my aunt and the white bitch? It was as if Aunt Mathilda, after having resigned herself to an odd life of service and duty, had found at last her equal. And as women-friends do, they carried on a life full of niceties and pleasing refinements. They ate bonbons that came in boxes wrapped frivolously with ribbons. My aunt arranged tangerines, pineapples and grapes in tall crystal bowls, while the bitch watched her as if on the point of criticizing her taste or offering a suggestion.

Often when I passed the door of her room, I heard a peal of laughter like the one which had overturned the order of her former life that night. Or I heard her engage in a dialogue with an interlocutor whose voice I did not hear. It was a new life. The bitch, the guilty one, slept in a hamper near her bed, an elegant, feminine hamper, ridiculous to my way of thinking, and followed her everywhere except into the dining-room. Entrance there was forbidden her, but waiting for her friend to come out again, she followed her to the billiard room and sat at her side on the sofa or on her lap, exchanging with her from time to time complicitory glances.

How as it possible, I used to ask myself? Why had she waited until now to go beyond herself and establish a dialogue? At times she appeared insecure about the bitch, fearful that, in the same way she had arrived one fine day, she might also go, leaving her with all this new abundance weighing on her hands. Or did she still fear for her health? These ideas, which now seem so clear, floated blurred in my imagination while I listened to the gravel of the path crunching under the wheels of my bicycle. What was not blurred, however, was my vehement desire to become gravely ill, to see if I might also succeed in harvesting some kind of relationship. Because the bitch's illness had been the cause of everything. If it had not been for that, my aunt might have never joined in league with her. But I had a constitution of iron, and furthermore, it was clear that Aunt Mathilda's heart did not have room for more than one love at a time.

My father and my uncles did not seem to notice any change. The bitch was very quiet, and abandoning her street ways, seemed to acquire manners more worthy of Aunt Mathilda. But still, she had somehow preserved all the sauciness of a female of the streets. It was clear that the hardships of her life had not been able to cloud either her good humor or her taste for adventure which, I felt, lay dangerously dormant inside her. For the men of the house it proved easier to accept her than to throw her out, since this would have forced them to revise their canons of security.

One night, when the pitcher of lemonade had already made its appearance on the console-table of the library, cooling that corner of the shadow, and the windows had been thrown open to the air, my father halted abruptly at the doorway of the billiard room:

"What is that?" he exclaimed, looking at the floor.

The three men stopped in consternation to look at a small, round pool on the waxed floor.

"Mathilda!" called Uncle Gustav.

She went to look and then reddened with shame. The bitch had taken refuge under the billiard table in the adjoining room. Walking over to the table my father saw her there, and changing direction sharply, he left the room, followed by his brothers.

Aunt Mathilda went upstairs. The bitch followed her. I stayed in the library with a glass of lemonade in my hand, and looked out at the summer sky, listening to some far-off siren from the sea, and to the murmur of the city stretched out under the stars. Soon I heard Aunt Mathilda coming down. She appeared with her hat on and with her keys chinking in her hand.

"Go up and go to bed," she said. "I'm going to take her for a walk on the street so that she can do her business."

Then she added something strange:

"It's such a lovely night."

And she went out.

From that night on, instead of going up after dinner to open her brothers' beds, she went to her room, put her hat tightly on her head and came downstairs again, chinking her keys. She went out with the bitch without explaining anything to anyone. And my uncles and my father and I stayed behind in the billiard room, and later we sat on the benches of the garden, with all the murmuring of the elm tree and the clearness of the sky weighing down on us. These nocturnal walks of Aunt Mathilda's were never spoken of by her brothers. They never showed any awareness of the change that had occurred inside our house.

In the beginning Aunt Mathilda was gone at the most for twenty minutes or half an hour, returning to take whatever refreshment there was and to exchange some trivial commentary. Later, her sorties were inexplicably prolonged. We began to realize, or I did at least, that she was no longer a woman taking her dog out for hygienic reasons: outside there, in the streets of the city, something was drawing her. When waiting, my father furtively eyed his pocket watch, and if the delay was very great Uncle Gustav went up to the second floor pretending he had forgotten something there, to spy for her from the balcony. But still they did not speak. Once, when Aunt Mathilda stayed out too long, my father paced back and forth along the path that wound between the hydrangeas. Uncle Gustav threw away a cigar which he could not light to his satisfaction, then another, crushing it with the heel of his shoe. Uncle Armand spilt a cup of coffee. I watched them, hoping that at long last they would explode, that they would finally say something to fill the minutes that were passing by one after another, getting longer and longer without the presence of Aunt Mathilda. It was twelve-thirty when she arrived.

"Why are you all waiting up for me?" she asked smiling.

She was holding her hat in her hand, and her hair, ordinarily so well-groomed, was mussed. I saw that a streak of mud was soiling her shoes.

"What happened to you?" asked Uncle Armand.

"Nothing," came her reply, and with it she shut off any right of her brothers to meddle in those unknown hours that were now her life. I say they were her life because, during the minutes she stayed with us before going up to her room with the bitch, I perceived an animation in her eyes, an excited restlessness like that in the eyes of the animal: it was as though they had been washed in scenes to which even our imagination lacked access. Those two were accomplices. The night protected them. They belonged to the murmuring sound of the city, to the sirens of the ships which, crossing the dark or illumined streets, the houses and factories and parks, reached my ears.

Her walks with the bitch continued for some time. Now we said good-night immediately after dinner, and each one went up to shut himself in his room, my father, Uncle Gustav, Uncle Armand and I. But no one went to sleep before she came in, late, sometimes terribly late, when the light of the dawn was already striking the top of our elm. Only after hearing her close the door of her bedroom did the pacing with which my father measured his room cease, or was the window in one of his brothers' rooms finally closed to exclude that fragment of the night which was no longer dangerous.

Once I heard her come up very late, and as I thought I heard her singing softly, I opened my door and peeked out. When she passed my room, with the white bitch nestled in her arms, her face seemed to me surprisingly young and unblemished, even though it was dirty, and I saw a rip in her skirt. I went to bed terrified, knowing this was the end.

I was not mistaken. Because one night, shortly after, Aunt Mathilda took the dog out for a walk after dinner, and did not return.

We stayed awake all night, each one in his room, and she did not come back. No one said anything the next day. They went—I presume—to their office, and I went to school. She wasn't home when we came back and we sat silently at our meal that night. I wonder if they found out something definite that very first day. But I think not, because we all, without seeming to, haunted the windows of the house, peering into the street.

"Your aunt went on a trip," the cook answered me when I finally dared to ask, if only her.

But I knew it was not true.

Life continued in the house just as if Aunt Mathilda were still living there. It is true that they used to gather in the library for hours and hours, and closeted there they may have planned ways of retrieving her out of that night which had swallowed her. Several times a visitor came who was clearly not of our world, a plain-clothesman perhaps, or the head of a stevedore's union come to pick up indemnification for some accident. Sometimes their voices rose a little, sometimes there was a deadened quiet, sometimes their voices became hard, sharp, as they fenced with the voice I did not know. But the library door was too thick, too heavy for me to hear what they were saying.

[1969]
Translated by
LORRAINE O'GRADY FREEMAN

Questions

1. Does Aunt Mathilda's escape from her brothers' household free her of her ugliness and make her beautiful, or are we to consider her escape as something less than genuine liberation?

2. What is the significance of the billiard ball game?

3. Why can't Aunt Mathilda express any emotions for the narrator/boy?

4. What will the narrator be like when he grows up—like his father and his uncles or more like Aunt Mathilda?

5. How do the several meanings of paseo apply to the story: walk, ride, parade, public park, boulevard?

Louise Erdrich
(b. 1954)
United States

L ouise Erdrich credits her parents with instilling in her an early love of reading and writing:

> My father used to give me a nickel for every story I wrote, and my mother wove strips
> of construction paper together and stapled them into book covers. So at an early age I
> felt myself to be a published author earning substantial royalties. Mine were wonderful
> parents: They got me excited about reading and writing in a lasting way.

Erdrich's German-born father taught for the Bureau of Indian Affairs, where her
Chippewa mother also worked. Erdrich frequently visited her maternal grandparents, who
lived on the Turtle Mountain Chippewa Reservation in North Dakota. Before she began
to turn those experiences into lyrical fiction, Erdrich attended Dartmouth and Johns
Hopkins; at Dartmouth, she met and later married Michael Dorris, an anthropologist
of Native American ancestry and also an author with whom she collaborated on a novel
based on Columbus's arrival in America, The Crown of Columbus (1991).

Love Medicine (1984), Erdrich's first novel (some critics consider it a collection
of short stories), won the National Book Critics Circle Award. The narrative, a
vivid, compelling portrait of a Turtle Mountain Chippewa community, employs multiple narrative voices: seven narrators from two interrelated families, the Lamartines
and the Kashpaws, tell 14 interlocking stories. Through their "oral" monologues, Erdrich conveys not only the complexity of her characters' family relationships but also
the tensions they feel within their tradition and with the white community. Through
experiences that are both comic and tragic, her characters ponder the meaning of circumstances ranging from poverty and despair, alcoholism, racism, and unrequited
love to spiritual strength, mystery, and mutuality. Toni Morrison commented that
"The beauty of Love Medicine saves us from being completely devastated by its
power." What binds Erdrich's characters is a deeply rooted capacity for love and survival, evoked through the author's rich, lyrical prose.

Erdrich has continued her imaginative recreation of Chippewa community life in
Beet Queen (1986), Tracks (1988), Bingo Palace (1994), Tales of Burning
Love (1996), and The Last Report on the Miracles at Little No Horse (2001).
She is also the author of two collections of poetry, Jacklight (1984) and Baptism of
Desire (1989).

LOVE MEDICINE

I never really done much with my life, I suppose. I never had a television. Grandma
Kashpaw had one inside her apartment at the Senior Citizens, so I used to go there
and watch my favorite shows. For a while she used to call me the biggest waste on the

reservation and hark back to how she saved me from my own mother, who wanted to tie me in a potato sack and throw me in a slough. Sure, I was grateful to Grandma Kashpaw for saving me like that, for raising me, but gratitude gets old. After a while, stale. I had to stop thanking her. One day I told her I had paid her back in full by staying at her beck and call. I'd do anything for Grandma. She knew that. Besides, I took care of Grandpa like nobody else could, on account of what a handful he'd gotten to be.

But that was nothing. I know the tricks of mind and body inside out without ever having trained for it, because I got the touch. It's a thing you got to be born with. I got secrets in my hands that nobody ever knew to ask. Take Grandma Kashpaw with her tired veins all knotted up in her legs like clumps of blue snails. I take my fingers and I snap them on the knots. The medicine flows out of me. The touch. I run my fingers up the maps of those rivers of veins or I knock very gentle above their hearts or I make a circling motion on their stomachs, and it helps them. They feel much better. Some women pay me five dollars.

I couldn't do the touch for Grandpa, though. He was a hard nut. You know, some people fall right through the hole in their lives. It's invisible, but they come to it after time, never knowing where. There is this woman here, Lulu Lamartine, who always had a thing for Grandpa. She loved him since she was a girl and always said he was a genius. Now she says that his mind got so full it exploded.

How can I doubt that? I know the feeling when your mental power builds up too far. I always used to say that's why the Indians got drunk. Even statistically we're the smartest people on the earth. Anyhow with Grandpa I couldn't hardly believe it, because all my youth he stood out as a hero to me. When he started getting toward second childhood he went through different moods. He would stand in the woods and cry at the top of his shirt. It scared me, scared everyone, Grandma worst of all.

Yet he was so smart—do you believe it?—that he *knew* he was getting foolish.

He said so. He told me that December I failed school and come back on the train to Hoopdance. I didn't have nowhere else to go. He picked me up there and he said it straight out: "I'm getting into my second childhood." And then he said something else I still remember: "I been chosen for it. I couldn't say no." So I figure that a man so smart all his life—tribal chairman and the star of movies and even pictured in the statehouse and on cans of snuff—would know what he's doing by saying yes. I think he was called to second childhood like anybody else gets a call for the priesthood or the army or whatever. So I really did not listen too hard when the doctor said this was some kind of disease old people got eating too much sugar. You just can't tell me that a man who went to Washington and gave them bureaucrats what for could lose his mind from eating too much Milky Way. No, he put second childhood on himself.

Behind those songs he sings out in the middle of Mass, and back of those stories that everybody knows by heart, Grandpa is thinking hard about life. I know the feeling. Sometimes I'll throw up a smokescreen to think behind. I'll hitch up to Winnipeg and play the Space Invaders for six hours, but all the time there and back I will be thinking some fairly deep thoughts that surprise even me, and I'm used to it. As for him, if it was just the thoughts there wouldn't be no problem. Smokescreen is what irritates the social structure, see, and Grandpa has done things that just distract people to the point they want to throw him in the cookie jar where they keep the mentally insane. He's far from that, I know for sure, but even Grandma had trouble keeping her patience once he started sneaking off to Lamartine's place. He's not supposed to have his candy, and Lulu feeds it to him. That's *one* of the reasons why he goes.

Grandma tried to get me to put the touch on Grandpa soon after he began stepping out. I didn't want to, but before Grandma started telling me again what a bad state my bare behind was in when she first took me home, I thought I should at least pretend.

I put my hands on either side of Grandpa's head. You wouldn't look at him and say he was crazy. He's a fine figure of a man, as Lamartine would say, with all his hair and half his teeth, a beak like a hawk, and cheeks like the blades of a hatchet. They put his picture on all the tourist guides to North Dakota and even copied his face for artistic paintings. I guess you could call him a monument all of himself. He started grinning when I put my hands on his templates, and I knew right then he knew how come I touched him. I knew the smokescreen was going to fall.

And I was right: just for a moment it fell.

"Let's pitch whoopee," he said across my shoulder to Grandma.

They don't use that expression much around here anymore, but for damn sure it must have meant something. It got her goat right quick.

She threw my hands off his head herself and stood in front of him, overmatching him pound for pound, and taller too, for she had a growth spurt in middle age while he had shrunk, so now the length and breadth of her surpassed him. She glared up and spoke her piece into his face about how he was off at all hours tomcatting and chasing Lamartine again and making a damn old fool of himself.

"And you got no more whoopee to pitch anymore anyhow!" she yelled at last, surprising me so my jaw just dropped, for us kids all had pretended for so long that those rustling sounds we heard from their side of the room at night never happened. She sure had pretended it, up till now, anyway. I saw that tears were in her eyes. And that's when I saw how much grief and love she felt for him. And it gave me a real shock to the system. You see I thought love got easier over the years so it didn't hurt so bad when it hurt, or feel so good when it felt good. I thought it smoothed out and old people hardly noticed it. I thought it curled up and died, I guess. Now I saw it rear up like a whip and lash.

She loved him. She was jealous. She mourned him like the dead.

And he just smiled into the air, trapped in the seams of his mind.

So I didn't know what to do. I was in a laundry then. They was like parents to me, the way they had took me home and reared me. I could see her point for wanting to get him back the way he was so at least she could argue with him, sleep with him, not be shamed out by Lamartine. She'd always love him. That hit me like a ton of bricks. For one whole day I felt this odd feeling that cramped my hands. When you have the touch, that's where longing gets you. I never loved like that. It made me feel all inspired to see them fight, and I wanted to go out and find a woman who I would love until one of us died or went crazy. But I'm not like that really. From time to time I heal a person all up good inside, however when it comes to the long shot I doubt that I got staying power.

And you need that, staying power, going out to love somebody. I knew this quality was not going to jump on me with no effort. So I turned my thoughts back to Grandma and Grandpa. I felt her side of it with my hands and my tangled guts, and I felt his side of it within the stretch of my mentality. He had gone out to lunch one day and never came back. He was fishing in the middle of Lake Turcot. And there was big thoughts on his line, and he kept throwing them back for even bigger ones that would explain to him, say, the meaning of how we got here and why we have to leave so soon. All in all, I could not see myself treating Grandpa with the touch, bringing him back, when the real part of him had chose to be off thinking somewhere. It was only the rest of him that stayed around causing trouble, after all, and we could handle most of it without any problem.

Besides, it was hard to argue with his reasons for doing some things. Take Holy Mass. I used to go there just every so often, when I got frustrated mostly, because even though I know the Higher Power dwells everyplace, there's something very calming about the cool greenish inside of our mission. Or so I thought, anyway. Grandpa was the one who stripped off my delusions in this matter, for it was he who busted right through what Father Upsala calls the sacred serenity of the place.

We filed in that time. Me and Grandpa. We sat down in our pews. Then the rosary got started up pre-Mass and that's when Grandpa filled up his chest and opened his mouth and belted out them words.

HAIL MARIE FULL OF GRACE.

He had a powerful set of lungs.

And he kept on like that. He did not let up. He hollered and he yelled them prayers, and I guess people was used to him by now, because they only muttered theirs and did not quit and gawk like I did. I was getting red-faced, I admit. I give him the elbow once or twice, but that wasn't nothing to him. He kept on. He shrieked to heaven and he pleaded like a movie actor and he pounded his chest like Tarzan in the Lord I Am Not Worthies. I thought he might hurt himself. Then after a while I guess I got used to it, and that's when I wondered: how come?

So afterwards I out and asked him. "How come? How come you yelled?"

"God don't hear me otherwise," said Grandpa Kashpaw.

I sweat. I broke right into a little cold sweat at my hairline because I knew this was perfectly right and for years not one damn other person had noticed it. God's been going deaf. Since the Old Testament, God's been deafening up on us. I read, see. Besides the dictionary, which I'm constantly in use of, I had this Bible once. I read it. I found there was discrepancies between then and now. It struck me. Here God used to raineth bread from clouds, smite the Phillipines, sling fire down on red-light districts where people got stabbed. He even appeared in person every once in a while. God used to pay attention, is what I'm saying.

Now there's your God in the Old Testament and there is Chippewa Gods as well. Indian Gods, good and bad, like tricky Nanabozho or the water monster, Missepeshu, who lives over in Lake Turcot. That water monster was the last God I ever heard to appear. It had a weakness for young girls and grabbed one of the Blues off her rowboat. She got to shore all right, but only after this monster had its way with her. She's an old lady now. Old Lady Blue. She still won't let her family fish that lake.

Our Gods aren't perfect, is what I'm saying, but at least they come around. They'll do a favor if you ask them right. You don't have to yell. But you do have to know, like I said, how to ask in the right way. That makes problems, because to ask proper was an art that was lost to the Chippewas once the Catholics gained ground. Even now, I have to wonder if Higher Power turned it back, if we got to yell, or if we just don't speak its language.

I looked around me. How else could I explain what all I had seen in my short life—King smashing his fist in things, Gordie drinking himself down to the Bismarck hospitals, or Aunt June left by a white man to wander off in the snow. How else to explain the times my touch don't work, and farther back, to the old-time Indians who was swept away in the outright germ warfare and dirty-dog killing of the whites. In those times, us Indians was so much kindlier than now.

We took them in.

Oh yes, I'm bitter as an old cutworm just thinking of how they done to us and doing still.

So Grandpa Kashpaw just opened my eyes a little there. Was there any sense relying on a God whose ears was stopped? Just like the government? I says then, right off, maybe we got nothing but ourselves. And that's not much, just personally speaking. I know I don't got the cold hard potatoes it takes to understand everything. Still, there's things I'd like to do. For instance, I'd like to help some people like my Grandpa and Grandma Kashpaw get back some happiness within the tail ends of their lives.

I told you once before I couldn't see my way clear to putting the direct touch on Grandpa's mind, and I kept my moral there, but something soon happened to make me think a little bit of mental adjustment wouldn't do him and the rest of us no harm.

It was after we saw him one afternoon in the sunshine courtyard of the Senior Citizens with Lulu Lamartine. Grandpa used to like to dig there. He had his little dandelion fork out, and he was prying up them dandelions right and left while Lamartine watched him.

"He's scratching up the dirt, all right," said Grandma, watching Lamartine watch Grandpa out the window.

Now Lamartine was about half the considerable size of Grandma, but you would never think of sizes anyway. They were different in an even more noticeable way. It was the difference between a house fixed up with paint and picky fence, and a house left to weather away into the soft earth, is what I'm saying. Lamartine was jacked up, latticed, shuttered, and vinyl sided, while Grandma sagged and bulged on her slipped foundations and let her hair go the silver gray of rain-dried lumber. Right now, she eyed the Lamartine's pert flowery dress with such a look it despaired me. I knew what this could lead to with Grandma. Alternating tongue storms and rock-hard silences was hard on a man, even one who didn't notice, like Grandpa. So I went fetching him.

But he was gone when I popped through the little screen door that led out on the courtyard. There was nobody out there either, to point which way they went. Just the dandelion fork quibbling upright in the ground. That gave me an idea. I snookered over to the Lamartine's door and I listened in first, then knocked. But nobody. So I went walking through the lounges and around the card tables. Still nobody. Finally it was my touch that led me to the laundry room. I cracked the door. I went in. There they were. And he was really loving her up good, boy, and she was going hell for leather. Sheets was flapping on the lines above, and washcloths, pillowcases, shirts was also flying through the air, for they was trying to clear out a place for themselves in a high-heaped but shallow laundry cart. The washers and the dryers was all on, chock full of quarters, shaking and moaning. I couldn't hear what Grandpa and the Lamartine was billing and cooing, and they couldn't hear me.

I didn't know what to do, so I went inside and shut the door.

The Lamartine wore a big curly light-brown wig. Looked like one of them squeaky little white-people dogs. Poodles they call them. Anyway, that wig is what saved us from the worse. For I could hardly shout and tell them I was in there, no more could I try and grab him. I was trapped where I was. There was nothing I could really do but hold the door shut. I was scared of somebody else upsetting in and really getting an eyeful. Turned out though, in the heat of the clinch, as I was trying to avert my eyes you see, the Lamartine's curly wig jumped off her head. And if you ever been in the midst of something and had a big change like that occur in the someone, you can't help know how it devastates your basic urges. Not only that, but her wig was almost with a life of its own. Grandpa's eyes were bugging at the change already, and swear to God if the thing didn't rear up and pop him in the face like it was going to start something. He scrambled up, Grandpa did, and the Lamartine jumped up after him all addled looking. They just stared at each other, huffing and puffing, with quizzical expression. The surprise seemed to drive all sense completely out of Grandpa's mind.

"The letter was what started the fire," he said. "I never would have done it."

"What letter?" said the Lamartine. She was stiff-necked now, and elegant, even bald, like some alien queen. I gave her back the wig. The Lamartine replaced it on her head, and whenever I saw her after that, I couldn't help thinking of her bald, with special powers, as if from another planet.

"That was a close call," I said to Grandpa after she had left.

But I think he had already forgot the incident. He just stood there all quiet and thoughtful. You really wouldn't think he was crazy. He looked like he was just about to say something important, explaining himself. He said something, all right, but it didn't have nothing to do with anything that made sense.

He wondered where the heck he put his dandelion fork. That's when I decided about the mental adjustment.

Now what was mostly our problem was not so much that he was not all there, but that what was there of him often hankered after Lamartine. If we could put a stop to that, I thought, we might be getting someplace. But here, see, my touch was of no use. For what could I snap my fingers at to make him faithful to Grandma? Like the quality of staying power, this faithfulness was invisible. I know it's something that you got to acquire, but I never known where from. Maybe there's no rhyme or reason to it, like my getting the touch, and then again maybe it's a kind of magic.

It was Grandma Kashpaw who thought of it in the end. She knows things. Although she will not admit she has a scrap of Indian blood in her, there's no doubt in my mind she's got some Chippewa. How else would you explain the way she'll be sitting there, in front of her TV story, rocking in her armchair and suddenly she turns on me, her brown eyes hard as lake-bed flint.

"Lipsha Morrissey," she'll say, "you went out last night and got drunk."

How did she know that? I'll hardly remember it myself. Then she'll say she just had a feeling or ache in the scar of her hand or a creak in her shoulder. She is constantly being told things by little aggravations in her joints or by her household appliances. One time she told Gordie never to ride with a crazy Lamartine boy. She had seen something in the polished-up tin of her bread toaster. So he didn't. Sure enough, the time came we heard how Lyman and Henry went out of control in their car, ending up in the river. Lyman swam to the top, but Henry never made it.

Thanks to Grandma's toaster, Gordie was probably spared.

Someplace in the blood Grandma Kashpaw knows things. She also remembers things, I found. She keeps things filed away. She's got a memory like them video games that don't forget your score. One reason she remembers so many details about the trouble I gave her in early life is so she can flash back her total when she needs to.

Like now. Take the love medicine. I don't know where she remembered that from. It came tumbling from her mind like an asteroid off the corner of the screen.

Of course she starts out by mentioning the time I had this accident in church and did she leave me there with wet overhalls? No she didn't. And ain't I glad? Yes I am. Now what you want now, Grandma?

But when she mentions them love medicines, I feel my back prickle at the danger. These love medicines is something of an old Chippewa specialty. No other tribe has got them down so well. But love medicines is not for the layman to handle. You don't just go out and get one without paying for it. Before you get one, even, you should go through one hell of a lot of mental condensation. You got to think it over. Choose the right one. You could really mess up your life grinding up the wrong little thing.

So anyhow, I said to Grandma I'd give this love medicine some thought. I knew the best thing was to go ask a specialist like Old Man Pillager, who lives up in a tangle of bush and never shows himself. But the truth is I was afraid of him, like everyone else. He was known for putting the twisted mouth on people, seizing up their hearts. Old Man Pillager was serious business, and I have always thought it best to steer clear of that whenever I could. That's why I took the powers in my own hands. That's why I did what I could.

I put my whole mentality to it, nothing held back. After a while I started to remember things I'd heard gossiped over.

I heard of this person once who carried a charm of seeds that looked like baby pearls. They was attracted to a metal knife, which made them powerful. But I didn't know where them seeds grew. Another love charm I heard about I couldn't go along with, because how was I suppose to catch frogs in the act, which it required. Them little creatures is slippery and fast. And then the powerfullest of all, the most extreme, involved nail clips and such. I wasn't anywhere near asking Grandma to provide me all the little body bits that this last love recipe called for. I went walking around for days just trying to think up something that would work.

Well I got it. If it hadn't been the early fall of the year, I never would have got it. But I was sitting underneath a tree one day down near the school just watching people's feet go by when something tells me, look up! Look up! So I look up, and I see two honkers, Canada geese, the kind with little masks on their faces, a bird what mates for life. I see them flying right over my head naturally preparing to land in some slough on the reservation, which they certainly won't get off of alive.

It hits me, anyway. Them geese, they mate for life. And I think to myself, just what if I went out and got a pair? And just what if I fed some part—say the goose heart—of the female to Grandma and Grandpa ate the other heart? Wouldn't that work? Maybe it's all invisible, and then maybe again it's magic. Love is a stony road. We know that for sure. If it's true that the higher feelings of devotion get lodged in the heart like people say, then we'd be home free. If not, eating goose heart couldn't harm nobody anyway. I thought it was worth my effort, and Grandma Kashpaw thought so, too. She had always known a good idea when she heard one. She borrowed me Grandpa's gun.

So I went out to this particular slough, maybe the exact same slough I never got thrown in by my mother, thanks to Grandma Kashpaw, and I hunched down in a good comfortable pile of rushes. I got my gun loaded up. I ate a few of these soft baloney sandwiches Grandma made me for lunch. And then I waited. The cattails blown back and forth above my head. Then stringy blue herons was spearing up their prey. The thing I know how to do best in this world, the thing I been training for all my life, is to wait. Sitting there and sitting there was no hardship on me. I got to thinking about some funny things that happened. There was this one time that Lulu Lamartine's little blue tweety bird, a paraclete, I guess you'd call it, flown up inside her dress and got lost within there. I recalled her running out into the hallway trying to yell something, shaking. She was doing a right good jig there, cutting the rug for sure, and the thing is it *never* flown out. To this day people speculate where it went. They fear she might perhaps of crushed it in her corsets. It sure hasn't ever yet been seen alive. I thought of funny things for a while, but then I used them up, and strange things that happened started weaseling their way into my mind.

I got to thinking quite naturally of the Lamartine's cousin named Wristwatch. I never knew what his real name was. They called him Wristwatch because he got his father's broken wristwatch as a young boy when his father passed on. Never in his whole life did Wristwatch take his father's watch off. He didn't care if it worked, although after a while he got sensitive when people asked what time it was, teasing him. He often put it to his ear like he was listening to the tick. But it was broken for good and forever, people said so, at least what's what they thought.

Well I saw Wristwatch smoking in his pickup one afternoon and by nine that evening he was dead.

He died sitting at the Lamartine's table, too. As she told it, Wristwatch had just eaten himself a good-size dinner and she said would he take seconds on the hot dish when he fell over to the floor. They turnt him over. He was gone. But here's the strange thing: when the Senior Citizen's orderly took the pulse he noticed that the wristwatch Wristwatch wore was now working. The moment he died the wristwatch started keeping perfect time. They buried him with the watch still ticking on his arm.

I got to thinking. What if some gravediggers dug up Wristwatch's casket in two hundred years and that watch was still going? I thought what question they would ask and it was this: Whose hand wound it?

I started shaking like a piece of grass at just the thought.

Not to get off the subject or nothing. I was still hunkered in the slough. It was passing late into the afternoon and still no honkers had touched down. Now I don't need to tell you that the waiting did not get to me, it was the chill. The rushes was very soft, but damp. I was getting cold and debating to leave, when they landed. Two geese swimming here and there as big as life, looking deep into each other's little pinhole eyes. Just the ones I was looking for. So I lifted Grandpa's gun to my shoulder and I aimed perfectly, and *Blam! Blam!* I delivered two accurate shots. But the thing is, them shots missed. I couldn't hardly believe it. Whether it was that the stock had warped or the barrel got bent someways, I don't quite know, but anyway them geese flown off into the dim sky, and Lipsha Morrissey was left there in the rushes with evening fallen and his two cold hands empty. He had before him just the prospect of another day of bone-cracking chill in them rushes, and the thought of it got him depressed.

Now it isn't my style, in no way, to get depressed.

So I said to myself, Lipsha Morrissey, you're a happy S.O.B. who could be covered up with weeds by now down at the bottom of this slough, but instead you're alive to tell the tale. You might have problems in life, but you still got the touch. You got the power, Lipsha Morrissey. Can't argue that. So put your mind to it and figure out how not to be depressed.

I took my advice. I put my mind to it. But I never saw at the time how my thoughts led me astray toward a tragic outcome none could have known. I ignored all the danger, all the limits, for I was tired of sitting in the slough and my feet were numb. My face was aching. I was chilled, so I played with fire. I told myself love medicine was simple. I told myself the old superstitions was just that—strange beliefs. I told myself to take the ten dollars Mary MacDonald had paid me for putting the touch on her arthritis joint, and the other five I hadn't spent yet from winning bingo last Thursday. I told myself to go down to the Red Owl store.

And here is what I did that made the medicine backfire. I took an evil shortcut. I looked at birds that was dead and froze.

All right. So now I guess you will say, "Slap a malpractice suit on Lipsha Morrissey."

I heard of those suits. I used to think it was a color clothing quack doctors had to wear so you could tell them from the good ones. Now I know better that it's law.

As I walked back from the Red Owl with the rock-hard, heavy turkeys, I argued to myself about malpractice. I thought of faith. I thought to myself that faith could be called belief against the odds and whether or not there's any proof. How does that sound? I thought how we might have to yell to be heard by Higher Power, but that's not saying it's not *there*. And that is faith for you. It's belief even when the goods don't deliver. Higher Power makes promises we all know they can't back up, but anybody ever go and slap an old malpractice suit on God? Or the U.S. government? No they don't. Faith might be stupid, but it gets us through. So what I'm heading at is this. I finally convinced myself that the real actual power to the love medicine was not the goose heart itself but the faith in the cure.

I didn't believe it, I knew it was wrong, but by then I had waded so far into my lie I was stuck there. And then I went one step further.

The next day, I cleaned the hearts away from the paper packages of gizzards inside the turkeys. Then I wrapped them hearts with a clean hankie and brung them both to get blessed up at the mission. I wanted to get official blessings from the priest, but when Father answered the door to the rectory, wiping his hands on a little towel, I could tell he was a busy man.

"Booshoo, Father," I said. "I got a slight request to make of you this afternoon."

"What is it?" he said.

"Would you bless this package?" I held out the hankie with the hearts tied inside it.

He looked at the package, questioning it.

"It's turkey hearts," I honestly had to reply.

A look of annoyance crossed his face.

"Why don't you bring this matter over to Sister Martin," he said. "I have duties."

And so, although the blessing wouldn't be as powerful, I went over to the Sisters with the package.

I rung the bell, and they brought Sister Martin to the door. I had her as a music teacher, but I was always so shy then. I never talked out loud. Now, I had grown taller than Sister Martin. Looking down, I saw that she was not feeling up to snuff. Brown circles hung under her eyes.

"What's the matter?" she said, not noticing who I was.

"Remember me, Sister?"

She squinted up at me.

"Oh, yes," she said after a moment. "I'm sorry, you're the youngest of the Kashpaws. Gordie's brother."

Her face warmed up.

"Lipsha," I said, "that's my name."

"Well, Lipsha," she said, smiling broad at me now, "what can I do for you?"

They always said she was the kindest-hearted of the Sisters up the hill, and she was. She brought me back into their own kitchen and made me take a big yellow wedge of cake and a glass of milk.

"Now tell me," she said, nodding at my package. "What have you got wrapped up so carefully in those handkerchiefs?"

Like before, I answered honestly.

"Ah," said Sister Martin. "Turkey hearts." She waited.

"I hoped you could bless them."

She waited some more, smiling with her eyes. Kindhearted though she was, I began to sweat. A person could not pull the wool down over Sister Martin. I stumbled through my mind for an explanation, quick, that wouldn't scare her off.

"They're a present," I said, "for Saint Kateri's statue."

"She's not a saint yet."

"I know," I stuttered on, "in the hopes they will crown her."

"Lipsha," she said, "I never heard of such a thing."

So I told her. "Well the truth is," I said, "it's a kind of medicine."

"For what?"

"Love."

"Oh Lipsha," she said after a moment, "you don't need any medicine. I'm sure any girl would like you exactly the way you are."

I just sat there. I felt miserable, caught in my pack of lies.

"Tell you what," she said, seeing how bad I felt, "my blessing won't make any difference anyway. But there is something you can do."

I looked up at her, hopeless.

"Just be yourself."

I looked down at my plate. I knew I wasn't much to brag about right then, and I shortly became even less. For as I walked out the door I stuck my fingers in the cup of holy water that was sacred from their touches. I put my fingers in and blessed the hearts, quick, with my own hand.

I went back to Grandma and sat down in her little kitchen at the Senior Citizens. I unwrapped them hearts on the table, and her hard agate eyes went soft. She said she wasn't even going to cook those hearts up but eat them raw so their power would go down strong as possible.

I couldn't hardly watch when she munched hers. Now that's true love. I was worried about how she would get Grandpa to eat his, but she told me she'd think of something and don't worry. So I did not. I was supposed to hide off in her bedroom while she put dinner on a plate for Grandpa and fixed up the heart so he'd eat it. I caught a glint of the plate she was making for him. She put that heart smack on a piece of lettuce like in a restaurant and then attached to it a little heap of boiled peas.

He sat down. I was listening in the next room.

She said, "Why don't you have some mash potato?" So he had some mash potato. Then she gave him a little piece of boiled meat. He ate that. Then she said, "Why you didn't never touch your salad yet. See that heart? I'm feeding you it because the doctor said your blood needs building up."

I couldn't help it, at that point I peeked through a crack in the door.

I saw Grandpa picking at that heart on his plate with a certain look. He didn't look appetized at all, is what I'm saying. I doubted our plan was going to work. Grandma was getting worried, too. She told him one more time, loudly, that he had to eat that heart.

"Swallow it down," she said. "You'll hardly notice it."

He just looked at her straight on. The way he looked at her made me think I was going to see the smokescreen drop a second time, and sure enough it happened.

"What you want me to eat this for so bad?" he asked her uncannily.

Now Grandma knew the jig was up. She knew that he knew she was working medicine. He put his fork down. He rolled the heart around his saucer plate.

"I don't want to eat this," he said to Grandma. "It don't look good."

"Why, it's fresh grade-A," she told him. "One hundred percent."

He didn't ask percent what, but his eyes took on an even more warier look.

"Just go on and try it," she said, taking the salt shaker up in her hand. She was getting annoyed. "Not tasty enough? You want me to salt it for you?" She waved the shaker over his plate.

"All right, skinny white girl!" She had got Grandpa mad. Oopsy-daisy, he popped the heart into his mouth. I was about to yawn loudly and come out of the bedroom. I was about ready for this clash of wills to be over, when I saw he was still up to his old tricks. First he rolled it into one side of his cheek. "Mmmmm," he said. Then he rolled it into the other side of his cheek. "Mmmmmmm," again. Then he stuck his tongue out with the heart on it and put it back, and there was no time to react. He had pulled Grandma's leg once too far. Her goat was got. She was so mad she hopped up quick as a wink and slugged him between the shoulderblades to make him swallow.

Only thing is, he choked.

He choked real bad. A person can choke to death. You ever sit down at a restaurant table and up above you there is a list of instructions what to do if something slides down the wrong pipe? It sure makes you chew slow, that's for damn sure. When Grandpa fell off his chair better believe me that little graphic illustrated poster fled into my mind. I jumped out the bedroom. I done everything within my power that I could do to unlodge what was choking him. I squeezed underneath his ribcage. I socked him in the back. I was desperate. But here's the factor of decision: he wasn't choking on the heart alone. There was more to it than that. It was other things that choked him as well. It didn't seem like he wanted to struggle or fight. Death came and tapped his chest, so he went just like that. I'm sorry all through my body at what I done to him with that heart, and there's those who will say Lipsha Morrissey is just excusing himself off the hook by giving song and dance about how Grandpa gave up.

Maybe I can't admit what I did. My touch had gone worthless, that is true. But here is what I seen while he lay in my arms.

You hear a person's life will flash before their eyes when they're in danger. It was him in danger, not me, but it was *his* life come over me. I saw him dying, and it was like someone pulled the shade down in a room. His eyes clouded over and squeezed shut, but just before that I looked in. He was still fishing in the middle of Lake Turcot. Big thoughts was on his line and he had half a case of beer in the boat. He waved at me, grinned, and then the bobber went under.

Grandma had gone out of the room crying for help. I bunched my force up in my hands and I held him. I was so wound up I couldn't even breathe. All the moments he had spent with me, all the times he had hoisted me on his shoulders or pointed into the leaves was concentrated in that moment. Time was flashing back and forth like a pinball machine. Lights blinked and balls hopped and rubber bands chirped, until suddenly I realized the last ball had gone down the drain and there was nothing. I felt his force leaving him, flowing out of Grandpa never to return. I felt his mind weakening. The bobber going under in the lake. And I felt the touch retreat back into the darkness inside my body, from where it came.

One time, long ago, both of us were fishing together. We caught a big old snapper what started towing us around like it was a motor. "This here fishline is pretty damn good," Grandpa said. "Let's keep this turtle on and see where he takes us." So we rode along behind that turtle, watching as from time to time it surfaced. The thing was just about the size of a washtub. It took us all around the lake twice, and as it was traveling, Grandpa said something as a joke. "Lipsha," he said, "we are glad your mother didn't want you because we was always looking for a boy like you who would tow us around the lake."

"I ain't no snapper. Snappers is so stupid they stay alive when their head's chopped off," I said.

"That ain't stupidity," said Grandpa. "Their brain's just in their heart, like yours is."

When I looked up, I knew the fuse had blown between my heart and my mind and that a terrible understanding was to be given.

Grandma got back into the room and I saw her stumble. And then she went down too. It was like a house you can't hardly believe has stood so long, through years of record weather, suddenly goes down in the worst yet. It makes sense, is what I'm saying, but you still can't hardly believe it. You think a person you know has got through death and illness and being broke and living on commodity rice will get through anything. Then they fold and you see how fragile were the stones that underpinned them. You see how instantly the ground can shift you thought was solid. You see the stop signs and the yellow dividing markers of roads you traveled and all the instructions you had played according to vanish. You see how all the everyday things you counted on was just a dream you had been having by which you run your whole life. She had been over me, like a sheer overhang of rock dividing Lipsha Morrissey from outer space. And now she went underneath. It was as though the banks gave way on the shores of Lake Turcot, and where Grandpa's passing was just the bobber swallowed under by his biggest thought, her fall was the house and the rock under it sliding after, sending half the lake splashing up to the clouds.

Where there was nothing.

You play them games never knowing what you see. When I fell into the dream alongside of both of them I saw that the dominions I had defended myself from anciently was but delusions of the screen. Blips of light. And I was scot-free now, whistling through space.

I don't know how I come back. I don't know from where. They was slapping my face when I arrived back at Senior Citizens and they was oxygenating her. I saw her chest move, almost unwilling. She sighed the way she would when somebody bothered her in the middle of a row of beads she was counting. I think it irritated her to no end that they brought her back. I knew from the way she looked after they took the mask off, she was not going to forgive them disturbing her restful peace. Nor was she forgiving Lipsha Morrissey. She had been stepping out onto the road of death, she told the children later at the funeral. I asked was there any stop signs or dividing markers on that road, but she clamped her lips in a vise the way she always done when she was mad.

Which didn't bother me. I knew when things had cleared out she wouldn't have no choice. I was not going to speculate where the blame was put for Grandpa's death. We was in it together. She had slugged him between the shoulders. My touch had failed him, never to return.

All the blood children and the took-ins, like me, came home from Minneapolis and Chicago, where they had relocated years ago. They stayed with friends on the reservation or with Aurelia or slept on Grandma's floor. They were struck down with grief and bereavement to be sure, every one of them. At the funeral I sat down in the back of the church with Albertine. She had gotten all skinny and ragged haired from cramming all her years of study into two or three. She had decided that to be a nurse was not enough for her so she was going to be a doctor. But the way she was straining her mind didn't look too hopeful. Her eyes were bloodshot from driving and crying. She took my hand. From the back we watched all the children and the mourners as they hunched over their prayers, their hands stuffed full of Kleenex. It was someplace in that long sad service that my vision shifted. I began to see things different, more clear. The family kneeling down turned to rocks in a field. It struck me how strong and reliable grief was, and death. Until the end of time, death would be our rock.

So I had perspective on it all, for death gives you that. All the Kashpaw children had done various things to me in their lives—shared their folks with me, loaned me cash, beat me up in secret—and I decided, because of death, then and there I'd call it quits. If I ever saw King again, I'd shake his hand. Forgiving somebody else made the whole thing easier to bear.

Everybody saw Grandpa off into the next world. And then the Kashpaws had to get back to their jobs, which was numerous and impressive. I had a few beers with them and I went back to Grandma, who had sort of got lost in the shuffle of everybody being sad about Grandpa and glad to see one another.

Zelda had sat beside her the whole time and was sitting with her now. I wanted to talk to Grandma, say how sorry I was, that it wasn't her fault, but only mine. I would have, but Zelda gave me one of her looks of strict warning as if to say, "I'll take care of Grandma. Don't horn in on the women."

If only Zelda knew, I thought, the sad realities would change her. But of course I couldn't tell the dark truth.

It was evening, late. Grandma's light was on underneath a crack in the door. About a week had passed since we buried Grandpa. I knocked first but there wasn't no answer, so I went right in. The door was unlocked. She was there but she didn't notice me at first. Her hands were tied up in her rosary, and her gaze was fully absorbed in the easy chair opposite her, the one that had always been Grandpa's favorite. I stood there, staring with her, at the little green nubs in the cloth and plastic armrest covers and the sad little hair-tonic stain he had made on the white doily where he laid his head. For the life of me I couldn't figure what she was staring at. Thin space. Then she turned.

"He ain't gone yet," she said.

Remember that chill I luckily didn't get from waiting in the slough? I got it now. I felt it start from the very center of me, where fear hides, waiting to attack. It spiraled outward so that in minutes my fingers and teeth were shaking and clattering. I knew she told the truth. She seen Grandpa. Whether or not he had been there is not the point. She had *seen* him, and that meant anybody else could see him, too. Not only that but, as is usually the case with these here ghosts, he had a certain uneasy reason to come back. And of course Grandma Kashpaw had scanned it out.

I sat down. We sat together on the couch watching his chair out of the corner of our eyes. She had found him sitting in his chair when she walked in the door.

"It's the love medicine, my Lipsha," she said. "It was stronger than we thought. He came back even after death to claim me to his side."

I was afraid. "We shouldn't have tampered with it," I said. She agreed. For a while we sat still. I don't know what she thought, but my head felt screwed on backward. I couldn't accurately consider the situation, so I told Grandma to go to bed. I would sleep on the couch keeping my eye on Grandpa's chair. Maybe he would come back and maybe he wouldn't. I guess I feared the one as much as the other, but I got to thinking, see, as I lay there in darkness, that perhaps even through my terrible mistakes some good might come. If Grandpa did come back, I thought he'd return in his right mind. I could talk with him. I could tell him it was all my fault for playing with power I did not understand. Maybe he'd forgive me and rest in peace. I hoped this. I calmed myself and waited for him all night.

He fooled me though. He knew what I was waiting for, and it wasn't what he was looking to hear. Come dawn I heard a blood-splitting cry from the bedroom and I rushed in there. Grandma turnt the lights on. She was sitting on the edge of the bed and her face looked harsh, pinched-up gray.

"He was here," she said. "He came and laid down next to me in bed. And he touched me."

Her heart broke down. She cried. His touch was so cold. She laid back in bed after a while, as it was morning, and I went to the couch. As I lay there, falling asleep, I suddenly felt Grandpa's presence and the barrier between us like a swollen river. I felt how I had wronged him. How awful was the place where I had sent him. Behind the wall of death, he'd watched the living eat and cry and get drunk. He was lonesome, but I understood he meant no harm.

"Go back," I said to the dark, afraid and yet full of pity. "You got to be with your own kind now," I said. I felt him retreating, like a sigh, growing less. I felt his spirit as it shrunk back through the walls, the blinds, the brick courtyard of Senior Citizens. "Look up Aunt June," I whispered as he left.

I slept late the next morning, a good hard sleep allowing the sun to rise and warm the earth. It was past noon when I awoke. There is nothing, to my mind, like a long sleep to make those hard decisions that you neglect under stress of wakefulness. Soon as I woke up that morning, I saw exactly what I'd say to Grandma. I had gotten humble in the past week, not just losing the touch but getting jolted into the understanding that would prey on me from here on out. Your life feels different on you, once you greet death and understand your heart's position. You wear your life like a garment from the mission bundle sale ever after—lightly because you realize you never paid nothing for it, cherishing because you know you won't ever come by such a bargain again. Also you have the feeling someone wore it before you and someone will after. I can't explain that, not yet, but I'm putting my mind to it.

"Grandma," I said, "I got to be honest about the love medicine."

She listened. I knew from then on she would be listening to me the way I had listened to her before. I told her about the turkey hearts and how I had them blessed. I told her what I used as love medicine was purely a fake, and then I said to her what my understanding brought me.

"Love medicine ain't what brings him back to you, Grandma. No, it's something else. He loved you over time and distance, but he went off so quick he never got the chance to tell you how he loves you, how he doesn't blame you, how he understands. It's true feeling, not no magic. No supermarket heart could have brung him back."

She looked at me. She was seeing the years and days I had no way of knowing, and she didn't believe me. I could tell this. Yet a look came on her face. It was like the look of mothers drinking sweetness from their children's eyes. It was tenderness.

"Lipsha," she said, "you was always my favorite."

She took the beads off the bedpost, where she kept them to say at night, and she told me to put out my hand. When I did this, she shut the beads inside of my fist and held them there a long minute, tight, so my hand hurt. I almost cried when she did this. I don't really know why. Tears shot up behind my eyelids, and yet it was nothing. I didn't understand, except her hand was so strong, squeezing mine.

The earth was full of life and there were dandelions growing out the window, thick as thieves, already seeded, fat as big yellow plungers. She let my hand go. I got up. "I'll go out and dig a few dandelions," I told her.

Outside, the sun was hot and heavy as a hand on my back. I felt it flow down my arms, out my fingers, arrowing through the ends of the fork into the earth. With every root I prized up there was return, as if I was kin to its secret lesson. The touch got stronger as I worked through the grassy afternoon. Uncurling from me like a seed out of the blackness where I was lost, the touch spread. The spiked leaves full of bitter mother's milk. A buried root. A nuisance people dig up and throw in the sun to wither. A globe of frail seeds that's indestructible.

[1982]

Questions

1. Consider the ways in which misunderstandings between people shape the events of the story.
2. What does Lipsha mean by the comment about his grandfather, "some people fall right through the hole in their lives?"
3. How does Lipsha's definition of faith as "belief against the odds" figure in the story? What other elements of belief—both Christian and Native American—are explored?
4. What is Lipsha's power? What is love medicine? Is it successful in producing love?
5. What aspects of the story are humorous? How does Erdrich balance the humorous and serious elements of the story?

William Faulkner

(1897–1962)
United States

By almost universal acclaim, William Faulkner is America's greatest novelist of the twentieth century, though many critics would expand the geographical context to the entire world. This distinction is twofold: first, because of the major novels of his career—The Sound and the Fury (1929), As I Lay Dying (1930), Light in August (1932), Absalom, Absalom! (1936), and The Hamlet (1940)—and, second, because of the setting of most of his major works—the mythical area of Mississippi that Faulkner called Yoknapatawpha County. When he won the Nobel Prize for literature in 1952, both of these aspects of his work were praised.

Born in New Albany, Mississippi, Faulkner moved with his family to Oxford (the location of the state university) five years later, where he lived most of his life. Faulkner's great grandfather was a novelist and an early source of inspiration for his work. By the time he was 10, Faulkner had already discovered that if he told stories to the boys in the neighborhood, he could get them to do his chores for him. Faulkner wanted to fight in World War I but never saw combat, although he joined the Canadian Royal Air Force (after fudging about his nationality). Later in life, Faulkner often claimed that he was wounded in the war and temporarily took on the affectations of an English count.

The stories about Faulkner's drinking are legion. What they indicate more than anything else is the unhappiness of his marriage, as well as his determination to support himself (and his extended family) by his writing. When royalties from his novels and short stories were insufficient, Faulkner wrote screenplays in Hollywood. When he was awarded the Nobel Prize in 1952, almost all of his work was out of print. (The award had been supported by a number of French critics who had admired his work for years.) Late in his life, Faulkner finally achieved financial security and the admiration of American critics and readers. Responding to Malcolm Cowley about the world he had created in Yoknapatawpha County, Faulkner said the following:

> I discovered that my own little postage stamp of native soil was worth writing about and that I would never live long enough to exhaust it, and that by sublimating the actual into the apocryphal I would have complete liberty to use whatever talent I might have to its absolute top.

Faulkner taught at the University of Virginia in 1957 and 1958. During those years and much of the rest of his life, he responded wittily and obliquely to the elaborate questions of numerous interviewers about his specific works. About "A Rose for Emily" he made several choice remarks, including the following:

> . . . there was the young girl with a young girl's normal aspirations to find love and then a husband and a family, who was brow-beaten and kept down by her father, a selfish man who didn't want her to leave home because he wanted a housekeeper . . . .
>
> She had been trained that you do not take a lover. You marry, you don't take a lover. She had broken all the laws of her tradition, her background. [from Faulkner in the University (1959), edited by Frederick Gwynn and Joseph Blotner]

A ROSE FOR EMILY

I

When Miss Emily Grierson died, our whole town went to her funeral: the men through a sort of respectful affection for a fallen monument, the women mostly out of curiosity to see the inside of her house, which no one save an old manservant—a combined gardener and cook—had seen in at least ten years.

It was a big, squarish frame house that had once been white, decorated with cupolas and spires and scrolled balconies in the heavily lightsome style of the seventies, set on what had once been our most select street. But garages and cotton gins had encroached and obliterated even the august names of that neighborhood; only Miss Emily's house was left, lifting its stubborn and coquettish decay above the cotton wagons and the gasoline pumps—an eyesore among eyesores. And now Miss Emily had gone to join the representatives of those august names where they lay in the cedar-bemused cemetery among the ranked and anonymous graves of Union and Confederate soldiers who fell at the battle of Jefferson.

Alive, Miss Emily had been a tradition, a duty, and a care; a sort of hereditary obligation upon the town, dating from that day in 1894 when Colonel Sartoris, the mayor—he who fathered the edict that no Negro woman should appear on the streets without an apron—remitted her taxes, the dispensation dating from the death of her father on into perpetuity. Not that Miss Emily would have accepted charity. Colonel Sartoris invented an involved tale to the effect that Miss Emily's father had loaned money to the town, which the town, as a matter of business, preferred this way of repaying. Only a man of Colonel Sartoris' generation and thought could have invented it, and only a woman could have believed it.

When the next generation, with its more modern ideas, became mayors and aldermen, this arrangement created some little dissatisfaction. On the first of the year they mailed her a tax notice. February came, and there was no reply. They wrote her a formal letter, asking her to call at the sheriff's office at her convenience. A week later the mayor wrote her himself, offering to call or to send his car for her, and received in reply a note on paper of an archaic shape, in a thin, flowing calligraphy in faded ink, to the effect that she no longer went out at all. The tax notice was also enclosed, without comment.

They called a special meeting of the Board of Aldermen. A deputation waited upon her, knocked at the door through which no visitor had passed since she ceased giving china-painting lessons eight or ten years earlier. They were admitted by the old Negro into a dim hall from which a stairway mounted into still more shadow. It smelled of dust and disuse—a close, dank smell. The Negro led them into the parlor. It was furnished in heavy, leather-covered furniture. When the Negro opened the blinds of one window, they could see that the leather was cracked; and when they sat down, a faint dust rose sluggishly about their thighs, spinning with slow motes in the single sun-ray. On a tarnished gilt easel before the fireplace stood a crayon portrait of Miss Emily's father.

They rose when she entered—a small, fat woman in black, with a thin gold chain descending to her waist and vanishing into her belt, leaning on an ebony cane with a tarnished gold head. Her skeleton was small and spare; perhaps that was why what would have been merely plumpness in another was obesity in her. She looked bloated, like a body long submerged in motionless water, and of that pallid hue. Her eyes, lost in the fatty ridges of her face, looked like two small pieces of coal pressed into a lump of dough as they moved from one face to another while the visitors stated their errand.

She did not ask them to sit. She just stood in the door and listened quietly until the spokesman came to a stumbling halt. Then they could hear the invisible watch ticking at the end of the gold chain.

Her voice was dry and cold. "I have no taxes in Jefferson. Colonel Sartoris explained it to me. Perhaps one of you can gain access to the city records and satisfy yourselves."

"But we have. We are the city authorities, Miss Emily. Didn't you get a notice from the sheriff, signed by him?"

"I received a paper, yes," Miss Emily said. "Perhaps he considers himself the sheriff. . . . I have no taxes in Jefferson."

"But there is nothing on the books to show that, you see. We must go by the—"

"See Colonel Sartoris. I have no taxes in Jefferson."

"But, Miss Emily—"

"See Colonel Sartoris." (Colonel Sartoris had been dead almost ten years.) "I have no taxes in Jefferson. Tobe!" The Negro appeared. "Show these gentlemen out."

II

So she vanquished them, horse and foot, just as she had vanquished their fathers thirty years before about the smell. That was two years after her father's death and a short time after her sweetheart—the one we believed would marry her—had deserted her. After her father's death she went out very little; after her sweetheart went away, people hardly saw her at all. A few of the ladies had the temerity to call, but were not received, and the only sign of life about the place was the Negro man—a young man then—going in and out with a market basket.

"Just as if a man—any man—could keep a kitchen properly," the ladies said; so they were not surprised when the smell developed. It was another link between the gross, teeming world and the high and mighty Griersons.

A neighbor, a woman, complained to the mayor, Judge Stevens, eighty years old.

"But what will you have me do about it, madam?" he said.

"Why, send her word to stop it," the woman said. "Isn't there a law?"

"I'm sure that won't be necessary," Judge Stevens said. "It's probably just a snake or a rat that nigger of hers killed in the yard. I'll speak to him about it."

The next day he received two more complaints, one from a man who came in diffident deprecation. "We really must do something about it, Judge. I'd be the last one in the world to bother Miss Emily, but we've got to do something." That night the Board of Aldermen met—three gray-beards and one younger man, a member of the rising generation.

"It's simple enough," he said. "Send her word to have her place cleaned up. Give her a certain time to do it in, and if she don't. . . ."

"Dammit, sir," Judge Stevens said, "will you accuse a lady to her face of smelling bad?"

So the next night, after midnight, four men crossed Miss Emily's lawn and slunk about the house like burglars, sniffing along the base of the brickwork and at the cellar openings while one of them performed a regular sowing motion with his hand out of a sack slung from his shoulder. They broke open the cellar door and sprinkled lime there, and in all the outbuildings. As they recrossed the lawn, a window that had been dark was lighted and Miss Emily sat in it, the light behind her, and her upright torso motionless as that of an idol. They crept quietly across the lawn and into the shadow of the locusts that lined the street. After a week or two the smell went away.

That was when people had begun to feel really sorry for her. People in our town, remembering how old lady Wyatt, her great-aunt, had gone completely crazy at last, believed that the Griersons held themselves a little too high for what they really were. None of the young men were quite good enough for Miss Emily and such. We had long thought of them as a tableau, Miss Emily a slender figure in white in the background, her father a spraddled silhouette in the foreground, his back to her and clutching a horsewhip, the two of them framed by the backflung front door. So when she got to be thirty and was still single, we were not pleased exactly, but vindicated; even with insanity in the family she wouldn't have turned down all of her chances if they had really materialized.

When her father died, it got about that the house was all that was left to her; and in a way, people were glad. At last they could pity Miss Emily. Being left alone, and a pauper, she had become humanized. Now she too would know the old thrill and the old despair of a penny more or less.

The day after his death all the ladies prepared to call at the house and offer condolence and aid, as is our custom. Miss Emily met them at the door, dressed as usual and with no trace of grief on her face. She told them that her father was not dead. She did that for three days, with the ministers calling on her, and the doctors, trying to persuade her to let them dispose of the body. Just as they were about to resort to law and force, she broke down, and they buried her father quickly.

We did not say she was crazy then. We believed she had to do that. We remembered all the young men her father had driven away, and we knew that with nothing left, she would have to cling to that which had robbed her, as people will.

III

She was sick for a long time. When we saw her again, her hair was cut short, making her look like a girl, with a vague resemblance to those angels in colored church windows—sort of tragic and serene.

The town had just let the contracts for paving the sidewalks, and in the summer after her father's death they began the work. The construction company came with niggers and mules and machinery, and a foreman named Homer Barron, a Yankee— a big, dark, ready man, with a big voice and eyes lighter than his face. The little boys would follow in groups to hear him cuss the niggers, and the niggers singing in time to the rise and fall of picks. Pretty soon he knew everybody in town. Whenever you heard a lot of laughing anywhere about the square, Homer Barron would be in the center of the group. Presently, we began to see him and Miss Emily on Sunday afternoons driving in the yellow-wheeled buggy and the matched team of bays from the livery stable.

At first we were glad that Miss Emily would have an interest, because the ladies all said, "Of course a Grierson would not think seriously of a Northerner, a day laborer." But there were still others, older people, who said that even grief could not cause a real lady to forget noblesse oblige—without calling it noblesse oblige. They just said, "Poor Emily. Her kinsfolk should come to her." She had some kin in Alabama; but years ago her father had fallen out with them over the estate of old lady Wyatt, the crazy woman, and there was no communication between the two families. They had not even been represented at the funeral.

And as soon as the old people said, "Poor Emily," the whispering began. "Do you suppose it's really so?" they said to one another. "Of course it is. What else could . . . ." This behind their hands; rustling of craned silk and satin behind jalousies closed upon the sun of Sunday afternoon as the thin, swift clop-clop-clop of the matched team passed: "Poor Emily."

She carried her head high enough—even when we believed that she was fallen. It was as if she demanded more than ever the recognition of her dignity as the last Grierson; as if it had wanted that touch of earthiness to reaffirm her imperviousness. Like when she bought the rat poison, the arsenic. That was over a year after they had begun to say "Poor Emily," and while the two female cousins were visiting her.

"I want some poison," she said to the druggist. She was over thirty then, still a slight woman, though thinner than usual, with cold, haughty black eyes in a face the flesh of which was strained across the temples and about the eyesockets as you imagine a lighthouse-keeper's face ought to look. "I want some poison," she said.

"Yes, Miss Emily. What kind? For rats and such? I'd recom ——"

"I want the best you have. I don't care what kind."

The druggist named several. "They'll kill anything up to an elephant. But what you want is ——"

"Arsenic," Miss Emily said. "Is that a good one?"

"Is . . . arsenic? Yes, ma'am. But what you want ——"

"I want arsenic."

The druggist looked down at her. She looked back at him, erect, her face like a strained flag. "Why, of course," the druggist said. "If that's what you want. But the law requires you to tell what you are going to use it for."

Miss Emily just stared at him, her head tilted back in order to look him eye for eye, until he looked away and went and got the arsenic and wrapped it up. The Negro delivery boy brought her the package; the druggist didn't come back. When she opened the package at home there was written on the box, under the skull and bones: "For rats."

IV

So the next day we all said, "She will kill herself"; and we said it would be the best thing. When she had first begun to be seen with Homer Barron, we had said, "She will marry him." Then we said, "She will persuade him yet," because Homer himself had remarked—he liked men, and it was known that he drank with the younger men in the Elks' Club—that he was not a marrying man. Later we said, "Poor Emily" behind the jalousies as they passed on Sunday afternoon in the glittering buggy, Miss Emily with her head high and Homer Barron with his hat cocked and a cigar in his teeth, reins and whip in a yellow glove.

Then some of the ladies began to say that it was a disgrace to the town and a bad example to the young people. The men did not want to interfere, but at last the ladies forced the Baptist minister—Miss Emily's people were Episcopal—to call upon her.

He would never divulge what happened during that interview, but he refused to go back again. The next Sunday they again drove about the streets, and the following day the minister's wife wrote to Miss Emily's relations in Alabama.

So she had blood-kin under her roof again and we sat back to watch develop-ments. At first nothing happened. Then we were sure that they were to be married. We learned that Miss Emily had been to the jeweler's and ordered a man's toilet set in silver, with the letters H.B. on each piece. Two days later we learned that she had bought a complete outfit of men's clothing, including a nightshirt, and we said, "They are married." We were really glad. We were glad because the two female cousins were even more Grierson than Miss Emily had ever been.

So we were not surprised when Homer Barron—the streets had been finished some time since—was gone. We were a little disappointed that there was not a pub-lic blowing-off, but we believed that he had gone on to prepare for Miss Emily's com-ing, or to give her a chance to get rid of the cousins. (By that time it was a cabal, and we were all Miss Emily's allies to help circumvent the cousins.) Sure enough, after an-other week they departed. And, as we had expected all along, within three days Homer Barron was back in town. A neighbor saw the Negro man admit him at the kitchen door at dusk one evening.

And that was the last we saw of Homer Barron. And of Miss Emily for some time. The Negro man went in and out with the market basket, but the front door remained closed. Now and then we would see her at the window for a moment, as the men did that night when they sprinkled the lime, but for almost six months she did not ap-pear on the streets. Then we knew that this was to be expected too; as if that quali-ty of her father which had thwarted her woman's life so many times had been too virulent and too furious to die.

When we next saw Miss Emily, she had grown fat and her hair was turning gray. During the next few years it grew grayer and grayer until it attained an even pepper-and-salt iron-gray, when it ceased turning. Up to the day of her death at seventy-four it was still that vigorous iron-gray, like the hair of an active man.

From that time on her front door remained closed, save during a period of six or seven years, when she was about forty, during which she gave lessons in china-painting. She fitted up a studio in one of the downstairs rooms, where the daugh-ters and granddaughters of Colonel Sartoris' contemporaries were sent to her with the same regularity and in the same spirit that they were sent to church on Sun-days with a twenty-five-cent piece for the collection plate. Meanwhile her taxes had been remitted.

Then the newer generation became the backbone and the spirit of the town, and the painting pupils grew up and fell away and did not send their children to her with boxes of color and tedious brushes and pictures cut from the ladies' magazines. The front door closed upon the last one and remained closed for good. When the town got free postal delivery, Miss Emily alone refused to let them fasten the metal num-bers above her door and attach a mailbox to it. She would not listen to them.

Daily, monthly, yearly we watched the Negro grow grayer and more stooped, going in and out with the market basket. Each December we sent her a tax notice, which would be returned by the post office a week later, unclaimed. Now and then we would see her in one of the downstairs windows—she had evidently shut up the top floor of the house—like the carven torso of an idol in a niche, looking or not looking at us, we could never tell which. Thus she passed from generation to generation—dear, inescapable, impervious, tranquil, and perverse.

And so she died. Fell ill in the house filled with dust and shadows, with only a doddering Negro man to wait on her. We did not even know she was sick; we had long since given up trying to get any information from the Negro. He talked to no one, probably not even to her, for his voice had grown harsh and rusty, as if from disuse.

She died in one of the downstairs rooms, in a heavy walnut bed with a curtain, her gray head propped on a pillow yellow and moldy with age and lack of sunlight.

V

The Negro met the first of the ladies at the front door and let them in, with their hushed, sibilant voices and their quick, curious glances, and then he disappeared. He walked right through the house and out the back and was not seen again.

The two female cousins came at once. They held the funeral on the second day, with the town coming to look at Miss Emily beneath a mass of bought flowers, with the crayon face of her father musing profoundly above the bier and the ladies sibilant and macabre; and the very old men—some in their brushed Confederate uniforms— on the porch and the lawn, talking of Miss Emily as if she had been a contemporary of theirs, believing that they had danced with her and courted her perhaps, confusing time with its mathematical progression, as the old do, to whom all the past is not a diminishing road but, instead, a huge meadow which no winter ever quite touches, divided from them now by the narrow bottleneck of the most recent decade of years.

Already we knew that there was one room in that region above stairs which no one had seen in forty years, and which would have to be forced. They waited until Miss Emily was decently in the ground before they opened it.

The violence of breaking down the door seemed to fill this room with pervading dust. A thin, acrid pall as of the tomb seemed to lie everywhere upon this room decked and furnished as for a bridal: upon the valance curtains of faded rose color, upon the rose-shaded lights, upon the dressing table, upon the delicate array of crystal and the man's toilet things backed with tarnished silver, silver so tarnished that the monogram was obscured. Among them lay a collar and tie, as if they had just been removed, which, lifted, left upon the surface a pale crescent in the dust. Upon a chair hung the suit, carefully folded; beneath it the two mute shoes and the discarded socks.

The man himself lay in the bed.

For a long while we just stood there, looking down at the profound and fleshless grin. The body had apparently once lain in the attitude of an embrace, but now the long sleep that outlasts love, that conquers even the grimace of love, had cuckolded him. What was left of him, rotted beneath what was left of the nightshirt, had become inextricable from the bed in which he lay; and upon him and upon the pillow beside him lay that even coating of the patient and biding dust.

Then we noticed that in the second pillow was the indentation of a head. One of us lifted something from it, and leaning forward, that faint and invisible dust dry and acrid in the nostrils, we saw a long strand of iron-gray hair.

[1931]

Questions

1. How do the five sections of "A Rose for Emily" contribute to its structure, its un-folding?
2. How are we to interpret the title?
3. How significant are the characters' names in this story?
4. What can be said about point of view in Faulkner's story?
5. Is the story geographically "locked" into its Southern context, or is it possible to as-sume the same events could happen in a Northern town?

Feng Jicai
(b. 1942)
China

F eng Jicai, born in Tianjin, China, began his first career as a painter but shifted to fiction when his "counterrevolutionary" art was unwelcome during China's Cultural Revolution of the 1960s and 1970s. For the same reason, he could not publish his fiction until after the death of Mao Zedong in 1976. Now a prolific writer (though not yet widely translated), he currently resides in Tianjin with his wife and son and holds major positions in Chinese writers' professional organizations.

One volume of Feng's stories and two novels have been translated into English: Chrysanthemums and Other Stories (1985), The Three-Inch Golden Lotus (1994), and Let One Hundred Flowers Bloom (1996). He has also published two volumes of oral history of the Chinese cultural revolution, the interval between 1966 and 1976 that dramatically affected the lives of ordinary Chinese people. The interviews, drawn from a broad representation of people, illuminate both the suffering and the heroism of that era.

Feng still precipitates controversy with his writing, however. His translator, Susan Wilff Chen, has noted that "The Street-Sweeping Show," originally published in 1982, is not reprinted in any of Feng's collections of short stories, because it resembled a real-life incident so closely that it caused objections when it first appeared.

THE STREET-SWEEPING SHOW

"National Cleanup Week starts today," said Secretary Zhao, "and officials everywhere are going out to join in the street sweeping. Here's our list of participants—all top city administrators and public figures. We've just had it mimeographed over at the office for your approval."

He looked like a typical upper-echelon secretary: the collar of his well-worn, neatly pressed Mao suit[1] was buttoned up military style; his complexion was pale; his glasses utilitarian. His gentle, deferential manner and pleasantly modulated voice concealed a shrewd, hard-driving personality.

The mayor pored over the list, as if the eighty names on it were those of people selected to go abroad. From time to time he glanced thoughtfully at the high white ceiling.

"Why isn't there anyone from the Women's Federation?" he asked.

---

[1]Mao   Mao ZeDong (also transliterated as Mao Tse-tung) (1893–1976); Communist leader and chairman of the Communist party of the People's Republic of China from 1949 until his death. Mao led the Cultural Revolution, 1966 to 1976, including the institution of a uniform code of dress.

Secretary Zhao thought for a moment. "Oh, you're right—there isn't! We've got the heads of every office in the city—the Athletic Committee, the Youth League Committee, the Federation of Trade Unions, the Federation of Literary and Art Circles— even some famous university professors. The only group we forgot is the Women's Federation."

"Women are the pillars of society. How can we leave out the women's representatives?" The mayor sounded smug rather than reproachful. Only a leader could think of everything. This was where true leadership ability came into play. Secretary Zhao was reminded of the time when the mayor had pointed out that the fish course was missing from the menu for a banquet in honor of some foreign guests.

"Add two names from the Women's Federation, and make sure you get people in positions of authority or who are proper representatives of the organization. 'International Working Women's Red Banner Pacesetters,' 'Families of Martyrs,' or 'Model Workers' would be fine." Like an elementary school teacher returning a poor homework paper to his student, the mayor handed the incomplete list back to his secretary.

"Yes, your honor, I'll do it right away. A complete list will be useful the next time something like this comes up. And I must contact everyone at once. The street sweeping is scheduled for two this afternoon in Central Square. Will you be able to go?"

"Of course. As mayor of the city, I have to set an example."

"The car will be at the gate for you at one-thirty. I'll go with you."

"All right," the mayor answered absentmindedly, scratching his forehead and looking away.

Secretary Zhao hurried out.

At one-thirty that afternoon the mayor was whisked to the square in his limousine. All office workers, shop clerks, students, housewives, and retirees were out sweeping the streets, and the air was thick with dust. Secretary Zhao hastily rolled up the window. Inside the car there was only a faint, pleasant smell of gasoline and leather.

At the square they pulled up beside a colorful assortment of limousines. In front of them a group of top city administrators had gathered to wait for the mayor's arrival. Someone had arranged for uniformed policemen to stand guard on all sides.

Secretary Zhao sprang out of the limousine and opened the door for his boss. The officials in the waiting crowd stepped forward with smiling faces to greet the mayor. Everyone knew him and hoped to be the first to shake his hand.

"Good afternoon—oh, nice to see you—good afternoon—" the mayor repeated as he shook hands with each of them.

An old policeman approached, followed by two younger ones pushing wheelbarrows full of big bamboo brooms. The old policeman selected one of the smaller, neater brooms and presented it respectfully to the mayor. When the other dignitaries had gotten their brooms, a marshal with a red armband led them all to the center of the square. Naturally the mayor walked at the head.

Groups of people had come from their workplaces to sweep the huge square. At the sight of this majestic, broom-carrying procession, with its marshal, police escort, and retinue of shutter-clicking photographers, they realized that they were in the presence of no ordinary mortals and gathered closer for a look. How extraordinary for a mayor to be sweeping the streets, thought Secretary Zhao, swelling with unconscious pride as he strutted along beside the mayor with his broom on his shoulder.

"Here we are," the marshal said when they had reached the designated spot.

All eighty-two dignitaries began to sweep.

The swelling crowd of onlookers, which was kept back by a police cordon, was buzzing with excitement:

"Look, he's the one over there."

"Which one? The one in black?"

"No. The bald fat one in blue."

"Cut the chitchat!" barked a policeman.

The square was so huge that no one knew where to sweep. The concrete pavement was clean to begin with; they pushed what little grit there was back and forth with their big brooms. The most conspicuous piece of litter was a solitary popsicle wrapper, which they all pursued like children chasing a dragonfly.

The photographers surrounded the mayor. Some got down on one knee to shoot from below, while others ran from side to side trying to get a profile. Like a cloud in a thunderstorm, the mayor was constantly illuminated by silvery flashes. Then a man in a visored cap, with a video camera, approached Secretary Zhao.

"I'm from the TV station," he said. "Would you please ask them to line up single file so they'll look neat on camera?"

Secretary Zhao consulted with the mayor, who agreed to this request. The dignitaries formed a long line and began to wield their brooms for the camera, regardless of whether there was any dirt on the ground.

The cameraman was about to start shooting, when he stopped and ran over to the mayor.

"I'm sorry, your honor," he said, "but you're all going to have to face the other way because you've got your backs to the sun. And I'd also like the entire line to be reversed so that you're at the head."

"All right," the mayor agreed graciously, and he led his entourage, like a line of dragon dancers, in a clumsy turn-around. Once in place, everyone began sweeping again.

Pleased, the cameraman ran to the head of the line, pushed his cap up, and aimed at the mayor. "All right," he said as the camera started to whir, "swing those brooms, all together now—put your hearts into it—that's it! Chin up please, your honor. Hold it—that's fine—all right!"

He stopped the camera, shook the mayor's hand, and thanked him for helping an ordinary reporter carry out his assignment.

Let's call it a day," the marshal said to secretary Zhao. Then he turned to the mayor. "You have victoriously accomplished your mission," he said.

"Very good—thank you for your trouble," the mayor replied routinely, smiling and shaking hands again.

Some reporters came running up to the mayor. "Do you have any instructions, your honor?" asked a tall, thin, aggressive one.

"Nothing in particular." The mayor paused for a moment. "Everyone should pitch in to clean up our city."

The reporters scribbled his precious words in their notebooks.

The policemen brought the wheelbarrows back, and everyone returned the brooms. Secretary Zhao replaced the mayor's for him.

It was time to go. The mayor shook hands with everyone again.

"Good-bye—good-bye—good-bye—"

The others waited until the mayor had gotten into his limousine before getting into theirs.

The mayor's limousine delivered him to his house, where his servant had drawn his bathwater and set out scented soap and fresh towels. He enjoyed a leisurely bath and emerged from the bathroom with rosy skin and clean clothes, leaving his grime and exhaustion behind him in the tub.

As he descended the stairs to eat dinner, his grandson hurriedly led him into the living room.

"Look, Granddad, you're on TV!"

There he was on the television screen, like an actor, putting on a show of sweeping the street. He turned away and gave his grandson a casual pat on the shoulder.

"It's not worth watching. Let's go have dinner."

[1982]
Translated by
SUSAN WILFF CHEN

Questions

1. What is the actual purpose of the street-sweeping ceremony?
2. What does the story suggest abut public rituals? About bureaucracy? About the media's role in such rituals? Compare this story with Isabel Allende's "And of Clay Are We Created."
3. What is the significance of the title?
4. Why does the mayor refuse to watch the ceremony on television?

F. Scott Fitzgerald

(1896–1940)
United States

A s innumerable critics have observed, it is difficult to think of the American Jazz Age, of the Lost Generation, without recalling F. Scott Fitzgerald's novels and short stories. Although the era has passed, it is preserved forever in Fitzgerald's work. As Charlie Wales muses toward the end of "Babylon Revisited," ". . . the snow of twenty-nine wasn't real snow. If you didn't want it to be snow, you just paid some money." Money grew on trees; anything could be had for a price, until the collapse of the stock market, when reality took hold of people's (but not all people's) lives.

Early in his career, shortly before the publication of his first novel, Fitzgerald made this observation about his writing:

> My idea is always to reach my generation. The wise writer, I think, writes for the youth of his own generation, the critic of the next and the schoolmasters of ever afterward. Granted the ability to improve what he imitates in the way of style, to choose from his own interpretation of the experiences around him what constitutes material, and we get the first-water genius.

As you read "Bernice Bobs Her Hair," consider the way that the three different audiences Fitzgerald identifies might respond to the story during both its own time and today.

Fitzgerald was born in St. Paul, Minnesota, in 1896. His most famous novel, The Great Gatsby, appeared in 1925. By the time of his death in 1940, he had published nearly 160 short stories as well as several other major novels, including This Side of Paradise (1920), The Beautiful and the Damned (1922), and Tender Is the Night (1934). His posthumous novel, The Last Tycoon, about Hollywood (where Fitzgerald had worked for years) appeared in 1940.

BERNICE BOBS HER HAIR

After dark on Saturday night one could stand on the first tee of the golf-course and see the country-club windows as a yellow expanse over a very black and wavy ocean. The waves of this ocean, so to speak, were the heads of many curious caddies, a few of the more ingenious chauffeurs, the golf professional's deaf sister—and there were usually several stray, diffident waves who might have rolled inside had they so desired. This was the gallery.

The balcony was inside. It consisted of the circle of wicker chairs that lined the wall of the combination clubroom and ballroom. At these Saturday-night dances it was largely feminine; a great babble of middle-aged ladies with sharp eyes and icy hearts behind lorgnettes and large bosoms. The main function of the balcony was critical. It occasionally showed grudging admiration, but never approval, for it is well known among ladies over thirty-five that when the younger set dance in the summertime it is with the very worst intentions in the world, and if they are not bombarded with stony eyes, stray couples will dance weird barbaric interludes in the corners, and the more popular, more dangerous girls will sometimes be kissed in the parked limousines of unsuspecting dowagers.

But, after all, this critical circle is not close enough to the stage to see the actors' faces and catch the subtler byplay. It can only frown and lean, ask questions and make satisfactory deductions from its set of postulates, such as the one which states that every young man with a large income leads the life of a hunted partridge. It never really appreciates the drama of the shifting, semicruel world of adolescence. No; boxes, orchestra-circle, principals, and chorus are represented by the medley of faces and voices that sway to the plaintive African rhythm of Dyer's dance orchestra.

From sixteen-year-old Otis Ormonde, who has two more years at Hill School, to G. Reese Stoddard, over whose bureau at home hangs a Harvard law diploma; from little Madeleine Hogue, whose hair still feels strange and uncomfortable on top of her head, to Bessie MacRae, who has been the life of the party a little too long—more than ten years—the medley is not only the centre of the stage but contains the only people capable of getting an unobstructed view of it.

With a flourish and a bang the music stops. The couples exchange artificial, effortless smiles, facetiously repeat "*la-de-dad-da* dum-*dum*," and then the clatter of young feminine voices soars over the burst of clapping.

A few disappointed stags caught in midfloor as they had been about to cut in subsided listlessly back to the walls, because this was not like the riotous Christmas dances—these summer hops were considered just pleasantly warm and exciting, where even the younger marrieds rose and performed ancient waltzes and terrifying fox trots to the tolerant amusement of their younger brothers and sisters.

Warren McIntyre, who casually attended Yale, being one of the unfortunate stags, felt in his dinner-coat pocket for a cigarette and strolled out onto the wide, semidark veranda, where couples were scattered at tables, filling the lantern-hung night with vague words and hazy laughter. He nodded here and there at the less absorbed and as he passed each couple some half-forgotten fragment of a story played in his mind, for it was not a large city and every one was Who's Who to every one else's past. There, for example, were Jim Strain and Ethel Demorest, who had been privately engaged for three years. Every one knew that as soon as Jim managed to hold a job for more than two months she would marry him. Yet how bored they both looked, and how wearily Ethel regarded Jim sometimes, as if she wondered why she had trained the vines of her affection on such a wind-shaken poplar.

Warren was nineteen and rather pitying with those of his friends who had gone East to college. But, like most boys, he bragged tremendously about the girls of his city when he was away from it. There was Genevieve Ormonde, who regularly made the rounds of dances, house-parties, and football games at Princeton, Yale, Williams, and Cornell; there was black-eyed Roberta Dillon, who was quite as famous to her own generation as Hiram Johnson or Ty Cobb; and, of course, there was Marjorie Harvey, who besides having a fairylike face and a dazzling, bewildering tongue was already justly celebrated for having turned five cart-wheels in succession during the last pump-and-slipper dance at New Haven.

Warren, who had grown up across the street from Marjorie, had long been "crazy about her." Sometimes she seemed to reciprocate his feeling with a faint gratitude, but she had tried him by her infallible test and informed him gravely that she did not love him. Her test was that when she was away from him she forgot him and had affairs with other boys. Warren found this discouraging, especially as Marjorie had been making little trips all summer, and for the first two or three days after each arrival home he saw great heaps of mail on the Harveys' hall table addressed to her in various masculine handwritings. To make matters worse, all during the month of August she had been visited by her cousin Bernice from Eau Claire, and it seemed impossible to see her alone. It was always necessary to hunt round and find some one to take care of Bernice. As August waned this was becoming more and more difficult.

Much as Warren worshipped Marjorie, he had to admit that Cousin Bernice was sorta dopeless. She was pretty, with dark hair and high color, but she was no fun on a party. Every Saturday night he danced a long arduous duty dance with her to please Marjorie, but he had never been anything but bored in her company.

"Warren"—a soft voice at his elbow broke in upon his thoughts, and he turned to see Marjorie, flushed and radiant as usual. She laid a hand on his shoulder and a glow settled almost imperceptibly over him.

"Warren," she whispered, "do something for me—dance with Bernice. She's been stuck with little Otis Ormonde for almost an hour."

Warren's glow faded.

"Why—sure," he answered half-heartedly.

"You don't mind, do you? I'll see that you don't get stuck."

"'Sall right."

Marjorie smiled—that smile that was thanks enough.

"You're an angel, and I'm obliged loads."

With a sigh the angel glanced round the veranda, but Bernice and Otis were not in sight. He wandered back inside, and there in front of the women's dressing-room he found Otis in the center of a group of young men who were convulsed with laughter. Otis was brandishing a piece of timber he had picked up, and discoursing volubly.

"She's gone in to fix her hair," he announced wildly. "I'm waiting to dance another hour with her."

Their laughter was renewed.

"Why don't some of you cut in?" cried Otis resentfully. "She likes more variety."

"Why, Otis," suggested a friend, "you've just barely got used to her."

"Why the two-by-four, Otis?" inquired Warren, smiling.

"The two-by four? Oh, this? This is a club. When she comes out I'll hit her on the head and knock her in again."

Warren collapsed on a settee and howled with glee.

"Never mind, Otis," he articulated finally. "I'm relieving you this time."

Otis simulated a sudden fainting attack and handed the stick to Warren.

"If you need it, old man," he said hoarsely.

No matter how beautiful or brilliant a girl may be, the reputation of not being frequently cut in on makes her position at a dance unfortunate. Perhaps boys prefer her company to that of the butterflies with whom they dance a dozen times an evening, but youth in this jazz-nourished generation is temperamentally restless, and the idea of fox-trotting more than one full fox trot with the same girl is distasteful, not to say odious. When it comes to several dances and the intermissions between she can be quite sure that a young man, once relieved, will never tread on her wayward toes again.

Warren danced the next full dance with Bernice, and finally, thankful for the intermission, he led her to a table on the veranda. There was a moment's silence while she did unimpressive things with her fan.

"It's hotter here than in Eau Claire," she said.

Warren stifled a sigh and nodded. It might be for all he knew or cared. He wondered idly whether she was a poor conversationalist because she got no attention or got no attention because she was a poor conversationalist.

"You going to be here much longer?" he asked, and then turned rather red. She might suspect his reasons for asking.

"Another week," she answered, and stared at him as if to lunge at his next remark when it left his lips.

Warren fidgeted. Then with a sudden charitable impulse he decided to try part of his line on her. He turned and looked at her eyes.

"You've got an awfully kissable mouth," he began quietly.

This was a remark that he sometimes made to girls at college proms when they were talking in just such half-dark as this. Bernice distinctly jumped. She turned an ungraceful red and became clumsy with her fan. No one had ever made such a remark to her before.

"Fresh!"—the word had slipped out before she realized it, and she bit her lip. Too late she decided to be amused, and offered him a flustered smile.

Warren was annoyed. Though not accustomed to have that remark taken seriously, still it usually provoked a laugh or a paragraph of sentimental banter. And he hated to be called fresh, except in a joking way. His charitable impulse died and he switched the topic.

"Jim Strain and Ethel Demorest sitting out as usual," he commented.

This was more in Bernice's line, but a faint regret mingled with her relief as the subject changed. Men did not talk to her about kissable mouths, but she knew that they talked in some such way to other girls.

"Oh, yes," she said, and laughed. "I hear they've been mooning round for years without a red penny. Isn't it silly?"

Warren's disgust increased. Jim Strain was a close friend of his brother's, and anyway he considered it bad form to sneer at people for not having money. But Bernice had had no intention of sneering. She was merely nervous.

II

When Marjorie and Bernice reached home at half after midnight they said good night at the top of the stairs. Though cousins, they were not intimates. As a matter of fact Marjorie had no female intimates—she considered girls stupid. Bernice on the contrary all through this parent-arranged visit had rather longed to exchange those confidences flavored with giggles and tears that she considered an indispensable factor in all feminine intercourse. But in this respect she found Marjorie rather cold; felt somehow the same difficulty in talking to her that she had in talking to men. Marjorie never giggled, was never frightened, seldom embarrassed, and in fact had very few of the qualities which Bernice considered appropriately and blessedly feminine.

As Bernice busied herself with toothbrush and paste this night she wondered for the hundredth time why she never had any attention when she was away from home. That her family were the wealthiest in Eau Claire, that her mother entertained tremendously, gave little dinners for her daughter before all dances and bought her a car of her own to drive round in, never occurred to her as factors in her home-town social success. Like most girls she had been brought up on the warm milk prepared by Annie Fellows Johnston and on novels in which the female was beloved because of certain mysterious womanly qualities, always mentioned but never displayed.

Bernice felt a vague pain that she was not at present engaged in being popular. She did not know that had it not been for Marjorie's campaigning she would have danced the entire evening with one man; but she knew that even in Eau Claire other girls with less position and less pulchritude were given a much bigger rush. She attributed this to something subtly unscrupulous in those girls. It had never worried her, and if it had her mother would have assured her that the other girls cheapened themselves and that men really respected girls like Bernice.

She turned out the light in her bathroom, and on an impulse decided to go in and chat for a moment with her aunt Josephine, whose light was still on. Her soft slippers bore her noiselessly down the carpeted hall, but hearing voices inside she stopped near the partly opened door. Then she caught her own name, and without any definite intention of eavesdropping lingered—and the thread of the conversation going on inside pierced her consciousness sharply as if it had been drawn through with a needle.

"She's absolutely hopeless!" It was Marjorie's voice. "Oh, I know what you're going to say! So many people have told you how pretty and sweet she is, and how she can cook! What of it? She has a bum time. Men don't like her."

"What's a little cheap popularity?"

Mrs. Harvey sounded annoyed.

"It's everything when you're eighteen," said Marjorie emphatically. "I've done my best. I've been polite and I've made men dance with her, but they just won't stand being bored. When I think of that gorgeous coloring wasted on such a ninny, and think what Martha Carey could do with it—oh!"

"There's no courtesy these days."

Mrs. Harvey's voice implied that modern situations were too much for her. When she was a girl all young ladies who belonged to nice families had glorious times.

"Well," said Marjorie, "no girl can permanently bolster up a lame-duck visitor, because these days it's every girl for herself. I've even tried to drop her hints about clothes and things, and she's been furious—given me the funniest looks. She's sensitive enough to know she's not getting away with much, but I'll bet she consoles herself by thinking that she's very virtuous and that I'm too gay and fickle and will come to a bad end. All unpopular girls think that way. Sour grapes! Sarah Hopkins refers to Genevieve and Roberta and me as gardenia girls! I'll bet she'd give ten years of her life and her European education to be a gardenia girl and have three or four men in love with her and be cut in on every few feet at dances."

"It seems to me," interrupted Mrs. Harvey rather wearily, "that you ought to be able to do something for Bernice. I know she's not very vivacious."

Marjorie groaned.

"Vivacious! Good grief! I've never heard her say anything to a boy except that it's hot or the floor's crowded or that she's going to school in New York next year. Sometimes she asks them what kind of car they have and tells them the kind she has. Thrilling!"

There was a short silence, and then Mrs. Harvey took up her refrain: "All I know is that other girls not half so sweet and attractive get partners. Martha Carey, for instance, is stout and loud, and her mother is distinctly common. Roberta Dillon is so thin this year that she looks as though Arizona were the place for her. She's dancing herself to death."

"But, mother," objected Marjorie impatiently, "Martha is cheerful and awfully witty and an awfully slick girl, and Roberta's a marvellous dancer. She's been popular for ages!"

Mrs. Harvey yawned.

"I think it's that crazy Indian blood in Bernice," continued Marjorie. "Maybe she's a reversion to type. Indian women all just sat round and never said anything."

"Go to bed, you silly child," laughed Mrs. Harvey. "I wouldn't have told you that if I'd thought you were going to remember it. And I think most of your ideas are perfectly idiotic," she finished sleepily.

There was another silence, while Marjorie considered whether or not convincing her mother was worth the trouble. People over forty can seldom be permanently convinced of anything. At eighteen our convictions are hills from which we look; at forty-five they are caves in which we hide.

Having decided this, Marjorie said good night. When she came out into the hall it was quite empty.

III

While Marjorie was breakfasting late next day Bernice came into the room with a rather formal good morning, sat down opposite, stared intently over and slightly moistened her lips.

"What's on your mind?" inquired Marjorie, rather puzzled.

Bernice paused before she threw her hand-grenade.

"I heard what you said about me to your mother last night."

Marjorie was startled, but she showed only a faintly heightened color and her voice was quite even when she spoke.

"Where were you?"

"In the hall. I didn't mean to listen—at first."

After an involuntary look of contempt Marjorie dropped her eyes and became very interested in balancing a stray corn-flake on her finger.

"I guess I'd better go back to Eau Claire—if I'm such a nuisance." Bernice's lower lip was trembling violently and she continued on a wavering note: "I've tried to be nice, and—and I've been first neglected and then insulted. No one ever visited me and got such treatment."

Marjorie was silent.

"But I'm in the way, I see. I'm a drag on you. Your friends don't like me." She paused, and then remembered another one of her grievances. "Of course I was furious last week when you tried to hint to me that that dress was unbecoming. Don't you think I know how to dress myself?"

"No," murmured Marjorie less than half-aloud.

"What?"

"I didn't hint anything," said Marjorie succinctly. "I said, as I remember, that it was better to wear a becoming dress three times straight than to alternate it with two frights."

"Do you think that was a very nice thing to say?"

"I wasn't trying to be nice." Then after a pause: "When do you want to go?"

Bernice drew in her breath sharply.

"Oh!" It was a little half-cry.

Marjorie looked up in surprise.

"Didn't you say you were going?"

"Yes, but——"

"Oh, you were only bluffing!"

They stared at each other across the breakfast-table for a moment. Misty waves were passing before Bernice's eyes, while Marjorie's face wore that rather hard expression that she used when slightly intoxicated undergraduates were making love to her.

"So you were bluffing," she repeated as if it were what she might have expected.

Bernice admitted it by bursting into tears. Marjorie's eyes showed boredom.

"You're my cousin," sobbed Bernice. "I'm v-v-visiting you. I was to stay a month, and if I go home my mother will know and she'll wah-wonder——"

Marjorie waited until the shower of broken words collapsed into little sniffles.

"I'll give you my month's allowance," she said coldly, "and you can spend this last week anywhere you want. There's a very nice hotel——"

Bernice's sobs rose to a flute note, and rising of a sudden she fled from the room.

An hour later, while Marjorie was in the library absorbed in composing one of those non-committal, marvellously elusive letters that only a young girl can write, Bernice reappeared, very red-eyed and consciously calm. She cast no glance at Marjorie but took a book at random from the shelf and sat down as if to read. Marjorie seemed absorbed in her letter and continued writing. When the clock showed noon Bernice closed her book with a snap.

"I suppose I'd better get my railroad ticket."

This was not the beginning of the speech she had rehearsed upstairs, but as Marjorie was not getting her cues—wasn't urging her to be reasonable; it's all a mistake—it was the best opening she could muster.

"Just wait till I finish this letter," said Marjorie without looking round. "I want to get it off in the next mail."

After another minute, during which her pen scratched busily, she turned round and relaxed with an air of "at your service." Again Bernice had to speak.

"Do you want me to go home?"

"Well," said Marjorie, considering, "I suppose if you're not having a good time you'd better go. No use being miserable."

"Don't you think common kindness——"

"Oh, please don't quote 'Little Women'!" cried Marjorie impatiently. "That's out of style."

"You think so?"

"Heavens, yes! What modern girl could live like those insane females?"

"They were the models for our mothers."

Marjorie laughed.

"Yes, they were—not! Besides, our mothers were all very well in their way, but they know very little about their daughters' problems."

Bernice drew herself up.

"Please don't talk about my mother."

Marjorie laughed.

"I don't think I mentioned her."

Bernice felt that she was being led away from her subject.

"Do you think you've treated me very well?"

"I've done my best. You're rather hard material to work with."

The lids of Bernice's eyes reddened.

"I think you're hard and selfish, and you haven't a feminine quality in you."

"Oh, my Lord!" cried Marjorie in desperation. "You little nut! Girls like you are responsible for all the tiresome colorless marriages; all those ghastly inefficiencies that pass as feminine qualities. What a blow it must be when a man with imagination marries the beautiful bundle of clothes that he's been building ideals around, and finds that she's just a weak, whining, cowardly mass of affectations!"

Bernice's mouth had slipped half open.

"The womanly woman!" continued Marjorie. "Her whole early life is occupied in whining criticisms of girls like me who really do have a good time."

Bernice's jaw descended farther as Marjorie's voice rose.

"There's some excuse for an ugly girl whining. If I'd been irretrievably ugly I'd never have forgiven my parents for bringing me into the world. But you're starting life without any handicap—" Marjorie's little fist clenched. "If you expect me to weep with you you'll be disappointed. Go or stay, just as you like." And picking up her letters she left the room.

Bernice claimed a headache and failed to appear at luncheon. They had a matinée date for the afternoon, but the headache persisting, Marjorie made explanation to a not very downcast boy. But when she returned late in the afternoon she found Bernice with a strangely set face waiting for her in her bedroom.

"I've decided," began Bernice without preliminaries, "that maybe you're right about things—possibly not. But if you'll tell me why your friends aren't—aren't interested in me I'll see if I can do what you want me to."

Marjorie was at the mirror shaking down her hair.

"Do you mean it?"

"Yes."

"Without reservations? Will you do exactly what I say?"

"Well, I——"

"Well nothing! Will you do exactly as I say?"

"If they're sensible things."

"They're not! You're no case for sensible things."

"Are you going to make—to recommend——"

"Yes, everything. If I tell you to take boxing-lessons you'll have to do it. Write home and tell your mother you're going to stay another two weeks."

"If you'll tell me——"

"All right—I'll just give you a few examples now. First, you have no ease of manner. Why? Because you're never sure about your personal appearance. When a girl feels that she's perfectly groomed and dressed she can forget that part of her. That's charm. The more parts of yourself you can afford to forget the more charm you have."

"Don't I look all right?"

"No; for instance, you never take care of your eyebrows. They're black and lustrous, but by leaving them straggly they're a blemish. They'd be beautiful if you'd take care of them in one-tenth the time you take doing nothing. You're going to brush them so that they'll grow straight."

Bernice raised the brows in question.

"Do you mean to say that men notice eyebrows?"

"Yes—subconsciously. And when you go home you ought to have your teeth straightened a little. It's almost imperceptible, still——"

"But I thought," interrupted Bernice in bewilderment, "that you despised little dainty feminine things like that."

"I hate dainty minds," answered Marjorie. "But a girl has to be dainty in person. If she looks like a million dollars she can talk about Russia, ping-pong, or the League of Nations and get away with it."

"What else?"

"Oh, I'm just beginning! There's your dancing."

"Don't I dance all right?"

"No, you don't—you lean on a man; yes, you do—ever so slightly. I noticed it when we were dancing together yesterday. And you dance standing up straight instead of bending over a little. Probably some old lady on the side-line once told you that you looked so dignified that way. But except with a very small girl it's much harder on the man, and he's the one that counts."

"Go on." Bernice's brain was reeling.

"Well, you've got to learn to be nice to men who are sad birds. You look as if you'd been insulted whenever you're thrown with any except the most popular boys. Why, Bernice, I'm cut in on every few feet—and who does most of it? Why, those very sad birds. No girl can afford to neglect them. They're the big part of any crowd. Young boys too shy to talk are the very best conversational practice. Clumsy boys are the best dancing practice. If you can follow them and yet look graceful you can follow a baby tank across a barb-wire sky-scraper."

Bernice sighed profoundly, but Marjorie was not through.

"If you go to a dance and really amuse, say, three sad birds that dance with you; if you talk so well to them that they forget they're stuck with you, you've done something. They'll come back next time, and gradually so many sad birds will dance with you that the attractive boys will see there's no danger of being stuck—then they'll dance with you."

"Yes," agreed Bernice faintly. "I think I begin to see."

"And finally," concluded Marjorie, "poise and charm will just come. You'll wake up some morning knowing you've attained it, and men will know it too."

Bernice rose.

"It's been awfully kind of you—but nobody's ever talked to me like this before, and I feel sort of startled."

Marjorie made no answer but gazed pensively at her own image in the mirror.

"You're a peach to help me," continued Bernice.

Still Marjorie did not answer, and Bernice thought she had seemed too grateful.

"I know you don't like sentiment," she said timidly.

Marjorie turned to her quickly.

"Oh, I wasn't thinking about that. I was considering whether we hadn't better bob your hair."

Bernice collapsed backward upon the bed.

IV

On the following Wednesday evening there was a dinner-dance at the country club. When the guests strolled in Bernice found her placecard with a slight feeling of irritation. Though at her right sat G. Reece Stoddard, a most desirable and distinguished young bachelor, the all-important left held only Charley Paulson. Charley lacked height, beauty, and social shrewdness, and in her new enlightenment Bernice decided that his only qualification to be her partner was that he had never been stuck with her. But this feeling of irritation left with the last of the soup-plates, and Marjorie's specific instruction came to her. Swallowing her pride she turned to Charley Paulson and plunged.

"Do you think I ought to bob my hair, Mr. Charley Paulson?"

Charley looked up in surprise.

"Why?"

"Because I'm considering it. It's such a sure and easy way of attracting attention."

Charley smiled pleasantly. He could not know this had been rehearsed. He replied that he didn't know much about bobbed hair. But Bernice was there to tell him.

"I want to be a society vampire, you see," she announced coolly, and went on to inform him that bobbed hair was the necessary prelude. She added that she wanted to ask his advice, because she had heard he was so critical about girls.

Charley, who knew as much about the psychology of women as he did of the mental states of Buddhist contemplatives, felt vaguely flattered.

"So I've decided," she continued, her voice rising slightly, "that early next week I'm going down to the Sevier Hotel barber-shop, sit in the first chair, and get my hair bobbed." She faltered, noticing that the people near her had paused in their conversation and were listening; but after a confused second Marjorie's coaching told, and she finished her paragraph to the vicinity at large. "Of course I'm charging admission, but if you'll all come down and encourage me I'll issue passes for the inside seats."

There was a ripple of appreciative laughter, and under cover of it G. Reece Stoddard leaned over quickly and said close to her ear: "I'll take a box right now."

She met his eyes and smiled as if he had said something surpassingly brilliant.

"Do you believe in bobbed hair?" asked G. Reece in the same undertone.

"I think it's unmoral," affirmed Bernice gravely. "But, of course, you've either got to amuse people or feed 'em or shock 'em." Marjorie had culled this from Oscar Wilde. It was greeted with a ripple of laughter from the men and a series of quick, intent looks from the girls. And then as though she had said nothing of wit or moment Bernice turned again to Charley and spoke confidentially in his ear.

"I want to ask you your opinion of several people. I imagine you're a wonderful judge of character."

Charley thrilled faintly—paid her a subtle compliment by overturning her water.

Two hours later, while Warren McIntyre was standing passively in the stag line abstractedly watching the dancers and wondering whither and with whom Marjorie had disappeared, an unrelated perception began to creep slowly upon him—a perception that Bernice, cousin of Marjorie, had been cut in on several times in the past five minutes. He closed his eyes, opened them and looked again. Several minutes back she had been dancing with a visiting boy, a matter easily accounted for; a visiting boy would know no better. But now she was dancing with some one else, and there was Charley Paulson headed for her with enthusiastic determination in his eye. Funny—Charley seldom danced with more than three girls an evening.

Warren was distinctly surprised when—the exchange having been effected—the man relieved proved to be none other than G. Reece Stoddard himself. And G. Reece seemed not at all jubilant at being relieved. Next time Bernice danced near, Warren regarded her intently. Yes, she was pretty, distinctly pretty; and to-night her face seemed really vivacious. She had that look that no woman, however histrionically proficient, can successfully counterfeit—she looked as if she were having a good time. He liked the way she had her hair arranged, wondered if it was brilliantine that made it glisten so. And that dress was becoming—a dark red that set off her shadowy eyes and high coloring. He remembered that he had thought her pretty when she first came to town, before he had realized that she was dull. Too bad she was dull—dull girls unbearable—certainly pretty though.

His thoughts zigzagged back to Marjorie. This disappearance would be like other disappearances. When she reappeared he would demand where she had been—would be told emphatically that it was none of his business. What a pity she was so sure of him! She basked in the knowledge that no other girl in town interested him; she defied him to fall in love with Genevieve or Roberta.

Warren sighed. The way to Marjorie's affections was a labyrinth indeed. He looked up. Bernice was again dancing with the visiting boy. Half unconsciously he took a step out from the stag line in her direction, and hesitated. Then he said to himself that it was charity. He walked toward her—collided suddenly with G. Reece Stoddard.

"Pardon me," said Warren.

But G. Reece had not stopped to apologize. He had again cut in on Bernice.

That night at one o'clock Marjorie, with one hand on the electric-light switch in the hall, turned to take a last look at Bernice's sparkling eyes.

"So it worked?"

"Oh, Marjorie, yes!" cried Bernice.

"I saw you were having a gay time."

"I did! The only trouble was that about midnight I ran short of talk. I had to repeat myself—with different men of course. I hope they won't compare notes."

"Men don't," said Marjorie, yawning, "and it wouldn't matter if they did—they'd think you were even trickier."

She snapped out the light, and as they started up the stairs Bernice grasped the banister thankfully. For the first time in her life she had been danced tired.

"You see," said Marjorie at the top of the stairs, "one man sees another man cut in and he thinks there must be something there. Well, we'll fix up some new stuff tomorrow. Good night."

"Good night."

As Bernice took down her hair she passed the evening before her in review. She had followed instructions exactly. Even when Charley Paulson cut in for the eighth time she had simulated delight and had apparently been both interested and flattered. She had not talked about the weather or Eau Claire or automobiles or her school, but had confined her conversation to me, you, and us.

But a few minutes before she fell asleep a rebellious thought was churning drowsily in her brain—after all, it was she who had done it. Marjorie, to be sure, had given her her conversation, but then Marjorie got much of her conversation out of things she read. Bernice had bought the red dress, though she had never valued it highly before Marjorie dug it out of her trunk—and her own voice had said the words, her own lips had smiled, her own feet had danced. Marjorie nice girl—vain, though—nice evening—nice boys—like Warren—Warren—Warren—what's-his-name—Warren——

She fell asleep.

V

To Bernice the next week was a revelation. With the feeling that people really enjoyed looking at her and listening to her came the foundation of self-confidence. Of course there were numerous mistakes at first. She did not know, for instance, that

Draycott Deyo was studying for the ministry; she was unaware that he had cut in on her because he thought she was a quiet, reserved girl. Had she known these things she would not have treated him to the line which began "Hello, Shell Shock!" and continued with the bathtub story—"It takes a frightful lot of energy to fix my hair in the summer—there's so much of it—so I always fix it first and powder my face and put on my hat; then I get into the bathtub, and dress afterward. Don't you think that's the best plan?"

Though Draycott Deyo was in the throes of difficulties concerning baptism by immersion and might possibly have seen a connection, it must be admitted that he did not. He considered feminine bathing an immoral subject, and gave her some of his ideas on the depravity of modern society.

But to offset that unfortunate occurrence Bernice had several signal successes to her credit. Little Otis Ormonde pleaded off from a trip East and elected instead to follow her with a puppylike devotion, to the amusement of his crowd and to the irritation of G. Reece Stoddard, several of whose afternoon calls Otis completely ruined by the disgusting tenderness of the glances he bent on Bernice. He even told her the story of the two-by-four and the dressing-room to show her how frightfully mistaken he and every one else had been in their first judgment of her. Bernice laughed off that incident with a slight sinking sensation.

Of all Bernice's conversation perhaps the best known and most universally approved was the line about the bobbing of her hair.

"Oh, Bernice, when you goin' to get the hair bobbed?"

"Day after to-morrow maybe," she would reply, laughing. "Will you come and see me? Because I'm counting on you, you know."

"Will we? You know! But you better hurry up."

Bernice, whose tonsorial intentions were strictly dishonorable, would laugh again. "Pretty soon now. You'd be surprised."

But perhaps the most significant symbol of her success was the gray car of the hypercritical Warren McIntyre, parked daily in front of the Harvey house. At first the parlor-maid was distinctly startled when he asked for Bernice instead of Marjorie; after a week of it she told the cook that Miss Bernice had gotta holda Miss Marjorie's best fella.

And Miss Bernice had. Perhaps it began with Warren's desire to rouse jealousy in Marjorie; perhaps it was the familiar though unrecognized strain of Marjorie in Bernice's conversation; perhaps it was both of these and something of sincere attraction besides. But somehow the collective mind of the younger set knew within a week that Marjorie's most reliable beau had made an amazing face-about and was giving an indisputable rush to Marjorie's guest. The question of the moment was how Marjorie would take it. Warren called Bernice on the phone twice a day, sent her notes, and they were frequently seen together in his roadster, obviously engrossed in one of those tense, significant conversations as to whether or not he was sincere.

Marjorie on being twitted only laughed. She said she was mighty glad that Warren had at last found some one who appreciated him. So the younger set laughed, too, and guessed that Marjorie didn't care and let it go at that.

One afternoon, when there were only three days left of her visit, Bernice was waiting in the hall for Warren, with whom she was going to a bridge party. She was in rather a blissful mood, and when Marjorie—also bound for the party—appeared beside her and began casually to adjust her hat in the mirror, Bernice was utterly unprepared for anything in the nature of a clash. Marjorie did her work very coldly and succinctly in three sentences.

"You may as well get Warren out of your head," she said coldly.

"What?" Bernice was utterly astounded.

"You may as well stop making a fool of yourself over Warren McIntyre. He doesn't care a snap of his fingers about you."

For a tense moment they regarded each other—Marjorie scornful, aloof; Bernice astounded, half-angry, half-afraid. Then two cars drove up in front of the house and there was a riotous honking. Both of them gasped faintly, turned, and side by side hurried out.

All through the bridge party Bernice strove in vain to master a rising uneasiness. She had offended Marjorie, the sphinx of sphinxes. With the most wholesome and innocent intentions in the world she had stolen Marjorie's property. She felt suddenly and horribly guilty. After the bridge game, when they sat in an informal circle and the conversation became general, the storm gradually broke. Little Otis Ormonde inadvertently precipitated it.

"When you going back to kindergarten, Otis?" some one had asked.

"Me? Day Bernice gets her hair bobbed."

"Then your education's over," said Marjorie quickly. "That's only a bluff of hers. I should think you'd have realized."

"That a fact?" demanded Otis, giving Bernice a reproachful glance.

Bernice's ears burned as she tried to think up an effectual comeback. In the face of this direct attack her imagination was paralyzed.

"There's a lot of bluffs in the world," continued Marjorie quite pleasantly. "I should think you'd be young enough to know that, Otis."

"Well," said Otis, "maybe so. But gee! With a line like Bernice's—"

"Really?" yawned Marjorie. "What's her latest bon mot?"

No one seemed to know. In fact, Bernice, having trifled with her muse's beau, had said nothing memorable of late.

"Was that really all a line?" asked Roberta curiously.

Bernice hesitated. She felt that wit in some form was demanded of her, but under her cousin's suddenly frigid eyes she was completely incapacitated.

"I don't know," she stalled.

"Splush!" said Marjorie. "Admit it!"

Bernice saw that Warren's eyes had left a ukulele he had been tinkering with and were fixed on her questioningly.

"Oh, I don't know!" she repeated steadily. Her cheeks were glowing.

"Splush!" remarked Marjorie again.

"Come through, Bernice," urged Otis. "Tell her where to get off."

Bernice looked round again—she seemed unable to get away from Warren's eyes.

"I like bobbed hair," she said hurriedly, as if he had asked her a question, "and I intend to bob mine."

"When?" demanded Marjorie.

"Any time."

"No time like the present," suggested Roberta.

Otis jumped to his feet.

"Good stuff!" he cried. "We'll have a summer bobbing party. Sevier Hotel barbershop, I think you said."

In an instant all were on their feet. Bernice's heart throbbed violently.

"What?" she gasped.

Out of the group came Marjorie's voice, very clear and contemptuous.

"Don't worry—she'll back out!"

"Come on, Bernice!" cried Otis, starting toward the door.

Four eyes—Warren's and Marjorie's—stared at her, challenged her, defied her. For another second she wavered wildly.

"All right," she said swiftly, "I don't care if I do."

An eternity of minutes later, riding down-town through the late afternoon beside Warren, the others following in Roberta's car close behind, Bernice had all the sensations of Marie Antoinette bound for the guillotine in a tumbrel. Vaguely she wondered why she did not cry out that it was all a mistake. It was all she could do to keep from clutching her hair with both hands to protect it from the suddenly hostile world. Yet she did neither. Even the thought of her mother was no deterrent now. This was the test supreme of her sportsmanship, her right to walk unchallenged in the starry heaven of popular girls.

Warren was moodily silent, and when they came to the hotel he drew up at the curb and nodded to Bernice to precede him out. Roberta's car emptied a laughing crowd into the shop, which presented two bold plate-glass windows to the street.

Bernice stood on the curb and looked at the sign, Sevier Barber-Shop. It was a guillotine indeed, and the hangman was the first barber, who, attired in a white coat and smoking a cigarette, leaned nonchalantly against the first chair. He must have heard of her; he must have been waiting all week, smoking eternal cigarettes beside that portentous, too-often-mentioned first chair. Would they blindfold her? No, but they would tie a white cloth round her neck lest any of her blood—nonsense—hair—should get on her clothes.

"All right, Bernice," said Warren quickly.

With her chin in the air she crossed the sidewalk, pushed open the swinging screen-door, and giving not a glance to the uproarious, riotous row that occupied the waiting bench, went up to the first barber.

"I want you to bob my hair."

The first barber's mouth slid somewhat open. His cigarette dropped to the floor.

"Huh?"

"My hair—bob it!"

Refusing further preliminaries, Bernice took her seat on high. A man in the chair next to her turned on his side and gave her a glance, half lather, half amazement. One barber started and spoiled little Willy Schuneman's monthly haircut. Mr. O'Reilly in the last chair grunted and swore musically in ancient Gaelic as a razor bit into his cheek. Two bootblacks became wide-eyed and rushed for her feet. No, Bernice didn't care for a shine.

Outside a passer-by stopped and stared; a couple joined him; half a dozen small boys' noses sprang into life, flattened against the glass; and snatches of conversation borne on the summer breeze drifted in through the screen-door.

"Lookada long hair on a kid!"

"Where'd yuh get 'at stuff? 'At's a bearded lady he just finished shavin'."

But Bernice saw nothing, heard nothing. Her only living sense told her that this man in the white coat had removed one tortoise-shell comb and then another; that his fingers were fumbling clumsily with unfamiliar hairpins; that this hair, this wonderful hair of hers, was going—she would never again feel its long voluptuous pull as it hung in a dark-brown glory down her back. For a second she was near breaking down, and then the picture before her swam mechanically into her vision—Marjorie's mouth curling in a faint ironic smile as if to say: "Give up and get down! You tried to buck me and I called your bluff. You see you haven't got a prayer."

And some last energy rose up in Bernice, for she clenched her hands under the white cloth, and there was a curious narrowing of her eyes that Marjorie remarked on to some one long afterward.

Twenty minutes later the barber swung her round to face the mirror, and she flinched at the full extent of the damage that had been wrought. Her hair was not curly, and now it lay in lank lifeless blocks on both sides of her suddenly pale face. It was ugly as sin—she had known it would be ugly as sin. Her face's chief charm had been a Madonna-like simplicity. Now that was gone and she was—well, frightfully mediocre—not stagy; only ridiculous, like a Greenwich Villager who had left her spectacles at home.

As she climbed down from the chair she tried to smile—failed miserably. She saw two of the girls exchange glances; noticed Marjorie's mouth curved in attenuated mockery—and that Warren's eyes were suddenly very cold.

"You see"—her words fell into an awkward pause—"I've done it."

"Yes, you've—done it," admitted Warren.

"Do you like it?"

There was a half-hearted "Sure" from two or three voices, another awkward pause, and then Marjorie turned swiftly and with serpentlike intensity to Warren.

"Would you mind running me down to the cleaners?" she asked. "I've simply got to get a dress there before supper. Roberta's driving right home and she can take the others."

Warren stared abstractedly at some infinite speck out the window. Then for an instant his eyes rested coldly on Bernice before they turned to Marjorie.

"Be glad to," he said slowly.

IV

Bernice did not fully realize the outrageous trap that had been set for her until she met her aunt's amazed glance just before dinner.

"Why, Bernice!"

"I've bobbed it, Aunt Josephine."

"Why, child!"

"Do you like it?"

"Why, Ber-nice!"

"I suppose I've shocked you."

"No, but what'll Mrs. Deyo think to-morrow night? Bernice, you should have waited until after the Deyos' dance—you should have waited if you wanted to do that."

"It was sudden, Aunt Josephine. Anyway, why does it matter to Mrs. Deyo particularly?"

"Why, child," cried Mrs. Harvey, "in her paper on 'The Foibles of the Younger Generation' that she read at the last meeting of the Thursday Club she devoted fifteen minutes to bobbed hair. It's her pet abomination. And the dance is for you and Marjorie!"

"I'm sorry."

"Oh, Bernice, what'll your mother say? She'll think I let you do it."

"I'm sorry."

Dinner was an agony. She had made a hasty attempt with a curling-iron, and burned her finger and much hair. She could see that her aunt was both worried and grieved, and her uncle kept saying, "Well, I'll be darned!" over and over in a hurt and faintly hostile tone. And Marjorie sat very quietly, intrenched behind a faint smile, a fainty mocking smile.

Somehow she got through the evening. Three boys called; Marjorie disappeared with one of them, and Bernice made a listless unsuccessful attempt to entertain the two others—sighed thankfully as she climbed the stairs to her room at half past ten. What a day!

When she had undressed for the night the door opened and Marjorie came in.

"Bernice," she said, "I'm awfully sorry about the Deyo dance. I'll give you my word of honor I'd forgotten all about it."

"'Sall right," said Bernice shortly. Standing before the mirror she passed her comb slowly through her short hair.

"I'll take you down-town to-morrow," continued Marjorie, "and the hairdresser'll fix it so you'll look slick. I didn't imagine you'd go through with it. I'm really mighty sorry."

"Oh, 'sall right!"

"Still it's your last night, so I suppose it won't matter much."

Then Bernice winced as Marjorie tossed her own hair over her shoulders and began to twist it slowly into two long blond braids until in her cream-colored negligée she looked like a delicate painting of some Saxon princess. Fascinated, Bernice watched the braids grow. Heavy and luxurious they were, moving under the supple fingers like restive snakes—and to Bernice remained this relic and the curling-iron and a to-morrow full of eyes. She could see G. Reece Stoddard, who liked her, assuming his Harvard manner and telling his dinner partner that Bernice shouldn't have been allowed to go to the movies so much; she could see Draycott Deyo exchanging glances with his mother and then being conscientiously charitable to her. But then perhaps by tomorrow Mrs. Deyo would have heard the news; would send round an icy little note requesting that she fail to appear—and behind her back they would all laugh and know that Marjorie had made a fool of her; that her chance at beauty had been sacrificed to the jealous whim of a selfish girl. She sat down suddenly before the mirror, biting the inside of her cheek.

"I like it," she said with an effort. "I think it'll be becoming."

Marjorie smiled.

"It looks all right. For heaven's sake, don't let it worry you!"

"I won't."

"Good night, Bernice."

But as the door closed something snapped within Bernice. She sprang dynamically to her feet, clenching her hands, then swiftly and noiselessly crossed over to her bed and from underneath it dragged out her suitcase. Into it she tossed toilet articles and a change of clothing. Then she turned to her trunk and quickly dumped in two drawerfuls of lingerie and summer dresses. She moved quietly, but with deadly efficiency, and in three-quarters of an hour her trunk was locked and strapped and she was fully dressed in a becoming new travelling suit that Marjorie had helped her pick out.

Sitting down at her desk she wrote a short note to Mrs. Harvey, in which she briefly outlined her reasons for going. She sealed it, addressed it, and laid it on her pillow. She glanced at her watch. The train left at one, and she knew that if she walked down to the Marborough Hotel two blocks away she could easily get a taxicab.

Suddenly she drew in her breath sharply and an expression flashed into her eyes that a practised character reader might have connected vaguely with the set look she had worn in the barber's chair—somehow a development of it. It was quite a new look for Bernice—and it carried consequences.

She went stealthily to the bureau, picked up an article that lay there, and turning out all the lights stood quietly until her eyes became accustomed to the darkness. Softly she pushed open the door to Marjorie's room. She heard the quiet, even breathing of an untroubled conscience asleep.

She was by the bedside now, very deliberate and calm. She acted swiftly. Bending over she found one of the braids of Marjorie's hair, followed it up with her hand to the point nearest the head, and then holding it a little slack so that the sleeper would feel no pull, she reached down with the shears and severed it. With the pigtail in her hand she held her breath. Marjorie had muttered something in her sleep. Bernice deftly amputated the other braid, paused for an instant, and then flitted swiftly and silently back to her own room.

Down-stairs she opened the big front door, closed it carefully behind her, and feeling oddly happy and exuberant stepped off the porch into the moonlight, swinging her heavy grip like a shopping-bag. After a minute's brisk walk she discovered that her left hand still held the two blond braids. She laughed unexpectedly—had to shut her mouth hard to keep from emitting an absolute peal. She was passing Warren's house now, and on the impulse she set down her baggage, and swinging the braids like pieces of rope flung them at the wooden porch, where they landed with a slight thud. She laughed again, no longer restraining herself.

"Huh!" she giggled wildly. "Scalp the selfish thing!"

Then picking up her suitcase she set off at a half-run down the moonlit street.

[1920]

Questions

1. Based on this story, how would you describe Fitzgerald's view of the elite in the 1920s when the story was first published? Has that picture changed substantially since the beginning of the new century?

2. What distinctions does the author make between Eau Clair, Wisconsin, and the East (i.e., between the mid-West and the East)? Are they important in this story?

3. Is the theme of the story "rivalry" between Bernice and Marjorie or something else?

4. For what is hair a metaphor in Fitzgerald's story?

Carlos Fuentes

(b. 1928)

Mexico

The scope of Carlos Fuentes's writing is so extensive that one is forced to conclude that he is a man who has simultaneously led several lives, only one of which is the writer of startling fiction. His visionary novel, Terra Nostra (1975), for example, assumes as its geography the entire world; the time spans from the beginning of written records—although the implications go back much further than that—to the foreseeable future. Perhaps equally startling, Terra Nostra includes characters who are fellow Latin American writers—part of the boom (explosion) in Latin American writing during the past 20 years.

Born in Mexico City in 1928, the young Fuentes spent numerous years as a child outside of Mexico because his father was a career diplomat. Although Fuentes studied law and international diplomacy, by 1952 he was devoting most of his energies to writing. Three early novels gave him an immediate international reputation: Where the Air Is Clear (1958); The Good Conscience (1959); and, perhaps his most famous novel, The Death of Artemio Cruz (1962). For a period of time, Fuentes served as his country's ambassador to France. The Old Gringo (1985) speculates on the life of Ambrose Bierce, who disappeared in Mexico in 1914. The novel was made into a successful Hollywood film. Subsequent works include Christopher Unborn (1989), The Orange Tree (1994), a series of interlocking novellas, The Crystal Frontier: A Novel in Nine Stories (1997), and The Years with Laura Díaz (1999).

In an interview with Mother Jones in 1986, Carlos Fuentes explained his reason for writing:

> The writer has to say things that would otherwise be silenced. This is the basic urge for this activity. . . . A writer is frightened of silence. Silence is death. It's terrible. I wish we didn't have repressive societies where a writer did not have to do this. It is terrible to have to mount a whole cultural expression, a whole artistic expression on the fact of silence and repression. I would prefer to have a happy society without good writers. But since that's not going to happen, we will need good writers.

THE DOLL QUEEN

I

I went because that card—such a strange card—reminded me of her existence. I found it in a forgotten book whose pages had revived the ghost associated with the childish calligraphy. For the first time in a long time I was rearranging my books. I met surprise after surprise since some, placed on the highest shelves, had not been read

for a long time. So long a time that the edges of the leaves were grainy, and a mixture of gold dust and greyish scale fell onto my open palm, reminiscent of the lacquer
covering certain bodies glimpsed first in dreams and later in the deceptive reality of
the first ballet performance to which we're taken. It was a book from my childhood—
perhaps from that of many children—that related a series of more or less truculent
exemplary tales which had the virtue of precipitating us upon our elders' knees to ask
them, over and over again: Why? Children who are ungrateful to their parents; maidens kidnapped by flashy horsemen and returned home in shame—as well as those
who willingly abandon hearth and home; old men who in exchange for an overdue
mortgage demand the hand of the sweetest and most long-suffering daughter of the
threatened family. . . . Why? I do not recall their answers. I only know that from
among the stained pages fell, fluttering, a white card in Amilamia's atrocious hand:
Amilamia wil not forget her good frend—com see me here lik I draw it.

And on the other side was that map of a path starting from an X that indicated,
doubtlessly, the park bench where I, an adolescent rebelling against prescribed and
tedious education, forgot my classroom schedule in order to spend several hours reading books which if not actually written by me, seemed to be: who could doubt that only
from *my* imagination could spring all those corsairs, those couriers of the tzar, all those
boys slightly younger than I who rowed all day up and down the great American rivers
on a raft. Clutching the arm of the park bench as if it were the frame of a magical saddle, at first I didn't hear the sound of the light steps and of the little girl who would
stop behind me after running down the graveled garden path. It was Amilamia, and I
don't know how long the child would have kept me silent company if her mischievous
spirit, one afternoon, had not chosen to tickle my ear with down from a dandelion she
blew towards me, her lips puffed out and her brow furrowed in a frown.

She asked my name and after considering it very seriously, she told me hers with
a smile while if not candid, was not too rehearsed. Quickly I realized that Amilamia
had discovered, if discovered is the word, a form of expression midway between the
ingenuousness of her years and the forms of adult mimicry that well-brought-up children have to know, particularly those for the solemn moments of introduction and
of leavetaking. Amilamia's seriousness, apparently, was a gift of nature, whereas her
moments of spontaneity, by contrast, seemed artificial. I like to remember her, afternoon after afternoon, in a succession of snapshots that in their totality sum up the
complete Amilamia. And it never ceases to surprise me that I cannot think of her as
she really was, or remember how she actually moved, light, questioning, constantly
looking around her. I must remember her fixed forever in time, as in a photograph
album. Amilamia in the distance, a point on the spot where the hill began to descend from a lake of clover towards the flat meadow where I, sitting on the bench,
used to read: a point of fluctuating shadow and sunshine and a hand that waved to
me from high on the hill. Amilamia frozen in her flight down the hill, her white skirt
billowing, the flowered panties gathered around her thighs with elastic, her mouth
open and eyes half-closed against the streaming air, the child crying with pleasure.
Amilamia sitting beneath the eucalyptus trees, pretending to cry so that I would go
over to her. Amilamia lying on her stomach with a flower in her hand: the petals of
a flower which I discovered later didn't grow in this garden, but somewhere else, perhaps in the garden of Amilamia's house, since the single pocket of her blue-checked
apron was often filled with those white blossoms. Amilamia watching me read, holding with both hands to the bars of the green bench, asking questions with her grey
eyes: I recall that she never asked me what I was reading, as if she could divine in my

eyes the images born of the pages. Amilamia laughing with pleasure when I lifted her by the waist and whirled her around my head; she seemed to discover a new perspective on the world in that slow flight. Amilamia turning her back to me and waving goodbye, her arm held high, the fingers waving excitedly. And Amilamia in the thousand postures she affected around my bench, hanging upside down, her bloomers billowing; sitting on the gravel with her legs crossed and her chin resting on her fist; lying on the grass baring her belly-button to the sun; weaving tree branches, drawing animals in the mud with a twig, licking the bars of the bench, hiding beneath the seat, silently breaking off the loose bark from the ancient treetrunks, staring at the horizon beyond the hill, humming with her eyes closed, imitating the voices of birds, dogs, cats, hens, and horses. All for me, and nevertheless, nothing. It was her way of being with me, all these things I remember, but at the same time her manner of being alone in the park. Yes, perhaps my memory of her is fragmentary because reading alternated with the contemplation of the chubby-cheeked child with smooth hair changing in the reflection of the light: now wheat-colored, now burnt chestnut. And it is only today that I think how Amilamia in that moment established the other point of support for my life, the one that created the tension between my own irresolute childhood and the open world, the promised land that was beginning to be mine through my reading.

Not then. Then I dreamed about the women in my books, about the quintessential female—the word distributed me—who assumed the disguise of the Queen in order to buy the necklace secretly, about the imagined beings of mythology—half recognizable, half white-breasted, damp-bellied salamanders—who awaited monarchs in their beds. And thus, imperceptibly, I moved from indifference towards my childish companion to an acceptance of the child's gracefulness and seriousness and from there to an unexpected rejection of a presence that became useless to me. She irritated me, finally. I who was fourteen was irritated by that child of seven who was not yet memory or nostalgia, but rather the past and its reality. I had let myself be dragged along by weakness. We had run together, holding hands, across the meadow. Together we had shaken the pines and picked up the cones that Amilamia guarded jealousy in her apron pocket. Together we had constructed paper boats and followed them, happy and gay, to the edge of the drain. And that afternoon amidst shouts of glee, when we tumbled together down the hill and rolled to a stop at its foot, Amilamia was on my chest, her hair between my lips; but when I felt her panting breath in my ear and her little arms sticky from sweets around my neck, I angrily pushed away her arms and let her fall. Amilamia cried, rubbing her wounded elbow and knee, and I returned to my bench. Then Amilamia went away and the following day she returned, handed me the paper without a word, and disappeared, humming, into the woods. I hesitated whether to tear up the card or keep it in the pages of the book: *Afternoons on the Farm*. Even my reading had become childish because of Amilamia. She did not return to the park. After a few days I left for my vacation and when I returned it was to the duties of my first year of prep school. I never saw her again.

II

And now, almost rejecting the image that is unaccustomed without being fantastic, but is all the more painful for being so real, I return to that forgotten park and stopping before the grove of pines and eucalyptus I recognize the smallness of the bosky enclosure that my memory has insisted on drawing with an amplitude that allowed sufficient space for the vast swell of my imagination. After all, Strogoff and Huckleberry, Milday de Winter and Geneviève de Brabante were born, lived and died here: in a little garden surrounded by mossy iron railings, sparsely planted with old, neglected trees, barely adorned by a concrete bench painted to look like wood that forces me to believe that my beautiful wrought-iron green-painted bench never existed, or else was a part of my orderly, retrospective delirium. And the hill. . . . How could I believe the promontory that Amilamia climbed and descended during her daily coming and going, that steep slope we rolled down together, was *this*. A barely elevated patch of dark stubble with no more heights and depths than those my memory had created.

Com see me here lik I draw it. So I would have to cross the garden, leave the woods behind, descend the hill in three loping steps, cut through that narrow grove of chestnuts—it was here, surely, where the child gathered the white petals—open the squeaking park gate and suddenly recall . . . know . . . find oneself in the street, realize that every afternoon of one's adolescence, as if by a miracle, he had succeeded in suspending the beat of the surrounding city, annulling that flood-tide of whistles, bells, voices, sobs, engines, radios, imprecations. Which was the true magnet, the silent garden or the feverish city?

I wait for the light to change and cross to the other sidewalk, my eyes never leaving the red iris detaining the traffic. I consult Amilamia's paper. After all, that rudimentary map is the true magnet of the moment I am living, and just thinking about it startles me. I was obliged, after the lost afternoons of my fourteenth year, to follow the channels of discipline; now I find myself, at twenty-nine, duly certified with a diploma, owner of an office, assured of a moderate income, a bachelor still, with no family to maintain, slightly bored with sleeping with secretaries, scarcely excited by an occasional outing to the country or to the beach, feeling the lack of a central attraction such as those once afforded me by my books, my park, and Amilamia. I walk down the street of this gray, low-buildinged suburb. The one-story houses with their doorways scaling paint succeed each other monotonously. Faint neighborhood sounds barely interrupt the general uniformity: the squeal of a knife-sharpener here, the hammering of a shoe-repairman there. The children of the neighborhood are playing in the dead-end streets. The music of an organ-grinder reaches my ears, mingled with the voices of children's rounds. I stop a moment to watch them with the sensation, also fleeting, that Amilamia must be among these groups of children, immodestly exhibiting her flowered panties, hanging by her knees from some balcony, still fond of acrobatic excesses, her apron pocket filled with white petals. I smile, and for the first time I am able to imagine the young lady of twenty-two who, even if she still lives at this address, will laugh at my memories, or who perhaps will have forgotten the afternoons spent in the garden.

The house is identical to all the rest. The heavy entry door, two grilled windows with closed shutters. A one-story house, topped by a false neo-classic balustrade that probably conceals the practicalities of the flat-roofed *azotea*:[1] clothes hanging on lines, tubs of water, servant's quarters, a chicken coop. Before I ring the bell, I want to free myself of any illusion. Amilamia no longer lives here. Why would she stay fifteen years in the same house? Besides, in spite of her precocious independence and

---

[1]*azotea* Spanish: roof.

aloneness, she seemed like a well-brought-up, well-behaved child, and this neighborhood is no longer elegant; Amilamia's parents, without doubt, have moved. But perhaps the new renters will know where.

I press the bell and wait. I ring again. Here is another contingency: no one is home. And will I feel the need again to look for my childhood friend? No. Because it will not be possible a second time to open a book from my adolescence and accidentally find Amilamia's card. I would return to my routine, I would forget the moment whose importance lay in its fleeting surprise.

I ring once more. I press my ear to the door and am surprised: I can hear a harsh and irregular breathing on the other side; the sound of labored breathing, accompanied by the disagreeable odor of stale tobacco, filters through the cracks in the hall.

"Good afternoon. Could you tell me . . .?"

As soon as he hears my voice, the person moves away with heavy and unsure steps. I press the bell again, shouting this time:

"Hey! Open up! What's the matter? Don't you hear me?"

No response. I continue ringing the bell, without result. I move back from the door, still staring at the small cracks, as if distance might give me perspective, or even penetration. With all my attention fixed on that damned door, I cross the street, walking backwards; a piercing scream, followed by a prolonged and ferocious blast of a whistle, saves me in time; dazed, I seek the person whose voice has just saved me. I see only the automobile moving down the street and I hang onto a lamp post, a hold that more than security offers me a point of support during the sudden rush of icy blood to my burning, sweaty skin. I look towards the house that had been, that was, that must be, Amilamia's. There, behind the balustrade, as I had known there would be, fluttering clothes are drying. I don't know what else is hanging there—skirts, pyjamas, blouses—I don't know. All I can see is that starched little blue-checked apron, clamped by clothespins to the long cord that swings between an iron bar and a nail in the white wall of the *azotea*.

III

In the Bureau of Records they have told me that the property is in the name of a Señor R. Valdivia, who rents the house. To whom? That they don't know. Who is Valdivia? He has declared himself a businessman. Where does he live? Who are *you*? the young lady asked me with haughty curiosity. I haven't been able to present a calm and sure appearance. Sleep has not relieved my nervous fatigue. Valdivia. As I leave the Bureau the sun offends me. I associate the repugnance provoked by the hazy sun sifting through the clouds—therefore all the more intense—with the desire to return to the damp, shadowy park. No. It is only the desire to know whether Amilamia lives in that house and why they refuse to let me enter. But the first thing I must do is reject the absurd idea that kept me awake all night. Having seen the apron drying on the flat roof, the one where she kept the flowers, and so believing that in that house lived a seven-year-old girl that I had known fourteen or fifteen years before. . . . She must have a little girl! Yes. Amilamia, at twenty-two, is the mother of a girl who dressed the same, looked the same, repeated the same games, and—who knows—perhaps even went to the same park. And deep in thought I again arrived at the door of the house. I ring the bell and await the whistling breathing on the other side of the door. I am mistaken. The door is opened by a woman who can't be more than about fifty. But wrapped in a shawl, dressed in black and in black low-heeled shoes, with no make-up and her salt and pepper hair pulled into a knot, she seems to have abandoned all illusion or pretext of youth; she is observing me with eyes so indifferent they seem almost cruel.

"You want something?"

"Señor Valdivia sent me." I cough and run my hand over my hair. I should have picked up my briefcase at the office. I realize that without it I cannot play my role very well.

"Valdivia?" the woman asks without alarm, without interest.

"Yes. The owner of this house."

One thing is clear. The woman will reveal nothing in her face. She looks at me, calmly.

"Oh, yes. The owner of the house."

"May I come in?"

I think that in bad comedies the traveling salesman sticks a foot in the door so they can't close the door in his face. I do the same, but the woman steps back and with a gesture of her hand invites me to come into what must have been a garage. On one side there is a glass-paned door, its paint faded. I walk towards the door over the yellow tiles of the entryway and ask again, turning towards the woman who follows me with tiny steps:

"This way?"

I notice for the first time that in her white hands she is carrying a chapelet which she toys with ceaselessly. I haven't seen one of those old-fashioned rosaries since my childhood and I want to comment on it, but the brusque and decisive manner with which the woman opens the door precludes any gratuitous conversation. We enter a long narrow room. The woman hastens to open the shutters. But because of four large perennial plants growing in porcelain and crusted glass pots the room remains in shadow. The only other objects in the room are an old high-backed cane-trimmed sofa and a rocking chair. But it is neither the plants nor the sparcity of the furniture that draws my attention.

The woman invites me to sit on the sofa before she sits in the rocking chair. Beside me, on the cane arm of the sofa, there is an open magazine.

"Señor Valdivia sends his apologies for not having come in person."

The woman rocks, unblinkingly. I peer at the comic book out of the corner of my eye.

"He sends his greetings and . . . ."

I stop, awaiting a reaction from the woman. She continues to rock. The magazine is covered with red-penciled scribbling.

". . . and asks me to inform you that he must disturb you for a few days . . . ."

My eyes search rapidly.

". . . A new evaluation of the house must be made for the tax lists. It seems it hasn't been done for . . . . You have been living here since . . . ?"

Yes. That is a stubby lipstick lying under the chair. If the woman smiles, it is only with the slow-moving hands caressing the chapelet; I sense, for an instant, a swift flash of ridicule that does not quite disturb her features. She still does not answer.

". . . for at least fifteen years, isn't that true?"

She does not agree. She does not disagree. And on the pale thin lips there is not the least sign of lipstick . . . .

". . . you, your husband, and . . . ?"

She stares at me, never changing expression, almost daring me to continue. We sit a moment in silence, she playing with the rosary, I leaning forwards, my hands on my knees. I rise.

"Well, then, I'll be back this afternoon with the papers . . . ."

The woman nods while, in silence, she picks up the lipstick and the comic book and hides them in the folds of her shawl.

IV

The scene has not changed. This afternoon, while I am writing down false figures in my notebook and feigning interest in establishing the quality of the dulled floor-boards and the length of the living room, the woman rocks, as the three decades of the chapelet whisper through her fingers. I sigh as I finish the supposed inventory of the living room and I ask her for permission to go to the other rooms in the house. The woman rises, bracing her long black-clad arms on the seat of the rocking chair and adjusting the shawl on her narrow bony shoulders.

She opens the opaque glass door and we enter a dining room with very little more furniture. But the table with the aluminum legs and the four nickel and plastic chairs lack even the slight hint of distinction of the living room furniture. Another window with wrought-iron grill and closed shutters must at times illuminate this bare-walled dining room, bare of either shelves or bureau. The only object on the table is a plastic fruit dish with a cluster of black grapes, two peaches, and a buzzing corona of flies. The woman, her arms crossed, her face expressionless, stops behind me. I take the risk of breaking the order of things: it is evident that these rooms will not tell me anything that I really want to know.

"Couldn't we go up to the roof?" I ask. "I believe that is the best way of measuring the total area."

The woman's eyes light up as she looks at me, or perhaps it is only the contrast with the penumbra of the dining room.

"What for?" she says finally. "Señor . . . Valdivia . . . knows the dimensions very well."

And those pauses, one before and one after the owner's name, are the first indications that something is at last perturbing the woman and forcing her, in defense, to resort to a certain irony.

"I don't know." I make an effort to smile. "Perhaps I prefer to go from top to bottom and not . . ." my false smile drains away, ". . . from bottom to top."

"You will go the way I show you," the woman says, her arms crossed across her chest, the silver cross hanging against her dark belly.

Before smiling weakly, I force myself to think how, in this shadow, my gestures are useless, not even symbolic. I open the notebook with a crunch of the cardboard cover and continue making my notes with the greatest possible speed, never glancing up, the numbers and estimates of this task whose fiction—the light flush in my cheeks and the perceptible dryness of my tongue tell me—is deceiving no one. And after filling the graph paper with absurd signs, with square roots and algebraic formulas, I ask myself what is preventing me from getting to the point, from asking about Amilamia and getting out of here with a satisfactory answer. Nothing. And nevertheless, I am sure that even if I obtained a response, the truth does not lie along this road. My slim and silent companion is a person I wouldn't look twice at in the street, but in this almost uninhabited house with the coarse furniture, she ceases to be an anonymous face in the crowd and is converted into a stock character of mystery. Such is the paradox, and if memories of Amilamia have once again awakened my appetite for the imaginary, I shall follow the rules of the game, I shall exhaust all the appearances, and I shall not rest until I find the answer—perhaps simple and clear, immediate and evident—that lies beyond the unexpected veils the señora of the rosary places in my path. Do I bestow a more-than-justified strangeness upon my reluctant Amphitryon? If that is so, I shall only take more pleasure in the labyrinths of my own invention. And the flies are still buzzing around the fruit dish, occasionally pausing on the damaged end of the peach, a nibbled bite—I lean closer using the pretext of my notes—where little teeth have left their mark in the velvety skin and ochre flesh of the fruit. I do not look towards the señora. I pretend I am taking notes. The fruit seems to be bitten but not touched. I crouch down to see it better, rest my hands upon the table, moving my lips closer as if I wished to repeat the act of biting without touching. I look down and I see another sign close to my feet: the track of two tires that seem to be bicycle tires, the paint of two rubber tires that come as far as the edge of the table and then lead away, growing fainter, the length of the room, towards the señora . . . .

I close my notebook.

"Let us continue, señora."

As I turn towards her, I find her standing with her hands resting on the back of a chair. Seated before her, coughing the smoke of his black cigarette, is a man with heavy shoulders and hidden eyes: these eyes, hardly visible behind swollen wrinkled lids as thick and droopy as the neck of an ancient turtle, seem nevertheless to follow my every movement. The half-shaven cheeks, criss-crossed by a thousand gray furrows, hang from protruding cheekbones, and his greenish hands are folded beneath his arms. He is wearing a coarse blue shirt, and his rumpled hair is so curly it looks like the bottom of a barnacle-covered ship. He does not move, and the true sign of his existence is that difficult whistling breathing (as if every breath must breach a flood-gate of phlegm, irritation, and abuse) that I had already heard through the chinks of the entry hall.

Ridiculously, he murmurs: "Good afternoon. . . ." and I am disposed to forget everything: the mystery, Amilamia, the assessment, the bicycle tracks. The apparition of this asthmatic old bear justifies a prompt retreat. I repeat "Good afternoon," this time with an inflection of farewell. The turtle's mask dissolves into an atrocious smile: every pore of that flesh seems fabricated of brittle rubber, of painted, peeling oilcloth. The arm reaches out and detains me.

"Valdivia died four years ago," says the man in a distant, choking voice that issues from his belly instead of his larynx: a weak, high-pitched voice.

Held by that strong, almost painful, claw, I tell myself it is useless to pretend. But the wax and rubber faces observing me say nothing and for that reason I am able, in spite of everything, to pretend one last time, to pretend that I am speaking to myself when I say:

"Amilamia . . . ."

Yes; no one will have to pretend any longer. The fist that clutches my arm affirms its strength for only an instant, immediately its grip loosens, then it falls, weak and trembling, before rising to take the waxen hand touching the shoulder: the señora, perplexed for the first time, looks at me with the eyes of a violated bird and sobs with a dry moan that does not disturb the rigid astonishment of her features. Suddenly the ogres of my imagination are two solitary, abandoned, wounded old people, scarcely able to console themselves in the shuddering clasp of hands that fills me with shame. My fantasy has brought me to this stark dining room to violate the intimacy and the secret of two human beings exiled from life by something I no longer have the right to share. I have never despised myself more. Never have words failed me in such a clumsy way. Any gesture of mine would be in vain: shall I approach them, shall I touch them, shall I caress the woman's head, shall I ask them to excuse my intrusion? I return the notebook to my jacket pocket. I toss into oblivion all the clues in my detective story: the comic book, the lipstick, the nibbled fruit, the bicycle tracks, the blue-checked apron. . . . I decide to leave this house in silence. The old man, from behind those thick eyelids, must have noticed me. The high breathy voice says:

"Did you know her?"

That past, so natural they must use it every day, finally destroys my illusions. There is the answer. Did you know her? How many years? How many years must the world have lived without Amilamia, assassinated first by my forgetfulness, and revived, scarcely yesterday, by a sad impotent memory? When did those serious gray eyes cease to be astonished by the delight of an always solitary garden? When did those lips cease to pout or press together thinly in that ceremonious seriousness with which, I now realize, Amilamia must have discovered and consecrated the objects and events of life that, she knew perhaps intuitively, was fleeting?

"Yes, we played together in the park. A long time ago."

"How old was she?" says the old man, his voice even more muffled.

"She must have been about seven. No, older than seven."

The woman's voice rises, along with the arms that seem to implore:

"What was she like, señor? Tell us what she was like, please."

I close my eyes. "Amilamia is my memory, too. I can only compare her to the things that she touched, that she brought, that she discovered in the park. Yes. Now I see her, coming down the hill. No. It isn't true that it was a barely elevated patch of stubble. It was a hill, with grass, and Amilamia's coming and going had traced a path, and she waved to me from the top before she started down, accompanied by the music, yes, the music I saw, the painting I smelled, the tastes I heard, the odors I touched . . . my hallucination. . . ." Do they hear me? "She came, waving, dressed in white, in a blue-checked apron . . . the one you have hanging on the *azotea*. . . ."

They take my arms and still I do not open my eyes.

"What was she like, señor?"

"Her eyes were gray and the color of her hair changed in the reflection of the sun and the shadow of the trees. . . ."

They lead me gently, the two of them; I hear the man's labored breathing, the cross on the rosary hitting against the woman's body.

"Tell us, please. . . ."

"The air brought tears to her eyes when she ran; when she reached my bench her cheeks were silvered with happy tears. . . ."

I do not open my eyes. Now we are going upstairs. Two, five, eight, nine, twelve steps. Four hands guide my body.

"What was she like, what was she like?"

"She sat beneath the eucalyptus and wove garlands from the branches and pretended to cry so I would quit my reading and go over to her. . . ."

Hinges creak. The odor overpowers everything else: it routs the other senses, it takes its seat like a yellow Mogol upon the throne of my hallucination; heavy as a coffin, insinuating as the slither of draped silk, ornamented as a Turkish sceptre, opaque as a deep, lost vein of ore, brilliant as a dead star. The hands no longer hold me. More than the sobbing, it is the trembling of the old people that envelops me. Slowly, I open my eyes: first through the dizzying liquid of my cornea then through the web of my eyelashes, the room suffocated in that enormous battle of perfumes is disclosed, effluvia and frosty, almost flesh-like petals; the presence of the flowers is so strong here they seem to take on the quality of living flesh—the sweetness of the jasmine, the nausea of the lilies, the tomb of the tuberose, the temple of the gardenia. Illuminated through the incandescent wax lips of heavy sputtering candles, the small windowless bed-room with its aura of wax and humid flowers assaults the very center of my plexus, and from there, only there at the solar center of life, am I able to revive and to per-ceive beyond the candles, among the scattered flowers, the accumulation of used toys: the colored hoops and wrinkled balloons, cherries dried to transparency, wood-en horses with scraggly manes, the scooter, blind and hairless dolls, bears spilling their sawdust, punctured oil-cloth ducks, moth-eaten dogs, wornout jumping ropes, glass jars of dried candy, wornout shoes, the tricycle (three wheels? no, two, and not like a bicycle—two *parallel* wheels below), little woolen and leather shoes; and, fac-ing me, within reach of my hand, the small coffin raised on paper flower-decorated blue boxes, flowers of life this time, carnations and sunflowers, poppies and tulips, but like the others, the ones of death, all part of a potion brewed by the atmosphere of this funeral hot-house in which reposes, inside the silvered coffin, between the black silk sheets, upon the pillow of white satin, that motionless and serene face framed in lace, highlighted with rose-colored tints, eyebrows traced by the lightest trace of pen-cil, closed lids, real eyelashes, thick, that cast a tenuous shadow on cheeks as healthy as those of the days in the park. Serious red lips, set almost in the angry pout that Amilamia feigned so I would come to play. Hands joined over the breast. A chapelet, identical to the mother's, strangling that cardboard neck. Small white shroud on the clean, pre-pubescent, docile body.

The old people, sobbing, have knelt.

I reach out my hand and run my fingers over the porcelain face of my friend. I feel the coldness of those painted features, of the doll-queen who presides over the pomp of this royal chamber of death. Porcelain, cardboard, and cotton. *Amilamia wil not for-get her good frend—com see me here lik I draw it.*

I withdraw my fingers from the false cadaver. Traces of my finger prints remain where I touched the skin of the doll.

And nausea crawls in my stomach where the candle smoke and the sweet stench of the lilies in the enclosed room have settled. I turn my back on Amilamia's sepul-chre. The woman's hand touches my arm. Her wildly staring eyes do not correspond with the quiet, steady voice.

"Don't come back, señor. If you truly loved her, don't come back again."

I touch the hand of Amilamia's mother. I see through nauseous eyes the old man's head buried between his knees, and I go out of the room to the stairway, to the liv-ing room, to the patio, to the street.

V

If not a year, nine or ten months have passed. The memory of that idolatry no longer frightens me. I have forgotten the odor of the flowers and the image of the petrified doll. The real Amilamia has returned to my memory and I have felt, if not content, sane again: the park, the living child, my hours of adolescent reading, have triumphed over the spectres of a sick cult. The image of life is the more powerful. I tell myself that I shall live forever with my real Amilamia, the conqueror of the caricature of death. And one day I dare look again at that notebook with graph paper where I wrote the information of the false assessment. And from its pages, once again, falls Amilamia's card with its terrible childish scrawl and its map for getting from the park to her house. I smile as I pick it up. I bite one of the edges, thinking that in spite of everything, the poor old people would accept this gift.

Whistling, I put on my jacket and knot my tie. Why not visit them and offer them this paper with the child's own writing?

I am running as I approach the one-story house. Rain is beginning to fall in large isolated drops that bring from the earth with magical immediacy an odor of damp benediction that seems to stir the humus and precipitate the fermentation of everything living with its roots in the dust.

I ring the bell. The shower increases and I become insistent. A shrill voice shouts: "I'm going!" and I wait for the figure of the mother with her eternal rosary to open the door for me. I turn up the collar of my jacket. My clothes, my body, too, smell different in the rain. The door opens:

"What do you want? How wonderful you've come!"

The misshapen girl sitting in the wheelchair lays one hand on the doorknob and smiles at me with an indecipherably wry grin. The hump on her chest converts the dress into a curtain over her body, a piece of white cloth that nonetheless lends an air of coquetry to the blue-checked apron. The little woman extracts a pack of cigarettes from her apron pocket and rapidly lights a cigarette, staining the end with orange-painted lips. The smoke causes the beautiful gray eyes to squint. She arranges the coppery, wheat-colored, permanently waved hair: She stares at me all the time with a desolate, inquisitive, and hopeful—but at the same time fearful—expression.

"No, Carlos. Go away. Don't come back."

And from the house, at the same moment, I hear the high breathy breathing of the old man, coming closer and closer.

"Where are you? Don't you know you're not supposed to answer the door? Go back! Devil's spawn! Do I have to beat you again?"

And the water from the rain trickles down my forehead, over my cheeks, and into my mouth, and the little frightened hands drop the comic book onto the damp stones.

[1974]
Translated by
MARGARET S. PEDEN

Questions

1. Is it possible to establish exactly what has happened to Carlos by the end of the story? What has happened to Amilamia? Why have her parents built the shrine for her? Of what is Amilamia guilty? Of what is Carlos guilty?

2. Why does Carlos wait so many years to visit Amilamia? What does her message mean: "Amilamia wil not forget her good frend—com see me here lik I draw it"?

3. Do Fuentes's remarks on "silence" quoted in the introductory notes have any bearing on the story's meaning?

Gabriel García Márquez

(b. 1928)

Colombia

I n recent years, Gabriel García Márquez has clearly become his continent's most famous writer—indeed, one of the most widely read writers in today's world. Born in a small coastal town in Colombia in 1928, García Márquez celebrated that heritage in One Hundred Years of Solitude (1967). The novel is often cited as the peak of the "boom," or explosion, in Latin American writing and as one of the most famous examples of magic realism. Equally memorable and fantastic, though for different reasons, are his later works, The Autumn of the Patriarch (1975), the study of a Latin American dictator's political abuses; Chronicle of a Death Foretold (1981); and Love in the Time of Cholera (1985). His Collected Stories were published in 1984. In addition to several volumes of non-fiction, subsequent acclaimed novels include The General in His Labyrinth (1990) and Of Love and Other Demons (1995). García Márquez was awarded the Nobel Prize for Literature in 1982.

Commenting on the relationship between art and life, Gabriel García Márquez once told the following anecdote:

> An electrician called at my house at eight in the morning and as soon as the door was open, he said: "You have to change the electric iron's cord." Immediately realizing that he had come to the wrong door, he apologized and left. Hours later, my wife connected the iron, and the cord caught fire. There is no need to go on. It is enough to read the papers, and open one's eyes, in order to feel willing to shout along with the French college students: "Power to the imagination."

BALTHAZAR'S MARVELOUS AFTERNOON

The cage was finished. Balthazar hung it under the eave, from force of habit, and when he finished lunch everyone was already saying that it was the most beautiful cage in the world. So many people came to see it that a crowd formed in front of the house, and Balthazar had to take it down and close the shop.

"You have to shave," Ursula, his wife, told him. "You look like a Capuchin."

"It's bad to shave after lunch," said Balthazar.

He had two weeks' growth, short, hard, and bristly hair like the mane of a mule, and the general expression of a frightened boy. But it was a false expression. In February he was thirty; he had been living with Ursula for four years, without marrying her and without having children, and life had given him many reasons to be on guard but none to be frightened. He did not even know that for some people the cage he had just made was the most beautiful one in the world. For him, accustomed to making cages since childhood, it had been hardly any more difficult than the others.

"Then rest for a while," said the woman. "With that beard you can't show yourself anywhere."

While he was resting, he had to get out of his hammock several times to show the cage to the neighbors. Ursula had paid little attention to it until then. She was annoyed because her husband had neglected the work of his carpenter's shop to devote himself entirely to the cage, and for two weeks had slept poorly, turning over and muttering incoherencies, and he hadn't thought of shaving. But her annoyance dissolved in the face of the finished cage. When Balthazar woke up from his nap, she had ironed his pants and a shirt; she had put them on a chair near the hammock and had carried the cage to the dining table. She regarded it in silence.

"How much will you charge?" she asked.

"I don't know," Balthazar answered. "I'm going to ask for thirty pesos to see if they'll give me twenty."

"Ask for fifty," said Ursula. "You've lost a lot of sleep in these two weeks. Furthermore, it's rather large. I think it's the biggest cage I've ever seen in my life."

Balthazar began to shave.

"Do you think they'll give me fifty pesos?"

"That's nothing for Mr. Chepe Montiel, and the cage is worth it," said Ursula. "You should ask for sixty."

The house lay in the stifling shadow. It was the first week of April and the heat seemed less bearable because of the chirping of the cicadas. When he finished dressing, Balthazar opened the door to the patio to cool off the house, and a group of children entered the dining room.

The news had spread. Dr. Octavio Giraldo, an old physician, happy with life but tired of his profession, thought about Balthazar's cage while he was eating lunch with his invalid wife. On the inside terrace, where they put the table on hot days, there were many flowerpots and two cages with canaries. His wife liked birds, and she liked them so much that she hated cats because they could eat them up. Thinking about her, Dr. Giraldo went to see a patient that afternoon, and when he returned he went by Balthazar's house to inspect the cage.

There were a lot of people in the dining room. The cage was on display on the table: with its enormous dome of wire, three stories inside, with passageways and compartments especially for eating and sleeping and swings in the space set aside for the birds' recreation, it seemed like a small-scale model of a gigantic ice factory. The doctor inspected it carefully, without touching it, thinking that in effect the cage was better than its reputation, and much more beautiful than any he had ever dreamed of for his wife.

"This is a flight of the imagination," he said. He sought out Balthazar among the group of people and, fixing his maternal eyes on him, added, "You would have been an extraordinary architect."

Balthazar blushed.

"Thank you," he said.

"It's true," said the doctor. He was smoothly and delicately fat, like a woman who had been beautiful in her youth, and he had delicate hands. His voice seemed like that of a priest speaking Latin. "You wouldn't even need to put birds in it," he said, making the cage turn in front of the audience's eyes as if he were auctioning it off. "It would be enough to hang it in the trees so it could sing by itself." He put it back on the table, thought a moment, looking at the cage, and said:

"Fine, then I'll take it."

"It's sold," said Ursula.

"It belongs to the son of Mr. Chepe Montiel," said Balthazar. "He ordered it specially."

The doctor adopted a respectful attitude.

"Did he give you the design?"

"No," said Balthazar. "He said he wanted a large cage, like this one, for a pair of troupials."

The doctor looked at the cage.

"But this isn't for troupials."

"Of course it is, Doctor," said Balthazar, approaching the table. The children surrounded him. "The measurements are carefully calculated," he said, pointing to the different compartments with his forefinger. Then he struck the dome with his knuckles, and the cage filled with resonant chords.

"It's the strongest wire you can find, and each joint is soldered outside and in," he said.

"It's even big enough for a parrot," interrupted one of the children.

"That it is," said Balthazar.

The doctor turned his head.

"Fine, but he didn't give you the design," he said. "He gave you no exact specifications, aside from making it a cage big enough for troupials. Isn't that right?"

"That's right," said Balthazar.

"Then there's no problem," said the doctor. "One thing is a cage big enough for troupials, and another is this cage. There's no proof that this one is the one you were asked to make."

"It's this very one," said Balthazar, confused. "That's why I made it."

The doctor made an impatient gesture.

"You could make another one," said Ursula, looking at her husband. And then, to the doctor: "You're not in any hurry."

"I promised it to my wife for this afternoon," said the doctor.

"I'm very sorry, Doctor," said Balthazar, "but I can't sell you something that's sold already."

The doctor shrugged his shoulders. Drying the sweat from his neck with a handkerchief, he contemplated the cage silently with the fixed, unfocused gaze of one who looks at a ship which is sailing away.

"How much did they pay you for it?"

Balthazar sought out Ursula's eyes without replying.

"Sixty pesos," she said.

The doctor kept looking at the cage. "It's very pretty." He sighed. "Extremely pretty." Then, moving toward the door, he began to fan himself energetically, smiling, and the trace of that episode disappeared forever from his memory.

"Montiel is very rich," he said.

In truth, José Montiel was not as rich as he seemed, but he would have been capable of doing anything to become so. A few blocks from there, in a house crammed with equipment, where no one had ever smelled a smell that couldn't be sold, he remained indifferent to the news of the cage. His wife, tortured by an obsession with death, closed the doors and windows after lunch and lay for two hours with her eyes opened to the shadow of the room, while José Montiel took his siesta. The clamor of many voices surprised her there. Then she opened the door to the living room and found a crowd in front of the house, and Balthazar with the cage in the middle of the crowd, dressed in white, freshly shaved, with that expression of decorous candor with which the poor approach the houses of the wealthy.

"What a marvelous thing!" José Montiel's wife exclaimed, with a radiant expression, leading Balthazar inside. "I've never seen anything like it in my life," she said, and added, annoyed by the crowd which piled up at the door:

"But bring it inside before they turn the living room into a grandstand."

Balthazar was no stranger to José Montiel's house. On different occasions, because of his skill and forthright way of dealing, he had been called in to do minor carpentry jobs. But he never felt at ease among the rich. He used to think about them, about their ugly and argumentative wives, about their tremendous surgical operations, and he always experienced a feeling of pity. When he entered their houses, he couldn't move without dragging his feet.

"Is Pepe home?" he asked.

He had put the cage on the dining-room table.

"He's at school," said José Montiel's wife. "But he shouldn't be long," and she added, "Montiel is taking a bath."

In reality, José Montiel had not had time to bathe. He was giving himself an urgent alcohol rub, in order to come out and see what was going on. He was such a cautious man that he slept without an electric fan so he could watch over the noises of the house while he slept.

"Adelaide?" he shouted. "What's going on?"

"Come and see what a marvelous thing!" his wife shouted.

José Montiel, obese and hairy, his towel draped around his neck, appeared at the bedroom window.

"What is that?"

"Pepe's cage," said Balthazar.

His wife looked at him perplexedly.

"Whose?"

"Pepe's," replied Balthazar. And then, turning toward José Montiel, "Pepe ordered it."

Nothing happened at that instant, but Balthazar felt as if someone had just opened the bathroom door on him. José Montiel came out of the bedroom in his underwear.

"Pepe!" he shouted.

"He's not back," whispered his wife, motionless.

Pepe appeared in the doorway. He was about twelve, and had the same curved eyelashes and was as quietly pathetic as his mother.

"Come here," José Montiel said to him. "Did you order this?"

The child lowered his head. Grabbing him by the hair, José Montiel forced Pepe to look him in the eye.

"Answer me."

The child bit his lip without replying.

"Montiel," whispered his wife.

José Montiel let the child go and turned toward Balthazar in a fury. "I'm very sorry, Balthazar," he said. "But you should have consulted me before going on. Only to you would it occur to contract with a minor." As he spoke, his face recovered its serenity. He lifted the cage without looking at it and gave it to Balthazar.

"Take it away at once, and try to sell it to whomever you can," he said. "Above all, I beg you not to argue with me." He patted him on the back and explained, "The doctor has forbidden me to get angry."

The child had remained motionless, without blinking, until Balthazar looked at him uncertainly with the cage in his hand. Then he emitted a guttural sound, like a dog's growl, and threw himself on the floor screaming.

José Montiel looked at him, unmoved, while the mother tried to pacify him. "Don't even pick him up," he said. "Let him break his head on the floor, and then put salt and lemon on it so he can rage to his heart's content." The child was shrieking tearlessly while his mother held him by the wrists.

"Leave him alone," José Montiel insisted.

Balthazar observed the child as he would have observed the death throes of a rabid animal. It was almost four o'clock. At that hour, at his house, Ursula was singing a very old song and cutting slices of onion.

"Pepe," said Balthazar.

He approached the child, smiling, and held the cage out to him. The child jumped up, embraced the cage which was almost as big as he was, and stood looking at Balthazar through the wirework without knowing what to say. He hadn't shed one tear.

"Balthazar," said José Montiel softly. "I told you already to take it away."

"Give it back," the woman ordered the child.

"Keep it," said Balthazar. And then, to José Montiel: "After all, that's what I made it for."

José Montiel followed him into the living room.

"Don't be foolish, Balthazar," he was saying, blocking his path. "Take your piece of furniture home and don't be silly. I have no intention of paying you a cent."

"It doesn't matter," said Balthazar. "I made it expressly as a gift for Pepe. I didn't expect to charge anything for it."

As Balthazar made his way through the spectators who were blocking the door, José Montiel was shouting in the middle of the living room. He was very pale and his eyes were beginning to get red.

"Idiot!" he was shouting. "Take your trinket out of here. The last thing we need is for some nobody to give orders in my house. Son of a bitch!"

In the pool hall, Balthazar was received with an ovation. Until that moment, he thought that he had made a better cage than ever before, that he'd had to give it to the son of José Montiel so he wouldn't keep crying, and that none of these things was particularly important. But then he realized that all of this had a certain importance for many people, and he felt a little excited.

"So they gave you fifty pesos for the cage."

"Sixty," said Balthazar.

"Score one for you," someone said. "You're the only one who has managed to get such a pile of money out of Mr. Chepe Montiel. We have to celebrate."

They bought him a beer, and Balthazar responded with a round for everybody. Since it was the first time he had ever been out drinking, by dusk he was completely drunk, and he was talking about a fabulous project of a thousand cages, at sixty pesos each, and then a million cages, till he had sixty million pesos. "We have to make a lot of things to sell to the rich before they die," he was saying, blind drunk. "All of them are sick, and they're going to die. They're so screwed up they can't even get angry any more." For two hours he was paying for the jukebox, which played without interruption. Everybody toasted Balthazar's health, good luck, and fortune, and the death of the rich, but at mealtime they left him alone in the pool hall.

Ursula had waited for him until eight, with a dish of fried meat covered with slices of onion. Someone told her that her husband was in the pool hall, delirious with happiness, buying beers for everyone, but she didn't believe it, because Balthazar had never got drunk. When she went to bed, almost at midnight, Balthazar was in a lighted room where there were little tables, each with four chairs, and an outdoor dance floor, where the plovers were walking around. His face was smeared with rouge, and since he couldn't take one more step, he thought he wanted to lie down with two women in the same bed. He had spent so much that he had had to leave his watch in pawn, with the promise to pay the next day. A moment later, spread-eagled in the street, he realized that his shoes were being taken off, but he didn't want to abandon the happiest dream of his life. The women who passed on their way to five-o'clock Mass didn't dare look at him, thinking he was dead.

[1962]
Translated by
J. S. BERNSTEIN

Questions

1. To what extent does "Balthazar's Marvelous Afternoon" imply a fusion of honor and machismo (masculinity)?
2. What function does Ursula play in the story? In what ways is she different from Balthazar?
3. Why does Balthazar lie to his friends in the bar?
4. Why does the story conclude with an image of death? Has comedy suddenly become tragedy?

Charlotte Perkins Gilman

(1860–1935)

United States

C harlotte Perkins Gilman was not only a writer of fiction but also a prominent social reformer and one of the leading intellectuals of the women's reform movement from the 1890s to 1920. Widely known throughout the United States and Europe
for her important studies of women's status and their role in society, she developed her
views both in sociological studies such as the central work, Women and Economics
(1898), and in several novels, including the utopian fiction Herland (1915).

Born in Hartford, Connecticut, Gilman suffered an unhappy childhood. Her father deserted the family soon after her birth; she and her mother and brother lived on
the edge of poverty and were compelled to move frequently. Her mother also starved
her emotionally, deliberately avoiding physical contact and affection in the belief that
she was preparing her daughter for life's hardships. Gilman studied art briefly and
earned money as a commercial artist by designing greeting cards. She married a fellow artist, Charles Stetson; their marriage later ended in divorce.

The birth of Gilman's first child, a daughter, precipitated a severe depression. Seeking the advice of the prominent physician S. Weir Mitchell, she was advised to avoid
all physical activity, especially writing. As she wrote later, the regimen of total isolation, bed rest, confinement, and proscription against writing nearly drove her crazy.
"The Yellow Wallpaper," based in part on her own experience, brilliantly highlights
the narrator's increasingly desperate state as well as castigating this abusive medical
treatment. First published in 1892, "The Yellow Wallpaper" was initially read as a
ghost story in the tradition of Edgar Allan Poe, complete with a haunted mansion and
a character deteriorating into madness. Contemporary readers see in Gilman's best-
known story not only a strong indictment of the social infantilization of women in the
late nineteenth century but also the nameless narrator's painful struggle to tell a story
whose telling both expresses and culminates in her own mental destruction.

THE YELLOW WALLPAPER

It is very seldom that mere ordinary people like John and myself secure ancestral halls
for the summer.

A colonial mansion, a hereditary estate, I would say a haunted house and reach
the height of romantic felicity—but that would be asking too much of fate!

Still I will proudly declare that there is something queer about it.

Else, why should it be let so cheaply? And why have stood so long untenanted?

John laughs at me, of course, but one expects that.

John is practical in the extreme. He has no patience with faith, an intense horror of superstition, and he scoffs openly at any talk of things not to be felt and seen and put down in figures.

John is a physician, and *perhaps*—(I would not say it to a living soul, of course, but this is dead paper and a great relief to my mind)—*perhaps* that is one reason I do not get well faster.

You see, he does not believe I am sick! And what can one do?

If a physician of high standing, and one's own husband, assures friends and relatives that there is really nothing the matter with one but temporary nervous depression— a slight hysterical tendency—what is one to do?

My brother is also a physician, and also of high standing, and he says the same thing.

So I take phosphates or phosphites—whichever it is—and tonics, and air and exercise, and journeys, and am absolutely forbidden to "work" until I am well again.

Personally, I disagree with their ideas.

Personally, I believe that congenial work, with excitement and change, would do me good.

But what is one to do?

I did write for a while in spite of them; but it *does* exhaust me a good deal—having to be so sly about it, or else meet with heavy opposition.

I sometimes fancy that in my condition, if I had less opposition and more society and stimulus—but John says the very worst thing I can do is to think about my condition, and I confess it always makes me feel bad.

So I will let it alone and talk about the house.

The most beautiful place! It is quite alone, standing well back from the road, quite three miles from the village. It makes me think of English places that you read about, for there are hedges and walls and gates that lock, and lots of separate little houses for the gardeners and people.

There is a *delicious* garden! I never saw such a garden—large and shady, full of box-bordered paths, and lined with long grape-covered arbors with seats under them.

There were greenhouses, but they are all broken now.

There was some legal trouble, I believe, something about the heirs and co-heirs; anyhow, the place has been empty for years.

That spoils my ghostliness, I am afraid, but I don't care—there is something strange about the house—I can feel it.

I even said so to John one moonlight evening, but he said what I felt was a draught, and shut the window.

I get unreasonably angry with John sometimes. I'm sure I never used to be so sensitive. I think it is due to this nervous condition.

But John says if I feel so I shall neglect proper self-control; so I take pains to control myself—before him, at least, and that makes me very tired.

I don't like our room a bit. I wanted one downstairs that opened onto the piazza and had roses all over the window, and such pretty old-fashioned chintz hangings! But John would not hear of it.

He said there was only one window and not room for two beds, and no near room for him if he took another.

He is very careful and loving, and hardly lets me stir without special direction.

I have a schedule prescription for each hour in the day; he takes all care from me, and so I feel basely ungrateful not to value it more.

He said he came here solely on my account, that I was to have perfect rest and all the air I could get. "Your exercise depends on your strength, my dear," said he, "and your food somewhat on your appetite; but air you can absorb all the time." So we took the nursery at the top of the house.

It is a big, airy room, the whole floor nearly, with windows that look all ways, and air and sunshine galore. It was nursery first, and then playroom and gymnasium, I should judge, for the windows are barred for little children, and there are rings and things in the walls.

The paint and paper look as if a boys' school had used it. It is stripped off—the paper—in great patches all around the head of my bed, about as far as I can reach, and in a great place on the other side of the room low down. I never saw a worse paper in my life. One of those sprawling, flamboyant patterns committing every artistic sin.

It is dull enough to confuse the eye in following, pronounced enough constantly to irritate and provoke study, and when you follow the lame uncertain curves for a little distance they suddenly commit suicide—plunge off at outrageous angles, destroy themselves in unheard-of contradictions.

The color is repellent, almost revolting: a smouldering unclean yellow, strangely faded by the slow-turning sunlight. It is a dull yet lurid orange in some places, a sickly sulphur tint in others.

No wonder the children hated it! I should hate it myself if I had to live in this room long.

There comes John, and I must put this away—he hates to have me write a word.

We have been here two weeks, and I haven't felt like writing before, since that first day.

I am sitting by the window now, up in this atrocious nursery, and there is nothing to hinder my writing as much as I please, save lack of strength.

John is away all day, and even some nights when his cases are serious.

I am glad my case is not serious!

But these nervous troubles are dreadfully depressing.

John does not know how much I really suffer. He knows there is no reason to suffer, and that satisfies him.

Of course it is only nervousness. It does weigh on me so not to do my duty in any way!

I meant to be such a help to John, such a real rest and comfort, and here I am a comparative burden already!

Nobody would believe what an effort it is to do what little I am able—to dress and entertain, and order things.

It is fortunate Mary is so good with the baby. Such a dear baby!

And yet I *cannot* be with him, it makes me so nervous.

I suppose John never was nervous in his life. He laughs at me so about this wallpaper!

At first he meant to repaper the room, but afterward he said that I was letting it get the better of me, and that nothing was worse for a nervous patient than to give way to such fancies.

He said that after the wallpaper was changed it would be the heavy bedstead, and then the barred windows, and then that gate at the head of the stairs, and so on.

"You know the place is doing you good," he said, "and really, dear, I don't care to renovate the house just for a three months' rental."

"Then do let us go downstairs," I said. "There are such pretty rooms there."

Then he took me in his arms and called me a blessed little goose, and said he would go down cellar, if I wished, and have it whitewashed into the bargain.

But he is right enough about the beds and windows and things.

It is as airy and comfortable a room as anyone need wish, and, of course, I would not be so silly as to make him uncomfortable just for a whim.

I'm really getting quite fond of the big room, all but that horrid paper.

Out of one window I can see the garden—those mysterious deep-shaded arbors, the riotous old-fashioned flowers, and bushes and gnarly trees.

Out of another I get a lovely view of the bay and a little private wharf belonging to the estate. There is a beautiful shaded lane that runs down there from the house. I always fancy I see people walking in these numerous paths and arbors, but John has cautioned me not to give way to fancy in the least. He says that with my imaginative power and habit of story-making, a nervous weakness like mine is sure to lead to all manner of excited fancies, and that I ought to use my will and good sense to check the tendency. So I try.

I think sometimes that if I were only well enough to write a little it would relieve the press of ideas and rest me.

But I find I get pretty tired when I try.

It is so discouraging not to have any advice and companionship about my work. When I get really well, John says we will ask Cousin Henry and Julia down for a long visit; but he says he would as soon put fireworks in my pillow-case as to let me have those stimulating people about now.

I wish I could get well faster.

But I must not think about that. This paper looks to me as if it *knew* what a vicious influence it had!

There is a recurrent spot where the pattern lolls like a broken neck and two bulbous eyes stare at you upside down.

I get positively angry with the impertinence of it and the everlastingness. Up and down and sideways they crawl, and those absurd unblinking eyes are everywhere. There is one place where two breadths didn't match, and the eyes go all up and down the line, one a little higher than the other.

I never saw so much expression in an inanimate thing before, and we all know how much expression they have! I used to lie awake as a child and get more entertainment and terror out of blank walls and plain furniture than most children could find in a toy-store.

I remember what a kindly wink the knobs of our big old bureau used to have, and there was one chair that always seemed like a strong friend.

I used to feel that if any of the other things looked too fierce I could always hop into that chair and be safe.

The furniture in this room is no worse than inharmonious, however, for we had to bring it all from downstairs. I suppose when this was used as a playroom they had to take the nursery things out, and no wonder! I never saw such ravages as the children have made here.

The wallpaper, as I said before, is torn off in spots, and it sticketh closer than a brother—they must have had perseverance as well as hatred.

Then the floor is scratched and gouged and splintered, the plaster itself is dug out here and there, and this great heavy bed, which is all we found in the room, looks as if it had been through the wars.

But I don't mind it a bit—only the paper.

There comes John's sister. Such a dear girl as she is, and so careful of me! I must not let her find me writing.

She is a perfect and enthusiastic housekeeper, and hopes for no better profession. I verily believe she thinks it is the writing which made me sick!

But I can write when she is out, and see her a long way off from these windows.

There is one that commands the road, a lovely shaded winding road, and one that just looks off over the country. A lovely country, too, full of great elms and velvet meadows.

This wallpaper has a kind of subpattern in a different shade, a particularly irritating one, for you can only see it in certain lights, and not clearly then.

But in the places where it isn't faded and where the sun is just so—I can see a strange, provoking, formless sort of figure that seems to skulk about behind that silly and conspicuous front design.

There's sister on the stairs!

Well, the Fourth of July is over! The people are all gone, and I am tired out. John thought it might do me good to see a little company, so we just had Mother and Nellie and the children down for a week.

Of course I didn't do a thing. Jennie sees to everything now.

But it tired me all the same.

John says if I don't pick up faster he shall send me to Weir Mitchell[1] in the fall.

But I don't want to go there at all. I had a friend who was in his hands once, and she says he is just like John and my brother, only more so!

Besides, it is such an undertaking to go so far.

I don't feel as if it was worthwhile to turn my hand over for anything, and I'm getting dreadfully fretful and querulous.

I cry at nothing, and cry most of the time.

Of course I don't when John is here, or anybody else, but when I am alone.

And I am alone a good deal just now. John is kept in town very often by serious cases, and Jennie is good and lets me alone when I want her to.

So I walk a little in the garden or down that lovely lane, sit on the porch under the roses, and lie down up here a good deal.

I'm getting really fond of the room in spite of the wallpaper. Perhaps *because* of the wallpaper.

It dwells in my mind so!

I lie here on this great immovable bed—it is nailed down, I believe—and follow that pattern about by the hour. It is as good as gymnastics, I assure you. I start, we'll say, at the bottom, down in the corner over there where it has not been touched, and I determine for the thousandth time that I *will* follow that pointless pattern to some sort of a conclusion.

I know a little of the principle of design, and I know this thing was not arranged on any laws of radiation, or alternation, or repetition, or symmetry, or anything else that I ever heard of.

It is repeated, of course, by the breadths, but not otherwise.

---

[1]*Weir Mitchell*   S. Weir Mitchell (1892–1914), a prominent Philadelphia neurologist who promoted the "rest cure" for his patients' (most of whom were female) nervous disorders. Gilman herself underwent the cure, which nearly drove her mad.

Looked at in one way, each breadth stands alone; the bloated curves and flourishes—a kind of "debased Romanesque" with delirium tremens[2] go waddling up and down in isolated columns of fatuity.

But, on the other hand, they connect diagonally, and the sprawling outlines run off in great slanting waves of optic horror, like a lot of wallowing sea-weeds in full chase.

The whole thing goes horizontally, too, at least it seems so, and I exhaust myself trying to distinguish the order of its going in that direction.

They have used a horizontal breadth for a frieze, and that adds wonderfully to the confusion.

There is one end of the room where it is almost intact, and there, when the crosslights fade and the low sun shines directly upon it, I can almost fancy radiation after all—the interminable grotesque seems to form around a common center and rush off in headlong plunges of equal distraction.

It makes me tired to follow it. I will take a nap, I guess.

I don't know why I should write this.

I don't want to.

I don't feel able.

And I know John would think it absurd. But I *must* say what I feel and think in some way—it is such a relief!

But the effort is getting to be greater than the relief.

Half the time now I am awfully lazy, and lie down ever so much. John says I mustn't lose my strength, and has me take cod liver oil and lots of tonics and things, to say nothing of ale and wines and rare meat.

Dear John! He loves me very dearly, and hates to have me sick. I tried to have a real earnest reasonable talk with him the other day, and tell him how I wish he would let me go and make a visit to Cousin Henry and Julia.

But he said I wasn't able to go, nor able to stand it after I got there; and I did not make out a very good case for myself, for I was crying before I had finished.

It is getting to be a great effort for me to think straight. Just this nervous weakness, I suppose.

And dear John gathered me up in his arms, and just carried me upstairs and laid me on the bed, and sat by me and read to me till it tired my head.

He said I was his darling and his comfort and all he had, and that I must take care of myself for his sake, and keep well.

He says no one but myself can help me out of it, that I must use my will and self-control and not let any silly fancies run away with me.

There's one comfort—the baby is well and happy, and does not have to occupy this nursery with the horrid wallpaper.

If we had not used it, that blessed child would have! What a fortunate escape! Why, I wouldn't have a child of mine, an impressionable little thing, live in such a room for worlds.

I never thought of it before, but it is lucky that John kept me here after all; I can stand it so much easier than a baby, you see.

---

[2]*delirium tremens*   frightening hallucinations and violent tremors induced by excessive drinking of alcoholic beverages.

Of course I never mention it to them any more—I am too wise—but I keep watch for it all the same.

There are things in the wallpaper that nobody knows about but me, or ever will.

Behind that outside pattern the dim shapes get clearer every day.

It is always the same shape, only very numerous.

And it is like a woman stooping down and creeping about behind that pattern. I don't like it a bit. I wonder—I begin to think—I wish John would take me away from here!

It is so hard to talk with John about my case, because he is so wise, and because he loves me so.

But I tried it last night.

It was moonlight. The moon shines in all around just as the sun does.

I hate to see it sometimes, it creeps so slowly, and always comes in by one window or another.

John was asleep and I hated to waken him, so I kept still and watched the moonlight on that undulating wallpaper till I felt creepy.

The faint figure behind seemed to shake the pattern, just as if she wanted to get out.

I got up softly and went to feel and see if the paper *did* move, and when I came back John was awake.

"What is it, little girl?" he said. "Don't go walking about like that—you'll get cold."

I thought it was a good time to talk, so I told him that I really was not gaining here, and that I wished he would take me away.

"Why, darling!" said he. "Our lease will be up in three weeks, and I can't see how to leave before.

"The repairs are not done at home, and I cannot possibly leave town just now. Of course, if you were in any danger, I could and would, but you really are better, dear, whether you can see it or not. I am a doctor, dear, and I know. You are gaining flesh and color, your appetite is better, I feel really much easier about you."

"I don't weigh a bit more," said I, "nor as much, and my appetite may be better in the evening when you are here but it is worse in the morning when you are away!"

"Bless her little heart!" said he with a big hug. "She shall be as sick as she pleases! But now let's improve the shining hours by going to sleep, and talk about it in the morning!"

"And you won't go away?" I asked gloomily.

"Why, how can I, dear? It is only three weeks more and then we will take a nice little trip for a few days while Jennie is getting the house ready. Really, dear, you are better!"

"Better in body perhaps—" I began, and stopped short, for he sat up straight and looked at me with such a stern, reproachful look that I could not say another word.

"My darling," said he, "I beg you, for my sake and for our child's sake, as well as for your own, that you will never for one instant let that idea enter your mind! There is nothing so dangerous, so fascinating, to a temperament like yours. It is a false and foolish fancy. Can you trust me as a physician when I tell you so?"

So of course I said no more on that score, and we went to sleep before long. He thought I was asleep first, but I wasn't, and lay there for hours trying to decide whether that front pattern and the back pattern really did move together or separately.

On a pattern like this, by daylight, there is a lack of sequence, a defiance of law, that is a constant irritant to a normal mind.

The color is hideous enough, and unreliable enough, and infuriating enough, but the pattern is torturing.

You think you have mastered it, but just as you get well under way in following, it turns a back-somersault and there you are. It slaps you in the face, knocks you down, and tramples upon you. It is like a bad dream.

The outside pattern is a florid arabesque, reminding one of a fungus. If you can imagine a toadstool in joints, an interminable string of toadstools, budding and sprouting in endless convolutions—why, that is something like it.

That is, sometimes!

There is one marked peculiarity about this paper, a thing nobody seems to notice but myself, and that is that it changes as the light changes.

When the sun shoots in through the east window—I always watch for that first long, straight ray—it changes so quickly that I never can quite believe it.

That is why I watch it always.

By moonlight—the moon shines in all night when there is a moon—I wouldn't know it was the same paper.

At night in any kind of light, in twilight, candlelight, lamplight, and worst of all by moonlight, it becomes bars! The outside pattern, I mean, and the woman behind it is as plain as can be.

I didn't realize for a long time what the thing was that showed behind, that dim subpattern, but now I am quite sure it is a woman.

By daylight she is subdued, quiet. I fancy it is the pattern that keeps her so still. It is so puzzling. It keeps me quiet by the hour.

I lie down ever so much now. John says it is good for me, and to sleep all I can.

Indeed he started the habit by making me lie down for an hour after each meal.

It is a very bad habit, I am convinced, for you see, I don't sleep.

And that cultivates deceit, for I don't tell them I'm awake—oh, no!

The fact is I am getting a little afraid of John.

He seems very queer sometimes, and even Jennie has an inexplicable look.

It strikes me occasionally, just as a scientific hypothesis, that perhaps it is the paper!

I have watched John when he did not know I was looking, and come into the room suddenly on the most innocent excuses, and I've caught him several times *looking at the paper!* And Jennie too. I caught Jennie with her hand on it once.

She didn't know I was in the room, and when I asked her in a quiet, a very quiet voice, with the most restrained manner possible, what she was doing with the paper, she turned around as if she had been caught stealing, and looked quite angry—asked me why I should frighten her so!

Then she said that the paper stained everything it touched, that she had found yellow smooches on all my clothes and John's and she wished we would be more careful!

Did not that sound innocent? But I know she was studying that pattern, and I am determined that nobody shall find it out but myself!

Life is very much more exciting now than it used to be. You see, I have something more to expect, to look forward to, to watch. I really do eat better, and am more quiet than I was.

John is so pleased to see me improve! He laughed a little the other day, and said I seemed to be flourishing in spite of my wallpaper.

I turned it off with a laugh. I had no intention of telling him it was *because* of the wallpaper—he would make fun of me. He might even want to take me away.

I don't want to leave now until I have found it out. There is a week more, and I think that will be enough.

I'm feeling so much better!

I don't sleep much at night, for it is so interesting to watch developments; but I sleep a good deal during the daytime.

In the daytime it is tiresome and perplexing.

There are always new shoots on the fungus, and new shades of yellow all over it. I cannot keep count of them, though I have tried conscientiously.

It is the strangest yellow, that wallpaper! It makes me think of all the yellow things I ever saw—not beautiful ones like buttercups, but old, foul, bad yellow things.

But there is something else about that paper—the smell! I noticed it the moment we came into the room, but with so much air and sun it was not bad. Now we have had a week of fog and rain, and whether the windows are open or not, the smell is here.

It creeps all over the house.

I find it hovering in the dining-room, skulking in the parlor, hiding in the hall, lying in wait for me on the stairs.

It gets into my hair.

Even when I go to ride, if I turn my head suddenly and surprise it—there is that smell!

Such a peculiar odor, too! I have spent hours in trying to analyze it, to find what it smelled like.

It is not bad—at first—and very gentle, but quite the subtlest, most enduring odor I ever met.

In this damp weather it is awful. I wake up in the night and find it hanging over me.

It used to disturb me at first. I thought seriously of burning the house—to reach the smell.

But now I am used to it. The only thing I can think of that it is like is the *color* of the paper! A yellow smell.

There is a very funny mark on this wall, low down, near the mopboard. A streak that runs round the room. It goes behind every piece of furniture, except the bed, a long, straight, even *smooch*, as if it had been rubbed over and over.

I wonder how it was done and who did it, and what they did it for.

Round and round and round—round and round and round—it makes me dizzy!

I really have discovered something at last.

Through watching so much at night, when it changes so, I have finally found out. The front pattern *does* move—and no wonder! The woman behind shakes it!

Sometimes I think there are a great many women behind, and sometimes only one, and she crawls around fast, and her crawling shakes it all over.

Then in the bright spots she keeps still, and in the very shady spots she just takes hold of the bars and shakes them hard.

And she is all the time trying to climb through. But nobody could climb through that pattern—it strangles so; I think that is why it has so many heads.

They get through and then the pattern strangles them off and turns them upside down, and makes their eyes white!

If those heads were covered or taken off it would not be half so bad.

I think that woman gets out in the daytime!

And I'll tell you why—privately—I've seen her!

I can see her out of every one of my windows!

It is the same woman, I know, for she is always creeping, and most women do not creep by daylight.

I see her in that long shaded lane, creeping up and down. I see her in those dark grape arbors, creeping all round the garden.

I see her on that long road under the trees, creeping along, and when a carriage comes she hides under the blackberry vines.

I don't blame her a bit. It must be very humiliating to be caught creeping by daylight!

I always lock the door when I creep by daylight. I can't do it at night, for I know John would suspect something at once.

And John is so queer now that I don't want to irritate him. I wish he would take another room! Besides, I don't want anybody to get that woman out at night but myself.

I often wonder if I could see her out of all the windows at once.

But, turn as fast as I can, I can only see out of one at one time.

And though I always see her, she *may* be able to creep faster than I can turn! I have watched her sometimes away off in the open country, creeping as fast as a cloud shadow in a wind.

If only that top pattern could be gotten off from the under one! I mean to try it, little by little.

I have found out another funny thing, but I shan't tell it this time! It does not do to trust people too much.

There are only two more days to get this paper off, and I believe John is beginning to notice. I don't like the look in his eyes.

And I heard him ask Jennie a lot of professional questions about me. She had a very good report to give.

She said I slept a good deal in the daytime.

John knows I don't sleep very well at night, for all I'm so quiet!

He asked me all sorts of questions too, and pretended to be very loving and kind. As if I couldn't see through him!

Still, I don't wonder he acts so, sleeping under this paper for three months.

It only interests me, but I feel sure John and Jennie are affected by it.

Hurrah! This is the last day, but it is enough. John is to stay in town over night, and won't be out until this evening.

Jennie wanted to sleep with me—the sly thing; but I told her I should undoubtedly rest better for a night all alone.

That was clever, for really I wasn't alone a bit! As soon as it was moonlight and that poor thing began to crawl and shake the pattern, I got up and ran to help her.

I pulled and she shook. I shook and she pulled, and before morning we had peeled off yards of that paper.

A strip about as high as my head and half around the room.

And then when the sun came and that awful pattern began to laugh at me, I declared I would finish it today!

We go away tomorrow, and they are moving all my furniture down again to leave things as they were before.

Jennie looked at the wall in amazement, but I told her merrily that I did it out of pure spite at the vicious thing.

She laughed and said she wouldn't mind doing it herself, but I must not get tired.

How she betrayed herself that time!

But I am here, and no person touches this paper but Me—not *alive!*

She tried to get me out of the room—it was too patent! But I said it was so quiet and empty and clean now that I believed I would lie down again and sleep all I could, and not to wake me even for dinner—I would call when I woke.

So now she is gone, and the servants are gone, and the things are gone, and there is nothing left but that great bedstead nailed down, with the canvas mattress we found on it.

We shall sleep downstairs tonight, and take the boat home tomorrow.

I quite enjoy the room, now it is bare again.

How those children did tear about here!

This bedstead is fairly gnawed!

But I must get to work.

I have locked the door and thrown the key down into the front path.

I don't want to go out, and I don't want to have anybody come in, till John comes.

I want to astonish him.

I've got a rope up here that even Jennie did not find. If that woman does get out, and tried to get away, I can tie her!

But I forgot I could not reach far without anything to stand on!

This bed will *not* move!

I tried to lift and push it until I was lame, and then I got so angry I bit off a little piece at one corner—but it hurt my teeth.

Then I peeled off all the paper I could reach standing on the floor. It sticks horribly and the pattern just enjoys it! All those strangled heads and bulbous eyes and waddling fungus growths just shriek with derision!

I am getting angry enough to do something desperate. To jump out of the window would be admirable exercise, but the bars are too strong even to try.

Besides I wouldn't do it. Of course not. I know well enough that a step like that is improper and might be misconstrued.

I don't like to *look* out of the windows even—there are so many of those creeping women, and they creep so fast.

I wonder if they all come out of that wallpaper as I did!

But I am securely fastened now by my well-hidden rope—you don't get *me* out in the road there!

I suppose I shall have to get back behind the pattern when it comes night, and that is hard!

It is so pleasant to be out in this great room and creep around as I please!

I don't want to go outside. I won't, even if Jennie asks me to.

For outside you have to creep on the ground, and everything is green instead of yellow.

But here I can creep smoothly on the floor, and my shoulder just fits in that long smooch around the wall, so I cannot lose my way.

Why, there's John at the door!

It is no use, young man, you can't open it!

How he does call and pound!

Now he's crying to Jennie for an axe.

It would be a shame to break down that beautiful door!

"John, dear!" said I in the gentlest voice. "The key is down by the front steps, under a plantain leaf!"

That silenced him for a few moments.

Then he said, very quietly indeed, "Open the door, my darling!"

"I can't," said I. "The key is down by the front door under a plantain leaf!" And then I said it again, several times, very gently and slowly, and said it so often that he had to go and see, and he got it of course, and came in. He stopped short by the door.

"What is the matter?" he cried. "For God's sake, what are you doing!"

I kept on creeping just the same, but I looked at him over my shoulder. "I've got out at last," said I, "in spite of you and Jane. And I've pulled off most of the paper, so you can't put me back!"

Now why should that man have fainted? But he did, and right across my path by the wall, so that I had to creep over him every time!

[1892]

Questions

1. What drives the narrator crazy? How are the stages of her emotional breakdown expressed in the story?

2. In what ways is the narrator's husband implicated as part of her predicament?

3. How does the point of view affect your understanding of what is happening to the narrator? Is she a reliable narrator?

4. How does the yellow wallpaper function symbolically in the story? What does it represent for the narrator? What does it represent for the reader? In what sense do the changes in the wallpaper express changes in the narrator?

5. In what sense has the woman "got out at last," as she exclaims at the end of the story?

Susan Glaspell

(1882–1948)
United States

Susan Glaspell bears a unique distinction in American drama of having not only written but also produced and occasionally acted in her own productions. She was the cofounder of the influential experimental theater group, the Provincetown Players, in a wharf theater on Cape Cod in 1915. In addition to writing and producing a number of plays, she was also a prolific writer of fiction, publishing 10 novels and a number of short stories. "A Jury of Her Peers" is based on (and was written shortly after) the dramatic version, the one-act play Trifles, one of the most frequently produced one-act plays in the United States.

Glaspell was born and raised in Davenport, Iowa. Following her graduation from Drake University, she became a reporter for the Des Moines Daily News, eventually writing her own column, "The News Girl." She soon began to write short fiction, publishing at least two stories a year from 1903 to 1922—mostly romances that appeared in popular journals like Ladies' Home Journal.

Glaspell's marriage in 1913 to George Cram Cook led to a life in Greenwich Village and a broadening of her writing to include playwriting. A number of her plays were staged by the Provincetown Players and by the actors of the Playwrights' Theatre in Greenwich Village, the avant-garde group that she and Cook also founded.

Glaspell herself appeared in the role of Mrs. Hale in the first performance of Trifles at the Wharf Theatre in 1916. Both the play and the short story have received renewed attention from students interested in female experience as a result of Glaspell's depiction of distinct domains of language, symbol, and meaning recognized by her male and female characters.

A JURY OF HER PEERS

When Martha Hale opened the storm-door and got a cut of the north wind, she ran back for her big woolen scarf. As she hurriedly wound that round her head her eye made a scandalized sweep of her kitchen. It was no ordinary thing that called her away—it was probably farther from ordinary than anything that had ever happened in Dickson County. But what her eye took in was that her kitchen was in no shape for leaving: her bread all ready for mixing, half the flour sifted and half unsifted.

She hated to see things half done; but she had been at that when the team from town stopped to get Mr. Hale, and then the sheriff came running in to say his wife wished Mrs. Hale would come too—adding, with a grin, that he guessed she was getting scarey and wanted another woman along. So she had dropped everything right where it was.

"Martha!" now came her husband's impatient voice. "Don't keep folks waiting out here in the cold."

She again opened the storm-door, and this time joined the three men and the one woman waiting for her in the big two-seated buggy.

After she had the robes tucked around her she took another look at the woman who sat beside her on the back seat. She had met Mrs. Peters the year before at the county fair, and the thing she remembered about her was that she didn't seem like a sheriff's wife. She was small and thin and didn't have a strong voice. Mrs. Gorman, sheriff's wife before Gorman went out and Peters came in, had a voice that somehow seemed to be backing up the law with every word. But if Mrs. Peters didn't look like a sheriff's wife, Peters made it up in looking like a sheriff. He was to a dot the kind of man who could get himself elected sheriff—a heavy man with a big voice, who was particularly genial with the law-abiding, as if to make it plain that he knew the difference between criminals and non-criminals. And right there it came into Mrs. Hale's mind, with a stab, that this man who was so pleasant and lively with all of them was going to the Wrights' now as a sheriff.

"The country's not very pleasant this time of year," Mrs. Peters at last ventured, as if she felt they ought to be talking as well as the men.

Mrs. Hale scarcely finished her reply, for they had gone up a little hill and could see the Wright place now, and seeing it did not make her feel like talking. It looked very lonesome this cold March morning. It had always been a lonesome-looking place. It was down in a hollow, and the poplar trees around it were lonesome-looking trees. The men were looking at it and talking about what had happened. The county attorney was bending to one side of the buggy, and kept looking steadily at the place as they drew up to it.

"I'm glad you came with me," Mrs. Peters said nervously, as the two women were about to follow the men in through the kitchen door.

Even after she had her foot on the door-step, her hand on the knob, Martha Hale had a moment of feeling she could not cross that threshold. And the reason it seemed she couldn't cross it now was simply because she hadn't crossed it before. Time and time again it had been in her mind, "I ought to go over and see Minnie Foster"—she still thought of her as Minnie Foster, though for twenty years she had been Mrs. Wright. And then there was always something to do and Minnie Foster would go from her mind. But *now* she could come.

The men went over to the stove. The women stood close together by the door. Young Henderson, the county attorney, turned around and said, "Come up to the fire, ladies."

Mrs. Peters took a step forward, then stopped. "I'm not—cold," she said.

And so the two women stood by the door, at first not even so much as looking around the kitchen.

The men talked for a minute about what a good thing it was the sheriff had sent his deputy out that morning to make a fire for them, and then Sheriff Peters stepped back from the stove, unbuttoned his outer coat, and leaned his hands on the kitchen table in a way that seemed to mark the beginning of official business. "Now, Mr. Hale," he said in a sort of semi-official voice, "before we move things about, you tell Mr. Henderson just what it was you saw when you came here yesterday morning."

The county attorney was looking around the kitchen.

"By the way," he said, "has anything been moved?" He turned to the sheriff. "Are things just as you left them yesterday?"

Peters looked from cupboard to sink; from that to a small worn rocker a little to one side of the kitchen table.

"It's just the same."

"Somebody should have been left here yesterday," said the county attorney.

"Oh—yesterday," returned the sheriff, with a little gesture as of yesterday having been more than he could bear to think of. "When I had to send Frank to Morris Center for that man who went crazy—let me tell you, I had my hands full *yesterday*. I knew you could get back from Omaha by to-day, George, and as long as I went over everything here myself—"

"Well, Mr. Hale," said the county attorney, in a way of letting what was past and gone go, "tell just what happened when you came here yesterday morning."

Mrs. Hale, still leaning against the door, had that sinking feeling of the mother whose child is about to speak a piece. Lewis often wandered along and got things mixed up in a story. She hoped he would tell this straight and plain, and not say unnecessary things that would just make things harder for Minnie Foster. He didn't begin at once, and she noticed that he looked queer—as if standing in that kitchen and having to tell what he had seen there yesterday morning made him almost sick.

"Yes, Mr. Hale?" the county attorney reminded.

"Harry and I had started to town with a load of potatoes," Mrs. Hale's husband began.

Harry was Mrs. Hale's oldest boy. He wasn't with them now, for the very good reason that those potatoes never got to town yesterday and he was taking them this morning, so he hadn't been home when the sheriff stopped to say he wanted Mr. Hale to come over to the Wright place and tell the county attorney his story there, where he could point it all out. With all Mrs. Hale's other emotions came the fear that maybe Harry wasn't dressed warm enough—they hadn't any of them realized how that north wind did bite.

"We come along this road," Hale was going on, with a motion of his hand to the road over which they had just come, "and as we got in sight of the house I says to Harry, 'I'm goin' to see if I can't get John Wright to take a telephone.' You see," he explained to Henderson, "unless I can get somebody to go in with me they won't come out this branch road except for a price I can't pay. I'd spoke to Wright about it once before; but he put me off, saying folks talked too much anyway; and all he asked was peace and quiet—guess you know about how much he talked himself. But I thought maybe if I went to the house and talked about it before his wife, and said all the women-folks liked the telephones, and that in this lonesome stretch of road it would be a good thing—well, I said to Harry that that was what I was going to say— though I said at the same time that I didn't know as what his wife wanted made much difference to John—"

Now, there he was!—saying things he didn't need to say. Mrs. Hale tried to catch her husband's eye, but fortunately the county attorney interrupted with:

"Let's talk about that a little later, Mr. Hale. I do want to talk about that, but I'm anxious now to get along to just what happened when you got here."

When he began this time, it was very deliberately and carefully:

"I didn't see or hear anything. I knocked at the door. And still it was all quiet inside. I knew they must be up—it was past eight o'clock. So I knocked again, louder, and I thought I heard somebody say 'Come in.' I wasn't sure—I'm not sure yet. But I opened the door—this door," jerking a hand toward the door by which the two women stood, "and there, in that rocker"—pointing to it—"sat Mrs. Wright."

Every one in the kitchen looked at the rocker. It came into Mrs. Hale's mind that that rocker didn't look in the least like Minnie Foster—the Minnie Foster of twenty years before. It was a dingy red, with wooden rungs up the back and the middle rung was gone, and the chair sagged to one side.

"How did she—look?" the county attorney was inquiring.

"Well," said Hale, "she looked—queer."

"How do you mean—queer?"

As he asked it he took out a note-book and pencil. Mrs. Hale did not like the sight of that pencil. She kept her eye fixed on her husband, as if to keep him from saying unnecessary things that would go into that note-book and make trouble.

Hale did speak guardedly, as if the pencil had affected him too.

"Well, as if she didn't know what she was going to do next. And kind of—done up."

"How did she seem to feel about your coming?"

"Why, I don't think she minded—one way or other. She didn't pay much attention. I said, 'Ho' do, Mrs. Wright? It's cold, ain't it?' And she said, 'Is it?'—and went pleatin' at her apron.

"Well, I was surprised. She didn't ask me to come up to the stove, or to sit down, but just set there, not even lookin' at me. And so I said: 'I want to see John.'

"And then she—laughed. I guess you would call it a laugh.

"I thought of Harry and the team outside, so I said, a little sharp, 'Can I see John?' 'No,' says she—kind of dull like. 'Ain't he home?' says I. Then she looked at me. 'Yes,' says she, 'he's home.' 'Then why can't I see him?' I asked her, out of patience with her now. 'Cause he's dead,' says she, just as quiet and dull—and fell to pleatin' her apron. 'Dead?' says I, like you do when you can't take in what you've heard.

"She just nodded her head, not getting a bit excited, but rockin' back and forth.

"'Why—where is he?' says I, not knowing *what* to say.

"She just pointed upstairs—like this"—pointing to the room above.

"I got up, with the idea of going up there myself. By this time I—didn't know what to do. I walked from there to here; then I says: 'Why, what did he die of?'

"'He died of a rope around his neck,' says she; and just went on pleatin' at her apron."

Hale stopped speaking, and stood staring at the rocker, as if he were still seeing the woman who had sat there the morning before. Nobody spoke; it was as if every one were seeing the woman who had sat there the morning before.

"And what did you do then?" the county attorney at last broke the silence.

"I went out and called Harry. I though I might—need help. I got Harry in, and we went upstairs." His voice fell almost to a whisper. "There he was—lying over the—"

"I think I'd rather have you go into that upstairs," the county attorney interrupted, "where you can point it all out. Just go on now with the rest of the story."

"Well, my first thought was to get that rope off. It looked—"

He stopped, his face twitching.

"But Harry, he went up to him, and he said, 'No, he's dead all right, and we'd better not touch anything.' So we went downstairs.

"She was still sitting that same way. 'Has anybody been notified?' I asked. 'No,' says she, unconcerned.

"'Who did this, Mrs. Wright?' said Harry. He said it business-like, and she stopped pleatin' at her apron. 'I don't know,' she says. 'You *don't know?*' says Harry. 'Weren't you sleepin' in the bed with him?' 'Yes,' says she, 'but I was on the inside.' 'Somebody slipped a rope around his neck and strangled him, and you didn't wake up?' says Harry. 'I didn't wake up,' she said after him.

"We may have looked as if we didn't see how that could be, for after a minute she said, 'I sleep sound.'

"Harry was going to ask her more questions, but I said maybe that weren't our business; maybe we ought to let her tell her story first to the coroner or the sheriff. So Harry went fast as he could over to High Road—the Rivers' place, where there's a telephone."

"And what did she do when she knew you had gone for the coroner?" The attorney got his pencil in his hand all ready for writing.

"She moved from that chair to this one over here"—Hale pointed to a small chair in the corner—"and just sat there with her hands held together and looking down. I got a feeling that I ought to make some conversation, so I said I had come in to see if John wanted to put in a telephone; and at that she started to laugh, and then she stopped and looked at me—scared."

At the sound of a moving pencil the man who was telling the story looked up.

"I dunno—maybe it wasn't scared," he hastened; "I wouldn't like to say it was. Soon Harry got back, and then Dr. Lloyd came, and you, Mr. Peters, and so I guess that's all I know that you don't."

He said that last with relief, and moved a little, as if relaxing. Every one moved a little. The county attorney walked toward the stair door.

"I guess we'll go upstairs first—then out to the barn and around there."

He paused and looked around the kitchen.

"You're convinced there was nothing important here?" he asked the sheriff. "Nothing that would—point to any motive?"

The sheriff too looked all around, as if to re-convince himself.

"Nothing here but kitchen things," he said, with a little laugh for the insignificance of kitchen things.

The county attorney was looking at the cupboard—a peculiar, ungainly structure, half closet and half cupboard, the upper part of it being built in the wall, and the lower part just the old-fashioned kitchen cupboard. As if its queerness attracted him, he got a chair and opened the upper part and looked in. After a moment he drew his hand away sticky.

"Here's a nice mess," he said resentfully.

The two women had drawn nearer, and now the sheriff's wife spoke.

"Oh—her fruit," she said, looking to Mrs. Hale for sympathetic understanding. She turned back to the county attorney and explained: "She worried about that when it turned so cold last night. She said the fire would go out and her jars might burst."

Mrs. Peters' husband broke into a laugh.

"Well, can you beat the women! Held for murder, and worrying about her preserves!"

The young attorney set his lips.

"I guess before we're through with her she may have something more serious than preserves to worry about."

"Oh, well," said Mrs. Hale's husband, with good-natured superiority, "women are used to worrying over trifles."

The two women moved a little closer together. Neither of them spoke. The county attorney seemed suddenly to remember his manners—and think of his future.

"And yet," said he, with the gallantry of a young politician, "for all their worries, what would we do without the ladies?"

The women did not speak, did not unbend. He went to the sink and began washing his hands. He turned to wipe them on the roller towel—whirled it for a cleaner place.

"Dirty towels! Not much of a housekeeper, would you say ladies?"

He kicked his foot against some dirty pans under the sink.

"There's a great deal of work to be done on a farm," said Mrs. Hale stiffly.

"To be sure. And yet"—with a little bow to her—"I know there are some Dickson County farm-houses that do not have such roller towels." He gave it a pull to expose its full length again.

"Those towels get dirty awful quick. Men's hands aren't always as clean as they might be."

"Ah, loyal to your sex, I see," he laughed. He stopped and gave her a keen look. "But you and Mrs. Wright were neighbors. I suppose you were friends, too."

Martha Hale shook her head.

"I've seen little enough of her of late years. I've not been in this house—it's more than a year."

"And why was that? You didn't like her?"

"I liked her well enough," she replied with spirit. "Farmers' wives have their hands full, Mr. Henderson. And then"—She looked around the kitchen.

"Yes?" he encouraged.

"It never seemed a very cheerful place," said she, more to herself than to him.

"No," he agreed; "I don't think any one would call it cheerful. I shouldn't say she had the home-making instinct."

"Well, I don't know as Wright had, either," she muttered.

"You mean they didn't get on very well?" he was quick to ask.

"No; I don't mean anything," she answered, with decision. As she turned a little away from him, she added: "But I don't think a place would be any the cheerfuler for John Wright's bein' in it."

"I'd like to talk to you about that a little later, Mrs. Hale," he said. "I'm anxious to get the lay of things upstairs now."

He moved toward the stair door, followed by the two men.

"I suppose anything Mrs. Peters does'll be all right?" the sheriff inquired. "She was to take in some clothes for her, you know—and a few little things. We left in such a hurry yesterday."

The county attorney looked at the two women whom they were leaving alone there among the kitchen things.

"Yes—Mrs. Peters," he said, his glance resting on the woman who was not Mrs. Peters, the big farmer woman who stood behind the sheriff's wife. "Of course Mrs. Peters is one of us," he said, in a manner of entrusting responsibility. "And keep your eye out, Mrs. Peters, for anything that might be of use. No telling; you women might come upon a clue to the motive—and that's the thing we need."

Mr. Hale rubbed his face after the fashion of a show man getting ready for a pleasantry.

"But would the women know a clue if they did come upon it?" he said; and, having delivered himself of this, he followed the others through the stair door.

The women stood motionless and silent, listening to the footsteps, first upon the stairs, then in the room above them.

Then, as if releasing herself from something strange, Mrs. Hale began to arrange the dirty pans under the sink, which the county attorney's disdainful push of the foot had deranged.

"I'd hate to have men comin' into my kitchen," she said testily—"snoopin' round and criticizin'."

"Of course it's no more than their duty," said the sheriff's wife, in her manner of timid acquiescence.

"Duty's all right," replied Mrs. Hale bluffly; "but I guess that deputy sheriff that come out to make the fire might have got a little of this on." She gave the roller towel a pull. "Wish I'd thought of that sooner! Seems mean to talk about her for not having things slicked up, when she had to come away in such a hurry."

She looked around the kitchen. Certainly it was not "slicked up." Her eye was held by a bucket of sugar on a low shelf. The cover was off the wooden bucket, and beside it was a paper bag—half full.

Mrs. Hale moved toward it.

"She was putting this in there," she said to herself—slowly.

She thought of the flour in her kitchen at home—half sifted, half not sifted. She had been interrupted and had left things half done. What had interrupted Minnie Foster? Why had that work been left half done? She made a move as if to finish it,—unfinished things always bothered her,—and then she glanced around and saw that Mrs. Peters was watching her—and she didn't want Mrs. Peters to get that feeling she had got of work begun and then—for some reason—not finished.

"It's a shame about her fruit," she said, and walked toward the cupboard that the county attorney had opened, and got on the chair, murmuring: "I wonder if it's all gone."

It was a sorry enough looking sight, but "Here's one that's all right," she said at last. She held it toward the light. "This is cherries, too." She looked again. "I declare I believe that's the only one."

With a sigh, she got down from the chair, went to the sink, and wiped off the bottle.

"She'll feel awful bad, after all her hard work in the hot weather. I remember the afternoon I put up my cherries last summer."

She set the bottle on the table, and, with another sigh, started to sit down in the rocker. But she did not sit down. Something kept her from sitting down in that chair. She straightened—stepped back, and, half turned away, stood looking at it, seeing the woman who sat there "pleatin' at her apron."

The thin voice of the sheriff's wife broke in upon her: "I must be getting those things from the front room closet." She opened the door into the other room, started in, stepped back. "You coming with me, Mrs. Hale?" she asked nervously. "You—you could help me get them."

They were soon back—the stark coldness of that shut-up room was not a thing to linger in.

"My!" said Mrs. Peters, dropping the things on the table and hurrying to the stove.

Mrs. Hale stood examining the clothes the woman who was being detained in town had said she wanted.

"Wright was close!" she exclaimed, holding up a shabby black skirt that bore the marks of much making over. "I think maybe that's why she kept so much to herself. I s'pose she felt she couldn't do her part; and then, you don't enjoy things when you feel shabby. She used to wear pretty clothes and be lively—when she was Minnie Foster, one of the town girls, singing in the choir. But that—oh, that was twenty years ago."

With a carefulness in which there was something tender, she folded the shabby clothes and piled them at one corner of the table. She looked at Mrs. Peters, and there was something in the other woman's look that irritated her.

"She don't care," she said to herself. "Much difference it makes to her whether Minnie Foster had pretty clothes when she was a girl."

Then she looked again, and she wasn't so sure; in fact, she hadn't at any time been perfectly sure about Mrs. Peters. She had that shrinking manner, and yet her eyes looked as if they could see a long way into things.

"This all you was to take in?" asked Mrs. Hale.

"No," said the sheriff's wife; "she said she wanted an apron. Funny thing to want," she ventured in her nervous little way, "for there's not much to get you dirty in jail, goodness knows. But I suppose just to make her feel more natural. If you're used to wearing an apron—. She said they were in the bottom drawer of this cupboard. Yes—here they are. And then her little shawl that always hung on the stair door."

She took the small gray shawl from behind the door leading upstairs, and stood a minute looking at it.

Suddenly Mrs. Hale took a quick step toward the other woman.

"Mrs. Peters!"

"Yes, Mrs. Hale?"

"Do you think she—did it?"

A frightened look blurred the other things in Mrs. Peters' eyes.

"Oh, I don't know," she said, in a voice that seemed to shrink away from the subject.

"Well, I don't think she did," affirmed Mrs. Hale stoutly. "Asking for an apron, and her little shawl. Worryin' about her fruit."

"Mr. Peters says—" Footsteps were heard in the room above; she stopped, looked up, then went on in a lowered voice: "Mr. Peters says—it looks bad for her. Mr. Henderson is awful sarcastic in a speech, and he's going to make fun of her saying she didn't—wake up."

For a moment Mrs. Hale had no answer. Then, "Well, I guess John Wright didn't wake up—when they was slippin' that rope under his neck," she muttered.

"No, it's *strange*," breathed Mrs. Peters. "They think it was such a—funny way to kill a man."

She began to laugh; at sound of the laugh, abruptly stopped.

"That's just what Mr. Hale said," said Mrs. Hale, in a resolutely natural voice. "There was a gun in the house. He says that's what he can't understand."

"Mr. Henderson said, coming out, that what was needed for the case was a motive. Something to show anger—or sudden feeling."

"Well, I don't see any signs of anger around here," said Mrs. Hale. "I don't—"

She stopped. It was as if her mind tripped on something. Her eye was caught by a dish-towel in the middle of the kitchen table. Slowly she moved toward the table. One half of it was wiped clean, the other half messy. Her eyes made a slow, almost unwilling turn to the bucket of sugar and the half empty bag beside it. Things begun—and not finished.

After a moment she stepped back, and said, in that manner of releasing herself:

"Wonder how they're finding things upstairs? I hope she had it a little more red up there. You know,"—she paused, and feeling gathered,—"it seems kind of *sneaking*; locking her up in town and coming out here to get her own house to turn against her!"

"But, Mrs. Hale," said the sheriff's wife, "the law is the law."

'I s'pose 'tis," answered Mrs. Hale shortly.

She turned to the stove, saying something about that fire not being much to brag of. She worked with it a minute, and when she straightened up she said aggressively:

"The law is the law—and a bad stove is a bad stove. How'd you like to cook on this?"—pointing with the poker to the broken lining. She opened the oven door and started to express her opinion of the oven; but she was swept into her own thoughts, thinking of what it would mean, year after year, to have the stove to wrestle with. The thought of Minnie Foster trying to bake in that oven—and the thought of her never going over to see Minnie Foster—.

She was startled by hearing Mrs. Peters say: "A person gets discouraged—and loses heart."

The sheriff's wife had looked from the stove to the sink—to the pail of water which had been carried in from outside. The two women stood there silent, above them the footsteps of the men who were looking for evidence against the woman who had worked in that kitchen. That look of seeing into things, of seeing through a thing to something else, was in the eyes of the sheriff's wife now. When Mrs. Hale next spoke to her, it was gently:

"Better loosen up your things, Mrs. Peters. We'll not feel them when we go out."

Mrs. Peters went to the back of the room to hang up the fur tippet she was wearing. A moment later she exclaimed, "Why, she was piecing a quilt," and held up a large sewing basket piled high with quilt pieces.

Mrs. Hale spread some of the blocks on the table.

"It's log-cabin pattern," she said, putting several of them together. "Pretty, isn't it?"

They were so engaged with the quilt that they did not hear the footsteps on the stairs. Just as the stair door opened Mrs. Hale was saying:

"Do you suppose she was going to quilt it or just knot it?"

The sheriff threw up his hands.

"They wonder whether she was going to quilt it or just knot it!"

There was a laugh for the ways of women, a warming of hands over the stove, and then the county attorney said briskly:

"Well, let's go right out to the barn and get that cleared up."

"I don't see as there's anything so strange," Mrs. Hale said resentfully, after the outside door had closed on the three men—"our taking up our time with little things while we're waiting for them to get the evidence. I don't see as it's anything to laugh about."

"Of course they've got awful important things on their minds," said the sheriff's wife apologetically.

They returned to an inspection of the blocks for the quilt. Mrs. Hale was looking at the fine, even sewing, preoccupied with thoughts of the woman who had done that sewing, when she heard the sheriff's wife say, in a queer tone:

"Why, look at this one."

She turned to take the block held out to her.

"The sewing," said Mrs. Peters, in a troubled way. "All the rest of them have been so nice and even—but—this one. Why, it looks as if she didn't know what she was about!"

Their eyes met—something flashed to life, passed between them; then, as if with an effort, they seemed to pull away from each other. A moment Mrs. Hale sat there, her hands folded over that sewing which was so unlike all the rest of the sewing. Then she had pulled a knot and drawn the threads.

"Oh, what are you doing, Mrs. Hale?" asked the sheriff's wife, startled.

"Just pulling out a stitch or two that's not sewed very good," said Mrs. Hale mildly.

"I don't think we ought to touch things," Mrs. Peters said, a little helplessly.

"I'd just finish up this end," answered Mrs. Hale, still in that mild, matter-of-fact fashion.

She threaded a needle and started to replace bad sewing with good. For a little while she sewed in silence. Then, in that thin, timid voice, she heard:

"Mrs. Hale!"

"Yes, Mrs. Peters?"

"What do you suppose she was so—nervous about?"

"Oh, *I* don't know," said Mrs. Hale, as if dismissing a thing not important enough to spend much time on. "I don't know as she was—nervous. I sew awful queer sometimes when I'm just tired."

She cut a thread, and out of the corner of her eye looked up at Mrs. Peters. The small, lean face of the sheriff's wife seemed to have tightened up. Her eyes had that look of peering into something. But the next moment she moved, and said in her thin, indecisive way:

"Well, I must get those clothes wrapped. They may be through sooner than we think. I wonder where I could find a piece of paper—and string."

"In that cupboard, maybe," suggested Mrs. Hale, after a glance around. One piece of the crazy sewing remained unripped. Mrs. Peters' back turned, Martha Hale now scrutinized that piece, compared it with the dainty, accurate sewing of the other blocks. The difference was startling. Holding this block made her feel queer, as if the distracted thoughts of the woman who had perhaps turned to it to try and quiet herself were communicating themselves to her.

Mrs. Peters' voice roused her.

"Here's a bird-cage," she said. "Did she have a bird, Mrs. Hale?"

"Why, I don't know whether she did or not." She turned to look at the cage Mrs. Peters was holding up. "I've not been here in so long." She sighed. "There was a man round last year selling canaries cheap—but I don't know as she took one. Maybe she did. She used to sing real pretty herself."

Mrs. Peters looked around the kitchen.

"Seems kind of funny to think of a bird here." She half laughed—an attempt to put up a barrier. "But she must have had one—or why would she have a cage? I wonder what happened to it."

"I suppose maybe the cat got it," suggested Mrs. Hale, resuming her sewing.

"No; she didn't have a cat. She's got that feeling some people have about cats—being afraid of them. When they brought her to our house yesterday, my cat got in the room, and she was real upset and asked me to take it out."

"My sister Bessie was like that," laughed Mrs. Hale.

The sheriff's wife did not reply. The silence made Mrs. Hale turn round. Mrs. Peters was examining the bird-cage.

"Look at this door," she said slowly. "It's broke. One hinge has been pulled apart."

Mrs. Hale came nearer.

"Looks as if some one must have been—rough with it."

Again their eyes met—startled, questioning, apprehensive. For a moment neither spoke nor stirred. Then Mrs. Hale, turning away, said brusquely:

"If they're going to find any evidence, I wish they'd be about it. I don't like this place."

"But I'm awful glad you came with me, Mrs. Hale." Mrs. Peters put the bird-cage on the table and sat down. "It would be lonesome for me—sitting here alone."

"Yes, it would, wouldn't it?" agreed Mrs. Hale, a certain determined naturalness in her voice. She picked up the sewing, but now it dropped in her lap, and she murmured in a different voice: "But I tell you what I *do* wish, Mrs. Peters. I wish I had come over sometimes when she was here. I wish—I had."

"But of course you were awful busy, Mrs. Hale. Your house—and your children."

"I could've come," retorted Mrs. Hale shortly. "I stayed away because it weren't cheerful—and that's why I ought to have come. I"—she looked around—"I've never liked this place. Maybe because it's down in a hollow and you don't see the road. I don't know what it is, but it's a lonesome place, and always was. I wish I had come over to see Minnie Foster sometimes. I can see now—" She did not put it into words.

"Well, you mustn't reproach yourself," counseled Mrs. Peters. "Somehow, we just don't see how it is with other folks till—something comes up."

"Not having children makes less work," mused Mrs. Hale, after a silence, "but it makes a quiet house—and Wright out to work all day—and no company when he did come in. Did you know John Wright, Mrs. Peters?"

"Not to know him. I've seen him in town. They say he was a good man."

"Yes—good," conceded John Wright's neighbor grimly. "He didn't drink, and kept his word as well as most, I guess, and paid his debts. But he was a hard man, Mrs. Peters. Just to pass the time of day with him—." She stopped, shivered a little. "Like a raw wind that gets to the bone." Her eye fell upon the cage on the table before her, and she added, almost bitterly: "I should think she would've wanted a bird!"

Suddenly she leaned forward, looking intently at the cage. "But what do you s'pose went wrong with it?"

"I don't know," returned Mrs. Peters; "unless it got sick and died."

But after she said it she reached over and swung the broken door. Both women watched it as if somehow held by it.

"You didn't know—her?" Mrs. Hale asked, a gentler note in her voice.

"Not till they brought her yesterday," said the sheriff's wife.

"She—come to think of it, she was kind of like a bird herself. Real sweet and pretty, but kind of timid and—fluttery. How—she—did—change."

That held her for a long time. Finally, as if struck with a happy thought and relieved to get back to everyday things, she exclaimed:

"Tell you what, Mrs. Peters, why don't you take the quilt in with you? It might take up her mind."

"Why, I think that's a real nice idea, Mrs. Hale," agreed the sheriff's wife, as if she too were glad to come into the atmosphere of a simple kindness. "There couldn't possibly be any objection to that, could there? Now, just what will I take? I wonder if her patches are in here—and her things."

They turned to the sewing basket.

"Here's some red," said Mrs. Hale, bringing out a roll of cloth. Underneath that was a box. "Here, maybe her scissors are in here—and her things." She held it up. "What a pretty box! I'll warrant that was something she had a long time ago—when she was a girl."

She held it in her hand a moment; then, with a little sigh, opened it.

Instantly her hand went to her nose.

"Why—!"

Mrs. Peters drew nearer—then turned away.

"There's something wrapped up in this piece of silk," faltered Mrs. Hale.

"This isn't her scissors," said Mrs. Peters in a shrinking voice.

Her hand not steady, Mrs. Hale raised the piece of silk. "Oh, Mrs. Peters!" she cried. "It's—"

Mrs. Peters bent closer.

"It's the bird," she whispered.

"But, Mrs. Peters!" cried Mrs. Hale. "*Look* at it! Its neck—look at its neck! It's all—other side *to*."

She held the box away from her.

The sheriff's wife again bent closer.

"Somebody wrung its neck," said she, in a voice that was slow and deep.

And then again the eyes of the two women met—this time clung together in a look of dawning comprehension, of growing horror. Mrs. Peters looked from the dead bird to the broken door of the cage. Again their eyes met. And just then there was a sound at the outside door.

Mrs. Hale slipped the box under the quilt pieces in the basket, and sank into the chair before it. Mrs. Peters stood holding to the table. The country attorney and the sheriff came in from outside.

"Well, ladies," said the county attorney, as one turning from serious things to little pleasantries, "have you decided whether she was going to quilt it or knot it?"

"We think," began the sheriff's wife in a flurried voice, "that she was going to—knot it."

He was too preoccupied to notice the change that came in her voice on that last.

"Well, that's very interesting, I'm sure," he said tolerantly. He caught sight of the bird-cage. "Has the bird flown?"

"We think the cat got it," said Mrs. Hale in a voice curiously even.

He was walking up and down, as if thinking something out.

"Is there a cat?" he asked absently.

Mrs. Hale shot a look up at the sheriff's wife.

"Well, not *now*," said Mrs. Peters. "They're superstitious, you know; they leave."

She sank into her chair.

The county attorney did not heed her. "No sign at all of any one having come in from the outside," he said to Peters, in the manner of continuing an interrupted conversation. "Their own rope. Now let's go upstairs again and go over it, piece by piece. It would have to have been some one who knew just the—"

The stair door closed behind them and their voices were lost.

The two women sat motionless, not looking at each other, but as if peering into something and at the same time holding back. When they spoke now it was as if they were afraid of what they were saying, but as if they could not help saying it.

"She liked that bird," said Martha Hale, low and slowly. "She was going to bury it in that pretty box."

"When I was a girl," said Mrs. Peters, under her breath, "my kitten—there was a boy took a hatchet, and before my eyes—before I could get there—" She covered her face an instant. "If they hadn't held me back I would have"—she caught herself, looked upstairs where footsteps were heard, and finished weakly—"hurt him."

Then they sat without speaking or moving.

"I wonder how it would seem," Mrs. Hale at last began, as if feeling her way over strange ground—"never to have had any children around?" Her eyes made a slow sweep of the kitchen, as if seeing what that kitchen had meant through all the years. "No, Wright wouldn't like the bird," she said after that—"a thing that sang. She used to sing. He killed that too." Her voice tightened.

Mrs. Peters moved uneasily.

"Of course we don't know who killed the bird."

"I knew John Wright," was Mrs. Hale's answer.

"It was an awful thing was done in this house that night, Mrs. Hale," said the sheriff's wife. "Killing a man while he slept—slipping a thing round his neck that choked the life out of him."

Mrs. Hale's hand went out to the bird-cage.

"His neck. Choked the life out of him."

"We don't *know* who killed him," whispered Mrs. Peters wildly. "We don't *know*."

Mrs. Hale had not moved. "If there had been years and years of—nothing, then a bird to sing to you, it would be awful—still—after the bird was still."

It was as if something within her not herself had spoken, and it found in Mrs. Peters something she did not know as herself.

"I know what stillness is," she said, in a queer, monotonous voice. "When we homesteaded in Dakota, and my first baby died—after he was two years old—and me with no other then—"

Mrs. Hale stirred.

"How soon do you suppose they'll be through looking for evidence?"

"I know what stillness is," repeated Mrs. Peters, in just the same way. Then she too pulled back. "The law has got to punish crime, Mrs. Hale," she said in her tight little way.

"I wish you'd seen Minnie Foster," was the answer, "when she wore a white dress with blue ribbons, and stood up there in the choir and sang."

The picture of that girl, the fact that she had lived neighbor to that girl for twenty years, and had let her die for lack of life, was suddenly more than she could bear.

"Oh, I *wish* I'd come over here once in a while!" she cried. "That was a crime! That was a crime! Who's going to punish that?"

"We mustn't take on," said Mrs. Peters, with a frightened look toward the stairs.

"I might 'a' *known* she needed help! I tell you, It's *queer*, Mrs. Peters. We live close together, and we live far apart. We all go through the same things—it's all just a different kind of the same thing! If it weren't why do you and I *understand*? Why do we *know*—what we know this minute?"

She dashed her hand across her eyes. Then, seeing the jar of fruit on the table, she reached out for it and choked out:

"If I was you I wouldn't *tell* her her fruit was gone! Tell her it *ain't*. Tell her it's all right—all of it. Here—take this in to prove it to her! She—she may never know whether it was broke or not."

She turned away.

Mrs. Peters reached out for the bottle of fruit as if she were glad to take it—as if touching a familiar thing, having something to do, could keep her from something else. She got up, looked about for something to wrap the fruit in, took a petticoat from the pile of clothes she had brought from the front room, and nervously started winding that round the bottle.

"My!" she began, in a high, false voice, "it's a good thing the men couldn't hear us! Getting all stirred up over a little thing like a—dead canary." She hurried over that. "As if that could have anything to do with—with—My, wouldn't they *laugh*?"

Footsteps were heard on the stairs.

"Maybe they would," muttered Mrs. Hale—"maybe they wouldn't."

"No, Peters," said the county attorney incisively; "it's all perfectly clear, except the reason for doing it. But you know juries when it comes to women. If there was some definite thing—something to show. Something to make a story about. A thing that would connect up with this clumsy way of doing it."

In a covert way Mrs. Hale looked at Mrs. Peters. Mrs. Peters was looking at her. Quickly they looked away from each other. The outer door opened and Mr. Hale came in.

"I've got the team round now," he said. "Pretty cold out there."

"I'm going to stay here awhile by myself," the county attorney suddenly announced. "You can send Frank out for me, can't you?" he asked the sheriff. "I want to go over everything. I'm not satisfied we can't do better."

Again, for one brief moment, the two women's eyes found one another.

The sheriff came up to the table.

"Did you want to see what Mrs. Peters was going to take in?"

The county attorney picked up the apron. He laughed.

"Oh, I guess they're not very dangerous things the ladies have picked out."

Mrs. Hale's hand was on the sewing basket in which the box was concealed. She felt that she ought to take her hand off the basket. She did not seem able to. He picked up one of the quilt blocks which she had piled on to cover the box. Her eyes felt like fire. She had a feeling that if he took up the basket she would snatch it from him.

But he did not take it up. With another little laugh, he turned away, saying:

"No; Mrs. Peters doesn't need supervising. For that matter, a sheriff's wife is married to the law. Ever think of it that way, Mrs. Peters?"

Mrs. Peters was standing beside the table. Mrs. Hale shot a look up at her; but she could not see her face. Mrs. Peters had turned away. When she spoke, her voice was muffled.

"Not—just that way," she said.

"Married to the law!" chuckled Mrs. Peters' husband. He moved toward the door into the front room, and said to the county attorney:

"I just want you to come in here a minute, George. We ought to take a look at these windows.

"We'll be right out, Mr. Hale," said the sheriff to the farmer, who was still waiting by the door.

Hale went to look after the horses. The sheriff followed the county attorney into the other room. Again—for one moment—the two women were alone in that kitchen.

Martha Hale sprang up, her hands tight together, looking at that other woman, with whom it rested. At first she could not see her eyes, for the sheriff's wife had not turned back, since she turned away at that suggestion of being married to the law. But now Mrs. Hale made her turn back. Her eyes made her turn back. Slowly, unwillingly, Mrs. Peters turned her head until her eyes met the eyes of the other woman. There was a moment when they held each other in a steady, burning look in which there was no evasion nor flinching. Then Martha Hale's eyes pointed the way to the basket in which was hidden the thing that would make certain the conviction of the other woman—that woman who was not there and yet who had been there with them all through the hour.

For a moment Mrs. Peters did not move. And then she did it. With a rush forward, she threw back the quilt pieces, got the box, tried to put it in her handbag. It was too big. Desperately she opened it, started to take the bird out. But there she broke—she could not touch the bird. She stood helpless, foolish.

There was the sound of a knob turning in the inner door. Martha Hale snatched the box from the sheriff's wife, and got it in the pocket of her big coat just as the sheriff and the county attorney came back into the kitchen.

"Well, Henry," said the county attorney facetiously, "at least we found out that she was not going to quilt it. She was going to—what is it you call it, ladies?"

Mrs. Hale's hand was against the pocket of her coat.

"We call it—knot it, Mr. Henderson."

[1917]

Questions

1. How do Mrs. Hale and Mrs. Peters discover Minnie Wright's motive for murder?
2. Mrs. Peters insists that "the law is the law"; what events persuade her to participate in the exoneration of Minnie Wright's crime? How does the story demonstrate the changes that occur in her and Mrs. Hale?
3. Consider how each of the following elements of the story carries a double meaning: knot, strangulation, crime, law, evidence, motive, jury.
4. What does the story imply in expressing different ways in which men and women interpret events and even objects in an environment? Are these differences exaggerated? How does the reader become a participant in interpretation and judgment?
5. What is the significance of the title? What conflicting views of the law are expressed in the story? Are they resolved?

Nikolai Gogol
(1809–1852)
Russia

Nikolai Vasilievich Gogol was born and raised in the Ukraine, the son of an amateur musician and playwright who suffered mental disorders and who died during Nikolai's childhood. Gogol's mother was only 15 when Nikolai was born; she went on to bear 11 more children. Steeped in folklore, she was an important source of the folk legends and superstitions of Ukrainian life in Gogol's early stories.

Gogol had hopes of being an actor, but his highly nervous nature and his fear of people made it difficult for him to succeed at that or most other professions. His defeats were exaggerated for him because of his high sense of purpose. He tried several jobs, including the civil service, and eventually acquired a position for which he had absolutely no qualifications, as a professor of medieval history at the University of St. Petersburg. His disastrous performance sounds like a situation he might have invented for one of his stories.

Eventually Gogol tried writing fiction based on Ukrainian fairy tales, legends, and romantic horror tales; the first volume, Evenings on a Farm Near Dikanka (1831), made his success and name immediately. He also wrote several plays, the best known of which, The Inspector General (1836), exposed the posturings and foibles of a cross section of Russian townspeople. His masterpiece, Dead Souls (1841), satirizes the greed and corruption of Russian landowners with epic sweep and humor. Although it might seem as if Gogol were a radical social critic, in fact he was politically conservative; he intended for Dead Souls (which he never completed) to end with his hero Chichikov's reform and the salvation of traditional Russia.

Gogol's mastery of the "comic grotesque"—the juxtaposition of humor and horror—is one of his unique contributions to narrative form. His mingling of the commonplace with the uncanny or supernatural, as in "The Overcoat," and his mastery of caricature are elements of his indelible style. Moreover, his poignant story of the plight of the little man marked a turning point in Russian literature: the character of the underdog or social misfit is understood not as a nuisance or a figure to be mocked but as a human being who is entitled to his share of happiness. However, he may not find that happiness, as Gogol himself did not. Split between his artistic gifts and his moral certainties, Gogol eventually died of melancholy, mental anguish, and self-starvation at the age of 41.

Gogol's influence on Russian literature was profound; he is regarded as the father of "Russian realism." Dostoevsky remarked, "We all emerged from the folds of Gogol's overcoat." The Russian writer Vladimir Nabokov observed the following in his Lectures on Russian Literature:

> "The Overcoat" is a grotesque and grim nightmare making black holes in the dim pattern of life. . . . After reading Gogol one's eyes may become gogolized and one is apt to see bits of his world in the most unexpected places. . . . [S]omething like Akaky Akakievich's overcoat has been the passionate dream of this or that chance acquaintance who never has heard about Gogol.

"The Overcoat," in its unique fusion of humor and suffering and in its stark rendering of the absurd universe that lurks just beneath the commonplace one, is unarguably one of the world's great masterpieces of short fiction.

THE OVERCOAT

In the department of . . . but I had better not mention which department. There is nothing in the world more touchy than a department, a regiment, a government office, and, in fact, any sort of official body. Nowadays every private individual considers all society insulted in his person. I have been told that very lately a complaint was lodged by a police inspector of which town I don't remember, and that in this complaint he set forth clearly that the institutions of the State were in danger and that his sacred name was being taken in vain; and, in proof thereof, he appended to his complaint an enormously long volume of some romantic work in which a police inspector appeared on every tenth page, occasionally, indeed, in an intoxicated condition. And so, to avoid any unpleasantness, we had better call the department of which we are speaking "a certain department."

And so, in a *certain department* there was a *certain clerk*; a clerk of whom it cannot be said that he was very remarkable; he was short, somewhat pockmarked, with rather reddish hair and rather dim, bleary eyes, with a small bald patch on the top of his head, with wrinkles on both sides of his cheeks and the sort of complexion which is usually described as hemorrhoidal . . . nothing can be done about that, it is the Petersburg climate. As for his grade in the civil service (for among us a man's rank is what must be established first) he was what is called a perpetual titular councilor, a class at which, as we all know, various writers who indulge in the praiseworthy habit of attacking those who cannot defend themselves jeer and jibe to their hearts' content. This clerk's surname was Bashmachkin. From the very name it is clear that it must have been derived from a shoe (*bashmak*); but when and under what circumstances it was derived from a shoe, it is impossible to say. Both his father and his grandfather and even his brother-in-law, and all the Bashmachkins without exception wore boots, which they simply resoled two or three times a year. His name was Akaky Akakievich.[1] Perhaps it may strike the reader as a rather strange and contrived name, but I can assure him that it was not contrived at all, that the circumstances were such that it was quite out of the question to give him any other name. Akaky Akakievich was born toward nightfall, if my memory does not deceive me, on the twenty-third of March. His mother, the wife of a government clerk, a very good woman, made arrangements in due course to christen the child. She was still lying in bed, facing the door, while on her right hand stood the godfather, an excellent man called Ivan Ivanovich Yeroshkin, one of the head clerks in the Senate, and the godmother, the wife of a police official and a woman of rare qualities, Arina Semeonovna Belobriushkova. Three names were offered to the happy mother for selection—Mokky, Sossy, or the name of the martyr Khozdazat. "No," thought the poor lady, "they are all such names!" To satisfy her, they opened the calendar at another page, and the names which turned up were: Trifily, Dula, Varakhasy. "What an infliction!" said the mother. "What names they all are! I really never heard such names. Varadat or Varukh would be bad enough, but Trifily and Varakhasy!" They turned over another page and the names were: Pavsikakhy and Vakhisy. "Well, I see," said the mother, "it is clear that it is his fate. Since that is how it is, he had better be named after his father; his father is Akaky; let the son be Akaky, too." This was how he came to be Akaky Akakievich. The baby was christened and cried and made sour faces during the ceremony, as though

---

[1] *Akaky Akakievich*   In Russian, *Akaky* is close to a child's word for excrement.

he foresaw that he would be a titular councilor. So that was how it all came to pass. We have reported it here so that the reader may see for himself that it happened quite inevitably and that to give him any other name was out of the question.

No one has been able to remember when and how long ago he entered the department, nor who gave him the job. Regardless of how many directors and higher officials of all sorts came and went, he was always seen in the same place, in the same position, at the very same duty, precisely the same copying clerk, so that they used to declare that he must have been born a copying clerk, uniform, bald patch, and all. No respect at all was shown him in the department. The porters, far from getting up from their seats when he came in, took no more notice of him than if a simple fly had flown across the reception room. His superiors treated him with a sort of despotic aloofness. The head clerk's assistant used to throw papers under his nose without even saying "Copy this" or "Here is an interesting, nice little case" or some agreeable remark of the sort, as is usually done in well-bred offices. And he would take it, gazing only at the paper without looking to see who had put it there and whether he had the right to do so; he would take it and at once begin copying it. The young clerks jeered and made jokes at him to the best of their clerkly wit, and told before his face all sorts of stories of their own invention about him; they would say of his landlady, an old woman of seventy, that she beat him, would ask when the wedding was to take place, and would scatter bits of paper on his head, calling them snow. Akaky Akakievich never answered a word, however, but behaved as though there were no one there. It had no influence on his work; in the midst of all this teasing, he never made a single mistake in his copying. It was only when the jokes became too unbearable, when they jolted his arm, and prevented him from going on with his work, that he would say: "Leave me alone! Why do you insult me?" and there was something touching in the words and in the voice in which they were uttered. There was a note in it of something that aroused compassion, so that one young man, new to the office, who, following the example of the rest, had allowed himself to tease him, suddenly stopped as though cut to the heart, and from that time on, everything was, as it were, changed and appeared in a different light to him. Some unseen force seemed to repel him from the companions with whom he had become acquainted because he thought they were well-bred and decent men. And long afterward, during moments of the greatest gaiety, the figure of the humble little clerk with a bald patch on his head appeared before him with his heart-rending words: "Leave me alone! Why do you insult me?" and within those moving words he heard others: "I am your brother." And the poor young man hid his face in his hands, and many times afterward in his life he shuddered, seeing how much inhumanity there is in man, how much savage brutality lies hidden under refined, cultured politeness, and, my God! even in a man whom the world accepts as a gentleman and a man of honor. . . .

It would be hard to find a man who lived for his work as did Akaky Akakievich. To say that he was zealous in his work is not enough; no, he loved his work. In it, in that copying, he found an interesting and pleasant world of his own. There was a look of enjoyment on his face; certain letters were favorites with him, and when he came to them he was delighted; he chuckled to himself and winked and moved his lips, so that it seemed as though every letter his pen was forming could be read in is face. If rewards had been given according to the measure of zeal in the service, he might to his amazement have even found himself a civil councilor; but all he gained in the service, as the wits, his fellow clerks, expressed it, was a button in his buttonhole and hemorrhoids where he sat. It cannot be said, however, that no notice had ever been taken of him. One director, being a good-natured man and anxious to reward him for his long service, sent him something a little more important than his ordinary copying; he was instructed to make some sort of report from a finished document for another office; the work consisted only of altering the headings and in places changing the first person into the third. This cost him so much effort that he was covered with perspiration; he mopped his brow and said at last, "No, I'd rather copy something."

From that time on they left him to his copying forever. It seemed as though nothing in the world existed for him except his copying. He gave no thought at all to his clothes; his uniform was—well, not green but some sort of rusty, muddy color. His collar was very low and narrow, so that, although his neck was particularly long, yet, standing out of the collar, it looked as immensely long as those of the dozens of plaster kittens, with nodding heads which foreigners carry about on their heads and peddle in Russia. And there were always things sticking to his uniform, either bits of hay or threads; moreover, he had a special knack of passing under a window at the very moment when various garbage was being flung out into the street, and so was continually carrying off bits of melon rind and similar litter on his hat. He had never once in his life noticed what was being done and what was going on in the street, all those things at which, as we all know, his colleagues, the young clerks, always stare, utilizing their keen sight so well that they notice anyone on the other side of the street with a strap hanging loose—an observation which always calls forth a sly grin. Whatever Akaky Akakievich looked at, he saw nothing but his clear, evenly written lines, and it was only perhaps when a horse suddenly appeared from nowhere and placed its head on his shoulder, and with its nostrils blew a real gale upon his cheek, that he would notice that he was not in the middle of his writing, but rather in the middle of the street.

On reaching home, he would sit down at once at the table, hurriedly eat his soup and a piece of beef with an onion; he did not notice the taste at all but ate it all with the flies and anything else that Providence happened to send him. When he felt that his stomach was beginning to be full, he would get up from the table, take out a bottle of ink, and begin copying the papers he had brought home with him. When he had none to do, he would make a copy especially for his own pleasure, particularly if the document were remarkable not for the beauty of its style but because it was addressed to some new or distinguished person.

Even at those hours when the gray Petersburg sky is completely overcast and the whole population of clerks have dined and eaten their fill, each as best he can, according to the salary he receives and his personal tastes; when they are all resting after the scratching of pens and bustle of the office, their own necessary work and other people's, and all the tasks that an overzealous man voluntarily sets himself even beyond what is necessary; when the clerks are hastening to devote what is left of their time to pleasure; some more enterprising are flying to the theater, others to the street to spend their leisure staring at women's hats, some to spend the evening paying compliments to some attractive girl, the star of a little official circle, while some—and this is the most frequent to fall—go simply to a fellow clerk's apartment on the third or fourth story, two little rooms with a hall or a kitchen, with some pretensions to style, with a lamp or some such article that has cost many sacrifices of dinners and excursions—at the time when all the clerks are scattered about the apartments of their friends, playing a stormy game of whist, sipping tea out of glasses, eating cheap biscuits, sucking in smoke from long pipes, telling, as the cards are dealt, some scandal that has floated down from higher circles, a pleasure which the Russian can never by any possibility deny himself, or, when there is nothing better to talk about, repeating the everlasting anecdote of the commanding officer who was told that the tail had been cut off the horse on the Falconet monument—in short, even when everyone was eagerly seeking entertainment, Akaky Akakievich did not indulge in any amusement. No one could say that they had ever seen him at an evening party. After working to his heart's content, he would go to bed, smiling at the thought of the next day and wondering what God would send him to copy. So flowed on the peaceful life of a man who knew how to be content with his fate on a salary of four hundred rubles, and so perhaps it would have flowed on to extreme old age, had it not been for the various disasters strewn along the road of life, not only of titular, but even of privy, actual court, and all other councilors, even those who neither give counsel to others nor accept it themselves.

There is in Petersburg a mighty foe of all who receive a salary of about four hundred rubles. That foe is none other than our northern frost, although it is said to be very good for the health. Between eight and nine in the morning, precisely at the hour when the streets are filled with clerks going to their departments, the frost begins indiscriminately giving such sharp and stinging nips at all their noses that the poor fellows don't know what to do with them. At that time, when even those in the higher grade have a pain in their brows and tears in their eyes from the frost, the poor titular councilors are sometimes almost defenseless. Their only protection lies in running as fast as they can through five or six streets in a wretched, thin little overcoat and then warming their feet thoroughly in the porter's room, till all their faculties and talents for their various duties thaw out again after having been frozen on the way. Akaky Akakievich had for some time been feeling that his back and shoulders were particularly nipped by the cold, although he did try to run the regular distance as fast as he could. He wondered at last whether there were any defects in his overcoat. After examining it thoroughly in the privacy of his home, he discovered that in two or three places, on the back and the shoulders, it had become a regular sieve; the cloth was so worn that you could see through it and the lining was coming out. I must note that Akaky Akakievich's overcoat had also served as a butt for the jokes of the clerks. It had even been deprived of the honorable name of overcoat and had been referred to as the "dressing gown." It was indeed of rather a peculiar make. Its collar had been growing smaller year by year as it served to patch the other parts. The patches were not good specimens of the tailor's art, and they certainly looked clumsy and ugly. On seeing what was wrong, Akaky Akakievich decided that he would have to take the overcoat to Petrovich, a tailor who lived on the fourth floor up a back staircase, and, in spite of having only one eye and being pockmarked all over his face, was rather successful in repairing the trousers and coats of clerks and others— that is, when he was sober, be it understood, and had no other enterprise on his mind. Of this tailor I ought not, of course, say much, but since it is now the rule that the character of every person in a novel must be completely described, well, there's nothing I can do but describe Petrovich too. At first he was called simply Grigory, and was a serf belonging to some gentleman or other. He began to be called Petrovich[2] from the time he got his freedom and began to drink rather heavily on every holiday, at

---

[2]Serfs were generally addressed by their first names only, while freemen were addressed by first name and patronymic (the middle name derived from the father's first name) or by patronymic only.

first only on the main holidays, but afterward, on all church holidays indiscriminately, wherever there was a cross in the calendar. In this he was true to the customs of his forefathers, and when he quarreled with his wife he used to call her a worldly woman and a German. Since we have now mentioned the wife, it will be necessary to say a few words about her, too, but unfortunately not much is known about her, except indeed that Petrovich had a wife and that she wore a cap and not a kerchief, but apparently she could not boast of beauty; anyway, none but soldiers of the guard peered under her cap when they met her, and they twitched their mustaches and gave vent to a rather peculiar sound.

As he climbed the stairs leading to Petrovich's—which, to do them justice, were all soaked with water and slops and saturated through and through with that smell of ammonia which makes the eyes smart, and is, as we all know, inseparable from the backstairs of Petersburg houses—Akaky Akakievich was already wondering how much Petrovich would ask for the job, and inwardly resolving not to give more than two rubles. The door was open, because Petrovich's wife was frying some fish and had so filled the kitchen with smoke that you could not even see the cockroaches. Akaky Akakievich crossed the kitchen unnoticed by the good woman, and walked at last into a room where he saw Petrovich sitting on a big, wooden, unpainted table with his legs tucked under him like a Turkish pasha. The feet, as is usual with tailors when they sit at work, were bare; and the first object that caught Akaky Akakievich's eye was the big toe, with which he was already familiar, with a misshapen nail as thick and strong as the shell of a tortoise. Around Petrovich's neck hung a skein of silk and another of thread and on his knees was a rag of some sort. He had for the last three minutes been trying to thread his needle, but could not get the thread into the eye and so was very angry with the darkness and indeed with the thread itself, muttering in an undertone: "She won't go in, the savage! You wear me out, you bitch." Akaky Akakievich was unhappy that he had come just at the minute when Petrovich was in a bad humor; he liked to give him an order when he was a little "elevated," or, as his wife expressed it, "had fortified himself with vodka, the one-eyed devil." In such circumstances Petrovich was as a rule very ready to give way and agree, and invariably bowed and thanked him. Afterward, it is true, his wife would come wailing that her husband had been drunk and so had asked too little, but adding a single ten-kopek piece would settle that. But on this occasion Petrovich was apparently sober and consequently curt, unwilling to bargain, and the devil knows what price he would be ready to demand. Akaky Akakievich realized this, and was, as the saying is, beating a retreat, but things had gone too far, for Petrovich was screwing up his solitary eye very attentively at him and Akaky Akakievich involuntarily said: "Good day, Petrovich!"

"I wish you a good day, sir," said Petrovich, and squinted at Akaky Akakievich's hands, trying to discover what sort of goods he had brought.

"Here I have come to you, Petrovich, do you see . . . !"

It must be noticed that Akaky Akakievich for the most part explained himself by apologies, vague phrases, and meaningless parts of speech which have absolutely no significance whatever. If the subject were a very difficult one, it was his habit indeed to leave his sentences quite unfinished, so that very often after a sentence had begun with the words, "It really is, don't you know . . ." nothing at all would follow and he himself would be quite oblivious to the fact that he had not finished his thought, supposing he had said all that was necessary.

"What is it?" said Petrovich, and at the same time with his solitary eye he scrutinized his whole uniform from the collar to the sleeves, the back, the skirts, the buttonholes—with all of which he was very familiar since they were all his own work. Such scrutiny is habitual with tailors; it is the first thing they do on meeting one.

"It's like this, Petrovich . . . the overcoat, the cloth . . . you see everywhere else it is quite strong; it's a little dusty and looks as though it were old, but it is new and it is only in one place just a little . . . on the back, and just a little worn on one shoulder and on this shoulder, too, a little . . . do you see? that's all, and it's not much work . . ."

Petrovich took the "dressing gown," first spread it out over the table, examined it for a long time, shook his head, and put his hand out to the window sill for a round snuffbox with a portrait on the lid of some general—which general I can't exactly say, for a finger had been thrust through the spot where a face should have been, and the hole had been pasted over with a square piece of paper. After taking a pinch of snuff, Petrovich held the "dressing gown" up in his hands and looked at it against the light, and again he shook his head; then he turned it with the lining upward and once more shook his head; again he took off the lid with the general pasted up with paper and snuffed a pinch into his nose, shut the box, put it away, and at last said: "No, it can't be repaired; a wretched garment!" Akaky Akakievich's heart sank at those words.

"Why can't it, Petrovich?" he said, almost in the imploring voice of a child. "Why, the only thing is, it is a bit worn on the shoulders; why, you have got some little pieces . . ."

"Yes, the pieces will be found all right," said Petrovich, "but it can't be patched, the stuff is rotten; if you put a needle in it, it would give way."

"Let it give way, but you just put a patch on it."

"There is nothing to put a patch on. There is nothing for it to hold on to; there is a great strain on it; it is not worth calling cloth; it would fly away at a breath of wind."

"Well, then, strengthen it with something—I'm sure, really, this is . . ."

"No," said Petrovich resolutely, "there is nothing that can be done, the thing is no good at all. You had far better, when the cold winter weather comes, make yourself leg wrappings out of it, for there is no warmth in stockings; the Germans invented them just to make money." (Petrovich enjoyed a dig at the Germans occasionally.) "And as for the overcoat, it is obvious that you will have to have a new one."

At the word "new" there was a mist before Akaky Akakievich's eyes, and everything in the room seemed blurred. He could see nothing clearly but the general with the piece of paper over his face on the lid of Petrovich's snuffbox.

"A new one?" he said, still feeling as though he were in a dream; "why, I haven't the money for it."

"Yes, a new one," Petrovich repeated with barbarous composure.

"Well, and if I did have a new one, how much would it . . . ?"

"You mean what will it cost?"

"Yes."

"Well, at least one hundred and fifty rubles," said Petrovich, and he compressed his lips meaningfully. He was very fond of making an effect; he was fond of suddenly disconcerting a man completely and then squinting sideways to see what sort of a face he made.

"A hundred and fifty rubles for an overcoat!" screamed poor Akaky Akakievich—it was perhaps the first time he had screamed in his life, for he was always distinguished by the softness of his voice.

"Yes," said Petrovich, "and even then it depends on the coat. If I were to put marten on the collar, and add a hood with silk linings, it would come to two hundred."

"Petrovich, please," said Akaky Akakievich in an imploring voice, not hearing and not trying to hear what Petrovich said, and missing all his effects, "repair it somehow, so that it will serve a little longer."

"No, that would be wasting work and spending money for nothing," said Petrovich, and after that Akaky Akakievich went away completely crushed, and when he had gone Petrovich remained standing for a long time with his lips pursed up meaningfully before he began his work again, feeling pleased that he had not demeaned himself or lowered the dignity of the tailor's art.

When he got into the street, Akaky Akakievich felt as though he was in a dream. "So that is how it is," he said to himself. "I really did not think it would be this way . . ." and then after a pause he added, "So that's it! So that's how it is at last! and I really could never have supposed it would be this way. And there . . ." There followed another long silence, after which he said: "So that's it! well, it really is so utterly unexpected . . . who would have thought . . . what a circumstance . . ." Saying this, instead of going home he walked off in quite the opposite direction without suspecting what he was doing. On the way a clumsy chimney sweep brushed the whole of his sooty side against him and blackened his entire shoulder; a whole hatful of plaster scattered upon him from the top of a house that was being built. He noticed nothing of this, and only after he had jostled against a policeman who had set his halberd down beside him and was shaking some snuff out of his horn into his rough fist, he came to himself a little and then only because the policeman said: "Why are you poking yourself right in one's face, haven't you enough room on the street?" This made him look around and turn homeward; only there he began to collect his thoughts, to see his position in a clear and true light, and began talking to himself no longer incoherently but reasonably and openly as with a sensible friend with whom one can discuss the most intimate and vital matters. "No," said Akaky Akakievich, "it is no use talking to Petrovich now; just now he really is . . . his wife must have been giving it to him. I had better go to him on Sunday morning; after Saturday night he will have a crossed eye and be sleepy, so he'll want a little drink and his wife won't give him a kopek. I'll slip ten kopeks into his hand and then he will be more accommodating and maybe take the overcoat. . . ."

So reasoning with himself, Akaky Akakievich cheered up and waited until the next Sunday; then, seeing from a distance Petrovich's wife leaving the house, he went straight in. Petrovich certainly had a crossed eye after Saturday. He could hardly hold his head up and was very drowsy; but, despite all that, as soon as he heard what Akaky Akakievich was speaking about, it seemed as though the devil has nudged him. "I can't," he said, "you must order a new one." Akaky Akakievich at once slipped a ten-kopek piece into his hand. "I thank you, sire, I will have just a drop to your health, but don't trouble yourself about the overcoat; it is no good for anything. I'll make you a fine new coat; you can have faith in me for that."

Akaky Akakievich would have said more about repairs, but Petrovich, without listening, said: "A new one I'll make you without fail; you can rely on that; I'll do my best. It could even be like the fashion that is popular, with the collar to fasten with silver-plated hooks under a flap."

Then Akaky Akakievich saw that there was no escape from a new overcoat and he was utterly depressed. How indeed, for what, with what money could he get it? Of course he could to some extent rely on the bonus for the coming holiday, but that

money had long been appropriated and its use determined beforehand. It was needed for new trousers and to pay the cobbler an old debt for putting some new tops on
some old boots, and he had to order three shirts from a seamstress as well as two
items of undergarments which it is indecent to mention in print; in short, all that
money absolutely must be spent, and even if the director were to be so gracious as
to give him a holiday bonus of forty-five or even fifty, instead of forty rubles, there
would be still left a mere trifle, which would be but a drop in the ocean compared
to the fortune needed for an overcoat. Though, of course, he knew that Petrovich
had a strange craze for suddenly demanding the devil knows what enormous price,
so that at times his own wife could not help crying out: "Why, you are out of your
wits, you idiot! Another time he'll undertake a job for nothing, and here the devil
has bewitched him to ask more than he is worth himself." Though, of course, he
knew that Petrovich would undertake to make it for eighty rubles, still where would
he get those eighty rubles? He might manage half of that sum; half of it could be
found, perhaps even a little more; but where could he get the other half? . . . But,
first of all, the reader ought to know where that first half was to be found. Akaky
Akakievich had the habit every time he spent a ruble of putting aside two kopeks
in a little box which he kept locked, with a slit in the lid for dropping in the money.
At the end of every six months he would inspect the pile of coppers there and change
them for small silver. He had done this for a long time, and in the course of many
years the sum had mounted up to forty rubles and so he had half the money in his
hands, but where was he to get the other half; where was he to get another forty
rubles? Akaky Akakievich thought and thought and decided at last that he would
have to diminish his ordinary expenses, at least for a year; give up burning candles
in the evening, and if he had to do any work he must go into the landlady's room
and work by her candle; that as he walked along the streets he must walk as lightly
and carefully as possible, almost on tiptoe, on the cobbles and flagstones, so that his
soles might last a little longer than usual; that he must send his linen to the wash
less frequently, and that, to preserve it from being worn, he must take it off every day
when he came home and sit in a thin cotton dressing gown, a very ancient garment
which Time itself had spared. To tell the truth, he found it at first rather difficult to
get used to these privations, but after a while it became a habit and went smoothly
enough—he even became quite accustomed to being hungry in the evening; on the
other hand, he had spiritual nourishment, for he carried ever in his thoughts the idea
of his future overcoat. His whole existence had in a sense become fuller, as though
he had married, as though some other person were present with him, as though he
were no longer alone but an agreeable companion had consented to walk the path
of life hand in hand with him, and that companion was none other than the new
overcoat with its thick padding and its strong, durable lining. He became, as it were,
more alive, even more strong-willed, like a man who has set before himself a definite goal. Uncertainty, indecision, in fact all the hesitating and vague characteristics, vanished from his face and his manners. At times there was a gleam in his eyes;
indeed, the most bold and audacious ideas flashed through his mind. Why not really have marten on the collar? Meditation on the subject always made him absent-
minded. On one occasion when he was copying a document, he very nearly made a
mistake, so that he almost cried out "ough" aloud and crossed himself. At least once
every month he went to Petrovich to talk about the overcoat: where it would be best
to buy the cloth, and what color it should be, and what price; and, though he returned home a little anxious, he was always pleased at the thought that at last the

time was at hand when everything would be bought and the overcoat would be made. Things moved even faster than he had anticipated. Contrary to all expectations, the director bestowed on Akaky Akakievich a bonus of no less than sixty rubles. Whether it was that he had an inkling that Akaky Akakievich needed a coat, or whether it happened by luck, owing to this he found he had twenty rubles extra. This circumstance hastened the course of affairs. Another two or three months of partial starvation and Akaky Akakievich had actually saved up nearly eighty rubles. His heart, as a rule very tranquil, began to throb.

The very first day he set out with Petrovich for the shops. They bought some very good cloth, and no wonder, since they had been thinking of it for more than six months, and scarcely a month had passed without their going out to the shop to compare prices; now Petrovich himself declared that there was no better cloth to be had. For the lining they chose calico, but of such good quality, that in Petrovich's words it was even better than silk, and actually as strong and handsome to look at. Marten they did not buy, because it was too expensive, but instead they chose cat fur, the best to be found in the shop—cat which in the distance might almost be taken for marten. Petrovich was busy making the coat for two weeks, because there was a great deal of quilting; otherwise it would have been ready sooner. Petrovich charged twelve rubles for the work; less than that it hardly could have been; everything was sewn with silk, with fine double seams, and Petrovich went over every seam afterwards with his own teeth, imprinting various patterns with them. It was . . . it is hard to say precisely on what day, but probably on the most triumphant day in the life of Akaky Akakievich, that Petrovich at last brought the overcoat. He brought it in the morning, just before it was time to set off for the department. The overcoat could not have arrived at a more opportune time, because severe frosts were just beginning and seemed threatening to become even harsher. Petrovich brought the coat himself as a good tailor should. There was an expression of importance on his face, such as Akaky Akakievich had never seen there before. He seemed fully conscious of having completed a work of no little importance and of having shown by his own example the gulf that separates tailors who only put in lining and do repairs from those who make new coats. He took the coat out of the huge handkerchief in which he had brought it (the handkerchief had just come home from the wash); he then folded it up and put it in his pocket for future use. After taking out the overcoat, he looked at it with much pride and holding it in both hands, threw it very deftly over Akaky Akakievich's shoulders, then pulled it down and smoothed it out behind with his hands; then draped it about Akaky Akakievich somewhat jauntily. Akaky Akakievich, a practical man, wanted to try it with his arms in the sleeves. Petrovich helped him to put it on, and it looked splendid with his arms in the sleeves, too. In fact, it turned out that the overcoat was completely and entirely successful. Petrovich did not let slip the occasion for observing that it was only because he lived in a small street and had no signboard, and because he had known Akaky Akakievich so long, that he had done it so cheaply, and that on Nevsky Prospekt they would have asked him seventy-five rubles for the tailoring alone. Akaky Akakievich had no inclination to discuss this with Petrovich; besides he was frightened of the big sums that Petrovich was fond of flinging airily about in conversation. He paid him, thanked him, and went off, with his new overcoat on, to the department. Petrovich followed him out and stopped in the street, staring for a long time at the coat from a distance and then purposely turned off and, taking a short cut through a side street, came back into the street, and got another view of the coat from the other side, that is, from the front.

Meanwhile Akaky Akakievich walked along in a gay holiday mood. Every second he was conscious that he had a new overcoat on his shoulders, and several times he actually laughed from inward satisfaction. Indeed, it had two advantages: one that it was warm and the other that it was good. He did not notice how far he had walked at all and he suddenly found himself in the department; in the porter's room he took off the overcoat, looked it over, and entrusted it to the porter's special care. I cannot tell how it happened, but all at once everyone in the department learned that Akaky Akakievich had a new overcoat and that the "dressing gown" no longer existed. They all ran out at once into the cloakroom to look at Akaky Akakievich's new overcoat; they began welcoming him and congratulating him so that at first he could do nothing but smile and then felt positively embarrassed. When, coming up to him, they all began saying that he must "sprinkle" the new overcoat and that he ought at least to buy them all a supper, Akaky Akakievich lost his head completely and did not know what to do, how to get out of it, nor what to answer. A few minutes later, flushing crimson, he even began assuring them with great simplicity that it was not a new overcoat at all, that it wasn't much, that it was an old overcoat. At last one of the clerks, indeed the assistant of the head clerk of the room, probably in order to show that he wasn't too proud to mingle with those beneath him, said: "So be it, I'll give a party instead of Akaky Akakievich and invite you all to tea with me this evening; as luck would have it, it is my birthday." The clerks naturally congratulated the assistant head clerk and eagerly accepted the invitation. Akaky Akakievich was beginning to make excuses, but they all declared that it was uncivil of him, that it would be simply a shame and a disgrace that he could not possibly refuse. So, he finally relented, and later felt pleased about it when he remembered that through this he would have the opportunity of going out in the evening, too, in his new overcoat. That whole day was for Akaky Akakievich the most triumphant and festive day in his life. He returned home in the happiest frame of mind, took off the overcoat, and hung it carefully on the wall, admiring the cloth and lining once more, and then pulled out his old "dressing gown," now completely falling apart, and put it next to his new overcoat to compare the two. He glanced at it and laughed: the difference was enormous! And long afterwards he went on laughing at dinner, as the position in which the "dressing gown" was placed recurred to his mind. He dined in excellent spirits and after dinner wrote nothing, no papers at all, but just relaxed for a little while on his bed, till it got dark; then, without putting things off, he dressed, put on his overcoat, and went out into the street. Where precisely the clerk who had invited him lived we regret to say we cannot tell; our memory is beginning to fail sadly, and everything there in Petersburg, all the streets and houses, are so blurred and muddled in our head that it is a very difficult business to put anything in orderly fashion. Regardless of that, there is no doubt that the clerk lived in the better part of the town and consequently a very long distance from Akaky Akakievich. At first Akaky Akakievich had to walk through deserted streets, scantily lighted, but as he approached his destination the streets became more lively, more full of people, and more brightly lighted; passersby began to be more frequent, ladies began to appear, here and there, beautifully dressed, and beaver collars were to be seen on the men. Cabmen with wooden, railed sledges, studded with brass-topped nails, were less frequently seen; on the other hand, jaunty drivers in raspberry-colored velvet caps, with lacquered sledges and bearskin rugs, appeared, and carriages with decorated boxes dashed along the streets, their wheels crunching through the snow.

Akaky Akakievich looked at all this as a novelty; for several years he had not gone out into the streets in the evening. He stopped with curiosity before a lighted shop window to look at a picture in which a beautiful woman was represented in the act of taking off her shoe and displaying as she did so the whole of a very shapely leg, while behind her back a gentleman with whiskers and a handsome imperial[1] on his chin was sticking his head in at the door. Akaky Akakievich shook his head and smiled and then went on his way. Why did he smile? Was it because he had come across something quite unfamiliar to him, though every man retains some instinctive feeling on the subject, or was it that he reflected, like many other clerks, as follows: "Well, those Frenchmen! It's beyond anything! If they go in for anything of the sort, it really is . . . !" Though possibly he did not even think that; there is no creeping into a man's soul and finding out all that he thinks. At last he reached the house in which the assistant head clerk lived in fine style; there was a lamp burning on the stairs, and the apartment was on the second floor. As he went into the hall Akaky Akakievich saw rows of galoshes. Among them in the middle of the room stood a hissing samovar puffing clouds of steam. On the walls hung coats and cloaks among which some actually had beaver collars or velvet lapels. From the other side of the wall there came noise and talk, which suddenly became clear and loud when the door opened and the footman came out with a tray full of empty glasses, a jug of cream, and a basket of biscuits. It was evident that the clerks had arrived long before and had already drunk their first glass of tea. Akaky Akakievich, after hanging up his coat with his own hands, went into the room, and at the same moment there flashed before his eyes a vision of candles, clerks, pipes, and card tables, together with the confused sounds of conversation rising up on all sides and the noise of moving chairs. He stopped very awkwardly in the middle of the room, looking about and trying to think of what to do, but he was noticed and received with a shout and they all went at once into the hall and again took a look at his overcoat. Though Akaky Akakievich was somewhat embarrassed, yet, being a simple-hearted man, he could not help being pleased at seeing how they all admired his coat. Then of course they all abandoned him and his coat, and turned their attention as usual to the tables set for whist. All this—the noise, the talk, and the crowd of people—was strange and wonderful to Akaky Akakievich. He simply did not know how to behave, what to do with his arms and legs and his whole body; at last he sat down beside the players, looked at the cards, stared first at one and then at another of the faces, and in a little while, feeling bored, began to yawn—especially since it was long past the time at which he usually went to bed. He tried to say goodbye to his hosts, but they would not let him go, saying that he absolutely must have a glass of champagne in honor of the new coat. An hour later supper was served, consisting of salad, cold veal, pastry and pies from the bakery, and champagne. They made Akaky Akakievich drink two glasses, after which he felt that things were much more cheerful, though he could not forget that it was twelve o'clock, and that he ought to have been home long ago. That his host might not take it into his head to detain him, he slipped out of the room, hunted in the hall for his coat, which he found, not without regret, lying on the floor, shook it, removed some fluff from it, put it on, and went down the stairs into the street. It was still light in the streets. Some little grocery shops, those perpetual clubs for servants and all sorts of people, were open; others which were closed showed, however, a long streak of light at every crack of the door, proving that they were not yet deserted, and probably maids and menservants were still finishing their conversation

---

[1]*imperial* A small pointed beard.

and discussion, driving their masters to utter perplexity as to their whereabouts. Akaky Akakievich walked along in a cheerful state of mind; he was even on the point of running, goodness knows why, after a lady of some sort who passed by like lightning with every part of her frame in violent motion. He checked himself at once, however, and again walked along very gently, feeling positively surprised at the inexplicable impulse that had seized him. Soon the deserted streets, which are not particularly cheerful by day and even less so in the evening, stretched before him. Now they were still more dead and deserted; the light of street lamps was scantier, the oil evidently running low; then came wooden houses and fences; not a soul anywhere; only the snow gleamed on the streets and the low-pitched slumbering hovels looked black and gloomy with their closed shutters. He approached the spot where the street was intersected by an endless square, which looked like a fearful desert with its houses scarcely visible on the far side.

In the distance, goodness knows where, there was a gleam of light from some sentry box which seemed to be at the end of the world. Akaky Akakievich's lightheartedness faded. He stepped into the square, not without uneasiness, as though his heart had a premonition of evil. He looked behind him and to both sides—it was as though the sea were all around him. "No, better not look," he thought, and walked on, shutting his eyes, and when he opened them to see whether the end of the square was near, he suddenly saw standing before him, almost under his very nose, some men with mustaches; just what they were like he could not even distinguish. There was a mist before his eyes, and a throbbing in his chest. "Why, that overcoat is mine!" said one of them in a voice like a clap of thunder, seizing him by the collar. Akaky Akakievich was on the point of shouting "Help" when another put a fist the size of a clerk's head against his lips, saying: "You just shout now." Akaky Akakievich felt only that they took the overcoat off, and gave him a kick with their knees, and he fell on his face in the snow and was conscious of nothing more. A few minutes later he recovered consciousness and got up on his feet, but there was no one there. He felt that it was cold on the ground and that he had no overcoat, and began screaming, but it seemed as though his voice would not carry to the end of the square. Overwhelmed with despair and continuing to scream, he ran across the square straight to the sentry box beside which stood a policeman leaning on his halberd and, so it seemed, looking with curiosity to see who the devil the man was who was screaming and running toward him from the distance. As Akaky Akakievich reached him, he began breathlessly shouting that he was asleep and not looking after his duty not to see that a man was being robbed. The policeman answered that he had seen nothing, that he had only seen him stopped in the middle of the square by two men, and supposed that they were his friends, and that, instead of abusing him for nothing, he had better go the next day to the police inspector, who would certainly find out who had taken the overcoat. Akaky Akakievich ran home in a terrible state: his hair, which was still comparatively abundant on his temples and the back of his head, was completely disheveled; his sides and chest and his trousers were all covered with snow. When his old landlady heard a fearful knock at the door, she jumped hurriedly out of bed and, with only one slipper on, ran to open it, modestly holding her chemise over her bosom; but when she opened it she stepped back, seeing in what a state Akaky Akakievich was. When he told her what had happened, she clasped her hands in horror and said that he must go straight to the district commissioner, because the local police inspector would deceive him, make promises, and lead him a dance;[2] that it would be best of all to go to the district

---

[2] *lead him a dance*   Lead him along without results.

commissioner, and that she knew him, because Anna, the Finnish girl who was once her cook, was now in service as a nurse at the commissioner's; and that she often saw him himself when he passed by their house, and that he used to be every Sunday at church too, saying his prayers and at the same time looking good-humoredly at everyone, and that therefore by every token he must be a kindhearted man. After listening to this advice, Akaky Akakievich made his way very gloomily to his room, and how he spent that night I leave to the imagination of those who are in the least able to picture the position of others.

Early in the morning he set off to the police commissioner's but was told that he was asleep. He came at ten o'clock, he was told again that he was asleep; he came at eleven and was told that the commissioner was not at home; he came at dinnertime, but the clerks in the anteroom would not let him in, and insisted on knowing what was the matter and what business had brought him and exactly what had happened; so that at last Akaky Akakievich for the first time in his life tried to show the strength of his character and said curtly that he must see the commissioner himself, and they dare not refuse to admit him, that he had come from the department on government business, and that if he made complaint of them they would see. The clerks dared say nothing to this, and one of them went to summon the commissioner. The latter received his story of being robbed of his overcoat in an extremely peculiar manner. Instead of attending to the main point, he began asking Akaky Akakievich questions: why had he been coming home so late? wasn't he going, or hadn't he been, to some bawdy house? so that Akaky Akakievich was overwhelmed with confusion, and went away without knowing whether or not the proper measures would be taken regarding his overcoat. He was absent from the office all that day (the only time that it had happened in his life). Next day he appeared with a pale face, wearing his old "dressing gown," which had become a still more pitiful sight. The news of the theft of the overcoat—though there were clerks who did not let even this chance slip of jeering at Akaky Akakievich—touched many of them. They decided on the spot to get up a collection for him, but collected only a very trifling sum, because the clerks had already spent a good deal contributing to the director's portrait and on the purchase of a book, at the suggestion of the head of their department, who was a friend of the author, and so the total realized was very insignificant. One of the clerks, moved by compassion, ventured at any rate to assist Akaky Akakievich with good advice, telling him not to go to the local police inspector, because, though it might happen that the latter might succeed in finding his overcoat because he wanted to impress his superiors, it would remain in the possession of the police unless he presented legal proofs that it belonged to him; he urged that by far the best thing would be to appeal to a Person of Consequence; that the Person of Consequence, by writing and getting into communication with the proper authorities, could push the matter through more successfully. There was nothing else to do. Akaky Akakievich made up his mind to go to the Person of Consequence. What precisely was the nature of the functions of the Person of Consequence has remained a matter of uncertainty. It must be noted that this Person of Consequence had only lately become a person of consequence, and until recently had been a person of no consequence. Though, indeed, his position even now was not reckoned of consequence in comparison with others of still greater consequence. But there is always to be found a circle of persons to whom a person of little consequence in the eyes of others is a person of consequence. It is true that he did his utmost to increase the consequence of his position in various ways, for instance by insisting that his subordinates should come out onto the stairs to meet him when he arrived at his office; that no one should venture to approach him directly but all proceedings should follow the strictest chain of command; that a collegiate registrar should report the matter to the governmental secretary; and the governmental secretary to the titular councilors or whomsoever it might be, and that business should only reach him through this channel. Everyone in Holy Russia has a craze for imitation; everyone apes and mimics his superiors. I have actually been told that a titular councilor who was put in charge of a small separate office, immediately partitioned off a special room for himself, calling it the head office, and posted lackeys at the door with red collars and gold braid, who took hold of the handle of the door and opened it for everyone who went in, though the "head office" was so tiny that it was with difficulty that an ordinary writing desk could be put into it. The manners and habits of the Person of Consequence were dignified and majestic, but hardly subtle. The chief foundation of his system was strictness; "strictness, strictness, and—strictness!" he used to say, and at the last word he would look very significantly at the person he was addressing, though, indeed, he had no reason to do so, for the dozen clerks who made up the whole administrative mechanism of his office stood in appropriate awe of him; any clerk who saw him in the distance would leave his work and remain standing at attention till his superior had left the room. His conversation with his subordinates was usually marked by severity and almost confined to three phrases: "How dare you? Do you know to whom you are speaking? Do you understand who I am?" He was, however, at heart a good-natured man, pleasant and obliging with his colleagues; but his advancement to a high rank had completely turned his head. When he received it, he was perplexed, thrown off his balance, and quite at a loss as to how to behave. If he chanced to be with his equals, he was still quite a decent man, a very gentlemanly man, in fact, and in many ways even an intelligent man; but as soon as he was in company with men who were even one grade below him, there was simply no doing anything with him: he sat silent and his position excited compassion, the more so as he himself felt that he might have been spending his time to so much more advantage. At times there could be seen in his eyes an intense desire to join in some interesting conversation, but he was restrained by the doubt whether it would not be too much on his part, whether it would not be too great a familiarity and lowering of his dignity, and in consequence of these reflections he remained everlastingly in the same mute condition, only uttering from time to time monosyllabic sounds, and in this way he gained the reputation of being a terrible bore.

So this was the Person of Consequence to whom our friend Akaky Akakievich appealed, and he appealed to him at a most unpropitious moment, very unfortunate for himself, though fortunate, indeed, for the Person of Consequence. The latter happened to be in his study, talking in the very best of spirits with an old friend of his childhood who had only just arrived and whom he had not seen for several years. It was at this moment that he was informed that a man called Bashmachkin was asking to see him. He asked abruptly, "What sort of man is he?" and received the answer, "A government clerk." Ah! he can wait. I haven't time now," said the Person of Consequence. Here I must observe that this was a complete lie on the part of the Person of Consequence; he had time; his friend and he had long ago said all they had to say to each other and their conversation had begun to be broken by very long pauses during which they merely slapped each other on the knee, saying, "So that's how things are, Ivan Abramovich!"—"So that's it, Stepan Varlamovich!" but, despite that, he told the clerk to wait in order to show his friend, who had left the civil service some years before and was living at home in the country, how long clerks had to wait for him. At last, after they had talked or rather been silent, to their heart's content and had smoked a cigar in very comfortable armchairs with sloping backs, he seemed suddenly to recollect, and said to the secretary, who was standing at the door with papers for his signature: "Oh, by the way, there is a clerk waiting, isn't there? tell him he can come in." When he saw Akaky Akakievich's meek appearance and old uniform, he turned to him at once and said: "What do you want?" in a firm and abrupt voice, which he had purposely rehearsed in his own room in solitude before the mirror for a week before receiving his present post and the grade of a general. Akaky Akakievich, who was overwhelmed with appropriate awe beforehand, was somewhat confused and, as far as his tongue would allow him, explained to the best of his powers, with even more frequent "ers" than usual, that he had had a perfectly new overcoat and now he had been robbed of it in the most inhuman way, and that now he had come to beg him by his intervention either to correspond with his honor, the head police commissioner, or anybody else, and find the overcoat. This mode of proceeding struck the general for some reason as too familiar. "What next, sir?" he went on abruptly. "Don't you know the way to proceed? To whom are you addressing yourself? Don't you know how things are done? You ought first to have handed in a petition to the office; it would have gone to the head clerk of the room, and to the head clerk of the section; then it would have been handed to the secretary and the secretary would have brought it to me. . . ."

"But, your Excellency," said Akaky Akakievich, trying to gather the drop of courage he possessed and feeling at the same time that he was perspiring all over, "I ventured, your Excellency, to trouble you because secretaries . . . er . . . are people you can't depend on. . . ."

"What? what? what?" said the Person of Consequence, "where did you get hold of that attitude? where did you pick up such ideas? What insubordination is spreading among young men against their superiors and their chiefs!" The Person of Consequence did not apparently observe that Akaky Akakievich was well over fifty, and therefore if he could have been called a young man it would only have been in comparison to a man of seventy. "Do you know to whom you are speaking? Do you understand who I am? Do you understand that, I ask you?" At this point he stamped, and raised his voice to such a powerful note that Akaky Akakievich was not the only one to be terrified. Akaky Akakievich was positively petrified; he staggered, trembling all over, and could not stand; if the porters had not run up to support him, he would have flopped on the floor; he was led out almost unconscious. The Person of Consequence, pleased that the effect had surpassed his expectations and enchanted at the idea that his words could even deprive a man of consciousness, stole a sideway glance at his friend to see how he was taking it, and perceived not without satisfaction that his friend was feeling very uncertain and even beginning to be a little terrified himself.

How he got downstairs, how he went out into the street—of all that Akaky Akakievich remembered nothing; he had no feeling in his arms or his legs. In all his life he had never been so severely reprimanded by a general, and this was by one of another department, too. He went out into the snowstorm that was whistling through the streets, with his mouth open, and as he went he stumbled off the pavement; the wind, as its way is in Petersburg, blew upon him from all points of the compass and from every side street. In an instant it had blown a quinsy into his throat, and when he got home he was not able to utter a word; he went to bed with a swollen face and throat. That's how violent the effects of an appropriate reprimand can be!

Next day he was in a high fever. Thanks to the gracious assistance of the Petersburg climate, the disease made more rapid progress than could have been expected, and when the doctor came, after feeling his pulse he could find nothing to do but prescribe a poultice, and that simply so that the patient might not be left without the benefit of medical assistance; however, two days later he informed him that his end was at hand, after which he turned to Akaky Akakievich's landlady and said: "And you had better lose no time, my good woman, but order him now a pine coffin, for an oak one will be too expensive for him." Whether Akaky Akakievich heard these fateful words or not, whether they produced a shattering effect upon him, and whether he regretted his pitiful life, no one can tell, for he was constantly in delirium and fever. Apparitions, each stranger than the one before, were continually haunting him: first he saw Petrovich and was ordering him to make an overcoat trimmed with some sort of traps for robbers, who were, he believed, continually under the bed, and he was calling his landlady every minute to pull out a thief who had even got under the quilt; then he kept asking why his old "dressing gown" was hanging before him when he had a new overcoat; then he thought he was standing before the general listening to the appropriate reprimand and saying, "I am sorry, your Excellency"; then finally he became abusive, uttering the most awful language, so that his old landlady positively crossed herself, having never heard anything of the kind from him before, and the more horrified because these dreadful words followed immediately upon the phrase "your Excellency." Later on, his talk was merely a medley of nonsense, so that it was quite unintelligible; all that was evident was that his incoherent words and thoughts were concerned with nothing but the overcoat. At last poor Akaky Akakievich gave up the ghost. No seal was put upon his room nor upon his things, because, in the first place, he had no heirs and, in the second, the property left was very small, to wit, a bundle of quills, a quire of white government paper, three pairs of socks, two or three buttons that had come off his trousers, and the "dressing gown" with which the reader is already familiar. Who came into all his wealth God only knows; even I who tell the tale must admit that I have not bothered to inquire. And Petersburg carried on without Akaky Akakievich, as though, indeed, he had never been in the city. A creature had vanished and departed whose cause no one had championed, who was dear to no one, of interest to no one, who never attracted the attention of a naturalist, though the latter does not disdain to fix a common fly upon a pin and look at him under the microscope—a creature who bore patiently the jeers of the office and for no particular reason went to his grave, though even he at the very end of his life was visited by an exalted guest in the form of an overcoat that for one instant brought color into his poor, drab life—a creature on whom disease fell as it falls upon the heads of the mighty ones of this world . . . !

Several days after his death, a messenger from the department was sent to his lodgings with instructions that he should go at once to the office, for his chief was asking for him; but the messenger was obliged to return without him, explaining that he could not come, and to the inquiry "Why?" he added, "Well, you see, the fact is he is dead; he was buried three days ago." This was how they learned at the office of the death of Akaky Akakievich, and the next day there was sitting in his seat a new clerk who was very much taller and who wrote not in the same straight handwriting but made his letters more slanting and crooked.

But who could have imagined that this was not all there was to tell about Akaky Akakievich, that he was destined for a few days to make his presence felt in the world after his death, as though to make up for his life having been unnoticed by anyone? But so it happened, and our little story unexpectedly finishes with a fantastic ending.

Rumors were suddenly floating about Petersburg that in the neighborhood of the Kalinkin Bridge and for a little distance beyond, a corpse had begun appearing at night in the form of a clerk looking for a stolen overcoat, and stripping from the shoulders of all passers-by, regardless of grade and calling, overcoats of all descriptions—trimmed with cat fur or beaver or padded, lined with raccoon, fox, and bear—made, in fact of all sorts of skin which men have adapted for the covering of their own. One of the clerks of the department saw the corpse with his own eyes and at once recognized it as Akaky Akakievich; but it excited in him such terror that he ran away as fast as his legs could carry him and so could not get a very clear view of him, and only saw him hold up his finger threateningly in the distance.

From all sides complaints were continually coming that backs and shoulders, not of mere titular councilors, but even of upper court councilors, had been exposed to catching cold, as a result of being stripped of their overcoats. Orders were given to the police to catch the corpse regardless of trouble or expense, dead or alive, and to punish him severely, as an example to others, and, indeed, they very nearly succeeded in doing so. The policeman of one district in Kiryushkin Alley snatched a corpse by the collar on the spot of the crime in the very act of attempting to snatch a frieze overcoat from a retired musician, who used, in his day, to play the flute. Having caught him by the collar, he shouted until he had brought two other policemen whom he ordered to hold the corpse while he felt just a minute in his boot to get out a snuffbox in order to revive his nose which had six times in his life been frostbitten, but the snuff was probably so strong that not even a dead man could stand it. The policeman had hardly had time to put his finger over his right nostril and draw up some snuff in the left when the corpse sneezed violently right into the eyes of all three. While they were putting their fists up to wipe their eyes, the corpse completely vanished, so that they were not even sure whether he had actually been in their hands. From that time forward, the policemen had such a horror of the dead that they were even afraid to seize the living and confined themselves to shouting from the distance. "Hey, you! Move on!" and the clerk's body began to appear even on the other side of the Kalinkin Bridge, terrorizing all timid people.

We have, however, quite neglected the Person of Consequence, who may in reality almost be said to be the cause of the fantastic ending of this perfectly true story. To begin with, my duty requires me to do justice to the Person of Consequence by recording that soon after poor Akaky Akakievich had gone away crushed to powder, he felt something not unlike regret. Sympathy was a feeling not unknown to him; his heart was open to many kindly impulses, although his exalted grade very often prevented them from being shown. As soon as his friend had gone out of his study, he even began brooding over poor Akaky Akakievich, and from that time forward, he was almost every day haunted by the image of the poor clerk who had been unable to survive the official reprimand. The thought of the man so worried him that a week later he actually decided to send a clerk to find out how he was and whether he really could help him in any way. And when they brought him word that Akaky Akakievich had died suddenly in a delirium and fever, it made a great impression on him; his conscience reproached him and he was depressed all day. Anxious to distract his mind and to forget the unpleasant incident, he went to spend the evening with one of his friends, where he found respectable company, and what was best of all, almost everyone was of the same grade so that he was able to be quite uninhibited. This had a wonderful effect on his spirits. He let himself go, became affable and genial—in short, spent a very agreeable evening. At supper he drank a couple of glasses of champagne—a proceeding which we all know is not a bad recipe for cheerfulness. The champagne made him inclined to do something unusual, and he decided not to go home yet but to visit a lady of his acquaintance, a certain Karolina Ivanovna—a lady apparently of German extraction, for whom he entertained extremely friendly feelings. It must be noted that the Person of Consequence was a man no longer young. He was an excellent husband, and the respectable father of a family. He had two sons, one already serving in an office, and a nice-looking daughter of sixteen with a rather turned-up, pretty little nose, who used to come every morning to kiss his hand, saying: "*Bon jour, Papa.*" His wife, who was still blooming and decidedly good-looking, indeed, used first to give him her hand to kiss and then turning his hand over would kiss it. But though the Person of Consequence was perfectly satisfied with the pleasant amenities of his domestic life, he thought it proper to have a lady friend in another quarter of the town. This lady friend was not a bit better looking nor younger than his wife, but these puzzling things exist in the world and it is not our business to criticize them. And so the Person of Consequence went downstairs, got into his sledge, and said to his coachman, "To Karolina Ivanovna." While luxuriously wrapped in his warm fur coat he remained in that agreeable frame of mind sweeter to a Russian than anything that could be invented, that is, when one thinks of nothing while thoughts come into the mind by themselves, one pleasanter than the other, without your having to bother following them or looking for them. Full of satisfaction, he recalled all the amusing moments of the evening he had spent, all the phrases that had started the intimate circle of friends laughing; many of them he repeated in an undertone and found then as amusing as before, and so, very naturally, laughed very heartily at them again. From time to time, however, he was disturbed by a gust of wind which, blowing suddenly, God knows why or where from, cut him in the face, pelting him with flakes of snow, puffing out his coat collar like a sail, or suddenly flinging it with unnatural force over his head and giving him endless trouble to extricate himself from it. All at once, the Person of Consequence felt that someone had clutched him very tightly by the collar. Turning around he saw a short man in a shabby old uniform, and not without horror recognized him as Akaky Akakievich. The clerk's face was white as snow and looked like that of a corpse, but the horror of the Person of Consequence was beyond all bounds when he saw the mouth of the corpse distorted into speech, and breathing upon him the chill of the grave, it uttered, the following words: "Ah, so here you are at last! At last I've . . . er . . . caught you by the collar. It's your overcoat I want; you refused to help me and abused me in the bargain! So now give me yours!" The poor Person of Consequence very nearly dropped dead. Resolute and determined as he was in his office and before subordinates in general, and though anyone looking at his manly air and figure would have said: "Oh, what a man of character!" yet in this situation he felt, like very many persons of heroic appearance, such terror that not without reason he began to be afraid he would have some sort of fit. He actually flung his overcoat off his shoulders as far as he could and shouted to his coachman in an unnatural voice: "Drive home! Let's get out of here!" The coachman, hearing the tone which he had only heard in critical moments and then accompanied by something even more tangible, hunched his shoulders up to his ears in case of worse following, swung his whip, and flew on like an arrow. In a little over six minutes, the Person of Consequence was at the entrance of his own house. Pale, panic-stricken, and without his overcoat, he arrived home instead of at Karolina Ivanovna's, dragged himself to his own room, and spent the night in great distress, so that next morning his daughter said to him at breakfast, "You look very pale today, Papa"; but her papa remained mute and said not a word to anyone of what had happened to him, where he had been, and where he had been going. The incident made a great impression upon him. Indeed, it happened far more rarely that he said to his subordinates, "How dare you? Do you understand who I am?" and he never uttered those words at all until he had first heard all the facts of the case.

What was even more remarkable is that from that time on the apparition of the dead clerk ceased entirely; apparently the general's overcoat had fitted him perfectly; anyway nothing more was heard of overcoats being snatched from anyone. Many restless and anxious people refused, however, to be pacified, and still maintained that in remote parts of the town the dead clerk went on appearing. One policeman, in Kolomna, for instance, saw with his own eyes an apparition appear from behind a house; but, being by natural constitution somewhat frail—so much so that on one occasion an ordinary grown-up suckling pig, making a sudden dash out of some private building, knocked him off his feet to the great amusement of the cabmen standing around, whom he fined two kopeks each for snuff for such disrespect—he did not dare to stop it, and so followed it in the dark until the apparition suddenly looked around and, stopping, asked him: "What do you want?" displaying a huge fist such as you never see among the living. The policeman said: "Nothing," and turned back on the spot. This apparition, however, was considerably taller and adorned with immense mustaches, and, directing its steps apparently toward Obukhov Bridge, vanished into the darkness of the night.

[1840]
Translated by
CONSTANCE GARNETT

Questions

1. How is Akaky characterized? On what basis does the reader sympathize with him? What is the narrator's attitude toward him? Why is he ridiculed by his office associates?

2. How would you describe the tone of the story? How does it contribute to one's understanding of Akaky's plight?

3. What does the overcoat symbolize?

4. How do the fantastic elements of the story's ending contribute to its meaning? What would be lost if the story ended with Akaky's death?

5. What does the story suggest about bureaucracy? About social justice? About the human condition?

Nadine Gordimer
(b. 1923)
South Africa

In an interview published in Women Writers Talk (1989), edited by Olga Kenyon, Nadine Gordimer had this to say about the political evolution of South Africa:

> [T]here are some extraordinary black and white people who are prepared to take a Pascalian wager on the fact that there is a way, that there must be a way. It goes beyond polarisation, it cannot happen while the situation is what it is. It can only be after the power structure has changed. But the fact is that if whites want to go on living in South Africa, they have to change. It's not a matter of just letting blacks in—white life is already dead, over. The big question is, given the kind of conditioning we've had for 300 years, is it possible to strike that down and make a common culture with the blacks?

Since 1953, when she published her first novel, The Lying Days, Nadine Gordimer has been aligned with the liberal white consciousness of South Africa. She was born in the Transvaal in 1923. Her father was a shopkeeper, her mother a housewife. A childhood illness kept Gordimer out of school until she was 14, by which time she was already an avid reader. By 15 she had published her first short story. It was not until she was somewhat older that she became aware of the South African political situation, and it was not until she was 30 that her first novel was published. Beginning with A World of Strangers (1958), Gordimer's novels focus directly on the South African racial situation. The most famous of these works include A Guest of Honor (1970), The Conservationist (1974), Burger's Daughter (1979), July's People (1981), A Sport of Nature (1987), My Son's Story (1990), None to Accompany Me (1994), and The House Gun (1998). Gordimer has also published 10 volumes of short stories, as well as several volumes of nonfiction. She was awarded the Nobel Prize for literature in 1991.

Asked by Olga Kenyon what it means to be a white South African, Gordimer responded as follows:

> You have to show that you support change. In my case that you support a complete revolution, if possible a peaceful one. I use revolution in a broad sense, a complete change of the whole political organisation, from grass roots. It's not enough for a white to say "Right, I'll be prepared to live under black majority rule," and sit back, waiting for it to come. You also have to work positively, in whatever way you can, as a human being.

"Country Lovers," from Soldier's Embrace (1975), a collection of short stories, was originally published paired with another story and jointly titled "Town and Country Lovers."

COUNTRY LOVERS

The farm children play together when they are small; but once the white children go away to school they soon don't play together any more, even in the holidays. Although most of the black children get some sort of schooling, they drop every year farther behind the grades passed by the white children; the childish vocabulary, the child's exploration of the adventurous possibilities of dam, koppies, mealie lands and veld—there comes a time when the white children have surpassed these with the vocabulary of boarding-school and the possibilities of interschool sports matches and the kind of adventures seen at the cinema. This usefully coincides with the age of twelve or thirteen; so that by the time early adolescence is reached, the black children are making, along with the bodily changes common to all, an easy transition to adult forms of address, beginning to call their old playmates *missus* and *baasie*—little master.

The trouble was Paulus Eysendyck did not seem to realize that Thebedi was now simply one of the crowd of farm children down at the kraal, recognizable in his sisters' old clothes. The first Christmas holidays after he had gone to boarding-school he brought home for Thebedi a painted box he had made in his wood-work class. He had to give it to her secretly because he had nothing for the other children at the kraal. And she gave him, before he went back to school, a bracelet she had made of thin brass wire and the grey-and-white beans of the castor-oil crop his father cultivated. (When they used to play together, she was the one who had taught Paulus how to make clay oxen for their toy spans.) There was a craze, even in the *platteland* towns like the one where he was at school, for boys to wear elephant-hair and other bracelets beside their watch-straps; his was admired, friends asked him to get similar ones for them. He said the natives made them on his father's farm and he would try.

When he was fifteen, six feet tall, and tramping round at school dances with the girls from the 'sister' school in the same town; when he had learnt how to tease and flirt and fondle quite intimately these girls who were the daughters of prosperous farmers like his father; when he had even met one who, at a wedding he had attended with his parents on a nearby farm, had let him do with her in a locked storeroom what people did when they made love—when he was as far from his childhood as all this, he still brought home from a shop in town a red plastic belt and gilt hoop ear-rings for the black girl, Thebedi. She told her father the missus had given these to her as a reward for some work she had done—it was true she sometimes was called to help out in the farmhouse. She told the girls in the kraal that she had a sweetheart nobody knew about, far away, away on another farm, and they giggled, and teased, and admired her. There was a boy in the kraal called Njabulo who said he wished he could have bought her a belt and ear-rings.

When the farmer's son was home for the holidays she wandered far from the kraal and her companions. He went for walks alone. They had not arranged this; it was an urge each followed independently. He knew it was she, from a long way off. She knew that his dog would not bark at her. Down at the dried-up river-bed where five or six years ago the children had caught a leguaan one great day—a creature that combined ideally the size and ferocious aspect of the crocodile with the harmlessness of the lizard—they squatted side by side on the earth bank. He told her traveller's tales: about school, about the punishments at school, particularly, exaggerating both their nature and his indifference to them. He told her about the town of Middleburg, which she had never seen. She had nothing to tell but she prompted with many questions, like any good listener. While he talked he twisted and tugged at the roots of white stinkwood and Cape willow trees that looped out of the eroded earth around them. It had always been a good spot for children's games, down there hidden by the mesh of old, ant-eaten trees held in place by vigorous ones, wild asparagus bushing up between the trunks, and here and there prickly-pear cactus sunken-skinned and bristly, like an old man's face, keeping alive sapless until the next rainy season. She punctured the dry hide of a prickly-pear again and again with a sharp stick while she listened. She laughed a lot at what he told her, sometimes dropping her face on her knees, sharing amusement with the cool shady earth beneath her bare feet. She put on her pair of shoes—white sandals, thickly Blanco-ed against the farm dust—when he was on the farm, but these were taken off and laid aside, at the river-bed.

One summer afternoon when there was water flowing there and it was very hot she waded in as they used to do when they were children, her dress bunched modestly and tucked into the legs of her pants. The schoolgirls he went swimming with at dams or pools on neighbouring farms wore bikinis but the sight of their dazzling bellies and thighs in the sunlight had never made him feel what he felt now, when the girl came up the bank and sat beside him, the drops of water beading off her dark legs the only points of light in the earth-smelling, deep shade. They were not afraid of one another, they had known one another always; he did with her what he had done that time in the storeroom at the wedding, and this time it was so lovely, so lovely, he was surprised . . . and she was surprised by it, too—he could see in her dark face that was part of the shade, with her big dark eyes, shiny as soft water, watching him attentively: as she had when they used to huddle over their teams of mud oxen, as she had when he told her about detention weekends at school.

They went to the river-bed often through those summer holidays. They met just before the light went, as it does quite quickly, and each returned home with the dark—she to her mother's hut, he to the farmhouse—in time for the evening meal. He did not tell her about school or town any more. She did not ask questions any longer. He told her, each time, when they would meet again. Once or twice it was very early in the morning; the lowing of the cows being driven to graze came to them where they lay, dividing them with unspoken recognition of the sound read in their two pairs of eyes, opening so close to each other.

He was a popular boy at school. He was in the second, then the first soccer team. The head girl of the 'sister' school was said to have a crush on him; he didn't particularly like her, but there was a pretty blonde who put up her long hair into a kind of doughnut with a black ribbon round it, whom he took to see films when the schoolboys and girls had a free Saturday afternoon. He had been driving tractors and other farm vehicles since he was ten years old, and as soon as he was eighteen he got a driver's licence and in the holidays, this last year of his school life, he took neighbours' daughters to dances and to the drive-in cinema that had just opened twenty kilometres from the farm. His sisters were married, by then; his parents often left him in charge of the farm over the weekend while they visited the young wives and grandchildren.

When Thebedi saw the farmer and his wife drive away on a Saturday afternoon, the boot of their Mercedes filled with fresh-killed poultry and vegetables from the garden that it was part of her father's work to tend, she knew that she must come not to the river-bed but up to the house. The house was an old one, thick-walled, dark against the heat. The kitchen was its lively thoroughfare, with servants, food supplies, begging cats and dogs, pots boiling over, washing being damped for ironing, and the big deep-freeze the missus had ordered from town, bearing a crocheted mat and a vase of plastic irises. But the dining-room with the bulging-legged heavy table was shut up in its rich, old smell of soup and tomato sauce. The sitting-room curtains were drawn and the T.V. set silent. The door of the parents' bedroom was locked and the empty rooms where the girls had slept had sheets of plastic spread over the beds. It was in one of these that she and the farmer's son stayed together whole nights—almost: she had to get away before the house servants, who knew her, came in at dawn. There was a risk someone would discover her or traces of her presence if he took her to his own bedroom, although she had looked into it many times when she was helping out in the house and knew well, there, the row of silver cups he had won at school.

When she was eighteen and the farmer's son nineteen and working with his father on the farm before entering a veterinary college, the young man Njabulo asked her father for her. Njabulo's parents met with hers and the money he was to pay in place of the cows it is customary to give a prospective bride's parents was settled upon. He had no cows to offer; he was a labourer on the Eysendyck farm, like her father. A bright youngster; old Eysendyck had taught him brick-laying and was using him for odd jobs in construction, around the place. She did not tell the farmer's son that her parents had arranged for her to marry. She did not tell him, either, before he left for his first term at the veterinary college, that she thought she was going to have a baby. Two months after her marriage to Njabulo, she gave birth to a daughter. There was no disgrace in that; among her people it is customary for a young man to make sure, before marriage, that the chosen girl is not barren, and Njabulo had made love to her then. But the infant was very light and did not quickly grow darker as most African babies do. Already at birth there was on its head a quantity of straight, fine floss, like that which carries the seeds of certain weeds in the veld. The unfocused eyes it opened were grey flecked with yellow. Njabulo was the matt, opaque coffee-grounds colour that has always been called black; the colour of Thebedi's legs on which beaded water looked oyster-shell blue, the same colour as Thebedi's face, where the black eyes, with their interested gaze and clear whites, were so dominant.

Njabulo made no complaint. Out of his farm labourer's earnings he bought from the Indian store a cellophane-windowed pack containing a pink plastic bath, six napkins, a card of safety pins, a knitted jacket, cap and bootees, a dress, and a tin of Johnson's Baby Powder, for Thebedi's baby.

When it was two weeks old Paulus Eysendyck arrived home from the veterinary college for the holidays. He drank a glass of fresh, still-warm milk in the childhood familiarity of his mother's kitchen and heard her discussing with the old house-servant where they could get a reliable substitute to help out now that the girl Thebedi had had a baby. For the first time since he was a small boy he came right into the kraal. It was eleven o'clock in the morning. The men were at work in the lands. He looked about him, urgently; the women turned away, each not wanting to be the one approached to point out where Thebedi lived. Thebedi appeared, coming slowly from the hut Njabulo had built in white man's style, with a tin chimney, and a proper window with glass panes set in straight as walls made of unfired bricks would allow. She greeted him with hands brought together and a token movement representing the respectful bob with which she was accustomed to acknowledge she was in the presence of his father or mother. He lowered his head under the doorway of her home and went in. He said, "I want to see. Show me."

She had taken the bundle off her back before she came out into the light to face him. She moved between the iron bedstead made up with Najbulo's checked blankets and the small wooden table where the pink plastic bath stood among food and kitchen pots, and picked up the bundle from the snugly-blanketed grocer's box where it lay. The infant was asleep; she revealed the closed, pale, plump tiny face, with a bubble of spit at the corner of the mouth, the spidery pink hands stirring. She took off the woollen cap and the straight fine hair flew up after it in static electricity, showing gilded strands here and there. He said nothing. She was watching him as she had done when they were little, and the gang of children had trodden down a crop in their games or transgressed in some other way for which he, as the farmer's son, the white one among them, must intercede with the farmer. She disturbed the sleeping face by scratching or tickling gently at a cheek with one finger, and slowly the eyes opened, saw nothing, were still asleep, and then, awake, no longer narrowed, looked out at them, grey with yellowish flecks, his own hazel eyes.

He struggled for a moment with a grimace of tears, anger and self-pity. She could not put out her hand to him. He said, "You haven't been near the house with it?"

She shook her head.

"Never?"

Again she shook her head.

"Don't take it out. Stay inside. Can't you take it away somewhere. You must give it to someone—"

She moved to the door with him.

He said, "I'll see what I will do. I don't know." And then he said: "I feel like killing myself."

Her eyes began to glow, to thicken with tears. For a moment there was the feeling between them that used to come when they were alone down at the river-bed.

He walked out.

Two days later, when his mother and father had left the farm for the day, he appeared again. The women were away on the lands, weeding, as they were employed to do as casual labour in summer; only the very old remained, propped up on the ground outside the huts in the flies and the sun. Thebedi did not ask him in. The child had not been well; it had diarrhoea. He asked where its food was. She said, 'The milk comes from me.' He went into Njabulo's house, where the child lay; she did not follow but stayed outside the door and watched without seeing an old crone who had lost her mind, talking to herself, talking to the fowls who ignored her.

She thought she heard small grunts from the hut, the kind of infant grunt that indicates a full stomach, a deep sleep. After a time, long or short she did not know, he came out and walked away with plodding stride (his father's gait) out of sight, towards his father's house.

The baby was not fed during the night and although she kept telling Njabulo it was sleeping, he saw for himself in the morning that it was dead. He comforted her with words and caresses. She did not cry but simply sat, staring at the door. Her hands were cold as dead chickens' feet to his touch.

Njabulo buried the little baby where farm workers were buried, in the place in the veld the farmer had given them. Some of the mounds had been left to weather away unmarked, others were covered with stones and a few had fallen wooden crosses. He was going to make a cross but before it was finished the police came and dug up the grave and took away the dead baby: someone—one of the other labourers? their women?—had reported that the baby was almost white, that, strong and healthy, it had died suddenly after a visit by the farmer's son. Pathological tests on the infant corpse showed intestinal damage not always consistent with death by natural causes.

Thebedi went for the first time to the country town where Paulus had been to school, to give evidence at the preparatory examination into the charge of murder brought against him. She cried hysterically in the witness box, saying yes, yes (the gilt hoop ear-rings swung in her ears), she saw the accused pouring liquid into the baby's mouth. She said he had threatened to shoot her if she told anyone.

More than a year went by before, in that same town, the case was brought to trial. She came to Court with a new-born baby on her back. She wore gilt hoop ear-rings; she was calm; she said she had not seen what the white man did in the house.

Paulus Eysendyck said he had visited the hut but had not poisoned the child.

The Defence did not contest that there had been a love relationship between the accused and the girl, or that intercourse had taken place, but submitted there was no proof that the child was the accused's.

The judge told the accused there was strong suspicion against him but not enough proof that he had committed the crime. The Court could not accept the girl's evidence because it was clear she had committed perjury either at this trial or at the preparatory examination. There was the suggestion in the mind of the Court that she might be an accomplice in the crime; but, again, insufficient proof.

The judge commended the honourable behaviour of the husband (sitting in court in a brown-and-yellow-quartered golf cap bought for Sundays) who had not rejected his wife and had "even provided clothes for the unfortunate infant out of his slender means."

The verdict on the accused was "not guilty."

The young white man refused to accept the congratulations of press and public and left the Court with his mother's raincoat shielding his face from photographers. His father said to the press, "I will try and carry on as best I can to hold up my head in the district."

Interviewed by the Sunday papers, who spelled her name in a variety of ways, the black girl, speaking in her own language, was quoted beneath her photograph: "It was a thing of our childhood, we don't see each other any more."

[1980]

Questions

1. Which character (Paulus or Thebedi) is more fully realized? Why?
2. Does the fall of *apartheid* suggest a change of any kind in the dynamics of the relationship depicted in Gordimer's story?
3. To what extent does this South African story mirror racial issues in the United States?

Judy Grahn
(b. 1940)

United States

The daughter of working-class parents in Chicago, Judy Grahn began writing poetry at the age of 10 but stopped and did not return to writing until years later. In the meantime, she left home at 17 and attended—and left—five different colleges before pursuing study at San Francisco State College. Subsequently, she spent a number of financially impoverished years working at various odd jobs until, after a nearly fatal illness, she began to write poetry seriously. Finding few sources of publication in the 1960s for her poetry, which candidly reflected her lesbian identity, Grahn cofounded and eventually also served as publisher, editor, and printer for the Women's Press Collective in Oakland, California.

Grahn's first volume of poetry, Edward the Dyke and Other Poems, was published in 1971. A second volume, The Queen of Wands (1982), received the American Book Award that year. In 1977 she published a collection of a decade of her poetry. Turning to nonfiction in Another Mother Tongue: Gay Words, Gay Worlds (1984), Grahn combined history, autobiography, linguistic inquiry, and storytelling to explore gay and lesbian experience in the past and in contemporary society.

Through her writing and teaching, Grahn celebrates female experience, hoping to increase public understanding of both lesbian and feminist issues. As she explained to an interviewer, she sees her audience as larger than the lesbian readers of her early work:

> I think of myself as a writer who writes out from that particular position of being a lesbian and also being a working-class woman from birth, as writing out into the world at large and about lots of women.

BOYS AT THE RODEO

A lot of people have spent time on some women's farm this summer of 1972 and one day six of us decide to go to the rodeo. We are all mature and mostly in our early thirties. We wear levis and shirts and short hair. Susan has shaved her head.

The man at the gate, who looks like a cousin of the sheriff, is certain we are trying to get in for free. It must have been something in the way we are walking. He stares into Susan's face. "I know you're at least fourteen," he says. He slaps her shoulder, in that comradely way men have with each other. That's when we know he thinks we are boys.

"You're over thirteen," he says to Wendy.

"You're over thirteen," he says to me. He examines each of us closely, and sees only that we have been outdoors, are muscled, and look him directly in the eye. Since we are too short to be men, we must be boys. Everyone else at the rodeo are girls.

We decide to play it straight, so to speak. We make up boys' names for each other. Since Wendy has missed the episode with Susan at the gate, I slap her on the shoulder to demonstrate. "This is what he did." Slam. She never missed a step. It didn't feel bad to me at all. We laugh uneasily. We have achieved the status of fourteen year old boys, what a disguise for travelling through the world. I split into two pieces for the rest of the evening, and have never decided if it is worse to be 31 years old and called a boy or to be 31 years old and called a girl.

Irregardless, we are starved so we decide to eat, and here we have the status of boys for real. It seems to us that all the men and all the women attached to the men and most of the children are eating steak dinner plates; and we are the only women not attached to men. We eat hot dogs, which cost one tenth as much. A man who has taken a woman to the rodeo on this particular day has to have at least $12.00 to spend. So he had charge of all of her money and some of our money too, for we average $3.00 apiece and have taken each other to the rodeo.

Hot dogs in hand we escort ourselves to the wooden stands, and first is the standing up ceremony. We are pledging allegiance for the way of life—the competition, the supposed masculinity and pretty girls. I stand up, cursing, pretending I'm in some other country. One which has not been rediscovered. The loudspeaker plays Anchors Aweigh, that's what I like about rodeos, always something unexpected. At the last one I attended in another state the men on horses threw candy and nuts to the kids, chipping their teeth and breaking their noses. Who is it, I wonder, that has put these guys in charge. Even quiet mothers raged over that episode.

Now it is time for the rodeo queen contest, and a display of four very young women on horses. They are judged for queen 30% on their horsemanship and 70% on the number of queen tickets which people bought on their behalf to "elect" them. Talk about stuffed ballot boxes. I notice the winner as usual is the one on the registered thoroughbred whose daddy owns tracts and tracts of something—lumber, minerals, animals. His family name is all over the county.

The last loser sits well on a scrubby little pony and lives with her aunt and uncle. I pick her for the dyke even though it is speculation without clues. I can't help it, it's a pleasant habit. I wish I could give her a ribbon. Not for being a dyke, but for sitting on her horse well. For believing there ever was a contest, for not being the daughter of anyone who owns thousands of acres of anything.

Now the loudspeaker announces the girls' barrel races, which is the only grown women's event. It goes first because it is not really a part of the rodeo, but more like a mildly athletic variation of a parade by women to introduce the real thing. Like us boys in the stand, the girls are simply bearing witness to someone else's act.

The voice is booming that barrel racing is a new, modern event, that these young women are the wives and daughters of cowboys, and barrel racing is a way for them to participate in their own right. How generous of these northern cowboys to have resurrected barrel racing for women and to have forgotten the hard roping and riding which women always used to do in rodeos when I was younger. Even though I was a town child, I heard thrilling rumors of the all-women's rodeo in Texas, including that the finest brahma bull rider in all of Texas was a forty year old woman who weighed a hundred pounds.

Indeed, my first lover's first lover was a big heavy woman who was normally slow as a cold python, but she was just hell when she got up on a horse. She could rope and tie a calf faster than any cowboy within 500 miles of Sweetwater, Texas. That's what the West Texas dykes said, and they never lied about anything as important to them as calf roping, or the differences between women and men. And what about that news story I had heard recently on the radio, about a bull rider who was eight months pregnant? The newsman just had apoplectic fits over her, but not me. I was proud of her. She makes me think of all of us who have had our insides so overly protected from jarring we cannot possibly get through childbirth without an anesthetic.

While I have been grumbling these thoughts to myself, three barrels have been set up in a big triangle on the field, and the women one by one have raced their horses around each one and back to start. The trick is to turn your horse as sharply as possible without overthrowing the barrel.

After this moderate display, the main bulk of the rodeo begins, with calf roping, bronco riding, bull riding. It's a very male show during which the men demonstrate their various abilities at immobilizing, cornering, maneuvering and conquering cattle of every age.

A rodeo is an interminable number of roped and tied calves, ridden and unridden broncoes. The repetition is broken by a few antics from the agile, necessary clown. His long legs nearly envelope the little jackass he is riding for the satire of it.

After a number of hours they produce an event I have never seen before—goat tying. This is for the girls eleven and twelve. They use one goat for fourteen participants. The goat is supposed to be held in place on a rope by a large man on horseback. Each girl rushes out in a long run half way across the field, grabs the animal, knocks it down, ties its legs together. Sometimes the man lets his horse drift so the goat pulls six or eight feet away from her, something no one would allow to happen in a male event. Many of the girls take over a full minute just to do their tying, and the fact that only one goat has been used makes everybody say, "poor goat, poor goat," and start laughing. This had become the real comedy event of the evening, and the purpose clearly is to show how badly girls do in the rodeo.

Only one has broken through this purpose to the other side. One small girl is not disheartened by the years of bad training, the ridiculous cross-field run, the laughing superior man on his horse, or the shape-shifting goat. She downs it in a beautiful flying tackle. This makes me whisper, as usual, "that's the dyke," but for the rest of it we watch the girls look ludicrous, awkward, outclassed and totally dominated by the large handsome man on horse. In the stands we six boys drink beer in disgust, groan and hug our breasts, hold our heads and twist our faces at each other in embarrassment.

As the calf roping starts up again, we decide to use our disguises to walk around the grounds. Making our way around to the cowboy side of the arena, we pass the intricate mazes of rail where the stock is stored, to the chutes where they are loading the bull riders onto the bulls.

I wish to report that although we pass by dozens of men, and although we have pressed against wild horses and have climbed on rails overlooking thousands of pounds of angry animal flesh, though we touch ropes and halters, we are never once warned away, never told that this is not the proper place for us, that we had better get back for our own good, are not safe, etc., none of the dozens of warnings and threats we would have gotten if we had been recognized as thirty one year old girls instead of fourteen year old boys. It is a most interesting way to wander around the world for the day.

We examine everything closely. The brahma bulls are in the chutes, ready to be released into the ring. They are bulky, kindly looking creatures with rolling eyes; they resemble overgrown pigs. One of us whispers, "Aren't those the same kind of cattle that walk around all over the streets in India and never hurt anybody?"

Here in the chutes made exactly their size, they are converted into wild antago-
nistic beasts by means of a nasty belt around their loins, squeezed tight to mash their
most tender testicles just before they are released into the ring. This torture is sup-
plemented by a jolt of electricity from an electric cattle prod to make sure they come
out bucking. So much for the rodeo as a great drama between man and nature.

A pale, nervous cowboy sits on the bull's back with one hand in a glove hooked
under a strap around the bull's midsection. He gains points by using his spurs during the ride. He has to remain on top until the timing buzzer buzzes a few seconds
after he and the bull plunge out of the gate. I had always considered it the most exciting event.

Around the fence sit many eager young men watching, helping, and getting in
the way. We are easily accepted among them. How depressing this can be.

Out in the arena a dismounted cowboy reaches over and slaps his horse fiercely on
the mouth because it has turned its head the wrong way.

I squat down peering through the rails where I see the neat, tight-fitting pants of
two young men standing provocatively chest to chest.

"Don't you think Henry's a queer," one says with contempt.

"Hell, I *know* he's a queer," the other says. They hold an informal spitting contest
for the punctuation. Meantime their eyes have brightened and their fronts are moving toward each other in their clean, smooth shirts. I realize they are flirting with
each other, using Henry to bring up the dangerous subject of themselves. I am remembering all the gay cowboys I ever knew. This is one of the things I like about cowboys. They don't wear those beautiful pearl button shirts and tight levis for nothing.

As the events inside the arena subside, we walk down to a roped off pavillion
where there is a dance. The band consists of one portly, bouncing enthusiastic man
of middle age who is singing with great spirit into the microphone. The rest of the
band are three grim, lean young men over fourteen. The drummer drums angrily,
while jerking his head behind himself as though searching the air for someone who
is already two hours late and had seriously promised to take him away from here. The
two guitar players are sleepwalking from the feet up with their eyes so glassy you could
read by them.

A redhaired man appears, surrounded by redhaired children who ask, "Are you
drunk, Daddy?"

"No, I am not drunk," Daddy says.

"Can we have some money?"

"No," Daddy says, "I am not drunk enough to give you any money."

During a break in the music the redhaired man asks the bandleader where he got
his band.

"Where did I get this band?" the bandleader puffs up, "I raised this band myself.
These are all my sons—I raised this band myself." The redhaired man is so very impressed he is nearly bowing and kissing the hand of the bandleader, as they repeat this
conversation two or three times. "This is *my* band," the bandleader says, and the two
guitar players exchange grim and glassy looks.

Next the bandleader has announced "Okie From Muskogee," a song intended to
portray the white country morality of cowboys. The crowd does not respond but he
sings enthusiastically anyway. Two of his more alert sons drag themselves to the microphone to wail that they don't smoke marijuana in Muskogee—as those hippies
down in San Francisco do, and they certainly don't. From the look of it they shoot
hard drugs and pop pills.

In the middle of the song a very drunk thirteen year old boy has staggered up to Wendy, pounding her on the shoulder and exclaiming, "Can you dig it, brother?" Later she tells me she has never been called brother before, and she likes it. Her first real identification as one of the brothers, in the brotherhood of man.

We boys begin to walk back to our truck, past a cowboy vomiting on his own pretty boots, past another lying completely under a car. Near our truck, a young man has calf-roped a young woman. She shrieks for him to stop, hopping weakly along behind him. This is the first bid for public attention I have seen from any woman here since the barrel race. I understand that this little scene is a re-enactment of the true meaning of the rodeo, and of the conquest of the west. And oh how much I do not want to be her; I do not want to be the conquest of the west.

I am remembering how the clown always seems to be tall and riding on an ass, that must be a way of poking fun at the small and usually dark people who tried to raise sheep or goats or were sod farmers and rode burros instead of tall handsome blond horses, and who were driven under by the beef raisers. And so today we went to a display of cattle handling instead of a sheep shearing or a goat milking contest—or to go into even older ghost territory, a corn dance, or acorn gathering. . . .

As we reach the truck, the tall man passes with the rodeo queen, who must surely be his niece, or something. All this non-contest, if it is for anyone, must certainly be for him. As a boy, I look at him. He is his own spitting image, of what is manly and white and masterly, so tall in his high heels, so *well horsed*. His manner portrays his theory of life as the survival of the fittest against wild beasts, and all the mythical rest of us who are too female or dark, not straight, or much too native to the earth to now be trusted as more than witnesses, flags, cheerleaders and unwilling stock.

As he passes, we step out of the way and I am glad we are in our disguise. I hate to step out of his way as a full grown woman, one who hasn't enough class status to warrant his thinly polite chivalry. He has knocked me off the sidewalk of too many towns, too often.

Yet somewhere in me I know I have always wanted to be manly, what I mean is having that expression of courage, control, coordination, ability I associate with men. To *provide*.

But here I am in this truck, not a man at all, a fourteen year old boy only. Tomorrow is my thirty-second birthday. We six snuggle together in the bed of this rickety truck which is our world for the time being. We are headed back to the bold and shakey adventures of our all-women's farm, our all-women's households and companies, our expanding minds, ambitions and bodies, we who are neither male nor female at this moment in the pageant world, who are not the rancher's wife, mother earth, Virgin Mary or the rodeo queen—we who are really the one who took her self seriously, who once took an all out dive at the goat believing that the odds were square and that she was truly in the contest.

And now that we know it is not a contest, just a play—we have run off with the goat ourselves to try another way of life.

Because I certainly do not want to be a 32 year old girl, or calf either, and I certainly also do always remember Gertrude Stein's beautiful dykely voice saying, what is the use of being a boy if you grow up to be a man.

[1978]

Questions

1. What do the women's disguises as boys enable them to do and see differently at the rodeo? Why? How is their status as "the only women not attached to men" significant?

2. What does the rodeo tradition imply about male and female roles? What does the story suggest about unconventional sexual identities?

3. How does Grahn develop the implicit relationship between the values that predominate at the rodeo and those that prevail in American society as a whole, particularly attitudes concerning race, class, gender roles, and sexual preference?

4. How are such phrases as "conquest of the West" and "survival of the fittest" used in the story?

Nathaniel Hawthorne
(1804–1864)
United States

O ne of the undisputed masters of nineteenth-century American literature, Nathaniel Hawthorne was born in Salem, Massachusetts, becoming both inheritor and explorer of the New England Puritan consciousness of an earlier era as well as his own. He attended Bowdoin College in Maine, where his classmates included the poet Henry Wadsworth Longfellow and Franklin Pierce, who later was elected to the American presidency. After graduating in 1825, Hawthorne returned to Salem and spent a reclusive life for the next 12 years. While working at the Boston Customhouse, he began to write the allegorical stories that initiate his preoccupation with the themes of moral responsibility, guilt, suffering, and human imperfection. His first volume of stories, Twice-Told Tales, was published in 1837, followed by two later volumes. His richly symbolic short stories anticipate themes and characters that are developed more fully in his longer narratives.

In 1842 Hawthorne married and moved to Concord, Massachusetts, where he became a neighbor of Emerson and Thoreau and the circle of Transcendentalists. After losing his position as a surveyor in the Salem Customhouse as a result of a change in political parties, Hawthorne wrote The Scarlet Letter (1850), the novel that finally gave him a measure of financial security while firmly establishing his literary reputation. In this historical romance set in seventeenth-century Puritan New England, Hawthorne masterfully probes the intertwined themes of human imperfection, moral responsibility, hidden guilt, and spiritual redemption through the psychologically complex characters Hester Prynne, Arthur Dimmesdale, and Roger Chillingworth.

Hawthorne's other major novels, The House of the Seven Gables (1851), The Blithedale Romance (1852), and The Marble Faun (1860), as well as his short stories, reflect the author's penetrating insight into human psychology and the moral realm. In "The Birthmark," Hawthorne explores the two domains of the natural order—matter and spirit—and the dangers that stem from confusing them.

THE BIRTHMARK

In the latter part of the last century there lived a man of science, an eminent proficient in every branch of natural philosophy, who not long before our story opens had made experience of a spiritual affinity more attractive than any chemical one. He had left his laboratory to the care of an assistant, cleared his fine countenance from the furnace smoke, washed the stain of acids from his fingers, and persuaded a beautiful woman to become his wife. In those days when the comparatively recent discovery of electricity and other kindred mysteries of Nature seemed to open paths into the region of miracle, it was not unusual for the love of science to rival the love of woman in its depth and absorbing energy. The higher intellect, the imagination, the spirit, and even the heart might all find their congenial ailment in pursuits which, as some of their ardent votaries believed, would ascend from one step of powerful intelligence to another, until the philosopher should lay his hand on the secret of creative force and perhaps make new worlds for himself. We know not whether Aylmer possessed this degree of faith in man's ultimate control over Nature. He had devoted himself, however, too unreservedly to scientific studies ever to be weaned from them by any second passion. His love for his young wife might prove the stronger of the two; but it could only be by intertwining itself with his love of science, and uniting the strength of the latter to his own.

Such a union accordingly took place, and was attended with truly remarkable consequences and a deeply impressive moral. One day, very soon after their marriage, Aylmer sat gazing at his wife with a trouble in his countenance that grew stronger until he spoke.

"Georgiana," said he, "has it never occurred to you that the mark upon your cheek might be removed?"

"No, indeed," said she, smiling; but perceiving the seriousness of his manner, she blushed deeply. "To tell the truth it has been so often called a charm that I was simple enough to imagine it might be so."

"Ah, upon another face perhaps it might," replied her husband; "but never on yours. No, dearest Georgiana, you came so nearly perfect from the hand of Nature that this slightest possible defect, which we hesitate whether to term a defect or a beauty, shocks me, as being the visible mark of earthly imperfection."

"Shocks you, my husband!" cried Georgiana, deeply hurt; at first reddening with momentary anger, but then bursting into tears. "Then why did you take me from my mother's side? You cannot love what shocks you!"

To explain this conversation it must be mentioned that in the centre of Georgiana's left cheek there was a singular mark, deeply interwoven, as it were, with the texture and substance of her face. In the usual state of her complexion—a healthy though delicate bloom—the mark wore a tint of deeper crimson, which imperfectly defined its shape amid the surrounding rosiness. When she blushed it gradually became more indistinct, and finally vanished amid the triumphant rush of blood that bathed the whole cheek with its brilliant glow. But if any shifting motion caused her to turn pale there was the mark again, a crimson stain upon the snow, in what Aylmer sometimes deemed an almost fearful distinctness. Its shape bore not a little similarity to the human hand, though of the smallest pygmy size. Georgiana's lovers were wont to say that some fairy at her birth hour had laid her tiny hand upon the infant's cheek, and left this impress there in token of the magic endowments that were to give her such sway over all hearts. Many a desperate swain would have risked life for the privilege of pressing his lips to the mysterious hand. It must not be concealed, however, that the impression wrought by this fairy sign manual varied exceedingly, according to the difference of temperament in the beholders. Some fastidious persons—but they were exclusively of her own sex—affirmed that the bloody hand, as they chose to call it, quite destroyed the effect of Georgiana's beauty, and rendered her countenance even hideous. But it would be as reasonable to say that one of those small blue stains which sometimes occur in the purest statuary marble would convert the

Eve of Powers[1] to a monster. Masculine observers, if the birthmark did not heighten their admiration, contented themselves with wishing it away, that the world might possess one living specimen of ideal loveliness without the semblance of a flaw. After his marriage,—for he thought little or nothing of the matter before,—Aylmer discovered that this was the case with himself.

Had she been less beautiful,—if Envy's self could have found aught else to sneer at,—he might have felt his affection heightened by the prettiness of this mimic hand, now vaguely portrayed, now lost, now stealing forth again and glimmering to and fro with every pulse of emotion that throbbed within her heart; but seeing her otherwise so perfect, he found this one defect grow more and more intolerable with every moment of their united lives. It was the fatal flaw of humanity which Nature, in one shape or another, stamps ineffaceably on all her productions, either to imply that they are temporary and finite, or that their perfection must be wrought by toil and pain. The crimson hand expressed the ineludible gripe[2] in which mortality clutches the highest and purest of earthly mould, degrading them into kindred with the lowest, and even with the very brutes, like whom their visible frames return to dust. In this manner, selecting it as the symbol of his wife's liability to sin, sorrow, decay, and death, Aylmer's sombre imagination was not long in rendering the birthmark a frightful object, causing him more trouble and horror than ever Georgiana's beauty, whether of soul or sense, had given him delight.

At all the seasons which should have been their happiest, he invariably and without intending it, nay, in spite of a purpose to the contrary, reverted to this one disastrous topic. Trifling as it at first appeared, it so connected itself with innumerable trains of thought and modes of feeling that it became the central point of all. With the morning twilight Aylmer opened his eyes upon his wife's face and recognized the symbol of imperfection; and when they sat together at the evening hearth his eyes wandered stealthily to her cheek, and beheld, flickering with the blaze of the wood fire, the spectral hand that wrote mortality where he would fain have worshipped. Georgiana soon learned to shudder at his gaze. It needed but a glance with the peculiar expression that his face often wore to change the roses of her cheek into a deathlike paleness, amid which the crimson hand was brought strongly out, like a bas-relief of ruby on the whitest marble.

Late one night when the lights were growing dim, so as hardly to betray the stain on the poor wife's cheek, she herself, for the first time, voluntarily took up the subject.

"Do you remember, my dear Aylmer," said she, with a feeble attempt at a smile, "have you any recollection of a dream last night about this odious hand?"

"None! none whatever!" replied Aylmer, starting; but then he added, in a dry, cold tone, affected for the sake of concealing the real depth of his emotion, "I might well dream of it; for before I fell asleep it had taken a pretty firm hold of my fancy."

"And you did dream of it?" continued Georgiana, hastily; for she dreaded lest a gush of tears should interrupt what she had to say. "A terrible dream! I wonder that you forget it. Is it possible to forget this one expression?—'It is in her heart now; we must have it out!' Reflect, my husband; for by all means I would have you recall that dream."

---

[1]*Hiram Powers* American sculptor (1805–1873); his nude statue, *Eve Tempted*, was both praised and condemned in its time.
[2]*gripe* Grip.

The mind is in a sad state when Sleep, the all-involving, cannot confine her spec-tres within the dim region of her sway, but suffers them to break forth, affrighting this actual life with secrets that perchance belong to a deeper one. Aylmer now re-membered his dream. He had fancied himself with his servant Aminadab, attempt-ing an operation for the removal of the birthmark; but the deeper went the knife, the deeper sank the hand, until at length its tiny grasp appeared to have caught hold of Georgiana's heart; whence, however, her husband was inexorably resolved to cut or wrench it away.

When the dream had shaped itself perfectly in his memory, Aylmer sat in his wife's presence with a guilty feeling. Truth often finds its way to the mind close muffled in robes of sleep, and then speaks with uncompromising directness of matters in regard to which we practise an unconscious self-deception during our waking moments. Until now he had not been aware of the tyrannizing influence acquired by one idea over his mind, and of the lengths which he might find in his heart to go for the sake of giving himself peace.

"Aylmer," resumed Georgiana, solemnly, "I know not what may be the cost to both of us to rid me of this fatal birthmark. Perhaps its removal may cause cureless deformity; or it may be the stain goes as deep as life itself. Again: do we know that there is a possibility, on any terms, of unclasping the firm gripe of this little hand which was laid upon me before I came into the world?"

"Dearest Georgiana, I have spent much thought upon the subject," hastily inter-rupted Aylmer. "I am convinced of the perfect practicability of its removal."

"If there be the remotest possibility of it," continued Georgiana, "let the attempt be made at whatever risk. Danger is nothing to me; for life, while this hateful mark makes me the object of your horror and disgust,—life is a burden which I would fling down with joy. Either remove this dreadful hand, or take my wretched life! You have deep science. All the world bears witness of it. You have achieved great wonders. Cannot you remove this little, little mark, which I cover with the tips of two small fingers? Is this beyond your power, for the sake of your own peace, and to save your poor wife from madness?"

"Noblest, dearest, tenderest wife," cried Aylmer, rapturously, "doubt not my power. I have already given this matter the deepest thought—thought which might almost have enlightened me to create a being less perfect than yourself. Georgiana, you have led me deeper than ever into the heart of science. I feel myself fully competent to ren-der this dear cheek as faultless as its fellow; and then, most beloved, what will be my triumph when I shall have corrected what Nature left imperfect in her fairest work! Pygmalion,[3] when his sculptured woman assumed life, felt not greater ecstasy than mine will be."

"It is resolved, then," said Georgiana, faintly smiling. "And, Aylmer, spare me not, though you should find the birthmark take refuge in my heart at last."

Her husband tenderly kissed her cheek—her right cheek—not that which bore the impress of the crimson hand.

The next day Aylmer apprised his wife of a plan that he had formed whereby he might have opportunity for the intense thought and constant watchfulness which the proposed operation would require; while Georgiana, likewise, would enjoy the

---

[3]*Pygmalion*   According to Greek legend, Pygmalion, King of Cyprus, fell in love with a female statue he had made; the goddess Aphrodite endowed the statue with life.

perfect repose essential to its success. They were to seclude themselves in the extensive apartments occupied by Aylmer as a laboratory, and where, during his toilsome youth, he had made discoveries in the elemental powers of Nature that had roused the admiration of all the learned societies in Europe. Seated calmly in this laboratory, the pale philosopher had investigated the secrets of the highest cloud region and of the profoundest mines; he had satisfied himself of the causes that kindled and kept alive the fires of the volcano; and had explained the mystery of fountains, and how it is that they gush forth, some so bright and pure, and others with such rich medicinal virtues, from the dark bosom of the earth. Here, too, at an earlier period, he had studied the wonders of the human frame, and attempted to fathom the very process by which Nature assimilates all her precious influences from earth and air, and from the spiritual world, to create and foster man, her masterpiece. The latter pursuit, however, Aylmer had long laid aside in unwilling recognition of the truth—against which all seekers sooner or later stumble—that our great creative Mother, while she amuses us with apparently working in the broadest sunshine, is yet severely careful to keep her own secrets, and, in spite of her pretended openness, shows us nothing but results. She permits us, indeed, to mar, but seldom to mend, and, like a jealous patentee, on no account to make. Now, however, Aylmer resumed these half-forgotten investigations; not, of course, with such hopes or wishes as first suggest them; but because they involved much physiological truth and lay in the path of his proposed scheme for the treatment of Georgiana.

As he led her over the threshold of the laboratory, Georgiana was cold and tremulous. Aylmer looked cheerfully into her face, with intent to reassure her, but was so startled with the intense glow of the birthmark upon the whiteness of her cheek that he could not restrain a strong convulsive shudder. His wife fainted.

"Aminadab! Aminadab!" shouted Aylmer, stamping violently on the floor.

Forthwith there issued from an inner apartment a man of low stature, but bulky frame, with shaggy hair hanging about his visage, which was grimed with the vapors of the furnace. This personage had been Aylmer's underworker during his whole scientific career, and was admirably fitted for that office by his great mechanical readiness, and the skill with which, while incapable of comprehending a single principle, he executed all the details of his master's experiments. With his vast strength, his shaggy hair, his smoky aspect, and the indescribable earthiness that incrusted him, he seemed to represent man's physical nature; while Aylmer's slender figure, and pale, intellectual face, were no less apt a type of the spiritual element.

"Throw open the door of the boudoir, Aminadab," said Aylmer, "and burn a pastil."[4]

"Yes, master," answered Aminadab, looking intently at the lifeless form of Georgiana; and then he muttered to himself, "If she were my wife, I'd never part with that birthmark."

When Georgiana recovered consciousness she found herself breathing an atmosphere of penetrating fragrance, the gentle potency of which had recalled her from her deathlike faintness. The scene around her looked like enchantment. Aylmer had converted those smoky, dingy, sombre rooms, where he had spent his brightest years in recondite pursuits, into a series of beautiful apartments not unfit to be the secluded abode of a lovely woman. The walls were hung with gorgeous curtains,

---

[4]*pastil* Modern spelling: *pastille*; a pellet of aromatic paste, used for fumigation.

which imparted the combination of grandeur and grace that no other species of adornment can achieve; and as they fell from the ceiling to the floor, their rich and ponderous folds, concealing all angles and straight lines, appeared to shut in the scene from infinite space. For aught Georgiana knew, it might be a pavilion among the clouds. And Aylmer, excluding the sunshine, which would have interfered with his chemical processes, had supplied its place with perfumed lamps, emitting flames of various hue, but all uniting in a soft, impurpled radiance. He now knelt by his wife's side, watching her earnestly, but without alarm; for he was confident in his science, and felt that he could draw a magic circle round her within which no evil might intrude.

"Where am I? Ah, I remember," said Georgiana, faintly; and she placed her hand over her cheek to hide the terrible mark from her husband's eyes.

"Fear not, dearest!" exclaimed he. "Do not shrink from me! Believe me, Georgiana, I even rejoice in this single imperfection, since it will be such a rapture to remove it."

"Oh, spare me!" sadly replied his wife. "Pray do not look at it again. I never can forget that convulsive shudder."

In order to soothe Georgiana, and, as it were, to release her mind from the burden of actual things, Aylmer now put in practice some of the light and playful secrets which science had taught him among its profounder lore. Airy figures, absolutely bodiless ideas, and forms of unsubstantial beauty came and danced before her, imprinting their momentary footsteps on beams of light. Though she had some indistinct idea of the method of these optical phenomena, still the illusion was almost perfect enough to warrant the belief that her husband possessed sway over the spiritual world. Then again, when she felt a wish to look forth from her seclusion, immediately, as if her thoughts were answered, the procession of external existence flitted across a screen. The scenery and the figures of actual life were perfectly represented, but with that bewitching, yet indescribable difference which always makes a picture, an image, or a shadow so much more attractive than the original. When wearied of this, Aylmer bade her cast her eyes upon a vessel containing a quantity of earth. She did so, with little interest at first; but was soon startled to perceive the germ of a plant shooting upward from the soil. Then came the slender stalk; the leaves gradually unfolded themselves; and amid them was a perfect and lovely flower.

"It is magical!" cried Georgiana. "I dare not touch it."

"Nay, pluck it," answered Aylmer,—"pluck it, and inhale its brief perfume while you may. The flower will wither in a few moments and leave nothing save its brown seed vessels; but thence may be perpetuated a race as ephemeral as itself."

But Georgiana had no sooner touched the flower than the whole plant suffered a blight, its leaves turning coal-black as if by the agency of fire.

"There was too powerful a stimulus," said Aylmer, thoughtfully.

To make up for this abortive experiment, he proposed to take her portrait by a scientific process of his own invention. It was to be effected by rays of light striking upon a polished plate of metal. Georgiana assented; but, on looking at the result, was affrighted to find the features of the portrait blurred and indefinable; while the minute figure of a hand appeared where the cheek should have been. Aylmer snatched the metallic plate and threw it into a jar of corrosive acid.

Soon, however, he forgot these mortifying failures. In the intervals of study and chemical experiment he came to her flushed and exhausted, but seemed invigorated by her presence, and spoke in glowing language of the resources of his art. He gave a history of the long dynasty of the alchemists, who spent so many ages in quest of the universal solvent by which the golden principle might be elicited from all things vile and base. Aylmer appeared to believe that, by the plainest scientific logic, it was altogether within the limits of possibility to discover this long-sought medium; "but," he added, "a philosopher who should go deep enough to acquire the power would attain too lofty a wisdom to stoop to the exercise of it." Not less singular were his opinions in regard to the elixir vitae.[5] He more than intimated that it was at his option to concoct a liquid that should prolong life for years, perhaps interminably; but that it would produce a discord in Nature which all the world, and chiefly the quaffer of the immortal nostrum, would find cause to curse.

"Aylmer, are you in earnest?" asked Georgiana, looking at him with amazement and fear. "It is terrible to possess such power, or even dream of possessing it."

"Oh, do not tremble, my love," said her husband. "I would not wrong either you or myself by working such inharmonious effects upon our lives; but I would have you consider how trifling, in comparison, is the skill requisite to remove this little hand."

At the mention of the birthmark, Georgiana, as usual, shrank as if a redhot iron had touched her cheek.

Again Aylmer applied himself to his labors. She could hear his voice in the distant furnace room giving directions to Aminadab, whose harsh, uncouth, misshapen tones were audible in response, more like the grunt or growl of a brute than human speech. After hours of absence, Aylmer reappeared and proposed that she should now examine his cabinet of chemical products and natural treasures of the earth. Among the former he showed her a small vial, in which, he remarked, was contained a gentle yet most powerful fragrance, capable of impregnating all the breezes that blow across a kingdom. They were of inestimable value, the contents of that little vial; and, as he said so, he threw some of the perfume into the air and filled the room with piercing and invigorating delight.

"And what is this?" asked Georgiana, pointing to a small crystal globe containing a gold-colored liquid. "It is so beautiful to the eye that I could imagine it the elixir of life."

"In one sense it is," replied Aylmer; "or, rather, the elixir of immortality. It is the most precious poison that ever was concocted in this world. By its aid I could apportion the lifetime of any mortal at whom you might point your finger. The strength of the dose would determine whether he were to linger out years, or drop dead in the midst of a breath. No king on his guarded throne could keep his life if I, in my private station, should deem that the welfare of millions justified me in depriving him of it."

"Why do you keep such a terrific drug?" inquired Georgiana in horror.

"Do not mistrust me, dearest," said her husband, smiling; "its virtuous potency is yet greater than its harmful one. But see! here is a powerful cosmetic. With a few drops of this in a vase of water, freckles may be washed away as easily as the hands are cleansed. A stronger infusion would take the blood out of the cheek, and leave the rosiest beauty a pale ghost."

"Is it with this lotion that you intend to bathe my cheek?" asked Georgiana, anxiously.

"Oh, no," hastily replied her husband; "this is merely superficial. Your case demands a remedy that shall go deeper."

---

[5] *elixir vitae*   An essence reputed by the alchemists to prolong life.

In his interviews with Georgiana, Aylmer generally made minute inquiries as to her sensations and whether the confinement of the rooms and the temperature of the atmosphere agreed with her. These questions had such a particular drift that Georgiana began to conjecture that she was already subjected to certain physical influences, either breathed in with the fragrant air or taken with her food. She fancied likewise, but it might be altogether fancy, that there was a stirring up of her system— a strange, indefinite sensation creeping through her veins, and tingling, half painfully, half pleasurably, at her heart. Still, whenever she dared to look into the mirror, there she beheld herself pale as a white rose and with the crimson birthmark stamped upon her cheek. Not even Aylmer now hated it so much as she.

To dispel the tedium of the hours which her husband found it necessary to devote to the processes of combination and analysis, Georgiana turned over the volumes of his scientific library. In many dark old tomes she met with chapters full of romance and poetry. They were the works of the philosophers of the middle ages, such as Albertus Magnus, Cornelius Agrippa, Paracelsus, and the famous friar who created the prophetic Brazen Head.[6] All these antique naturalists stood in advance of their centuries, yet were imbued with some of their credulity, and therefore were believed, and perhaps imagined themselves to have acquired from the investigation of Nature a power above Nature, and from physics a sway over the spiritual world. Hardly less curious and imaginative were the early volumes of the Transactions of the Royal Society, in which the members, knowing little of the limits of natural possibility, were continually recording wonders or proposing methods whereby wonders might be wrought.

But to Georgiana the most engrossing volume was a large folio from her husband's own hand, in which he had recorded every experiment of his scientific career, its original aim, the methods adopted for its development, and its final success or failure, with the circumstances to which either event was attributable. The book, in truth, was both the history and emblem of his ardent, ambitious, imaginative, yet practical and laborious life. He handled physical details as if there were nothing beyond them; yet spiritualized them all, and redeemed himself from materialism by his strong and eager aspiration towards the infinite. In his grasp the veriest clod of earth assumed a soul. Georgiana, as she read, reverenced Aylmer and loved him more profoundly than ever, but with a less entire dependence on his judgment than heretofore. Much as he had accomplished, she could not but observe that his most splendid successes were almost invariably failures, if compared with the ideal at which he aimed. His brightest diamonds were the merest pebbles, and felt to be so by himself, in comparison with the inestimable gems which lay hidden beyond his reach. The volume, rich with achievements that had won renown for its author, was yet as melancholy a record as ever mortal hand had penned. It was the sad confession and continual exemplification of the shortcomings of the composite man, the spirit burdened with clay and working in matter, and of the despair that assails the higher nature at finding itself so miserably thwarted by the earthly part. Perhaps every man of genius in whatever sphere might recognize the image of his own experience in Aylmer's journal.

---

[6]*Albertus Magnus*, etc.   Medieval alchemists and philosophers whose work anticipated modern science. The friar who created the Brazen Head was Roger Bacon (1214?–1294?), a philosopher and alchemist who was reputed to have created a talking head that would respond to his questions concerning the progress of his enterprises.

So deeply did these reflections affect Georgiana that she laid her face upon the open volume and burst into tears. In this situation she was found by her husband.

"It is dangerous to read in a sorcerer's books," said he, with a smile, though his countenance was uneasy and displeased. "Georgiana, there are pages in that volume which I can scarcely glance over and keep my senses. Take heed lest it prove as detrimental to you."

"It has made me worship you more than ever," said she.

"Ah, wait for this one success," rejoined he, "then worship me if you will. I shall deem myself hardly unworthy of it. But come, I have sought you for the luxury of your voice. Sing to me, dearest."

So she poured out the liquid music of her voice to quench the thirst of his spirit. He then took his leave with a boyish exuberance of gayety, assuring her that her seclusion would endure but a little longer, and that the result was already certain. Scarcely had he departed when Georgiana felt irresistibly impelled to follow him. She had forgotten to inform Aylmer of a symptom which for two or three hours past had begun to excite her attention. It was a sensation in the fatal birthmark, not painful, but which induced a restlessness throughout her system. Hastening after her husband, she intruded for the first time into the laboratory.

The first thing that struck her eye was the furnace, that hot and feverish worker, with the intense glow of its fire, which by the quantities of soot clustered above it seemed to have been burning for ages. There was a distilling apparatus in full operation. Around the room were retorts, tubes, cylinders, crucibles, and other apparatus of chemical research. An electrical machine stood ready for immediate use. The atmosphere felt oppressively close, and was tainted with gaseous odors which had been tormented forth by the processes of science. The severe and homely simplicity of the apartment, with its naked walls and brick pavement, looked strange, accustomed as Georgiana had become to the fantastic elegance of her boudoir. But what chiefly, indeed almost solely, drew her attention, was the aspect of Aylmer himself.

He was pale as death, anxious and absorbed, and hung over the furnace as if it depended upon his utmost watchfulness whether the liquid which it was distilling should be the draught of immortal happiness or misery. How different from the sanguine and joyous mien that he had assumed for Georgiana's encouragement!

"Carefully now, Aminadab; carefully, thou human machine; carefully, thou man of clay!" muttered Aylmer, more to himself than his assistant. "Now, if there be a thought too much or too little, it is all over."

"Ho! ho!" mumbled Aminadab. "Look, master! look!"

Aylmer raised his eyes hastily, and at first reddened, then grew paler than ever, on beholding Georgiana. He rushed towards her and seized her arm with a gripe that left the print of his fingers upon it.

"Why do you come hither? Have you no trust in your husband?" cried he, impetuously. "Would you throw the blight of that fatal birthmark over my labors? It is not well done. Go, prying woman, go!"

"Nay, Aylmer," said Georgiana with the firmness of which she possessed no stinted endowment, "it is not you that have a right to complain. You mistrust your wife; you have concealed the anxiety with which you watch the development of this experiment. Think not so unworthily of me, my husband. Tell me all the risk we run, and fear not that I shall shrink; for my share in it is far less than your own."

"No, no, Georgiana!" said Aylmer, impatiently; "it must not be."

"I submit," replied she calmly. "And Aylmer, I shall quaff whatever draught you bring me; but it will be on the same principle that would induce me to take a dose of poison if offered by your hand."

"My noble wife," said Aylmer, deeply moved, "I knew not the height and depth of your nature until now. Nothing shall be concealed. Know, then, that this crimson hand, superficial as it seems, has clutched its grasp into your being with a strength of which I had no previous conception. I have already administered agents powerful enough to do aught except to change your entire physical system. Only one thing remains to be tried. If that fail us we are ruined."

"Why did you hesitate to tell me this?" asked she.

"Because, Georgiana," said Aylmer, in a low voice, "there is danger."

"Danger? There is but one danger—that this horrible stigma shall be left upon my cheek!" cried Georgiana. "Remove it, remove it, whatever be the cost, or we shall both go mad!"

"Heaven knows your words are too true," said Aylmer, sadly. "And now, dearest, return to your boudoir. In a little while all will be tested."

He conducted her back and took leave of her with a solemn tenderness which spoke far more than his words how much was now at stake. After his departure Georgiana became rapt in musings. She considered the character of Aylmer, and did it completer justice than at any previous moment. Her heart exulted, while it trembled, at his honorable love—so pure and lofty that it would accept nothing less than perfection nor miserably make itself contented with an earthlier nature than he had dreamed of. She felt how much more precious was such a sentiment than that meaner kind which would have borne with the imperfection for her sake, and have been guilty of treason to holy love by degrading its perfect idea to the level of the actual; and with her whole spirit she prayed that, for a single moment, she might satisfy his highest and deepest conception. Longer than one moment she well knew it could not be; for his spirit was ever on the march, ever ascending, and each instant required something that was beyond the scope of the instant before.

The sound of her husband's footsteps aroused her. He bore a crystal goblet containing a liquor colorless as water, but bright enough to be the draught of immortality. Aylmer was pale; but it seemed rather the consequence of a highly-wrought state of mind and tension of spirit than of fear or doubt.

"The concoction of the draught has been perfect," said he, in answer to Georgiana's look. "Unless all my science have deceived me, it cannot fail."

"Save on your account, my dearest Aylmer," observed his wife, "I might wish to put off this birthmark of mortality by relinquishing mortality itself in preference to any other mode. Life is but a sad possession to those who have attained precisely the degree of moral advancement at which I stand. Were I weaker and blinder it might be happiness. Were I stronger, it might be endured hopefully. But, being what I find myself, methinks I am of all mortals the most fit to die."

"You are fit for heaven without tasting death!" replied her husband. "But why do we speak of dying? The draught cannot fail. Behold its effect upon this plant."

On the window seat there stood a geranium diseased with yellow blotches, which had overspread all its leaves. Aylmer poured a small quantity of the liquid upon the soil in which it grew. In a little time, when the roots of the plant had taken up the moisture, the unsightly blotches began to be extinguished in a living verdure.

"There needed no proof," said Georgiana, quietly. "Give me the goblet. I joyfully stake all upon your word."

"Drink, then, thou lofty creature!" exclaimed Aylmer, with fervid admiration. "There is no taint of imperfection on thy spirit. Thy sensible frame, too, shall soon be all perfect."

She quaffed the liquid and returned the goblet to his hand.

"It is grateful," said she with a placid smile. "Methinks it is like water from a heavenly fountain; for it contains I know not what of unobtrusive fragrance and deliciousness. It allays a feverish thirst that had parched me for many days. Now, dearest, let me sleep. My earthly senses are closing over my spirit like the leaves around the heart of a rose at sunset.

She spoke the last words with a gentle reluctance, as if it required almost more energy than she could command to pronounce the faint and lingering syllables. Scarcely had they loitered through her lips ere she was lost in slumber. Aylmer sat by her side, watching her aspect with the emotions proper to a man the whole value of whose existence was involved in the process now to be tested. Mingled with this mood, however, was the philosophic investigation characteristic of the man of science. Not the minutest symptom escaped him. A heightened flush of the cheek, a slight irregularity of breath, a quiver of the eyelid, a hardly perceptible tremor through the frame,—such were the details which, as the moments passed, he wrote down in his folio volume. Intense thought had set its stamp upon every previous page of that volume, but the thoughts of years were all concentrated upon the last.

While thus employed, he failed not to gaze often at the fatal hand, and not without a shudder. Yet once, by a strange and unaccountable impulse, he pressed it with his lips. His spirit recoiled, however, in the very act; and Georgiana, out of the midst of her deep sleep, moved uneasily and murmured as if in remonstrance. Again Aylmer resumed his watch. Nor was it without avail. The crimson hand, which at first had been strongly visible upon the marble paleness of Georgiana's cheek, now grew more faintly outlined. She remained not less pale than ever; but the birthmark, with every breath that came and went, lost somewhat of its former distinctness. Its presence had been awful; its departure was more awful still. Watch the stain of the rainbow fading out the sky, and you will know how that mysterious symbol passed away.

"By Heaven! it is well-nigh gone!" said Aylmer to himself, in almost irrepressible ecstasy. "I can scarcely trace it now. Success! success! And now it is like the faintest rose color. The lightest flush of blood across her cheek would overcome it. But she is so pale!"

He drew aside the window curtain and suffered the light of natural day to fall into the room and rest upon her cheek. At the same time he heard a gross, hoarse chuckle, which he had long known as his servant Aminadab's expression of delight.

"Ah, clod! ah, earthly mass!" cried Aylmer, laughing in a sort of frenzy, "you have served me well! Matter and spirit—earth and heaven—have both done their part in this! Laugh, thing of the senses! You have earned the right to laugh."

These exclamations broke Georgiana's sleep. She slowly unclosed her eyes and gazed into the mirror which her husband had arranged for that purpose. A faint smile flitted over her lips when she recognized how barely perceptible was now that crimson hand which had once blazed forth with such disastrous brilliancy as to scare away all their happiness. But then her eyes sought Aylmer's face with a trouble and anxiety that he could by no means account for.

"My poor Aylmer!" murmured she.

"Poor? Nay, richest, happiest, most favored!" exclaimed he. "My peerless bride, it is successful! You are perfect!"

"My poor Aylmer," she repeated, with a more than human tenderness, "you have aimed loftily; you have done nobly. Do not repent that with so high and pure a feeling, you have rejected the best the earth could offer. Aylmer, dearest Aylmer, I am dying!"

Alas! it was too true! The fatal hand had grappled with the mystery of life, and was the bond by which an angelic spirit kept itself in union with a mortal frame. As the last crimson tint of the birthmark—that sole token of human imperfection—faded from her cheek, the parting breath of the now perfect woman passed into the atmosphere; and her soul, lingering a moment near her husband, took its heavenward flight. Then a hoarse, chuckling laugh was heard again! Thus ever does the gross fatality of earth exult in its invariable triumph over the immortal essence which, in this dim sphere of half development, demands the completeness of a higher state. Yet, had Aylmer reached a profounder wisdom, he need not thus have flung away the happiness which would have woven his mortal life of the selfsame texture with the celestial. The momentary circumstance was too strong for him; he failed to look beyond the shadowy scope of time, and, living once for all in eternity, to find the perfect future in the present.

[1843]

Questions

1. What is the birthmark? What does it come to symbolize by the end of the story?

2. What attitudes toward nature and science are explored in the story? Why are Aylmer's love of science and his love for his wife in conflict? Why do his successful experiments fail when he tries to repeat them for Georgiana?

3. Consider "The Birthmark" as an exploration of different kinds of power. What is Aylmer's power? What is Georgiana's?

4. Is the story more concerned with the abuse of science or with female imperfection?

5. What moral values or attitudes toward nature do Aylmer, Georgiana, and Aminadab represent? What moral perspective does Hawthorne express through the story's conclusion?

Ernest Hemingway

(1898–1961)

United States

Because Ernest Hemingway lived the kind of colorful, adventurous, even legendary life that most writers only write about, it is difficult to separate the legends from his celebrated fiction. A journalist who traveled widely—living in Cuba, Spain, Africa, France, Italy, and several parts of the United States—Hemingway wrote for American newspapers, first as a reporter for the Kansas City Star and later as a foreign correspondent. He saw action in World War I with the American Red Cross Ambulance Corps (sustaining a serious injury) when he was only 19, was involved with the Loyalists in Spain, and lived on the Paris Left Bank along with other American expatriate writers such as Ezra Pound and Gertrude Stein. During World War II, he served as a war correspondent, flying missions with the Royal Air Force and covering the Normandy landing. He was injured in a plane crash during an African safari. During those years, he was married four times.

Hemingway's adventurous, risk-taking life unquestionably provided both the inspiration and the substance for his fiction. His early novel, The Sun Also Rises (1926), explores a group of disillusioned Americans, part of the Lost Generation of expatriates in Spain after the war. A Farewell to Arms (1929) draws its energy from encounters with war that Hemingway knew intimately. For Whom the Bell Tolls (1940), set during the Spanish Civil War, is among Hemingway's masterpieces.

Hemingway's early novels and stories immediately established his reputation as the master of a distinctive and original style, characterized by spare, lucid, precise prose in which his characters reveal themselves through dialogue and action rather than authorial commentary. In Death in the Afternoon, Hemingway commented that "Prose is architecture, not interior decoration, and the Baroque is over." When pressed to describe the function of his writing for a Paris Review interview, he described it as follows:

> From things that have happened and from things as they exist and from all things that you know and all those you cannot know, you make something through your invention that is not a representation but a whole new thing truer than anything true and alive, and you make it alive, and if you make it well enough, you give it immortality.

Writing was Hemingway's way of discovering himself and of making sense of the pessimism he imbibed as part of the collapse of values precipitated by two harrowing wars. His male characters often seek to model their behavior according to rules derived from specialized contexts like bullfighting and hunting. The Hemingway "code," characterized by courage, self-discipline, and "grace under pressure," was the source of dignity and meaning for his male heroes, who regarded the world as otherwise absurd or harsh. Hemingway's female characters, caught in the same atmosphere of despair but excluded from participation in these male rituals, are often portrayed as helpless or destructive.

Hemingway received the Pulitzer Prize for The Old Man and the Sea in 1953; in 1954, he was awarded the Nobel Prize for Literature. In 1961, in poor physical and emotional health and haunted by the memory of his father's suicide years earlier, Hemingway fatally shot himself.

HILLS LIKE WHITE ELEPHANTS

The hills across the valley of the Ebro were long and white. On this side there was no shade and no trees and the station was between two lines of rails in the sun. Close against the side of the station there was the warm shadow of the building and a curtain, made of strings of bamboo beads, hung across the open door into the bar, to keep out flies. The American and the girl with him sat at a table in the shade, outside the building. It was very hot and the express from Barcelona would come in forty minutes. It stopped at this junction for two minutes and went on to Madrid.

"What should we drink?" the girl asked. She had taken off her hat and put it on the table.

"It's pretty hot," the man said.

"Let's drink beer."

"Dos cervezas," the man said into the curtain.

"Big ones?" a woman asked from the doorway.

"Yes. Two big ones."

The woman brought two glasses of beer and two felt pads. She put the felt pads and the beer glasses on the table and looked at the man and the girl. The girl was looking off at the line of hills. They were white in the sun and the country was brown and dry.

"They look like white elephants," she said.

"I've never seen one," the man drank his beer.

"No, you wouldn't have."

"I might have," the man said. "Just because you say I wouldn't have doesn't prove anything."

The girl looked at the bead curtain. "They've painted something on it," she said. "What does it say?"

"Anis del Toro. It's a drink."

"Could we try it?"

The man called "Listen" through the curtain. The woman came out from the bar.

"Four reales."

"We want two Anis del Toro."

"With water?"

"Do you want it with water?"

"I don't know," the girl said. "Is it good with water?"

"It's all right."

"You want them with water?" asked the woman.

"Yes, with water."

"It tastes like licorice," the girl said and put the glass down.

"That's the way with everything."

"Yes," said the girl. "Everything tastes of licorice. Especially all the things you've waited so long for, like absinthe."

"Oh, cut it out."

"You started it," the girl said. "I was being amused. I was having a fine time."

"Well, let's try and have a fine time."

"All right. I was trying. I said the mountains looked like white elephants. Wasn't that bright?"

"That was bright."

"I wanted to try this new drink. That's all we do, isn't it—look at things and try new drinks?"

"I guess so."

The girl looked across at the hills.

"They're lovely hills," she said. "They don't really look like white elephants. I just meant the coloring of their skin through the trees."

"Should we have another drink?"

"All right."

The warm wind blew the bead curtain against the table.

"The beer's nice and cool," the man said.

"It's lovely," the girl said.

"It's really an awfully simple operation, Jig," the man said. "It's not really an operation at all."

The girl looked at the ground the table legs rested on.

"I know you wouldn't mind it, Jig. It's really not anything. It's just to let the air in."

The girl did not say anything.

"I'll go with you and I'll stay with you all the time. They just let the air in and then it's all perfectly natural."

"Then what will we do afterward?"

"We'll be fine afterward. Just like we were before."

"What makes you think so?"

"That's the only thing that bothers us. It's the only thing that's made us unhappy."

The girl looked at the bead curtain, put her hand out and took hold of two of the strings of beads.

"And you think then we'll be all right and be happy."

"I know we will. You don't have to be afraid. I've known lots of people that have done it."

"So have I," said the girl. "And afterward they were all so happy."

"Well," the man said, "if you don't want to you don't have to. I wouldn't have you do it if you didn't want to. But I know it's perfectly simple."

"And you really want to?"

"I think it's the best thing to do. But I don't want you to do it if you don't really want to."

"And if I do it you'll be happy and things will be like they were and you'll love me?"

"I love you now. You know I love you."

"I know. But if I do it, then it will be nice again if I say things are like white elephants, and you'll like it?"

"I'll love it. I love it now but I just can't think about it. You know how I get when I worry."

"If I do it you won't ever worry?"

"I won't worry about that because it's perfectly simple."

"Then I'll do it. Because I don't care about me."

"What do you mean?"

"I don't care about me."

"Well, I care about you."

"Oh, yes. But I don't care about me. And I'll do it and then everything will be fine."

"I don't want you to do it if you feel that way."

The girl stood up and walked to the end of the station. Across, on the other side, were fields of grain and trees along the banks of the Ebro. Far away, beyond the river, were mountains. The shadow of a cloud moved across the field of grain and she saw the river through the trees.

"And we could have all this," she said. "And we could have everything and every day we make it more impossible."

"What did you say?"

"I said we could have everything."

"We can have everything."

"No, we can't."

"We can have the whole world."

"No, we can't."

"We can go everywhere."

"No, we can't. It isn't ours any more."

"It's ours."

"No, it isn't. And once they take it away, you never get it back."

"But they haven't taken it away."

"We'll wait and see."

"Come on back in the shade," he said. "You mustn't feel that way."

"I don't feel any way," the girl said. "I just know things."

"I don't want you to do anything that you don't want to do——"

"Nor that isn't good for me," she said. "I know. Could we have another beer?"

"All right. But you've got to realize——"

"I realize," the girl said. "Can't we maybe stop talking?"

They sat down at the table and the girl looked across at the hills on the dry side of the valley and the man looked at her and at the table.

"You've got to realize," he said, "that I don't want you to do it if you don't want to. I'm perfectly willing to go through with it if it means anything to you."

"Doesn't it mean anything to you? We could get along."

"Of course it does. But I don't want anybody but you. I don't want any one else. And I know it's perfectly simple."

"Yes, you know it's perfectly simple."

"It's all right for you to say that, but I did know it."

"Would you do something for me now?"

"I'd do anything for you."

"Would you please please please please please please please stop talking?"

He did not say anything but looked at the bags against the wall of the station. There were labels on them from all the hotels where they had spent nights.

"But I don't want you to," he said, "I don't care anything about it."

"I'll scream," the girl said.

The woman came out through the curtains with two glasses of beer and put them down on the damp felt pads. "The train comes in five minutes," she said.

"What did she say?" asked the girl.

"That the train is coming in five minutes."

The girl smiled brightly at the woman, to thank her.

"I'd better take the bags over to the other side of the station," the man said. She smiled at him.

"All right. Then come back and we'll finish the beer."

He picked up the two heavy bags and carried them around the station to the other tracks. He looked up the tracks but could not see the train. Coming back, he walked through the barroom, where people waiting for the train were drinking. He drank an Anis at the bar and looked at the people. They were all waiting reasonably for the train. He went out through the bead curtain. She was sitting at the table and smiled at him.

"Do you feel better?" he asked.

"I feel fine," she said. "There's nothing wrong with me. I feel fine."

[1927]

Questions

1. What significance can be made of Hemingway's title? Why does the woman say the hills look like white elephants and then later say they don't?
2. Does the story move beyond the stereotype of a young man trying to convince a young woman that his position is the more important one?
3. In spite of the economy of the dialogue, what is left unspoken?

Langston Hughes

(1902–1967)

United States

Y ears before his death in 1967, Langston Hughes had earned the respect and admiration of black America and had been labeled "The Poet Laureate of the Negro People." It is impossible to consider African-American literature without thinking of Hughes's lifelong contribution as poet, novelist, journalist, editor, translator, playwright, and one-man support group for black artistry in general—from the Harlem Renaissance during the 1920s until the New Black Arts Movement of the 1960s. If Hughes's short stories are less widely known than his poems, the explanation may be in large part due to the vagaries of American publishing. Black readers were familiar with Hughes's Jesse Simple stories for years, beginning with their appearance in The Chicago Defender in 1943. Most mainstream readers had to wait until the stories were collected in the various Simple volumes, starting with Simple Speaks His Mind in 1950. The story included here, "Thank You, M'am," was written in 1953, although the context for its origin no doubt goes back much earlier, to "The Need for Heroes," an essay Hughes published in The Crisis in 1941:

> The written word is the only record we will have of this our present, or our past, to leave behind for future generations. . . . We have a need for heroes. We have a need for books and plays that will encourage and inspire our youth, set for them patterns of conduct, move and stir them to be forthright, strong, clear-thinking and unafraid. . . . It is the social duty of Negro writers to reveal to the people the deep reservoirs of heroism within the race. . . . We need in literature the kind of black men and women all of us know exist in life; who are not afraid to claim our rights as human beings and as Americans.

THANK YOU, M'AM

She was a large woman with a large purse that had everything in it but hammer and nails. It had a long strap and she carried it slung across her shoulder. It was about eleven o'clock at night, and she was walking alone, when a boy ran up behind her and tried to snatch her purse. The strap broke with the single tug the boy gave it from behind. But the boy's weight, and the weight of the purse combined caused him to lose his balance so, instead of taking off full blast as he had hoped, the boy fell on his back on the sidewalk, and his legs flew up. The large woman simply turned around and kicked him right square in his blue jeaned sitter. Then she reached down, picked the boy up by the shirt front, and shook him until his teeth rattled.

After that the woman said, "Pick up my pocketbook, boy, and give it here."

She still held him. But she bent down enough to permit him to stoop and pick up her purse. Then she said, "Now ain't you ashamed of yourself?"

Firmly gripped by his shirt front, the boy said, "Yes'm."

The woman said, "What did you want to do it for?"

The boy said, "I didn't aim to."

She said, "You a lie!"

By that time two or three people passed, stopped, turned to look, and some stood watching.

"If I turn you loose, you will run?" asked the woman.

"Yes'm," said the boy.

"Then I won't turn you loose," said the woman. She did not release him.

"I'm very sorry, lady, I'm sorry," whispered the boy.

"Um-hum! And your face is dirty. I got a great mind to wash your face for you. Ain't you got nobody home to tell you to wash your face?"

"No'm," said the boy.

"Then it will get washed this evening," said the large woman starting up the street, dragging the frightened boy behind her.

He looked as if he were fourteen or fifteen, frail and willow-wild, in tennis shoes and blue jeans.

The woman said, "You ought to be my son. I would teach you right from wrong. Least I can do right now is to wash your face. Are you hungry?"

"No'm," said the being-dragged boy. "I just want you to turn me loose."

"Was I bothering *you* when I turned that corner?" asked the woman.

"No'm."

"But you put yourself in contact with *me*," said the woman. "If you think that that contact is not going to last awhile, you got another thought coming. When I get through with you, sir, you are going to remember Mrs. Luella Bates Washington Jones."

Sweat popped out on the boy's face and he began to struggle. Mrs. Jones stopped, jerked him around in front of her, put a half-nelson about his neck, and continued to drag him up the street. When she got to her door, she dragged the boy inside, down a hall, and into a large kitchenette-furnished room at the rear of the house. She switched on the light and left the door open. The boy could hear other roomers, laughing and talking in the large house. Some of their doors were open, too, so he knew he and the woman were not alone. The woman still had him by the neck in the middle of her room.

She said, "What is your name?"

"Roger," answered the boy.

"Then, Roger, you go to that sink and wash your face," said the woman, where-upon she turned him loose—at last. Roger looked at the door—looked at the woman—looked at the door—*and went to the sink.*

"Let the water run until it gets warm," she said. "here's a clean towel."

"You gonna take me to jail?" asked the boy, bending over the sink.

"Not with that face, I would not take you nowhere," said the woman. "Here I am trying to get home to cook me a bite to eat and you snatch my pocketbook! Maybe you ain't been to your supper either, late as it be. Have you?"

"There's nobody home at my house," said the boy.

"Then we'll eat," said the woman. "I believe you're hungry—or been hungry—to try to snatch my pocketbook."

"I wanted a pair of blue suede shoes," said the boy.

"Well, you didn't have to snatch *my* pocketbook to get some suede shoes," said Mrs. Luella Bates Washington Jones. "You could of asked me."

"M'am?"

The water dripping from his face, the boy looked at her. There was a long pause. A very long pause. After he had dried his face and not knowing what else to do dried it again, the boy turned around, wondering what next. The door was open. He could make a dash for it down the hall. He could run, run, run, run, *run*!

The woman was sitting on the day-bed. After awhile she said, "I were young once and I wanted things I could not get."

There was another long pause. The boy's mouth opened. Then he frowned, but not knowing he frowned.

The woman said, "Um-hum! You thought I was going to say *but*, didn't you? You thought I was going to say, *but I didn't snatch people's pocketbooks*. Well, I wasn't going to say that." Pause. Silence. "I have done things, too, which I would not tell you, son—neither tell God, if he didn't already know. So you set down while I fix us something to eat. You might run that comb through your hair so you will look presentable."

In another corner of the room behind a screen was a gas plate and an icebox. Mrs. Jones got up and went behind the screen. The woman did not watch the boy to see if he was going to run now, nor did she watch her purse which she left behind her on the day-bed. But the boy took care to sit on the far side of the room where he thought she could easily see him out of the corner of her eye, if she wanted to. He did not trust the woman *not* to trust him. And he did not want to be mistrusted now.

"Do you need somebody to go to the store," asked the boy, "maybe to get some milk or something?"

"Don't believe I do," said the woman, "unless you just want sweet milk yourself. I was going to make cocoa out of this canned milk I got here."

"That will be fine," said the boy.

She heated some lima beans and ham she had in the icebox, made the cocoa, and set the table. The woman did not ask the boy anything about where he lived, or his folks, or anything else that would embarrass him. Instead, as they ate, she told him about her job in a hotel beauty-shop that stayed open late, what the work was like, and how all kinds of women came in and out, blondes, red-heads, and Spanish. Then she cut him a half of her ten-cent cake.

"Eat some more, son," she said.

When they were finished eating she got up and said, "Now, here, take this ten dollars and buy yourself some blue suede shoes. And next time, do not make the mistake of latching onto *my* pocketbook *nor nobody else's*—because shoes come by devilish like that will burn your feet. I got to get my rest now. But I wish you would behave yourself, son, from here on in."

She led him down the hall to the front door and opened it. "Goodnight! Behave yourself, boy!" she said, looking out into the street.

The boy wanted to say something else other than, "Thank you m'am," to Mrs. Luella Bates Washington Jones, but he couldn't do so as he turned at the barren stoop and looked back at the large woman in the door. He barely managed to say, "Thank you," before she shut the door. And he never saw her again.

[1953]

Questions

1. Is Langston Hughes guilty of romanticizing the incident in his story? Why? Why not?
2. For contrast, read BarbaraNeely's "Spilled Salt," also included in this volume. In what ways do the two stories mirror or complement each other?
3. Why does Hughes refer to the woman in the story as Mrs. Luella Bates Washington Jones and not simply as Mrs. Jones?

Zora Neale Hurston

(1891–1960)
United States

Z ora Neale Hurston has probably influenced contemporary African-American women's fiction more than any other earlier black writer; and, indeed, until Toni Morrison published Beloved (1987), Hurston was our country's most prolific African-American woman writer. Her classic novel, Their Eyes Were Watching God (1937), demonstrated that black lives are not marked solely by responses to racism in the United States (a theme that is also present in "The Gilded Six-Bits"). In addition to her fiction, Ms. Hurston is also regarded as one of the most important collectors of African-American folklore of this century. According to Robert Hemenway, her biographer, Hurston defined folklore as "the art people create before they find out there is such a thing as art."

Hurston's life was rarely typified by the financial stability she so greatly deserved. She was always a bit of a rebel. Her wit and charm apparently sustained her during the most painful of times. On an occasion when she was arrested for crossing the street on a red light, she finagled herself out of the ticket by exclaiming that she had observed white folks cross on green and assumed that red was for black people. Although part of the Harlem Renaissance of the 1920s (whose writers she referred to as the "niggerati"), her writing did not appear until the decade thereafter. She died in 1960 in a poorhouse, without funds to pay for her funeral.

Because interest in Hurston's work has swelled in recent years, her books are now available in a uniform Perennial Library edition, edited by Henry Louis Gates, Jr.: Mules and Men (1935), Their Eyes Were Watching God (1937), Moses, Man of the Mountain (1939), Dust Tracks on the Road (1942), and Seraph on the Suwanee (1948).

THE GILDED SIX-BITS

It was a Negro yard around a Negro house in a Negro settlement that looked to the payroll of the G and G Fertilizer works for its support. But there was something happy about the place. The front yard was parted in the middle by a sidewalk from gate to door-step, a sidewalk edged on either side by quart bottles driven neck down into the ground on a slant. A mess of homey flowers planted without a plan but blooming cheerily from their helter-skelter places. The fence and house were whitewashed. The porch and steps scrubbed white.

The front door stood open to the sunshine so that the floor of the front room could finish drying after its weekly scouring. It was Saturday. Everything clean from the front gate to the privy house. Yard raked so that the strokes of the rake would make a pattern. Fresh newspaper cut in fancy edge on the kitchen shelves.

Missie May was bathing herself in the galvanized washtub in the bedroom. Her dark-brown skin glistened under the soapsuds that skittered down from her wash rag. Her stiff young breasts thrust forward aggressively like broad-based cones with the tips lacquered in black.

She heard men's voices in the distance and glanced at the dollar clock on the dresser.

"Humph! Ah'm way behind time to'day! Joe gointer be heah 'fore Ah git mah clothes on if Ah don't make haste."

She grabbed the clean meal sack at hand and dried herself hurriedly and began to dress. But before she could tie her slippers, there came the ring of singing metal on wood. Nine times.

Missie May grinned with delight. She had not seen the big tall man come stealing in the gate and creep up the walk grinning happily at the joyful mischief he was about to commit. But she knew that it was her husband throwing silver dollars in the door for her to pick up and pile beneath her plate at dinner. It was this way every Saturday afternoon. The nine dollars hurled into the open door, he scurried to a hiding place behind the cape jasmine bush and waited.

Missie May promptly appeared at the door in mock alarm.

"Who dat chuckin' money in ma do'way?" she demanded. No answer from the yard. She leaped off the porch and began to search the shrubbery. She peeped under the porch and hung over the gate to look up and down the road. While she did this, the man behind the jasmine darted to the china berry tree. She spied him and gave chase.

"Nobody ain't gointer be chuckin' money at me and Ah not do 'em nothin'," she shouted in mock anger. He ran around the house with Missie May at his heels. She overtook him at the kitchen door. He ran inside but could not close it after him before she crowded in and locked with him in a rough and tumble. For several minutes the two were a furious mass of male and female energy. Shouting, laughing, twisting, turning, tussling, tickling each other in the ribs; Missie May clutching Joe and Joe trying, but not too hard, to get away.

"Missie May, take yo' hand out mah pocket!" Joe shouted out between laughs.

"Ah ain't, Joe, not lessen you gwine gimme whateve' it is good you got in you' pocket. Turn it go, Joe, do Ah'll tear yo' clothes."

"Go on tear 'em. You de one dat pushes de needles around heah. Move yo' hand, Missie May."

"Lemme git dat paper sack out yo' pocket. Ah bet it's candy kisses."

"Tain't. Move yo' hand. Woman ain't got no business in a man's clothes nohow. Go away."

"Unhhunh! Ah got it. It 'tis so candy kisses. Ah knowed you had something' for me in yo' clothes. Now Ah got to see whut's in every pocket you got."

Joe smiled indulgently and let his wife go through all of his pockets and take out the things that he had hidden there for her to find. She bore off the chewing gum, the cake of sweet soap, the pocket handkerchief as if she had wrested them from him, as if they had not been bought for the sake of this friendly battle.

"Whew! dat play-fight done got me all warmed up," Joe exclaimed. "Got me some water in de kittle?"

"Yo' water is on de fire and yo' clean things is cross de bed. Hurry up and wash yo'-self and git changed so we kin eat. Ah'm hongry." As Missie said this, she bore the steaming kettle into the bedroom.

"You ain't hongry, sugar," Joe contradicted her. "Youse jes' a little empty. Ah'm de one whut's hongry. Ah could eat up camp meeting', back off 'ssociation, and drink Jurdan dry. Have it on de table when 'ah git out de tub."

"Don't you mess wid mah business, man. You git in yo' clothes. Ah'm a real wife, not no dress and breath. Ah might not look lak one, but if you burn me, you won't git a thing but wife ashes."

Joe splashed in the bedroom and Missie May fanned around in the kitchen. A fresh red and white checked cloth on the table. Big pitcher of buttermilk beaded with pale drops of butter from the churn. Hot fried mullet, crackling bread, ham hock atop a mound of string beans and new potatoes, and perched on the window-sill a pone of spicy potato pudding.

Very little talk during the meal but that little consisted of banter that pretended to deny affection but in reality flaunted it. Like when Missie May reached for a second helping of the tater pone. Joe snatched it out of her reach.

After Missie May had made two or three unsuccessful grabs at the pan, she begged, "Ah, Joe, gimme some mo' dat tater pone."

"Nope, sweetenin' is for us men-folks. Y'all pritty lil frail eels don't need nothin' lak dis. You too sweet already."

"Please, Joe."

"Naw, naw. Ah don't want you to git no sweeter than whut you is already. We goin' down de road a lil piece t'night so you go put on yo' Sunday-go-to-meetin' things."

Missie May looked at her husband to see if he was planing some prank. "Sho nuff, Joe?"

"Yeah. We goin' to de ice cream parlor."

"Where de ice cream parlor at, Joe?"

"A new man done come heah from Chicago and he done got a place and took and opened it up for a ice cream parlor, and being' as it's real swell, Ah wants you to be one de first ladies to walk in dere and have some set down."

"Do Jesus, Ah ain't knowed nothin' 'bout it. Who de man done it?"

"Mister Otis D. Slemmons, of spots and places—Memphis, Chicago, Jacksonville, Philadelphia and so on."

"Dat heavy-set man wid his mouth full of good teethes?"

"Yeah, Where did you see 'im at?"

"Ah went down to de sto' tuh git a box of lye and Ah seen 'im standin' on de corner talkin' to some of de mens, and Ah come on back and went to scrubbin' de floor, and he passed and tipped his hat whilst Ah was scourin' de steps. Ah thought Ah never seen *him* befo'."

Joe smiled pleasantly. "Yeah, he's up to date. He got de finest clothes Ah ever seen on a colored man's back."

"Aw, he don't look no better in his clothes than you do in yourn. He got a puzzle gut on 'im and he so chuckle-headed, he got a pone behind his neck."

Joe looked down at his own abdomen and said wistfully, "Wisht Ah had a build on me lak he got. He ain't puzzle-gutted, honey. He jes' got a corperation. Dat make 'im look lak a rich white man. All rich mens is got some belly on 'em."

"Ah seen de pitchers of Henry Ford and he's a spare-built man and Rockefeller look lak he ain't got but one gut. But Ford and Rockefeller and dis Slemmons and all de rest kin be as many-gutted as dey please, Ah'm satisfied wid you jes' lak you is, baby. God took pattern after a pine tree and built you noble. Youse a pritty man, and if Ah knowed any way to make you mo' pritty still Ah'd take and do it."

Joe reached over gently and toyed with Missie May's ear. "You jes' say dat cause you love me, but Ah know Ah can't hold no light to Otis D. Slemmons. Ah ain't never been nowhere and Ah ain't got nothing' but you."

Missie May got on his lap and kissed him and he kissed back in kind. Then he went on. "All de womens is crazy 'bout 'im everywhere he go."

"How do you know dat, Joe?"

"He tole us so hisself."

"Dat don't make it so. His mouf is cut cross-ways, ain't it? Well, he kin lie jes' lak anybody else."

"Good Lawd, Missie? You womens sho is hard to sense into things. He's got a five-dollar gold piece for a stick-pin and he got a ten-dollar gold piece on his watch chain and his mouf is jes' crammed full of gold teethes. Sho wisht it wuz mine. And whut make it so cool, he got money 'cumulated. And womens give it all to 'im."

"Ah don't see whut de womens see on 'im. Ah wouldn't give 'im a wink if de sheriff wuz after 'im."

"Well, he tole us how de white womens in Chicago give 'im all dat gold money. So he don't 'low nobody to touch it at all. Not even put dey finger on it. Dey tole 'im not to. You kin make 'miration at it, but don't tetch it."

"Whyn't he stay up dere where dey so crazy 'bout 'im?"

"Ah reckon dey done made 'im vast-rich and he wants to travel some. He says dey wouldn't leave 'im hit a lick of work. He got mo' lady people crazy 'bout him than he kin shake a stick at."

"Joe, Ah hates to see you so dumb. Dat stray nigger jes' tell y'all anything and y'all b'lieve it."

"Go 'head on now, honey and put on yo' clothes. He takin' 'bout his pritty womens— Ah want 'im to see *mine*."

Missie May went off to dress and Joe spent the time trying to make his stomach punch out like Slemmons' middle. He tried the rolling swagger of the stranger, but found that his tall bone-and-muscle stride fitted ill with it. He just had time to drop back into his seat before Missie May came in dressed to go.

On the way home that night Joe was exultant. "Didn't Ah say ole Otis was swell? Can't he talk Chicago talk? Wuzn't dat funny whut he said when great big fat ole Ida Armstrong come in? He asted me, 'Who is dat broad wid de forte shake?' Dat's a new word. Us always thought forty was a set of figgers but he showed us where it means a whole heap of things. Sometimes he don't say forty, he jes' says thirty-eight and two and dat mean de same thing. Know whut he tole me when Ah wuz payin' for our ice cream? He say, 'Ah have to hand it to you, Joe. Dat wife of yours is jes' thirty-eight and two. Yessuh, she's forte?' Ain't he killin'?"

"He'll do in case of a rush. But he sho is got uh heap uh gold on 'im. Dats de first time Ah ever seed gold money. It lookted good on him sho nuff, but it'd look a whole heap better on you."

"Who me? Missie May youse crazy! Where would a po' man lak me git gold money from?"

Missie May was silent for a time, then she said, "Us might find some goin' long de road some time. Us could."

"Who would be losin' gold money round heah? We ain't ever seen none dese white folks wearin' no gold money on dey watch chain. You must be friggerin' Mister Packard or Mister Cadillac goin' pass through heah."

"You don't know whut been lost 'round heah. Maybe somebody way back in memorial times lost they gold money and went on off and it ain't never been found. And then if we wuz to find it, you could wear some 'thout havin' no gang of womens lak dat Slemmons say he got."

Joe laughed and hugged her. "Don't be so wishful 'bout me. Ah'm satisfied de way Ah is. So long as Ah be yo' husband, Ah don't keer 'bout nothin' else. Ah'd ruther all de other womens in de world to be dead than for you to have de toothache. Less we go to bed and git our night rest."

It was Saturday night once more before Joe could parade his wife in Slemmon's ice cream parlor again. He worked the night shift and Saturday was his only night off. Every other evening around six o'clock he left home, and dying dawn saw him hustling home around the lake where the challenging sun flung a flaming sword from east to west across the trembling water.

That was the best part of life—going home to Missie May. Their white-washed house, the mock battle on Saturday, the dinner and ice cream parlor afterwards, church on Sunday nights when Missie outdressed any other woman in town—all, everything was right.

One night around eleven the acid ran out at the G. and G. The foreman knocked off the crew and let the steam die down. As Joe rounded the lake on his way home, a lean moon rode the lake in a silver boat. If anybody had asked Joe about the moon on the lake, he would have said he hadn't paid it any attention. But he saw it with his feelings. It made him yearn painfully for Missie. Creation obsessed him. He thought about children. They ought to be making little feet for shoes. A little boy child would be about right.

He saw a dim light in the bedroom and decided to come in through the kitchen door. He could wash the fertilizer dust off himself before presenting himself to Missie May. It would be nice for her not to know that he as there until he slipped into his place in bed and hugged her back. She always liked that.

He eased the kitchen door open slowly and silently, but when he went to set his dinner bucket on the table he bumped it into a pile of dishes, and something crashed to the floor. He heard his wife gasp in fright and hurried to reassure her.

"Iss me, honey. Don't git skeered."

There was a quick, large movement in the bedroom. A rustle, a thud and a stealthy silence. The light went out.

What? Robbers? Murderers? Some varmit attacking his helpless wife, perhaps. He struck a match, threw himself on guard and stepped over the door-sill into the bedroom.

The great belt on the wheel of Time slipped and eternity stood still. By the match light he could see the man's legs fighting with his breeches in is frantic desire to get them on. He had both chance and time to kill the intruder in his helpless condition—half in and half out of his pants—but he was too weak to take action. The shapeless enemies of humanity that live in the hours of Time had waylaid Joe. He was assaulted in his weakness. Like Samson awakening after his haircut. So he just opened his mouth and laughed.

The match went out and he struck another and lit the lamp. A howling wind raced across his heart, but underneath its fury he heard his wife sobbing and Slemmons pleading for his life. Offering to buy it with all that he had. "Please, suh, don't kill me. Sixty-two dollars at de sto'. Gold money."

Joe just stood. Slemmons looked at the window, but it was screened. Joe stood like a rough-backed mountain between him and the door. Barring him from escape, from sunrise, from life.

He considered a surprise attack upon the big clown that stood there laughing like a chessy cat. But before his fist could travel an inch, Joe's own rushed out to crush him like a battering ram. Then Joe stood over him.

"Git into yo' damn rags, Slemmons, an dat quick."

Slemmons scrambled to his feet and into his vest and coat. As he grabbed his hat, Joe's fury overrode his intentions and he grabbed at Slemmons with his left hand and struck at him with his right. The right landed. The left grazed the front of his vest. Slemmons was knocked a somersault into the kitchen and fled through the open door. Joe found himself alone with Missie May, with the golden watch charm clutched in his left fist. A short bit of broken chain dangled between his fingers.

Missie May was sobbing. Wails of weeping without words. Joe stood, and after awhile he found out that he had something in his hand. And then he stood and felt without thinking and without seeing with his natural eyes. Missie May kept on crying and Joe kept on feeling so much and not knowing what to do with all his feelings, he put Slemmons watch charm in his pants pocket and took a good laugh and went to bed.

"Missie May, whut you cryin' for?"

"Cause Ah love you so hard and Ah know you don't love *me* no mo'."

Joe sank his face into the pillow for a spell then he said huskily, "You don't know de feelings of dat yet, Missie May."

"Oh Joe, honey, he said he wuz gointer give me dat gold money and he jes' kept on after me—"

Joe was very still and silent for a long time. Then he said, "Well, don't cry no mo', Missie May. Ah got yo' gold piece for you."

The hours went past on their rusty ankles. Joe still and quiet on one bed-rail and Missie May wrung dry of sobs on the other. Finally the sun's tide crept upon the shore of night and drowned all its hours. Missie May with her face stiff and streaked towards the window saw the dawn come into her yard. It was day. Nothing more. Joe wouldn't be coming home as usual. No need to fling open the front door and sweep off the porch, making it nice for Joe. Never no more breakfast to cook; no more washing and starching of Joe's jumper-jackets and pants. No more nothing. So why get up?

With this strange man in her bed, she felt embarrassed to get up and dress. She decided to wait till he had dressed and gone. Then she would get up, dress quickly and be gone forever beyond reach of Joe's looks and laughs. But he never moved. Red light turned to yellow, then white.

From beyond the no-man's land between them came a voice. A strange voice that yesterday had been Joe's.

"Missie May, ain't you gonna fix me no breakfus'?"

She sprang out of bed. "Yeah, Joe. Ah didn't reckon you wuz hongry."

No need to die today. Joe needed her for a few more minutes anyhow.

Soon there was a roaring fire in the cook stove. Water bucket full and two chickens killed. Joe loved fried chicken and rice. She didn't deserve a thing and good Joe was letting her cook him some breakfast. She rushed hot biscuits to the table as Joe took his seat.

He ate with his eyes in his plate. No laughter, no banter.

"Missie May, you ain't eatin' yo' breakfus'."

"Ah don't choose none, Ah thank yuh."

His coffee cup was empty. She sprang to refill it. When she turned from the stove and bent to set the cup beside Joe's plate, she saw the yellow coin on the table be-tween them.

She slumped into her seat and wept into her arms.

Presently Joe said calmly, "Missie May, you cry too much. Don't look back lak Lot's wife and turn to salt."

The sun, the hero of every day, the impersonal old man that beams as brightly on death as on birth, came up every morning and raced across the blue dome and dipped into the sea of fire every evening. Water ran down hill and birds nested.

Missie knew why she didn't leave Joe. She couldn't. She loved him too much, but she could not understand why Joe didn't leave her. He was polite, even kind at times, but aloof.

There were no more Saturday romps. No ringing silver dollars to stack beside her plate. No pockets to rifle. In fact the yellow coin in his trousers was like a monster hiding in the cave of his pockets to destroy her.

She often wondered if he still had it, but nothing could have induced her to ask nor yet to explore his pockets to see for herself. Its shadow was in the house whether or no.

One night Joe came home around midnight and complained of pains in the back. He asked Missie to rub him down with liniment. It had been three months since Missie had touched his body and it all seemed strange. But she rubbed him. Grateful for the chance. Before morning, youth triumphed and Missie exulted. But the next day, as she joyfully made up their bed, beneath her pillow she found the piece of money with the bit of chain attached.

Alone to herself, she looked at the thing with loathing, but look she must. She took it into her hands with trembling and saw first thing that it was no gold piece. It was a gilded half dollar. Then she knew why Slemmons had forbidden anyone to touch his gold. He trusted village eyes at a distance not to recognize his stick-pin as a gild-ed quarter, and his watch charm as a four-bit piece.

She was glad at first that Joe had left it there. Perhaps he was through with her pun-ishment. They were man and wife again. Then another thought came clawing at her. He had come home to buy from her as if she were any woman in the long house. Fifty cents for her love. As if to say that he could pay as well as Slemmons. She slid the coin into his Sunday pants pocket and dressed herself and left his house.

Half way between her house and the quarters she met her husband's mother, and after a short talk she turned and went back home. Never would she admit defeat to that woman who prayed for it nightly. If she had not the substance of marriage she had the outside show. Joe must leave *her*. She let him see she didn't want his old gold four-bits too.

She saw no more of the coin for some time though she knew that Joe could not help finding it in his pocket. But his health kept poor, and he came home at least every ten days to be rubbed.

The sun swept around the horizon, trailing its robes of weeks and days. One morn-ing as Joe came in from work, he found Missie May chopping wood. Without a word he took the ax and chopped a huge pile before he stopped.

"You ain't got no business choppin' wood, and you know it."

"How come? Ah been choppin' it for de last longest."

"Ah ain't blind. You makin' feet for shoes."

"Won't you be glad to have a lil baby chile, Joe?"

"You know dat 'thout astin' me."

"Iss gointer be a boy chile, and de very spit of you."

"You reckon, Missie May?"

"Who else could it look lak?"

Joe said nothing, but he thrust his hand deep into his pocket and fingered something there.

It was almost six months later Missie May took to bed and Joe went and got his mother to come wait on the house.

Missie May was delivered of a fine boy. Her travail was over when Joe came in from work one morning. His mother and the old women were drinking great bowls of coffee around the fire in the kitchen.

The minute Joe came into the room his mother called him aside.

"How did Missie May make out?" he asked quickly.

"Who, dat gal? She strong as a ox. She gointer have plenty mo'. We done fixed her wid de sugar and lard to sweeten her for de nex' one."

Joe stood silent awhile.

"You ain't ast 'bout de baby, Joe. You oughter be mighty proud cause he sho is de spittin' imagine of yuh, son. Dat's yourn all right, if you never git another one, dat un is yourn. And you know Ah'm mighty proud too, son, cause Ah never thought well of you marryin' Missie May cause her ma used tuh fan her foot round right smart and Ah been mighty skeered dat Missie May wuz gointer git misput on her road."

Joe said nothing. He fooled around the house till late in the day then just before he went to work, he went and stood at the foot of the bed and asked his wife how she felt. He did this every day during the week.

On Saturday he went to Orlando to make his market. It had been a long time since he had done that.

Meat and lard, meal and flour, soap and starch. Cans of corn and tomatoes. All the staples. He fooled around town for a while and bought bananas and apples. Way after while he went around to the candy store.

"Hello, Joe," the clerk greeted him. "Ain't seen you in a long time."

"Nope, Ah ain't been heah. Been round in spots and places."

"Want some of them molasses kisses you always buy?"

"Yessuh." He threw the gilded half dollar on the counter. "Will dat spend?"

"Whut is it, Joe? Well, I'll be doggone! A gold-plated four-bit piece. Where'd you git it, Joe?"

"Offen a stray nigger dat come through Eatonville. He had it on his watch chain for a charm—goin' round making out iss gold money. Ha ha! He had a quarter on his tie pin and it wuz all golded up too. Tryin' to fool people. Makin' out he so rich and everything. Ha! Ha! Tryin' to tole off folkses wives from home."

"How did you git it, Joe? Did he fool you, too?"

"Who, me? Naw suh! He ain't fooled me none. Know what Ah done? He come round me wid his smart talk. Ah hauled off and knocked 'im down and took his old four-bits way from 'im. Gointer buy my wife some good ole lasses kisses wid it. Gimme fifty cents worth of dem candy kisses."

"Fifty cents buys a mighty lot of candy kisses, Joe. Why don't you split it up and take some chocolate bars, too. They eat good, too."

"Yessuh, dey do, but Ah wants all dat in kisses. Ah got a lil boy chile home now. Tain't a week old yet, but he kin suck a sugar tit and maybe eat one them kisses hisself."

Joe got his candy and left the store. The clerk turned to the next customer. "Wist I could be like these darkies. Laughin' all the time. Nothin' worries 'em."

Back in Eatonville, Joe reached his own front door. There was the ring of singing metal on wood. Fifteen times. Missie May couldn't run to the door, but she crept there as quickly as she could.

"Joe Banks, Ah hear you chuckin' money in mah do'way. You wait till ah get mah strength back and Ah'm gointer fix you for dat."

[1933]

Questions

1. Are the references to gold throughout the story intended to be taken seriously as criticisms of a material society or as something else?

2. What can be said of Hurston's use of images throughout the story, such as the one of the sun: "The sun, the hero of every day, the impersonal old man that beams as brightly on death as on birth, came up every morning and raced across the blue dome and dipped into the sea of fire every evening"?

3. Is "The Gilded Six-Bits" a happy story of African-American life or is there a streak of pessimism beneath the surface narrative?

Shirley Jackson

(1919–1965)

United States

Shirley Jackson might almost be said to have led two lives: one as the wife of a noted literary critic and professor, Stanley Edgar Hyman, and mother of their four children, and the other as the author of fiction, at least one story of which has assured her permanent place in literature. Her fictional oeuvre also branches into two directions: one cluster focuses on family life and domestic comedy; the other, far darker in tone, explores dimensions of madness, terror, moral innocence, and evil.

Jackson spent her early years in California, where she showed an early interest in writing: She won a poetry prize before she was 13. She attended the University of Rochester briefly (leaving because of an attack of depression—an illness that returned intermittently during her adult life) and later the University of Syracuse, where she met and married Hyman in 1940. While there, she wrote short stories that were published in a student journal they founded together, presciently named The Spectre (prescient, because a number of her stories and novels were to include ghostly or supernatural elements). She continued to write fiction while raising a growing family, establishing a daily discipline that enabled her to produce six novels and a number of short stories despite the domestic claims on her time.

Jackson's most famous and frequently anthologized and dramatized story, "The Lottery," disturbingly links ancient ritual with archetypal possibilities for evil. Jackson herself was surprised at the intensity of response to this story when it first appeared in The New Yorker in 1948. As she later summarized the flood of letters expressing outrage sent to the editor (more than for any other piece of fiction the magazine had ever published), she identified three recurring themes, "bewilderment, speculation, and plain old-fashioned abuse. . . . The general tone of the early letters, however, was a kind of wide-eyed, shocked innocence. People at first were not so much concerned with what the story meant; what they wanted to know was where these lotteries were held, and whether they could go there and watch." When pressed for an interpretation of "The Lottery," Jackson answered that such an explanation was "very difficult." She phrased her response this way:

> I suppose I hoped, by setting a particularly brutal ancient rite in the present and in my own village, to shock the story's readers with a graphic dramatization of the pointless violence and general inhumanity in their own lives. . . . I gather that in some cases the mind just rebels. The number of people who expected [the winner of the lottery] to win a Bendix washer at the end would amaze you.

THE LOTTERY

The morning of June 27th was clear and sunny, with the fresh warmth of a full-summer day; the flowers were blossoming profusely and the grass was richly green. The people of the village began to gather in the square, between the post office and the bank, around ten o'clock; in some towns there were so many people that the lottery took two days and had to be started on June 26th, but in this village, where there were only about three hundred people, the whole lottery took less than two hours, so it could begin at ten o'clock in the morning and still be through in time to allow the villagers to get home for noon dinner.

The children assembled first, of course. School was recently over for the summer, and the feeling of liberty sat uneasily on most of them; they tended to gather together quietly for a while before they broke into boisterous play, and their talk was still of the classroom and teacher, of books and reprimands. Bobby Martin had already stuffed his pockets full of stones, and the other boys soon followed his example, selecting the smoothest and roundest stones; Bobby and Harry Jones, and Dickie Delacroix—the villagers pronounced this name "Dellacroy"—eventually made a great pile of stones in one corner of the square and guarded it against the raids of the other boys. The girls stood aside, talking among themselves, looking over their shoulders at the boys, and the very small children rolled in the dust or clung to the hands of their older brothers or sisters.

Soon the men began to gather, surveying their own children, speaking of planting and rain, tractors and taxes. They stood together, away from the pile of stones in the corner, and their jokes were quiet and they smiled rather than laughed. The women, wearing faded house dresses and sweaters, came shortly after their menfolk. They greeted one another and exchanged bits of gossip as they went to join their husbands. Soon the women, standing by their husbands, began to call to their children, and the children came reluctantly, having to be called four or five times. Bobby Martin ducked under his mother's grasping hand and ran, laughing, back to the pile of stones. His father spoke up sharply, and Bobby came quickly and took his place between his father and his oldest brother.

The lottery was conducted—as were the square dances, the teenage club, the Halloween program—by Mr. Summers, who had time and energy to devote to civic activities. He was a round-faced, jovial man and he ran the coal business, and people were sorry for him, because he had no children and his wife was a scold. When he arrived in the square, carrying the black wooden box, there was a murmur of conversation among the villagers, and he waved and called, "Little late today, folks." The postmaster, Mr. Graves, followed him, carrying a three-legged stool, and the stool was put in the center of the square and Mr. Summers set the black box down on it. The villagers kept their distance, leaving a space between themselves and the stool, and when Mr. Summers said, "Some of you fellows want to give me a hand?" there was a hesitation before two men, Mr. Martin and his oldest son, Baxter, came forward to hold the box steady on the stool while Mr. Summers stirred up the papers inside it.

The original paraphernalia for the lottery had been lost long ago, and the black box now resting on the stool had been put into use even before Old Man Warner, the oldest man in town, was born. Mr. Summers spoke frequently to the villagers about making a new box, but no one liked to upset even as much tradition as was represented by the black box. There was a story that the present box had been made with some pieces of the box that had preceded it, the one that had been constructed when the first people settled down to make a village here. Every year, after the lottery, Mr. Summers began talking again about a new box, but every year the subject was allowed to fade off without anything's being done. The black box grew shabbier each year; by now it was no longer completely black but splintered badly along one side to show the original wood color, and in some places faded or stained.

Mr. Martin and his oldest son, Baxter, held the black box securely on the stool until Mr. Summers had stirred the papers thoroughly with his hand. Because so much of the ritual had been forgotten or discarded, Mr. Summers had been successful in having slips of paper substituted for the chips of wood that had been used for generations. Chips of wood, Mr. Summers had argued, had been all very well when the village was tiny, but now that the population was more than three hundred and likely to keep on growing, it was necessary to use something that would fit more easily into the black box. The night before the lottery, Mr. Summers and Mr. Graves made up the slips of paper and put them in the box, and it was then taken to the safe of Mr. Summers's coal company and locked up until Mr. Summers was ready to take it to the square next morning. The rest of the year, the box was put away, sometimes one place, sometimes another; it had spent one year in Mr. Graves's barn and another year underfoot in the post office, and sometimes it was set on a shelf in the Martin grocery and left there.

There was a great deal of fussing to be done before Mr. Summers declared the lottery open. There were the lists to make up—of heads of families, heads of households in each family, members of each household in each family. There was the proper swearing-in of Mr. Summers by the postmaster, as the official of the lottery; at one time, some people remembered, there had been a recital of some sort, performed by the official of the lottery, a perfunctory, tuneless chant that had been rattled off duly each year; some people believed that the official of the lottery used to stand just so when he said or sang it, others believed that he was supposed to walk among the people, but years and years ago this part of the ritual had been allowed to lapse. There had been, also, a ritual salute, which the official of the lottery had had to use in addressing each person who came up to draw from the box, but this also had changed with time, until now it was felt necessary only for the official to speak to each person approaching. Mr. Summers was very good at all this; in his clean white shirt and blue jeans, with one hand resting carelessly on the black box, he seemed very proper and important as he talked interminably to Mr. Graves and the Martins.

Just as Mr. Summers finally left off talking and turned to the assembled villagers, Mrs. Hutchinson came hurriedly along the path to the square, her sweater thrown over her shoulders, and slid into place in the back of the crowd. "Clean forgot what day it was," she said to Mrs. Delacroix, who stood next to her, and they both laughed softly. "Thought my old man was out back stacking wood," Mrs. Hutchinson went on, "and then I looked out the window and the kids was gone, and then I remembered it was the twenty-seventh and came a-running." She dried her hands on her apron, and Mrs. Delacroix said, "You're in time, though. They're still talking away up there."

Mrs. Hutchinson craned her neck to see through the crowd and found her husband and children standing near the front. She tapped Mrs. Delacroix on the arm as a farewell and began to make her way through the crowd. The people separated good-humoredly to let her through; two or three people said, in voices just loud enough to be heard across the crowd, "Here comes your Missus, Hutchinson," and "Bill, she made it after all." Mrs. Hutchinson reached her husband, and Mr. Summers, who had been waiting, said cheerfully, "Thought we were going to have to get on without you, Tessie." Mrs. Hutchinson said, grinning, "Wouldn't have me leave m'dishes in the sink, now, would you, Joe?" and soft laughter ran through the crowd as the people stirred back into position after Mrs. Hutchinson's arrival.

"Well, now," Mr. Summers said soberly, "guess we better get started, get this over with, so's we can go back to work. Anybody ain't here?"

"Dunbar," several people said. "Dunbar, Dunbar."

Mr. Summers consulted his list. "Clyde Dunbar," he said. "That's right. He's broke his leg, hasn't he? Who's drawing for him?"

"Me, I guess," a woman said, and Mr. Summers turned to look at her. "Wife draws for her husband," Mr. Summers said. "Don't you have a grown boy to do it for you, Janey?" Although Mr. Summers and everyone else in the village knew the answer perfectly well, it was the business of the official of the lottery to ask such questions formally. Mr. Summers waited with an expression of polite interest while Mrs. Dunbar answered.

"Horace's not but sixteen yet," Mrs. Dunbar said regretfully. "Guess I gotta fill in for the old man this year."

"Right," Mr. Summers said. He made a note on the list he was holding. Then he asked, "Watson boy drawing this year?"

A tall boy in the crowd raised his hand. "Here," he said. "I'm drawing for m' mother and me." He blinked his eyes nervously and ducked his head as several voices in the crowd said things like "Good fellow, Jack," and "Glad to see your mother's got a man to do it."

"Well," Mr. Summers said, "guess that's everyone. Old Man Warner make it?"

"Here," a voice said, and Mr. Summers nodded.

A sudden hush fell on the crowd as Mr. Summers cleared his throat and looked at the list. "All ready?" he called. "Now, I'll read the names—heads of families first—and the men come up and take a paper out of the box. Keep the paper folded in your hand without looking at it until everyone has had a turn. Everything clear?"

The people had done it so many times that they only half listened to the directions; most of them were quiet, wetting their lips, not looking around. Then Mr. Summers raised one hand high and said, "Adams." A man disengaged himself from the crowd and came forward. "Hi, Steve," Mr. Summers said, and Mr. Adams said, "Hi, Joe." They grinned at one another humorlessly and nervously. Then Mr. Adams reached into the black box and took out a folded paper. He held it firmly by one corner as he turned and went hastily back to his place in the crowd, where he stood a little apart from his family, not looking down at his hand.

"Allen," Mr. Summers said, "Anderson . . . Bentham."

"Seems like there's no time at all between lotteries any more," Mrs. Delacroix said to Mrs. Graves in the back row. "Seems like we got through with the last one only last week."

"Time sure goes fast," Mrs. Graves said.

"Clark . . . Delacroix."

"There goes my old man," Mrs. Delacroix said. She held her breath while her husband went forward.

"Dunbar," Mr. Summers said, and Mrs. Dunbar went steadily to the box while one of the women said, "Go on, Janey," and another said, "There she goes."

"We're next," Mrs. Graves said. She watched while Mr. Graves came around from the side of the box, greeted Mr. Summers gravely, and selected a slip of paper from the box. By now, all through the crowd there were men holding the small folded papers in their large hands, turning them over and over nervously. Mrs. Dunbar and her two sons stood together, Mrs. Dunbar holding the slip of paper.

"Harburt . . . Hutchinson."

"Get up there, Bill," Mrs. Hutchinson said, and the people near her laughed.

"Jones."

"They do say," Mr. Adams said to Old Man Warner, who stood next to him, "that over in the north village they're talking of giving up the lottery."

Old Man Warner snorted. "Pack of crazy fools," he said "Listening to the young folks, nothing's good enough for *them*. Next thing you know, they'll be wanting to go back to living in caves, nobody work any more, live *that* way for a while. Used to be a saying about 'Lottery in June, corn be heavy soon.' First thing you know, we'd all be eating stewed chickweed and acorns. There's *always* been a lottery," he added petulantly. "Bad enough to see young Joe Summers up there joking with everybody."

"Some places have already quit lotteries," Mrs. Adams said.

"Nothing but trouble in *that*," Old Man Warner said stoutly. "Pack of young fools."

"Martin." And Bobby Martin watched his father go forward. "Overdyke . . . Percy."

"I wish they'd hurry," Mrs. Dunbar said to her older son. "I wish they'd hurry."

"They're almost through," her son said.

"You get ready to run tell Dad," Mrs. Dunbar said.

Mr. Summers called his own name and then stepped forward precisely and selected a slip from the box. The he called, "Warner."

"Seventy-seventh year I been in the lottery," Old Man Warner said as he went through the crowd. "Seventy-seventh time."

"Watson." The tall boy came awkwardly through the crowd. Someone said. "Don't be nervous, Jack," and Mr. Summers said, "Take your time, son."

"Zanini."

After that, there was a long pause, a breathless pause, until Mr. Summers, holding his slip of paper in the air, said, "All right, fellows." For a minute, no one moved, and then all the slips of paper were opened. Suddenly, all the women began to speak at once, saying, "Who is it?" "Who's got it?" "Is it the Dunbars?" "Is it the Watsons?" Then the voices began to say, "It's Hutchinson. It's Bill . . . Bill Hutchinson's got it."

"Go tell your father," Mrs. Dunbar said to her older son.

People began to look around to see the Hutchinsons. Bill Hutchinson was standing quiet, staring down at the paper in his hand. Suddenly, Tessie Hutchinson shouted to Mr. Summers, "You didn't give him time enough to take any paper he wanted. I saw you. It wasn't fair!"

"Be a good sport, Tessie," Mrs. Delacroix called, and Mrs. Graves said, "All of us took the same chance."

"Shut up, Tessie," Bill Hutchinson said.

"Well, everyone," Mr. Summers said, "that was done pretty fast, and now we've got to be hurrying a little more to get done in time." He consulted his next list. "Bill," he said, "you draw for the Hutchinson family. You got any other households in the Hutchinsons?"

"There's Don and Eva," Mrs. Hutchinson yelled. "Make *them* take their chance!"

"Daughters drew with their husbands' families, Tessie," Mr. Summers said gently. "You know that as well as anyone else."

"It wasn't *fair*," Tessie said.

"I guess not, Joe," Bill Hutchinson said regretfully. "My daughter draws with her husband's family, that's only fair. And I've got no other family except the kids."

"Then, as far as drawing for families is concerned, it's you," Mr. Summers said in explanation, "and as far as drawing for households is concerned, that's you, too. Right?"

"Right," Bill Hutchinson said.

"How many kids, Bill?" Mr. Summers asked formally.

"Three," Bill Hutchinson said. "There's Bill, Jr., and Nancy, and little Dave. And Tessie and me."

"All right, then," Mr. Summers said. "Harry, you got their tickets back?"

Mr. Graves nodded and held up the slips of paper. "Put them in the box, then," Mr. Summers directed. "Take Bill's and put it in."

"I think we ought to start over," Mrs. Hutchinson said, as quietly as she could. "I tell you it wasn't *fair*. You didn't give him time enough to choose. *Every*body saw that."

Mr. Graves had selected the five slips and put them in the box, and he dropped all the papers but those onto the ground, where the breeze caught them and lifted them off.

"Listen, everybody," Mrs. Hutchinson was saying to the people around her.

"Ready, Bill?" Mr. Summers asked, and Bill Hutchinson, with one quick glance around at his wife and children, nodded.

"Remember," Mr. Summers said, "take the slips and keep them folded until each person has taken one. Harry, you help little Dave." Mr. Graves took the hand of the little boy, who came willingly with him up to the box. "Take a paper out of the box, Davy," Mr. Summers said. Davy put his hand into the box and laughed. "Take just *one* paper," Mr. Summers said. "Harry, you hold it for him." Mr. Graves took the child's hand and removed the folded paper from the tight fist and held it while little Dave stood next to him and looked up at him wonderingly.

"Nancy next," Mr. Summers said. Nancy was twelve, and her school friends breathed heavily as she went forward, switching her skirt, and took a slip daintily from the box. "Bill, Jr.," Mr. Summers said, and Billy, his face red and his feet overlarge, nearly knocked the box over as he got a paper out. "Tessie," Mr. Summers said. She hesitated for a minute, looking around defiantly, and then set her lips and went up to the box. She snatched a paper out and held it behind her.

"Bill," Mr. Summers said, and Bill Hutchinson reached into the box and felt around, bringing his hand out at last with the slip of paper in it.

The crowd was quiet. A girl whispered, "I hope it's not Nancy," and the sound of the whisper reached the edges of the crowd.

"It's not the way it used to be," Old Man Warner said clearly. "People ain't the way they used to be."

"All right," Mr. Summers said. "Open the papers. Harry, you open little Dave's."

Mr. Graves opened the slip of paper and there was a general sigh through the crowd as he held it up and everyone could see that it was blank. Nancy and Bill, Jr., opened theirs at the same time, and both beamed and laughed, turning around to the crowd and holding their slips of paper above their heads.

"Tessie," Mr. Summers said. There was a pause, and then Mr. Summers looked at Bill Hutchinson, and Bill unfolded this paper and showed it. It was blank.

"It's Tessie," Mr. Summers said, and his voice was hushed. "Show us her paper, Bill."

Bill Hutchinson went over to his wife and forced the slip of paper out of her hand. It had a black spot on it, the black spot Mr. Summers had made the night before with the heavy pencil in the coal-company office. Bill Hutchinson held it up and there was a stir in the crowd.

"All right, folks," Mr. Summers said. "Let's finish quickly."

Although the villagers had forgotten the ritual and lost the original black box, they still remembered to use stones. The pile of stones the boys had made earlier was ready; there were stones on the ground with the blowing scraps of paper that had come out of the box. Mrs. Delacroix selected a stone so large she had to pick it up with both hands and turned to Mrs. Dunbar. "Come on," she said. "Hurry up."

Mrs. Dunbar had small stones in both hands, and she said, gasping for breath, "I can't run at all. You'll have to go ahead and I'll catch up with you."

The children had stones already, and someone gave little Davy Hutchinson a few pebbles.

Tessie Hutchinson was in the center of a cleared space by now, and she held her hands out desperately as the villagers moved in on her. "It isn't fair," she said. A stone hit her on the side of the head.

Old Man Warner was saying, "Come on, come on, everyone." Steve Adams was in the front of the crowd of villagers, with Mrs. Graves beside him.

"It isn't fair, it isn't right," Mrs. Hutchinson screamed and then they were upon her.

[1948]

Questions

1. How does the story achieve its impact? How is suspense sustained? When do you begin to suspect the outcome?
2. How do the setting, tone, and point of view contribute to the effectiveness of the story? Why does the author use an omniscient narrator rather than one of the characters' perspectives?
3. What is the purpose of the lottery?
4. What is the theme of the story?

Svava Jakobsdóttir

(b. 1930)

Iceland

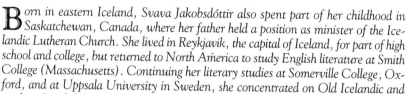

Born in eastern Iceland, Svava Jakobsdóttir also spent part of her childhood in Saskatchewan, Canada, where her father held a position as minister of the Icelandic Lutheran Church. She lived in Reykjavik, the capital of Iceland, for part of high school and college, but returned to North America to study English literature at Smith College (Massachusetts). Continuing her literary studies at Somerville College, Oxford, and at Uppsala University in Sweden, she concentrated on Old Icelandic and modern Swedish literatures.

From the study of literature, Jakobsdóttir turned to its creation, publishing her first collection of stories, Twelve Women, in 1965. She has also published a novel and several other collections of short stories, as well as three plays and several radio scripts. In her writing, Jakobsdóttir frequently focuses on women's roles and expectations in contemporary society.

Jakobsdóttir has also served in several capacities within the political and diplomatic profession: first in Iceland's Foreign Ministry and later as an elected member of the Icelandic Parliament, a delegate to the United Nations, and a member of the Nordic Committee whose goal was the promotion of gender equality. After serving several terms in office, she gave up her political career to be a full-time writer. She is married to a folklorist, Jon Hnefill Adalsteinsson, and has one son.

A STORY FOR CHILDREN

For as long as she could remember she had resolved to be true to her nature and devote all her energies to her home and her children. There were several children now and from morning till night she was swamped with work, doing the household chores and caring for the children. She was now preparing supper and waiting for the potatoes to boil. A Danish women's magazine lay on the kitchen bench as if it had been tossed there accidentally; in fact, she kept it there on purpose and sneaked a look at it whenever she got a chance. Without letting the pot of potatoes out of her mind she picked up the magazine and skimmed over Fru Ensom's[1] advice column. This was by no means the column that seemed most interesting to her, but it was usually short. It was possible that it would last just long enough so that the potatoes would be boiling when she finished reading it. The first letter in the column was short: Dear Fru Ensom, I have never lived for anything other than my children and have done everything for them. Now I am left alone and they never visit me. What should I do? Fru Ensom answered: Do more for them.

---

[1]*Fru Ensom*   Danish: Mrs. Lonesome.

This was the logical answer, of course. It was perfectly clear that nothing else was possible. She hoped that she wouldn't start writing to the magazines about such obvious things when the time came. No, these columns where people moaned and groaned were not to her liking. The columns which discussed childrearing and the role of the mother—or rather, *the* column, since both subjects were discussed in one and the same column—were much more positive. The fundamental aspects of child-rearing had of course been familiar to her for quite some time now, but it did happen that she felt weak and fatigued at times. At that point she would leaf through the columns on child-rearing seeking courage and confirmation that she was on the right track in life. She only regretted having less and less time to read.

The uncleaned fish awaited her in the sink and she withstood the temptation to read the child-rearing column this time. She closed the magazine and stood up. She limped a little bit ever since the children had cut off the big toe on her right foot. They had wanted to find out what happened if someone had only nine toes. Within herself she was proud of her limp and of her children's eagerness to learn, and sometimes she limped even more than was necessary. She now turned the heat down under the potatoes and began cleaning the fish. The kitchen door opened and her little son, who was six years old and had blue eyes and light curly hair, came up to her.

"Mama," he said, and stuck a pin in her arm. She started and almost cut herself with the knife.

"Yes, dear," she said, and reached out her other arm so the child could stick it, too.

"Mama, tell me a story."

She put the knife down, dried her hands and sat down with the child in her lap to tell him a story. She was just about halfway through the story when it occurred to her that one of the other children might suffer psychological harm from not getting supper on time. In the boy's face she tried to see how he would take it if she stopped telling the story. She felt the old indecisiveness taking hold of her and she became distracted from the story. This inability of hers to make decisions had increased with the number of children and the ever-increasing chores. She had begun to fear those moments which interrupted her usual rush from morning to night. More and more often she lost her poise if she stopped to make a decision. The child-rearing columns gave little or no help at such moments, though she tried to call them to mind. They only discussed one problem and one child at a time. Other problems always had to wait until next week.

This time she was spared making a decision. The door opened and all the children crowded into the kitchen. Stjáni, the oldest, was in the lead. At an early age he had shown an admirable interest in both human and animal biology. The boy who had been listening to the story now slid out of her lap and took up a position among his brothers and sisters. They formed a semicircle around her and she looked over each of them one after the other.

"Mama, we want to see what a person's brain looks like."

She looked at the clock.

"Right now?" she asked.

Stjáni didn't answer his mother's question. With a nod of his head and a sharp glance he gave his younger brother a sign, and the younger brother went and got a rope, while Stjáni fastened the saw blade to the handle. The rope was then wrapped around the mother. She felt how the little hands fumbled at her back while the knot was tied. The rope was loose and it wouldn't take much effort to get free. But she was careful not to let it be noticed. He had always been sensitive about how clumsy he was with his hands. Just as Stjáni raised the saw up to her head the image of the children's father came into her mind. She saw him in front of her just as he would appear in a little while: on the threshold of the front door with his briefcase in one hand and his hat in the other. She never saw him except in the front doorway, either on his way out or on his way in. She had once been able to imagine him outside the house among other people or at the office, but now, after the children had been born, they had moved into a new house and he into a new office, and she had lost her bearings. He would come home soon and she still hadn't started frying the fish. The blood had now begun to flow down her head. Stjáni had gotten through with the saw. It seemed to be going well, and fairly quickly. Now and then he stopped as if he were measuring with his eyes just how big the hole had to be. Blood spurted into his face and a curse crossed his lips. He nodded his head and the young brother went immediately and got the mop bucket. They placed it under the hole and soon it was half full. The procedure was over at the exact moment the father appeared in the doorway. He stood motionless for a while and pondered the sight which presented itself to him: his wife tied up, with a hole in her head, the eldest son holding a gray brain in his hand, the curious group of children huddled together, and only one pot on the stove.

"Kids! How can you think of doing this when it's already suppertime?"

He picked up the piece of his wife's skull and snapped it back in just as she was about to bleed to death. Then he took over and soon the children were busy tidying up after themselves. He wiped most of the blood stains off the walls himself before he checked on the pot on the stove. There was a suspicious sound coming from it. The water had boiled away and he took the pot off the stove and set it on the metal counter next to the sink. When he saw the half-cleaned fish in the sink he realized that his wife had still not gotten up from the chair. Puzzled, he knit his brow. It wasn't usual for her to be sitting down when there was so much to do. He went over to her and looked at her attentively. He noticed then that they had forgotten to untie her.

When he had freed her they looked into each other's eyes and smiled. Never was their harmony more deeply felt than when their eyes met in mutual pride over the children.

"Silly urchins," he said, and his voice was filled with the concern and affection that he felt for his family.

Soon afterward they sat down at the table. Everyone except Stjáni. He was in his room studying the brain under a microscope. Meanwhile, his mother kept his supper warm for him in the kitchen. They were all hungry and took to their food briskly; this was an unusually late supper. There was no change to be seen in the mother. She had washed her hair and combed it over the cut before she sat down. Her mild expression displayed the patience and self-denial usual at mealtimes. This expression had first appeared during those years when she served her children first and kept only the smallest and most meager piece for herself. Now the children were big enough so that they could take the best pieces themselves and the expression was actually unnecessary, but it had become an inseparable part of the meal. Before the meal was over Stjáni came in and sat down. The mother went to get his supper. In the kitchen she boned the fish thoroughly before putting it on the plate. When she picked up the garbage pail to throw the bones away she let out a scream. The brain was right on top of the pail.

The rest of the family rushed out as soon as her scream reached the dining room. The father was in the lead and was quick to discover what was wrong when he saw his wife staring down into the garbage pail. Her scream had died out, but it could still be seen in the contours of her face.

"You think it's a shame to throw it out, don't you, dear?" he asked.

"I don't know," she said and looked at him apologetically. "I didn't think."

"Mama didn't think, mama didn't think, mama didn't think," chanted one of the children who had an especially keen sense of humor.

They all burst out laughing and the laughter seemed to solve the problem. The father said he had an idea; they didn't have to throw the brain out, they could keep it in alcohol.

With that, he put the brain into a clear jar and poured alcohol over it. They brought the jar into the living room and found a place for it on a shelf of knick-knacks. They all agreed it fit well there. Then they finished eating.

There were no noticeable changes in the household routine due to the brain loss. At first a lot of people came to visit. They came to see the brain, and those who had prided themselves on their grandmother's old spinning wheel in the corner of their living room now looked with envy upon the brain upon the shelf. She felt no changes in herself either at first. It hadn't become a bit more difficult for her to do housework or to understand the Danish magazines. Many things even turned out to be easier than before, and situations that earlier had caused her to rack her brain no longer did so. But gradually she began to feel a heaviness in her chest. It seemed as if her lungs no longer had room enough to function and after a year had passed she went to the doctor. A thorough examination revealed that her heart had grown larger *usus innaturalis et adsidui causa.*[2] She asked the doctor to excuse her for having forgotten all the Latin she had learned in school, and patiently he explained to her how the loss of one organ could result in changes in another. Just as a man who loses his sight will acquire a more acute sense of hearing, her heart had increased its activity a good deal when her brain was no longer available. This was a natural development, *lex vitae,*[3] if one may say so—and at that, the doctor laughed—there was no need to fear that such a law could be anything but just. Therefore she didn't have to be afraid. She was in the best of health.

She felt relieved at these words. Lately she had even been afraid that she had only a short time to live, and this fear had become an increasingly loud voice within her breast which said: What will become of them if I die? But now she realized that this voice, whose strength and clarity grew steadily, was no prophecy, but rather the voice of her heart. This knowledge made her happy because the voice of one's heart could be trusted.

The years passed and her heart's voice showed her the way: from the children's rooms and her husband's study to the kitchen and the bedroom. This route was dear to her, and no gust of wind that blew through the front door was ever strong enough to sweep away her tracks. Only one thing aroused fear in her: unexpected changes in the world. The year they changed counter girls at the milk store five times she was never quite all right. But the children grew up. She awoke with a bad dream when her oldest child, Stjáni, began to pack his suitcase to go out into the world. With uncontrollable vehemence she threw herself over the threshold to block his exit. A sucking sound could be heard as the boy stepped on her on his way out. He thought

---

[2]*usus innaturalis et adsidui causa*   Latin: a case involving unnatural and persistent use.
[3]*lex vitae*   Latin: law of life.

she was moaning and paused a moment and said that she herself was to blame. No one had asked her to lie down there. She smiled as she got up because what he had said wasn't quite right. Her heart had told her to lie there. She had heard the voice clearly and now, as she watched him walk down the street, the voice spoke to her again and said that she could still be glad that she had softened his first steps out into the world. Later on they all left one after the other and she was left alone. She no longer had anything to do in the children's rooms and she would often sit in the easy chair in the living room now. If she looked up, the jar on the shelf came into view, where the brain had stood all these years and, in fact, was almost completely forgotten. Custom had made it commonplace. Sometimes she pondered over it. As far as she could see, it had kept well. But she got less and less pleasure out of looking at it. It reminded her of her children. And gradually she felt that a change was again taking place within herself, but she couldn't bring herself to mention it to her husband. She saw him so seldom lately, and whenever he appeared at home she got up from the chair in a hurry, as if a guest had arrived. One day he brought up the question himself of whether she wasn't feeling well. Pleased, she looked up, but when she saw that he was figuring the accounts at the same time, she became confused in answering (she had never been particularly good in figuring). In her confusion she said she didn't have enough to do. He looked at her amazed and said there were enough things to be done if people only used their brain. Of course he said this without thinking. He knew very well that she didn't have a brain, but she nevertheless took him literally. She took the jar down from the shelf, brought it to the doctor and asked if he thought the brain was still useable. The doctor didn't exclude the possibility of its being of some use, but on the other hand, all organs atrophied after being preserved in alcohol for a long time. Therefore it would be debatable whether it would pay to move it at all; in addition, the *nervi cerebrales*[4] had been left in rather poor shape, and the doctor asked whether some clumsy dolt had actually done the surgery.

"He was so little then, the poor thing," the woman said.

"By the way," said the doctor, "I recall that you had a highly developed heart."

The woman avoided the doctor's inquiring look and a faint pang of conscience gripped her. And she whispered to the doctor what she hadn't dared hint of to her husband:

"My heart's voice has fallen silent."

As she said this she realized why she had come. She unbuttoned her blouse, took it off and laid it neatly on the back of the chair. Her bra went the same way. Then she stood ready in front of the doctor, naked from the waist up. He picked up a scalpel and cut, and a moment later he handed her the gleaming, red heart. Carefully he placed it in her palm and her hands closed around it. Its hesitant beat resembled the fluttering of a bird in a cage. She offered to pay the doctor, but he shook his head and, seeing that she was having difficulty, helped her get dressed. He then offered to call her a taxi since she had so much to carry. She refused, stuffed the brain jar into her shopping bag and slipped the bag over her arm. Then she left with the heart in her hands.

Now began the long march from one child to the next. She first went to see her sons, but found none of them at home. They had all gotten a berth on the ship of state

---

[4]*nervi cerebrales* Latin: cerebral nerves.

and it was impossible to tell when they would return. Furthermore, they never stayed in home port long enough for there to be time for anything other than begetting children. She withdrew from the bitterness of her daughters-in-law and went to see her oldest daughter, who opened the door herself. A look of astonishment and revulsion came over her face when she saw the slimy, red heart pulsating in her mother's palm, and in her consternation, she slammed the door. This was of course an involuntary reaction and she quickly opened the door again, but she made it clear to her mother that she didn't care at all about her heart; and she wasn't sure it would go with the new furniture in the living room. The mother then realized that it was pointless to continue the march, because her younger daughters had even newer furniture. So she went home. There she filled a jar with alcohol and dropped the heart into it. A deep sucking sound, like a gasp within a human breast, could be heard as the heart sank to the bottom. And now they each stood on the shelf in their own jars, her brain and her heart. But no one came to view them. And the children never came to visit. Their excuse always was that they were too busy. But the truth was that they didn't like the sterile smell that clung to everything in the house.

[1975]
Translated by
DENNIS AUBURN HILL

Questions

1. At what point do you realize that the story is not strictly realistic? How do the ironic, grotesque, and exaggerated elements enhance the story's effectiveness?
2. What aspects of the story are humorous? How is the humor balanced with its more serious implications?
3. How do you understand the "fact" that the mother lacks a brain but has a "highly developed heart"?
4. What views of motherhood and childhood are explored in the story?
5. How do you interpret the ending?

Henry James
(1843–1916)
United States/England

Henry James changed the shape of American fiction by giving it an international perspective as well as a highly refined form. He was born in New York City, the second son of Henry James, Sr., a radical theologian who moved freely among his contemporaries, including Ralph Waldo Emerson and Thomas Carlyle. James's older brother, William, became one of the country's most famous philosophers. Both sons were privately educated and, as children, traveled extensively in Europe. Henry made one formal attempt at education by attending Harvard Law School in 1862, without completing his degree. Three years later, his stories began appearing in The Atlantic. In 1871, he published his first novel, The Passionate Pilgrim. In The American (1877), he developed his major theme: the conflict between a robust American, naive and rich, and decadent Europeans, steeped in tradition but unwilling to sacrifice heritage for dollars. To this international theme, varied in dozens of subsequent short stories and novels, James was shortly to add a more complex form, altering the point of view and the psychological depiction of his characters. It is impossible to think of American and British fiction of the late nineteenth and early twentieth centuries without considering Henry James's influence on the genre.

James wrote so many short stories about artists (especially painters and writers) that they have been collected as Stories of Writers and Artists. An early story, "Greville Fane" (1892), may hit closer to home than many of the writer's other artist stories. James was a prolific writer, yet his popularity was restricted by a limited number of readers. Rarely did the royalties from his work add up to a significant amount of money, while other, less talented writers were often financially rewarded for their popular work. After the turn of the century, in an attempt to solidify his reputation, James spent several years rewriting many of his earlier works, which were then reissued in the uniform New York Edition. Shortly thereafter, the combined royalties for all of these books amounted to $211.00. Edith Wharton secretly subsidized the advance James received for his last, unfinished novel.

GREVILLE FANE

Coming in to dress for dinner, I found a telegram: "Mrs Stormer dying; can you give us half a column for to-morrow evening? Let her off easy, but not too easy." I was late; I was in a hurry; I had very little time to think, but at a venture I dispatched a reply: "Will do what I can." It was not till I had dressed and was rolling away to dinner that, in the hansom, I bethought myself of the difficulty of the condition attached. The difficulty was not of course in letting her off easy but in qualifying that indulgence. "I simply won't qualify it," I said to myself. I didn't admire her, but I liked her, and I had known her so long that I almost felt heartless in sitting down at such an hour to a feast of indifference. I must have seemed abstracted, for the early years of my acquaintance with her came back to me. I spoke of her to the lady I had taken down, but the lady I had taken down had never heard of Greville Fane. I tried my other neighbour, who pronounced her books "too vile." I had never thought them very good, but I should let her off easier than that.

I came away early, for the express purpose of driving to ask about her. The journey took time, for she lived in the northwest district, in the neighbourhood of Primrose Hill. My apprehension that I should be too late was justified in a fuller sense than I had attached to it—I had only feared that the house would be shut up. There were lights in the windows, and the temperate tinkle of my bell brought a servant immediately to the door, but poor Mrs Stormer had passed into a state in which the resonance of no earthly knocker was to be feared. A lady, in the hall, hovering behind the servant, came forward when she heard my voice. I recognised Lady Luard, but she had mistaken me for the doctor.

"Excuse my appearing at such an hour," I said; "it was the first possible moment after I heard."

"It's all over," Lady Luard replied. "Dearest mamma!"

She stood there under the lamp with her eyes on me; she was very tall, very stiff, very cold, and always looked as if these things, and some others beside, in her dress, her manner and even her name, were an implication that she was very admirable. I had never been able to follow the argument, but that is a detail. I expressed briefly and frankly what I felt, while the little mottled maidservant flattened herself against the wall of the narrow passage and tried to look detached without looking indifferent. It was not a moment to make a visit, and I was on the point of retreating when Lady Luard arrested me with a queer, casual, drawling "Would you—a—would you, perhaps, be *writing* something?" I felt for the instant like an interviewer, which I was not. But I pleaded guilty to this intention, on which she rejoined: "I'm so very glad—but I think my brother would like to see you." I detested her brother, but it wasn't an occasion to act this out; so I suffered myself to be inducted, to my surprise, into a small back room which I immediately recognised as the scene, during the later years, of Mrs Stormer's imperturbable industry. Her table was there, the battered and blotted accessory to innumerable literary lapses, with its contracted space for the arms (she wrote only from the elbow down) and the confusion of scrappy, scribbled sheets which had already become literary remains. Leolin was also there, smoking a cigarette before the fire and looking impudent even in his grief, sincere as it well might have been.

To meet him, to greet him, I had to make a sharp effort; for the air that he wore to me as he stood before me was quite that of his mother's murderer. She lay silent for ever upstairs—as dead as an unsuccessful book, and his swaggering erectness was a kind of symbol of his having killed her. I wondered if he had already, with his sister, been calculating what they could get for the poor papers on the table; but I had not long to wait to learn, for in reply to the scanty words of sympathy I addressed him he puffed out: "It's miserable, miserable, yes; but she has left three books complete." His words had the oddest effect; they converted the cramped little room into a seat of trade and made the "book" wonderfully feasible. He would certainly get all that could be got for the three. Lady Luard explained to me that her husband had been with them but had had to go down to the House. To her brother she explained that I was going to write something, and to me again she made it clear that she hoped I would "do mamma justice." She added that she didn't think this had ever been done.

She said to her brother: "Don't you think there are some things he ought thoroughly to understand?" and on his instantly exclaiming "Oh, thoroughly—thoroughly!" she went on, rather austerely: "I mean about mamma's birth."

"Yes, and her connections," Leolin added.

I professed every willingness, and for five minutes I listened, but it would be too much to say that I understood. I don't even now, but it is not important. My vision was of other matters than those they put before me, and while they desired there should be no mistake about their ancestors I became more and more lucid about themselves. I got away as soon as possible, and walked home through the great dusky, empty London—the best of all conditions for thought. By the time I reached my door my little article was practically composed—ready to be transferred on the morrow from the polished plate of fancy. I believe it attracted some notice, was thought "graceful" and was said to be by some one else. I had to be pointed without being lively, and it took some tact. But what I said was much less interesting than what I thought—especially during the half-hour I spent in my armchair by the fire, smoking the cigar I always light before going to bed. I went to sleep there, I believe; but I continued to moralise about Greville Fane. I am reluctant to lose that retrospect altogether, and this is a dim little memory of it, a document not to "serve." The dear woman had written a hundred stories, but none so curious as her own.

When first I knew her she had published half-a-dozen fictions, and I believe I had also perpetrated a novel. She was more than a dozen years older than I, but she was a person who always acknowledged her relativity. It was not so very long ago, but in London, amid the big waves of the present, even a near horizon gets hidden. I met her at some dinner and took her down, rather flattered at offering my arm to a celebrity. She didn't look like one, with her matronly, mild, inanimate face, but I supposed her greatness would come out in her conversation. I gave it all the opportunities I could, but I was not disappointed when I found her only a dull, kind woman. This was why I liked her—she rested me so from literature. To myself literature was an irritation, a torment; but Greville Fane slumbered in the intellectual part of it like a Creole in a hammock. She was not a woman of genius, but her faculty was so special, so much a gift out of hand, that I have often wondered why she fell below that distinction. This was doubtless because the transaction, in her case, had remained incomplete; genius always pays for the gift, feels the debt, and she was placidly unconscious of obligation. She could invent stories by the yard, but she couldn't write a page of English. She went down to her grave without suspecting that though she had contributed volumes to the diversion of her contemporaries she had not contributed a sentence to the language. This had not prevented bushels of criticism from being heaped upon her head; she was worth a couple of columns any day to the weekly papers, in which it was shown that her pictures of life were dreadful but her style really charming. She asked me to come and see her, and I went. She lived then in Montpellier Square; which helped me to see how dissociated her imagination was from her character.

An industrious widow, devoted to her daily stint, to meeting the butcher and baker and making a home for her son and daughter, from the moment she took her pen in her hand she became a creature of passion. She thought the English novel deplorably wanting in that element, and the task she had cut out for herself was to supply the deficiency. Passion in high life was the general formula of this work, for her imagination was at home only in the most exalted circles. She adored, in truth, the aristocracy, and they constituted for her the romance of the world or, what is more to the point, the prime material of fiction. Their beauty and luxury, their loves and revenges, their temptations and surrenders, their immoralities and diamonds were as familiar to her as the blots on her writing-table. She was not a belated producer of the old fashionable novel, she had a cleverness and a modernness of her own, she had freshened up the fly-blown tinsel. She turned off plots by the hundred—and so far as her flying quill could convey her—was perpetually going abroad. Her types, her illustrations, her tone were nothing if not cosmopolitan. She recognised nothing less provincial than European society, and her fine folk knew each other and made love to each other from Doncaster to Bucharest. She had an idea that she resembled Balzac, and her favourite historical characters were Lucien de Rubempré and the Vidame de Pamiers. I must add that when I once asked her who the latter personage was she was unable to tell me. She was very brave and healthy and cheerful, very abundant and innocent and wicked. She was clever and vulgar and snobbish, and never so intensely British as when she was particularly foreign.

This combination of qualities had brought her early success, and I remember having heard with wonder and envy of what she "got," in those days, for a novel. The revelation gave me a pang: it was such a proof that, practising a totally different style, I should never make my fortune. And yet when, as I knew her better, she told me her real tariff and I saw how rumour had quadrupled it, I liked her enough to be sorry. After a while I discovered too that if she got less it was not that *I* was to get any more. My failure never had what Mrs Stormer would have called the banality of being relative—it was always admirably absolute. She lived at ease however in those days—ease is exactly the word, though she produced three novels a year. She scorned me when I spoke of difficulty—it was the only thing that made her angry. If I hinted that a work of art required a tremendous licking into shape she thought it a pretension and a *pose*. She never recognised the "torment of form"; the furthest she went was to introduce into one of her books (in satire her hand was heavy) a young poet who was always talking about it. I couldn't quite understand her irritation on this score, for she had nothing at stake in the matter. She had a shrewd perception that form, in prose at least, never recommended any one to the public we were condemned to address, and therefore she lost nothing (putting her private humiliation aside) by not having any. She made no pretence of producing works of art, but had comfortable tea-drinking hours in which she freely confessed herself a common pastrycook, dealing in such tarts and puddings as would bring customers to the shop. She put in plenty of sugar and of cochineal, or whatever it is that gives these articles a rich and attractive colour. She had a serene superiority to observation and opportunity which constituted an inexpugnable strength and would enable her to go on indefinitely. It is only real success that wanes, it is only solid things that melt. Greville Fane's ignorance of life was a resource still more unfailing than the most approved receipt. On her saying once that the day would come when she should have written herself out I answered: "Ah, you look into fairyland, and the fairies love you, and *they* never change. Fairyland is always there; it always was from the beginning of time, and it always will be to the end. They've given you the key and you can always open the door. With me it's different; I try, in my clumsy way, to be in some direct relation to life." "Oh, bother your direct relation to life!" she used to reply, for she was always annoyed by the phrase—which would not in the least prevent her from using it when she wished to try for style. With no more prejudices than an old sausage-mill, she would give forth again with patient punctuality any poor verbal scrap that had been dropped into her. I cheered her with saying that the dark day, at the end, would be for the like of *me*; inasmuch as, going in our small way by experience and observation, we depended not on a revelation, but on a little tiresome process. Observation depended on opportunity, and where should we be when opportunity failed?

One day she told me that as the novelist's life was so delightful and during the good years at least such a comfortable support (she had these staggering optimisms) she meant to train up her boy to follow it. She took the ingenious view that it was a profession like another and that therefore everything was to be gained by beginning young and serving an apprenticeship. Moreover the education would be less expensive than any other special course, inasmuch as she could administer it herself. She didn't profess to keep a school, but she could at least teach her own child. It was not that she was so very clever, but (she confessed to me as if she were afraid I would laugh at her) that *he* was. I didn't laugh at her for that, for I thought the boy sharp— I had seen him at sundry times. He was well grown and good-looking and unabashed, and both he and his sister made me wonder about their defunct papa, concerning whom the little I knew was that he had been a clergyman. I explained them to myself by suppositions and imputations possibly unjust to the departed; so little were they—superficially at least—the children of their mother. There used to be, on an easel in her drawing-room, an enlarged photograph of her husband, done by some horrible post-humous "process" and draped, as to its florid frame, with a silken scarf, which testified to the candour of Greville Fane's bad taste. It made him look like an unsuccessful tragedian; but it was not a thing to trust. He may have been a successful comedian. Of the two children the girl was the elder, and struck me in all her younger years as singularly colourless. She was only very long, like an undecipherable letter. It was not till Mrs Stormer came back from a protracted residence abroad that Ethel (which was this young lady's name) began to produce the effect, which was afterwards remarkable in her, of a certain kind of high resolution. She made one apprehend that she meant to do something for herself. She was long-necked and near-sighted and striking, and I thought I had never seen sweet seventeen in a form so hard and high and dry. She was cold and affected and ambitious, and she carried an eyeglass with a long handle, which she put up whenever she wanted not to see. She had come out, as the phrase is, immensely; and yet I felt as if she were surrounded with a spiked iron railing. What she meant to do for herself was to marry, and it was the only thing, I think, that she meant to do for any one else; yet who would be inspired to clamber over that bristling barrier? What flower of tenderness or of intimacy would such an adventurer conceive as his reward?

This was for Sir Baldwin Luard to say; but he naturally never confided to me the secret. He was a joyless, jokeless young man, with the air of having other secrets as well, and a determination to get on politically that was indicated by his never having been known to commit himself—as regards any proposition whatever—beyond an exclamatory "Oh!" His wife and he must have conversed mainly in prim ejaculations, but they understood sufficiently that they were kindred spirits. I remember being angry with Greville Fane when she announced these nuptials to me as magnificent; I remember asking her what splendour there was in the union of the daughter of a woman of genius with an irredeemable mediocrity. "Oh! he's awfully clever," she said; but she blushed for the maternal fib. What she meant was that though Sir Baldwin's estates were not vast (he had a dreary house in South Kensington and a still drearier "Hall" somewhere in Essex, which was let), the connection was a "smarter" one than a child of hers could have aspired to form. In spite of the social bravery of her novels she took a very humble and dingy view of herself, so that of all her productions "my daughter

Lady Luard" was quite the one she was proudest of. That personage thought her mother very vulgar and was distressed and perplexed by the occasional license of her pen, but had a complicated attitude in regard to this indirect connection with literature. So far as it was lucrative her ladyship approved of it, and could compound with the inferiority of the pursuit by doing practical justice to some of its advantages. I had reason to know (my reason was simply that poor Mrs Stormer told me) that she suffered the inky fingers to press an occasional banknote into her palm. On the other hand she deplored the "peculiar style" to which Greville Fane had devoted herself, and wondered where an author who had the convenience of so lady-like a daughter could have picked up such views about the best society. "She might know better, with Leolin and me," Lady Luard had been known to remark; but it appeared that some of Greville Fane's superstitions were incurable. She didn't live in Lady Luard's society, and the best was not good enough for her—she must make it still better.

I could see that this necessity grew upon her during the years she spent abroad, when I had glimpses of her in the shifting sojourns that lay in the path of my annual ramble. She betook herself from Germany to Switzerland and from Switzerland to Italy; she favoured cheap places and set up her desk in the smaller capitals. I took a look at her whenever I could, and I always asked how Leolin was getting on. She gave me beautiful accounts of him, and whenever it was possible the boy was produced for my edification. I had entered from the first into the joke of his career—I pretended to regard him as a consecrated child. It had been a joke for Mrs Stormer at first, but the boy himself had been shrewd enough to make the matter serious. If his mother accepted the principle that the intending novelist cannot begin too early to see life, Leolin was not interested in hanging back from the application of it. He was eager to qualify himself, and took to cigarettes at ten, on the highest literary grounds. His poor mother gazed at him with extravagant envy and, like Desdemona, wished heaven had made *her* such a man. She explained to me more than once that in her profession she had found her sex a dreadful drawback. She loved the story of Madame George Sand's early rebellion against this hindrance, and believed that if she had worn trousers she could have written as well as that lady. Leolin had for the career at least the qualification of trousers, and as he grew older he recognised its importance by laying in an immense assortment. He grew up in gorgeous apparel, which was his way of interpreting his mother's system. Whenever I met her I found her still under the impression that she was carrying this system out and that Leolin's training was bearing fruit. She was giving him experience, she was giving him impressions, she was putting a *gagne-pain*[1] into his hand. It was another name for spoiling him with the best conscience in the world. The queerest pictures come back to me of this period of the good lady's life and of the extraordinarily virtuous, muddled, bewildering tenor of it. She had an idea that she was seeing foreign manners as well as her petticoats would allow; but, in reality she was not seeing anything, least of all fortunately how much she was laughed at. She drove her whimsical pen at Dresden and at Florence, and produced in all places and at all times the same romantic and ridiculous fictions. She carried about her box of properties and fished out promptly the familiar, tarnished old puppets. She believed in them when others couldn't, and as they were like nothing that was to be seen under the sun it was impossible to prove by comparison that they were wrong. You can't compare birds and fishes; you could only feel

---

[1]*gagne-pain*   French: livelihood.

that, as Greville Fane's characters had the fine plumage of the former species, human beings must be of the latter.

It would have been droll if it had not been so exemplary to see her tracing the loves of the duchesses beside the innocent cribs of her children. The immoral and the maternal lived together in her diligent days on the most comfortable terms, and she stopped curling the mustaches of her Guardsmen to pat the heads of her babes. She was haunted by solemn spinsters who came to tea from continental *pensions*,[2] and by unsophisticated Americans who told her she was just loved in *their* country. "I had rather be just paid there," she usually replied; for this tribute of transatlantic opinion was the only thing that galled her. The Americans went away thinking her coarse; though as the author of so many beautiful love-stories she was disappointing to most of these pilgrims, who had not expected to find a shy, stout, ruddy lady in a cap like a crumbled pyramid. She wrote about the affections and the impossibility of controlling them, but she talked of the price of *pension* and the convenience of an English chemist. She devoted much thought and many thousands of francs to the education of her daughter, who spent three years at a very superior school at Dresden, receiving wonderful instruction in sciences, arts and tongues, and who, taking a different line from Leolin, was to be brought up wholly as a *femme du monde*.[3] The girl was musical and philological; she made a specialty of languages and learned enough about them to be inspired with a great contempt for her mother's artless accents. Greville Fane's French and Italian were droll; the imitative faculty had been denied her, and she had an unequalled gift, especially pen in hand, of squeezing big mistakes into small opportunities. She knew it, but she didn't care; correctness was the virtue in the world that, like her heroes and heroines, she valued least. Ethel, who had perceived in her pages some remarkable lapses, undertook at one time to revise her proofs; but I remember her telling me a year after the girl had left school that this function had been very briefly exercised. "She can't read me," said Mrs Stormer; "I offend her taste. She tells me that at Dresden—at school—I was never allowed." The good lady seemed surprised at this, having the best conscience in the world about her lucubrations. She had never meant to fly in the face of anything, and considered that she grovelled before the Rhadamanthus of the English literary tribunal, the celebrated and awful Young Person. I assured her, as a joke, that she was frightfully indecent (she hadn't in fact that reality any more than any other) my purpose being solely to prevent her from guessing that her daughter had dropped her not because she was immoral but because she was vulgar. I used to figure her children closeted together and asking each other while they exchanged a gaze of dismay: "Why should she *be* so—and so *fearfully* so—when she has the advantage of our society? Shouldn't *we* have taught her better?" Then I imagined their recognising with a blush and a shrug that she was unreachable, irreformable. Indeed she was, poor lady; but it is never fair to read by the light of taste things that were not written by it. Greville Fane had, in the topsy-turvy, a serene good faith that ought to have been safe from allusion, like a stutter or a *faux pas*.[4]

She didn't make her son ashamed of the profession to which he was destined, however; she only made him ashamed of the way she herself exercised it. But he bore

---

[2]*pension* French: boarding-house or small hotel.
[3]*femme du monde* French: woman of the world.
[4]*faux pas* French: social error.

his humiliation much better than his sister, for he was ready to take for granted that he should one day restore the balance. He was a canny and farseeing youth, with appetites and aspirations, and he had not a scruple in his composition. His mother's theory of the happy knack he could pick up deprived him of the wholesome discipline required to prevent young idlers from becoming cads. He had, abroad, a casual tutor and a snatch or two of a Swiss school, but no consecutive study, no prospect of a university or a degree. It may be imagined with what zeal, as the years went on, he entered into the pleasantry of there being no manual so important to him as the massive book of life. It was an expensive volume to peruse, but Mrs Stormer was willing to lay out a sum in what she would have called her *premiers frais.*[5] Ethel disapproved—she thought this education far too unconventional for an English gentleman. Her voice was for Eton and Oxford, or for any public school (she would have resigned herself) with the army to follow. But Leolin never was afraid of his sister, and they visibly disliked, though they sometimes agreed to assist, each other. They could combine to work the oracle—to keep their mother at her desk.

When she came back to England, telling me she had got all the continent could give her, Leolin was a broad-shouldered, red-faced young man, with an immense wardrobe and an extraordinary assurance of manner. She was fondly obstinate about her having taken the right course with him, and proud of all that he knew and had seen. He was now quite ready to begin, and a little while later she told me he *had* begun. He had written something tremendously clever, and it was coming out in the *Cheapside.* I believe it came out; I had no time to look for it; I never heard anything about it. I took for granted that if this contribution had passed through his mother's hands it had practically become a specimen of her own genius, and it was interesting to consider Mrs Stormer's future in the light of her having to write her son's novels as well as her own. This was not the way she looked at it herself; she took the charming ground that he would help her to write hers. She used to tell me that he supplied passages of the greatest value to her own work—all sorts of technical things, about hunting and yachting and wine—that she couldn't be expected to get very straight. It was all so much practice for him and so much alleviation for her. I was unable to identify these pages, for I had long since ceased to "keep up" with Greville Fane; but I was quite able to believe that the wine-question had been put, by Leolin's good offices, on a better footing, for the dear lady used to mix her drinks (she was perpetually serving the most splendid suppers) in the queerest fashion. I could see that he was willing enough to accept a commission to look after that department. It occurred to me indeed, when Mrs Stormer settled in England again, that by making a shrewd use of both her children she might be able to rejuvenate her style. Ethel had come back to gratify her young ambition, and if she couldn't take her mother into society, she would at least go into it herself. Silently, stiffly, almost grimly, this young lady held up her head, clenched her long teeth, squared her lean elbows and made her way up the staircases she had elected. The only communication she ever made to me, the only effusion of confidence with which she ever honoured me, was when she said: "I don't want to know the people mamma knows; I mean to know others." I took due note of the remark, for I was not one of the "others." I couldn't trace therefore the steps of her process; I could only admire it at a distance and congratulate her mother on the results. The results were that Ethel went to "big" parties and got people to take her.

---

[5]*premier frais*   French: initial costs.

Some of them were people she had met abroad, and others were people whom the people she had met abroad had met. They ministered alike to Miss Ethel's convenience, and I wondered how she extracted so many favours without the expenditure of a smile. Her smile was the dimmest thing in the world, diluted lemonade, without sugar, and she had arrived precociously at social wisdom, recognising that if she was neither pretty enough nor rich enough nor clever enough, she could at least in her muscular youth be rude enough. Therefore if she was able to tell her mother what really took place in the mansions of the great, give her notes to work from, the quill could be driven at home to better purpose and precisely at a moment when it would have to be more active than ever. But if she did tell, it would appear that poor Mrs Stormer didn't believe. As regards many points this was not a wonder; at any rate I heard nothing of Greville Fane's having developed a new manner. She had only one manner from start to finish, as Leolin would have said.

She was tired at last, but she mentioned to me that she couldn't afford to pause. She continued to speak of Leolin's work as the great hope of their future (she had saved no money) though the young man wore to my sense an aspect more and more professional if you like, but less and less literary. At the end of a couple of years there was something monstrous in the impudence with which he played his part in the comedy. When I wondered how she could play *her* part I had to perceive that her good faith was complete and that what kept it so was simply her extravagant fondness. She loved the young impostor with a simple, blind, benighted love, and of all the heroes of romance who had passed before her eyes he was by far the most brilliant. He was at any rate the most real—she could touch him, pay for him, suffer for him, worship him. He made her think of her princes and dukes, and when she wished to fix these figures in her mind's eye she thought of her boy. She had often told me she was carried away by her own creations, and she was certainly carried away by Leolin. He vivified, by potentialities at least, the whole question of youth and passion. She held, not unjustly, that the sincere novelist should feel the whole flood of life; she acknowledged with regret that she had not had time to feel it herself, and it was a joy to her that the deficiency might be supplied by the sight of the way it was rushing through this magnificent young man. She exhorted him, I suppose, to let it rush; she wrung her own flaccid little sponge into the torrent. I knew not what passed between them in her hours of tuition, but I gathered that she mainly impressed on him that the great thing was to live, because that gave you material. He asked nothing better; he collected material, and the formula served as a universal pretext. You had only to look at him to see that, with his rings and breastpins, his cross-barred jackets, his early *embonpoint*,[6] his eyes that looked like imitation jewels, his various indications of a dense, full-blown temperament, his idea of life was singularly vulgar; but he was not so far wrong as that his response to his mother's expectations was not in a high degree practical. If she had imposed a profession on him from his tenderest years it was exactly a profession that he followed. The two were not quite the same, inasmuch as *his* was simply to live at her expense; but at least she couldn't say that he hadn't taken a line. If she insisted on believing in him he offered himself to the sacrifice. My impression is that her secret dream was that he should have a *liaison*[7] with a countess, and he persuaded her without difficulty that he had one. I don't know what countesses are capable of, but I have a clear notion of what Leolin was.

---

[6]*embonpoint*   French: stoutness, plumpness.
[7]*liaison*   French: connection (usually amorous).

He didn't persuade his sister, who despised him—she wished to work her mother in her own way, and I asked myself why the girl's judgment of him didn't make me like her better. It was because it didn't save her after all from a mute agreement with him to go halves. There were moments when I couldn't help looking hard into his atrocious young eyes, challenging him to confess his fantastic fraud and give it up. Not a little tacit conversation passed between us in this way, but he had always the best of it. If I said: "Oh, come now, with *me* you needn't keep it up; plead guilty, and I'll let you off," he wore the most ingenuous, the most candid expression, in the depths of which I could read: "Oh, yes, I know it exasperates you—that's just why I do it." He took the line of earnest inquiry, talked about Balzac and Flaubert, asked me if I thought Dickens *did* exaggerate and Thackeray *ought* to be called a pessimist. Once he came to see me, at his mother's suggestion he declared, on purpose to ask me how far, in my opinion, in the English novel, one really might venture to "go." He was not resigned to the usual pruderies—he suffered under them already. He struck out the brilliant idea that nobody knew how far we might go, for nobody had ever tried. Did I think *he* might safely try—would it injure his mother if he did? He would rather disgrace himself by his timidities than injure his mother, but certainly some one ought to try. Wouldn't *I* try—couldn't I be prevailed upon to look at it as a duty? Surely the ultimate point ought to be fixed—he was worried, haunted by the question. He patronised me unblushingly, made me feel like a foolish amateur, a helpless novice, inquired into my habits of work and conveyed to me that I was utterly *vieux jeu*[8] and had not had the advantage of an early training. I had not been brought up from the germ, I knew nothing of life—didn't go at it on *his* system. He had dipped into French feuilletons and picked up plenty of phrases, and he made a much better show in talk than his poor mother, who never had time to read anything and could only be vivid with her pen. If I didn't kick him down-stairs it was because he would have alighted on her at the bottom.

When she went to live at Primrose Hill I called upon her and found her weary and wasted. It had waned a good deal, the elation caused the year before by Ethel's marriage; the foam on the cup had subsided and there was a bitterness in the draught. She had had to take a cheaper house and she had to work still harder to pay even for that. Sir Baldwin was obliged to be close; his charges were fearful, and the dream of her living with her daughter (a vision she had never mentioned to me) must be renounced. "I would have helped with things, and I could have lived perfectly in one room," she said; "I would have paid for everything, and—after all—I'm some one, ain't I? But I don't fit in, and Ethel tells me there are tiresome people she *must* receive. I can help them from here, no doubt, better than from there. She told me once, you know, what she thinks of my picture of life. 'Mamma, your picture of life is preposterous!' No doubt it is, but she's vexed with me for letting my prices go down; and I had to write three novels to pay for all her marriage cost me. I did it very well—I mean the outfit and the wedding; but that's why I'm here. At any rate she doesn't want a dingy old woman in her house. I should give it an atmosphere of literary glory, but literary glory is only the eminence of nobodies. Besides, she doubts my glory—she knows I'm glorious only at Peckham and Hackney. She doesn't want her friends to ask if I've never known nice people. She can't tell them I've never been in society. She tried to teach me better once, but I couldn't learn. It would seem too as if Peckham and Hackney had had enough of me; for (don't tell any one!) I've had to take less for my last than

---

[8]*vieux jeu*   French: old-fashioned.

I ever took for anything." I asked her how little this had been, not from curiosity, but in order to upbraid her, more disinterestedly than Lady Luard had done, for such concessions. She answered "I'm ashamed to tell you," and then she began to cry.

I had never seen her break down, and I was proportionately moved; she sobbed, like a frightened child, over the extinction of her vogue and the exhaustion of her vein. Her little work-room seemed indeed a barren place to grow flowers, and I wondered, in the after years (for she continued to produce and publish) by what desperate and heroic process she dragged them out of the soil. I remember asking her on that occasion what had become of Leolin, and how much longer she intended to allow him to amuse himself at her cost. She rejoined with spirit, wiping her eyes, that he was down at Brighton hard at work—he was in the midst of a novel—and that he *felt* life so, in all its misery and mystery, that it was cruel to speak of such experiences as a pleasure. "He goes beneath the surface," she said, "and he *forces* himself to look at things from which he would rather turn away. Do you call that amusing yourself? You should see his face sometimes! And he does it for me as much as for himself. He tells me everything—he comes home to me with his *trouvailles*.[9] We are artists together, and to the artist all things are pure. I've often heard you say so yourself." The novel that Leolin was engaged in at Brighton was never published, but a friend of mine and of Mrs Stormer's who was staying there happened to mention to me later that he had seen the young apprentice to fiction driving, in a dogcart, a young lady with a very pink face. When I suggested that she was perhaps a woman of title with whom he was conscientiously flirting my informant replied: "She is indeed, but do you know what her title is?" He pronounced it—it was familiar and descriptive—but I won't reproduce it here. I don't know whether Leolin mentioned it to his mother: she would have needed all the purity of the artist to forgive him. I hated so to come across him that in the very last years I went rarely to see her, though I knew that she had come pretty well to the end of her rope. I didn't want her to tell me that she had fairly to give her books away—I didn't want to see her cry. She kept it up amazingly, and every few months, at my club, I saw three new volumes, in green, in crimson, in blue, on the book-table that groaned with light literature. Once I met her at the Academy soirée, where you meet people you thought were dead, and she vouchsafed the information, as if she owed it to me in candour, that Leolin had been obliged to recognise insuperable difficulties in the question of *form*, he was so fastidious; so that she had now arrived at a definite understanding with him (it was such a comfort) that *she* would do the form if he would bring home the substance. That was now his position—he foraged for her in the great world at a salary. "He's my 'devil,' don't you see? as if I were a great lawyer: he gets up the case and I argue it." She mentioned further that in addition to his salary he was paid by the piece: he got so much for a striking character, so much for a pretty name, so much for a plot, so much for an incident, and had so much promised him if he would invent a new crime.

"He *has* invented one," I said, "and he's paid every day of his life."

"What is it?" she asked, looking hard at the picture of the year, "Baby's Tub," near which we happened to be standing.

I hesitated a moment. "I myself will write a little story about it, and then you'll see."

But she never saw; she had never seen anything, and she passed away with her fine blindness unimpaired. Her son published every scrap of scribbled paper that could be

---

[9]*trouvailles* French: discoveries, lucky finds.

extracted from her table-drawers, and his sister quarrelled with him mortally about the proceeds, which showed that she only wanted a pretext, for they cannot have been great. I don't know what Leolin lives upon, unless it be on a queer lady many years older than himself, whom he lately married. The last time I met him he said to me with his infuriating smile: "Don't you think we can go a little further still—just a little?" He really goes too far.

[1892]

Questions

1. What can be said of the characters' names in James's story: Mrs. Stormer/Greville Fane, Ethel, Leolin?
2. What is Mrs. Stormer's relationship with her children? Consider, by way of contrast, the relationships in Jakobsdóttir's "A Story for Children."
3. What specifically is being satirized in James's short story and how does it apply to the writer's own literary career?
4. What does James imply about the relationship between artistry and family?

Sarah Orne Jewett
(1849–1909)
United States

S arah Orne Jewett was born in South Berwick, Maine, into a wealthy old New England family of shipowners, merchants, and physicians. Her father was a doctor; her mother was distantly related to the Puritan poet Anne Bradstreet. Although Jewett was educated at the Berwick Academy, she felt that she received her real education from her father, who was well versed in the classics and in nature and who allowed her to accompany him on house calls.

Jewett published her first story at the age of 18, under a pseudonym. Eventually she published nearly 150 stories and sketches in the leading journals of her time; she also wrote nearly two dozen stories for children. Once considered a regional or "local color" writer, Jewett is now more fully appreciated for her rich understanding and portrayal of local manners and characters as well as her vivid depictions of the natural landscape of rural New England, all of which she observed with great depth of insight. The collection of stories for which she is best known, The Country of Pointed Firs (1896), a series of sketches of the inhabitants of a seaport village in Maine, is striking and unusual in its focus on older characters, most of whom are women over 60. She also wrote several novels, including Deephaven (1877) and A Country Doctor (1884). Jewett remained unmarried by choice, declaring that "marriage would only be a hindrance"; however, she maintained enduring relationships with a number of female friends.

"A White Heron," Jewett's best-known and most frequently anthologized story, demonstrates her lyrical exploration of the relationship between the human and natural worlds.

A WHITE HERON

I

The woods were already filled with shadows one June evening, just before eight o'-clock, though a bright sunset still glimmered faintly among the trunks of the trees. A little girl was driving home her cow, a plodding, dilatory, provoking creature in her behavior, but a valued companion for all that. They were going away from the western light, and striking deep into the dark woods, but their feet were familiar with the path, and it was no matter whether their eyes could see it or not.

There was hardly a night the summer through when the old cow could be found waiting at the pasture bars; on the contrary, it was her greatest pleasure to hide herself away among the high huckleberry bushes, and though she wore a loud bell she had made the discovery that if one stood perfectly still it would not ring. So Sylvia had to hunt for her until she found her and call Co'! Co'! with never an answering Moo, until her childish patience was quite spent. If the creature had not given good milk and plenty of it, the case would have seemed very different to her owners. Besides, Sylvia had all the time there was, and very little use to make of it. Sometimes in pleasant weather it was a consolation to look upon the cow's pranks as an intelligent attempt to play hide and seek, and as the child had no playmates she lent herself to this amusement with a good deal of zest. Though this chase had been so long that the wary animal herself had given an unusual signal of her whereabouts, Sylvia had only laughed when she came upon Mistress Moolly at the swamp-side, and urged her affectionately homeward with a twig of birch leaves. The old cow was not inclined to wander farther, she even turned in the right direction for once as they left the pasture, and stepped along the road at a good pace. She was quite ready to be milked now, and seldom stopped to browse. Sylvia wondered what her grandmother would say because they were so late. It was a great while since she had left home at half past five o'clock, but everybody knew the difficulty of making this errand a short one. Mrs. Tilley had chased the horned torment too many summer evenings herself to blame any one else for lingering, and was only thankful as she waited that she had Sylvia, nowadays, to give such valuable assistance. The good woman suspected that Sylvia loitered occasionally on her own account; there never was such a child for straying about out-of-doors since the world was made! Everybody said that it was a good change for a little maid who had tried to grow for eight years in a crowded manufacturing town, but, as for Sylvia herself, it seemed as if she never had been alive at all before she came to live at the farm. She thought often with wistful compassion of a wretched dry geranium that belonged to a town neighbor.

"'Afraid of folks,'" old Mrs. Tilley said to herself, with a smile, after she had made the unlikely choice of Sylvia from her daughter's houseful of children, and was returning to the farm. "'Afraid of folks,' they said! I guess she won't be troubled no great with 'em up to the old place!" When they reached the door of the lonely house and stopped to unlock it, and the cat came to purr loudly, and rub against them, a deserted pussy, indeed, but fat with young robins, Sylvia whispered that this was a beautiful place to live in, and she never should wish to go home.

The companions followed the shady wood-road, the cow taking slow steps, and the child very fast ones. The cow stopped long at the brook to drink, as if the pasture were not half a swamp, and Sylvia stood still and waited, letting her bare feet cool themselves in the shoal water, while the great twilight moths struck softly against her. She waded on through the brook as the cow moved away, and listened to the thrushes with a heart that beat fast with pleasure. There was a stirring in the great boughs overhead. They were full of little birds and beasts that seemed to be wide-awake, and going about their world, or else saying good-night to each other in sleepy twitters. Sylvia herself felt sleepy as she walked along. However, it was not much farther to the house, and the air was soft and sweet. She was not often in the woods so late as this, and it made her feel as if she were a part of the gray shadows and the moving leaves. She was just thinking how long it seemed since she first came to the farm a year ago, and wondering if everything went on in the noisy town just the same as when she was there; the thought of the great red-faced boy who used to chase and frighten her made her hurry along the path to escape from the shadow of the trees.

Suddenly this little woods-girl is horror-stricken to hear a clear whistle not very far away. Not a bird's whistle, which would have a sort of friendliness, but a boy's whistle, determined, and somewhat aggressive. Sylvia left the cow to whatever sad fate might await her, and stepped discreetly aside into the bushes, but she was just too late. The enemy had discovered her, and called out in a very cheerful and persuasive tone, "Halloa, little girl, how far is it to the road?" and trembling Sylvia answered almost inaudibly, "A good ways."

She did not dare to look boldly at the tall young man, who carried a gun over his shoulder, but she came out of her bush and again followed the cow, while he walked alongside.

"I have been hunting for some birds," the stranger said kindly, "and I have lost my way, and need a friend very much. Don't be afraid," he added gallantly. "Speak up and tell me what your name is, and whether you think I can spend the night at your house, and go out gunning early in the morning."

Sylvia was more alarmed than before. Would not her grandmother consider her much to blame? But who could have foreseen such an accident as this? It did not appear to be her fault, and she hung her head as if the stem of it were broken, but managed to answer, "Sylvy," with much effort when her companion again asked her name.

Mrs. Tilley was standing in the doorway when the trio came into view. The cow gave a loud moo by way of explanation.

"Yes, you'd better speak up for yourself, you old trial! Where'd she tucked herself away this time, Sylvy?" Sylvia kept an awed silence; she knew by instinct that her grandmother did not comprehend the gravity of the situation. She must be mistaking the stranger for one of the farmer-lads of the region.

The young man stood his gun beside the door, and dropped a heavy game-bag beside it; then he bade Mrs. Tilley good-evening, and repeated his wayfarer's story, and asked if he could have a night's lodging.

"Put me anywhere you like," he said. "I must be off early in the morning, before day; but I am very hungry, indeed. You can give me some milk at any rate, that's plain."

"Dear sakes, yes," responded the hostess, whose long slumbering hospitality seemed to be easily awakened. "You might fare better if you went out on the main road a mile or so, but you're welcome to what we've got. I'll milk right off, and you make yourself at home. You can sleep on husks or feathers," she proffered graciously. "I raised them all myself. There's good pasturing for geese just below here towards the ma'sh. Now step round and set a plate for the gentleman, Sylvy!" And Sylvia promptly stepped. She was glad to have something to do, and she was hungry herself.

It was a surprise to find so clean and comfortable a little dwelling in this New England wilderness. The young man had known the horrors of its most primitive housekeeping, and the dreary squalor of that level of society which does not rebel at the companionship of hens. This was the best thrift of an old-fashioned farmstead, though on such a small scale that it seemed like a hermitage. He listened eagerly to the old woman's quaint talk, he watched Sylvia's pale face and shining gray eyes with ever growing enthusiasm, and insisted that this was the best supper he had eaten for a month; then, afterward, the new-made friends sat down in the doorway together while the moon came up.

Soon it would be berry-time, and Sylvia was a great help at picking. The cow was a good milker, though a plaguy thing to keep track of, the hostess gossiped frankly, adding presently that she had buried four children, so that Sylvia's mother, and a son (who might be dead) in California were all the children she had left. "Dan, my boy, was a great hand to go gunning," she explained sadly. "I never wanted for pa'tridges or gray squer'ls while he was to home. He's been a great wand'rer, I expect, and he's no hand to write letters. There, I don't blame him, I'd ha' seen the world myself if it had been so I could.

"Sylvia takes after him," the grandmother continued affectionately, after a minute's pause. "There ain't a foot o' ground she don't know her way over, and the wild creatur's counts her one o' themselves. Squer'ls she'll tame to come an' feed right out o' her hands, and all sorts o' birds. Last winter she got the jay-birds to bangeing here, and I believe she'd 'a' scanted herself of her own meals to have plenty to throw out amongst 'em, if I hadn't kep' watch. Anything but crows, I tell her, I'm willin' to help support,—though Dan he went an' tamed one o' them that did seem to have reason same as folks. It was round here a good spell after he went away. Dan an' his father they didn't hitch,—but he never held up his head ag'in after Dan had dared him an' gone off."

The guest did not notice this hint of family sorrows in his eager interest in something else.

"So Sylvy knows all about birds, does she?" he exclaimed, as he looked round at the little girl who sat, very demure but increasingly sleepy, in the moonlight. "I am making a collection of birds myself. I have been at it ever since I was a boy." (Mrs. Tilley smiled.) "There are two or three very rare ones I have been hunting for these five years. I mean to get them on my own ground if they can be found."

"Do you cage 'em up?" asked Mrs. Tilley doubtfully, in response to this enthusiastic announcement.

"Oh, no, they're stuffed and preserved, dozens and dozens of them," said the ornithologist, "and I have shot or snared every one myself. I caught a glimpse of a white heron three miles from here on Saturday, and I have followed it in this direction. They have never been found in this district at all. The little white heron, it is," and he turned again to look at Sylvia with the hope of discovering that the rare bird was one of her acquaintances.

But Sylvia was watching a hop-toad in the narrow footpath.

"You would know the heron if you saw it," the stranger continued eagerly. "A queer tall white bird with soft feathers and long thin legs. And it would have a nest perhaps in the top of a high tree, made of sticks, something like a hawk's nest."

Sylvia's heart gave a wild beat; she knew that strange white bird, and had once stolen softly near where it stood in some bright green swamp grass, away over at the other side of the woods. There was an open place where the sunshine always seemed strangely yellow and hot, where tall, nodding rushes grew, and her grandmother had warned her that she might sink in the soft black mud underneath and never be heard of more. Not far beyond were the salt marshes and beyond those was the sea, the sea which Sylvia wondered and dreamed about, but never had looked upon, though its great voice could often be heard above the noise of the woods on stormy nights.

"I can't think of anything I should like so much as to find that heron's nest," the handsome stranger was saying. "I would give ten dollars to anybody who could show it to me," he added desperately, "and I mean to spend my whole vacation hunting for it if need be. Perhaps it was only migrating, or had been chased out of its own region by some bird of prey."

Mrs. Tilley gave amazed attention to all this, but Sylvia still watched the toad, not divining, as she might have done at some calmer time, that the creature wished to get to its hole under the doorstep, and was much hindered by the unusual spectators at that hour of the evening. No amount of thought, that night, could decide how many wished-for treasures the ten dollars, so lightly spoken of, would buy.

The next day the young sportsman hovered about the woods, and Sylvia kept him company, having lost her first fear of the friendly lad, who proved to be most kind and sympathetic. He told her many things about the birds and what they knew and where they lived and what they did with themselves. And he gave her a jack-knife, which she thought as great a treasure as if she were a desert-islander. All day long he did not once make her troubled or afraid except when he brought down some unsuspecting singing creature from its bough. Sylvia would have liked him vastly better without his gun; she could not understand why he killed the very birds he seemed to like so much. But as the day waned, Sylvia still watched the young man with loving admiration. She had never seen anybody so charming and delightful; the woman's heart, asleep in the child, was vaguely thrilled by a dream of love. Some premonition of that great power stirred and swayed these young foresters who traversed the solemn woodlands with soft-footed silent care. They stopped to listen to a bird's song; they pressed forward again eagerly, parting the branches—speaking to each other rarely and in whispers; the young man going first and Sylvia following, fascinated, a few steps behind, with her gray eyes dark with excitement.

She grieved because the longed-for white heron was elusive, but she did not lead the guest, she only followed, and there was no such thing as speaking first. The sound of her own unquestioned voice would have terrified her—it was hard enough to answer yes or no when there was need of that. At last evening began to fall, and they drove the cow home together, and Sylvia smiled with pleasure when they came to the place where she heard the whistle and was afraid only the night before.

II

Half a mile from home, at the farthest edge of the woods, where the land was highest, a great pine-tree stood, the last of its generation. Whether it was left for a boundary mark, or for what reason, no one could say; the woodchoppers who had felled its mates were dead and gone long ago, and a whole forest of sturdy trees, pines and oaks and maples, had grown again. But the stately head of this old pine towered above them all and made a landmark for sea and shore miles and miles away. Sylvia knew it well. She had always believed that whoever climbed to the top of it could see the ocean; and the little girl had often laid her hand on the great rough trunk and looked up wistfully at those dark boughs that the wind always stirred, no matter how hot and still the air might be below. Now she thought of the tree with a new excitement, for why, if one climbed it at break of day, could not one see all the world, and easily discover whence the white heron flew, and mark the place, and find the hidden nest?

What a spirit of adventure, what wild ambition! What fancied triumph and delight and glory for the later morning when she could make known the secret! It was almost too real and too great for the childish heart to bear.

All night the door of the little house stood open, and the whippoorwills came and sang upon the very step. The young sportsman and his old hostess were sound asleep, but Sylvia's great design kept her broad awake and watching. She forgot to think of sleep. The short summer night seemed as long as the winter darkness, and at last when the whippoorwills ceased, and she was afraid the morning would after all come too soon, she stole out of the house and followed the pasture path through the woods, hastening toward the open ground beyond, listening with a sense of comfort and companionship to the drowsy twitter of a half-awakened bird, whose perch she had jarred in passing. Alas, if the great wave of human interest which flooded for the first time this dull little life should sweep away the satisfactions of an existence heart to heart with nature and the dumb life of the forest!

There was the huge tree asleep yet in the paling moonlight, and small and hopeful Sylvia began with utmost bravery to mount to the top of it, with tingling, eager blood coursing the channels of her whole frame, with her bare feet and fingers, that pinched and held like bird's claws to the monstrous ladder reaching up, up, almost to the sky itself. First she must mount the white oak tree that grew alongside, where she was almost lost among the dark branches and the green leaves heavy and wet with dew; a bird fluttered off its nest, and a red squirrel ran to and fro and scolded pettishly at the harmless housebreaker. Sylvia felt her way easily. She had often climbed there, and knew that higher still one of the oak's upper branches chafed against the pine trunk, just where its lower boughs were set close together. There, when she made the dangerous pass from one tree to the other, the great enterprise would really begin.

She crept out along the swaying oak limb at last, and took the daring step across into the old pine-tree. The way was harder than she thought; she must reach far and hold fast, the sharp dry twigs caught and held her and scratched her like angry talons, the pitch made her thin little fingers clumsy and stiff as she went round and round the tree's great stem, higher and higher upward. The sparrows and robins in the woods below were beginning to wake and twitter to the dawn, yet it seemed much lighter there aloft in the pine-tree, and the child knew that she must hurry if her project were to be of any use.

The tree seemed to lengthen itself out as she went up, and to reach farther and farther upward. It was like a great main-mast to the voyaging earth; it must truly have been amazed that morning through all its ponderous frame as it felt this determined spark of human spirit creeping and climbing from higher branch to branch. Who knows how steadily the least twigs held themselves to advantage this light, weak creature on her way! The old pine must have loved his new dependent. More than all the hawks, and bats, and moths, and even the sweet-voiced thrushes, was the brave, beating heart of the solitary gray-eyed child. And the tree stood still and held away the winds that June morning while the dawn grew bright in the east.

Sylvia's face was like a pale star, if one had seen it from the ground, when the last thorny bough was past, and she stood trembling and tired but wholly triumphant, high in the tree-top. Yes, there was the sea with the dawning sun making a golden dazzle over it, and toward that glorious east flew two hawks with slow-moving pinions. How low they looked in the air from that height when before one had only seen them far up, and dark against the blue sky. Their gray feathers were as soft as moths; they seemed only a little way from the tree, and Sylvia felt as if she too could go flying away among the clouds. Westward, the woodlands and farms reached miles and miles into the distance; here and there were church steeples, and white villages; truly it was a vast and awesome world.

The birds sang louder and louder. At last the sun came up bewilderingly bright. Sylvia could see the white sails of ships out at sea, and the clouds that were purple and rose-colored and yellow at first began to fade away. Where was the white heron's nest in the sea of green branches, and was this wonderful sight and pageant of the world the only reward for having climbed to such a giddy height? Now look down

again, Sylvia, where the green marsh is set among the shining birches and dark hem-
locks; there where you saw the white heron once you will see him again; look, look!
a white spot of him like a single floating feather comes up from the dead hemlock and
grows larger, and rises, and comes close at last, and goes by the landmark pine with
steady sweep of wing and outstretched slender neck and crested head. And wait!
wait! do not move a foot or a finger, little girl, do not send an arrow of light and consciousness from your two eager eyes, for the heron has perched on a pine bough not
far beyond yours, and cries back to his mate on the nest, and plumes his feathers for
the new day!

The child gives a long sigh a minute later when a company of shouting cat-birds
comes also to the tree, and vexed by their fluttering and lawlessness the solemn heron
goes away. She knows his secret now, the wild, light, slender bird that floats and wa-
vers, and goes back like an arrow presently to his home in the green world beneath.
Then Sylvia, well satisfied, makes her perilous way down again, not daring to look far
below the branch she stands on, ready to cry sometimes because her fingers ache and
her lamed feet slip. Wondering over and over again what the stranger would say to
her, and what he would think when she told him how to find his way straight to the
heron's nest.

"Sylvy, Sylvy!" called the busy old grandmother again and again, but nobody answered, and the small husk bed was empty, and Sylvia had disappeared.

The guest waked from a dream, and remembering his day's pleasure hurried to
dress himself that it might sooner begin. He was sure from the way the shy little girl
looked once or twice yesterday that she had at least seen the white heron, and now
she must really be persuaded to tell. Here she comes now, paler than ever, and her
worn old frock is torn and tattered, and smeared with pine pitch. The grandmother
and the sportsman stand in the door together and question her, and the splendid moment had come to speak of the dead hemlock-tree by the green marsh.

But Sylvia does not speak after all, though the old grandmother fretfully rebukes
her, and the young man's kind appealing eyes are looking straight in her own. He
can make them rich with money; he has promised it, and they are poor now. He is so
well worth making happy, and he waits to hear the story she can tell.

No, she must keep silence! What is it that suddenly forbids her and makes her
dumb? Has she been nine years growing, and now, when the great world for the first
time puts out a hand to her, must she thrust it aside for a bird's sake? The murmur of
the pine's green branches is in her ears, she remembers how the white heron came flying through the golden air and how they watched the sea and the morning together,
and Sylvia cannot speak; she cannot tell the heron's secret and give its life away.

Dear loyalty, that suffered a sharp pang as the guest went away disappointed later in
the day, that could have served and followed him and loved him as a dog loves! Many
a night Sylvia heard the echo of his whistle haunting the pasture path as she came
home with the loitering cow. She forgot even her sorrow at the sharp report of his gun
and the piteous sight of thrushes and sparrows dropping silent to the ground, their
songs hushed and their pretty feathers stained and wet with blood. Were the birds better friends than their hunter might have been,—who can tell? Whatever treasures
were lost to her, woodlands and summertime, remember! Bring your gifts and graces
and tell your secrets to this lonely country child!

[1886]

Questions

1. What is Sylvia's attitude toward nature? What is the ornithologist's attitude? Why is Sylvia initially frightened by the ornithologist?
2. What is the central conflict in the story? Why does Sylvia make the choice she makes?
3. What is the "initiation" that Sylvia undergoes? How does the narrator convey Sylvia's changing perspective?
4. What is the narrator's relation to the story? How do the shifts in point of view and tense contribute to the unfolding of the narrative?
5. What is the theme of the story?

Elizabeth Jolley

(b. 1923)

England/Australia

Born in Birmingham, England, of a mother from the impoverished Austrian aristocracy who became a nurse, and an English father who was a science teacher, Elizabeth Jolley grew up in England but spoke only German at home until she was six. Because her father did not want his daughters to attend school, Elizabeth and her sister were educated at home by French and German governesses and British Broadcasting System school programs. As Jolley writes, these formative experiences contributed to her eventual vocation as a writer: "Children who do not go to school and whose family speak a foreign language are exiles in their own street. Like all lonely children we retreated into fantasy and imagination." Later, when her father finally sent Elizabeth to a Quaker boarding school, she tried to subdue her homesickness by writing stories. Jolley notes the following:

> All my life I have kept journals in which I write about people and places; dwelling on, perhaps, some detail of human effort or the way in which a tree might change in the changing light of an afternoon.

Later trained as a nurse, Jolley did not begin to submit her stories for publication until she and her husband, a librarian, emigrated to western Australia in 1959. While raising a family, teaching, and managing an orchard and a goose farm, Jolley continued to write and to publish novels and stories, a number of which she had been working on for years. (Sadly, the goose farm was lost in bushfires that swept the area in 1996.) As she commented in an interview, "The thing about writing is that you do several things alongside, and that writing is only one part of your life. If you made it your whole life, you might go entirely mad, especially if you didn't succeed . . . ."

Jolley's stories, distinguished by their fresh blend of offbeat humor, satire, and pathos, are collected in four volumes, including Five Acre Virgin and other Stories (1976), The Traveling Entertainer and Other Stories (1979), Woman in a Lampshade (1983), and Fellow Passengers (1997). Her novels, including (among others), Miss Peabody's Inheritance (1983), Foxbaby (1985), The Orchard Thieves (1995), and An Accommodating Spouse (1999), have received a number of prizes and awards. In 1998, Jolley was named one of Australia's Living Treasures.

ANOTHER HOLIDAY FOR THE PRINCE

We're having this dumb play at school Falstaff or something I was supposed to be the Sheriff of London but the bell went before my part came on and as it was the long weekend Hot Legs let us go before the bell stopped. I went down and hung around the Deli for a while with the others and when I got home Mother was already there.

407

"Don't bang the door," she said, "He's still in bed."

"Sorry!"

"He's sleeping," she went on, she seemed relieved. "Sleep's the best thing he can have. I wish *he'd* eat!" She watched me as I took bread and spread the butter thick, she was never mean about butter, when we didn't have other things we always had plenty of butter. I ate my pieces quickly before she could tell me not to spoil my tea.

Mother always called him the Prince, she worried about him all the time. I couldn't think why. He was only my brother and a drop-out at that. Dropped out from school and then dropping in and out of one job after another, sometimes not even staying long enough in one place to get his pay. I could always tell by Mother's face when I came in.

"He's back, was back when I came home," and she would sit in a heap at the kitchen table. And after a bit I'd say, "What's for tea?" and that brightened her.

"What do you think the Prince would like?" and she'd go up the terrace for liver-wurst or something tasty to fry up.

My brother smoked and drank and coughed and watched telly with the blinds drawn day in and day out and half the night too.

"He's resting," Mother comforted herself. "Boys outgrow their strength. They need extra rest. If only he'd eat and go outdoors in the air, though!"

Saturday mornings I often went with her to her work to get her finished up as quick as possible.

Mother said it was a revelation every time she got off the bus and walked round the corner and saw the wide river below shining so peaceful with the far bank dark with trees and all the lovely homes piled up on this side of the hill. It was like a great big continental post card. The stillness and the blue misty light on the smooth water made her feel rested she said and she felt she was a better person every time she saw it.

We had the house to ourselves, it was all vinyl and bathrooms. She wouldn't ever let me do out the study.

"There's big cigars in there and sex drinks and books with titles," she said and she sent me to hang out the washing. There was nothing in the *Seducer's Cook Book* to upset her she said and dusting those nude drawings didn't affect her, she was too worn out and faded for that kind of thing.

We seemed to get on really quick with the work and when we sat down to have our cocoa she looked out at the river approving of the calm.

"They'll stay out in their boat the weekend," she said, sipping gratefully.

"I don't like you going out to work," I said.

"You don't want to mind about that," she said. "Everyone's got to work at some time or other, it's best to like it," she said. "Otherwise you'll have to spend most of your life not liking what you've got to do," she said. "My Mrs. Lady is a lovely woman, such a good mother too, you saw all that nice washing! really sets an example, so clean you could do an operation in any room in this house. And don't you ever forget those nice dresses and jumpers you've had from her."

"But you're going for your life all the time."

"Hard work never hurt any one. It's good for me, helps to fight off the menopause."

"What's that?" Mother used big words. She read too much.

"It's when your life changes, you'll find out later," she said, and then she said, "and where else could I have an avocado pear with my cocoa."

"Ugh! Avocado pear!"

"It's an acquired taste," and she waltzed off with the broom. Later while I was wiping out the saucepan cupboard I could hear her queer singing above the noise of the floor polisher. She seemed to get quicker and younger as she worked.

As we were about to go home Mother took a little key off a hook in the kitchen. "I've a very nice surprise for you," she said, twirling it on her bony finger.

"That why you were singing then?"

"Oh was I singing?" Her cheeks were suddenly bright red and her eyes seemed to be full of tears as if an idea was trying to burst out of them.

"What do you think! Mrs. Lady has left me the use of her car and some money so we can go away for the weekend!" Oh I felt an excitement, I hugged Mother.

"It's a wonder you didn't die keeping the secret all morning." I hugged her again.

"My! Mind my living daylights," she gasped for breath.

"The Prince," Mother said. "We'll get him to that nice motel again right on the sea front. He won't be able to avoid breathing the sea air if he's right in it."

Of course my brother growled. He was in a terrible mood. Mother pleaded with him through the clouds of smoke.

"Only pack up a few things and just come. I have the car. Come and see."

Grudgingly he looked. It took all the afternoon to persuade him.

"Look at the roo bar,[1] and see, there's a radio," Mother urged him, she fretted at the waste of time. She promised to let him drive once we got down into the country to try to make him come.

"But what about a license?" I asked.

"Hold your shit Bogfart!" He gave me a shove.

"Now just you watch your language!" Mother was severe. "Mrs. Lady has fixed everything. Only be quick and let's go!" She had had a shower and her wet hair was flat on her head. She urged and pleaded and threatened and we set off very late, about half past five.

Next day he stayed in the motel room watching T.V. and Mother fretted on the beach.

"Come in!" I called her from the water. "It's beaut in!" And it really was considering the time of the year. But she couldn't get up any enthusiasm, she couldn't bear to see all that lovely sunshine wasted because he wouldn't come out.

Lunch time my brother was still disagreeable. It spoiled the meal and he refused to eat his sweets. But Mother said afterwards not to take any notice when he growled, it was only because he had used his pudding spoon for his soup and she knew it wasn't any use telling him with that snooty waitress looking on.

The motel was really gas! There was so much hot water Mother washed out all our clothes and we both washed our hair again. I got out my social studies. Hot Legs has this idea about a test every Wednesday.

"Shit head!" My brother started picking on me. "Why don't you get out before they chuck you out. That's all crap," he said, knocking the book across the floor. "You'll only fail your exam and they don't want failures, spoils their bloody numbers. They'll ask you to leave, see if they don't."

I sat there and howled out loud, though I didn't want to, not in front of him.

Mother was furious, her face went bright red.

---

[1]*roo bar*   A metal bar surrounding the front grill of a car to protect it against collisions with animals such as kangaroos.

"Why you son of a bitch!" she screamed, I really thought she was going to go for him, she looked that mad.

And he put on a real idiot's face and turned his eyes up so only the whites showed and he said in a furry thick voice like as if he was drunk, "Well if I'm the son of a bitch dear lady you must be the bitch," and what with his daft face and Mother standing there all towelled up there really was a funny side to it and we all laughed our heads off. I wasn't sure if Mother was laughing or crying, anyway she got dressed and went off down into the town, we heard her crash the gears at the corner, it's been a while since she drove anything. She came back quite soon with steakburgers and chips and ice cream and Coke and we had a really good evening watching the T.V.

On the Monday just when we should have been setting off for home, my brother said, "What's the beach like?"

And Mother couldn't get him there quick enough. Oh he was a scream. He kept sitting backwards into the water just as a wave came and he went under as if he was drowning with only his thin white fingers reaching up out of the water as it swirled back. I thought Mother would kill herself laughing. She was really enjoying herself.

"Halp!" My brother sat back disappearing again into the sea and his wet white fingers grasped the froth of the wave. Mother played in the water like a girl. "Give you a race!" She swam splashing and choking. She could only do about five strokes of anything.

I don't think I've ever seen her so happy.

We were nearly the last to leave the beach. We saw the sun go, leaving only a long red sky far out over the water which was boiling up dark along the sand.

"Come on!" My brother was nervous and irritable.

"Our Prince is cold and hungry." Mother hurried me in the change rooms.

"We'll get a chicken and eat it on the way home."

She seemed anxious suddenly. Her agitation was worse at the Chicken Bar, we had to wait as there'd been a little rush on chickens. She paced up and down the narrow shop and she kept looking anxiously out at the car. My brother was sitting there, we could see his white face through the dark, he was listening to the radio. We were all hungry.

"Smells all right!" He even smiled as we got back into the car. Mother tore up the chicken dividing it on bits of paper between the three of us.

"I'll have to step on it," she said. "I don't want to inconvenience Mrs. Lady over her car."

We were just about to start on the food when it seemed we were surrounded by the police. There they were poking their heads in at the windows, I felt a real fool.

"Eat!" Mother commanded, but of course we couldn't and neither could she.

"It was me! I took the bloody car!" I didn't recognize my brother's voice, I couldn't believe the words were really coming from his white face. He lit a cigarette blowing smoke all over his ragged bits of chicken. I could see his hands shaking.

"You filthy bloody liar. You shut up!" Mother screamed. "Don't listen to that son of a bitch he's . . ."

"If you're not careful Missis," the cop said, "I'll have to book you for obscene language too," and then he seemed to remember something. He looked hard at Mother.

"You don't vary much in your sort of crimes do you Missis. Wasn't it just about here in similar circumstances a few weeks back, if my memory isn't playing tricks."

"This is the only sort of crime, as you put it, as I need to do," Mother replied with quiet haughtiness. "It so happens it was a different car and it was a whole year ago. Time must pass very for some people!" she added.

Mother cried when she knew she had to go to gaol,[2] she never could stand unbleached calico next to her skin she said. And she felt so bad about Mrs. Lady too. She'd hoped to get the car back before they got in off their boat and of course she'd intended to work off the cheque she'd written for herself. She would have liked to have the chance to explain to Mrs. Lady.

After a bit she stopped crying.

"It'll be better for the Prince," she said. "A more regular life, and they'll see he eats." This seemed to comfort her.

"Be a good girl at the Home," she said to me. "You won't be so strange as there's sure to be a few you'll know. And everything will all come right," she said. "A change is as good as a rest they say."

It was awful hearing my brother cry later. I didn't know it was him at first, he sounded like a man crying. In his room he'd got this big box of chocolates all wrapped up ready for Mother's Day, it wouldn't go in his case with all his things and he didn't know what to do.

"I'll help you," I said to him.

"Oh go to hell and get stuffed!" he said and banged his door on me.

In Pottery Class I'm making a jar with a lid. If it comes out all right I think I'll use it for a jewel box as we don't ever eat marmalade.

[1976]

Questions

1. Through which details and events does the reader discover the actual social and financial circumstances of the mother and her children?
2. Why does the mother take such a risk on behalf of her son?
3. Is the story humorous? If so, which elements contribute to its humor?
4. Why is the story told from the daughter's point of view? What is her attitude toward her mother and her brother? From what is only hinted at in her narrative, can you reconstruct the recent history of this family?
5. How does the story illuminate issues concerning social class?

---

[2]*gaol* Jail.

James Joyce
(1882–1941)
Ireland

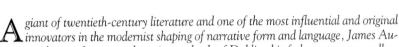

A giant of twentieth-century literature and one of the most influential and original innovators in the modernist shaping of narrative form and language, James Augustine Aloysius Joyce was born in a suburb of Dublin; his father was a tax collector, his mother was a pianist. At one point Joyce seemed destined to follow his mother's vocation: possessed of a fine tenor voice, he considered a career in music. Even in his writing, music is a prominent structural motif.

Joyce's influence on twentieth-century literature is formidable and definitive: His experiments with language, subject, point of view, and formal structure established entirely new conventions and conceptions of literary expression. Each of Joyce's major works reflects his extension of the boundaries of traditional narrative forms. The 15 stories in Dubliners (1914), begun in 1904 when Joyce was in his early twenties, already show his departure from tradition. One of his guiding strategies was the inclusion of what he termed "epiphanies": brief but significant moments of insight, illumination, or revelation for his characters.

Rejecting the deeply conservative moral and intellectual climate of Catholic Ireland as inhospitable to his art as well as his private life, Joyce chose voluntary exile, leaving his country in 1904 with Nora Barnacle (his eventual wife) to accept a teaching position in Trieste, Switzerland. Although he continued to write about Dublin, he rarely returned to Ireland during his lifetime. As he commented to a friend about this apparent anomaly, "I always write about Dublin, because if I can get to the heart of Dublin I can get to the heart of all the cities of the world. In the particular is contained the universal."

In A Portrait of the Artist as a Young Man (1916), Joyce explores the values and impressions of childhood, adolescence, and young adulthood as they reflect and shape the developing consciousness of a fledgling writer, Stephen Dedalus—who, like his creator, decides to leave Ireland. The novel concludes with Dedalus's passionate declaration of artistic independence: "I go to encounter for the millionth time the reality of experience and to forge in the smithy of my soul the uncreated conscience of my race."

Joyce's masterpieces, Ulysses (1922) and Finnegans Wake (1939), are radical in their structural and narrative innovations. Ulysses incorporates the structure of Homer's Odyssey as the ironic counterpoint to the lives of three characters as they crisscross Dublin during a single June day in 1904. Each of the chapters is narrated in a different style; several sequences demonstrate Joyce's brilliant use of the stream-of-consciousness technique he originated as a method of entering and directly reproducing the apparently random (but in fact highly controlled) flow of his characters' consciousnesses. Finnegans Wake, Joyce's last work, encompasses both particular characters and universal experiences and themes, unfolding as a dream vision of Dublin within the mind of one character and simultaneously within the larger contexts of history, metaphysics, and myth. Language itself is broken and reconstituted; Joyce's allusive, digressive, and punning play with words is part of the novel's self-conscious exploration of language and consciousness.

In "Eveline," from Dubliners, *Joyce demonstrates his sympathetic understanding of ordinary young people who represent a cross-section of contemporary urban life in Dublin. At the same time, it is the nature of their inner moral lives that determines their perceptions of the world and the choices that follow from them.*

EVELINE

She sat at the window watching the evening invade the avenue. Her head was leaned against the window curtains and in her nostrils was the odour of dusty cretonne. She was tired.

Few people passed. The man out of the last house passed on his way home; she heard his footsteps clacking along the concrete pavement and afterwards crunching on the cinder path before the new red houses. One time there used to be a field there in which they used to play every evening with other people's children. Then a man from Belfast bought the field and built houses in it—not like their little brown houses but bright brick houses with shining roofs. The children of the avenue used to play together in that field—the Devines, the Waters, the Dunns, little Keogh the cripple, she and her brothers and sisters. Ernest, however, never played: he was too grown up. Her father used often to hunt them in out of the field with his blackthorn stick; but usually little Keogh used to keep *nix* and call out when he saw her father coming. Still they seemed to have been rather happy then. Her father was not so bad then; and besides, her mother was alive. That was a long time ago; she and her brothers and sisters were all grown up; her mother was dead. Tizzie Dunn was dead, too, and the Waters had gone back to England. Everything changes. Now she was going to go away like the others, to leave her home.

Home! She looked round the room, reviewing all its familiar objects which she had dusted once a week for so many years, wondering where on earth all the dust came from. Perhaps she would never see again those familiar objects from which she had never dreamed of being divided. And yet during all those years she had never found out the name of the priest whose yellowing photograph hung on the wall above the broken harmonium beside the coloured print of the promises made to Blessed Margaret Mary Alacoque. He had been a school friend of her father. Whenever he showed the photograph to a visitor her father used to pass it with a casual word:

—He is in Melbourne now.

She had consented to go away, to leave her home. Was that wise? She tried to weigh each side of the question. In her home anyway she had shelter and food; she had those whom she had known all her life about her. Of course she had to work hard, both in the house and at business. What would they say of her in the Stores when they found out that she had run away with a fellow? Say she was a fool, perhaps; and her place would be filled up by advertisement. Miss Gavan would be glad. She had always had an edge on her, especially whenever there were people listening.

—Miss Hill, don't you see these ladies are waiting?

—Look lively, Miss Hill, please.

She would not cry many tears at leaving the Stores.

But in her new home, in a distant unknown country, it would not be like that. Then she would be married—she, Eveline. People would treat her with respect then. She would not be treated as her mother had been. Even now, though she was over nineteen, she sometimes felt herself in danger of her father's violence. She knew it was that that had given her the palpitations. When they were growing up he had never gone for her, like he used to go for Harry and Ernest, because she was a girl; but latterly he had begun to threaten her and say what he would do to her only for her dead mother's sake. And now she had nobody to protect her. Ernest was dead and Harry, who was in the church decorating business, was nearly always down somewhere in the country. Besides, the invariable squabble for money on Saturday nights had begun to weary her unspeakably. She always gave her entire wages—seven shillings—and Harry always sent up what he could but the trouble was to get any money from her father. He said she used to squander the money, that she had no head, that he wasn't going to give her his hard-earned money to throw about the streets, and much more, for he was usually fairly bad of a Saturday night. In the end he would give her the money and ask her had she any intention of buying Sunday's dinner. Then she had to rush out as quickly as she could and do her marketing, holding her black leather purse tightly in her hand as she elbowed her way through the crowds and returning home late under her load of provisions. She had hard work to keep the house together and to see that the two young children who had been left to her charge went to school regularly and got their meals regularly. It was hard work—a hard life—but now that she was about to leave it she did not find it a wholly undesirable life.

She was about to explore another life with Frank. Frank was very kind, manly, open-hearted. She was to go away with him by the night-boat to be his wife and to live with him in Buenos Aires where he had a home waiting for her. How well she remembered the first time she had seen him; he was lodging in a house on the main road where she used to visit. It seemed a few weeks ago. He was standing at the gate, his peaked cap pushed back on his head and his hair tumbled forward over a face of bronze. Then they had come to know each other. He used to meet her outside the Stores every evening and see her home. He took her to see *The Bohemian Girl* and she felt elated as she sat in an unaccustomed part of the theatre with him. He was awfully fond of music and sang a little. People knew that they were courting and, when he sang about the lass that loves a sailor, she always felt pleasantly confused. He used to call her Poppens out of fun. First of all it had been an excitement for her to have a fellow and then she had begun to like him. He had tales of distant countries. He had started as a deck boy at a pound a month on a ship of the Allan Line going out to Canada. He told her the names of the ships he had been on and the names of the different services. He had sailed through the Straits of Magellan and he told her stories of the terrible Patagonians.[1] He had fallen on his feet in Buenos Aires, he said,

---

[1] *terrible Patagonians*   Legends based on nomadic tribes that lived at the Southern tip of Argentina (known as Patagonia); the Straits of Magellan—the channel between the South American mainland and Tierra del Fuego.

and had come over to the old country just for a holiday. Of course, her father had found out the affair and had forbidden her to have anything to say to him.

—I know these sailor chaps, he said.

One day he had quarrelled with Frank and after that she had to meet her lover secretly.

The evening deepened in the avenue. The white of two letters in her lap grew indistinct. One was to Harry; the other was to her father. Ernest had been her favourite but she liked Harry too. Her father was becoming old lately, she noticed; he would miss her. Sometimes he could be very nice. Not long before, when she had been laid up for a day, he had read her out a ghost story and made toast for her at the fire. Another day, when their mother was alive, they had all gone for a picnic to the Hill of Howth. She remembered her father putting on her mother's bonnet to make the children laugh.

Her time was running out but she continued to sit by the window, leaning her head against the window curtain, inhaling the odour of dusty cretonne. Down far in the avenue she could hear a street organ playing. She knew the air. Strange that it should come that very night to remind her of the promise to her mother, her promise to keep the home together as long as she could. She remembered the last night of her mother's illness; she was again in the close dark room at the other side of the hall and outside she heard a melancholy air of Italy. The organ-player had been ordered to go away and given sixpence. She remembered her father strutting back into the sickroom saying:

—Damned Italians! coming over here!

As she mused the pitiful vision of her mother's life laid its spell on the very quick of her being—that life of commonplace sacrifices closing in final craziness. She trembled as she heard again her mother's voice saying constantly with foolish insistence:

—Derevaun Seraun! Derevaun Seraun![2]

She stood up in a sudden impulse of terror. Escape! She must escape! Frank would save her. He would give her life, perhaps love, too. But she wanted to live. Why should she be unhappy? She had a right to happiness. Frank would take her in his arms, fold her in his arms. He would save her.

She stood among the swaying crowd in the station at the North Wall. He held her hand and she knew that he was speaking to her, saying something about the passage over and over again. The station was full of soldiers with brown baggages. Through the wide doors of the sheds she caught a glimpse of the black mass of the boat, lying in beside the quay wall, with illumined portholes. She answered nothing. She felt her cheek pale and cold and, out of a maze of distress, she prayed to God to direct her, to show her what was her duty. The boat blew a long mournful whistle into the mist. If she went, tomorrow she would be on the sea with Frank, steaming towards Buenos Aires. Their passage had been booked. Could she still draw back after all he had done for her? Her distress awoke a nausea in her body and she kept moving her lips in silent fervent prayer.

---

[2]*"Derevaun Seraun!"*   An expression of uncertain translation, possibly corrupt Gaelic for "the end of pleasure is pain" [William Y. Tindall].

A bell clanged upon her heart. She felt him seize her hand:

—Come!

All the seas of the world tumbled about her heart. He was drawing her into them: he would drown her. She gripped with both hands at the iron railing.

—Come!

No! No! No! It was impossible. Her hands clutched the iron in frenzy. Amid the seas she sent a cry of anguish!

—Eveline! Evvy!

He rushed beyond the barrier and called to her to follow. He was shouted at to go on but he still called to her. She set her white face to him, passive, like a helpless animal. Her eyes gave him no sign of love or farewell or recognition.

[1914]

Questions

1. What is the conflict in the story?
2. What attracts Eveline to Frank? Why does she decide not to go with him?
3. What attitudes toward her parents and her family do you discover through Eveline's thoughts? How do those attitudes influence her decision to remain in Ireland?

Franz Kafka
(1883–1924)
Czechoslovakia

Although Franz Kafka's works have been translated into more than a hundred languages, during his own lifetime he was never to know the extent of his genius. The first child of a German-speaking Jewish family in Prague, Czechoslovakia, Kafka suffered a lonely childhood (two younger brothers died during childhood and his three sisters were much younger than he). Even more critical for Kafka's own emotional life, he feared his father, a successful but authoritarian businessman. Issues of authority and difficulties in Kafka's relationships with women (he was engaged three times—twice to the same woman—but never married) preoccupied him for most of his life.

Kafka studied law and earned a doctorate in jurisprudence at the German University of Prague. Working as a civil service lawyer in the dreary office of the state Workmans' Accident Insurance Institute and investigating claims during the day, he began to write at night and eventually quit his job. In 1917 his health complications were officially diagnosed as tuberculosis (for which there was no cure at the time). His illness tormented him, but it also became a source of spiritual discovery and confirmed his determination to pursue his writing to the virtual exclusion of other activities. He phrased it this way in his diary:

> My talent for portraying my dreamlike inner life has thrust all other matters into the background. . . . Nothing else will ever satisfy me. But the strength I can muster for that portrayal is not to be counted on: perhaps it has already vanished forever. . . . (Diary, August 6, 1914).

As his friend Milena Jesenska wrote in his obituary, he suffered from a lung disease "which he cherished and fostered even while accepting treatment. . . . It endowed him with a delicacy of feeling that bordered on the ridiculous, and with a spiritual purity uncompromising to the point of horror. . . ."

Kafka wrote three novels, all technically unfinished at his death and all published posthumously: The Trial (1925), The Castle (1926), and Amerika (1927). He had instructed his friend and literary executor, Max Brod, to destroy his manuscripts at his death; Brod, torn between loyalty to Kafka's final wishes and recognition of his friend's literary genius, published his works, which include, in addition to the novels, volumes of short stories, parables, aphorisms, diaries, and reflections. The characters Joseph K (The Trial) and K (The Castle), trapped in labyrinths of legal or bureaucratic incomprehensibility and paralyzed by spiritual uncertainty, are unforgettable central figures in the landscape of twentieth-century literature. In fact, Franz Kafka, above and beyond his unique and profound literary explorations of modern anxiety, accomplished something that, as George Steiner phrases it, "no other writer in the history of language and of literature had accomplished: He . . . made indelibly his own . . . a letter of the alphabet. K is now Kafka's." Moreover, the term "Kafkaesque" is an equally indelible part of the twentieth-century vocabulary as a term for the absurd and incomprehensible entanglements of everyday life.

Kafka's voice is absolutely unique in modern literature. His visionary capacity to turn dreamlike events—or, more accurately, the stuff of nightmares—into symbolic narrative results in the often bizarre, grotesque, and paradoxical characteristics of his fiction and parables, which unfold in an ironic, understated tone. Despite his Jewish background, Kafka was haunted by the idea of Original Sin as well as by the connections among guilt, punishment, and authority. Although at one time critics regarded Kafka as a neurotic genius who poured his psychological preoccupations into his writing, more recently scholars and readers have recognized the way in which Kafka gave form not simply to his own anxieties but also to those of an entire age; he seems to have prophetically anticipated some of the darkest historical events of the twentieth century, including the Holocaust. The ideas of alienation and the "absurd," the human longing for the infinite in the face of spiritual doubt, have no more brilliant spokesman than Kafka.

A REPORT TO AN ACADEMY

GENTLEMEN OF THE ACADEMY:
You have honored me with your invitation to submit a report to the Academy about my former life as an ape.

Taking this invitation in its literal sense, I am unfortunately unable to comply with it. Nearly five years stand between me and my apehood, a period that may be short in terms of the calendar but is an infinitely long one to gallop through as I have done, accompanied for certain stretches by excellent people, advice, applause and band music, but fundamentally on my own, because, to remain within the metaphor, all that accompaniment never got very close to the rail. This achievement would have been impossible if I had willfully clung to my origins, to the memories of my youth. In fact, avoidance of all willfulness was the supreme commandment I had imposed on myself; I, a free ape, accepted that yoke. Thereby, however, my memories were in turn increasingly lost to me. If at first a return to the past, should the humans have so wished, was as wide open to me as the universal archway the sky forms over the earth, at the same time my wildly accelerated development made this archway increasingly low and narrow; I felt more at ease and sheltered in the human world; the storm winds that blew out of my past grew calm; today there is only a breeze that cools my heels; and the hole in the distance through which it issues, and from which I once issued, has become so small that, if I ever had sufficient strength and desire to run all the way back there, I would have to scrape the hide off my body to squeeze through. Speaking frankly (although I enjoy using figures of speech for these matters), speaking frankly: your own apehood, gentlemen, to the extent that there is anything like that in your past, cannot be more remote from you than mine is from me. But every wanderer on earth feels a tickling in his heels: the little chimpanzee and great Achilles. In the most limited sense, however, I may be able to satisfy your demands, and, in fact, I do so with great pleasure. The first thing I learned was shaking hands;

shaking hands indicates candidness; today, when I am at the pinnacle of my career, why not add my candid words to that first handshake? My report will not teach the Academy anything basically new and will fall far short of what has been asked of me, which, with the best will in the world, I am unable to tell you—nevertheless, it is meant to show the guidelines by which a former ape has burst into the human world and established himself there. But I certainly would not have the right to make even the insignificant statement that follows, if I were not completely sure of myself and had not secured a truly unassailable position on all the great vaudeville stages of the civilized world.

I come from the Gold Coast. For the story of how I was captured rely on the reports of others. A hunting expedition of the Hagenbeck[1] firm—incidentally, since then I've drained many a fine bottle of red wine with its leader—was lying in wait in the brush by the shore when I ran down to the watering place one evening in the midst of a pack of apes. They fired; I was the only one hit; I was wounded in two places.

One wound was in the cheek; that was slight, but left behind a large, red, hairless scar, which won me the repulsive, totally unsuitable name of Red Peter, which must have been invented by an ape!—as if the red spot on my cheek were the only difference between me and the trained ape Peter, who had a local reputation here and there and who kicked the bucket recently. But that's by the by.

The second bullet hit me below the hip. It was a serious wound and the cause of my limping a little even today. Not long ago I read in an article by one of ten thousand windbags[2] who gab about me in the papers, saying my ape nature is not yet suppressed; the proof being that, when visitors come, I'm fond of taking off my trousers to show where the bullet hit me. That guy should have every last finger of the hand he writes with individually blasted off! I, I have the right to drop my pants in front of anyone I feel like; all they'll see there is a well-tended coat of fur and the scar left over from—here let us choose a specific word for a specific purpose, but a word I wouldn't want misunderstood—the scar left over from an infamous shot. Everything is open and aboveboard; there's nothing to hide; when it comes to the truth, every high-minded person rejects namby-pamby etiquette. On the other hand, if that writer were to take his trousers off when company came, you can be sure it would look quite different, and I'm ready to accept it as a token of his good sense that he refrains from doing so. But then he shouldn't bedevil me with his delicate sensibilities!

After those shots I woke up—and here my own recollections gradually begin—in a cage between decks on the Hagenbeck steamer. It wasn't a four-sided cage with bars all around; instead, there were only three barred sides attached to a crate, so that the crate formed the fourth wall. The whole thing was too low for standing erect in, and too narrow for sitting down in. And so I squatted with bent, constantly trembling knees, and, since at first I probably didn't want to see anyone and felt like being in the dark all the time, I faced the crate, while behind me the bars cut into my flesh. This way of keeping wild animals right after their capture is considered advantageous, and, with the experience I have today, I can't deny that, in a human sense, it is really the case.

---

[1] Carl Hagenbeck of Hamburg was a pioneering zoo director, circus entrepreneur, and supplier of live animals for exhibitions of all kinds.—Trans.

[2] One of Kafka's animal jokes is irretrievably lost in translation here: The word he uses for "windbags" also means "greyhounds."—Trans.

But at that time I didn't think about it. For the first time in my life I had no way out, or at least not straight ahead of me; right in front of me was the crate, each board tightly joined to the next. True, between the boards there was a gap running right through, and when I first discovered it I greeted it with a joyful howl of ignorance, but this gap wasn't even nearly wide enough for me to push my tail through,[3] and all my ape's strength couldn't widen it.

They told me later on that I made unusually little noise, from which they concluded that I would either go under, or else, if I managed to live through the first, critical period, I would be extremely trainable. I lived through that period. Muffled sobbing, painful searching for fleas, weary licking of a coconut, banging the side of the crate with my cranium, sticking out my tongue whenever someone approached—those were my first occupations in my new life. But, throughout it all, only that one feeling: no way out. Today, naturally, I can only sketch from hindsight, and in human words, what I then felt as an ape, and therefore I am sketching it incorrectly, but even if I can no longer attain the old apish truth, my description isn't basically off course, and no doubt about it.

And yet, up to then, I had had so many ways out and now no longer one. I had boxed myself in. If I had been nailed down that couldn't have subtracted from my freedom of action. Why so? Scratch the skin between your toes till it bleeds, and you still won't find the reason. Press yourself backwards against the bars until they nearly cut you in two, you won't find the reason. I had no way out, but had to create one for myself, because without it I couldn't live. Always up against the side of that crate—I would definitely have dropped dead. But, for Hagenbeck, apes belong at the side of the crate—so I stopped being an ape. A lucid, elegant train of thought, which I must have somehow hatched out with my belly, because apes think with their belly.

I'm afraid that it may not be clearly understood what I mean by "a way out." I am using the phrase in its most common and most comprehensive sense. I purposely do not say "freedom." I don't mean that expansive feeling of freedom on all sides. As an ape I might have known it, and I've met human beings who long for it. As for me, however, I didn't desire freedom then, and I don't now. Incidentally: human beings fool themselves all too often on the subject of freedom. And just as freedom counts among the loftiest feelings, so does the corresponding delusion count among the loftiest. Often in vaudeville houses, before my act came on, I've seen some pair of artists do their trapeze routine way up near the ceiling. They swung to and fro, they rocked back and forth, they made leaps, they floated into each other's arms, one held the other by the hair with his teeth. "That, too, is human freedom," I would muse, "movement achieved in sovereign self-confidence." You mockery of holy Nature! No building would remain unshaken by the laughter of the ape world at that sight.

No, it wasn't freedom I wanted. Only a way out; to the right, to the left, in any direction at all; I made no other demands; even if the way out were a delusion; the demand was a small one, the delusion wouldn't be any bigger. To move forward, to move forward! Anything but standing still with raised arms, flattened against the side of a crate.

---

[3]There are several indications in the story, and in posthumously published deleted fragments, that Kafka meant Red Peter to be a chimpanzee; he either didn't know or didn't care that chimpanzees have no tail. (The German *Affe* that Kafka mainly uses means either ape or monkey indiscriminately.)—Trans.

Today I see it clearly: without the utmost inner calm I would never have been able to save myself And, in reality, I may owe everything that I've achieved to the calm that came over me after the first few days there on the ship. But, in turn, I probably owe that calm to the people on the ship.

They're good sorts, despite everything. Even today I enjoy recalling the sound of their heavy steps, which at the time reechoed in my half-slumber. They had the habit of tackling everything as slowly as possible. If one of them wanted to rub his eyes, he would lift his hand as if it were a hanging weight. Their jokes were coarse but hearty. Their laughter was always mingled with a coughing sound that sounded dangerous but was insignificant. They always had something in their mouth they could spit out and they didn't care a bit where they spat it. They were always complaining that my fleas were jumping onto them; but they were never seriously mad at me for it; they were perfectly well aware that fleas thrive in my fur and that fleas jump; they reconciled themselves to it. When they had no duties, sometimes a few of them would sit down in a semicircle around me; they rarely spoke but just mumbled to one another like pigeons cooing; they would stretch out on crates and smoke their pipes; they would slap their knees the minute I made the slightest movement; and from time to time one of them would take a stick and tickle me where I liked it. If I were to be invited today to take part in a voyage on that ship, I would certainly decline the invitation, but it is equally certain that the memories I could muse over from my days between the decks there are not all unpleasant.

The calm I acquired in the company of those people restrained me especially from any attempt to escape. From the vantage point of today, it seems to me I had at least a vague notion that I had to find a way out if I were to survive, but that the way out was not to be attained by escape. I no longer know for certain whether escape was possible, but I think so; an ape probably always has some means of escape. With my teeth as they are today, I have to be careful even when cracking an ordinary nut, but at the time I would probably certainly have managed to bite through the lock on the door in a matter of time. I didn't. What would I have gained if I had? They would have caught me again the minute I stuck my head out and locked me in a cage that was worse yet; or else I might have escaped unnoticed and run over to other animals, for instance the giant snakes opposite me, and breathed my last in their embraces; or I might even have successfully stolen away onto the top deck and jumped overboard; in that case, I would have rocked on the ocean for a while and then drowned. Deeds of desperation. My calculations weren't that human, but under the influence of my environment I behaved as if I had calculated it all.

I didn't calculate, but I did observe things very calmly. I watched those human beings walk back and forth, always the same faces, the same motions; it often seemed to me as if it was just a single person. Well, that person or those persons were walking around unmolested. A lofty goal hazily entered my mind. Nobody promised me that, if I became like them, the bars would be removed. Promises like that based on apparently impossible terms just aren't made. But if the terms are met, later on the promises turn up exactly where they were formerly sought in vain. Now, there was nothing about these humans in themselves that allured me all that much. If I were a devotee of that above-mentioned freedom, I would certainly have chosen the ocean over the kind of way out that offered itself to me in the dull eyes of those people. At any rate, I had already been observing them long before I thought about such things; in fact, it was the accumulation of observations that first pushed me in the chosen direction.

It was so easy to imitate people. I could already spit within the first few days. Then we would mutually spit in each other's faces; the only difference being that I licked my face clean afterwards, and they didn't. I was soon smoking a pipe like an old hand; if, when doing so, I still stuck my thumb into the bowl, everyone between the decks whooped with joy; it was only the difference between the empty and filled pipe that I didn't understand for a long time.

It was the liquor bottle that gave me most trouble. The smell was torture to me; I forced myself with all my strength; but weeks went by before I overcame the resistance. Oddly, it was these inward struggles that the people took more seriously than anything else about me. Although in my recollections I can't tell the people apart, there was one of them who came again and again, alone or with comrades, by day and night, at the most varied hours; he would place himself in front of me with the bottle and give me instruction. He couldn't comprehend me, he wanted to solve the riddle of my being. Slowly he uncorked the bottle and then looked at me to see if I had understood; I confess, I always watched him with frantic, exaggerated attention; no human teacher will ever find such a human pupil anywhere on earth; after the bottle was uncorked, he lifted it to his mouth; my eyes followed him all the way into his gullet; he nodded, contented with me, and put the bottle to his lips; I, delighted by dawning knowledge, then squeal and scratch myself all over wherever I feel the need; he is happy, presses the bottle against his mouth and takes a swallow; I, impatient and desperate to emulate him, soil myself in my cage, and this, too, gives him great satisfaction; and now, holding the bottle far away from himself and lifting it toward himself again briskly, he bends backwards with pedagogical exaggeration and empties it in one draught. I, worn out by the excess of my desire, am unable to follow any longer and hang weakly on the bars while he concludes the theoretical instruction by rubbing his stomach and grinning.

Only now does the practical exercise begin. Am I not too exhausted already by the theoretical part? Far too exhausted, most likely. That's how my destiny goes. All the same, I do the best I can as I reach for the bottle he holds out to me; trembling, I uncork it; as I succeed, I gradually acquire new strength; I lift the bottle, by this time imitating my model so closely that there's hardly any difference; I put it to my mouth and—and with loathing, with loathing, even though it's empty and only the smell is left, with loathing I throw it on the ground. To my teacher's sorrow, to my own greater sorrow; I fail to make things right with either him or myself when, even after throwing away the bottle, I don't forget to do an excellent job of rubbing my stomach and grinning at the same time.

Things went that way all too often during my course of instruction. And to my teacher's credit: he wasn't angry with me; true, he sometimes held his lit pipe against my fur until it started to get singed in some spot that was very hard to reach, but then he would put it out again himself with his gigantic, kindly hand; he wasn't angry with me, he realized that we were both fighting as allies against ape nature, and the difficulty was more on my side.

What a victory it was, then, for him and for me, when one evening, before a large group of spectators—maybe it was a party, a gramophone was playing, an officer was walking about among the men—when on that evening, while no one was observing me, I grasped a liquor bottle that had been accidentally left in front of my cage, uncorked it according to all the rules as the people paid increasingly greater attention, put it to my mouth and, without hesitating, without twisting my lips, like a drinker from way back, with rolling eyes and gurgling throat, really and truly emptied the bottle; threw it away, no longer like someone in despair, but like an artiste; did actually forget to rub my stomach; but, instead, because I simply had to, because I had the urge to, because my senses were in an uproar—in a word, I called out "Hello," breaking into human speech, leaping into the human community by means of that outcry, and feeling its echo, "Listen, he's talking," like a kiss all over my sweat-soaked body.

I repeat: I didn't imitate human beings because they appealed to me; I imitated because I was looking for a way out, for no other reason. And that victory still didn't amount to much. My speaking voice failed me again immediately, and it took months for it to come back; my aversion to the liquor bottle returned and was even stronger than before. But, all the same, my course was set once and for all.

When I was handed over to the first trainer in Hamburg, I immediately recognized the two possibilities that were open to me: zoo or vaudeville. I didn't hesitate. I told myself: make every effort to get into vaudeville; that's the way out; the zoo is just another cage; once you land there, you're lost.

And I learned, gentlemen. Oh, you learn when you have to; you learn when you want a way out; you learn regardless of all else. You observe yourself, whip in hand; you lacerate yourself at the least sign of resistance. My ape nature, turning somersaults, raged out of me and away, so that my first teacher nearly became apelike himself, and soon had to give up the instruction and go to a sanatorium. Fortunately he came out again before long.

But I used up many teachers, sometimes a few teachers simultaneously. When I had become more sure of my abilities, when the public was following my progress and my future began to look bright, I took on teachers on my own, sat them down in five successive rooms and took lessons from all of them at once, uninterruptedly leaping from one room to another.

That progress! That penetration of rays of knowledge from all sides into my awakening brain! I won't deny it: it made me happy. But I also admit: I didn't overestimate it, not even then, let alone today. Through an effort that hasn't found its match on earth to the present day, I have attained the educational level of an average European. Perhaps that wouldn't be anything by itself, but it is really something when you consider that it helped me out of my cage and gave me this particular way out, this human way out. There's an excellent German expression: *sich in die Büsche schlagen*, to steal away secretly. That's what I did, I stole away secretly. I had no other way, always presupposing that I couldn't choose freedom.

When I survey my development and the goal it has had up to now, I am neither unhappy nor contented. My hands in my trousers pockets, the wine bottle on the table, I half recline, half sit, in my rocking chair and look out the window. When a visitor comes, I receive him in a proper manner. My impresario sits in the anteroom; when I ring, he comes and listens to what I have to say. There's a performance almost every evening, and my success probably can't get much greater. When I come home late at night from banquets, learned societies or friendly gatherings, a little half-trained female chimpanzee is waiting for me and I have a good time with her, ape fashion; in the daytime I don't want to see her, because her eyes have that deranged look which bewildered trained animals have; I'm the only one who recognizes it, and I can't stand it.

All in all, however, I have achieved what I wanted to achieve. Let nobody say that it wasn't worth the trouble. Anyway, I don't want any human being's opinion, I merely wish to disseminate information; I am merely making a report; even to you, gentlemen of the Academy, I have merely made a report.

[1917]
Translated by
STANLEY APPELBAUM

Questions

1. What characteristics define the "humanness" of the narrator? What characteristics are associated with his animal nature? What has he discovered in the process of his transformation from ape to human?
2. What does the story suggest about captivity and the narrator's desire not so much for "freedom" but for "a way out" of his ape nature?
3. What is the meaning of the narrator's "report" and to what kind of "academy" is he reporting?
4. Is the story a satire? If so, what is being satirized?

Ghassan Kanafani
(1936–1972)
Palestine

In his introduction to Ghassan Kanafani's collection of short stories, Men in the Sun, Hilary Kilpatrick, the author's translator, describes the writer as follows: "Ghassan Kanafani was known in the West as the spokesman for the Popular Front for the Liberation of Palestine, and the editor of its weekly, Al-Hadaf. But in the Arab world he was also considered a leading novelist, and one of the foremost Palestinian writers in prose." During his short life as a writer, Kanafani was not only a professional journalist but also the author of 10 volumes of fiction (five collections of short stories and five novels), two plays, and two critical studies of Palestinian literature. He was born in Acre in 1936 and died in an automobile explosion in 1972, the result of a booby trap. At the time of his death, Kanafani's widow wrote, "His inspiration for writing and working unceasingly was the Palestinian-Arab struggle. . . . He always stressed that the Palestine problem could not be solved in isolation from the Arab world's whole social and political situation."

Much of Kanafani's fiction (including "A Hand in the Grave") is free of the ideological concerns of his political life. He attempted to separate the two. Yet one cannot help noting Edward W. Said's description of the author's novella, Men in the Sun, commented on at the time of the Iraqi invasion of Kuwait in the summer of 1990: "a prescient parable of three Palestinian refugees trying to smuggle themselves from Iraq to Kuwait in a tank truck, [and] dying of asphyxiation and heat at the border post."

In 2000, a new edition of Kanafani's short fiction appeared in the United States: Palestine's Children: Returning to Haifa and Other Stories.

A HAND IN THE GRAVE

I woke up very early that day. I could hear my father repeating. "God be praised as he prepared to perform his prayers. Later he came past me:

"Your eyes look tired. What's happened? Didn't you sleep well last night?"

I nodded, turning the soap over in my hand, and began to look at my face in the mirror with its silver back peeling away at the edges, without replying to my father's questions. I did not turn my head, but I realized that he had hung the towel round his neck and put on his sandals. He began to yawn, stretching his arms as far as they would go. As I soaped my face I heard my sister ask my father:

"What's happened?"

"Nothing. Your brother's face looks as though it's been bleached; he definitely didn't sleep last night. Do you know when he came home yesterday?"

"Yes. He wasn't late."

"You're lying. You always tell lies, when it's something to do with Nabil."

I began to rinse my face with water, and though the conversation seemed to threaten a nasty storm I felt that I was outside it all. I heard my sister say:

"I told you that he came home early last night. You just don't want to believe it. Will you drink your coffee?"

"I don't want any coffee. I don't want to be poisoned. Can he tell me why his face is so pale if he went to bed early?"

I dried my face and turned towards him. I knew he was looking for a reason to explode. That is how he appeared every morning, doing nothing the whole time before breakfast except search for a pretext to unburden himself of his rage; today I represented his first attempt. He looked hard at me and then repeated his question, his lips quivering:

"If you went to bed early, young man, why is your face so pale?"

I circled round him, and when my shoulder was level with his I observed quietly:

"Facial pallor has a number of causes. It may be due to worms in the stomach, or a heavy meal the night before, or excessive smoking. And there are more serious causes, anaemia for instance, TB, or the onset of hemiplegia."[1]

What I expected did not occur, for my father did not get in the least upset. Instead he gave me a side-long admiring glance. Perhaps he was remembering that he had supported me for more than ten years so that I could enter the medical faculty, and here I was giving him scientific answers in all seriousness, which brought joy to his heart. But he did not want to give way so easily.

"You woke up early this morning. Did you give the call to the dawn prayer then?"

I had reached my room, and flung the towel over the bed. Without turning to face my father and sister who were standing in the doorway, I answered in a calm tone:

"I woke up early to rob a grave."

"To rob what?"

"A grave." I turned and faced him, trembling. "To rob a grave. Yes. Is that strange? In the faculty we need a skeleton, and Suhail and I have been told to provide it."

My father was still incapable of taking in the whole picture, and he stood there repeating without being aware of it:

"To rob a grave?"

"Yes, to rob a grave, and steal the skeleton of some man who has been dead more than twenty years because I want to study it."

My sister closed the door between us and left me alone. When I could hear no sound on the other side of the door I put on my clothes. The sack and shovel I had already prepared, and it was up to Suhail to provide a small pick. I bent down to pick up my things, but my sister opened the door before I could straighten up and gave me an affectionate rebuke.

"Why did you upset him, Nabil? You're not yourself this morning. Why did you lie to him?"

"I wasn't lying. I mean to rob a grave."

My father had joined her, and was looking over her shoulder. I noticed that he was trembling, and that he burst out shouting:

"God curse the hour when I enrolled you in the medical faculty. You want to steal a corpse, do you? Thief! Godless sinner! Haven't you read what God said in . . . ?"

---

[1]*hemiplegia*   Paralysis of one side of the body.

"I have. I've read all God's Word, but God isn't against the medical faculty. They require me to provide a skeleton, just as the sheikh used to require you to know the section 'Ain Min'."[2]

He gave me a look of disapproval for intruding into his past with this levity, then quickly came up with an angry question:

"Are all the students of the medical faculty going to rob people's graves this morning? You won't leave a single corpse in the graveyards! Tell me, are all the students going to rob graves?"

I threw the shovel into the sack, twisted it round my wrist, and went up to him:

"Certainly not! A skeleton costs seventy-five lire. Have you got seventy-five lire? That's why Suhail and I mean to steal, because you can't give me seventy-five lire, and his uncle can't give it him either!"

I pressed my lips together and glared angrily at him. He was gazing at me, completely at a loss, and I lifted the sack, thrusting it into his face.

"And now, let me go before the sun rises and gives us away."

He moved out of my way, baffled, unable to take his eyes from my face. His mouth was hanging open, although he was incapable of uttering a word, as I passed him on my way to the door.

Suhail was waiting for me close to the corner. In the twilight before dawn he resembled a black ghost lurking in a corner to frighten a naughty child.

"Is it you?" he whispered in the gloom, and drew his arm through mine. I knew, without looking at his face, that he was as frightened as I was. We took a few steps, then he stopped.

"He hasn't given you seventy-five lire, eh?" he asked in the tone of someone wanting to say that he too had been unable to obtain the seventy-five lire. I shook my head and then explained.

"I left everything till this morning. And apparently surprise prevented him from even thinking of it. So I went out, expecting him to shout to me before I left that he would give me the seventy-five lire. But he stood there, flabbergasted. What happened to you?"

Suhail said, nodding:

"My uncle thought that I wanted to fool him out of seventy-five lire, but when I assured him that that's how things really were he told me that he was prepared to pay the expenses of the living but not the cost of the dead. Then he said I was young and brave, so what prevented me robbing a grave and saving the money?"

We walked on a little, then turned into the street which led out of the city. I heard his whisper:

"So that's how it is."

"What?"

"We'll rob a grave. The attempts at begging have failed. Your father would sell his own skeleton for less than seventy-five lire; as for my uncle, he'd sell his for the price of one breakfast. It's no good, we must rob a grave."

I stopped, and gripped his shoulder.

"Don't say you're afraid! If you are, go back, and I'll go on alone."

---

[2]*Ain Min*   The Quran is divided into 30 sections for purposes of recitation, and each section is numbered according to letters of the Arabic alphabet [Translator's note].

"I? Afraid? Ha! *I'm* not frightened. But I don't like making my way through the end of the night to steal a corpse. How do you think you look, on your way to rob the dead?"

There was no doubt about it, he was frightened, more frightened than I. We walked on silently, our heads bowed. There was a cemetery outside the city, an old cemetery with low graves built out of brown earth. It was not walled, and was generally quite unguarded. It was a graveyard such as is found in some remote spot, inexplicably, as though it were the remains of an ancient battle between strangers who had come from afar and perished without anyone bothering to give them a proper burial.

Our steps had a funereal ring. When we approached the cemetery I felt my chest shaking, so violently was my heart beating, and I fancied that something, a ghost perhaps, was perched on my shoulder. I did not look at Suhail, out of fear that he would think that I was scared, and I seemed to hear the whistle of his breathing as he trod heavily and silently beside me.

"Here we are." I spoke after I had gathered all my forces together, and shifting the sack from one shoulder to the other I stood still. "We must choose a good grave."

He did not reply. In the distance an ugly light was silently spreading above the top of the mountain. The incubus was still perched on my shoulder, and my chest was shaken by violent spasms. I turned to Suhail, who was gazing in front of him, motionless.

"Listen, Suhail! If you are frightened, let's go back."

He glanced at me for a moment, then walked in front of me up the slight incline to the cemetery. Panting as he climbed, he began to speak:

"I? Frightened? If you want, *you* go back. But I'll carry on. What do you think of this grave? It looks solid, and old, and it's large. Don't you think it's suitable?"

I didn't expect Suhail to be so courageous. What he said caught me by surprise, and made me want to prove to him that I was equally brave.

"This one? It looks to me more like a bull's grave, but it's fine so long as it takes your fancy."

As soon as I finished speaking I was terrified, and I made the sudden discovery that Suhail, too, was terrified, and that he was looking at me in utter disbelief that I could speak such ill of the dead. I was trying hard to put the sack on the ground and get out the shovel, but I had the feeling that the sack was too heavy to move and my arm was a numb, empty shell. I could hear Suhail whispering to himself:

"Seventy-five lire! Only seventy-five lire! For heaven's sake!"

I saw him throw his small pick on the ground, take off his jacket with a nervous gesture, and turn to me:

"Don't stand there like a fool. Let's start before it gets any lighter. Don't tell me you're frightened! It was your idea."

I put the sack down. Suhail had gone to work forcefully and quickly and had broken away the mound of earth. He leaned on the pick as I shovelled the soil away. We could both feel our blood beginning to flow again.

"There's still the stone slab. What do you think? Shall we drag it away?"

I glanced at him as he panted for breath. In the light of dawn he took on a mythical aspect. "We're almost there," I said to myself making an effort to appear normal. It was clear to me that Suhail was relying on my courage; at the same time I had to earn my reputation in the faculty when Suhail related the event the next day. I felt the slab with my fingers, then raised my head to him.

"I don't think we'll be able to move it away. Let's make a hole in it."

"But we may break part of the skeleton."

"No, when a corpse is buried they usually place the stone some way away from it. Haven't you ever seen a burial in your life?"

He lifted up his pick with a curt "No."

I took the pick from him when he tired, and he in turn took it from me. We worked quickly, out of fear that the columns of peasants would begin to reach the city. It was growing lighter, an ashen, cold, ugly light, and we each of us could make out the expression on his companion's face without difficulty. So, come what might, we busied ourselves with the work.

Suddenly a small cry burst from Suhail. The head of the pick had made a small black hole in the stone and stuck itself into it. We raised the pick together, and he lifted his head and looked at me when our hands touched. I smiled and began to widen the opening as I felt him looking beyond me fearfully.

"You won't be able to get it out of that little hole. You must make it wider," said Suhail behind me, his voice trembling. I was gasping as I enlarged it, and I found it preferable to talk so that my fear would lose itself in the panting brought on by exertion.

"We won't get anything out now. We just want to be sure that it's there, and then we can widen the hole."

"And which of us will stick his hand in?" he asked in a quiet but scared voice, while I began to clean the edges of the hole. It gave forth a strong stench of decay. I ignored his question.

"Who will put his hand in?" he repeated, and this time I stood up and faced him.

"Either of us. You aren't afraid, are you? Do you know what's inside? A skull like the ones which the students pick up every morning in the faculty. That's all."

"Then you put your hand in," he said in a desperate tone. He was as terrified as it is possible to be, and had reached a point when he could no longer go on with the game. For my part I could not imagine that we should give in after all we had achieved, so I gave a calm reply:

"Yes. I'll put my hand in."

I knelt down, put my arm through the hole, and groped inside the grave for several minutes without being able to feel anything. I stood up.

"I couldn't reach the bottom. You're thinner than I am. How would you like to put your arm in? You've seen with your own eyes. There's nothing to be afraid of."

He glanced at me in silent doubt for a moment, then stepped forward, bent down till he was kneeling, and stretched his arm through the hole. His face was white, but then his colour returned, and I guessed that he had found nothing.

"I haven't got to the bottom," he said with a certain cheerfulness. Meanwhile I bent down opposite him, saying:

"Bend your shoulder down farther. We mustn't go back empty-handed. Try!"

Suhail slid his arm farther in, and began to squeeze his shoulder through as he lay on his side, stretched out, with his face touching the ground.

"Have you felt anything?"

He gave a jerky "No!" in reply.

I stood up, putting my hand on my hip. He was obviously keen, and making sustained, violent efforts.

I cannot recall what distracted my attention from him the next moment, but all of a sudden I was brought back to my surroundings by a terrible scream which did not stop. In the tide of swift fear which I felt flow through my limbs I saw Suhail turn over, his face grazing the gravestone, as he made a hysterical attempt to pull his arm out of the hole. I glimpsed his eyes as I dragged at his other arm in an effort to free him, and I shall never forget the sight of them, stretched open as far as they could go. His blue lips trembled while he choked out the scream of a slaughtered beast between his teeth, and his whole body trembled on the stone as though the awful hand of an unseen demon was shaking him savagely. Even when I could get his arm out of the hole he did not stop screaming. The jagged edges of the opening had cut deep scratches in his shoulder and forearm and they were beginning to ooze blood.

Without stopping those hideous loud screams Suhail stood up, while I in turn had begun to shiver and had no idea what I ought to do. I tried to grasp his shoulders and shake him, but he was turning round and round, trembling as though he were having convulsions. All at once he fell silent, and it was as if he was not the person who had been screaming a moment before. Pressing his bluish lips together obstinately, he turned to face me. There was no colour in his face, and his eyes were reddened circles. On his forehead beads of sweat mingled with the fine dust of the tombstone. He stared at me as though he were looking through me at some loathsome vision, but then he opened his lips and shouted in my face, forcing the words out between his teeth:

"My fingers! My fingers! I stuck them in its eyes!"

I was trembling, but more out of fear of Suhail than anything else. I gripped him by the shoulders and shook him fiercely, shouting:

"You idiot! This is an old grave . . . it's more than fifty years old!"

He gave me a stupid look; clearly he had not heard me. He started repeating:

"His eyes . . . I stuck my fingers in his eyes!"

The rest of Suhail's story is not very strange. And why not admit now that the idea was mine? And that it was not expected that in the first year of the medical faculty we should buy a skeleton? But we, Suhail and I, wanted to acquire a skeleton, so as to have the feeling that we had joined the medical faculty.

Suhail and I went back to the university that afternoon. I was ill. Suhail, however, began to tell the story to the other students, trembling like a leaf as he did so. In the days which followed, he continued to tell the story to anyone he came across, explaining in amazing detail how he had put his fingers into the eyes of the corpse. The university found itself obliged to expel him from the medical faculty after all hope of curing him had been abandoned. Everyone thought he had gone mad. I, for my part, transferred to the faculty of law after I discovered that I could not stand the sight of a skeleton.

Today, after more than seven years have passed since that incident, fate has proved that it was both just and stupid. I remember how Suhail's uncle told me the next day that he hoped that Suhail would not be able to get to the cemetery, and expected that he would come back to him panic-stricken, after which he would give him the price of the skeleton. My father, on the other hand, praised God at length when he heard the story, and observed to my sister that the thieves had received their due reward from the grave and the dead man. Thus he came to believe that the grave which we had desecrated was that of a saint and took to visiting it every dawn to receive blessing from its earth and sand and pray beside it.

Yes, it was both a just and a foolish fate. For only yesterday, after more than seven years had passed, I learned by chance the story of the graveyard we had visited.

It was not a real graveyard. It was a kind of waste land belonging to a Turkish peasant who, during the periods of famine, had taken the trouble to construct earthen graves which were actually no more than covers for small storage spaces where he kept wheat and flour to avoid its being stolen or confiscated. The Turk had left a will which was only opened yesterday, when he died, and the secret was contained in that will.

Only yesterday, the heirs took possession of the ground to remove the graves and begin cultivating it.

The city's newspapers published the news on their front pages.

[1962]
Translated by
HILARY KILPATRICK

Questions

1. Is the tension between the narrator and his father of significance for the story's later unfolding?
2. What kind of conflict develops between the two medical students?
3. Does Kanafani make any moral judgments about the attempted grave robbery?
4. In what way is the story a horror story reminiscent of the tales of Edgar Allan Poe? (See Poe's "The Cask of Amontillado" in this volume.)

John Kasaipwalova

(b. 1949)

Papua New Guinea

Much of the background to John Kasaipwalova's "Betel Nut Is Bad Magic for Airplanes" is recent history. When Kasaipwalova published his short story in 1972 (in The Night Warrior and Other Stories from Papua New Guinea, edited by Ulli Beier), the country was in the last stages of Australian administration as a United Nations trusteeship. Although the situation might not have been "colonial" in the manner in which England and France governed their colonies, in practice the context was quite similar. Australian officials were disliked, and their actions often were regarded as petty attempts to maintain the status quo.

In "Betel Nut Is Bad Magic for Airplanes," the conflict between the Aussies and the Papua New Guineans is largely verbal, a linguistic exercise of wit, which we see as soon as the narrator talks to the policemen in standard English. Although he may not be able to articulate his dilemma precisely, the narrator demonstrates a concerted effort to remain a part of his culture, his tradition. One way of retaining that context is verbally, by refusing to give in and use the oppressor's language, except in the instance of necessity. (In Papua New Guinea, there are roughly 715 indigenous languages. English is spoken by only 1 or 2 percent of the population, though Pidgin English, used throughout much of the story, is widespread.) As for the regulation concerning betel nuts, the problem is not the nuts themselves but the chewer's need to spit.

John Kasaipwalova was born in Okaidoka Village on Kiriwina Island of the Trobriand Island Group, Milne Bay Province, in 1949. He was handed over to his maternal uncle to be brought up and trained as a chief. However, the boy's father (a Catholic convert) foiled the plan by sending him to a Catholic school. As a result of his excellent academic record, Kasaipwalova earned a scholarship at the University of Queensland to study Veterinary Science. That degree was never completed. In 1970, Kasaipwalova enrolled at the University of Papua New Guinea, where he was active in both literary groups and politics. He published two volumes of poems: Hanuabada (1972) and Reluctant Flame (1972). With Greg Murphy he collaborated on a folk opera called Sail the Midnight Sun (1980). In recent years, he has been active politically and involved in several business ventures.

BETEL NUT IS BAD MAGIC FOR AIRPLANES

One Saturday afternoon in May 22 this year some of we university students went to meet our people at Jacksons Airport in Seven Mile. They arrived and we happy very much. Then we all comes to that backyard corner. That one place where Ansett and TAA[1] capsize boxes for native people who go by plane.

---

[1]*Ansett and TAA*   Ansett Airline and Trans-Australian Airline.

We was standing about thirty of we, waiting to catch our things. We was chewing plenty buwa[2] like civilized people. We was not spitting or making rubbish. Only feeling very good from the betel nuts our people had bringed to Moresby.

Then for nothing somebody in brown uniform with cap like pilot, and wearing boots like dimdim[3] and black belt, he comes up to one our people and he gives some Motu and English. That one our people didn't understood. So soon that uniform man was redding his eyes and rubbing his teeths just like white man's puppy dog. Maybe something like five minutes died but still he talk. Bloody bastard! He wanted our people to stop chewing buwa because TAA and Ansett jets had come and plenty plenty white people inside the terminal. They must not be offended to see us chew betel nut. Anyways, this brown puppy dog of white man angried himself for nothing. His anger now made big big pumpkin inside his throat for because he was "educated native" and he didn't wanted kanaka[4] natives doing like that in front of Europeans.

Soon quickly one native uni. gel[5] student seen what's happening. She goes and she asks why he was giving Motu and English to our people. He whyed. She seen quickly that his why is no good. So the uni. gel student she says to him to go away. Chewing buwa is our custom for many, many civilizations. Bloody bastard! Maybe this one first time natives talked him like that way, because quickly he becomes more angry. He started talking big and making his fingers round like hard cricket ball.

I seen what's hairpin too and I fright really true. But I walks over and I asks. The uni. gel she explains and he talks also. We talk loud and many peoples they see us too and he say, "Stop being cheeky. Just shut up and do what I tell you. You are breaking the law!" So I says, "What law are we breaking? Tell me! What ordinance are we breaking?"

The puppy he gets very angry and he say "Don't be smart! Just shut up and stop chewing betel nut. You are breaking the law!"

Then my anger really wanted to stand its feet, so I says "Bull shit. We are neither spitting nor throwing rubbish. Black people never made that law and this is black people's land. There's no such law."

"All right you think you smart! You want me to report the boss?"

"I don't know your boss. Run to him if you want to smell his boots. Go on report if you want!"

His face smoked and he walked away to get his boss. I says good words to our people and we continue chewing our buwa. We was really getting tired. Our boxes sleeping somewhere we donno. I chewed my buwa but little bit my stomach was frighten because the security man will bring his boss. Then maybe big trouble! Bloody bastard!

Not long. Soon the brown puppy dog comes with their white papa dog and two other brown puppy dogs too. They was all wearing khaki uniforms, caps, boots and black belts. They seen us and we seen them too. They come to us. My heart started winking and breathing very fast. The white papa dog, his face like one man I seen one day near Boroko R. S. L. Club.[6]

---

[2]*buwa*   Betel nut.
[3]*dimdim*   White man.
[4]*kanaka*   Native.
[5]*uni. gel*   University girl.
[6]*Boroko R. S. L. Club*   Boroko Return Service League Club.

O sori! I looks at him and truly my chest wanted to run away. His bigness, his face red and especially his big big beer stomach, they frighten me already. Maybe if you seen him too, ei, you will really laugh. Bloody bastard! His stomach was too big for him. I can seen how his belt was trying its best to hold the big swelling together. His brown shirt was really punished and all of we can sees how it wanted to break. But no matter, because the stomach was trying to fall down over the black belt like one full up bilum[7] bag.

Me, it was already nearly too much. I straighten my legs quickly because something like water was falling down my leg inside my long trousers. I dunno what something and maybe only my fright trying his luck on me. But I didn't look at my long trousers. Too many people watching and also my head was boding sweat from the hotness.

Anyways, the security guards came to us. But now we three university students, we was standing together and looking them very proudly. Too late now. We was not going to run any more. We decided to defend our rights. At first they didn't know what to say and only they talked quietly inside their throats. Then their boss, the Australian papa with big stomach, he started showing we his teeths. Oi, we was frighten by his hard voice. He says to me, "Listen boy, who gave you permission to chew betel nut here? You are breaking the law, the legal laws of this land. And when they (pointing to his puppies) told you to stop, you said you didn't believe in the law and will continue to break the law!"

Straightaway my face blooded because many black, white and yellow people, they was watching us too and this white papa dog, he was talking bad like that way to me. Plenty times I hear white people calling black men "bois" so this time I hear it and my mind was already fire. I wanted to give him some. Maybe good English or maybe little bit Strine.[8] So I says loudly to him, "All right white man, on what moral grounds is it unlawful for me to chew betel nut here? This is a free country of which we black people are citizens and unless you can show me the moral basis for your 'so called laws' I cannot recognize and therefore comply to that law!"

Well, he was very very angry now because one black man answering him in very good English. Maybe he didn't understand what I say.

"Listen boy, don't be smart. You are breaking the law and the law is laid down by the lawful government in the book."

I knows straightaway that he is another one of those ignorant, uneducated white men. I getting very angry too.

"O.K. then, show me that ordinance which specifically lays down that we natives are not allowed to chew betel nut within the precincts of an air terminal, in our own country. As a citizen I have at least the right to be shown that law before you crassly accuse me of breaking the law. Until such times as you do so we shall consider you a liar and one using his delegated authority to intimidate the black people of Niugini."

"Shut up! You are nothing more than a cheeky brat!"

"Your resorting to insults is unwarranted here. All I'm demanding from you is the proof for the existence of such a law. Come on show me the exact ordinance."

"I don't have to show you the written ordinance. The lawful authority is vested in me as an officer to arrest you if I want to. It's written in Commonwealth Safety Regulations Act, section 32."

---

[7]*bilum*   Local string bag.
[8]*Strine*   Australian.

"Bull shit. I want to see it with my own eyes! Listen mate. Why aren't you arresting those white kids inside the terminal for chewing P. K.?[9] What's the difference between their P. K. inside the terminal and our betel nut outside on the road pavement?"

"Shut up you cheeky brat!" Then he wanted to grab my little neck. I was only short so I jumped back and he missed. But his face was red fire. "Since you are not going to obey, we shall arrest you!"

He was making we feel like we was some "bad cowboys" or criminals. All we three university students we was already hotted up and we was arguing with him very loudly. But when he tried that one on me, that was finish for everything. I lost my manners. I lost my calmness and also my boiling anger and fear. My heart was knocking my chest very hard. Only one thing I wanted to be—a true kanaka. So I threw my voice at him nearly spitting his face.

"Don't you dare lay hands on me white boi. This is black man's country and we have the right to make our laws to suit us. Commonwealth government is not the Nuigini House of Assembly. If you think your laws are justified, you are nothing more than a bloody white racist! A bloody white racist, you hear!"

I was shaking. The overseas people who was arrived and also black people, they was watching. Our people was just waiting for him to hit me and then they would finish him on the spot. Maski[10] Bomana.[11] We will only eat rice and have good times there. The Australian papa dog, he seen too many black faces around him. Too much for him. I think our argument already full him up. He starts walking away and threatening we.

"We'll fix you, you cheeky brat! Don't you run away. I'm going to ring the police."

"Ring the police if you want to! Always like you white racists. Each time you know you are wrong or want to bully us black people, you have to use the police on us."

The brown puppy dogs didn't know what to do so they followed their white boss, the papa dog with big stomach. I think all the water in my blood was all red now. I breathing very fast but maybe that was because I already frighten about the coming of the police. I seen many times how they do to protect white men's lives or property. Only last week I seen them hitting some Chimbu men because they was enjoying life from drinks. I wanted to throw some stones at the police cars but they was too fast and they took the Chimbu men away to kalabus.[12]

Then something maybe like five minutes and we hear big siren noise. Two blue polis cars and one big lorry. That one had gorilla wire all around it and truly big enough to capture maybe twenty or thirty natives inside it. The cars and the lorry was all for we three university students. They stopped the traffic and about six black polis bois jumped down. I was really frighten. But papa dog he gets his courage and they march to us. We was standing calmly, because we was ready now. Any time! The polis bois they seen us not making big trouble so they run away with the big lorry, but they stopped the two blue cars.

They comes marching up to we and our people. Also university bus already come and we busy loading up the boxes, bags of yams and drums. But papa dog he no play now. Bloody bastard! His teeths was already making noise to the polis bois.

"Officer I want you to charge him now."

---

[9]*P. K.* A brand of chewing gum.
[10]*Maski* Never mind.
[11]*Bomana* Location of prison.
[12]*kalabus* Prison.

The polis bois they look very stupid because they didn't know what's up. Only I can seen their eyes. They was very hungry and truly wanted to catch us because white man he said to them. My anger comes back to my head very quickly. I happy little bit, but, because the polis bois was black men and not white.

"Officer before you charge me, I would like to know what you are charging me for and perhaps, allow me to give my side of the story."

The officer he stands very stupidly. He has no words to say. So white papa dog he tells him more.

"Officer, I want you to charge him with the use of obscene language in public and also breach of the Commonwealth Safety Regulations Act, section thirty-two."

All of we was too surprised and we make one big whistle because he was already lying.

"Obscene language, my foot! All right if you reckon I used obscene language, just exactly what words did I use? Go on, tell the officer the exact words I used."

"Officer charge him. I wouldn't even repeat the words in front of the lady, in any case.

The lady who papa dog was pointing to, she was the university gel student with us. So she says, "Officer I don't mind at all, just ask him to prove to us what obscene words we used."

The polis bois they says nothing only wanting to take us away to kalabus.

"Officer they have breached the law under section 32 of the Commonwealth Safety Regulations Act and he was using very insulting language something like 'this is bloody, black fella's country.' I have my witnesses here." He showed them his puppy dogs.

We knewed fully he was truly telling lie. He only want to kalabus we because we was opened our mouths against him.

"Look officer this man is lying and we have here at least thirty witnesses to tell you exactly what I said. I called him a bloody white racist which is what he really is. I had simply questioned him his rights to force us to stop chewing betel nut here. We weren't throwing rubbish or spitting."

The polis bois was getting very annoyed and they wanted to catch me. But I was only very small and I jumped back. Then one officer he say, "You have to come to the police station."

"What for?" I asks very angry. "We've done nothing wrong. If you are going to believe the word of this white man against our thirty witnesses right here, then I suggest that you are nothing more than puppet tools for white man."

My words hit their shame because many black people was watching them too. Quickly they didn't like me. Bloody bastards! They want to friend with white man.

"Just shut up and come to the police station!"

Truly by now I wanted to give them some. But oi, their size and also their big boots! If they give me one, I will really have many holes in my bottom. But I says maski.

"You can't arrest me without telling me what the charges are. Let go my hands! We came to see that our people get to the university and I'm not going anywhere until our people are comfortably seen back to the university!"

I run away free and we start our people into the bus. The polis bois and the white papa dog, they didn't know what to do, so they was standing there like bamboo, all empty. Soon our peoples they come back to university in the bus and we three university students, we goes and we argue some more.

In the end, they tells we three to get into the police car. We goes in but then we sees how the polis bois was going to leave the papa dog behind and take us to Boroko Police Station. So we quickly opens the doors and we runs out. They catch us very quickly again then I says loudly, "We are not going to the police station unless that white man also comes with us. It's hardly justifiable for the police to be his spokesman because this will conveniently screen him from any embarrassment."

What can they do? They knows they was wrong so they calls him back. They pushed we into the back seat, then they opens the front door for the papa dog. So I talks loudly and strong.

"Get in there white man!"

He blooded more and we laugh inside. The polis they was all very silent. We speeded to Boroko Police Station. I knows that place often.

They bringed us to one big table and many police men behind it. The papa dog he didn't waste time. He open one book and he show them.

"I want you to charge them for trespassing under section thirty-two. Under this regulation I have the authority to arrest or have arrested any persons I see to be causing danger to the safety of aeroplanes . . . .

Then I know he was truly telling more lies and I shout straightaway. "What a lot of rubbish. We weren't carrying anything inflammable. We were simply chewing betel nut on the road pavement outside the terminal."

The white sergeant police, he turns fastly and like one lion's mouth, he yells me, "Listen boy, keep your mouth shut!"

His voice was too big for me. His eyes wanted to shoot and his blue uniform swelling from his fatness. I wanted to say more. But too late! I sees his bigness and I hear his voice and that one finished me up quick. Anyways we was very tired now and we shut up good. Maybe we let him give us some now and maybe later we fight him inside court house. So the papa dog gives more lies.

"I also want to charge him with the use of obscene language in a public place. He was using the words and I quote 'this is fuckin black fellas' country.'"

He tell them more and he shows them more from his book. But the police sergeant and his bois didn't knew what means "obscene language." They look for one dictionary and we was standing there like five or maybe ten minutes waiting for them. They didn't find what means that word. I seen the sergeant pull one telephone and talks to it.

Like two minutes later, we was took to one office inside, near the back. That one office, his name CIB[13] office. We walks in, the four of we and we seen one man sitting inside. He looks like very important man. Long trousers, shoes and tie. We sit down and again the papa dog he starts more talking. Ei, he talks very long, and this making me feel like one real "bad" cowboy or something. Finally the important man shut him up.

"You can either charge him with one or the other. With regards to the section thirty-two, a similar case took place in Lae last year and I remember clearly the new precedent set then. If you want to charge him with that you have to write away for the Controller General's permission from Melbourne."

The papa dog, he nearly cried because he knewed and we knewed that he wronged all the time. Then my turn for explain. I told him about the argument and everything.

---

[13]*CIB* Criminal Investigation Branch.

"I have my two witnesses here to testify. I didn't use 'fuckin black fellas' country."
I do admit having spoken to him in a firm voice but what I called him was a 'bloody
white racist.' As far as I'm concerned these are not obscene words. They are political terms which I often ascribe to persons committing injustice to others, and I would
just as readily call a black man a 'bloody black racist' if I saw him committing an injustice to a man of another ethnic origin."

The important man held his head for long time and we wait like sleeping pigs.
Then he looks up and writes down the white man's name, address and phone. After
that he told him to go. I wanted to say something but my mouth shut very quickly.
The important man, he writes our names in his book then he say, "I will notify you
on Monday as to what the charge will be. In the meantime you may go."

We walk out and we was feeling little bit happy. But I remember we have no money
for bus to Waigani. The police they should pay us. So I walks back to the CIB office.
"Sir the police had inconvenienced us in the first place and I think it is only right they
should take us back to the university."

The important man walk out with us to the front office and he called on sergeant.
"Sergeant, arrange for a car to take these students safely to the university, will you?"

That one sergeant same one before. He didn't like it, to treat us good. We three
university students, we come back to Waigani. We was chewing our betel nut on
the way.

[1972]

Questions

1. Is the protest by the students a success or a failure? Do they gain anything or do
   they lose?
2. Why does the narrator keep using Western expressions such as "bad cowboy"?
3. If chewing betel nut is offensive to the Europeans, what equivalent object and/or
   custom by the Australians might be offensive to the Papua New Guineans?

Khamsing Srinawk

(b. 1930)

Thailand

K hamsing Srinawk, who has written under the pseudonym Lao Khamhawm, was born in 1930 in a small village in northeastern Thailand. Although his family was poor and uneducated, he was encouraged by an uncle who was a monk to pursue his intellectual interests. As his translator, Domnern Garden, notes, when Khamsing completed secondary school, "his older brother gave him a pair of shoes so he could go to Bangkok to pursue his driving ambition to be a writer." Khamsing studied economics at Thammasart University in Bangkok and briefly studied journalism while supporting himself through writing news and feature articles for local newspapers. Before pursuing his literary career in earnest, he served as a forest ranger in northern Thailand and as an assistant to a group of anthropological researchers in a village near Bangkok. His first collection of short stories, No Barriers, was published in 1958; The Politician and Other Stories appeared in 1973.

Srinawk spent a year in the United States working with a publishing house and subsequently traveled in Europe and Africa as an official guest of several governments, as an observer in both literary and agricultural capacities. He currently resides on his farm in Korat Province, Thailand, with his family.

THE GOLD-LEGGED FROG

The sun blazed as if determined to burn every living thing in the broad fields to a crisp. Now and again the tall, straight, isolated *sabang* and shorea trees let go of some of their dirty leaves. He sat exhausted against a tree trunk, his dark blue shirt wet with sweat. The expanse round him expressed total dryness. He stared at the tufts of dull grass and bits of straw spinning in a column to the sky. The whirlwind sucked brown earth up into the air casting a dark pall over everything. He recalled the old people had told him this was the portent of drought, want, disaster, and death, and he was afraid. He was now anxious to get home; he could already see the tips of the bamboo thickets surrounding the house far ahead like blades of grass. But he hesitated. A moment before reaching the shade of the tree he felt his ears buzz and his eyes blur and knew it meant giddiness and sunstroke. He looked at the soles of his feet blistered from the burning sandy ground and became indescribably angry—angry at the weather capable of such endless torture. In the morning the cold had pierced his bones, but now it was so hot he felt his head would break into pieces. As he recalled the biting cold of the morning, he thought again of his little son.

That very morning he and two of his small children went out into the dry paddy fields near the house to look for frogs for the morning meal. The air was chilly. The two children on either side of him shivered as they stopped to look for frogs hiding in the cracks of the parched earth. Each time they saw two bright eyes in a deep crack, they would shout, "Pa, here's another one. Pa, this crack has two. Gold-legged ones! Hurry, Pa."

He had hopped from place to place as the voices called him, prying up the dry clods with his hoe. He caught some of the frogs immediately, but a few jumped away as soon as he began digging. It was the children's job to give chase and pounce on them. Some they got. Some jumped into other fissures, obliging him to pry up a new cake of earth. Besides the frog, if his luck were good, he would unearth a land snail or razor clam waiting for the rains. He would take these as well.

The air had started to warm and already he had had enough frogs to eat with the morning rice. The sound of drumming, the village chief's call for a meeting, had sounded faintly from the village. Vague anger again spilled over as his thoughts returned to that moment. If only he had gone home then, the poor child would be all right now. It was really the last crack. As soon as he had poked it, the ground broke apart. A fully-grown gold-legged frog as big as a thumb leaped past the older child. The younger raced after it for about twelve yards when it dodged into a deep hoof-print of a water buffalo. The child groped for it. And then he was shocked almost senseless by the trembling cry of his boy, "Pa, a snake, a snake bit my hand."

A cobra spread its hood, hissing. When finally able to act, the father with all his strength had slammed the handle of his hoe three times down onto the back of the serpent, leaving its tail twitching. He carried his child and the basket of frogs home without forgetting to tell the other to drag the snake along as well.

On the way back his son had cried softly and moaned, beating his chest with his fists and complaining he could not breathe. At home, the father summoned all the faith-healers and herbalists whose names he could think of and the turmoil began.

"Chop up a frog and put it on the wound," a neighbour called out.

When another shouted, "Give him the toasted liver of the snake to eat," he hurriedly slit open the snake to look for the liver while his wife sat by crying. The later it got, the bigger the crowd grew. On hearing the news, all the neighbours attending the village chief's meeting joined the others. One of them told him he had to go to the District Office in town that very day because the village chief told them the government was going to hand out money to those with five or more children, and he was one who had just five. It was a new shock.

"Can't you see my boy's gasping out his life? How can I go?" he cried resentfully.

"What difference will it make? You've called in a lot of doctors, all of them expert."

"Go, you fool. It's two hundred baht[1] they're giving. You've never had that much in your whole life. Two hundred!"

"Pardon my saying it," another added, "but if something should happen and the boy dies, you'd be out, that's all."

"I won't go," he yelled. "My kid can't breathe and you tell me to go. Why can't they hand it out some other day? It's true I've never had two hundred baht since I was born, but I'm not going. I'm not going."

"Jail," another interjected. "If you don't go, you simply go to jail. Whoever disobeyed the authorities? If they decide to give, you have to take. If not, jail."

The word "jail" repeated like that unnerved him, but still he resisted.

---

[1]*baht*   Monetary unit of Thailand.

"Whatever it is, I said I'm not going. I don't want it. How can I leave the kid when he's dying?" He raised his voice. "No, I won't go."

"You go. Don't go against the government. We're subjects." He turned to find the village chief standing grimly at his side.

"If I don't go, will it really be jail?" he asked in a voice suddenly become hoarse.

"For sure," the village chief replied sternly. "Maybe for life."

That did it. In a daze, he asked the faith-healers and neighbors to take care of his son and left the house.

He reached the District Office almost at eleven and found some of his neighbors who had also come for the money already sitting in a group. They told him to address the old deputy district officer which he did.

"I am Mr. Nak Na-ngam, sir. I have come for the money, the many-children money."

The deputy district officer raised his fat face to stare at him for a moment, then spoke heavily. "Idiot, don't you have eyes to see people are working. Get out! Get out and wait outside."

"But, sir, my boy is dying . . ." However, he cut himself short when he thought perhaps if the official suspected that his child might be dead there would be trouble. The deputy officer looked down at his paper and went on scribbling. Nak dejectedly joined the group outside. "All you do is suffer if you're born a rice farmer and a subject," he thought. "You're poor and helpless, your mouth gets stained from eating roots when the rice has run out, you're at the end of your tether and you turn to the authorities only to be put down."

The official continued to write as if there were no peasants waiting anxiously. A few minutes after twelve, he strode from the office but had the kindness to say a few words. "It's noon already. Time for a break. Come back at one o'clock for it."

Nak and his neighbors sat there waiting until one o'clock. The taciturn deputy on returning called them all to sit on the floor near him. He began by asking each of them why they had so many children. The awkward replies of the peasants brought guffaws from the other officials who turned to listen to the embarrassed answers. At last his turn came.

"Who is Mr. Nak Na-ngam?"

"I am sir," he responded with humility.

"And now, why do we have such a lot of children?"

Several people tittered.

"Oh, when you're poor, sir," he burst out, his exasperation uncontrollable.

"What the hell's it got to do with being poor?" the deputy officer questioned in a voice that showed disappointment with the answer.

"We're awful poor and no money to buy a blanket. So no matter how bad the smell is always, I gotta use my wife for a blanket and the kids just keep comin'."

Instead of laughter, dead silence, finally broken by the dry voice of the blank-faced deputy, "Bah! This joker uses his wife for a blanket."

The wind gusted again. The *sabang* and shorea trees threw off another lot of leaves. The spears of sunlight still dazzled him. The whirlwind still hummed in the middle of the empty ricefield ahead. Nak left the shade of the tall tree and headed through the flaming afternoon sunshine towards his village.

"Hey, Nak . . ." The voice came from a group of neighbors passing in the opposite direction. Another topped it.

"You sure are lucky." The words raised his spirits. He smiled a little before repeating expectantly, "How am I lucky—in what way?"

"The two hundred baht. You got it, didn't you?"

"I got it. It's right here." He patted his pocket.

"What luck! You sure have good luck, Nak. One more day and you'd have been out two hundred baht."

[1958]

Translated by

Domnern Garden

Questions

1. What is the conflict in the story? How does it reveal Nak's economic position and the limits of his choices?

2. In what way is the ending of the story ironic? How is "luck" defined?

3. How does the detailed description of the setting contribute to your understanding of the exigencies of poverty faced by Nak's family and their neighbors?

4. Compare this story with Mark Twain's "Luck."

Jamaica Kincaid

(b. 1949)

Antigua/United States

The daughter of a carpenter/cabinet maker and his wife, Jamaica Kincaid was born Elaine Potter Richardson in St. Johns, Antigua. At the age of 17, she left the island to become an au pair in New York City; she remained there to study photography at the New School for Social Research and at Franconia College in New Hampshire. Subsequently, she married Allen Shawn, a composer and professor of music at Bennington College; they have two children.

Kincaid began her career in writing as a journalist and later as a staff writer for The New Yorker magazine. Encouraged by her editors, she published her first fiction in that magazine. At the Bottom of the River (1983), parts of which were published in installments in The New Yorker, focuses on a young girl in Antigua and demonstrates elements of Kincaid's distinctive style: a detailed attention to the mundane and prosaic, rendered through a lyrical and poetic language that captures inner states of consciousness, fantasy, dream, and myth. With Annie John (1985)—variously described as a novel and a set of interlinked stories—Kincaid continued to draw on her West Indian experiences, recounting the coming of age of a young girl in Antigua. That volume, like Lucy (1990) and The Autobiography of My Mother (1995), also reveals Kincaid's preoccupation with the emotionally complex mother-daughter relationship as it becomes further complicated by cultural, political, and geographical matters.

Of the stories in At the Bottom of the River—which includes "My Mother"— Patricia Ismond observes in World Literature Written in English, "The preoccupation with childhood lies at the core of Kincaid's work and represents a very special achievement. In exploring it, she renews our understanding of the meaning of innocence and the value and possibilities of our first world. . . . It is not a state free from stain and imperfection."

MY MOTHER

Immediately on wishing my mother dead and seeing the pain it caused her, I was sorry and cried so many tears that all the earth around me was drenched. Standing before my mother, I begged her forgiveness, and I begged so earnestly that she took pity on me, kissing my face and placing my head on her bosom to rest. Placing her arms around me, she drew my head closer and closer to her bosom, until finally I suffocated. I lay on her bosom, breathless, for a time uncountable, until one day, for a reason she has kept to herself, she shook me out and stood me under a tree and I started to breathe again. I cast a sharp glance at her and said to myself, "So." Instantly I grew my own bosoms, small mounds at first, leaving a small, soft place between them, where, if ever necessary, I could rest my own head. Between my mother and me now were the tears I had cried, and I gathered up some stones and banked them in so that they formed a small pond. The water in the pond was thick and black and poisonous, so that only unnamable invertebrates could live in it. My mother and I now watched each other carefully, always making sure to shower the other with words and deeds of love and affection.

I was sitting on my mother's bed trying to get a good look at myself. It was a large bed and it stood in the middle of a large, completely dark room. The room was completely dark because all the windows had been boarded up and all the crevices stuffed with black cloth. My mother lit some candles and the room burst into a pink-like, yellow-like glow. Looming over us, much larger than ourselves, were our shadows. We sat mesmerized because our shadows had made a place between themselves, as if they were making room for someone else. Nothing filled up the space between them, and the shadow of my mother sighed. The shadow of my mother danced around the room to a tune that my own shadow sang, and then they stopped. All along, our shadows had grown thick and thin, long and short, had fallen at every angle, as if they were controlled by the light of day. Suddenly my mother got up and blew out the candles and our shadows vanished. I continued to sit on the bed, trying to get a good look at myself.

My mother removed her clothes and covered thoroughly her skin with a thick gold-colored oil, which had recently been rendered in a hot pan from the livers of reptiles with pouched throats. She grew plates of metal-colored scales on her back, and light, when it collided with this surface, would shatter and collapse into tiny points. Her teeth now arranged themselves into rows that reached all the way back to her long white throat. She uncoiled her hair from her head and then removed her hair altogether. Taking her head into her large palms, she flattened it so that her eyes, which were by now ablaze, sat on top of her head and spun like two revolving balls. Then, making two lines on the soles of each foot, she divided her feet into crossroads. Silently, she had instructed me to follow her example, and now I too traveled along on my white underbelly, my tongue darting and flickering in the hot air. "Look," said my mother.

My mother and I were standing on the seabed side by side, my arms laced loosely around her waist, my head resting securely on her shoulder, as if I needed the support. To make sure she believed in my frailness, I sighed occasionally—long soft sighs, the kind of sigh she had long ago taught me could evoke sympathy. In fact, how I really felt was invincible. I was no longer a child but I was not yet a woman. My skin had just blackened and cracked and fallen away and my new impregnable carapace had taken full hold. My nose had flattened; my hair curled in and stood out straight from my head simultaneously; my many rows of teeth in their retractable trays were in place. My mother and I wordlessly made an arrangement—I sent out my beautiful sighs, she received them; I leaned ever more heavily on her for support, she offered her shoulder, which shortly grew to the size of a thick plank. A long time passed, at the end of which I had hoped to see my mother permanently cemented to the seabed. My mother reached out to pass a hand over my head, a pacifying gesture, but I laughed and, with great agility, stepped aside. I let out a horrible roar, then a self-pitying whine. I had grown big, but my mother was bigger, and that would always be so. We walked to the Garden of Fruits and there ate to our hearts' satisfaction. We departed through the southwesterly gate, leaving as always, in our trail, small colonies of worms.

With my mother, I crossed, unwillingly, the valley. We saw a lamb grazing and when it heard our footsteps it paused and looked up at us. The lamb looked cross and miserable. I said to my mother, "The lamb is cross and miserable. So would I be, too, if I had to live in a climate not suited to my nature." My mother and I now entered the cave. It was the dark and cold cave. I felt something growing under my feet and I bent down to eat it. I stayed that way for years, bent over eating whatever I found growing under my feet. Eventually, I grew a special lens that would allow me to see in the darkest of darkness; eventually, I grew a special coat that kept me warm in the coldest of coldness. One day I saw my mother sitting on a rock. She said, "What a strange expression you have on your face. So cross, so miserable, as if you were living in a climate not suited to your nature." Laughing, she vanished. I dug a deep, deep hole. I built a beautiful house, a floorless house, over the deep, deep hole. I put in lattice windows, most favored of windows by my mother, so perfect for looking out at people passing by without her being observed. I painted the house itself yellow, the windows green, colors I knew would please her. Standing just outside the door, I asked her to inspect the house. I said, "Take a look. Tell me if it's to your satisfaction." Laughing out of the corner of a mouth I could not see, she stepped inside. I stood just outside the door, listening carefully, hoping to hear her land with a thud at the bottom of the deep, deep hole. Instead, she walked up and down in every direction, even pounding her heel on the air. Coming outside to greet me, she said, "It is an excellent house. I would be honored to live in it," and then vanished. I filled up the hole and burnt the house to the ground.

My mother has grown to an enormous height. I have grown to an enormous height also, but my mother's height is three times mine. Sometimes I cannot see from her breasts on up, so lost is she in the atmosphere. One day, seeing her sitting on the seashore, her hand reaching out in the deep to caress the belly of a striped fish as he swam through a place where two seas met, I glowed red with anger. For a while then I lived alone on the island where there were eight full moons and I adorned the face of each moon with expressions I had seen on my mother's face. All the expressions favored me. I soon grew tired of living in this way and returned to my mother's side. I remained, though glowing red with anger, and my mother and I built houses on opposite banks of the dead pond. The dead pond lay between us; in it, only small invertebrates with poisonous lances lived. My mother behaved toward them as if she had suddenly found herself in the same room with relatives we had long since risen above. I cherished their presence and gave them names. Still I missed my mother's close company and cried constantly for her, but at the end of each day when I saw her return to her house, incredible and great deeds in her wake, each of them singing loudly her praises, I glowed and glowed again, red with anger. Eventually, I wore myself out and sank into a deep sleep, the only dreamless sleep I have ever had.

One day my mother packed my things in a grip and, taking me by the hand, walked me to the jetty, placed me on board a boat, in care of the captain. My mother, while caressing my chin and cheeks, said some words of comfort to me because we had never been apart before. She kissed me on the forehead and turned and walked away. I cried so much my chest heaved up and down, my whole body shook at the sight of her back turned toward me, as if I had never seen her back turned toward me before. I started to make plans to get off the boat, but when I saw that the boat was encased in a large green bottle, as if it were about to decorate a mantelpiece, I fell asleep, until I reached my destination, the new island. When the boat stopped, I got off and I saw a woman with feet exactly like mine, especially around the arch of the instep. Even though the face was completely different from what I was used to, I recognized this woman as my mother. We greeted each other at first with great caution and politeness, but as we walked along, our steps became one, and as we talked, our voices became one voice, and we were in complete union in every other way. What peace came over me then, for I could not see where she left off and I began, or where I left off and she began.

My mother and I walk through the rooms of her house. Every crack in the floor holds a significant event: here, an apparently healthy young man suddenly dropped dead; here a young woman defied her father and, while riding her bicycle to the forbidden lovers' meeting place, fell down a precipice, remaining a cripple for the rest of a very long life. My mother and I find this a beautiful house. The rooms are large and empty, opening on to each other, waiting for people and things to fill them up. Our white muslin skirts billow up around our ankles, our hair hangs straight down our backs as our arms hang straight at our sides. I fit perfectly in the crook of my mother's arm, on the curve of her back, in the hollow of her stomach. We eat from the same bowl, drink from the same cup; when we sleep, our heads rest on the same pillow. As we walk through the rooms, we merge and separate, merge and separate; soon we shall enter the final stage of our evolution.

The fishermen are coming in from sea; their catch is bountiful, my mother has seen to that. As the waves plop, plop against each other, the fishermen are happy that the sea is calm. My mother points out the fishermen to me, their contentment is a source of my contentment. I am sitting in my mother's enormous lap. Sometimes I sit on a mat she has made for me from her hair. The lime trees are weighed down with limes— I have already perfumed myself with their blossoms. A hummingbird has nested on my stomach, a sign of my fertileness. My mother and I live in a bower made from flowers whose petals are imperishable. There is the silvery blue of the sea, crisscrossed with sharp darts of light, there is the warm rain falling on the clumps of castor bush, there is the small lamb bounding across the pasture, there is the soft ground welcoming the soles of my pink feet. It is in this way my mother and I have lived for a long time now.

[1983]

Questions

1. How does the narrator feel about her mother? How are her feelings expressed?
2. How do language, imagery, exaggeration, and fantasy contribute to the story's effect and meaning? How do realistic and fantastic details shape the story?
3. What does the final sentence suggest?

Margaret Laurence

(1926–1987)

Canada

O ne of Canada's most distinguished novelists, Margaret Wemyss Laurence was born in the provincial prairie town of Neepawa, Manitoba—a place she recreated in her fiction as Manawaka. Before she could celebrate its moral rootedness and castigate its snobbery and narrow-mindedness (as she does in her novels), she had to leave it. She studied English at United College, Winnipeg, while writing for the college paper and later the city paper. She married a civil engineer, Jack Laurence, whose work took them to England and West Africa. Laurence's African experiences in the 1950s, as a witness to the rough political transition from colonial satellites to independent states, form the subject of her early narratives, including This Side Jordan (1960).

Laurence, subsequently divorced, eventually returned to Canada, settling in Ontario, and wrote the novels that have made her distinguished reputation: The Stone Angel (1964), A Jest of God (1966), The Fire-Dwellers (1969), A Bird in the House (1970), and The Diviners (1974). A Jest of God was made into the film Rachel, Rachel. In her strong and introspective but often inwardly divided female characters, Laurence anticipated contemporary feminist issues, unerringly framing the dilemmas that mid-twentieth-century North American women had begun to face in seeking to define themselves through personal independence as well as significant relationships. In The Diviners (considered by most critics to be Laurence's masterpiece), the river that flows in two directions is a fitting symbol for the divided pulls of her characters.

A BIRD IN THE HOUSE

The parade would be almost over by now, and I had not gone. My mother had said in a resigned voice, "All right, Vanessa, if that's the way you feel," making me suffer twice as many jabs of guilt as I would have done if she had lost her temper. She and Grandmother MacLeod had gone off, my mother pulling the low boxsleigh with Roddie all dolled up in his new red snowsuit, just the sort of little kid anyone would want people to see. I sat on the lowest branch of the birch tree in our yard, not minding the snowy wind, even welcoming its punishment. I went over my reasons for not going, trying to believe they were good and sufficient, but in my heart I felt I was betraying my father. This was the first time I had stayed away from the Remembrance Day parade. I wondered if he would notice that I was not there, standing on the sidewalk at the corner of River and Main while the parade passed, and then following to the Court House grounds where the service was held.

I could see the whole thing in my mind. It was the same every year. The Manawaka Civic Band always led the way. They had never been able to afford full uniforms, but they had peaked navy-blue caps and sky-blue chest ribbons. They were joined on Remembrance Day by the Salvation Army band, whose uniforms seemed too ordinary for a parade, for they were the same ones the bandsmen wore every Saturday night when they played "Nearer My God to Thee" at the foot of River Street. The two bands never managed to practise quite enough together, so they did not keep in time too well. The Salvation Army band invariably played faster, and afterwards my father would say irritably, "They play those marches just like they do hymns, blast them, as though they wouldn't get to heaven if they didn't hustle up." And my mother, who had great respect for the Salvation Army because of the good work they did, would respond chidingly, "Now, now, Ewen—" I vowed I would never say "Now, now" to my husband or children, not that I ever intended having the latter, for I had been put off by my brother Roderick, who was now two years old with wavy hair, and everyone said what a beautiful child. I was twelve, and no one in their right mind would have said what a beautiful child, for I was big-boned like my Grandfather Connor and had straight lanky black hair like a Blackfoot or Cree.

After the bands would come the veterans. Even thinking of them at this distance, in the white and withdrawn quiet of the birch tree, gave me a sense of painful embarrassment. I might not have minded so much if my father had not been among them. How could he go? How could he not see how they all looked? It must have been a long time since they were soldiers, for they had forgotten how to march in step. They were old—that was the thing. My father was bad enough, being almost forty, but he wasn't a patch on Howard Tully from the drugstore, who was completely grey-haired and also fat, or Stewart MacMurchie, who was bald at the back of his head. They looked to me like imposters, plump or spindly caricatures of past warriors. I almost hated them for walking in that limping column down Main. At the Court House, everyone would sing *Lord God of Hosts, be with us yet, lest we forget, lest we forget*. Will Masterson would pick up his old Army bugle and blow the last Post. Then it would be over and everyone could start gabbling once more and go home.

I jumped down from the birch bough and ran to the house, yelling, making as much noise as I could.

I'm a poor lonesome cowboy
An' a long way from home—

I stepped inside the front hall and kicked off my snow boots. I slammed the door behind me, making the dark ruby and emerald glass shake in the small leaded panes. I slid purposely on the hall rug, causing it to bunch and crinkle on the slippery polished oak of the floor. I seized the newel post, round as a head, and spun myself to and fro on the bottom stair.

I ain't got no father
To buy the clothes I wear.
I'm a poor lonesome—

At this moment my shoulders were firmly seized and shaken by a pair of hands, white and delicate and old, but strong as talons.

"Just what do you think you're doing, young lady?" Grandmother MacLeod enquired, in a voice like frost on a windowpane, infinitely cold and clearly etched.

I went limp and in a moment she took her hands away. If you struggled, she would always hold on longer.

"Gee, I never knew you were home yet."

"I would have thought that on a day like this you might have shown a little respect and consideration," Grandmother MacLeod said, "even if you couldn't make the effort to get cleaned up enough to go to the parade."

I realised with surprise that she imagined this to be my reason for not going. I did not try to correct her impression. My real reason would have been even less acceptable.

"I'm sorry," I said quickly.

In some families, *please* is described as the magic word. In our house, however, it was *sorry*.

"This isn't an easy day for any of us," she said.

Her younger son, my Uncle Roderick, had been killed in the Great War.[1] When my father marched, and when the hymn was sung, and when that unbearably lonely tune was sounded by the one bugle and everyone forced themselves to keep absolutely still, it would be that boy of whom she was thinking. I felt the enormity of my own offence.

"Grandmother—I'm sorry."

"So you said."

I could not tell her I had not really said it before at all. I went into the den and found my father there. He was sitting in the leather-cushioned armchair beside the fireplace. He was not doing anything, just sitting and smoking. I stood beside him, wanting to touch the light-brown hairs on his forearm, but thinking he might laugh at me or pull his arm away if I did.

"I'm sorry," I said, meaning it.

"What for, honey?"

"For not going."

"Oh—that. What was the matter?"

I did not want him to know, and yet I had to tell him, make him see.

"They look silly," I blurted. "Marching like that."

For a minute I thought he was going to be angry. It would have been a relief to me if he had been. Instead, he drew his eyes away from mine and fixed them above the mantelpiece where the sword hung, the handsome and evil-looking crescent in its carved bronze sheath that some ancestor had once brought from the Northern Frontier of India.

"Is that the way it looks to you?" he said.

I felt in his voice some hurt, something that was my fault. I wanted to make everything all right between us, to convince him that I understood, even if I did not. I prayed that Grandmother MacLeod would stay put in her room, and that my mother would take a long time in the kitchen, giving Roddie his lunch. I wanted my father to myself, so I could prove to him that I cared more about him than any of the others did. I wanted to speak in some way that would be more poignant and comprehending than anything of which my mother could possibly be capable. But I did not know how.

---

[1]*Great War*   World War 1 (1914–1918).

"You were right there when Uncle Roderick got killed, weren't you?" I began uncertainly.

"Yes."

"How old was he, Dad?"

"Eighteen," my father said.

Unexpectedly, that day came into intense being for me. He had had to watch his own brother die, not in the antiseptic calm of some hospital, but out in the open, the stretches of mud I had seen in his snapshots. He would not have known what to do. He would just have had to stand there and look at it, whatever that might mean. I looked at my father with a kind of horrified awe, and then I began to cry. I had forgotten about impressing him with my perception. Now I needed him to console me for this unwanted glimpse of the pain he had once known.

"Hey, cut it out, honey," he said, embarrassed. "It was bad, but it wasn't all as bad as that part. There were a few other things."

"Like, what?" I said, not believing him.

"Oh—I don't know," he replied evasively. "Most of us were pretty young, you know, I and the boys I joined up with. None of us had ever been away from Manawaka before. Those of us who came back mostly came back here, or else went no further away from town than Winnipeg. So when we were overseas that was the only time most of us were ever a long way from home."

"Did you want to be?" I asked, shocked.

"Oh well—" my father said uncomfortably. "It was kind of interesting to see a few other places for a change, that's all."

Grandmother MacLeod was standing in the doorway.

"Beth's called you twice for lunch, Ewen. Are you deaf, you and Vanessa?"

"Sorry," my father and I said simultaneously.

Then we went upstairs to wash our hands.

That winter my mother returned to her old job as nurse in my father's medical practice. She was able to do this only because of Noreen.

"Grandmother MacLeod says we're getting a maid," I said to my father, accusingly, one morning. "We're not, are we?"

"Believe you me, on what I'm going to be paying her," my father growled, "she couldn't be called anything as classy as a maid. Hired girl would be more like it."

"Now, now, Ewen," my mother put in, "it's not as if we were cheating her or anything. You know she wants to live in town, and I can certainly see why, stuck out there on the farm, and her father hardly ever letting her come in. What kind of life is that for a girl?"

"I don't like the idea of your going back to work, Beth," my father said. "I know you're fine now, but you're not exactly the robust type."

"You can't afford to hire a nurse any longer. It's all very well to say the Depression won't last forever—probably it won't, but what else can we do for now?"

"I'm damned if I know," my father admitted. "Beth—"

"Yes?"

They both seemed to have forgotten about me. It was at breakfast, which we always ate in the kitchen, and I sat rigidly on my chair, pretending to ignore and thus snub their withdrawal from me. I glared at the window, but it was so thickly plumed and scrolled with frost that I could not see out. I glanced back to my parents. My father had not replied, and my mother was looking at him in that anxious and half-frowning way she had recently developed.

"What is it, Ewen?" Her voice had the same nervous sharpness it bore sometimes when she would say to me, "For mercy's sake, Vanessa, what is it *now?*" as though whatever was the matter, it was bound to be the last straw.

My father spun his sterling silver serviette ring, engraved with his initials, slowly around on the table.

"I never thought things would turn out like this, did you?"

"Please—" my mother said in a low strained voice, "please, Ewen, let's not start all this again. I can't take it."

"All right," my father said. "Only—"

"The MacLeods used to have money and now they don't," my mother cried. "Well, they're not alone. Do you think all that matters to me, Ewen? What I can't bear is to see you forever reproaching yourself. As if it were your fault."

"I don't think it's the comedown," my father said. "If I were somewhere else, I don't suppose it would matter to me, either, except where you're concerned. But I suppose you'd work too hard wherever you were—it's bred into you. If you haven't got anything to slave away at, you'll sure as hell invent something."

"What do you think I should do, let the house go to wrack and ruin? That would go over well with your mother, wouldn't it?"

"That's just it," my father said. "It's the damned house all the time. I haven't only taken on my father's house, I've taken on everything that goes with it, apparently. Sometimes I really wonder—"

"Well, it's a good thing I've inherited some practicality even if you haven't," my mother said. "I'll say that for the Connors—they aren't given to brooding, thank the Lord. Do you want your egg poached or scrambled?"

"Scrambled," my father said. "All I hope is that this Noreen doesn't get married straightaway, that's all."

"She won't," my mother said. "Who's she going to meet who could afford to marry?"

"I marvel at you, Beth," my father said. "You look as though a puff of wind would blow you away. But underneath, by God, you're all hardwood."

"Don't talk stupidly," my mother said. "All I hope is that she won't object to taking your mother's breakfast up on a tray."

"That's right," my father said angrily. "Rub it in."

"Oh Ewen, I'm sorry!" my mother cried, her face suddenly stricken. "I don't know why I say these things. I don't mean to."

"I know," my father said. "Here, cut it out, honey. Just for God's sake please don't cry."

"I'm sorry," my mother repeated, blowing her nose.

"We're both sorry," my father said. "Not that that changes anything."

After my father had gone, I got down from my chair and went to my mother.

"I don't want you to go back to the office. I don't want a hired girl here. I'll hate her."

My mother sighed, making me feel that I was placing an intolerable burden on her, and yet making me resent having to feel this weight. She looked tired, as she often did these days. Her tiredness bored me, made me want to attack her for it.

"Catch me getting along with a dumb old hired girl," I threatened.

"Do what you like," my mother said abruptly. "What can I do about it?"

And then, of course, I felt bereft, not knowing which way to turn. My father need not have worried about Noreen getting married. She was, as it turned out, interested not in boys but in God. My mother was relieved about the boys but alarmed about God.

"It isn't natural," she said, "for a girl of seventeen. Do you think she's all right mentally, Ewen?"

When my parents, along with Grandmother MacLeod, went to the United Church every Sunday, I was made to go to Sunday school in the church basement, where there were small red chairs which humiliatingly resembled kindergarten furniture, and pictures of Jesus wearing a white sheet and surrounded by a whole lot of well-dressed kids whose mothers obviously had not suffered them to come unto Him until every face and ear was properly scrubbed. Our religious observances also included grace at meals, when my father would mumble "For what we are about to receive the Lord make us truly thankful Amen," running the words together as though they were one long word. My mother approved of these rituals, which seemed decent and moderate to her. Noreen's religion, however, was a different matter. Noreen belonged to the Tabernacle of the Risen and Reborn, and she had got up to testify no less than seven times in the past two years, she told us. My mother, who could not imagine anyone's voluntarily making a public spectacle of themselves, was profoundly shocked by this revelation.

"Don't worry," my father soothed her. "She's all right. She's just had kind of a dull life, that's all."

My mother shrugged and went on worrying and trying to help Noreen without hurting her feelings, by tactful remarks about the advisability of modulating one's voice when singing hymns, and the fact that there was plenty of hot water so Noreen really didn't need to hesitate about taking a bath. She even bought a razor and a packet of blades and whispered to Noreen that any girl who wore transparent blouses so much would probably like to shave under her arms. None of these suggestions had the slightest effect on Noreen. She did not cease belting out hymns at the top of her voice, she bathed once a fortnight, and the sorrel-coloured hair continued to bloom like a thicket of Indian paintbrush in her armpits.

Grandmother MacLeod refused to speak to Noreen. This caused Noreen a certain amount of bewilderment until she finally hit on an answer.

"Your poor grandma," she said. "She is deaf as a post. These things are sent to try us here on earth, Vanessa. But if she makes it into Heaven, I'll bet you anything she will hear clear as a bell."

Noreen and I talked about Heaven quite a lot, and also Hell. Noreen had an intimate and detailed knowledge of both places. She not only knew what they looked like—she even knew how big they were. Heaven was seventy-seven thousand miles square and it had four gates, each one made out of a different kind of precious jewel. The Pearl Gate, the Topaz Gate, the Amethyst Gate, the Ruby Gate—Noreen would reel them off, all the gates of Heaven. I told Noreen they sounded like poetry, but she was puzzled by my reaction and said I shouldn't talk that way. If you said poetry, it sounded like it was just made up and not really so, Noreen said.

Hell was larger than Heaven, and when I asked why, thinking of it as something of a comedown for God, Noreen said naturally it had to be bigger because there were a darn sight more people there than in Heaven. Hell was one hundred and ninety million miles deep and was in perpetual darkness, like a cave or under the sea. Even the flames (this was the awful thing) *did not give off any light.*

I did not actually believe in Noreen's doctrines, but the images which they conjured up began to inhabit my imagination. Noreen's fund of exotic knowledge was not limited to religion, although in a way it all seemed related. She could do many things which had a spooky tinge to them. Once when she was making a cake, she found we had run out of eggs. She went outside and gathered a bowl of fresh snow and used it instead. The cake rose like a charm, and I stared at Noreen as though she were a sorceress. In fact, I began to think of her as a sorceress, someone not quite of this earth. There was nothing unearthly about her broad shoulders and hips and her forest of dark red hair, but even these features took on a slightly sinister significance to me. I no longer saw her through the eyes or the expressed opinions of my mother and father, as a girl who had quit school at grade eight and whose life on the farm had been endlessly drab. I knew the truth—Noreen's life had not been drab at all, for she dwelt in a world of violent splendours, a world filled with angels whose wings of delicate light bore real feathers, and saints shining like the dawn, and prophets who spoke in ancient tongues, and the ecstatic souls of the saved, as well as denizens of the lower regions—mean-eyed imps and crooked cloven-hoofed monsters and beasts with the bodies of swine and the human heads of murderers, and lovely depraved jezebels torn by dogs through all eternity. The middle layer of Creation, our earth, was equally full of grotesque presences, for Noreen believed strongly in the visitation of ghosts and the communication with spirits. She could prove this with her Ouija board. We would both place our fingers lightly on the indicator, and it would skim across the board and spell out answers to our questions. I did not believe wholeheartedly in the Ouija board, either, but I was cautious about the kind of question I asked, in case the answer would turn out unfavourable and I would be unable to forget it.

One day Noreen told me she could also make a table talk. We used the small table in my bedroom, and sure enough, it lifted very slightly under our fingertips and tapped once for *Yes*, twice for *No*. Noreen asked if her Aunt Ruthie would get better from the kidney operation, and the table replied *No*. I withdrew my hands.

"I don't want to do it any more."

"Gee, what's the matter, Vanessa?" Noreen's plain placid face creased in a frown. "We only just begun."

"I have to do my homework."

My heart lurched as I said this. I was certain Noreen would know I was lying, and that she would know not by any ordinary perception, either. But her attention had been caught by something else, and I was thankful, at least until I saw what it was.

My bedroom window was not opened in the coldest weather. The storm window, which was fitted outside as an extra wall against the winter, had three small circular holes in its frame so that some fresh air could seep into the house. The sparrow must have been floundering in the new snow on the roof, for it had crawled in through one of these holes and was now caught between the two layers of glass. I could not bear the panic of the trapped bird, and before I realised what I was doing, I had thrown open the bedroom window. I was not releasing the sparrow into any better a situation, I soon saw, for instead of remaining quiet and allowing us to catch it in order to free it, it began flying blindly around the room, hitting the lampshade, brushing against the walls, its wings seeming to spin faster and faster.

I was petrified. I thought I would pass out if those palpitating wings touched me. There was something in the bird's senseless movements that revolted me. I also thought it was going to damage itself, break one of those thin wing-bones, perhaps, and then it would be lying on the floor, dying, like the pimpled and horribly featherless baby birds we saw sometimes on the sidewalks in the spring when they had fallen out of their nests. I was not any longer worried about the sparrow. I wanted only to avoid the sight of it lying broken on the floor. Viciously, I thought that if Noreen said, *God sees the little sparrow fall*, I would kick her in the shins. She did not, how-ever, say this.

"A bird in the house means a death in the house," Noreen remarked.

Shaken, I pulled my glance away from the whirling wings and looked at Noreen. "What?"

"That's what I've heard said, anyhow."

The sparrow had exhausted itself. It lay on the floor, spent and trembling. I could not bring myself to touch it. Noreen bent and picked it up. She cradled it with great gentleness between her cupped hands. Then we took it downstairs, and when I had opened the back door, Noreen set the bird free.

"Poor little scrap," she said, and I felt struck to the heart, knowing she had been concerned all along about the sparrow, while I, perfidiously, in the chaos of the moment, had been concerned only about myself.

"Wanna do some with the Ouija board, Vanessa?" Noreen asked.

I shivered a little, perhaps only because of the blast of cold air which had come into the kitchen when the door was opened.

"No thanks, Noreen. Like I said, I got my homework to do. But thanks all the same."

"That's okay," Noreen said in her guileless voice. "Any time."

But whenever she mentioned the Ouija board or the talking table, after that, I al-ways found some excuse not to consult these oracles.

"Do you want to come to church with me this evening, Vanessa?" my father asked.

"How come you're going to the evening service?" I enquired.

"Well, we didn't go this morning. We went snowshoeing instead, remember? I think your grandmother was a little bit put out about it. She went alone this morn-ing. I guess it wouldn't hurt you and me to go now."

We walked through the dark, along the white streets, the snow squeaking dryly under our feet. The streetlights were placed at long intervals along the sidewalks, and around each pole the circle of flimsy light created glistening points of blue and crystal on the crusted snow. I would have liked to take my father's hand, as I used to do, but I was too old for that now. I walked beside him, taking long steps so he would not have to walk more slowly on my account.

The sermon bored me, and I began leafing through the Hymnary for entertainment. I must have drowsed, for the next thing I knew, my father was prodding me and we were on our feet for the closing hymn.

Near the Cross, near the Cross,
Be my glory ever,
Till my ransomed soul shall find
Rest beyond the river.

I knew the tune well, so I sang loudly for the first verse. But the music to that hymn is sombre, and all at once the words themselves seemed too dreadful to be sung. I stopped singing, my throat knotted. I thought I was going to cry, but I did not know why, except that the song recalled to me my Grandmother Connor, who had been dead only a year now. I wondered why her soul needed to be ransomed. If God did not think she was good enough just as she was, then I did not have much use for His opinion. *Rest beyond the river*—was that what had happened to her? She had believed in Heaven, but I did not think that rest beyond the river was quite what she had in mind. To think of her in Noreen's flashy Heaven, though—that was even worse.

Someplace where nobody ever got annoyed or had to be smoothed down and placated, someplace where there were never any family scenes—that would have suited my Grandmother Connor. Maybe she wouldn't have minded a certain amount of rest beyond the river, at that.

When we had the silent prayer, I looked at my father. He sat with his head bowed and his eyes closed. He was frowning deeply, and I could see the pulse in his temple. I wondered then what he believed. I did not have any real idea what it might be. When he raised his head, he did not look uplifted or anything like that. He merely looked tired. Then Reverend McKee pronounced the benediction, and we could go home.

"What do you think about all that stuff, Dad?" I asked hesitantly, as we walked.

"What stuff, honey?"

"Oh, Heaven and Hell, and like that."

My father laughed. "Have you been listening to Noreen too much? Well, I don't know. I don't think they're actual places. Maybe they stand for something that happens all the time here, or else doesn't happen. It's kind of hard to explain. I guess I'm not so good at explanations."

Nothing seemed to have been made any clearer to me. I reached out and took his hand, not caring that he might think this a babyish gesture.

"I hate that hymn!"

"Good Lord," my father said in astonishment. "Why, Vanessa?"

But I did not know and so could not tell him.

Many people in Manawaka had flu that winter, so my father and Dr. Cates were kept extremely busy. I had flu myself, and spent a week in bed, vomiting only the first day and after that enjoying poor health, as my mother put it, with Noreen bringing me ginger ale and orange juice, and each evening my father putting a wooden tongue-depressor into my mouth and peering down my throat, then smiling and saying he thought I might live after all.

Then my father got sick himself, and had to stay at home and go to bed. This was such an unusual occurrence that it amused me.

"Doctors shouldn't get sick," I told him.

"You're right," he said. "That was pretty bad management."

"Run along now, dear," my mother said.

That night I woke and heard voices in the upstairs hall. When I went out, I found my mother and Grandmother MacLeod, both in their dressing-gowns. With them was Dr. Cates. I did not go immediately to my mother, as I would have done only a year before. I stood in the doorway of my room, squinting against the sudden light.

"Mother—what is it?"

She turned, and momentarily I saw the look on her face before she erased it and put on a contrived calm.

"It's all right," she said. "Dr. Cates has just come to have a look at Daddy. You go on back to sleep."

The wind was high that night, and I lay and listened to it rattling the storm windows and making the dry and winter-stiffened vines of the Virginia creeper scratch like small persistent claws against the red brick. In the morning, my mother told me that my father had developed pneumonia.

Dr. Cates did not think it would be safe to move my father to the hospital. My mother began sleeping in the spare bedroom, and after she had been there for a few nights, I asked if I could sleep in there too. I thought she would be bound to ask me why, and I did not know what I would say, but she did not ask. She nodded, and in some way her easy agreement upset me.

That night Dr. Cates came again, bringing with him one of the nurses from the hospital. My mother stayed upstairs with them. I sat with Grandmother MacLeod in the living room. That was the last place in the world I wanted to be, but I thought she would be offended if I went off. She sat as straight and rigid as a totem pole, and embroidered away at the needlepoint cushion cover she was doing. I perched on the edge of the chesterfield and kept my eyes fixed on *The White Company* by Conan Doyle, and from time to time I turned a page. I had already read it three times before, but luckily Grandmother MacLeod did not know that. At nine o'clock she looked at her gold brooch watch, which she always wore pinned to her dress, and told me to go to bed, so I did that.

I wakened in darkness. At first, it seemed to me that I was in my own bed, and everything was as usual, with my parents in their room, and Roddie curled up in the crib in his room, and Grandmother MacLeod sleeping with her mouth open in her enormous spool bed, surrounded by half a dozen framed photos of Uncle Roderick and only one of my father, and Noreen snoring fitfully in the room next to mine, with the dark flames of her hair spreading out across the pillow, and the pink and silver motto cards from the Tabernacle stuck with adhesive tape onto the wall beside her bed— *Lean on Him, Emmanuel Is My Refuge, Rock of Ages Cleft for Me.*

Then in the total night around me, I heard a sound. It was my mother, and she was crying, not loudly at all, but from somewhere very deep inside her. I sat up in bed. Everything seemed to have stopped, not only time but my own heart and blood as well. Then my mother noticed that I was awake.

I did not ask her, and she did not tell me anything. There was no need. She held me in her arms, or I held her, I am not certain which. And after a while the first mourning stopped, too, as everything does sooner or later, for when the limits of endurance have been reached, then people must sleep.

In the days following my father's death, I stayed close beside my mother, and this was only partly for my own consoling. I also had the feeling that she needed my protection. I did not know from what, nor what I could possibly do, but something held me there. Reverend McKee called, and I sat with my grandmother and my mother in the living room. My mother told me I did not need to stay unless I wanted to, but I refused to go. What I thought chiefly was that he would speak of the healing power of prayer, and all that, and it would be bound to make my mother cry again. And in fact, it happened in just that way, but when it actually came, I could not protect her from this assault. I could only sit.

My mother tried not to cry unless she was alone or with me. I also tried, but neither of us was entirely successful. Grandmother MacLeod, on the other hand, was never seen crying, not even the day of my father's funeral. But that day, when we had returned to the house and she had taken off her black velvet overshoes and her heavy sealskin coat with its black fur that was the softest thing I had ever touched, she stood in the hallway and for the first time she looked unsteady. When I reached out instinctively towards her, she sighed.

"That's right," she said. "You might just take my arm while I go upstairs, Vanessa."

That was the most my Grandmother MacLeod ever gave in, to anyone's sight. I left her in her bedroom, sitting on the straight chair beside her bed and looking at the picture of my father that had been taken when he graduated from medical college. Maybe she was sorry now that she had only the one photograph of him, but whatever she felt, she did not say.

I went down into the kitchen. I had scarcely spoken to Noreen since my father's death. This had not been done on purpose. I simply had not seen her. I had not really seen anyone except my mother. Looking at Noreen now, I suddenly recalled the sparrow. I felt physically sick, remembering the fearful darting and plunging of those wings, and the fact that it was I who had opened the window and let it in. Then an inexplicable fury took hold of me, some terrifying need to hurt, burn, destroy. Absolutely without warning, either to her or to myself, I hit Noreen as hard as I could. When she swung around, appalled, I hit out at her once more, my arms and legs flailing. Her hands snatched at my wrists, and she held me, but still I continued to struggle, fighting blindly, my eyes tightly closed, as though she were a prison all around me and I was battling to get out. Finally, too shocked at myself to go on, I went limp in her grasp and she let me drop to the floor.

"Vanessa! I never done one single solitary thing to you, and here you go hitting and scratching me like that! What in the world has got into you?"

I began to say I was sorry, which was certainly true, but I did not say it. I could not say anything.

"You're not yourself, what with your dad and everything," she excused me. "I been praying every night that your dad is with God, Vanessa. I know he wasn't actually saved in the regular way, but still and all—"

"Shut up," I said.

Something in my voice made her stop talking. I rose from the floor and stood in the kitchen doorway.

"He didn't need to be saved," I went on coldly, distinctly. "And he is not in Heaven, because there is no Heaven. And it doesn't matter, see? *It doesn't matter!*"

Noreen's face looked peculiarly vulnerable now, her high wide cheekbones and puzzled childish eyes, and the thick russet tangle of her hair. I had not hurt her much before, when I hit her. But I had hurt her now, hurt her in some inexcusable way. Yet I sensed, too, that already she was gaining some satisfaction out of feeling sorrowful about my disbelief.

I went upstairs to my room. Momentarily I felt a sense of calm, almost of acceptance. *Rest beyond the river.* I knew now what that meant. It meant Nothing. It meant only silence, forever.

Then I lay down on my bed and spent the last of my tears, or what seemed then to be the last. Because, despite what I had said to Noreen, it did matter. It mattered, but there was no help for it.

Everything changed after my father's death. The MacLeod house could not be kept up any longer. My mother sold it to a local merchant who subsequently covered the deep red of the brick over, with yellow stucco. Something about the house had always made me uneasy—that tower room where Grandmother MacLeod's potted plants drooped in a lethargic and lime-green confusion, those long stairways and hidden places, the attic which I had always imagined to be dwelt in by the spirits of the family dead, that gigantic portrait of the Duke of Wellington at the top of the stairs. It was never an endearing house. And yet when it was no longer ours, and when the Virginia creeper had been torn down and the dark walls turned to a light marigold, I went out of my way to avoid walking past, for it seemed to me that the house had lost the stern dignity that was its very heart.

Noreen went back to the farm. My mother and brother and myself moved into Grandfather Connor's house. Grandmother MacLeod went to live with Aunt Morag in Winnipeg. It was harder for her than for anyone, because so much of her life was bound up with the MacLeod house. She was fond of Aunt Morag, but that hardly counted. Her men were gone, her husband and her sons, and a family whose men are gone is no family at all. The day she left, my mother and I did not know what to say. Grandmother MacLeod looked even smaller than usual in her fur coat and her black velvet toque. She became extremely agitated about trivialities, and fussed about the possibility of the taxi not arriving on time. She had forbidden us to accompany her to the station. About my father, or the house, or anything important, she did not say a word. Then, when the taxi had finally arrived, she turned to my mother.

"Roddie will have Ewen's seal ring, of course, with the MacLeod crest on it," she said. "But there is another seal as well, don't forget, the larger one with the crest and motto. It's meant to be worn on a watch chain. I keep it in my jewel-box. It was Roderick's. Roddie's to have that, too, when I die. Don't let Morag talk you out of it."

During the Second World War, when I was seventeen and in love with an airman who did not love me, and desperately anxious to get away from Manawaka and from my grandfather's house, I happened one day to be going through the old mahogany desk that had belonged to my father. It had a number of small drawers inside, and I accidentally pulled one of these all the way out. Behind it there was another drawer, one I had not known about. Curiously, I opened it. Inside there was a letter written on almost transparent paper in a cramped angular handwriting. It began—*Cher Monsieur Ewen*—That was all I could make out, for the writing was nearly impossible to read and my French was not good. It was dated 1919. With it, there was a picture of a girl, looking absurdly old-fashioned to my eyes, like the faces on long-discarded calendars or chocolate boxes. But beneath the dated quality of the photograph, she seemed neither expensive nor cheap. She looked like what she probably had been—an ordinary middle-class girl, but in another country. She wore her hair in long ringlets, and her mouth was shaped into a sweetly sad posed smile like Mary Pickford's. That was all. There was nothing else in the drawer.

I looked for a long time at the girl, and hoped she had meant some momentary and unexpected freedom. I remembered what he had said to me, after I hadn't gone to the Remembrance Day parade.

"What are you doing, Vanessa?" my mother called from the kitchen.

"Nothing," I replied.

I took the letter and picture outside and burned them. That was all I could do for him. Now that we might have talked together, it was many years too late. Perhaps it would not have been possible anyway. I did not know.

As I watched the smile of the girl turn into scorched paper, I grieved for my father as though he had just died now.

[1970]

Questions

1. What aspects of religious faith and doubt, as well as conceptions of heaven and hell, trouble Vanessa MacLeod? How does she resolve her spiritual questions?
2. What is Noreen's role in the story?
3. What kind of childhood and family are depicted in the story?
4. Why does Vanessa burn the photograph and letter that had belonged to her father?

Ursula K. Le Guin

(b. 1929)
United States

Ursula Le Guin is the daughter of two distinguished parents: anthropologist Alfred Kroeber, an expert on the Indians of California, and Theodora Kroeber, a writer. Le Guin acknowledges that the form her own career took bears the influence of both of her parents. Her father sought out other cultures, including their myths, legends, and languages; she has preferred to invent cultures, creating their myths, legends, and languages. Growing up in Berkeley, California, within a highly literate and intellectual environment, Le Guin later went on to study literature at Radcliffe and received her M.A. from Columbia (1952). On a Fulbright grant to France, she met and later married historian Charles Le Guin.

Le Guin's early fiction was a mixture of elements of fantasy and science fiction, and her protagonists were mostly male. Her writing reached a turning point with The Left Hand of Darkness (1969), in which she provocatively explored the issue of gender itself: In the invented chilly world of Gethen, biologically androgynous beings may choose to mother as well as to father children. Eventually Le Guin distinguished between her pure fantasy writing—what she calls "Inner Lands"—and her science fiction—the realm of "Outer Space." Her books in both genres have frequently been honored by Nebula and Hugo awards; she received the National Book Award in 1973 for her novel The Farthest Shore (1972), the final novel of the Earthsea fantasy trilogy for children (also including A Wizard of Earthsea, 1968, and The Tombs of Atuan, 1971).

Much of Le Guin's fiction, whether classified as fantasy or science fiction, challenges cultural assumptions. By imaginatively altering reality, whether through ideas concerning gender and male–female relationships, time and space, or language and other element's of culture, Le Guin examines pressing issues within our own cultural reality. As she phrases it, "Realism is perhaps the least adequate means of understanding or portraying the incredible realities of our existence. . . ." In fact, through her diverse "alien" characters and creatures, she expresses her profound moral vision and her concern for decidedly human dilemmas. Her most recent novel, The Telling (2000), despite its extraterrestrial setting and alternate time, is really about the way we live in this world and at this time.

Critics have identified as a central vision in Le Guin's writing—both fantasy and science fiction—the ideal of wholeness or integration as well as the pursuit of a balance between the individual and society. Expressing the moral vision that underlies all of her fiction, Le Guin made the following comment in her acceptance speech for the National Book Award in 1973:

> The fantasist, whether he uses the ancient archetypes of myth and legend or the younger ones of science and technology, may be talking as seriously as any sociologists—and a good deal more directly—about human life as it is lived, and as it might be lived, and as it ought to be lived. For after all, as great scientists have said and all children know, it is above all by the imagination that we achieve perception, and compassion, and hope.

The Map in the Attic

SUR[1]

A Summary Report of the Yelcho Expedition to the Antarctic, 1909–1910

Although I have no intention of publishing this report, I think it would be nice if a grandchild of mine, or somebody's grandchild, happened to find it some day; so I shall keep it in the leather trunk in the attic, along with Rosita's christening dress and Juanito's silver rattle and my wedding shoes and finneskos.[2]

---

[1]*sur* Spanish: south.
[2]*finneskos* Reindeer-skin boots.

The first requisite for mounting an expedition—money—is normally the hardest to come by. I grieve that even in a report destined for a trunk in the attic of a house in a very quiet suburb of Lima I dare not write the name of the generous benefactor, the great soul without whose unstinting liberality the *Yelcho* Expedition would never have been more than the idlest excursion into daydream. That our equipment was the best and most modern—that our provisions were plentiful and fine—that a ship of the Chilean Government, with her brave officers and gallant crew, was twice sent halfway round the world for our convenience: all this is due to that benefactor whose name, alas! I must not say, but whose happiest debtor I shall be till death.

When I was little more than a child my imagination was caught by a newspaper account of the voyage of the *Belgica*, which, sailing south from Tierra del Fuego, became beset by ice in the Bellingshausen Sea and drifted a whole year with the floe, the men aboard her suffering a great deal from want of food and from the terror of the unending winter darkness. I read and reread that account, and later followed with excitement the reports of the rescue of Dr. Nordenskjold from the South Shetland Isles by the dashing Captain Irizar of the *Uruguay*, and the adventures of the *Scotia* in the Weddell Sea. But all these exploits were to me but forerunners of the British National Antarctic Expedition of 1902–1904, in the *Discovery*, and the wonderful account of that expedition by Captain Scott.[3] This book, which I ordered from London and reread a thousand times, filled me with longing to see with my own eyes that strange continent, last Thule[4] of the South, which lies on our maps and globes like a white cloud, a void, fringed here and there with scraps of coastline, dubious capes, supposititious islands, headlands that may or may not be there: Antarctica. And the desire was as pure as the polar snows: to go, to see—no more, no less. I deeply respect the scientific accomplishments of Captain Scott's expedition, and have read with passionate interest the findings of physicists, meteorologists, biologists, etc.; but having had no training in any science, nor any opportunity for such training, my ignorance obliged me to forego any thought of adding to the body of scientific knowledge concerning Antarctica; and the same is true for all the members of my expedition. It seems a pity; but there was nothing we could do about it. Our goal was limited to observation and exploration. We hoped to go a little farther, perhaps, and see a little more; if not, simply to go and to see. A simple ambition, I think, and essentially a modest one.

Yet it would have remained less than an ambition, no more than a longing, but for the support and encouragement of my dear cousin and friend Juana————(I use no surnames, lest this report fall into strangers' hands at last, and embarrassment or unpleasant notoriety thus be brought upon unsuspecting husbands, sons, etc.). I had lent Juana my copy of *The Voyage of the Discovery*, and it was she who, as we strolled beneath our parasols across the Plaza de Armas after Mass one Sunday in 1908, said, "Well, if Captain Scott can do it, why can't we?"

It was Juana who proposed that we write Carlota————in Valparaiso. Through Carlota we met our benefactor, and so obtained our money, our ship, and even the plausible pretext of going on retreat in a Bolivian convent, which some of us were

---

[3]*Robert Falcon Scott* (1868–1912) British explorer and naval officer who commanded an expedition to explore the Ross Sea region of Antarctica (1901–1904).

[4]*Thule* Among the ancients, the northernmost region of the world, also understood as the ultimate or furthest goal, "Ultima Thule."

forced to employ (while the rest of us said we were going to Paris for the winter season). And it was my Juana who in the darkest moments remained resolute, unshaken in her determination to achieve our goal.

And there were dark moments, especially in the early months of 1909—times when I did not see how the Expedition would ever become more than a quarter ton of pemmican gone to waste and a lifelong regret. It was so very hard to gather our expeditionary force together! So few of those we asked even knew what we were talking about—so many thought we were mad, or wicked, or both! And of those few who shared our folly, still fewer were able, when it came to the point, to leave their daily duties and commit themselves to a voyage of at least six months, attended with not inconsiderable uncertainty and danger. An ailing parent; an anxious husband beset by business cares; a child at home with only ignorant or incompetent servants to look after it: these are not responsibilities lightly to be set aside. And those who wished to evade such claims were not the companions we wanted in hard work, risk, and privation.

But since success crowned our efforts, why dwell on the setbacks and delays, or the wretched contrivances and downright lies that we all had to employ? I look back with regret only to those friends who wished to come with us but could not, by any contrivance, get free—those we had to leave behind to a life without danger, without uncertainty, without hope.

On the seventeenth of August, 1909, in Punta Arenas, Chile, all the members of the Expedition met for the first time: Juana and I, the two Peruvians; from Argentina, Zoe, Berta, and Teresa; and our Chileans, Carlota and her friends Eva, Pepita, and Dolores. At the last moment I had received word that Maria's husband, in Quito, was ill, and she must stay to nurse him, so we were nine, not ten. Indeed, we had resigned ourselves to being but eight, when, just as night fell, the indomitable Zoe arrived in a tiny pirogue manned by Indians, her yacht having sprung a leak just as it entered the Strait of Magellan.

That night before we sailed we began to get to know one another; and we agreed, as we enjoyed our abominable supper in the abominable seaport inn of Punta Arenas, that if a situation arose of such urgent danger that one voice must be obeyed without present question, the unenviable honor of speaking with that voice should fall first upon myself: if I were incapacitated, upon Carlota: if she, then upon Berta. We three were then toasted as "Supreme Inca," "La Araucana,"[5] and "The Third Mate," among a lot of laughter and cheering. As it came out, to my very great pleasure and relief, my qualities as a "leader" were never tested; the nine of us worked things out amongst us from beginning to end without any orders being given by anybody, and only two or three times with recourse to a vote by voice or show of hands. To be sure, we argued a good deal. But then, we had time to argue. And one way or another the arguments always ended up in a decision, upon which action could be taken. Usually at least one person grumbled about the decision, sometimes bitterly. But what is life without grumbling, and the occasional opportunity to say, "I told you so"? How could one bear housework, or looking after babies, let alone the rigors of sledge-hauling in Antarctica, without grumbling? Officers—as we came to understand aboard the *Yelcho*—are forbidden to grumble; but we nine were, and are, by birth and upbringing, unequivocally, all crew.

---

[5]*Inca, La Araucana*   Indians who occupied Chile before the Spanish conquest.

Though our shortest course to the southern continent, and that originally urged upon us by the captain of our good ship, was to the South Shetlands and the Bellingshausen Sea, or else by the South Orkneys into the Weddell Sea, we planned to sail west to the Ross Sea, which Captain Scott had explored and described, and from which the brave Ernest Shackleton[6] had returned only the previous autumn. More was known about this region than any other portion of the coast of Antarctica, and though that more was not much, yet it served as some insurance of the safety of the ship, which we felt we had no right to imperil. Captain Pardo had fully agreed with us after studying the charts and our planned itinerary; and so it was westward that we took our course out of the Strait next morning.

Our journey half round the globe was attended by fortune. The little *Yelcho* steamed cheerily along through gale and gleam, climbing up and down those seas of the Southern Ocean that run unbroken round the world. Juana, who had fought bulls and the far more dangerous cows on her family's *estancia*, called the ship "*la vaca valiente*"[7] because she always returned to the charge. Once we got over being seasick we all enjoyed the sea voyage, though oppressed at times by the kindly but officious protectiveness of the captain and his officers, who felt that we were only "safe" when huddled up in the three tiny cabins which they had chivalrously vacated for our use.

We saw our first iceberg much farther south than we had looked for it, and saluted it with Veuve Clicquot[8] at dinner. The next day we entered the ice pack, the belt of floes and bergs, broken loose from the land ice and winter-frozen seas of Antarctica, which drifts northward in the spring. Fortune still smiled on us: our little steamer, incapable, with her unreinforced metal hull, of forcing a way into the ice, picked her way from lane to lane without hesitation, and on the third day we were through the pack, in which ships have sometimes struggled for weeks and been obliged to turn back at last. Ahead of us now lay the dark grey waters of the Ross Sea, and beyond that, on the horizon, the remote glimmer, the cloud-reflected whiteness of the Great Ice Barrier.

Entering the Ross Sea a little east of Longitude West 160°, we came in sight of the Barrier at the place where Captain Scott's party, finding a bight in the vast wall of ice, had gone ashore and sent up their hydrogen-gas balloon for reconnaissance and photography. The towering face of the Barrier, its sheer cliffs and azure and violet waterworn caves, all were as described, but the location had changed: instead of a narrow bight there was a considerable bay, full of the beautiful and terrific orca whales playing and spouting in the sunshine of that brilliant southern spring.

Evidently masses of ice many acres in extent had broken away from the Barrier (which—at least for most of its vast extent—does not rest on land but floats on water) since the *Discovery's* passage in 1902. This put our plan to set up camp on the Barrier itself in a new light; and while we were discussing alternatives, we asked Captain Pardo to take the ship west along the Barrier face towards Ross Island and McMurdo Sound. As the sea was clear of ice and quite calm, he was happy to do so, and, when we sighted the smoke plume of Mount Erebus, to share in our celebration—another half case of Veuve Clicquot.

---

[6]*Ernest Shackleton* (1874–1922)   Member of the British Antarctic expedition led by Scott.
[7]*la vaca valiente*   Spanish: the fine cow; *estancia*   Spanish: cattle ranch.
[8]*Veuve Cliquot*   Expensive French champagne.

The *Yelcho* anchored in Arrival Bay, and we went ashore in the ship's boat. I cannot describe my emotions when I set foot on the earth, on that earth, the barren, cold gravel at the foot of the long volcanic slope. I felt elation, impatience, gratitude, awe, familiarity. I felt that I was home at last. Eight Adélie penguins immediately came to greet us with many exclamations of interest not unmixed with disapproval. "Where on earth have you been? What took you so long? The Hut is around this way. Please come this way. Mind the rocks!" They insisted on our going to visit Hut Point, where the large structure built by Captain Scott's party stood, looking just as in the photographs and drawings that illustrate his book. The area about it, however, was disgusting—a kind of graveyard of seal skins, seal bones, penguin bones, and rubbish, presided over by the mad, screaming skua gulls. Our escorts waddled past the slaughterhouse in all tranquility, and one showed me personally to the door, though it would not go in.

The interior of the hut was less offensive, but very dreary. Boxes of supplies had been stacked up into a kind of room within the room; it did not look as I had imagined it when the *Discovery* party put on their melodramas and minstrel shows in the long night. (Much later, we learned that Sir Ernest had rearranged it a good deal when he was there just a year before us.) It was dirty, and had about it a mean disorder. A pound tin of tea was standing open. Empty meat tins lay about; biscuits were spilled on the floor; a lot of dog turds were underfoot—frozen, of course, but not a great deal improved by that. No doubt the last occupants had had to leave in a hurry, perhaps even in a blizzard. All the same, they could have closed the tea tin. But housekeeping, the art of the infinite, is no game for amateurs.

Teresa proposed that we use the hut as our camp. Zoe counterproposed that we set fire to it. We finally shut the door and left it as we had found it. The penguins appeared to approve, and cheered us all the way to the boat.

McMurdo Sound was free of ice, and Captain Pardo now proposed to take us off Ross Island and across to Victoria Land, where we might camp at the foot of the Western Mountains, on dry and solid earth. But those mountains, with their storm-darkened peaks and hanging cirques and glaciers, looked as awful as Captain Scott had found them on his western journey, and none of us felt much inclined to seek shelter among them.

Aboard the ship that night we decided to go back and set up our base as we had originally planned, on the Barrier itself. For all available reports indicated that the clear way south was across the level Barrier surface until one could ascend one of the confluent glaciers to the high plateau which appears to form the whole interior of the continent. Captain Pardo argued strongly against this plan, asking what would become of us if the Barrier "calved"—if our particular acre of ice broke away and started to drift northward. "Well," said Zoe, "then you won't have to come so far to meet us." But he was so persuasive on this theme that he persuaded himself into leaving one of the *Yelcho*'s boats with us when we camped, as a means of escape. We found it useful for fishing, later on.

My first steps on Antarctic soil, my only visit to Ross Island, had not been pleasure unalloyed. I thought of the words of the English poet:

Though every prospect pleases,
and only Man is vile.

But then, the backside of heroism is often rather sad; women and servants know that. They know also that the heroism may be no less real for that. But achievement is smaller than men think. What is large is the sky, the earth, the sea, the soul. I looked back as the ship sailed east again that evening. We were well into September now, with ten hours or more of daylight. The spring sunset fingered on the twelve-thousand-foot peak of Erebus and shone rosy gold on her long plume of steam. The steam from our own small funnel faded blue on the twilit water as we crept along under the towering pale wall of ice.

On our return to "Orca Bay"—Sir Ernest, we learned years later, had named it the Bay of Whales—we found a sheltered nook where the Barrier edge was low enough to provide fairly easy access from the ship. The *Yelcho* put out her ice anchor, and the next long, hard days were spent in unloading our supplies and setting up our camp on the ice, a half kilometer in from the edge: a task in which the *Yelcho's* crew lent us invaluable aid and interminable advice. We took all the aid gratefully, and most of the advice with salt.

The weather so far had been extraordinarily mild for spring in this latitude; the temperature had not yet gone below—20° Fahrenheit, and there was only one blizzard while we were setting up camp. But Captain Scott had spoken feelingly of the bitter south winds on the Barrier, and we had planned accordingly. Exposed as our camp was to every wind, we built no rigid structures above ground. We set up tents to shelter in while we dug out a series of cubicles in the ice itself, lined them with hay insulation and pine boarding, and roofed them with canvas over bamboo poles, covered with snow for weight and insulation. The big central room was instantly named Buenos Aires by our Argentineans, to whom the center, wherever one is, is always Buenos Aires. The heating and cooking stove was in Buenos Aires. The storage tunnels and the privy (called Punta Arenas) got some back heat from the stove. The sleeping cubicles opened off Buenos Aires, and were very small, mere tubes into which one crawled feet first; they were lined deeply with hay and soon warmed by one's body warmth. The sailors called them "coffins" and "wormholes," and looked with horror on our burrows in the ice. But our little warren or prairie-dog village served us well, permitting us as much warmth and privacy as one could reasonably expect under the circumstances. If the *Yelcho* was unable to get through the ice in February, and we had to spend the winter in Antarctica, we certainly could do so, though on very limited rations. For this coming summer, our base—Sudamérica del Sur, South South America, but we generally called it the Base—was intended merely as a place to sleep, to store our provisions, and to give shelter from blizzards.

To Berta and Eva, however, it was more than that. They were its chief architect-designers, its most ingenious builder-excavators, and its most diligent and contented occupants, forever inventing an improvement in ventilation, or learning how to make skylights, or revealing to us a new addition to our suite of rooms, dug in the living ice. It was thanks to them that our stores were stowed so handily, that our stove drew and heated so efficiently, and that Buenos Aires, where nine people cooked, ate, worked, conversed, argued, grumbled, painted, played the guitar and banjo, and kept the Expedition's library of books and maps, was a marvel of comfort and convenience. We lived there in real amity; and if you simply had to be alone for a while, you crawled into your sleeping hole head first.

Berta went a little farther. When she had done all she could to make South South America livable, she dug out one more cell just under the ice surface, leaving a nearly transparent sheet of ice like a greenhouse roof; and there, alone, she worked at sculptures. They were beautiful forms, some like a blending of the reclining human figure with the subtle curves and volumes of the Weddell seal, others like the fantastic shapes of ice cornices and ice caves. Perhaps they are there still, under the snow, in the bubble in the Great Barrier. There where she made them they might last as long as stone. But she could not bring them north. That is the penalty for carving in water.

Captain Pardo was reluctant to leave us, but his orders did not permit him to hang about the Ross Sea indefinitely, and so at last, with many earnest injunctions to us to stay put—make no journeys—take no risks—beware of frostbite—don't use edge tools—look out for cracks in the ice—and a heartfelt promise to return to Orca Bay on the twentieth of February, or as near that date as wind and ice would permit, the good man bade us farewell, and his crew shouted us a great goodbye cheer as they weighed anchor. That evening, in the long orange twilight of October, we saw the top-mast of the *Yelcho* go down the north horizon, over the edge of the world, leaving us to ice, and silence, and the Pole.

That night we began to plan the Southern journey.

The ensuing month passed in short practice trips and depotlaying. The life we had led at home, though in its own way strenuous, had not fitted any of us for the kind of strain met with in sledge-hauling at ten or twenty degrees below freezing. We all needed as much working-out as possible before we dared undertake a long haul.

My longest exploratory trip, made with Dolores and Carlota, was southwest towards Mount Markham, and it was a nightmare—blizzards and pressure ice all the way out, crevasses and no view of the mountains when we got there, and white weather and sastrugi[9] all the way back. The trip was useful, however, in that we could begin to es-timate our capacities; and also in that we had started out with a very heavy load of provisions, which we depoted at 100 and 130 miles SSW of Base. Thereafter other parties pushed on farther, till we had a line of snow cairns and depots right down to Latitude 83°43', where Juana and Zoe, on an exploring trip, had found a kind of stone gateway opening on a great glacier leading south. We established these depots to avoid, if possible, the hunger that had bedevilled Captain Scott's Southern Party, and the consequent misery and weakness. And we also established to our own satis-faction—intense satisfaction—that we were sledgehaulers at least as good as Cap-tain Scott's husky dogs. Of course we could not have expected to pull as much or as fast as his men. That we did so was because we were favored by much better weath-er than Captain Scott's party ever met on the Barrier; and also the quantity and qual-ity of our food made a very considerable difference. I am sure that the fifteen percent of dried fruits in our pemmican helped prevent scurvy; and the potatoes, frozen and dried according to an ancient Andean Indian method, were very nourishing yet very light and compact—perfect sledging rations. In any case, it was with considerable confidence in our capacities that we made ready at last for the Southern journey.

The Southern Party consisted of two sledge teams: Juana, Dolores, and myself; Carlota, Pepita, and Zoe. The support team of Berta, Eva, and Teresa set out before us with a heavy load of supplies, going right up onto the glacier to prospect routes and leave depots of supplies for our return journey. We followed five days behind them, and met them returning between Depot Ercilla and Depot Miranda (see map). That "night"—of course there was no real darkness—we were all nine together in the heart of the level plain of ice. It was the fifteenth of November, Dolores's birthday. We cel-ebrated by putting eight ounces of pisco[10] in the hot chocolate, and became very

---

[9]*sastrugi* Wavelike ridges of hard snow.
[10]*pisco* Peruvian brandy.

merry. We sang. It is strange now to remember how thin our voices sounded in that great silence. It was overcast, white weather, without shadows and without visible horizon or any feature to break the level; there was nothing to see at all. We had come to that white place on the map, that void, and there we flew and sang like sparrows.

After sleep and a good breakfast the Base Party continued north, and the Southern Party sledged on. The sky cleared presently. High up, thin clouds passed over very rapidly from southwest to northeast, but down on the Barrier it was calm and just cold enough, five or ten degrees below freezing, to give a firm surface for hauling.

On the level ice we never pulled less than eleven miles, seventeen kilometers, a day, and generally fifteen or sixteen miles, twenty-five kilometers. (Our instruments, being British made, were calibrated in feet, miles, degrees Fahrenheit, etc., but we often converted miles to kilometers because the larger numbers sounded more encouraging.) At the time we left South America, we knew only that Mr. Shackleton had mounted another expedition to the Antarctic in 1908, had tried to attain the Pole but failed, and had returned to England in June of the current year, 1909. No coherent report of his explorations had yet reached South America when we left; we did not know what route he had gone, or how far he had got. But we were not altogether taken by surprise when, far across the featureless white plain, tiny beneath the mountain peaks and the strange silent flight of the rainbow-fringed cloud wisps, we saw a fluttering dot of black. We turned west from our course to visit it: a snow heap nearly buried by the winter's storms—a flag on a bamboo pole, a mere shred of threadbare cloth—an empty oilcan—and a few footprints standing some inches above the ice. In some conditions of weather the snow compressed under one's weight remains when the surrounding soft snow melts or is scoured away by the wind; and so these reversed footprints had been left standing all these months, like rows of cobbler's lasts—a queer, sight.

We met no other such traces on our way. In general I believe our course was somewhat east of Mr. Shackleton's. Juana, our surveyor, had trained herself well and was faithful and methodical in her sightings and readings, but our equipment was minimal—a theodolite on tripod legs, a sextant with artificial horizon, two compasses, and chronometers. We had only the wheel meter on the sledge to give distance actually travelled.

In any case, it was the day after passing Mr. Shackleton's waymark that I first saw clearly the great glacier among the mountains to the southwest, which was to give us a pathway from the sea level of the Barrier up to the altiplano,[11] ten thousand feet above. The approach was magnificent: a gateway formed by immense vertical domes and pillars of rock. Zoe and Juana had called the vast ice river that flowed through that gateway the Florence Nightingale Glacier, wishing to honor the British, who had been the inspiration and guide of our expedition; that very brave and very peculiar lady seemed to represent so much that is best, and strangest, in the island race. On maps, of course, this glacier bears the name Mr. Shackleton gave it, the Beardmore.

The ascent of the Nightingale was not easy. The way was open at first, and well marked by our support party, but after some days we came among terrible crevasses, a maze of hidden cracks, from a foot to thirty feet wide and from thirty to a thousand feet deep. Step by step we went, and step by step, and the way always upward now. We were fifteen days on the glacier. At first the weather was hot, up to 20° F., and

---

[11]*altiplano*   High plateau.

the hot nights without darkness were wretchedly uncomfortable in our small tents. And all of us suffered more or less from snowblindness just at the time when we wanted clear eyesight to pick our way among the ridges and crevasses of the tortured ice, and to see the wonders about and before us. For at every day's advance more great, nameless peaks came into view in the west and southwest, summit beyond summit, range beyond range, stark rock and snow in the unending noon.

We gave names to these peaks, not very seriously, since we did not expect our discoveries to come to the attention of geographers. Zoe had a gift for naming, and it is thanks to her that certain sketch maps in various suburban South American attics bear such curious features as "Bolívar's Big Nose," "I Am General Rosas,"[12] "The Cloudmaker," "Whose Toe?" and "Throne of Our Lady of the Southern Cross." And when at last we got up onto the altiplano, the great interior plateau, it was Zoe who called it the pampa, and maintained that we walked there among vast herds of invisible cattle, transparent cattle pastured on the spindrift snow, their gauchos[13] the restless, merciless winds. We were by then all a little crazy with exhaustion and the great altitude—twelve thousand feet—and the cold and the wind blowing and the luminous circles and crosses surrounding the suns, for often there were three or four suns in the sky, up there.

That is not a place where people have any business to be. We should have turned back; but since we had worked so hard to get there, it seemed that we should go on, at least for a while.

A blizzard came with very low temperatures, so we had to stay in the tents, in our sleeping bags, for thirty hours, a rest we all needed; though it was warmth we needed most, and there was no warmth on that terrible plain anywhere at all but in our veins. We huddled close together all that time. The ice we lay on is two miles thick.

It cleared suddenly and became, for the plateau, good weather: twelve below zero and the wind not very strong. We three crawled out of our tent and met the others crawling out of theirs. Carlota told us then that her group wished to turn back. Pepita had been feeling very ill; even after the rest during the blizzard, her temperature would not rise above 90°. Carlota was having trouble breathing. Zoe was perfectly fit, but much preferred staying with her friends and lending them a hand in difficulties to pushing on towards the Pole. So we put the four ounces of pisco which we had been keeping for Christmas into the breakfast cocoa, and dug out our tents, and loaded our sledges, and parted there in the white daylight on the bitter plain.

Our sledge was fairly light by now. We pulled on to the south. Juana calculated our position daily. On the twenty-second of December, 1909, we reached the South Pole. The weather was, as always, very cruel. Nothing of any kind marked the dreary whiteness. We discussed leaving some kind of mark or monument, a snow cairn, a tent pole and flag; but there seemed no particular reason to do so. Anything we could do, anything we were, was insignificant in that awful place. We put up the tent for shelter for an hour and made a cup of tea, and then struck "90° Camp." Dolores, standing patient as ever in her sledging harness, looked at the snow; it was so hard frozen that it showed no trace of our footprints coming, and she said, "Which way?"

"North," said Juana.

---

[12]*General Rosas* Juan Manuel de Rosas (1793–1877), Argentinian dictator; *Simon Bolívar* (1783–1830) Soldier-leader of the South American revolution for independence from Spain.
[13]*gauchos* cattlemen; *pampa* South American plains.

It was a joke, because at that particular place there is no other direction. But we did not laugh. Our lips were cracked with frostbite and hurt too much to let us laugh. So we started back, and the wind at our backs pushed us along, and dulled the knife edges of the waves of frozen snow.

All that week the blizzard wind pursued us like a pack of mad dogs. I cannot describe it. I wished we had not gone to the Pole. I think I wish it even now. But I was glad even then that we had left no sign there, for some man longing to be first might come some day, and find it, and know then what a fool he had been, and break his heart.

We talked, when we could talk, of catching up to Carlota's party, since they might be going slower than we. In fact they had used their tent as a sail to catch the following wind and had got far ahead of us. But in many places they had built snow cairns or left some sign for us; once Zoe had written on the lee side of a ten-foot sastruga, just as children write on the sand of the beach at Miraflores, "This Way Out!" The wind blowing over the frozen ridge had left the words perfectly distinct.

In the very hour that we began to descend the glacier, the weather turned warmer, and the mad dogs were left to howl forever tethered to the Pole. The distance that had taken us fifteen days going up we covered in only eight days going down. But the good weather that had aided us descending the Nightingale became a curse down on the Barrier ice, where we had looked forward to a kind of royal progress from depot to depot, eating our fill and taking our time for the last three hundred-odd miles. In a tight place on the glacier I lost my goggles—I was swinging from my harness at the time in a crevasse—and then Juana had broken hers when we had to do some rock climbing coming down to the Gateway. After two days in bright sunlight with only one pair of snow goggles to pass amongst us, we were all suffering badly from snowblindness. It became acutely painful to keep lookout for landmarks or depot flags, to take sightings, even to study the compass, which had to be laid down on the snow to steady the needle. At Concolorcorvo Depot, where there was a particularly good supply of food and fuel, we gave up, crawled into our sleeping bags with bandaged eyes, and slowly boiled alive like lobsters in the tent exposed to the relentless sun. The voices of Berta and Zoe were the sweetest sound I ever heard. A little concerned about us, they had skied south to meet us. They led us home to Base.

We recovered quite swiftly, but the altiplano left its mark. When she was very little, Rosita asked if a dog "had bitted Mama's toes." I told her Yes, a great, white, mad dog named Blizzard! My Rosita and my Juanito heard many stories when they were little, about that fearful dog and how it howled, and the transparent cattle of the invisible gauchos, and a river of ice eight thousand feet high called Nightingale, and how Cousin Juana drank a cup of tea standing on the bottom of the world under seven suns, and other fairy tales.

We were in for one severe shock when we reached Base at last. Teresa was pregnant. I must admit that my first response to the poor girl's big belly and sheepish look was anger—rage—fury. That one of us should have concealed anything, and such a thing, from the others! But Teresa had done nothing of the sort. Only those who had concealed from her what she most needed to know were to blame. Brought up by servants, with four years' schooling in a convent, and married at sixteen, the poor girl was still so ignorant at twenty years of age that she had thought it was "the cold weather" that made her miss her periods. Even this was not entirely stupid, for all of us on the Southern journey had seen our periods change or stop altogether as we experienced increasing cold, hunger, and fatigue. Teresa's appetite had begun to draw general attention; and then she had begun, as she said pathetically, "to get fat." The others were worried at the thought of all the sledge-hauling she had done, but she flourished, and the only problem was her positively insatiable appetite. As well as could be determined from her shy references to her last night on the hacienda with her husband, the baby was due at just about the same time as the *Yelcho*, the twentieth of February. But we had not been back from the Southern Journey two weeks when, on February 14, she went into labor.

Several of us had borne children and had helped with deliveries, and anyhow most of what needs to be done is fairly self-evident; but a first labor can be long and trying, and we were all anxious, while Teresa was frightened out of her wits. She kept calling for her José till she was as hoarse as a skua.[14] Zoe lost all patience at last and said, "By God, Teresa, if you say 'José!' once more I hope you have a penguin!" But what she had, after twenty long hours, was a pretty little red-faced girl.

Many were the suggestions for that child's name from her eight proud midwife-aunts: Polita, Penguina, McMurdo, Victoria. . . . But Teresa announced, after she had had a good sleep and a large serving of pemmican, "I shall name her Rosa—Rosa del Sur," Rose of the South. That night we drank the last two bottles of Veuve Clicquot (having finished the pisco at 88°30' South) in toasts to our little Rose.

On the nineteenth of February, a day early, my Juana came down into Buenos Aires in a hurry. "The ship," she said, "the ship has come," and she burst into tears—she who had never wept in all our weeks of pain and weariness on the long haul.

Of the return voyage there is nothing to tell. We came back safe.

In 1912 all the world learned that the brave Norwegian Amundsen[15] had reached the South Pole; and then, much later, came the accounts of how Captain Scott and his men had come there after him, but did not come home again.

Just this year, Juana and I wrote to the captain of the *Yelcho*, for the newspapers have been full of the story of his gallant dash to rescue Sir Ernest Shackleton's men from Elephant Island, and we wished to congratulate him, and once more to thank him. Never one word has he breathed of our secret. He is a man of honor, Luis Pardo.

I add this last note in 1929. Over the years we have lost touch with one another. It is very difficult for women to meet, when they live so far apart as we do. Since Juana died, I have seen none of my old sledgemates, though sometimes we write. Our little Rosa del Sur died of the scarlet fever when she was five years old. Teresa had many other children. Carlota took the veil in Santiago ten years ago. We are old women now, with old husbands, and grown children, and grandchildren who might some day like to read about the Expedition. Even if they are rather ashamed of having such a crazy grandmother, they may enjoy sharing in the secret. But they must not let Mr. Amundsen know! He would be terribly embarrassed and disappointed. There is no need for him or anyone else outside the family to know. We left no footprints, even.

[1982]

---

[14]*skua*   Predatory seagull.
[15]*Roald Amundsen* (1872–1928)   Norwegian explorer; first man to reach the South Pole.

Questions

1. What motivates the women's expedition? What are their goals? Are the ways in which they organize their group effort unusual or distinctive?
2. Why does the narrator feel that the women's expedition must remain unknown to history. Why do the women "leave no footprints, even"?
3. What does the narrator mean when she says that "achievement is smaller than men think. What is large is the sky, the earth, the sea, the soul."
4. Through which details does Le Guin impart a realistic quality to the story? What elements reveal it to be fantasy?

Doris Lessing

(b. 1919)

Rhodesia/England

Doris Lessing's life is literally as well as geographically and politically diverse. Born Doris May Tayler in Persia (now Iran) to English parents who moved from there to southern Africa, she grew up on a farm in Southern Rhodesia (now Zimbabwe). Apart from a brief period at school in Salisbury, she was self-educated at home; she began work as a secretary in Salisbury at the age of 16. Deeply sensitized to the inequities of the oppression of blacks in southern Africa, Lessing became actively involved in leftist politics for a time. Eventually, following two marriages that ended in divorce, she left Africa for England, where she has since resided.

Lessing's early fiction, begun in Africa, not only chronicles the political and social divisions of her time and place but also articulates the struggle for self-realization and independence of complex female characters, beginning with Mary Turner of her first novel, The Grass Is Singing (1950). As Lessing expressed her evolution as a writer in an interview with Minda Bikman, "I think most writers have to start very realistically because that's a way of establishing what they are, particularly women. . . . When you've found out [who you are], you can start making things up." Of the more than 20 novels Lessing has published, one of the most highly regarded is The Golden Notebook (1962), which anticipated central issues of the women's movement of the 1960s in an innovative, experimental narrative form. Other major novels include the five-novel series Children of Violence (1952–1969).

Turning to science fiction frameworks to express her concerns about the future, Lessing published Briefing for a Descent into Hell (1971), The Memoirs of a Survivor (1974), and the five-novel series Canopus at Argos: Archives (1979–1983). In her subsequent novels, including The Diaries of Jane Somers (1983–1984, originally published under the pseudonym Jane Somers), The Good Terrorist (1985), and The Fifth Child (1988), Lessing returned to more realistic narrative forms to explore contemporary moral and social issues. The Habit of Loving (1957), A Man and Two Women (1963), African Stories (1964), and several other collections of stories demonstrate the diversity of Lessing's subjects and the versatility of her style. Her most recent novel is Ben, in the World (2000), the sequel to The Fifth Child.

Throughout her writing—which includes not only short stories and novels but also poetry, plays, and essays—Lessing has remained passionately committed to social justice and individual dignity. Her work frequently has anticipated and chronicled central contemporary social movements and issues, including mental illness, terrorism, war, women's rights, sexuality, mysticism, aging, and speculation on the future.

THE OLD CHIEF MSHLANGA

They were good, the years of ranging the bush over her father's farm which, like every white farm, was largely unused, broken only occasionally by small patches of cultivation. In between, nothing but trees, the long sparse grass, thorn and cactus and gully, grass and outcrop and thorn. And a jutting piece of rock which had been thrust up from the warm soil of Africa unimaginable eras of time ago, washed into hollows and whorls by sun and wind that had travelled so many thousands of miles of space and bush, would hold the weight of a small girl whose eyes were sightless for anything but a pale willowed river, a pale gleaming castle—a small girl singing: "Out flew the web and floated wide, the mirror cracked from side to side . . ."

Pushing her way through the green aisles of the mealie stalks, the leaves arching like cathedrals veined with sunlight far overhead, with the packed red earth underfoot, a fine lace of red starred witchweed would summon up a black bent figure croaking premonitions: the Northern witch, bred of cold Northern forests, would stand before her among the mealie[1] fields, and it was the mealie fields that faded and fled, leaving her among the gnarled roots of an oak, snow fall thick and soft and white, the woodcutter's fire glowing red welcome through crowding tree trunks.

A white child, opening its eyes curiously on a sun-suffused landscape, a gaunt and violent landscape, might be supposed to accept it as her own, to take the msasa trees and the thorn trees as familiars, to feel her blood running free and responsive to the swing of the seasons.

This child could not see a msasa tree, or the thorn, for what they were. Her books held tales of alien fairies, her rivers ran slow and peaceful, and she knew the shape of the leaves of an ash or an oak, the names of the little creatures that lived in English streams, when the words "the veld"[2] meant strangeness, though she could remember nothing else.

Because of this, for many years, it was the veld that seemed unreal; the sun was a foreign sun, and the wind spoke a strange language.

The black people on the farm were as remote as the trees and the rocks. They were an amorphous black mass, mingling and thinning and massing like tadpoles, faceless, who existed merely to serve, to say "Yes, Baas," take their money and go. They changed season by season, moving from one farm to the next, according to their outlandish needs, which one did not have to understand, coming from perhaps hundreds of miles north or east, passing on after a few months—where? Perhaps even as far away as the fabled gold mines of Johannesburg, where the pay was so much better than the few shillings a month and the double handful of mealie meal twice a day which they earned in that part of Africa.

The child was taught to take them for granted: the servants in the house would come running a hundred yards to pick up a book if she dropped it. She was called "Nkosikaas"—Chieftainess, even by the black children her own age.

Later, when the farm grew too small to hold her curiosity, she carried a gun in the crook of her arm and wandered miles a day, from vlei to vlei,[3] from *kopje to*

---

[1]*mealie*   Africaans: maize.
[2]*veld*   Africaans: open countryside, grasslands.
[3]*vlei*   Africaans: valley, often with water running through it.

kopje,[4] accompanied by two dogs: the dogs and the gun were an armour against fear. Because of them she never felt fear.

If a native came into sight along the kaffir[5] paths half a mile away, the dogs would flush him up a tree as if he were a bird. If he expostulated (in his uncouth language which was by itself ridiculous) that was cheek. If one was in a good mood, it could be a matter for laughter. Otherwise one passed on, hardly glancing at the angry man in the tree.

On the rare occasions when white children met together they could amuse themselves by hailing a passing native in order to make a buffoon of him; they could set the dogs on him and watch him run; they could tease a small black child as if he were a puppy—save that they would not throw stones and sticks at a dog without a sense of guilt.

Later still, certain questions presented themselves in the child's mind; and because the answers were not easy to accept, they were silenced by an even greater arrogance of manner.

It was even impossible to think of the black people who worked about the house as friends, for if she talked to one of them, her mother would come running anxiously: "Come away; you mustn't talk to natives."

It was this instilled consciousness of danger, of something unpleasant, that made it easy to laugh out loud, crudely, if a servant made a mistake in his English or if he failed to understand an order—there is a certain kind of laughter that is fear, afraid of itself.

One evening, when I was about fourteen, I was walking down the side of a mealie field that had been newly ploughed, so that the great red clods showed fresh and tumbling to the vlei beyond, like a choppy red sea; it was that hushed and listening hour, when the birds send long sad calls from tree to tree, and all the colours of earth and sky and leaf are deep and golden. I had my rifle in the curve of my arm, and the dogs were at my heels.

In front of me, perhaps a couple of hundred yards away, a group of three Africans came into sight around the side of a big antheap. I whistled the dogs close in to my skirts and let the gun swing in my hand, and advanced, waiting for them to move aside, off the path, in respect for my passing. But they came on steadily, and the dogs looked up at me for the command to chase. I was angry. It was "cheek" for a native not to stand off a path, the moment he caught sight of you.

In front walked an old man, stooping his weight on to a stick, his hair grizzled white, a dark red blanket slung over his shoulders like a cloak. Behind him came two young men, carrying bundles of pots, assegais,[6] hatchets.

The group was not a usual one. They were not natives seeking work. These had an air of dignity, of quietly following their own purpose. It was the dignity that checked my tongue. I walked quietly on, talking softly to the growling dogs, till I was ten paces away. Then the old man stopped, drawing his blanket close.

"Morning, Nkosikaas," he said, using the customary greeting for any time of the day.

"Good morning," I said. "Where are you going?" My voice was a little truculent.

The old man spoke in his own language, then one of the young men stepped forward politely and said in careful English: "My Chief travels to see his brothers beyond the river."

---

[4]*kopje*   Africaans: hill.
[5]*kaffir*   Africaans: derogatory term for African native person.
[6]*assegai*   Africaans: slender spear with an iron tip.

A Chief! I thought, understanding the pride that made the old man stand before me like an equal—more than an equal, for he showed courtesy, and I showed none.

The old man spoke again, wearing dignity like an inherited garment, still standing ten paces off, flanked by his entourage, not looking at me (that would have been rude) but directing his eyes somewhere over my head at the trees.

"You are the little Nkosikaas from the farm of Baas Jordan?"

"That's right," I said.

"Perhaps your father does not remember," said the interpreter for the old man, "but there was an affair with some goats. I remember seeing you when you were . . ." The young man held his hand at knee level and smiled.

We all smiled.

"What is your name?" I asked.

"This is Chief Mshlanga," said the young man.

"I will tell my father that I met you," I said.

The old man said: "My greetings to your father, little Nkosikaas."

"Good morning," I said politely, finding the politeness difficult, from lack of use.

"Morning, little Nkosikaas," said the old man, and stood aside to let me pass.

I went by, my gun hanging awkwardly, the dogs sniffing and growling, cheated of their favourite game of chasing natives like animals.

Not long afterwards I read in an old explorer's book the phrase: "Chief Mshlanga's country." It went like this: "Our destination was Chief Mshlanga's country, to the north of the river; and it was our desire to ask his permission to prospect for gold in his territory."

The phrase "ask his permission" was so extraordinary to a white child, brought up to consider all natives as things to use, that it revived those questions, which could not be suppressed: they fermented slowly in my mind.

On another occasion one of those old prospectors who still move over Africa looking for neglected reefs, with their hammers and tents, and pans for sifting gold from crushed rock, came to the farm and, in talking of the old days, used that phrase again: "This was the Old Chief's country," he said. "It stretched from those mountains over there way back to the river, hundreds of miles of country." That was his name for our district: "The Old Chief's Country"; he did not use our name for it—a new phrase which held no implication of usurped ownership.

As I read more books about the time when this part of Africa was opened up, not much more than fifty years before, I found Old Chief Mshlanga had been a famous man, known to all the explorers and prospectors. But then he had been young; or maybe it was his father or uncle they spoke of—I never found out.

During that year I met him several times in the part of the farm that was traversed by natives moving over the country. I learned that the path up the side of the big red field where the birds sang was the recognized highway for migrants. Perhaps I even haunted it in the hope of meeting him: being greeted by him, the exchange of courtesies, seemed to answer the questions that troubled me.

Soon I carried a gun in a different spirit; I used it for shooting food and not to give me confidence. And now the dogs learned better manners. When I saw a native approaching, we offered and took greetings; and slowly that other landscape in my mind faded, and my feet struck directly on the African soil, and I saw the shapes of tree and hill clearly, and the black people moved back, as it were, out of my life: it was as if I stood aside to watch a slow intimate dance of landscape and men, a very old dance, whose steps I could not learn.

But I thought: this is my heritage, too; I was bred here; it is my country as well as the black man's country; and there is plenty of room for all of us, without elbowing each other off the pavements and roads.

It seemed it was only necessary to let free that respect I felt when I was talking with old Chief Mshlanga, to let both black and white people meet gently, with tolerance for each other's differences: it seemed quite easy.

Then, one day, something new happened. Working in our house as servants were always three natives: cook, houseboy, garden boy. They used to change as the farm natives changed: staying for a few months,, then moving on to a new job, or back home to their kraals.[7] They were thought of as "good" or "bad" natives; which meant: how did they behave as servants? Were they lazy, efficient, obedient, or disrespectful? If the family felt good-humoured, the phrase was: "What can you expect from raw black savages?" If we were angry, we said: "These damned niggers, we would be much better off without them."

One day, a white policeman was on his rounds of the district, and he said laughingly: "Did you know you have an important man in your kitchen?"

"What!" exclaimed my mother sharply. "What do you mean?"

"A Chief's son." The policeman seemed amused. "He'll boss the tribe when the old man dies."

"He'd better not put on a Chief's son act with me," said my mother.

When the policeman left, we looked with different eyes at our cook: he was a good worker, but he drank too much at week-ends—that was how we knew him.

He was a tall youth, with very black skin, like black polished metal, his tightly growing black hair parted white man's fashion at one side, with a metal comb from the store stuck into it; very polite, very distant, very quick to obey an order. Now that it had been pointed out, we said: "Of course, you can see. Blood always tells."

My mother became strict with him now she knew about his birth and prospects. Sometimes, when she lost her temper, she would say: "You aren't the Chief yet, you know." And he would answer her very quietly, his eyes on the ground: "Yes, Nkosikaas."

One afternoon he asked for a whole day off, instead of the customary half-day, to go home next Sunday.

"How can you go home in one day?"

"It will take me half an hour on my bicycle," he explained.

I watched the direction he took; and the next day I went off to look for this kraal; I understood he must be Chief Mshlanga's successor: there was no other kraal near enough our farm.

Beyond our boundaries on that side the country was new to me. I followed unfamiliar paths past *kopjes* that till now had been part of the jagged horizon, hazed with distance. This was Government land, which had never been cultivated by white men; at first I could not understand why it was that it appeared, in merely crossing the boundary, I had entered a completely fresh type of landscape. It was a wide green valley, where a small river sparkled, and vivid water-birds darted over the rushes. The grass was thick and soft to my calves, the trees stood tall and shapely.

I was used to our farm, whose hundreds of acres of harsh eroded soil bore trees that had been cut for the mine furnaces and had grown thin and twisted, where the

---

[7]*kraal* Africaans: native village; also, an enclosure for cattle, goats, or other animals.

cattle had dragged the grass flat, leaving innumerable criss-crossing trails that deepened each season into gullies, under the force of the rains.

This country had been left untouched, save for prospectors whose picks had struck a few sparks from the surface of the rocks as they wandered by; and for migrant natives whose passing had left, perhaps, a charred patch on the trunk of a tree where their evening fire had nestled.

It was very silent: a hot morning with pigeons cooing throatily, the midday shadows lying dense and thick with clear-yellow spaces of sunlight between and in all that wide green park-like valley, not a human soul but myself.

I was listening to the quick regular tapping of a woodpecker when slowly a chill feeling seemed to grow up from the small of my back to my shoulders, in a constricting spasm like a shudder, and at the roots of my hair a tingling sensation began and ran down over the surface of my flesh, leaving me goosefleshed and cold, though I was damp with sweat. Fever? I thought; then uneasily, turned to look over my shoulder; and realized suddenly that this was fear. It was extraordinary, even humiliating. It was a new fear. For all the years I had walked by myself over this country I had never known a moment's uneasiness; in the beginning because I had been supported by a gun and the dogs, then because I had learnt an easy friendliness for the Africans I might encounter.

I had read of this feeling, how the bigness and silence of Africa, under the ancient sun, grows dense and takes shape in the mind, till even the birds seem to call menacingly, and a deadly spirit comes out of the trees and the rocks. You move warily, as if your very passing disturbs something old and evil, something dark and big and angry that might suddenly rear and strike from behind. You look at groves of entwined trees, and picture the animals that might be lurking there; you look at the river running slowly, dropping from level to level through the vlei, spreading into pools where at night the bucks come to drink, and the crocodiles rise and drag them by their soft noses into underwater caves. Fear possessed me. I found I was turning round and round, because of that shapeless menace behind me that might reach out and take me; I kept glancing at the files of *kopies* which, seen from a different angle, seemed to change with every step so that even known landmarks, like a big mountain that had sentinelled my world since I first became conscious of it, showed an unfamiliar sunlit valley among its foothills. I did not know where I was. I was lost. Panic seized me. I found I was spinning round and round, staring anxiously at this tree and that, peering up at the sun which appeared to have moved into an eastern slant, shedding the sad yellow light of sunset. Hours must have passed! I looked at my watch and found that this state of meaningless terror had lasted perhaps ten minutes.

The point was that it was meaningless. I was not ten miles from home: I had only to take my way back along the valley to find myself at the fence; away among the foothills of the *kopjes* gleamed the roof of a neighbour's house, and a couple of hours' walking would reach it. This was the sort of fear that contracts the flesh of a dog at night and sets him howling at the full moon. It had nothing to do with what I thought or felt; and I was more disturbed by the fact that I could become its victim than of the physical sensation itself: I walked steadily on, quietened, in a divided mind, watching my own pricking nerves and apprehensive glances from side to side with a disgusted amusement. Deliberately I set myself to think of this village I was seeking, and what I should do when I entered it—if I could find it, which was doubtful, since I was walking aimlessly and it might be anywhere in the hundreds of thousands of acres of bush that stretched about me. With my mind on that village, I realized that a new sensation was added to the fear: loneliness. Now such a terror of isolation invaded me that I could hardly walk; and if it were not that I came over the crest of a small rise and saw a village below me, I should have turned and gone home. It was a cluster of thatched huts in a clearing among trees. There were neat patches of mealies and pumpkins and millet, and cattle grazed under some trees at a distance. Fowls scratched among the huts, dogs lay sleeping on the grass, and goats friezed a *kopje* that jutted up beyond a tributary of the river lying like an enclosing arm round the village.

As I came close I saw the huts were lovingly decorated with patterns of yellow and red and ochre mud on the walls; and the thatch was tied in place with plaits of straw.

This was not at all like our farm compound, a dirty and neglected place, a temporary home for migrants who had no roots in it.

And now I did not know what to do next. I called a small black boy, who was sitting on a lot playing a stringed gourd, quite naked except for the strings of blue beads round his neck, and said: "Tell the Chief I am here." The child stuck his thumb in his mouth and stared shyly back at me.

For minutes I shifted my feet on the edge of what seemed a deserted village, till at last the child scuttled off, and then some women came. They were draped in bright cloths, with brass glinting in their ears and on their arms. They also stared, silently; then turned to chatter among themselves.

I said again: "Can I see Chief Mshlanga?" I saw they caught the name; they did not understand what I wanted. I did not understand myself.

At last I walked through them and came past the huts and saw a clearing under a big shady tree, where a dozen old men sat crosslegged on the ground, talking. Chief Mshlanga was leaning back against the tree, holding a gourd in his hand, from which he had been drinking. When he saw me, not a muscle of his face moved, and I could see he was not pleased: perhaps he was afflicted with my own shyness, due to being unable to find the right forms of courtesy for the occasion. To meet me, on our own farm, was one thing; but I should not have come here. What had I expected? I could not join them socially: the thing was unheard of. Bad enough that I, a white girl, should be walking the veld alone as a white man might: and in this part of the bush where only Government officials had the right to move.

Again I stood, smiling foolishly, while behind me stood the groups of brightly clad, chattering women, their faces alert with curiosity and interest, and in front of me sat the old men, with old lined faces, their eyes guarded, aloof. It was a village of ancients and children and women. Even the two young men who kneeled beside the Chief were not those I had seen with him previously: the young men were all away working on the white men's farms and mines, and the Chief must depend on relatives who were temporarily on holiday for his attendants.

"The small white Nkosikaas is far from home," remarked the old man at last.

"Yes," I agreed, "it is far." I wanted to say: "I have come to pay you a friendly visit, Chief Mshlanga." I could not say it. I might now be feeling an urgent helpless desire to get to know these men and women as people, to be accepted by them as a friend, but the truth was I had set out in a spirit of curiosity: I had wanted to see the village that one day our cook, the reserved and obedient young man who got drunk on Sundays, would one day rule over.

"The child of Nkosi Jordan is welcome," said Chief Mshlanga.

"Thank you," I said, and could think of nothing more to say. There was a silence, while the flies rose and began to buzz around my head; and the wind shook a little in the thick green tree that spread its branches over the old men.

"Good morning," I said at last. "I have to return now to my home."

"Morning, little Nkosikaas," said Chief Mshlanga.

I walked away from the indifferent village, over the rise past the staring amber-eyed goats, down through the tall stately trees into the great rich green valley where the river meandered and the pigeons cooed tales of plenty and the woodpecker tapped softly.

The fear had gone; the loneliness had set into stiff-necked stoicism; there was now a queer hostility in the landscape, a cold, hard, sullen indomitability that walked with me, as strong as a wall, as intangible as smoke; it seemed to say to me: you walk here as a destroyer. I went slowly homewards, with an empty heart: I had learned that if one cannot call a country to heel like a dog, neither can one dismiss the past with a smile in an easy gush of feeling, saying: I could not help it, I am also a victim.

I only saw Chief Mshlanga once again.

One night my father's big red land was trampled down by small sharp hooves, and it was discovered that the culprits were goats from Chief Mshlanga's kraal. This had happened once before, years ago.

My father confiscated all the goats. Then he sent a message to the old Chief that if he wanted them he would have to pay for the damage.

He arrived at our house at the time of sunset one evening, looking very old and bent now, walking stiffly under his regally-draped blanket, leaning on a big stick. My father sat himself down in his big chair below the steps of the house; the old man squatted carefully on the ground before him, flanked by his two young men.

The palaver was long and painful, because of the bad English of the young man who interpreted, and because my father could not speak dialect, but only kitchen kaffir.

From my father's point of view, at least two hundred pounds' worth of damage had been done to the crop. He knew he could not get the money from the old man. He felt he was entitled to keep the goats. As for the old chief, he kept repeating angrily: "Twenty goats! My people cannot lose twenty goats! We are not rich, like the Nkosi Jordan, to lose twenty goats at once."

My father did not think of himself as rich, but rather as very poor. He spoke quickly and angrily in return, saying that the damage done meant a great deal to him, and that he was entitled to the goats.

At last it grew so heated that the cook, the Chief's son, was called from the kitchen to be interpreter, and now my father spoke fluently in English, and our cook translated rapidly so that the old man could understand how very angry my father was. The young man spoke without emotion, in a mechanical way, his eyes lowered, but showing how he felt his position by a hostile uncomfortable set of the shoulders.

It was now in the late sunset, the sky a welter of colours, the birds singing their last songs, and the cattle, lowing peacefully, moving past us towards their sheds for the night. It was the hour when Africa is most beautiful; and here was this pathetic, ugly scene, doing no one any good.

At last my father stated finally: "I'm not going to argue about it. I am keeping the goats."

The old Chief flashed back in his own language: "That means that my people will go hungry when the dry season comes."

"Go to the police, then," said my father, and looked triumphant.

There was, of course, no more to be said.

The old man sat silent, his head bent, his hands dangling helplessly over his withered knees. Then he rose, the young men helping him, and he stood facing my father. He spoke once again, very stiffly; and turned away and went home to his village.

"What did he say?" asked my father of the young man, who laughed uncomfortably and would not meet his eyes.

"What did he say?" insisted my father.

Our cook stood straight and silent, his brows knotted together. Then he spoke. "My father says: All this land, this land you call yours, is his land, and belongs to our people."

Having made this statement, he walked off into the bush after his father, and we did not see him again.

Our next cook was a migrant from Nyasaland,[8] with no expectations of greatness.

Next time the policeman came on his rounds he was told this story. He remarked: "That kraal has no right to be there; it should have been moved long ago. I don't know why no one has done anything about it. I'll have a chat with the Native Commissioner next week. I'm going over for tennis on Sunday, anyway."

Some time later we heard that Chief Mshlanga and his people had been moved two hundred miles east, to a proper Native Reserve; the Government land was going to be opened up for white settlement soon.

I went to see the village again, about a year afterwards. There was nothing there. Mounds of red mud, where the huts had been, had long swathes of rotting thatch over them, veined with the red galleries of the white ants. The pumpkin vines rioted everywhere, over the bushes, up the lower branches of trees so that the great golden balls rolled underfoot and dangled overhead: it was a festival of pumpkins. The bushes were crowding up, the new grass sprang vivid green.

The settler lucky enough to be allotted the lush warm valley (if he chose to cultivate this particular section) would find, suddenly, in the middle of a mealie field, the plants were growing fifteen feet tall, the weight of the cobs dragging at the stalks, and wonder what unsuspected vein of richness he had struck.

[1951]

Questions

1. How does the setting contribute to the story's central conflict?
2. Why does the narrator go to visit the Old Chief Mshlanga? What is the effect or consequence of her visit?
3. What do the narrator and the reader learn about the relationship between races in southern Africa during *apartheid*?
4. What does the narrator mean when she remarks, "I am also a victim"? Of what is she a victim?

---

[8]*Nyasaland*   Former name of the country now called Malawi.

Catherine Lim
(b. 1942)
Singapore

Catherine Lim has often been identified as Singapore's most important writer, prompting superlatives from a number of international critics. She has published two widely praised collections of short stories: Little Ironies—Stories of Singapore (1978) and Or Else, the Lightning God and Other Stories (1980). Of Little Ironies, Austin Coates has written the following:

> The stories are riveting; there is no other word for them. In their Singapore Chinese context they rank with the best of Guy de Maupassant and Alphonse Daudet. Each story has the same sureness of observation, clarity in the presentation of character, and finely judged economy both of words and emotion. . . . Her knowledge of Chinese ways of living and habits of thought is masterly. It may sound absurd to say this, but so few people are able, as she is, to draw back and look at it objectively. She exposes men and women with a mixture of complacent ruthlessness and compassion.

Lim has published two novels, The Serpent's Tooth (1983) and The Bondmaid (1997), the latter perhaps her most famous work with American readers. Identifying the themes of her fiction, Susan Ang has written: "Lim's main themes are the clashes between generations and cultures, the disparity of attitudes and lifestyles found amongst the various income-groups, and the discrepancy between society's ever-improving economic profile and its state of moral poverty."

OR ELSE, THE LIGHTNING GOD

Whenever Margaret didn't have the opportunity to talk to Suan Choo in the office about the problems with her mother-in-law, she telephoned her friend in the evening. And she did so now, reclining on the bed, freshly bathed and talcumed. Eng Kiat wasn't home, and the old one was in her room downstairs, so it was all right to speak as freely as she wanted to Suan Choo. Suan Choo had a mother-in-law too, equally troublesome, and so understood her problem perfectly. Margaret knew that the old one, though she spoke no English, understood the meanings of certain words when she heard them; her small eyes would flash, she would look up sharply when she caught words such as "mother-in-law," "money," "servant," "nuisance," convinced that she was being talked about and criticised. So Margaret, in her conversations with Suan Choo had evolved a new set of terms intended to put the old lady off the scent. "Mother-in-law" became "dowager" or "antique," "servant" was "domestic." Sometimes failure to find appropriate alternatives forced Margaret to spell out the word, but the element of unnaturalness introduced into the conversation in this way made the old lady, who was very sharp indeed, pause to listen suspiciously.

"Suan Choo, guess what I saw when I came back from work today," she said, managing to light a cigarette with one hand while holding the receiver with the other. "Or rather, what I smelt. There was a foul smell coming from the kitchen. I rushed to see and there was an earthenpot of the Dowager's herbal medicine a-brewing as usual. The stuff had boiled over and was trickling down the sides of my poor cooker. Luckily I came back in time. Otherwise, that wretched thing would have ruined my whole kitchen. This is the third time this week, Choo, that the Dowager's left her Chinese medicine brewing while she goes off I don't know where. Later she came back and had the audacity to ask who had turned off the flame when her medicine wasn't yet properly brewed!"

Suan Choo was able to furnish a similar story of outrageous mother-in-law behaviour, and the two laughed loud and long over the phone. Margaret's cheerful mood was due partly to the doctor's assurance, when she paid one of her regular calls that morning, that he thought her chances for the baby were very much improved by the administration of the new drug. "When Doctor Lee told me to relax and have plenty of rest, I nearly said, 'You must be joking, Doctor. How can anyone relax with a mother-in-law like mine about the place?'" said Margaret and she laughed again. Not all complaints ended on such a cheerful note.

"Suan Choo, would you believe it, the Dowager actually invited a medium to my house?" cried Margaret shortly after, clutching her friend's arm. "A temple medium, one of those weird men who go into a trance and froth at the mouth? She actually made arrangements for a séance in my house! It seemed she wanted to communicate with my dead father-in-law. Imagine my fury. To make my house a den for those eerie people with their joss-sticks and prayer paper and I don't know what else! A good thing I came back in time. I nearly threw away those horrible prayer things of theirs."

No less than a full delivery of her tirade could have eased the pressure of mounting anger, and after Margaret had finished giving an account of the offence, she went into more details.

"They were going to use her room for the purpose. I saw a table already laid out with those evil-looking candles and joss-sticks and glasses of water and what have you. My father-in-law's photo was on the wall—you know, the one taken of him a month before he died—that unnatural ghostly look—you remarked once how eerie it looked, and how the old man's eyes seemed to be following you, remember? Well, they had the photo on the wall, and a paper effigy of the old man, I think, on the table, against the wall—and I don't know what other rubbish. Fortunately, I came home in time to prevent it. Imagine, Choo, calling up the dead in my house. It makes my flesh creep all over. That mother-in-law of mine is driving me crazy, and Dr. Lee tells me to relax—relax, my God!"

Suan Choo, more interested this time in exploring the subject of the supernatural than in contributing to tirades against mothers-in-law, said that her aunt once conjured the spirit of her uncle in a seance and spoke to the dead one through the medium for half an hour. The aunt maintained that the medium's features had taken on those of her dead husband; she swore it was her husband sitting in the room talking to her.

"Why can't these old people leave their dead alone?" cried Margaret in exasperation. "Why must they cause trouble to others by delving into these dark, sinister things which are best left alone? Anyway, I think those people my mother-in-law associates with are a bunch of cheats, that's all. They foist upon her all sorts of herbal medicines and charms and other such rubbish, and she pays through her nose for them. And where does her money come from? Eng Kiat and me, of course! Do you know, Choo, we give that old fool two hundred dollars a month for pocket money, and she still complains it's not enough! She lives with us, there's a servant to attend to her needs, even her new clothes and slippers and umbrellas are bought for her, and she dares complain the two hundred dollars isn't enough!"

The subject of money had become a very sore one, and here Suan Choo was able to join in the complaints with equal energy, for her mother-in-law sponged outrageously on her husband, demanding money for this or for that all the time.

Margaret's anger extended to the brothers-in-law who refused to carry out their share of the duty of supporting the old one.

"There's Eng Loong, I've told you of his miserly ways so often. His business is thriving, and his wife, I hear, is making tons of money in the Stock Exchange, but they don't give one cent to the old lady. It's only the occasional *ang pow*[1] for the Chinese New Year or the birthday, and they think they're hell of a filial," cried Margaret angrily. "Then there's that good-for-nothing Eng Chian—always flitting from one job to another. I suspect he's been borrowing money from Kiat again, but of course that husband of mine will never tell me anything. So everyone comes to Kiat stretching out a long arm and here am I slaving like a fool in the office, helping to support a host of parasites!" Margaret lit a cigarette furiously, then stubbed it out.

"I forgot," she told her friend in a softened tone. "The doctor says I'm not to smoke during this period. Hey, Choo," a smile appeared on her face, "I may have good news to tell you soon. I'm keeping my fingers crossed!"

When her husband returned from his business trip abroad, Margaret was indeed able to tell him the good news and husband and wife rejoiced, for at last, after six years of marriage, Margaret was to have a child.

"There's no need to tell the old lady yet," said Margaret. "We'll tell her only when we're perfectly sure."

They told her a month later, and Margaret was rankled by the cold indifference of her mother-in-law's response.

"Well, it is good for you," she said stiffly. "You've waited six years for a child, and now you're going to have one."

Margaret recollected the old lady's solicitous anxiety when Eng Loong's wife was pregnant; she fussed, she recommended this food and that food, she made bird's nest soup with expensive rare herbs, she was so concerned. And Mee Lian never bought her any jewellery or even a new dress. Margaret heaved in anger at the unjust antagonism of the old one.

But, she told Suan Choo and her other friends, she couldn't care a jot. She was not of that old breed who trembled in the presence of a mother-in-law and sought to please all the time.

"Today things are different," cried Margaret with spirited defiance. "It's not like in the old days when women were subject to their mothers-in-law. I remember my mum telling me that her mother-in-law nagged and scolded her everyday, and if my father wanted to take her out to the *wayang*,[2] he had to get permission from the old gorgon. Today, it's no longer like this, ah, no more! Today, we're working wives drawing good

---

[1] *ang pow*   A gift of money (in a red envelope) for Chinese New Year.
[2] *wayang*   A show; entertainment.

salaries, we're independent, we're educated. Today, *they* depend on us, *they* stretch out their hands for their monthly money. So what is there to be afraid of?" Margaret described, with animation, her happy position, free of any ties of obligation to the old.

"Number One, we're financially secure, we made it on our own without any help from my husband's family," she said. "Kiat's parents didn't spend a cent on his higher education, for he got scholarships and bursaries all the way. I wouldn't want to be in Diana Lau's position. She's living with her rich in-laws; you know that famous big house in Marine Vista with the two huge stone lions at the entrance? That's the family home, and I hear Diana is scared as hell of offending her old father-in-law and mother-in-law. You know the old lady whom we met in Tai Sing Goldsmith the other day, the one glittering with diamonds? Well, I'm glad I don't have a rich mother-in-law like that; it makes things more difficult. Like this, I'm independent, I'm free, I'm not afraid of anybody!"

Suan Choo had two small children and whenever she had problems with the servant, her mother-in-law came to help.

"She's quite useless with the children," said Suan Choo, "but at least I have someone in the house with the kids while Gerard and I are at work. I don't have to leave the children at a friend's, like Gek Eng does whenever the servant plays her out."

"Number Two, I don't depend on my mother-in-law to help in the house," said Margaret with energetic triumph. "My Ah Chan is most reliable and manages perfectly, and I don't have children as yet. When my baby arrives, I'm going to get Ah Chan to take care of the baby, and another servant to do the housework. My mother-in-law will never have the occasion to say, 'See, these young people depend on us their elders to see to this and that.'"

Margaret's mother, a small-sized, timid-looking woman, who was rather in awe of her strong-willed, efficient daughter, nevertheless took her aside one morning when she came on a visit, and gravely spoke about respect for the old.

"You mustn't quarrel with your mother-in-law, Margaret," she said with grave solicitousness. "Young people must heed the old; they must not raise their voice against the old. It is not good, Margaret."

Margaret said impatiently, "Mother, I agree with you. I agree with you when the old are reasonable and considerate in their behaviour. But when they are unreasonable and hypocritical and spiteful, when they are never satisfied no matter how much you do for them and criticise you behind your back, then they don't deserve the respect of the young!"

"Margaret, it is not good to talk like this, it is not good at all," said the elderly woman, with a melancholy shake of her head. "I respected my mother-in-law because of her grey hairs though she was cruel to me. The young must respect the old, Margaret, or they will be punished." And she spoke of that punishment reserved for those guilty of filial impiety, the ultimate transgression: they would be struck by the Lightning God. The Lightning God in Heaven heeds the cries of the old.

"What nonsense!" cried Margaret, and now she was really angry. She said sharply to her mother, "Mother, this is the new age. This is not the old age, when you were scared of your mother-in-law and allowed her to trample on you. There is no Lightning God today, Mother—no Lightning God or Thunder God or Kitchen God. They all died long ago."

Margaret had never seethed with such indignation before. She went out and decided to take her mind off the problems besetting her by doing some shopping. She needed some cleansing cream, and if she found something she liked to put in the baby's room, which was almost ready, she would get it, regardless of cost. For, Margaret thought, why should I stinge on myself and the baby, and let all the money go the spongers? I will not be so foolish.

The shopping afforded her much pleasure, and she bought a very large and very expensive panda for the baby. She wished Kiat were home, so she could show him the delightful toy. Kiat was a good, loving husband, only too soft when it came to his family. She rang Suan Choo to tell her about the shopping and uttered a little scream of surprise and delight when Suan Choo confided that she too was going to have a baby; the doctor had just confirmed it.

"I hope it'll be a boy this time, Choo," said Margaret, very glad for her friend.

"I'm thinking of the servant problem," said Suan Choo. "My mother-in-law's in one of her cranky moods again, and the earlier I get a reliable servant, the better."

And Margaret, rejoicing with her best friend, was in a sufficiently good mood to withstand her mother-in-law's latest assault upon her nerves: the old lady was making a patchwork blanket, and strewn all over her nice, clean marble floor downstairs were small pieces of cloth and bits of thread. The servant Ah Chan complained that that was the third time she had to sweep up the stuff that morning, but Margaret said, "Oh, leave her alone, Ah Chan. Otherwise, she will have something more to complain to the neighbours about." The neighbour who irritated Margaret most was the next-door washerwoman who was always talking to her mother-in-law over the fence. The two women's habit of lowering their voices and nudging each other, each time they thought Margaret was approaching, was most annoying. She was positive the old one talked about her to the next-door gossip, and she was furious. She had complained about this to her husband, but in his characteristic casual manner, he had said, "Aw, leave them alone. They're idle gossips, that's all."

Oh, when will I be rid of my burden? thought Margaret. She knew the old one would always be staying with them for Eng Loong's wife would not have her, and Eng Chian was a good-for-nothing who had difficulty supporting himself. Her Eng Kiat, because he had a good-natured disposition, was taken advantage of by all. Margaret had the idea, as yet not carefully defined as a strategy, of getting rid of the troublesome old one once her baby arrived. There must be some excuse which the coming of the baby could furnish for making arrangements for the old one to live elsewhere. It would be some months before the baby arrived; meanwhile, she would have to put up with the old lady whose ways were becoming intolerable.

"One of these days I shall blow up, I don't care what Kiat says," cried poor Margaret. "The old one's Lightning God can strike me dead if he likes!" She took some comfort from the thought that Suan Choo was also having much trouble with her mother-in-law. Suan Choo had confided, the night before, in a voice shrill with exasperation, that her mother-in-law had unreasonably quarrelled with her new servant. The servant had been proving to be so reliable and efficient. Now the servant had left, and she had to start looking all over again for another one. And she was feeling so sick these days, with her frequent vomiting.

"Choo, we are in the same boat," said Margaret. "I keep telling everybody, one of these days I'm going to blow up."

She blew up shortly after this. It happened this way. Margaret was having lunch with an office colleague, who knew her next-door neighbours. It seemed that her mother-in-law had complained to the washerwoman of being ill-treated by Margaret. She was left alone in the house most of the time, she said, and she didn't have proper food.

"No proper food!" gasped Margaret and she could hardly believe what she had just heard. Her refrigerator was always full, her groceries store was stocked to the ceiling with tinned food and dried stuff for the old one to help herself to, and she was complaining of not having enough food!

It seemed, continued the colleague, the washerwoman went over one morning to see the old lady who was sitting at the table eating a bowl of rice porridge with nothing in it but soya sauce. The washerwoman was shocked and asked her why she was eating such meagre food, food not fit for a beggar, whereupon the old one started to weep. It was so pitiful that the washerwoman wept with her.

"Oh, I can't stand this, I can't stand it anymore!" cried Margaret, white with anger. "She gives me endless trouble, I load her with gifts and food and money and she goes around telling people I ill-treat her and starve her! How can I stand this? That gossipy washerwoman has no business to interfere in our affairs. I'm not going to let this pass, I promise you!" Margaret was now weeping in vexed distress. Her friend grew alarmed, for Margaret was six months pregnant now, and it was bad for a woman in her condition to be so distressed.

Margaret stormed home and confronted her mother-in-law. It was raining heavily and she got wet running from the taxi into the house, but she did not bother to dry herself; she went straight in search of the old one who was in the kitchen, and confronted her. Her words of accusation came out in angry torrents; she accused her mother-in-law of ingratitude, of deceit, of injustice to her. Her voice quavered in her anger, her knees trembled beneath her and her hands were cold, for such a situation was something new and, in retrospect, frightening to her. But she stood, firm and strong now, shrill with hurt and fury.

The old one looked up from the table where she was drinking a cup of coffee; she stared at her, first with disbelief, then with silent malevolence. Her mouth was gathered in tight lines of cold fury. Then she stood up. She said to Margaret, "So you dare speak this way to your old mother-in-law? You see the grey hairs on my head, and you dare speak to me in this way? You, who are going to be a mother yourself? You take care!" She pointed a finger at Margaret, her small grey eyes flashing with anger, but Margaret was not to be cowed easily.

"I'm not afraid of you!" she cried in quivering indignation. "I've had enough trouble from you, and so you get out of my house!"

The old one glared at her, the small grey eyes glittering menacingly.

"You wouldn't dare do this to me if my son were here," she said slowly.

"This is MY house, it was bought in MY name, and I tell you to get out," shrieked Margaret, the hot tears rushing to her eyes.

The old one stood up to her full height, and she said, in a clear, shrill voice, "All right. Listen, then, daughter-in-law. In this house you have treated me like dirt, you have made me feel worse than a prisoner. You follow me about with your eyes when I want to speak to my son, and you are not happy when my son is good to me and gives me money. Don't think I'm not aware of all this! So I leave now, but before I go, let me tell you this. Those who are cruel to their elders will never prosper! They are cursed. I curse you now; you are bearing a child, but I curse you!"

The roar of the rain outside almost drowned her words, but Margaret heard, and a thrill of terror ran through her. But she remained in the standing posture of defiance, though her heart was beating violently. The old one went into her room, put some things into a paper bag and left with an umbrella, in the pouring rain.

By herself, Margaret ran up to her room, threw herself upon the bed and wept bitterly. Oh, how hateful everything was! How simply hateful! Why was she so unlucky as to be suffering all this? In her distress, she put a long distance call to her husband to come home.

When he arrived, the next evening, he found her inert on the bed, the tears falling silently down her cheeks. She clung to him, crying dismally. He was alarmed on the baby's account and soothed her as best he could, but inwardly he was irked: "These women—will they never stop their nonsense." Unable to criticise his wife or mother, he lashed out in full fury against the washerwoman, now seen as the cause of all the trouble.

His task, after he had soothed Margaret and made her comfortable, was to look for his mother and make sure she had come to no harm. And he groaned again to himself, and shook his head, "These women—they give endless trouble."

He was relieved to find that the old one had gone to Eng Loong's house and was now under the care of Eng Loong and Mee Lian. He explained as best he could, the two brothers shook their heads, and Mee Lian bustled about to make her old mother-in-law comfortable, for she had caught cold in the rain.

"So it's me, the villainess, sending out an old white-haired woman into the rain and storm," cried Margaret with a sharp laugh, when Eng Kiat returned and told her of what had happened.

She felt unwell and lay in bed for a long time. She fretted and grew irritable, and snapped at her husband and servant. The nights were more distressful for she couldn't sleep—her head swarmed with troubling thoughts and her heart was charged with troubling feelings. Again and again she saw the old one, standing upright, with hand raised and finger pointing upwards, and heard her shrill cry ring out, "I curse you! You are with child, but still I curse you!"

The glint of malevolence in the old eyes Margaret could never forget. She trembled each time she recollected that glare of malice in the old face, the white hair that had loosened from the knot at the back of her head and floated in stiff strands about the face. It was ghastly. It was horrible. Margaret closed her eyes tight to shut off that evil scene, but it would come back, again and again. In her dreams, it took on a vividness and monstrosity that caused her to wake up screaming; in her dreams, the old one's features assumed a demonic leer and her voice a demonic shriek so that the curse rang piercingly in Margaret's ears. She woke up screaming and clung to her husband sobbing.

"She cursed me, your mother cursed me, and I'm already seven months with child," she sobbed in her fear. Eng Kiat, haggard with sleeplessness, tried his best to soothe her. He kept reassuring her that everything would be all right, that old people, especially uneducated ones like his mother, cursed when they were angry, and said all sorts of bizarre things.

"Her curse was terrible, she meant every word of it," said Margaret. "Yesterday and today," she continued with a sob, "the child inside me did not move. Didn't even stir once. I swear to you, Kiat, our baby hasn't moved for two days!"

A tremor of terror ran through the husband, but he only said, with feigned casualness, "Now, now, that's being morbid, darling, and that's not like you at all. You had a bad experience and are now imagining all sorts of things. I'll take you to see Dr. Lee tomorrow morning. You'll see that everything is all right."

Dr. Lee said that there was nothing wrong. Mother and child were doing well, and all Margaret needed was a lot of rest. On reaching home, Margaret told her husband she noticed that Dr. Lee looked worried; perhaps he had discovered something about her baby but was not willing to tell her? Eng Kiat said impatiently, "What nonsense!" but Margaret insisted that he took longer than usual to examine her and there was a frown on his face.

She had lost her appetite and was feeling utterly wretched. A frightened look had come into her eyes; in one of her dreams, her baby was stillborn, in another it had arms but no legs. Margaret sat up in bed in the darkness, and put her hands to her mouth to stifle the sobs, for she did not want to disturb her husband in his sleep.

Suan Choo rang up. Margaret hadn't spoken to Suan Choo for days and was glad to hear her friend's voice. Suan Choo spoke weakly. She was in hospital, recovering from a miscarriage. When she hung up, Margaret stood still, her eyes dilated in terror, her hands cold. Suan Choo had quarrelled with her mother-in-law, and this was her punishment. The power of the curse of the old! Margaret picked up the phone again, rang frantically for Suan Choo, and told her, in stricken whispers, what she thought.

"But that's impossible. The quarrel was some time ago, and besides, my mother-in-law never cursed me. Anyway, we are okay now, and she's helping out with the kids," said Suan Choo, terrified nevertheless by the possibility.

"No, no, Choo, you don't believe it, but it's true! I tell you it's true, their curse is powerful!" sobbed Margaret.

She grew distracted, not wanting her husband to be out of her sight, and she told Dr. Lee tearfully that she felt the child was dying inside her or would be born to torment her.

"On the day she cursed me, there was thunder and lightning," she said in an awestricken voice.

She was in a dark building, which was a temple, for there were red pillars and niches in the walls in which a number of gods sat brooding. Some of them were hidden in the shadows, but she knew they were watching her. The smell of smoke from the giant joss-sticks in a large gold urn on the floor stung her eyes and made her cough a little, and when the tears cleared, she saw, curled round the joss-sticks, snakes of a variety of sizes and colours. They were dull-eyed and their bodies moved slowly, lugubriously, on the joss-sticks, as if drowsed by the fumes. A long time ago, when she was a little girl, she had gone with her mother and aunt to a Chinese temple which housed hundreds of snakes that were supposed to be holy, and she had hidden behind her mother and cried when a snake slowly lifted its head and cast a beady eye on her. Now she looked upon the snakes on the joss-sticks unafraid, for she knew the poison had been taken out of them long ago. They continued to move slowly, ponderously, and then they slithered down to the floor towards her and were all over her, so that she gasped and choked and tried to pull them off. She saw her mother-in-law at a distance, holding a bunch of small joss-sticks in her hand and getting ready to stick them into the ash in an urn on the temple altar. She called to her mother-in-law to help her pull off the snakes; the old one didn't appear to hear her and went on arranging the joss-sticks neatly in the urn, then some oranges on a plate, and some fragrant flowers in a vase, in readiness for an offering to the temple gods. One of the gods in the niches stirred to life; Margaret called to him to help her disengage the snakes which seemed to have increased in number; two were around her neck; a multitude were on her arms, bosom, legs.

"Please—," she choked and the god who had awakened stepped out and advanced upon her. She looked pleadingly at him; his visage was now her mother-in-law's, with the glinting eyes and stiff white hair streaming in the storm, now her father-in-law's, with the malevolent leer.

"Please—," sobbed Margaret, and she put her arms protectively round her swollen belly, afraid her child would be harmed.

She woke up, panting, her wet hair clinging to her face and neck.

Dr. Lee took Eng Kiat aside to discuss Margaret's illness and to recommend psychiatric treatment.

"She's under some obsession which is driving her to distraction; it will be bad for the baby," said the doctor and for the first time, Eng Kiat, under enormous pressure for weeks, broke down and wept.

Margaret's mother consulted a temple medium. In a trance, he said that the only thing that could save Margaret's sanity and the child's life was to have the mother-in-law write certain words on a prayer paper which should then be burnt and the ashes put in water for Margaret to drink. Only in this way would the curse be lifted and Margaret's peace of mind restored.

When told of the temple medium's advice, Margaret, drawn, haggard and hollow-eyed, asked in a small pleading voice, "Do you think it'll work? Do you think it'll save my baby?"

The mother-in-law, recovering from her illness in Eng Loong's house and attended by Mee Lian, refused to write the words for the prayer paper.

"Don't ask me to do anything for her, and don't mention her name in my hearing again," she snapped, sitting in a chair in a corner of the room from which she seldom stirred. There was a look of hard resolution in her eyes.

Margaret herself came to plead. She had grown very thin, but her belly was huge and heavy. She was wearing a long housecoat, and a faded woollen cardigan. Eng Kiat had his arm protectively round her shoulders. When she was brought in front of the old lady, she immediately went up with a sob, but the old one turned aside sharply, and refused to look at her.

"Mother, please," sobbed Margaret and could not go on. Her mother and Mee Lian wept with her, and the sons pleaded with the old one to grant them the favour.

She sat still and unmoved, her lips tightly compressed, her brow dark with displeasure. When they continued pleading, she moved a hand impatiently and cried out, in shrill petulance, "All right! Give me the paper to write and be gone! Leave me in peace!" The brush was put in her hand, the temple medium's words were dictated by Margaret's mother, and in a few seconds she had finished.

"Now go, all of you!" she cried imperiously. And according to the temple medium's instructions, the prayer paper was burnt, the ashes were dropped into a glass of water, and Margaret drank gratefully, reverently, to the last drop.

[1980]

Questions

1. Margaret and Suan Choo take pride in being modern, independent women. Are they really that independent?

2. What tone does the author employ throughout her story?

3. Why does Margaret start believing in the curse? Does the author want us to believe that the mother-in-law's traditions are better than Margaret's?

Arnost Lustig

(b. 1926)

Czechoslovakia/United States

Arnost Lustig grew up in Prague, Czechoslovakia, where he was born in 1926. During World War II, he was interned in three concentration camps: Theresienstadt, Buchenwald, and Auschwitz. His novel Darkness Casts No Shadow (1976) describes the harrowing account of two boys' escape from one of those camps. It was made into a widely praised Czech film, for which Lustig wrote the screenplay. His earlier novel, A Prayer for Katerina Horovitzova (1974), won the Clement Gottwald State Prize (1967) and, in the English version, was nominated for a National Book Award. "The Lemon," from Diamonds of the Night (1976), prompted the reviewer in the London Times Literary Supplement to write, "No one reading [these tales] could ever feel they were only stories." On the publication of Indecent Dreams (1988), Josef Skvorecky compared Arnost Lustig to several other great Czech writers, including Franz Kafka and Milan Kundera. These and other volumes of Lustig's works (several awaiting translation into English) have earned him praise as the major writer of the Holocaust. (Dates refer to the English translations.)

Lustig has written this about the story included here:

"The Lemon" was one of my first stories. I wrote it after the war, in the fall of '45, for Diamonds of the Night, a collection of stories. The impulse came from a picnic I attended on the riverbanks near Prague. Everybody was singing, dancing, and enjoying themselves, except for a friend of mine. Later that night I asked him what was wrong. In response, he asked me, "Did you know my father, mother, and sister, little Sonitschka?" I nodded. He told me how they had died in a Lodz ghetto, where the hunger was worse than in Auschwitz-Birkenau, and the humiliation unbearable.

In order to save his mother and sister, he had to knock out the gold tooth from the mouth of his dead father before someone else would. He did it. He felt awful. I told him that I was glad I hadn't had to do it, but if I had been in his shoes I would have done the same since, under the circumstances, it was the best and only way to help his mother and little sister. His story spoiled my mood, too. The next day, I wrote this story. I wanted to express the truths in my heart: that human nobility can walk around in dirty rags; that heroism has many faces; that the feeling of human solidarity is stronger than the selfishness that society forces upon us; that even in the corrupted, you can find diamonds of a pure heart.

War brings about horrible things, but also moments of extraordinary beauty where humanity wins over indifference, courage over cowardice, and hope over resignation. This story aspires, like the entire collection, to be a poem about the moral purity of a man of our time; a song about the purity inside the hearts of the spoiled.

Arnost Lustig left Czechoslovakia after the Soviet occupation in 1968. In 1970, he began teaching at American University, in Washington, D.C. Since the fall of communism, he has remained active in the Czech literary scene. Other major works translated into English include Dita Saxova (1980), Street of Lost Brothers (1990), and The House of Returned Echoes (2001).

THE LEMON

Ervin was scowling. His feline eyes, set in a narrow skull, shifted nervously and his lips were pressed angrily into a thin blue arch. He hardly answered Chicky's greeting. Under his arm he was clutching a pair of pants rolled into a bundle.

"What'll you give me for these?" he demanded, unrolling the trousers, which were made of a thin nut-brown cloth. The seat and knees were shiny.

Chicky grinned. "Ye gods, where did you pick those up?" He inspected the cuffs and seams. "Jesus Christ himself wouldn't be caught dead in such a low-class shroud."

Ervin ignored the sneer. "I'm only interested in one thing, Chicky, and that's what I can get for them." He spoke fast.

"Listen, not even a resurrected Jesus Christ on the crummiest street in Lodz would wear a pair of pants like that," Chicky went on with the air of an expert.

He noticed the nerve twitching in Ervin's jaw. "Well, the knees still look pretty good, though," he reconsidered. "Where did you get them?"

It was cloudy and the sun was like a big translucent ball. The barn swallows were flying low. Ervin looked up at the sky and at the swallows swooping toward unseen nests. He'd been expecting Chicky to ask that and he'd prepared himself on the way.

He displayed his rather unimpressive wares again. He knew he had to go through with it now, even if the pants were full of holes. The skin on Chicky's face was thin, almost transparent; he had a small chin and rheumy eyes.

A member of the local security force came around the corner.

"Hey, you little brats," he snapped, casting a quick glance at their skinny bodies, "go on, get out of here!"

They turned around. Fortunately, a battered yellow streetcar that was set aside for the Jews came along just then and diverted the security guard's attention.

"Don't tell me it's a big secret!" Chicky said. "Anybody can easily see those pants belonged to some grown-up. What're you so scared of?"

"What should I be scared of?" Ervin retorted, clutching the trousers close. "I've got to cash in on them, that's all."

"They're rags."

"They're English material, they're no rags."

"Well, I might see what I can do for you," Chicky relented. "But on a fifty-fifty basis."

Ervin handed over the bundle, and Chicky took a piece of twine from his pocket and tied up the trousers to suit himself, making a fancy knot. He looked up and down the street.

The security guard was at the other end of the street with his back to the boys. They were on the corner of an alley which hadn't had a name for a long time. It was intermittently paved with cobblestones. People hurried on; Ervin and Chicky moved closer to the wall. The streetcar now took a different route. The next stop was out of sight.

Chicky, the smaller of the two, the one with the shaved head, was clutching the brown checkered pants under his arm as Ervin had done.

"But don't you go having second thoughts, Ervin. Don't let me go ahead and work my ass off and then. . . ."

"My dad died," Ervin said.

"Hm . . . well," Chicky remarked. "It's taken a lot of people these last few weeks," he observed.

"Now there's only one important thing, and that's how you're going to cash in on those pants."

It occurred to Chicky that Ervin might want a bigger share of the take because the pants had been his father's.

"Who's your customer, Chicky?"

"Old Moses," Chicky lied.

"Do I know him?"

"Little short guy."

"First time I've heard of him."

"He just comes up as high as my waist. He's absolutely the biggest bastard in town. But he kind of likes me. Maybe it's because I remind him of somebody."

"He's interested in pants?"

"He's interested in absolutely everything, Ervin."

"Funny I never heard of him."

"Well, I guess I'd better be going," Chicky said.

"What do you suppose your friend would give me for these pants?" Ervin asked.

"Give *us*, you mean," Chicky corrected.

"Anyway, go on and see what you can do," said Ervin, dodging a direct answer.

"He might cough up some bread in exchange for these pants. Or a couple ounces of flour." He unrolled the trousers again. "Like I told you, the knees are still pretty good and the lining's passable. The fly isn't stained yellow like it is in old men's pants. In that respect, these trousers are in good shape and that tells you something about the person who wore them. I'll try to get as much as I can for them, Ervin." He bared his teeth in a tiger grin.

"I need a lemon, Chicky."

"What about a big hunk of nothing?"

"I'm not joking," Ervin said curtly. "All right, then half a lemon, if you can't get a whole one." The expression on Chicky's face changed.

"You know what *I* need, Ervin?" he began. "I need an uncle in Florida where the sun shines all year long and trained fish dance in the water. I need an uncle who would send me an affidavit and money for my boat ticket so I could go over there and see those fish and talk to them." He paused. "A *lemon!* Listen, Ervin, where do you get those ideas, huh, tell me, will you?"

Chicky gazed up into the sky and imagined a blue and white ocean liner and elegant fish poking their noses up out of the silver water, smiling at him, wishing him bon voyage.

Swallows, white-breasted and sharp-winged, darted across the sullen sky. Chicky whistled at them, noticing that Ervin didn't smile.

"That lemon's not for me," said Ervin.

"Where do you think you are? Where do you think Old Moses'd get a lemon? It's harder to find a lemon in this place than. . . ."

But he couldn't think of a good comparison.

Chicky's expression changed to one of mute refusal. He thought to himself, Ervin is something better than I am. His father died, Ervin took his trousers, so now he can talk big about lemons. Chicky's mouth dropped sourly.

"It's for Miriam," Ervin said flatly. "If she doesn't get a lemon, she's finished."

"What's wrong with her?"

"I'm not sure. . . ."

"Just in general. I know you're no doctor."

"Some kind of vitamin deficiency, but it's real bad."

"Are her teeth falling out?"

"The doctor examined her this morning when he came to see my mother. The old man was already out in the hall. There's no point talking about it."

"It's better to be healthy, I grant you that," Chicky agreed. He rolled up the pants again. "At best, I may be able to get you a piece of bread." He tied the twine into a bow again. "If there were four of us getting a share of this rag, Ervin—your mom, your sister, and you and me, nobody would get anything out of it in the end."

"If I didn't need it, I'd keep my mouth shut," Ervin repeated.

"I can tell we won't see eye to eye, even on judgment Day."

A Polish streetcar rattled and wheezed along behind them. The town was divided into Polish and Jewish sectors. The streetcar line always reminded Ervin that there were still people who could move around and take a streetcar ride through the ghetto, even if it was just along a corridor of barbed wire with sentries in German uniforms so nobody would get any ideas about jumping off—or on.

"It's got to be something more than that. Everybody's got a vitamin deficiency here. What if it's something contagious, Ervin, and here I am fussing around with these pants of yours?" He gulped back his words. "And I've already caught whatever it is?"

"Nobody knows *what* it is," said Ervin.

"Well, I'm going, Ervin. . . ."

"When are you coming back?"

"What if we both went to see what we could do?"

"No," said Ervin quietly.

"Why not?"

Ervin knew what it was he had been carrying around inside him on his way to meet Chicky. *It was everything that had happened when he'd stripped off those trousers. His father's body had begun to stiffen and it felt strange. He kept telling himself it was all right, that it didn't matter.* Instead, he kept reciting the alphabet and jingles.

This was your father, a living person. And now he's dead. Chicky was the only one he could have talked to.

"I haven't got a dad or a mother even," Chicky said suddenly. A grin flickered. "That's my tough luck. They went up the chimney long ago."[1]

The sky above the low rooftops was like a shallow, stagnant sea.

Chicky lingered, uncertain.

It was just his body, Ervin told himself. *Maybe memory is like the earth and sky and ocean, like all the seashores and the mountains, like a fish swimming up out of the water to some island, poking out its big glassy eyes just to see how things look. Like that fish Chicky had been talking about. Nobody knows, not even the smartest rabbi in the world. And not the bad rabbis either. But while he was taking his father's trousers off, he knew what he was doing. He wasn't thinking about his father, but about an old Italian tune he used to sing and which Miriam loved. Father sang off key, but it sounded pretty. Prettier than a lot of other things. It was about love and flowers and his father had learned it during the war when he fought in the Piave campaign.*

He already had the trousers halfway off. And he knew the reasons he loved his father would never go away.

---

[1] *went up the chimney long ago*   Incinerated by the Nazis long ago.

  The swallows flew quietly in low, skidding arches. Ervin looked around to see how the weather was, and finally his gaze dropped. The rounded cobblestones melted away.

  "All right then, I'll bring it around to your place later," Chicky said.

  "By when do you think you can do it?"

  "In two or three hours."

  "But, Chicky. . . ."

  Chicky turned and disappeared around the corner as another streetcar came clanging along.

  Now Ervin could think ahead, instead of going back to what had been on his mind before. He set off down the alley in the opposite direction, toward the house where he and his family had been living for two years.

  The tiny shops upstairs and in the basement had been hardly more than market stalls which had been converted into apartments for several families.

  He remembered how he discovered that his father no longer wore underpants. The stringy thighs. The darkened penis, the reddish pubic hair. Rigid legs. Scars on the shin bone. His father had gotten those scars when he was wounded fighting in Italy.

  Then that old tune came back to him, sung off key again, the song from somewhere around Trieste that he and Miriam had liked so much.

  Hell, who needed those pants more than they did? Father had probably traded in his underpants long ago. Who knows for what?

  So Father died, he is no more, Ervin thought to himself.

  He reached home, one of the dwarfish shops where he and his mother and sister lived.

  The corrugated iron shutter over the entry had broken a spring, so it wouldn't go all the way up or down. He could see a mouse.

  He squeezed through a crack in the wall. Mother was scared of mice, so he'd repaired the wall boards through which the mice came in and out. Pressing against the wall, Ervin was suddenly aware of his body, and that reminded him of his father again.

  "It's me," he called out.

  It had occurred to him that there was nothing to be proud of, being unable to cash in on the trousers *himself.* (Even so, his mother must have known what he had done.) He had to take a deep breath and adjust to the musty smell in the room. It was easier to get used to the difference between the light outside and the darkness inside.

  Mother greeted him with a snore. She had long since lost any resemblance to the woman who had come here with him. He peered around him. He had been almost proud of having such a pretty mother. On top of everything else, her legs had swollen. She hadn't been able to get out of bed for the past eight weeks. She'd waited on everything for Father, and now for him.

  "Where've you been?" his mother asked.

  "Out," he answered.

  He crawled into his corner where he could turn his back on everything, including his father who lay out in the hall wrapped in a blanket. Miriam, too, was curled up next to the wall, so he couldn't see her face. He heard her coughing.

  He bundled his legs into the tattered rug that used to be his father's. *He'd always had the worst covers. He didn't want to admit he was a loser, and as long as he was able to give up something for them, maybe it wasn't so obvious. The dim light made its way through the thin fabric of dust and dampness and the breath of all three of them. When he lost, he put on the smile of a beautiful woman. He was making a point of being a graceful loser. As if it made any difference to anybody except himself.*

"Did you find anything?" his mother asked.

"No. . . ."

"What are we going to do?"

"Maybe this afternoon," he said, his face to the wall.

"Miriam!" his mother called out to his sister. "Don't cough! It wears you out."

"Mirrie," Ervin said. "Miriam!" She didn't answer.

"Can't she speak?" he asked his mother.

"It wears her out," she repeated. "You really ought to look around and see if you can't scrape up something."

"There's no point so early in the afternoon."

"You ought to try at least," his mother insisted.

That's how it used to be with Father, Ervin recalled. *She always kept sending him somewhere. But Father had gone out just as he'd done now, and, like him, he almost felt better outside; he also may have believed that just by going out he was getting back in shape, that he'd be able to do what he used to do in the beginning. Then Mother started saying things couldn't get any worse. She never went wrong about that. That's because there is no limit to what's "worse." The limit was in his father. And now Ervin had to find it, just like his father.*

"I already told you, I can't find anything just now," he said.

"You ought to go out and try, dear," his mother went on. *This was what Father had had to put up with.* "You see how Miriam looks, don't you?" his mother persisted.

"I can see her," he answered. "But I can't find anything now."

"This can't help but finish badly."

"Oh, cut it out! I'm not going anywhere," Ervin declared flatly. "I've already tried. There's nothing to be had."

"For God's sake, listen to me!" his mother cried sharply. "Go on out and *try!* Miriam hasn't had a thing to eat today."

The stains on the plaster were close to his eyes. The room was damp, and it almost swallowed up the sound of his mother's voice and his own. The dampness didn't bother him, though. He could hear faint scratching noises in the walls.

The boards he'd put up didn't help much. He almost envied mice. Just as he'd felt a certain envy for trees when he was outside. Ervin suddenly wished he could catch one of those sad little animals. Pet it, then kill it. Father had told them about the time they were besieged during the First World War and the soldiers ate mice.

To kill and caress. Or simply kill, so you're not always bothered by something or somebody.

But if Chicky was right, a trained mouse should get along great.

"I wonder if I shouldn't air out the room a bit," he said into the silence.

"Have they been here already?" he asked after a while.

"No."

"They're taking their time about it."

Now, in her turn, his mother was silent. "Who knows how many calls they have to make today?"

"Why don't you want to go out, son?"

"I will. In a while," he answered gently. "It doesn't make any sense now, though."

"Ervin, son. . . ."

The room was quiet, the silence broken only by Miriam's coughing.

Ervin put his head between his knees, trying to guess where the mouse was and what it was doing. He stuck his fingers in his ears. The scratching continued. *So Father's still lying out there in the hall. He doesn't have any pants and Mother doesn't even know it. He's naked, but that doesn't bother his old Piave scars. Mother could use that extra blanket now,* he thought to himself. *But he left it around his father for some reason which he didn't know himself. So I don't have the feeling that I've stolen everything from him, including our second tattered blanket,* he thought to himself. *It was lucky she couldn't get out of bed now, even if she wanted to. Her legs wouldn't support her. She'd see that Father had no pants. They'll probably take him along with the blanket. What the hell? They were certainly taking their time. They should have been here an hour ago. It was a regulation of the commanding officer and the self-government committee that corpses must be removed promptly. Everybody was scared of infection. The corpse collectors were kept busy. They probably didn't miss a chance to take anything they could get. Everybody knew they stole like bluejays.*

Miriam would probably have been afraid to sleep with a dead person in the same room, even if it was Father, Ervin decided.

"There's some rabbi here who works miracles, I heard," his mother said. "Why don't you go and see him?"

"What would I say to him?"

"Tell him that I'm your mother."

"I don't have any idea where he lives. And even if he could perform a miracle, he certainly won't put himself out to come over here. He waits for people to come to him."

"I feel so weak," his mother told him.

Suddenly it occurred to him that maybe his mother would have been better off lying out in the hall beside his father. It would be better for Miriam too. Mother's gestures and the things she told him were getting more and more indecisive.

"Why don't you want to go anywhere?" Mother said.

"Because there's no point," he replied, "I'd be wearing myself out in vain. I'll find something, but not until this afternoon."

"Miriam won't last long. She can hardly talk anymore."

"Miriam?" Ervin called out.

Miriam was silent and his mother added: "You know how it was with Daddy."

"He'd been sick for a long time."

And when her son said nothing, she tried again. "Ervin. . . ."

"It doesn't make any sense," he growled. "I'm not going anywhere now. Not till later."

He sat quite still for a while, staring at the blotches and shadows moving on the wall. He could hear mice scampering across the floor toward the mattress where Mother and Miriam were lying. Mother screeched, then Miriam.

Ervin was bored.

It might be more comfortable and pleasant to wait outside. But there was something in here that made him stay. He remembered how he and Chicky used to play poker. They always pretended there was some stake. That made it more interesting. You could bluff and pretend to have a full house when you didn't even have a pair. But there was always the chance—which they'd invented—that you might win something.

He remembered how he and Miriam used to go ice-skating. She was little and her knees were wobbly. He'd drag her around the rink for a while, then take her into the restaurant where you could have a cup of tea for ten hellers. Miriam's nose would be running, and she'd stay there for an hour with her tea so he could have a good time out on the ice. Once his mother had given them money to buy two ham sandwiches. His arches always ached when he'd been skating. So did Miriam's.

If they'd come for Father—and he wished it were over with—he wouldn't have to worry that the body would start to decay or that his mother would find out he didn't have any pants on.

"Why don't you go out and see that miracle rabbi?"

"Because it doesn't make any sense."

At first, Mother only had trouble with her legs. And Miriam hadn't coughed *quite* as much.

The sentries along the streetcar line always looked comfortably well-fed, with nice round bellies, as though they had everything they needed. When these sentries passed through the ghetto, they acted as though victory was already theirs, even if they might lose this little skirmish with the Jews. *Daddy once said that this was their world, whether they won or lost.*

Ervin's stomach growled. It was like the noise the mice made. He stretched and waited for his mother to start nagging him again. But she didn't, and it was almost as though something were missing. *He didn't want to think about his father's body wrapped in that blanket out in the hall. Daddy had been sick long enough. He was certainly better off this way.*

After a while, he wasn't sure whether his stomach was making the noise or the mice. His mother groaned. He thought about a nap. Just then he heard someone banging on the iron shutter. He got up.

"Well, I'll be on my way," he said.

"Come back soon," his mother replied. "Come back safe and sound."

"Sure," he answered. As he approached the shutter, he asked, "Is that you, Chicky?"

"No," a voice replied. "It's the miracle-working rabbi with a pitcher of milk."

Ervin pushed the broken shutter and slipped through. It was easy. His body was nothing but skin and bones now. He had a long narrow skull, with bulging greenish blue eyes. He could feel his mother's eyes on him as he squeezed out. Outside in the courtyard he pulled down his shirt and his bones cracked. Chicky was waiting on the sidewalk.

"So?" asked Ervin.

"Even with those stains on the seat," Chicky started.

"What're you trying to tell me?"

"He gave me more than I expected." He smiled slyly and happily.

Chicky produced a piece of bread, carefully wrapped in a dirty scarf. He handed it to Ervin. "This is for you. I already ate my share on the way, like we agreed."

"Just this measly piece?"

"Maybe you forgot those stains on the seat of those pants."

"Such a little hunk?"

"What else did you expect, hm? Or maybe you think I ought to come back with a whole moving van full of stuff for one pair of pants?"

Chicky wiped his nose, offended.

"You just better not forget about those stains on the seat. Besides, almost everybody's selling off clothes now."

Ervin took the bread. Neither one mentioned the lemon. Ervin hesitated before crawling back into the room, half-hoping Chicky was going to surprise him. Chicky liked to show off.

"Wait here for me," he blurted. "I'll be right back."

Ervin squinted through the dimness to where his mother lay on the mattress.

"Here, catch," he said maliciously. He threw the bread at her. It struck her face, bounced, and slid away. He could hear her groping anxiously over the blanket and across the floor. As soon as she had grabbed it, she began to wheeze loudly.

She broke the bread into three pieces in the dark.

"Here, this is for you," she said.

"I don't want it."

"Why not?" she asked. He heard something else in her voice. "Ervin?"

He stared at the cracks in the wall where the mice crawled through. He was afraid his mother was going to ask him again.

"My God, Ervin, don't you hear me?"

"I've already had mine," he said.

"How much did you take?"

"Don't worry, just my share." He felt mice paws pattering across the tops of his shoes. Again, he had the urge to catch one and throw it on the bed.

"Miriam!" his mother called.

Ervin left before he could hear his sister's reply. He knew what his mother was thinking.

Chicky was waiting, his hands in his pockets, leaning against the wall. He was picking his teeth. He was looking up at the sky trying to guess which way the clouds were going. There must be wind currents that kept changing.

For a while the two boys strolled along in silence. Then just for something to say, Chicky remarked: "You know what that little crook told me? He says you can't take everything away from everybody."

Everything melted together: father, bread, mother, sister, the moment he was imagining what Chicky might bring back for them. Mice.

"He says we can *hope* without *believing.*" Chicky laughed, remembering something else.

"Do you feel like bragging all day?"

"If you could see into me the way I can see into you, you could afford to talk. When my dad went up the chimney, I told myself I was still lucky to have my mother. And when I lost Mother, I told myself that at least I was lucky to have a brother left. He was weaker than a fly. And I said to myself, it's great to have your health at least."

Ervin was silent, so Chicky continued: "Still, we're pretty lucky, Ervin. Even if that's what my little businessman says too. Don't get the idea the world's going to stop turning just because one person in it is feeling miserable at this particular moment. You'd be exaggerating."

They didn't talk about it anymore. They could walk along like this together, so close their elbows or shoulders almost touched, and sometimes as they took a step together, their hips. The mice and the chameleon were gone; Chicky was really more like a barn swallow. Chicky was just slightly crooked. The thought suddenly put him in a better mood. Like when the sun came out or when he looked at a tree or the blue sky.

"He's full of wise sayings," Chicky resumed. "According to him, we have to pay for everything. And money and *things* aren't the worst way to pay."

"Aw, forget it. You're sticking as close to me as a fag."

"What about you?" Chicky's little face stretched.

"They haven't come to get him yet, the bastards."

"I can probably tell you why," Chicky declared. "Would you believe it, my dad's beard grew for two days after he was already dead?"

"Do you ever think you might have been a swallow?"

"Say, you're really outdoing yourself today," Chicky remarked. "But if you want to know something, I *have* thought about it."

Ervin looked up into the sky again. He might have known Chicky would have ideas like that. Ervin himself sometimes had the feeling that he was up there being blown around among the raindrops when there was a thunderstorm. The sky looked like an iron shutter. Sometimes he could also imagine himself jumping through the sky, using his arms and legs to steer with.

"Ervin. . . ." Chicky interrupted.

"What?"

"That old guy gave me a tremendous piece of advice."

"So be glad."

"No, Ervin, I mean it."

"Who's arguing?"

"Aren't you interested? He asked me if your old man had anything else."

"What else could he have?"

"He was just hinting."

"These have been hungry days for us. That crooked second-hand man of yours, his brains are going soft. I hope he can tell the difference between dogs and cats."

"Considering we're not their people, Ervin, what he told me wasn't just talk."

"My dad was the cleanest person in this whole dump," said Ervin.

"He didn't mean that and neither did I, Ervin."

"What's with all this suspense?"

"Just say you're not interested and we'll drop it," Chicky said.

"Come on, spill it, will you? What *did* he mean then?"

"Maybe there was a ring or something?"

"Do you really think he'd have let Mother and Miriam die right in front of his eyes if he'd had anything like a ring?"

"He wasn't talking only about a ring. He meant gold."

"Dad had to turn over everything he had that was even gilded."

"He hinted at it only after I tried to explain to him about the lemon."

"You know how it was. Mother doesn't have anything either."

"He only hinted at it when I told him how important it was for you to have that lemon, Ervin."

"Well, what was it he hinted, then?" Ervin noticed the expectant look on Chicky's face.

"He hinted that it wasn't impossible, but only in exchange for something made of pure gold. And that he didn't care what it was."

"Don't be a bastard," said Ervin slowly. "Forget it. My dad didn't have anything like that. Go on, get lost!"

"He even indicated exactly *what* and *how*."

"Look, come on—kindly spill it," Ervin said with irritation. *Once again he saw his father lying there wrapped in the blanket. It flooded through him in a dark tide, like when his mother didn't believe that he hadn't taken more than his share of the bread. He'd known right from the start what Chicky was talking about.*

Ervin didn't say anything.

"Gold teeth, for instance. It's simply something in the mouth he doesn't need anymore, something nobody needs except maybe you and me."

Ervin remained silent.

"Well, I wasn't the one who said anything about a lemon," he concluded.

Ervin stopped and so did Chicky. Then Ervin turned and looked him up and down, eyes bulging.

"Aw, cut it out," Chicky said wearily. "Don't look at me as though I killed your dad."

Suddenly Ervin slapped him. Chicky's face was small and triangular, tapering off crookedly at the top. It was very obvious because his head was shaved. Then Ervin slapped him again and began to punch his face and chest. When his fist struck Chicky's Adam's apple, Ervin could feel how fragile everything about him was.

Again he saw himself stripping those brown checkered trousers off his father's body. The undertakers would be coming along any minute. [They should have been here long ago.] He thought of how he'd managed to do that before they came and how he'd probably manage to do even this if he wanted to. And he knew that he couldn't have swallowed that piece of bread even if his mother had given it to him without those second thoughts of hers. He kept pounding his fists into Chicky, and it was as if he were striking at himself and his mother. *He kept telling himself that his father was dead anyway and that it didn't matter much and that it didn't have any bearing on the future either.*

Then he felt everything slowing down. Chicky began to fight back. Ervin got in two fast punches, one on the chin, the other in the belly. Chicky hit Ervin twice before people gathered and tried to break it up, threatening to call the security guards.

Ervin picked himself up off the sidewalk as fast as he could. He shook himself like a dog and went home through the courtyard.

"Ervin?" his mother called out. "Is that you?"

"Yeah," he answered.

"Did you find anything else?"

He was shivering as he sometimes did when he was cold because he'd loaned his blanket to his mother or Miriam.

"Mirrie. . . ." he tried.

He bundled himself up into the rug. He was glad Chicky had hit him back. It was hard to explain why. It was different from wanting to catch a mouse and kill it. He touched his cheek and chin, fingering the swollen places. Again he waited for his mother to say something. But she didn't. Mother only knows as much as I tell her, he said to himself. Mother's quite innocent, Ervin decided. Despite everything she's still innocent. Would she have been able to do what she had criticized him for? He wished she'd say something, give at least an echo. He thought of Miriam. For a moment he could see her, tall and slender, her breasts and blond hair.

The twilight began to melt into the dampness of the cellar. The spider webs disappeared in the darkness. He wished they'd muffle the edge of his mother's voice. He waited for Miriam's cough. The silence was like a muddy path where nobody wants to walk. *And his father was still lying out there in the hall.*

When someone dies, Ervin thought to himself, *it means not expecting, not worrying about anything, not hoping for something that turns out to be futile. It means not forcing yourself into something you don't really want, while you go on behaving as though you did. It means not being dependent on anybody or anything. It means being rid of what's bothering you. It's like when you close your eyes and see things and people in your own way.*

That idea of a path leading from the dead to the living and back again is just a lot of foolishness I thought up by myself. To be dead means to expect nothing, not to expect somebody to say something, not to wait for someone's voice. Not to stare enviously after a streetcar going somewhere from somewhere else.

He looked around. Miriam had begun to cough again. She's coughing almost gently, he thought to himself. She probably doesn't have enough strength left to cough anymore.

My God, that lying, thieving, sly old man, that bastard who's fed for six thousand years on Jewish wisdom and maybe would for another half an hour—but maybe not even that long!

That dirty louse, full of phony maxims and dreams as complicated as clockwork, lofty as a rose, rank as an onion, who perhaps wasn't quite as imaginary as I wanted to think he was, judging from Chicky's descriptions which made him sound as though he'd swallowed all the holy books. That slimy crook with his miserable messages, that you have to pay for everything and that money and things aren't the most precious currency. But he also said you can't take everything away from everybody, as though he wanted to confuse you by contradicting himself in the same breath. Where did he get those ideas?

"No, I don't have anything," he said suddenly, as if he knew his mother was still waiting for an answer.

He heard her sigh. From his sister's bed he heard a stifled cough. (She's probably ashamed of coughing by now.)

Nothing's plaguing Father anymore either. Not even the craving for a bowl of soup. He wasn't looking forward anymore to seeing Ervin dash out onto the field in a freshly laundered uniform and shiny football boots, which he took care of, in front of crowds of people waiting for entertainment and thrills and a chance to yell their lungs out. If they come for Father now, they'll do just what Chicky said they would. Anyway, the undertakers themselves do it to the old people. He remembered his father's smile which got on his mother's nerves.

He stared into the darkness. His mother was bandaging her swollen legs. Her eyes were very bright. She's probably feverish, he thought. She made a few inexplicable gestures. *What if the rabbis are right and there is some afterwards? Then his father must be able to see him. Where do you suppose he really is, Ervin wondered, and where am I? Does anybody know? Inwardly he tried to smile at his father. It would be nice if I could really smile at him. To be on the safe side, Ervin tried smiling at his father again.*

"I'm going out and take another look around," he said.

Mother ceased her strange movements. "Where do you want to go in the dark?"

"I want to have a look at something."

"Be careful, child."

He went out into the hall and the place he had avoided before, so he wouldn't have to look at the wall beside which his father's body was still lying. He was squeezing through the crack in the wall. For a short while an insurance agent had lived in the corner shop. *But this isn't your father anymore, he told himself; he was only until yesterday. Now there is nothing but a weight and the task of carrying it away, he reminded himself immediately. But I'll think of him only in good ways. And Mother and Miriam will think about him as if nothing's happened.*

He threw off the old blanket. He closed his eyes for a second. *I won't be able to eat very much, he realized, as though he wanted to convince himself that this was the only difference it would make.* Everything moved stiffly. He had to turn the head and open its mouth. He grabbed it by the chin and hair and that was how he managed. He couldn't remember exactly which tooth it was. He tried one after another. He was hurrying. He didn't want Chicky and the men with the coffins to catch him at it. Instead, he tried to imagine that lemon. It was like a yellow sphere at the end of the hall. Suddenly he couldn't remember where lemons came from, except that it was somewhere in the south, and whether they grew on trees or bushes. He'd never really known anyway.

He picked up a sharp stone. He had a sticky feeling as though he were robbing somebody. He tried to decide which was the best way to knock it out. He tried several times without success. Then he stopped trying to get at just that one tooth.

Finally something in the jaw loosened. Ervin could smell his own breath. He tossed the stone away. He was glad nobody had seen him. Into the palm of his hand he scooped what he'd been seeking. (He was squatting and the head dropped back to the floor.)

Ervin stood up slowly. He felt as though his body and thoughts were flowing into a dark river, and he didn't know where it came from and where it was going. He wiped his hands on his pants. The cellar was dark, like the last place a person can retreat to. For a moment he closed his eyes. He had to take it out into the light. He headed for the other end of the corridor.

He'd hardly stepped out into the street when he saw Chicky's face in the twilight. There, you see, Ervin said to himself. He was keeping watch after all. Chicky would have done what he'd just done if he'd had the chance.

"Hello, kid," Chicky began. "Hello, you Jew bastard." Then Chicky exploded: "You lousy hyena! You son of a bitch! I suppose you've come to apologize. At least I hope so."

Ervin was clutching the thing tightly in his fist. He stared at Chicky for a long time.

"But I got in two good punches, didn't I? Like Max Schmeling." Chicky sounded pleased with himself. His eyes shone.

But then he noticed that the skin under Ervin's eyes was bluer than any bruise could have made it. He noticed, too, the pale blotches on Ervin's face. And how he kept his hand in his pocket.

"No hard feelings," Chicky said.

"I have it."

"I was sure you'd manage. . . ."

Ervin pulled his hand out of his pocket and Chicky's glance shifted swiftly.

"Bring me that lemon, Chicky, but the whole thing!" He unclenched his fist. It lay there cupped in his palm, a rather unattractive shell of gold the color of old copper, and very dirty.

"You won't take the tiniest slice for yourself."

"If it's pure, Ervin, you're in luck," Chicky said.

When Ervin did not respond he continued: "Sometimes it's just iron or some ersatz. Then it's worn through on top. The old man warned me about that in advance. But if it isn't, then you're damned lucky, Ervin, honest."

"When will you bring me that lemon?" Ervin asked, getting to the point.

"First hand it over and let me take a look."

Impatiently, Chicky inspected the crown, acting as though he hadn't heard Ervin. He scraped away the blood that had dried around the root and removed bits of cement. He blew on it and rubbed the dull gold between his fingers, then let it rest in his palm again.

"For this, the old runt will jump like a toad."

"I hope so."

"But first, Ervin, it's fifty-fifty."

"The hell it is," he answered firmly.

"I'll only do it for half."

"If Miriam doesn't get that lemon, she won't even last out till evening."

"Why shouldn't she last out? I'm keeping half."

"You're not keeping anything," repeated Ervin. "Now get going before it's too late."

Ervin glared at him, but there was a question in his eyes. Chicky acted calm. None of his self-satisfaction had filtered through to Ervin. His throat tightened. He began to shiver. He could feel the goose pimples on his neck and arms. It wasn't the way he wanted to think it was, *that his father had died and otherwise everything was just the same as before*. And when Chicky looked at him, Ervin could read in his eyes that instead of bringing a lemon or some kind of pills that have the same effect as lemons, Chicky would probably bring another piece of bread.

Ervin heard a quiet gurgle rising in his throat. He tried thinking about that runty second-hand dealer.

"I'd be crazy to do it for nothing," said Chicky slowly. He squinted warily and his nostrils flared. He bared his teeth. There were big gaps between them.

"Either we go halves or I tell your mom how you're treating me."

"You're not such a bastard, Chicky, are you?"

"Well, I'd have to be," replied Chicky.

"Get going," Ervin said.

"That sounds more like it."

"I'll wait at home."

"All right."

"And hurry up. Honestly, it's very important."

"Fast as a dog can do you know what," grinned Chicky.

Small and nimble, he dodged among the pedestrians. In the meantime, two men with tubs had appeared. Chicky must have passed them. The tubs were covered with tattered sheets and something bulged underneath. Everybody stepped aside as the porters passed. They knew what they were carrying.

Ervin didn't feel like going back home. He crawled into the opening of a cement culvert pipe. His long skinny head stuck out as he sat there watching the sun set behind the clouds. It dropped slowly. The barn swallows were flying lower now than they had been earlier that afternoon, flying in flocks, suddenly soaring up, then back toward earth.

He kept looking up and down the alley so he wouldn't miss Chicky when he came back.

It all began to melt together before his eyes: the silhouettes of the buildings and the cobblestones that had been pounded into the earth and then washed loose by long-gone rains. He watched the sky which was full of barn swallows and the sun disappeared. Rain was gathering in the clouds as their colors changed.

I ought to be like a rock, he told himself. Even harder than a rock.

And he wept, quietly and without tears, in some little crevice which was inside.

[1945]
Translated by
JEANNE NĚMCOVÁ

Questions

1. What kind of relationship do the two boys have with each other? How old are they? What are their differences?

2. What tactics have the boys perfected for survival in the ghetto?

3. One of Lustig's major themes has been the difficulty that human beings have recognizing evil in the world in which they live. Is this story about evil or about one of its opposites—love?

Naguib Mahfouz
(b. 1911)
Egypt

Naguib Mahfouz was awarded the Nobel Prize for Literature in 1988. He was the first Arab writer to win the prestigious award and only the second from the African continent (Wole Soyinka, a Nigerian, had won two years earlier). At the time of the citation, Mahfouz was nearly 80 years old (he was born in Cairo on December 11, 1911) and the most famous writer of fiction in the Arab world. However, his reputation with Arab readers has not always been secure. Although he held a position as a civil servant in the Ministry of Culture for many years and worked as a journalist, several of his novels have been banned. In 1989, when the Iranian Ayatollah Ruholla Khomeini placed the death sentence on Salman Rushdie for his novel The Satanic Verses, it was Mahfouz who, among Moslems, rose to his defense. His support of Rushdie led to a new round of threats against the Egyptian novelist: Moslem fundamentalists threatened to kill Mahfouz also, for what they considered blasphemy in his writings.

Mahfouz's undergraduate degree was in philosophy. He has remarked about his shift to literature, "I studied philosophy, and, until I was twenty-five, I wanted to continue. Then, I had a crisis and chose literature. But philosophy was important; it prevented me, I think, from becoming sentimental in a time when all my teachers were romantics." A prolific writer, by the time of the Nobel Prize Mahfouz had written nearly 25 novels and a dozen volumes of short stories, in addition to several plays and screenplays. In English, his most popular works have been Midag Alley (1981), Miramar (1983), and the more recently translated volumes of his Cairo Trilogy: Palace Walk (1990), Palace of Desire (1991), and Sugar Street (1992). The story reprinted here, "Half a Day," is from The Time and the Place and Other Stories (1991). Echoes of an Autobiography was published in 1997. (These dates are for the English translations.)

Commenting on Mahfouz's career, Roger Allen in World Literature Today has written the following:

> Alongside a concern with the mundane but crucial issues of survival in the inimical environment of the modern city, Mahfouz shows a continuing and particular concern for such questions as the nature of madness, the alienation of modern man and his search for consolation, and the role of religion in contemporary societies dominated by humanistic values. His choice of venue for the various fictional worlds he has created has been the city, with a particular concentration on Cairo. . . . Unlike other Egyptian novelists . . . he has not used the countryside and its peasant population as a focus for criticism of the course of socialist policies in his country, but has concentrated instead on the sector with which he is extremely familiar: the bureaucrat class in the city.

HALF A DAY

I proceeded alongside my father, clutching his right hand, running to keep up with the long strides he was taking. All my clothes were new: the black shoes, the green school uniform, and the red tarboosh.[1] My delight in my new clothes, however, was not altogether unmarred, for this was no feast day but the day on which I was to be cast into school for the first time.

My mother stood at the window watching our progress, and I would turn toward her from time to time, as though appealing for help. We walked along a street lined with gardens; on both sides were extensive fields planted with crops, prickly pears, henna trees, and a few date palms.

"Why school?" I challenged my father openly. "I shall never do anything to annoy you."

"I'm not punishing you," he said, laughing. "School's not a punishment. It's the factory that makes useful men out of boys. Don't you want to be like your father and brothers?"

I was not convinced. I did not believe there was really any good to be had in tearing me away from the intimacy of my home and throwing me into this building that stood at the end of the road like some huge, high-walled fortress, exceedingly stern and grim.

When we arrived at the gate we could see the courtyard, vast and crammed full of boys and girls. "Go in by yourself," said my father, "and join them. Put a smile on your face and be a good example to others."

I hesitated and clung to his hand, but he gently pushed me from him. "Be a man," he said. "Today you truly begin life. You will find me waiting for you when it's time to leave."

I took a few steps, then stopped and looked but saw nothing. Then the faces of boys and girls came into view. I did not know a single one of them, and none of them knew me. I felt I was a stranger who had lost his way. But glances of curiosity were directed toward me, and one boy approached and asked, "Who brought you?"

"My father," I whispered.

"My father's dead," he said quite simply.

I did not know what to say. The gate was closed, letting out a pitiable screech. Some of the children burst into tears. The bell rang. A lady came along, followed by a group of men. The men began sorting us into ranks. We were formed into an intricate pattern in the great courtyard surrounded on three sides by high buildings of several floors; from each floor we were overlooked by a long balcony roofed in wood.

"This is your new home," said the woman. "Here too there are mothers and fathers. Here there is everything that is enjoyable and beneficial to knowledge and religion. Dry your tears and face life joyfully."

We submitted to the facts, and this submission brought a sort of contentment. Living beings were drawn to other living beings, and from the first moments my heart made friends with such boys as were to be my friends and fell in love with such girls as I was to be in love with, so that it seemed my misgivings had had no basis. I had

---

[1]*tarboosh*   A tassled cap often worn by Muslim men and made from felt or cloth.

never imagined school would have this rich variety. We played all sorts of different games: swings, the vaulting horse, ball games. In the music room we chanted our first songs. We also had our first introduction to language. We saw a globe of the Earth, which revolved and showed the various continents and countries. We started learning the numbers. The story of the Creator of the universe was read to us, we were told of His present world and of His Hereafter, and we heard examples of what He said. We ate delicious food, took a little nap, and woke up to go on with friendship and love, play and learning.

As our path revealed itself to us, however, we did not find it as totally sweet and unclouded as we had presumed. Dust-laden winds and unexpected accidents came about suddenly, so we had to be watchful, at the ready, and very patient. It was not all a matter of playing and fooling around. Rivalries could bring about pain and hatred or give rise to fighting. And while the lady would sometimes smile, she would often scowl and scold. Even more frequently she would resort to physical punishment.

In addition, the time for changing one's mind was over and gone and there was no question of ever returning to the paradise of home. Nothing lay ahead of us but exertion, struggle, and perseverance. Those who were able took advantage of the opportunities for success and happiness that presented themselves amid the worries.

The bell rang announcing the passing of the day and the end of work. The throngs of children rushed toward the gate, which was opened again. I bade farewell to friends and sweethearts and passed through the gate. I peered around but found no trace of my father, who had promised to be there. I stepped aside to wait. When I had waited for a long time without avail, I decided to return home on my own. After I had taken a few steps, a middle-aged man passed by, and I realized at once that I knew him. He came toward me, smiling, and shook me by the hand, saying, "It's a long time since we last met—how are you?"

With a nod of my head, I agreed with him and in turn asked, "And you, how are you?"

"As you can see, not all that good, the Almighty be praised!"

Again he shook me by the hand and went off. I proceeded a few steps, then came to a startled halt. Good Lord! Where was the street lined with gardens? Where had it disappeared to? When did all these vehicles invade it? And when did all these hordes of humanity come to rest upon its surface? How did these hills of refuse come to cover its sides? And where were the fields that bordered it? High buildings had taken over, the street surged with children, and disturbing noises shook the air. At various points stood conjurers showing off their tricks and making snakes appear from baskets. Then there was a band announcing the opening of a circus, with clowns and weight lifters walking in front. A line of trucks carrying central security troops crawled majestically by. The siren of a fire engine shrieked, and it was not clear how the vehicle would cleave its way to reach the blazing fire. A battle raged between a taxi driver and his passenger, while the passenger's wife called out for help and no one answered. Good God! I was in a daze. My head spun. I almost went crazy. How could all this have happened in half a day, between early morning and sunset? I would find the answer at home with my father. But where was my home? I could see only tall buildings and hordes of people. I hastened on to the crossroads between the gardens and Abu Khoda. I had to cross Abu Khoda to reach my house, but the stream of cars would not let up. The fire engine's siren was shrieking at full pitch as it moved at a snail's pace, and I said to myself, "Let the fire take its pleasure in what it con-sumes." Extremely irritated, I wondered when I would be able to cross. I stood there a long time, until the young lad employed at the ironing shop on the corner came up to me. He stretched out his arm and said gallantly, "Grandpa, let me take you across."

[1989]
Translated by
DENYS JOHNSON-DAVIES

Questions

1. What kind of person is the narrator's father?
2. At what point in the story does it become apparent that the story covers more than the narrator's first day in school? How does Mahfouz employ the journey motif in his narrative?
3. What is the story's theme?
4. How is the fire at the end of the story significant? What is the importance of other events reported in the final paragraph?

Bernard Malamud

(1914–1986)

United States

Bernard Malamud was born in Brooklyn and died in Manhattan. His education was at City College of New York (B.A.) and at Columbia University (M.A.). During his years as a writer, he taught at Harlem High School, at Oregon State University, and from 1961 to 1986 at Bennington College. His novels include The Natural (1952); The Assistant (1957); The Fixer (1961), which won the Pulitzer Prize; and Dublin's Lives (1979). He published several volumes of short stories, including The Magic Barrel (1958), which won the National Book Award, and Idiots First (1963). The Stories of Bernard Malamud appeared in 1983.

Malamud's parents were Russian-Jewish immigrants, upon whose experiences the writer drew for both his novels and his short stories. So strong are Jewish themes in his work that the editors of Contemporary Authors wrote, at the time of his death, that "Each of [Malamud's] first three novels features a schlemiel figure who tries to restore a Wasteland to a Paradise against a Jewish background." Although the novels tend to be serious, even tragic, many of the author's stories (such as "The Jewbird") are essentially satiric or comic. Malamud has often been praised for his mastery of dialogue, especially his complex use of Jewish-American speech patterns.

Malamud was 60 when he agreed to a Paris Review interview. To Daniel Stern's question, "Are you a Jewish writer?" Malamud gave the following reply:

> I'm an American, I'm a Jew, and write for all men. A novelist has to, or he's built himself a cage. I write about Jews, when I write about Jews, because they set my imagination going. I know something about their history, the quality of their experience and belief, and of their literature, though not as much as I would like.

Asked if he preferred writing short stories instead of novels, he replied as follows:

> Just as much, though the short story has its own pleasures. I like packing a self or two into a few pages, predicating lifetimes. The drama is terse, happens faster, and is often outlandish. A short story is a way of indicating the complexity of life in a few pages, producing the surprise and effect of a profound knowledge in a short time.

THE JEWBIRD

The window was open so the skinny bird flew in. Flappity-flap with its frazzled black wings. That's how it goes. It's open, you're in. Closed, you're out and that's your fate. The bird wearily flapped through the open kitchen window of Harry Cohen's top-floor apartment on First Avenue near the lower East River. On a rod on the wall hung an escaped canary cage, its door wide open, but this black-type long-beaked bird—its ruffled head and small dull eyes, crossed a little, making it look like a dissipated crow—landed if not smack on Cohen's thick lamb chop, at least on the table, close by. The frozen foods salesman was sitting at supper with his wife and young son on a hot August evening a year ago. Cohen, a heavy man with hairy chest and beefy shorts; Edie, in skinny yellow shorts and red halter; and their ten-year-old Morris (after his father)—Maurie, they called him, a nice kid though not overly bright—were all in the city after two weeks out, because Cohen's mother was dying. They had been enjoying Kingston, New York, but drove back when Mama got sick in her flat in the Bronx.

"Right on the table," said Cohen, putting down his beer glass and swatting at the bird. "Son of a bitch."

"Harry, take care with your language," Edie said, looking at Maurie, who watched every move.

The bird cawed hoarsely, and with a flap of its bedraggled wings—feathers tufted this way and that—rose heavily to the top of the open kitchen door, where it perched staring down.

"Gevalt,[1] a pogrom!"

"It's a talking bird," said Edie in astonishment.

"In Jewish," said Maurie.

"Wise guy," muttered Cohen. He gnawed on his chop, then put down the bone. "So if you can talk, say what's your business. What do you want here?"

"If you can't spare a lamb chop," said the bird, "I'll settle for a piece of herring with a crust of bread. You can't live on your nerve forever."

"This ain't a restaurant," Cohen replied. "All I'm asking is what brings you to this address?"

"The window was open," the bird sighed; adding after a moment, "I'm running. I'm flying but I'm also running."

"From whom?" asked Edie with interest.

"Anti-Semeets."

"Anti-Semites?" they all said.

"That's from who."

"What kind of anti-Semites bother a bird?" Edie asked.

"Any kind," said the bird, "also including eagles, vultures, and hawks. And once in a while some crows will take your eyes out."

"But aren't you a crow?"

"Me? I'm a Jewbird."

Cohen laughed heartily. "What do you mean by that?"

The bird began dovening. He prayed without Book or tallith, but with passion. Edie bowed her head though not Cohen. And Maurie rocked back and forth with the prayer, looking up with one wide-open eye.

When the prayer was done Cohen remarked, "No hat, no phylacteries?"

"I'm an old radical."

"You're sure you're not some kind of a ghost of dybbuk?"

"Not a dybbuk," answered the bird, "though one of my relatives had such an experience once. It's all over now, thanks God. They freed her from a former lover, a crazy jealous man. She's now the mother of two wonderful children."

---

[1]*Gevalt* A cry of amazement.

"Birds?" Cohen asked slyly.

"Why not?"

"What kind of birds?"

"Like me. Jewbirds."

Cohen tipped back in his chair and guffawed. "That's a big laugh. I've heard of a Jewfish but not a Jewbird."

"We're once removed." The bird rested on one skinny leg, then on the other. "Please, could you spare maybe a piece of herring with a small crust of bread?"

Edie got up from the table.

"What are you doing?" Cohen asked her.

"I'll clear the dishes."

Cohen turned to the bird. "So what's your name, if you don't mind saying?"

"Call me Schwartz."

"He might be an old Jew changed into a bird by somebody," said Edie, removing a plate.

"Are you?" asked Harry, lighting a cigar.

"Who knows?" answered Schwartz. "Does God tell us everything?"

Maurie got up on his chair. "What kind of herring?" he asked the bird in excitement.

"Get down, Maurie, or you'll fall," ordered Cohen.

"If you haven't got matjes, I'll take schmaltz,"[2] said Schwartz.

"All we have is marinated, with slices of onion—in a jar," said Edie.

"If you'll open for me the jar I'll eat marinated. Do you have also, if you don't mind, a piece of rye bread—the spitz?"[3]

Edie thought she had.

"Feed him out on the balcony," Cohen said. He spoke to the bird. "After that take off."

Schwartz closed both bird eyes. "I'm tired and it's a long way."

"Which direction are you headed, north or south?"

Schwartz, barely lifting his wings, shrugged.

"You don't know where you're going?"

"Where there's charity I'll go."

"Let him stay, papa," said Maurie. "He's only a bird."

"So stay the night," Cohen said, "but no longer."

In the morning Cohen ordered the bird out of the house but Maurie cried, so Schwartz stayed for a while. Maurie was still on vacation from school and his friends were away. He was lonely and Edie enjoyed the fun he had, playing with the bird.

"He's no trouble at all," she told Cohen, "and besides his appetite is very small."

"What'll you do when he makes dirty?"

"He flies across the street in a tree when he makes dirty, and if nobody passes below, who notices?"

"So all right," said Cohen, "but I'm dead set against it. I warn you he ain't gonna stay here long."

"What have you got against the poor bird?"

"Poor bird, my ass. He's a foxy bastard. He thinks he's a Jew."

"What difference does it make what he thinks?"

"A Jewbird, what a chutzpah. One false move and he's out on his drumsticks."

---

[2] *matjes* and *schmaltz* Expensive herring or something lesser.

[3] *spitz* The heel (of a loaf of bread).

At Cohen's insistence Schwartz lived out on the balcony in a new wooden bird-house Edie had bought him.

"With many thanks," said Schwartz, "though I would rather have a human roof over my head. You know how it is at my age. I like the warm, the windows, the smell of cooking. I would also be glad to see once in a while the *Jewish Morning Journal* and have now and then a schnapps because it helps my breathing, thanks God. But whatever you give me, you won't hear complaints."

However, when Cohen brought home a bird feeder full of dried corn, Schwartz said, "Impossible."

Cohen was annoyed. "What's the matter, crosseyes, is your life getting too good for you? Are you forgetting what it means to be migratory? I'll bet a helluva lot of crows you happen to be acquainted with, Jews or otherwise, would give their eyeteeth to eat this corn."

Schwartz did not answer. What can you say to a grubber yung?[4]

"Not for my digestion," he later explained to Edie. "Cramps. Herring is better even if it makes you thirsty. At least rainwater don't cost anything." He laughed sadly in breathy caws.

And herring, thanks to Edie, who knew where to shop, was what Schwartz got, with an occasional piece of potato pancake, and even a bit of soupmeat when Cohen wasn't looking.

When school began in September, before Cohen would once again suggest giving the bird the boot, Edie prevailed on him to wait a little while until Maurie adjusted.

"To deprive him right now might hurt his school work, and you know what trouble we had last year."

"So okay, but sooner or later the bird goes. That I promise you."

Schwartz, though nobody had asked him, took on full responsibility for Maurie's performance in school. In return for favors granted, when he was let in for an hour or two at night, he spent most of his time overseeing the boy's lessons. He sat on top of the dresser near Maurie's desk as he laboriously wrote out his homework. Maurie was a restless type and Schwartz gently kept him to his studies. He also listened to him practice his screechy violin, taking a few minutes off now and then to rest his ears in the bathroom. And they afterwards played dominoes. The boy was an indifferent checker player and it was impossible to teach him chess. When he was sick, Schwartz read him comic books though he personally disliked them. But Maurie's work improved in school and even his violin teacher admitted his playing was better. Edie gave Schwartz credit for these improvements though the bird pooh-poohed them.

Yet he was proud there was nothing lower than C minuses on Maurie's report card, and on Edie's insistence celebrated with a little schnapps.

"If he keeps up like this," Cohen said, "I'll get him in any Ivy League college for sure."

"Oh I hope so," sighed Edie.

But Schwartz shook his head. "He's a good boy—you don't have to worry. He won't be a shicker[5] or a wifebeater, God forbid, but a scholar he'll never be, if you know what I mean, although maybe a good mechanic. It's no disgrace in these times."

"If I were you," Cohen said, angered, "I'd keep my big snoot out of other people's private business."

---

[4]*grubber yung*   Plump joker.
[5]*shicker*   A drinker.

"Harry, please," said Edie.

"My goddamn patience is wearing out. That crosseyes butts into everything."

Though he wasn't exactly a welcome guest in the house, Schwartz gained a few ounces although he did not improve in appearance. He looked bedraggled as ever, his feathers unkempt, as though he had just flown out of a snowstorm. He spent, he admitted, little time taking care of himself. Too much to think about. "Also outside plumbing," he told Edie. Still there was more glow to his eyes so that though Cohen went on calling him crosseyes he said it less emphatically.

Liking his situation, Schwartz tried tactfully to stay out of Cohen's way, but one night when Edie was at the movies and Maurie was taking a hot shower, the frozen foods salesman began a quarrel with the bird.

"For Christ sake, why don't you wash yourself sometimes? Why must you always stink like a dead fish?"

"Mr. Cohen, if you'll pardon me, if somebody eats garlic he will smell from garlic. I eat herring three times a day. Feed me flowers and I will smell like flowers."

"Who's obligated to feed you anything at all? You're lucky to get herring."

"Excuse me, I'm not complaining," said the bird. "You're complaining."

"What's more," said Cohen, "Even from out on the balcony I can hear you snoring away like a pig. It keeps me awake at night."

"Snoring," said Schwartz, "isn't a crime, thanks God."

"All in all you are a goddamn pest and free loader. Next thing you'll want to sleep in bed next to my wife."

"Mr. Cohen," said Schwartz, "on this rest assured. A bird is a bird."

"So you say, but how do I know you're a bird and not some kind of a goddamn devil?"

"If I was a devil you would know already. And I don't mean because your son's good marks."

"Shut up, you bastard bird," shouted Cohen.

"Grubber yung," cawed Schwartz, rising to the tips of his talons, his long wings outstretched.

Cohen was about to lunge for the bird's scrawny neck but Maurie came out of the bathroom, and for the rest of the evening until Schwartz's bedtime on the balcony, there was pretended peace.

But the quarrel had deeply disturbed Schwartz and he slept badly. His snoring woke him, and awake, he was fearful of what would become of him. Wanting to stay out of Cohen's way, he kept to the birdhouse as much as possible. Cramped by it, he paced back and forth on the balcony ledge, or sat on the birdhouse roof, staring into space. In evenings, while overseeing Maurie's lessons, he often fell asleep. Awakening, he nervously hopped around exploring the four corners of the room. He spent much time in Maurie's closet, and carefully examined his bureau drawers when they were left open. And once when he found a large paper bag on the floor, Schwartz poked his way into it to investigate what possibilities were. The boy was amused to see the bird in the paper bag.

"He wants to build a nest," he said to his mother.

Edie, sensing Schwartz's unhappiness, spoke to him quietly.

"Maybe if you did some of the things my husband wants you, you would get along better with him."

"Give me a for instance," Schwartz said.

"Like take a bath, for instance."

"I'm too old for baths," said the bird. "My feathers fall out without baths."

"He says you have a bad smell."

"Everybody smells. Some people smell because of their thoughts or because who they are. My bad smell comes from the food I eat. What does his come from?"

"I better not ask him or it might make him mad," said Edie.

In late November Schwartz froze on the balcony in the fog and cold, and especially on rainy days he woke with stiff joints and could barely move his wings. Already he felt twinges of rheumatism. He would have liked to spend more time in the warm house, particularly when Maurie was in school and Cohen at work. But though Edie was good-hearted and might have sneaked him in in the morning, just to thaw out, he was afraid to ask her. In the meantime Cohen, who had been reading articles about the migration of birds, came out on the balcony one night after work when Edie was in the kitchen preparing pot roast, and peeking into the birdhouse, warned Schwartz to be on his way soon if he knew what was good for him. "Time to hit the flyways."

"Mr. Cohen, why do you hate me so much?" asked the bird. "What did I do to you?"

"Because you're an A-number-one trouble maker, that's why. What's more, whoever heard of a Jewbird! Now scat or it's open war."

But Schwartz stubbornly refused to depart so Cohen embarked on a campaign of harassing him, meanwhile hiding it from Edie and Maurie. Maurie hated violence and Cohen didn't want to leave a bad impression. He thought maybe if he played dirty tricks on the bird he would fly off without being physically kicked out. The vacation was over, let him make his easy living off the fat of somebody else's land. Cohen worried about the effect of the bird's departure on Maurie's schooling but decided to take the chance, first, because the boy now seemed to have the knack of studying—give the black bird-bastard credit—and second, because Schwartz was driving him bats by being there always, even in his dreams.

The frozen foods salesman began his campaign against the bird by mixing watery cat food with the herring slices in Schwartz's dish. He also blew up and popped numerous paper bags outside the birdhouse as the bird slept, and when he got Schwartz good and nervous, though not enough to leave, he brought a full-grown cat into the house, supposedly a gift for little Maurie, who had always wanted a pussy. The cat never stopped springing up at Schwartz whenever he saw him, one day managing to claw out several of his tailfeathers. And even at lesson time, when the cat was usually excluded from Maurie's room, though somehow or other he quickly found his way in at the end of the lesson, Schwartz was desperately fearful of his life and flew from pinnacle to pinnacle—light fixture to clothes-tree to door-top—in order to elude the beast's wet jaws.

Once when the bird complained to Edie how hazardous his existence was, she said, "Be patient, Mr. Schwartz. When the cat gets to know you better he won't try to catch you any more."

"When he stops trying we will both be in Paradise," Schwartz answered. "Do me a favor and get rid of him. He makes my whole life worry. I'm losing feathers like a tree loses leaves."

"I'm awfully sorry but Maurie likes the pussy and sleeps with it."

What could Schwartz do? He worried but came to no decision, being afraid to leave. So he ate the herring garnished with cat food, tried hard not to hear the paper bags bursting like fire crackers outside the birdhouse at night, and lived terror-stricken closer to the ceiling than the floor, as the cat, his tail flicking, endlessly watched him.

Weeks went by. Then on the day after Cohen's mother had died in her flat in the Bronx, when Maurie came home with a zero on an arithmetic test, Cohen, enraged, waited until Edie had taken the boy to his violin lesson, then openly attacked the bird. He chased him with a broom on the balcony and Schwartz frantically flew back and forth, finally escaping into his birdhouse. Cohen triumphantly reached in, and grabbing both skinny legs, dragged the bird out, cawing loudly, his wings wildly beating. He whirled the bird around and around his head. But Schwartz, as he moved in circles, managed to swoop down and catch Cohen's nose in his beak, and hung on for dear life. Cohen cried out in great pain, punched the bird with his fist, and tugging at its legs with all his might, pulled his nose free. Again he swung the yawking Schwartz around until the bird grew dizzy, then with a furious heave, flung him into the night. Schwartz sank like stone into the street. Cohen then tossed the birdhouse and feeder after him, listening at the ledge until they crashed on the sidewalk below. For a full hour, broom in hand, his heart palpitating and nose throbbing with pain, Cohen waited for Schwartz to return but the broken-hearted bird didn't.

That's the end of that dirty bastard, the salesman thought and went in. Edie and Maurie had come home.

"Look," said Cohen, pointing to his bloody nose swollen three times its normal size, "what that sonofabitch bird did. It's a permanent scar."

"Where is he now?" Edie asked, frightened.

"I threw him out and he flew away. Good riddance."

Nobody said no, though Edie touched a handkerchief to her eyes and Maurie rapidly tried the nine times table and found he knew approximately half.

In the spring when the winter's snow had melted, the boy, moved by a memory, wandered in the neighborhood, looking for Schwartz. He found a dead black bird in a small lot near the river, his two wings broken, neck twisted, and both bird-eyes plucked clean.

"Who did it to you, Mr. Schwartz?" Maurie wept.

"Anti-Semeets," Edie said later.

[1963]

Questions

1. Why is Cohen so uptight about Schwartz? Is it what Edie says at the end of the story or something else?
2. What kind of comparison can be made between "The Jewbird" and Albert Camus's "The Guest"?
3. Can the satire of the story be appreciated only by someone from the same ethnic group? Is racial prejudice a fitting theme for satire?
4. Who is the main character in the story?

Katherine Mansfield

(1888–1923)
New Zealand/England

Born near Wellington, New Zealand, Katherine Mansfield Beauchamp left home early to study the cello in England, but turned to writing instead. Although she returned to New Zealand briefly, publishing her earliest stories in New Zealand and Australian magazines, in 1908 she chose to pursue her life as a writer in London with the help of a small allowance from her father. One of the stories she submitted to a London magazine caught the attention of John Middleton Murry, an editor and critic who became her mentor and eventually her husband.

Mansfield's first collection of stories, In a German Pension, was published in 1911. Several other volumes followed, including Bliss and Other Stories (1920) and The Garden Party (1922). During the last five years of her life, Mansfield suffered from tuberculosis; she was tormented by her deteriorating health, which impeded her profound desire to be "rooted in life" as well as her ability to write. She sought a miracle by taking residence in a spiritual healing community at Fountainbleau, where she died at the age of 34.

Mansfield wrote 88 stories (of which 26 were unfinished). Many of her stories hold a lasting place in twentieth-century fiction because of her influential innovations in form. Like her model, Chekhov, Mansfield reduced the significance of plot, instead emphasizing moments of emotional discovery and epiphany that directly revealed her characters' inner lives. Her eye for the telling detail, vignettes of character, and impressionistic depictions of settings as the backdrops for her characters' visions particularly distinguish her exemplary New Zealand stories.

HER FIRST BALL

Exactly when the ball began Leila would have found it hard to say. Perhaps her first real partner was the cab. It did not matter that she shared the cab with the Sheridan girls and their brother. She sat back in her own little corner of it, and the bolster on which her hand rested felt like the sleeve of an unknown young man's dress suit; and away they bowled, past waltzing lampposts and houses and fences and trees.

"Have you really never been to a ball before, Leila? But, my child, how too weird—" cried the Sheridan girls.

"Our nearest neighbor was fifteen miles," said Leila softly, gently opening and shutting her fan.

Oh, dear, how hard it was to be indifferent like the others! She tried not to smile too much; she tried not to care. But every single thing was so new and exciting . . . Meg's tuberoses, Jose's long loop of amber, Laura's little dark head, pushing above her white fur like a flower through snow. She would remember for ever. It even gave her a pang to see her cousin Laurie throw away the wisps of tissue paper he pulled from the fastening of his new gloves. She would like to have kept those wisps as a keepsake, as a remembrance. Laurie leaned forward and put his hand on Laura's knee.

"Look here, darling," he said. "The third and the ninth as usual. Twig?"

Oh, how marvellous to have a brother! In her excitement Leila felt that if there had been time, if it hadn't been impossible, she couldn't have helped crying because she was an only child, and no brother had ever said "Twig?" to her; no sister would ever say, as Meg said to Jose that moment, "I've never known your hair go up more successfully than it has tonight!"

But, of course, there was no time. They were at the drill hall already; there were cabs in front of them and cabs behind. The road was bright on either side with moving fan-like lights, and on the pavement gay couples seemed to float through the air; little satin shoes chased each other like birds.

"Hold on to me, Leila; you'll get lost," said Laura.

"Come on, girls, let's make a dash for it," said Laurie.

Leila put two fingers on Laura's pink velvet cloak, and they were somehow lifted past the big gold lantern, carried along the passage, and pushed into the little room marked "Ladies." Here the crowd was so great there was hardly space to take off their things; the noise was deafening. Two benches on either side were stacked high with wraps. Two old women in white aprons ran up and down tossing fresh armfuls. And everybody was pressing forward trying to get at the little dressing table and mirror at the far end.

A great quivering jet of gas lighted the ladies' room. It couldn't wait; it was dancing already. When the door opened again and there came a burst of tuning from the drill hall, it leaped almost to the ceiling.

Dark girls, fair girls were patting their hair, tying ribbons again, tucking handkerchiefs down the front of their bodices, smoothing marble-white gloves. And because they were all laughing it seemed to Leila that they were all lovely.

"Aren't there any invisible hairpins?" cried a voice. "How most extraordinary! I can't see a single invisible hairpin."

"Powder my back, there's a darling," cried some one else.

"But I must have a needle and cotton. I've torn simply miles and miles of the frill," wailed a third.

Then, "Pass them along, pass them along!" The straw basket of programs was tossed from arm to arm. Darling little pink-and-silver programs, with pink pencils and fluffy tassels. Leila's fingers shook as she took one out of the basket. She wanted to ask someone, "Am I meant to have one too?" but she had just time to read: "Waltz 3. *Two, Two in a Canoe*. Polka 4. *Making the Feathers Fly*," when Meg cried, "Ready, Leila?" and they pressed their way through the crush in the passage towards the big double doors of the drill hall.

Dancing had not begun yet, but the band had stopped tuning, and the noise was so great it seemed that when it did begin to play it would never be heard. Leila, pressing close to Meg, looking over Meg's shoulder, felt that even the little quivering colored flags strung across the ceiling were talking. She quite forgot to be shy; she forgot how in the middle of dressing she had sat down on the bed with one shoe off and one shoe on and begged her mother to ring up her cousins and say she couldn't go after all. And the rush of longing she had had to be sitting on the veranda of their forsaken upcountry home, listening to the baby owls crying "More pork" in the moonlight, was changed to a rush of joy so sweet that it was hard to bear alone. She clutched her fan, and, gazing at the gleaming, golden floor, the azaleas, the lanterns, the stage at one end with its red carpet and gilt chairs and the band in a corner, she thought breathlessly, "How heavenly; how simply heavenly!"

All the girls stood grouped together at one side of the doors, the men at the other, and the chaperones in dark dresses, smiling rather foolishly, walked with little careful steps over the polished floor towards the stage.

"This is my little country cousin Leila. Be nice to her. Find her partners; she's under my wing," said Meg, going up to one girl after another.

Strange faces smiled at Leila—sweetly, vaguely. Strange voices answered, "Of course, my dear." But Leila felt the girls didn't really see her. They were looking towards the men. Why didn't the men begin? What were they waiting for? There they stood, smoothing their gloves, patting their glossy hair and smiling among themselves. Then, quite suddenly, as if they had only just made up their minds that that was what they had to do, the men came gliding over the parquet. There was a joyful flutter among the girls. A tall, fair man flew up to Meg, seized her program, scribbled something; Meg passed him on to Leila. "May I have the pleasure?" He ducked and smiled. There came a dark man wearing an eyeglass, then cousin Laurie with a friend, and Laura with a little freckled fellow whose tie was crooked. Then quite an old man—fat, with a big bald patch on his head—took her program and murmured, "Let me see, let me see!" And he was a long time comparing his program, which looked black with names, with hers. It seemed to give him so much trouble that Leila was ashamed. "Oh, please don't bother," she said eagerly. But instead of replying the fat man wrote something, glanced at her again. "Do I remember this bright little face?" he said softly. "Is it known to me of yore?" At that moment the band began playing; the fat man disappeared. He was tossed away on a great wave of music that came flying over the gleaming floor, breaking the groups up into couples, scattering them, sending them spinning. . . .

Leila had learned to dance at boarding school. Every Saturday afternoon the boarders were hurried off to a little corrugated iron mission hall where Miss Eccles (of London) held her "select" classes. But the difference between that dusty-smelling hall—with calico texts on the walls, the poor terrified little woman in a brown velvet toque with rabbit's ears thumping the cold piano, Miss Eccles poking the girls' feet with her long white wand—and this was so tremendous that Leila was sure if her partner didn't come and she had to listen to that marvelous music and to watch the others sliding, gliding over the golden floor, she would die at least, or faint, or lift her arms and fly out of one of those dark windows that showed the stars.

"Ours, I think—" Some one bowed, smiled, and offered her his arm; she hadn't to die after all. Some one's hand pressed her waist, and she floated away like a flower that is tossed into a pool.

"Quite a good floor, isn't it?" drawled a faint voice close to her ear.

"I think it's most beautifully slippery," said Leila.

"Pardon!" The faint voice sounded surprised. Leila said it again. And there was a tiny pause before the voice echoed, "Oh, quite!" and she was swung round again.

He steered so beautifully. That was the great difference between dancing with girls and men, Leila decided. Girls banged into each other, and stamped on each other's feet; the girl who was gentleman always clutched you so.

The azaleas were separate flowers no longer; they were pink and white flags streaming by.

"Were you at the Bells' last week?" the voice came again. It sounded tired. Leila wondered whether she ought to ask him if he would like to stop.

"No, this is my first dance," said she.

Her partner gave a little gasping laugh. "Oh, I say," he protested.

"Yes, it is really the first dance I've ever been to." Leila was most fervent. It was such a relief to be able to tell somebody. "You see, I've lived in the country all my life up until now. . . ."

At that moment the music stopped, and they went to sit on two chairs against the wall. Leila tucked her pink satin feet under and fanned herself, while she blissfully watched the other couples passing and disappearing through the swing doors.

"Enjoying yourself, Leila?" asked Jose, nodding her golden head.

Laura passed and gave her the faintest little wink; it made Leila wonder for a moment whether she was quite grown up after all. Certainly her partner did not say very much. He coughed, tucked his handkerchief away, pulled down his waistcoat, took a minute thread off his sleeve. But it didn't matter. Almost immediately the band started, and her second partner seemed to spring from the ceiling.

"Floor's not bad," said the new voice. Did one always begin with the floor? And then, "Were you at the Neaves' on Tuesday?" And again Leila explained. Perhaps it was a little strange that her partners were not more interested. For it was thrilling. Her first ball! She was only at the beginning of everything. It seemed to her that she had never known what the night was like before. Up till now it had been dark, silent, beautiful very often—oh, yes—but mournful somehow. Solemn. And now it would never be like that again—it had opened dazzling bright.

"Care for an ice?" said her partner. And they went through the swing doors, down the passage, to the supper room. Her cheeks burned, she was fearfully thirsty. How sweet the ices looked on little glass plates, and how cold the frosted spoon was, iced too! And when they came back to the hall there was the fat man waiting for her by the door. It gave her quite a shock again to see how old he was; he ought to have been on the stage with the fathers and mothers. And when Leila compared him with her other partners he looked shabby. His waistcoat was creased, there was a button off his glove, his coat looked as if it was dusty with French chalk.

"Come along, little lady," said the fat man. He scarcely troubled to clasp her, and they moved away so gently, it was more like walking than dancing. But he said not a word about the floor. "Your first dance, isn't it?" he murmured.

"How *did* you know?"

"Ah," said the fat man, "that's what it is to be old!" He wheezed faintly as he steered her past an awkward couple. "You see, I've been doing this kind of thing for the last thirty years."

"Thirty years?" cried Leila. Twelve years before she was born!

"It hardly bears thinking about, does it?" said the fat man gloomily. Leila looked at his bald head, and she felt quite sorry for him.

"I think it's marvelous to be still going on," she said kindly.

"Kind little lady," said the fat man, and he pressed her a little closer, and hummed a bar of the waltz. "Of course," he said, "you can't hope to last anything like as long as that. No-o," said the fat man, "long before that you'll be sitting up there on the stage, looking on, in your nice black velvet. And these pretty arms will have turned into little short fat ones, and you'll beat time with such a different kind of fan—a black bony one." The fat man seemed to shudder. "And you'll smile away like the poor old dears up there, and point to your daughter, and tell the elderly lady next to you how

some dreadful man tried to kiss her at the club ball. And your heart will ache, ache"—
the fat man squeezed her closer still, as if he really was sorry for that poor heart—"because no one wants to kiss you now. And you'll say how unpleasant these polished
floors are to walk on, how dangerous they are. Eh, Mademoiselle Twinkletoes?" said
the fat man softly.

Leila gave a light little laugh, but she did not feel like laughing. Was it—could it
all be true? It sounded terribly true. Was this first ball only the beginning of her last
ball after all? At that the music seemed to change; it sounded sad, sad it rose upon a
great sigh. Oh, how quickly things changed! Why didn't happiness last for ever? For
ever wasn't a bit too long.

"I want to stop," she said in a breathless voice. The fat man led her to the door.

"No," she said, "I won't go outside. I won't sit down. I'll just stand here, thank
you." She leaned against the wall, tapping with her foot, pulling up her gloves and
trying to smile. But deep inside her a little girl threw her pinafore over her head and
sobbed. Why had he spoiled it all?

"I say, you know," said the fat man, "you mustn't take me seriously, little lady."

"As if I should!" said Leila, tossing her small dark head and sucking her underlip. . . .

Again the couples paraded. The swing doors opened and shut. Now new music was
given out by the bandmaster. But Leila didn't want to dance any more. She wanted
to be home, or sitting on the veranda listening to those baby owls. When she looked
through the dark windows at the stars, they had long beams like wings. . . .

But presently a soft, melting, ravishing tune began, and a young man with curly
hair bowed before her. She would have to dance, out of politeness, until she could find
Meg. Very stiffly she walked into the middle; very haughtily she put her hand on his
sleeve. But in one minute, in one turn, her feet glided, glided. The lights, the azaleas,
the dresses, the pink faces, the velvet chairs, all became one beautiful flying wheel.
And when her next partner bumped her into the fat man and he said, "Pardon," she
smiled at him more radiantly than ever. She didn't even recognize him again.

[1922]

Questions

1. How is Leila different from her city cousins? How are these differences important
   to the story?
2. What are Leila's feelings about the ball? Do they change during the evening?
3. What role does the fat man play in Leila's perceptions of the ball? How does Leila
   respond to his cynical observations?
4. Compare this story to "The Kiss" by Anton Chekhov. In what ways are the naive
   young protagonists similar? In what ways are the stories similar in theme?

René Marqués
(1919–1979)
Puerto Rico

The myth of the American Dream tells us (among other things) that immigrants adjust to their new lives in the United States and share in the country's bounty. Although René Marqués's story questions that myth, in a larger sense his story asks whether Puerto Rico (his country of birth) will ever be independent from the United States or will continue to be dominated by the American presence. No doubt these are questions sharpened in Marqués's consciousness as a result of the periods of his own life when he lived and studied in the United States.

Born in Arecibo, Puerto Rico, in 1919, Marqués initially trained as an agricultural engineer. He subsequently worked as an agronomist for the Department of Agriculture, as the manager of a department store, and as an English teacher. Though he was a prolific writer, only a few of his works have been translated into English: the story that follows, a play titled The Oxcart (1969), and a novel, The Look (1975). In her study of Marquéz, Eleanor Martin observes that his work is "a mirror of his time; it is particularly a reflection of his intervention in Puerto Rico's economy, culture, and politics" during the twentieth century.

ISLAND OF MANHATTAN

> "Cordelia of the waves,
> Bitter Cordelia."
>
> —Gabriela Mistral

Juanita raised the collar of her wool jacket and took a deep breath. She would never get used to this subterranean life. Every time she came out of the subway station, she felt an irrepressible relief.

She stood in the middle of the sidewalk, stepping aside to avoid the avalanche of people. Even so, a huge man brutally pushed against her.

"Animal," she whispered.

The man stopped in his tracks, looked at her and said, almost smiling, "Take it easy, spik." Then, as she walked away quickly, he began to follow her.

She didn't know if it were the insult or the mocking smile that made her shake with anger.

"Yankee! Brute!" she shouted. But the man did not even look back this time.

Juanita looked at her watch. Twenty-five to ten. She had time. She absent-mindedly wound her watch and thought about the five payments she still owed on it. She straightened her shoulders and began to walk towards Madison.

She was walking slowly, as if she were strolling around the little plaza in Lares. She laughed to herself at the beauty of it. The memory of Lares seemed a dream. Or was this the total dream!

The important thing was that she was not in a hurry. For the first time in four years she was not in a hurry. Twenty-five minutes in which to walk three blocks. She stopped next to an overflowing garbage can to straighten her stockings. She pulled the garter down and snapped it over the stocking. She noticed that there was a run.

"Damn it! And a new pair!"

At that moment she heard a whistle. She quickly lowered her skirt and looked up to see a young man leaning against the railing. She looked him up and down.

"You have a long way to go before you can whistle like a man," she mocked.

The youngster turned tomato-red, but was Don Juan enough to say, "With you I could learn in a day."

She laughed loudly, nervously, and walked on. To learn in one day. Without knowing why, she stopped laughing. No. Perhaps not in one day. But one learns quickly. A year in Rio Piedras, two in San Juan, four in New York. Yes, above all, these years. How far I've come! The farm in San Isidro where the old man was a tenant farmer. The humid shade of the guamas. The little plaza. The moldy vestments of the big-bellied priest. The white candle of the first communion.

She felt a sweet sadness, tranquil, without anxiety or bitterness. The candle of her first communion. The white candle that today she wasn't going to have. Perhaps if she had shared that thought with someone she would not have laughed so loudly just then. No, there would be no white candle, nor lights, nor flowers. Nor a big-bellied priest.

"Goddammit! That bag is mine. You spik! Let it go! You dirty Portorican!"

"I made that bag myself, coño. It's mine, you half of a man, you Yankee!"

The two little boys wrestled furiously on the sidewalk, blocking her way. She was tempted to intervene, but she saw that the small, dark one with kinky hair was winning.

She smiled. "Take advantage of this, jibarito! There won't be many times when you'll be on top!" she shouted as she walked past.

"At ten in front of Joe's Bar," Nico had said. To meet him or not—she had given a lot of thought to this. Nico knew everything about her life—the year at the University, her work in radio, the shame in New York. Yes, above all, that. Still he kept insisting. Jenny felt confused.

"Why do you call yourself Nick instead of Nico?"

"Because I'm a foreman. This way everyone respects me."

"Wouldn't they respect you if they called you Nico?"

"Don't ask too many questions, baby. . . ." And he laughed showing shining teeth against his dark complexion.

How could he speak seriously of marriage? This thought unsettled her. She experienced a rare feeling of sin, of being immoral and yet accepting a moral solution.

"Do you know what I am, Nico?"

"Sure, you are my Jenny."

"I'm a prostitute."

"You are my Jenny."

And to her it didn't seem natural that a man—a real man—would accept the situation like that.

"You don't seem Puerto Rican."

"I'm an American citizen."

"You're from Quebradillas."

"But still an American citizen."

She was also an American citizen, but there was a huge abyss between her American citizenship and her Puerto Rican heritage.

"Nico, sometimes I believe I could understand an American better than I understand you."

"But, baby, you don't have to understand anything. The only thing you have to do is love me."

Did I love him ever? Yes, that had to be love. I had never loved anyone like that before, except that Lareño from San Isidro, barefoot and pale. It had been such a long time ago.

She probably began to love Nico during her only year at the University. He was in his second year of Industrial Arts and she, with a scholarship and the dream of a rural school, was in her freshman year. It was through Nico that she had gotten involved in the strike at the University.

"Man and woman, side by side, must protest against injustice," he had said.

When they were both expelled for protesting, she fully understood what Nico had meant. The street of Rio Piedras had seemed wide and frank with its real immediacy.

And she remembered clearly the university carrillon behind her repeating the sonorous melody—"London Bridge is falling down, falling down. . . ."

But it was not the English bridge that was falling in her life, but the dream of a rural school near San Isidro.

A beer bottle fell on the sidewalk breaking into a thousand pieces. Juanita jumped back surprised. From the window came the voice of a woman—shrill, strident, hysterical, like an uncontainable torrent.

"And if you like to drink beer, go to the bar! I am fed up with cleaning up your vomit! Do you hear me? Fed up! What I have here is not a house, but a pigpen! We live like pigs! And as if it weren't enough, you come here with your drunken vomit! When I get a few pennies together, I'm going back to Puerto Rico. And I'm taking the children with me!"

The voice of the man—thick, hoarse, stuttering sadly.

"But, Negra, don't be like this. If we can find something better? . . ."

"You can look for something, but don't count on me." And Juanita heard a door slam, furiously, and with finality.

She kicked the pieces of glass with her foot, looked again at the vacant window and straightening her shoulders, walked on.

Yes, Nico was a winner. In seven years he had conquered the city. Already he was a foreman. And he called himself Nick and spoke English. Juanita admired that capacity for adjusting. But she was suspicious. She had a peasant fear of that extraordinary ability to submit to New York. "It isn't natural," she thought.

"You've changed so much, Nico," she had told him.

"Nonsense, I am the same." And he had affirmed this with a long kiss.

Was he the same? Or was she the one who had changed? Six years was a long time. And she remembered his voice burning with indignation when they had been expelled from the University.

"I'm going to New York. Here on the island there is no feeling for justice."

With Nico's departure, she found herself lost and she almost returned to Lares. But an awakening instinct to fight back kept her in San Juan. She kept herself alive selling hot dogs and Coca-Colas until she got the job at the radio station. It all began with her reciting a poem by Llorens on an amateur program. The rest just happened, like rain falling from heaven. She began acting in soap operas.

Her acting in radio programs didn't carry her to stardom, but those obscure roles of perverse women gave her room and board and the cotton dresses she made herself. She owed this opportunity to Nico too. It was he who had insisted on correcting her country accent. By the time Nico had left for the states, she was able to tighten her teeth to let out sibilant "eses." And she had also learned not to pronounce "i" for "e." Nico's lessons had prepared her for radio. She began to receive fan letters, one of them even from Lares.

Now, in the cold air of the city, she could laugh at the soap operas in San Juan. But at that time, no. Justice always triumphed in the scripts. And the unjust were justly punished. Nevertheless, her position was precarious. When a villainess died, she no longer had a job. And although her honor wanted the death of the villainess, her stomach wanted to prolong the life of that despicable being.

Then came the strike and its clamor of confused voices.

"Our right. . . . Justice. . . . The law. . . . Our rights. . . . Justice. . . . The owner. . . . Justice. . . . The owner. . . . Justice. . . . the worker. . . ."

And thinking of Nico, she went on strike. Another time, on strike!

She wrote him in New York, sure that he would approve of her decision. But the letter was returned. The great city had swallowed him up.

The day when she fainted, carrying a picket sign in front of the radio station, the strike ended. It was the fourth month of abstinence, of almost fasting. The fourth month of picket lines, of insults from scabs. And she raised a prayer to heaven for returning "our daily bread." But she soon found out that "our daily bread" doesn't always come from heaven.

The strike had been a success. Justice had triumphed, said some. But others, the owners of the station, didn't say anything. The owners of the station smiled, kindly patronizing smiles. And the scabs replaced the ex-strikers.

Juanita remembered how on another occasion the street had appeared wide and frank in its immediacy. And how as she had left the station, the amplifiers in the vestibule repeated the melody, "Enjoy yourself. It's later than you think."

Late? If it were too late to enjoy yourself, it was not too late to escape.

And so the noise of the plane's motors united the group of immigrants in a huge uncertainty of space of the earth they seemed to leave behind and gain again.

At that moment the noise of a passing bus brought her back to reality. She was at Madison. She walked one block to the right and stopped to cross the street. Joe's Bar was on the other side. She saw a crowd of people exactly in the spot where she was to meet Nico. What was happening. Were the Irish police at it again or was it only an accident? The green light changed and she crossed the Avenue rapidly. Then she noticed the flags and the speakers' platform. It was another meeting. Meetings were boring to her. But there was no way to avoid it. Had Nico arrived yet? She looked around for him. No, he wasn't there. Well, she would have to wait. She stood in front of the bar where there were fewer people. She opened her purse and took out a mirror to touch up her lipstick.

At the beginning the English words didn't mean anything to her. She was thinking in Spanish, which made her deaf to the foreign language. Still, little by little, her brain began to perceive the English words. Later, the fiery speech began to make itself intelligible to her. She put away her lipstick, closed her purse and looked toward the rostrum.

A man was speaking about eight black men condemned to death for having tried to rape a blonde woman. Juanita at the beginning believed that she had heard it incorrectly. No, no, it was not possible. But the man went on repeating it and repeating it. Nevertheless, the whole idea of this stuck in her craw. To kill eight men for having tried to rape a woman? My God . . . Eight lives! And only for trying! What would have happened to the eight black men had they actually destroyed that delicate virginal tissue? Well, they could not do more to them after killing them. No, but they could do something before. Perhaps they could tear their flesh piece by piece with great red-hot tongs, like the print in the sacristy of the church in Lares. But no, the man was saying that they were only going to be hanged.

She tried to imagine the eight hanging by ropes, hanging from the branch of a tamarind tree. Would it be from a tree that they would hang them? "No, it isn't natural," she said.

And she thought of her own virginity. It was the day of her visit to the Insular Office in New York. The woman who was filling out the forms had stopped her suddenly and had looked fixedly at her.

"You were a striker at the University?"

Surprised, she had nodded her head.

"And a striker at the radio station in Puerto Rico?" She felt the need to talk, to explain something. But she didn't know what to say. Again, she just nodded her head. The woman got up and disappeared behind a green glass door marked Private. Juanita began to look at the posters announcing educational films. "A Voice in the Mountain," read one. She thought of how abandoned her own voice sounded in this mountain of steel and armored cement.

Then the woman returned and, sitting down, continued her work filling out forms.

"Sign here," she said, handing her the fountain pen.

Juanita signed and sat there waiting.

"That is all," said the other.

"They will get in touch with me if there is something?" she asked tentatively.

"Of course," said the woman.

But she left the office with the certainty that it was all useless, that they would not help her find work here. She didn't know why she had this certainty. She didn't know if the questions about the strike were personal questions of the employer or something official which could hurt her. She didn't know anything. But she felt a terrible and total hopelessness. She began to think that this was the end.

For that reason, she was almost thankful for the impertinence of the blonde man in the street. She needed the company of someone, the warmth of another voice. She needed the presence of another human being to whom she could communicate the feeling that she was alive, that she did exist. So she let herself be led. They went to Palisades Park. He was reasonably attentive to her. He made her play the Wheel of Fortune and she won a canary. A canary that didn't sing, but was alive. A canary living locked up in his cage.

They returned late to Manhattan. And they drank whiskey. It was the first time she had drunk whiskey. But she didn't make a big fuss about it. She drank it slowly with the same resignation with which she would have taken a laxative. Her hopelessness was drowning in a dense cloud. Then suddenly she found herself in a narrow and bad-smelling little room. The canary slept in his cage. And the man undressed her with hot, impatient hands. She wanted to fight, but she felt weak. The panic and the horror, more than the whiskey, had paralyzed her.

Hours later, she found herself on a dark street, leaning against a brick wall with the stabbing cold of the morning sneaking in through the tears in her dress. And when she raised her hand to her mouth to choke a sob, she discovered the bill in her clenched fist.

They didn't hang anyone then. The police were not aware that there was one less virgin around. Only Doña Casilda, the Cuban in Harlem, knew it, she who performed the abortion. The rest had been easy, too easy.

And suddenly Juanita began to feel a tremendous burning in her blood. It was like a blaze which rose and rose. And the word *Justice* in the mouth of the speaker began to take on a special meaning. And the word *Injustice* too. She thought of the white, blonde woman. She thought of the eight black men too. And she understood. She understood with clarity the language and almost with horror the ideas. Her hard, peasant guts had finally perceived something monstrous.

And that perception warmed her soul. And shook her conscience. Virgin of Carmen! Was it possible?

She forgot the platform and the meeting. She didn't see the people surrounding her. She saw instead herself as if projected on a screen. And she saw the blonde and the eight men. And now she heard the words of the speaker in a different way. It was almost as if she had not heard them. As if those words were conceived in her brain and spoken by another. She was not able to say if it was what she was thinking now in English or what the other man was saying in Spanish.

But there was no longer any language barrier. For that matter when the speaker was asking in English that justice be done for the eight men, she shouted in Spanish, "Yes, we are going to do it!" But she could have sworn that she had said it in English.

On hearing the shout in Spanish, many faces turned towards her . . . smiling, hostile, impassive. But Juanita didn't see the faces. She knew that they were there, but she didn't see them. She only saw the piece of paper that began to circulate from the platform among the crowd. She saw the paper appear and disappear from hand to hand, the distance between it and her gradually decreasing.

Suddenly she felt two strong hands on her shoulders. "What the hell are you doing here?"

She recognized the voice, but wasn't surprised nor did she have any interest in turning around. The paper continued within her eyeshot. Did she have a pencil in her purse? She opened her purse and looked for it . . . only a lipstick.

"Do you have a pencil?" she asked, half turning her head.

"Come on," she heard Nico say. Later his voice became urgent, almost hopeless. "Come on. Let's get out of here." And she felt that he was trying to drag her outside the circle of spectators.

Juanita brusquely shook his hands off her shoulders. "Leave me alone," she said. And once free, she was face to face with him. She saw that he was pale and in anguish. His face was soaked with perspiration in spite of the cool air of the Avenue.

"What has happened to you?" she asked.

He looked again at the people surrounding him. He came near her again and whispered in a tone of supplication that she had never known before, "Let's get away from here, for the love of God! Come on!"

He said this in Spanish. And what was strange, in a Spanish with a Puerto Rican accent, free from the North American accent that he had acquired in his six years in the city. Seeing that she just looked at him saying nothing, he tried to pretend anguish, smiling.

"Remember, today we get married."

"Married?" Yes, that was right. Today they were getting married.

After six years they had found each other in New York.

"You see what I am now," she had said then with a brutal frankness to hide her shame.

But he wasn't ashamed. Nico was a conqueror. She believed that they had found each other too late. But he, no. Nick was a man of the city. And she had conquered his scruples. She had fastened herself to this man who had been her only inspiration when she had arrived in Rio Piedras saying "Lari" and swallowing her "eses."

Marry. Yes, Nico was there. And today they were getting married. But it wasn't haste for the wedding that she now saw in him. It was something that she didn't understand.

"I'm not leaving yet. Wait for me." And she turned from him.

The paper with the petition for a new trial for the black men was coming nearer. She felt his body behind her, the hands compulsively grabbing her two arms, his breath burning in her right ear.

"Please, you don't understand. This is dangerous."

"Dangerous?" She was bothered by the pressure of Nico's hands on her arms.

"Don't hold me so tight," she said.

His voice continued in Spanish, more urgently, more brokenly.

"Are you crazy? Look at that flag. We'll find ourselves in the police files. Come on, come on, I tell you."

She looked towards the platform and she finally understood. The breeze had begun to softly unfurl one of the two flags, withered and quiet until that instant, the same instant in which the petition reached her hands. And the voice of the man in her ears, like a deaf shout. "Let it go! Pass it on, so they don't see you with it!"

But the voice didn't strike her consciousness. What did a flag matter to her? What mattered in this instance was justice. And justice was that piece of paper which was in her hands for the first time in her life. For that reason, his voice sounded strange, remote, indifferent.

A woman offered her a stump of a pencil. She took it and looked at the blunt point. She almost simultaneously felt that they were going to snatch the paper from her hands.

She turned around and looked at Nico grabbing the paper away from her convulsively. She saw his disjointed features, his pale lips, his forehead perspiring and contracted. She lowered her eyes to look at the paper crumpled in his hands and raised her eyes again to look at the livid face. In that short time she discovered the strange trembling in her body.

She had the impression that she wasn't looking at a human being. And she discovered what she hadn't discovered moments before. Nico's fear. An almost animal fear, an infra-human fear coming through his eyes, through his soul, through his pores. And she understood. For the second time that morning she had understood with a painful clarity. She understood Nico also, almost suddenly. She saw how much humanity he had had to give up to become foreman. She understood the price of his triumph in the city. And she understood his fear. But the understanding disgusted her. She felt such a violent loathing that it almost brought on a contraction in her stomach.

And again Juanita began to feel a tremendous warmth in her blood. It was like a blaze that rose and rose. She had to exert an extraordinary strength to contain the fire that burned at her lips. Remembering him and lowering her voice she was able to condense to a brief threat all the tumult of her feelings. "Give me that paper or I'll tear your face to shreds."

Also to him this Juanita was different from his sweet "Jenny." If the new dread of the threat hadn't added up to all his fears, he would have felt deceived. But only horror reigned in him now.

"If you sign that, I'll never marry you."

She wanted to laugh, but she controlled herself. She took the paper and pressing her made-up face close to his livid one, she almost spat out the words, "If I were a decent woman, I could afford the luxury of saying, 'I would rather become a whore than marry you!'"

She began to laugh finally and, seeing his expression, she added in a voice that was almost a shout, "But as I am what I am, I can only say to you, 'Coward! I don't ever want to see you again!'"

And she turned her back on him. She held the paper against her purse and signed it with the blunt pencil. In that instant a little band next to the platform began to play a tune she had never heard before. She handed the paper and pencil on to a black man and began to make her way through the crowd. Only when she came to the comer of 114th Street did she stop. The street opened wide and frank in its real immediacy. She raised the collar of her wool jacket and breathed deeply.

The fresh air gave her a rare sensation of joy this time. She felt that the justice that would free the eight condemned men had given her back her own freedom. And she began to walk down the street. A clock in a drugstore told her it was twelve o'clock. Seeing the two clock hands together, she instinctively made the sign of the cross, as if here in the city the angelus of the church of Lares was ringing.

[1974]
Translated by
FAYE EDWARDS and GLADYS ORITZ

Questions

1. Is the subway mentioned at the beginning of the story of any significance in your interpretation of Marqués's tale?
2. Does the reversal of traditional masculine and feminine roles add anything to your understanding of Puerto Rico's relationship to the United States? Or about gender roles and stereotypes?
3. What, specifically, does the title suggest?
4. If Juanita's story had been written by a woman writer, would it be substantially different?

Bobbie Ann Mason

(b. 1940)

United States

B obbie Ann Mason was born in Mayfield, Kentucky, and grew up on her parents' dairy farm. Majoring in journalism at the University of Kentucky, she went on to receive a Ph.D. in English at the University of Connecticut and taught English at a college in Pennsylvania. She began her writing career by publishing sketches of such teen stars as Annette Funicello in slick teen fan magazines such as Movie Stars, Movie Life, and T.V. Star Parade. In an entirely different vein, in 1975 she published The Girl Sleuth: A Feminist Guide to the Bobbsey Twins, Nancy Drew, and Their Sisters. Mason gave the following description of the unlikely trajectory of her career as a writer:

> After graduating from the University of Kentucky I went to New York City and worked
> as a writer on some fan magazines. . . . It wasn't the writing career I had had in mind
> when I was an iconoclastic columnist on the University of Kentucky Kernel, so I went
> off to graduate school to study literature and that took a long time. When I finally came
> to my senses after finishing the dissertation . . . [on Vladimir Nabokov's novel Ada], I
> lapsed back into my childhood and started reading Nancy Drew books. Life has been
> steady progress since then.

Mason published her first short story in The New Yorker in 1980. Not long afterward, her collection of stories, Shiloh and Other Stories (1982), received high praise, including its recognition with the Ernest Hemingway Foundation Award. She has published three additional collections of stories, Love Life (1989), Midnight Magic (1998), and Zigzagging Down a Wild Trail (2001), as well as three novels, In Country (1985), Spence and Lila (1988), and Feather Crowns (1993).

In her stories and novels, Mason focuses on ordinary working-class people from the milieu of her own origins in rural western Kentucky, characters who are on the lower margins of the middle class and trying to move up. With an unerring eye for both the material and the psychological environments of her characters, Mason explores the ways in which they are caught, like flies in amber, in a world paradoxically static and rapidly changing before their very eyes.

SHILOH

Leroy Moffitt's wife, Norma Jean, is working on her pectorals. She lifts three-pound dumbbells to warm up, then progresses to a twenty-pound barbell. Standing with her legs apart, she reminds Leroy of Wonder Woman.

"I'd give anything if I could just get these muscles to where they're real hard," says Norma Jean. "Feel this arm. It's not as hard as the other one."

"That's cause you're right-handed," says Leroy, dodging as she swings the barbell in an arc.

"Do you think so?"

"Sure."

Leroy is a truckdriver. He injured his leg in a highway accident four months ago, and his physical therapy, which involves weights and a pulley, prompted Norma Jean to try building herself up. Now she is attending a body-building class. Leroy has been collecting temporary disability since his tractor-trailer jackknifed in Missouri, badly twisting his left leg in its socket. He has a steel pin in his hip. He will probably not be able to drive his rig again. It sits in the backyard, like a gigantic bird that has flown home to roost. Leroy has been home in Kentucky for three months, and his leg is almost healed, but the accident frightened him and he does not want to drive any more long hauls. He is not sure what to do next. In the meantime, he makes things from craft kits. He started by building a miniature log cabin from notched Popsicle sticks. He varnished it and placed it on the TV set, where it remains. It reminds him of a rustic Nativity scene. Then he tried string art (sailing ships on black velvet), a macramé owl kit, a snap-together B-17 Flying Fortress, and a lamp made out of a model truck, with a light fixture screwed in the top of the cab. At first the kits were diversions, something to kill time, but now he is thinking about building a full-scale log house from a kit. It would be considerably cheaper than building a regular house, and besides, Leroy has grown to appreciate how things are put together. He has begun to realize that in all the years he was on the road he never took time to examine anything. He was always flying past scenery.

"They won't let you build a log cabin in any of the new subdivisions," Norma Jean tells him.

"They will if I tell them it's for you," he says, teasing her. Ever since they were married, he has promised Norma Jean he would build her a new home one day. They have always rented, and the house they live in is small and nondescript. It does not even feel like a home, Leroy realizes now.

Norma Jean works at the Rexall drugstore, and she has acquired an amazing amount of information about cosmetics. When she explains to Leroy the three stages of complexion care, involving creams, toners, and moisturizers, he thinks happily of other petroleum products—axle grease, diesel fuel. This is a connection between him and Norma Jean. Since he has been home, he has felt unusually tender about his wife and guilty over his long absences. But he can't tell what she feels about him. Norma Jean has never complained about his traveling; she has never made hurt remarks, like calling his truck a "widow-maker." He is reasonably certain she has been faithful to him, but he wishes she would celebrate his permanent homecoming more happily. Norma Jean is often startled to find Leroy at home, and he thinks she seems a little disappointed about it. Perhaps he reminds her too much of the early days of their marriage, before he went on the road. They had a child who died as an infant, years ago. They never speak about their memories of Randy, which have almost faded, but now that Leroy is home all the time, they sometimes feel awkward around each other, and Leroy wonders if one of them should mention the child. He has the feeling that they are waking up out of a dream together—that they must create a new marriage, start afresh. They are lucky they are still married. Leroy has read that for most people losing a child destroys the marriage—or else he heard this on *Donahue*. He can't always remember where he learns things anymore.

At Christmas, Leroy bought an electric organ for Norma Jean. She used to play the piano when she was in high school. "It don't leave you," she told him once. "It's like riding a bicycle."

The new instrument had so many keys and buttons that she was bewildered by it at first. She touched the keys tentatively, pushed some buttons, then pecked out "Chopsticks." It came out in an amplified fox-trot rhythm, with marimba sounds.

"It's an orchestra!" she cried.

The organ had a pecan-look finish and eighteen preset chords, with optional flute, violin, trumpet, clarinet, and banjo accompaniments. Norma Jean mastered the organ almost immediately. At first she played Christmas songs. Then she bought *The Sixties Songbook* and learned every tune in it, adding variations to each with the rows of brightly colored buttons.

"I didn't like these old songs back then," she said. "But I have this crazy feeling I missed something."

"You didn't miss a thing," said Leroy.

Leroy likes to lie on the couch and smoke a joint and listen to Norma Jean play "Can't Take My Eyes Off You" and "I'll Be Back." He is back again. After fifteen years on the road, he is finally settling down with the woman he loves. She is still pretty. Her skin is flawless. Her frosted curls resemble pencil trimmings.

Now that Leroy has come home to stay, he notices how much the town has changed. Subdivisions are spreading across western Kentucky like an oil slick. The sign at the edge of town says "Pop: 11,500"—only seven hundred more than it said twenty years before. Leroy can't figure out who is living in all the new houses. The farmers who used to gather around the courthouse square on Saturday afternoons to play checkers and spit tobacco juice have gone. It has been years since Leroy has thought about the farmers, and they have disappeared without his noticing.

Leroy meets a kid named Stevie Hamilton in the parking lot at the new shopping center. While they pretend to be strangers meeting over a stalled car, Stevie tosses an ounce of marijuana under the front seat of Leroy's car. Stevie is wearing orange jogging shoes and a T-shirt that says CHATTAHOOCHEE SUPER-RAT. His father is a prominent doctor who lives in one of the expensive subdivisions in a new white-columned brick house that looks like a funeral parlor. In the phone book under his name there is a separate number, with the listing "Teenagers."

"Where do you get this stuff?" asks Leroy. "From your pappy?"

"That's for me to know and you to find out," Stevie says. He is slit-eyed and skinny.

"What else you got?"

"What you interested in?"

"Nothing special. Just wondered."

Leroy used to take speed on the road. Now he has to go slowly. He needs to be mellow. He leans back against the car and says, "I'm aiming to build me a log house, soon as I get time. My wife, though, I don't think she likes the idea."

"Well, let me know when you want me again," Stevie says. He has a cigarette in his cupped palm, as though sheltering it from the wind. He takes a long drag, then stomps it on the asphalt and slouches away.

Stevie's father was two years ahead of Leroy in high school. Leroy is thirty-four. He married Norma Jean when they were both eighteen, and their child Randy was born a few months later, but he died at the age of four months and three days. He would be about Stevie's age now. Norma Jean and Leroy were at the drive-in, watching a double feature (*Dr. Strangelove* and *Lover Come Back*), and the baby was sleeping in the back seat. When the first movie ended, the baby was dead. It was the sudden infant death syndrome. Leroy remembers handing Randy to a nurse at the emergency room, as though he were offering her a large doll as a present. A dead baby feels like a sack of flour. "It just happens sometimes," said the doctor, in what Leroy always recalls as a nonchalant tone. Leroy can hardly remember the child anymore, but he still sees vividly a scene from *Dr. Strangelove* in which the President of the United States was talking in a folksy voice on the hot line to the Soviet premier about the bomber accidentally headed toward Russia. He was in the War Room, and the world map was lit up. Leroy remembers Norma Jean standing catatonically beside him in the hospital and himself thinking: Who is this strange girl? He had forgotten who she was. Now scientists are saying that crib death is caused by a virus. Nobody knows anything, Leroy thinks. The answers are always changing.

When Leroy gets home from the shopping center, Norma Jean's mother, Mabel Beasley, is there. Until this year, Leroy has not realized how much time she spends with Norma Jean. When she visits, she inspects the closets and then the plants, informing Norma Jean when a plant is droopy or yellow. Mabel calls the plants "flowers," although there are never any blooms. She always notices if Norma Jean's laundry is piling up. Mabel is a short, overweight woman whose tight, brown-dyed curls look more like a wig than the actual wig she sometimes wears. Today she has brought Norma Jean an off-white dust ruffle she made for the bed; Mabel works in a custom-upholstery shop.

"This is the tenth one I made this year," Mabel says. "I got started and couldn't stop."

"It's real pretty," says Norma Jean.

"Now we can hide things under the bed," says Leroy, who gets along with his mother-in-law primarily by joking with her. Mabel has never really forgiven him for disgracing her by getting Norma Jean pregnant. When the baby died, she said that fate was mocking her.

"What's that thing?" Mabel says to Leroy in a loud voice, pointing to a tangle of yarn on a piece of canvas.

Leroy holds it up for Mabel to see. "It's my needlepoint," he explains. "This is a *Star Trek* pillow cover."

"That's what a woman would do," says Mabel. "Great day in the morning!"

"All the big football players on TV do it," he says.

"Why, Leroy, you're always trying to fool me. I don't believe you for one minute. You don't know what to do with yourself—that's the whole trouble. Sewing!"

"I'm aiming to build us a log house," says Leroy. "Soon as my plans come."

"Like *heck* you are," says Norma Jean. She takes Leroy's needlepoint and shoves it into a drawer. "You have to find a job first. Nobody can afford to build now anyway."

Mabel straightens her girdle and says, "I still think before you get tied down y'all ought to take a little run to Shiloh."

"One of these days, Mama," Norma Jean says impatiently.

Mabel is talking about Shiloh, Tennessee. For the past few years, she has been urging Leroy and Norma Jean to visit the Civil War battleground there. Mabel went there on her honeymoon—the only real trip she ever took. Her husband died of a perforated ulcer when Norma Jean was ten, but Mabel, who was accepted into the United Daughters of the Confederacy in 1975, is still preoccupied with going back to Shiloh.

"I've been to kingdom come and back in that truck out yonder," Leroy says to Mabel, "but we never yet set foot in that battleground. Ain't that something? How did I miss it?"

"It's not even that far," Mabel says.

After Mabel leaves, Norma Jean reads to Leroy from a list she has made. "Things you could do," she announces. "You could get a job as a guard at Union Carbide, where they'd let you set on a stool. You could get one at the lumberyard. You could do a little carpenter work, if you want to build so bad. You could—"

"I can't do something where I'd have to stand up all day."

"You ought to try standing up all day behind a cosmetics counter. It's amazing that I have strong feet, coming from two parents that never had strong feet at all." At the moment Norma Jean is holding on to the kitchen counter, raising her knees one at a time as she talks. She is wearing two-pound ankle weights.

"Don't worry," says Leroy. "I'll do something."

"You could truck calves to slaughter for somebody. You wouldn't have to drive any big old truck for that."

"I'm going to build you this house," says Leroy. "I want to make you a real home."

"I don't want to live in any log cabin."

"It's not a cabin. It's a house."

"I don't care. It looks like a cabin."

"You and me together could lift those logs. It's just like lifting weights."

Norma Jean doesn't answer. Under her breath, she is counting. Now she is marching through the kitchen. She is doing goose steps.

Before his accident, when Leroy came home he used to stay in the house with Norma Jean, watching TV in bed and playing cards. She would cook fried chicken, picnic ham, chocolate pie—all his favorites. Now he is home alone much of the time. In the mornings, Norma Jean disappears, leaving a cooling place in the bed. She eats a cereal called Body Buddies, and she leaves the bowl on the table, with soggy tan balls floating in a milk puddle. He sees things about Norma Jean that he never realized before. When she chops onions, she stares off into a corner, as if she can't bear to look. She puts on her house slippers almost precisely at nine o'clock every evening and nudges her jogging shoes under the couch. She saves bread heels for the birds. Leroy watches the birds at the feeder. He notices the peculiar way goldfinches fly past the window. They close their wings, then fall, then spread their wings to catch and lift themselves. He wonders if they close their eyes when they fall. Norma Jean closes her eyes when they are in bed. She wants the lights turned out. Even then, he is sure she closes her eyes.

He goes for long drives around town. He tends to drive a car rather carelessly. Power steering and an automatic shift make a car feel so small and inconsequential that his body is hardly involved in the driving process. His injured leg stretches out comfortably. Once or twice he has almost hit something, but even the prospect of an accident seems minor in a car. He cruises the new subdivisions, feeling like a criminal rehearsing for a robbery. Norma Jean is probably right about a log house being inappropriate here in the new subdivisions. All the houses look grand and complicated. They depress him.

One day when Leroy comes home from a drive he finds Norma Jean in tears. She is in the kitchen making a potato and mushroom-soup casserole, with grated-cheese topping. She is crying because her mother caught her smoking.

"I didn't hear her coming. I was standing here puffing away pretty as you please," Norma Jean says, wiping her eyes.

"I knew it would happen sooner or later," says Leroy, putting his arm around her.

"She don't know the meaning of the word 'knock,'" says Norma Jean. "It's a wonder she hadn't caught me years ago."

"Think of it this way," Leroy says. "What if she caught me with a joint?"

"You better not let her!" Norma Jean shrieks. "I'm warning you, Leroy Moffitt!"

"I'm just kidding. Here, play me a tune. That'll help you relax."

Norma Jean puts the casserole in the oven and sets the timer. Then she plays a ragtime tune, with horns and banjo, as Leroy lights up a joint and lies on the couch, laughing to himself about Mabel's catching him at it. He thinks of Stevie Hamilton—a doctor's son pushing grass. Everything is funny. The whole town seems crazy and small. He is reminded of Virgil Mathis, a boastful policeman Leroy used to shoot pool with. Virgil recently led a drug bust in a back room at a bowling alley, where he seized ten thousand dollars' worth of marijuana. The newspaper had a picture of him holding up the bags of grass and grinning widely. Right now, Leroy can imagine Virgil breaking down the door and arresting him with a lungful of smoke. Virgil would probably have been alerted to the scene because of all the racket Norma Jean is making. Now she sounds like a hard-rock band. Norma Jean is terrific. When she switches to a latin-rhythm version of "Sunshine Superman," Leroy hums along. Norma Jean's foot goes up and down, up and down.

"Well, what do you think?" Leroy says, when Norma Jean pauses to search through her music.

"What do I think about what?"

His mind has gone blank. Then he says, "I'll sell my rig and build us a house." That wasn't what he wanted to say. He wanted to know what she thought—what she *really* thought—about them.

"Don't start in on that again," says Norma Jean. She begins playing "Who'll Be the Next in Line?"

Leroy used to tell hitchhikers his whole life story—about his travels, his hometown, the baby. He would end with a question: "Well, what do you think?" It was just a rhetorical question. In time, he had the feeling that he'd been telling the same story over and over to the same hitchhikers. He quit talking to hitchhikers when he realized how his voice sounded—whining and self-pitying, like some teenage-tragedy song. Now Leroy has the sudden impulse to tell Norma Jean about himself, as if he had just met her. They have known each other so long they have forgotten a lot about each other. They could become reacquainted. But when the oven timer goes off and she runs to the kitchen, he forgets why he wants to do this.

The next day, Mabel drops by. It is Saturday and Norma Jean is cleaning. Leroy is studying the plans of his log house, which have finally come in the mail. He has them spread out on the table—big sheets of stiff blue paper, with diagrams and numbers printed in white. While Norma Jean runs the vacuum, Mabel drinks coffee. She sets her coffee cup on a blueprint.

"I'm just waiting for time to pass," she says to Leroy, drumming her fingers on the table.

As soon as Norma Jean switches off the vacuum, Mabel says in a loud voice, "Did you hear about the datsun dog that killed the baby?"

Norma Jean says, "The word is 'dachshund.'"

"They put the dog on trial. It chewed the baby's legs off. The mother was in the next room all the time." She raises her voice. "They thought it was neglect."

Norma Jean is holding her ears. Leroy manages to open the refrigerator and get some Diet Pepsi to offer Mabel. Mabel still has some coffee and she waves away the Pepsi.

"Datsuns are like that," Mabel says. "They're jealous dogs. They'll tear a place to pieces if you don't keep an eye on them."

"You better watch out what you're saying, Mabel," says Leroy.

"Well, facts is facts."

Leroy looks out the window at his rig. It is like a huge piece of furniture gathering dust in the backyard. Pretty soon it will be an antique. He hears the vacuum cleaner. Norma Jean seems to be cleaning the living room rug again.

Later, she says to Leroy, "She just said that about the baby because she caught me smoking. She's trying to pay me back."

"What are you talking about?" Leroy says, nervously shuffling blueprints.

"You know good and well," Norma Jean says. She is sitting in a kitchen chair with her feet up and her arms wrapped around her knees. She looks small and helpless. She says, "The very idea, her bringing up a subject like that! Saying it was neglect."

"She didn't mean that," Leroy says.

"She might not have *thought* she meant it. She always says things like that. You don't know how she goes on."

"But she didn't really mean it. She was just talking."

Leroy opens a king-sized bottle of beer and pours it into two glasses, dividing it carefully. He hands a glass to Norma Jean and she takes it from him mechanically. For a long time, they sit by the kitchen window watching the birds at the feeder.

Something is happening. Norma Jean is going to night school. She has graduated from her six-week bodybuilding course and now she is taking an adult-education course in composition at Paducah Community College. She spends her evenings outlining paragraphs.

"First you have a topic sentence," she explains to Leroy. "Then you divide it up. Your secondary topic has to be connected to your primary topic."

To Leroy, this sounds intimidating. "I never was any good in English," he says.

"It makes a lot of sense."

"What are you doing this for, anyhow?"

She shrugs. "It's something to do." She stands up and lifts her dumbbells a few times.

"Driving a rig, nobody cared about my English."

"I'm not criticizing your English."

Norma Jean used to say, "If I lose ten minutes' sleep, I just drag all day." Now she stays up late, writing compositions. She got a B on her first paper—a how-to theme on soup-based casseroles. Recently Norma Jean has been cooking unusual foods—tacos, lasagna, Bombay chicken. She doesn't play the organ anymore, though her second paper was called "Why Music Is Important to Me." She sits at the kitchen table, concentrating on her outlines, while Leroy plays with his log house plans, practicing with a set of Lincoln Logs. The thought of getting a truckload of notched, numbered logs scares him, and he wants to be prepared. As he and Norma Jean work together at the kitchen table, Leroy has the hopeful thought that they are sharing something, but he knows he is a fool to think this. Norma Jean is miles away. He knows he is going to lose her. Like Mabel, he is just waiting for time to pass.

One day, Mabel is there before Norma Jean gets home from work, and Leroy finds himself confiding in her. Mabel, he realizes, must know Norma Jean better than he does.

"I don't know what's got into that girl," Mabel says. "She used to go to bed with the chickens. Now you say she's up all hours. Plus her a-smoking. I like to died."

"I want to make her this beautiful home," Leroy says, indicating the Lincoln Logs. "I don't think she even wants it. Maybe she was happier with me gone."

"She don't know what to make of you, coming home like this."

"Is that it?"

Mabel takes the roof off his Lincoln Log cabin. "You couldn't get *me* in a log cabin," she says. "I was raised in one. It's no picnic, let me tell you."

"They're different now," says Leroy.

"I tell you what," Mabel says, smiling oddly at Leroy.

"What?"

"Take her on down to Shiloh. Y'all need to get out together, stir a little. Her brain's all balled up over them books."

Leroy can see traces of Norma Jean's features in her mother's face. Mabel's face has the texture of crinkled cotton, but suddenly she looks pretty. It occurs to Leroy that Mabel has been hinting all along that she wants them to take her with them to Shiloh.

"Let's all go to Shiloh," he says. "You and me and her. Come Sunday."

Mabel throws up her hands in protest. "Oh, no, not me. Young folks want to be by theirselves."

When Norma Jean comes in with groceries, Leroy says excitedly, "Your mama here's been dying to go to Shiloh for thirty-five years. It's about time we went, don't you think?"

"I'm not going to butt in on anybody's second honeymoon," Mabel says.

"Who's going on a honeymoon, for Christ's sake?" Norma Jean says loudly.

"I never raised no daughter of mine to talk that-a-way," Mabel says.

"You ain't seen nothing yet," says Norma Jean. She starts putting away boxes and cans, slamming cabinet doors.

"There's a log cabin at Shiloh." Mabel says, "It was there during the battle. There's bullet holes in it."

"When are you going to *shut up* about Shiloh, Mama?" asks Norma Jean.

"I always thought Shiloh was the prettiest place, so full of history," Mabel goes on. "I just hoped y'all could see it once before I die, so you could tell me about it." Later, she whispers to Leroy, "You do what I said. A little change is what she needs."

"Your name means 'the king,'" Norma Jean says to Leroy that evening. He is trying to get her to go to Shiloh, and she is reading a book about another century.

"Well, I reckon I ought to be right proud."

"I guess so."

"Am I still king around here?"

Norma Jean flexes her biceps and feels them for hardness. "I'm not fooling around with anybody, if that's what you mean," she says.

"Would you tell me if you were?"

"I don't know."

"What does *your* name mean?"

"It was Marilyn Monroe's real name."

"No kidding!"

"Norma comes from the Normans. They were invaders," she says. She closes her book and looks hard at Leroy. "I'll go to Shiloh with you if you'll stop staring at me."

On Sunday, Norma Jean packs a picnic and they go to Shiloh. To Leroy's relief, Mabel says she does not want to come with them. Norma Jean drives, and Leroy, sitting beside her, feels like some boring hitchhiker she has picked up. He tries some conversation, but she answers him in monosyllables. At Shiloh, she drives aimlessly through the park, past bluffs and trails and steep ravines. Shiloh is an immense place, and Leroy cannot see it as a battleground. It is not what he expected. He thought it would look like a golf course. Monuments are everywhere, showing through the thick clusters of trees. Norma Jean passes the log cabin Mabel mentioned. It is surrounded by tourists looking for bullet holes.

"That's not the kind of log house I've got in mind," says Leroy apologetically.

"I know *that*."

"This is a pretty place. Your mama was right."

"It's O.K.," says Norma Jean. "Well, we've seen it. I hope she's satisfied."

They burst out laughing together.

At the park museum, a movie on Shiloh is shown every half hour, but they decide that they don't want to see it. They buy a souvenir Confederate flag for Mabel, and then they find a picnic spot near the cemetery. Norma Jean has brought a picnic cooler, with pimento sandwiches, soft drinks, and Yodels. Leroy eats a sandwich and then smokes a joint, hiding it behind the picnic cooler. Norma Jean has quit smoking altogether. She is picking cake crumbs from the cellophane wrapper, like a fussy bird.

Leroy says, "So the boys in gray ended up in Corinth. The Union soldiers zapped 'em finally. April 7, 1862."

They both know that he doesn't know any history. He is just talking about some of the historical plaques they have read. He feels awkward, like a boy on a date with an older girl. They are still just making conversation.

"Corinth is where Mama eloped to," says Norma Jean.

They sit in silence and stare at the cemetery for the Union dead and, beyond, at a tall cluster of trees. Campers are parked nearby, bumper to bumper, and small children in bright clothing are cavorting and squealing. Norma Jean wads up the cake wrapper and squeezes it tightly in her hand. Without looking at Leroy, she says, "I want to leave you."

Leroy takes a bottle of Coke out of the cooler and flips off the cap. He holds the bottle poised near his mouth but cannot remember to take a drink. Finally he says, "No, you don't."

"Yes, I do."

"I won't let you."

"You can't stop me."

"Don't do me that way."

Leroy knows Norma Jean will have her own way. "Didn't I promise to be home from now on?" he says.

"In some ways, a woman prefers a man who wanders," says Norma Jean. "That sounds crazy, I know."

"You're not crazy."

Leroy remembers to drink from his Coke. Then he says, "Yes, you *are* crazy. You and me could start all over again. Right back at the beginning."

"We *have* started all over again," says Norma Jean. "And this is how it turned out."

"What did I do wrong?"

"Nothing."

"Is this one of those women's lib things?" Leroy asks.

"Don't be funny."

The cemetery, a green slope dotted with white markers, looks like a subdivision site. Leroy is trying to comprehend that his marriage is breaking up, but for some reason he is wondering about white slabs in a graveyard.

"Everything was fine till Mama caught me smoking," says Norma Jean, standing up. "That set something off."

"What are you talking about?"

"She won't leave me alone—*you* won't leave me alone." Norma Jean seems to be crying, but she is looking away from him. "I feel eighteen again. I can't face that all over again." She starts walking away. "No, it *wasn't* fine. I don't know what I'm saying. Forget it."

Leroy takes a lungful of smoke and closes his eyes as Norma Jean's words sink in. He tries to focus on the fact that thirty-five hundred soldiers died on the grounds around him. He can only think of that war as a board game with plastic soldiers. Leroy almost smiles, as he compares the Confederates' daring attack on the Union camps and Virgil Mathis's raid on the bowling alley. General Grant, drunk and furious, shoved the Southerners back to Corinth, where Mabel and Jet Beasley were married years later, when Mabel was still thin and good-looking. The next day, Mabel and Jet visited the battleground, and then Norma Jean was born, and then she married Leroy and they had a baby, which they lost, and now Leroy and Norma Jean are here at the same battleground. Leroy knows he is leaving out a lot. He is leaving out the insides of history. History was always just names and dates, to him. It occurs to him that building a house out of logs is similarly empty—too simple. And the real inner workings of a marriage, like most of history, have escaped him. Now he sees that building a log house is the dumbest idea he could have had. It was clumsy of him to think Norma Jean would want a log house. It was a crazy idea. He'll have to think of something else, quickly. He will wad the blueprints into tight balls and fling them into the lake. Then he'll get moving again. He opens his eyes. Norma Jean has moved away and is walking through the cemetery, following a serpentine brick path.

Leroy gets up to follow his wife, but his good leg is asleep and his bad leg still hurts him. Norma Jean is far away, walking rapidly toward the bluff by the river, and he tries to hobble toward her. Some children run past him, screaming noisily. Norma Jean has reached the bluff, and she is looking out over the Tennessee River. Now she turns toward Leroy and waves her arms. Is she beckoning to him? She seems to be doing an exercise for her chest muscles. The sky is unusually pale—the color of the dust ruffle Mabel made for their bed.

[1982]

Questions

1. Which details of the story contribute to your understanding of Norma Jean and Leroy's values and tastes? How are these values important to the outcome of the story?

2. Why does Norma Jean decide to leave Leroy? What does she hope to find?

3. Is there humor in the story? If so, where is it and how is it used? Does Mason seem to be mocking her characters or sympathizing with them?

4. What role does Norma Jean's mother play in the story?

5. How does history—both the history of Norma Jean and Leroy's marriage and Civil War history—contribute to the story's meaning? How are the two contexts related?

William Somerset Maugham
(1874–1965)
England

William Somerset Maugham, born in Paris of an English diplomat father and a mother who died when he was eight, was educated in Germany and England. After qualifying to become a doctor, he began a second career as an author, writing a number of light comedies in the mode of Noel Coward. In 1908, four of his plays were staged simultaneously in London. In 1917, Maugham married Syrie Wellcome, a talented interior designer, two years after their daughter Liza was born.

Of his novels, Maugham's best-known and most accomplished work is the partly autobiographical novel Of Human Bondage (1915). The novel follows the life of the lame and sensitive Philip Carey, who is determined to be both a doctor and an artist (and, through limited talent, nearly fails at both) and who suffers through a disastrous love affair. Among Maugham's other novels are The Moon and Sixpence (1919), based on the life of the French painter Gauguin and on Maugham's first-hand knowledge of Tahiti, and Cakes and Ale (1930), probably modeled on the life of English writer Thomas Hardy. Several of his novels and stories focus on the competing claims of duty and art or the disappointing recognition of limited artistic talent.

In a sense, this theme embodies Maugham's own situation in the world of letters. Although he achieved financial success and an enormous popular following—Christopher Morley called him "the most continually readable storyteller of our lifetime"—he never achieved the higher distinctions of critical acclaim. Candidly acknowledging the limits of his reputation, he observed, "In my youth I had accepted the challenge of writing and literature to idealize them; in my age I see the magnitude of the attempt and wonder at my audacity."

THE APPOINTMENT IN SAMARRA

Death speaks: There was a merchant in Baghdad who sent his servant to market to buy provisions and in a little while the servant came back, white and trembling, and said, Master, just now when I was in the market-place I was jostled by a woman in the crowd and when I turned I saw it was Death that jostled me. She looked at me and made a threatening gesture; now, lend me your horse, and I will ride away from this city and avoid my fate. I will go to Samarra and there Death will not find me. The merchant lent him his horse, and the servant mounted it, and he dug his spurs in its flanks and as fast as the horse could gallop he went. Then the merchant went down to the market-place and he saw me standing in the crowd and he came to me and said, Why did you make a threatening gesture to my servant when you saw him this morning? That was not a threatening gesture, I said, it was only a start of surprise. I was astonished to see him in Baghdad, for I had an appointment with him tonight in Samarra.

[1933]

Questions

1. Who tells this story? How does the point of view contribute to its meaning? How would the meaning of the story change if it were told from another perspective?
2. What is the "moral" of the story?
3. How are differences of interpretation of the events built into the narrative itself?
4. How does the story achieve its effect as a fable?

Guy de Maupassant
(1850–1893)
France

In his relatively brief life, Guy de Maupassant produced an astonishing oeuvre of over 300 short stories, in addition to six novels, more than 200 sketches for newspapers and magazines, essays on travel, and dramatic adaptations. In fact, he was a born storyteller whose stories reveal a sharp eye for vivid detail and social observation, a balance of detachment and sympathy, and the controlled use of irony.

Born to middle-class parents in Rouen, Normandy, de Maupassant studied law and served as a soldier in the Franco-Prussian War from 1870 to 1871. In Paris, he supported himself by writing for newspapers and working as a government bureaucrat in the Ministries of the Navy and Education while he tried to write plays; eventually he discovered that his true form was the short story. His literary apprenticeship was significantly furthered by his mentors, Gustave Flaubert, Emile Zola, and other established writers. Flaubert encouraged de Maupassant to write stories, advising him to choose his subjects carefully by finding some aspect that had not been previously explored; many of his stories were first published in newspapers as contes, or short tales, including his earliest ones, horror stories in the tradition of Edgar Allan Poe. "The Necklace," one of his most accomplished ironic treatments of bourgeois illusions, was published in 1884. While in Paris, de Maupassant lived a somewhat dissolute life, contracting syphilis, which led to years of deteriorating health and his untimely death at the age of 42.

De Maupassant contributed definitively to the aesthetics of the modern story form. By omitting narrative digressions and moral judgments, he pared the form to its essential elements, a technical strategy that significantly influenced most of his successors. In an important statement about writing, de Maupassant revealed his own view of the selective processes essential to literary creation:

> [The writer's goal] is not to tell us a story, to entertain or to move us, but to make us think and to make us understand the deep and hidden meaning of events. . . . To move us, as he has been moved himself by the spectacle of life, [the author] must reproduce it before our eyes with a scrupulous accuracy. He should compose his work so adroitly, and with such dissimulation and apparent simplicity, that it is impossible to uncover its plan or to perceive his intentions. . . . In giving every detail its exact degree of shading in accordance with its importance, the author produces the profound impression of the particular truth he wishes to point out.
>
> . . . Each of us makes, individually, a personal illusion of the world. It may be a poetic, sentimental, joyful, melancholy, sordid, or dismal one, according to our nature. The writer's goal is to reproduce this illusion of life faithfully, using all the literary techniques at his disposal.

THE NECKLACE

She was one of those pretty and charming girls who are sometimes, as if by a mistake of destiny, born in a family of clerks. She had no dowry, no expectations, no means of being known, understood, loved, wedded by any rich and distinguished man; and she let herself be married to a little clerk at the Ministry of Public Instruction.

She dressed plainly because she could not dress well, but she was as unhappy as though she had really fallen from her proper station, since with women there is neither caste nor rank: and beauty, grace and charm act instead of family and birth. Natural fineness, instinct for what is elegant, suppleness of wit, are the sole hierarchy, and make from women of the people the equals of the very greatest ladies.

She suffered ceaselessly, feeling herself born for all the delicacies and all the luxuries. She suffered from the poverty of her dwelling, from the wretched look of the walls, from the worn-out chairs, from the ugliness of the curtains. All those things, of which another woman of her rank would never even have been conscious, tortured her and made her angry. The sight of the little Breton peasant who did her humble housework aroused in her regrets which were despairing, and distracted dreams. She thought of the silent antechambers hung with Oriental tapestry, lit by tall bronze candelabra, and of the two great footmen in knee breeches who sleep in the big armchairs, made drowsy by the heavy warmth of the hot-air stove. She thought of the long *salons*[1] fitted up with ancient silk, of the delicate furniture carrying priceless curiosities, and of the coquettish perfumed boudoirs made for talks at five o'clock with intimate friends, with men famous and sought after, whom all women envy and whose attention they all desire.

When she sat down to dinner, before the round table covered with a tablecloth three days old, opposite her husband, who uncovered the soup tureen and declared with an enchanted air, "Ah, the good *pot-au-feu*![2] I don't know anything better than that," she thought of dainty dinners, of shining silverware, of tapestry which peopled the walls with ancient personages and with strange birds flying in the midst of a fairy forest; and she thought of delicious dishes served on marvelous plates, and of the whispered gallantries which you listen to with a sphinxlike smile, while you are eating the pink flesh of a trout or the wings of a quail.

She had no dresses, no jewels, nothing. And she loved nothing but that; she felt made for that. She would so have liked to please, to be envied, to be charming, to be sought after.

She had a friend, a former schoolmate at the convent, who was rich, and whom she did not like to go and see any more, because she suffered so much when she came back.

But one evening, her husband returned home with a triumphant air, and holding a large envelope in his hand.

"There," said he. "Here is something for you."

---

[1] *salons* Fashionable drawing rooms.
[2] *pot-au-feu* Soup or stew.

She tore the paper sharply, and drew out a printed card which bore these words:

"The Minister of Public Instruction and Mme. Georges Ramponneau request the honor of M. and Mme. Loisel's company at the palace of the Ministry on Monday evening, January eighteenth."

Instead of being delighted, as her husband hoped, she threw the invitation on the table with disdain, murmuring:

"What do you want me to do with that?"

"But, my dear, I thought you would be glad. You never go out, and this is such a fine opportunity. I had awful trouble to get it. Everyone wants to go; it is very select, and they are not giving many invitations to clerks. The whole official world will be there."

She looked at him with an irritated glance, and said, impatiently:

"And what do you want me to put on my back?"

He had not thought of that; he stammered:

"Why, the dress you go to the theater in. It looks very well, to me."

He stopped, distracted, seeing his wife was crying. Two great tears descended slowly from the corners of her eyes toward the corners of her mouth. He stuttered:

"What's the matter? What's the matter?"

But, by violent effort, she had conquered her grief, and she replied, with a calm voice, while she wiped her wet cheeks:

"Nothing. Only I have no dress and therefore I can't go to this ball. Give your card to some colleague whose wife is better equipped than I."

He was in despair. He resumed:

"Come, let us see, Mathilde. How much would it cost, a suitable dress, which you could use on other occasions, something very simple?"

She reflected several seconds, making her calculations and wondering also what sum she could ask without drawing on herself an immediate refusal and a frightened exclamation from the economical clerk.

Finally, she replied, hesitatingly:

"I don't know exactly, but I think I could manage it with four hundred francs."

He had grown a little pale, because he was laying aside just that amount to buy a gun and treat himself to a little shooting next summer on the plain of Nanterre, with several friends who went to shoot larks down there, of a Sunday.

But he said:

"All right. I will give you four hundred francs. And try to have a pretty dress."

The day of the ball drew near, and Mme. Loisel seemed sad, uneasy, anxious. Her dress was ready, however. Her husband said to her one evening:

"What is the matter? Come, you've been so queer these last three days."

And she answered:

"It annoys me not to have a single jewel, not a single stone, nothing to put on. I shall look like distress. I should almost rather not go at all."

He resumed:

"You might wear natural flowers. It's very stylish at this time of the year. For ten francs you can get two or three magnificent roses."

She was not convinced.

"No; there's nothing more humiliating than to look poor among other women who are rich."

But her husband cried:

"How stupid you are! Go look up your friend Mme. Forestier, and ask her to lend you some jewels. You're quite thick enough with her to do that."

She uttered a cry of joy:

"It's true. I never thought of it."

The next day she went to her friend and told of her distress.

Mme. Forestier went to a wardrobe with a glass door, took out a large jewel-box, brought it back, opened it, and said to Mme. Loisel:

"Choose, my dear."

She saw first of all some bracelets, then a pearl necklace, then a Venetian cross, gold and precious stones of admirable workmanship. She tried on the ornaments before the glass, hesitated, could not make up her mind to part with them, to give them back. She kept asking:

"Haven't you any more?"

"Why, yes. Look. I don't know what you like."

All of a sudden she discovered, in a black satin box, a superb necklace of diamonds, and her heart began to beat with an immoderate desire. Her hands trembled as she took it. She fastened it around her throat, outside her high-necked dress, and remained lost in ecstasy at the sight of herself.

Then she asked, hesitating, filled with anguish:

"Can you lend me that, only that?"

"Why, yes, certainly."

She sprang upon the neck of her friend, kissed her passionately, then fled with her treasure.

The day of the ball arrived. Mme. Loisel made a great success. She was prettier than them all, elegant, gracious, smiling, and crazy with joy. All the men looked at her, asked her name, endeavored to be introduced. All the attachés of the Cabinet wanted to waltz with her. She was remarked by the minister himself.

She danced with intoxication, with passion, made drunk by pleasure, forgetting all, in the triumph of her beauty, in the glory of her success, in a sort of cloud of happiness composed of all this homage, of all this admiration, of all these awakened desires, and of that sense of complete victory which is so sweet to a woman's heart.

She went away about four o'clock in the morning. Her husband had been sleeping since midnight, in a little deserted anteroom, with three other gentlemen whose wives were having a very good time. He threw over her shoulders the wraps which he had brought, modest wraps of common life, whose poverty contrasted with the elegance of the ball dress. She felt this, and wanted to escape so as not to be remarked by the other women, who were enveloping themselves in costly furs.

Loisel held her back.

"Wait a bit. You will catch cold outside. I will go and call a cab."

But she did not listen to him, and rapidly descended the stairs. When they were in the street they did not find a carriage; and they began to look for one, shouting after the cabmen whom they saw passing by at a distance.

They went down toward the Seine, in despair, shivering with cold. At last they found on the quay one of those ancient noctambulant coupés which, exactly as if they were ashamed to show their misery during the day, are never seen round Paris until after nightfall.

It took them to their door in the Rue des Martyrs, and once more, sadly, they climbed up homeward. All was ended, for her. And as to him, he reflected that he must be at the Ministry at ten o'clock.

She removed the wraps which covered her shoulders, before the glass, so as once more to see herself in all her glory. But suddenly she uttered a cry. She no longer had the necklace around her neck!

Her husband, already half undressed, demanded:

"What is the matter with you?"

She turned madly towards him:

"I have—I have—I've lost Mme. Forestier's necklace."

He stood up, distracted.

"What!—how?—impossible!"

And they looked in the folds of her dress, in the folds of her cloak, in her pockets, everywhere. They did not find it.

He asked:

"You're sure you had it on when you left the ball?"

"Yes, I felt it in the vestibule of the palace."

"But if you had lost it in the street we should have heard it fall. It must be in the cab."

"Yes. Probably. Did you take his number?"

"No. And you, didn't you notice it?"

"No."

They looked, thunderstruck, at one another. At last Loisel put on his clothes.

"I shall go back on foot," said he, "over the whole route which we have taken to see if I can find it."

And he went out. She sat waiting on a chair in her ball dress, without strength to go to bed, overwhelmed, without fire, without a thought.

Her husband came back about seven o'clock. He had found nothing.

He went to Police Headquarters, to the newspaper offices, to offer a reward; he went to the cab companies—everywhere, in fact, whither he was urged by the least suspicion of hope.

She waited all day, in the same condition of mad fear before this terrible calamity.

Loisel returned at night with a hollow, pale face; he had discovered nothing.

"You must write to your friend," said he, "that you have broken the clasp of her necklace and that you are having it mended. That will give us time to turn round."

She wrote at his dictation.

At the end of a week they had lost all hope.

And Loisel, who had aged five years, declared:

"We must consider how to replace that ornament."

The next day they took the box which had contained it, and they went to the jeweler whose name was found within. He consulted his books.

"It was not I, madame, who sold that necklace; I must simply have furnished the case."

Then they went from jeweler to jeweler, searching for a necklace like the other, consulting their memories, sick both of them with chagrin and anguish.

They found, in a shop at the Palais Royal, a string of diamonds which seemed to them exactly like the one they looked for. It was worth forty thousand francs. They could have it for thirty-six.

So they begged the jeweler not to sell it for three days yet. And they made a bargain that he should buy it back for thirty-four thousand francs, in case they found the other one before the end of February.

Loisel possessed eighteen thousand francs which his father had left him. He would borrow the rest.

He did borrow, asking a thousand francs of one, five hundred of another, five louis[3] here, three louis there. He gave notes, took up ruinous obligations, dealt with usurers and all the race of lenders. He compromised all the rest of his life, risked his signature without even knowing if he could meet it; and, frightened by the pains yet to come, by the black misery which was about to fall upon him, by the prospect of all the physical privation and of all the moral tortures which he was to suffer, he went to get the new necklace, putting down upon the merchant's counter thirty-six thousand francs.

When Mme. Loisel took back the necklace, Mme. Forestier said to her, with a chilly manner:

"You should have returned it sooner; I might have needed it."

She did not open the case, as her friend had so much feared. If she had detected the substitution, what would she have thought, what would she have said? Would she not have taken Mme. Loisel for a thief?

Mme. Loisel now knew the horrible existence of the needy. She took her part, moreover, all of a sudden, with heroism. That dreadful debt must be paid. She would pay it. They dismissed their servant; they changed their lodgings; they rented a garret under the roof.

She came to know what heavy housework meant and the odious cares of the kitchen. She washed the dishes, using her rosy nails on the greasy pots and pans. She washed the dirty linen, the shirts, and the dishcloths, which she dried upon a line; she carried the slops down to the street every morning, and carried up the water, stopping for breath at every landing. And, dressed like a woman of the people, she went to the fruiterer, the grocer, the butcher, her basket on her arm, bargaining, insulted, defending her miserable money sou by sou.

Each month they had to meet some notes, renew others, obtain more time.

Her husband worked in the evening making a fair copy of some tradesman's accounts, and late at night he often copied manuscript for five sous a page.

And this life lasted for ten years.

At the end of ten years, they had paid everything, everything, with the rates of usury, and the accumulations of the compound interest.

Mme. Loisel looked old now. She had become the woman of impoverished households—strong and hard and rough. With frowsy hair, skirts askew, and red hands, she talked loud while washing the floor with great swishes of water. But sometimes, when her husband was at the office, she sat down near the window, and she thought of that gay evening of long ago, of the ball where she had been so beautiful and so fêted.

What would have happened if she had not lost that necklace? Who knows? Who knows? How life is strange and changeful! How little a thing is needed for us to be lost or to be saved!

But, one Sunday, having gone to take a walk in the Champs Elysées to refresh herself from the labor of the week, she suddenly perceived a woman who was leading a child. It was Mme. Forestier, still young, still beautiful, still charming.

Mme. Loisel felt moved. Was she going to speak to her? Yes, certainly. And now that she had paid, she was going to tell her all about it. Why not?

She went up.

"Good-day, Jeanne."

---

[3]A *louis* was worth 20 francs.

The other, astonished to be familiarly addressed by this plain goodwife, did not recognize her at all, and stammered:

"But—madam!—I do not know—You must be mistaken."

"No. I am Mathilde Loisel."

Her friend uttered a cry.

"Oh, my poor Mathilde! How you are changed!"

"Yes, I have had days hard enough, since I have seen you, days wretched enough—and that because of you!"

"Of me! How so?"

"Do you remember that diamond necklace which you lent me to wear at the ministerial ball?"

"Yes. Well?"

"Well, I lost it."

"What do you mean? You brought it back."

"I brought you back another just like it. And for this we have been ten years paying. You can understand that it was not easy for us, us who had nothing. At last it is ended, and I am very glad."

Mme. Forestier had stopped.

"You say that you bought a necklace of diamonds to replace mine?"

"Yes. You never noticed it, then! They were very like."

And she smiled with a joy which was proud and naïve at once.

Mme. Forestier, strongly moved, took her two hands.

"Oh, my poor Mathilde! Why, my necklace was paste.[4] It was worth at most five hundred francs!"

[1884]
Translated by
MARJORIE LAURIE

Questions

1. What values motivate Mme. Loisel? Does the story suggest that she is appropriately chastened or that she pays too dearly for her social aspirations?

2. How does Mme. Loisel change during the 10 years after she loses the necklace? What might her life have been if the misfortune had not occurred?

3. Why does the story conclude before Mme. Loisel responds to Mme. Forestier's revelation about the necklace? Try to imagine her response.

4. What elements of the story are ironic? How does de Maupassant suggest the gap between appearances and reality?

5. What do you learn about the values and manners of the society in which the story is set? Is the author's judgment of those values revealed in the story?

---

[4]*paste* Gems made from a hard, brilliant glass containing oxide of lead.

Richard McCann

(b. 1949)

United States

R ichard McCann grew up in Silver Spring, Maryland. His fiction and poetry have appeared in numerous periodicals, including The Atlantic, Esquire, and Shenandoah, and have been reprinted in Editor's Choice: Best New Short Fiction for 1987, Men on Men 2: Best New Gay Fiction, and Poets for Life: 76 Poets Respond to AIDS. He is a contributor to and co-editor of Things Shaped in Passing: More 'Poets for Life' Writing for the AIDS Pandemic (1994). He is also the author of three books of poetry: Dream of the Traveler (1976), Nights of 1990 (1994), and Ghost Letters (1994), which received the Beatrice Hawley Award. His essay, "The Resurrectionist," appears in Best American Essays 2000.

When asked to comment on the genesis of "My Mother's Clothes," McCann provided the following information:

> My father was our household's official orator. He twice took evening courses in public speaking at a nearby Catholic college. Each time he was scheduled to give a speech, he wore his army uniform to class.
>
> But my mother believed that only secrets were real. Her stories were fraught with painful losses; her stories were suffused with griefs that couldn't be healed. She told me her father was an alcoholic who had died of exposure in an alleyway. She told me her mother had died in a sanatorium she had entered for depression. She died because she was sad, my mother explained. She died because she couldn't stop crying.
>
> "When I was a girl," she said, "I had a gold brush and comb set. When I was a girl, I had a silver fox coat." She said her parents had looked just like Scott and Zelda Fitzgerald.
>
> Sometimes, my mother showed photos of herself when she was young, taken during her first marriage. One had almost appeared in Life. On its back she had written, "I looked like Merle Oberon."
>
> She told me that if I was lucky I would inherit "the gift of gab."
>
> From her, I inherited the impulse toward fiction—an anxious dread of loss, and a fear that reality was obscure and best approached obliquely. But I was almost thirty-three before I tried to write stories of my own. Until then, for complicated reasons, I had only been trying to retell my mother's stories. In order to write fiction, however, I had to become willing to tell my own secrets on my own terms, even if those secrets were sometimes about my mother and me.

MY MOTHER'S CLOTHES: THE SCHOOL OF BEAUTY AND SHAME

Like every corner house in Carroll Knolls, the corner house on our block was turned backward on its lot, a quirk introduced by the developer of the subdivision, who, having run short of money, sought variety without additional expense.

The turned-around houses, as we kids called them, were not popular, perhaps because they seemed too public, their casement bedroom windows cranking open onto sunstruck asphalt streets. In actuality, however, it was the rest of the houses that were public, their picture windows offering dioramic glimpses of early-American sofas and Mediterranean-style pole lamps whose mottled globes hung like iridescent melons from wrought-iron chains. In order not to be seen walking across the living room to the kitchen in our pajamas, we had to close the venetian blinds. The corner house on our block was secretive, as though it had turned its back on all of us, whether in superiority or in shame, refusing to acknowledge even its own unkempt yard of yellowing zoysia grass. After its initial occupants moved away, the corner house remained vacant for months.

The spring I was in sixth grade, it was sold. When I came down the block from school, I saw a moving van parked at its curb. "Careful with that!" a woman was shouting at a mover as he unloaded a tiered end table from the truck. He stared at her in silence. The veneer had already been splintered from the table's edge, as though someone had nervously picked at it while watching TV. Then another mover walked from the truck carrying a child's bicycle, a wire basket bolted over its thick rear tire, brightly colored plastic streamers dangling from its handlebars.

The woman looked at me. "What have you got there? In your hand."

I was holding a scallop shell spray-painted gold, with imitation pearls glued along its edges. Mrs. Eidus, the art teacher who visited our class each Friday, had showed me how to make it.

"A hatpin tray," I said. "It's for my mother."

"It's real pretty." She glanced up the street as though trying to guess which house I belonged to. "I'm Mrs. Tyree," she said, "and I've got a boy about your age. His daddy's bringing him tonight in the new Plymouth. I bet you haven't sat in a new Plymouth."

"We have a Ford." I studied her housedress, tiny blue and purple flowers imprinted on thin cotton, a line of white buttons as large as Necco Wafers marching toward its basted hemline. She was the kind of mother my mother laughed at for cutting recipes out of *Woman's Day*. Staring from our picture window, my mother would sometimes watch the neighborhood mothers drag their folding chairs into a circle on someone's lawn. "There they go," she'd say, "a regular meeting of the Daughters of the Eastern Star!" "They're hardly even *women*," she'd whisper to my father, "and their *clothes*." She'd criticize their appearance—their loud nylon scarves tied beneath their chins, their disintegrating figures stuffed into pedal pushers—until my father, worried that my brother, Davis, and I could hear, although laughing himself, would beg her, "Stop it, Maria, please stop; it isn't funny." But she wouldn't stop, not ever. "Not even thirty and they look like they belong to the DAR! They wear their pearls inside their bosoms in case the rope should break!" She was the oldest mother on the block but she was the most glamorous, sitting alone on the front lawn in her sleek kick-pleated skirts and cashmere sweaters, reading her thick paperback novels, whose bindings had split. Her hair was lightly hennaed, so that when I saw her pillowcases piled atop the washer, they seemed dusted with powdery rouge. She had once lived in New York City.

After dinner, when it was dark, I joined the other children congregated beneath the streetlamp across from the turned-around house. Bucky Trueblood, an eighth-grader who had once twisted the stems off my brother's eyeglasses, was crouched in the center, describing his mother's naked body to us elementary school children gathered around him, our faces slightly upturned, as though searching for a distant constellation, or for the bats that Bucky said would fly into our hair. I sat at the edge, one half of my body within the circle of light, the other half lost to darkness. When Bucky described his mother's nipples, which he'd glimpsed when she bent to kiss him good-night, everyone giggled; but when he described her genitals, which he'd seen by dropping his pencil on the floor and looking up her nightie while her feet were propped on a hassock as she watched TV, everyone huddled nervously together, as though listening to a ghost story that made them fear something dangerous in the nearby dark. "I don't believe you," someone said; "I'm telling you," Bucky said, "*that's what it looks like.*"

I slowly moved outside the circle. Across the street a cream-colored Plymouth was parked at the curb. In a lighted bedroom window Mrs. Tyree was hanging café curtains. Behind the chain link fence, within the low branches of a willow tree, the new child was standing in his yard. I could see his white T-shirt and the pale oval of his face, a face deprived of detail by darkness and distance. Behind him, at the open bedroom window, his mother slowly fiddled with a valance. Behind me the children sat spellbound beneath the light. Then Bucky jumped up and pointed in the new child's direction—"Hey, you, you want to hear something really *good?*"—and even before the others had a chance to spot him, he vanished as suddenly and completely as an imaginary playmate.

The next morning, as we waited at our bus stop, he loitered by the mailbox on the opposite corner, not crossing the street until the yellow school bus pulled up and flung open its door. Then he dashed aboard and sat down beside me. "I'm Denny," he said. Denny: a heavy, unbeautiful child, who, had his parents stayed in their native Kentucky, would have been a farm boy, but who in Carroll Knolls seemed to belong to no particular world at all, walking past the identical ranch houses in his overalls and Keds, his whitish-blond hair close-cropped all around except for the distinguishing, stigmatizing feature of a wave that crested perfectly just above his forehead, a wave that neither rose nor fell, a wave he trained with Hopalong Cassidy hair tonic, a wave he tended fussily, as though it were the only loveliness he allowed himself.

What in Carroll Knolls might have been described by someone not native to those parts—a visiting expert, say—as *beautiful,* capable of arousing terror and joy? The brick ramblers strung with multicolored Christmas lights? The occasional front-yard plaster Virgin entrapped within a chicken-wire grotto entwined with plastic roses? The spring Denny moved to Carroll Knolls, I begged my parents to take me to a nightclub, had begged so hard for months, in fact, that by summer they finally agreed to a Sunday matinee. Waiting in the backseat of our Country Squire, a red bow tie clipped to my collar, I watched our house float like a mirage behind the sprinkler's web of water. The front door opened, and a white dress fluttered within the mirage's ascending waves. Slipping on her sunglasses, my mother emerged onto the concrete stoop, adjusted her shoulder strap, and teetered across the wet grass in new spectator shoes. Then my father stepped out and cut the sprinkler off. We drove—the warm breeze inside the car sweetened by my mother's Shalimar—past ranch houses tethered to yards by chain link fences; past the Silver Spring Volunteer Fire Department and Carroll Knolls Elementary School; past the Polar Bear Soft-Serv stand, its white stucco siding shimmery with mirror shards; past a bulldozed red-clay field where a weathered billboard advertised IF YOU LIVED HERE YOU'D BE HOME BY NOW, until we arrived at the border—a line of cinder-block discount liquor stores, a traffic light—of

Washington, D.C. The light turned red. We stopped. The breeze died and the Shalimar fell from the air. Exhaust fumes mixed with the smell of hot tar. A drunk man stumbled into the crosswalk, followed by an old woman shielding herself from the sun with an orange umbrella, and two teenaged boys dribbling a basketball back and forth between them. My mother put down her sun visor. "Lock your door," she said.

Then the light changed, releasing us into another country. The station wagon sailed down boulevards of Chinese elms and flowering Bradford pears, through hot, dense streets where black families sat on wooden chairs at curbs, along old streetcar tracks that caused the tires to shimmy and the car to swerve, onto Pennsylvania Avenue, past the White House, encircled by its fence of iron spears, and down 14th Street, past the Treasury Building, until at last we reached the Neptune Room, a cocktail lounge in the basement of a shabbily elegant hotel.

Inside, the Neptune Room's walls were painted with garish mermaids reclining seductively on underwater rocks, and human frogmen who stared longingly through their diving helmets' glass masks at a loveliness they could not possess on dry earth. On stage, leaning against the baby grand piano, a *chanteuse* (as my mother called her) was singing of her grief, her wrists weighted with rhinestone bracelets, a single blue spotlight making her seem like one who lived, as did the mermaids, underwater.

I was transfixed. I clutched my Roy Rogers cocktail (the same as a Shirley Temple, but without the cheerful, girlish grenadine) tight in my fist. In the middle of "The Man I Love" I stood and struggled toward the stage.

I strayed into the spotlight's soft-blue underwater world. Close up, from within the light, the singer was a boozy, plump peroxide blonde in a tight black cocktail dress; but these indiscretions made her yet more lovely, for they showed what she had lost, just as her songs seemed to carry her backward into endless regret. When I got close to her, she extended one hand—red nails, a huge glass ring—and seized one of mine.

"Why, what kind of little sailor have we got here?" she asked the audience.

I stared through the border of blue light and into the room, where I saw my parents gesturing, although whether they were telling me to step closer to her microphone or to step farther away, I could not tell. The whole club was staring.

"Maybe he knows a song!" a man shouted from the back.

"Sing with me," she whispered. "What can you sing?"

I wanted to lift her microphone from its stand and bow deeply from the waist, as Judy Garland did on her weekly TV show. But I could not. As she began to sing, I stood voiceless, pressed against the protection of her black dress; or, more accurately, I stood beside her, silently lip-syncing to myself. I do not recall what she sang, although I do recall a quick, farcical ending in which she falsettoed, like Betty Boop, "Gimme a Little Kiss, Will Ya, Huh?" and brushed my forehead with pursed red lips.

That summer, humidity enveloping the landfill subdivision, Denny, "the new kid," stood on the boundaries, while we neighborhood boys played War, a game in which someone stood on Stanley Allen's front porch and machine-gunned the rest of us, who one by one clutched our bellies, coughed as if choking on blood, and rolled in exquisite death throes down the grassy hill. When Stanley's father came up the walk from work, he ducked imaginary bullets. "Hi, Dad," Stanley would call, rising from the dead to greet him. Then we began the game again: Whoever died best in the last round got to kill in the next. Later, after dusk, we'd smear the wings of balsa planes with glue, ignite them, and send them flaming through the dark on kamikaze missions.

Long after the streets were deserted, we children sprawled beneath the corner street-lamp, praying our mothers would not call us—"*Time to come in!*"—back to our oven-like houses; and then sometimes Bucky, hoping to scare the elementary school kids, would lead his solemn procession of junior high "hoods" down the block, their penises hanging from their unzipped trousers.

Denny and I began to play together, first in secret, then visiting each other's houses almost daily, and by the end of the summer I imagined him to be my best friend. Our friendship was sealed by our shared dread of junior high school. Davis, who had just finished seventh grade, brought back reports of corridors so long that one could get lost in them, of gangs who fought to control the lunchroom and the bathrooms. The only safe place seemed to be the Health Room, where a pretty nurse let you lie down on a cot behind a folding screen. Denny told me about a movie he'd seen in which the children, all girls, did not have to go to school at all but were taught at home by a beautiful governess, who, upon coming to their rooms each morning, threw open their shutters so that sunlight fell like bolts of satin across their beds, whispered their pet names while kissing them, and combed their long hair with a silver brush. "She never got mad," said Denny, beating his fingers up and down through the air as though striking a keyboard, "except once when some old man told the girls they could never play piano again."

With my father at work in the Pentagon and my mother off driving the two-tone Welcome Wagon Chevy to new subdivisions, Denny and I spent whole days in the gloom of my living room, the picture window's venetian blinds closed against an August sun so fierce that it bleached the design from the carpet. Dreaming of fabulous prizes—sets of matching Samsonite luggage, French Provincial bedroom suites, Corvettes, jet flights to Hawaii—we watched Jan Murray's "Treasure Hunt" and Bob Barker's "Truth or Consequences" (a name that seemed strangely threatening). We watched "The Loretta Young Show," worshipping yet critiquing her elaborate gowns. When "The Early Show" came on, we watched old Bette Davis, Gene Tierney, and Joan Crawford movies—*Dark Victory, Leave Her to Heaven, A Woman's Face.* Hoping to become their pen pals, we wrote long letters to fading movie stars, who in turn sent us autographed photos we traded between ourselves. We searched the house for secrets, like contraceptives, Kotex, and my mother's hidden supply of Hershey bars. And finally, Denny and I, running to the front window every few minutes to make sure no one was coming unexpectedly up the sidewalk, inspected the secrets of my mother's dresser: her satin nightgowns and padded brassieres, folded atop pink drawer liners and scattered with loose sachet; her black mantilla, pressed inside a shroud of lilac tissue paper; her heart-shaped candy box, a flapper doll strapped to its lid with a ribbon, from which spilled galaxies of cocktail rings and cultured pearls. Small shrines to deeper intentions, private grottoes of yearning: her triangular cloisonné earrings, her brooch of enameled butterfly wings.

Because beauty's source was longing, it was infused with romantic sorrow; because beauty was defined as "feminine," and therefore as "other," it became hopelessly confused with my mother: Mother, who quickly sorted through new batches of photographs, throwing unflattering shots of herself directly into the fire before they could be seen. Mother, who dramatized herself, telling us and our playmates, "My name is Maria Dolores; in Spanish, that means 'Mother of Sorrows,'" Mother, who had once wished to be a writer and who said, looking up briefly from whatever she was reading, "Books are my best friends." Mother, who read aloud from Whitman's *Leaves of Grass* and O'Neill's *Long Day's Journey Into Night* with a voice so grave I could not tell the difference between them. Mother, who lifted cut-glass vases and antique clocks from her obsessively dusted curio shelves to ask, "If this could talk, what story would it tell?"

And more, always more, for she was the only woman in our house, a "people-watcher," a "talker," a woman whose mysteries and moods seemed endless: Our Mother of the White Silk Gloves; Our Mother of the Veiled Hats; Our Mother of the Paper Lilacs; Our Mother of the Sighs and Heartaches; Our Mother of the Gorgeous Gypsy Earrings; Our Mother of the Late Movies and the Cigarettes; Our Mother whom I adored and who, in adoring, I ran from, knowing it "wrong" for a son to wish to be like his mother; Our Mother who wished to influence us, passing the best of herself along, yet who held the fear common to that era, the fear that by loving a son too intensely she would render him unfit—"Momma's boy," "tied to apron strings"—and who therefore alternately drew us close and sent us away, believing a son needed "male influence" in large doses, that female influence was pernicious except as a final finishing, like manners; Our Mother of the Mixed Messages; Our Mother of Sudden Attentiveness; Our Mother of Sudden Distances; Our Mother of Anger; Our Mother of Apology. The simplest objects of her life, objects scattered accidentally about the house, became my shrines to beauty, my grottoes of romantic sorrow: her Revlon lipstick tubes, "Cherries in the Snow"; her Art Nouveau atomizers on the blue mirror top of her vanity; her pastel silk scarves knotted to a wire hanger in her closet; her white handkerchiefs blotted with red mouths. Voiceless objects; silences. The world halved with a cleaver: "masculine," "feminine." In these ways was the plainest ordinary love made complicated and grotesque. And in these ways was beauty, already confused with the "feminine," also confused with shame, for all these longings were secret, and to control me all my brother had to do was to threaten to expose that Denny and I were dressing ourselves in my mother's clothes.

Denny chose my Mother's drabbest outfits, as though he were ruled by the deepest of modesties, or by his family's austere Methodism: a pink wraparound skirt from which the color had been laundered, its hem almost to his ankles; a sleeveless white cotton blouse with a Peter Pan collar; a small straw summer clutch. But he seemed to challenge his own primness, as though he dared it with his "effects": an undershirt worn over his head to approximate cascading hair; gummed hole-punch reinforcements pasted to his fingernails so that his hands, palms up, might look like a woman's—flimsy crescent moons waxing above his fingertips.

He dressed slowly, hesitantly, but once dressed, he was a manic Proteus metamorphosing into contradictory, half-realized forms, throwing his "long hair" back and balling it violently into a French twist; tapping his paper nails on the glass-topped vanity as though he were an important woman kept waiting at a cosmetics counter; stabbing his nails into the air as though he were an angry teacher assigning an hour of detention; touching his temple as though he were a shy schoolgirl tucking back a wisp of stray hair; resting his fingertips on the rim of his glass of Kool-Aid as though he were an actress seated over an ornamental cocktail—a Pink Lady, say, or a Silver Slipper. Sometimes, in an orgy of jerky movement, his gestures overtaking him with greater and greater force, a dynamo of theatricality unleashed, he would hurl himself across the room like a mad girl having a fit, or like one possessed; or he would snatch the chenille spread from my parents' bed and drape it over his head to fashion for himself the long train of a bride. "Do you like it?" he'd ask anxiously, making me his mirror. "Does it look *real?*" He wanted, as did I, to become something he'd neither yet seen nor dreamed of, something he'd recognize the moment he saw it: himself. Yet he was constantly confounded, for no matter how much he adorned himself with scarves and jewelry, he could not understand that this was himself, as was also and at the same time the boy in overalls and Keds. He was split in two pieces—as who was not?—the blond wave cresting rigidly above his close-cropped hair.

"He makes me nervous," I heard my father tell my mother one night as I lay in bed. They were speaking about me. That morning I'd stood awkwardly on the front lawn— "Maybe you should go help your father," my mother had said—while he propped an extension ladder against the house, climbed up through power lines he separated with his bare hands, and staggered across the pitched roof he was reshingling. When his hammer slid down the incline, catching on the gutter, I screamed, "You're falling!" Startled, he almost fell.

"He needs to spend more time with you," I heard my mother say.

I couldn't sleep. Out in the distance a mother was calling her child home. A screen door slammed. I heard cicadas, their chorus as steady and loud as the hum of a power line. *He needs to spend more time with you.* Didn't she know? Saturday mornings, when he stood in his rubber hip boots fishing off the shore of Triadelphia Reservoir, I was afraid of the slimy bottom and could not wade after him; for whatever reasons of his own—something as simple as shyness, perhaps—he could not come to get me. I sat in the parking lot drinking Tru-Ade and reading *Betty and Veronica*, wondering if Denny had walked alone to Wheaton Plaza, where the weekend manager of Port-o'-Call allowed us to Windex the illuminated glass shelves that held Lladro figurines, the porcelain ballerina's hands so realistic one could see tiny life and heart lines etched into her palms. *He needs to spend more time with you.* Was she planning to discontinue the long summer afternoons that she and I spent together when there were no new families for her to greet in her Welcome Wagon car? "I don't feel like being alone today," she'd say, inviting me to sit on their chenille bedspread and watch her model new clothes in her mirror. Behind her an oscillating fan fluttered nylons and scarves she'd heaped, discarded, on a chair. "Should I wear the red belt with this dress or the black one?" she'd ask, turning suddenly toward me and cinching her waist with her hands.

Afterward we would sit together at the rattan table on the screened-in porch, holding cocktail napkins around sweaty glasses of iced Russian tea and listening to big-band music on the Zenith.

"You look so pretty," I'd say. Sometimes she wore outfits I'd selected for her from her closet-pastel chiffon dresses, an apricot blouse with real mother-of-pearl buttons.

One afternoon she leaned over suddenly and shut off the radio. "You know you're going to leave me one day," she said. When I put my arms around her, smelling the dry carnation talc she wore in hot weather, she stood up and marched out of the room. When she returned, she was wearing Bermuda shorts and a plain cotton blouse. "Let's wait for your father on the stoop," she said.

Late that summer—the summer before he died—my father took me with him to Fort Benjamin Harrison, near Indianapolis, where, as a colonel in the U.S. Army Reserves, he did his annual tour of duty. On the propjet he drank bourbon and read newspapers while I made a souvenir packet for Denny: an airsickness bag, into which I placed the Chiclets given me by the stewardess to help pop my ears during take-off, and the laminated white card that showed the location of emergency exits. Fort Benjamin Harrison looked like Carroll Knolls: hundreds of acres of concrete and sun-scorched shrubbery inside a cyclone fence. Daytimes I waited for my father in the dining mess with the sons of other officers, drinking chocolate milk that came from a silver machine, and desultorily setting fires in ashtrays. When he came to collect me, I walked behind him—gold braid hung from his epaulets—while enlisted men saluted us and opened doors. At night, sitting in our BOQ room, he asked me questions about myself: "Are you looking forward to seventh grade?" "What do you think you'll want to be?" When these topics faltered—I stammered what I hoped were right answers—we watched TV, trying to preguess lines of dialogue on reruns of his favorite shows, "The Untouchables" and "Rawhide." "That Della Street," he said as we watched "Perry Mason," "is almost as pretty as your mother." On the last day, eager to make the trip memorable, he brought me a gift: a glassine envelope filled with punched IBM cards that told me my life story as his secretary had typed it into the office computer. Card One: *You live at 10406 Lillians Mill Court, Silver Spring, Maryland*. Card Two: *You are entering seventh grade*. Card Three: *Last year your teacher was Mrs. Dillard*. Card Four: *Your favorite color is blue*. Card Five: *You love the Kingston Trio*. Card Six: *You love basketball and football*. Card Seven: *Your favorite sport is swimming*.

Whose son did these cards describe? The address was correct, as was the teacher's name and the favorite color; and he'd remembered that one morning during breakfast I'd put a dime in the jukebox and played the Kingston Trio's song about "the man who never returned." But whose fiction was the rest? Had I, who played no sport other than kickball and Kitty-Kitty-Kick-the-Can, lied to him when he asked me about myself? Had he not heard from my mother the outcome of the previous summer's swim lessons? At the swim club a young man in black trunks had taught us, as we held hands, to dunk ourselves in water, surface, and then go down. When he had told her to let go of me, I had thrashed across the surface, violently afraid I'd sink. But perhaps I had not lied to him; perhaps he merely did not wish to see. It was my job, I felt, to reassure him that I was the son he imagined me to be, perhaps because the role of reassurer gave me power. In any case, I thanked him for the computer cards. I thanked him the way a father thanks a child for a well-intentioned gift he'll never use—a set of handkerchiefs, say, on which the embroidered swirls construct a monogram of no particular initial, and which thus might be used by anyone.

As for me, when I dressed in my mother's clothes, I seldom moved at all: I held myself rigid before the mirror. The kind of beauty I'd seen practiced in movies and in fashion magazines was beauty attained by lacquered stasis, beauty attained by fixed poses—"ladylike stillness," the stillness of mannequins, the stillness of models "caught" in mid-gesture, the stillness of the passive moon around which active meteors orbited and burst. My costume was of the greatest solemnity: I dressed like the *chanteuse* in the Neptune Room, carefully shimmying my mother's black slip over my head so as not to stain it with Brylcreem, draping her black mantilla over my bare shoulders, dipping her rhinestone dangles to my ears. Had I at that time already seen the movie in which French women who had fraternized with German soldiers were made to shave their heads and walk through the streets, jeered by their fellow villagers? And if so, did I imagine myself to be one of the collaborators, or one of the villagers, taunting her from the curb? I ask because no matter how elaborate my costume, I made no effort to camouflage my crew cut or my male body.

How did I perceive myself in my mother's triple-mirrored vanity, its endless repetitions? I saw myself as doubled—both an image and he who studied it. I saw myself as beautiful, and guilty: The lipstick made my mouth seem the ripest rose, or a wound; the small rose on the black slip opened like my mother's heart disclosed, or like the Sacred Heart of Mary, aflame and pierced by arrows; the mantilla transformed me into a Mexican penitent or a Latin movie star, like Dolores Del Rio. The mirror was a silvery stream: On the far side, in a clearing, stood the woman who was icily immune from the boy's terror and contempt; on the close side, in the bedroom, stood the boy who feared and yet longed after her inviolability. (Perhaps, it occurs to me now, this doubleness is the source of drag queens' vulnerable ferocity.) Sometimes, when I saw that person in the mirror, I felt as though I had at last been lifted from that dull, locked room, with its mahogany bedroom suite and chalky blue walls. But other times, particularly when I saw Denny and me together, so that his reality shattered my fantasies, we seemed merely ludicrous and sadly comic, as though we were dressed in the garments of another species, like dogs in human clothes. I became aware of my spatulate hands, my scarred knees, my large feet; I became aware of the drooping, unfilled bodice of my slip. Like Denny, I could neither dispense with images nor take their flexibility as pleasure, for the idea of self I had learned and was learning still was that one was constructed by one's images—"When boys cross their legs, they cross one ankle atop the knee"—so that one finally sought the protection of believing in one's own image and, in believing in it as reality, condemned oneself to its poverty.

(That locked room. My mother's vanity; my father's highboy. If Denny and I, still in our costumes, had left that bedroom, its floor strewn with my mother's shoes and handbags, and gone through the darkened living room, out onto the sunstruck porch, down the sidewalk, and up the street, how would we have carried ourselves? Would we have walked boldly, chattering extravagantly back and forth between ourselves, like drag queens refusing to acknowledge the stares of contempt that are meant to halt them? Would we have walked humbly, with the calculated, impervious piety of the condemned walking barefoot to the public scaffold? Would we have walked simply, as deeply accustomed to the normalcy of our own strangeness as Siamese twins? Or would we have walked gravely, a solemn procession, like Bucky Trueblood's gang, their manhood hanging from their unzipped trousers?)

(We were eleven years old. Why now, more than two decades later, do I wonder for the first time how we would have carried ourselves through a publicness we would have neither sought nor dared? I am six feet two inches tall; I weigh 198 pounds. Given my size, the question I am most often asked about my youth is "What football position did you play?" Overseas I am most commonly taken to be a German or a Swede. Right now, as I write this, I am wearing L. L. Bean khaki trousers, a LaCoste shirt, Weejuns: the anonymous American costume, although partaking also of certain signs of sexual orientation, this costume having become the standard garb of the urban American gay man. Why do I tell you these things? Am I trying—not subtly—to inform us of my "maleness," to reassure us that I have "survived" without noticeable "complexes"? Or is this my urge, my constant urge, to complicate my portrait of myself to both of us, so that I might layer my selves like so many multicolored crinoline slips, each rustling as I walk? When the wind blows, lifting my skirt, I do not know which slip will be revealed.)

Sometimes, while Denny and I were dressing up, Davis would come home unexpectedly from the bowling alley, where he'd been hanging out since entering junior high. At the bowling alley he was courting the protection of Bucky's gang.

"Let me in!" he'd demand, banging fiercely on the bedroom door, behind which Denny and I were scurrying to wipe the makeup off our faces with Kleenex.

"We're not doing anything," I'd protest, buying time.

"Let me in this minute or I'll tell!"

Once in the room, Davis would police the wreckage we'd made, the emptied hatboxes, the scattered jewelry, the piled skirts and blouses. "You'd better clean this up right now," he'd warn. "You two make me *sick*."

Yet his scorn seemed modified by awe. When he helped us rehang the clothes in the closet and replace the jewelry in the candy box, a sullen accomplice destroying someone else's evidence, he sometimes handled the garments as though they were infused with something of himself, although at the precise moment when he seemed to find them loveliest, holding them close, he would cast them down.

After our dress-up sessions Denny would leave the house without good-byes. I was glad to see him go. We would not see each other for days, unless we met by accident; we never referred to what we'd done the last time we'd been together. We met like those who have murdered are said to meet, each tentatively and warily examining the other for signs of betrayal. But whom had we murdered? The boys who walked into that room? Or the women who briefly came to life within it? Perhaps this metaphor has outlived its meaning. Perhaps our shame derived not from our having killed but from our having created.

In early September, as Denny and I entered seventh grade, my father became ill. Over Labor Day weekend he was too tired to go fishing. On Monday his skin had vaguely yellowed; by Thursday he was severely jaundiced. On Friday he entered the hospital, his liver rapidly failing; Sunday he was dead. He died from acute hepatitis, possibly acquired while cleaning up after our sick dog, the doctor said. He was buried at Arlington National Cemetery, down the hill from the Tomb of the Unknown Soldier. After the twenty-one-gun salute, our mother pinned his colonel's insignia to our jacket lapels. I carried the flag from his coffin to the car. For two weeks I stayed home with my mother, helping her write thank-you notes on small white cards with black borders; one afternoon, as I was affixing postage to the square, plain envelopes, she looked at me across the dining room table. "You and Davis are all I have left," she said. She went into the kitchen and came back. "Tomorrow," she said, gathering up the note cards, "you'll have to go to school." Mornings I wandered the long corridors alone, separated from Denny by the fate of our last names, which had cast us into different homerooms and daily schedules. Lunchtimes we sat together in silence in the rear of the cafeteria. Afternoons, just before gym class, I went to the Health Room, where, lying on a cot, I'd imagine the Phys. Ed. coach calling my name from the class roll, and imagine my name, unclaimed, unanswered to, floating weightlessly away, like a balloon that one jumps to grab hold of but that is already out of reach. Then I'd hear the nurse dial the telephone. "He's sick again," she'd say. "Can you come pick him up?" At home I helped my mother empty my father's highboy. "No, we want to save that," she said when I folded his uniform into a huge brown bag that read GOODWILL INDUSTRIES; I wrapped it in a plastic dry-cleaner's bag and hung it in the hall closet.

After my father's death my relationship to my mother's things grew yet more complex, for as she retreated into her grief, she left behind only her mute objects as evidence of her life among us: objects that seemed as lonely and vulnerable as she was, objects that I longed to console, objects with which I longed to console myself—a tangled gold chain, thrown in frustration on the mantel; a wineglass, left unwashed in the sink. Sometimes at night Davis and I heard her prop her pillow up against her bedroom wall, lean back heavily, and tune her radio to a call-in show: "*Nightcaps, what are you thinking at this late hour?"* Sunday evenings, in order to help her prepare for the next day's job hunt, I stood over her beneath the bare basement bulb, the same bulb that first illuminated my father's jaundice. I set her hair, sticking each wet strand with gel and rolling it, inventing gossip that seemed to draw us together, a beautician and his customer.

"You have such pretty hair," I'd say.

"At my age, don't you think I should cut it?" She was almost fifty.

"No, never."

That fall Denny and I were caught. One evening my mother noticed something out of place in her closet. (Perhaps now that she no longer shared it, she knew where every belt and scarf should have been.)

I was in my bedroom doing my French homework, dreaming of one day visiting Au Printemps, the store my teacher spoke of so excitedly as she played us the Edith Piaf records that she had brought back from France. In the mirror above my desk I saw my mother appear at my door.

"Get into the living room," she said. Her anger made her small, reflected body seem taut and dangerous.

In the living room Davis was watching TV with Uncle Joe, our father's brother, who sometimes came to take us fishing. Uncle Joe was lying in our father's La-Z-Boy recliner.

"There aren't going to be any secrets in this house," she said. "You've been in my closet. What were you doing there?"

"No, we weren't," I said. "We were watching TV all afternoon."

"*We?* Was Denny here with you? Don't you think I've heard about that? Were you and Denny going through my clothes? Were you wearing them?"

"No, Mom," I said.

"Don't lie!" She turned to Uncle Joe, who was staring at us. "Make him stop! He's lying to me!"

She slapped me. Although I was already taller than she, she slapped me over and over, slapped me across the room until I was backed against the TV. Davis was motionless, afraid. But Uncle Joe jumped up and stood between my mother and me, holding her until her rage turned to sobs. "I can't, I can't be both a mother and a father," she said to him. "I can't do it." I could not look at Uncle Joe, who, although he was protecting me, did not know I was lying.

She looked at me. "We'll discuss this later," she said. "Get out of my sight."

We never discussed it. Denny was outlawed. I believe, in fact, that it was I who suggested he never be allowed in our house again. I told my mother I hated him. I do not think I was lying when I said this. I truly hated him—hated him, I mean, for being me.

For two or three weeks Denny tried to speak with me at the bus stop, but whenever he approached, I busied myself with kids I barely knew. After a while Denny found a new best friend, Lee, a child despised by everyone, for Lee was "effeminate." His clothes were too fastidious; he often wore his cardigan over his shoulders, like an old woman feeling a chill. Sometimes, watching the street from our picture window, I'd see Lee walking toward Denny's house. "What a queer," I'd say to whoever might be listening. "He walks like a *girl*." Or sometimes, at the junior high school, I'd see him and Denny walking down the corridor, their shoulders pressed together as if they were telling each other secrets, or as if they were joined in mutual defense. Sometimes when I saw them, I turned quickly away, as though I'd forgotten something important in my locker. But when I felt brave enough to risk rejection, for I belonged to no group, I joined Bucky Trueblood's gang, sitting on the radiator in the main hall, and waited for Lee and Denny to pass us. As Lee and Denny got close, they stiffened and looked straight ahead.

"Faggots," I muttered.

I looked at Bucky, sitting in the middle of the radiator. As Lee and Denny passed, he leaned forward from the wall, accidentally disarranging the practiced severity of his clothes, his jeans puckering beneath his tooled belt, the breast pocket of his T-shirt drooping with the weight of a pack of Pall Malls. He whistled. Lee and Denny flinched. He whistled again. Then he leaned back, the hard lines of his body reasserting themselves, his left foot striking a steady beat on the tile floor with the silver V-tap of his black loafer.

[1986]

Questions

1. Why is so much detail given over to Carroll Knolls at the beginning of the story?
2. Would "Mother" be an equally appropriate title for the story? Why does McCann give his story a subtitle ("The School of Beauty and Shame")?
3. If the paragraph in parentheses (describing the narrator's future) had been omitted, would your interpretation of the story and understanding of the narrator be significantly altered?
4. What importance does Davis play in the story?
5. Why does the narrator turn so strongly against Denny at the end of the story?

John McCluskey

(b. 1944)

United States

Beginning with Frederick Douglass, there is hardly a major African-American writer who hasn't written about the significance of music in black lives. In earlier literature, these remarks might have been about spirituals or the blues; more recently black writers have often focused on jazz. In "Living with Music," for example, Ralph Ellison wrote the following:

> These jazzmen, many of them now world-famous, lived for and with music intensely. Their driving motivation was neither money nor fame, but the will to achieve the most eloquent expression of idea-emotions through the technical mystery of their instruments . . . and the give and take, the subtle rhythmical shaping and blending of idea, tone and imagination demanded of group improvisation. The delicate balance struck between strong individual personality and the group during these early jam sessions was a marvel of social organization.

As you read John McCluskey's "Lush Life," consider whether his story is a tale of individual musicians or of group dynamics.

John McCluskey has written two novels: Look What They Done to My Song (1974), about a young black musician, and Mr. America's Last Season Blues (1983), about a black athlete. He has also edited several volumes of African-American fiction and history. About his work, he has commented: "As a writer, my commitment is to that level of creative excellence so ably demonstrated by Afro-American artists as diverse as Ralph Ellison, Romare Bearden, and Miles Davis. Hoping to avoid any fashionable ambiguity and pedantry, I want my fiction and essays to heighten the appreciation of the complexities of Afro-American literature and life." McCluskey teaches at Indiana University at Bloomington.

LUSH LIFE

Dayton, Ohio

Behind the dance hall the first of the car doors were banging shut, motors starting up, and from somewhere—a backyard, an alley—dogs barked. The band's bus was parked at one darkened corner of the parking lot. Empty, it was a mute and hulking barn in this hour. Along its side in slanted, bold-red letters was painted a sign: EARL FERGUSON AND AMERICA'S GREATEST BAND.

Suddenly the back door to the dance hall swung open and loud laughter rushed out on a thick pillow of cigarette smoke. Ahead of others, two men in suits—the taller one in plaids and the other in stripes—walked quickly, talking, smoking. They stopped at a convertible, a dark-red Buick, dew already sprouting across its canvas top. Other men, all members of the band, in twos or threes, would come up, slap their backs, share a joke or two, then drift toward the bus. In the light over the back door, moths played.

The shorter man, Billy Cox, took off his glasses, fogged the lenses twice, then cleaned them with his polka-dot silk square. He reached a hand toward Tommy, the bassist, approaching.

"I'm gone say, 'See y'all further up the road in Cleveland,'" Tommy said. "But after a night like tonight, it's gone be one hell of a struggle to tear ourselves from this town. Am I right about that, Billy C.?"

Tommy laughed, gold tooth showing, and patted his impeccable "do." More than once it had been said that Tommy sweated ice water. With his face dry, hair in place, tie straightened after three hours of furious work, no one could doubt it now.

Tommy spoke again, this time stern, wide-legged, and gesturing grandly. "Just you two don't get high and dry off into some damn ditch." His usual farewell slid toward a cackle. Billy waved him off.

In the Scout Car, Billy and Earl Ferguson would drive through the night to the next date. Throughout the night they would stay at least an hour or so ahead of the bus. They would breakfast and be nearly asleep by the time the bus pulled into the same hotel parking lot, the men emerging, looking stunned from a fitful sleep on a noisy bus.

From a nearby car a woman's throaty laugh lit up the night. They turned to see Pretty Horace leaning into a car, the passenger's side, smoothing down the back edges of his hair and rolling his rump as he ran his game.

"Man, stop your lying!" came her voice. She, too, was with the ends of her hair, dyed bright red and glowing in that light. Her friend from the driver's seat, with nothing better to do perhaps, leaned to hear, to signify, her face round as the moon's.

Moving with a pickpocket's stealth and slow grin spreading, Poo moved up to the driver's side of the car and whispered something. The driver jerked back, then gave him her best attention, smiling. One hand to her throat, she moistened her lips, glistened a smile.

In unison, Billy and Earl shook their heads while watching it all. Billy slid one hand down a lapel, pulled a cigarette from the corner of his mouth. "Some of the boys gone make a long night of this one."

Earl nodded. "Some mean mistreaters fixing to hit that bus late and do a whole lot of shucking, man."

Yes, some would dare the bus's deadline by tipping into an after-hours party, by following some smiling woman home. The rules were simple, however: if you missed the bus and could not make practice the next day, you were fined fifty dollars. If you missed the date because you missed the bus or train, you were fired. Daring these, you could seek adventure that broke the monotony of long road trips. You could bring stories that released bubbles of laughter throughout an overheated and smoke-filled bus.

Cars were rolling out of the side parking lot and, passing members of the band, the drivers honked in appreciation. Earl bowed slowly and waved an arm wide and high toward his men, some still walking out of the back door of the dance hall. Then he embraced Billy, mugged, and pointed to Billy's chest as if branding there all the credit for a magnificent night. After all, they had done Basie and Ellington to perfection. Their own original tunes had been wonders to behold. From the very beginning the audience had been with them and danced and danced, heads bobbing and shoulders rocking, cheering every solo. The dancers had fun on the stair step of every melody; hugging tightly, they did the slow grind to the promise of every ballad. Now they thanked the band again with the toot of their horns, shouts, and the wave of their hands.

Within an hour the bus would start up, all the equipment packed and stored below. Then it would roll slowly out of the parking lot. Some of the men would already be snoring. By the outskirts of town, a car might catch up to it, tires squealing as the car rocked to a stop. One of the men—usually McTee or "Rabbit" Ousley, as myth might have it—would climb out and blow a kiss to some grinning woman behind the wheel and strut onto the bus like some wide-legged conqueror. The doors to the bus would close behind him, sealing his stories from any verification and sealing them against the long, long night.

But it was the Buick, Earl and Billy inside, pulling away first. They would leave before these tales of triumph, outright lies about quick and furious love in a drafty back room or tales of a young wife whispering, "Run! Run!" and the scramble for a window after the husband's key slid into the lock downstairs. Yes, before all that, Earl and Billy would pull from the parking lot and start away, slow at first, like they had all the time in the world.

Well before the edge of town, they would have checked for cigarettes, surely, and from some magical place on a side street, a jukebox blaring and the smell of fried chicken meeting them at the door with its judas hole, they would find their coffee in Mason jars, coffee heavily sugared and creamed, and steaming chicken sandwiches wrapped neatly in waxed paper.

Older women, who would do double duty at Sunday church dinners, would smile and wipe their hands on their aprons. And bless them, these good and prodigal sons with conked hair. Then, moving toward the door, Billy and Earl would be greeted by achingly beautiful women with late night joy lacing their hoarse voices. Billy and Earl would take turns joking and pulling each other away, then, outside and laughing, climb back into the car for the journey through the night.

For the first few minutes, the lights of Dayton thinning, used car lots and a roller rink as outposts, they were silent before nervous energy swept over them. It was that unsettling bath of exhaustion and exuberance, rising to a tingle at the base of the neck, so familiar at the end of a performance. With Earl at the wheel, they began to harmonize and scat their way through "Take the A Train," "One O'Clock Jump," and their own wonderful collaboration, "October Mellow." In this way they would ride for a while. They would sing in ragged breaths before they gave out in laughter. The radio might go on, and there would be mostly the crackle of static, or, faintly, a late night gospel concert with harmonies rising and falling, like a prayer song tossed to the wind. Stray cars would rush past in the next lane, headed back toward Dayton. They passed a trailer groaning under its load, one or two squat Fords, then settled back. The night's first chapter was closed behind them with the noise from the motor, with smears of light.

Like a sudden tree in the car's lights, a sign sprouted and announced the city limits of Springfield.

Billy started nodding as if answering some ancient question. "Springfield got more fine women than they got in two St. Louises or five New Orleanses, I'm here to tell you."

"Wake up, Billy. Find me a place with women finer than they got in St. Louis or New Orleans or Harlem—think I'm gone let Harlem slide?—find me such a place and you got a easy one-hundred-dollar bill in your hand and I'll be in heaven. I'm talking serious now."

Billy snorted, sitting up straight and shaking his head. "I ain't hardly sleeping. Just remembering is all. See, I ain't been through here since 1952, but I can call some preacher's daughter right now—brown skin and about yeah-tall—yeah, at this very hour. Lord, she would be so fine that you and me both would run up the side of a mountain and holler like a mountain jack."

Then Earl blew a smoke ring and watched its rise; maybe it would halo the rearview mirror. "Well, okay, I'll take your word for it now, but if we're ever back through here, I definitely want to stop and see if these women are as pretty as you say."

"They pretty, they mamas pretty, they grandmamas pretty. . . ."

Earl laughed his high-pitched laugh. "You get crazier every day, Billy Cox." He pushed the accelerator, slamming them deeper into their seats.

Earl leveled off at sixty and for minutes was content to enjoy the regular beat of the wheels hitting the seams across the pavement, pa-poom, pa-poom, pa-poom. It was on the next stretch of road, ten miles outside of Springfield, that they truly sensed the flatness of the place. In the darkness there were no distant hills promising contour, variety, or perspective. Fields to the left? Woods to the right? They were silent for a minute or so. Crackling music flared up once again from the radio, then died.

"What do you think of the new boy's work tonight?" Billy asked.

"Who, 'Big City'? Not bad, man. Not bad at all." Earl snapped his fingers. "He's swinging more now. Matter of fact, he's driving the entire trumpet section, Big Joe included. You get the prize on that one, you brought him in. I remember you kept saying he could play the sweetest ballads, could curl up inside something like Strayhorn's 'Daydream' as easy as a cat curl up on a bed."

Billy nodded and looked out the side window. "I knew he had it in him the first time I heard him. His problem was hanging around Kansas City too long with that little jive band and just playing careful music. Sometimes you can't tell what's on the inside—just fast or slow, just hard or soft, just mean or laughing sweet. Can't never tell with some. But I had that feeling, know what I'm saying? Had the feeling that if we cut him loose, let him roam a little taste, that he could be all them combinations, that he could be what a tune needed him to be."

Earl tossed a cigarette stub out the window. He remembered the night he had met young Harold. The band was on break, and Harold walked up slowly, head down. The trumpet player had been nervous in his too-tight suit. Earl had later confided to Billy that he looked like he had just come in from plowing a cornfield and that if he joined the band he would have to learn how to dress, to coordinate his colors of his ties and suits, shine his shoes. When you joined the Ferguson band, you joined class. Style was more than your sound. It was your walk, the way you sat during the solos by others, the way you met the night. Earl had promptly nicknamed him "Big City."

"He said meeting you was like meeting God," Billy had said the next morning over hash browns and lukewarm coffee.

Earl smiled now. He was not God, true. He did know that among bandleaders roaming with their groups across this country, he was one of the best. He knew, too, that soft-spoken Billy Cox, five years younger, was the best composer in the business, period. Together they worked an easy magic. Few could weave sounds the way they could, few could get twelve voices, twelve rambunctious personalities, to shout or moan as one. And with it all was the trademark sound: the perfect blend of brass and reeds. Basie might have had a stronger reed section, with the force of a melodic hurricane; Ellington, a brass section with bite and unmatchable brightness. But they had the blend. Within the first few notes you knew that it was Earl Ferguson's band and nobody else's. Now and then players would leave to join other caravans inching across the continent, but the sound, their mix, stayed the same.

The scattered lights of Springfield were far behind them now, merged to a dull electric glow in the rearview mirror. And out from the town there were only occasional lights along State Route 42, one or two on front porches, lights bathing narrow, weathered, and wooded fronts, wood swings perfectly still in that time. Tightly closed shutters, silences inside. Both tried to imagine the front of the houses at noon—children pushing the porch swing? A dog napping in the shade nearby? Clothes flapping on a line running from behind the house? Gone suddenly, a blur to pinpoint, then out.

From a pocket Billy had taken out a matchbook. A few chord progressions had been scribbled on the inside cover. Then, drawing out a small lined tablet from beneath the seat, he quickly drew a bass staff and started humming.

"You got something going?" Earl asked.

"I think, yeah. A little light something, you know, like bright light and springtime and whatnot."

Earl tapped the wheel lightly with the palm of his free hand. "Toss in a small woman's bouncy walk, and I might get excited with you."

"Well, help me then. This time you use the woman—tight yellow skirt, right?— and I'll use the light, the light of mid-May, and when they don't work together, I think we'll both know."

"Solid. What you got so far?"

Billy did not answer. He kept a finger to his ear, staring from the matchbook cover to the tablet. Earl let it run. You don't interrupt when the idea is so young.

More often than not, Billy and Earl brought opposites or, at least, unlikely combinations together. One of the band's more popular numbers, a blues, was the result of Billy's meditations on the richly perfumed arms of a large and fleshy woman, arms tightly holding a man who mistook her short laugh for joy. To this, Earl had brought the memory of a rainy night and a long soft moan carried on the wind, something heard from the end of an alley. They used only the colors and sounds from these images, and only later, when the songs were fully arranged, did the smell and the touch of them sweep in. There had been other songs that resolved the contrasts, the differences, between the drone of a distant train and an empty glass of gin, a lipstick print at its rim, fingerprints around it. A baby's whimpering, and a man grinning as he counted a night's big take from the poker table, painted bright red fingernails tapping lightly down a lover's arm, and the cold of a lonely apartment. How much did the dancing couples, those whispering and holding close as second skins or those bouncing and whirling tirelessly, feel these things, too? Or did they bring something entirely different to the rhythms, something of their own?

Earl and Billy had talked about this many times. They had concluded that it was enough to bring contexts to dreams, to strengthen those who listened and danced. And there were those moments, magical, alive, when the dance hall was torn from the night and whirled, spinning like a top, a half mile from heaven.

Billy started whistling and tapping his thigh. Then he hummed a fragment of a song loudly.

Earl was nodding. "Nice. Already I can hear Slick Harry taking off with Ousley just under him with the alto. In triplets? Let's see, go through it again right quick."

Again Billy hummed and Earl brought in high triplets, nervous wings snagged to the thread of the melody, lifting the piece toward brightness. They stopped, and Billy, smiling now, worked quickly, a draftsman on fire, adding another line or two, crossing out, scribbling notes. He would look up to follow the front edges of the car's lights, then away to the darkness and back to the page.

"Listen up." Billy gave the next lines, flats predominating, while offering harsh counterpoint to the first two lines and snatching the song away from a tender playfulness for a moment. He scratched his chin and nodded. Pointed to the darkness.

"This is what I got so far." And he sang the line in a strong tenor voice, his melody now seeming to double the notes from the last line, though the rhythm did not vary. It was the kind of thing Art Tatum might do with "Tea for Two" or something equally simple. The song moved swiftly from a lyrical indulgence to a catch-me-if-you-can show of speed.

"Watch it now," Earl said, "or they will figure us for one of those beboppers." He chuckled. The woman in his mind walked faster, traffic about her thickened, the streets sent up jarring sounds. Those would be trumpets, probably. Surroundings leaned in. Trombones and tenor saxophones playing in the lowest octaves announced their possibilities.

Earl offered a line of his own. His woman walked quickly up the steps of a brownstone. In. Common enough sequence, but no surprise there. Whatever prompted it, though, was fleeting. Gone. Then he said, "Okay, forget mine for now. Let's stay with what you got."

Billy shrugged and marked off another staff, then glanced again to the match cover. He let out a long, low whistle. "Now we come to the bridge."

"This is when we need a piano, Earl. I bet the closest one to here is probably some ol' beat-up thing in one of these country churches out here. Or something sitting in the front parlor of one of these farmer's houses, and the farmer's daughter playing 'Jingle Bells' after bringing in the eggs."

Hip and arrogant city was in their laughter, they of funky cafés where fights might break out and beer bottles fly as the piano man bobbed and weaved, keeping time on a scarred piano that leaned and offered sticky keys in the lowest and highest octaves.

Then the Earl of Ferguson told the story of a piano search years before Billy had joined the band. With two other men in the car and barely an hour east of St. Louis, when the puzzle of a chord progression struck with the force of a deep stomach cramp. Spotting one light shining in the wilderness, a small neon sign still shining over a door, he ordered the car stopped. Trotting up, Earl noticed the sign blink off. He banged on the door, the hinges straining from each blow. Nobody turned off a sign in his face. The door swung open and up stepped an evil-looking, red-haired farmer in overalls, a man big enough to fill the doorway.

"I said to this giant, 'Quick, I got to get on your piano.' Not 'I got to find your toilet,' or 'I got to use your phone,' but 'I got to use your piano.'" He shook his head as he laughed now.

"That giant rocked on his heels like I had punched him square in the chest. He left just enough room for me to squeeze in and sure enough there was a little raggedy piano in the corner of his place.

"P. M. had enough sense to offer to buy some of the man's good whiskey while I'm sitting there playing and trying to figure out the good chord. P. M. always did have good common sense. Most folks try to remember what just happened, but Past was already on what's happening next. I'm forgetting you never knew P. M. The guys called him

Past Midnight because he was so dark-skinned. The shadow of a shadow. Next thing they calling him Past, then one day Rabbit showed up calling him P. M., and it stuck. His real name was Wiley Reed, and he was one of the best alto players in the world."

He paused now, glanced out his side window. "Anyway, he showed him class that night. The giant steady looking around suspiciouslike at first. I mean, he didn't know us from Adam, didn't know how many more of us was waiting outside to rush in and turn out the joint. But he loosened up and took his mess of keys out and go to his cabinet. I'm just playing away because this is the greatest song of my life, don't care if it is in some country roadhouse way out in Plumb Nelly. I'm cussing, too, Billy, because this song is giving me fits, do you hear me? It just wouldn't let me go. All I wanted was to make it through the bridge. I figured the rest would come soon as I'm back in the car.

"Well, P. M. and the man making small talk, and Leon trying to get slick on everybody and tipping over to get him a few packs of Old Golds. I'm checking all this, see, and closing in on something solid and oh-so-sweet, and hearing the big guy go on and on about getting home because his wife already thinking he's sniffing around the new waitress—I remember that part clear as I'm sitting here—when, *boom!* Leon open up the closet, a mop and a jug of moonshine fell out and this woman inside trying to button up her blouse. She give a scream like she done seen the boogeyman. All hell commence to break loose. Next thing you know Leon backing off and telling the woman he ain't meant no harm, just trying to get some cigarettes, he lie. Big Boy running over and telling me we got to take our whiskey and go, song or no song. I look up, and two white guys running down the steps from just over our heads, one of them holding some cards in his hands. The other one run to the telephone like he reporting a robbery. I mean from the outside it's just a little-bitty place on the side of the road, but inside all kinds of shit going on. Well, I found the chords I wanted, did a quick run-through and called out to the fellows to haul ass. If some man's wife or some woman's man don't come in there shooting up the place, then the sheriff might raid the place for all-night gambling. Either way we lose."

Earl was laughing now. A light rain had started to fall just as he ended his tale. The windshield wipers clicked rhythmically; the bump of the road seemed a grace note: *bachoo-choo, bachoo-choo.*

"Never know when you get the tune down right. Go too early and you pluck it raw. Go too late and you got rotten fruit." Earl coughed. "Don't go at all and you put a bad hurt on yourself."

From across the highway a rabbit darted toward them, then cut away. Earl had turned the car just slightly before straightening it without letting up on the accelerator.

"Almost had us one dead rabbit."

Billy did not answer. He was tapping his pencil on the tablet. Up ahead and to the east they would discover the electric glow of Columbus. Beyond that they would have three more hours before Cleveland and breakfast at the Majestic Hotel on Carnegie Avenue. There might be a new singer or two waiting to try out with the band. Who knows? Somebody—another Billy or Sassy Sarah—might get lucky and ride back with them to New York, her life changed forever. Some young woman, prettier than she would ever know, would otherwise be serving up beef stew or spareribs in some tiny smoky place on Cedar Avenue, notes running through her head or thoughts of a sickly mother and two children she and her husband were trying to feed. How many times Billy and Earl had seen it, how many times they had heard the hope there, the sweat mustaches sprouting, the need to escape the routine nights. It was common ground. They had all been there, falling to sleep in clothes that smelled of cigarette smoke, the world a place of slow mornings with traffic starting and a door slamming, a baby crying, and an "Oh, goddamn, one more funky morning, but I'm alive to see it through anyhow."

There was a bump beneath the car. "You clipped something for sure that time, sportey-otee."

"All kinds of stuff out here at night," Earl said. "They like the warm road. Coons, possums, snakes, cows."

"Cows?"

"Yeah, cows." Billy had lit a cigarette. Earl tapped the end of the fresh one he had just placed in his mouth, and Billy reached to light it. "Thanks. Don't tell me you done forgot that cow we nicked on the road up to Saratoga Springs."

Yes, yes, Billy remembered. "Cow must have thought we was the Midnight Special, much noise as I was making trying to scare him off the road. Probably just out to get him a little side action in the next field." The car had knocked it to one knee before it struggled back up and, in the rearview mirror, slipped into the darkness.

They were quiet for long moments. After music, after hours, different thoughts could struggle to life. If there was an easiness earlier, swift terror could strike them in the darkest hours before dawn. They could grow suddenly uneasy in the silences. They could sense it together like a bone-deep chill starting. For now Billy pushed the wing shut on his side, rolled his window up another inch.

In a small town just west of Columbus, they passed a café, the lone light in that stretch. A man behind a long counter—white apron, white T-shirt—was scrubbing the counter and talking with a customer. He stopped his work to make a point, head moving from side to side. The customer nodded. Another man stood over a table at the window, dunking a doughnut. With his free hand, he waved as the car passed. Surprised, Earl honked once, then turned to glance back.

"That back there reminds me of something."

"Huh?"

"That man right back there waving. You didn't see him? Standing back there, waving at us and probably every car coming through here this late."

"Don't tell me you want to get some food," Billy said. "Hell, Earl, I thought those chicken sandwiches and pound cake—"

"No, no. That ain't what I'm thinking. Had a guy in the band by the name of Boonie years ago, way before you joined the band. Boonie could play him some mean trombone, I'm here to tell you. Fact, he could play trumpet and cornet, too. Probably would have played the tuba if I would have asked him to. Like you, he was the master of horns. Anyway, something happened—could have been bad gin or something else nobody will ever know about. He just snapped, and they found him one morning standing on a corner cussing at folks and swearing up and down that he was the governor of Africa. They took him to the jailhouse first, then the crazy house. They didn't keep him there long, six, seven months maybe.

"I went up to see him, way out in the country, Billy, you know where they put those places. Well, just past the gate was this man, and he waved at me when I first came in, and, while I was walking around with Boonie, he waved a couple more times. At first I thought he was just part of the staff because he was all over the place. But then I noticed he's wearing the same kind of clothes as Boonie. And he keeps smiling, you know? By the time I left, he was back out by the gate and waving again. It didn't take me long to figure out that all he had to do was wave at whatever was new and moving by. Like that man back there waving at the night."

Billy only glanced at him, then looked back to his notebook. Earl shook his head and chuckled. "Governor of Africa, can you beat that? Boonie was lucky, though; I mean, the way he wound up. He never got his chops back after he got out. He worked around a little, then finally left the life. He got a foundry job and raised his family in Detroit. Others ain't been so lucky."

Earl glanced ahead to more lights showing up through the rain. He knew some who entered hospitals, never to emerge. And many, too many, died before the age of fifty. Just last March, young "Bird" Parker had died in New York, not yet thirty-five. He whose notes surprised like shooting stars. Playing this music could be as risky as working in a steel mill or coal mine. But what were the choices? What could he do about it, leader of some? Perhaps only show them a lesson or two through his example. Now he did limit himself to one large and long drink per night—one part scotch and three parts water—from an oversized coffee mug. Soon he would cut down on his cigarettes. Beyond that he let the rules pronounce the purpose: you needed a clear head and a sound body to play the music he lived for.

Their talk of work and women—the incomplete song still a bright ribbon over their heads—pulled them well beyond the glow of Columbus. Coffee and sandwiches finished, they were down to three cigarettes each and figured there was nothing open between Columbus and Cleveland. Billy took over at the wheel. Twenty miles or so north of Columbus, they neared a car in trouble at the side of the road. The hood was up and in the swath of the front headlights was a man— very young, thin, white—kneeling at the back tire.

"Keep going, Billy. That cracker'll get help."

Billy slowed. "Well, Earl, it won't hurt. . . ."

Earl stared at him, hard. "You getting softhearted on me? That boy could be the Klan, see? You remember what happened to the Purnell band down in Tennessee just last month? Huh, remember that stuff. Got beat up by a bunch of rednecks, one of them getting his nose broke, and they still winding up in jail for disturbing the peace and impersonating a band? No, let him get help from his own kind."

Billy pulled the car off the road. "He's just a kid, Earl."

"You go without me, then." He watched Billy leave, then quickly felt under his seat.

Billy was approaching the car, and Earl could hear him ask, "Need a hand?"

"Sure do," the boy said loudly. "If you got a jack on you, we can do this in no time."

Beneath his seat in the Buick, Earl had found the gun wrapped in a towel. He opened the glove compartment and placed it inside, unwrapping the towel and leaving the small door open. He began to hum the new song slowly, softly, watching his friend, smiling Billy, trusting Billy, help a stranger.

Billy brought the jack from their trunk and set it up. He could smell alcohol on the boy, and, straightening up, he saw a girl in the car sip from a flask. Neither could have been older than eighteen. She was trying to hum something, missing, then tried again.

"Dumb me out here without a jack, I swear," the boy said. Billy only nodded as they set the jack under the frame.

The boy called the girl out of the car, and she stood apart shyly, both hands holding up the collar of her light coat.

"Your friend back there under the weather?" the boy asked.

"He just don't need the exercise," Billy said. "How about her? She feeling all right?"

The boy looked up in surprise, then he smiled. "No, she all right. She don't need no exercise either." He leaned closer to Billy as they pulled off the wheel and started to set the spare. "Course, me and her just about exercised out." Then he laughed. "Whoo-ee!"

The tire was on now, and the boy was tightening the lugs. "Pretty nice car you got back there. You a undertaker or a preacher?"

"No, neither one. I'm a musician."

The boy whistled low. "Musicians make enough for a car like that? I need to learn me some music. You get to travel a lot and see them big-city women and all like that?"

"Sure do."

The boy glanced at the girl and said loudly, "Course, a man could go all over the world and never find a woman sweet as my Josie there."

Her hair needed a brush, her dress was wrinkled, and her shoes were old and run-over. She was plain and drunk. In the morning she might be in the choir of a tiny church and by evening making biscuits to the staccato of radio news broadcasts. Billy was folding up the jack and turning away.

"Ain't she about the prettiest doggone thing a man could ever see?"

"I know how you feel, sport. I got one just as sweet back in New York."

Billy walked away and waved good-bye with his back turned. He slammed the trunk closed, then settled behind the wheel. He pulled the car back onto the highway.

Earl was whistling. "Feel better?" he asked, not looking up.

"What's that for?" Billy pointed to the gun.

"I thought about cleaning it. Ain't been cleaned in a year." Then: "My daddy told me once that it takes more than a smile and a good heart to get through this world. Told me sometimes you can reach out a helping hand and get it chopped off."

Billy was shivering. "Hide it, Earl. Please."

"Okay, okay. Look, while you were playing the Good Samaritan with Jethro back there, I finished the song. Listen up, young-blood."

Earl hummed through the opening key, stretching the note, then moved through the bright afternoon of the melody, repeated the line in the thinning light of its early evening. The song soon lifted to the bridge, a vivid golden stair step on which to linger briefly. Then the return to the opening line that suggested new possibilities: the smell of a pine forest after a rain, a meadow, too, a deer or two frozen at one edge. There was a street, glistening, a small oil slick catching dull rainbows, and a stranger's laughter like a bright coin spinning at their feet. Yes, all of that.

The small and proud woman walking, her hips working against yellow wool, had been lost to Earl. She would return, surely, to move through another song, walking to a different rhythm. For now she had brought Earl excited to Billy's first thoughts. Provided a spirit. Together, they hummed the song through, speeding it up, slowing. Each time, they tried different harmonies—the bass stronger here, the trombones higher there. Most of the parts had been worked through by the time they noticed the hills near Medina taking shape.

"Got it," Billy said finally. He slapped the wheel with relief.

"It's nice," Earl said.

"Think the people will like it?" Billy asked.

Earl yawned and looked out the window. Maybe he could get twenty minutes or so of sleep before they touched the edges of the city. "You worry too much, Billy. Course they gone like it. They got no choice. We did the best we could. We'll run through it this afternoon, do it again in Pittsburgh, and maybe have it ready by the time we hit Philly. Can't you just hear Big City's solo already?" He settled back, eyes closed.

Cars, trees, cornfields just harvested were explosions of dull colors. Signs placed one hundred feet apart, a shaving cream ad suddenly claimed Billy's attention. *The big blue tube's/Just like Louise/You get a thrill/From every squeeze.* He laughed aloud, then started whistling. Then the car roared into a stretch of light fog. Billy leaned forward, his head almost touching the windshield. Then he stiffened.

"Earl, wake up. I got something to tell you."

"Let it slide. Tell me over grits and coffee." Earl kept his eyes closed.

"No, it can't wait. It happened back there in Dayton. I just now remembered. You know on that second break? Well, I stepped outside to get a little air, take a smoke, you understand. A couple folk stroll past and tell me how much they like our playing, so I'm talking with them a while and then I see this woman—short with a red wig and she standing off to the side. She look up every now and then like she want to come over and say something. But she wait until nobody's around and she walk over real quick-like. Something about her make me think about a bird hopping, then resting, hopping some more. She told me she really like the music, like some of the songs really get a hold of her. . . ."

Earl opened one eye. "Yeah, and she just want to take a cute little man like you home to make music to her all the time."

"No, no, no. Nothing like that, but you better believe I was hoping for some action."

Forehead still to the windshield, Billy fumbled for words, worked a hand like he was flagging down a car. "No, she's smiling but not smiling, if you know what I mean. We talk about a lot of things, then she gets down to the thing she really wanted to talk about, I figure. She told me about her baby. She told me about hearing her baby screaming one day and she rush from her ironing and found him in the next room bleeding. He fell on a stick or glass or something, cut his belly, and blood going every which way. Said her son's belly was thin, like a balloon, but not going down when it's poked. She put her hand there, she said, and could feel each beat of the heart. Every time the heart beat, more blood would spurt out between her fingers. She screamed for help, screamed for her neighbors next door, just screamed and screamed. Blood was all over her, too, she said, but she never saw that until later. All she could do is tell her child not to die and press on that thin belly. And pray and pray, even after he in the ambulance. She told me that baby was all she got in this world."

Billy shook his head slowly. "What could I say to all that? Here I go outside for some fresh air and a draw or two on my Lucky Strikes. She brings me this story when I want to know whether my shoes are shined, my front still holding up, or whether some big-legged woman want to pull me home with her. I touched her on the shoulder, was all I could do. She told me the baby lived, and she smiled this dopey smile. Then she left."

Earl's eyes were closed. He waved his hand as if shooing a fly from his forehead. "It's this music we play, Billy. It opens people up, makes them give up secrets. Better than whiskey or dope for that. It don't kill you, and you can't piss it away. You can whistle it the next day in new places. You can loan it to strangers, and they thank you for it."

Then he shrugged. "It's what keeps us going all night."

Sitting back, fog thinning, Billy nodded and started back whistling. Before long they would sight the giant mills pumping smoke into the gray morning. At Lakewood Billy might swing closer to the gray and glassy Erie. Then he would pick up speed and head toward the east side, through a world raging to light outside their windows. Finally they would gain Carnegie Avenue and weave their way among the early church traffic. They would find the Majestic Hotel, breakfast, and attempt sleep, two wizards before the band.

[1990]

Questions

1. Why does McCluskey refer to Earl as "The Earl of Ferguson"?
2. What is the significance of the roadside incident involving a vehicle with a flat tire?
3. To what extent does Billy's account (near the end of the story) of the woman with the sick child enhance our understanding of "Lush Life"?

Katherine Min
(b. 1959)
Korea/United States

K atherine Min's heritage is Korean-American. She was born in the United States, of parents who came to America after the Korean War, yet as a teenager she lived in Seoul. After attending Amherst College (where she majored in English) and Columbia (where she earned an M.A. in journalism), she returned to Korea and worked for the Korea Herald. Subsequently married and back in the United States, she worked at Dartmouth and the University of Virginia, while writing dozens of short stories and—as she says—acquiring 200 rejection slips.

"The One Who Goes Farthest Away" was published in Special Report: Fiction in 1990. The story was prompted by her father's consideration to move back to Korea. "My writing the story came of my trying to make the decision for him," she said. "But I finally decided I couldn't impose my will on him."

Currently she is working on a novel.

THE ONE WHO GOES FARTHEST AWAY

Thirty-five years ago the street had been dirt, narrow and rutted; there had been stables along it with tired ponies, all their ribs showing through dull, matted coats. Now, as he walked along the red-tiled sidewalk, he watched the cars glide over the smooth black tar, watched the men on bicycles, loaded in back with toilet paper, chickens, and ice, weave in and out of traffic with the intensity of racers.

He couldn't help comparing the world he had known with what he now saw; ever since he'd come back, he'd felt this curious simultaneity in his mind, as though the past lay superimposed on the present, playing itself out in phantom traces across the city. Thirty-five years ago there had been oxen to carry the loads, lumbering down the dusty streets attended by thin, indolent men. There had been bicycles too, but not for commerce, ridden by schoolchildren in their starched uniforms who had been freed from the basements of the war.

Entering a small courtyard, Kyoungsu marveled at how much the city had changed. The skyscrapers pressed in all around the older, shorter buildings, making them seem not so much like buildings as footstools. When he'd left, the city had been devastated, a dry, gray plain filled with rubble and debris, crowded with starving refugees from the North. *Like a phoenix*, Kyoungsu thought, *the city has rebuilt itself*. He shook his head at the aptness of the image. Out of the ashes.

He slipped off his polished black shoes and placed them next to the other identical pairs, which sat in a row on the wooden stoop outside the house. His were the newest-looking.

A tall woman in a green dress greeted him at the door and bowed slightly. "Welcome, professor," she said, her smile widening to reveal bad teeth. She ushered him into a narrow foyer. "This way, please," she indicated. "Your friends are waiting." She slid open a door of paper and wood and motioned for him to enter.

"Ah, Kyoungsu is here at last!" boomed a jovial male voice.

Three men rose from their cushions on the floor. They embraced Kyoungsu one after the other, slapping him on the back and laughing, all talking at once.

"Let's sit down, why don't we," Jae Shik said, "and Kyoungsu can tell us all about himself." This brought renewed laughter, as it was so typically Jae Shik to organize them all.

On the low black lacquer table were some glasses, an open bottle of whiskey, and two plates of nuts, dried cuttlefish, and raisins. The sight of it made Kyoungsu feel welcome. He settled onto a blue silk cushion beside his friends. He smelled the oiled paper, which covered the floor, heated underneath by hot air pipes. It had a musty odor.

"Ja," Young Bae said, picking up the bottle.

Kyoungsu held out his glass formally, with two hands, and Young Bae poured into it.

"To Kyoungsu." Jae Shik lifted his glass, and the others followed suit. "On his return to his homeland."

"To us," Kyoungsu replied with emotion. "To old friends."

They all drank up. Jae Shik refilled their glasses.

"Ah," Young Bae sighed. "We *are* old, aren't we? Look at you, Kyoungsu. Your hair has gone white."

"At least I still have hair," Kyoungsu observed.

Young Bae fingered the bald dome of his head, smoothing down the one lock of hair that still clung there like a faint wisp of smoke. "Bald men are considered sexy," he said.

"Fat men, too?" Hyun Ki asked. They laughed. Young Bae had always been fat, but his bulk had lost its firmness since the last time Kyoungsu had seen him; his stomach sagged unhealthily downward.

They looked older, it was true. Young Bae's baldness showed mottled brown patches on his scalp, patches that repeated on the backs of his large hands. Hyun Ki was thinner than ever, skeletal; his eyes had worsened, and the glasses he wore seemed an inch thick. Even Jae Shik had aged, his boyish face lined with creases.

Kyoungsu felt saddened to see his friends so changed. In his mind they were always teenagers together, their faces bright with an unknown future, bodies restless, flowing with adrenaline. The time intervening seemed insubstantial. Why then, did they look so old? Kyoungsu gulped the whiskey in his glass. It burrowed warmth inside him as he drank.

"So, you've come back, Kyoungsu," Young Bae said, the cigarette in his mouth wavering in the air as he spoke.

"Well, I haven't decided yet," Kyoungsu replied, shrugging. "I've been down in Kwangju for three months now, at the university. They've offered me a permanent position, but I have to go back to the States for at least a year, whatever I decide."

"Of course you're coming back," Jae Shik said, popping pine nuts into his mouth one by one.

"I don't know." Kyoungsu shook his head. "It's a difficult decision."

"Why difficult?" asked Young Bae. "You are Korean. You belong in Korea. You've been away too long already."

"In America, he has it made," Hyun Ki retorted. His eyes blinked enormously behind thick lenses. "Why should he come back here?"

"Because Korea is his homeland," Jae Shik said simply.

Kyoungsu nodded. "I'm quite comfortable with life in the States," he said. "My kids are there, and I've got tenure. Jun Hee has a good job that she enjoys. But as I get older—I don't know—I think more and more about returning." He smiled at them.

"You know, Kyoungsu," Young Bae remarked suddenly, "you have an accent!" He pointed his cigarette toward Jae Shik, laughing. "Doesn't he? Doesn't he, Jae Shik? You sound like a foreigner, Kyoungsu!"

"Of course he has an accent," said Jae Shik. "He's lived abroad more than he's lived here."

Kyoungsu smiled sadly. "The Americans say the same thing," he said. "I guess between learning English and losing Korean I don't really have a language." The poignancy of this struck him, and he knew that it was true, that for him neither language was entirely comfortable anymore. In his mind he thought in a mishmash of the two, groping back and forth, often not distinguishing between them.

"Anyway, I can still understand you," said Hyun Ki, patting Kyoungsu on the back. "Tell us about your job in Kwangju, Godforsaken place," he said.

"Oh, it's not so bad," Kyoungsu shrugged. "They're treating me very well, of course, because they want me to stay. And the students are very sharp, but they're afraid to speak up in class. I have to really work to draw them out; they're so deferential to authority."

Young Bae snorted. "The same students who throw rocks at the police. Very nice, very deferential."

"And why shouldn't they throw rocks at the police?" Kyoungsu snapped. "When the police slaughter them by the thousands. You know what they did. . . ."

Jae Shik held up a hand. His voice was quiet, almost a whisper, but there was urgency behind it. "Kyoungsu, please! This isn't America!"

Kyoungsu held his tongue. Jae Shik had always hated political discussion. More than this, he hated when Kyoungsu and Young Bae bickered, something they had done constantly since grade school.

"Anyway, things are changing, Kyoungsu," Hyun Ki spoke up, his enormous eyes focusing and unfocusing behind his glasses. "Korean kids are following your Western example. Don't be fooled by their behavior in class. Young kids—my kids included—they don't follow the Confucian rules anymore." To Kyoungsu, his gaunt face looked bitter, unhappy, like the face of a disillusioned monk.

"Still, they must be better behaved than those American kids," reflected Jae Shik. "You see them on TV, so wild-looking with those strange clothes and weird hair. Some of the boys even wear earrings!" He scratched his hairless cheek in wonder.

"Yes," Kyoungsu nodded. "Korean kids are still much more easily managed." He was thinking of his own children, the battles he had had with them growing up. Jane's sullen face appeared to him as it had looked when she'd been thirteen: straight black hair hanging in her eyes, hands thrust deep in the pockets of worn-out jeans. "You think you're still in Korea," she would accuse him, when he wouldn't allow her to date or wear makeup like the other girls in her class. "But it's not fair, Dad. This is America."

Young Bae was laughing, shaking his head over something. "You were the hotheaded one, though, Kyoungsu," he was saying. "A madman! Do you remember the time you attacked me? What had I done to offend you? I can't remember. Jae Shik and Sang Chul had to pull you off before the principal came and found us."

"I remember," said Jae Shik soberly, watching Kyoungsu's face with apprehension. "You deserved it, Young Bae. You and your tongue."

Kyoungsu also remembered. He saw Young Bae as he'd been in high school, a sallow boy in a black school uniform stretched tight across his fat stomach. They used to call him Lord Buddha until Jae Shik, in a religious phase, had told them it was irreverent. Kyoungsu hadn't liked Young Bae as much as the others. He'd been hard even then, his round face set in a tough way, with narrow eyes that looked almost closed, and a mouth curling downward that had been attached to a cigarette since he was thirteen. He used to bribe Kyoungsu into doing his homework for him, offering marbles and money for roasted yams. Then, out of shame, he would insult Kyoungsu, belittle his family name. Once, that one time, Kyoungsu had punched him for it, blackening his eye with the knuckles of one fist.

"Do you remember?" Hyun Ki said, his voice distant with the past. "Do you remember the time we all cut class and went to Inchon to eat abalone porridge? When we were around fifteen, I think. What a beautiful day that was!"

Kyoungsu nodded. "In June, wasn't it?" His glass paused at his lips. "We got that fisherman to take us out on his boat."

"Yes, yes," Jae Shik said, "and he let us take turns steering."

Hyun Ki removed his glasses. Without them, his eyes looked tiny. He began to clean the lenses on a corner of his handkerchief. "It was Sang Chul's idea," he said quietly.

They fell silent.

"Did I ever tell you," Kyoungsu said, "about the time in the army when Sang Chul and I were on leave together?"

The men shook their heads slowly, each lost in his own private memory of their friend. Kyoungsu spoke and they listened intently.

"We were drinking in a small bar somewhere in Pusan with a day left on leave, and this old guy next to us started to buy us beer. He said he was a fortune-teller, that he would tell us what we wanted to know about our futures. Well, Sang Chul, you can guess, was pretty keen, so the man took his palm and gazed into it for a long time."

Kyoungsu felt his own palms grow wet. He rubbed them absently on his pants legs. "After a while, the man just turned to me and asked to see my palm. He told me I would leave Korea and live somewhere far away. He said I would be successful, and though I wouldn't be rich, I would be comfortable. And he said I would die an old man."

He saw Sang Chul's face, that smirking combination of eagerness and scorn, both eyes trained steadily on the fortuneteller's face. "Sang Chul kept asking the man, 'What about my fortune? Why don't you tell me what's in store for me, old man?' But he just shook his head. I remember his eyes looked frightened, and he shrank away from us. . . ." Kyoungsu stopped and gazed reflectively into his glass.

"Sang Chul laughed and called the old man a lot of names, and then we both forgot about it and I said good-bye to him." Kyoungsu bowed his head, tracing the lines in a rumpled napkin with his finger.

"Poor bastard," Young Bae muttered.

"He was the best of all of us," Hyun Ki said gloomily, and they all fell silent.

Jae Shik clapped his hands. "Ja," he said, smiling with visible effort. "Let's order more whiskey."

The hostess brought the bottle on a tray and placed it on the table, then backed out of the room slowly, her eyes cast down on the floor. It was such a feminine gesture,

Kyoungsu observed, demure and graceful—very Korean; it stirred a tenderness in him, and he thought of his wife, Jun Hee.

"Still," said Hyun Ki, "it's a wonder any of us survived. Jae Shik was wounded. Young Bae, you almost got sent to the North. And, Kyoungsu, remember when the bomb landed on the outhouse right after you had left it?"

"Good thing you weren't constipated!" Young Bae laughed huskily, then was silent.

How lucky we are, thought Kyoungsu, and he wanted to weep, to cry out. The war had claimed one-third of their classmates. It had divided families. It had seemed to Kyoungsu once that the world would never right itself, that he would never know the quiet pleasures of a normal life. And look at them now. They were the survivors. He felt an overwhelming affection for them all.

"A toast to Sang Chul," he said, raising his glass.

"To our generation," someone shouted. They tossed the whiskey down their throats and wiped the tears from their eyes.

"Did you know," Hyun Ki said after a moment, "they tore down that house, Kyoungsu, your father's old one? They turned it into a shop—antiques for tourists."

"It survived the war and got torn down for progress," muttered Hyun Ki.

"They tore down all the old houses," Jae Shik said, mopping the lacquer table with a napkin. "For the Olympics. New hotels. New shops."

"They tore it down?" Kyoungsu repeated dully. He remembered playing in the courtyard with the little Chindo dog his father kept. Sometimes his father would come in after being out all night and ruffle Kyoungsu's hair with a rough hand. He would give him a 500-hwan note for lunch and wander off to bed, and Kyoungsu would stare after him—at the distant man in the homburg and the English-looking suit—then go off and spend the money on cigarettes and comic books.

"It's changed so much here," Kyoungsu said quietly. He pulled his crossed legs toward his body, rocking back and forth.

"I remember," he murmured, his eyes on his glass, "how homesick I was when I first arrived in America. I was the first Korean at Amherst College, right out of the war; all the other freshmen were four years younger, and my English was poor. I remember the Americans were all so kind to me. My roommate invited me to his house for Thanksgiving; the dean of the college invited me to Christmas dinner. But I missed Korean food so badly. Especially kimchi."

The others nodded, their faces straining to comprehend a place lacking in this staple, the spicy fermented cabbage they had eaten three times a day for their entire lives.

"Once I tried to cook an egg in my room over vacation," Kyoungsu went on. "I wanted it hard-boiled, so I put the egg in my sock and held it under the hot-water faucet for about 20 minutes. It came out raw."

The men chuckled.

Kyoungsu continued. He was aware of the sound his voice made as he talked, of the silence surrounding it. "It was never a conscious decision to stay," he said. "Just one day leading to the next, to the next, faster and faster, until one day I woke up and I was fifty-six and living in a foreign country. I had two grown-up kids who didn't even speak Korean."

The others listened shyly, looking down at their socked feet. Kyoungsu felt his own surprise as he thought of how much time had passed.

"Why did you leave, anyway?" said Young Bae with sudden harshness. "The war ruined everything. You were the smartest in our class. The country needed you."

"Oh, come on, Young Bae," Kyoungsu retorted. "You wanted to go too, but your mother threatened to go on a hunger strike if you left her!"

"That's right," Hyun Ki laughed. "That's right, Young Bae, I remember. She told my mother she would rather die than lose her oldest son."

Young Bae took a surly gulp of whiskey, his Adam's apple working like a pump. He grimaced. "Anyway," he said, "I didn't go. And I'm glad I didn't."

"And you did very well, Young Bae," said Jae Shik, patting him on the shoulder. "And Kyoungsu did well in America. And now he's coming back, and we'll all be together."

Hyun Ki poured the last of the whiskey into Kyoungsu's glass.

"Do you remember?" Kyoungsu laughed, upsetting the plate of nuts with his sleeve. "Do you remember," he repeated eagerly, "the time we went up to the temple at sunrise?"

"Which one?" Jae Shik asked.

Kyoungsu thought. "I don't know. The one on Kwanaksan? We were trying to be better Buddhists then."

"I don't remember," said Hyun Ki.

Young Bae shook his head. "I wasn't there."

"Yes, you were. All of us were," Kyoungsu insisted. "Don't you remember, Jae Shik? It was your idea. We must have been twelve or thirteen. We climbed up on a Sunday morning, very early, with our lunches packed, and when we got to the top, we vowed we would all go to America."

"Did we do that?" Jae Shik asked.

"Did we?" Young Bae echoed, a note of wonder in his voice.

"The one who goes the farthest away remembers the most," mused Hyun Ki.

Young Bae laughed. "Or makes it up," he said, coughing. "Fantasies."

They all chuckled, but Kyoungsu saw it all very clearly, the five of them in their identical school uniforms with their crew cuts and black knapsacks, hiking up Kwanaksan in the streaked light of dawn, discussing Buddhism and America with the same eagerness and mystification. They would all go to America; they had decided—a notion one of them had come up with—but only he had gone. And why was that?

Kyoungsu chewed thoughtfully on the end of a shredded piece of dried cuttlefish, savoring the fishy sweetness that he liked so much. It reminded him of the movie theater they used to go to sometimes when they were skipping school. It was a dingy place with sticky floors and a torn velvet curtain where they had first seen the old Tarzan movies and Errol Flynn, mistaking the Hollywood images of Africa or the high seas for a vision of America. It had been in Sam-chong-dong, hadn't it? Surely it wasn't there any longer. He thought if he had the time he might go see.

The smells of his childhood: sesame oil, garlic, and hot pepper in the earthen kitchen of his mother's house, the kerosene and roasting chestnuts from the street vendors' carts—the sounds: the tinny voice of the calisthenics instructor blaring from the loudspeaker in the courtyard of their school, "Ready, begin, one, two, one, two . . ."; the hollow, wooden pounding of the Buddhist drums; the dry rasp of his father's cough—the feeling: timeless afternoons playing war games with Jae Shik when he was seven or eight in the courtyard at Insadong; then the real thing, lying face-down in a damp trench, eighteen but really still a boy, fingering the rifle in his hands with a reluctant fascination and terror. He realized sadly, his stomach tightening, that he remembered these times in his life more vividly than any recent memory.

"I know why I wanted to come back," he said quietly. He shook his head in wonder at himself. "Because I wanted to die here."

"But you are a long way from dying, Kyoungsu," said Jae Shik.

He nodded. He wanted to say that America was a country where there was only the future. From the day he had arrived, with twenty-five dollars in his pocket, he had been swept forward into tomorrow and the next day, awed by the driving possibilities of life without tradition, without the past. There were no memories for him in America.

But here the past swirled with smell and sound, with texture and shape; it spoke to him in many voices, arresting him, crowding up against him as he revolved through the city, more real than the concrete buildings, than the newly laid highways, more resonant than the traffic noise, than the voices in the streets. He could not tell his friends that for him his homeland was a dead land, inhabited by ghosts, by stunning visions of the past. He could not tell them.

"Ah," Hyun Ki was getting to his feet slowly, a bit unsteadily. "Forgive me, but I must go," he said. "It's after two, and I have to go in to work tomorrow." He reached for Kyoungsu's hand. "Come back to us, Kyoungsu, and quit this talk of death," he said, looking with concern at his friend.

The others started to get up also. Young Bae yawned. "I'm off as well," he said. "It's past my bedtime."

"Stay a little longer, Hyun Ki," Kyoungsu protested. "Jae Shik? We can go to a tent restaurant and have some *kooksoo*."[1]

"No, no," Jae Shik shook his head. "Your wife is in the States, Kyoungsu, or you would know better."

Young Bae belched, rubbing a hand underneath his belt. "*Ajuma!*"[2] he called out. "The bill, please!"

Hyun Ki dug his wallet from his back pocket. "Oh, no, you don't, Young Bae," he said. "My treat."

Kyoungsu reached for his own wallet. "I wish you'd let me pay," he said. "I am the visitor, after all."

Young Bae waved them aside with both arms. "I am the richest one here," he said, taking the bills from his wallet. He laughed, shaking his finger at Kyoungsu. "Mr. Professor, sit. You used to do my homework, too. And I am the wealthiest one of all of us."

The hostess appeared, and Young Bae paid her. "And this is for you," he said, handing her an additional 10,000-won note.

They slipped on their shoes, after much arguing over whose were whose, and walked out into the small courtyard. Neon lights cast a yellow vapor across the city sky. Kyoungsu noted all the English names flashing in Korean letters: Crown, Ambassador, Venus.

Jae Shik embraced Kyoungsu, patting his back several times. "When you come back," he said, "we will meet every week to drink together."

Kyoungsu pressed his friend's hand, nodding absently.

"Your wife isn't so Americanized she will beat you for going out with us, is she?" Hyun Ki teased, shaking Kyoungsu's hand, then holding it with his own.

---

[1]*kooksoo*   Soup with noodles.
[2]*Ajuma!*   Waitress!

Kyoungsu grinned. "She is so Americanized, she will go out drinking with her friends also!"

He laughed and the others did, too, but Kyoungsu knew that to them it was hilarious because it seemed absurd; to him it was funny precisely because it was true.

"We argue," Young Bae said, clapping a hand on Kyoungsu's shoulder. "My God, how I've missed fighting with you!"

Kyoungsu hugged him. "Fat man," he whispered, affection choking his words. *What good men they all are*, he thought, *such good men*. His oldest friends.

"Going back to your brother's place?" Jae Shik asked him. "Share a cab?"

Kyoungsu shook his head. "No, no," he said. "I'm all right. I think I'll walk."

"Okay then."

Kyoungsu waved. As he watched his classmates retreat into the shadows, he saw their young faces clearly: smooth, except for Hyun Ki's acne, blinking with an innocence that bestowed upon the world a newness, an even light, their mouths calling to him in childish voices, speaking of boyhood games, of manly achievements, their smiles like promises made to one another. He realized how much it had cost him to leave them, how much it would continue to cost him.

[1990]

Questions

1. Why can't Kyoungsu return to live in Korea?
2. In the story, Young Bae remarks that the one who goes farthest away makes up his past. Is this true of Kyoungsu? Are his memories of the past distorted?
3. Is Kyoungsu a cultural half-caste?

Susan Minot

(b. 1956)

United States

S usan Minot was born in Manchester, Massachusetts, in 1956. She grew up in that area, eventually attending Concord Academy and Boston University, later transferring to Brown, where she began her writing. The title of her first novel, Monkeys (1986), refers to a mother's term for her children. The novel covers a period of 13 years and describes the maturation of the children of the Vincent family, ending with their mother's death. The structure of the work—as well as that of her second novel, Evening (1998)—is that of a series of interconnected stories, a relatively loose form that can be seen in some of Minot's other work, such as her story "Lust," included here.

Many of the stories in Lust and Other Stories (1989) were written during an extended stay in Italy. When Minot was on her way back to the United States, her automobile was vandalized in Milan and all of the stories were stolen. Minot began the arduous task of reconstructing them from scratch. When they were published as a collection, they prompted Kelli Pryor to write, "The stories that make up Lust are about desire's smaller wounds."

LUST

Leo was from a long time ago, the first one I ever saw nude. In the spring before the Hellmans filled their pool, we'd go down there in the deep end, with baby oil, and like that. I met him the first month away at boarding school. He had a halo from the campus light behind him. I flipped.

Roger was fast. In his illegal car, we drove to the reservoir, the radio blaring, talking fast, fast, fast. He was always going for my zipper. He got kicked out sophomore year.

By the time the band got around to playing "Wild Horses," I had tasted Bruce's tongue. We were clicking in the shadows on the other side of the amplifier, out of Mrs. Donovan's line of vision. It tasted like salt, with my neck bent back, because we had been dancing so hard before.

Tim's line: "I'd like to see you in a bathing suit." I knew it was his line when he said the exact same thing to Annie Hines.

You'd go on walks to get off campus. It was raining like hell, my sweater as sopped as a wet sheep. Tim pinned me to a tree, the woods light brown and dark brown, a white house half-hidden with the lights already on. The water was as loud as a crowd hissing. He made certain comments about my forehead, about my cheeks.

We started off sitting at one end of the couch and then our feet were squished against the armrest and then he went over to turn off the TV and came back after he had taken off his shirt and then we slid onto the floor and he got up again to close the door, then came back to me, a body waiting on the rug.

You'd try to wipe off the table or to do the dishes and Willie would untuck your shirt and get his hands up under in front, standing behind you, making puffy noises in your ear.

He likes it when I wash my hair. He covers his face with it and if I start to say something, he goes, "Shush."

For a long time, I had Philip on the brain. The less they noticed you, the more you got them on the brain.

My parents had no idea. Parents never really know what's going on, especially when you're away at school most of the time. If she met them, my mother might say, "Oliver seems nice" or "I like that one" without much of an opinion. If she didn't like them, "He's a funny fellow, isn't he?" or "Johnny's perfectly nice but a drink of water." My father was too shy to talk to them at all, unless they played sports and he'd ask them about that.

The sand was almost cold underneath because the sun was long gone. Eben piled a mound over my feet, patting around my ankles, the ghostly surf rumbling behind him in the dark. He was the first person I ever knew who died, later that summer, in a car crash. I thought about it for a long time.

"Come here," he says on the porch.
    I go over to the hammock and he takes my wrist with two fingers.
    "What?"
    He kisses my palm then directs my hand to his fly.

Songs went with whichever boy it was. "Sugar Magnolia" was Tim, with the line "Rolling in the rushes/down by the riverside." With "Darkness Darkness," I'd picture Philip with his long hair. Hearing "Under my Thumb" there'd be the smell of Jamie's suede jacket.

We hid in the listening rooms during study hall. With a record cover over the door's window, the teacher on duty couldn't look in. I came out flushed and heady and back at the dorm was surprised how red my lips were in the mirror.

One weekend at Simon's brother's, we stayed inside all day with the shades down, in bed, then went out to Store 24 to get some ice cream. He stood at the magazine rack and read through MAD while I got butterscotch sauce, craving something sweet.

I could do some things well. Some things I was good at, like math or painting or even sports, but the second a boy put his arm around me, I forget about wanting to do anything else, which felt like a relief at first until it became like sinking into a muck.

It was different for a girl.

When we were little, the brothers next door tied up our ankles. They held the door of the goat house and wouldn't let us out till we showed them our underpants. Then they'd forget about being after us and when we played whiffle ball, I'd be just as good as them.

Then it got to be different. Just because you have on a short skirt, they yell from the cars, slowing down for a while and if you don't look, they screech off and call you a bitch.

"What's the matter with me?" they say, point-blank.

Or else, "Why won't you go out with me? I'm not asking you to get married," about to get mad.

Or it'd be, trying to be reasonable, in a regular voice, "Listen, I just want to have a good time."

So I'd go because I couldn't think of something to say back that wouldn't be obvious, and if you go out with them, you sort of have to do something.

I sat between Mack and Eddie in the front seat of the pickup. They were having a fight about something. I've a feeling about me.

Certain nights you'd feel a certain surrender, maybe if you'd had wine. The surrender would be forgetting yourself and you'd put your nose to his neck and feel like a squirrel, safe, at rest, in a restful dream. But then you'd start to slip from that and the dark would come in and there'd be a cave. You make out the dim shape of the windows and feel yourself become a cave, filled absolutely with air, or with a sadness that wouldn't stop.

Teenage years. You know just what you're doing and don't see the things that start to get in the way.

Lots of boys, but never two at the same time. One was plenty to keep you in a state. You'd start to see a boy and something would rush over you like a fast storm cloud and you couldn't possibly think of anyone else. Boys took it differently. Their eyes perked up at any little number that walked by. You'd act like you weren't noticing.

The joke was that the school doctor gave out the pill like aspirin. He didn't ask you anything. I was fifteen. We had a picture of him in assembly, holding up an IUD shaped like a T. Most girls were on the pill, if anything, because they couldn't handle a diaphragm. I kept the dial in my top drawer like my mother and thought of her each time I tipped out the yellow tablets in the morning before chapel.

If they were too shy, I'd be more so. Andrew was nervous. We stayed up with his family album, sharing a pack of Old Golds. Before it got light, we turned on the TV. A man was explaining how to plant seedlings. His mouth jerked to the side in a tic. Andrew thought it was a riot and kept imitating him. I laughed to be polite. When we finally dozed off, he dared to put his arm around me but that was it.

You wait till they come to you. With half fright, half swagger, they stand one step down. They dare to touch the button on your coat then lose their nerve and quickly drop their hand so you—you'd do anything for them. You touch their cheek.

The girls sit around in the common room and talk about boys, smoking their heads off.

"What are you complaining about?" says Jill to me when we talk about problems.

"Yeah," says Giddy. "You always have a boyfriend."

I look at them and think, As if.

I thought the worst thing anyone could call you was a cock-teaser. So, if you flirted, you had to be prepared to go through with it. Sleeping with someone was perfectly normal once you had done it. You didn't really worry about it. But there were other problems. The problems had to do with something else entirely.

Mack was during the hottest summer ever recorded. We were renting a house on an island with all sorts of other people. No one slept during the heat wave, walking around the house with nothing on which we were used to because of the nude beach. In the living room, Eddie lay on top of a coffee table to cool off. Mack and I, with the bedroom door open for air, sweated and sweated all night.

"I can't take this," he said at 3 A.M. "I'm going for a swim." He and some guys down the hall went to the beach. The heat put me on edge. I sat on a cracked chest by the open window and smoked and smoked till I felt even worse, waiting for something—I guess for him to get back.

One was on a camping trip in Colorado. We zipped our sleeping bags together, the coyotes' hysterical chatter far away. Other couples murmured in other tents. Paul was up before sunrise, starting a fire for breakfast. He wasn't much of a talker in the daytime. At night, his hand leafed about in the hair at my neck.

There'd be times when you overdid it. You'd get carried away. All the next day, you'd be in a total fog, delirious, absent-minded, crossing the street and nearly getting run over.

The more girls a boy has, the better. He has a bright look, having reaped fruits, blooming. He stalks around, sure-shouldered, and you have the feeling he's got more in him, a fatter heart, more stories to tell. For a girl, with each boy it's like a petal gets plucked each time.

Then you start to get tired. You begin to feel diluted, like watered-down stew.

Oliver came skiing with us. We lolled by the fire after everyone had gone to bed. Each creak you'd think was someone coming downstairs. The silver-loop bracelet he gave me had been a present from his girlfriend before.

On vacations, we went skiing, or you'd go south if someone invited you. Some people had apartments in New York that their families hardly ever used. Or summer houses, or older sisters. We always managed to find some place to go. We made the plan at coffee hour. Simon snuck out and met me at Main Gate after lights-out. We crept to the chapel and spent the night in the balcony. He tasted like onions from a submarine sandwich.

The boys are one of two ways: either they can't sit still or they don't move. In front of the TV, they won't budge. On weekends they play touch football while we sit on the sidelines, picking blades of grass to chew on, and watch. We're always watching them run around. We shiver in the stands, knocking our boots together to keep our toes warm and they whizz across the ice, chopping their sticks around the puck. When they're in the rink, they refuse to look at you, only eyeing each other beneath low helmets. You cheer for them but they don't look up, even if it's a face-off when nothing's happening, even if they're doing drills before any game has started at all.

Dancing under the pink tent, he bent down and whispered in my ear. We slipped away to the lawn on the other side of the hedge. Much later, as he was leaving the buffet with two plates of eggs and sausage, I saw the grass stains on the knees of his white pants.

Tim's was shaped like a banana, with a graceful curve to it. They're all different. Willie's like a bunch of walnuts when nothing was happening, another's as thin as a thin hot dog. But it's like faces; you're never really surprised.

Still, you're not sure what to expect.

I look into his face and he looks back. I look into his eyes and they look back at mine. Then they look down at my mouth so I look at his mouth, then back to his eyes then, backing up, at his whole face. I think, Who? Who are you? His head tilts to one side.
    I say, "Who are you?"
    "What do you mean?"
    "Nothing."
    I look at his eyes again, deeper. Can't tell who he is, what he thinks.
    "What?" he says. I look at his mouth.
    "I'm just wondering," I say and go wandering across his face. Study the chin line. It's shaped like a persimmon.
    "Who are you? What are you thinking?"
    He says, "What the hell are you talking about?"

Then they get mad after when you say enough is enough. After, when it's easier to explain that you don't want to. You wouldn't dream of saying that maybe you weren't really ready to in the first place.

Gentle Eddie. We waded into the sea, the waves round and plowing in, buffalo-headed, slapping our thighs. I put my arms around his freckled shoulders and he held me up, buoyed by the water, and rocked me like a sea shell.

I had no idea whose party it was, the apartment jam-packed, stepping over people in the hallway. The room with the music was practically empty, the bare floor, me in red shoes. This fellow slides onto one knee and takes me around the waist and we rock to jazzy tunes, with my toes pointing heavenward, and waltz and spin and dip to "Smoke Gets in Your Eyes" or "I'll Love You Just for Now." He puts his head to my chest, runs a sweeping hand down my inside thigh and we go loose-limbed and sultry and as smooth as silk and I stamp my red heels and he takes me into a swoon. I never saw him again after that but I thought, I could have loved that one.

You wonder how long you can keep it up. You begin to feel like you're showing through, like a bathroom window that only lets in grey light, the kind you can't see out of.

They keep coming around. Johnny drives up at Easter vacation from Baltimore and I let him in the kitchen with everyone sound asleep. He has friends waiting in the car.

"What are you crazy? It's pouring out there," I say.

"It's okay," he says. "They understand."

So he gets some long kisses from me, against the refrigerator, before he goes because I hate those girls who push away a boy's face as if she were made out of Ivory soap, as if she's that much greater than he is.

The note on my cubby told me to see the headmaster. I had no idea for what. He had received complaints about my amorous displays on the town green. It was Willie that spring. The headmaster told me he didn't care what I did but that Casey Academy had a reputation to uphold in the town. He lowered his glasses on his nose. "We've got twenty acres of woods on this campus," he said. "Smooch with your boyfriend there."

Everybody'd get weekend permissions for different places then we'd all go to someone's house whose parents were away. Usually there'd be more boys than girls. We raided the liquor closet and smoked pot at the kitchen table and you'd never know who would end up where, or with whom. There were always disasters. Ceci got bombed and cracked her head open on the banister and needed stitches. Then there was the time Wendel Blair walked through the picture window at the Lowe's and got slashed to ribbons.

He scared me. In bed, I didn't dare look at him. I lay back with my eyes closed, luxuriating because he knew all sorts of expert angles, his hands never fumbling, going over my whole body, pressing the hair up and off the back of my head, giving an extra hip shove, as if to say *There*. I parted my eyes slightly, keeping the screen of my lashes low because it was too much to look at him, his mouth loose and pink and parted, his eyes looking through my forehead, or kneeling up, looking through my throat. I was ashamed but couldn't look him in the eye.

You wonder about things feeling a little off-kilter. You begin to feel like a piece of pounded veal.

At boarding school, everyone gets depressed. We go in and see the housemother, Mrs. Gunther. She got married when she was eighteen. Mr. Gunther was her high-school sweetheart, the only boyfriend she ever had.

"And you knew you wanted to marry him right off?" we ask her.

She smiles and says, "Yes."

"They always want something from you," says Jill, complaining about her boyfriend.

"Yeah," says Giddy. "You always feel like you have to deliver something."

"You do," says Mrs. Gunther. "Babies."

After sex, you curl up like a shrimp, something deep inside you ruined, slammed in a place that sickens at slamming, and slowly you fill up with an overwhelming sadness, an elusive gaping worry. You don't try to explain it, filled with the knowledge that it's nothing after all, everything filling up finally and absolutely with death. After the briskness of loving, loving stops. And you roll over with death stretched out alongside you like a feather boa, or a snake, light as air, and you . . . you don't even ask for anything or try to say something to him because it's obviously your own damn fault. You haven't been able to—to what? To open your heart. You open your legs but can't, or don't dare anymore, to open your heart.

It starts this way:
    You stare into their eyes. They flash like all the stars are out. They look at you seriously, their eyes at a low burn and their hands no matter what starting off shy and with such a gentle touch that the only thing you can do is take that tenderness and let yourself be swept away. When, with one attentive finger they tuck the hair behind your ear, you—
    You do everything they want.

Then comes after. After when they don't look at you. They scratch their balls, stare at the ceiling. Or if they do turn, their gaze is altogether changed. They are surprised. They turn casually to look at you, distracted, and get a mild distracted surprise. You're gone. Their black look tells you that the girl they were fucking is not there anymore. You seem to have disappeared.

[1984]

Questions

1. Are the form and the content of Susan Minot's story related?
2. Although the narrator of "Lust" gives us a composite picture of her own feelings and emotions, what can be said about the men in her story?
3. Does the narrator like herself?
4. Where exactly does the theme of the story change from lust (sex) to something else? What is that something else?
5. Would "Sex" be an equally appropriate title for Minot's story?

Mishima Yukio
(1925–1970)
Japan

Western readers of Japanese fiction have often erroneously concluded that the country's contemporary writers are obsessed with death. The widow of Yasunari Kawabata, a Nobel-prize writer, attempted to suppress the publication of a book that argued that her 72-year-old husband had committed suicide because the housemaid had decided to stop working for him. Others have argued that Kawabata committed suicide because his young friend, Mishima Yukio, had already beaten him to it. Whatever the case, the images of death and ritual suicide (of the samurai) often permeate the fiction of several of the country's most famous writers. (Consider, for example, Mishima's short story "Patriotism.")

Mishima was born in Tokyo in 1925. At the time of his death in 1970, he was probably his country's most famous writer—both internationally and at home. During the course of his prolific career, he published novels, short stories, dramas, and essays. Shortly before his suicide, Mishima told Donald Keene that he had written "enough for one lifetime," that he had put everything into his last book (The Sea of Fertility) and had "nothing left to do but to die." Keene made the following additional comment:

> Mishima meant it literally, and it must have seemed particularly appropriate to die on the day that he delivered to the publisher the concluding installment of his culminating work. It was not that Mishima feared a waning of his creative powers. He knew he could go on writing better than anyone else in Japan, almost without effort. But there was nothing more he wanted to say. He chose to end his career at his peak.

SWADDLING CLOTHES

He was always busy, Toshiko's husband. Even tonight he had to dash off to an appointment, leaving her to go home alone by taxi. But what else could a woman expect when she married an actor—an attractive one? No doubt she had been foolish to hope that he would spend the evening with her. And yet he must have known how she dreaded going back to their house, unhomely with its Western-style furniture and with the bloodstains still showing on the floor.

Toshiko had been oversensitive since girlhood: that was her nature. As the result of constant worrying she never put on weight, and now, an adult woman, she looked more like a transparent picture than a creature of flesh and blood. Her delicacy of spirit was evident to her most casual acquaintance.

Earlier that evening, when she had joined her husband at a night club, she had been shocked to find him entertaining friends with an account of "the incident." Sitting there in his American-style suit, puffing at a cigarette, he had seemed to her almost a stranger.

"It's a fantastic story," he was saying, gesturing flamboyantly as if in an attempt to outweigh the attractions of the dance band. "Here this new nurse for our baby arrives from the employment agency, and the very first thing I noticed about her is her stomach. It's enormous as if she had a pillow stuck under her kimono! No wonder, I thought, for I soon saw that she could eat more than the rest of us put together. She polished off the contents of our rice bin like that. . . ." He snapped his fingers. " 'Gastric dilation'—that's how she explained her girth and her appetite. Well, the day before yesterday we heard groans and moans coming from the nursery. We rushed in and found her squatting on the floor, holding her stomach in her two hands, and moaning like a cow. Next to her our baby lay in his cot, scared out of his wits and crying at the top of his lungs. A pretty scene, I can tell you!"

"So the cat was out of the bag?" suggested one of their friends, a film actor like Toshiko's husband.

"Indeed it was! And it gave me the shock of my life. You see, I'd completely swallowed that story about 'gastric dilation.' Well, I didn't waste any time. I rescued our good rug from the floor and spread a blanket for her to lie on. The whole time the girl was yelling like a stuck pig. By the time the doctor from the maternity clinic arrived, the baby had already been born. But our sitting room was a pretty shambles!"

"Oh, that I'm sure of!" said another of their friends, and the whole company burst into laughter.

Toshiko was dumbfounded to hear her husband discussing the horrifying happening as though it were no more than an amusing incident which they chanced to have witnessed. She shut her eyes for a moment and all at once she saw the newborn baby lying before her: on the parquet floor the infant lay, and his frail body was wrapped in bloodstained newspapers.

Toshiko was sure that the doctor had done the whole thing out of spite. As if to emphasize his scorn for his mother who had given birth to a bastard under such sordid conditions, he had told his assistant to wrap the baby in some loose newspapers, rather than proper swaddling. This callous treatment of the newborn child had offended Toshiko. Overcoming her disgust at the entire scene, she had fetched a brand-new piece of flannel from her cupboard and, having swaddled the baby in it, had laid him carefully in an armchair.

This all had taken place in the evening after her husband had left the house. Toshiko had told him nothing of it, fearing that he would think her oversoft, oversentimental; yet the scene had engraved itself deeply in her mind. Tonight she sat silently thinking back on it, while the jazz orchestra brayed and her husband chatted cheerfully with his friends. She knew that she would never forget the sight of the baby, wrapped in stained newspapers and lying on the floor—it was a scene fit for a butchershop. Toshiko, whose own life had been spent in solid comfort, poignantly felt the wretchedness of the illegitimate baby.

I am the only person to have witnessed its shame, the thought occurred to her. The mother never saw her child lying there in its newspaper wrappings, and the baby itself of course didn't know. I alone shall have to preserve that terrible scene in my memory. When the baby grows up and wants to find out about his birth, there will be no one to tell him, so long as I preserve silence. How strange that I should have this feeling of guilt! After all, it was I who took him up from the floor, swathed him properly in flannel, and laid him down to sleep in the armchair.

They left the night club and Toshiko stepped into the taxi that her husband had called for her. "Take this lady to Ushigomé," he told the driver and shut the door from the outside. Toshiko gazed through the window at her husband's smiling face and noticed his strong, white teeth. Then she leaned back in the seat, oppressed by the knowledge that their life together was in some way too easy, too painless. It would have been difficult for her to put her thoughts into words. Through the rear window of the taxi she took a last look at her husband. He was striding along the street toward his Nash car, and soon the back of his rather garish tweed coat had blended with the figures of the passersby.

The taxi drove off, passed down a street dotted with bars and then by a theatre, in front of which the throngs of people jostled each other on the pavement. Although the performance had only just ended, the lights had already been turned out and in the half dark outside it was depressingly obvious that the cherry blossoms decorating the front of the theatre were merely scraps of white paper.

Even if that baby should grow up in ignorance of the secret of his birth, he can never become a respectable citizen, reflected Toshiko, pursuing the same train of thoughts. Those soiled newspaper swaddling clothes will be the symbol of his entire life. But why should I keep worrying about him so much? Is it because I feel uneasy about the future of my own child? Say twenty years from now, when our boy will have grown up into a fine, carefully educated young man, one day by a quirk of fate he meets that other boy, who then will also have turned twenty. And say that the other boy, who has been sinned against, savagely stabs him with a knife. . . .

It was a warm, overcast April night, but thoughts of the future made Toshiko feel cold and miserable. She shivered on the back seat of the car. No, when the time comes I shall take my son's place, she told herself suddenly. Twenty years from now I shall be forty-three. I shall go to that young man and tell him straight out about everything—about his newspaper swaddling clothes, and about how I went and wrapped him in flannel.

The taxi ran along the dark wide road that was bordered by the park and by the Imperial Palace moat. In the distance Toshiko noticed the pinpricks of light which came from the blocks of tall office buildings.

Twenty years from now that wretched child will be in utter misery. He will be living a desolate, hopeless, poverty-stricken existence—a lonely rat. What else could happen to a baby who has had such a birth? He'll be wandering through the streets by himself, cursing his father, loathing his mother.

No doubt Toshiko derived a certain satisfaction from her somber thoughts: she tortured herself with them without cease. The taxi approached Hanzomon and drove past the compound of the British Embassy. At that point the famous rows of cherry trees were spread out before Toshiko in all their purity. On the spur of the moment she decided to go and view the blossoms by herself in the dark night. It was a strange decision for a timid and unadventurous young woman, but then she was in a strange state of mind and she dreaded the return home. That evening all sorts of unsettling fancies had burst open in her mind.

She crossed the wide street—a slim, solitary figure in the darkness. As a rule when she walked in the traffic Toshiko used to cling fearfully to her companion, but tonight she darted alone between the cars and a moment later had reached the long narrow park that borders the Palace moat. Chidorigafuchi, it is called—the Abyss of the Thousand Birds.

Tonight the whole park had become a grove of blossoming cherry trees. Under the calm cloudy sky the blossoms formed a mass of solid whiteness. The paper lanterns that hung from wires between the trees had been put out; in their place electric light bulbs, red, yellow, and green, shone dully beneath the blossoms. It was well past ten o'clock and most of the flower-viewers had gone home. As the occasional passersby strolled through the park, they would automatically kick aside the empty bottles or crush the waste paper beneath their feet.

Newspapers, thought Toshiko, her mind going back once again to those happenings. Bloodstained newspapers. If a man were ever to hear of that piteous birth and know that it was he who had lain there, it would ruin his entire life. To think that I, a perfect stranger, should from now on have to keep such a secret—the secret of a man's whole existences. . . .

Lost in these thoughts, Toshiko walked on through the park. Most of the people still remaining there were quiet couples; no one paid her any attention. She noticed two people sitting on a stone bench beside the moat, not looking at the blossoms, but gazing silently at the water. Pitch black it was, and swathed in heavy shadows. Beyond the moat the somber forest of the Imperial Palace blocked her view. The trees reached up, to form a solid dark mass against the night sky. Toshiko walked slowly along the path beneath the blossoms hanging heavily overhead.

On a stone bench, slightly apart from the others, she noticed a pale object—not, as she had at first imagined, a pile of cherry blossoms, nor a garment forgotten by one of the visitors to the park. Only when she came closer did she see that it was a human form lying on the bench. Was it, she wondered, one of those miserable drunks often to be seen sleeping in public places? Obviously not, for the body had been systematically covered with newspapers, and it was the whiteness of those papers that had attracted Toshiko's attention. Standing by the bench, she gazed down at the sleeping figure.

It was a man in a brown jersey who lay there, curled up on layers of newspapers, other newspapers covering him. No doubt this had become his normal night residence now that spring had arrived. Toshiko gazed down at the man's dirty, unkempt hair, which in places had become hopelessly matted. As she observed the sleeping figure wrapped in its newspapers, she was inevitably reminded of the baby who had lain on the floor in its wretched swaddling clothes. The shoulder of the man's jersey rose and fell in the darkness in time with his heavy breathing.

It seemed to Toshiko that all her fears and premonitions had suddenly taken concrete form. In the darkness the man's pale forehead stood out, and it was a young forehead, though carved with wrinkles of long poverty and hardship. His khaki trousers had been slightly pulled up; on his sockless feet he wore a pair of battered gym shoes. She could not see his face and suddenly had an overmastering desire to get one glimpse of it.

She walked to the head of the bench and looked down. The man's head was half buried in his arms, but Toshiko could see that he was surprisingly young. She noticed the thick eyebrows and the fine bridge of his nose. His slightly open mouth was alive with youth.

But Toshiko had approached too close. In the silent night the newspaper bedding rustled, and abruptly the man opened his eyes. Seeing the young woman standing directly beside him, he raised himself with a jerk, and his eyes lit up. A second later a powerful hand reached out and seized Toshiko by her slender wrist.

She did not feel in the least afraid and made no effort to free herself. In a flash the thought had struck her, Ah, so the twenty years have already gone by! The forest of the Imperial Palace was pitch dark and utterly silent.

[1966]
Translated by
IVAN MORRIS

Questions

1. Two major images of the story are cherry tree blossoms and newspapers. In what way are they related?
2. Are the men in Toshiko's life (her actor husband, the child in swaddling clothes, the man on the bench) all part and parcel of the same unresolved problem for her, or do they represent something else? Why is she the one who feels guilt and shame?
3. What are we to make of the many Western objects in the story: clothing, furniture, cars? Do they contribute to Toshiko's crisis?
4. What happens to Toshiko at the end of the story?
5. Is "Swaddling Clothes" a story about death or about something else?

Lorrie Moore
(b. 1957)
United States

Born Marie Lorena Moore, Lorrie Moore grew up and was educated in upstate New York, receiving a B.A. from St. Lawrence University and an M.F.A. from Cornell. Her first work of fiction won first prize in Seventeen magazine's fiction contest before she turned twenty. Since 1985, when she published her first collection of stories, Self-Help, she has garnered critical acclaim for fiction distinguished by a wry sense of humor, ironic tone, and scalpel-sharp language. Jay McInerney, borrowing some of Moore's own tone to review the first volume of her stories, jested in a review in The New York Times Book Review that "anyone who doesn't like it should consult a doctor." Readers of "People Like That Are the Only People Here: Canonical Babbling in Peed Onk," first published in The New Yorker and later in Birds of America (1998), were startled by the daring manner in which Moore transformed the circumstances of her infant son's life-threatening disease and surgery into a story that renders not only the seriousness of the subject but also, improbably, its occasional comic moments.

In addition to three collections of stories, Moore has published two novels, Anagrams (1986) and Who Will Run the Frog Hospital? (1994). Of her fiction, Michiko Kakutani, writing in The New York Times, observes that the writer shares some of her characters' qualities, including "a wry, crackly voice" and "an askew sense of humor." "How to Become a Writer" amply illustrates both of these qualities.

HOW TO BECOME A WRITER

First, try to be something, anything, else. A movie star/astronaut. A movie star/missionary. A movie star/kindergarten teacher. President of the World. Fail miserably. It is best if you fail at an early age—say, fourteen. Early, critical disillusionment is necessary so that at fifteen you can write long haiku sequences about thwarted desire. It is a pond, a cherry blossom, a wind brushing against sparrow wing leaving for mountain. Count the syllables. Show it to your mom. She is tough and practical. She has a son in Vietnam and a husband who may be having an affair. She believes in wearing brown because it hides spots. She'll look briefly at your writing, then back up at you with a face blank as a donut. She'll say: "How about emptying the dishwasher?" Look away. Shove the forks in the fork drawer. Accidentally break one of the freebie gas station glasses. This is the required pain and suffering. This is only for starters.

In your high school English class look only at Mr. Killian's face. Decide faces are important. Write a villanelle about pores. Struggle. Write a sonnet. Count the syllables:

nine, ten, eleven, thirteen. Decide to experiment with fiction. Here you don't have to count syllables. Write a short story about an elderly man and woman who accidentally shoot each other in the head, the result of an inexplicable malfunction of a shotgun which appears mysteriously in their living room one night. Give it to Mr. Killian as your final project. When you get it back, he has written on it: "Some of your images are quite nice, but you have no sense of plot." When you are home, in the privacy of your own room, faintly scrawl in pencil beneath his black-inked comments: "Plots are for dead people, pore-face."

Take all the babysitting jobs you can get. You are great with kids. They love you. You tell them stories about old people who die idiot deaths. You sing them songs like "Blue Bells of Scotland," which is their favorite. And when they are in their pajamas and have finally stopped pinching each other, when they are fast asleep, you read every sex manual in the house, and wonder how on earth anyone could ever do those things with someone they truly loved. Fall asleep in a chair reading Mr. McMurphy's *Playboy*. When the McMurphys come home, they will tap you on the shoulder, look at the magazine in your lap, and grin. You will want to die. They will ask you if Tracey took her medicine all right. Explain, yes, she did, that you promised her a story if she would take it like a big girl and that seemed to work out just fine. "Oh, marvelous," they will exclaim.

Try to smile proudly.

Apply to college as a child psychology major.

As a child psychology major, you have some electives. You've always liked birds. Sign up for something called "The Ornithological Field Trip." It meets Tuesdays and Thursdays at two. When you arrive at Room 134 on the first day of class, everyone is sitting around a seminar table talking about metaphors. You've heard of these. After a short, excruciating while, raise your hand and say diffidently, "Excuse me, isn't this Bird-watching One-oh-one?" The class stops and turns to look at you. They seem to all have one face—giant and blank as a vandalized clock. Someone with a beard booms out, "No, this is Creative Writing." Say: "Oh—right," as if perhaps you knew all along. Look down at your schedule. Wonder how the hell you ended up here. The computer, apparently, has made an error. You start to get up to leave and then don't. The lines at the registrar this week are huge. Perhaps you should stick with this mistake. Perhaps your creative writing isn't all that bad. Perhaps it is fate. Perhaps this is what your dad meant when he said, "It's the age of computers, Francie, it's the age of computers."

Decide that you like college life. In your dorm you meet many nice people. Some are smarter than you. And some, you notice, are dumber than you. You will continue, unfortunately, to view the world in exactly these terms for the rest of your life.

The assignment this week in creative writing is to narrate a violent happening. Turn in a story about driving with your Uncle Gordon and another one about two old people who are accidentally electrocuted when they go to turn on a badly wired desk lamp. The teacher will hand them back to you with comments: "Much of your writing is smooth and energetic. You have, however, a ludicrous notion of plot." Write another story about a man and a woman who, in the very first paragraph, have their lower torsos accidentally blitzed away by dynamite. In the second paragraph, with the insurance money, they buy a frozen yogurt stand together. There are six more paragraphs. You read the whole thing out loud in class. No one likes it. They say your sense of plot is outrageous and incompetent. After class someone asks you if you are crazy.

Decide that perhaps you should stick to comedies. Start dating someone who is funny, someone who has what in high school you called a "really great sense of humor" and what now your creative writing class calls "self-contempt giving rise to comic form." Write down all of his jokes, but don't tell him you are doing this. Make up anagrams of his old girlfriend's name and name all of your socially handicapped characters with them. Tell him his old girlfriend is in all of your stories and then watch how funny he can be, see what a really great sense of humor he can have.

Your child psychology advisor tells you you are neglecting courses in your major. What you spend the most time on should be what you're majoring in. Say yes, you understand.

In creative writing seminars over the next two years, everyone continues to smoke cigarettes and ask the same things: "But does it work?" "Why should we care about this character?" "Have you earned this cliché?" These seem like important questions.

On days when it is your turn, you look at the class hopefully as they scour your mimeographs for a plot. They look back up at you, drag deeply, and then smile in a sweet sort of way.

You spend too much time slouched and demoralized. Your boyfriend suggests bicycling. Your roommate suggests a new boyfriend. You are said to be self-mutilating and losing weight, but you continue writing. The only happiness you have is writing something new, in the middle of the night, armpits damp, heart pounding, something no one has yet seen. You have only those brief, fragile, untested moments of exhilaration when you know: you are a genius. Understand what you must do. Switch majors. The kids in your nursery project will be disappointed, but you have a calling, an urge, a delusion, an unfortunate habit. You have, as your mother would say, fallen in with a bad crowd.

Why write? Where does writing come from? These are questions to ask yourself. They are like: Where does dust come from? Or: Why is there war? Or: If there's a God, then why is my brother now a cripple?

These are questions that you keep in your wallet, like calling cards. These are questions, your creative writing teacher says, that are good to address in your journals but rarely in your fiction.

The writing professor this fall is stressing the Power of the Imagination. Which means he doesn't want long descriptive stories about your camping trip last July. He wants you to start in a realistic context but then to alter it. Like recombinant DNA. He wants you to let your imagination sail, to let it grow big-bellied in the wind. This is a quote from Shakespeare.

Tell your roommate your great idea, your great exercise of imaginative power: a transformation of Melville to contemporary life. It will be about monomania and the fish-eat-fish world of life insurance in Rochester, New York. The first line will be "Call me Fishmeal," and it will feature a menopausal suburban husband named Richard, who because he is so depressed all the time is called "Mopey Dick" by his witty wife Elaine. Say to your roommate: "Mopey Dick, get it?" Your roommate looks at you, her face blank as a large Kleenex. She comes up to you, like a buddy, and puts an arm around your burdened shoulders. "Listen, Francie," she says, slow as speech therapy. "Let's go out and get a big beer."

The seminar doesn't like this one either. You suspect they are beginning to feel sorry for you. They say: "You have to think about what is happening. Where is the story here?"

The next semester the writing professor is obsessed with writing from personal experience. You must write from what you know, from what has happened to you. He wants deaths, he wants camping trips. Think about what has happened to you. In three years there have been three things: you lost your virginity; your parents got divorced; and your brother came home from a forest ten miles from the Cambodian border with only half a thigh, a permanent smirk nestled into one corner of his mouth.

   About the first you write: "It created a new space, which hurt and cried in a voice that wasn't mine, 'I'm not the same anymore, but I'll be okay.'"

   About the second you write an elaborate story of an old married couple who stumble upon an unknown land mine in their kitchen and accidentally blow themselves up. You call it: "For Better or for Liverwurst."

   About the last you write nothing. There are no words for this. Your typewriter hums. You can find no words.

At undergraduate cocktail parties, people say, "Oh, you write? What do you write about?" Your roommate, who has consumed too much wine, too little cheese, and no crackers at all, blurts: "Oh, my god, she always writes about her dumb boyfriend."

   Later on in life you will learn that writers are merely open, helpless texts with no real understanding of what they have written and therefore must half-believe anything and everything that is said of them. You, however, have not yet reached this stage of literary criticism. You stiffen and say, "I do not," the same way you said it when someone in the fourth grade accused you of really liking oboe lessons and your parents really weren't just making you take them.

   Insist you are not very interested in any one subject at all, that you are interested in the music of language, that you are interested in—in—syllables, because they are the atoms of poetry, the cells of the mind, the breath of the soul. Begin to feel woozy. Stare into your plastic wine cup.

   "Syllables?" you will hear someone ask, voice trailing off, as they glide slowly toward the reassuring white of the dip.

Begin to wonder what you do write about. Or if you have anything to say. Or if there even is such a thing as a thing to say. Limit these thoughts to no more than ten minutes a day; like sit-ups, they can make you thin.

   You will read somewhere that all writing has to do with one's genitals. Don't dwell on this. It will make you nervous.

Your mother will come visit you. She will look at the circles under your eyes and hand you a brown book with a brown briefcase on the cover. It is entitled: *How to Become a Business Executive*. She has also brought the *Names for Baby* encyclopedia you asked for; one of your characters, the aging clown–school teacher, needs a new name. Your mother will shake her head and say: "Francie, Francie, remember when you were going to be a child psychology major?"

Say: "Mom, I like to write."

She'll say: "Sure you like to write. Of course. Sure you like to write."

Write a story about a confused music student and title it: "Schubert Was the One with the Glasses, Right?" It's not a big hit, although your roommate likes the part where the two violinists accidentally blow themselves up in a recital room. "I went out with a violinist once," she says, snapping her gum.

Thank god you are taking other courses. You can find sanctuary in nineteenth-century ontological snags and invertebrate courting rituals. Certain globular mollusks have what is called "Sex by the Arm." The male octopus, for instance, loses the end of one arm when placing it inside the female body during intercourse. Marine biologists call it "Seven Heaven." Be glad you know these things. Be glad you are not just a writer. Apply to law school.

From here on in, many things can happen. But the main one will be this: you decide not to go to law school after all, and, instead, you spend a good, big chunk of your adult life telling people how you decided not to go to law school after all. Somehow you end up writing again. Perhaps you go to graduate school. Perhaps you work odd jobs and take writing courses at night. Perhaps you are working on a novel and writing down all the clever remarks and intimate personal confessions you hear during the day. Perhaps you are losing your pals, your acquaintances, your balance.

You have broken up with your boyfriend. You now go out with men who, instead of whispering "I love you," shout: "Do it to me, baby." This is good for your writing.

Sooner or later you have a finished manuscript more or less. People look at it in a vaguely troubled sort of way and say, "I'll bet becoming a writer was always a fantasy of yours, wasn't it?" Your lips dry to salt. Say that of all the fantasies possible in the world, you can't imagine being a writer even making the top twenty. Tell them you were going to be a child psychology major. "I bet," they always sigh, "you'd be great with kids." Scowl fiercely. Tell them you're a walking blade.

Quit classes. Quit jobs. Cash in old savings bonds. Now you have time like warts on your hands. Slowly copy all of your friends' addresses into a new address book. Vacuum. Chew cough drops. Keep a folder full of fragments.

An eyelid darkening sideways.

World as conspiracy.

Possible plot? A woman gets on a bus.

Suppose you threw a love affair and nobody came.

At home drink a lot of coffee. At Howard Johnson's order the cole slaw. Consider how it looks like the soggy confetti of a map: where you've been, where you're going—"You Are Here," says the red star on the back of the menu.

Occasionally a date with a face blank as a sheet of paper asks you whether writers often become discouraged. Say that sometimes they do and sometimes they do. Say it's a lot like having polio.

"Interesting," smiles your date, and then he looks down at his arm hairs and starts to smooth them, all, always, in the same direction.

[1985]

Questions

1. What is the effect of the second-person ("you") point of view? To whom is the narrator speaking?
2. How do language, style, and tone shape the story? How does the author achieve humor and irony?
3. How does the author play with the concept of the "self-help manual"?
4. How does the story challenge traditional elements of narrative?
5. Compare this story with Rudolfo A. Anaya's "B. Traven Is Alive and Well in Cuernavaca."

Toni Morrison

(b. 1931)

United States

Toni Morrison was born in Lorain, Ohio, as Chloe Anthony Wofford. The second of four children of a steel mill worker who migrated from Georgia and a musically talented homemaker whose parents were Alabama sharecroppers, she acquired the nickname Toni during her years as an undergraduate at Howard University. Following her graduation with a B.A. in English, she earned a M.A. in English at Cornell University. She was briefly married to a Jamaican architect; when the marriage ended, Morrison supported her two young sons as a book editor and wrote fiction at night. As she commented in a Chicago Tribune interview, "Writing was something I did privately at night like women with families who use their off hours for creative projects. . . . I didn't call myself a writer. I just did it to pass the time, and I enjoyed it." For nearly twenty years beginning in the 1970s, she was an editor at Random House; she supported, encouraged, and inspired many new writers, including a number of African-American women writers such as Gloria Naylor and Alice Walker. Morrison has also taught English and humanities at several universities; currently, she holds a Distinguished Chair in the Humanities at Princeton.

Beginning with The Bluest Eye (1970), Morrison deeply engages the reader through her exploration of vital moral issues, sharply realized characters, luminous language, and attention to a variety of dimensions of African-American experience, sometimes drawn from collective historical circumstances such as slavery and the Great Migration. Her other novels include Sula (1974); Song of Solomon (1977), awarded the National Book Critics' Circle Award; Tar Baby (1981); Beloved (1987), awarded the Pulitzer Prize for Fiction along with several other major literary awards; Jazz (1992); and Paradise (1998). Beloved, inspired by a contemporary newspaper account of a runaway slave who killed her young daughter to save her from servitude, indelibly renders the experience of slavery through the character of Sethe and her ghost-daughter, Beloved. Of this novel, Morrison has commented in a Belles Lettres interview that she wanted to "insert" into fiction the erased "interior life" of slaves as well as memories of slavery that were "unbearable and unspeakable" in order to bring about healing. In 1993, she was awarded the Nobel Prize for Literature—the first African-American author to receive the honor.

One of Morrison's few published short stories, "Recitatif" is a powerful expression of the author's conviction—expressed in her essay, "Rootedness: The Ancestor as Foundation"—that "the best art is political and you ought to be able to make it unquestionably political and irrevocably beautiful at the same time." What is deliberately omitted from the story—the racial identities of the two central characters—obliges readers to ponder, among other things, their own assumptions about race in American culture.

RECITATIF

My mother danced all night and Roberta's was sick. That's why we were taken to St. Bonny's. People want to put their arms around you when you tell them you were in a shelter, but it really wasn't bad. No big long room with one hundred beds like Bellevue. There were four to a room, and when Roberta and me came, there was a shortage of state kids, so we were the only ones assigned to 406 and could go from bed to bed if we wanted to. And we wanted to, too. We changed beds every night and for the whole four months we were there we never picked one out as our own permanent bed.

It didn't start out that way. The minute I walked in and the Big Bozo introduced us, I got sick to my stomach. It was one thing to be taken out of your own bed early in the morning—it was something else to be stuck in a strange place with a girl from a whole other race. And Mary, that's my mother, she was right. Every now and then she would stop dancing long enough to tell me something important and one of the things she said was that they never washed their hair and they smelled funny. Roberta sure did. Smell funny, I mean. So when the Big Bozo (nobody ever called her Mrs. Itkin, just like nobody ever said St. Bonaventure)—when she said, "Twyla, this is Roberta. Roberta, this is Twyla. Make each other welcome," I said, "My mother won't like you putting me in here."

"Good," said Bozo. "Maybe then she'll come and take you home."

How's that for mean? If Roberta had laughed I would have killed her, but she didn't. She just walked over to the window and stood with her back to us.

"Turn around," said the Bozo. "Don't be rude. Now Twyla. Roberta. When you hear a loud buzzer, that's the call for dinner. Come down to the first floor. Any fights and no movie." And then, just to make sure we knew what we would be missing, "*The Wizard of Oz.*"

Roberta must have thought I meant that my mother would be mad about my being put in the shelter. Not about rooming with her, because as soon as Bozo left she came over to me and said, "Is your mother sick too?"

"No," I said. "She just likes to dance all night."

"Oh." She nodded her head and I liked the way she understood things so fast. So for the moment it didn't matter that we looked like salt and pepper standing there and that's what the other kids called us sometimes. We were eight years old and got F's all the time. Me because I couldn't remember what I read or what the teacher said. And Roberta because she couldn't read at all and didn't even listen to the teacher. She wasn't good at anything except jacks, at which she was a killer: pow scoop pow scoop pow scoop.

"We didn't like each other all that much at first, but nobody else wanted to play with us because we weren't real orphans with beautiful dead parents in the sky. We were dumped. Even the New York City Puerto Ricans and the upstate Indians ignored us. All kinds of kids were in there, black ones, white ones, even two Koreans. The food was good, though. At least I thought so. Roberta hated it and left whole pieces of things on her plate: Spam, Salisbury steak—even Jell-O with fruit cocktail in it, and she didn't care if I ate what she wouldn't. Mary's idea of supper was popcorn and a can of Yoo-Hoo. Hot mashed potatoes and two weenies was like Thanksgiving for me.

It really wasn't bad, St. Bonny's. The big girls on the second floor pushed us around now and then. But that was all. They wore lipstick and eyebrow pencil and wobbled their knees while they watched TV. Fifteen, sixteen, even, some of them were. They were put-out girls, scared runaways most of them. Poor little girls who fought their uncles off but looked tough to us, and mean. God, did they look mean. The staff tried to keep them separate from the younger children, but sometimes they caught us watching them in the orchard where they played radios and danced with each other. They'd light out after us and pull our hair or twist our arms. We were scared of them, Roberta and me, but neither of us wanted the other one to know it. So we got a good list of dirty names we could shout back when we ran from them through the orchard. I used to dream a lot and almost always the orchard was there. Two acres, four maybe, of these little apple trees. Hundreds of them. Empty and crooked like beggar women when I first came to St. Bonny's but fat with flowers when I left. I don't know why I dreamt about that orchard so much. Nothing really happened there. Nothing all that important, I mean. just the big girls and playing the radio. Roberta and me watching. Maggie fell down there once. The kitchen woman with legs like parentheses. And the big girls laughed at her. We should have helped her up, I know, but we were scared of those girls with lipstick and eyebrow pencil. Maggie couldn't talk. The kids said she had her tongue cut out, but I think she was just born that way: mute. She was old and sandy-colored and she worked in the kitchen. I don't know if she was nice or not. I just remember her legs like parentheses and how she rocked when she walked. She worked from early in the morning till two o'clock, and if she was late, if she had too much cleaning and didn't get out till two-fifteen or so, she'd cut through the orchard so she wouldn't miss her bus and have to wait another hour. She wore this really stupid little hat—a kid's hat with ear flaps—and she wasn't much taller than we were. A really awful little hat. Even for a mute, it was dumb—dressing like a kid and never saying anything at all.

"But what about if somebody tries to kill her?" I used to wonder about that. "Or what if she wants to cry? Can she cry?"

"Sure," Roberta said. "But just tears. No sounds come out."

"She can't scream?"

"Nope. Nothing."

"Can she hear?"

"I guess."

"Let's call her," I said. And we did.

"Dummy! Dummy!" She never turned her head.

"Bow legs! Bow legs!" Nothing. She just rocked on, the chin straps of her baby-boy hat swaying from side to side. I think we were wrong. I think she could hear and didn't let on. And it shames me even now to think there was somebody in there after all who heard us call her those names and couldn't tell on us.

We got along all right, Roberta and me. Changed beds every night, got F's in civics and communication skills and gym. The Bozo was disappointed in us, she said. Out of 130 of us state cases, 90 were under twelve. Almost all were real orphans with beautiful dead parents in the sky. We were the only ones dumped and the only ones with F's in three classes including gym. So we got along—what with her leaving whole pieces of things on her plate and being nice about not asking questions.

I think it was the day before Maggie fell down that we found out our mothers were coming to visit us on the same Sunday. We had been at the shelter twenty-eight days (Roberta twenty-eight and a half) and this was their visit with us. Our mothers would come at ten o'clock in time for chapel, then lunch with us in the teacher's lounge. I thought if my dancing mother met her sick mother it might be good for her. And

Roberta thought her sick mother would get a big bang out of a dancing one. We got excited about it and curled each other's hair. After breakfast we sat on the bed watching the road from the window. Roberta's socks were still wet. She washed them the night before and put them on the radiator to dry. They hadn't, but she put them on anyway because their tops were so pretty—scalloped in pink. Each of us had a purple construction-paper basket that we had made in craft class. Mine had a yellow crayon rabbit on it. Roberta's had eggs with wiggly lines of color. Inside were cellophane grass and just the jelly beans because I'd eaten the two marshmallow eggs they gave us. The Big Bozo came herself to get us. Smiling she told us we looked very nice and to come downstairs. We were so surprised by the smile we'd never seen before, neither of us moved.

"Don't you want to see your mommies?"

I stood up first and spilled the jelly beans all over the floor. Bozo's smile disappeared while we scrambled to get the candy up off the floor and put it back in the grass.

She escorted us downstairs to the first floor, where the other girls were lining up to file into the chapel. A bunch of grown-ups stood to one side. Viewers mostly. The old biddies who wanted servants and the fags who wanted company looking for children they might want to adopt. Once in a while a grandmother. Almost never anybody young or anybody whose face wouldn't scare you in the night. Because if any of the real orphans had young relatives they wouldn't be real orphans. I saw Mary right away. She had on those green slacks I hated and hated even more now because didn't she know we were going to chapel? And that fur jacket with the pocket linings so ripped she had to pull to get her hands out of them. But her face was pretty—like always—and she smiled and waved like she was the little girl looking for her mother, not me.

I walked slowly, trying not to drop the jelly beans and hoping the paper handle would hold. I had to use my last Chiclet because by the time I finished cutting everything out, all the Elmer's was gone. I am left-handed and the scissors never worked for me. It didn't matter, though; I might just as well have chewed the gum. Mary dropped to her knees and grabbed me, mashing the basket, the jelly beans, and the grass into her ratty fur jacket.

"Twyla, baby. Twyla, baby!"

I could have killed her. Already I heard the big girls in the orchard the next time saying, "Twyyyyyla, baby!" But I couldn't stay mad at Mary while she was smiling and hugging me and smelling of Lady Esther dusting powder. I wanted to stay buried in her fur all day.

To tell the truth I forgot about Roberta. Mary and I got in line for the traipse into chapel and I was feeling proud because she looked so beautiful even in those ugly green slacks that made her behind stick out. A pretty mother on earth is better than a beautiful dead one in the sky even if she did leave you all alone to go dancing.

I felt a tap on my shoulder, turned, and saw Roberta smiling. I smiled back, but not too much lest somebody think this visit was the biggest thing that ever happened in my life. Then Roberta said, "Mother, I want you to meet my roommate, Twyla. And that's Twyla's mother."

I looked up it seemed for miles. She was big. Bigger than any man and on her chest was the biggest cross I'd ever seen. I swear it was six inches long each way. And in the crook of her arm was the biggest Bible ever made.

Mary, simpleminded as ever, grinned and tried to yank her hand out of the pocket with the raggedy lining—to shake hands, I guess. Roberta's mother looked down at me and then looked down at Mary too. She didn't say anything, just grabbed Roberta with her Bible-free hand and stepped out of line, walking quickly to the rear of it. Mary was still grinning because she's not too swift when it comes to what's really going on. Then this light bulb goes off in her head and she says "That bitch!" really loud and us almost in the chapel now. Organ music whining; the Bonny Angels singing sweetly. Everybody in the world turned around to look. And Mary would have kept it up—kept calling names if I hadn't squeezed her hands as hard as I could. That helped a little, but she still twitched and crossed and uncrossed her legs all through service. Even groaned a couple of times. Why did I think she would come there and act right? Slacks. No hat like the grandmothers and viewers, and groaning all the while. When we stood for hymns she kept her mouth shut. Wouldn't even look at the words on the page. She actually reached in her purse for a mirror to check her lipstick. All I could think of was that she really needed to be killed. The sermon lasted a year, and I knew the real orphans were looking smug again.

We were supposed to have lunch in the teacher's lounge, but Mary didn't bring anything, so we picked fur and cellophane grass off the mashed jelly beans and ate them. I could have killed her. I sneaked a look at Roberta. Her mother had brought chicken legs and ham sandwiches and oranges and a whole box of chocolate-covered grahams. Roberta drank milk from a thermos while her mother read the Bible to her.

Things are not right. The wrong food is always with the wrong people. Maybe that's why I got into waitress work later—to match up the right people with the right food. Roberta just let those chicken legs sit there, but she did bring a stack of grahams up to me later when the visit was over. I think she was sorry that her mother would not shake my mother's hand. And I liked that and I liked the fact that she didn't say a word about Mary groaning all the way through the service and not bringing any lunch.

Roberta left in May when the apple trees were heavy and white. On her last day we went to the orchard to watch the big girls smoke and dance by the radio. It didn't matter that they said, "Twyyyyyla, baby." We sat on the ground and breathed. Lady Esther. Apple blossoms. I still go soft when I smell one or the other. Roberta was going home. The big cross and the big Bible was coming to get her and she seemed sort of glad and sort of not. I thought I would die in that room of four beds without her and I knew Bozo had plans to move some other dumped kid in there with me. Roberta promised to write every day, which was really sweet of her because she couldn't read a lick so how could she write anybody? I would have drawn pictures and sent them to her but she never gave me her address. Little by little she faded. Her wet socks with the pink scalloped tops and her big serious-looking eyes—that's all I could catch when I tried to bring her to mind.

I was working behind the counter at the Howard Johnson's on the Thruway just before the Kingston exit. Not a bad job. Kind of a long ride from Newburgh, but okay once I got there. Mine was the second night shift, eleven to seven. Very light until a Greyhound checked in for breakfast around six-thirty. At that hour the sun was all the way clear of the hills behind the restaurant. The place looked better at night—more like shelter—but I loved it when the sun broke in, even if it did show all the cracks in the vinyl and the speckled floor looked dirty no matter what the mop boy did.

It was August and a bus crowd was just unloading. They would stand around a long while: going to the john, and looking at gifts and junk-for-sale machines, reluctant to sit down so soon. Even to eat. I was trying to fill the coffeepots and get them all situated on the electric burners when I saw her. She was sitting in a booth smoking a cigarette with two guys smothered in head and facial hair. Her own hair was so big and wild I could hardly see her face. But the eyes. I would know them anywhere. She had on a powder-blue halter and shorts outfit and earrings the size of bracelets. Talk about lipstick and eyebrow pencil. She made the big girls look like nuns. I couldn't get off the counter until seven o'clock, but I kept watching the booth in case they got up to leave before that. My replacement was on time for a change, so I counted and stacked my receipts as fast as I could and signed off. I walked over to the booth, smiling and wondering if she would remember me. Or even if she wanted to remember me. Maybe she didn't want to be reminded of St. Bonny's or to have anybody know she was ever there. I know I never talked about it to anybody.

I put my hands in my apron pockets and leaned against the back of the booth facing them.

"Roberta? Roberta Fisk?"

She looked up. "Yeah?"

"Twyla."

She squinted for a second and then said, "Wow."

"Remember me?"

"Sure. Hey. Wow."

"It's been awhile," I said, and gave a smile to the two hairy guys.

"Yeah. Wow. You work here?"

"Yeah," I said. "I live in Newburgh."

"Newburgh? No kidding?" She laughed then, a private laugh that included the guys but only the guys, and they laughed with her. What could I do but laugh too and wonder why I was standing there with my knees showing out from under that uniform. Without looking I could see the blue-and-white triangle on my head, my hair shapeless in a net, my ankles thick in white oxfords. Nothing could have been less sheer than my stockings. There was this silence that came down right after I laughed. A silence it was her turn to fill up. With introductions, maybe, to her boyfriends or an invitation to sit down and have a Coke. Instead she lit a cigarette off the one she'd just finished and said, "We're on our way to the Coast. He's got an appointment with Hendrix." She gestured casually toward the boy next to her.

"Hendrix? Fantastic," I said. "Really fantastic. What's she doing now?"

Roberta coughed on her cigarette and the two guys rolled their eyes up at the ceiling.

"Hendrix. Jimi Hendrix, asshole. He's only the biggest—Oh, wow. Forget it."

I was dismissed without anyone saying good-bye, so I thought I would do it for her.

"How's your mother?" I asked. Her grin cracked her whole face. She swallowed. "Fine," she said. "How's yours?"

"Pretty as a picture," I said and turned away. The backs of my knees were damp. Howard Johnson's really was a dump in the sunlight.

James is as comfortable as a house slipper. He liked my cooking and I liked his big loud family. They have lived in Newburgh all of their lives and talk about it the way people do who have always known a home. His grandmother has a porch swing older than his father and when they talk about streets and avenues and buildings they call them names they no longer have. They still call the A&P Rico's because it stands on property once a mom-and-pop store owned by Mr. Rico. And they call the new community college Town Hall because it once was. My mother-in-law puts up jelly and cucumbers and buys butter wrapped in cloth from a dairy. James and his father talk about fishing and baseball and I can see them all together on the Hudson in a raggedy skiff. Half the population of Newburgh is on welfare now, but to my husband's family it was still some upstate paradise of a time long past. A time of ice houses and vegetable wagons, coal furnaces and children weeding gardens. When our son was born my mother-in-law gave me the crib blanket that had been hers.

But the town they remembered had changed. Something quick was in the air. Magnificent old houses, so ruined they had become shelter for squatters and rent risks, were bought and renovated. Smart IBM people moved out of their suburbs back into the city and put shutters up and herb gardens in their backyards. A brochure came in the mail announcing the opening of a Food Emporium. Gourmet food, it said— and listed items the rich IBM crowd would want. It was located in a new mall at the edge of town and I drove out to shop there one day—just to see. It was late in June. After the tulips were gone and the Queen Elizabeth roses were open everywhere. I trailed my cart along the aisle tossing in smoked oysters and Robert's sauce and things I knew would sit in my cupboard for years. Only when I found some Klondike ice cream bars did I feel less guilty about spending James's fireman's salary so foolishly. My father-in-law ate them with the same gusto little Joseph did.

Waiting in the checkout line I heard a voice say, "Twyla!"

The classical music piped over the aisles had affected me and the woman leaning toward me was dressed to kill. Diamonds on her hand, a smart white summer dress. "I'm Mrs. Benson," I said.

"Ho. Ho. The Big Bozo," she sang.

For a split second I didn't know what she was talking about. She had a bunch of asparagus and two cartons of fancy water.

"Roberta!"

"Right."

"For heaven's sake. Roberta."

"You look great," she said.

"So do you. Where are you? Here? In Newburgh?"

"Yes. Over in Annandale."

We both giggled. Really giggled. Suddenly, in just a pulse beat, twenty years disappeared and all of it came rushing back. The big girls (whom we called gar girls— Roberta's misheard word for the evil stone faces described in a civics class) there dancing in the orchard, the ploppy mashed potatoes, the double weenies, the Spam with pineapple. We went into the coffee shop holding on to one another and I tried to think why we were glad to see each other this time and not before. Once, twelve years ago, we passed like strangers. A black girl and a white girl meeting in a Howard Johnson's on the road and having nothing to say. One in a blue-and-white triangle waitress hat, the other on her way to see Hendrix. Now we were behaving like sisters separated for much too long. Those four short months were nothing in time. Maybe it was the thing itself. Just being there, together. Two little girls who knew what nobody else in the world knew—how not to ask questions. How to believe what had to be believed. There was politeness in that reluctance and generosity as well. Is your mother sick too? No, she dances all night. Oh—and an understanding nod.

We sat in a booth by the window and fell into recollection like veterans.

"Did you ever learn to read?"

"Watch." She picked up the menu. "Special of the day. Cream of corn soup. Entrées. Two dots and a wriggly line. Quiche. Chef salad, scallops . . ."

I was laughing and applauding when the waitress came up.

"Remember the Easter baskets?"

"And how we tried to *introduce* them?"

"Your mother with that cross like two telephone poles."

"And yours with those tight slacks."

We laughed so loudly heads turned and made the laughter hard to suppress.

"What happened to the Jimi Hendrix date?"

Roberta made a blow-out sound with her lips.

"When he died I thought about you."

"Oh, you heard about him finally?"

"Finally. Come on, I was a small-town country waitress."

"And I was a small-town country dropout. God, were we wild. I still don't know how I got out of there alive."

"But you did."

"I did. I really did. Now I'm Mrs. Kenneth Norton."

"Sounds like a mouthful."

"It is."

"Servants and all?"

Roberta held up two fingers.

"Ow! What does he do?"

I was opening my mouth to say more when the cashier called my attention to her empty counter.

"Meet you outside." Roberta pointed her finger and went into the express line.

I placed the groceries and kept myself from glancing around to check Roberta's progress. I remembered Howard Johnson's and looking for a chance to speak only to be greeted with a stingy "wow." But she was waiting for me and her huge hair was sleek now, smooth around a small, nicely shaped head. Shoes, dress, everything lovely and summery and rich. I was dying to know what happened to her, how she got from Jimi Hendrix to Annandale, a neighborhood full of doctors and IBM executives. Easy, I thought. Everything is so easy for them. They think they own the world.

"How long," I asked her. "How long have you been here?"

"A year. I got married to a man who lives here. And you, you're married too, right? Benson, you said."

"Yeah. James Benson."

"And is he nice?"

"Oh, is he nice?"

"Well, is he?" Roberta's eyes were steady as though she really meant the question and wanted an answer.

"He's wonderful, Roberta. Wonderful."

"So you're happy."

"Very."

"That's good," she said and nodded her head. "I always hoped you'd be happy. Any kids? I know you have kids."

"One. A boy. How about you?"

"Four."

"Four?"

She laughed. "Step kids. He's widower."

"Oh."

"Got a minute? Let's have a coffee."

I thought about the Klondikes melting and the inconvenience of going all the way to my car and putting the bags in the trunk. Served me right for buying all that stuff I didn't need. Roberta was ahead of me.

"Put them in my car. It's right here."

And then I saw the dark blue limousine.

"You married a Chinaman?"

"No." She laughed. "He's the driver."

"Oh, my. If the Big Bozo could see you now."

"Computers and stuff. What do I know?"

"I don't remember a hell of a lot from those days, but Lord, St. Bonny's is as clear as daylight. Remember Maggie? The day she fell down and those gar girls laughed at her?"

Roberta looked up from her salad and stared at me. "Maggie didn't fall," she said.

"Yes, she did. You remember."

"No, Twyla. They knocked her down. Those girls pushed her down and tore her clothes. In the orchard."

"I don't—that's not what happened."

"Sure it is. In the orchard. Remember how scared we were?"

"Wait a minute. I don't remember any of that."

"And Bozo was fired."

"You're crazy. She was there when I left. You left before me."

"I went back. You weren't there when they fired Bozo."

"What?"

"Twice. Once for a year when I was about ten, another for two months when I was fourteen. That's when I ran away."

"You ran away from St. Bonny's?"

"I had to. What do you want? Me dancing in that orchard?"

"Are you sure about Maggie?"

"Of course I'm sure. You've blocked it, Twyla. It happened. Those girls had behavior problems, you know."

"Didn't they, though. But why can't I remember the Maggie thing?"

"Believe me. It happened. And we were there."

"Who did you room with when you went back?" I asked her as if I would know her. The Maggie thing was troubling me.

"Creeps. They tickled themselves in the night."

My ears were itching and I wanted to go home suddenly. This was all very well but she couldn't just comb her hair, wash her face, and pretend everything was hunky-dory. After the Howard Johnson's snub. And no apology. Nothing.

"Were you on dope or what that time at Howard Johnson's?" I tried to make my voice sound friendlier than I felt.

"Maybe, a little. I never did drugs much. Why?"

"I don't know, you acted sort of like you didn't want to know me then."

"Oh, Twyla, you know how it was in those days: black—white. You know how everything was."

But I didn't know. I thought it was just the opposite. Busloads of blacks and whites came into Howard Johnson's together. They roamed together then: students, musicians, lovers, protesters. You got to see everything at Howard Johnson's, and blacks were very friendly with whites in those days. But sitting there with nothing on my plate but two hard tomato wedges wondering about the melting Klondikes it seemed childish remembering the slight. We went to her car and, with the help of the driver, got my stuff into my station wagon.

"We'll keep in touch this time," she said.

"Sure," I said. "Sure. Give me a call."

"I will," she said, and then, just as I was sliding behind the wheel, she leaned into the window. "By the way. Your mother. Did she ever stop dancing?"

I shook my head. "No. Never."

Roberta nodded.

"And yours? Did she ever get well?"

She smiled a tiny sad smile. "No. She never did. Look, call me, okay?"

"Okay," I said, but I knew I wouldn't. Roberta had messed up my past somehow with that business about Maggie. I wouldn't forget a thing like that. Would I?

Strife came to us that fall. At least that's what the paper called it. Strife. Racial strife. The word made me think of a bird—a big shrieking bird out of 1,000,000,000 B.C. Flapping its wings and cawing. Its eye with no lid always bearing down on you. All day it screeched and at night it slept on the rooftops. It woke you in the morning, and from the *Today* show to the eleven o'clock news it kept you an awful company. I couldn't figure it out from one day to the next. I knew I was supposed to feel something strong, but I didn't know what, and James wasn't any help. Joseph was on the list of kids to be transferred from the junior high school to another one at some far-out-of-the-way place and I thought it was a good thing until I heard it was a bad thing. I mean I didn't know. All the schools seemed dumps to me, and the fact that one was nicer looking didn't hold much weight. But the papers were full of it and then the kids began to get jumpy. In August, mind you. Schools weren't even open yet. I thought Joseph might be frightened to go over there, but he didn't seem scared so I forgot about it, until I found myself driving along Hudson Street out there by the school they were trying to integrate and saw a line of women marching. And who do you suppose was in line, big as life, holding a sign in front of her bigger than her mother's cross? MOTHERS HAVE RIGHTS TOO! it said.

I drove on and then changed my mind. I circled the block, slowed down, and honked my horn.

Roberta looked over and when she saw me she waved. I didn't wave back, but I didn't move either. She handed her sign to another woman and came over to where I was parked.

"Hi."

"What are you doing?"

"Picketing. What's it look like?"

"What for?"

"What do you mean, 'What for?' They want to take my kids and send them out of the neighborhood. They don't want to go."

"So what if they go to another school? My boy's being bussed too, and I don't mind. Why should you?"

"It's not about us, Twyla. Me and you. It's about our kids."

"What's more *us* than that?"

"Well, it is a free country."

"Not yet, but it will be."

"What the heck does that mean? I'm not doing anything to you."

"You really think that?"

"I know it."

"I wonder what made me think you were different."

"I wonder what made me think you were different."

"Look at them," I said. "Just look. Who do they think they are? Swarming all over the place like they own it. And now they think they can decide where my child goes to school. Look at them, Roberta. They're Bozos."

Roberta turned around and looked at the women. Almost all of them were standing still now, waiting. Some were even edging toward us. Roberta looked at me out of some refrigerator behind her eyes. "No, they're not. They're just mothers."

"And what am I? Swiss cheese?"

"I used to curl your hair."

"I hated your hands in my hair."

The women were moving. Our faces looked mean to them of course and they looked as though they could not wait to throw themselves in front of a police car or, better yet, into my car and drag me away by my ankles. Now they surrounded my car and gently, gently began to rock it. I swayed back and forth like a sideways yo-yo. Automatically I reached for Roberta, like the old days in the orchard when they saw us watching them and we had to get out of there, and if one of us fell the other pulled her up and if one of us was caught the other stayed to kick and scratch, and neither would leave the other behind. My arm shot out of the car window but no receiving hand was there. Roberta was looking at me sway from side to side in the car and her face was still. My purse slid from the car seat down under the dashboard. The four policemen who had been drinking Tab in their car finally got the message and strolled over, forcing their way through the women. Quietly, firmly they spoke. "Okay, ladies. Back in line or off the streets."

Some of them went away willingly; others had to be urged away from the car doors and the hood. Roberta didn't move. She was looking steadily at me. I was fumbling to turn on the ignition, which wouldn't catch because the gearshift was still in drive. The seats of the car were a mess because the swaying had thrown my grocery coupons all over and my purse was sprawled on the floor.

"Maybe I am different now, Twyla. But you're not. You're the same little state kid who kicked a poor old black lady when she was down on the ground. You kicked a black lady and you have the nerve to call me a bigot."

The coupons were everywhere and the guts of my purse were bunched under the dashboard. What was she saying? Black? Maggie wasn't black.

"She wasn't black," I said.

"Like hell she wasn't, and you kicked her. We both did. You kicked a black lady who couldn't even scream."

"Liar!"

"You're the liar! Why don't you just go on home and leave us alone, huh?"

She turned away and I skidded away from the curb.

The next morning I went into the garage and cut the side out of the carton our portable TV had come in. It wasn't nearly big enough, but after a while I had a decent sign: red spray-painted letters on a white background—AND SO DO CHILDREN****. I meant just to go down to the school and tack it up somewhere so those cows on the picket line across the street could see it, but when I got there, some ten or so others had already assembled—protesting the cows across the street. Police permits and everything. I got in line and we strutted in time on our side while Roberta's group strutted on theirs. That first day we were all dignified, pretending the other side didn't exist. The second day there was name calling and finger gestures. But that was about all. People changed signs from time to time, but Roberta never did and neither did I. Actually my sign didn't make sense without Roberta's. "And so do children what?" one of the women on my side asked me. Have rights, I said, as though it was obvious.

Roberta didn't acknowledge my presence in any way, and I got to thinking maybe she didn't know I was there. I began to pace myself in the line, jostling people one minute and lagging behind the next, so Roberta and I could reach the end of our respective lines at the same time and there would be a moment in our turn when we would face each other. Still, I couldn't tell whether she saw me and knew my sign was for her. The next day I went early before we were scheduled to assemble. I waited until she got there before I exposed my new creation. As soon as she hoisted her MOTHERS HAVE RIGHTS TOO I began to wave my new one, which said, HOW WOULD YOU KNOW? I know she saw that one, but I had gotten addicted now. My signs got crazier each day, and the women on my side decided that I was a kook. They couldn't make heads or tails out of my brilliant screaming posters.

I brought a painted sign in queenly red with huge black letters that said, IS YOUR MOTHER WELL? Roberta took her lunch break and didn't come back for the rest of the day or any day after. Two days later I stopped going too and couldn't have been missed because nobody understood my signs anyway.

It was a nasty six weeks. Classes were suspended and Joseph didn't go to anybody's school until October. The children—everybody's children—soon got bored with that extended vacation they thought was going to be so great. They looked at TV until their eyes flattened. I spent a couple of mornings tutoring my son, as the other mothers said we should. Twice I opened a text from last year that he had never turned in. Twice he yawned in my face. Other mothers organized living room sessions so the kids would keep up. None of the kids could concentrate, so they drifted back to *The Price Is Right* and *The Brady Bunch*. When the school finally opened there were fights once or twice and some sirens roared through the streets every once in a while. There were a lot of photographers from Albany. And just when ABC was about to send up a news crew, the kids settled down like nothing in the world had happened. Joseph hung my HOW WOULD YOU KNOW? sign in his bedroom. I don't know what became of AND SO DO CHILDREN***. I think my father-in-law cleaned some fish on it. He was always puttering around in our garage. Each of his five children lived in Newburgh, and he acted as though he had five extra homes.

I couldn't help looking for Roberta when Joseph graduated from high school, but I didn't see her. It didn't trouble me much what she had said to me in the car. I mean the kicking part. I know I didn't do that, I couldn't do that. But I was puzzled by her telling me Maggie was black. When I thought about it I actually couldn't be certain. She wasn't pitch-black, I knew, or I would have remembered that. What I remember was the kiddie hat and the semicircle legs. I tried to reassure myself about the race thing for a long time until it dawned on me that the truth was already there, and Roberta knew it. I didn't kick her, I didn't join in with the gar girls and kick that lady, but I sure did want to. We watched and never tried to help her and never called for help. Maggie was my dancing mother. Deaf, I thought, and dumb. Nobody inside. Nobody who would hear you if you cried in the night. Nobody who could tell you anything important that you could use. Rocking, dancing, swaying as she walked.

And when the gar girls pushed her down and started roughhousing, I knew she wouldn't scream, couldn't—just like me—and I was glad about that.

We decided not to have a tree, because Christmas would be at my mother-in-law's house, so why have a tree at both places? Joseph was at SUNY New Paltz and we had to economize, we said. But at the last minute, I changed my mind. Nothing could be that bad. So I rushed around town looking for a tree, something small but wide. By the time I found a place, it was snowing and very late. I dawdled like it was the most important purchase in the world and the tree man was fed up with me. Finally I chose one and had it tied onto the trunk of the car. I drove away slowly because the sand trucks were not out yet and the streets could be murder at the beginning of a snow-fall. Downtown the streets were wide and rather empty except for a cluster of people coming out of the Newburgh Hotel. The one hotel in town that wasn't built out of cardboard and Plexiglas. A party, probably. The men huddled in the snow were dressed in tails and the women had on furs. Shiny things glittered from underneath their coats. It made me tired to look at them. Tired, tired, tired. On the next corner was a small diner with loops and loops of paper bells in the window. I stopped the car and went in. Just for a cup of coffee and twenty minutes of peace before I went home and tried to finish everything before Christmas Eve.

"Twyla?"

There she was. In a silvery evening gown and dark fur coat. A man and another woman were with her, the man fumbling for change to put in the cigarette machine. The woman was humming and tapping on the counter with her fingernails. They all looked a little bit drunk.

"Well. It's you."

"How are you?"

I shrugged. "Pretty good. Frazzled. Christmas and all."

"Regular?" called the woman from the counter.

"Fine," Roberta called back and then, "Wait for me in the car."

She slipped into the booth beside me. "I have to tell you something, Twyla. I made up my mind if I ever saw you again, I'd tell you."

"I'd as soon not hear anything, Roberta. It doesn't matter now, anyway."

"No," she said. "Not about that."

"Don't be long," said the woman. She carried two regulars to go and the man peeled his cigarette pack as they left.

"It's about St. Bonny's and Maggie."

"Oh, please."

"Listen to me. I really did think she was black. I didn't make that up. I really thought so. But now I can't be sure. I just remember her as old, so old. And because she couldn't talk—well, you know, I thought she was crazy. She'd been brought up in an institution like my mother was and like I thought I would be too. And you were right. We didn't kick her. It was the gar girls. Only them. But, well, I wanted to. I re-ally wanted them to hurt her. I said we did it, too. You and me, but that's not true. And I don't want you to carry that around. It was just that I wanted to do it so bad that day—wanting to is doing it."

Her eyes were watery from the drinks she'd had, I guess. I know it's that way with me. One glass of wine and I start bawling over the littlest thing.

"We were kids, Roberta."

"Yeah. Yeah. I know, just kids."

"Eight."

"Eight."

"And lonely."

"Scared, too."

She wiped her cheeks with the heel of her hand and smiled. "Well, that's all I wanted to say."

I nodded and couldn't think of any way to fill the silence that went from the diner past the paper bells on out into the snow. It was heavy now. I thought I'd better wait for the sand trucks before starting home.

"Thanks, Roberta."

"Sure."

"Did I tell you? My mother, she never did stop dancing."

"Yes. You told me. And mine, she never got well." Roberta lifted her hands from the tabletop and covered her face with her palms. When she took them away she really was crying. "Oh, shit, Twyla. Shit, shit, shit. What the hell happened to Maggie?"

[1983]

Questions

1. How are the two main characters similar? How are they different? How does Morrison convey the changes that occur both within each girl and in each girl's view of the other? What is the effect of not knowing the central characters' racial identities?

2. How are social and cultural references used in the story?

3. What is the effect of having the story narrated by Twyla? Does the reader learn Roberta's point of view as well? If so, how?

4. Why is Maggie important to the story?

5. *Recitatif* is a musical term that refers to the performance of certain prose parts and dialogues in operas and oratorios. The singer declaims the words using the rhythm and tempo of speech but uttered in musical tones. What does the title mean in relation to Morrison's story?

Kermit Moyer

(b. 1943)

United States

K ermit Moyer was born in Harrisburg, Pennsylvania, in 1943. An army brat, he grew up in Hawaii, Okinawa, Georgia, Pennsylvania, and Texas. He has taught at American University in Washington, D.C., since 1970, where he also began writing short stories and teaching in the creative writing program. When Tumbling, his first collection of short stories, was published in 1988, it was cited by the reviewer in The New York Times Book Review as one of the most significant volumes to appear in the 13-year history of the Illinois Short Fiction Series.

Asked to comment about the story, Moyer gave the following response:

At its most abstract, I suppose that "Tumbling" is about the way the imagination mediates our experience. As their nursery-rhyme names may suggest, Jack and Jill are also intended to express something elemental about male and female. By the end of the story, Jill discovers how radically entangled she's become in the masculine Oedipal scenarios that, wittingly or unwittingly, she's been helping to enact. With this discovery, the seemingly solid ground of reality opens up beneath her feet and, like her namesake, she goes tumbling. But, as we know, a fall can also be a genesis, and acrobats routinely turn tumbling into a demonstration of human resiliency and grace. I should add that, although I had some of these ideas in mind when I started the story, the act of writing tends to focus microscopically on the concrete unfolding of a particular moment rather than on anything so generalized as an idea or a "theme." In this sense, writing the story seemed less like the working out of a thesis than like the transcription of a dream.

TUMBLING

Early one rainy morning just about a week ago, Jack and me were sitting in a laundromat in this little town where we'd spent the night in an unlocked car. We sleep in cars a lot of times, it's not as bad as you might think. A little cramped maybe, but if there's a radio and a key to make it work, we don't mind too much. Like that night we were in a big new-smelling Cadillac in a used-car lot. Jack said they could make it smell that way with an aerosol can. Plenty of room and everything clean and shiny. The radio picked up stations from as far away as Chicago and Fort Wayne, Indiana, and we sang along with the top forty and listened to one of those shows where people call in. Jacky tried to get a station from back home to see if there was anything on about us, but he couldn't find one. He said the signals were probably too weak to reach as far as we were by then. He was sitting behind the wheel smoking Camels because it was Daddy's brand. I hated for him to get that clean ashtray dirty. I don't know why. I said we should think of the folks that might want to buy that car. Jack just laughed and said maybe a few cigarette butts might give them a chance to think about us. "But wouldn't that be leaving evidence?" I said. That's one of the things Jacky talks about sometimes: covering our tracks, he calls it. He wipes our finger-prints off the radio knobs and the steering wheels, and he's always careful to use a handkerchief to open and close the doors. Well, that morning dawned so rainy-gray and drizzly you didn't even want to move. Jacky let me sleep with the duffel bag for a pillow and I just rolled myself up with my hands pressed between my knees and tried to keep what was happening in my dream from slipping away. It was a birthday party and it was you, Mom, not Jacky, helping me blow out the candles. I was wear-ing my blue print dress with the puffy sleeves and the white lace collar, and Jacky was saying, "Let me, let me." There was pink icing on the cake and I wanted to see if maybe Daddy was there too. I thought he might be because we were still little in my dream. But Jack was shaking my shoulder and telling me to rise and shine, we had to get out of there before they opened up. So I combed my hair in the rearview mirror, and then we scooted out and found this laundromat, which was either already open or else hadn't ever closed. We were wet from the rain by that time, so we got behind the machines and changed into some dry clothes. We put a wash in and then just sat around, watching the raindrops slide down the windows and reading magazines. We had the place all to ourselves, and it made me feel kind of blue, looking out at noth-ing but the rain and two or three parked cars. There was a Woolworth's right across the street that hadn't opened up yet. It was only about six o'clock in the morning. I could see a BACK TO SCHOOL sign in one window and I wondered if come September we'd be going back to school or not. My dream was still with me, too, but all scattered and floating away from where it came from. A foggy picture would come in front of my mind's eye, and I'd think it was something I was about to remember, something that really happened, and then I'd realize it was only my dream, and that'd make me feel like I'd lost something. The fat sound of the washer going chugga-*whoosh*-chugga-*whoosh* and the little pinging noise of the dryer had put me into sort of a hypnotic trance anyway. But not Jacky. He was reading a *Time* magazine, making noises to himself whenever he'd find something interesting. "Hey, listen to this," he says. "Re-member what I told you? *Scientists now believe that the universe has been expanding from a single fixed point for millions of years. If we trace back the motion of the galaxies, we ar-rive at a point in the distant past when they were a single unified mass, a time when the uni-verse must have been very different from its present disseminated state.*" I turned away from the window and said, "What do you mean, 'remember what I told you'? I don't remember anything like that." "Come on, Jill," he says, "everything's always moving away, I always said that, and we're going against the current anytime we try to keep them, you know, from flying apart, or anytime we try to get them back together again. That's why it's so hard, and that's why we have to be so careful all the time." "Oh, yeah," I said. "Sure. We're just like the galaxies."

It was right then that this big fat lady comes into the laundromat. She's got a whole wick-er basket full of dirty laundry, so she pushes the door open with her shoulder and sort of backs in. When she turns around and sees us she flinches. "Land sakes," she says. "You give me a fright. I never expected a soul in here this early." Her face was one of those bright lit-up country kind with rosy apple cheeks—made red from bunches of tiny lit-tle broken veins I saw later—a face just as shiny wet from the rain as if she'd been cry-ing her eyes out, except she looked so pleased with everything you couldn't believe she'd even know how to cry. She had round arms with freckles and her hair was just like yours, Mom—reddish strawberry-blonde—all twisted up in braids at the back of her head and against her neck. I was glad she was here because now I thought maybe I could get out of feeling so blue. Jacky'd be sure to put on one of his shows, and that meant I'd have to play along. Which usually I get a kick out of. Anytime we talk to somebody I have to wait and see who we're going to be this time. Real life is always so ordinary on the one hand and so complicated on the other, but Jacky's stories can make it all seem just as simple and easy as filling in a coloring book. "Can you tell us about how far we are from the Maryland line?" he says. The fat lady is still standing there with her arms hooped around this big basket of laundry. Jacky's got that funny way of being able to get your attention, and I could see her sort of tilt her head like she's having trouble hearing what he's trying to tell her. She says, "Not far—only about fifty miles, I guess. just take Route 15 south out of town. Do you all have family in Maryland?" Jacky looks up at her and directly into her eyes. He sort of waves his hand over toward me and says, "This is Peggy Sue." *Peggy Sue?* I thought. He's got to be kidding. I just sat there with my hands folded in my lap and looked sort of lost—which was easy enough because that's just exactly how I felt, we'd been on the road almost two weeks by then, sticking to the back roads. In a way I was in the same boat as the fat lady, just waiting to find out what the story would be so I could play along. So then Jack says, "We're on our way to Maryland to get married." I closed my eyes for a second and tried to take that one in. When I looked up, the fat lady is staring at me and resting her basket on the formica table between the row of washers on one side and the row of dryers on the other. "Why, you're just kids," she says. If I turned slightly toward the window, I could see my reflection in the glass. It was all wavery from the rain. "Just a couple of kids," she says. I'm watching her in the reflection on the window and I can see right through her to the five-and-ten across the street. "You don't want to hear any of this," Jacky says. He's staring down at his hands and shaking his head back and forth. I can see him in the window too—our reflections have a sharp edge to them but the raindrops, sliding crooked down the glass, make everything outside blurry. "Look here," she says out of the blue, her head tilted and her voice going all kindly and soft. "You're in a family way, isn't that right child?" When I turned around she was watching me with a sly, sort of happy look. Jacky sits up straight, like he's suddenly got everything under control. "We're all right. We can take care of ourselves," he says. The fat lady's watching Jacky again, and she narrows her eyes and says, "How old are you kids? Where're you from?" "We're old enough, you don't have to worry about that," Jacky says right away. Then he says, "At least we're old enough in Maryland—we're just passing through here." He got that line from a movie we'd seen where somebody had to go to Maryland to get married because they were under-age. We go to movies a lot on the road, for the simple reason that movie theaters turned out to be a good place to spend the night. "What about you?" she says to me. "Are you old enough too?" I circled my arms around my stomach and said, "It looks like I am." The fat lady nods her head and turns back to Jacky. "Well then I guess you better get yourselves a map the next time you fill up," she says. For a second it looked like that was the end of the conversation, but then Jacky says, "We're not driving, we don't have a car." He stops short, and then he blurts out, "We've been hitchhiking." Which was true enough, that's for sure—one of the problems is being too young to have a driver's license much less a car. All we have is the money we got from cashing Daddy's check— which I'm real sorry about, Mom, but Jacky made out a good case it was his and mine in the first place. And we decided, or rather I should say he did, that we'd pretty much have to forget about riding on buses or trains or anything like that because otherwise we'd be sure to get picked up. So there we were sitting in a laundromat at six in the morning. For some reason, I remember, I kept listening to the rain. The light in that laundromat was real yellow against all the gray outside, and since this fat lady came in, the sound of the rain made it, I don't know, sort of cozy and warm-feeling somehow. "So you'll be looking for a ride then I guess," she says to Jacky. "I want you to know I think you're doing the right thing. I know it's bound to be hard for a spell, but you'll be just fine if you really love one another." She smiles in a way that makes it hard not to believe her. I immediately started to brighten up. Then she says, "Are you hungry, have you two had any breakfast yet? You must be starved." I felt like we were turning a corner when she said that. I don't know why, except it made me think of you asking that same question the time you didn't get back from your date until early Sunday morning and we were already up. You were still dressed fancy from Saturday night and you tried to tell us you'd been to church already. I could just see you in that navy blue cocktail dress with the bow at the bust whipping up jelly omelets and French toast and once in a while tossing your hair out of your eyes the way you do when your hands are full. Standing by the stove in your stocking feet after you'd kicked off your heels. Remembering that made me feel like a little kid, and here I was supposed to be pregnant and everything. When we don't answer her, the fat lady looks at Jack and tells him, "You need to make sure this girl eats on a regular schedule. She's a little lady now, and she'll have to keep her strength up." Then she turns to me and says, "Don't worry, I wouldn't tell your secret to a soul, but you'll have to eat enough for the baby too, that's the first thing." She smiled and I nodded and she says, "Good. Now just let me get this wash started. Our dryer's all right, but the Bendix's been on the fritz, so here I am. Well. We'll have to see about getting some nourishment into you. It's not healthy to be as skinny as you are in your condition." To tell the truth, I *was* just about starved, and I was also glad to let this fat lady take charge for a while—even if it was under false pretenses. I was avoiding Jacky's eyes because I didn't want to be reminded of that at all. I just wanted to be taken care of for a little while. Maybe I'd even get to take a bath. In my dream there were lots and lots of candles on the cake even though we were little, and when I couldn't blow them all out you blew out the rest, so I knew all my wishes were going to come true. Jacky was crying and he kept saying, "Let me, let me," but that didn't really matter. The feeling I had in my dream was this: I didn't know what my wishes were, but I just had a feeling they were all going to come true.

I think it was something about the fat lady herself that made Jack come up with that particular story. The trick Jacky has is he can pretty much hook up the right story with the right person. He just lets them make it up with him. That's where the fat lady was a natural. She really loved the idea of us running off because we had to get married. It might be a speck scandalous, she said, but that's all right, these things always happened this way. She expected we'd be as happy as anybody else and, besides, the baby was a sure sign. So now I had to play my part in this hot teenage romance she and Jack cooked up. Star-struck lovers and everything. And that's probably right where it all started, from then on it's just been one thing after another. Like running off to find Daddy in the first place. If you look at it from a distance, I guess it's pretty ridiculous. But each step of the way it seemed perfectly natural and, the funny thing is, after a while the reasons why hardly seemed to matter. I knew you'd be worried about us, but I also knew you'd be all right and I wasn't so sure about Jacky. And anyway at first I thought I'd be able to steer him home before you even got back from your weekend in the city. But the plan of how to do each step of the thing somehow took over. Each step always makes sense—even if the whole thing doesn't. Daddy's supposed to be in Brunswick, Georgia, so that's where we're going. And of course running off was a good way to make you feel sorry too. Jacky's sure you spent the weekend with that guy from work, the one that brought you home after the office party. I guess you never knew it, but Jacky saw the two of you kissing or something in the kitchen that night. Those things don't matter to me, but where you're concerned Jacky can't even stand the idea of stuff like that. So going off to find Daddy was a bright light for Jacky—he *had* to follow it. And I just had to go along. I guess I've always felt like I had to look after Jacky, even if he is eight minutes older than me. I don't only mean take care of him exactly—I mean more like I have to follow him with my mind and with my feelings. He gets so worked up about stuff sometimes, and really, things like that just never mattered to me. What's actually happening matters a lot more than anything you might merely think about it, don't you agree?

You should have seen the fat lady's house. But of course she wasn't the fat lady by then. We found out her name was Mrs. Spicer, and she had a whole flock of kids, most of them grown now, and grandchildren—the youngest was only about four years old. Well, it didn't take long before Jack had Mrs. Spicer eating out of his hand. He'd tease her and make her laugh and pretty soon she's treating him like he's her favorite son or something. But I don't think she ever pictured me as one of her daughters though. I was more like somebody she used to be herself, that's what she told me. We got in the front seat of this Chevrolet station wagon she had, and then she drove us just barely outside of town to a big old pink house with blue shutters and lots of peaks and chimneys and three wide porches, a screened one up on the second floor just for sleeping—all of it set back on a low hill you couldn't even see from the highway because of all the trees. Everything surrounded by cornfields and peach orchards and a flower garden big enough to walk through, almost like a little park. just to get there you had to go up a long driveway, really an actual road, between tall rows of evergreen trees. We weren't that far from the mountains—Jacky's pointed them out from the road, and I'd already felt the temperature drop. He showed me on the map how close we were to where the color changed from yellow to long fingers of brown. Those were the Blue Ridge Mountains, he said. One of Jacky's ideas was to take the Appalachian Trail down to Georgia. Brunswick's over on the coast though, about an inch-and-a-half down from Savannah. According to the mileage chart, an inch-and-a-half is about seventy-five miles. Jacky kept changing his mind between going through the mountains and then cutting east along what he called "Sherman's march to the sea" or going along the coast through all the Navy bases and ocean cities as we made our way down to Brunswick. It was a hard decision, and we were right at the turning point that day. He liked to read out the names of the towns and cities between here and there, saying them over while he moved his fingertip along the different paths: Winchester or Norfolk? Asheville or Southport? Atlanta or Charleston, South Carolina? Jacky always pays attention to the names of places. To Jacky it's like the name of each little town we come to—especially if they have funny ones like Buffalo Mills or Mann's Choice or Rainsburg, Pennsylvania—like each little town is his to put away and keep, or like us just knowing the names of those places is what's making them come true. That's why I thought we might end up going east after all: there's just more names in that direction, and going off toward the blue edge of the map seemed more definite to Jacky than just trailing down through the mountains, I could tell. I was sure hoping so anyway, even though I never imagined for a minute we'd find Daddy either way. I just figured if we stayed close to people we'd be okay, but if we went off into the woods who knows what might happen? We don't even have sleeping bags, just a worn-out Navy blanket and that ratty old wedding-ring quilt you remember was my favorite. I like woods and open country, but what I like best is coming into a town, seeing the billboards, passing the first house with a painted fence and a mowed lawn, then maybe coming to an Esso station and a Dairy Queen. We'd always stop for one of those ice-cream cones with a curl-on-the-top, and Jacky'd already be studying the map, looking for the crookedest line between this town and the next one and licking away at the mustache of vanilla on his upper lip.

We stayed with Mrs. Spicer for two entire days, and during the whole time Jack was Buddy and I was Peggy Sue. That's one of our favorite songs, "Peggy Sue," and those names were sort of a secret joke to Jacky. He especially liked it that Mrs. Spicer probably never even heard of that record or of Buddy Holly either (which I found out later she had, on her own radio). I keep hearing that song in my mind because of those names—*I love you, Peggy Sue, with a love so rare and true, uh-oh Peg-gy, my Peg-gy Sue-uh-ooo, uh-ooo-ooo*. That's what I mean about the way Jacky can always get you to thinking exactly what he wants. I mean it was fine with me, that's what we'd been doing all along anyway—and it's fun too, always acting out some story or other. Jack says we have to stay incognito because we can never be sure if anyone's after us or not. We're runaways, he says, and it's safer to keep changing identities. Sometimes I'm his sister and other times I'm not—sometimes I'm his sidekick or his leading lady. But there's always some story going along with it. Even looking for Daddy. That's real, I guess, I mean that's something we're *doing*, but it's really just another story too. The stuff that actually happens, day by day, that stuff doesn't have anything to do with Daddy. Like Mrs. Spicer. Can you feature her taking us into her bedroom to ask us about our "hygiene practices"? That's what she called it. She said we were right to leave such things up to God Almighty. She said she thanked the Lord for all of her children. She wasn't a heathen and she could see we weren't either. "Oh, yes, ma'am," Jacky says, looking over at me sort of moony. "Our love is holy, we know that." Mrs. Spicer just widens her eyes and says, "Amen."

After we got to her house that first morning, she fixed us some corn fritters—these little things like pancakes with whole kernels of corn in them—all we could possibly eat—along with thick country sausage and a big round blue pitcher of milk. We always use the carton at home, so I remember that pitcher, round as a peony and with a kind of pinched-in spout like a flower petal. It was the sort of thing anybody'd love to have themselves someday—that house too, lots of nooks and crannies, so perfectly homey you could hardly believe it, little touches like embroidered cushions on the window seats of these bay windows at all the stairway landings—I bet the house Jacky and me are staying in right now used to be a lot like that, except this one's falling apart and there's no furniture to speak of, only this broken-down rocking chair I'm sitting in and what we managed to pull together out of cardboard boxes and some old wooden milk crates Jack found in the cellar. But I'm sure this used to be a really fabulous mansion though, back in the Gay Nineties or the Roaring Twenties or whatever. We're right next to the ocean, I can hear the surf against the stone wall across the road this very minute. Maryland, or maybe Delaware, I think. It's hard to know exactly which state you're in where we are now.

You might have liked Mrs. Spicer, she was wonderful in a lot of ways, but I doubt that you would have. You don't like anybody sitting in judgment all the time, no matter how kindly they try to tell you what you're doing wrong. I'm like you, my feeling is:

whatever anybody else says, I've got my own reasons. But even if Mrs. Spicer could get on your nerves a little bit, you still had to hand it to her. Picture this: the three of us're sitting in this big old country kitchen—four long windows looking out on a vegetable garden where you can see bulging red tomatoes in chicken-wire cages and leafy, purple-colored cabbages. Copper pots and pans are hanging on the wall, and there's this great stone fireplace. The kitchen table's covered with a bright blue-check oilcloth. We're just finishing breakfast and Jack's drinking a cup of coffee—which he taught himself to like after we went on the road, the same with smoking. It goes along with his idea of how he ought to be. So Jacky's drinking his coffee, and Mrs. Spicer's over at the sink looking through the window at something outside. She leans up against the rim of the sink and raps on the middle part of the window—it's open at both the top and the bottom—and she calls out through the screen, "Here, Wendell, you better let sleeping dogs lie—old Bertha's not going to like that. Why don't you and William go on over to your tree house and read some comic books?" Over her shoulder she says, "William's from down the road, he just got a new tricycle." Then through the screen she calls, "You heard me now, you better not tease Bertha like that—" and from over on the other side of the kitchen, farthest from the sink, a deep voice pipes in: "Oh, Mama, let 'em be. A little scrimmage with Bertha might do 'em good." When I turned around to see who's here now, I notice Jacky's still got his eye on Mrs. Spicer. Before he looks he's waiting to see what her reaction's going to be, just as crafty as a fox. I figured whoever's in the doorway's probably Mister Spicer, which it turned out he was, only not Mister but Major. I'm just trying to kind of slide a glance by him, I don't want to give anything away, but he locks onto my eyes, bang, and gives me a big wink—like we know a secret that makes everybody else look like fools, or like he's telling me this fat lady's harmless so we might as well play along. When I look back down at my plate, I see there's only a stub of fried sausage left—which I stick with my fork and smear around in the maple syrup before putting it in my mouth. Mrs. Spicer was a great cook, you'd have thought so too—that sausage was probably the best I ever had, and the corn fritters were entirely out of this world. We'd been pretty much living on french fries and popcorn and Coke for days by then. I'm starting to pour myself some more milk from the blue pitcher, when Jacky stands up and says, "Good morning, sir!"— like a military cadet or something. That's exactly how long it took Jacky to figure him out. "At ease, son, at ease," the guy says. "Sit down and finish your coffee. And you, young lady," he says to me, "you must be little sister, is that right?" I smiled and shook my head and waited for Jack to explain our story, but he never had to—Mrs. Spicer charges right in and does it for him, all in one breath nearly, leaving out the part about me being pregnant, and finishing up with, "So I thought you might take them down to Hagerstown on Saturday when you and Sam Healey go in to the races." Then she turns toward us and says, "This is my husband, Major Spicer." "Pleased to meet you, sir," Jacky chimes in right away, offering his hand. I said, "Same here," and gave him back a wink of my own. I don't know why. I guess I thought at least the two of us might have our feet on the ground, even if nobody else did.

It turned out I was wrong about that—was I ever—but the guy did give you the impression of being absolutely no-nonsense and in-charge—very distinguished looking, but with this crinkly little smile around the edges that seemed to bring him right down to earth and make it sort of a joke that anybody of our intelligence, his and mine I mean, would actually have to tolerate the kind of foolishness we had to put up with.

I mean you felt like he was including you in the winner's circle with him—at least that's how he made me feel. And then the story Mrs. Spicer reeled off was such a crock of beans. I mean talk about corny, I thought the Major'd see right through us in a flash and pretty soon we'd be on a bus back home. But instead, he says, sort of sly like he knows it's all just so much bull but he likes the careful planning it takes anyway, he says, "Well, well, I see," and puts his hands behind his back. He's got a newspaper rolled up in one fist and he rocks back on his heels and taps his leg with it—this way you can tell he's thinking, like when he'd smoke his pipe and you'd know it'd be an interruption to say anything to him. "I see," he says again, and, "Understood," like he's really thought it through. "Mind you," he says, "I don't necessarily agree with you in principle, but if that's your choice, I have to admire your tactical skills. Did Mrs. Spicer say you found her—or, I'm sorry, *she* found *you*—at the laundromat in town? Have I got that right?" He's looking at Jacky, but then his eyes shift back to mine like he's giving me a signal. That's when I started giggling, I mean I couldn't help it, even though there was supposedly nothing at all to laugh about— so I started coughing instead. Major Spicer steps over beside my chair and starts patting me on the back, like congratulations or something, and that makes it even funnier. So to stop laughing, like I've got to clear my throat, I take a sip of milk— which of course is a big mistake. The next second I'm spitting a white stream across the table, holding onto the edge and wrinkling up the smooth oilcloth to keep from falling over. Jack's wiping milk off his face with a blue napkin, real cloth, and he's glaring at me, and the Major's stroking my back now, almost like some guy looking to see if you're wearing a bra, and saying, "That's all right, go ahead and laugh, little sister. It's a good release." That's what he called me the whole time, except maybe once— "little sister." Did he know me and Jacky weren't really lovers but brothers and sisters instead? Maybe not, but he sure gave you the feeling that whatever anybody else said, it was all just so much bull—you and him knew what the real score was. But keeping up appearances was part of the game, like one of the rules or something. I mean he never said anything rude and he never lost that stiff Army posture of his either, the way he'd bend over from the waist, his back just as straight as a doll's anytime he'd reach down to scratch one of the family dogs or cats that were all over the place, laying around with their heads on their paws or sitting there staring up at you like you're going to give them something good, maybe a crunchy dog biscuit or a pat on the rear. It was real homey the way the dogs rubbed up against you, panting and grinning like they were just tickled to death you were there. If you think the yellow light in that laundromat was cozy, this was something entirely else. After a while that house really gave you the feeling of living in a beehive—Mrs. Spicer was this bustling queen bee with all these other bees buzzing around making honey—and Major Spicer off to one side, maybe, like the beekeeper with the net helmet to keep the bees from stinging him and getting in his eyes. Nothing ever really seemed to faze Major Spicer— no matter what crazy stuff was going on, he was above it all, outside of it entirely. For instance, the next thing we knew there was a lot of barking outside and some little kid is screaming his head off, but the Major doesn't even move. "There, what did I tell you?" Mrs. Spicer says. "Bertha won't put up with that kind of nonsense, they should have known better." Major Spicer laughs and says, "If they don't, they're finding out now, aren't they. Experience, Rhea, that's the only way we ever learn anything in life—as our adventurous young couple here bear witness. Those boys will pay closer attention in the future. A good object lesson if you ask me." Mrs. Spicer might have been listening to all this but I doubt it—she was already on her way out the door. In another second we could see her through the window waving at little Wendell and William with a broomstick she must have picked up on the back porch. We couldn't see the kids from where we were, but we could sure hear them. The barking had stopped as soon as Mrs. Spicer yelled, "*No*, Bertha, *bad* dog," but the screams were just getting louder, and we could hear the other kid, who turned out to be Wendell, the four-year-old, saying things like, "I *told* him *not* to," and "We didn't even *touch* her, we just wanted to *play*." Mrs. Spicer bangs the broomstick down on the porch and says, "Mind your own business, sir, and leave Bertha to mind hers," and in a different voice she says, "There, there, you're all right, William, Bertha's not going to bite you." Major Spicer is chuckling and he's still standing beside me with his hand on my shoulder. I could smell his particular odor, like the smell of a pillow, beneath the other odor of tobacco and Old Spice shaving lotion that I can recognize anywhere and that always makes me think of Daddy. His fingers were absentmindedly stroking the back of my neck under my hair, the same way you might pet a dog. It didn't feel personal at all, just friendly and offhand, so I didn't mind it, I like to have the back of my neck stroked, who doesn't? But Jacky looks over and lifts his eyebrows, so when I see nobody's looking, I stick my tongue out at him. Jacky just smiles and shakes his head like as far as he's concerned I'm some kind of moron. That look of his always makes me mad, but in one way I guess it turned out he was right. And I have to admit I never expected anything like what happened—in fact, I get so embarrassed I feel like one big blush whenever I think about it. This is getting into the stuff I'm not sure how to put in my letter—if Jacky ever lets me write one. The thing is, I don't want to just break the news to you, I want to tell you exactly how everything actually happened so you'll see it wasn't really anybody's fault. I mean finding fault is just picturing things according to some story where one way is automatically right and the other way is automatically wrong, but what I'm saying is that these particular things just naturally happened the way they happened, that's all. It made me feel sort of confused, but, honestly, in another way I really didn't mind, I was following right along with it. That was the next afternoon, after we'd spent the night there and eaten four more meals: lunch and dinner the first day, and then another breakfast and another lunch the next. Mrs. Spicer came up with the solution of whether she should let me and Jacky sleep together—because of course we weren't married yet, even if I *was* supposed to be pregnant. What she did was put us in bunk beds out on the sleeping porch with about half-a-dozen visiting grandchildren. It would've felt like a summer camp except it was all one big family, and they treated Jacky and me just like honorary members of the tribe. Major Spicer even asked me to say grace over lunch the next day. We were sitting at a long oval-shaped table, Jacky and me and about umpteen grown-ups and kids, out on what they called the dining porch. In front of us were these big yellow bowls of chicken-corn soup—really more like a chicken and corn and dumpling stew (Mrs. Spicer said they always ate a lot of corn in the summer)—and besides that there was sour-cream cabbage slaw, and sliced tomatoes in vinegar and sugar, and fresh-baked rolls, and—set out in these special little scallop-edged serving dishes— home-canned apple butter and molasses. It was great. Everything about that place made you feel terrific, it really did.

What happened was that after lunch that day Mrs. Spicer took Jacky along to help her pick some peaches, and, well, Major Spicer and me didn't even hear them when they got back. There were always people going in and out anyway, and we were upstairs way over on the other side of the house in the Major's personal study. I liked

Major Spicer, and it's true he reminded me a little bit of Daddy. But I don't think I could ever really confuse the two of them, at least not the way the Major mixed me up with the girl in the picture. He was showing me through this big album of photographs at the time. Lots of old black-and-white pictures, starting with ones of his family and then going on to what he called his overseas tours in the military—this one I particularly remember of him standing in a flat bright place with his hands behind his back and wearing one of those helmets like Ramar of the jungle. That was in North Africa during the war, he told me. The album was a kind of personal scrapbook. There was a dim, brownish one near the beginning of his mother and father— her standing in an ankle-length dress near the spout of an old hand pump, an arm held up to shade her eyes as if what she was looking at was too bright for her to look at straight-on—him standing beside the pump handle in a three-piece suit, one foot forward and a hand stuck into the arm hole of his vest like he's about to make a speech on the Fourth of July. There was page after page of newspaper clippings about Major Spicer from the sports pages and large group-portrait shots where he was a member of some team or other. In a specially clear one he was sitting at the center of the first row of his hometown baseball team holding a bat. Everyone had on a striped shirt and knee-socks, and they were all arranged on the seats of a wooden bleacher. To the sides and behind them you could see the trunks of trees, the tiny little crooked lines in the bark focused so sharp the trees took your attention almost as much as the faces. When Jacky walked in, we'd been looking at a photograph of a girl sitting in a tree swing. She had on a long white dress and was sitting sort of sideways, leaning against the rope so one knee rose up against her skirt. Her arms were stretched kind of lazy-like across her lap, a branch of wild flowers in one hand, maybe blue chicory or ironweed or some kind of aster, the stalk dangling so a blossom almost touched the ground. Her hair caught the light and was held back from her face by a wide, dark ribbon. This was someone I reminded him of, that's what he was telling me, someone he knew when he was still in school, before he joined the Army, way back before the war. And she really did look like me, she could have been my old-fashioned double. Her name was Audrey Cavanagh, his first love, so ethereal, he said, like a little faun, and she was built like you, he said, a fine round bottom for such a narrow girl, and his hand moves from my waist where he's been occasionally touching me to help direct my attention to some particular photograph, him seated in the swivel chair, me standing there beside the desk, and he slides his hand down over my rear end just like that, like he's sculpting clay. And I still don't move, not even when after a while his hand strokes up the inside of my leg and I feel his finger and thumb slip up inside my shorts—I was wearing those loose khaki ones with the wide cuffs and the big pockets. I put one hand on his shoulder like I was trying to keep my balance, that's all I did. He was touching me so lightly I almost had to push against him to be sure he was there. Him talking all the time, and me still listening—as if the other thing with his hand is happening to somebody else. One minute he's talking to the girl in the photograph, saying things like, "Ah, Audrey, you're still as lovely as an angel, perched there in your swing," and the next minute it's as if he's talking to me, calling me by her name and at the same time feeling me up like it's open season on ducks or something. The way the desk was facing out a window meant we had our backs to the door, which also must have been unlatched, because neither one of us even heard it when Jacky came in. There's no telling how long he'd been standing there watching us, but long enough I guess. I bet we made a pretty picture from over by the doorway. It wasn't until the Major turned so he could nuzzle up against my chest that we saw Jack. He's just standing there pop-eyed in the door-way, like he's suddenly re-membered something important he forgot to do. You almost expected him to snap his fingers. We were all frozen that way for a second, caught in this burst of something, not light but almost as bright and quick as when a flashbulb goes off. And then every-thing picks up again all of a sudden right where it left off, and there's voices and sounds again and everybody's moving in different directions. Me, I've got myself backed up against this big globe of the world on a wooden stand right there beside the desk. The globe was so big it came up to my waist, and I had my hands behind me holding onto it. I'm spinning it slowly, feeling the relief map of the mountain ranges slide by beneath my fingers, and I'm thinking, almost like a joke: even if part of me *is* in the United States of America, the other part of me is probably over in China somewhere, all the way over on the other side of the world.

What happened next was, one of the married daughters—everybody called her Sissy—I think her married name was Northman or Newman or something like that, she was little Wendell's mother but she'd left her husband just a couple weeks before, it was a big family scandal at the moment—anyway, Sissy comes waltzing in right behind Jacky and she must have bumped up against him or something because both of them jumped like they'd been hit by electricity. When Jacky jumped, it startled me so I pushed the globe right out of its socket and it bounces once and then rolls over across the floor to-ward where the Major'd come to a halt after he'd left his chair. All of us are looking at this big colored globe of the world, blue and green and brown and yellow, and the Major bends down and lifts it up off the floor with both hands to see if any damage has been done. "Is it okay?" I ask. I feel like I have to say *something*, so I say, "I didn't know it could slip out like that." "Just a slight dent, hardly noticeable," says the Major. "Right smack in the middle of Greenland. Nothing there anyway." Jacky looks up at him and smiles, just as cool, as if butter wouldn't melt in his mouth. "You can probably get it to pop out again if you just apply a little heat," he says. "Like holding a match to a ping-pong ball." Sissy laughs and says in a little-girl voice, "Will Daddy kiss the world and make it all better?" And the rest of us laughed too. Ha, ha, ha. Everything seemed like it was just hanging there again for a second, and then Sissy says, "It's so hot, I sent Buddy up to bring down one of your picture puzzles, preferably a snowy Currier and Ives. We're going to take it out on the east porch and try to cool off a little. Then I remembered Mama put all those old puzzles up in the attic. Sorry to barge in and startle everybody. My, it's warm in here, isn't it? Daddy, you ought to turn on the window fan if you're going to spend any time up here. Peggy Sue?" she says to me, "you look like you could use something with ice in it." So Jacky went first and then Sissy followed me and him out the door, and we left the Major still standing there holding his globe in his arms. The way he was holding it made the world look like a big Buddha's belly. The little dent where Greenland was could've been its navel.

So Jacky and me never really had a chance to talk right then. Sissy sent him up to the attic for a jigsaw puzzle and then she says to me, "How would you like some good old country lemonade?" and grabs my hand, and the next thing I know the three of us are out on the porch on the shady side of the house sipping ice-cold lemonade through straws. There's a big cut-glass pitcher all fogged-up and sweaty sitting beside us, and we're scattering out the cardboard pieces of the puzzle on a folding table, each piece glazed and colored on one side and dull pink on the other. We're trying to separate all the edge pieces first, looking for straight lines against all the knobs and sockets of the regular pieces. Because of how we're sitting, I'm working on a side edge, Sissy's working on the snow-covered bottom part, and Jacky's got all the blue pieces of sky. The picture's called "An American Homestead Winter," and there's lots of white, but there's other colors too: a few reds and lots of greens and browns and yellows, and about a million different tones of grayish-blue shadow. The picture on the cover of the box shows these sort of waxy-looking people going about their chores, gathering wood, carrying a bucket, feeding cows and ducks in the snow. A brown dog that looks a lot like old Bertha, but younger, is prancing along beside the man carrying the kindling, and to his right there's a red horse-drawn sleigh with a man in a blue coat holding the reins, and next to him a lady, probably his wife, with some kind of a pink bonnet tied under her chin. They're passing a farmhouse set on a low hill by the road. It reminded me of the Spicers' house a little bit. I was thinking it looked like their house might look after a snowfall. I'm concentrating as hard as I can on the puzzle so I won't have to think about the other stuff. I'm looking for pieces of twisty brown forest with a straight edge on one side. I don't even glance over at Jacky because I'm not ready to meet his eyes yet, I'm not sure how he expects me to act. But what the heck, nothing much really happened. And why should *I* be embarrassed? I didn't do anything. That's what I think, but there's no telling what Jacky thinks, which is what always throws me off. But we're all working on the puzzle so we don't really get a chance to look at each other much anyway. Instead, we're looking back and forth from the picture on the box to the skinny sections of connected puzzle pieces in front of us. It's like we're working on three different puzzles instead of one big one. OVER FIVE HUNDRED PIECES, it says on the box, SCROLL-CUT AND INTERLOCKING. "So I see Daddy's been showing you his trophies," Sissy says to me. "That's a sure sign of favor—if you can sit through it. There!" she says, pushing a piece of shadowy snow into one of her little sections. "A corner! Now we're starting to get somewhere. All we need is the corner on your side, Peggy Sue, and we'll have almost half the frame! Buddy, I hate to say anything, but your sky appears to be upside down." "Hah!" Jacky snorts. "From where I'm sitting it's everything else that's upside down." Sissy laughs like she's been taken by surprise. "You're absolutely right," she says, "Everything *is* relative." She's got on glasses with turquoise frames, and she points a finger between her eyebrows to push them back up her nose. Her hair's so brown it's almost black and it's cut short and curly. She reminds me a little of Audrey Hepburn—real thin-boned and aristocratic-looking. She must be distracted about something though because she lights a new cigarette before the last one's finished burning. When she exhales, her nostrils flare out, and then she reaches up and picks a fleck of tobacco off her tongue. "Well, it's almost Wedding Day Eve! You love birds must feel like you've got the world on a string, sittin' on a rainbow—isn't that the way the song goes?" She moves a piece of puzzle around and when she can't find a fit tosses it back onto her little pile. "I bet you can't wait to get into Maryland and tie the knot that binds, right? Make it official in the eyes of God, man, and the PTA." Jacky just laughs and says, "It'll probably take a couple of days once we get to Maryland to get a license and everything." "Well," she says, "I wish you all the luck. At your stage, it's all bill-and-coo and rub-a-dub-dub. Believe me, I know all about it, and I say enjoy it while it lasts. Seize the day. Just don't take all that hot britches stuff too seriously. I'm not saying this to shock you, but—look take my advice and go to a good drugstore instead of a justice of the peace. Go ahead and have all the fun you want—just don't get married unless you absolutely have to." She's found a piece that fits and she taps it in with a clear-polished fingernail. Her nails aren't long but they're so perfect they make me curl my fingers.

My own nails are pretty raggedy-looking, even though I've been trying to only chew them when they need trimming. Her fingers have yellow tobacco stains though. She'll forget she's holding a cigarette and it'll burn right down to the skin. "What makes you think we've got such 'hot britches?'" Jacky asks. He's got his elbow on his knee and his chin in his hand and he's looking up at Sissy like she's the light at the end of the tunnel. "I mean, why do you think that?" Over across the yard we can hear some kids playing guns in the woods. "Pa'*dow*! Pa'*dow*!" one of them yells. "I *gotcha*" "You did *not*!" "I did *so*!" Sissy gives her surprised laugh and raises her glasses to the top of her head so she can look at Jacky eye to eye. "Because, as my mother always says—and what higher authority can there be?—'when peaches get ripe they fall off the tree.'" She raises her eyebrows and nods her head in a quick gesture she uses a lot—it's like her mother's "Amen." "I'm not saying you're wrong," Jacky smiles. "In fact, I'd have to say you're probably right, but is that just a generalization or are you talking about me and Peggy Sue in particular?" "Well, if the shoe fits . . .," Sissy smiles back, ". . . it might as well be yours—no?" She lowers her glasses again and looks down at the puzzle. "Peggy Sue, what do you think?" she asks. "Does the shoe fit?" "I guess it both does and doesn't," I say. I'm a regular little diplomat. "I'm not exactly sure what shoe you're talking about," I say, "but it probably doesn't fit as good as this," and I push another piece into a string of about ten or twelve that was my main section of edge, twice as long as any of theirs. Sissy falls back into her rocking chair and takes a drag on her cigarette. "Don't be too sure," she says. She rests her elbow on the arm of her chair and touches the tip of her cigarette to the tip of her thumb, and as she breathes out smoke she just openly sizes Jacky up—the way somebody might look at something they wanted to draw. "I just meant that you're, you know, young and healthy and in love, and there's bound to be a certain, let's say . . . physical attraction, *n'est-ce pas?*"[1] Jacky doesn't say anything for a second. They're both just staring at each other. I mean I almost felt like a third wheel. "Is that how it was with you and your husband?" Jacky finally says. "But of course!" laughs Sissy. "That part was sheer bliss. At least it was at first. But as it turned out, we really didn't have much else in common. When the other wore out, there wasn't a hell of a whole lot left." "The other?" Jacky asks. I can sense Sissy smiling at him more than I can actually see her. "Hot britches," she says: "Rub-a-dub-dub." And she wags her cigarette back and forth with her thumb. "Uh-huh, uh-huh," Jacky says, nodding his head. I'm still working quietly away on my pile of edges when Sissy suddenly sits up straight and reaches for her lemonade. She rattles the ice, then purses her lips to the straw and sips the lemonade down until it sputters in the ice cubes like a little motor. She's got her eyes back on the puzzle now, and she says, "Look at Peggy Sue! She's found the other corner!" Then, after studying her own sections of white bottom pieces for a minute, she taps a piece with the pink nail of her middle finger and says, "If this fits that, I think we can join sides." She places it real gently and pushes it in. "Yes! Perfect fit! How's that? Now we've got the bottom and one side—all we need is Buddy's blue sky and we're halfway home!"

I don't know where the Major was. Maybe he was still in his study, staring at Greenland. The three of us sat there working on the puzzle all afternoon and at one time or another almost everybody else in the family stopped by to put in a couple of pieces, but we never saw hide nor hair of the Major. We worked on the puzzle until it was

---

[1]*n'cest-ce pas?* French: is it not?

almost suppertime. There were lightning bugs under the trees across the lawn by then, and it was getting hard to see. We could have turned on a lamp I guess, but nobody thought to. All we had left to fill in was some of the snow and a section of the sky. Except for that, the picture was almost done. It could have been either a sundown or a daybreak scene because there was a lot of pink in the sky, along with the blue. I tried to figure out which it was, morning or evening, but you couldn't really tell. It probably didn't matter. When I asked Sissy what she thought, she said, "Who knows? Maybe it's one of those long winter twilights that last all day. You know the kind I mean? Mmmmm . . . days like that always make me feel so romantic." She arches her back like one of the cats stretching and then suddenly widens her eyes and laughs. "Don't misunderstand," she says. "I only mean days like that make me want to curl up on a davenport somewhere next to a crackling fire with a pot of steaming tea and a good, long novel—something Victorian maybe—although, come to think of it, there's not a wisp of smoke coming from any of these chimneys . . . I wonder why." "Where there's no smoke, there's no fire," Jacky says, whatever that's supposed to mean, and we're all three sitting there in the dark giggling like idiots when Mrs. Spicer calls through the window screen: "Supper's near about ready, Sissy, if you fellows want to wash your hands." "Thanks, Mama," Sissy says, and then she looks across the table at Jacky and me, raises her glasses to the top of her head, and grins. "Oh, *screw*," she says in a way that sounds really sexy. "It looks like we won't get to finish what we started. And we came so close too." Nobody says anything for a second. Jacky leans back from the table, and right at that instant the crickets started up, like a ringing in your ears. It was a real warm evening. The stars were coming out and the sky was a thick, deep purple. There wasn't a breeze to be had, and the skin under my leg kept sticking to the cane seat of my chair. Through the window we can hear people moving around inside, chairs scraping against the floor, a drawer opening and then the sound of silverware. "Mom?" somebody's calling. "Where *are* you? Ma-a-um!" Sissy sighs and says, "Well, it was nice while it lasted, wasn't it?" Then she calls inside, "Here, lover, mother's out here, just a sec." She turns back to us and says, "He probably fell in the creek. He's always getting his feet wet. From wet diapers to wet sneakers," and she laughs. "You'll find out, Peggy Sue. You'll be me before you know it." Right then, click, a lamp goes on inside the window and some of the light spills out onto the card table. Except for where the table shows black through the unfilled holes, the light makes the glazed surface of the picture puzzle shine so that the snow looks almost real.

When we went in to supper, there was the Major sitting at the head of the table just as if nothing had ever happened at all. He's smiling that same crinkly smile and sniffing at the ham roast like he's posing for the cover of the *Saturday Evening Post*. Real wholesome and homey. When he said grace, he ended the prayer with: "And thank You too, Lord, for the sweet gift of love that is so deeply impressed, by Thy will, in the bosom of each and every one of Thy children . . . In Christ's name, Amen." I mean you had to hand it to the guy. And Jacky and me are playing right along—except Jacky's voice gets this little edge sometimes. He'll say stuff that means one thing to him and me and Sissy, another thing to him and me and the Major, and something else entirely to everybody else. Like when we had fresh sliced peaches with sugar and cream for dessert, and Jacky says, "Peaches may fall off the tree when they're ripe enough, but we picked these, didn't we, Mrs. Spicer? Sissy, how do yours taste? How about yours, Major? Ripe enough?" I think Jacky might have made him nervous, because right after supper the Major offered to take everybody into town to see *Ben-Hur*, which they'd all been dying to see for weeks, I guess. Me and Jacky'd already seen it twice, so when it looks like Sissy's going to have to stay home with little Wendell, Jacky volunteers us to babysit. "We'd just like to repay some of the hospitality we've been shown," he says. "Goodness, what a young gentleman!" says Mrs. Spicer. So Sissy got to go to the movies with the rest, and we ended up having to put Wendell and his little friend William to bed. William had gotten permission to stay over and keep Wendell company. Anyway, it wasn't until they finally fell asleep after a last drink of water and a Peter Pan storybook and a pillow fight that Jacky and me had a chance to be alone. And I could see right away he didn't want to talk about me and the Major at all. Instead, he looks up and says, "Want to see something neat?" We're sitting at the kitchen table eating a second helping of peaches and cream, which we'd brought out of the refrigerator as soon as we knew the coast was clear. "Sure . . . like what?" I say. "Like follow me, I'll show you," Jacky says. We drop our plates into the soapy water in the sink, and Jacky grabs a long red flashlight from a shelf near the back door. I figure we're going outside and I start to turn the knob, but Jacky shakes his head and says, "This way, little sister, this way." I didn't like him calling me that, but I followed him anyway. We went out the kitchen to the hallway and then up the front stairs to the second floor. We're tiptoeing past the door to the sleeping porch where the kids are and Jacky's got the flashlight in one hand and he puts a finger to his lips with the other, and I suddenly felt like we were robbers. I got a sort of butterflies feeling like I had to go to the bathroom. We're passing another door when Jacky stops, turns, and pushes it open. It's a lady's bedroom, you could tell just by the way it smelled. "I think Sissy sleeps in here. Want to look around?" he says. "Is this what you wanted to show me?" I asked. "What's so neat about this?" "Shhh!" he whispers. "Keep your pants on." Then instead of turning on a lamp, he switches on the flashlight and shines it around the room. The beam of light was almost like something solid, like a stick that Jack could poke around with. He pokes it over some stuff on the night table—a crocheted doily, an empty glass, a Kleenex box with a white tissue puffed out part way through the opening—pokes it on over to the bunched-up pillows against the headboard, then on down the bed itself—which has a purply patchwork comforter that looks like somebody's been laying on it—on down across the floor to a little pile of clothes near the dresser. On top are the navy blue shorts Sissy was wearing earlier—inside-out now with the pocket linings showing—and a pair of pearl-colored panties. "What are we doing?" I asked. "Just looking," Jacky says. "Well, I'm getting out of here," I told him. Sissy'd been nice to us and I didn't like nosing around in her room that way. So I turned around and walked out, and after another second here comes Jacky too. "Okay, let's go," he says, switching off the flashlight and pulling the door closed to where it was.

I have no idea what's on his mind at this point. I'm just hoping he doesn't want to steal anything. Our money was getting low and I was wondering how we planned to get some more—which I still am wondering in fact. But Jacky walks on down the hall and doesn't stop at any more bedrooms. Instead he takes me around a turn at the end of the hallway and we immediately come to a dead end at this closed door. The turn in the hall is really just a little nook with the door tucked in it. Jacky turns the knob and sweeps out his arm in this sort of cramped imitation of Reginald Van Gleason[2] the Third ushering me into some fabulous mansion. All I can see is a staircase going

---

[2]*Reginald Van Gleason*   One of Jackie Gleason's personas on his 1950s TV show.

up. It's like a tunnel, no wider than the door, and it's real steep. The stairs are made out of unfinished boards, so rough they look almost fuzzy, and they march up one after another into the dark. When Jacky points the flashlight, I can see ceiling rafters through the opening at the top of the stairway but that's all. While I'm poking my head through the door, Jacky leans over and—real quiet but right in my eardrum—says, "The *Shadow* kno-o-ows," and then he does this spooky laugh. Eeyow, it gave me the creeps, and I didn't want to go nosing around in anybody's attic with a flashlight anyway—there'd probably be spiderwebs all over the place up there and who knew what all else, maybe even bats for all I knew. Even down there in the doorway I could smell the dust, and something else too, like the insides of certain old books, or like the woods. It was a smell that had layers to it, the way it might be if the smells of a whole lot of different rooms were piled all into one another. "Come on, Jill," Jacky says. He puts his hand on my arm and points the flashlight: "Look!" he says. "There's the signpost up ahead! Your next stop—The Twilight Zone!" He's got Rod Serling's voice down pat, and I'm laughing now, ready to go up and take a look. The spookiness isn't real anymore, it's like being inside a fun house now, and while we're climbing the stairs Jacky's doing his Mr. Magoo voice, saying stuff like, "Eh-eh-eh . . . yes, by Gad, the old homestead . . . I'd recognize it anywhere . . . chuckle-chuckle-chuckle" and I'm just laughing away, not even thinking about the stuff with the Major or anything else now. When we come up the stairs through the opening at the top, our eyes are at floor level, and from this angle especially the attic is pitch-black. We can only see where the flashlight makes a hole in the dark. There's a lot we can't see. Things just pop into sight wherever Jack happens to shine the flashlight. It's like he's showing his own movie with that light and also following along wherever it takes us. He's shining it around like he can lick up everything he sees with it or like he's pouring all this stuff out of the flashlight itself instead of finding what's already there.

From what I could tell, it was just an ordinary attic, but bigger and more crowded with junk—old bicycle wheels hanging from the rafters and all different kinds of chairs, stacks of *Life* magazines and *National Geographics*, wooden chests and mirrors and a huge bamboo birdcage in a metal hoop at the top of its own floor stand. "Can you believe this place?" Jacky says. "Isn't this incredible? When I was up here this afternoon I couldn't believe it. They must've been storing stuff up here since before the flood!" He's really revved up about it, and I can see what he means. I've never been in any place quite like it in my life, not really. It seemed like an ordinary attic at first just because it looked exactly the way I'd always pictured an attic *would* look, without ever really thinking about it or anything. Jacky moves his searchlight in a circle around the room and we can see the junk piled everywhere, with little aisles winding through it all, like paths in the woods, leading off to other sections of the attic we can't even begin to see from here. Piles of books and boxes, green steamer trunks with white stenciling and half a dozen tennis rackets, a pair of black rubber hip boots and a straw fishing reel hung up by a leather strap next to an old-fashioned baby buggy with a sun canopy and big, spoked wheels. Stuff even crowding into where the eaves of the roof come down close to the floor and make low little passageways and crawl spaces around the edges of the room. I bet we weren't up there more than a minute when we heard a sort of low stomach rumble of thunder. For a split second, the little half-moon windows in the gables of the attic all lit up like jack-o'-lanterns and almost at the same instant there's a giant crash of thunder that makes the whole attic sort of shake and creak and jingle. "Too much!" Jacky says. "What a great place for a ghost story!" He's whispering and probably doesn't even realize it. The windows light up again right then and there's another clap of thunder and then suddenly it's raining, the sound of it loud and steady, drumming on the roof right over our heads. We can hear it whishing against the sides of the house and gurgling down the drainpipes—a lot of little sounds that melt into one big one. Funny thing is, instead of making it spookier, the rain makes the attic seem all protected and snug, like someplace where it's always King's-X and bad things can't happen. "What if everything you ever had all ended up in one place?" Jacky says. "Like you could find anything you'd ever lost up here no matter where you lost it." "Yeah," I said, "that'd be neat. What'd you look for first?" "No, you don't get it," he says, "I mean you'd never even *need* to look for anything because it'd all be there already, like your whole life, all in one place, not spread out everywhere. That would be you—everything that was part of you all together." Jacky can go on like that all night, talking about some dumb theory or other, like the one about the galaxies expanding. Sometimes you think he's got to be kidding and it turns out he's dead serious. So Jacky's talking away and we're moving into some deeper part of the attic, almost like another room that the main one opens up into, when suddenly I see somebody standing there against the wall. It was like having the breath knocked out of you. I couldn't even scream, I just grabbed Jacky's arm and pointed, and when he shined the light over we saw it was only one of those sewing dummies in the shape of a woman. Whoever it was had a good figure too, maybe as nice as yours, Mom—and it was sort of like seeing them naked. That might sound weird but it's true. It could've been Mrs. Spicer before she got fat. Looking at it gave me almost the same feeling of spying I had in Sissy's bedroom. Jacky couldn't take his eyes off it. "Well, what have we here?" he says. He goes over and sets the flashlight down on top of a shelf so he's got his hands free, then he comes up to the dummy and cups his palms over the dummy's breasts. "Oh, baby," he moans. He puts his hands around its rear end and pulls the dummy up against him and starts humping away like he's a dog going at your leg. Then he says to me, "What if this was Sissy? Oh, man! Wouldn't that be something! . . . Just like you and the Major." Finally, I thought, here it comes. I was beginning to wonder if he'd seen anything or not. "Why'd you let him do it?" Jacky says. "Did you like it?" I didn't know what to answer, so for a second I just listened to the rain drumming on the roof. If this was winter, I was thinking, the rain would be snow and in the morning everything would look shiny and white, just like the picture on the jigsaw puzzle. Jacky turns away from the dummy and I'm thinking he's going to ask me again and I won't be able to avoid it forever, but instead he says, "What if I did that to Sissy. Do you think she'd like it?" I'm standing next to something soft, and when Jacky shines the light over at me I see it's an old daybed with piles of woolen coats and old uniforms and stuff on it. "I guess so," I tell him. "I think she might have a crush on you." I figure if I can keep on his good side about Sissy he won't want to talk about me. "Yeah?" he says. "Would you let me if you were Sissy?" "Sure," I said. "What would it be like?" he says—then, "Let's pretend you're Sissy and I'm me, like when you taught me how to slow-dance. Show me," he says. And he puts the flashlight down on some kind of old hope chest so the light makes our shadows real long—they go all the way across the floor and halfway up the opposite wall, like giants. Jacky comes up until he's standing right next to me and he reaches up and touches his fingers to my breast, real soft. I wasn't really, you know, excited or anything like that, but my breast started to get all tingly, and I guess he could feel the tip of it perk up, because he looks at me funny and says, "That's it, isn't it? . . . does that feel good?" I sort of gulped and nodded and he kept on doing it and then in a few minutes he started kissing me and putting his tongue in my mouth, and I swear that's about the time I knew I was lost. But then he stops all of a sudden and reaches in his pocket. I thought he was only trying to straighten himself out down there—I mean I could feel how stretched he was and how tight his jeans must be, but instead he pulls something out of his pocket and holds it over to the light. It's the pair of panties we saw in Sissy's bedroom. I couldn't believe it. "Would you put these on?" he says. "Oh, man, that'd really be something." I was getting excited too by then, and I bet I never really do put this part in my letter, but I loved the way it felt to get *Jacky* so excited. I mean when he saw me in those panties he starts moaning an groaning and then he's got his hands all over me and he pushes me down onto the pile of coats. I could feel a button on one of the uniforms poking up against my back. By now Jacky's pants are down and he's got my legs apart, and then, just like that, we're actually doing it. It hurt like anything at first, but pretty soon I got sort of numb and it was okay. The whole time, I could smell wool and I could hear these springs somewhere under us squeaking like little birds in a shrub tree. Compared to that, the sound of the rain seemed to come from real far off. It all happened so fast, but it seemed to take a long time too. I was thinking how much I loved Jacky and how good it felt to have him so close inside me, wanting me so much, when I hear him whispering in my ear, "Sissy," he's saying. "Oh, God, Sissy, you just love it . . . you just love it. . . ." *Sissy, Sissy*, he kept calling me, over and over again—until after a while I started to cry, I couldn't help it, and pretty soon the tears were coming like they might never stop.

The next morning we hugged everybody good-bye—everybody except the Major, that is, who never touched me again, not once after that one time—and we promised to write, and then Major Spicer and this old Army buddy of his drove us to Hagerstown and left us off at a Howard Johnson's motel. That was a couple of days ago and now we're in this falling-down old mansion I told you about—in Delaware or Maryland or maybe even Virginia. It's hard to tell exactly what state you're in around here, but we're right next to the ocean. The sound of the surf comes and goes just like somebody breathing. So now I keep thinking, maybe I really *am* pregnant. Can that happen between brothers and sisters, between twins? Or if it can, do you have to do it more than once? Because we only did it that one time, and since then we never even mention it and Jacky's gotten so he's real self-conscious about any kind of touching at all. It seems like we might as well be strangers—that's the worst part about the whole thing. I guess if I don't get my period that'll mean I'm probably pregnant. We'll just have to wait and see, right? If I *am* pregnant though, then maybe we can finally stop this wild-goose chase after Daddy and turn around. Sometimes I almost wish I *was* pregnant, because I'd really love to come home. Where we are now, there's always this fishy salt smell in the air. It'll go away but then it'll come back and you'll notice it again. Sometimes it smells great and other times it smells just like garbage. The ocean makes a steady whishing sound like rain against the rocks on the other side of the stone wall across the road. Jacky's out there somewhere trying to catch a bluefish. There's a lot of tall grass around here that looks like wheat. The feathery tips are a silver color, and I spend a lot of time just sitting here watching the way the wind ripples through them like they were made out of water.

[1986]

Questions

1. How far are we supposed to take the parallels between "Tumbling" and the "Jack and Jill" nursery rhyme? Does Moyer imply some kind of archetypal enactment of basic human patterns of action, or do the parallels between the two tales suggest something quite different?

2. When Moyer refers to "the masculine Oedipal scenario" in reference to Jill's tumble, does he imply that the primary theme of the story is her search for her father? If that is so, why is the entire story addressed to her mother?

3. Why is so much detail devoted to the description of Major and Mrs. Spicer's household? Why is the setting of the final scene (the attic) equally detailed? Why is so much detail given over to the Currier and Ives jigsaw puzzle?

4. Jill seems content to accept her brother's decisions for their journey in search of their father. Is the reader equally trusting of Jack's authority?

Es'kia Mphahlele
(b. 1919)
South Africa

E s'kia Mphahlele has been such a force in South African literature for so many years that he is often referred to as the "Dean of African Letters." He was one of the founding editors and writers of the South African literary journal Drum (1950). It is impossible to think of life under apartheid without considering Mphahlele's autobiography, Down Second Avenue (1959). That book and other early works by the writer were banned in South Africa, and Mphahlele was forced into exile for many years. His pioneer volume, The African Image (1962), codified black artistry from an African perspective at a time when most commentaries were Western. In the stories, novels, and critical works that have followed, Dr. Mphahlele (he has a Ph.D. in English from the University of Denver) has widened our perspective of life in South Africa and explained the black aesthetic in such a manner as to make African writing accessible to the Western reader. More recently, his collected stories have been published in a volume called Renewal Time (1989).

Writing in The African Image about the emergence of the Drum writers of the 1950s, Dr. Mphahlele had this to say:

> These South African writers are fashioning an urban literature on terms that are unacceptable to the white ruling class. They are detribalized or Coloured (of mixed blood), not accepted as an integral part of the country's culture (a culture in a chaotic state). But, like every other non-white, they keep on, digging their feet into an urban culture of their own making. This is a fugitive culture: borrowing here, incorporating there, retaining this, rejecting that. But it is a virile culture. The clamour of it is going to keep beating on the walls surrounding the already fragmented culture of the whites until they crumble.

MRS. PLUM

I

My madam's name was Mrs. Plum. She loved dogs and Africans and said that everyone must follow the law even if it hurt. These were three big things in Madam's life.

I came to work for Mrs. Plum in Greenside, not very far from the centre of Johannesburg, after leaving two white families. The first white people I worked for as a cook and laundry woman were a man and his wife in Parktown North. They drank too much and always forgot to pay me. After five months I said to myself No. I am going to leave these drunks. So that was it. That day I was as angry as a red-hot iron when it meets water. The second house I cooked and washed for had five children who were badly brought up. This was in Belgravia. Many times they called me You Black

632

Girl and I kept quiet. Because their mother heard them and said nothing. Also I was only new from Phokeng my home, far away near Rustenburg, I wanted to learn and know the white people before I knew how far to go with the others I would work for afterwards. The thing that drove me mad and made me pack and go was a man who came to visit them often. They said he was cousin or something like that. He came to the kitchen many times and tried to make me laugh. He patted me on the buttocks. I told the master. The man did it again and I asked the madam that very day to give me my money and let me go.

These were the first nine months after I had left Phokeng to work in Johannesburg. There were many of us girls and young women from Phokeng, from Zeerust, from Shuping, from Kosten, and many other places who came to work in the cities. So the suburbs were full of blackness. Most of us had already passed Standard Six and so we learned more English where we worked. None of us liked to work for white farmers, because we know too much about them on the farms near our homes. They do not pay well and they are cruel people.

At Easter time so many of us went home for a long weekend to see our people and to eat chicken and sour milk and *morogo*—wild spinach. We also took home sugar and condensed milk and tea and coffee and sweets and custard powder and tinned foods.

It was a home-girl of mine, Chimane, who called me to take a job in Mrs. Plum's house, just next door to where she worked. This is the third year now. I have been quite happy with Mrs. Plum and her daughter Kate. By this I mean that my place as a servant in Greenside is not as bad as that of many others. Chimane too does not complain much. We are paid six pounds a month with free food and free servant's room. No one can ever say that they are well paid, so we go on complaining somehow. Whenever we meet on Thursday afternoons, which is time off for all of us black women in the suburbs, we talk and talk and talk: about our people at home and their letters; about their illnesses; about bad crops; about a sister who wanted a school uniform and books and school fees; about some of our madams and masters who are good, or stingy with money or food, or stupid, or full of nonsense, or who kill themselves and each other, or who are dirty—and so many things I cannot count them all.

Thursday afternoons we go to town to look at the shops, to attend a woman's club, to see our boy friends, to go to bioscope some of us. We turn up smart, to show others the clothes we bought from the black men who sell soft goods to servants in the suburbs. We take a number of things and they come round every month for a bit of money until we finish paying. Then we dress the way of many white madams and girls. I think we look really smart. Sometimes we catch the eyes of a white woman looking at us and we laugh and laugh until we nearly drop on the ground because we feel good inside ourselves.

II

What did the girl next door call you? Mrs. Plum asked me the first day I came to her. Jane, I replied. Was there not an African name? I said yes, Karabo. All right, Madam said. We'll call you Karabo, she said. She spoke as if she knew a name is a big thing. I knew so many whites who did not care what they called black people as long as it was all right for their tongue. This pleased me, I mean Mrs. Plum's use of *Karabo*; because the only time I heard the name was when I was home or when my friends spoke to me. Then she showed me what to do: meals, meal times, washing, and where all the things were that I was going to use.

My daughter will be here in the evening, Madam said. She is at school. When the daughter came, she added, she would tell me some of the things she wanted me to do for her every day.

Chimane, my friend next door, had told me about the daughter Kate, how wild she seemed to be, and about Mr. Plum who had killed himself with a gun in a house down the street. They had left the house and come to this one.

Madam is a tall woman. Not slender, not fat. She moves slowly, and speaks slowly. Her face looks very wise, her forehead seems to tell me she has a strong liver: she is not afraid of anything. Her eyes are always swollen at the lower eyelids like a white person who has not slept for many many nights or like a large frog. Perhaps it is because she smokes too much, like wet wood that will not know whether to go up in flames or stop burning. She looks me straight in the eyes when she talks to me, and I know she does this with other people too. At first this made me fear her, now I am used to her. She is not a lazy woman, and she does many things outside, in the city and in the suburbs.

This was the first thing her daughter Kate told me when she came and we met. Don't mind mother, Kate told me. She said, She is sometimes mad with people for very small things. She will soon be all right and speak nicely to you again.

Kate, I like her very much, and she likes me too. She tells me many things a white woman does not tell a black servant. I mean things about what she likes and does not like, what her mother does or does not do, all these. At first I was unhappy and wanted to stop her, but now I do not mind.

Kate looks very much like her mother in the face. I think her shoulders will be just as round and strong-looking. She moves faster than Madam. I asked her why she was still at school when she was so big. She laughed. Then she tried to tell me that the school where she was was for big people, who had finished with lower school. She was learning big things about cooking and food. She can explain better, me I cannot. She came home on weekends.

Since I came to work for Mrs. Plum Kate has been teaching me plenty of cooking. I first learned from her and Madam the word *recipes*. When Kate was at the big school, Madam taught me how to read cookery books. I went on very slowly at first, slower than an ox-wagon. Now I know more. When Kate came home, she found I had read the recipe she left me. So we just cooked straight-away. Kate thinks I am fit to cook in a hotel. Madam thinks so too. Never never! I thought. Cooking in a hotel is like feeding oxen. No one can say thank you to you. After a few months I could cook the Sunday lunch and later I could cook specials for Madam's or Kate's guests.

Madam did not only teach me cooking. She taught me how to look after guests. She praised me when I did very very well; not like the white people I had worked for before. I do not know what runs crooked in the heads of other people. Madam also had classes in the evenings for servants to teach them how to read and write. She and two other women in Greenside taught in a church hall.

As I say, Kate tells me plenty of things about Madam. She says to me she says, My mother goes to meetings many times. I ask her I say, What for? She says to me she says, For your people. I ask her I say, My people are in Phokeng far away. They have got mouths, I say. Why does she want to say something for them? Does she know what my mother and what my father want to say? They can speak when they want to. Kate raises her shoulders and drops them and says, How can I tell you Karabo? I don't say your people—your family only. I mean all the black people in the country. I say Oh! What do the black people want to say? Again she raises her shoulders and drops them, taking a deep breath.

I ask her I say, With whom is she in the meeting?

She says, With other people who think like her.

I ask her I say, Do you say there are people in the world who think the same things? She nods her head.

I ask, What things?

So that a few of your people should one day be among those who rule this country, get more money for what they do for the white man, and—what did Kate say again? Yes, that Madam and those who think like her also wanted my people who have been to school to choose those who must speak for them in the—I think she said it looks like a *Kgotla* at home who rule the villages.

I say to Kate I say, Oh I see now. I say, Tell me Kate why is Madam always writing on the machine, all the time everyday nearly?

She replies she says, Oh my mother is writing books.

I ask, You mean a book like those?—pointing at the books on the shelves.

Yes, Kate says.

And she told me how Madam wrote books and other things for newspapers and she wrote for the newspapers and magazines to say things for the black people who should be treated well, be paid more money, for the black people who can read and write many things to choose those who want to speak for them.

Kate also told me she said, My mother and other women who think like her put on black belts over their shoulders when they are sad and they want to show the white government they do not like the things being done by whites to blacks. My mother and the others go and stand where the people in government are going to enter or go out of a building.

I ask her I say, Does the government and the white people listen and stop their sins? She says No. But my mother is in another group of white people.

I ask, Do the people of the government give the women tea and cakes? Kate says, Karabo! How stupid; oh!

I say to her I say, Among my people if someone comes and stands in front of my house I tell him to come in and I give him food. You white people are wonderful. But they keep standing there and the government people do not give them anything.

She replies, You mean strange. How many times have I taught you not to say *wonderful* when you mean *strange*! Well, Kate says with a short heart and looking cross and she shouts, Well they do not stand there the whole day to ask for tea and cakes stupid. Oh dear!

Always when Madam finished to read her newspapers she gave them to me to read to help me speak and write better English. When I had read she asked me to tell her some of the things in it. In this way, I did better and better and my mind was opening and opening and I was learning and learning many things about the black people inside and outside the towns which I did not know in the least. When I found words that were too difficult or I did not understand some of the things I asked Madam. She always told me You see this, you see that, eh? with a heart that can carry on a long way. Yes, Madam writes many letters to the papers. She is always sore about the way the white police beat up black people; about the way black people who work for whites are made to sit at the Zoo Lake with their hearts hanging, because the white people say our people are making noise on Sunday afternoon when they want to rest in their houses and gardens; about many ugly things that happen when some white people meet black man on the pavement or street. So Madam writes to the papers to let others know, to ask the government to be kind to us.

In the first year Mrs. Plum wanted me to eat at table with her. It was very hard, one because I was not used to eating at table with a fork and knife, two because I heard of no other kitchen worker who was handled like this. I was afraid. Afraid of everybody, of Madam's guests if they found me doing this. Madam said I must not be silly. I must show that African servants can also eat at table. Number three, I could not eat some of the things I loved very much: mealie-meal porridge with sour milk or *morogo*, stamped mealies mixed with butter beans, sour porridge for breakfast and other things. Also, except for morning porridge, our food is nice when you eat with the hand. So nice that it does not stop in the mouth or the throat to greet anyone before it passes smoothly down.

We often had lunch together with Chimane next door and our garden boy—Ha! I must remember never to say *boy* again when I talk about a man. This makes me think of a day during the first few weeks in Mrs. Plum's house. I was talking about Dick her garden man and I said "garden boy." And she says to me she says, Stop talking about a "boy," Karabo. Now listen here, she says, You Africans must learn to speak properly about each other. And she says White people won't talk kindly about you if you look down upon each other.

I say to her I say Madam, I learned the word from the white people I worked for, and all the kitchen maids say 'boy.'

She replies she says to me, Those are white people who know nothing, just lowclass whites. I say to her I say I thought white people know everything.

She said, You'll learn, my girl, and you must start in this house, hear? She left me there thinking, my mind mixed up.

I learned. I grew up.

III

If any woman or girl does not know the Black Crow Club in Bree Street, she does not know anything. I think nearly everything takes place inside and outside that house. It is just where the dirty part of the City begins, with factories and the market. After the market is the place where Indians and Coloured people live. It is also at the Black Crow that the buses turn round and back to the black townships. Noise, noise, noise all the time. There are women who sell hot sweet potatoes and fruit and monkey nuts and boiled eggs in the winter, boiled mealies and the other things in the summer, all these on the pavements. The streets are always full of potato and fruit skins and monkey nut shells. There is always a strong smell of roast pork. I think it is because of Piel's cold storage down Bree Street.

Madam said she knew the black people who work in the Black Crow. She was happy that I was spending my afternoon on Thursday in such a club. You will learn sewing, knitting, she said, and other things that you like. Do you like to dance? I told her I said, Yes, I want to learn. She paid the two shillings fee for me each month.

We waited on the first floor, we the ones who were learning sewing; waiting for the teacher. We talked and laughed about madams and masters, and their children and their dogs and birds and whispered about our boy friends.

Sies![1] My Madam you do not know—*mojuta oa'nete*[2]—a real miser . . .

Jo—jo—jo![3] you should see our new dog. A big thing like this. People! Big in a foolish way . . .

What! Me, I take a master's bitch by the leg, me, and throw it away so that it keeps howling, *tjwe—tjwe! ngo—wu ngo—wu!*[4] I don't play about with them, me . . .

Shame, poor thing! God sees you, true. . . .!

They wanted me to take their dog out for a walk every afternoon and I told them I said it is not my work in other houses the garden man does it. I just said to my-self I said they can go to the chickens. Let them bite their elbow before I take out a dog, I am not so mad yet. . . .

Hei![5] It is not like the child of my white people who keeps a big white rat and you know what? He puts it on his bed when he goes to school. And let the blan-kets just begin to smell of urine and all the nonsense and they tell me to wash them. *Hei*, people . . .!

Did you hear about Rebone, people? Her Madam put her out, because her master was always tapping her buttocks with his fingers. And yesterday the madam saw the master press Rebone against himself. . . .

Jo—jo—jo! people . . .!

Dirty white man!

No, not dirty. The madam smells too old for him.

Hei! Go and wash your mouth with soap, this girl's mouth is dirty. . . .

Jo, Rebone, daughter of the people! We must help her to find a job before she thinks of going back home.

The teacher came. A woman with strong legs, a strong face, and kind eyes. She had short hair and dressed in a simple but lovely floral frock. She stood well on her legs and hips. She had a black mark between the two top front teeth. She smiled as if we were her children. Our group began with games, and then Lilian Ngoyi took us for sewing. After this she gave a brief talk to all of us from the different classes.

I can never forget the things this woman said and how she put them to us. She told us that the time had passed for black girls and women in the suburbs to be satisfied with working, sending money to our people and going to see them once a year. We were to learn, she said, that the world would never be safe for black people until they were in the government with the power to make laws. The power should be given by the Africans who were more than the whites.

We asked her questions and she answered them with wisdom. I shall put some of them down in my own words as I remember them.

Shall we take the place of the white people in the government?

Some yes. But we shall be more than they as we are more in the country. But also the people of all colours will come together and there are good white men we can choose and there are Africans some white people will choose to be in the government.

There are good madams and masters and bad ones. Should we take the good ones for friends?

---

[1] *Sies!* Shame!
[2] *mojuta oa'nete* Cheap; a real miser.
[3] *Jo—jo—jo!* You, you, you!
[4] *tjwe—tjwe! ngo—wu ngo—wu!* He belongs to us.
[5] *Hei!* Hi!

A master and a servant can never be friends. Never, so put that out of your head, will you! You are not even sure if the ones you say are good are not like that because they cannot breathe or live without the work of your hands. As long as you need their money, face them with respect. But you must know that many sad things are happening in our country and you, all of you, must always be learning, adding to what you already know, and obey us when we ask you to help us.

At other times Lilian Ngoyi told us she said, Remember your poor people at home and the way in which the whites are moving them from place to place like sheep and cattle. And at other times again she told us she said, Remember that a hand cannot wash itself, it needs another to do it.

I always thought of Madam when Lilian Ngoyi spoke. I asked myself, What would she say if she knew that I was listening to such words. Words like: A white man is looked after by his black nanny and his mother when he is a baby. When he grows up the white government looks after him, sends him to school, makes it impossible for him to suffer from the great hunger, keeps a job ready and open for him as soon as he wants to leave school. Now Lilian Ngoyi asked she said, How many white people can be born in a white hospital, grow up in white streets, be clothed in lovely cotton, lie on white cushions; how many whites can live all their lives in a fenced place away from people of other colours and then, as men and women learn quickly the correct ways of thinking, learn quickly to ask questions in their minds, big questions that will throw over all the nice things of a white man's life? How many? Very, very few! For those whites who have not begun to ask, it is too late. For those who have begun and are joining us with both feet in our house, we can only say Welcome!

I was learning. I was growing up. Every time I thought of Madam, she became more and more like a dark forest which one fears to enter, and which one will never know. But there were several times when I thought, This woman is easy to understand, she is like all other white women. What else are they teaching you at the Black Crow, Karabo?

I tell her I say, nothing, Madam. I ask her I say Why does Madam ask?

You are changing.

What does Madam mean?

Well, you are changing.

But we are always changing Madam.

And she left me standing in the kitchen. This was a few days after I had told her that I did not want to read more than one white paper a day. The only magazines I wanted to read, I said to her, were those from overseas, if she had them. I told her that white papers had pictures of white people most of the time. They talked mostly about white people and their gardens, dogs, weddings and parties. I asked her if she could buy me a Sunday paper that spoke about my people. Madam bought it for me. I did not think she would do it.

There were mornings when, after hanging the white people's washing on the line Chimane and I stole a little time to stand at the fence and talk. We always stood where we could be hidden by our rooms.

Hei, Karabo, you know what? That was Chimane.

No—what? Before you start, tell me, has Timi come back to you?

Ach, I do not care. He is still angry. But boys are fools, they always come back dragging themselves on their empty bellies. Hei you know what?

Yes?

The Thursday past I saw Moruti K. K. I laughed until I dropped on the ground. He is standing in front of the Black Crow. I believe his big stomach was crying from hunger.

Now he has a small dog in his armpit, and is standing before a woman selling boiled eggs and—*hei* home-girl!—tripe and intestines are boiling in a pot—oh—the smell! you could fill a hungry belly with it, the way it was good. I think Moruti K. K. is waiting for the woman to buy a boiled egg. I do not know what the woman was still doing. I am standing nearby. The dog keeps wriggling and pushing out its nose, looking at the boiling tripe. Moruti keeps patting it with his free hand, not so? Again the dog wants to spill out of Moruti's hand and it gives a few sounds through the nose. *Hei* man, home-girl! One two three the dog spills out to catch some of the good meat! It misses falling into the hot gravy in which the tripe is swimming I do not know how. Moruti K. K. tries to chase it. It has tumbled on to the woman's eggs and potatoes and all are in the dust. She stands up and goes after K. K. She is shouting to him to pay, not so? Where am I at that time? I am nearly dead with laughter the tears are coming down so far.

I was myself holding tight on the fence so as not to fall through laughing. I held my stomach to keep back a pain in the side.

I ask her I say, Did Moruti K. K. come back to pay for the wasted food?

Yes, he paid.

The dog?

He caught it. That is a good African dog. A dog must look for its own food when it is not time for meals. Not these stupid spoiled angels the whites keep giving tea and biscuits.

Hmm.

Dick our garden man joined us, as he often did. When the story was repeated to him the man nearly rolled on the ground laughing.

He asks who is Reverend K. K.

I say he is the owner of the Black Crow.

Oh!

We reminded each other, Chimane and I, of the round minister. He would come into the club, look at us with a smooth smile on his smooth round face. He would look at each one of us, with that smile on all the time, as if he had forgotten that I was there. Perhaps he had, because as he looked at us, almost stripping us naked with his watery shining eyes—funny—he could have been a farmer looking at his ripe corn, thinking many things.

K. K. often spoke without shame about what he called ripe girls—*matjitjana*—with good firm breasts. He said such girls were pure without any nonsense in their heads and bodies. Everybody talked a great deal about him and what they thought he must be doing in his office whenever he called in so-and-so.

The Reverend K. K. did not belong to any church. He baptised, married, and buried people for a fee, who had no church to do such things for them. They said he had been driven out of the Presbyterian Church. He had formed his own, but it did not go far. Then he later came and opened the Black Crow. He knew just how far to go with Lilian Ngoyi. She said although he used his club to teach us things that would help us in life, she could not go on if he was doing any wicked things with the girls in his office. Moruti K. K. feared her, and kept his place.

IV

When I began to tell my story I thought I was going to tell you mostly about Mrs. Plum's two dogs. But I have been talking about people. I think Dick is right when he says What is a dog! And there are so many dogs cats and parrots in Greenside and other places that Mrs. Plum's dogs do not look special. But there was something special in the dog business in Madam's house. The way in which she loved them, maybe.

Monty[6] is a tiny animal with long hair and small black eyes and a face nearly like that of an old woman. The other, Malan, is a bit bigger, with brown and white colours. It has small hair and looks naked by the side of the friend. They sleep in two separate baskets which stay in Madam's bedroom. They are to be washed often and brushed and sprayed and they sleep on pink linen. Monty has a pink ribbon which stays on his neck most of the time. They both carry a cover on their backs. They make me fed up when I see them in their baskets, looking fat, and as if they knew all that was going on everywhere.

It was Dick's work to look after Monty and Malan, to feed them, and to do everything for them. He did this together with garden work and cleaning of the house. He came at the beginning of this year. He just came, as if from nowhere, and Madam gave him the job as she had chased away two before him, she told me. In both those cases, she said that they could not look after Monty and Malan.

Dick had a long heart, even although he told me and Chimane that European dogs were stupid, spoiled. He said One day those white people will put ear rings and toe rings and bangles on their dogs. That would be the day he would leave Mrs. Plum. For, he said, he was sure that she would want him to polish the rings and bangles with Brasso.

Although he had a long heart, Madam was still not sure of him. She often went to the dogs after a meal or after a cleaning and said to them Did Dick give you food sweethearts? Or, Did Dick wash you sweethearts? Let me see. And I could see that Dick was blowing up like a balloon with anger. These things called white people! he said to me. Talking to dogs!

I say to him I say, People talk to oxen at home do I not say so?

Yes, he says, but at home do you not know that a man speaks to an ox because he wants to make it pull the plough or the wagon or to stop or to stand still for a person to inspan it. No one simply goes to an ox looking at him with eyes far apart and speaks to it. Let me ask you, do you ever see a person where we come from take a cow and press it to his stomach or his cheek? Tell me!

And I say to Dick I say, We were talking about an ox, not a cow.

He laughed with his broad mouth until tears came out of his eyes. At a certain point I laughed aloud too.

One day when you have time, Dick says to me, he says, you should look into Madam's bedroom when she has put a notice outside her door.

Dick, what are you saying? I ask.

I do not talk, me. I know deep inside me.

Dick was about our age, I and Chimane. So we always said *moshiman'o*[7] when we spoke about his tricks. Because he was not too big to be a boy to us. He also said to us *Hei, lona banyana kelona*—Hey you girls, you! His large mouth always seemed to be making ready to laugh. I think Madam did not like this. Many times she would say What is there to make you laugh here? Or in the garden she would say This is a flower and when it wants water that is not funny! Or again, if you did more work and stopped

[6]*Monty and Malan* Dr. D. F. Malan, a leading figure of the Dutch Reformed Church and subsequent leader of the Nationalist party, which ushered in the worst phase of apartheid in 1948. Monty may be a reference to British Field Marshall B. L. ("Monty") Montgomery.
[7]*moshiman'o* This boy.

trying to water my plants with your smile you would be more useful. Even when Dick did not mean to smile. What Madam did not get tired of saying was, If I left you to look after my dogs without anyone to look after you at the same time you would drown the poor things.

Dick smiled at Mrs. Plum. Dick hurt Mrs. Plum's dogs? Then cows can fly. He was really—really afraid of white people, Dick. I think he tried very hard not to feel afraid. For he was always showing me and Chimane in private how Mrs. Plum walked, and spoke. He took two bowls and pressed them to his chest, speaking softly to them as Madam speaks to Monty and Malan. Or he sat at Madam's table and acted the way she sits when writing. Now and again he looked back over his shoulder, pulled his face long like a horse's making as if he were looking over his glasses while telling me something to do. Then he would sit on one of the armchairs, cross his legs and act the way Madam drank her tea; he held the cup he was thinking about between his thumb and the pointing finger, only letting their nails meet. And he laughed after every act. He did these things, of course, when Madam was not home. And where was I at such times? Almost flat on my stomach, laughing.

But oh how Dick trembled when Mrs. Plum scolded him! He did his house-cleaning very well. Whatever mistake he made, it was mostly with the dogs; their linen, their food. One white man came into the house one afternoon to tell Madam that Dick had been very careless when taking the dogs out for a walk. His own dog was waiting on Madam's stoop. He repeated that he had been driving down our street; and Dick had let loose Monty and Malan to cross the street. The white man made plenty of noise about this and I think wanted to let Madam know how useful he had been. He kept on saying just one inch, *just* one inch. It was lucky I put on my brakes quick enough. . . . But your boy kept on smiling—Why? Strange. My boy would only do it twice and only twice and then . . . ! His pass. The man moved his hand like one writing, to mean that he could sign his servant's pass for him to go and never come back. When he left, the white man said Come on Rusty, the boy is waiting to clean you. Dogs with names, men without, I thought.

Madam climbed on top of Dick for this, as we say.

Once one of the dogs, I don't know which—Malan or Monty—tore my stocking—brand new, you hear—and tore it with its teeth and paws. When I told Madam about it, my anger as high as my throat, she gave me money to buy another pair. It happened again. This time she said she was not going to give me money because I must also keep my stockings where the two gentlemen would not reach them. Mrs. Plum did not want us ever to say *Voetsek* when we wanted the dogs to go away. Me I said this when they came sniffing at my legs or fingers. I hate it.

In my third year in Mrs. Plum's house, many things happened, most of them all bad for her. There was trouble with Kate; Chimane had big trouble; my heart was twisted by two loves; and Monty and Malan became real dogs for a few days.

Madam had a number of suppers and parties. She invited Africans to some of them. Kate told me the reasons for some of the parties. Like her mother's books when finished, a visitor from across the seas and so on. I did not like the black people who came here to drink and eat. They spoke such difficult English like people who were full of all the books in the world. They looked at me as if I were right down there whom they thought little of—me a black person like them.

One day I heard Kate speak to her mother. She says I don't know why you ask so many Africans to the house. A few will do at a time. She said something about the government which I could not hear well. Madam replies she says to her You know some of them do not meet white people often, so far away in their dark houses. And she says to Kate that they do not come because they want her as a friend but they just want drink for nothing.

I simply felt that I could not be the servant of white people and of blacks at the same time. At my home or in my room I could serve them without a feeling of shame. And now, if they were only coming to drink!

But one of the black men and his sister always came to the kitchen to talk to me. I must have looked unfriendly the first time, for Kate talked to me about it afterwards as she was in the kitchen when they came. I know that at that time I was not easy at all. I was ashamed and I felt that a white person's house was not the place for me to look happy in front of other black people while the white man looked on.

Another time it was easier. The man was alone. I shall never forget that night, as long as I live. He spoke kind words and I felt my heart grow big inside me. It caused me to tremble. There were several other visits. I knew that I loved him, I could never know what he really thought of me, I mean as a woman and he as a man. But I loved him, and I still think of him with a sore heart. Slowly I came to know the pain of it. Because he was a doctor and so full of knowledge and English I could not reach him. So I knew he could not stoop down to see me as someone who wanted him to love me.

Kate turned very wild. Mrs. Plum was very much worried. Suddenly it looked as if she were a new person, with new ways and new everything. I do not know what was wrong or right. She began to play the big gramophone aloud, as if the music were for the whole of Greenside. The music was wild and she twisted her waist all the time, with her mouth half-open. She did the same things in her room. She left the big school and every Saturday night now she went out. When I looked at her face, there was something deep and wild there on it, and when I thought she looked young she looked old, and when I thought she looked old she was young. We were both 22 years of age. I think that I could see the reason why her mother was so worried, why she was suffering.

Worse was to come.

They were now openly screaming at each other. They began in the sitting-room and went upstairs together, speaking fast hot biting words, some of which I did not grasp. One day Madam comes to me and says You know Kate loves an African, you know the doctor who comes to supper here often. She says he loves her too and they will leave the country and marry outside. Tell me, Karabo, what do your people think of this kind of thing between a white woman and a black man? It *cannot* be right is it?

I reply and I say to her We have never seen it happen before where I come from.

That's right, Karabo, it is just madness.

Madam left. She looked like a hunted person.

These white women, I say to myself I say these white women, why do not they love their own men and leave us to love ours!

From that minute I knew that I would never want to speak to Kate. She appeared to me as a thief, as a fox that falls upon a flock of sheep at night. I hated her. To make it worse, he would never be allowed to come to the house again.

Whenever she was home there was silence between us. I no longer wanted to know anything about what she was doing, where or how.

I lay awake for hours on my bed. Lying like that, I seemed to feel parts of my body beat and throb inside me, the way I have seen big machines doing, pounding and pounding and pushing and pulling and pouring some water into one hole which came out at another end. I stretched myself so many times so as to feel tired and sleepy.

When I did sleep, my dreams were full of painful things.

One evening I made up my mind, after putting it off many times. I told my boy-friend that I did not want him any longer. He looked hurt, and that hurt me too. He left.

The thought of the African doctor was still with me and it pained me to know that I should never see him again; unless I met him in the street on a Thursday afternoon. But he had a car. Even if I did meet him by luck, how could I make him see that I loved him? Ach, I do not believe he would even stop to think what kind of woman I am. Part of that winter was a time of longing and burning for me. I say part because there are always things to keep servants busy whose white people go to the sea for the winter.

To tell the truth, winter was the time for servants; not nannies, because they went with their madams so as to look after the children. Those like me stayed behind to look after the house and dogs. In winter so many families went away that the dogs remained the masters and madams. You could see them walk like white people in the streets. Silent but with plenty of power. And when you saw them you knew that they were full of more nonsense and fancies in the house.

There was so little work to do.

One week word was whispered round that a home-boy of ours was going to hold a party in his room on Saturday. I think we all took it for a joke. How could the man be so bold and stupid? The police were always driving about at night looking for black people; and if the whites next door heard the party noise—*oho!* But still, we were full of joy and wanted to go. As for Dick, he opened his big mouth and nearly fainted when he heard of it and that I was really going.

During the day on the big Saturday Kate came.

She seemed a little less wild. But I was not ready to talk to her. I was surprised to hear myself answer her when she said to me Mother says you do not like a marriage between a white girl and a black man, Karabo.

Then she was silent.

She says But I want to help him, Karabo.

I ask her I say You want to help him to do what?

To go higher and higher, to the top.

I knew I wanted to say so much that was boiling in my chest. I could not say it. I thought of Lilian Ngoyi at the Black Crow, what she said to us. But I was mixed up in my head and in my blood.

You still agree with my mother?

All I could say was I said to your mother I had never seen a black man and a white woman marrying, you hear me? What I think about it is my business.

I remembered that I wanted to iron my party dress and so I left her. My mind was full of the party again and I was glad because Kate and the doctor would not worry my peace that day. And the next day the sun would shine for all of us, Kate or no Kate, doctor or no doctor.

The house where our home-boy worked was hidden from the main road by a number of trees. But although we asked a number of questions and counted many fingers of bad luck until we had no more hands for fingers, we put on our best pay-while-you-wear dresses and suits and clothes bought from boys who had stolen them, and went to our home-boy's party. We whispered all the way while we climbed up to the house. Someone who knew told us that the white people next door were away for the winter. Oh, so that is the thing! we said.

We poured into the garden through the back and stood in front of his room laughing quietly. He came from the big house behind us, and were we not struck dumb when he told us to go into the white people's house! Was he mad? We walked in with slow footsteps that seemed to be sniffing at the floor, not sure of anything. Soon we were standing and sitting all over on the nice warm cushions and the heaters were on. Our home-boy turned the lights low. I counted fifteen people inside. We saw how we loved one another's evening dress. The boys were smart too.

Our home-boy's girl-friend Naomi was busy in the kitchen preparing food. He took out glasses and cold drinks—fruit juice, tomato juice, ginger beers, and so many other kinds of soft drink. It was just too nice. The tarts, the biscuits, the snacks, the cakes, woo, that was a party, I tell you. I think I ate more ginger cake than I had ever done in my life. Naomi had baked some of the things. Our home-boy came to me and said I do not want the police to come here and have reason to arrest us, so I am not serving hot drinks, not even beer. There is no law that we cannot have parties, is there? So we can feel free. Our use of this house is the master's business. If I had asked him he would have thought me mad.

I say to him I say, You have a strong liver to do such a thing.

He laughed.

He played pennywhistle music on gramophone records—Miriam Makeba, Dorothy Masuka, and other African singers and players. We danced and the party became more and more noisy and more happy. Hai, those girls Miriam and Dorothy, they can sing, I tell you! We ate more and laughed more and told more stories. In the middle of the party, our home-boy called us to listen to what he was going to say. Then he told us how he and a friend of his in Orlando collected money to bet on a horse for the July Handicap in Durban. They did this each year but lost. Now they had won two hundred pounds. We all clapped hands and cheered. Two hundred pounds woo!

You should go and sit at home and just eat time, I say to him. He laughs and says You have no understanding not one little bit.

To all of us he says Now my brothers and sisters enjoy yourselves. At home I should slaughter a goat for us to feast and thank our ancestors. But this is town life and we must thank them with tea and cake and all those sweet things. I know some people think I must be so bold that I could be midwife to a lion that is giving birth, but enjoy yourselves and have no fear.

Madam came back looking strong and fresh.

The very week she arrived the police had begun again to search servants' rooms. They were looking for what they called loafers and men without passes who they said were living with friends in the suburbs against the law. Our dog's-meat boys became scarce because of the police. A boy who had a girl-friend in the kitchens, as we say, always told his friends that he was coming for dog's meat when he meant he was visiting his girl. This was because we gave our boy-friends part of the meat the white people bought for the dogs and us.

One night a white and a black policeman entered Mrs. Plum's yard. They said they had come to search. She says no, they cannot. They say Yes, they must do it. She answers No. They forced their way to the back, to Dick's room and mine. Mrs. Plum took the hose that was running in the front garden and quickly went round to the back. I cut across the floor to see what she was going to say to the men. They were talking to Dick, using dirty words. Mrs. Plum did not wait, she just pointed the hose at the two policemen. This seemed to surprise them. They turned round and she pointed it into their faces. Without their seeing me I went to the tap at the corner of the house and opened it more. I could see Dick, like me, was trying to keep down his laughter. They shouted and tried to wave the water away, but she kept the hose pointing at them, now moving it up and down. They turned and ran through the back gate, swearing the while.

That fixes them, Mrs. Plum said.

The next day the morning paper reported it.

They arrived in the afternoon—the two policemen—with another. They pointed out Mrs. Plum and she was led to the police station. They took her away to answer for stopping the police while they were doing their work.

She came back and said she had paid bail.

At the magistrate's court, Madam was told that she had done a bad thing. She would have to pay a fine or else go to prison for fourteen days. She said she would go to jail to show that she felt she was not in the wrong.

Kate came and tried to tell her that she was doing something silly going to jail for a small thing like that. She tells Madam she says This is not even a thing to take to the high court. Pay the money. What is £5?

Madam went to jail.

She looked very sad when she came out. I thought of what Lilian Ngoyi often said to us: You must be ready to go to jail for the things you believe are true and for which you are taken by the police. What did Mrs. Plum really believe about me, Chimane, Dick, and all the other black people? I asked myself. I did not know. But from all those things she was writing for the papers and all those meetings she was going to where white people talked about black people and the way they are treated by the government, from what those white women with black bands over their shoulders were doing standing where a white government man was going to pass, I said to myself I said This woman, *hai*, I do not know she seems to think very much of us black people. But why was she so sad?

Kate came back home to stay after this. She still played the big gramophone loud-loud-loud and twisted her body at her waist until I thought it was going to break. Then I saw a young white man come often to see her. I watched them through the opening near the hinges of the door between the kitchen and the sitting-room where they sat. I saw them kiss each other for a long time. I saw him lift up Kate's dress and her white-white legs begin to tremble, and—oh I am afraid to say more, my heart was beating hard. She called him Jim. I thought it was funny because white people in the shops call black men Jim.

Kate had begun to play with Jim when I met a boy who loved me and I loved. He was much stronger than the one I sent away and I loved him more, much more. The face of the doctor came to my mind often, but it did not hurt me so any more. I stopped looking at Kate and her Jim through openings. We spoke to each other, Kate and I, almost as freely as before but not quite. She and her mother were friends again.

Hallo, Karabo, I heard Chimane call me one morning as I was starching my apron. I answered. I went to the line to hang it. I saw she was standing at the fence, so I knew she had something to tell me. I went to her.

Hallo!

Hallo, Chimane!

O *kae?*

Ke teng. *Wena?*

At that moment a woman came out through the back door of the house where Chimane was working.

I have not seen that one before, I say, pointing with my head.

Chimane looked back. Oh, that one. *Hei*, daughter-of-the-people, *Hei*, you have not seen miracles. You know this is Madam's mother-in-law as you see her there. Did I never tell you about her?

No, never.

White people, nonsense. You know what? That poor woman is here now for two days. She has to cook for herself and I cook for the family.

On the same stove?

Yes, She comes after me when I have finished.

She has her own food to cook?

Yes, Karabo. White people have no heart no sense.

What will eat them up if they share their food?

Ask me, just ask me. God! She clapped her hands to show that only God knew, and it was His business, not ours.

Chimane asks me she says, Have you heard from home?

I tell her I say, Oh daughter-of-the-people, more and more deaths. Something is finishing the people at home. My mother has written. She says they are all right, my father too and my sisters, except for the people who have died. Malebo, the one who lived alone in the house I showed you last year, a white house, he is gone. Then teacher Sedimo. He was very thin and looked sick all the time. He taught my sisters not me. His mother-in-law you remember I told you died last year—no, the year before. Mother says also there is a woman she does not think I remember because I last saw her when I was a small girl she passed away in Zeerust she was my mother's greatest friend when they were girls. She would have gone to her burial if it was not because she has swollen feet.

How are the feet?

She says they are still giving her trouble. I ask Chimane, How are your people at Nokaneng? They have not written?

She shook her head.

I could see from her eyes that her mind was on another thing and not her people at that moment.

Wait for me Chimane eh, forgive me, I have scones in the oven, eh! I will just take them out and come back, eh!

When I came back to her Chimane was wiping her eyes. They were wet.

Karabo, you know what?

E—e. I shook my head.

I am heavy with child.

Hau!

There was a moment of silence.

Who is it, Chimane?

Timi. He came back only to give me this.

But he loves you. What does he say have you told him?

I told him yesterday. We met in town.

I remembered I had not seen her at the Black Crow.

Are you sure, Chimane? You have missed a month?

She nodded her head.

Timi himself—he did not use the thing?

I only saw after he finished, that he had not.

Why? What does he say?

He tells me he says I should not worry I can be his wife.

Timi is a good boy, Chimane. How many of these boys with town ways who know too much will even say Yes it is my child?

Hai, Karabo, you are telling me other things now. Do you not see that I have not worked long enough for my people? If I marry now who will look after them when I am the only child?

Hm. I hear your words. It is true. I tried to think of something soothing to say.

Then I say You can talk it over with Timi. You can go home and when the child is born you look after it for three months and when you are married you come to town to work and can put your money together to help the old people while they are looking after the child.

What shall we be eating all the time I am at home? It is not like those days gone past when we had land and our mother could go to the fields until the child was ready to arrive.

The light goes out in my mind and I cannot think of the right answer. How many times have I feared the same thing! Luck and the mercy of the gods that is all I live by. That is all we live by—all of us.

Listen, Karabo. I must be going to make tea for Madam. It will soon strike half-past ten.

I went back to the house. As Madam was not in yet, I threw myself on the divan in the sitting-room. Malan came sniffing at my legs. I put my foot under its fat belly and shoved it up and away from me so that it cried *tjunk—tjunk—tjunk* as it went out. I say to it I say Go and tell your brother what I have done to you and tell him to try it and see what I will do. Tell your grandmother when she comes home too.

When I lifted my eyes he was standing in the kitchen door, Dick. He says to me he says *Hau!* now you have also begun to speak to dogs!

I did not reply I just looked at him, his mouth ever stretched out like the mouth of a bag, and I passed to my room.

I sat on my bed and looked at my face in the mirror. Since the morning I had been feeling as if a black cloud were hanging over me, pressing on my head and shoulders. I do not know how long I sat there. Then I smelled Madam. What was it? Where was she? After a few moments I knew what it was. My perfume and scent. I used the same cosmetics as Mrs. Plum's. I should have been used to it by now. But this morning— why did I smell Mrs. Plum like this? Then, without knowing why, I asked myself I said, Why have I been using the same cosmetics as Madam? I wanted to throw them all out. I stopped. And then I took all the things and threw them into the dustbin. I was going to buy other kinds on Thursday; finished!

I could not sit down. I went out and into the white people's house. I walked through and the smell of the house made me sick and seemed to fill up my throat. I went to the bathroom without knowing why. It was full of the smell of Madam. Dick was cleaning the bath. I stood at the door and looked at him cleaning the dirt out of the bath, dirt from Madam's body. *Sies!* I said aloud. To myself I said, Why cannot people wash the dirt of their own bodies out of the bath? Before Dick knew I was near I went out. Ach, I said again to myself, why should I think about it now when I have been doing their washing for so long and cleaned the bath many times when Dick was ill. I had held worse things from her body times without number. . . .

I went out and stood midway between the house and my room, looking into the next yard. The three-legged grey cat next door came to the fence and our eyes met. I do not know how long we stood like that looking at each other. I was thinking,

Why don't you go and look at your grandmother like that? when it turned away and mewed hopping on the three legs. Just like someone who feels pity for you.

In my room I looked into the mirror on the chest of drawers. I thought, Is this Karabo this?

Thursday came, and the afternoon off. At the Black Crow I did not see Chimane. I wondered about her. In the evening I found a note under my door. It told me if Chimane was not back that evening I should know that she was at 660 3rd Avenue, Alexandra Township. I was not to tell the white people.

I asked Dick if he could not go to Alexandra with me after I had washed the dishes. At first he was unwilling. But I said to him I said, Chimane will not believe that you refused to come with me when she sees me alone. He agreed.

On the bus Dick told me much about his younger sister whom he was helping with money to stay at school until she finished; so that she could become a nurse and a midwife. He was very fond of her, as far as I could find out. He said he prayed always that he should not lose his job, as he had done many times before, after staying a few weeks only at each job; because of this he had to borrow monies from people to pay his sister's school fees, to buy her clothes and books. He spoke of her as if she were his sweetheart. She was clever at school, pretty (she was this in the photo Dick had shown me before). She was in Orlando Township. She looked after his old people, although she was only thirteen years of age. He said to me he said Today I still owe many people because I keep losing my job. You must try to stay with Mrs. Plum, I said.

I cannot say that I had all my mind on what Dick was telling me. I was thinking of Chimane: what could she be doing? Why that note?

We found her in bed. In that terrible township where night and day are full of knives and bicycle chains and guns and the barking of hungry dogs and of people in trouble. I even held my heart in my hands. She was in pain and her face, even in the candlelight, was grey. She turned her eyes at me. A fat woman was sitting in a chair. One arm rested on the other and held her chin in its palm. She had hardly opened the door for us after we had shouted our names when she was on her bench again as if there were nothing else to do.

She snorted, as if to let us know that she was going to speak. She said There is your friend. There she is my own-own niece who comes from the womb of my own sister, my sister who was made to spit out my mother's breast to give way for me. Why does she go and do such an evil thing. Ao! you young girls of today you do not know children die so fast these days that you have to thank God for sowing a seed in your womb to grow into a child. If she had let the child be born I should have looked after it or my sister would have been so happy to hold a grandchild on her lap, but what does it help? She has allowed a worm to cut the roots, I don't know.

Then I saw that Chimane's aunt was crying. Not once did she mention her niece by her name, so sore her heart must have been. Chimane only moaned.

Her aunt continued to talk, as if she was never going to stop for breath, until her voice seemed to move behind me, not one of the things I was thinking: trying to remember signs, however small, that could tell me more about this moment in a dim little room in a cruel township without street lights, near Chimane. Then I remembered the three-legged cat, its grey-green eyes, its *miau*. What was this shadow that seemed to walk about us but was not coming right in front of us?

I thanked the gods when Chimane came to work at the end of the week. She still looked weak, but that shadow was no longer there. I wondered Chimane had never told me about her aunt before. Even now I did not ask her.

I told her I told her white people that she was ill and had been fetched to Noka-neng by a brother. They would never try to find out. They seldom did, these people. Give them any lie, and it will do. For they seldom believe you whatever you say. And how can a black person work for white people and be afraid to tell them lies. They are always asking the questions, you are always the one to give the answers.

Chimane told me all about it. She had gone to a woman who did these things. Her way was to hold a sharp needle, cover the point with the finger, and guide it into the womb. She then fumbled in the womb until she found the egg and then pierced it. She gave you something to ease the bleeding. But the pain, spirits of our forefathers!

Mrs. Plum and Kate were talking about dogs one evening at dinner. Every time I brought something to table I tried to catch their words. Kate seemed to find it funny, because she laughed aloud. There was a word I could not hear well which began with *sem*—: whatever it was, it was to be for dogs. This I understood by putting a few words together. Mrs. Plum said it was something that was common in the big cities of Amer-ica, like New York. It was also something Mrs. Plum wanted and Kate laughed at the thought. Then later I was to hear that Monty and Malan could be sure of a nice burial.

Chimane's voice came up to me in my room the next morning, across the fence. When I come out she tells me she said *Hei* child-of-my-father, here is something to tickle your ears. You know what? What? I say. She says, These white people can do things that make the gods angry. More godless people I have not seen. The madam of our house says the people of Greenside want to buy ground where they can bury their dogs. I heard them talk about it in the sitting-room when I was giving them coffee last night. *Hei*, people, let our forefathers come and save us!

Yes, I say, I also heard the madam of our house talk about it with her daughter. I just heard it in pieces. By my mother one day these dogs will sit at table and use knife and fork. These things are to be treated like people now, like children who are never going to grow up.

Chimane sighed and she says *Hela batho*,[8] why do they not give me some of that money they will spend on the ground and on gravestones to buy stockings! I have nothing to put on, by my mother.

Over her shoulder I saw the cat with three legs. I pointed with my head. When Chi-mane looked back and saw it she said *Hm*, even *they* live like kings. The mother-in-law found it on a chair and the madam said the woman should not drive it away. And there was no other chair, so the woman went to her room.

Hela!

I was going to leave when I remembered what I wanted to tell Chimane. It was that five of us had collected a £1 each to lend her so that she could pay the woman of Alexandra for having done that thing for her. When Chimane's time came to re-ceive money we collected each month and which we took in turns, she would pay us back. We were ten women and each gave £2 at a time. So one waited ten months to receive £20. Chimane thanked us for helping her.

I went to wake up Mrs. Plum as she had asked me. She was sleeping late this morn-ing. I was going to knock at the door when I heard strange noises in the bedroom. What is the matter with Mrs. Plum? I asked myself. Should I call her, in case she is ill? No, the noises were not those of a sick person. They were happy noises but like those a person makes in a dream, the voice full of sleep. I bent a little to peep through

---

[8]*Hela batho*   Oh gosh, people!

the keyhole. What is this? I kept asking myself. Mrs. Plum! Malan! What is she doing this one? Her arm was round Malan's belly and pressing its back against her stomach at the navel, Mrs. Plum's body in a nightdress moving in jerks like someone in fits . . . her leg rising and falling . . . Malan silent like a thing to be owned without any choice it can make to belong to another.

The gods save me! I heard myself saying, the words sounding like wind rushing out of my mouth. So this is what Dick said I would find out for myself!

No one could say where it all started; who talked about it first; whether the police wanted to make a reason for taking people without passes and people living with servants and working in town or not working at all. But the story rushed through Johannesburg that servants were going to poison the white people's dogs. Because they were too much work for us: that was the reason. We heard that letters were sent to the newspapers by white people asking the police to watch over the dogs to stop any wicked things. Some said that we the servants were not really bad, we were being made to think of doing these things by evil people in town and in the locations. Others said the police should watch out lest we poison madams and masters because black people did not know right from wrong when they were angry. We were still children at heart, others said. Mrs. Plum said that she had also written to the papers.

Then it was the police came down on the suburbs like locusts on a cornfield. There were lines and lines of men who were arrested hour by hour in the day. They liked this very much, the police. Everybody they took, everybody who was working was asked, Where's the poison eh? Where did you hide it? Who told you to poison the dogs eh? If you tell us we'll leave you to go free, you hear? and so many other things.

Dick kept saying It is wrong this thing they want to do to kill poor dogs. What have these things of God done to be killed for? Is it the dogs that make us carry passes? Is it dogs that make the laws that give us pain? People are just mad they do not know what they want, stupid! But when white policeman spoke to him, Dick trembled and lost his tongue and the things he thought. He just shook his head. A few moments after they had gone through his pockets he still held his arms stretched out, like the man of straw who frightens away birds in a field. Only when I hissed and gave him a sign did he drop his arms. He rushed to a corner of the garden to go on with his work.

Mrs. Plum had put Monty and Malan in the sitting-room, next to her. She looked very much worried. She called me. She asked me she said Karabo, you think Dick is a boy we can trust? I did not know how to answer. I did not know whom she was talking about when she said we. Then I said I do not know, Madam. You know! she said. I looked at her. I said I do not know what Madam thinks. She said she did not think anything, that was why she asked. I nearly laughed because she was telling a lie this time and not I.

At another time I should have been angry if she lied to me, perhaps. She and I often told each other lies, as Kate and I also did. Like when she came back from jail, after that day when she turned a hosepipe on two policemen. She said life had been good in jail. And yet I could see she was ashamed to have been there. Not like our black people who are always being put in jail and only look at it as the white man's evil game. Lilian Ngoyi often told us this, and Mrs. Plum showed me how true those words are. I am sure that we have kept to each other by lying to each other.

There was something in Mrs. Plum's face as she was speaking which made me fear her and pity her at the same time. I had seen her when she had come from prison; I had seen her when she was shouting at Kate and the girl left the house; now there was this thing about dog poisoning. But never had I seen her face like this before. The eyes, the nostrils, the lips, the teeth seemed to be full of hate, tired, fixed on doing something bad; and yet there was something on that face that told me she wanted me on her side.

Dick is all right Madam, I found myself saying. She took Malan and Monty in her arms and pressed them to herself, running her hands over their heads. They looked so safe, like a child in a mother's arm.

Mrs. Plum said All right you may go. She said Do not tell anybody what I have asked about Dick eh?

When I told Dick about it, he seemed worried.

It is nothing, I told him.

I had been thinking before that I did not stand with those who wanted to poison the dogs, Dick said. But the police have come out, I do not care what happens to the dumb things, now.

I asked him I said Would you poison them if you were told by someone to do it? No. But I do not care, he replied.

The police came again and again. They were having a good holiday, everyone could see that. A day later Mrs. Plum told Dick to go because she would not need his work any more.

Dick was almost crying when he left. Is Madam so unsure of me? he asked. I never thought a white person could fear me! And he left.

Chimane shouted from the other yard. She said, *Hei ngoana'rona,*[9] the boers are fire-hot eh!

Mrs. Plum said she would hire a man after the trouble was over.

A letter came from my parents in Phokeng. In it they told me my uncle had passed away. He was my mother's brother. The letter also told me of other deaths. They said I would not remember some, I was sure to know the others. There were also names of sick people.

I went to Mrs. Plum to ask her if I could go home. She asks she says When did he die? I answer I say It is three days, Madam. She says So that they have buried him? I reply Yes Madam. Why do you want to go home then? Because my uncle loved me very much Madam. But what are you going to do there? To take my tears and words of grief to his grave and to my old aunt, Madam. No you cannot go, Karabo. You are working for me you know? Yes, Madam. I, and not your people pay you. I must go Madam, that is how we do it among my people, Madam. She paused. She walked into the kitchen and came out again. If you want to go, Karabo, you must lose the money for the day you will be away. Lose my pay, Madam? Yes, Karabo.

The next day I went to Mrs. Plum and told her I was leaving for Phokeng and was not coming back to her. Could she give me a letter to say that I worked for her. She did, with her lips shut tight. I could feel that something between us was burning like raw chillies. The letter simply said that I had worked for Mrs. Plum for three years. Nothing more. The memory of Dick being sent away was still an open sore in my heart.

The night before the day I left, Chimane came to see me in my room. She had her own story to tell me. Timi, her boy-friend, had left her—for good. Why? Because I killed his baby. Had he not agreed that you should do it? No. Did he show he was worried when you told him you were heavy? He was worried, like me as you saw me, Karabo. Now he says if I kill one I shall eat all his children up when we are married.

---

[9]*ngoana'rona* Child.

You think he means what he says? Yes, Karabo. He says his parents would have been very happy to know that the woman he was going to marry can make his seed grow.

Chimane was crying, softly.

I tried to speak to her, to tell her that if Timi left her just like that, he had not wanted to marry her in the first place. But I could not, no, I could not. All I could say was Do not cry, my sister, do not cry. I gave her my handkerchief.

Kate came back the morning I was leaving, from somewhere very far I cannot remember where. Her mother took no notice of what Kate said asking her to keep me, and I was not interested either.

One hour later I was on the Railway bus to Phokeng. During the early part of the journey I did not feel anything about the Greenside house I had worked in. I was not really myself, my thoughts dancing between Mrs. Plum, my uncle, my parents, and Phokeng, my home. I slept and woke up many times during the bus ride. Right through the ride I seemed to see, sometimes in sleep, sometimes between sleep and waking, a red car passing our bus, then running behind us. Each time I looked out it was not there.

Dreams came and passed. He tells me he says You have killed my seed I wanted my mother to know you are a woman in whom my seed can grow. . . . Before you make the police take you to jail make sure that it is for something big you should go to jail for, otherwise you will come out with a heart and mind that will bleed inside you and poison you. . . .

The bus stopped for a short while, which made me wake up.

The Black Crow, the club women . . . *Hei*, listen! I lie to the madam of our house and I say I had a telegram from my mother telling me she is very very sick. I show her a telegram my sister sent me as if Mother were writing. So I went home for a nice weekend. . . .

The laughter of the women woke me up, just in time for me to stop a line of saliva coming out over my lower lip. The bus was making plenty of dust now as it was running over part of the road they were digging up. I was sure the red car was just behind us, but it was not there when I woke.

Any one of you here who wants to be baptized or has a relative without a church who needs to be can come and see me in the office. . . . A round man with a fat tummy and sharp hungry eyes, a smile that goes a long, long way . . . .

The bus was going uphill, heavily and noisily.

I kick a white man's dog, me, or throw it there if it has not been told the black people's law. . . . This is Mister Monty and this is Mister Malan. Now get up you lazy boys and meet Mister Kate. Hold out your hands and say hallo to him. . . . Karabo, bring two glasses there. . . . Wait a bit—What will you chew boys while Mister Kate and I have a drink? Nothing? Sure?

We were now going nicely on a straight tarred road and the trees rushed back. Mister Kate. What nonsense, I thought.

Look Karabo, Madam's dogs are dead. What? Poison. I killed them. She drove me out of a job did she not? For nothing. Now I want her to feel she drove me out for something. I came back when you were in your room and took the things and poisoned them. . . . And you know what? She has buried them in clean pink sheets in the garden. Ao, clean clean good sheets. I am going to dig them out and take one sheet do you want the other one? Yes, give me the other one I will send it to my mother. . . . *Hei*, Karabo, see here they come. Monty and Malan. The bloody fools they do not want to stay in their hole. Go back you silly fools. Oh you do not want to move eh?

Come here, now I am going to throw you in the big pool. No, Dick! No Dick! no, no! Dick! They cannot speak do not kill things that cannot speak. Madam can speak for them she always does. No! Dick . . . !

I woke up with a jump after I had screamed Dick's name, almost hitting the window. My forehead was full of sweat. The red car also shot out of my sleep and was gone. I remembered a friend of ours who told us how she and the garden man had saved two white sheets in which their white master had buried their two dogs. They went to throw the dogs in a dam.

When I told my parents my story Father says to me he says, So long as you are in good health my child, it is good. The worker dies, work does not. There is always work. I know when I was a boy a strong sound body and a good mind were the biggest things in life. Work was always there, and the lazy man could never say there was no work. But today people see work as something bigger than everything else, bigger than health, because of money.

I reply I say, Those days are gone Papa. I must go back to the city after resting a little to look for work. I must look after you. Today people are too poor to be able to help you.

I knew when I left Greenside that I was going to return to Johannesburg to work. Money was little, but life was full and it was better than sitting in Phokeng and watching the sun rise and set. So I told Chimane to keep her eyes and ears open for a job.

I had been at Phokeng for one week when a red car arrived. Somebody was sitting in front with the driver, a white woman. At once I knew it to be that of Mrs. Plum. The man sitting beside her was showing her the way, for he pointed towards our house in front of which I was sitting. My heart missed a few beats. Both came out of the car. The white woman said Thank you to the man after he had spoken a few words to me.

I did not know what to do and how to look at her as she spoke to me. So I looked at the piece of cloth I was sewing pictures on. There was a tired but soft smile on her face. Then I remembered that she might want to sit. I went inside to fetch a low bench for her. When I remembered it afterwards, the thought came to me that there are things I never think white people can want to do at our homes when they visit for the first time: like sitting, drinking water or entering the house. This is how I thought when the white priest came to see us. One year at Easter Kate drove me home as she was going to the north. In the same way I was at a loss what to do for a few minutes.

Then Mrs. Plum says, I have come to ask you to come back to me, Karabo. Would you like to?

I say I do not know, I must think about it first.

She says, Can you think about it today? I can sleep at the town hotel and come back tomorrow morning, and if you want to you can return with me.

I wanted her to say she was sorry to have sent me away, I did not know how to make her say it because I know white people find it too much for them to say Sorry to a black person. As she was not saying it, I thought of two things to make it hard for her to get me back and maybe even lose me in the end.

I say, You must ask my father first, I do not know, should I call him?

Mrs. Plum says, Yes.

I fetched both Father and Mother. They greeted her while I brought benches. Then I told them what she wanted.

Father asks Mother and Mother asks Father. Father asks me. I say if they agree, I will think about it and tell her the next day.

Father says, It goes by what you feel my child.

I tell Mrs. Plum I say, if you want me to think about it I must know if you will want to put my wages up from £6 because it is too little.

She asks me, How much will you want?

Up by £4.

She looked down for a few moments.

And then I want two weeks at Easter and not just the weekend. I thought if she really wanted me she would want to pay for it. This would also show how sorry she was to lose me.

Mrs. Plum says, I can give you one week. You see you already have something like a rest when I am in Durban in the winter.

I tell her I say I shall think about it.

She left.

The next day she found me packed and ready to return with her. She was very much pleased and looked kinder than I had ever known her. And me, I felt sure of myself, more than I had ever done.

Mrs. Plum says to me, You will not find Monty and Malan.

Oh?

Yes, they were stolen the day after you left. The police have not found them yet. I think they are dead myself.

I thought of Dick . . . my dream. Could he? And she . . . did this woman come to ask me to return because she had lost two animals she loved?

Mrs. Plum says to me she says, You know, I like your people, Karabo, the Africans.

And Dick and Me? I wondered.

[1967]

Questions

1. Why is the story called "Mrs. Plum" and not "Karabo"?
2. It is clear that Karabo is significantly changed by the end of the story. Can the same be said of Mrs. Plum?
3. Do you think that a person like Mrs. Plum would have helped or hindered the struggle to abolish *apartheid*?
4. What does the substory involving Chimane and her boyfriend tell us?
5. One of the ideas that Karabo learns from Lilian Ngoyi is that "a master and a servant can never be friends." Is this true?
6. Is Mphahlele's metaphor of fear (as the barrier that separates South African racial groups) a suitable one for his story?

Sławomir Mrożek

(b. 1930)

Poland

S lawomir Mrożek is Poland's preeminent contemporary satirist and playwright. Born in Borzęcin, Poland, Mrożek studied architecture and oriental culture in Kraków. Later he was a caricaturist and journalist for newspapers, besides directing, editing, and producing several films. Mrożek's gift for capturing in exaggerated form the essential details of a person's behavior and style through caricature served him well when he changed to the written word. His satirical short stories have been widely translated, including two volumes in English (The Elephant and The Ugupu Bird). His plays, including The Police and Tango (English titles), are frequently performed. Through satire, Mrożek frequently mocks the reigning political institutions and communist doctrines of his country, for which reason he left Poland for the West when his work was banned in 1968. Despite the political liberalization of Poland since the 1970s, Mrożek has chosen to live in France and Italy.

Mrożek's English translator, Konrad Syrop, praises the author's wit, his poetic language, his ability to compress several layers of meaning within brief narratives, and "his style, which ranges from the austere to the ornate, depending on the demands of the story."

THE ELEPHANT

The director of the Zoological Gardens had shown himself to be an upstart. He regarded his animals simply as stepping stones on the road of his own career. He was indifferent to the educational importance of his establishment. In his zoo the giraffe had a short neck, the badger had no burrow and the whistlers, having lost all interest, whistled rarely and with some reluctance. These shortcomings should not have been allowed, especially as the zoo was often visited by parties of schoolchildren.

The zoo was in a provincial town, and it was short of some of the most important animals, among them the elephant. Three thousand rabbits were a poor substitute for the noble giant. However, as our country developed, the gaps were being filled in a well-planned manner. On the occasion of the anniversary of the liberation, on 22nd July, the zoo was notified that it had at long last been allocated an elephant. All the staff, who were devoted to their work, rejoiced at this news. All the greater was their surprise when they learned that the director had sent a letter to Warsaw, renouncing the allocation and putting forward a plan for obtaining an elephant by more economic means.

"I, and all the staff," he had written, "are fully aware how heavy a burden falls upon the shoulders of Polish miners and foundry men because of the elephant. Desirous of reducing our costs, I suggest that the elephant mentioned in your communication should be replaced by one of our own procurement. We can make an elephant out of rubber, of the correct size, fill it with air and place it behind railings. It will be carefully painted the correct color and even on close inspection will be indistinguishable from the real animal. It is well known that the elephant is a sluggish animal and it does not run and jump about. In the notice on the railings we can state that this particular elephant is particularly sluggish. The money saved in this way can be turned to the purchase of a jet plane or the conservation of some church monument.

"Kindly note that both the idea and its execution are my modest contribution to the common task and struggle.

"I am, etc."

This communication must have reached a soulless official, who regarded his duties in a purely bureaucratic manner and did not examine the heart of the matter but, following only the directive about reduction of expenditure, accepted the director's plan. On hearing the Ministry's approval, the director issued instructions for the making of the rubber elephant.

The carcass was to have been filled with air by two keepers blowing into it from opposite ends. To keep the operation secret the work was to be completed during the night because the people of the town, having heard that an elephant was joining the zoo, were anxious to see it. The director insisted on haste also because he expected a bonus, should his idea turn out to be a success.

The two keepers locked themselves in a shed normally housing a workshop, and began to blow. After two hours of hard blowing they discovered that the rubber skin had risen only a few inches above the floor and its bulge in no way resembled an elephant. The night progressed. Outside, human voices were stilled and only the cry of the jackass interrupted the silence. Exhausted, the keepers stopped blowing and made sure that the air already inside the elephant should not escape. They were not young and were unaccustomed to this kind of work.

"If we go on at this rate," said one of them, "we shan't finish by morning. And what am I to tell my missus? She'll never believe me if I say that I spent the night blowing up an elephant."

"Quite right," agreed the second keeper. "Blowing up an elephant is not an everyday job. And it's all because our director is a leftist."

They resumed their blowing, but after another half-hour they felt too tired to continue. The bulge on the floor was larger but still nothing like the shape of an elephant.

"It's getting harder all the time," said the first keeper.

"It's an uphill job, all right," agreed the second. "Let's have a little rest."

While they were resting, one of them noticed a gas pipe ending in a valve. Could they not fill the elephant with gas? He suggested it to his mate.

They decided to try. They connected the elephant to the gas pipe, turned the valve, and to their joy in a few minutes there was a full-sized beast standing in the shed. It looked real: the enormous body, legs like columns, huge ears and the inevitable trunk. Driven by ambition the director had made sure of having in his zoo a very large elephant indeed.

"First class," declared the keeper who had the idea of using gas. "Now we can go home."

In the morning the elephant was moved to a special run in a central position, next to the monkey cage. Placed in front of a large real rock it looked fierce and magnificent. A big notice proclaimed: "Particularly sluggish. Hardly moves."

Among the first visitors that morning was a party of children from the local school. The teacher in charge of them was planning to give them an object-lesson about the elephant. He halted the group in front of the animal and began:

"The elephant is a herbivorous mammal. By means of its trunk it pulls out young trees and eats their leaves."

The children were looking at the elephant with enraptured admiration. They were waiting for it to pull out a young tree, but the beast stood still behind its railings.

" . . . The elephant is a direct descendant of the now-extinct mammoth. It's not surprising, therefore, that it's the largest living land animal."

The more conscientious pupils were making notes.

" . . . Only the whale is heavier than the elephant, but then the whale lives in the sea. We can safely say that on land the elephant reigns supreme."

A slight breeze moved the branches of the trees in the zoo.

" . . . The weight of a fully grown elephant is between nine and thirteen thousand pounds."

At that moment the elephant shuddered and rose in the air. For a few seconds it swayed just above the ground, but a gust of wind blew it upward until its mighty silhouette was against the sky. For a short while people on the ground could see the four circles of its feet, its bulging belly and the trunk, but soon, propelled by the wind, the elephant sailed above the fence and disappeared above the treetops. Astonished monkeys in the cage continued staring into the sky.

They found the elephant in the neighboring botanical gardens. It had landed on a cactus and punctured its rubber hide.

The schoolchildren who had witnessed the scene in the zoo soon started neglecting their studies and turned into hooligans. It is reported that they drink liquor and break windows. And they no longer believe in elephants.

[1962]
Translated by
Konrad Syrop

Questions

1. Why does the zoo director prefer a fake elephant to a real one? How do his motives provide insight into the social and political institutions in Poland? How are these institutions satirized in the story?

2. What meanings are suggested by the inflatable elephant? Consider Konrad Syrop's (Mrożek's translator's) suggestion that the story is an allegory in which "the rubber elephant represents communist doctrine."

3. Why do the school children who witness the airborne elephant start "neglecting their studies and turn[ing] into hooligans"?

Bharati Mukherjee

(b. 1940)

India/United States

Bharati Mukherjee was born in Calcutta, the daughter of a pharmaceutical chemist and businessman. Before coming to North America in 1961, she attended a postcolonial British convent school, studied English at the University of Calcutta, and received an M.A. in English and ancient Indian culture at the University of Baroda. While pursuing a Ph.D. in English at the University of Iowa, she met and married Canadian writer Clark Blaise. Mukherjee lived in Canada for 15 years, during which time she taught at McGill University in Toronto. As a result of the racism she experienced in Canada, she left in 1980 to resettle in the United States.

Mukherjee's first novel, Tiger's Daughter (1972), was followed by Wife (1975), Jasmine (1989), The Holder of the World (1993), and Leave It to Me (1997). She has also published two collections of short stories, Darkness (1985) and The Middleman and Other Stories (1988); the latter book, which won the National Book Critics Circle Award, brought her to the attention of American readers. Mukherjee and her husband have collaborated on several books, including Days and Nights in Calcutta (1977), a journalistic account that registers their complementary perspectives during their year-long stay in India: Mukherjee as an exile returning to her country to confront the ambivalent feelings and impressions it generated for her, particularly concerning the oppressive situation of women, and Blaise as an American responding to India for the first time, both fascinated by its cultural richness and troubled by its poverty. As Mukherjee observed in an essay for The Writer on Her Work: New Essays in New Territory, "I am aware of myself as a four-hundred-year-old woman, born in the captivity of a colonial, pre-industrial oral culture and living now as a contemporary New Yorker."

In her early stories and novels, Mukherjee explores the difficulty for Indian immigrants to establish both personal and cultural identities in North America against a setting of racism, sexism, and cultural misunderstanding—the "unsettled magma between two worlds." More recently, Mukherjee's canvas has broadened to reflect the immigrant experiences of other ethnic groups in America. As Polly Shulman describes Mukherjee's focus on contemporary multicultural reality, "everyone is living in a new world, even those who never left home. As traditions break down, the characters must try to make lives out of the pieces." Mukherjee has described her artistic focus in an interview for Belles Lettres:

> I see my job as a writer to make my complicated and unfamiliar world understandable to the mainstream reader. That is what good fiction does. If my writing is strong enough, then even unexplained cultural details about the Indian community in Queens or the Korean community in New York will become accessible.
>
> I want to give voice to the new pioneers in this country. . . . We have big stories to tell. We have lived 300 years of our own history very quickly because most of us [have] come from either postcolonial countries or countries with a lot of civil and religious strife. Now we are rapidly learning 200 years of American history and acculturating into American society. Our lives are extraordinary, even grand and heroic.
>
> I try to show this in my fiction.

A FATHER

One Wednesday morning in mid-May Mr. Bhowmick woke up as he usually did at 5:43 A.M., checked his Rolex against the alarm clock's digital readout, punched down the alarm (set for 5:45), then nudged his wife awake. She worked as a claims investigator for an insurance company that had an office in a nearby shopping mall. She didn't really have to leave the house until 8:30, but she liked to get up early and cook him a big breakfast. Mr. Bhowmick had to drive a long way to work. He was a naturally dutiful, cautious man, and he set the alarm clock early enough to accommodate a margin for accidents.

While his wife, in a pink nylon negligee she had paid for with her own MasterCard card, made him a new version of French toast from a clipping ("Eggs-cellent Recipes!") Scotchtaped to the inside of a kitchen cupboard, Mr. Bhowmick brushed his teeth. He brushed, he gurgled with the loud, hawking noises that he and his brother had been taught as children to make in order to flush clean not merely teeth but also tongue and palate.

After that he showered, then, back in the bedroom again, he recited prayers in Sanskrit to Kali, the patron goddess of his family, the goddess of wrath and vengeance. In the pokey flat of his childhood in Ranchi, Bihar, his mother had given over a whole bedroom to her collection of gods and goddesses. Mr. Bhowmick couldn't be that extravagant in Detroit. His daughter, twenty-six and an electrical engineer, slept in the other of the two bedrooms in his apartment. But he had done his best. He had taken Woodworking I and II at a nearby recreation center and built a grotto for the goddess. Kali-Mata was eight inches tall, made of metal and painted a glistening black so that the metal glowed like the oiled, black skin of a peasant woman. And though Kali-Mata was totally nude except for a tiny gilt crown and a garland strung together from sinners' chopped off heads, she looked warm, cozy, *pleased*, in her makeshift wooden shrine in Detroit. Mr. Bhowmick had gathered quite a crowd of admiring, fellow woodworkers in those final weeks of decoration.

"Hurry it up with the prayers," his wife shouted from the kitchen. She was an agnostic, a believer in ambition, not grace. She frequently complained that his prayers had gotten so long that soon he wouldn't have time to go to work, play duplicate bridge with the Ghosals, or play the *tabla*[1] in the Bengali Association's one Sunday per month musical soirees. Lately she'd begun to drain him in a wholly new way. He wasn't praying, she nagged; he was shutting her out of his life. There'd be no peace in the house until she hid Kali-Mata in a suitcase.

She nagged, and he threatened to beat her with his shoe as his father had threatened his mother: it was the thrust and volley of marriage. There was no question of actually taking off a shoe and applying it to his wife's body. She was bigger than he was. And, secretly, he admired her for having the nerve, the agnosticism, which as a college boy in backward Bihar he too had claimed.

"I have time," he shot at her. He was still wrapped in a damp terry towel.

"You have time for everything but domestic life."

It was the fault of the shopping mall that his wife had started to buy pop psychology paperbacks. These paperbacks preached that for couples who could sit down and

---

[1]*tabla* Indian musical instrument, a kind of drum.

talk about their "relationship," life would be sweet again. His engineer daughter was on his wife's side. She accused him of holding things in.

"Face it, Dad," she said. "You have an affect deficit."

But surely everyone had feelings they didn't want to talk about or talk over. He definitely did not want to blurt out anything about the sick-in-the-guts sensations that came over him most mornings and that he couldn't bubble down with Alka-Seltzer or smother with Gas-X. The women in his family were smarter than him. They were cheerful, outgoing, more American somehow.

How could he tell these bright, mocking women that in the 5:43 A.M. darkness, he sensed invisible presences: gods and snakes frolicked in the master bedroom, little white sparks of cosmic static crackled up the legs of his pajamas. Something was out there in the dark, something that could invent accidents and coincidences to remind mortals that even in Detroit they were no more than mortal. His wife would label this paranoia and dismiss it. Paranoia, premonition: whatever it was, it had begun to undermine his composure.

Take this morning. Mr. Bhowmick had woken up from a pleasant dream about a man taking a Club Med vacation, and the postdream satisfaction had lasted through the shower, but when he'd come back to the shrine in the bedroom, he'd noticed all at once how scarlet and saucy was the tongue that Kali-Mata stuck out at the world. Surely he had not lavished such alarming detail, such admonitory colors on that flap of flesh.

Watch out, ambulatory sinners. Be careful out there, the goddess warned him, and not with the affection of Sergeant Esterhaus, either.

"French toast must be eaten hot-hot," his wife nagged. "Otherwise they'll taste like rubber."

Mr. Bhowmick laid the trousers of a two-trouser suit he had bought on sale that winter against his favorite tweed jacket. The navy stripes in the trousers and the small, navy tweed flecks in the jacket looked quite good together. So what if the Chief Engineer had already started wearing summer cottons?

"I am coming, I am coming," he shouted back. "You want me to eat hot-hot, you start the frying only when I am sitting down. You didn't learn anything from Mother in Ranchi?"

"Mother cooked French toast from fancy recipes? I mean French Sandwich Toast with complicated filling?"

He came into the room to give her his testiest look. "You don't know the meaning of complicated cookery. And mother had to get the coal fire of the *chula*[2] going first."

His daughter was already at the table. "Why don't you break down and buy her a microwave oven? That's what I mean about sitting down and talking things out." She had finished her orange juice. She took a plastic measure of Slim-Fast out of its can and poured the powder into a glass of skim milk. "It's ridiculous."

Babli was not the child he would have chosen as his only heir. She was brighter certainly than the sons and daughters of the other Bengalis he knew in Detroit, and she had been the only female student in most of her classes at Georgia Tech, but as she sat there in her beige linen business suit, her thick chin dropping into a polka-dotted cravat, he regretted again that she was not the child of his dreams. Babli would be able to help him out moneywise if something happened to him, something so bad

---

[2]*chula*   Clay oven.

that even his pension plans and his insurance policies and his money market schemes wouldn't be enough. But Babli could never comfort him. She wasn't womanly or ten-der the way that unmarried girls had been in the wistful days of his adolescence. She could sing Hindi film songs, mimicking exactly the high, artificial voice of Lata Mungeshkar, and she had taken two years of dance lessons at Sona Devi's Dance Academy in Southfield, but these accomplishments didn't add up to real femininity. Not the kind that had given him palpitations in Ranchi.

Mr. Bhowmick did his best with his wife's French toast. In spite of its filling of marsh-mallows, apricot jam and maple syrup, it tasted rubbery. He drank two cups of Dar-jeeling tea, said, "Well, I'm off," and took off.

All might have gone well if Mr. Bhowmick hadn't fussed longer than usual about putting his briefcase and his trenchcoat in the backseat. He got in behind the wheel of his Oldsmobile, fixed his seatbelt and was just about to turn the key in the igni-tion when his neighbor, Al Stazniak, who was starting up his Buick Skylark, sneezed. A sneeze at the start of a journey brings bad luck. Al Stazniak's sneeze was fierce, made up of five short bursts, too loud to be ignored.

Be careful out there! Mr. Bhowmick could see the goddess's scarlet little tongue tip wagging at him.

He was a modern man, an intelligent man. Otherwise he couldn't have had the options in life that he did have. He couldn't have given up a good job with perks in Bombay and found a better job with General Motors in Detroit. But Mr. Bhowmick was also a prudent enough man to know that some abiding truth lies bunkered with-in each wanton Hindu superstition. A sneeze was more than a sneeze. The heedless are carried off in ambulances. He had choices to make. He could ignore the sneeze, and so challenge the world unseen by men. Perhaps Al Stazniak had hayfever. For a sneeze to be a potent omen, surely it had to be unprovoked and terrifying, a thun-derclap cleaving the summer skies. Or he could admit the smallness of mortals, undo the fate of the universe by starting over, and go back inside the apartment, sit for a second on the sofa, then re-start his trip.

Al Stazniak rolled down his window. "Everything okay?"

Mr. Bhowmick nodded shyly. They weren't really friends in the way neighbors can sometimes be. They talked as they parked or pulled out of their adjacent parking stalls. For all Mr. Bhowmick knew, Al Stazniak had no legs. He had never seen the man out of his Skylark.

He let the Buick back out first. Everything was okay, yes, please. All the same he undid his seatbelt. Compromise, adaptability, call it what you will. A dozen times a day he made these small trade-offs between new-world reasonableness and old-world beliefs.

While he was sitting in his parked car, his wife's ride came by. For fifty dollars a month, she was picked up and dropped off by a hard up, newly divorced woman who worked at a florist's shop in the same mall. His wife came out the front door in brown K-Mart pants and a burgundy windbreaker. She waved to him, then slipped into the passenger seat of the florist's rusty Japanese car.

He was a metallurgist. He knew about rust and ways of preventing it, secret ways, thus far unknown to the Japanese.

Babli's fiery red Mitsubishi was still in the lot. She wouldn't leave for work for an-other eight minutes. He didn't want her to know he'd been undone by a sneeze. Babli wasn't tolerant of superstitions. She played New Wave music in her tapedeck. If asked about Hinduism, all she'd ever said to her American friends was that "it's neat." Mr.

Bhowmick had heard her on the phone years before. The cosmos balanced on the head of a snake was like a beachball balanced on the snout of a circus seal. "This Hindu myth stuff," he'd heard her say, "is like a series of super graphics."

He'd forgiven her. He could probably forgive her anything. It was her way of surviving high school in a city that was both native to her, and alien.

There was no question of going back where he'd come from. He hated Ranchi. Ranchi was no place for dreamers. All through his teenage years, Mr. Bhowmick had dreamed of success abroad. What form that success would take he had left vague. Success had meant to him escape from the constant plotting and bitterness that wore out India's middle class.

Babli should have come out of the apartment and driven off to work by now. Mr. Bhowmick decided to take a risk, to dash inside and pretend held left his briefcase on the coffee table.

When he entered the living room, he noticed Babli's spring coat and large vinyl pocketbook on the sofa. She was probably sorting through the junk jewelry on her dresser to give her business suit a lift. She read hints about dressing in women's magazines and applied them to her person with seriousness. If his luck held, he could sit on the sofa, say a quick prayer and get back to the car without her catching on.

It surprised him that she didn't shout out from her bedroom, "Who's there?" What if he had been a rapist?

Then he heard Babli in the bathroom. He heard unladylike squawking noises. She was throwing up. A squawk, a spitting, then the horrible gurgle of a waterfall.

A revelation came to Mr. Bhowmick. A woman vomiting in the privacy of the bathroom could mean many things. She was coming down with the flu. She was nervous about a meeting. But Mr. Bhowmick knew at once that his daughter, his untender, unloving daughter whom he couldn't love and hadn't tried to love, was not, in the larger world of Detroit, unloved. Sinners are everywhere, even in the bosom of an upright, unambitious family like the Bhowmicks. It was the goddess sticking out her tongue at him.

The father sat heavily on the sofa, shrinking from contact with her coat and pocketbook. His brisk, bright engineer daughter was pregnant. Someone had taken time to make love to her. Someone had thought her tender, feminine. Someone even now was perhaps mooning over her. The idea excited him. It was so grotesque and wondrous. At twenty-six Babli had found the man of her dreams; whereas at twenty-six Mr. Bhowmick had given up on truth, beauty and poetry and exchanged them for two years at Carnegie Tech.

Mr. Bhowmick's tweed-jacketed body sagged against the sofa cushions. Babli would abort, of course. He knew his Babli. It was the only possible option if she didn't want to bring shame to the Bhowmick family. All the same, he could see a chubby baby boy on the rug, crawling to his granddaddy. Shame like that was easier to hide in Ranchi. There was always a barren womb sanctified by marriage that could claim sudden fructifying by the goddess Parvati. Babli would do what she wanted. She was headstrong and independent and he was afraid of her.

Babli staggered out of the bathroom. Damp stains ruined her linen suit. It was the first time he had seen his daughter look ridiculous, quite unprofessional. She didn't come into the living room to investigate the noises he'd made. He glimpsed her shoeless stockinged feet flip-flop on collapsed arches down the hall to her bedroom.

"Are you all right?" Mr. Bhowmick asked, standing in the hall. "Do you need Sinutab?"

She wheeled around. "What're you doing here?"

He was the one who should be angry. "I'm feeling poorly too," he said. "I'm taking the day off."

"I feel fine," Babli said.

Within fifteen minutes Babli had changed her clothes and left. Mr. Bhowmick had the apartment to himself all day. All day for praising or cursing the life that had brought him along with its other surprises an illegitimate grandchild.

It was his wife that he blamed. Coming to America to live had been his wife's idea. After the wedding, the young Bhowmicks had spent two years in Pittsburgh on his student visa, then gone back home to Ranchi for nine years. Nine crushing years. Then the job in Bombay had come through. All during those nine years his wife had screamed and wept. She was a woman of wild, progressive ideas—she'd called them her "American" ideas—and she'd been martyred by her neighbors for them. American *memsahib. Markin mem, Markin mem.*[3] In bazaars the beggar boys had trailed her and hooted. She'd done provocative things. She'd hired a *chamar*[4] woman who by caste rules was forbidden to cook for higher caste families, especially for widowed mothers of decent men. This had caused a blowup in the neighborhood. She'd made other, lesser errors. While other wives shopped and cooked every day, his wife had cooked the whole week's menu on weekends.

"What's the point of having a refrigerator, then?" She'd been scornful of the Ranchi women.

His mother, an old-fashioned widow, had accused her of trying to kill her by poisoning. "You are in such a hurry? You want to get rid of me quick-quick so you can go back to the States?"

Family life had been turbulent.

He had kept aloof, inwardly siding with his mother. He did not love his wife now, and he had not loved her then. In any case, he had not defended her. He felt some affection, and he felt guilty for having shunned her during those unhappy years. But he had thought of it then as revenge. He had wanted to marry a beautiful woman. Not being a young man of means, only a young man with prospects, he had had no right to yearn for pure beauty. He cursed his fate and after a while, settled for a barrister's daughter, a plain girl with a wide, flat plank of a body and myopic eyes. The barrister had sweetened the deal by throwing in an all-expenses-paid two years' study at Carnegie Tech to which Mr. Bhowmick had been admitted. Those two years had changed his wife from pliant girl to ambitious woman. She wanted America, nothing less.

It was his wife who had forced him to apply for permanent resident status in the U.S. even though he had a good job in Ranchi as a government engineer. The putting together of documents for the immigrant visa had been a long and humbling process. He had had to explain to a chilly clerk in the Embassy that, like most Indians of his generation, he had no birth certificate. He had to swear out affidavits, suffer through police checks, bribe orderlies whose job it was to move his dossier from desk to desk. The decision, the clerk had advised him, would take months, maybe years. He hadn't dared hope that merit might be rewarded. Merit could collapse under bad luck. It was for grace that he prayed.

While the immigration papers were being processed, he had found the job in Bombay. So he'd moved his mother in with his younger brother's family, and left

---

[3]*memsahib* Mrs.; *Markin mem*—American Mrs.
[4]*chamar* A person of one of the lower castes in the Indian caste (class) system.

his hometown for good. Life in Bombay had been lighthearted, almost fulfilling. His wife had thrown herself into charity work with the same energy that had offended the Ranchi women. He was happy to be in a big city at last. Bombay was the Rio de Janeiro of the East; he'd read that in a travel brochure. He drove out to Nariman Point at least once a week to admire the necklace of municipal lights, toss coconut shells into the dark ocean, drink beer at the Oberoi-Sheraton where overseas Indian girls in designer jeans beckoned him in sly ways. His nights were full. He played duplicate bridge, went to the movies, took his wife to Bingo nights at his club. In Detroit he was a lonelier man.

Then the green card[5] had come through. For him, for his wife, and for the daughter who had been born to them in Bombay. He sold what he could sell, and put in his brother's informal trust what he couldn't to save on taxes. Then he had left for America, and one more start.

All through the week, Mr. Bhowmick watched his daughter. He kept furtive notes on how many times she rushed to the bathroom and made hawking, wrenching noises, how many times she stayed late at the office, calling her mother to say she'd be taking in a movie and pizza afterwards with friends.

He had to tell her that he knew. And he probably didn't have much time. She shouldn't be on Slim-Fast in her condition. He had to talk things over with her. But what would he say to her? What position could he take? He had to choose between public shame for the family, and murder.

For three more weeks he watched her and kept his silence. Babli wore shifts to the office instead of business suits, and he liked her better in those garments. Perhaps she was dressing for her young man, not from necessity. Her skin was pale and blotchy by turn. At breakfast her fingers looked stiff, and she had trouble with silverware.

Two Saturdays running, he lost badly at duplicate bridge. His wife scolded him. He had made silly mistakes. When was Babli meeting this man? Where? He must be American; Mr. Bhowmick prayed only that he was white. He pictured his grandson crawling to him, and the grandson was always fat and brown and buttery-skinned, like the infant Krishna. An American son-in-law was a terrifying notion. Why was she not mentioning men, at least, preparing the way for the major announcement? He listened sharply for men's names, rehearsed little lines like, "Hello, Bob, I'm Babli's old man," with a cracked little laugh. Bob, Jack, Jimmy, Tom. But no names surfaced. When she went out for pizza and a movie it was with the familiar set of Indian girls and their strange, unpopular, American friends, all without men. Mr. Bhowmick tried to be reasonable. Maybe she had already gotten married and was keeping it secret. "Well, Bob, you and Babli sure had Mrs. Bhowmick and me going there, heh-heh," he mumbled one night with the Sahas and Ghosals, over cards. "Pardon?" asked Pronob Saha. Mr. Bhowmick dropped two tricks, and his wife glared. "Such stupid blunders," she fumed on the drive back. A new truth was dawning; there would be no marriage for Babli. Her young man probably was not so young and not so available. He must be already married. She must have yielded to passion or been raped in the office. His wife seemed to have noticed nothing. Was he a murderer, or a conspirator? He kept his secret from his wife; his daughter kept her decision to herself.

---

[5]*green card*   American certification of an immigrant's legal resident status.

Nights, Mr. Bhowmick pretended to sleep, but as soon as his wife began her snoring—not real snores so much as loud, gaspy gulpings for breath—he turned on his side and prayed to Kali-Mata.

In July, when Babli's belly had begun to push up against the waistless dresses she'd bought herself, Mr. Bhowmick came out of the shower one weekday morning and found the two women screaming at each other. His wife had a rolling pin in one hand. His daughter held up a *National Geographic* as a shield for her head. The crazy look that had been in his wife's eyes when she'd shooed away beggar kids was in her eyes again.

"Stop it!" His own boldness overwhelmed him. "Shut up! Babli's pregnant, so what? It's your fault, you made us come to the States."

Girls like Babli were caught between rules, that's the point he wished to make. They were too smart, too impulsive for a backward place like Ranchi, but not tough nor smart enough for sex-crazy places like Detroit.

"My fault?" his wife cried. "I told her to do hanky-panky with boys? I told her to shame us like this?"

She got in one blow with the rolling pin. The second glanced off Babli's shoulder and fell on his arm which he had stuck out for his grandson's sake.

"I'm calling the police," Babli shouted. She was out of the rolling pin's range. "This is brutality. You can't do this to me."

"Shut up! Shut your mouth, foolish woman." He wrenched the weapon from his wife's fist. He made a show of taking off his shoe to beat his wife on the face.

"What do you know? You don't know anything." She let herself down slowly on a dining chair. Her hair, curled overnight, stood in wild whorls around her head. "Nothing."

"And you do!" He laughed. He remembered her tormentors, and laughed again. He had begun to enjoy himself. Now *he* was the one with the crazy, progressive ideas.

"Your daughter is pregnant, yes," she said, "any fool knows that. But ask her the name of the father. Go, ask."

He stared at his daughter who gazed straight ahead, eyes burning with hate, jaw clenched with fury.

"Babli?"

"Who needs a man?" she hissed. "The father of my baby is a bottle and a syringe. Men louse up your lives. I just want a baby. Oh, don't worry—he's a certified fit donor. No diseases, college graduate, above average, and he made the easiest twenty-five dollars of his life—"

"Like animals," his wife said. For the first time he heard horror in her voice. His daughter grinned at him. He saw her tongue, thick and red, squirming behind her row of perfect teeth.

"Yes, yes, yes," she screamed, "like livestock. Just like animals. You should be happy—that's what marriage is all about, isn't it? Matching bloodlines, matching horoscopes, matching castes, matching, matching, matching . . ." and it was difficult to know if she was laughing or singing, or mocking and like a madwoman.

Mr. Bhowmick lifted the rolling pin high above his head and brought it down hard on the dome of Babli's stomach. In the end, it was his wife who called the police.

[1985]

Questions

1. How do Mr. and Mrs. Bhowmick and their daughter exemplify distinctly different responses to American life and culture? How are these differences significant for the story's development and its resolution?
2. What does the goddess Kali-Mata represent in Mr. Bhowmick's system of belief? What is the connection between the goddess and his daughter Babli?
3. In what way is Babli's pregnancy a reaction to her family's values and their cultural dislocation? What does Mukherjee's story suggest about cultural assimilation?

Carmen Naranjo

(b. 1931)

Costa Rica

Author, editor, social critic, museum director, and cultural ambassador (among other positions), Carmen Naranjo understands the people and institutions of Costa Rica from a variety of perspectives. She studied public administration at the Autonomous University of Mexico and literature at the University of Iowa. As the most visible woman in public office in her country, she has served as secretary of culture and ambassador to Israel and currently is director of Editorial Universitaria Centroamericana press, the major publishing company of Central America. Naranjo is also the multitalented author of seven novels and seven volumes of short stories, as well as four collections of essays. Apart from one collection of stories, There Never Was a Once Upon a Time (1985), most of her work has not been translated into English.

In her fiction, Naranjo employs a variety of modes from realism to fantasy to explore psychological themes as well as social issues and to experiment with nontraditional forms, particularly with narrative perspectives. She has received several national literary awards and prizes for her fiction and poetry in addition to Costa Rica's highest award for public service.

AND WE SOLD THE RAIN

"This is a royal fuck-up," was all the treasury minister could say a few days ago as he got out of the jeep after seventy kilometers of jouncing over dusty rutted roads and muddy trails. His advisor agreed: there wasn't a cent in the treasury, the line for foreign exchange wound four times around the capital, and the IMF[1] was stubbornly insisting that the country could expect no more loans until the interest had been paid up, public spending curtailed, salaries frozen, domestic production increased, imports reduced, and social programs cut.

The poor were complaining, "We can't even buy beans—they've got us living on radish tops, bananas and garbage; they raise our water bills but don't give us any water even though it rains every day, and on top of that they add on a charge for excess consumption for last year, even though there wasn't any water in the pipes then either."

"Doesn't anyone in this whole goddamned country have an idea that could get us out of this?" asked the president of the republic, who shortly before the elections, surrounded by a toothily smiling, impeccably tailored meritocracy, had boasted that by virtue of his university-trained mind (Ph.D. in developmental economics) he was the best candidate. Someone proposed to him that he pray to La Negrita; he did and

---

[1]IMF International Monetary Fund.

nothing happened. Somebody else suggested that he reinstate the Virgin of Ujarrás. But after so many years of neglect, the pretty little virgin had gone deaf and ignored the pleas for help, even though the entire cabinet implored her, at the top of their lungs, to light the way to a better future and a happier tomorrow.

The hunger and poverty could no longer be concealed: the homeless, pockets empty, were squatting in the Parque Central, the Parque Nacional, and the Plaza de la Cultura. They were camping along Central and Second Avenues and in a shanty-town springing up on the plains outside the city. Gangs were threatening to invade the national theater, the Banco Central, and all nationalized banking headquarters. The Public Welfare Agency was rationing rice and beans as if they were medicine. In the marketplace, robberies increased to one per second, and homes were burgled at the rate of one per half hour. Business and government were sinking in sleaze; drug lords operated uncontrolled, and gambling was institutionalized in order to launder dollars and attract tourists. Strangely enough, the prices of a few items went down: whiskey, caviar and other such articles of conspicuous consumption.

The sea of poverty that was engulfing cities and villages contrasted with the grow-ing number of Mercedes Benzes, BMWs and a whole alphabet of trade names of gleaming new cars.

The minister announced to the press that the country was on the verge of bank-ruptcy. The airlines were no longer issuing tickets because so much money was owed them, and travel became impossible; even official junkets were eliminated. There was untold suffering of civil servants suddenly unable to travel even once a month to the great cities of the world! A special budget might be the solution, but tax rev-enues were nowhere to be found, unless a compliant public were to go along with the president's brilliant idea of levying a tax on air—a minimal tax, to be sure, but, after all, the air was a part of the government's patrimony. Ten *colones*[2] per breath would be a small price to pay.

July arrived, and one afternoon a minister without portfolio and without umbrel-la, noticing that it had started to rain, stood watching people run for cover. "Yes," he thought, "here it rains like it rains in Comala, like it rains in Macondo. It rains day and night, rain after rain, like a theater with the same movie, sheets of water. Poor people without umbrellas, without a change of clothes, they get drenched, people living in leaky houses, without a change of shoes for when they're shipwrecked. And here, all my poor colleagues with colds, all the poor deputies with laryngitis, the pres-ident with that worrisome cough, all this on top of the catastrophe itself. No TV sta-tion is broadcasting; all of them are flooded, along with the newspaper plants and the radio stations. A people without news is a lost people, because they don't know that everywhere else, or almost everywhere else, things are even worse. If we could only export the rain," thought the minister.

Meanwhile, the people, depressed by the heavy rains, the dampness, the lack of news, the cold, and their hunger and despair without their sitcoms and soap operas, began to rain inside and to increase the baby population—that is, to try to increase the odds that one of their progeny might survive. A mass of hungry, naked babies began to cry in concert every time it rained.

When one of the radio transmitters was finally repaired, the president was able to broadcast a message: He had inherited a country so deeply in debt that it could no

---

[2]*colones*   Monetary unit of Costa Rica.

longer obtain credit and could no longer afford to pay either the interest or the amortization on loans. He had to dismiss civil servants, suspend public works, cut off services, close offices, and spread his legs somewhat to transnationals. Now even these lean cows were dying; the fat ones were on the way, encouraged by the International Monetary Fund, the AID and the IDB, not to mention the EEC.[3] The great danger was that the fat cows had to cross over the neighboring country on their way, and it was possible that they would be eaten up—even though they came by air, at nine thousand feet above the ground, in a first class stable in a pressurized, air-conditioned cabin. Those neighbors were simply not to be trusted.

The fact was that the government had faded in the people's memory. By now no one remembered the names of the president or his ministers; people remembered them as "the one with glasses who thinks he's Tarzan's mother," or "the one who looks like the baby hog someone gave me when times were good, maybe a little uglier."

The solution came from the most unexpected source. The country had organized the Third World contest to choose "Miss Underdeveloped," to be elected, naturally, from the multitudes of skinny, dusky, round-shouldered, short-legged, half-bald girls with cavity-pocked smiles, girls suffering from parasites and God knows what else. The prosperous Emirate of the Emirs sent its designée, who in sheer amazement at how it rained and rained, widened her enormous eyes—fabulous eyes of harem and Koran delights—and was unanimously elected reigning Queen of Underdevelopment. Lacking neither eyeteeth nor molars, she was indeed the fairest of the fair. She returned in a rush to the Emirate of the Emirs, for she had acquired, with unusual speed, a number of fungal colonies that were taking over the territory under her toenails and fingernails, behind her ears, and on her left cheek.

"Oh, Father Sultan, my lord, lord of the moons and of the suns, if your Arabian highness could see how it rains and rains in that country, you would not believe it. It rains day and night. Everything is green, even the people; they are green people, innocent and trusting, who probably have never even thought about selling their most important resource, the rain. The poor fools think about coffee, rice, sugar, vegetables, and lumber, and they hold Ali Baba's treasure in their hands without even knowing it. What we would give to have such abundance!"

Sultan Abun dal Tol let her speak and made her repeat the part about the rain from dawn to dusk, dusk to dawn, for months on end. He wanted to hear over and over about that greenness that was forever turning greener. He loved to think of it raining and raining, of singing in the rain, of showers bringing forth flowers. . . .

A long distance phone call was made to the office of the export minister from the Emirate of the Emirs, but the minister wasn't in. The trade minister grew radiant when Sultan Abun dal Tol, warming to his subject, instructed him to buy up rain and construct an aqueduct between their countries to fertilize the desert. Another call. Hello, am I speaking with the country of rain, not the rain of marijuana or cocaine, not that of laundered dollars, but the rain that falls naturally from the sky and makes the sandy desert green? Yes, yes, you are speaking with the export minister, and we are willing to sell you our rain. Of course, its production costs us nothing; it is a resource as natural to us as your petroleum. We will make you a fair and just agreement.

---

[3]AID, Agency for International Development; IDB, International Development Bank; EEC, European Economic Community.

The news filled five columns during the dry season, when obstacles like floods and dampness could be overcome. The president himself made the announcement: We will sell rain at ten dollars per cc. The price will be reviewed every ten years. Sales will be unlimited. With the earnings we will regain our independence and our self-respect.

The people smiled. A little less rain would be agreeable to everyone, and the best part was not having to deal with the six fat cows, who were more than a little oppressive. The IMF, the World Bank, the AID, the Embassy, the International Development Bank and perhaps the EEC would stop pushing the cows on them, given the danger that they might be stolen in the neighboring country, air-conditioned cabin, first class stable and all. Moreover, one couldn't count on those cows really being fat, since accepting them meant increasing all kinds of taxes, especially those on consumer goods, lifting import restrictions, spreading one's legs completely open to the transnationals, paying the interest, which was now a little higher, and amortizing the debt that was increasing at a rate only comparable to the spread of an epidemic. And as if this were not enough, it would be necessary to structure the cabinet a certain way, as some ministers were viewed by some legislators as potentially dangerous, as extremists.

The president added with demented glee, his face garlanded in sappy smiles, that French technicians, those guardians of European meritocracy, would build the rain funnels and the aqueduct, a guarantee of honesty, efficiency and effective transfer of technology.

By then we had already sold, to our great disadvantage, the tuna, the dolphins, and the thermal dome, along with the forests and all Indian artifacts. Also our talent, dignity, sovereignty, and the right to traffic in anything and everything illicit.

The first funnel was located on the Atlantic coast, which in a few months looked worse than the dry Pacific. The first payment from the emir arrived—in dollars!—and the country celebrated with a week's vacation. A little more effort was needed. Another funnel was added in the north and one more in the south. Both zones immediately dried up like raisins. The checks did not arrive. What happened? The IMF garnisheed them for interest payments. Another effort: a funnel was installed in the center of the country, where formerly it had rained and rained. It now stopped raining forever, which paralyzed brains, altered behavior, changed the climate, defoliated the corn, destroyed the coffee, poisoned aromas, devastated canefields, dessicated palm trees, ruined orchards, razed truck gardens, and narrowed faces, making people look and act like rats, ants, and cockroaches, the only animals left alive in large numbers.

To remember what we once had been, people circulated photographs of an enormous oasis with great plantations, parks, and animal sanctuaries full of butterflies and flocks of birds, at the bottom of which was printed, "Come and visit us. The Emirate of Emirs is a paradise."

The first one to attempt it was a good swimmer who took the precaution of carrying food and medicine. Then a whole family left, then whole villages, large and small. The population dropped considerably. One fine day there was nobody left, with the exception of the president and his cabinet. Everyone else, even the deputies, followed the rest by opening the cover of the aqueduct and floating all the way to the cover at the other end, doorway to the Emirate of the Emirs.

In that country we were second-class citizens, something we were already accustomed to. We lived in a ghetto. We got work because we knew about coffee, sugar cane, cotton, fruit trees, and truck gardens. In a short time we were happy and felt as if these things too were ours, or at the very least, that the rain still belonged to us.

A few years passed; the price of oil began to plunge and plunge. The emir asked for a loan, then another, then many; eventually he had to beg and beg for money to service the loans. The story sounds all too familiar. Now the IMF has taken possession of the aqueducts. They have cut off the water because of a default in payments and because the sultan had the bright idea of receiving as a guest of honor a representative of that country that is a neighbor of ours.

[1988]
Translated by
JO ANNE ENGELBERT

Questions

1. What political and social institutions and values does Naranjo satirize? What details contribute to the story's humor? How would you describe the tone of the story?
2. What are the implications of the story's conclusion?
3. What relationship is suggested between developing and developed countries?
4. Compare this story with R. K. Narayan's "A Horse and Two Goats."

R. K. Narayan
(1907–2001)
India

Born into an old Brahmin family to the headmaster of a distinguished secondary school in Madras, Rasipuram Krisnaswami Narayan spent a rather lonely childhood in the home of his grandmother and uncle. Privy to the library of his father's school, he developed an early love of British novelists such as Dickens, Scott, and Hardy. He was later educated at the University of Mysore but, failing at the profession he had assumed he would pursue as a teacher of English, Narayan turned to free-lance writing while working as a journalist for a Madras newspaper.

Although he is one of the most widely read and loved writers of the Indian subcontinent, Narayan initially had difficulty in finding a publisher for his fiction. Graham Greene was influential in securing for Narayan a British publisher for his first four novels. Narayan's greatest audience is in the United States, where his novels were typically published before they appeared in India.

Like William Faulkner's mythic Yoknapatawpha County, Narayan's Malgudi is an entire world in microcosm: a fictional transformation of Mysore, where the author spent most of his life. Through a deeply humane comic vision, Narayan traces the struggles of his sensitive and often doubting characters—middle-class men who are professionally involved in teaching, journalism, or commerce—to find moral equilibrium and spiritual peace within the framework of public life. The formation and testing of character are central preoccupations of his 15 novels, including Swami and Friends (1935), The Bachelor of Arts (1937), and The Painter of Signs (1976). His collections of short stories include A Horse and Two Goats (1970), from which the title story is included here, and The Grandmother's Tale and Selected Stories (1999).

In 1939 Narayan's marriage ended tragically when his wife died suddenly of typhoid. His autobiographical novel, Grateful to Life and Death (1945), masterfully traces his recovery from bereavement through telepathic communication with his deceased wife. The mystical communication he experienced radically transformed his view of personality to something far larger than traditional notions encompass:

> [T]he full view of a personality would extend from the infant curled up in the womb and before it, and beyond it, and ahead of it, into infinity. Our normal view is limited to a physical perception in a condition restricted in time, like the flashing of a torchlight on a spot, the rest of the area being in darkness. If one could have a total view of oneself and others, one would see all in their full stature, through all the stages of evolution and growth, ranging from childhood to old age, in this life, the next one, and the previous ones. [My Days]

A HORSE AND TWO GOATS

Of the seven hundred thousand villages dotting the map of India, in which the majority of India's five hundred million live, flourish, and die, Kritam was probably the tiniest, indicated on the district survey map by a microscopic dot, the map being meant more for the revenue official out to collect tax than for the guidance of the motorist, who in any case could not hope to reach it since it sprawled far from the highway at the end of a rough track furrowed up by the iron-hooped wheels of bullock carts. But its size did not prevent its giving itself the grandiose name Kritam, which meant in Tamil "coronet" or "crown" on the brow of this subcontinent. The village consisted of less than thirty houses, only one of them built with brick and cement. Painted a brilliant yellow and blue all over with gorgeous carvings of gods and gargoyles on its balustrade, it was known as the Big House. The other houses, distributed in four streets, were generally of bamboo thatch, straw, mud, and other unspecified material. Muni's was the last house in the fourth street, beyond which stretched the fields. In his prosperous days Muni had owned a flock of forty sheep and goats and sallied forth every morning driving the flock to the highway a couple of miles away. There he would sit on the pedestal of a clay statue of a horse while his cattle grazed around. He carried a crook at the end of a bamboo pole and snapped foliage from the avenue trees to feed his flock; he also gathered faggots and dry sticks, bundled them, and carried them home for fuel at sunset.

His wife lit the domestic fire at dawn, boiled water in a mud pot, threw into it a handful of millet flour, added salt, and gave him his first nourishment for the day. When he started out, she would put in his hand a packed lunch, once again the same millet cooked into a little ball, which he could swallow with a raw onion at midday. She was old, but he was older and needed all the attention she could give him in order to be kept alive.

His fortunes had declined gradually, unnoticed. From a flock of forty which he drove into a pen at night, his stock had now come down to two goats, which were not worth the rent of a half rupee a month the Big House charged for the use of the pen in their back yard. And so the two goats were tethered to the trunk of a drumstick tree which grew in front of his hut and from which occasionally Muni could shake down drumsticks. This morning he got six. He carried them in with a sense of triumph. Although no one could say precisely who owned the tree, it was his because he lived in its shadow.

She said, "If you were content with the drumstick leaves alone, I could boil and salt some for you."

"Oh, I am tired of eating those leaves. I have a craving to chew the drumstick out of sauce, I tell you."

"You have only four teeth in your jaw, but your craving is for big things. All right, get the stuff for the sauce, and I will prepare it for you. After all, next year you may not be alive to ask for anything. But first get me all the stuff, including a measure of rice or millet, and I will satisfy your unholy craving. Our store is empty today. Dhall,[1]

---

[1]*dhall*   A kind of lentil.

chili, curry leaves, mustard, coriander, gingelley oil, and one large potato. Go out and get all this." He repeated the list after her in order not to miss any item and walked off to the shop in the third street.

He sat on an upturned packing case below the platform of the shop. The shopman paid no attention to him. Muni kept clearing his throat, coughing, and sneezing until the shopman could not stand it any more and demanded, "What ails you? You will fly off that seat into the gutter if you sneeze so hard, young man." Muni laughed inordinately, in order to please the shopman, at being called "young man." The shopman softened and said, "You have enough of the imp inside to keep a second wife busy, but for the fact the old lady is still alive." Muni laughed appropriately again at this joke. It completely won the shopman over; he liked his sense of humour to be appreciated. Muni engaged his attention in local gossip for a few minutes, which always ended with a reference to the postman's wife who had eloped to the city some months before.

The shopman felt most pleased to hear the worst of the postman, who had cheated him. Being an itinerant postman, he returned home to Kritam only once in ten days and every time managed to slip away again without passing the shop in the third street. By thus humouring the shopman, Muni could always ask for one or two items of food, promising repayment later. Some days the shopman was in a good mood and gave in, and sometimes he would lose his temper suddenly and bark at Muni for daring to ask for credit. This was such a day, and Muni could not progress beyond two items listed as essential components. The shopman was also displaying a remarkable memory for old facts and figures and took out an oblong ledger to support his observations. Muni felt impelled to rise and flee. But his self-respect kept him in his seat and made him listen to the worst things about himself. The shopman concluded, "If you could find five rupees[2] and a quarter, you will have paid off an ancient debt and then could apply for admission to swarga.[3] How much have you got now?"

"I will pay you everything on the first of the next month."

"As always, and whom do you expect to rob by then?"

Muni felt caught and mumbled, "My daughter has sent word that she will be sending me money."

"Have you a daughter?" sneered the shopman. "And she is sending you money! For what purpose, may I know?"

"Birthday, fiftieth birthday," said Muni quietly.

"Birthday! How old are you?"

Muni repeated weakly, not being sure of it himself, "Fifty." He always calculated his age from the time of the great famine when he stood as high as the parapet around the village well, but who could calculate such things accurately nowadays with so many famines occurring? The shopman felt encouraged when other customers stood around to watch and comment. Muni thought helplessly, "My poverty is exposed to everybody. But what can I do?"

"More likely you are seventy," said the shopman. "You also forget that you mentioned a birthday five weeks ago when you wanted castor oil for your holy bath."

"Bath! Who can dream of a bath when you have to scratch the tank-bed for a bowl of water? We would all be parched and dead but for the Big House, where they

---

[2]*rupee* Monetary unit of India.
[3]*swarga* Heaven.

let us take a pot of water from their well." After saying this Muni unobtrusively rose and moved off.

He told his wife, "That scoundrel would not give me anything. So go out and sell the drumsticks for what they are worth."

He flung himself down in a corner to recoup from the fatigue of his visit to the shop. His wife said, "You are getting no sauce today, nor anything else. I can't find anything to give you to eat. Fast till the evening, it'll do you good. Take the goats and be gone now," she cried and added, "Don't come back before the sun is down." He knew that if he obeyed her she would somehow conjure up some food for him in the evening. Only he must be careful not to argue and irritate her. Her temper was undependable in the morning but improved by evening time. She was sure to go out and work—grind corn in the Big House, sweep or scrub somewhere, and earn enough to buy foodstuff and keep a dinner ready for him in the evening.

Unleashing the goats from the drumstick tree, Muni started out, driving them ahead and uttering weird cries from time to time in order to urge them on. He passed through the village with his head bowed in thought. He did not want to look at anyone or be accosted. A couple of cronies lounging in the temple corridor hailed him, but he ignored their call. They had known him in the days of affluence when he lorded over a flock of fleecy sheep, not the miserable gawky goats that he had today. Of course he also used to have a few goats for those who fancied them, but real wealth lay in sheep; they bred fast and people came and bought the fleece in the shearing season; and then that famous butcher from the town came over on the weekly market days bringing him betel leaves, tobacco, and often enough some bhang,[4] which they smoked in a hut in the coconut grove, undisturbed by wives and well-wishers. After a smoke one felt light and elated and inclined to forgive everyone including that brother-in-law of his who had once tried to set fire to his home. But all this seemed like the memories of a previous birth. Some pestilence afflicted his cattle (he could of course guess who had laid his animals under a curse), and even the friendly butcher would not touch one at half the price . . . and now here he was left with the two scraggy creatures. He wished someone would rid him of their company too. The shopman had said that he was seventy. At seventy, one only waited to be summoned by God. When he was dead what would his wife do? They had lived in each other's company since they were children. He was told on their day of wedding that he was ten years old and she was eight. During the wedding ceremony they had had to recite their respective ages and names. He had thrashed her only a few times in their career, and later she had the upper hand. Progeny, none. Perhaps a large progeny would have brought him the blessing of the gods. Fertility brought merit. People with fourteen sons were always so prosperous and at peace with the world and themselves. He recollected the thrill he had felt when he mentioned a daughter to that shopman; although it was not believed, what if he did not have a daughter?—his cousin in the next village had many daughters, and any one of them was as good as his; he was fond of them all and would buy them sweets if he could afford it. Still, everyone in the village whispered behind their backs that Muni and his wife were a barren couple. He avoided looking at anyone; they all professed to be so high up, and everyone else in the village had more money than he. "I am the poorest fellow in our caste and no wonder that they spurn me, but I won't look at them either," and so he passed

[4]*bhang* Marijuana.

on with his eyes downcast along the edge of the street, and people left him also very much alone, commenting only to the extent, "Ah, there he goes with his two goats; if he slits their throats, he may have more peace of mind." "What has he to worry about anyway? They live on nothing and have none to worry about." Thus people commented when he passed through the village. Only on the outskirts did he lift his head and look up. He urged and bullied the goats until they meandered along to the foot of the horse statue on the edge of the village. He sat on its pedestal for the rest of the day. The advantage of this was that he could watch the highway and see the lorries[5] and buses pass through to the hills, and it gave him a sense of belonging to a larger world. The pedestal of the statue was broad enough for him to move around as the sun travelled up and westward; or he could also crouch under the belly of the horse, for shade.

The horse was nearly life-size, moulded out of clay, baked, burnt, and brightly coloured, and reared its head proudly, prancing its forelegs in the air and flourishing its tail in a loop; beside the horse stood a warrior with scythe-like mustachios, bulging eyes, and aquiline nose. The old image-makers believed in indicating a man of strength by bulging out his eyes and sharpening his moustache tips, and also decorated the man's chest with beads which looked today like blobs of mud through the ravages of sun and wind and rain (when it came), but Muni would insist that he had known the beads to sparkle like the nine gems at one time in his life. The horse itself was said to have been as white as a dhobi-washed[6] sheet, and had had on its back a cover of pure brocade of red and black lace, matching the multicoloured sash around the waist of the warrior. But none in the village remembered the splendour as no one noticed its existence. Even Muni, who spent all his waking hours at its foot, never bothered to look up. It was untouched even by the young vandals of the village who gashed tree trunks with knives and tried to topple off milestones and inscribed lewd designs on all walls. This statue had been closer to the population of the village at one time, when this spot bordered the village; but when the highway was laid through (or perhaps when the tank and wells dried up completely here) the village moved a couple of miles inland.

Muni sat at the foot of the statue, watching his two goats graze in the arid soil among the cactus and lantana bushes. He looked at the sun; it had tilted westward no doubt, but it was not the time yet to go back home; if he went too early his wife would have no food for him. Also he must give her time to cool off her temper and feel sympathetic, and then she would scrounge and manage to get some food. He watched the mountain road for a time signal. When the green bus appeared around the bend he could leave, and his wife would feel pleased that he had let the goats feed long enough.

He noticed now a new sort of vehicle coming down at full speed. It looked like both a motor car and a bus. He used to be intrigued by the novelty of such spectacles, but of late work was going on at the source of the river on the mountain and an assortment of people and traffic went past him, and he took it all casually and described to his wife, later in the day, everything he saw. Today, while he observed the yellow vehicle coming down, he was wondering how to describe it later to his wife when it sputtered and stopped in front of him. A red-faced foreigner, who had been driving it, got

---

[5]*lorries* Trucks.
[6]*dhobi* Servant who washes clothes.

down and went round it, stooping, looking, and poking under the vehicle; then he straightened himself up, looked at the dashboard, stared in Muni's direction, and approached him. "Excuse me, is there a gas station nearby, or do I have to wait until another car comes—" He suddenly looked up at the clay horse and cried, "Marvellous," without completing his sentence. Muni felt he should get up and run away, and cursed his age. He could not readily put his limbs into action; some years ago he could out-run a cheetah, as happened once when he went to the forest to cut fuel and it was then that two of his sheep were mauled—a sign that bad times were coming. Though he tried, he could not easily extricate himself from his seat, and then there was also the problem of the goats. He could not leave them behind.

The red-faced man wore khaki clothes—evidently a policeman or a soldier. Muni said to himself, "He will chase or shoot if I start running. Some dogs chase only those who run—oh, Shiva protect me. I don't know why this man should be after me." Meanwhile the foreigner cried, "Marvellous!" again, nodding his head. He paced around the statue with his eyes fixed on it. Muni sat frozen for a while, and then fidgeted and tried to edge away. Now the other man suddenly pressed his palms together in a salute, smiled, and said, "Namaste![7] How do you do?"

At which Muni spoke the only English expressions he had learnt, "Yes, no." Having exhausted his English vocabulary, he started in Tamil: "My name is Muni. These two goats are mine, and no one can gainsay it—though our village is full of slander-ers these days who will not hesitate to say that what belongs to a man doesn't belong to him." He rolled his eyes and shuddered at the thought of evil-minded men and women peopling his village.

The foreigner faithfully looked in the direction indicated by Muni's fingers, gazed for a while at the two goats and the rocks, and with a puzzled expression took out his silver cigarette case and lit a cigarette. Suddenly remembering the courtesies of the season, he asked, "Do you smoke?" Muni answered, "Yes, no." Whereupon the red-faced man took a cigarette and gave it to Muni, who received it with surprise, having had no offer of a smoke from anyone for years now. Those days when he smoked bhang were gone with his sheep and the large-hearted butcher. Nowadays he was not able to find even matches, let alone bhang. (His wife went across and borrowed a fire at dawn from a neighbour.) He had always wanted to smoke a cigarette; only once did the shopman give him one on credit, and he remembered how good it had tasted. The other flicked the lighter open and offered a light to Muni. Muni felt so confused about how to act that he blew on it and put it out. The other, puzzled but undaunted, flourished his lighter, presented it again, and lit Muni's cigarette. Muni drew a deep puff and started coughing; it was racking, no doubt, but extremely pleas-ant. When his cough subsided he wiped his eyes and took stock of the situation, un-derstanding that the other man was not an Inquisitor of any kind. Yet, in order to make sure, he remained wary. No need to run away from a man who gave him such a po-tent smoke. His head was reeling from the effect of one of those strong American cig-arettes made with roasted tobacco. The man said, "I come from New York," took out a wallet from his hip pocket, and presented his card.

Muni shrank away from the card. Perhaps he was trying to present a warrant and arrest him. Beware of khaki, one part of his mind warned. Take all the cigarettes or bhang or whatever is offered, but don't get caught. Beware of khaki. He wished he

---

[7]*Namaste!*   Greeting: Hello!

weren't seventy as the shopman had said. At seventy one didn't run, but surrendered to whatever came. He could only ward off trouble by talk. So he went on, all in the chaste Tamil for which Kritam was famous. (Even the worst detractors could not deny that the famous poetess Avvaiyar was born in this area, although no one could say whether it was in Kritam or Kuppam, the adjoining village.) Out of this heritage the Tamil language gushed through Muni in an unimpeded flow. He said, "Before God, sir, Bhagwan, who sees everything, I tell you, sir, that we know nothing of the case. If the murder was committed, whoever did it will not escape. Bhagwan is all-seeing. Don't ask me about it. I know nothing." A body had been found mutilated and thrown under a tamarind tree at the border between Kritam and Kuppam a few weeks before, giving rise to much gossip and speculation. Muni added an explanation. "Anything is possible there. People over there will stop at nothing." The foreigner nodded his head and listened courteously though he understood nothing.

"I am sure you know when this horse was made," said the red man and smiled ingratiatingly.

Muni reacted to the relaxed atmosphere by smiling himself, and pleaded, "Please go away, sir, I know nothing. I promise we will hold him for you if we see any bad character around, and we will bury him up to his neck in a coconut pit if he tries to escape; but our village has always had a clean record. Must definitely be the other village."

Now the red man implored, "Please, please, I will speak slowly, please try to understand me. Can't you understand even a single word of English? Everyone in this country seems to know English. I have gotten along with English everywhere in this country, but you don't speak it. Have you any religious or spiritual scruples against English speech?"

Muni made some indistinct sounds in his throat and shook his head. Encouraged, the other went on to explain at length, uttering each syllable with care and deliberation. Presently he sidled over and took a seat beside the old man, explaining, "You see, last August, we probably had the hottest summer in history, and I was working in shirt-sleeves in my office on the fortieth floor of the Empire State Building. We had a power failure one day, you know, and there I was stuck for four hours, no elevator, no air conditioning. All the way in the train I kept thinking, and the minute I reached home in Connecticut, I told my wife Ruth, 'We will visit India this winter, it's time to look at other civilizations.' Next day she called the travel agent first thing and told him to fix it, and so here I am. Ruth came with me but is staying back at Srinagar, and I am the one doing the rounds and joining her later."

Muni looked reflective at the end of this long oration and said, rather feebly, "Yes, no," as a concession to the other's language, and went on in Tamil, "When I was this high"—he indicated a foot high—"I had heard my uncle say . . ."

No one can tell what he was planning to say, as the other interrupted him at this stage to ask, "Boy, what is the secret of your teeth? How old are you?"

The old man forgot what he had started to say and remarked, "Sometimes we too lose our cattle. Jackals or cheetahs may sometimes carry them off, but sometimes it is just theft from over in the next village, and then we will know who has done it. Our priest at the temple can see in the camphor flame the face of the thief, and when he is caught . . ." He gestured with his hands a perfect mincing of meat.

The American watched his hands intently and said, "I know what you mean. Chop something? Maybe I am holding you up and you want to chop wood? Where is your axe? Hand it to me and show me what to chop. I do enjoy it, you know, just a hobby. We get a lot of driftwood along the backwater near my house, and on Sundays I do nothing but chop wood for the fireplace. I really feel different when I watch the fire in the fireplace, although it may take all the sections of the Sunday *New York Times* to get a fire started." And he smiled at this reference.

Muni felt totally confused but decided the best thing would be to make an attempt to get away from this place. He tried to edge out, saying, "Must go home," and turned to go. The other seized his shoulder and said desperately, "Is there no one, absolutely no one here, to translate for me?" He looked up and down the road, which was deserted in this hot afternoon; a sudden gust of wind churned up the dust and dead leaves on the roadside into a ghostly column and propelled it towards the mountain road. The stranger almost pinioned Muni's back to the statue and asked, "Isn't this statue yours? Why don't you sell it to me?"

The old man now understood the reference to the horse, thought for a second, and said in his own language, "I was an urchin this high when I heard my grandfather explain this horse and warrior, and my grandfather himself was this high when he heard his grandfather, whose grandfather . . ."

The other man interrupted him. "I don't want to seem to have stopped here for nothing. I will offer you a good price for this," he said, indicating the horse. He had concluded without the least doubt that Muni owned this mud horse. Perhaps he guessed by the way he sat on its pedestal, like other souvenir sellers in this country presiding over their wares.

Muni followed the man's eyes and pointing fingers and dimly understood the subject matter and, feeling relieved that the theme of the mutilated body had been abandoned at least for the time being, said again, enthusiastically, "I was this high when my grandfather told me about this horse and the warrior, and my grandfather was this high when he himself . . ." and he was getting into a deeper bog of reminiscence each time he tried to indicate the antiquity of the statue.

The Tamil that Muni spoke was stimulating even as pure sound, and the foreigner listened with fascination. "I wish I had my tape-recorder here," he said, assuming the pleasantest expression. "Your language sounds wonderful. I get a kick out of every word you utter, here"—he indicated his ears—"but you don't have to waste your breath in sales talk. I appreciate the article. You don't have to explain its points."

"I never went to a school, in those days only Brahmin went to schools, but we had to go out and work in the fields morning till night, from sowing to harvest time . . . and when Pongal came and we had cut the harvest, my father allowed me to go out and play with others at the tank, and so I don't know the Parangi language you speak, even little fellows in your country probably speak the Parangi language, but here only learned men and officers know it. We had a postman in our village who could speak to you boldly in your language, but his wife ran away with someone and he does not speak to anyone at all nowadays. Who would if a wife did what she did? Women must be watched; otherwise they will sell themselves and the home." And he laughed at his own quip.

The foreigner laughed heartily, took out another cigarette, and offered it to Muni, who now smoked with ease, deciding to stay on if the fellow was going to be so good as to keep up his cigarette supply. The American now stood up on the pedestal in the attitude of a demonstrative lecturer and said, running his finger along some of the carved decorations around the horse's neck, speaking slowly and uttering his words syllable by syllable, "I could give a sales talk for this better than anyone else. . . . This is a marvellous combination of yellow and indigo, though faded now. . . . How do you people of this country achieve these flaming colours?"

Muni, now assured that the subject was still the horse and not the dead body, said, "This is our guardian, it means death to our adversaries. At the end of Kali Yuga, this world and all other worlds will be destroyed, and the Redeemer will come in the shape of a horse called 'Kalki'; this horse will come to life and gallop and trample down all bad men. As he spoke of bad men the figures of his shopman and his brother-in-law assumed concrete forms in his mind, and he revelled for a moment in the predicament of the fellow under the horse's hoof: served him right for trying to set fire to his home. . . .

While he was brooding on this pleasant vision, the foreigner utilized the pause to say, "I assure you that this will have the best home in the U.S.A. I'll push away the bookcase, you know I love books and am a member of five book clubs, and the choice and bonus volumes mount up to a pile really in our living room, as high as this horse itself. But they'll have to go. Ruth may disapprove, but I will convince her. The T.V. may have to be shifted too. We can't have everything in the living room. Ruth will probably say what about when we have a party. I'm going to keep him right in the middle of the room. I don't see how that can interfere with the party—we'll stand around him and have our drinks."

Muni continued his description of the end of the world. "Our pundit discoursed at the temple once how the oceans are going to close over the earth in a huge wave and swallow us—this horse will grow bigger than the biggest wave and carry on its back only the good people and kick into the floods the evil ones—plenty of them about—" he said reflectively. "Do you know when it is going to happen?" he asked.

The foreigner now understood by the tone of the other that a question was being asked and said, "How am I transporting it? I can push the seat back and make room in the rear. That van can take in an elephant"—waving precisely at the back of the seat.

Muni was still hovering on visions of avatars and said again, "I never missed our pundit's discourses at the temple in those days during every bright half of the month, although he'd go on all night, and he told us that Vishnu is the highest god. Whenever evil men trouble us, he comes down to save us. He has come many times. The first time he incarnated as a great fish, and lifted the scriptures on his back when the floods and sea waves . . ."

"I am not a millionaire, but a modest businessman. My trade is coffee."

Amidst all this wilderness of obscure sound Muni caught the word "coffee" and said, "If you want to drink 'kapi,' drive further up, in the next town, they have Friday market, and there they open 'kapi-otels'—so I learn from passersby. Don't think I wander about. I go nowhere and look for nothing." His thoughts went back to the avatars. "The first avatar was in the shape of a little fish in a bowl of water, but every hour it grew bigger and bigger and became in the end a huge whale which the seas could not contain, and on the back of the whale the holy books were supported, saved and carried." Once he had launched on the first avatar, it was inevitable that he should go on to the next, a wild boar on whose tusk the earth was lifted when a vicious conqueror of the earth carried it off and hid it at the bottom of the sea. After describing this avatar Muni concluded, "God will always save us whenever we are troubled by evil beings. When we were young we staged at full moon the story of the avatars. That's how I know the stories; we played them all night until the sun rose, and sometimes the European collector would come to watch, bringing his own chair. I had a good voice and so they always taught me songs and gave me the women's roles. I was always Goddess Lakshmi, and they dressed me in a brocade sari, loaned from the Big House. . . ."

The foreigner said, "I repeat I am not a millionaire. Ours is a modest business; after all, we can't afford to buy more than sixty minutes of T.V. time in a month, which works out to two minutes a day, that's all, although in the course of time we'll maybe sponsor a one-hour show regularly if our sales graph continues to go up. . . ."

Muni was intoxicated by the memory of his theatrical days and was about to explain how he had painted his face and worn a wig and diamond earrings when the visitor, feeling that he had spent too much time already, said, "Tell me, will you accept a hundred rupees or not for the horse? I'd love to take the whiskered soldier also but no space for him this year. I'll have to cancel my air ticket and take a boat home, I suppose. Ruth can go by air if she likes, but I will go with the horse and keep him in my cabin all the way if necessary." And he smiled at the picture of himself voyaging across the seas hugging this horse. He added, "I will have to pad it with straw so that it doesn't break. . . ."

"When we played *Ramayana*,[8] they dressed me as Sita," added Muni. "A teacher came and taught us the songs for the drama and we gave him fifty rupees. He incarnated himself as Rama, and He alone could destroy Ravana, the demon with ten heads who shook all the worlds; do you know the story of *Ramayana?*"

"I have my station wagon as you see. I can push the seat back and take the horse in if you will just lend me a hand with it."

"Do you know *Mahabharata?*[9] Krishna was the eighth avatar of Vishnu, incarnated to help the Five Brothers regain their kingdom. When Krishna was a baby he danced on the thousand-hooded giant serpent and trampled it to death; and then he suckled the breasts of the demoness and left them flat as a disc though when she came to him her bosoms were large, like mounds of earth on the banks of a dug up canal." He indicated two mounds with his hands. The stranger was completely mystified by the gesture. For the first time he said, "I really wonder what you are saying because your answer is crucial. We have come to the point when we should be ready to talk business."

"When the tenth avatar comes, do you know where you and I will be?" asked the old man.

"Lend me a hand and I can lift off the horse from its pedestal after picking out the cement at the joints. We can do anything if we have a basis of understanding."

At this stage the mutual mystification was complete, and there was no need even to carry on a guessing game at the meaning of words. The old man chattered away in a spirit of balancing off the credits and debits of conversational exchange, and said in order to be on the credit side, "Oh, honourable one, I hope God has blessed you with numerous progeny. I say this because you seem to be a good man, willing to stay beside an old man and talk to him, while all day I have none to talk to except when somebody stops by to ask for a piece of tobacco. But I seldom have it, tobacco is not what it used to be at one time, and I have given up chewing. I cannot afford it nowadays." Noting the other's interest in his speech, Muni felt encouraged to ask, "How many children have you?" with appropriate gestures with his hands. Realizing that a question was being asked, the red man replied, "I said a hundred," which encouraged Muni to go into details. "How many of your children are boys and how many girls?

---

[8]*Ramayana*   One of the two great epics of India, written in Sanscrit and describing the adventures of the hero Rama; *Sita*—Rama's wife.

[9]*Mahabharata*   The other great epic of India, written in Sanscrit about 200 B.C.E.

Where are they? Is your daughter married? Is it difficult to find a son-in-law in your country also?"

In answer to these questions the red man dashed his hand into his pocket and brought forth his wallet in order to take immediate advantage of the bearish trend in the market. He flourished a hundred-rupee currency note and said, "Well, this is what I meant."

The old man now realized that some financial element was entering their talk. He peered closely at the currency note, the like of which he had never seen in his life; he knew the five and ten by their colours although always in other people's hands, while his own earning at any time was in coppers and nickels. What was this man flourishing the note for? Perhaps asking for change. He laughed to himself at the notion of anyone coming to him for changing a thousand- or ten-thousand-rupee note. He said with a grin, "Ask our village headman, who is also a money-lender; he can change even a lakh[10] of rupees in gold sovereigns if you prefer it that way; he thinks nobody knows, but dig the floor of his puja[11] room and your head will reel at the sight of the hoard. The man disguises himself in rags just to mislead the public. Talk to the headman yourself because he goes mad at the sight of me. Someone took away his pumpkins with the creeper and he, for some reason, thinks it was me and my goats . . . that's why I never let my goats be seen anywhere near the farms." His eyes travelled to his goats nosing about, attempting to wrest nutrition from minute greenery peeping out of rock and dry earth.

The foreigner followed his look and decided that it would be a sound policy to show an interest in the old man's pets. He went up casually to them and stroked their backs with every show of courteous attention. Now the truth dawned on the old man. His dream of a lifetime was about to be realized. He understood that the red man was actually making an offer for the goats. He had reared them up in the hope of selling them some day and, with the capital, opening a small shop on this very spot. Sitting here, watching towards the hills, he had often dreamt how he would put up a thatched roof here, spread a gunny sack out on the ground, and display on it fried nuts, coloured sweets, and green coconut for the thirsty and famished wayfarers on the highway, which was sometimes very busy. The animals were not prize ones for a cattle show, but he had spent his occasional savings to provide them some fancy diet now and then, and they did not look too bad. While he was reflecting thus, the red man shook his hand and left on his palm one hundred rupees in tens now, suddenly realizing that this was what the old man was asking. "It is all for you or you may share it if you have a partner."

The old man pointed at the station wagon and asked, "Are you carrying them off in that?"

"Yes, of course," said the other, understanding the transportation part of it.

The old man said, "This will be their first ride in a motor car. Carry them off after I get out of sight, otherwise they will never follow you, but only me even if I am travelling on the path to Yama Loka."[12] He laughed at his own joke, brought his palms together in a salute, turned round and went off, and was soon out of sight beyond a clump of thicket.

---

[10]*lakh*   100,000 of an item (as American speakers use "a million").

[11]*puja*   A room for private prayer.

[12]*Yama Loka*   The afterlife, according to Hindu belief. Yama is the judge of human beings and king of the invisible world after death.

The red man looked at the goats grazing peacefully. Perched on the pedestal of the horse, as the westerly sun touched off the ancient faded colours of the statue with a fresh splendour, he ruminated, "He must be gone to fetch some help, I suppose!" and settled down to wait. When a truck came downhill, he stopped it and got the help of a couple of men to detach the horse from its pedestal and place it in his station wagon. He gave them five rupees each, and for a further payment they siphoned off gas from the truck, and helped him to start his engine.

Muni hurried homeward with the cash securely tucked away at his waist in his dhoti. He shut the street door and stole up softly to his wife as she squatted before the lit oven wondering if by a miracle food would drop from the sky. Muni displayed his fortune for the day. She snatched the notes from him, counted them by the glow of the fire, and cried, "One hundred rupees! How did you come by it? Have you been stealing?"

"I have sold our goats to a red-faced man. He was absolutely crazy to have them, gave me all this money and carried them off in his motor car!"

Hardly had these words left his lips when they heard bleating outside. She opened the door and saw the two goats at her door. "Here they are!" she said. "What's the meaning of all this?"

He muttered a great curse and seized one of the goats by its ears and shouted, "Where is that man? Don't you know you are his? Why did you come back?" The goat only wriggled in his grip. He asked the same question of the other too. The goat shook itself off. His wife glared at him and declared, "If you have thieved, the police will come tonight and break your bones. Don't involve me. I will go away to my parents. . . ."

[1970]

Questions

1. What assumptions does each man make about the other? How do these assumptions reveal their respective cultural situations and personal values?
2. What does the story suggest about cross-cultural communication? How do the comments made by Muni and the American tourist form a kind of conversation despite their different languages? Consider the accuracy of the American's observation, "We can do anything if we have a basis of understanding."
3. What are the sources of the story's humor?
4. Compare this story with Carmen Naranjo's "And We Sold the Rain" and Joseph Conrad's "Amy Foster."

Ngugi wa Thiong'o
(b. 1938)
Kenya

Ngugi wa Thiong'o is East Africa's most accomplished writer. Born in Kenya, he is the author of a half dozen novels, including Weep Not, Child (1964), A Grain of Wheat (1967), Petals of Blood (1977), and Devil on the Cross (1980). He has also written numerous short stories, plays, and critical essays. Although he has written compellingly about his country's struggle for independence, in recent years Ngugi has exerted much of his energy against neocolonialism. Sadly, his political opinions have not been tolerated by his country's leaders. He was imprisoned for a year by his government and shortly after his release went into exile. His account of his incarceration was published in 1981: Detained: A Writer's Diary.

His essay "Church, Culture and Politics," from Homecoming (1972), helps to illuminate "A Meeting in the Dark," which was written at the beginning of his literary career:

> The coming of Christianity . . . set in motion a process of social change, involving rapid disintegration of the tribal set-up and the frame-work of social norms and values by which people had formerly ordered their lives and their relationships to others. This was especially true of Central Province, where the Church of Scotland Mission, which has a highly strict puritan tradition, could not separate the strictly Christian dogma or doctrine from the European scale of values, and from European customs. The evidence that you were saved was not whether you were a believer in and follower of Christ, and accepted all men as equal: the measure of your Christian love and charity was in preserving the outer signs and symbols of a European way of life; whether you dressed as Europeans did, whether you had acquired European good manners, liked European hymns and tunes, and of course whether you had refused to have your daughter circumcised.

A MEETING IN THE DARK

His mother used to tell him stories. "Once upon a time there was a young girl who lived with her father and mother in a lonely house that was hidden by a hill. The house was old but strong. When the rains came and the winds blew, the house remained firm. Her father and mother liked her, but they quarrelled sometimes and she would cry. Otherwise, she was happy. Nobody knew of the house. So nobody came to see them. Then one day a stranger came. He was tall and handsome. He had milk-white teeth. Her mother gave him food. Then he told them of a beautiful country beyond the hill. The girl wanted to go there. Secretly, she followed the man. They had not gone very far when the stranger turned into an Irimu. He became ugly and he had another mouth at the back which was hidden by his long hair. Occasionally, the hair was blown by the wind. Flies were taken in and the mouth would be shut.

The girl ran back. The bad Irimu followed her. She ran hard, hard, and the Irimu could not catch her. But he was getting nearer her all the time. When she came close to her home, she found the Irimu had stopped running. But the house was no longer there. She had no home to go to and she could not go forward to the beautiful land, to see all the good things, because the Irimu was on the way."

How did the story end? John wondered. He thought: "I wish I were young again in our old home, then I would ask my mother about it." But now he was not young; not young any more. And he was not a man yet!

He stood at the door of the hut and saw his old, frail but energetic father coming along the village street, with a rather dirty bag made out of strong calico swinging by his side. His father always carried this bag. John knew what it contained: a Bible, a hymn book, and probably a notebook and a pen. His father was a preacher. It must have been he who had stopped his mother from telling him stories. His mother had stopped telling him stories long ago. She would say, "Now, don't ask for any more stories. Your father may come." So he feared his father. John went in and warned his mother of his father's coming. Then his father came in. John stood aside, then walked towards the door. He lingered there doubtfully, then he went out.

"John, hei, John!"

"Baba!"

"Come back."

He stood doubtfully in front of his father. His heart beat faster and an agitated voice within him seemed to ask: Does he know?

"Sit down. Where are you going?"

"For a walk, Father," he answered evasively.

"To the village?"

"Well—yes—no. I mean nowhere in particular." John saw his father look at him hard, seeming to read his face. John sighed a very slow sigh. He did not like the way his father eyed him. He always looked at him as though John was a sinner, one who had to be watched all the time. "I am," his heart told him. John guiltily refused to meet the old man's gaze and looked past him and appealingly to his mother who was quietly peeling potatoes. But she seemed to be oblivious of everything around her.

"Why do you look away? What have you done?"

John shrank within himself with fear. But his face remained expressionless. However, he could hear the loud beats of his heart. It was like an engine pumping water. He felt no doubt his father knew all about it. He thought: "Why does he torture me? Why does he not at once say he knows?" Then another voice told him: "No, he doesn't know, otherwise he would have already jumped at you." A consolation. He faced his thoughtful father with courage.

"When is the journey?"

Again John thought—why does he ask? I have told him many times. Aloud, he said, "Next week, Tuesday."

"Right. Tomorrow we go to the shops, hear?"

"Yes, Father."

"You can go."

"Thank you, Father." He began to move.

"John!"

"Yes?" John's heart almost stopped beating. That second, before his father's next words, was an age.

"You seem to be in hurry. I don't want to hear of you loitering in the village. I know you young men, going to show off just because you are going away! I don't want to hear of trouble in the village."

Much relieved, he went out. He could guess what his father meant by not wanting trouble in the village. How did the story end? Funny, but he could not remember how his mother had ended it. It had been so long ago. Her home was not there. Where did she go? What did she do?

"Why do you persecute the boy so much?" Susan spoke for the first time. Apparently she had carefully listened to the whole drama without a word. Now was her time to speak. She looked at her tough old preacher who had been a companion for life. She had married him a long time ago. She could not tell the number of years. They had been happy. Then the man became a convert. And everything in the home put on a religious tone. He even made her stop telling stories to the child. "Tell him of Jesus. Jesus died for you. Jesus died for the child. He must know the Lord." She too had been converted. But she was never blind to the moral torture he inflicted on the boy (that's what she always called John), so that the boy had grown up mortally afraid of him. She always wondered if it was love for the son. Or could it be a resentment because, well, they two had "sinned" before marriage? John had been the result of that sin. But that had not been John's fault. It was the boy who ought to complain. She often wondered if the boy had . . . but no. The boy had been very small when they left Fort Hall. She looked at her husband. He remained mute, though his left hand did, rather irritably, feel about his face.

"It is as if he was not your son. Or do you . . ."

"Hm, sister." The voice was pleading. She was seeking a quarrel but he did not feel equal to one. Really, women could never understand. Women were women, whether saved or not. Their son had to be protected against all evil influences. He must be made to grow in the footsteps of the Lord. He looked at her, frowning a little. She had made him sin but that had been a long time ago. And he had been saved. John must not follow the same road.

"You ought to tell us to leave. You know I can go away. Go back to Fort Hall. And then everybody . . ."

"Look, sister." He hastily interrupted. He always called her sister. Sister-in-the-Lord, in full. But he sometimes wondered if she had been truly saved. In his heart, he prayed: Lord, be with our sister Susan. Aloud, he continued, "You know I want the boy to grow in the Lord."

"But you torture him so! You make him fear you!"

"Why! He should not fear me. I have really nothing against him."

"It is you. You. You have always been cruel to him. . . ." She stood up. The peelings dropped from her frock and fell in a heap on the floor.

"Stanley!"

"Sister." He was startled by the vehemence in her voice. He had never seen her like this. Lord, take the devil out of her. Save her this minute. She did not say what she wanted to say. Stanley looked away from her. It was a surprise, but it seemed he feared his wife. If you had told people in the village about this, they would not have believed you. He took his Bible and began to read. On Sunday he would preach to a congregation of brethren and sisters.

Susan, a rather tall, thin woman, who had once been beautiful, sat down again and went on with her work. She did not know what was troubling her son. Was it the coming journey?

Outside, John strolled aimlessly along the path that led from his home. He stood near the wattle tree which was a little way from his father's house, and surveyed the whole village. They lay before his eyes—crammed—rows and rows of mud and grass huts, ending in sharp sticks that pointed to heaven. Smoke was coming out of various huts, an indication that many women had already come from the *shambas*. Night would soon fall. To the west, the sun was hurrying home behind the misty hills. Again, John looked at the crammed rows and rows of huts that formed Makeno Village, one of the new mushroom "towns" that grew up all over the country during the Mau Mau war. It looked so ugly. A pang of pain rose in his heart and he felt like crying—I hate you, I hate you. You trapped me alive. Away from you, it would never have happened. He did not shout. He just watched.

A woman was coming towards where he stood. A path into the village was just near there. She was carrying a big load of *kuni* which bent her into an Akamba-bow shape. She greeted him.

"Is it well with you, Njooni?"

"It is well with me, mother." There was no trace of bitterness in his voice. John was by nature polite. Everyone knew of this. He was quite unlike the other proud, educated sons of the tribe—sons who came back from the other side of the waters with white or Negro wives who spoke English. And they behaved just like Europeans! John was a favourite, a model of humility and moral perfection. Everyone knew that though a clergyman's son, John would never betray the tribe.

"When are you going to—to—"

"Makerere?"

"Makelele." She laughed. The way she pronounced the name was funny. And the way she laughed too. She enjoyed it. But John felt hurt. So everyone knew of this.

"Next week."

"I wish you well."

"Thank you, mother."

She said quietly—as if trying to pronounce it better—"Makelele." She laughed at herself again but she was tired. The load was heavy.

"Stay well, son."

"Go well and in peace, mother."

And the woman who all the time had stood, moved on, panting like a donkey, but obviously pleased with John's kindness.

John remained long looking at her. What made such a woman live on day to day, working hard, yet happy? Had she much faith in life? Or was her faith in the tribe? She and her kind, who had never been touched by ways of the white man, looked as though they had something to cling to. As he watched her disappear, he felt proud that they should think well of him. He felt proud that he had a place in their esteem. And then came the pang. *Father will know. They will know.* He did not know what he feared most; the action his father would take when he knew, or the loss of the little faith the simple villagers had placed in him, when they knew.

He went down to the small local teashop. He met many people who wished him well at the college. All of them knew that the Pastor's son had finished all the white man's learning in Kenya. He would now go to Uganda; they had read this in the *Baraza*, a Swahili weekly paper. John did not stay long at the shop. The sun had already gone to rest and now darkness was coming. The evening meal was ready. His tough father was still at the table reading his Bible. He did not look up when John entered. Strange silence settled in the hut.

"You look unhappy." His mother first broke the silence. John laughed. It was a nervous little laugh.

"No, mother," he hastily replied, nervously looking at his father. He secretly hoped that Wamuhu had not blabbed.

"Then I am glad."

She did not know. He ate his dinner and went out to his hut. A man's hut. Every young man had his own hut. John was never allowed to bring any girl visitor in there. He did not want "trouble." Even to be seen standing with one was a crime. His father could easily thrash him. He wished he had rebelled earlier like all the other young educated men. He lit the lantern. He took it in his hand. The yellow light flickered dangerously and then went out. He knew his hands were shaking. He lit it again and hurriedly took his big coat and a huge *Kofia* which were lying on the unmade bed. He left the lantern burning, so that his father would see it and think him in. John bit his lower lip spitefully. He hated himself for being so girlish. It was unnatural for a boy of his age.

Like a shadow, he stealthily crossed the courtyard and went on to the village street.

He met young men and women, lining the streets. They were laughing, talking, whispering. They were obviously enjoying themselves. John thought, they are more free than I am. He envied their exuberance. They clearly stood outside or above the strict morality that the educated ones had to be judged by. Would he have gladly changed places with them? He wondered. At last, he came to the hut. It stood at the very heart of the village. How well he knew it—to his sorrow. He wondered what he would do! Wait for her outside? What if her mother came out instead? He decided to enter.

"*Hodi!*"

"Enter. We are in."

John pulled down his hat before he entered. Indeed they were all there—all except she whom he wanted. The fire in the hearth was dying. Only a small flame from a lighted lantern vaguely illuminated the whole hut. The flame and the giant shadow created on the wall seemed to be mocking him. He prayed that Wamuhu's parents would not recognize him. He tried to be "thin," and to disguise his voice as he greeted them. They recognized him and made themselves busy on his account. To be visited by such an educated one who knew all about the white man's world and knowledge, and who would now go to another land beyond, was not such a frequent occurrence that it could be taken lightly. Who knew but he might be interested in their daughter? Stranger things had happened. After all, learning was not the only thing. Though Wamuhu had no learning, yet charms she had and she could be trusted to captivate any young man's heart with her looks and smiles.

"You will sit down. Take that stool."

"No!" He noticed with bitterness that he did not call her "mother."

"Where is Wamuhu?" The mother threw a triumphant glance at her husband. They exchanged a knowing look. John bit his lips again and felt like bolting. He controlled himself with difficulty.

"She has gone out to get some tea leaves. Please sit down. She will cook you some tea when she comes."

"I am afraid . . ." he muttered some inaudible words and went out. He almost collided with Wamuhu.

In the hut:

"Didn't I tell you? Trust a woman's eye!"

"You don't know these young men."

"But you see John is different. Everyone speaks well of him and he is a clergyman's son."

"Y-e-e-s! A clergyman's son? You forgot your daughter is circumcised." The old man was remembering his own day. He had found for himself a good, virtuous woman, initiated in all the tribe's ways. And she had known no other man. He had married her. They were happy. Other men of his *Rika* had done the same. All their girls had been virgins, it being a taboo to touch a girl in that way, even if you slept in the same bed, as indeed so many young men and girls did. Then the white men had come, preaching a strange religion, strange ways, which all men followed. The tribe's code of behaviour was broken. The new faith could not keep the tribe together. How could it? The men who followed the new faith would not let the girls be circumcised. And they would not let their sons marry circumcised girls. Puu! Look at what was happening. Their young men went away to the land of the white men. What did they bring? White women. Black women who spoke English. Aaa—bad. And the young men who were left just did not mind. They made unmarried girls their wives and then left them with fatherless children.

"What does it matter?" his wife was replying. "Is Wamuhu not as good as the best of them? Anyway, John is different."

"Different! different! Puu! They are all alike. Those coated with the white clay of the white man's ways are the worst. They have nothing inside. Nothing—nothing here." He took a piece of wood and nervously poked the dying fire. A strange numbness came over him. He trembled. And he feared; he feared for the tribe. For now he said it was not only the educated men who were coated with strange ways, but the whole tribe. The tribe had followed a false Irimu like the girl in the story. For the old man trembled and cried inside, mourning for a tribe that had crumbled. The tribe had nowhere to go to. And it could not be what it was before. He stopped poking and looked hard at the ground.

"I wonder why he came. I wonder." Then he looked at his wife and said, "Have you seen strange behaviour with your daughter?"

His wife did not·answer. She was preoccupied with her own great hopes. . . .

John and Wamuhu walked on in silence. The intricate streets and turns were well known to them both. Wamuhu walked with quick light steps; John knew she was in a happy mood. His steps were heavy and he avoided people even though it was dark. But why should he feel ashamed? The girl was beautiful, probably the most beautiful girl in the whole of Limuru. Yet he feared being seen with her. It was all wrong. He knew that he could have loved her, even then he wondered if he did not love her. Perhaps it was hard to tell but had he been one of the young men he had met, he would not have hesitated in his answer.

Outside the village he stopped. She too stopped. Neither had spoken a word all through. Perhaps the silence spoke louder than words. Each was only too conscious of the other.

"Do they know?" Silence. Wamuhu was probably considering the question. "Don't keep me waiting. Please answer me," he implored. He felt weary, very weary, like an old man who had suddenly reached his journey's end.

"No. You told me to give you one more week. A week is over today."

"Yes. That's why I came!" John hoarsely whispered.

Wamuhu did not speak. John looked at her. Darkness was now between them. He was not really seeing her; before him was the image of his father—haughtily religious and dominating. Again he thought: I John, a priest's son, respected by all and going to college, will fall, fall to the ground. He did not want to contemplate the fall.

"It was your fault." He found himself accusing her. In his heart he knew he was lying.

"Why do you keep on telling me that? Don't you want to marry me?"

John sighed. He did not know what to do.

Once upon a time there was a young girl . . . she had no home to go to . . . she could not go forward to the beautiful land and see all the good things because the Irimu was on the way. . . .

"When will you tell them?"

"Tonight." He felt desperate. Next week he would go to the college. If he could persuade her to wait, he might be able to get away and come back when the storm and consternation had abated. But then the government might withdraw his bursary. He was frightened and there was a sad note of appeal as he turned to her and said:

"Look, Wamuhu, how long have you been pre—I mean like this?"

"I have told you over and over again. I have been pregnant for three months and mother is being suspicious. Only yesterday she said I breathed like a woman with a child."

"Do you think you could wait for three weeks more?" She laughed. Ah! the little witch! She knew his trick. Her laughter always aroused many emotions in him.

"All right. Give me just tomorrow. I'll think up something. Tomorrow I'll let you know all."

"I agree. Tomorrow. I cannot wait any more unless you mean to marry me."

Why not marry her? She is beautiful! Why not marry her? And do I or don't I love her?

She left. John felt as if she was deliberately blackmailing him. His knees were weak and lost strength. He could not move but sank on the ground in a heap. Sweat poured profusely down his cheeks, as if he had been running hard under a strong sun. But this was cold sweat. He lay on the grass; he did not want to think. Oh! No! He could not possibly face his father. Or his mother. Or Rev. Thomas Carstone who had had such faith in him. John realized that he was not more secure than anybody else, in spite of his education. He was no better than Wamuhu. *Then why don't you marry her?* He did not know. John had grown up under a Calvinistic father and learnt under a Calvinistic headmaster—a missionary! John tried to pray. But to whom was he praying? To Carstone's God? It sounded false. It was as if he was blaspheming. Could he pray to the God of the tribe? His sense of guilt crushed him.

He woke up. Where was he? Then he understood. Wamuhu had left him. She had given him one day. He stood up; he felt good. Weakly, he began to walk back home. It was lucky that darkness blanketed the whole earth, and him in it. From the various huts, he could hear laughter, heated talks or quarrels. Little fires could be seen flickeringly red through the open doors. Village stars—John thought. He raised up his eyes. The heavenly stars, cold and distant, looked down on him, impersonally. Here and there, groups of boys and girls could be heard laughing and shouting. For them life seemed to go on as usual. John consoled himself by thinking that they too would come to face their day of trial.

John was shaky. Why! Why! Why could he not defy all expectations, all prospects of a future, and marry the girl? No. No. It was impossible. She was circumcised, and he knew that his father and the church would never consent to such a marriage. She had no learning, or rather she had not gone beyond Standard 4. Marrying her would probably ruin his chances of ever going to a University. . . .

He tried to move briskly. His strength had returned. His imagination and thought took flight. He was trying to explain his action before an accusing world—he had done so many times before, ever since he knew of this. He still wondered what he could have done. The girl had attracted him. She was graceful and her smile had been very bewitching. There was none who could equal her and no girl in the village had any pretence to any higher standard of education. Women's education was very low. Perhaps that was why so many Africans went "away" and came back married. He too wished he had gone with the others, especially in the last giant student airlift to America. If only Wamuhu had learning . . . and she was uncircumcised . . . then he might probably rebel. . . .

The light still shone in his mother's hut. John wondered if he should go in for the night prayers. But he thought against it; he might not be strong enough to face his parents. In his hut, the light had gone out. He hoped his father had not noticed it. . . .

John woke up early. He was frightened. He was normally not superstitious but still he did not like the dreams of the night. He dreamt of circumcision; he had just been initiated in the tribal manner. Somebody—he could not tell his face—came and led him because he took pity on him. They went, went into a strange land. Somehow, he found himself alone. The somebody had vanished. A ghost came. He recognized it as the ghost of the home he had left. It pulled him back; then another ghost came. It was the ghost of the land he had come to. It pulled him from the front. The two contested. Then came other ghosts from all sides and pulled him from all sides so that his body began to fall into pieces. And the ghosts were insubstantial. He could not cling to any. Only they were pulling him, and he was becoming nothing, nothing . . . he was now standing a distance away. It had not been him. But he was looking at the girl, the girl in the story. She had nowhere to go. He thought he would go to help her; he would show her the way. But as he went to her, he lost his way . . . he was all alone . . . something destructive was coming towards him, coming, coming . . . He woke up. He was sweating all over—

Dreams about circumcision were no good. They portended death. He dismissed the dream with a laugh. He opened the window only to find the whole country clouded in mist. It was perfect July weather in Limuru. The hills, ridges, valleys and plains that surrounded the village were lost in the mist. It looked such a strange place. But there was almost a magic fascination in it. Limuru was a land of contrasts and evoked differing emotions, at different times. Once, John would be fascinated, and would yearn to touch the land, embrace it or just be on the grass. At another time he would feel repelled by the dust, the strong sun and the pot-holed roads. If only his struggle were just against the dust, the mist, the sun and the rain, he might feel content. Content to live here. At least he thought he would never like to die and be buried anywhere else but at Limuru. But there was the human element whose vices and betrayal of other men were embodied as the new ugly villages. The last night's incident rushed into his mind like a flood, making him weak again. He came out of his blankets and went out. Today he would go to the shops. He was uneasy. An odd feeling was coming to him, in fact had been coming, that his relationship with his father was perhaps unnatural. But he dismissed the thought. Tonight would be the "day of reckoning." He shuddered to think of it. It was unfortunate that this scar had come into his life at this time when he was going to Makerere and it would have brought him closer to his father.

They went to the shops. All day long, John remained quiet as they moved from shop to shop buying things from the lanky but wistful Indian traders. And all day long, John wondered why he feared his father so much. He had grown up fearing him, trembling whenever he spoke or gave commands. John was not alone in this. Stanley was feared by all.

He preached with great vigour, defying the very gates of hell. Even during the Emergency, he had gone on preaching, scolding, judging and condemning. All those who were not saved were destined for hell. Above all, Stanley was known for his great moral observances—a bit too strict, rather pharisaical in nature. None noticed this; certainly not the sheep he shepherded. If an elder broke any of the rules, he was liable to be expelled, or excommunicated. Young men and women, seen standing together "in a manner prejudicial to church and God's morality" (they were one anyway), were liable to be excommunicated. And so, many young men tried to serve two masters, by seeing their girls at night and going to church by day. The alternative was to give up church-going altogether. . . .

Stanley took a fatherly attitude to all the people in the village. You must be strict with what is yours. And because of all this, he wanted his house to be a good example. That is why he wanted his son to grow up right. But motives behind many human actions may be mixed. He could never forget that he had also fallen before his marriage. Stanley was also a product of the disintegration of the tribe due to the new influences.

The shopping took a long time. His father strictly observed the silences between them and neither by word nor by hint did he refer to last night. They reached home and John was thinking that all was well when his father called him.

"John."

"Yes, Father."

"Why did you not come for prayers last night?"

"I forgot—"

"Where were you?"

Why do you ask me? What right have you to know where I was? One day I am going to revolt against you. But immediately, John knew that this act of rebellion was something beyond him—not unless something happened to push him into it. It needed someone with something he lacked.

"I-I-I mean, I was—"

"You should not sleep so early before prayers. Remember to be there tonight."

"I will."

Something in the boy's voice made the father look up. John went away relieved. All was still well.

Evening came. John dressed like the night before and walked with faltering steps towards the fatal place. The night of reckoning had come. And he had not thought of anything. After this night all would know. Even Rev. Thomas Carstone would hear of it. He remembered Mr. Carstone and the last words of blessing he had spoken to him. No! he did not want to remember. It was no good remembering these things; and yet the words came. They were clearly written in the air, or in the darkness of his mind. "You are going into the world. The world is waiting even like a hungry lion, to swallow you, to devour you. Therefore, beware of the world. Jesus said, Hold fast unto . . ." John felt a pain—a pain that wriggled through his flesh as he remembered these words. He contemplated the coming fall. Yes! He, John would fall from the Gates of Heaven down through the open waiting gates of Hell. Ah! He could see it all, and what people would say. Everybody would shun his company, would give him oblique looks that told so much. The trouble with John was that his imagination magnified the fall from the heights of "goodness" out of proportion. And fear of people and consequences ranked high in the things that made him contemplate the fall with so much horror.

John devised all sorts of punishment for himself. And when it came to thinking of a way out, only fantastic and impossible ways of escape came into his head. He simply could not make up his mind. And because he could not and he feared father and people, and he did not know his true attitude to the girl, he came to the agreed spot having nothing to tell the girl. Whatever he did looked fatal to him. Then suddenly he said—

"Look Wamuhu. Let me give you money. You might then say that someone else was responsible. Lots of girls have done this. Then that man may marry you. For me, it is impossible. You know that."

"No. I cannot do that. How can you, you—"

"I will give you two hundred shillings."

"No!"

"Three hundred!"

"No!" She was almost crying. It pained her to see him so.

"Four hundred, five hundred, six hundred!" John had begun calmly but now his voice was running high. He was excited. He was becoming more desperate. Did he know what he was talking about? He spoke quickly, breathlessly, as if he was in a hurry. The figure was rapidly rising—nine thousand, ten thousand, twenty thousand. . . . He is mad. He is foaming. He is quickly moving towards the girl in the dark. He has laid his hands on her shoulders and is madly imploring her in a hoarse voice. Deep inside him, something horrid that assumes the threatening anger of his father and the village, seems to be pushing him. He is violently shaking Wamuhu, while his mind tells him that he is patting her gently. Yes. He is out of his mind. The figure has now reached fifty thousand shillings and is increasing. Wamuhu is afraid, extricates herself from him, the mad, educated son of a religious clergyman, and she runs. He runs after her and holds her, calling her by all sorts of endearing words. But he is shaking her, shake, shake, her, her—he tries to hug her by the neck, presses . . . She lets out one horrible scream and then falls on the ground. And so all of a sudden, the struggle is over, the figures stop and John stands there trembling like the leaf of a tree on a windy day.

John, in the grip of fear, ran homeward. Soon everyone would know.

[1964]

Questions

1. What is the significance of the Irimu, mentioned in the opening paragraph? (When considering this question, you might want to compare the opening of Ngugi's story and Amos Tutuola's "The Complete Gentleman," also found in this volume.)

2. In what sense is darkness the predominant metaphor of Ngugi's story?

3. Given the fact that Wamuhu has been circumcised but John has not gone through the similar "rites of passage," how important is the following statement at the end of the second paragraph: "And he was not a man yet!"

4. How different would John's dilemma be if the story had an American setting, perhaps during the past century, and John and his girlfriend were of different religions?

Joyce Carol Oates

(b. 1938)

United States

Joyce Carol Oates is one of the most respected and prolific American writers of her generation. Since the publication of her first collection of short stories, By the North Gate (1963), and her first novel, With Shuddering Fall (1964), hardly a year has passed without the publication of a new Oates novel, collection of stories, or volume of poems. She has published more than 35 novels, 25 volumes of short stories, and 15 volumes of poetry, in addition to a number of plays and non-fiction works. Her most popular novels include Them (1969), which won the National Book Award for fiction; Expensive People (1969); A Garden of Earthly Delights (1970); All the Good People I've Left Behind (1979); Bellefleur (1980); Mysteries of Winterthurn (1984); You Must Remember This (1987); Because It Is Bitter and Because It Is My Heart (1990); Broken Heart Blues (1999); and Blonde (2000). Her short stories, which total several hundred, have frequently been anthologized in Martha Foley's annual Best American Short Stories and in the annual O. Henry Awards volumes.

Joyce Carol Oates was born in Lockport, New York, in 1938, where from 1945 to 1952 she attended a one-room rural school. She graduated from Syracuse University in 1960 and the following year completed an M.A. in English from the University of Wisconsin. Beginning in 1963, she taught at a number of universities in the United States and Canada. Since 1978, she has been writer-in-residence and professor of English at Princeton.

Often accused of creating a dark, almost perverse world of violence and gothic horror, Oates has answered to the charge on a number of occasions. Responding to Joe David Bellamy's question about violence in an interview published in The Atlantic (1972), Oates replied as follows:

> Am I personally haunted by the fear of violence, the need for violence, or do I reflect everyone else's feelings about it? I sense it around me, both the fear and the desire, and perhaps I simply have appropriated it from other people.

Responding more angrily to a similar question in 1981 (in an essay she wrote for the New York Times Book Review), she said that the question was insulting and sexist, that it would never be asked of a male writer:

> War, rape, murder, and the more colorful minor crimes evidently fall within the exclusive province of the male writer, just as, generally, they fall within the exclusive province of male action.

"Where Are You Going, Where Have You Been?" was made into a film in 1986: Smooth Talk, directed by Joyce Chopra.

WHERE ARE YOU GOING, WHERE HAVE YOU BEEN?

For Bob Dylan

Her name was Connie. She was fifteen and she had a quick nervous giggling habit of craning her neck to glance into mirrors, or checking other people's faces to make sure her own was all right. Her mother, who noticed everything and knew everything and who hadn't much reason any longer to look at her own face, always scolded Connie about it. "Stop gawking at yourself, who are you? You think you're so pretty?" she would say. Connie would raise her eyebrows at these familiar complaints and look right through her mother, into a shadowy vision of herself as she was right at that moment: she knew she was pretty and that was everything. Her mother had been pretty once too, if you could believe those old snapshots in the album, but now her looks were gone and that was why she was always after Connie.

"Why don't you keep your room clean like your sister? How've you got your hair fixed—what the hell stinks? Hair spray? You don't see your sister using that junk."

Her sister June was twenty-four and still lived at home. She was a secretary in the high school Connie attended, and if that wasn't bad enough—with her in the same building—she was so plain and chunky and steady that Connie had to hear her praised all the time by her mother and her mother's sisters. June did this, June did that, she saved money and helped clean the house and cooked and Connie couldn't do a thing, her mind was all filled with trashy daydreams. Their father was away at work most of the time and when he came home he wanted supper and he read the newspaper at supper and after supper he went to bed. He didn't bother talking much to them, but around his bent head Connie's mother kept picking at her until Connie wished her mother was dead and she herself was dead and it was all over. "She makes me want to throw up sometimes," she complained to her friends. She had a high, breathless, amused voice which made everything she said a little forced, whether it was sincere or not.

There was one good thing: June went places with girl friends of hers, girls who were just as plain and steady as she, and so when Connie wanted to do that her mother had no objections. The father of Connie's best girl friend drove the girls the three miles to town and left them off at a shopping plaza, so that they could walk through the stores or go to a movie, and when he came to pick them up again at eleven he never bothered to ask what they had done.

They must have been familiar sights, walking around that shopping plaza in their shorts and flat ballerina slippers that always scuffed the sidewalk, with charm bracelets jingling on their thin wrists; they would lean together to whisper and laugh secretly if someone passed by who amused or interested them. Connie had long dark blond hair that drew anyone's eye to it, and she wore part of it pulled up on her head and puffed out and the rest of it she let fall down her back. She wore a pullover jersey blouse that looked one way when she was at home and another way when she was away from home. Everything about her had two sides to it, one for home and one for anywhere that was not home: her walk that could be childlike and bobbing, or languid enough to make anyone think she was hearing music in her head, her mouth which was pale and smirking most of the time, but bright and pink on these evenings out, her laugh which was cynical and drawling at home—"Ha, ha, very funny"—but high-pitched and nervous anywhere else, like the jingling of the charms on her bracelet.

Sometimes they did go shopping or to a movie, but sometimes they went across the highway, ducking fast across the busy road, to a drive-in restaurant where older kids hung out. The restaurant was shaped like a big bottle, though squatter than a real bottle, and on its cap was a revolving figure of a grinning boy who held a hamburger aloft. One night in mid-summer they ran across, breathless with daring, and right away someone leaned out a car window and invited them over, but it was just a boy from high school they didn't like. It made them feel good to be able to ignore him. They went up through the maze of parked and cruising cars to the bright-lit, fly-infested restaurant, their faces pleased and expectant as if they were entering a sacred building that loomed out of the night to give them what haven and what blessing they yearned for. They sat at the counter and crossed their legs at the ankles, their thin shoulders rigid with excitement and listened to the music that made everything so good: the music was always in the background like music at a church service, it was something to depend upon.

A boy named Eddie came in to talk with them. He sat backwards on his stool, turning himself jerkily around in semi-circles and then stopping and turning again, and after a while he asked Connie if she would like something to eat. She said she did and so she tapped her friend's arm on her way out—her friend pulled her face up into a brave droll look—and Connie said she would meet her at eleven, across the way. "I just hate to leave her like that," Connie said earnestly, but the boy said that she wouldn't be alone for long. So they went out to his car and on the way Connie couldn't help but let her eyes wander over the windshields and faces all around her, her face gleaming with the joy that had nothing to do with Eddie or even this place; it might have been the music. She drew her shoulders up and sucked in her breath with the pure pleasure of being alive, and just at that moment she happened to glance at a face just a few feet from hers. It was a boy with shaggy black hair, in a convertible jalopy painted gold. He stared at her and then his lips widened into a grin. Connie slit her eyes at him and turned away, but she couldn't help glancing back and there he was still watching her. He wagged a finger and laughed and said, "Gonna get you, baby," and Connie turned away again without Eddie noticing anything.

She spent three hours with him, at the restaurant where they ate hamburgers and drank Cokes in wax cups that were always sweating, and then down an alley a mile or so away, and when he left her off at five to eleven only the movie house was still open at the plaza. Her girl friend was there, talking with a boy. When Connie came up the two girls smiled at each other and Connie said, "How was the movie?" and the girl said, "You should know." They rode off with the girl's father, sleepy and pleased, and Connie couldn't help but look at the darkened shopping plaza with its big empty parking lot and its signs that were faded and ghostly now, and over at the drive-in restaurant where cars were still circling tirelessly. She couldn't hear the music at this distance.

Next morning June asked her how the movie was and Connie said, "So-so."

She and that girl and occasionally another girl went out several times a week that way, and the rest of the time Connie spent around the house—it was summer vacation—getting in her mother's way and thinking, dreaming, about the boys she met. But all the boys fell back and dissolved into a single face that was not even a face, but an idea, a feeling, mixed up with the urgent insistent pounding of the music and the humid night air of July. Connie's mother kept dragging her back to the daylight by finding things for her to do or saying suddenly, "What's this about the Pettinger girl?" And Connie would say nervously, "Oh, her. That dope." She always drew thick clear lines between herself and such girls, and her mother was simple and kindly enough to believe her. Her mother was so simple, Connie thought, that it was maybe cruel to fool her so much. Her mother went scuffling around the house in old bedroom slippers and complained over the telephone to one sister about the other, then the other called up and the two of them complained about the third one. If June's name was mentioned her mother's tone was approving, and if Connie's name was mentioned it was disapproving. This did not really mean she disliked Connie and actually Connie thought that her mother preferred her to June because she was prettier, but the two of them kept up a pretense of exasperation, a sense that they were tugging and struggling over something of little value to either of them. Sometimes, over coffee, they were almost friends, but something would come up—some vexation that was like a fly buzzing suddenly around their heads—and their faces went hard with contempt.

One Sunday Connie got up at eleven—none of them bothered with church—and washed her hair so that it could dry all day long, in the sun. Her parents and sister were going to a barbecue at an aunt's house and Connie said no, she wasn't interested, rolling her eyes, to let mother know just what she thought of it. "Stay home alone then," her mother said sharply. Connie sat out back in a lawn chair and watched them drive away, her father quiet and bald, hunched around so that he could back the car out, her mother with a look that was still angry and not at all softened through the windshield, and in the back seat poor old June all dressed up as if she didn't know what a barbecue was, with all the running yelling kids and the flies. Connie sat with her eyes closed in the sun, dreaming and dazed with the warmth about her as if this were a kind of love, the caresses of love, and her mind slipped over onto thoughts of the boy she had been with the night before and how nice he had been, how sweet it always was, not the way someone like June would suppose but sweet, gentle, the way it was in movies and promised in songs; and when she opened her eyes she hardly knew where she was, the back yard ran off into weeds and a fenceline of trees and behind it the sky was perfectly blue and still. The asbestos "ranch house" that was now three years old startled her—it looked small. She shook her head as if to get awake.

It was too hot. She went inside the house and turned on the radio to drown out the quiet. She sat on the edge of her bed, barefoot, and listened for an hour and a half to a program called XYZ Sunday jamboree, record after record of hard, fast, shrieking songs she sang along with, interspersed by exclamations from "Bobby King": "An' look here you girls at Napoleon's—Son and Charley want you to pay real close attention to this song coming up!"

And Connie paid close attention herself, bathed in a glow of slow-pulsed joy that seemed to rise mysteriously out of the music itself and lay languidly about the airless little room, breathed in and breathed out with each gentle rise and fall of her chest.

After a while she heard a car coming up the drive. She sat up at once, startled, because it couldn't be her father so soon. The gravel kept crunching all the way in from the road—the driveway was long—and Connie ran to the window. It was a car she didn't know. It was an open jalopy, painted a bright gold that caught the sun opaquely. Her heart began to pound and her fingers snatched at her hair, checking it, and she whispered "Christ. Christ," wondering how bad she looked. The car came to a stop at the side door and the horn sounded four short taps as if this were a signal Connie knew.

She went into the kitchen and approached the door slowly, then hung out the screen door, her bare toes curling down off the step. There were two boys in the car and now she recognized the driver: he had shaggy, shabby black hair that looked crazy as a wig and he was grinning at her.

"I ain't late, am I?" he said.

"Who the hell do you think you are?" Connie said.

"Toldja I'd be out, didn't I?"

"I don't even know who you are."

She spoke sullenly, careful to show no interest or pleasure, and he spoke in a fast bright monotone. Connie looked past him to the other boy, taking her time. He had fair brown hair, with a lock that fell onto his forehead. His sideburns gave him a fierce, embarrassed look, but so far he hadn't even bothered to glance at her. Both boys wore sunglasses. The driver's glasses were metallic and mirrored everything in miniature.

"You wanta come for a ride?" he said.

Connie smirked and let her hair fall loose over one shoulder.

"Don'tcha like my car? New paint job," he said. "Hey."

"What?"

"You're cute."

She pretended to fidget, chasing flies away from the door.

"Don'tcha believe me, or what?" he said.

"Look, I don't even know who you are," Connie said in disgust.

"Hey, Ellie's got a radio, see. Mine's broke down." He lifted his friend's arm and showed her the little transistor the boy was holding, and now Connie began to hear the music. It was the same program that was playing inside the house.

"Bobby King?" she said.

"I listen to him all the time. I think he's great."

"He's kind of great," Connie said reluctantly.

"Listen, that guy's *great*. He knows where the action is."

Connie blushed a little, because the glasses made it impossible for her to see just what this boy was looking at. She couldn't decide if she liked him or if he was just a jerk, and so she dawdled in the doorway and wouldn't come down or go back inside. She said, "What's all that stuff painted on your car?"

"Can'tcha read it?" He opened the door very carefully, as if he was afraid it might fall off. He slid out just as carefully, planting his feet firmly on the ground, the tiny metallic world in his glasses slowing down like gelatine hardening and in the midst of it Connie's bright green blouse. "This here is my name, to begin with," he said. ARNOLD FRIEND was written in tar-like black letters on the side, with a drawing of a round grinning face that reminded Connie of a pumpkin, except it wore sunglasses. "I wanta introduce myself, I'm Arnold Friend and that's my real name and I'm gonna be your friend, honey, and inside the car's Ellie Oscar, he's kinda shy." Ellie brought his transistor up to his shoulder and balanced it there. "Now these numbers are a secret code, honey," Arnold Friend explained. He read off the numbers 33, 19, 17 and raised his eyebrows at her to see what she thought of that, but she didn't think much of it. The left rear fender had been smashed and around it was written, on the gleaming gold background: DONE BY CRAZY WOMAN DRIVER. Connie had to laugh at that. Arnold Friend was pleased at her laughter and looked up at her. "Around the other side's a lot more—you wanta come and see them?"

"No."

"Why not?"

"Why should I?"

"Don'tcha wanta see what's on the car? Don'tcha wanta go for a ride?"

"I don't know."

"Why not?"

"I got things to do."

"Like what?"

"Things."

He laughed as if she had said something funny. He slapped his thighs. He was standing in a strange way, leaning back against the car as if he were balancing himself. He wasn't tall, only an inch or so taller than she would be if she came down to him. Connie liked the way he was dressed, which was the way all of them dressed: tight faded jeans stuffed into black, scuffed boots, a belt that pulled his waist in and showed how lean he was, and a white pull-over shirt that was a little soiled and showed the hard small muscles of his arms and shoulders. He looked as if he probably did hard work, lifting and carrying things. Even his neck looked muscular. And his face was a familiar face, somehow: the jaw and chin and cheeks slightly darkened, because he hadn't shaved for a day or two, and the nose long and hawk-like, sniffing as if she were a treat he was going to gobble up and it was all a joke.

"Connie, you ain't telling the truth. This is your day set aside for a ride with me and you know it," he said, still laughing. The way he straightened and recovered from his fit of laughing showed that it had been all fake.

"How do you know what my name is?" she said suspiciously.

"It's Connie."

"Maybe and maybe not."

"I know my Connie," he said, wagging his finger. Now she remembered him even better, back at the restaurant, and her cheeks warmed at the thought of how she sucked in her breath just at the moment she passed him—how she must have looked to him. And he had remembered her. "Ellie and I come out here especially for you," he said. "Ellie can sit in back. How about it?"

"Where?"

"Where what?"

"Where're we going?"

He looked at her. He took off the sunglasses and she saw how pale the skin around his eyes was, like holes that were not in shadow but instead in light. His eyes were like chips of broken glass that catch the light in an amiable way. He smiled. It was as if the idea of going for a ride somewhere, to some place, was a new idea to him.

"Just for a ride, Connie sweetheart."

"I never said my name was Connie," she said.

"But I know what it is. I know your name and all about you, lots of things," Arnold Friend said. He had not moved yet but stood still leaning back against the side of his jalopy. "I took a special interest in you, such a pretty girl, and found out all about you like I know your parents and sister are gone somewheres and I know where and how long they're going to be gone, and I know who you were with last night, and your best friend's name is Betty. Right?"

He spoke in a simple lilting voice, exactly as if he were reciting the words to a song. His smile assured her that everything was fine. In the car Ellie turned up the volume on his radio and did not bother to look around at them.

"Ellie can sit in the back seat," Arnold Friend said. He indicated his friend with a casual jerk of his chin, as if Ellie did not count and she could not bother with him.

"How'd you find out all that stuff?" Connie said.

"Listen! Betty Schultz and Tony Fitch and Jimmy Pettinger and Nancy Pettinger," he said, in a chant. "Raymond Stanley and Bob Hutter—"

"Do you know all those kids?"

"I know everybody."

"Look, you're kidding. You're not from around here."

"Sure."

"But—how come we never saw you before?"

"Sure you saw me before," he said. He looked down at his boots, as if he were a little offended. "You just don't remember."

"I guess I'd remember you," Connie said.

"Yeah?" He looked up at this, beaming. He was pleased. He began to mark time with the music from Ellie's radio, tapping his fists lightly together. Connie looked away from his smile to the car, which was painted so bright it almost hurt her eyes to look at it. She looked at that name, ARNOLD FRIEND. And up at the front fender was an expression that was familiar—MAN THE FLYING SAUCERS. It was an expression kids had used the year before, but didn't use this year. She looked at it for a while as if the words meant something to her that she did not yet know.

"What're you thinking about? Huh?" Arnold Friend demanded. "Not worried about your hair blowing around in the car, are you?"

"No."

"Think I maybe can't drive good?"

"How do I know?"

"You're a hard girl to handle. How come?" he said. "Don't you know I'm your friend? Didn't you see me put my sign in the air when you walked by?"

"What sign?"

"My sign." And he drew an X in the air, leaning out toward her. They were maybe ten feet apart. After his hand fell back to his side the X was still in the air, almost visible. Connie let the screen door close and stood perfectly still inside it, listening to the music from her radio and the boy's blend together. She stared at Arnold Friend. He stood there so stiffly relaxed, pretending to be relaxed, with one hand idly on the door handle as if he were keeping himself up that way and had no intention of ever moving again. She recognized most things about him, the tight jeans that showed his thighs and buttocks and the greasy leather boots and the tight shirt, and even that slippery friendly smile of his, that sleepy dreamy smile that all the boys used to get across ideas they didn't want to put into words. She recognized all this and also the singsong way he talked, slightly mocking, kidding, but serious and a little melancholy, and she recognized the way he tapped one fist against the other in homage to the perpetual music behind him. But all these things did not come together.

She said suddenly, "Hey, how old are you?"

His smile faded. She could see then that he wasn't a kid, he was much older—thirty, maybe more. At this knowledge her heart began to pound faster.

"That's a crazy thing to ask. Can'tcha see I'm your own age?"

"Like hell you are."

"Or maybe a coupla years older, I'm eighteen."

"Eighteen?" she said doubtfully.

He grinned to reassure her and lines appeared at the corners of his mouth. His teeth were big and white. He grinned so broadly his eyes became slits and she saw how thick the lashes were, thick and black as if painted with a black tar-like material. Then he seemed to become embarrassed, abruptly, and looked over his shoulder at Ellie. "*Him*, he's crazy," he said. "Ain't he a riot, he's a nut, a real character." Ellie was still listening to the music. His sunglasses told nothing about what he was thinking. He wore a bright orange shirt unbuttoned halfway to show his chest, which was a pale, bluish chest and not muscular like Arnold Friend's. His shirt collar was turned up all around and the very tips of the collar pointed out past his chin as if they were protecting him. He was pressing the transistor radio up against his ear and sat there in a kind of daze, right in the sun.

"He's kinda strange," Connie said.

"Hey, she says you're kinda strange! Kinda strange!" Arnold Friend cried. He pounded on the car to get Ellie's attention. Ellie turned for the first time and Connie saw with shock that he wasn't a kid either—he had a fair, hairless face, cheeks reddened slightly as if the veins grew too close to the surface of his skin, the face of a forty-year-old baby. Connie felt a wave of dizziness rise in her at this sight and she stared at him as if waiting for something to change the shock of the moment, make it all right again. Ellie's lips kept shaping words, mumbling along with the words blasting his ear.

"Maybe you two better go away," Connie said faintly.

"What? How come?" Arnold Friend cried. "We come out here to take you for a ride. It's Sunday." He had the voice of the man on the radio now. It was the same voice, Connie thought. "Don'tcha know it's Sunday all day and honey, no matter who you were with last night today you're with Arnold Friend and don't you forget it!—Maybe you better step out here," he said, and this last was in a different voice. It was a little flatter, as if the heat was finally getting to him.

"No. I got things to do."

"Hey."

"You two better leave."

"We ain't leaving until you come with us."

"Like hell I am—"

"Connie, don't fool around with me. I mean, I mean, don't fool *around*," he said, shaking his head. He laughed incredulously. He placed his sunglasses on top of his head, carefully, as if he were indeed wearing a wig, and brought the stems down behind his ears. Connie stared at him, another wave of dizziness and fear rising in her so that for a moment he wasn't even in focus but was just a blur, standing there against his gold car, and she had the idea that he had driven up the driveway all right but had come from nowhere before that and belonged nowhere and that everything about him and even the music that was so familiar to her was only half real.

"If my father comes and sees you—"

"He ain't coming. He's at a barbecue."

"How do you know that?"

"Aunt Tillie's. Right now they're—uh—they're drinking. Sitting around," he said vaguely, squinting as if he were staring all the way to town and over to Aunt Tillie's back yard. Then the vision seemed to clear and he nodded energetically. "Yeah. Sitting around. There's your sister in a blue dress, huh? And high heels, the poor sad bitch—nothing like you, sweetheart! And your mother's helping some fat woman with the corn, they're cleaning the corn—husking the corn—"

"What fat woman?" Connie cried.

"How do I know what fat woman. I don't know every goddamn fat woman in the world!" Arnold Friend laughed.

"Oh, that's Mrs. Hornby. . . . Who invited her?" Connie said. She felt a little light-headed. Her breath was coming quickly.

"She's too fat. I don't like them fat. I like them the way you are, honey," he said, smiling sleepily at her. They stared at each other for a while, through the screen door. He said softly, "Now what you're going to do is this: you're going to come out that door. You're going to sit up front with me and Ellie's going to sit in the back, the hell with Ellie, right? This isn't Ellie's date. You're my date. I'm your lover, honey."

"What? You're crazy—"

"Yes, I'm your lover. You don't know what that is but you will," he said. "I know that too. I know all about you. But look: it's real nice and you couldn't ask for nobody better than me, or more polite. I always keep my word. I'll tell you how it is, I'm always nice at first, the first time. I'll hold you so tight you won't think you have to try to get away or pretend anything because you'll know you can't. And I'll come inside you where it's all secret and you'll give in to me and you'll love me—"

"Shut up! You're crazy!" Connie said. She backed away from the door. She put her hands against her ears as if she'd heard something terrible, something not meant for her. "People don't talk like that, you're crazy," she muttered. Her heart was almost too big now for her chest and its pumping made sweat break out all over her. She looked out to see Arnold Friend pause and then take a step toward the porch lurching. He almost fell. But, like a clever drunken man, he managed to catch his balance. He wobbled in his high boots and grabbed hold of one of the porch posts.

"Honey?" he said. "You still listening?"

"Get the hell out of here!"

"Be nice, honey. Listen."

"I'm going to call the police—"

He wobbled again and out of the side of his mouth came a fast spat curse, an aside not meant for her to hear. But even this "Christ!" sounded forced. Then he began to smile again. She watched this smile come, awkward as if he were smiling from inside a mask. His whole face was a mask, she thought wildly, tanned down onto his throat but then running out as if he had plastered make-up on his face but had forgotten about his throat.

"Honey—? Listen, here's how it is. I always tell the truth and I promise you this: I ain't coming in that house after you."

"You better not! I'm going to call the police if you—if you don't—"

"Honey," he said, talking right through her voice, "honey, I'm not coming in there but you are coming out here. You know why?"

She was panting. The kitchen looked like a place she had never seen before, some room she had run inside but which wasn't good enough, wasn't going to help her. The kitchen window had never had a curtain, after three years, and there were dishes in the sink for her to do—probably—and if you ran your hand across the table you'd probably feel something sticky there.

"You listening, honey? Hey?"

"—going to call the police—"

"Soon as you touch the phone I don't need to keep my promise and can come inside. You won't want that."

She rushed forward and tried to lock the door. Her fingers were shaking. "But why lock it," Arnold Friend said gently, talking right into her face. "It's just a screen door.

It's just nothing." One of his boots was at a strange angle, as if his foot wasn't in it. It pointed out to the left, bent at the ankle. "I mean, anybody can break through a screen door and glass and wood and iron or anything else if he needs to, anybody at all and specially Arnold Friend. If the place got lit up with a fire, honey, you'd come running out into my arms, right into my arms and safe at home—like you knew I was your lover and'd stopped fooling around, I don't mind a nice shy girl but I don't like no fooling around." Part of those words were spoken with a slight rhythmic lilt, and Connie somehow recognized them—the echo of a song from last year, about a girl rushing into her boy friend's arms and coming home again—

Connie stood barefoot on the linoleum floor, staring at him. "What do you want?" she whispered.

"I want you," he said.

"What?"

"Seen you that night and thought, that's the one, yes sir. I never needed to look any more."

"But my father's coming back. He's coming to get me. I had to wash my hair first—" She spoke in a dry, rapid voice, hardly raising it for him to hear.

"No, your daddy is not coming and yes, you had to wash your hair and you washed it for me. It's nice and shining and all for me, I thank you, sweetheart," he said, with a mock bow, but again he almost lost his balance. He had to bend and adjust his boots. Evidently his feet did not go all the way down; the boots must have been stuffed with something so that he would seem taller. Connie stared out at him and behind him Ellie in the car, who seemed to be looking off toward Connie's right, into nothing. This Ellie said, pulling the words out of the air one after another as if he were just discovering them, "You want me to pull out the phone?"

"Shut your mouth and keep it shut," Arnold Friend said, his face red from bending over or maybe from embarrassment because Connie had seen his boots. "This ain't none of your business."

"What—what are you doing? What do you want?" Connie said. "If I call the police they'll get you, they'll arrest you—"

"Promise was not to come in unless you touch that phone, and I'll keep that promise," he said. He resumed his erect position and tried to force his shoulders back. He sounded like a hero in a movie, declaring something important. He spoke too loudly and it was as if he were speaking to someone behind Connie. "I ain't made plans for coming in that house where I don't belong but just for you to come out to me, the way you should. Don't you know who I am?"

"You're crazy," she whispered. She backed away from the door but did not want to go into another part of the house, as if this would give him permission to come through the door. "What do you. . . . You're crazy, you. . . ."

"Huh? What're you saying, honey?"

Her eyes darted everywhere in the kitchen. She could not remember what it was, this room.

"This is how it is, honey: you come out and we'll drive away, have a nice ride. But if you don't come out we're gonna wait till your people come home and then they're all going to get it."

"You want that telephone pulled out?" Ellie said. He held the radio away from his ear and grimaced, as if without the radio the air was too much for him.

"I toldja shut up, Ellie." Arnold Friend said, "You're deaf, get a hearing aid, right? Fix yourself up. This little girl's no trouble and's gonna be nice to me, so Ellie keep to yourself, this ain't your date—right? Don't hem in on me. Don't hog. Don't crush. Don't bird dog. Don't trail me," he said in a rapid meaningless voice, as if he were running through all the expressions he'd learned but was no longer sure which one of them was in style, then rushing on to new ones, making them up with his eyes closed, "Don't crawl under my fence, don't squeeze in my chipmunk hole, don't sniff my glue, suck my popsicle, keep your own greasy fingers on yourself" He shaded his eyes and peered in at Connie, who was backed against the kitchen table. "Don't mind him, honey, he's just a creep. He's a dope. Right? I'm the boy for you and like I said you come out here nice like a lady and give me your hand, and nobody else gets hurt, I mean, your nice old bald-headed daddy and your mummy and your sister in her high heels. Because listen: why bring them in this?"

"Leave me alone," Connie whispered.

"Hey, you know that old woman down the road, the one with the chickens and stuff—you know her?"

"She's dead!"

"Dead? What? You know her?" Arnold Friend said.

"She's dead—"

"Don't you like her?"

"She's dead—she's—she isn't here any more—"

"But don't you like her, I mean, you got something against her? Some grudge or something?" Then his voice dipped as if he were conscious of rudeness. He touched the sunglasses on top of his head as if to make sure they were still there. "Now you be a good girl."

"What are you going to do?"

"Just two things, or maybe three," Arnold Friend said. "But I promise it won't last long and you'll like me that way you get to like people you're close to. You will. It's all over for you here, so come on out. You don't want your people in any trouble, do you?"

She turned and bumped against a chair or something, hurting her leg, but she ran into the back room and picked up the telephone. Something roared in her ear, a tiny roaring, and she was so sick with fear that she could do nothing but listen to it—the telephone was clammy and very heavy and her fingers groped down to the dial but were too weak to touch it. She began to scream into the phone, into the roaring. She cried out, she cried for her mother, she felt her breath start jerking back and forth in her lungs as if it were something Arnold Friend were stabbing her with again and again with no tenderness. A noisy sorrowful wailing rose all about her and she was locked inside it the way she was locked inside this house.

After a while she could hear again. She was sitting on the floor, with her wet back against the wall.

Arnold Friend was saying from the door, "That's a good girl. Put the phone back."

She kicked the phone away from her.

"No, honey. Pick it up. Put it back right."

She picked it up and put it back. The dial tone stopped.

"That's a good girl. Now you come outside."

She was hollow with what had been fear, but what was now just an emptiness. All that screaming had blasted it out of her. She sat, one leg cramped under her, and deep inside her brain was something like a pinpoint of light that kept going and would not let her relax. She thought, I'm not going to see my mother again. She thought, I'm not going to sleep in my bed again. Her bright green blouse was all wet.

Arnold Friend said, in a gentle-loud voice that was like a stage voice. "The place where you came from ain't there any more, and where you had in mind to go is cancelled out. This place you are now—inside your daddy's house—is nothing but a cardboard box I can knock down any time. You know that and always did know it. You hear me?"

She thought, I have got to think. I have to know what to do.

"We'll go out to a nice field, out in the country here where it smells so nice and it's sunny," Arnold Friend said. "I'll have my arms tight around you so you won't need to try to get away and I'll show you what love is like, what it does. The hell with this house! It looks solid all right," he said. He ran a fingernail down the screen and the noise did not make Connie shiver, as it would have the day before. "Now put your hand on your heart, honey. Feel that? That feels solid too but we know better, be nice to me, be sweet like you can because what else is there for a girl like you but to be sweet and pretty and give in?—and get away before her people come back?"

She felt her pounding heart. Her hands seemed to enclose it. She thought for the first time in her life that it was nothing that was hers, that belonged to her, but just a pounding, living thing inside this body that wasn't hers either.

"You don't want them to get hurt," Arnold Friend went on. "Now get up, honey. Get up all by yourself."

She stood.

"Now turn this way. That's right. Come over to me—Ellie, put that away, didn't I tell you? You dope. You miserable creepy dope," Arnold Friend said. His words were not angry but only part of an incantation. The incantation was kindly. "Now come out through the kitchen to me honey and let's see a smile, try it, you're a brave sweet little girl and now they're eating corn and hotdogs cooked to bursting over an outdoor fire, and they don't know one thing about you and never did and honey you're better than them because not one of them would have done this for you."

Connie felt the linoleum under her feet; it was cool. She brushed her hair back out of her eyes. Arnold Friend let go of the post tentatively and opened his arms for her, his elbows pointing up toward each other and his wrist limp, to show that this was an embarrassed embrace and a little mocking, he didn't want to make her self-conscious.

She put out her hand against the screen. She watched herself push the door slowly open as if she were safe back somewhere in the other doorway, watching this body and this head of long hair moving out into the sunlight where Arnold Friend waited.

"My sweet little blue-eyed girl," he said, in a half-sung sigh that had nothing to do with her brown eyes but was taken up just the same by the vast sunlit reaches of the land behind him and on all sides of him, so much land that Connie had never seen before and did not recognize except to know that she was going to it.

[1970]

Questions

1. Does Connie give in to the stranger as a result of her awakening sexuality or her fear of what he may do to her family—that is, as a result of weakness or strength in protecting her family?

2. Is Oates's story intended to be interpreted as Connie's encounter with the Devil?

3. What function does Ellie play in the narrative?

4. Why is the story dedicated to Bob Dylan?

Ōba Minako

(b. 1930)

Japan

I n The Showa Anthology: Modern Japanese Short Stories, Van C. Gessel and Tomone Matsumoto, the editors, describe Ōba Minako's work as follows:

> The author sometimes uses straightforward narrative but more often prefers a montage technique. . . . [Her] stories of love and death [are] full of vivid imagery that is sometimes beautiful, often grotesque. Ōba's subtle and complex literary world provides no answers, but casts a fresh and occasionally disturbing light on the human condition.

Ōba Minako's literary career began in 1968 with a short story called "The Three Crabs." In that story and in others that were soon to follow, she creates a world in which reality and imagination flow into one another, often making it impossible for the reader to determine what is real in her characters' world. As you read "The Pale Fox," try to determine which parts of the story the narrator actually experiences and which ones she imagines.

THE PALE FOX

"It's been a long time," said the Pale Fox.

Seven years ago, when they were lovers, a melancholy look in the man's downcast face had reminded her of a fox. Sometimes, in the pale light of the moon, or washed perhaps by the light of a neon sign, his face took on a bluish cast, and since that time she had referred to him in her mind as the Pale Fox. His sharp, narrow chin resembled a fox—a fox pausing in a moonlit forest, head cocked toward the moon.

"These white flowers smell nice," said the Pale Fox, "but the thistles, roses, and nettles are a nuisance."

Turning away from the light, the Fox's eyes shone amber, like glowing charcoal or Christmas tree lights.

"It's been seven years, hasn't it?"

The Pale Fox was like a priest who performed the ritual with faultless precision. The priest's eyes were too far apart for a fox, and each drifted independently. For some reason she enjoyed running the tip of her finger down between his eyebrows to the bridge of his nose.

"That's a vulnerable spot. It gives me the shivers when you do that; it makes me feel I'm about to be stabbed by an assassin." The Pale Fox disliked her doing this, but was reluctant to brush the woman's finger away.

The Fox's nose was moist in the moonlight.

The woman thought: I wonder why Father says this is the grave where Mother is buried? It is such a splendid and majestic tomb. It might have been the grave of some venerable priest clothed in rich, brocaded vestments, or a great warrior in full armor and helmet, or a grand minister of state with drooping moustaches.

The funeral must surely have been splendid, too, with much fanfare and a service carried out in the glare of footlights, attended by joyous throngs of celebrities. The choreographer of this spectacle would have been called the Priest of Heaven, and would have led the reading of the scriptures and the voluptuous sobbing of the mourners. Yes, this was the funeral it must have been.

By now, of course, the grave was encrusted with moss and lichen, and it was impossible to read the inscription carved on it. All she could make out was a single Chinese character that seemed to be the word for "great." Yet once it had been a glittering and elaborate tomb.

Though the flesh in the casket had decayed and putrefied, beautiful women had gathered in attendance. Ladies who had flinched at the smell of corruption had risked being thrown into prison. It was a grave of writhing anguish.

This was a grave that wielded power, that threw back its shoulders in pride; this was a grave that laughed arrogantly with cold eyes and a thin smile. But this was all vanity now, for the corpse had rotted and the tomb was crumbling.

The forest was heavy with gloom. When the black birds started up with a mournful cry, cold drops fell from the trees and she looked up. Far away, between the overlapping leaves, was the violet sky.

The path was slippery with mud, and fungi that reminded her of withered and broken oranges grew from the fallen tree trunks. There were others with plump, fleshy umbrellas that spread wide like patches of snow.

Each time her father stumbled, he clutched at her. His hands were cold, and the daughter felt that a corpse was touching her. Still, she was curious about this landscape of death being shown her by a corpse, and she appreciated each stop they made.

"I found Mother's grave. I looked for it everywhere and couldn't find it, but then all of a sudden I saw it, thanks to the way the light was shining."

It was like the abalone clinging to the rocks. Somewhere down among the forest of gently waving sea tangle there comes the glitter of a fish's belly, and suddenly you see it, the tight, tender flesh of the abalone enclosed in its shell, deep within the lush growth of moss.

Her father was delighted. From his youth he had been happiest gathering abalone and edible fungi. He was a metal craftsman by trade who had brought his workshop to the rocky shore of this island and devoted the greater part of each year to making metal objects. Toward the end of the year, he would take everything he had made to the city to sell; but apart from that one annual journey, he remained on the island. The children enjoyed spending several months there with their father during the summer. Stretching out like a backdrop behind the rocky shore was a pine forest where all sorts of fungi flourished.

His eyes were as sharp as an animal's when he probed for abalone trembling beneath the surface of the sea, or the thin, white stalks of fungi hidden in the forest under fallen leaves. He would find each mollusc among the seaweed and pull its living flesh from the rocks where it clung fast. The woman imagined the old man's twisted jaw and superimposed the image on the sharp jaw of the Pale Fox.

"It was a place like this, your mother's grave."

Her father had discovered the grave deep in the inner recesses of an ancient temple on the edge of the pine forest. At the back of the tomb he had found a small door leading to the crypt. He had tried to open it, but it was choked with moss and would not move. Some grass with small, white flowers grew in a crack in the stone that marked the door to the crypt. There were also ferns.

"Your mother is sitting in there. I could see her knee," said her father. "The swelling in her shins seems to have subsided. The color of her earlobes isn't good, though. "

Mother had to have her ears pierced to wear the earrings that Father made for her. The daughter remembered from her childhood that when Mother's ears had been pierced, Father had disinfected them so they would not fester.

The shells of the abalone were hidden by sea moss; the tomb was covered with forest moss. When she bent to examine the moss more closely, the beauty of a microcosmic world spread out before her. The stone tomb beneath it became an illusion; the vision of elegance vanished.

Clutching his cane of polished rose root, her father resembled a gaunt, white cat. He smiled and his eyes gleamed with a small, blue flame.

"Shall we burn a cigarette instead of incense?"

Searching in her handbag, she found two cigarettes; they were all she had left. She lit one and put it on the moss. The white paper absorbed some moisture and she watched it go out, leaving only a wisp of smoke. She lit the remaining cigarette and inhaled, turning aside to keep the smoke from getting in her eyes. Then, as though her mother were a patient lying on the tombstone, she held the cigarette out between her fingers so that the sick woman could take it in her mouth. She stayed like that for a while, waiting for the ash to lengthen and fall off.

After all, it was tobacco that had killed her mother, and now that she was dead, her father frequently offered cigarettes at the family altar.

She felt as though she were playing house with her father. It was as though they had joined hands and were dancing around some ancient tomb, playing a children's game. In the shadow of the tombstone, a toad sat watching.

For seven years she had heard no news at all, then suddenly, one day, a man came to see her and it was the Fox. His arrival was totally unexpected, like waking in the morning to find a single leaf by her pillow.

The Pale Fox was smoother than the polished rose root. He believed he had a very beautiful body; he liked to stand straight and walk slowly. She realized he was probably waiting for some word of praise, but felt it was too much trouble to try and find a compliment to satisfy his vanity. At the same time, she was ashamed of her own indifference.

The Pale Fox told her that during the seven years they had been apart, he had married, lived with his wife for four years, and then left her.

"She was like one of those dolls that can shed tears. Whenever I came home, I would find her sitting in the same place, in the same position. In the end she became like a moth, the large sort that crawl around on walls."

"First you say she's a crying doll, and then she's just a dried-up moth stuck to the wall."

"Finally that's all she was, just a spot on the wall. She was the sort of woman who dreams of finding happiness in ordinary family life. She had done nothing wrong, that's why it was such a shame. I even changed my mind after we had separated, and we tried meeting several times, but we never talked about anything. We slept together each time we met, but we couldn't talk about things. I'd leave again as soon as our lovemaking was done. At that point she changed from a moth into a butter-fly sitting with its wings folded. As she sat, dust would rise from her wings and make me wheeze."

He paused, then tried to explain his own silence by saying, "Some people talk a lot. I think they lose something when they talk too much."

The woman gazed with admiration at the Pale Fox, who spoke as little as possible in order not to lose anything.

He was, however, the sort of man who could never suit his actions to his words, or his deeds to his thoughts, and so he always ended up talking when the woman re-mained silent. Nevertheless, he apparently felt obliged to explain what he had done during those seven years.

"I was exhausted the whole time we were married. The constant weariness made my bones ache as though I was carrying a load with straps cutting into my shoulders. I always do what I want, and yet while my own life-style was selfish, I felt some re-sponsibility toward my thoroughly unselfish partner. At the bottom of my heart I suppose what I really want is a woman who'll be a slave to me."

"I'm sure there are women in the world who'd be happy to be your slave. But if you ever encountered one, you'd start dreaming of a woman you could treat as an equal. You really would. Haven't you learned yet that the tyrant is always bound by the tyrant's debt? In your case, the only way to free yourself is to free the other per-son as well."

"But women all renounce their freedom; it's a way of binding their men to them." Somewhere in his heart the Pale Fox dreamed of having a slave, but in reality he could never manipulate women in that way.

Seven years ago he had asked her to marry him, saying that he intended to be a good husband. The expression on his face had revealed the pathetic determination of someone who was throwing his own freedom away. This frightened the woman and she recoiled from him. She could imagine him saying the same thing to his for-mer wife before their marriage, and she pitied him. To make unrealistic promises, to make promises he could not keep, could only lead to hopelessness in the long run.

It was when he was completely beaten that he dreamed of possessing a slave. If a woman chooses to be a slave, presumably the man's guilt is resolved and this allows him to behave as he pleases. The woman understood this man's fantasy very well; he wanted her to fall on her knees and embrace him, but she felt it was too much both-er. Again she felt ashamed of her indifference.

"You are too fond of women. That's why it's impossible either to pledge yourself to one single woman or to treat us simply as objects. But, you know, you're probably fond of women because women are fond of men. If women were not allowed to know men, if the person you married were not allowed to know any man but yourself, she still wouldn't necessarily become the sort of woman you want. A woman can't be treated as a woman if she's lost whatever makes her one. The sort of marriage you had in mind depends too much on someone who's lost her identity as a woman."

In an encounter like this, mood is more important than logic. And so, solemnly, ten-derly, they proceeded with their ritual, devoting themselves to it wholeheartedly, and when the ceremony had reached its climax and ended, they were left clinging to the altar like a pair of bats, physically and emotionally drained. Once the ceremony was over, her earlier indifference returned, and she became embarrassed by her lack of en-thusiasm. In the end she compromised by telling herself that different people just have different ideas, and that it does no good to ignore other ways of thinking.

The Pale Fox dozed. His arms, twined around her waist, went limp. She could see one ugly, swollen wart on a stubby finger; it reminded her of the skin near the ears of lizards she had seen the previous day at the botanical gardens. They had kissed for the first time in seven years standing in front of a pair of lizards locked in a motionless sexual embrace. The immobile lizards looked like stuffed animals in a specimen case.

His warty finger also appeared to be stuffed. The wart seemed to spread and grow until it resembled a crater. Countless white fungus stalks grew out of this crater.

Her father called again from the island. He had called twice while she was out. Praying Mantis, the man she was living with, passed on the information that he had phoned, but she did not feel like returning his call, and left again.

Her father was in the habit of ringing his seven children one after the other, making the same call to each. The woman was usually the last to be called. She was, after all, the youngest child. Apparently he had said the rocks on the island were covered with abalone, but that was long ago, and now the rocks were covered only by moss. Whatever phase the moon was in, there was only moss that may have looked like abalone shells clinging to the rocks.

"I told her you called, but she left again in a hurry," explained Praying Mantis when her father phoned yet again. The following day, before she had decided whether or not to return his call, there was a fourth phone call from the island, and when she picked up the receiver, she heard her father's hoarse voice.

"We're having lovely weather here on the island. Why don't you come for a visit? The place is full of abalone. There's a new moon now and there are always plenty of them around then."

Unable to endure this senile fantasy, she said, "As usual, the Mantis has a guest here just now."

"I see. A guest is it? I remember in the old days your mother and I used to think up all sorts of excuses for declining our parents' invitations to visit, because we wanted to meet each other instead. . . . I'll go to your mother's grave again and offer a cigarette from you. It occurs to me that you're the only one of the children who knows where that grave is, so I want you to remember how to find it." Her father hung up the phone.

Her mother had borne seven children, and not one of them had provided a monument for her grave. In her will the mother had requested that her ashes be scattered over the sea. The children had some notion that the surging waves would transform her into various shapes. But the father was disappointed by the children's devotion to their mother's will.

Soon the Pale Fox awoke. He drew the woman to him, but it was clear he did so only because he felt obliged to. Even while he longed for a woman slave, the Fox continued to treat women with respect. Understanding this pathetic dream, the woman playfully scratched his beautiful body all over and tugged at his hair.

Like a child on a visit somewhere who wants to go home, the woman longed to return to Praying Mantis. He was a strange man, devoted to that form of ecstasy peculiar to the mantis in which the male is killed and devoured by the female. He enjoyed hearing women talk about other men they had known. He was curious about women only if they displayed curiosity about men. Searching now for words that would flatter the Pale Fox, she moved about the room making gestures, throwing glances that might appeal to him. She did not have the patience for anything more; all she wanted now was to sleep, to sleep next to the Mantis with her leg thrown over his stomach. (The woman could not sleep unless her legs were slightly elevated.)

It would not do to stay with the Pale Fox until morning, and she realized that this feeling confirmed once again the reason she had recoiled from living with him seven years ago.

If he were a real fox, she could put a collar on him and fasten it to the bedpost. Yet, even then, in the morning she might find that he had disappeared, leaving only the collar lying on the bed, the chain still attached. The Pale Fox, it seemed, was always changing into something else. The woman was indifferent to the gallant youth he sometimes became; what captivated her was his true form, a fox sniffing out his prey. She liked his beautiful blue fur, his erect ears, sharp jaw, moist nose, his surprisingly long, pink tongue, bushy tail, and glittering, golden eyes. But the Fox in his true form always eluded her, escaping to the forest; she only caught glimpses of him.

Just as she was getting dressed, the Fox, too, felt a longing for his home in the forest. "We should probably be going now," he said. "I'm leaving town tomorrow," he added, "so it would be better if I went back to my own hotel tonight. I have to pack my things."

As he got up, the Pale Fox said, "Shall we go out for something to eat?" He was looking at the key that lay on the bedside table. They no longer had any use for it, since they would not be coming back to this room.

They locked the door as they went out, leaving the key behind. Outside a warm, muggy wind blew, and the large, red sun perched on the horizon directly in front of them, wrapped in a cloak of gray smog. Groups of people hurried along in the gullies through forests of tall buildings. From the expressions on their faces, they seemed to have forgotten what a dreary business it is to be faithful. In the stores where the stench of the city was blown away by air conditioners, people kept their sullen, bloated faces downturned, and shuffled aimlessly like caged animals.

The man and the woman carried on an absurd conversation. They spoke of buying a villa together on the island. Neither of them had any money, of course, and even as they talked of buying a villa, both were thinking how impossible it would be for them to live there together. As they talked, each fantasized about imaginary slaves.

While they ate their meal of raw, spiced meat, the woman saw a reflection of herself in a wall mirror. It showed a cruel, voracious insect that only slightly resembled her elderly father. The insect appeared covered with a veil of spider web, while the Fox had transformed himself into a beetle. Their wings tangled together and their conversation was meaningless.

Mother's earlobes, she remembered, had been discolored and unhealthy-looking. Had it been her sister who retrieved Mother's earrings from the ashes after the body had been cremated?

When she arrived home, the Mantis said, "There was a phone call from your sister. Something about your father. It seems something has happened. She said he was taken into protective custody yesterday by the island police. Did he seem normal the last time you saw him?"

"I didn't notice anything wrong," said the woman.

"Your sister says he should be put in an institution."

"Oh."

The father had seven children. None of those seven children was opposed to the idea of putting their father in an institution. What they had in mind was a mental hospital located on top of a hill on the island. In its advertising, the hospital used pictures of the surrounding fields in spring, clothed in a haze of yellow blossoms.

Crested white butterflies fluttered over the yellow fields, and there in the midst of them stood a white building, rising like some fantastic castle. It seemed to float above the ground; a white-clad ghost without feet.

When she awoke the next morning the woman realized she had left behind at the hotel an ornamental hairpin her father had made when he was young. Her mother had given it to her as a keepsake. It was not yet check-out time, so she hurriedly caught a taxi and set off for the hotel. When she explained to the desk clerk that she had left the key in the room and locked herself out, he rang for the bellboy, but then, remembering, said, "Oh, wait a minute. Your husband came back a little while ago. I gave the key to him."

The woman was heading for the elevator when it occurred to her that he should be at his hotel packing and that he hadn't originally planned to come back. She went to the house phone and dialed.

Soft and light as a feather, the voice at the other end was clearly the Fox's. He was not a beetle now.

"Hello, it's me. I left my hairpin there, on the shelf in the bathroom. It's silver and shaped like a fish; the eyes are inlaid bits of black coral. It's a keepsake from my mother. Could you bring it to me before you check out? Or send it by registered mail."

The woman listened carefully, straining for any sign that he had another woman in the room with him, but she heard nothing. Without a word in reply the Pale Fox put down the receiver.

Two or three days later the hairpin arrived safely in a small, registered envelope. There was not even a note to go with it.

[1973]
Translated by
STEPHEN W. KOHL

Questions

1. What are the narrator's feelings toward her deceased mother? How are they manipulated by her father?
2. What connects the story of the Pale Fox (her ex-lover) with the story of her parents?
3. Is the father actually insane or is his insanity something else?
4. Why do the narrator's lovers have the names she has given them?
5. How does the story reveal attitudes about sexual and gender roles?

Tim O'Brien
(b. 1946)
United States

W hen people discuss the books they have read about the war in Vietnam, Tim O'Brien is certain to be mentioned, either for his fiction or non-fictional accounts of his experiences there. From 1968–1970, O'Brien served in Vietnam, eventually becoming a sergeant. After his return to the States, he almost immediately began to write about the war, both as a reporter for the Washington Post and in his first published book, If I Die in a Combat Zone, Box Me Up and Ship Me Home (1973). That memoir was followed by Northern Lights (1975), a novel about a returned vet, and then by what many critics believe is his finest work, Going after Cacciato (1978), which won the National Book Award. Cacciato can be read either as a collection of short stories or as a novel. The war in Vietnam also looms significantly in The Nuclear Age (1981), which focuses on an anti-war, draft-dodger/terrorist.

After a hiatus of several years, O'Brien returned to the loose form he had employed so successfully in Going after Cacciato and concentrated again on the common soldier in The Things They Carried: A Work of Fiction (1990). In 1994, O'Brien returned briefly to Vietnam and—as a result of that trip—wrote still another oblique account of his real and imaginary experiences there—In the Lake of the Woods (1994), a meditation on the My Lai massacre. Purged, perhaps, of the war, O'Brien said after the publication of that volume that he'd been on a kind of search to understand himself and the world as he'd known it.

Bobbie Ann Mason, the author's contemporary, has written the following about "The Things They Carried":

> By using the simplicity of a list and trying to categorize the simple items the soldiers carried, O'Brien reveals the real terror of the war itself. And the categories go from the tangible—foot powder, photographs, chewing gum—to the intangible. They carried disease; memory. When it rained, they carried the sky. The weight of what they carried moves expansively, opens out, grows from the stuff in the rucksack to the whole weight of the American war chest, with its litter of ammo and packaging through the landscape of Vietnam. And then it moves back, away from the huge outer world, back into the interior of the self. The story details the way they carried themselves (dignity, laughter, words) as well as what they carried inside (fear, "emotional baggage"). (You've Got to Read This, edited by Ron Hansen and Jim Shepard)

THE THINGS THEY CARRIED

First Lieutenant Jimmy Cross carried letters from a girl named Martha, a junior at Mount Sebastian College in New Jersey. They were not love letters, but Lieutenant Cross was hoping, so he kept them folded in plastic at the bottom of his rucksack. In the late afternoon after a day's march, he would dig his foxhole, wash his hands under a canteen, unwrap the letters, hold them with the tips of his fingers, and spend the last hour of light pretending. He would imagine romantic camping trips into the White Mountains in New Hampshire. He would sometimes taste the envelope flaps, knowing her tongue had been there. More than anything, he wanted Martha to love him as he loved her, but the letters were mostly chatty, elusive on the matter of love. She was a virgin, he was almost sure. She was an English major at Mount Sebastian, and she wrote beautifully about her professors and roommates and midterm exams, about her respect for Chaucer and her great affection for Virginia Woolf. She often quoted lines of poetry; she never mentioned the war, except to say, Jimmy, take care of yourself. The letters weighed 10 ounces. They were signed Love, Martha but Lieutenant Cross understood that Love was only a way of signing and did not mean what he sometimes pretended it meant. At dusk, he would carefully return the letters to his rucksack. Slowly, a bit distracted, he would get up and move among his men, checking the perimeter, then at full dark he would return to his hole and watch the night and wonder if Martha was a virgin.

The things they carried were largely determined by necessity. Among the necessities or near-necessities were P-38 can openers, pocket knives, heat tabs, wristwatches, dog tags, mosquito repellent, chewing gum, candy, cigarettes, salt tablets, packets of Kool-Aid, lighters, matches, sewing kits, Military Payment Certificates, C rations, and two or three canteens of water. Together, these items weighed between 15 and 20 pounds, depending upon a man's habits or rate of metabolism. Henry Dobbins, who was a big man, carried extra rations; he was especially fond of canned peaches in heavy syrup over pound cake. Dave Jensen, who practiced field hygiene, carried a toothbrush, dental floss, and several hotel-sized bars of soap he'd stolen on R&R in Sydney, Australia. Ted Lavender, who was scared, carried tranquilizers until he was shot in the head outside the village of Than Khe in mid-April. By necessity, and because it was SOP,[1] they all carried steel helmets that weighted 5 pounds including the liner and camouflage cover. They carried the standard fatigue jackets and trousers. Very few carried underwear. On their feet they carried jungle boots—2.1 pounds— and Dave Jensen carried three pairs of socks and a can of Dr. Scholl's foot powder as a precaution against trench foot. Until he was shot, Ted Lavender carried six or seven ounces of premium dope, which for him was a necessity. Mitchell Sanders, the RTO,[2] carried condoms. Norman Bowker carried a diary. Rat Kiley carried comic books. Kiowa, a devout Baptist, carried an illustrated New Testament that had been presented to him by his father, who taught Sunday school in Oklahoma City, Oklahoma. As a hedge against bad times, however, Kiowa also carried his grandmother's distrust of the white man, his grandfather's old hunting hatchet. Necessity dictated. Because the land was mined and booby-trapped, it was SOP for each man to carry a steel-centered, nylon-covered flak jacket which weighed 6.7 pounds, but which on hot days seemed much heavier. Because you could die so quickly, each man carried at least one large compress bandage, usually in the helmet band for easy access. Because the nights were cold, and because the monsoons were wet, each carried a green plastic poncho that could be used as a raincoat or groundsheet or makeshift tent. With its quilted liner, the poncho weighed almost two pounds, but it was worth every

---

[1]SOP   Standard Operating Procedure.
[2]RTO   Radiotelephone Operator.

ounce. In April, for instance, when Ted Lavender was shot, they used his poncho to wrap him up, then to carry him across the paddy, then to lift him into the chopper that took him away.

They were called legs or grunts.

To carry something was to hump it, as when Lieutenant Jimmy Cross humped his love for Martha up the hills and through the swamps. In its intransitive form, to hump meant to walk, or to march, but it implied burdens far beyond the intransitive.

Almost everyone humped photographs. In his wallet, Lieutenant Cross carried two photographs of Martha. The first was a Kodacolor snapshot signed Love, though he knew better. She stood against a brick wall. Her eyes were gray and neutral, her lips slightly open as she stared straight-on at the camera. At night, sometimes, Lieutenant Cross wondered who had taken the picture, because he knew she had boyfriends, because he loved her so much, and because he could see the shadow of the picture-taker spreading out against the brick wall. The second photograph had been clipped from the 1968 Mount Sebastian yearbook. It was an action shot—women's volleyball—and Martha was bent horizontal to the floor, reaching, the palms of her hands in sharp focus, the tongue taut, the expression frank and competitive. There was no visible sweat. She wore white gym shorts. Her legs, he thought, were almost certainly the legs of a virgin, dry and without hair, the left knee cocked and carrying her entire weight, which was just over one hundred pounds. Lieutenant Cross remembered touching that left knee. A dark theater, he remembered, and the movie was *Bonnie and Clyde*, and Martha wore a tweed skirt, and during the final scene, when he touched her knee, she turned and looked at him in a sad, sober way that made him pull his hand back, but he would always remember the feel of the tweed skirt and the knee beneath it and the sound of the gunfire that killed Bonnie and Clyde, how embarrassing it was, how slow and oppressive. He remembered kissing her good night at the dorm door. Right then, he thought, he should've done something brave. He should've carried her up the stairs to her room and tied her to the bed and touched that left knee all night long. He should've risked it. Whenever he looked at the photographs, he thought of new things he should've done.

What they carried was partly a function of rank, partly of field specialty.

As a first lieutenant and platoon leader, Jimmy Cross carried a compass, maps, code books, binoculars, and a .45-caliber pistol that weighed 2.9 pounds fully loaded. He carried a strobe light and the responsibility for the lives of his men.

As an RTO, Mitchell Sanders carried the PRC-25 radio, a killer, 26 pounds with its battery.

As a medic, Rat Kiley carried a canvas satchel filled with morphine and plasma and malaria tablets and surgical tape and comic books and all the things a medic must carry, including M&M's for especially bad wounds, for a total weight of nearly 20 pounds.

As a big man, therefore a machine gunner, Henry Dobbins carried the M-60, which weighed 23 pounds unloaded, but which was almost always loaded. In addition, Dobbins carried between 10 and 15 pounds of ammunition draped in belts across his chest and shoulders.

As PFCs or Spec 4s, most of them were common grunts and carried the standard M-16 gas-operated assault rifle. The weapon weighed 7.5 pounds unloaded, 8.2 pounds with its full 20-round magazine. Depending on numerous factors, such as topography and psychology, the riflemen carried anywhere from 12 to 20 magazines, usually in cloth bandoliers, adding on another 8.4 pounds at minimum, 14 pounds at maximum. When it was available, they also carried M-16 maintenance gear—rods and steel brushes and swabs and tubes of LSA oil—all of which weighed about a pound. Among the grunts, some carried the M-79 grenade launcher, 5.9 pounds unloaded, a reasonably light weapon except for the ammunition, which was heavy. A single round weighed 10 ounces. The typical load was 25 rounds. But Ted Lavender, who was scared, carried 34 rounds when he was shot and killed outside Than Khe, and he went down under an exceptional burden, more than 20 pounds of ammunition, plus the flak jacket and helmet and rations and water and toilet paper and tranquilizers and all the rest, plus the unweighed fear. He was dead weight. There was no twitching or flopping. Kiowa, who saw it happen, said it was like watching a rock fall, or a big sandbag or something—just boom, then down—not like the movies where the dead guy rolls around and does fancy spins and goes ass, over teakettle—not like that, Kiowa said, the poor bastard just flat-fuck fell. Boom. Down. Nothing else. It was a bright morning in mid-April. Lieutenant Cross felt the pain. He blamed himself. They stripped off Lavender's canteens and ammo, all the heavy things, and Rat Kiley said the obvious, the guy's dead, and Mitchell Sanders used his radio to report one U.S. KIA and to request a chopper. Then they wrapped Lavender in his poncho. They carried him out to a dry paddy, established security, and sat smoking the dead man's dope until the chopper came. Lieutenant Cross kept to himself. He pictured Martha's smooth young face, thinking he loved her more than anything, more than his men, and now Ted Lavender was dead because he loved her so much and could not stop thinking about her. When the dustoff arrived, they carried Lavender aboard. Afterward they burned Than Khe. They marched until dusk, then dug their holes, and that night Kiowa kept explaining how you had to be there, how fast it was, how the poor guy just dropped like so much concrete. Boom-down, he said. Like cement.

In addition to the three standard weapons—the M-60, M-16, and M-79—they carried whatever presented itself, or whatever seemed appropriate as a means of killing or staying alive. They carried catch-as-catch-can. At various times, in various situations, they carried M-14s and CAR-15s and Swedish Ks and grease guns and captured AK-47s and Chi-Coms and RPGs and Simonov carbines and black market Uzis and .38-caliber Smith & Wesson handguns and 66 mm LAWs and shotguns and silencers and blackjacks and bayonets and C-4 plastic explosives. Lee Strunk carried a slingshot; a weapon of last resort, he called it. Mitchell Sanders carried brass knuckles. Kiowa carried his grandfather's feathered hatchet. Every third or fourth man carried a Claymore antipersonnel mine—3.5 pounds with its firing device. They all carried fragmentation grenades—14 ounces each. They all carried at least one M-18 colored smoke grenade—24 ounces. Some carried CS or tear gas grenades. Some carried white phosphorus grenades. They carried all they could bear, and then some, including a silent awe for the terrible power of the things they carried.

In the first week of April, before Lavender died, Lieutenant Jimmy Cross received a good-luck charm from Martha. It was a simple pebble, an ounce at most. Smooth to the touch, it was a milky white color with flecks of orange and violet, oval-shaped, like a miniature egg. In the accompanying letter, Martha wrote that she had found the pebble on the Jersey shoreline, precisely where the land touched water at high tide, where things came together but also separated. It was this separate-but-together quality, she wrote, that had inspired her to pick up the pebble and to carry it in her breast pocket for several days, where it seemed weightless, and then to send it through the mail, by air, as a token of her truest feelings for him. Lieutenant Cross found this romantic. But he wondered what her truest feelings were, exactly, and what she meant by separate-but-together. He wondered how the tides and waves had come into play on that afternoon along the Jersey shoreline when Martha saw the pebble and bent down to rescue it from geology. He imagined bare feet. Martha was a poet, with the poet's sensibilities, and her feet would be brown and bare, the toenails unpainted, the eyes chilly and, somber like the ocean in March, and though it was painful, he wondered who had been with her that afternoon. He imagined a pair of shadows moving along the strip of sand where things came together but also separated. It was phantom jealousy, he knew, but he couldn't help himself. He loved her so much. On the march, through the hot days of early April, he carried the pebble in his mouth, turning it with his tongue, tasting sea salt and moisture. His mind wandered. He had difficulty keeping his attention on the war. On occasion he would yell at his men to spread out the column, to keep their eyes open, but then he would slip away into daydreams, just pretending, walking barefoot along the Jersey shore, with Martha carrying nothing. He would feel himself rising. Sun and waves and gentle winds, all love and lightness.

What they carried varied by mission.

When a mission took them to the mountains, they carried mosquito netting, machetes, canvas tarps, and extra bug juice.

If a mission seemed especially hazardous, or if it involved a place they knew to be bad, they carried everything they could. In certain heavily mined AOs,[3] where the land was dense with Toe Poppers and Bouncing Betties, they took turns humping a 28-pound mine detector. With its headphones and big sensing plate, the equipment was a stress on the lower back and shoulders, awkward to handle, often useless because of the shrapnel in the earth, but they carried it anyway, partly for safety, partly for the illusion of safety.

On ambush, or other night missions, they carried peculiar little odds and ends. Kiowa always took along his New Testament and a pair of moccasins for silence. Dave Jensen carried night-sight vitamins high in carotene. Lee Strunk carried his slingshot; ammo, he claimed, would never be a problem. Rat Kiley carried brandy and M&M's candy. Until he was shot, Ted Lavender carried the starlight scope, which weighed 6.3 pounds with its aluminum carrying case. Henry Dobbins carried his girlfriend's pantyhose wrapped around his neck as a comforter. They all carried ghosts. When dark came, they would move out single file across the meadows and paddies to their ambush coordinates, where they would quietly set up the Claymores[4] and lie down and spend the night waiting.

Other missions were more complicated and required special equipment. In mid-April, it was their mission to search out and destroy the elaborate tunnel complexes in the Than Khe area south of Chu Lai. To blow the tunnels, they carried one-pound blocks of pentrite high explosives, four blocks to a man, 68 pounds in all. They carried wiring, detonators, and battery-powered clackers. Dave Jensen carried earplugs. Most often, before blowing the tunnels, they were ordered by higher command to

---

[3]*AOs*   Areas of operations.
[4]*Claymores*   Claymore Antipersonnel Mine.

search them, which was considered bad news, but by and large they just shrugged and carried out orders. Because he was a big man, Henry Dobbins was excused from tunnel duty. The others would draw numbers. Before Lavender died there were 17 men in the platoon, and whoever drew the number 17 would strip off his gear and crawl in headfirst with a flashlight and Lieutenant Cross's .45-caliber pistol. The rest of them would fan out as security. They would sit down or kneel, not facing the hole, listening to the ground beneath them, imagining cobwebs and ghosts, whatever was down there—the tunnel walls squeezing in—how the flashlight seemed impossibly heavy in the hand and how it was tunnel vision in the very strictest sense, compression in all ways, even time, and how you had to wiggle in—ass and elbows—a swallowed-up feeling—and how you found yourself worrying about odd things: Will your flashlight go dead? Do rats carry rabies? If you screamed, how far would the sound carry? Would your buddies hear it? Would they have the courage to drag you out? In some respects, though not many, the waiting was worse than the tunnel itself. Imagination was a killer.

On April 16, when Lee Strunk drew the number 17, he laughed and muttered something and went down quickly. The morning was hot and very still. Not good, Kiowa said. He looked at the tunnel opening, then out across a dry paddy toward the village of Than Khe. Nothing moved. No clouds or birds or people. As they waited, the men smoked and drank Kool-Aid, not talking much, feeling sympathy for Lee Strunk but also feeling the luck of the draw. You win some, you lose some, said Mitchell Sanders, and sometimes you settle for a rain check. It was a tired line and no one laughed.

Henry Dobbins ate a tropical chocolate bar. Ted Lavender popped a tranquilizer and went off to pee.

After five minutes, Lieutenant Jimmy Cross moved to the tunnel, leaned down, and examined the darkness. Trouble, he thought—a cave-in maybe. And then suddenly, without willing it, he was thinking about Martha. The stresses and fractures, the quick collapse, the two of them buried alive under all that weight. Dense, crushing love. Kneeling, watching the hole, he tried to concentrate on Lee Strunk and the war, all the dangers, but his love was too much for him, he felt paralyzed, he wanted to sleep inside her lungs and breathe her blood and be smothered. He wanted her to be a virgin and not a virgin, all at once. He wanted to know her. Intimate secrets: Why poetry? Why so sad? Why that grayness in her eyes? Why so alone? Not lonely, just alone—riding her bike across campus or sitting off by herself in the cafeteria—even dancing, she danced alone—and it was the aloneness that filled him with love. He remembered telling her that one evening. How she nodded and looked away. And how, later, when he kissed her, she received the kiss without returning it, her eyes wide open, not afraid, not a virgin's eyes, just flat and uninvolved.

Lieutenant Cross gazed at the tunnel. But he was not there. He was buried with Martha under the white sand at the Jersey shore. They were pressed together, and the pebble in his mouth was her tongue. He was smiling. Vaguely, he was aware of how quiet the day was, the sullen paddies, yet he could not bring himself to worry about matters of security. He was beyond that. He was just a kid at war, in love. He was twenty-four years old. He couldn't help it.

A few moments later Lee Strunk crawled out of the tunnel. He came up grinning, filthy but alive. Lieutenant Cross nodded and closed his eyes while the others clapped Strunk on the back and made jokes about rising from the dead.

Worms, Rat Kiley said. Right out of the grave. Fuckin' zombie.

The men laughed. They all felt great relief.

Spook city, said Mitchell Sanders.

Lee Strunk made a funny ghost sound, a kind of moaning, yet very happy, and right then, when Strunk made that high happy moaning sound, when he went *Ahhooooo*, right then Ted Lavender was shot in the head on his way back from peeing. He lay with his mouth open. The teeth were broken. There was a swollen black bruise under his left eye. The cheekbone was gone. Oh shit, Rat Kiley said, the guy's dead. The guy's dead, he kept saying, which seemed profound—the guy's dead. I mean really.

The things they carried were determined to some extent by superstition. Lieutenant Cross carried his good-luck pebble. Dave Jensen carried a rabbit's foot. Norman Bowker, otherwise a very gentle person, carried a thumb that had been presented to him as a gift by Mitchell Sanders. The thumb was dark brown, rubbery to the touch, and weighed four ounces at most. It had been cut from a VC corpse, a boy of fifteen or sixteen. They'd found him at the bottom of an irrigation ditch, badly burned, flies in his mouth and eyes. The boy wore black shorts and sandals. At the time of his death he had been carrying a pouch of rice, a rifle, and three magazines of ammunition.

You want my opinion, Mitchell Sanders said, there's a definite moral here.

He put his hand on the dead boy's wrist. He was quiet for a time, as if counting a pulse, then he patted the stomach, almost affectionately, and used Kiowa's hunting hatchet to remove the thumb.

Henry Dobbins asked what the moral was.

Moral?

You know. *Moral*.

Sanders wrapped the thumb in toilet paper and handed it across to Norman Bowker. There was no blood. Smiling, he kicked the boy's head, watched the flies scatter, and said, It's like with that old TV show—Paladin. Have gun, will travel.

Henry Dobbins thought about it.

Yeah, well, he finally said. I don't see no moral.

There it *is*, man.

Fuck off.

They carried USO stationery and pencils and pens. They carried Sterno, safety pins, trip flares, signal flares, spools of wire, razor blades, chewing tobacco, liberated joss sticks and statuettes of the smiling Buddha, candles, grease pencils, *The Stars and Stripes*, fingernail clippers, Psy Ops leaflets, bush hats, bolos, and much more. Twice a week, when the resupply choppers came in, they carried hot chow in green mermite cans and large canvas bags filled with iced beer and soda pop. They carried plastic water containers, each with a two-gallon capacity. Mitchell Sanders carried a set of starched tiger fatigues for special occasions. Henry Dobbins carried Black Flag insecticide. Dave Jensen carried empty sandbags that could be filled at night for added protection. Lee Strunk carried tanning lotion. Some things they carried in common. Taking turns, they carried the big PRC-77 scrambler radio, which weighed 30 pounds with its battery. They shared the weight of memory. They took up what others could no longer bear. Often, they carried each other, the wounded or weak. They carried infections. They carried chess sets, basketballs, Vietnamese-English dictionaries, insignia of rank, Bronze Stars and Purple Hearts, plastic cards imprinted with the Code of Conduct. They carried diseases, among them malaria and dysentery. They carried lice and ringworm and leeches and paddy algae and various rots and molds. They carried the land itself—Vietnam, the place, the soil—a powdery orange-red dust that covered their boots and fatigues and faces. They carried the sky. The whole atmosphere, they carried it, the humidity, the monsoons, the stink of fungus and decay, all of it, they carried gravity. They moved like mules. By daylight they took sniper fire, at night they were mortared, but it was not battle, it was just the endless march, village to village, without purpose, nothing won or lost. They marched for the sake of the march. They plodded along slowly, dumbly, leaning forward against the heat, unthinking, all blood and bone, simple grunts, soldiering with their legs, toiling up the hills and down into the paddies and across the rivers and up again and down, just humping, one step and then the next and then another, but no volition, no will, because it was automatic, it was anatomy, and the war was entirely a matter of posture and carriage, the hump was everything, a kind of inertia, a kind of emptiness, a dullness of desire and intellect and conscience and hope and human sensibility. Their principles were in their feet. Their calculations were biological. They had no sense of strategy or mission. They searched the villages without knowing what to look for, not caring, kicking over jars of rice, frisking children and old men, blowing tunnels, sometimes setting fires and sometimes not, then forming up and moving on to the next village, then other villages, where it would always be the same. They carried their own lives. The pressures were enormous. In the heat of early afternoon, they would remove their helmets and flak jackets, walking bare, which was dangerous but which helped ease the strain. They would often discard things along the route of march. Purely for comfort, they would throw away rations, blow their Claymores and grenades, no matter, because by nightfall the resupply choppers would arrive with more of the same, then a day or two later still more, fresh watermelons and crates of ammunition and sunglasses and woolen sweaters—the resources were stunning—sparklers for the Fourth of July, colored eggs for Easter—it was the great American war chest—the fruits of science, the smokestacks, the canneries, the arsenals at Hartford, the Minnesota forests, the machine shops, the vast fields of corn and wheat—they carried like freight trains; they carried it on their backs and shoulders—and for all the ambiguities of Vietnam, all the mysteries and unknowns, there was at least the single abiding certainty that they would never be at a loss for things to carry.

After the chopper took Lavender away, Lieutenant Jimmy Cross led his men into the village of Than Khe. They burned everything. They shot chickens and dogs, they trashed the village well, they called in artillery and watched the wreckage, then they marched for several hours through the hot afternoon, and then at dusk, while Kiowa explained how Lavender died, Lieutenant Cross found himself trembling.

He tried not to cry. With his entrenching tool, which weighed five pounds, he began digging a hole in the earth.

He felt shame. He hated himself. He had loved Martha more than his men, and as a consequence Lavender was now dead, and this was something he would have to carry like a stone in his stomach for the rest of the war.

All he could do was dig. He used his entrenching tool like an ax, slashing, feeling both love and hate, and then later, when it was full dark, he sat at the bottom of his foxhole and wept. It went on for a long while. In part, he was grieving for Ted Lavender, but mostly it was for Martha, and for himself, because she belonged to another world, which was not quite real, and because she was a junior at Mount Sebastian

College in New Jersey, a poet and a virgin and uninvolved, and because he realized she did not love him and never would.

Like cement, Kiowa whispered in the dark. I swear to God—boom, down. Not a word.
I've heard this, said Norman Bowker.
A pisser, you know? Still zipping himself up. Zapped while zipping.
All right, fine. That's enough.
Yeah, but you had to see it, the guy just—
I *heard*, man. Cement. So why not shut the fuck *up?*
Kiowa shook his head sadly and glanced over at the hole where Lieutenant Jimmy Cross sat watching the night. The air was thick and wet. A warm dense fog had settled over the paddies and there was the stillness that precedes rain.
After a time Kiowa sighed.
One thing for sure, he said. The lieutenant's in some deep hurt. I mean that crying jag—the way he was carrying on—it wasn't fake or anything, it was real heavy-duty hurt. The man cares.
Sure, Norman Bowker said.
Say what you want, the man does care.
We all got problems.
Not Lavender.
No, I guess not, Bowker said. Do me a favor, though.
Shut up?
That's a smart Indian. Shut up.
Shrugging, Kiowa pulled off his boots. He wanted to say more, just to lighten up his sleep, but instead he opened his New Testament and arranged it beneath his head as a pillow. The fog made things seem hollow and unattached. He tried not to think about Ted Lavender, but then he was thinking how fast it was, no drama, down and dead, and how it was hard to feel anything except surprise. It seemed unchristian. He wished he could find some great sadness, or even anger, but the emotion wasn't there and he couldn't make it happen. Mostly he felt pleased to be alive. He liked the smell of the New Testament under his cheek, the leather and ink and paper and glue, whatever the chemicals were. He liked hearing the sounds of night. Even his fatigue, it felt fine, the stiff muscles and the prickly awareness of his own body, a floating feeling. He enjoyed not being dead. Lying there, Kiowa admired Lieutenant Jimmy Cross's capacity for grief. He wanted to share the man's pain, he wanted to care as Jimmy Cross cared. And yet when he closed his eyes, all he could think was Boom-down, and all he could feel was the pleasure of having his boots off and the fog curling in around him and the damp soil and the Bible smells and the plush comfort of night.
After a moment Norman Bowker sat up in the dark.
What the hell, he said. You want to talk, *talk.* Tell it to me.
Forget it.
No, man, go, on. One thing I hate, it's a silent Indian.

For the most part they carried themselves with poise, a kind of dignity. Now and then, however, there were times of panic, when they squealed or wanted to squeal but couldn't, when they twitched and made moaning sounds and covered their heads and said Dear Jesus and flopped around on the earth and fired their weapons blindly and cringed and sobbed and begged for the noise to stop and went wild and made stupid promises to themselves and to God and to their mothers and fathers, hoping not to die. In different ways, it happened to all of them. Afterward, when the firing ended, they would blink and peek up. They would touch their bodies, feeling shame, then quickly hiding it. They would force themselves to stand. As if in slow motion, frame by frame, the world would take on the old logic—absolute silence, then the wind, then sunlight, then voices. It was the burden of being alive. Awkwardly, the men would reassemble themselves, first in private, then in groups, becoming soldiers again. They would repair the leaks in their eyes. They would check for casualties, call in dustoffs, light cigarettes, try to smile, clear their throats and spit and begin cleaning their weapons. After a time someone would shake his head and say, No lie, I almost shit my pants, and someone else would laugh, which meant it was bad, yes, but the guy had obviously not shit his pants, it wasn't that bad, and in any case nobody would ever do such a thing and then go ahead and talk about it. They would squint into the dense, oppressive sunlight. For a few moments, perhaps, they would fall silent, lighting a joint and tracking its passage from man to man, inhaling, holding in the humiliation. Scary stuff, one of them might say. But then someone else would grin or flick his eyebrows and say, Roger-dodger, almost cut me a new asshole, *almost*.

There were numerous such poses. Some carried themselves with a sort of wistful resignation, others with pride or stiff soldierly discipline or good humor or macho zeal. They were afraid of dying but they were even more afraid to show it.

They found jokes to tell.

They used a hard vocabulary to contain the terrible softness. *Greased* they'd say. *Offed, lit up, zapped while zipping.* It wasn't cruelty, just stage presence. They were actors. When someone died, it wasn't quite dying, because in a curious way it seemed scripted, and because they had their lines mostly memorized, irony mixed with tragedy, and because they called it by other names, as if to encyst and destroy the reality of death itself. They kicked corpses. They cut off thumbs. They talked grunt lingo. They told stories about Ted Lavender's supply of tranquilizers, how the poor guy didn't feel a thing, how incredibly tranquil he was.

There's a moral here, said Mitchell Sanders.

They were waiting for Lavender's chopper, smoking the dead man's dope.

The moral's pretty obvious, Sanders said, and winked. Stay away from drugs. No joke, they'll ruin your day every time.

Cute, said Henry Dobbins.

Mind blower, get it? Talk about wiggy. Nothing left, just blood and brains.

They made themselves laugh.

There it is, they'd say. Over and over—there it is, my friend, there it is—as if the repetition itself were an act of poise, a balance between crazy and almost crazy, knowing without going, there it is, which meant be cool, let it ride, because Oh yeah, man, you can't change what can't be changed, there it is, there it absolutely and positively and fucking well *is*.

They were tough.

They carried all the emotional baggage of men who might die. Grief, terror, love, longing—these were intangibles, but the intangibles had their own mass and specific gravity, they had tangible weight. They carried shameful memories. They carried the common secret of cowardice barely restrained, the instinct to run or freeze or hide, and in many respects this was the heaviest burden of all, for it could never be put down, it required perfect balance and perfect posture. They carried their reputations. They carried the soldier's greatest fear, which was the fear of blushing. Men killed, and died, because they were embarrassed not to. It was what had brought them to the war in the first place, nothing positive, no dreams of glory or honor, just to avoid the blush of dishonor. They died so as not to die of embarrassment. They crawled into tunnels and walked point and advanced under fire. Each morning, despite the unknowns, they made their legs move. They endured. They kept humping. They did not submit to the obvious alternative, which was simply to close the eyes and fall. So easy, really. Go limp and tumble to the ground and let the muscles unwind and not speak and not budge until your buddies picked you up and lifted you into the chopper that would roar and dip its nose and carry you off to the world. A mere matter of falling, yet no one ever fell. It was not courage, exactly; the object was not valor. Rather, they were too frightened to be cowards.

By and large they carried these things inside, maintaining the masks of composure. They sneered at sick call. They spoke bitterly about guys who had found release by shooting off their own toes or fingers. Pussies, they'd say. Candy-asses. It was fierce, mocking talk, with only a trace of envy or awe, but even so the image played itself out behind their eyes.

They imagined the muzzle against flesh. So easy: squeeze the trigger and blow away a toe. They imagined it. They imagined the quick, sweet pain, then the evacuation to Japan, then a hospital with warm beds and cute geisha nurses.

And they dreamed of freedom birds.

At night, on guard, staring into the dark, they were carried away by jumbo jets. They felt the rush of takeoff. *Gone!* they yelled. And then velocity—wings and engines—a smiling stewardess—but it was more than a plane, it was a real bird, a big sleek silver bird with feathers and talons and high screeching. They were flying. The weights fell off; there was nothing to bear. They laughed and held on tight, feeling the cold of wind and altitude, soaring, thinking *It's over, I'm gone!*—they were naked, they were light and free—it was all lightness, bright and fast and buoyant, light as light, a helium buzz in the brain, a giddy bubbling in the lungs as they were taken up over the clouds and the war, beyond duty, beyond gravity and mortification and global entanglements—*Sin loi!*[5] they yelled. *I'm sorry, mother-fuckers, but I'm out of it, I'm goofed, I'm on a space cruise, I'm gone!*—and it was a restful, unencumbered sensation, just riding the light waves, sailing that big silver freedom bird over the mountains and oceans, over America, over the farms and great sleeping cities and cemeteries and highways and the golden arches of McDonald's, it was flight, a kind of fleeing, a kind of falling, falling higher and higher, spinning off the edge of the earth and beyond the sun and through the vast, silent vacuum where there were no burdens and where everything weighed exactly nothing—*Gone!* they screamed. *I'm sorry but I'm gone!*—and so at night, not quite dreaming, they gave themselves over to lightness, they were carried, they were purely borne.

On the morning after Ted Lavender died, First Lieutenant Jimmy Cross crouched at the bottom of his foxhole and burned Martha's letters. Then he burned the two photographs. There was a steady rain falling, which made it difficult, but he used heat tabs and Sterno to build a small fire, screening it with his body, holding the photographs over the tight blue flame with the tips of his fingers.

---

[5]*Sin loi* "Sorry about that!"

He realized it was only a gesture. Stupid, he thought. Sentimental, too, but mostly just stupid.

Lavender was dead. You couldn't burn the blame.

Besides, the letters were in his head. And even now, without photographs, Lieutenant Cross could see Martha playing volleyball in her white gym shorts and yellow T-shirt. He could see her moving in the rain.

When the fire died out, Lieutenant Cross pulled his poncho over his shoulders and ate breakfast from a can.

There was no great mystery, he decided.

In those burned letters Martha had never mentioned the war, except to say, Jimmy, take care of yourself. She wasn't involved. She signed the letters Love, but it wasn't love, and all the fine lines and technicalities did not matter. Virginity was no longer an issue. He hated her. Yes, he did. He hated her. Love, too, but it was a hard, hating kind of love.

The morning came up wet and blurry. Everything seemed part of everything else, the fog and Martha and the deepening rain.

He was a soldier, after all.

Half smiling, Lieutenant Jimmy Cross took out his maps. He shook his head hard, as if to clear it, then bent forward and began planning the day's march. In ten minutes, or maybe twenty, he would rouse the men and they would pack up and head west, where the maps showed the country to be green and inviting. They would do what they had always done. The rain might add some weight, but otherwise it would be one more day layered upon all the other days.

He was realistic about it. There was that new hardness in his stomach. He loved her but he hated her.

No more fantasies, he told himself.

Henceforth, when he thought about Martha, it would be only to think that she belonged elsewhere. He would shut down the daydreams. This was not Mount Sebastian, it was another world, where there were no pretty poems or midterm exams, a place where men died because of carelessness and gross stupidity. Kiowa was right. Boom-down, and you were dead, never partly dead.

Briefly, in the rain, Lieutenant Cross saw Martha's gray eyes gazing back at him.

He understood.

It was very sad, he thought. The things men carried inside. The things men did or felt they had to do.

He almost nodded at her, but didn't.

Instead he went back to his maps. He was now determined to perform his duties firmly and without negligence. It wouldn't help Lavender, he knew that, but from this point on he would comport himself as an officer. He would dispose of his good-luck pebble. Swallow it, maybe, or use Lee Strunk's slingshot, or just drop it along the trail. On the march he would impose strict field discipline. He would be careful to send out flank security, to prevent straggling or bunching up, to keep his troops moving at the proper pace and at the proper interval. He would insist on clean weapons. He would confiscate the remainder of Lavender's dope. Later in the day, perhaps, he would call the men together and speak to them plainly. He would accept the blame for what had happened to Ted Lavender. He would be a man about it. He would look them in the eyes, keeping his chin level, and he would issue the new SOPS in a calm, impersonal tone of voice, a lieutenant's voice, leaving no room for argument or discussion. Commencing immediately, he'd tell them, they would no longer abandon equipment along the route of march. They would police up their acts. They would get their shit together, and keep it together, and maintain it neatly and in good working order.

He would not tolerate laxity. He would show strength, distancing himself.

Among the men there would be grumbling, of course, and maybe worse, because their days would seem longer and their loads heavier, but Lieutenant Jimmy Cross reminded himself that his obligation was not to be loved but to lead. He would dispense with love; it was not now a factor. And if anyone quarreled or complained, he would simply tighten his lips and arrange his shoulders in the correct command posture. He might give a curt little nod. Or he might not. He might just shrug and say, Carry on, then they would saddle up and form into a column and move out toward the villages west of Than Khe.

[1986]

Questions

1. Why does Martha write to Lieutenant Cross?
2. Does the order in which the physical objects (the things) that are carried have significance? What about the intangible objects?
3. What constitutes "weight" in O'Brien's story?

Flannery O'Connor

(1925–1964)

United States

Much has been made of Flannery O'Connor's Catholic upbringing, especially in the way that religion plays such a strong importance in her novels and short stories. In "A Good Man Is Hard to Find"—probably O'Connor's most famous story—readers have often been fascinated by a kind of ironic reversal within the main characters, as if the seemingly good character (the grandmother) has lost her faith and the bad one (the Misfit) has somehow embraced a basic Christian truth: Remain true to your convictions. As V. S. Pritchett has written of O'Connor's religion:

> She was an old Catholic, not a convert, in the South of the poor white of the Bible Belt, and this gave her a critical skirmishing power. But the symbolism of religion, rather than the acrimonies of sectarian dispute, fed her violent imagination—the violence is itself oddly early Protestant—as if she had seen embers of the burning Bible-fed imagery in the minds of her own characters. . . . The essence of Flannery O'Connor's vision is that she sees terror as a purification—unwanted, of course: it is never the sadomasochist's intended indulgence. The moment of purification may actually destroy; it will certainly show someone changed.

O'Connor was born in Savannah, Georgia, in 1925. She attended Georgia State College for Women in Milledgeville and subsequently attended the writer's workshop at the University of Iowa, where her talent was so obvious to other students in the program that some of them are said to have suffered from instant writer's block. In 1950 she was diagnosed as having the autoimmune disease lupus (from which her father died nine years earlier) and, as a result, returned to Milledgeville, where she lived with her mother. Her first novel, Wise Blood, appeared in 1952, followed by a volume of stories, A Good Man Is Hard to Find, in 1955. These works were followed by The Violent Bear It Away, a novel published in 1964 (the year she died of lupus), and Everything That Rises Must Converge, published the following year. O'Connor's Collected Stories, published in 1972, won the National Book Award for fiction. Her entire Collected Works (including essays and letters) were published in a single-volume edition by The Library of America (1988).

In an essay called "The Grotesque in Southern Fiction," O'Connor wrote:

> Whenever I'm asked why Southern writers particularly have a penchant for writing about freaks, I say it is because we are still able to recognize one. To be able to recognize a freak, you have to have some conception of the whole man, and in the South the general conception of man is still, in the main, theological. That is a large statement, and it is dangerous to make it, for almost anything you say about Southern belief can be denied in the next breath with equal propriety. But approaching the subject from the standpoint of the writer, I think it is safe to say that while the South is hardly Christ-centered, it is most certainly Christ-haunted. The Southerner who isn't convinced of it is very much afraid that he may have been formed in the image and likeness of God. Ghosts can be fierce and instructive. They cast strange shadows, particularly in our literature. In any case, it is when the freak can be sensed as a figure of our essential displacement that it attains some depth in literature.

A Good Man Is Hard to Find

The dragon is by the side of the road, watching those who pass. Beware lest he devour you. We go to the Father of Souls, but it is necessary to pass by the dragon.

—St. Cyril of Jerusalem

The grandmother didn't want to go to Florida. She wanted to visit some of her connections in east Tennessee and she was seizing at every chance to change Bailey's mind. Bailey was the son she lived with, her only boy. He was sitting on the edge of his chair at the table, bent over the orange sports section of the *Journal*. "Now look here, Bailey," she said, "see here, read this," and she stood with one hand on her thin hip and the other rattling the newspaper at his bald head. "Here this fellow that calls himself The Misfit is aloose from the Federal Pen and headed toward Florida and you read here what it says he did to these people. Just you read it. I wouldn't take my children in any direction with a criminal like that aloose in it. I couldn't answer to my conscience if I did."

Bailey didn't look up from his reading so she wheeled around then and faced the children's mother, a young woman in slacks, whose face was as broad and innocent as a cabbage and was tied around with a green headkerchief that had two points on the top like a rabbit's ears. She was sitting on the sofa, feeding the baby his apricots out of a jar. "The children have been to Florida before," the old lady said. "You all ought to take them somewhere else for a change so they would see different parts of the world and be broad. They never have been to east Tennessee."

The children's mother didn't seem to hear her but the eight-year-old boy, John Wesley, a stocky child with glasses, said, "If you don't want to go to Florida, why dontcha stay at home?" He and the little girl, June Star, were reading the funny papers on the floor.

"She wouldn't stay at home to be queen for a day," June Star said without raising her yellow head.

"Yes and what would you do if this fellow, The Misfit, caught you?" the grandmother asked.

"I'd smack his face," John Wesley said.

"She wouldn't stay at home for a million bucks," June Star said. "Afraid she'd miss something. She has to go everywhere we go."

"All right, Miss," the grandmother said. "Just remember that the next time you want me to curl your hair."

June Star said her hair was naturally curly.

The next morning the grandmother was the first one in the car, ready to go. She had her big black valise that looked like the head of a hippopotamus in one corner, and underneath it she was hiding a basket with Pitty Sing, the cat, in it. She didn't intend for the cat to be left alone in the house for three days because he would miss her too much and she was afraid he might brush against one of the gas burners and accidentally asphyxiate himself. Her son, Bailey, didn't like to arrive at a motel with a cat.

She sat in the middle of the back seat with John Wesley and June Star on either side of her. Bailey and the children's mother and the baby sat in front and they left Atlanta at eight forty-five with the mileage on the car at 55890. The grandmother wrote this down because she thought it would be interesting to say how many miles they had been when they got back. It took them twenty minutes to reach the outskirts of the city.

The old lady settled herself comfortably, removing her white cotton gloves and putting them up with her purse on the shelf in front of the back window. The children's mother still had on slacks and still had her head tied up in a green kerchief, but the grandmother had on a navy blue straw sailor hat with a bunch of white violets on the brim and a navy blue dress with a small white dot in the print. Her collars and cuffs were white organdy trimmed with lace and at her neckline she had pinned a purple spray of cloth violets containing a sachet. In case of an accident, anyone seeing her dead on the highway would know at once that she was a lady.

She said she thought it was going to be a good day for driving, neither too hot nor too cold, and she cautioned Bailey that the speed limit was fifty-five miles an hour and that the patrolmen hid themselves behind billboards and small clumps of trees and sped out after you before you had a chance to slow down. She pointed out interesting details of the scenery: Stone Mountain; the blue granite that in some places came up to both sides of the highway; the brilliant red clay banks slightly streaked with purple; and the various crops that made rows of green lace-work on the ground. The trees were full of silver-white sunlight and the meanest of them sparkled. The children were reading comic magazines and their mother had gone back to sleep.

"Let's go through Georgia fast so we won't have to look at it much," John Wesley said.

"If I were a little boy," said the grandmother, "I wouldn't talk about my native state that way. Tennessee has the mountains and Georgia has the hills."

"Tennessee is just a hillbilly dumping ground," John Wesley said, "and Georgia is a lousy state too."

"You said it," June Star said.

"In my time," said the grandmother, folding her thin veined fingers, "children were more respectful of their native states and their parents and everything else. People did right then. Oh look at the cute little pickaninny!" she said and pointed to a Negro child standing in the door of a shack. "Wouldn't that make a picture, now?" she asked and they all turned and looked at the little Negro out of the back window. He waved.

"He didn't have any britches on," June Star said.

"He probably didn't have any," the grandmother explained. "Little niggers in the country don't have things like we do. If I could paint, I'd paint that picture," she said.

The children exchanged comic books.

The grandmother offered to hold the baby and the children's mother passed him over the front seat to her. She set him on her knee and bounced him and told him about the things they were passing. She rolled her eyes and screwed up her mouth and stuck her leathery thin face into his smooth bland one. Occasionally he gave her a faraway smile. They passed a large cotton field with five or six graves fenced in the middle of it, like a small island. "Look at the graveyard!" the grandmother said, pointing it out. "That was the old family burying ground. That belonged to the plantation."

"Where's the plantation?" John Wesley asked.

"Gone with the Wind," said the grandmother. "Ha. Ha."

When the children finished all the comic books they had brought, they opened the lunch and ate it. The grandmother ate a peanut butter sandwich and an olive and would not let the children throw the box and the paper napkins out the window. When there was nothing else to do they played a game by choosing a cloud and making the other two guess what shape it suggested. John Wesley took one the shape of a cow and June Star guessed a cow and John Wesley said, no, an automobile, and June Star said he didn't play fair, and they began to slap each other over the grandmother.

The grandmother said she would tell them a story if they would keep quiet. When she told a story, she rolled her eyes and waved her head and was very dramatic. She said once when she was a maiden lady she had been courted by a Mr. Edgar Atkins Teagarden from Jasper, Georgia. She said he was a very good-looking man and a gentleman and that he brought her a watermelon every Saturday afternoon with his initials cut in it, E. A. T. Well, one Saturday, she said, Mr. Teagarden brought the watermelon and there was nobody at home and he left it on the front porch and returned in his buggy to Jasper, but she never got the watermelon, she said, because a nigger boy ate it when he saw the initials, E. A. T.! This story tickled John Wesley's funny bone and he giggled and giggled but June Star didn't think it was any good. She said she wouldn't marry a man that just brought her a watermelon on Saturday. The grandmother said she would have done well to marry Mr. Teagarden because he was a gentleman and had bought Coca-Cola stock when it first came out and that he had died only a few years ago, a very wealthy man.

They stopped at The Tower for barbecued sandwiches. The Tower was a part stucco and part wood filling station and dance hall set in a clearing outside of Timothy. A fat man named Red Sammy Butts ran it and there were signs stuck here and there on the building and for miles up and down the highway saying, TRY RED SAMMY'S FAMOUS BARBECUE. NONE LIKE FAMOUS RED SAMMY'S! RED SAM! THE FAT BOY WITH THE HAPPY LAUGH. A VETERAN! RED SAMMY'S YOUR MAN!

Red Sammy was lying on the bare ground outside the Tower with his head under a truck while a gray monkey about a foot high, chained to a small chinaberry tree, chattered nearby. The monkey sprang back into the tree and got on the highest limb as soon as he saw the children jump out of the car and run toward him.

Inside, The Tower was a long dark room with a counter at one end and tables at the other and dancing space in the middle. They all sat down at a board table next to the nickelodeon and Red Sam's wife, a tall burnt-brown woman with hair and eyes lighter than her skin, came and took their order. The children's mother put a dime in the machine and played "The Tennessee Waltz," and the grandmother said that tune always made her want to dance. She asked Bailey if he would like to dance but he only glared at her. He didn't have a naturally sunny disposition like she did and trips made him nervous. The grandmother's brown eyes were very bright. She swayed her head from side to side and pretended she was dancing in her chair. June Star said play something she could tap to so the children's mother put in another dime and played a fast number and June Star stepped out onto the dance floor and did her tap routine.

"Ain't she cute?" Red Sam's wife said, leaning over the counter. "Would you like to come be my little girl?"

"No I certainly wouldn't," June Star said. "I wouldn't live in a broken-down place like this for a million bucks!" and she ran back to the table.

"Ain't she cute?" the woman repeated, stretching her mouth politely.

"Aren't you ashamed?" hissed the grandmother.

Red Sam came in and told his wife to quit lounging on the counter and hurry up with these people's order. His khaki trousers reached just to his hip bones and his stomach hung over them like a sack of meal swaying under his shirt. He came over and sat down at a table nearby and let out a combination sigh and yodel. "You can't win," he said. "You can't win," and he wiped his sweating red face off with a gray handkerchief. "These days you don't know who to trust," he said. "Ain't that the truth?"

"People are certainly not nice like they used to be," said the grandmother.

"Two fellers come in here last week," Red Sammy said, "driving a Chrysler. It was a old beat-up car but it was a good one and these boys looked all right to me. Said they worked at the mill and you know I let them fellers charge the gas they bought? Now why did I do that?"

"Because you're a good man!" the grandmother said at once.

"Yes'm, I suppose so," Red Sam said as if he were struck with this answer.

His wife brought the orders, carrying the five plates all at once without a tray, two in each hand and one balanced on her arm. "It isn't a soul in this green world of God's that you can trust," she said. "And I don't count nobody out of that, not nobody," she repeated, looking at Red Sammy.

"Did you read about that criminal, The Misfit, that's escaped?" asked the grandmother.

"I wouldn't be a bit surprised if he didn't attack this place right here," said the woman. "If he hears about it being here, I wouldn't be none surprised to see him. If he hears it's two cent in the cash register, I wouldn't be a tall surprised if he . . . "

"That'll do," Red Sam said. "Go bring these people their Co'-Colas," and the woman went off to get the rest of the order.

"A good man is hard to find," Red Sammy said. "Everything is getting terrible. I remember the day you could go off and leave your screen door unlatched. Not no more."

He and the grandmother discussed better times. The old lady said that in her opinion Europe was entirely to blame for the way things were now. She said the way Europe acted you would think we were made of money and Red Sam said it was no use talking about it, she was exactly right. The children ran outside into the white sunlight and looked at the monkey in the lacy chinaberry tree. He was busy catching fleas on himself and biting each one carefully between his teeth as if it were a delicacy.

They drove off again into the hot afternoon. The grandmother took cat naps and woke up every few minutes with her own snoring. Outside of Toombsboro she woke up and recalled an old plantation that she had visited in this neighborhood once when she was a young lady. She said the house had six white columns across the front and that there was an avenue of oaks leading up to it and two little wooden trellis arbors on either side in front where you sat down with your suitor after a stroll in the garden. She recalled exactly which road to turn off to get to it. She knew that Bailey would not be willing to lose any time looking at an old house, but the more she talked bout it, the more she wanted to see it once again and find out if the little twin arbors were still standing. "There was a secret panel in this house," she said craftily, not telling the truth but wishing that she were, "and the story went that all the family silver was hidden in it when Sherman came through but it was never found. . . ."

"Hey!" John Wesley said. "Let's go see it! We'll find it! We'll poke all the woodwork and find it! Who lives there? Where do you turn off at? Hey Pop, can't we turn off there?"

"We never have seen a house with a secret panel!" June Star shrieked. "Let's go to the house with the secret panel! Hey Pop, can't we go see the house with the secret panel!"

"It's not far from here, I know," the grandmother said. "It won't take over twenty minutes."

Bailey was looking straight ahead. His jaw was as rigid as a horseshoe. "No." he said.

The children began to yell and scream that they wanted to see the house with the secret panel. John Wesley kicked the back of the front seat and June Star hung over her mother's shoulder and whined desperately into her ear that they never had any fun even on their vacation, that they could never do what THEY wanted to do. The baby began to scream and John Wesley kicked the back of the seat so hard that his father could feel the blows in his kidney.

"All right!" he shouted and drew the car to a stop at the side of the road. "Will you all shut up? Will you all just shut up for one second? If you don't shut up, we won't go anywhere."

"It would be very educational for them," the grandmother murmured.

"All right," Bailey said, "but get this: this is the only time we're going to stop for anything like this. This is the one and only time."

"The dirt road that you have to turn down is about a mile back," the grandmother directed. "I marked it when we passed."

"A dirt road," Bailey groaned.

After they had turned around and were headed toward the dirt road, the grandmother recalled other points about the house, the beautiful glass over the front doorway and the candle-lamp in the hall. John Wesley said that the secret panel was probably in the fireplace.

"You can't go inside this house," Bailey said. "You don't know who lives there."

"While you all talk to the people in front, I'll run around behind and get in a window," John Wesley suggested.

"We'll all stay in the car," his mother said.

They turned onto the dirt road and the car raced roughly along in a swirl of pink dust. The grandmother recalled the times when there were no paved roads and thirty miles was a day's journey. The dirt road was hilly and there were sudden washes in it and sharp curves on dangerous embankments. All at once they would be on a hill, looking down over the blue tops of trees for miles around, then the next minute, they would be in a red depression with the dust-coated trees looking down on them.

"This place had better turn up in a minute," Bailey said, "or I'm going to turn around."

The road looked as if no one had traveled on it for months.

"It's not much farther," the grandmother said and just as she said it, a horrible thought came to her. The thought was so embarrassing that she turned red in the face and her eyes dilated and her feet jumped up, upsetting her valise in the corner. The instant the valise moved, the newspaper top she had over the basket under it rose with a snarl and Pitty Sing, the cat, sprang onto Bailey's shoulder.

The children were thrown to the floor and their mother, clutching the baby was thrown out the door onto the ground, the old lady was thrown into the front seat. The car turned over once and landed right-side-up in a gulch off the side of the road. Bailey remained in the driver's seat with the cat—gray-striped with a broad white face and an orange nose—clinging to his neck like a caterpillar.

As soon as the children saw they could move their arms and legs, they scrambled out of the car, shouting, "We've had an ACCIDENT!" The grandmother was curled up under the dashboard, hoping she was injured so that Bailey's wrath would not come down on her all at once. The horrible thought she had before the accident was that the house she had remembered so vividly was not in Georgia but in Tennessee.

Bailey removed the cat from his neck with both hands and flung it out the window against the side of a pine tree. Then he got out of the car and started looking for the children's mother. She was sitting against the side of the red gutted ditch, holding the screaming baby, but she only had a cut down her face and a broken shoulder. "We've had an ACCIDENT!" the children screamed in a frenzy of delight.

"But nobody's killed," June Star said with disappointment as the grandmother limped out of the car, her hat still pinned to her head but the broken front brim standing up at a jaunty angle and the violet spray hanging off the side. They all sat down in the ditch, except the children, to recover from the shock. They were all shaking.

"Maybe a car will come along," said the children's mother hoarsely.

"I believe I have injured an organ," said the grandmother, pressing her side, but no one answered her. Bailey's teeth were clattering. He had on a yellow sport shirt with bright blue parrots designed in it and his face was as yellow as the shirt. The grandmother decided that she would not mention that the house was in Tennessee.

The road was about ten feet above and they could only see the tops of the trees on the other side of it. Behind the ditch they were sitting in there were more woods, tall and dark and deep. In a few minutes they saw a car some distance away on top of a hill, coming slowly as if the occupants were watching them. The grandmother stood up and waved both arms dramatically to attract their attention. The car continued to come on slowly, disappeared around a bend and appeared again, moving even slower, on top of the hill they had gone over. It was a big black battered hearse-like automobile. There were three men in it.

It came to a stop just over them and for some minutes, the driver looked down with a steady expressionless gaze to where they were sitting, and didn't speak. Then he turned his head and muttered something to the other two and they got out. One was a fat boy in black trousers and a red sweat shirt with a silver stallion embossed on the front of it. He moved around on the right side of them and stood staring, his mouth partly open in a kind of loose grin. The other had on khaki pants and a blue striped coat and a gray hat pulled very low, hiding most of his face. He came around slowly on the left side. Neither spoke.

The driver got out of the car and stood by the side of it, looking down at them. He was an older man than the other two. His hair was just beginning to gray and he wore silver-rimmed spectacles that gave him a scholarly look. He had a long creased face and didn't have on any shirt or undershirt. He had on blue jeans that were too tight for him and was holding a black hat and a gun. The two boys also had guns.

"We've had an ACCIDENT!" the children screamed.

The grandmother had the peculiar feeling that the bespectacled man was someone she knew. His face was as familiar to her as if she had known him all her life but she could not recall who he was. He moved away from the car and began to come down the embankment, placing his feet carefully so that he wouldn't slip. He had on tan and white shoes and no socks, and his ankles were red and thin. "Good afternoon," he said. "I see you all had you a little spill."

"We turned over twice!" said the grandmother.

"Oncet," he corrected. "We seen it happen. Try their car and see will it run, Hiram," he said quietly to the boy with the gray hat.

"What you got that gun for?" John Wesley asked. "Whatcha gonna do with that gun?"

"Lady," the man said to the children's mother, "would you mind calling them children to sit down by you? Children make me nervous. I want you all to sit down right together there where you're at."

"What are you telling US what to do for?" June Star asked.

Behind them the line of woods gaped like a dark open mouth. "Come here," said the mother.

"Look here now," Bailey said suddenly, "we're in a predicament! We're in . . ."

The grandmother shrieked. She scrambled to her feet and stood staring. "You're The Misfit!" she said. "I recognized you at once!"

"Yes'm," the man said, smiling slightly as if he were pleased in spite of himself to be known, "but it would have been better for all of you, lady, if you hadn't of reckernized me."

Bailey turned his head sharply and said something to his mother that shocked even the children. The old lady began to cry and The Misfit reddened.

"Lady," he said, "don't you get upset. Sometimes a man says things he don't mean. I don't reckon he meant to talk to you thataway."

"You wouldn't shoot a lady, would you?" the grandmother said and removed a clean handkerchief from her cuff and began to slap at her eyes with it.

The Misfit pointed the toe of his shoe into the ground and made a little hole and then covered it up again. "I would hate to have to," he said.

"Listen," the grandmother almost screamed, "I know you're a good man. You don't look a bit like you have common blood. I know you must come from nice people!"

"Yes mam," he said, "finest people in the world." When he smiled he showed a row of strong white teeth. "God never made a finer woman than my mother and my daddy's heart was pure gold," he said. The boy with the red sweat shirt had come around behind them and was standing with his gun at his hip. The Misfit squatted down on the ground. "Watch them children, Bobby Lee," he said. "You know they make me nervous." He looked at the six of them huddled together in front of him and he seemed to be embarrassed as if he couldn't think of anything to say. "Ain't a cloud in the sky," he remarked, looking up at it. "Don't see no sun but don't see no cloud neither."

"Yes, it's a beautiful day," said the grandmother. "Listen," she said, "You shouldn't call yourself The Misfit because I know you're a good man at heart. I can just look at you and tell."

"Hush!" Bailey yelled. "Hush! Everybody shut up and let me handle this!" He was squatting in the position of a runner about to sprint forward but he didn't move.

"I pre-chate that, lady," The Misfit said and drew a little circle in the ground with the butt of his gun.

"It'll take a half a hour to fix this here car," Hiram called, looking over the raised hood of it.

"Well, first you and Bobby Lee get him and that little boy to step over yonder with you." The Misfit said, pointing to Bailey and John Wesley, "The boys want to ast you something," he said to Bailey. "Would you mind stepping back in them woods there with them?"

"Listen," Bailey began, "we're in a terrible predicament! Nobody realizes what this is," and his voice cracked. His eyes were as blue and intense as the parrots in his shirt and he remained perfectly still.

The grandmother reached up to adjust her hat brim as if she were going to the woods with him but it came off in her hand. She stood staring at it and after a second she let it fall to the ground. Hiram pulled Bailey up by the arm as if he were assisting an old man. John Wesley caught hold of his father's hand and Bobby Lee followed. They went off toward the woods and just as they reached the dark edge, Bailey turned and supporting himself against a gray naked pine trunk, he shouted, "I'll be back in a minute, Mamma, wait on me!"

"Come back this instant!" his mother shrilled but they all disappeared into the woods.

"Bailey Boy!" the grandmother called in a tragic voice but she found she was looking at The Misfit squatting on the ground in front of her. "I just know you're a good man," she said desperately. "You're not a bit common!"

"Nome, I ain't a good man," The Misfit said after a second as if he had considered her statement carefully, "but I ain't the worst in the world neither. My daddy said I was a different breed of dog from my brothers and sisters. 'You know,' Daddy said, 'it's some that can live their whole life out without asking about it and it's others has to know why it is, and this boy is one of the latters. He's going to be into everything!'" He put on his black hat and looked up suddenly and then away deep into the woods as if he were embarrassed again. "I'm sorry I don't have on a shirt before you ladies," he said, hunching his shoulders slightly. "We buried our clothes that we had on when we escaped and we're just making do until we can get better. We borrowed these from some folks we met," he explained.

"That's perfectly all right," the grandmother said. "Maybe Bailey has an extra shirt in his suitcase."

"I'll look and see terrectly," The Misfit said.

"Where are they taking him?" the children's mother screamed.

"Daddy was a card himself," The Misfit said. "You couldn't put anything over on him. He never got in trouble with the Authorities though. Just had the knack of handling them."

"You could be honest too if you'd only try," said the grandmother. "Think how wonderful it would be to settle down and live a comfortable life and not have to think about somebody chasing you all the time."

The Misfit kept scratching in the ground with the butt of his gun as if he were thinking about it. "Yes'm, somebody is always after you," he murmured.

The grandmother noticed how thin his shoulder blades were just behind his hat because she was standing up looking down at him. "Do you ever pray?" she asked.

He shook his head. All she saw was the black hat wiggle between his shoulder blades. "Nome," he said.

There was a pistol shot from the woods, followed closely by another. Then silence. The old lady's head jerked around. She could hear the wind move through the tree tops like a long satisfied insuck of breath. "Bailey Boy!" she called.

"I was a gospel singer for a while," The Misfit said. "I been most everything. Been in the arm service, both land and sea, at home and abroad, been twict married, been an undertaker, been with the railroads, plowed Mother Earth, been in a tornado, seen a man burnt alive oncet," and he looked up at the children's mother and the little girl who were sitting close together, their faces white and their eyes glassy; "I even seen a woman flogged," he said.

"Pray, pray," the grandmother began, "pray, pray. . . ."

"I never was a bad boy that I remember of," The Misfit said in an almost dreamy voice, "but somewheres along the line I done something wrong and got sent to the penitentiary. I was buried alive," and he looked up and held her attention to him by a steady stare.

"That's when you should have started to pray," she said. "What did you do to get sent to the penitentiary, that first time?"

"Turn to the right, it was a wall," The Misfit said, looking up again at the cloudless sky. "Turn to the left, it was a wall. Look up it was a ceiling, look down it was a floor. I forgot what I done, lady. I set there and set there, trying to remember what it was I done and I ain't recalled it to this day. Oncet in a while, I would think it was coming to me, but it never come."

"Maybe they put you in by mistake," the old lady said vaguely.

"Nome," he said. "It wasn't no mistake. They had the papers on me."

"You must have stolen something," she said.

The Misfit sneered slightly. "Nobody had nothing I wanted," he said. "It was a head-doctor at the penitentiary said what I had done was kill my daddy but I known that for a lie. My daddy died in nineteen ought nineteen of the epidemic flu and I never had a thing to do with it. He was buried in the Mount Hopewell Baptist church-yard and you can see for yourself."

"If you would pray," the old lady said, "Jesus would help you."

"That's right," The Misfit said.

"Well then, why don't you pray?" she asked trembling with delight suddenly.

"I don't want no hep," he said. "I'm doing all right by myself."

Bobby Lee and Hiram came ambling back from the woods. Bobby Lee was drag-ging a yellow shirt with bright blue parrots in it.

"Throw me that shirt, Bobby Lee," The Misfit said. The shirt came flying at him and landed on his shoulder and he put it on. The grandmother couldn't name what the shirt reminded her of. "No, lady," The Misfit said while he was buttoning it up, "I found out the crime don't matter. You can do one thing or you can do another, kill a man or take a tire off his car, because sooner or later you're going to forget what it was you done and just be punished for it."

The children's mother had begun to make heaving noises as if she couldn't get her breath. "Lady," he asked, "would you and that little girl like to step off yonder with Bobby Lee and Hiram and join your husband?"

"Yes, thank you," the mother said faintly. Her left arm dangled helplessly and she was holding the baby, who had gone to sleep, in the other. "Hep that lady up, Hiram," The Misfit said as she struggled to climb out of the ditch, "and Bobby Lee, you hold onto that little girl's hand."

"I don't want to hold hands with him," June Star said. "He reminds me of a pig."

The fat boy blushed and laughed and caught her by the arm and pulled her off into the woods after Hiram and her mother.

Alone with The Misfit, the grandmother found that she had lost her voice. There was not a cloud in the sky nor any sun. There was nothing around her but woods. She wanted to tell him that he must pray. She opened and closed her mouth several times before anything came out. Finally she found herself saying, "Jesus, Jesus," meaning, Jesus will help you, but the way she was saying it, it sounded as if she might be cursing.

"Yes'm," The Misfit said as if he agreed. "Jesus thown everything off balance. It was the same case with Him as with me except He hadn't committed any crime and they could prove I had committed one because they had the papers on me. Of course," he said, "they never shown me my papers. That's why I sign myself now. I said long ago, you get your signature and sign everything you do and keep a copy of it. Then you'll know what you done and you can hold up the crime to the punishment and see do they match and in the end you'll have something to prove you ain't been treated right. I call myself The Misfit," he said, "because I can't make what all I done wrong fit what all I gone through in punishment."

There was a piercing scream from the woods, followed closely by a pistol report. "Does it seem right to you, lady, that one is punished a heap and another ain't pun-ished at all?"

"Jesus!" the old lady cried. "You've got good blood! I know you wouldn't shoot a lady! I know you come from nice people! Pray! Jesus, you ought not to shoot a lady. I'll give you all the money I've got!"

"Lady," The Misfit said, looking beyond her far into the woods, "there never was a body that give the undertaker a tip."

There were two more pistol reports and the grandmother raised her head like a parched old turkey hen crying for water and called, "Bailey Boy, Bailey Boy!" as if her heart would break.

"Jesus was the only One that ever raised the dead," The Misfit continued, "and He shouldn't have done it. He thrown everything off balance. If He did what He said, then it's nothing for you to do but throw away everything and follow Him, and if He didn't, then it's nothing for you to do but enjoy the few minutes you got left the best you can—by killing somebody or burning down his house or doing some other meanness to him. No pleasure but meanness," he said and his voice had become almost a snarl.

"Maybe He didn't raise the dead," the old lady mumbled, not knowing what she was saying and feeling so dizzy that she sank down in the ditch with her legs twisted under her.

"I wasn't there so I can't say He didn't," The Misfit said. "I wisht I had of been there," he said, hitting the ground with his fist. "It ain't right I wasn't there because if I had of been there I would of known. Listen lady," he said in a high voice, "if I had of been there I would of known and I wouldn't be like I am now." His voice seemed about to crack and the grandmother's head cleared for an instant. She saw the man's face twisted close to her own as if he were going to cry and she murmured, "Why you're one of my babies. You're one of my own children!" She reached out and touched him on the shoulder. The Misfit sprang back as if a snake had bitten him and shot her three times through the chest. Then he put his gun down on the ground and took off his glasses and began to clean them.

Hiram and Bobby Lee returned from the woods and stood over the ditch, looking down at the grandmother who half sat and half lay in a puddle of blood with her legs crossed under her like a child's and her face smiling up at the cloudless sky.

Without his glasses, The Misfit's eyes were red-rimmed and pale and defenseless-looking. "Take her off and throw her where you thrown the others," he said, picking up the cat that was rubbing itself against his leg.

"She was a talker, wasn't she?" Bobby Lee said, sliding down the ditch with a yodel.

"She would of been a good woman," The Misfit said, "if it had been somebody there to shoot her every minute of her life."

"Some fun!" Bobby Lee said.

"Shut up, Bobby Lee," The Misfit said. "It's no real pleasure in life."

[1955]

Questions

1. At what place in the story do your sympathies with the grandmother turn against her?
2. What is the Misfit's philosophy of life?
3. Is there too much coincidence in the story?
4. What does the final dialogue between Bobby Lee and the Misfit (after the grandmother's death) mean?
5. What is O'Connor's concept of a good man?

Ōe Kenzaburo

(b. 1935)

Japan

Although he doesn't use the term, John Nathan (Ōe Kenzaburo's American translator) describes the writer in his introduction to Teach Us to Outgrow Our Madness as the enfant terrible of contemporary Japanese writing. Ōe's novels have won him every major Japanese literary prize, and yet his work is still relatively unknown in the United States. The loss is ours, because Ōe's affinities with American writing and his fascination with American culture should guarantee a natural bond. In "Prize Stock," for example—a story influenced by Mark Twain's Huckleberry Finn—the main character is a young Japanese boy during World War II who takes care of an American GI who has crash-landed his airplane in the boy's village. The fascination of the story, and, indeed, its power to thoroughly engage us, is due to the fact that the GI is an African American and that the boy/narrator learns to distrust the adults around him, just as Huck does in Mark Twain's masterpiece.

For an understanding of "Aghwee the Sky Monster," it is important to know that Ōe's first child was born with brain damage in 1964. John Nathan tells it as follows:

> [T]he baby boy, whom he called "Pooh," altered his world with the force of an exploding sun. I won't presume to describe Ōe's relationship with the child. . . . Suffice it to say that over the years as Pooh grew up, a fierce, exclusive, isolating bond developed between father and son. In a fervent, painful way, Ōe and his fragile, autistic child became one another's best, embracing one another as if they were each other's fate. Shortly after Pooh was born, Ōe ordered two gravestones erected side by side in the cemetery in his native village. He has told me many times that he would die when Pooh died.

Ōe Kenzaburo was born in 1935. He majored in French at Tokyo University and has often been regarded as an unofficial spokesman for the New Left. He was awarded the Nobel Prize for Literature in 1994. His most recent books translated into English include A Quiet Life (1996), which he refers to as semi-fiction, and An Echo of Heaven (1996), a novel.

AGHWEE THE SKY MONSTER

Alone in my room, I wear a piratical black patch over my right eye. The eye may look all right, but the truth is I have scarcely any sight in it. I say scarcely, it isn't totally blind. Consequently, when I look at this world with both eyes I see two worlds perfectly superimposed, a vague and shadowy world on top of one that's bright and vivid. I can be walking down a paved street when a sense of peril and unbalance will stop me like a rat just scurried out of a sewer, dead in my tracks. Or I'll discover a film of unhappiness and fatigue on the face of a cheerful friend and clog the flow of an easy chat with my stutter. I suppose I'll get used to this eventually. If I don't, I intend to

737

wear my patch not only in my room when I'm alone but on the street and with my friends. Strangers may pass with condescending smiles—what an old-fashioned joke!—but I'm old enough not to be annoyed by every little thing.

The story I intend to tell is about my first experience earning money; I began with my right eye because the memory of that experience ten years ago revived in me abruptly and quite out of context when violence was done to my eye last spring. Remembering, I should add, I was freed from the hatred uncoiling in my heart and beginning to fetter me. At the very end I'll talk about the accident itself.

Ten years ago I had twenty-twenty vision. Now one of my eyes is ruined. *Time* shifted, launched itself from the springboard of an eyeball squashed by a stone. When I first met that sentimental madman I had only a child's understanding of *time*. I was yet to have the cruel awareness of *time* drilling its eyes into my back and *time* lying in wait ahead.

Ten years ago I was eighteen, five feet six, one hundred and ten pounds, had just entered college and was looking for a part-time job. Although I still had trouble reading French, I wanted a cloth-bound edition in two volumes of *L'Âme Enchanté*.[1] It was a Moscow edition, with not only a foreword but footnotes and even the colophon in Russian and wispy lines like bits of thread connecting the letters of the French text. A curious edition to be sure, but sturdier and more elegant than the French, and much cheaper. At the time I discovered it in a bookstore specializing in East European publications I had no interest in Romain Rolland, yet I went immediately into action to make the volumes mine. In those days I often succumbed to some weird passion and it never bothered me, I had the feeling there was nothing to worry about so long as I was sufficiently obsessed.

As I had just entered college and wasn't registered at the employment center, I looked for work by making the rounds of people I knew. Finally my uncle introduced me to a banker who came up with an offer. "Did you happen to see a movie called *Harvey?*" he asked. I said yes, and tried for a smile of moderate but unmistakable dedication, appropriate for someone about to be employed for the first time. *Harvey* was that Jimmy Stewart film about a man living with an imaginary rabbit as big as a bear; it had made me laugh so hard I thought I would die. "Recently, my son has been having the same sort of delusions about living with a monster." The banker didn't return my smile. "He's stopped working and stays in his room. I'd like him to get out from time to time but of course he'd need a—companion. Would you be interested?"

I knew quite a bit about the banker's son. He was a young composer whose avant-garde music had won prizes in France and Italy and who was generally included in the photo roundups in the weekly magazines, the kind of article they always called "Japan's Artists of Tomorrow." I had never heard his major works, but I had seen several films he had written the music for. There was one about the adventures of a juvenile delinquent that had a short, lyrical theme played on the harmonica. It was beautiful. Watching the picture, I remember feeling vaguely troubled by the idea of an adult nearly thirty years old (in fact, the composer was twenty-eight when he hired me, my present age), working out a theme for the harmonica, I suppose because my own harmonica had become my little brother's property when I had entered elementary school. And possibly because I knew more about the composer, whose name was D, than just public facts; I knew he had created a scandal. Generally I have nothing but

---

[1]*L'Âme Enchanté*   French: *The Enchanted Soul.*

contempt for scandals, but I knew that the composer's infant child had died, that he had gotten divorced as a result, and that he was rumored to be involved with a certain movie actress. I hadn't known that he was in the grips of something like the rabbit in Jimmy Stewart's movie, or that he had stopped working and secluded himself in his room. How serious was his condition, I wondered, was it a case of nervous breakdown, or was he clearly schizophrenic?

"I'm not certain I know just what you mean by companion," I said, reeling in my smile. "Naturally, I'd like to be of service if I can." This time, concealing my curiosity and apprehension I tried to lend my voice and expression as much sympathy as possible without seeming forward. It was only a part-time job, but it was the first chance of employment I had had and I was determined to do my accommodating best.

"When my son decides he wants to go somewhere in Tokyo, you go along—just that. There's a nurse at the house and she has no trouble handling him, so you don't have to worry about violence." The banker made me feel like a soldier whose cowardice had been discovered. I blushed and said, trying to recover lost ground, "I'm fond of music, and I respect composers more than anyone, so I look forward to accompanying D and talking with him."

"All he thinks about these days is this thing in his head, and apparently that's all he talks about!" The banker's brusqueness made my face even redder. "You can go out to see him tomorrow," he said.

"At—your house?"

"That's right, did you think he was in an asylum?" From the banker's tone of voice I could only suppose that he was at bottom a nasty man.

"If I should get the job," I said with my eyes on the floor, "I'll drop by again to thank you." I could easily have cried.

"No, he'll be hiring you (All right then, I resolved defiantly, I'll call D my employer), so that won't be necessary. All I care about is that he doesn't get into any trouble outside that might develop into a scandal. . . . There's his career to think about. Naturally, what he does reflects on me—"

So that was it! I thought, so I was to be a moral sentinel guarding the banker's family against a second contamination by the poisons of scandal. Of course I didn't say a thing, I only nodded dependably, anxious to warm the banker's chilly heart with the heat of reliance on me. I didn't even ask the most pressing question, something truly difficult to ask: This monster haunting your son, sir, is it a rabbit like Harvey, nearly six feet tall? A creature covered in bristly hair like an Abominable Snowman? What kind of a monster is it? In the end I remained silent and consoled myself with the thought that I might be able to pry the secret out of the nurse if I made friends with her.

Then I left the executive's office, and as I walked along the corridor grinding my teeth in humiliation as if I were Julien Sorel after a meeting with someone important I became self-conscious to the tips of my fingers and tried assessing my attitude and its effectiveness. When I got out of college I chose not to seek nine-to-five employment, and I do believe the memory of my dialogue with that disagreeable banker played a large part in my decision.

Even so, when classes were over the next day I took a train out to the residential suburb where the composer lived. As I passed through the gate of that castle of a house, I remember a roaring of terrific beasts, as at a zoo in the middle of the night. I was dismayed, I cowered, what if those were the screams of my employer? A good thing it didn't occur to me then that those savage screams might have been coming from the monster haunting D like Jimmy Stewart's rabbit. Whatever they were, it was so clear that the screaming had rattled me that the maid showing me the way was indiscreet enough to break into a laugh. Then I discovered someone else laughing, voicelessly, in the dimness beyond a window in an annex in the garden. It was the man who was supposed to employ me; he was laughing like a face in a movie without a sound track. And boiling all around him was that howling of wild beasts. I listened closely and realized that several of the same animals were shrieking in concert. And in voices too shrill to be of this world. Abandoned by the maid at the entrance to the annex, I decided the screaming must be part of the composer's tape collection, regained my courage, straightened up and opened the door.

Inside, the annex reminded me of a kindergarten. There were no partitions in the large room, only two pianos, an electric organ, several tape recorders, a record player, something we had called a "mixer" when I was in the high-school radio club—there was hardly room to step. A dog asleep on the floor, for example, turned out to be a tuba of reddish brass. It was just as I had imagined a composer's studio; I even had the illusion I had seen the place before. His father had said D had stopped working and secluded himself in his room, could he have been mistaken?

The composer was just bending to switch off the tape recorder. Enveloped in a chaos that was not without its own order, he moved his hands swiftly and in an instant those beastly screams were sucked into a dark hole of silence. Then he straightened and turned to me with a truly tranquil smile.

Having glanced around the room and seen that the nurse was not present I was a little wary, but the composer gave me no reason in the world to expect that he was about to get violent.

"My father told me about you. Come in, there's room over there," he said in a low, resonant voice.

I took off my shoes and stepped up onto the rug without putting on slippers. Then I looked around for a place to sit, but except for a round stool in front of the piano and the organ, there wasn't a bit of furniture in the room, not even a cushion. So I brought my feet together between a pair of bongo drums and some empty tape boxes and there I stood uncomfortably. The composer stood there too, arms hanging at his sides. I wondered if he ever sat down. He didn't ask me to be seated either, just stood there silent and smiling.

"Could those have been monkey voices?" I said, trying to crack a silence that threatened to set more quickly than any cement.

"Rhinoceros—they sounded that way because I speeded the machine up. And I had the volume way up, too. At least I think they're rhinoceros—rhino is what I asked for when I had this tape made—of course I can't really be sure. But now that you're here, I'll be able to go to the zoo myself."

"I may take that to mean that I'm employed?"

"Of course! I didn't have you come out here to test you. How can a lunatic test a normal person?" The man who was to be my employer said this objectively and almost as if he were embarrassed. Which made me feel disgusted with the obsequiousness of what I had said—I may take that to mean that I'm employed? I had sounded like a shopkeeper! The composer was different from his businessman father and I should have been more direct with him.

"I wish you wouldn't call yourself a lunatic. It's awkward for me." Trying to be frank was one thing, but what a brainless remark! But the composer met me half way, "All right, if that's how you feel. I suppose that would make work easier."

Work is a vague word, but, at least during those few months when I was visiting him once a week, the composer didn't get even as close to work as going to the zoo to record a genuine rhino for himself. All he did was wander around Tokyo in various conveyances or on foot and visit a variety of places. When he mentioned work, he must therefore have had me in mind. And I worked quite a lot; I even went on a mission for him all the way to Kyoto.

"Then when should I begin?" I said.

"Right away if it suits you. Now."

"That suits me fine."

"I'll have to get ready—would you wait outside?"

Head lowered cautiously, as though he were walking in a swamp, my employer picked his way to the back of the room past musical instruments and sound equipment and piles of manuscript to a black wooden door which he opened and then closed behind him. I got a quick look at a woman in a nurse's uniform, a woman in her early forties with a longish face and heavy shadows on her cheeks that might have been wrinkles or maybe scars. She seemed to encircle the composer with her right arm as she ushered him inside, while with her left hand she closed the door. If this was part of the routine, I would never have a chance to talk with the nurse before I went out with my employer. Standing in front of the closed door, in the darkest part of that dim room, I shuffled into my shoes and felt my anxiety about this job of mine increase. The composer had smiled the whole time and when I had prompted him he had replied. But he hadn't volunteered much. Should I have been more reserved? Since outside might have meant two things and since I was determined that everything should be perfect on my first job, I decided to wait just inside the main gate, from where I could see the annex in the garden.

D was a small, thin man, but with a head that seemed larger than most. To make the bony cliff of his forehead look a little less forbidding he combed his pale, well-washed, and fluffy hair down over his brow. His mouth and jaw were small, and his teeth were horribly irregular. And yet, probably due to the color of his deeply recessed eyes, there was a static correctness about his face that went well with a tranquil smile. As for the overall impression, there was something canine about the man. He wore flannel trousers and a sweater with stripes like fleas. His shoulders were a little stooped, his arms outlandishly long.

When he came out of the back door of the annex, my employer was wearing a blue wool cardigan over his other sweater and a pair of white tennis shoes. He reminded me of a grade-school music teacher. In one hand he held a black scarf, and as if he were puzzling whether to wrap it around his neck, there was perplexity in his grin to me as I waited at the gate. For as long as I knew D, except at the very end when he was lying in a hospital bed, he was always dressed this way. I remember his outfit so well because I was always struck by something comical about an adult man wearing a cardigan around his shoulders, as if he were a woman in disguise. Its shapelessness and nondescript color made that sweater perfect for him. As the composer pigeon-toed toward me past the shrubbery, he absently lifted the hand that held the scarf and signaled me with it. Then he wrapped the scarf resolutely around his neck. It was already four in the afternoon and fairly cold out-of-doors.

D went through the gate, and as I was following him (our relationship was already that of employer and employee) I had the feeling I was being watched and turned around: behind the same window through which I had discovered my employer, that forty-year-old nurse with the scarred—or were they wrinkles?—cheeks was watching us the way a soldier remaining behind might see a deserter off, her lips clamped shut like a turtle's. I resolved to get her alone as soon as I could to question her about D's condition. What was wrong with the woman, anyway? Here she was taking care of a young man with a nervous condition, maybe a madman, yet when her charge went out she had nothing to say to his companion! Wasn't that professional negligence? Wasn't she at least obliged to fill in the new man on the job? Or was my employer a patient so gentle and harmless that nothing had to be said?

When he got to the sidewalk D shuttered open his tired-looking eyes in their deep sockets and glanced swiftly up and down the deserted, residential street. I didn't know whether it was an indication of madness or what—sudden action without any continuity seemed to be a habit of his. The composer looked up at the clear, end-of-autumn sky, blinking rapidly. Though they were sunken, there was something remarkably expressive about his deep brown eyes. Then he stopped blinking and his eyes seemed to focus, as though he were searching the sky. I stood obliquely behind him, watching, and what impressed me most vividly was the movement of his Adam's apple, which was large as any fist. I wondered if he had been destined to become a large man; perhaps something had impeded his growth in infancy and now only his head from the neck up bespoke the giant he was meant to be.

Lowering his gaze from the sky, my employer found and held my puzzled eyes with his own and said casually, but with a gravity that made objection impossible, "On a clear day you can see things floating up there very well. He's up there with them, and frequently he comes down to me when I go outdoors."

Instantly I felt threatened. Looking away from my employer, I wondered how to survive this first ordeal that had confronted me so quickly. Should I pretend to believe in "him," or would that be a mistake? Was I dealing with a raving madman, or was the composer just a poker-faced humorist trying to have some fun with me? As I stood there in distress, he extended me a helping hand: "I know you can't see the figures floating in the sky, and I know you wouldn't be aware of him even if he were right here at my side. All I ask is that you don't act amazed when he comes down to earth, even if I talk to him. Because you'd upset him if you were to break out laughing all of a sudden or tried to shut me up. And if you happen to notice when we're talking that I want some support from you, I'd appreciate it if you'd chime right in and say something, you know, affirmative. You see, I'm explaining Tokyo to him as if it were a paradise. It might seem a lunatic paradise to you, but maybe you could think of it as a satire and be affirmative anyway, at least when he's down here with me."

I listened carefully and thought I could make out at least the contours of what my employer expected of me. Then was he a rabbit as big as a man after all, nesting in the sky? But that wasn't what I asked; I permitted myself to ask only: "How will I know when he's down here with you?"

"Just by watching me; he only comes down when I'm outside."

"How about when you're in a car?"

"In a car or a train, as long as I'm next to an open window he's likely to show up. There have been times when he's appeared when I was in the house, just standing next to an open window."

"And . . . right now?" I asked uncomfortably. I must have sounded like the class dunce who simply cannot grasp the multiplication principle.

"Right now it's just you and me," my employer said graciously. "Why don't we ride in to Shinjuku today; I haven't been on a train in a long time."

We walked to the station, and all the way I kept an eye peeled for a sign that something had appeared at my employer's side. But before I knew it we were on the train and, so far as I could tell, nothing had materialized. One thing I did notice: the composer ignored the people who passed us on the street even when they greeted him. As if he himself did not exist, as if the people who approached with hellos and how-are-yous were registering an illusion which they mistook for him, my employer utterly ignored all overtures to contact.

The same thing happened at the ticket window; D declined to relate to other people. Handing me one thousand yen he told me to buy tickets, and then refused to take his own even when I held it out to him. I had to stop at the gate and have both our tickets punched while D swept through the turnstile onto the platform with the freedom of the invisible man. Even on the train, he behaved as if the other passengers were no more aware of him than of the atmosphere; huddling in a seat in the farthest corner of the car, he rode in silence with his eyes closed. I stood in front of him and watched in growing apprehension for whatever it was to float in through the open window and settle at his side. Naturally, I didn't believe in the monster's existence. It was just that I was determined not to miss the instant when D's delusions took hold of him; I felt I owed him that much in return for the money he was paying me. But, as it happened, he sat like some small animal playing dead all the way to Shinjuku Station, so I could only surmise that he hadn't had a visit from the sky. Of course, supposition was all it was: as long as other people were around us, my employer remained a sullen oyster of silence. But I learned soon enough that my guess had been correct. Because when the moment came it was more than apparent (from D's reaction, I mean) that something was visiting him.

We had left the station and were walking down the street. It was that time of day a little before evening when not many people are out, yet we ran across a small crowd gathered on a corner. We stopped to look; surrounded by the crowd, an old man was turning around and around in the street without a glance at anyone. A dignified-looking old man, he was spinning in a frenzy, clutching a briefcase and an umbrella to his breast, mussing his gray, pomaded hair a little as he stamped his feet and barked like a seal. The faces in the watching crowd were lusterless and dry in the evening chill that was stealing into the air; the old man's face alone was flushed, and sweating, and seemed about to steam.

Suddenly I noticed that D, who should have been standing at my side, had taken a few steps back and had thrown one arm around the shoulders of an invisible something roughly his own height. Now he was peering affectionately into the space slightly above the empty circle of his arm. The crowd was too intent on the old man to be concerned with D's performance, but I was terrified. Slowly the composer turned to me, as if he wanted to introduce me to a friend. I didn't know how to respond; all I could do was panic and blush. It was like forgetting your silly lines in the junior high school play. The composer continued to stare at me, and now there was annoyance in his eyes. He was seeking an explanation for that intent old man turning single-mindedly in the street for the benefit of his visitor from the sky. A paradisical explanation! But all I could do was wonder stupidly whether the old man might have been afflicted with Saint Vitus' dance.

When I sadly shook my head in silence, the light of inquiry went out of my employer's eyes. As if he were taking leave of a friend, he dropped his arm. Then he slowly shifted his gaze skyward until his head was all the way back and his large Adam's apple stood out in bold relief. The phantom had soared back into the sky and I was ashamed; I hadn't been equal to my job. As I stood there with my head hanging, the composer stepped up to me and indicated that my first day of work was at an end: "We can go home, now. He's come down today already, and you must be pretty tired." I did feel exhausted after all that tension.

We rode back in a taxi with the windows rolled up, and as soon as I'd been paid for the day, I left. But I didn't go straight to the station; I waited behind a telephone pole diagonally across from the house. Dusk deepened, the sky turned the color of a rose, and just as the promise of night was becoming fact, the nurse, in a short-skirted, one-piece dress of a color indistinct in the dimness, appeared through the main gate pushing a brand-new bicycle in front of her. Before she could get on the bicycle, I ran over to her. Without her nurse's uniform, she was just an ordinary little woman in her early forties; vanished from her face was the mystery I had discovered through the annex window. And my appearance had unsettled her. She couldn't climb on the bike and pedal away, but neither would she stand still; she had begun to walk the bike along when I demanded that she explain our mutual employer's condition. She resisted, peevishly, but I had a good grip on the bicycle seat and so in the end she gave in. When she began to talk, her formidable lower jaw snapped shut at each break in the sentence; she was absolutely a talking turtle.

"He says it's a fat baby in a white cotton nightgown. Big as a kangaroo, he says. It's supposed to be afraid of dogs and policemen and it comes down out of the sky. He says its name is Aghwee! Let me tell you something, if you happen to be around when that spook gets hold of him, you'd better just play dumb, you can't afford to get involved. Don't forget, you're dealing with a looney! And another thing, don't you take him anyplace funny, even if he wants to go. On top of everything else, a little gonorrhea is all we need around here!"

I blushed and let go of the bicycle seat. The nurse, jangling her bell, pedaled away into the darkness as fast as she could go with legs as round and thin as handlebars. Ah, a fat baby in a white cotton nightgown, big as a kangaroo!

When I showed up at the house the following week, the composer fixed me with those clear brown eyes of his and rattled me by saying, though not especially in reproof, "I hear you waited for the nurse and asked her about my visitor from the sky. You really take your work seriously."

That afternoon we took the same train in the opposite direction, into the country for half an hour to an amusement park on the banks of the Tama river. We tried all kinds of rides and, luckily for me, the baby as big as a kangaroo dropped out of the sky to visit D when he was up by himself in the Sky Sloop, wooden boxes shaped like boats that were hoisted slowly into the air on the blades of a kind of windmill. From a bench on the ground, I watched the composer talking with an imaginary passenger at his side. And until his visitor had climbed back into the sky, D refused to come down; again and again a signal from him sent me running to buy him another ticket.

Another incident that made an impression on me that day occurred as we were crossing the amusement park toward the exit, when D accidentally stepped in some wet cement. When he saw that his foot had left an imprint he became abnormally irritated, and until I had negotiated with the workmen, paid them something for their pains and had the footprint troweled away, he stubbornly refused to move from the spot. This was the only time the composer ever revealed to me the least violence in his nature. On the way home on the train, I suppose because he regretted having barked at me, he excused himself in this way: "I'm not living in present time anymore, at least not consciously. Do you know the rule that governs trips into the past in a time machine? For example, a man who travels back ten thousand years in time doesn't dare do anything in that world that might remain behind him. Because he doesn't exist in time ten thousand years ago, and if he left anything behind him there the result would be a warp, infinitely slight maybe but still a warp, in all of history from then until now, ten thousand years of it. That's the way the rule goes, and since I'm not living in present time, I mustn't do anything here in this world that might remain or leave an imprint."

"But why have you stopped living in present time?" I asked, and my employer sealed himself up like a golf ball and ignored me. I regretted my loose tongue; I had finally exceeded the limits permitted me, because I was too concerned with D's problem. Maybe the nurse was right; playing dumb was the only way, and I couldn't afford to get involved. I resolved not to.

We walked around Tokyo a number of times after that, and my new policy was a success. But the day came when the composer's problems began to involve me whether I liked it or not. One afternoon we got into a cab together and, for the first time since I had taken the job, D mentioned a specific destination, a swank apartment house designed like a hotel in Daikan Yama. When we arrived, D waited in the coffee shop in the basement while I went up the elevator alone to pick up a package that was waiting for me. I was to be given the package by D's former wife, who was living alone in the apartment now.

I knocked on a door that made me think of the cell blocks at Sing Sing (I was always going to the movies in those days; I have the feeling about ninety-five percent of what I knew came directly from the movies) and it was opened by a short woman with a pudgy red face on top of a neck that was just as pudgy and as round as a cylinder. She ordered me to take my shoes off and step inside, and pointed to a sofa near the window where I was to sit. This must be the way high society receives a stranger, I remember thinking at the time. For me, the son of a poor farmer, refusing her invitation and asking for the package at the door would have taken the courage to defy Japanese high society, the courage of that butcher who threatened Louis XIV. I did as I was told, and stepped for the first time in my life into a studio apartment in the American style.

The composer's former wife poured me some beer. She seemed somewhat older than D, and although she gestured grandly and intoned when she spoke, she was too round and overweight to achieve dignity. She was wearing a dress of some heavy cloth with the hem of the skirt unraveled in the manner of a squaw costume, and her necklace of diamonds set in gold looked like the work of an Inca craftsman (now that I think about it, these observations, too, smell distinctly of the movies). Her window overlooked the streets of Shibuya, but the light pouring through it into the room seemed to bother her terrifically; she was continually shifting in her chair, showing me legs as round and bloodshot as her neck, while she questioned me in the voice of a prosecutor. I suppose I was her only source of information about her former husband. Sipping my black, bitter beer as if it were hot coffee, I answered her as best I could, but my knowledge of D was scant and inaccurate and I couldn't satisfy her. Then she started asking about D's actress girl friend, whether she came to see him and things like that, and there was nothing I could say. Annoyed, I thought to myself, what business was it of hers, didn't she have any woman's pride?

"Does D still see that Phantom?"

"Yes, it's a baby the size of a kangaroo in a white cotton nightgown and he says its name is Aghwee, the nurse was telling me about it," I said enthusiastically, glad to encounter a question I could do justice to. "It's usually floating in the sky, but sometimes it flies down to D's side."

"Aghwee, you say. Then it must be the ghost of our dead baby. You know why he calls it Aghwee? Because our baby spoke only once while it was alive and that was what it said—Aghwee. That's a pretty mushy way to name the ghost that's haunting you, don't you think?" The woman spoke derisively; an ugly, corrosive odor reached me from her mouth. "Our baby was born with a lump on the back of its head that made it look as if it had two heads. The doctor diagnosed it as a brain hernia. When D heard the news he decided to protect himself and me from a catastrophe, so he got together with the doctor and they killed the baby—I think they only gave it sugar water instead of milk no matter how loud it screamed. My husband killed the baby because he didn't want us to be saddled with a child who could only function as a vegetable, which is what the doctor had predicted! So he was acting out of fantastic egotism more than anything else. But then there was an autopsy and the lump turned out to be a benign tumor. That's when D began seeing ghosts; you see he'd lost the courage he needed to sustain his egotism, so he declined to live his own life, just as he had declined to let the baby go on living. Not that he committed suicide, he just fled from reality into a world of phantoms. But once your hands are all bloody with a baby's murder, you can't get them clean again just by running from reality, anybody knows that. So here he is, hands as filthy as ever and carrying on about Aghwee."

The cruelness of her criticism was hard to bear, for my employer's sake. So I turned to her, redder in the face than ever with the excitement of her own loquacity, and struck a blow for D. "Where were you while all this was going on? You were the mother, weren't you?"

"I had a Caesarean, and for a week afterwards I was in a coma with a high fever. It was all over when I woke up," said D's former wife, leaving my gauntlet on the floor. Then she stood up and moved toward the kitchen. "I guess you'll have some more beer?"

"No, thank you, I've had enough. Would you please give me the package I'm supposed to take to D?"

"Of course, just let me gargle. I have to gargle every ten minutes, for pyorrhea—you must have noticed the smell?"

D's former wife put a brass key into a business envelope and handed it to me. Standing behind me while I tied my shoes, she asked what school I went to and then said proudly: "I hear there's not even one subscriber to the T———Times in the dormitories there. You may be interested to know that my father will own that paper soon."

I let silence speak for my contempt.

I was about to get into the elevator when doubt knifed through me as though my chest were made of butter. I had to think. I let the elevator go and decided to use the stairs. If his former wife had described D's state of mind correctly, how could I be sure he wouldn't commit suicide with a pinch of cyanide or something taken from a box this key unlocked? All the way down the stairs I wondered what to do, and then I was standing in front of D's table and still hadn't arrived at a conclusion. The composer sat there with his eyes tightly shut, his tea untouched on the table. I suppose it wouldn't do for him to be seen drinking materials from this time now that he had stopped living in it and had become a traveler from another.

"I saw her," I began, resolved all of a sudden to lie, "and we were talking all this time but she wouldn't give me anything."

My employer looked up at me placidly and said nothing, though doubt clouded his puppy eyes in their deep sockets. All the way back in the cab I sat in silence at his side, secretly perturbed. I wasn't sure whether he had seen through my lie. In my shirt pocket the key was heavy.

But I only kept it for a week. For one thing, the idea of D's suicide began to seem silly; for another, I was worried he might ask his wife about the key. So I put it in a different envelope and mailed it to him special delivery. The next day I went out to the house a little worried and found my employer in the open space in front of the annex, burning a pile of scores in manuscript. They must have been his own compositions: that key had unlocked the composer's music.

We didn't go out that day. Instead I helped D incinerate his whole opus. We had burned everything and had dug a hole and I was burying the ashes when suddenly D began to whisper. The phantom had dropped out of the sky. And until it left I continued working, slowly burying those ashes. That afternoon Aghwee (and there was no denying it was a mushy name) the monster from the sky remained at my employer's side for fully twenty minutes.

From that day on, since I either stepped to one side or dropped behind whenever the baby phantom appeared, the composer must have realized that I was complying with only the first of his original instructions, not to act amazed, while his request that I back him up with something affirmative was consistently ignored. Yet he seemed satisfied, and so my job was made easier. I couldn't believe D was the kind of person to create a disturbance in the street; in fact his father's warning began to seem ridiculous, our tours of Tokyo together continued so uneventfully. I had already purchased the Moscow edition of *L'Âme Enchanté* I wanted, but I no longer had any intention of giving up such a wonderful job. My employer and I went everywhere together. D wanted to visit all the concert halls where works of his had been performed and all the schools he had ever been to. We would make special trips to places he had once enjoyed himself—bars, movie theaters, indoor swimming pools—and then we would turn back without going inside. And the composer hid a passion for all of Tokyo's many forms of public transportation: I'm sure we rode the entire metropolitan subway system. Since the monster baby couldn't descend from the sky while we were underground, I could enjoy the subway in peace of mind. Naturally, I tensed whenever we encountered dogs or officers of the law, remembering what the nurse had told me, but those encounters never coincided with an appearance by Aghwee. I discovered that I was loving my job. Not loving my employer or his phantom baby the size of a kangaroo. Simply loving my job.

One day the composer approached me about making a trip for him. He would pay traveling expenses, and my daily wage would be doubled; since I would have to stay overnight in a hotel and wouldn't be back until the second day, I would actually be earning four times what I usually made. Not only that, the purpose of the trip was to meet D's former girlfriend the movie actress in D's place. I accepted eagerly, I was delighted. And so began that comic and pathetic journey.

D gave me the name of the hotel the actress had mentioned in a recent letter and the date she was expecting him to arrive. Then he had me learn a message to the girl: my employer was no longer living in present time; he was like a traveler who had arrived here in a time machine from a world ten thousand years in the future. Accordingly, he couldn't permit himself to create a new existence with his own signature on it through such acts as writing letters.

I memorized the message, and then it was late at night and I was sitting opposite a movie actress in the basement bar of a hotel in Kyoto, with a chance first to explain why D hadn't come himself, next to persuade his mistress of his conception of time, and finally to deliver his message. I concluded: "D would like you to be careful not to confuse his recent divorce with another divorce he once promised you he would get; and since he isn't living in present time anymore, he says it's only natural that he won't be seeing you again." I felt my face color; for the first time I had the sensation that I had a truly difficult job.

"Is that what D-boy says? And what do you say? How do you feel about all this that you'd run an errand all the way to Kyoto?"

"Frankly, I think D is being mushy."

"That's the way he is—I'd say he's being pretty mushy with you, too, asking this kind of favor!"

"I'm employed; I get paid by the day for what I do."

"What are you drinking there? Have some brandy."

I did. Until then I'd been drinking the same dark beer D's former wife had given me, with an egg in it to thin it down. By some queer carom of a psychological billiard, I'd been influenced by a memory from D's former wife's apartment while waiting to meet his mistress. The actress had been drinking brandy all along. It was the first imported brandy I'd ever had.

"And what's all this about D-boy seeing a ghost, a baby as big as a kangaroo? What did you call it, Raghbee?"

"Aghwee! The baby only spoke once before it died and that was what it said."

"And D thought it was telling him its name? Isn't that darling! If that baby had been normal, it was all decided that D was going to get a divorce and marry me. The day the baby was born we were in bed together in a hotel room and there was a phone call and then we knew something awful had happened. D jumped out of bed and went straight to the hospital. Not a word from him since—" The actress gulped her brandy down, filled her glass to the brim from the bottle of Hennessy on the table as if she were pouring fruit juice, and drained her glass again.

Our table was hidden from the bar by a display case full of cigarettes. Hanging on the wall above my shoulder was a large color poster with the actress's picture on it, a beer advertisement. The face in the poster glittered like gold, no less than the beer. The girl sitting opposite me was not quite so dazzling, there was even a depression in her forehead, just below the hairline, that looked deep enough to contain an adult thumb. But it was precisely the fault that made her more appealing than her picture.

She couldn't get the baby off her mind.

"Look, wouldn't it be terrifying to die without memories or experiences because you'd never done anything human while you were alive? That's how it would be if you died as an infant—wouldn't that be terrible"

"Not to the baby, I don't imagine," I said deferentially.

"But think about the world after death!" The actress's logic was full of leaps.

"The world after death?"

"If there is such a thing, the souls of the dead must live there with their memories for all eternity. But what about the soul of a baby who never knew anything and never had any experiences? I mean what memories can it have?"

At a loss, I drank my brandy in silence.

"I'm terribly afraid of death so I'm always thinking about it—you don't have to be disgusted with yourself because you don't have a quick answer for me. But you know what I think? The minute that baby died, I think D-boy decided not to create any new memories for himself, as if he had died, too, and that's why he stopped living, you know, positively, in present time. And I bet he calls that baby ghost down to earth all over Tokyo so he can create new memories for it!"

At the time I thought she must be right. This tipsy movie actress with a dent in her forehead big enough for a thumb is quite an original psychologist, I thought to myself. And much more D's type, I thought, than the pudgy, tomato-faced daughter of a newspaper baron. All of a sudden I realized that, even here in Kyoto with hundreds of miles between us, I, the model of a faithful employee, was thinking exclusively about D. No, there was something else, too, there was D's phantom. I realized that the baby whose appearance I waited for nervously every time my employer and I went out together hadn't been off my mind for a minute.

It was time for the bar to close and I didn't have a room. I'd managed to get as old as I was without ever staying in a hotel and I knew nothing about reservations. Luckily, the actress was known at the hotel, and a word from her got me a room. We went up in the elevator together, and I started to get off at my floor when she suggested we have one last drink and invited me to her room. It was from that point that memories of the evening get comic and pathetic. When she had seated me in a chair, the actress returned to the door and looked up and down the hall, then went through a whole series of nervous motions, flounced on the bed as if to test the springs, turned lights on and switched them off, ran a little water in the tub. Then she poured me the brandy she had promised and, sipping a Coca-Cola, she told me about another man who had courted her during her affair with D, and finally going to bed with him, and D slapping her so hard the teeth rattled in her mouth. Then she asked if I thought today's college students went in for "heavy petting"? It depended on the student, I said—suddenly the actress had become a mother scolding a child for staying up too late and was telling me to find my own room and go to sleep. I said good night, went downstairs, and fell asleep immediately. I woke up at dawn with a fire in my throat.

The most comic and pathetic part was still to come. I understood the minute I opened my eyes that the actress had invited me to her room intending to seduce a college student who was wild for heavy petting. And with that understanding came rage and abject desire. I hadn't slept with a woman yet, but this humiliation demanded that I retaliate. I was drunk on what must have been my first Hennessy VSOP, and I was out of my head with the kind of poisonous desire that goes with being eighteen. It was only five o'clock in the morning and there was no sign of life in the halls. Like a panther wild with rage I sped to her door on padded feet. It was ajar. I stepped inside and found her seated at the dresser mirror with her back to me. Creeping up directly behind her (to this day I wonder what I was trying to do), I lunged at her neck with both hands. The actress whirled around with a broad smile on her face, rising as she turned, and then she had my hands in her own and was pumping them happily up and down as if she were welcoming a guest and sing-songing, "Good morning! Good morning! Good morning!" Before I knew it I had been seated in a chair and we were sharing her toast and morning coffee and reading the newspaper together. After a while the movie actress said in a tone of voice she might have used to discuss the weather: "You were trying to rape me just now, weren't you!" She went back to her makeup and I got out of there, fled downstairs to my own room and burrowed back into bed, trembling as though I had malaria. I was afraid that a report of this incident might reach D, but the subject of the movie actress never came up again. I continued to enjoy my job.

Winter had come. Our plan that afternoon was to bicycle through D's residential neighborhood and the surrounding fields. I was on a rusty old bike and my employer had borrowed the nurse's shiny new one. Gradually we expanded the radius of a circle around D's house, riding into a new housing development and coasting down hills in the direction of the fields. We were sweating, relishing the sensation of liberation, more and more exhilarated. I say "we" and include D because that afternoon it was evident that he was in high spirits, too. He was even whistling a theme from a Bach sonata for flute and harpsichord called Siciliana. I happened to know that because when I was in high school I had played flute. I never learned to play well but I did develop a habit of thrusting out my upper lip the way a tapir does. Naturally, I had friends who insisted my buck teeth were to blame. But the fact is, flutists frequently look like tapirs.

As we pedaled down the street, I picked up the tune and began to whistle along with D. Siciliana is a sustained and elegant theme, but I was out of breath from pedaling and my whistle kept lapsing into airy sibilance. Yet D's phrasing was perfect, absolutely legato. I stopped whistling then, ashamed to go on, and the composer glanced over at me with his lips still pursed in a whistle like a carp puckering up to breathe and smiled his tranquil smile. Granted there was a difference in the bikes, it was still unnatural and pathetic that an eighteen-year-old student, skinny maybe, but tall, should begin to tire and run short of breath before a twenty-eight-year-old composer who was a little man and sick besides. Unjust is what it was, and infuriating. My mood clouded instantly and I felt disgusted with the whole job. So I stood up on the pedals all of a sudden and sped away as furiously as a bicycle racer. I even turned down a narrow gravel path between two vegetable fields purposely. When I looked back a minute later, my employer was hunched over the handle bars, his large, round head nodding above his narrow shoulders, churning the gravel beneath his wheels in hot pursuit of me. I coasted to a stop, propped a foot on the barbed wire fence that bordered the field and waited for D to catch up. I was already ashamed of my childishness.

His head still bobbing, my employer was approaching fast. And then I knew the phantom was with him. D was racing his bike down the extreme left of the gravel path, his face twisted to the right so that he was almost looking over his right shoulder, and the reason his head appeared to bob was that he was whispering encouragement to something running, or maybe flying, alongside the bicycle. Like a marathon coach pacing one of his runners. Ah, I thought, he's doing that on the premise that Aghwee is neck and neck with his speeding bike. The monster as large as a kangaroo, the fat, funny baby in a white cotton nightgown was bounding—like a kangaroo!—down that gravel path. I shuddered, then I kicked the barbed wire fence and slowly pedaled away, waiting for my employer and the monster in his imagination to catch up.

Don't think I had let myself begin to believe in Aghwee's existence. I had taken the nurse's advice, sworn not to lose sight of the anchor on my common sense as in those slightly solemn slapstick comedies where, for example, the keeper of the mad house goes mad; consciously derisive, I was thinking to myself that the neurotic composer was putting on a show with his bicycle just to follow up a lie he had told me once, and what a lot of trouble to go to? In other words, I was keeping a clinical distance between myself and D's phantom monster. Even so, there occurred a strange alteration in my state of mind.

It began this way: D had finally caught up and was biking along a few feet behind me when, as unexpectedly as a cloudburst, and as inescapably, we were enveloped by the belting of a pack of hounds. I looked up and saw them racing toward me down the gravel path, young adult Dobermans that stood two feet high, more than ten of them. Running breathlessly behind the pack, the thin black leather leashes grasped in one hand, was a man in overalls, chasing the dogs perhaps, or maybe they were dragging him along. Jet-black Dobermans, sleek as wet seals, with just a dusting of dry chocolate on their chests and jowls and pumping haunches. And down on us they howled, filling the gravel path, keening for the attack at such a forward tilt they looked about to topple on their foaming snouts. There was a meadow on the other side of the field; the man in overalls must have been training the beasts there and now he was on his way home with them.

Trembling with fear, I got off my bike and helplessly surveyed the field on the other side of the fence. The barbed wire came up to my chest. I might have had a chance myself but I would never have been able to boost the little composer to safety on the other side. The poisons of terror were beginning to numb my head, but for one lucid instant I could see the catastrophe that was bound to occur in a few seconds. As the Dobermans neared, D would sense that Aghwee was being attacked by a pack of the animals it most feared. He would probably hear the baby's frightened crying. And certainly he would meet the dogs head-on, in defense of his baby. Then the Dobermans would rip him to pieces. Or he would try to escape with the baby and make a reckless leap to clear the fence and be just as cruelly torn. I was rocked by the pity of what I knew must happen. And while I stood there dumbly without a plan, those giant black-and-chocolate devils were closing in on us, snapping in the air with awful jaws, so close by now that I could hear their alabaster claws clicking on the gravel. Suddenly I knew I could do nothing for D and his baby, and with that knowledge I went limp, unresisting as a pervert when he is seized in the subway, and was swallowed whole in the darkness of my fear. I backed off the gravel path until the barbed wire was a fire in my back, pulled my bike in front of me as if it were a wall, and shut my eyes tight. An animal stench battered me, together with the howling of the dogs and the pounding of their feet, and I could feel tears seeping past my eyelids. I abandoned myself to a wave of fear and it swept me away. . . .

On my shoulder was a hand gentle as the essence of all gentleness; it felt like Aghwee touching me. But I knew it was my employer; he had let those fiendish dogs pass and no catastrophe of fear had befallen him. I continued crying anyway, with my eyes closed and my shoulders heaving. I was too old to cry in front of other people, I suppose the shock of fright had induced some kind of infantile regression in me. When I stopped crying, we walked our bikes past that barbed wire fence like prisoners in a concentration camp, in silence, our heads hanging, to the meadow beyond the field where strangers were playing ball and exercising dogs (D wasn't occupied with Aghwee anymore, the baby must have left while I was crying). We laid our bikes down and then sprawled on the grass ourselves. My tears had flooded away my pretensions and my rebelliousness and the perverse suspicion in my heart. And D was no longer wary of me. I lay back on the grass and clasped my hands beneath my head, curiously light and dry after all that crying. Then I closed my eyes and listened quietly while D peered down at me with his chin in his hand and spoke to me of Aghwee's world.

"Do you know a poem called 'Shame' by Chuya Nakahara? Listen to the second verse:

The mournful sky
High where branches tangle
Teems with dead baby souls;

I blinked and saw
above the distant fields
fleece knit into a dream
of mastodons.

"That's one aspect of the world of the dead baby I see. There are some Blake engravings, too, especially one called 'Christ Refusing the Banquet Offered by Satan'—have you ever seen it? And there's another, 'The Morning Stars Singing Together.' In both there are figures in the sky who have the same reality about them as the people on the ground, and whenever I look at them I'm sure Blake was hinting at an aspect of this other world. I once saw a Dali painting that was close, too, full of opaque beings floating in the sky about a hundred yards above the ground and glowing with an ivory white light. Now that's exactly the world I see. And you know what those glowing things are that fill the sky? Beings we've lost from our lives down here on earth, and now they float up there in the sky about a hundred yards above the ground, quietly glowing like amoebas under a microscope. And sometimes they descend the way our Aghwee does (my employer said it and I didn't protest, which doesn't mean I acquiesced). But it takes a sacrifice worthy of them to acquire the eyes to see them floating there and the ears to detect them when they descend to earth, and yet there are moments when suddenly we're endowed with that ability without any sacrifice or even effort on our part. I think that's what happened to you a few minutes ago."

Without any sacrifice or even effort on my part, just a few tears of expiation, my employer seemed to have wanted to say. The truth was I had shed tears out of fear and helplessness and a kind of vague terror about my future (my first job, an experiment in a kind of microcosm of life, was guarding this mad composer, and since I had failed to do that adequately, it was predictable that situations I couldn't cope with would recur as one of the patterns of my life), but instead of interrupting with a protest, I continued to listen docilely.

"You're still young, probably you haven't lost sight of anything in this world that you can never forget, that's so dear to you you're aware of its absence all the time. Probably the sky a hundred yards or so above your head is still nothing more than sky to you. But all that means is that the storehouse happens to be empty at the moment. Or have you lost anything that was really important to you?"

The composer paused for my answer, and I found myself remembering his former mistress, that movie actress with a dent in her forehead as big as an adult thumb. Naturally, no crucial loss of mine could have had anything to do with her, all that crying had eroded my head and a sentimental honey was seeping into the crevices.

"Well, have you?" For the first time since we had met, my employer was insistent. "Have you lost anything that was important to you?"

Suddenly I had to say something silly to cover my embarrassment.

"I lost a cat," I tried.

"A Siamese or what?"

"Just an ordinary cat with orange stripes; he disappeared about a week ago."

"If it's only been a week he might come back. Isn't it the season for them to wander?"

"That's what I thought, too, but now I know he won't be back."

"Why?"

"He was a tough tom with his own territory staked out. This morning I saw a weak-looking cat walking up and down his block and it wasn't even on its guard—my cat won't be coming back." When I'd stopped talking I realized I'd told a story intended for laughs in a voice that was hoarse with sadness.

"Then there's a cat floating in your sky," my employer said solemnly.

Through closed eyes I pictured an opaque cat as large as an ad balloon, glowing with an ivory-white light as it floated through the sky. It was a comical flight all right, but it also made me wistful.

"The figures floating in your sky begin to increase at an accelerating rate. That's why I haven't been living in present time ever since that incident with the baby, so I could stop that spreading. Since I'm not living in our time, I can't discover anything new, but I don't lose sight of anything, either—the state of my sky never changes." There was profound relief in the composer's voice.

But was my own sky really empty except for one bloated cat with orange stripes? I opened my eyes and started to look up at the clear, now almost evening sky, when dread made me close my eyes again. Dread of myself, for what if I had seen a glowing herd of numberless beings I had lost from time down here on earth!

We lay on the grass in that meadow for quite a while, ringed by the passive affinity two people have for one another when the same gloom is gripping them. And gradually I began to get my perspective back. I reproached myself: how unlike the eighteen-year-old pragmatist I really was to have let myself be influenced by a mad composer! I'm not suggesting my equilibrium was perfectly restored. The day I succumbed to that strange panic, I drew closer than ever to the sentiments of my employer and to that glowing herd in the sky one hundred yards above the ground. To an extent, what you might call the aftereffects remained with me.

And then the final day came. It was Christmas Eve. I'm certain about the date because D gave me a wristwatch with a little apology about being a day early. And I remember that a powdery snow fell for about an hour just after lunch. We went down to the Ginza together but it was already getting crowded, so we decided to walk out to Tokyo harbor. D wanted to see a Chilean freighter that was supposed to have docked that day. I was eager to go, too; I pictured a ship with snow blanketing her decks. We had left the Ginza crowds and were just passing the Kabuki Theater when D looked up at the dark and still snowy sky. And Aghwee descended to his side. As usual, I walked a few steps behind the composer and his phantom. We came to a wide intersection. D and the baby had just stepped off the curb when the light changed. D stopped, and a fleet of trucks as bulky as elephants heaved into motion with their Christmas freight. That was when it happened. Suddenly D cried out and thrust both arms in front of him as if he were trying to rescue something; then he leaped in among those trucks and was struck to the ground. I watched stupidly from the curb.

"That was suicide; he just killed himself!" said a shaky voice at my side.

But I had no time to wonder whether it might have been suicide. In a minute that intersection had become backstage at a circus, jammed with milling trucks like elephants, and I was kneeling at D's side, holding his bloody body in my arms and trembling like a dog. I didn't know what to do, a policeman had dashed up and then disappeared on the run again.

D wasn't dead; it was more awful than that. He was dying, lying there in the filthy wet that had been a light snow, oozing blood and something like tree-sap. The dark and snowy pattern of the sky ripped open and the stately light of a Spanish pieta made my employer's blood glisten like silly fat. By that time a crowd had gathered, snatches of "Jingle Bells" wheeled above our heads like panic-stricken pigeons, and I knelt at D's side listening hard for nothing in particular and hearing screaming in the distance. But the crowd just stood there silently in the cold, as if indifferent to the screams. I have never listened so hard on a street corner again, nor again heard screams like that.

An ambulance finally arrived and my employer was lifted inside unconscious. He was caked with blood and mud, and shock seemed to have withered his body. In his white tennis shoes, he looked like an injured blind man. I climbed into the ambulance with a doctor and an orderly and a young man about my age who seemed haughty and aloof. He turned out to be the driver's helper on the long-distance truck that had hit D. The congestion was getting worse all the time as the ambulance cut across the Ginza (according to some statistics I saw recently, there were record crowds that Christmas Eve). Those who heard the siren and stopped to watch us pass, nearly all of them, shared a look of circumspectly solemn concern. In one corner of my dazed head I reflected that the so-called inscrutable Japanese smile, while it seemed likely to exist, did not. Meanwhile D lay unconscious on that wobbly stretcher, bleeding his life away.

When we arrived at the hospital, two orderlies who didn't even pause to change out of shoes into slippers rushed D away to some recess of the building. The same policeman as before appeared out of nowhere again and calmly asked me a lot of questions. Then I was permitted to go to D. The young worker from the truck had already found the room and was sitting on a bench in the corridor next to the door. I sat down next to him and we waited for a long time. At first he would only mutter about all the deliveries he still had to make, but when two hours had passed he began to complain that he was hungry in a surprisingly young voice, and my hostility toward him dwindled. We waited some more, then the banker arrived with his wife and three daughters, who were all dressed up to go to a party. Ignoring us, they went inside. All four of the women had fat, squat bodies and red faces; they reminded me of D's former wife. I continued to wait. It had been hours by then, and the whole time I had been tormented by suspicion—hadn't my employer intended to kill himself from the beginning? Before taking his life he had settled things with his ex-wife and former mistress, burned his manuscripts, toured the city saying goodbye to places he would miss—hadn't he hired me because he needed some good-natured help with those chores? Kept me from seeing his plan by inventing a monster baby floating in the sky? In other words, wasn't it the case that my only real function had been to help D commit suicide? The young laborer had fallen asleep with his head on my shoulder and every minute or two he would convulse as though in pain. He must have been dreaming about running over a man with a truck.

It was pitch black outside when the banker appeared in the door and called me. I eased my shoulder from under the worker's head and stood up. The banker paid me my salary for the day and then let me into the room. D lay on his back with rubber tubes in his nostrils as in a joke. His face gave me pause: it was black as smoked meat. But I couldn't help voicing the doubt that had me so afraid. I called out to my dying employer: "Did you hire me just so you could commit suicide? Was all that about Aghwee just a cover-up?" Then my throat was clogged with tears and I was surprised to hear myself shouting, "I was about to believe in Aghwee!"

At that moment, as my eyes filled with tears and things began to dim, I saw a smile appear on D's darkened, shriveled face. It might have been a mocking smile and it might have been a smile of friendly mischief. The banker led me out of the room. The young man from the truck was stretched out on the bench asleep. On my way out, I slipped the thousand yen I had earned into his jacket pocket. I read in the evening paper the next day that the composer was dead.

And then it was this spring and I was walking down the street when a group of frightened children suddenly started throwing stones. It was so sudden and unprovoked, I don't know what I had done to threaten them. Whatever it was, fear had turned those children into killers, and one of them hit me in the right eye with a rock as big as a fist. I went down on one knee, pressed my hand to my eye and felt a lump of broken flesh. With my good eye I watched my dripping blood draw in the dirt in the street as though magnetically. It was then that I sensed a being I knew and missed leave the ground behind me like a kangaroo and soar into the teary blue of a sky that retained its winter brittleness. Goodbye, Aghwee, I heard myself whispering in my heart. And then I knew that my hatred of those frightened children had melted away and that time had filled my sky during those ten years with figures that glowed with an ivory-white light, I suppose not all of them purely innocent. When I was wounded by those children and sacrificed my sight in one eye, so clearly a gratuitous sacrifice, I had been endowed, if for only an instant, with the power to perceive a creature that had descended from the heights of my sky.

[1977]
Translated by
John Nathan

Questions

1. What are the sources of D's guilt?
2. Is the narrator correct when he concludes that D has tolerated him because he needed a companion as he wraps up the matters of his life? Or is there another reason?
3. Why is Aghwee referred to as a "monster," when his duties appear to be more protective than harmful?
4. Why does the narrator finally believe in Aghwee?

Ben Okri
(b. 1959)
Nigeria

One of Africa's most prolific and celebrated writers, Ben Okri was awarded the prestigious Booker Prize in 1991 for The Famished Road, the story of an abiku (a spirit-child) named Azaro, fated to a cycle of deaths and rebirths. The powerful story describes Azaro's mother's almost pathological anguish that he will never be of this world, though the child himself describes his condition in much more benign terms. The Famished Road is the first volume of a trilogy, continuing with Songs of Enchantment (1993) and Infinite Riches (1998).

Okri was born in Minna, Nigeria, in 1959. His education included Urhobo College, in Warri, and later the University of Essex, in England. His first novel, Flowers and Shadows, written before he turned twenty, was published in 1980. That volume was quickly followed by another novel, The Landscapes Within (1981), and a collection of short stories, Incidents at the Shrine (1986). Okri's poetry includes An African Elegy (1992) and Mental Flight (1999), written for the millennium and read before Queen Elizabeth on that occasion.

Often referred to as a mystic—see Astonishing the Gods (1995)—Okri is equally well known for his anti-war writings. As a child he witnessed firsthand his nation's civil war (also referred to as the Biafran war). The following passage from his short story, "A Prayer from the Living," first published on the op-ed page of The New York Times in 1993, is a vivid response to the arrival of the American troops in Somalia:

> And the dead were all about me, smiling, serene. They didn't urge me on; they were just quietly and intensely joyful. They did not ask me to hurry to them, but left it to me. What could I choose? Human life—full of greed and bitterness, dim, low-oxygenated, judgmental and callous, gentle, too, and wonderful as well, but . . . human life had betrayed me. And besides, there was nothing left to save in me. Even my soul was dying of starvation.

IN THE SHADOW OF WAR

That afternoon three soldiers came to the village. They scattered the goats and chickens. They went to the palm-frond bar and ordered a calabash of palm-wine. They drank amidst the flies.

Omovo watched them from the window as he waited for his father to go out. They both listened to the radio. His father had bought the old Grundig cheaply from a family that had to escape the city when the war broke out. He had covered the radio with a white cloth and made it look like a household fetish. They listened to the news of bombings and air raids in the interior of the country. His father combed his hair, parted it carefully, and slapped some aftershave on his unshaven face. Then he struggled into the shabby coat that he had long outgrown.

Omovo stared out of the window, irritated with his father. At that hour, for the past seven days, a strange woman with a black veil over her head had been going past the house. She went up the village paths, crossed the Express road, and disappeared into the forest. Omovo waited for her to appear.

The main news was over. The radio announcer said an eclipse of the moon was expected that night. Omovo's father wiped the sweat off his face with his palm and said, with some bitterness:

"As if an eclipse will stop this war."

"What is an eclipse?" Omovo asked.

"That's when the world goes dark and strange things happen."

"Like what?"

His father lit a cigarette.

"The dead start to walk about and sing. So don't stay out late, eh."

Omovo nodded.

"Heclipses hate children. They eat them."

Omovo didn't believe him. His father smiled, gave Omovo his ten kobo allowance, and said:

"Turn off the radio. It's bad for a child to listen to news of war."

Omovo turned it off. His father poured a libation at the doorway and then prayed to his ancestors. When he had finished he picked up his briefcase and strutted out briskly. Omovo watched him as he threaded his way up the path to the bus-stop at the main road. When a danfo bus came, and his father went with it, Omovo turned the radio back on. He sat on the window-sill and waited for the woman. The last time he saw her she had glided past with agitated flutters of her yellow smock. The children stopped what they were doing and stared at her. They had said that she had no shadow. They had said that her feet never touched the ground. As she went past, the children began to throw things at her. She didn't flinch, didn't quicken her pace, and didn't look back.

The heat was stupefying. Noises dimmed and lost their edges. The villagers stumbled about their various tasks as if they were sleep-walking. The three soldiers drank palm-wine and played draughts beneath the sun's oppressive glare. Omovo noticed that whenever children went past the bar the soldiers called them, talked to them, and gave them some money. Omovo ran down the stairs and slowly walked past the bar. The soldiers stared at him. On his way back one of them called him.

"What's your name" he asked.

Omovo hesitated, smiled mischievously, and said:

"Heclipse."

The soldier laughed, spraying Omovo's face with spit. He had a face crowded with veins. His companions seemed uninterested. They swiped flies and concentrated on their game. Their guns were on the table. Omovo noticed that they had numbers on them. The man said:

"Did your father give you that name because you have big lips?"

His companions looked at Omovo and laughed. Omovo nodded.

"You are a good boy," the man said. He paused. Then he asked, in a different voice:

"Have you seen that woman who covers her face with a black cloth?"

"No."

The man gave Omovo ten kobo and said:

"She is a spy. She helps our enemies. If you see her come and tell us at once, you hear?"

Omovo refused the money and went back upstairs. He re-positioned himself on the window-sill. The soldiers occasionally looked at him. The heat got to him and soon he fell asleep in a sitting position. The cocks, crowing dispiritedly, woke him up. He could feel the afternoon softening into evening. The soldiers dozed in the bar. The hourly news came on. Omovo listened without comprehension to the day's casualties. The announcer succumbed to the stupor, yawned, apologized, and gave further details of the fighting.

Omovo looked up and saw that the woman had already gone past. The men had left the bar. He saw them weaving between the eaves of the thatch houses, stumbling through the heat-mists. The woman was further up the path. Omovo ran downstairs and followed the men. One of them had taken off his uniform top. The soldier behind had buttocks so big they had begun to split his pants. Omovo followed them across the Express road. When they got into the forest the men stopped following the woman, and took a different route. They seemed to know what they were doing. Omovo hurried to keep the woman in view.

He followed her through the dense vegetation. She wore faded wrappers and a grey shawl, with the black veil covering her face. She had a red basket on her head. He completely forgot to determine if she had a shadow, or whether her feet touched the ground.

He passed unfinished estates, with their flaking ostentatious signboards and their collapsing fences. He passed an empty cement factory: blocks lay crumbled in heaps and the workers' sheds were deserted. He passed a baobab tree, under which was the intact skeleton of a large animal. A snake dropped from a branch and slithered through the undergrowth. In the distance, over the cliff edge, he heard loud music and people singing war slogans above the noise.

He followed the woman till they came to a rough camp on the plain below. Shadowy figures moved about in the half-light of the cave. The woman went to them. The figures surrounded her and touched her and led her into the cave. He heard their weary voices thanking her. When the woman reappeared she was without the basket. Children with kwashiorkor stomachs and women wearing rags led her half-way up the hill. Then, reluctantly, touching her as if they might not see her again, they went back.

He followed her till they came to a muddied river. She moved as if an invisible force were trying to blow her away. Omovo saw capsized canoes and trailing water-logged clothes on the dark water. He saw floating items of sacrifice: loaves of bread in Polythene wrappings, gourds of food, Coca-Cola cans. When he looked at the canoes again they had changed into the shapes of swollen dead animals. He saw outdated currencies on the riverbank. He noticed the terrible smell in the air. Then he heard the sound of heavy breathing from behind him, then someone coughing and spitting. He recognized the voice of one of the soldiers urging the others to move faster. Omovo crouched in the shadow of a tree. The soldiers strode past. Not long afterwards he heard a scream. The men had caught up with the woman. They crowded round her.

"Where are the others?" shouted one of them.

The woman was silent.

"You dis witch! You want to die, eh? Where are they?"

She stayed silent. Her head was bowed. One of the soldiers coughed and spat towards the river.

"Talk! Talk!" he said, slapping her.

The fat soldier tore off her veil and threw it to the ground. She bent down to pick it up and stopped in the attitude of kneeling, her head still bowed. Her head was bald, and disfigured with a deep corrugation. There was a livid gash along the side of her face. The bare-chested soldier pushed her. She fell on her face and lay still. The lights changed over the forest and for the first time Omovo saw that the dead animals on the river were in fact the corpses of grown men. Their bodies were tangled with river-weed and their eyes were bloated. Before he could react, he heard another scream. The woman was getting up, with the veil in her hand. She turned to the fat soldier, drew herself to her fullest height, and spat in his face. Waving the veil in the air, she began to howl dementedly. The two other soldiers backed away. The fat soldier wiped his face and lifted the gun to the level of her stomach. A moment before Omovo heard the shot a violent beating of wings just above him scared him from his hiding place. He ran through the forest screaming. The soldiers tramped after him. He ran through a mist which seemed to have risen from the rocks. As he ran he saw an owl staring at him from a canopy of leaves. He tripped over the roots of a tree and blacked out when his head hit the ground.

When he woke up it was very dark. He waved his fingers in front of his face and saw nothing. Mistaking the darkness for blindness he screamed, thrashed around, and ran into a door. When he recovered from his shock he heard voices outside and the radio crackling on about the war. He found his way to the balcony, full of wonder that his sight had returned. But when he got there he was surprised to find his father sitting on the sunken cane chair, drinking palm-wine with the three soldiers. Omovo rushed to his father and pointed frantically at the three men.

"You must thank them," his father said. "They brought you back from the forest."

Omovo, overcome with delirium, began to tell his father what he had seen. But his father, smiling apologetically at the soldiers, picked up his son and carried him off to bed.

[1988]

Questions

1. What does the mysterious woman represent? Why does she have no shadow? What is the shadow of war?

2. Okri uses an epigraph from Christopher Okigbo at the beginning of *Stars of the New Curfew* (1988), his collection of short stories that begins with "In the Shadow of War":

   We carry in our worlds that flourish
   Our worlds that have failed.

   How does the quotation illuminate Okri's story?

3. In what way do the stories in this volume by Amos Tutuola and Chinua Achebe further illuminate Okri's story?

Tillie Olsen

(b. 1913)
United States

The daughter of politically active Russian-Jewish immigrants, Tillie Lerner Olsen was born in Omaha, Nebraska. As a result of her family's limited means and the economic hardships of the depression years, she entered the work force at an early age, holding a series of manual and clerical jobs; she never attended college. Influenced by her father's socialist politics, she was active in leftist and unionist causes and was arrested twice for actions associated with her activism. In 1936 she married Jack Olsen, a longshoreman and union activist. Although she began to write before she married, the demands of being a working mother—eventually, of four daughters—compelled Olsen to set her creative work aside for many years. Beginning her first novel, Yonnondio: From the Thirties, in 1932, she did not complete and publish it until 1974, following her enrollment in a creative writing course at San Francisco State University and fellowship support from Stanford University. The novel, set during the depression, is regarded by many critics as one of the most important works about the 1930s.

In Silences (1978), a collection of essays and speeches, Olsen ponders the fact of the relatively small number of women writers and, extrapolating from her own experience, concludes that the demands of mothering while earning a living have "silenced" innumerable women, impeding them from actualizing their creative potential. As she phrases it, "The power and the need to create, over and beyond reproduction, is native in both women and men. Where the gifted among women (and men) have remained mute, or have never attained full capacity, it is because of circumstances, inner or outer, which oppose the needs of creation." Of Olsen's small but important body of fiction, Margaret Atwood remarked in The New York Times Book Review, "few writers have gained such wide respect on such a small body of published work. . . . Among women writers in the United States, 'respect' is too pale a word: 'reverence' is more like it. This is presumably because women writers, even more than their male counterparts, recognize what a heroic feat it is to have held down a job, raised four children, and still somehow managed to become and to remain a writer."

Both a feminist and an activist for working-class women, Olsen often focuses, in both her fiction and non-fictional writings, on the cumulative effects of adversity: poverty, illness, loneliness, and thwarted ambition. Other themes include the humanity and heroism of working-class people and the centrality of the mother-daughter relationship. Her most critically acclaimed story, the novella-length "Tell Me a Riddle," received the O. Henry Award as the best American story of 1961 and was later published with three other stories—including "I Stand Here Ironing"—under the novella's title. In each of her stories, Olsen's mastery of narrative realism, imagistic language, authentic dialogue, and closely observed psychological nuances combine to produce unanticipated and lingering emotional effects.

I STAND HERE IRONING

I stand here ironing, and what you asked me moves tormented back and forth with the iron.

"I wish you would manage the time to come in and talk with me about your daughter. I'm sure you can help me understand her. She's a youngster who needs help and whom I'm deeply interested in helping."

"Who needs help." . . . Even if I came, what good would it do? You think because I am her mother I have a key, or that in some way you could use me as a key? She has lived for nineteen years. There is all that life that has happened outside of me, beyond me.

And when is there time to remember, to sift, to weigh, to estimate, to total? I will start and there will be an interruption and I will have to gather it all together again. Or I will become engulfed with all I did or did not do, with what should have been and what cannot be helped.

She was a beautiful baby. The first and only one of our five that was beautiful at birth. You do not guess how new and uneasy her tenancy in her now-loveliness. You did not know her all those years she was thought homely, or see her poring over her baby pictures, making me tell her over and over how beautiful she had been—and would be, I would tell her—and was now, to the seeing eye. But the seeing eyes were few or nonexistent. Including mine.

I nursed her. They feel that's important nowadays. I nursed all the children, but with her, with all the fierce rigidity of first motherhood, I did like the books then said. Though her cries battered me to trembling and my breasts ached with swollenness, I waited till the clock decreed.

Why do I put that first? I do not even know if it matters, or if it explains anything.

She was a beautiful baby. She blew shining bubbles of sound. She loved motion, loved light, loved color and music and textures. She would lie on the floor in her blue overalls patting the surface so hard in ecstasy her hands and feet would blur. She was a miracle to me, but when she was eight months old I had to leave her daytimes with the woman downstairs to whom she was no miracle at all, for I worked or looked for work and for Emily's father, who "could no longer endure" (he wrote in his good-bye note) "sharing want with us."

I was nineteen. It was the pre-relief, pre-WPA world of the depression. I would start running as soon as I got off the streetcar, running up the stairs, the place smelling sour, and awake or asleep to startle awake, when she saw me she would break into a clogged weeping that could not be comforted, a weeping I can hear yet.

After a while I found a job hashing at night so I could be with her days, and it was better. But it came to where I had to bring her to his family and leave her.

It took a long time to raise the money for her fare back. Then she got chicken pox and I had to wait longer. When she finally came, I hardly knew her, walking quick and nervous like her father, looking like her father, thin, and dressed in a shoddy red that yellowed her skin and glared at the pockmarks. All the baby loveliness gone.

She was two. Old enough for nursery school they said, and I did not know then what I know now—the fatigue of the long day, and the lacerations of group life in the kinds of nurseries that are only parking places for children.

Except that it would have made no difference if I had known. It was the only place there was. It was the only way we could be together, the only way I could hold a job.

And even without knowing, I knew. I knew the teacher that was evil because all these years it has curdled into my memory, the little boy hunched in the corner, her rasp, "why aren't you outside, because Alvin hits you? that's no reason, go out, scaredy." I knew Emily hated it even if she did not clutch and implore "don't go Mommy" like the other children, mornings.

She always had a reason why we should stay home. Momma, you look sick. Momma, I feel sick. Momma, the teachers aren't there today, they're sick. Momma, we can't go, there was a fire there last night. Momma, it's a holiday today, no school, they told me.

But never a direct protest, never rebellion. I think of our others in their three-, four-year-oldness—the explosions, the tempers, the denunciations, the demands—and I feel suddenly ill. I put the iron down. What in me demanded that goodness in her? And what was the cost, the cost to her of such goodness?

The old man living in the back once said in his gentle way: "You should smile at Emily more when you look at her." What *was* in my face when I looked at her? I loved her. There were all the acts of love.

It was only with the others I remembered what he said, and it was the face of joy, and not of care or tightness or worry I turned to them—too late for Emily. She does not smile easily, let alone almost always as her brothers and sisters do. Her face is closed and sombre, but when she wants, how fluid. You must have seen it in her pantomimes, you spoke of her rare gift for comedy on the stage that rouses a laughter out of the audience so dear they applaud and applaud and do not want to let her go.

Where does it come from, that comedy? There was none of it in her when she came back to me that second time, after I had had to send her away again. She had a new daddy now to learn to love, and I think perhaps it was a better time.

Except when we left her alone nights, telling ourselves she was old enough.

"Can't you go some other time, Mommy, like tomorrow?" she would ask. "Will it be just a little while you'll be gone? Do you promise?"

The time we came back, the front door open, the clock on the floor in the hall. She rigid awake. "It wasn't just a little while. I didn't cry. Three times I called you, just three times, and then I ran downstairs to open the door so you could come faster. The clock talked loud. I threw it away, it scared me what it talked."

She said the clock talked loud again that night I went to the hospital to have Susan. She was delirious with the fever that comes before red measles, but she was fully conscious all the week I was gone and the week after we were home when she could not come near the new baby or me.

She did not get well. She stayed skeleton thin, not wanting to eat, and night after night she had nightmares. She would call for me, and I would rouse from exhaustion to sleepily call back: "You're all right, darling, go to sleep, it's just a dream," and if she still called, in a sterner voice, "Now go to sleep, Emily, there's nothing to hurt you." Twice, only twice, when I had to get up for Susan anyhow, I went in to sit with her.

Now when it is too late (as if she would let me hold and comfort her like I do the others) I get up and go to her at once at her moan or restless stirring. "Are you awake, Emily? Can I get you something?" And the answer is always the same: "No, I'm all right, go back to sleep, Mother."

They persuaded me at the clinic to send her away to a convalescent home in the country where "she can have the kind of food and care you can't manage for her, and you'll be free to concentrate on the new baby." They still send children to that place. I see pictures on the society page of sleek young women planning affairs to raise money for it, or dancing at the affairs, or decorating Easter eggs or filling Christmas stockings for the children.

They never have a picture of the children so I do not know if the girls still wear those gigantic red bows and the ravaged looks on the every other Sunday when parents can come to visit "unless otherwise notified"—as we were notified the first six weeks.

Oh it is a handsome place, green lawns and tall trees and fluted flower beds. High up on the balconies of each cottage the children stand, the girls in their red bows and white dresses, the boys in white suits and giant red ties. The parents stand below shrieking up to be heard and the children shriek down to be heard, and between them the invisible wall "Not To Be Contaminated by Parental Germs or Physical Affection."

There was a tiny girl who always stood hand in hand with Emily. Her parents never came. One visit she was gone. "They moved her to Rose Cottage" Emily shouted in explanation. "They don't like you to love anybody here."

She wrote once a week, the labored writing of a seven-year-old. "I am fine. How is the baby. If I write my letter nicely I will have a star. Love." There never was a star. We wrote every other day, letters she could never hold or keep but only hear read—once. "We simply do not have room for children to keep any personal possessions," they patiently explained when we pieced one Sunday's shrieking together to plead how much it would mean to Emily, who loved so to keep things, to be allowed to keep her letters and cards.

Each visit she looked frailer. "She isn't eating," they told us.

(They had runny eggs for breakfast or mush with lumps, Emily said later, I'd hold it in my mouth and not swallow. Nothing ever tasted good, just when they had chicken.)

It took us eight months to get her released home, and only the fact that she gained back so little of her seven lost pounds convinced the social worker.

I used to try to hold and love her after she came back, but her body would stay stiff, and after a while she'd push away. She ate little. Food sickened her, and I think much of life too. Oh she had physical lightness and brightness, twinkling by on skates, bouncing like a ball up and down up and down over the jump rope, skimming over the hill; but these were momentary.

She fretted about her appearance, thin and dark and foreign-looking at a time when every little girl was supposed to look or thought she should look a chubby blond replica of Shirley Temple. The doorbell sometimes rang for her, but no one seemed to come and play in the house or be a best friend. Maybe because we moved so much.

There was a boy she loved painfully through two school semesters. Months later she told me how she had taken pennies from my purse to buy him candy. "Licorice was his favorite and I brought him some every day, but he still liked Jennifer better'n me. Why, Mommy?" The kind of question for which there is no answer.

School was a worry to her. She was not glib or quick in a world where glibness and quickness were easily confused with ability to learn. To her overworked and exasperated teachers she was an overconscientious "slow learner" who kept trying to catch up and was absent entirely too often.

I let her be absent, though sometimes the illness was imaginary. How different from my now-strictness about attendance with the others. I wasn't working. We had a new baby, I was home anyhow. Sometimes, after Susan grew old enough, I would keep her home from school, too, to have them all together.

Mostly Emily had asthma, and her breathing, harsh and labored, would fill the house with a curiously tranquil sound. I would bring the two old dresser mirrors and her boxes of collections to her bed. She would select beads and single earrings, bottle tops and shells, dried flowers and pebbles, old postcards and scraps, all sorts of oddments; then she and Susan would play Kingdom, setting up landscapes and furniture, peopling them with action.

Those were the only times of peaceful companionship between her and Susan. I have edged away from it, that poisonous feeling between them, that terrible balancing of hurts and needs I had to do between the two, and did so badly, those earlier years.

Oh there are conflicts between the others too, each one human, needing, demanding, hurting, taking—but only between Emily and Susan, no, Emily toward Susan that corroding resentment. It seems so obvious on the surface, yet it is not obvious. Susan, the second child, Susan, golden- and curly-haired and chubby, quick and articulate and assured, everything in appearance and manner Emily was not; Susan, not able to resist Emily's precious things, losing or sometimes clumsily breaking them; Susan telling jokes and riddles to company for applause while Emily sat silent (to say to me later: that was my riddle, Mother, I told it to Susan); Susan, who for all the five years' difference in age was just a year behind Emily in developing physically.

I am glad for that slow physical development that widened the difference between her and her contemporaries, though she suffered over it. She was too vulnerable for that terrible world of youthful competition, of preening and parading, of constant measuring of yourself against every other, of envy, "If I had that copper hair," "If I had that skin. . . ." She tormented herself enough about not looking like the others, there was enough of the unsureness, the having to be conscious of words before you speak, the constant caring—what are they thinking of me? without having it all magnified by the merciless physical drives.

Ronnie is calling. He is wet and I change him. It is rare there is such a cry now. That time of motherhood is almost behind me when the ear is not one's own but must always be racked and listening for the child cry, the child call. We sit for a while and I hold him, looking out over the city spread in charcoal with its soft aisles of light. "Shoogily," he breathes and curls closer. I carry him back to bed, asleep. Shoogily. A funny word, a family word, inherited from Emily, invented by her to say: comfort.

In this and other ways she leaves her seal, I say aloud. And startle at my saying it. What do I mean? What did I start to gather together, to try and make coherent? I was at the terrible, growing years. War years. I do not remember them well. I was working, there were four smaller ones now, there was not time for her. She had to help be a mother, and housekeeper, and shopper. She had to set her seal. Mornings of crisis and near hysteria trying to get lunches packed, hair combed, coats and shoes found, everyone to school or Child Care on time, the baby ready for transportation. And always the paper scribbled on by a smaller one, the book looked at by Susan then mislaid, the homework not done. Running out to that huge school where she was one, she was lost, she was a drop; suffering over her unpreparedness, stammering and unsure in her classes.

There was so little time left at night after the kids were bedded down. She would struggle over books, always eating (it was in those years she developed her enormous appetite that is legendary in our family) and I would be ironing, or preparing food for the next day, or writing V-mail to Bill, or tending the baby. Sometimes, to make me laugh, or out of her despair, she would imitate happenings or types at school.

I think I said once: "Why don't you do something like this in the school amateur show?" One morning she phoned me at work, hardly understandable through the weeping: "Mother, I did it. I won, I won; they gave me first prize; they clapped and clapped and wouldn't let me go."

Now suddenly she was Somebody, and as imprisoned in her difference as she had been in her anonymity.

She began to be asked to perform at other high schools, even in colleges, then at city and statewide affairs. The first one we went to, I only recognized her that first moment when thin, shy, she almost drowned herself into the curtains. Then: Was this Emily? The control, the command, the convulsing and deadly clowning, the spell, then the roaring, stamping audience, unwilling to let this rare and precious laughter out of their lives.

Afterwards: You ought to do something about her with a gift like that—but without money or knowing how, what does one do? We have left it all to her, and the gift has as often eddied inside, clogged and clotted, as been used and growing.

She is coming. She runs up the stairs two at a time with her light graceful step, and I know she is happy tonight. Whatever it was that occasioned your call did not happen today.

"Aren't you ever going to finish the ironing, Mother? Whistler painted his mother in a rocker. I'd have to paint mine standing over an ironing board." This is one of her communicative nights and she tells me everything and nothing as she fixes herself a plate of food out of the icebox.

She is so lovely. Why did you want me to come in at all? Why were you concerned? She will find her way.

She starts up the stairs to bed. "Don't get *me* up with the rest in the morning." "But I thought you were having midterms." "Oh, those," she comes back in, kisses me, and says quite lightly, "in a couple of years when we'll all be atom-dead they won't matter a bit."

She has said it before. She *believes* it. But because I have been dredging the past, and all that compounds a human being is so heavy and meaningful in me, I cannot endure it tonight.

I will never total it all. I will never come in to say: She was a child seldom smiled at. Her father left me before she was a year old. I had to work her first six years when there was work, or I sent her home and to his relatives. There were years she had care she hated. She was dark and thin and foreign-looking in a world where the prestige went to blandness and curly hair and dimples; she was slow where glibness was prized. She was a child of anxious, not proud, love. We were poor and could not afford for her the soil of easy growth. I was a young mother, I was a distracted mother. There were the other children pushing up, demanding. Her younger sister seemed all that she was not. There were years she did not let me touch her. She kept too much in herself, her life was such she had to keep too much in herself. My wisdom came too late. She has much to her and probably little will come of it. She is a child of her age, of depression, of war, of fear.

Let her be. So all that is in her will not bloom—but in how many does it? There is still enough left to live by. Only help her to know—help make it so there is cause for her to know—that she is more than this dress on the ironing board, helpless before the iron.

[1953]

Questions

1. Whose story is it—the daughter's or the mother's?
2. What happens in the story? Is anything resolved by the end?
3. How do the tone and the manner in which the story is told contribute to its emotional effect?
4. How does the final paragraph contribute to the story's meaning?
5. Compare "I Stand Here Ironing" with Elizabeth Jolley's story, "Another Holiday for the Prince."

Sembene Ousmane

(b. 1923)

Senegal

*I*n contemporary Africa, Sembene Ousmane is more widely known as a filmmaker than as a writer. His film version of the story reprinted here launched him on a successful new career midway through an already significant one as a writer of fiction. (The film won a prize at the Cannes Film Festival in 1967.) Ousmane's decision to turn to the cinema was based in large part on his realization that in Africa in the 1960s his audience would be greatly extended. By using film as a medium of communication, he would no longer be dependent on the literacy rates of his people across the continent. Since the film version of "Black Girl," Ousmane has made nearly a dozen additional films, widely shown in Africa as well as outside of the continent. At times his work has provoked the hostility of officials within his native Senegal because of its strong political context. Yet Ousmane has continued to pursue his dual careers, in spite of attempts to censor his work.

In an interview he gave to The New York Times in 1969, Ousmane made the following statement:

> The thing I was trying to do in it [his film Mandabi] was show Africans some of the deplorable conditions under which they themselves live. When one creates, one doesn't think of the world; one thinks of his own country. It is, after all, the Africans who will ultimately bring about change in Africa—not the Americans, or the French or the Russians or the Chinese.

These comments appear to be equally valid for "Black Girl," although the story is set in the colonial era.

BLACK GIRL

It was the morning of the 23rd of June in the year of our Lord nineteen hundred fifty-eight. At Antibes, along the Riviera, neither the fate of the French Republic, nor the future of Algeria nor the state of the colonial territories preoccupied those who swarmed across the beaches below La Croisette.

Above, on the road leading to the Hermitage, two old-style Citroëns, one behind the other, were moving up the mountain. They stopped and several men quickly got out, rushing down the gravel walk towards a house on which a worn sign spelled out "Villa of Green Happiness." The men were the police chief of the town of Grasse, a medical officer, and two police inspectors from Antibes, flanked by officers in uniform.

There was nothing green about the Villa of Green Happiness except its name. The garden was kept in the French manner, the walks covered with gravel, set off by a couple of palm trees with drooping fronds. The Chief looked closely at the house, his eyes stopping at the third window, the broken glass, the ladder.

Inside were other inspectors and a photographer. Three people who seemed to be reporters were looking with rather absent-minded interest at the African statues, masks, animal skins, and ostrich eggs set here and there on the walls. Entering the living-room was like violating the privacy of a hunter's lair.

Two women were hunched together, sobbing. They looked very much alike, the same straight forehead, the same curved nose, the same dark circles about eyes reddened from crying. The one in the pale dress was speaking: "After my nap, I felt like taking a bath. The door was locked from the inside"—blowing her nose—"and I thought to myself, it's the maid taking her bath. I say 'the maid,'" she corrected, "but we never called her anything else but her name, Diouana. I waited for more than an hour, but didn't see her come out. I went back and called, knocking on the door. There was no answer. Then I phoned our neighbour, the Commodore. . . ."

She stopped, wiped her nose, and began to cry again. Her sister, the younger of the two, hair cut in a boyish style, sat hanging her head.

"You're the one who discovered the body?"

"Yes . . . that is, when Madame Pouchet called and told me that the black girl had locked herself in the bathroom, I thought it was a joke. I spent thirty-five years at sea, you know. I've roamed the seven seas. I'm retired from the Navy."

"Yes, yes, we know."

"Yes, well, when Madame Pouchet called I brought my ladder."

"You brought the ladder?"

"No. It was Mademoiselle Dubois, Madame's sister, who suggested the idea. And when I got to the window, I saw the black girl swimming in blood."

"Where is the key to the door?"

"Here it is, your Honour," said the inspector.

"Just wanted to see it."

"I've checked the window," said the other inspector.

"I'm the one who opened it, after breaking the pane," said the retired navy man.

"Which pane did you break?"

"Which pane?" he repeated. He was wearing white linen trousers and a blue jacket.

"Yes, I saw it, but I'd like to ask precisely."

"The second from the top," answered the sister.

At this, two stretcher-bearers came down, carrying a body wrapped in a blanket. Blood dripped on the steps. The magistrate lifted a corner of the blanket and frowned. A black girl lay dead on the stretcher, her throat cut from one ear to the other.

"It was with this knife. A kitchen knife," said another man, from the top of the stairs.

"Did you bring her from Africa or did you hire her here?"

"We brought her back from Africa, in April. She came by boat. My husband is with aerial navigation in Dakar, but the company only pays air passage for the family. She worked for us in Dakar. For two and a half or three years."

"How old is she?"

"I don't know exactly."

"According to her passport, she was born in 1927."

"Oh! The natives don't know when they are born," offered the naval officer, plunging his hands in his pockets.

"I don't know why she killed herself. She was well treated here, she ate the same food, shared the same rooms as my children."

"And your husband, where is he?"

"He left for Paris the day before yesterday."

"Ah!" said the inspector, still looking at the knickknacks. "Why do you think it was suicide?"

"Why?" said the retired officer . . . "Oh! Who do you think would make an attempt on the life of a Negro girl? She never went out. She didn't know anyone, except for Madame's children."

The reporters were getting impatient. The suicide of a maid—even if she were black—didn't amount to a hill of beans. There was nothing newsworthy in it.

"It must have been homesickness. Because lately, she'd been behaving very strangely. She wasn't the same."

The police magistrate went upstairs, accompanied by one of the inspectors. They examined the bathroom, the window.

"Some boomerang, this story," said the inspector.

The others waited in the living-room.

"We'll let you know when the coroner is finished," said the inspector, on his way out with the police magistrate an hour after their arrival.

The cars and the reporters left. In the Villa of Green Happiness the two women and the retired naval officer remained silent.

Bit by bit, Madame Pouchet searched her memory. She thought back to Africa and her elegant villa on the road to Hann. She remembered Diouana pushing open the iron gate and signalling to the German shepherd to stop barking.

It was there, in Africa, that everything had started. Diouana had made the six-kilometre round trip on foot three times a week. For the last month she had made it gaily, enraptured, her heart beating as if she were in love for the first time. Beginning at the outskirts of Dakar, brand-new houses were scattered like jewels in a landscape of cactus, bougainvillea and jasmine. The asphalt of the Avenue Gambetta stretched out like a long black ribbon. Joyous and happy as usual, the little maid had no complaints about the road or her employers. Though it was a long way, it had no longer seemed so far the past month, ever since Madame had announced she would take her to France. France! Diouana shouted the word in her head. Everything around her had become ugly, the magnificent villas she had so often admired seemed shabby.

In order to be able to travel, in order to go to France, since she was originally from the Casamance, she had needed an identity card. All her paltry savings went to get one. "So what?" she thought. "I'm on my way to France!"

"Is that you, Diouana?"

"*Viye*,[1] Madame," came her answer in the Senegalese accent. She spoke from the vestibule, nicely dressed in her light coloured cotton, her hair neatly combed.

"Good! Monsieur is in town. Will you look after the children?"

"*Viye*, Madame," she agreed in her childish voice.

Though her identity card read "born in 1927," Diouana was not yet thirty. But she must have been over twenty-one. She went to find the children. Every room was in the same condition. Parcels packed and tied with strings, boxes piled here and there. After ten whole days of washing and ironing, there wasn't much left for

---

[1]*Viye*   Yes.

Diouana to do. In the proper sense of her duties, she was a laundress. There was a cook, a houseboy and herself. Three people. The servants.

"Diouana . . . Diouana," Madame called.

"Madame?" she answered, emerging from the children's room.

Madame was standing with a notebook in her hands making an inventory of the baggage. The movers would be coming at any moment.

"Have you been to see your parents? Do you think they will be happy?"

"*Viye*, Madame. The whole family is agreed. I tell Mama for myself. Also tell Papa Boutoupa," she said.

Her face, which had been radiant with happiness, fixed on the empty walls, and began to fade. Her heartbeat slowed. She would be ill if Madame changed her mind. Ready to plead her case, Diouana's ebony-black face grew gloomy, she lowered her eyes.

"You're not going to tell me at the last moment, on this very day, that you're leaving us in the lurch?"

"No, Madame, me go."

They were not speaking the same language. Diouana wanted to see France, this country whose beauty, richness, and joy of living everyone praised. She wanted to see it and make a triumphal return. This was where people got rich. Already, without having left African soil, she could see herself on the dock, returning from France, wealthy to the millions, with gifts of clothes for everyone. She dreamed of the freedom to go where she wished, without having to work like a beast of burden. If Madame should change her mind, refuse to take her, it would truly make her ill.

As for Madame, she was remembering the last few holidays she had spent in France. Three of them. And then she had only had two children. In Africa, Madame had acquired bad habits when it came to servants. In France when she hired a maid not only was the salary higher, but the maid demanded a day off to boot. Madame had had to let her go and hired another. The next one was no different from the first, if not worse. She answered Madame tit for tat. "Anyone who is capable of having children should take a turn with them herself. I can't live in. I have my own children to take care of and a husband too," she declared.

Used to being waited on hand and foot, Madame had yielded to her wifely duties, and clumsily fulfilled the role of mother. As for a real vacation, she had hardly had any. She soon persuaded her husband to return to Africa.

On her return, grown thin and thoroughly exasperated, she had conceived a plan for her next vacation. She put want ads in all the newspapers. A hundred young girls answered. Her choice fell on Diouana, newly arrived from her native bush. Producing two more children during the three years that Diouana worked for her, between her last holiday and the one to come, Madame sang the praises of France. For three thousand francs a month, any young African girl would have followed her to the end of the earth. And to top it off, from time to time, especially lately, Madame would give Diouana little gifts of this and that, old clothes, shoes that could be mended.

This was the insurmountable moat that separated the maid and her employer.

"Did you give Monsieur your identity card?"

"*Viye*, Madame."

"You may go back to your work. Tell the cook to give the three of you a good meal."

"*Merci*, Madame," she answered, and went off to the kitchen.

Madame continued her inventory.

Monsieur returned on the stroke of noon, his arrival announced by the barking of the dog. Getting out of his Peugeot 403, he found his wife, indefatigable, pencil in hand.

"Haven't the baggage men come yet?" she said nervously.

"They'll be here at a quarter to two. Our bags will be on top. That way they'll be out first when we land in Marseille. And what about Diouana? Diouana!"

The eldest of the children ran to fetch her. She was under the trees with the littlest one.

"*Viye*, Madame."

"It's Monsieur who was calling you."

"That's fine. Here are your ticket and your identity card."

Diouana held out a hand to take them.

"You keep the identity card, I'll take care of the ticket. The Duponts are returning on the same ship, they'll look after you. Are you glad to be going to France?"

"*Viye*, Monsieur."

"Good. Where are your bags?"

"At Rue Escarfait, Monsieur."

"After I've had lunch we'll go fetch them in the car."

"Bring the children in, Diouana, it's time for their nap."

"*Viye*, Madame."

Diouana wasn't hungry. The cook's helper, two years younger than she, brought the plates and took the empty ones away, noiselessly. The cook was sweating heavily. He wasn't happy. He was going to be out of work. This was how the departure affected him. And for this reason he was a bit resentful of the maid. Leaning out the wide window overlooking the sea, transported, Diouana watched the birds flying high above in the immense expanse of blue. In the distance she could barely make out the Island of Gorée.[2] She was holding her identity card, turning it over and over, examining it and smiling quietly to herself. The picture was a gloomy one. She wasn't pleased with the pose or with the exposure. "What does it matter? I'm leaving!" she thought.

"Samba," said Monsieur, who had come to the kitchen, "the meal was excellent today. You outdid yourself. Madame is very pleased with you."

The cook's helper stood at attention. Samba, the cook, adjusted his tall white hat and made an effort to smile.

"Thank you very much, Monsieur," he said. "I too am happy, very happy, because Monsieur and Madame are happy. Monsieur very nice. My family big, unhappy. Monsieur leave, me no more work."

"We'll be back, my good man. And then, with your talent you'll soon find another job!"

Samba, the cook, wasn't so sure. The Whites were stingy. And in a Dakar filled with country people each claiming to be a master cook, it wouldn't be easy to find a job.

"We'll be back, Samba. Maybe sooner than you think. The last time we stayed only two and a half months."

To these consoling words from Madame, who had joined her husband in the kitchen, Samba could only answer: "*Merci*, Madame. Madame very nice lady."

---

[2]*Gorée*   An island off the coast of Senegal from which hundreds of thousands of slaves were sent to the New World.

Madame was glad. She knew from experience what it meant to have a good reputation with the servants.

"You can go home this afternoon at four with Monsieur. I'll pack up the rest. When we come back I promise to hire you again. Are you pleased?"

"*Merci*, Madame."

Madame and Monsieur were gone. Samba gave Diouana a slap. She hit him back angrily.

"Hey! Careful. Careful. You're going away today. So we shouldn't fight."

"That hurt!" she said.

"And Monsieur, does he hurt you too?"

Samba suspected a secret liaison between the maid and her employer.

"They're calling for you, Diouana. I hear the car starting."

She left without even saying goodbye.

The car moved along the highway. Diouana didn't often have the privilege of being driven by Monsieur. Her very look invited the pedestrians' admiration, though she dared not wave a hand or shout while going past, "I'm on my way to France!" Yes, France! She was sure her happiness was plain to see. The subterranean sources of this tumultuous joy made her a bit shaky. When the car stopped in front of the house at Rue Escarfait, she was surprised. "Already?" she thought. Next door to her humble house, at the Gay Navigator Café, a few customers were seated at the tables and several were talking quietly on the sidewalk.

"Is it today you're leaving, little one?" asked Tive Correa. Already tipsy, he steadied himself, legs apart, holding his bottle by the neck. His clothes were rumpled.

Diouana would have nothing to do with the drunkard. She didn't listen to Tive Correa's advice. An old sailor, Tive Correa had come home from Europe after twenty years absence. He had left, rich with youth, full of ambition, and come home a wreck. From having wanted everything he had returned with nothing but an excessive love for the bottle. For Diouana he predicted nothing but misfortune. Once, when she had asked his advice, his opinion had been that she shouldn't go. In spite of his serious state of inebriety, he made a few steps towards Monsieur, bottle still in hand.

"Is it true that Diouana's leaving with you Monsieur?"

Monsieur did not answer. He took out a cigarette and lit it, blew the smoke through the car door, and looked Tive Correa over from head to toe. What a bum he was, greasy clothes, stinking of palm wine. Correa leaned over, putting a hand on the car door.

"I was there. I lived in France for twenty years," he began, with a note of pride in his voice. "I, whom you see this way, ruin though I am today, I know France better than you do. During the war I lived in Toulon, and the Germans sent us with the other Africans to Aix-en-Provence, to the mines at Gardanne. I've been against her going."

"We haven't forced her to go! She wants to," Monsieur answered dryly.

"Certainly. What young African doesn't dream of going to France? Unfortunately, they confuse living in France with being a servant in France. I come from the village next to Diouana's, in Casamance. There, we don't say the way you do that it is the light that attracts the butterfly, but the other way round. In my country, Casamance, we say that the darkness pursues the butterfly."

In the meantime, Diouana returned, escorted by several women. They were chatting along, each begging for a little souvenir. Diouana promised happily; she was smiling, her white teeth gleaming.

"The others are at the dock," said one. "Don't forget my dress."

"For me, some shoes for the children. You've got the size in your suitcase. And remember the sewing machine."

"The petticoats, too."

"Write and tell me how much the hair straightening irons cost and also the price of a red jacket with big buttons, size 44."

"Don't forget to send a little money to your mother in Boutoupa. . . ."

Each one had something to tell her, some request to make of her; Diouana promised. Her face was radiant. Tive Correa took the suitcase, pushing it drunkenly but not roughly into the car.

"Let her go, girls. Do you think money grows on trees in France? She'll have something to say about that when she gets back."

Loud protests from the women.

"Goodbye, little cousin. Take care of yourself. You have the address of the cousin in Toulon. Write to him as soon as you get there, he will help you. Come give me a kiss."

They all kissed each other goodbye. Monsieur was getting impatient. He started up the motor to indicate politely that he wished they'd be done with it.

The Peugeot was moving. Everyone waved.

At the dock it was the same; relatives, friends, little commissions. Everyone pressed around her. Always under the watchful eye of Monsieur. She embarked.

A week at sea. "No news," she would have written if she'd been keeping a diary, in which case she'd also have had to know how to read and write. Water in front, behind, to port, to starboard. Nothing but a sheet of liquid, and above it, the sky.

When the boat landed, Monsieur was there. After the formalities, they quickly made their way to the Côte d'Azur. She devoured everything with her eyes, marvelling, astonished. She packed every detail into her head. It was beautiful. Africa seemed a sordid slum by comparison. Towns, buses, trains, trucks went by along the coastal highway. The heaviness of the traffic surprised her.

"Did you have a good crossing?"

"*Viye*, Monsieur," she would have answered, if Monsieur had asked the question.

After a two-hour drive, they were in Antibes.

Days, weeks and the first month went by. The third month began. Diouana was no longer the joyous young girl with the ready laugh, full of life. Her eyes were beginning to look hollow, her glance was less alert, she no longer noticed details. She had a lot more work to do here than in Africa. At first her fretting was hardly noticeable. Of France, "La Belle France," she had only a vague idea, a fleeting vision. French gardens, the hedges of the other villas, the crests of roofs appearing above the green trees, the palms. Everyone lived his own life, isolated, shut up in his own house. Monsieur and Madame went out a good deal, leaving her with the four children. The children quickly organized a mafia and persecuted her. "You've got to keep them happy," Madame would say. The oldest, a real scamp, recruited others of like inclination and they played explorer. Diouana was the "savage." The children pestered her. Once in a while the eldest got a good spanking. Having picked up phrases from the conversations of mama, papa or the neighbours back in Africa—phrases in which notions of racial prejudice played a part—he made exaggerated remarks to his pals. Without the knowledge of his parents, they would turn up, chanting, "Black Girl, Black Girl. She's as black as midnight."

Perpetually harassed, Diouana began to waste away. In Dakar she had never had to think about the colour of her skin. With the youngsters teasing she began to question it. She understood that here she was alone. There was nothing that connected her with the others. And it aggravated her, poisoned her life, the very air she breathed.

Everything grew blunt; her old dreams, her contentment eroded. She did a lot of hard work. It was she who did all the cooking, laundry, babysitting, ironing. Madame's sister came to stay at the villa, making seven people to look after. At night, as soon as she went up to bed, Diouana slept like a log.

The venom was poisoning her heart. She had never hated anything. Everything became monotonous. Where was France? The beautiful cities she had seen at the movies in Dakar, the rare foods, the interesting crowds? The population of France reduced itself to these spiteful monsters, Monsieur, Madame and Mademoiselle, who had become strangers to her. The country seemed limited to the immediate surroundings of the villa. Little by little she was drowning. The wide horizons of a short while ago stopped now at the colour of her skin, which suddenly filled her with an invincible terror. Her skin. Her blackness. Timidly, she retreated into herself.

With no one from her universe to exchange ideas with, she held long moments of palaver with herself. A week ago, Monsieur and Madame had cleverly taken her along to visit their relatives in Cannes.

"Tomorrow we'll go to Cannes. My parents have never tasted African food. You'll do us African honour with your cooking," Madame had said. She was nearly bare, and getting bronzed from the sun.

"*Viye*, Madame."

"I've ordered some rice and two chickens. . . . You'll be careful not to spice it too much?"

"*Viye*, Madame."

Answering this way, her heart hardened. It seemed the hundredth time that she'd been trailed from villa to villa. To this one's house and then to that one's. It was at the Commodore's—everyone called him the Commodore—that she had rebelled the first time. Some silly people, who followed her about, hanging on her heels in the kitchen, had been there for dinner. Their presence was an oppressive shadow on her slightest movement. She had the feeling of not knowing how to do anything. These strange, self-centred, sophisticated beings never stopped asking her idiotic questions about how African women do their cooking. She kept herself under control.

The three women were still chirping when she waited on them at the table, testing the first spoonful on the tip of their tongues, then gluttonously devouring the rest.

"This time, at my parents, you must outdo yourself."

"*Viye*, Madame."

Restored to her kitchen, her thoughts went to Madame's former kindness. She detested it. Madame had been good to her, but in a self-seeking way. The only reason for her attentiveness had been to wind the strings round Diouana, the better to make her sweat. She loathed everything. Back in Dakar, Diouana used to gather Monsieur and Madame's leftovers to take home to Rue Escarfait. She had taken pride then in working for "important white people." Now she was so alone their meals made her sick to her stomach. The resentment spoiled her relations with her employers. She stood her ground, they stood theirs. They no longer exchanged any remarks but those of a business nature.

"Diouana, will you do the washing today?"

"*Viye*, Madame."

"Last time you didn't do a good job on my slips. The iron was too hot. And the collars of Monsieur's shirts were scorched. Do pay attention to what you're doing, will you?"

"*Viye*, Madame."

"Oh, I forgot. There are some buttons missing on Monsieur's shirts and his shorts."

Every little job was Diouana's. And then Madame started speaking to her in pidgin French, even in front of guests. And this was the only thing she did with honesty. In the end, no one in the house ever spoke to the maid any more except in terms of "Missie." Senegalese pidgin talk. Bewildered by her inadequacies in French, Diouana closed herself into a sort of solitary confinement. After long, lonely moments of meditation she came to the conclusion first of all that she was nothing but a useful object, and furthermore that she was being put on exhibit like a trophy. At parties, when Monsieur or Madame made remarks about "native" psychology, Diouana was taken as an illustration. The neighbours would say: "It's the Pouchets' black girl. . . ." She wasn't "the African girl" in her own right, but theirs. And that hurt.

The fourth month began. Things got worse. Her thoughts grew more lucid every day. She had work and work to spare. All week long. Sunday was Mademoiselle's favourite day for asking friends over. There were lots of them. The weeks began and ended with them.

Everything became clear. Why had Madame wanted her to come? Her generosities had been premeditated. Madame no longer took care of her children. She kissed them every morning, that was all. And where was "La Belle France?" These questions kept repeating themselves. "I am cook, nursemaid, chambermaid; I do all the washing and ironing and for a mere three thousand francs a month. I do housework for six people. What am I doing here?"

Diouana gave way to her memories. She compared her "native bush" to these dead shrubs. How different from the forest of her home in Casamance. The memory of her village, of the community life, cut her off from the others even more. She bit her lips, sorry to have come. And on this film of the past, a thousand other details were projected.

Returning to these surroundings, where she was doubly an outsider, her feelings hardened. She thought often of Tive Correa. His predictions had come cruelly true. She would have liked to write to him, but couldn't. Since arriving in France, she had had only two letters from her mother. She didn't have the time to answer, even though Madame had promised to write for her. Was it possible to tell Madame what she was thinking? She was angry with herself. Her ignorance made her mute. It was infuriating. And besides, Mademoiselle had made off with her stamps.

A pleasant idea crossed her mind though, and raised a smile. This evening only Monsieur was at home, watching television. She decided to take advantage of the opportunity. Then, unexpectedly finding Madame there too, Diouana stopped abruptly and left the room.

"Sold, sold. Bought, bought," she repeated to herself. "They've bought me. For three thousand francs I do all this work. They lured me, tied me to them, and I'm stuck here like a slave." She was determined now. That night she opened her suitcase, looked at the objects in it and wept. No one cared.

Yet she went through the same motions and remained as sealed off from the others as an oyster at low tide on the beach of her native Casamance.

"Douna"—it was Mademoiselle calling her. Why was it impossible for her to say Di-ou-a-na?

Her anger redoubled. Mademoiselle was even lazier than Madame: "Come take this away"—"There is such-and-such to be done, Douna"—"Why don't you do this, Douna?"—"Douna, now and then please rake the garden." For an answer Mademoiselle would receive an incendiary glance. Madame complained about her to Monsieur.

"What is the matter with you, Diouana? Are you ill or something?" he asked.

She no longer opened her mouth.

"You can tell me what's the matter. Perhaps you'd like to go to Toulon. I haven't had the time to go, but tomorrow I'll take you with me."

"Anyone would think we disgust her," said Madame.

Three days later Diouana took her bath. Returning home after a morning of shopping, Madame Pouchet went in the bathroom and quickly emerged.

"Diouana! Diouana!" she called. "You *are* dirty, in spite of everything. You might have left the bathroom clean."

"No me, Madame. It was the children, *viye.*"

"The children! The children are tidy. It may be that you're fed up with them. But to find you telling lies, like a native, *that* I don't like. I don't like liars and you are a liar!"

Diouana kept silent, though her lips were trembling. She went upstairs to the bathroom, and took her clothes off. It was there they found her, dead.

"Suicide," the investigators concluded. The case was closed.

The next day, in the newspaper on page four, column six, hardly noticeable, was a small headline:

"Homesick African Girl Cuts Throat in Antibes."

[1962]

Translated by

ELLEN CONROY KENNEDY

Questions

1. Are the Pouchets guilty of murder?
2. Is the newspaper headline at the end of the story an accurate summary of what has happened to Diouana?
3. The French title of the story ("La Noire de . . .") is literally translated as "The Black Girl from. . . ." Is this a more accurate title than "Black Girl"?
4. What is Tive Correa's function in the story?

Amos Oz
(b. 1939)
Israel

F or most of his adult life, Amos Oz has lived at Kibbutz Hupa, a collective community in Israel. A sabra—a first-generation Israeli—he was born Amos Klaus-
ner to prosperous Zionist parents who immigrated to Israel. His father was a librarian,
writer, and scholar of comparative literature. During adolescence, Oz rebelled against
his family's middle-class values by deciding to join directly in the Israeli social experiment. He changed his surname, joined a kibbutz, and undertook the essential but me-
nial work required of kibbutzim residents, from driving a tractor to working in
agricultural production. Oz also served in the Israeli army, seeing action in two wars.

   Pursuing higher education at Hebrew University and Oxford, Oz subsequently returned to the Kibbutz Hulda and began to write fiction. (His royalty income goes to
the kibbutz.) He acknowledges the irony of his life:

> In the end, when I look at myself, I am doing exactly what my father wanted me to do.
> In the kibbutz I look like one of the members, and yet I follow my forefathers. I deal with
> words. My escape was a full circle.

   In his novels, stories, essays, and interviews about the State (and state) of Israel,
Oz has become an imaginative witness and recorder of the darker side of a unique but
troubled social and political experiment: Jews who struggle to survive in a desert landscape that symbolizes both the physical and the emotional siege under which they live.
Oz phrased it this way in an essay for Partisan Review:

> [Life in a kibbutz] waked and fed my curiosity about the strange phenomenon of flawed,
> tormented human beings dreaming about perfection, aching for the Messiah, aspiring to
> change human nature. This perpetual paradox of magnanimous dream and unhappy re-
> ality is indeed one of the main threads in my writing.

   Among his nine novels and several collections of stories, all originally written in
Hebrew, are Elsewhere, Perhaps (1966); My Michael (1968); A Perfect Peace
(1983); Where the Jackals Howl (1965, revised 1976), from which the title story
is included here; Black Box (1988); To Know a Woman (1992); and Fima (1993).
In his collection of essays and commentaries on life in his homeland, Israel, Palestine,
and Peace (1995), Oz proposes that the first step toward peace in the Middle East
should be the erection of "a monument to our mutual stupidity." Describing the special area that Oz has carved out as his subject and theme, Ruth Wisse made the following observation:

> [Oz has taken] the great myths with which modern Israel is associated—the noble ex-
> periment of the kibbutz, the reclamation of the soil, the wars against the British and the
> Arabs, the phoenix-like rise of the Jewish spirit out of the ashes of the Holocaust—and
> shown us their underside: bruised, dazed, and straying characters who move in an at-
> mosphere of almost unalleviated depression.

NOMAD AND VIPER

I

The famine brought them.

They fled north from the horrors of famine, together with their dusty flocks. From September to April the desert had not known a moment's relief from drought. The loess[1] was pounded to dust. Famine had spread through the nomads' encampments and wrought havoc among their flocks.

The military authorities gave the situation their urgent attention. Despite certain hesitations, they decided to open the roads leading north to the Bedouins. A whole population—men, women, and children—could not simply be abandoned to the horrors of starvation.

Dark, sinuous, and wiry, the desert tribesmen trickled along the dirt paths, and with them came their emaciated flocks. They meandered along gullies hidden from town dwellers' eyes. A persistent stream pressed northward, circling the scattered settlements, staring wide-eyed at the sights of the settled land. The dark flocks spread into the fields of golden stubble, tearing and chewing with strong, vengeful teeth. The nomads' bearing was stealthy and subdued; they shrank from watchful eyes. They took pains to avoid encounters. Tried to conceal their presence.

If you passed them on a noisy tractor and set billows of dust loose on them, they would courteously gather their scattered flocks and give you a wide passage, wider by far than was necessary. They stared at you from a distance, frozen like statues. The scorching atmosphere blurred their appearance and gave a uniform look to their features: a shepherd with his staff, a woman with her babes, an old man with his eyes sunk deep in their sockets. Some were half-blind, or perhaps feigned half-blindness from some vague alms-gathering motive. Inscrutable to the likes of you.

How unlike our well-tended sheep were their miserable specimens: knots of small, skinny beasts huddling into a dark, seething mass, silent and subdued, humble as their dumb keepers.

The camels alone spurn meekness. From atop tall necks they fix you with tired eyes brimming with scornful sorrow. The wisdom of age seems to lurk in their eyes, and a nameless tremor runs often through their skin.

Sometimes you manage to catch them unawares. Crossing a field on foot, you may suddenly happen on an indolent flock standing motionless, noon-struck, their feet apparently rooted in the parched soil. Among them lies the shepherd, fast asleep, dark as a block of basalt. You approach and cover him with a harsh shadow. You are startled to find his eyes wide open. He bares most of his teeth in a placatory smile. Some of them are gleaming, others decayed. His smell hits you. You grimace. Your grimace hits him like a punch in the face. Daintily he picks himself up, trunk erect, shoulders hunched. You fix him with a cold blue eye. He broadens his smile and utters a guttural syllable. His garb is a compromise: a short, patched European jacket over a white desert robe. He cocks his head to one side. An appeased gleam crosses his face. If you do not upbraid him, he suddenly extends his left hand and asks for a cigarette in rapid

---

[1]*loess*   Fine, yellowish-brown loam deposited by wind.

Hebrew. His voice has a silken quality, like that of a shy woman. If your mood is generous, you put a cigarette to your lips and toss another into his wrinkled palm. To your surprise, he snatches a gilt lighter from the recesses of his robe and offers a furtive flame. The smile never leaves his lips. His smile lasts too long, is unconvincing. A flash of sunlight darts off the thick gold ring adorning his finger and pierces your squinting eyes.

Eventually you turn your back on the nomad and continue on your way. After a hundred, two hundred paces, you may turn your head and see him standing just as he was, his gaze stabbing your back. You could swear that he is still smiling, that he will go on smiling for a long while to come.

And then, their singing in the night. A long-drawn-out, dolorous wail drifts on the night air from sunset until the early hours. The voices penetrate to the gardens and pathways of the kibbutz[2] and charge our nights with an uneasy heaviness. No sooner have you settled down to sleep than a distant drumbeat sets the rhythm of your slumber like the pounding of an obdurate heart. Hot are the nights, and vapor-laden. Stray clouds caress the moon like a train of gentle camels, camels without any bells.

The nomads' tents are made up of dark drapes. Stray women drift around at night, barefoot and noiseless. Lean, vicious nomad hounds dart out of the camp to challenge the moon all night long. Their barking drives our kibbutz dogs insane. Our finest dog went mad one night, broke into the henhouse, and massacred the young chicks. It was not out of savagery that the watchmen shot him. There was no alternative. Any reasonable man would justify their action.

II

You might imagine that the nomad incursion enriched our heat-prostrated nights with a dimension of poetry. This may have been the case for some of our unattached girls. But we cannot refrain from mentioning a whole string of prosaic, indeed unaesthetic disturbances, such as foot-and-mouth disease, crop damage, and an epidemic of petty thefts.

The foot-and-mouth disease came out of the desert, carried by their livestock, which had never been subjected to any proper medical inspection. Although we took various early precautions, the virus infected our sheep and cattle, severely reducing the milk yield and killing off a number of animals.

As for the damage to the crops, we had to admit that we had never managed to catch one of the nomads in the act. All we ever found were the tracks of men and animals among the rows of vegetables, in the hayfields, and deep inside the carefully fenced orchards. And wrecked irrigation pipes, plot markers, farming implements left out in the fields, and other objects.

We are not the kind to take such things lying down. We are no believers in forbearance or vegetarianism. This is especially true of our younger men. Among the veteran founders there are a few adherents of Tolstoyan ideas and such like. Decency constrains me not to dwell in detail on certain isolated and exceptional acts of reprisal

---

[2]*kibbutz*   Communal settlement in Israel, organized as a collective.

conducted by some of the youngsters whose patience had expired, such as cattle rustling, stoning a nomad boy, or beating one of the shepherds senseless. In defense of the perpetrators of the last-mentioned act of retaliation I must state clearly that the shepherd in question had an infuriatingly sly face. He was blind in one eye, broken-nosed, drooling; and his mouth—on this the men responsible were unanimous—was set with long, curved fangs like a fox's. A man with such an appearance was capable of anything. And the Bedouins would certainly not forget this lesson.

The pilfering was the most worrisome aspect of all. They laid hands on the unripe fruit in our orchards, pocketed the faucets, whittled away piles of empty sacks in the fields, stole into the henhouses, and even made away with the modest valuables from our little houses.

The very darkness was their accomplice. Elusive as the wind, they passed through the settlement, evading both the guards we had posted and the extra guards we had added. Sometimes you would set out on a tractor or a battered jeep toward midnight to turn off the irrigation faucets in an outlying field and your headlights would trap fleeting shadows, a man or a night beast. An irritable guard decided one night to open fire, and in the dark he managed to kill a stray jackal.

Needless to say, the kibbutz secretariat did not remain silent. Several times Etkin, the secretary, called in the police, but their tracking dogs betrayed or failed them. Having led their handlers a few paces outside the kibbutz fence, they raised their black noses, uttered a savage howl, and stared foolishly ahead.

Spot raids on the tattered tents revealed nothing. It was as if the very earth had decided to cover up the plunder and brazenly outstare the victims. Eventually the elder of the tribe was brought to the kibbutz office, flanked by a pair of inscrutable nomads. The short-tempered policemen pushed them forward with repeated cries of "Yallah, yallah."

We, the members of the secretariat, received the elder and his men politely and respectfully. We invited them to sit down on the bench, smiled at them, and offered them steaming coffee prepared by Geula at Etkin's special request. The old man responded with elaborate courtesies, favoring us with a smile which he kept up from the beginning of the interview till its conclusion. He phrased his remarks in careful, formal Hebrew.

It was true that some of the youngsters of his tribe had laid hands on our property. Why should he deny it. Boys would be boys, and the world was getting steadily worse. He had the honor of begging our pardon and restoring the stolen property. Stolen property fastens its teeth in the flesh of the thief, as the proverb says. That was the way of it. What could one do about the hotheadedness of youth? He deeply regretted the trouble and distress we had been caused.

So saying, he put his hand into the folds of his robe and drew out a few screws, some gleaming, some rusty, a pair of pruning hooks, a stray knife-blade, a pocket flashlight, a broken hammer, and three grubby bank notes, as a recompense for our loss and worry.

Etkin spread his hands in embarrassment. For reasons best known to himself, he chose to ignore our guest's Hebrew and to reply in broken Arabic, the residue of his studies during the time of the riots and the siege. He opened his remarks with a frank and clear statement about the brotherhood of nations—the cornerstone of our ideology—and about the quality of neighborliness of which the peoples of the East had long been justly proud, and never more so than in these days of bloodshed and groundless hatred.

To Etkin's credit, let it be said that he did not shrink in the slightest from reciting a full and detailed list of the acts of theft, damage, and sabotage that our guest—as the result of oversight, no doubt—had refrained from mentioning in his apology. If all the stolen property were returned and the vandalism stopped once and for all, we would be wholeheartedly willing to open a new page in the relations of our two neighboring communities. Our children would doubtless enjoy and profit from an educational courtesy visit to the Bedouin encampment, the kind of visit that broadens horizons. And it went without saying that the tribe's children would pay a return visit to our kibbutz home, in the interest of deepening mutual understanding.

The old man neither relaxed nor broadened his smile, but kept it sternly at its former level as he remarked with an abundance of polite phrases that the gentlemen of the kibbutz would be able to prove no further thefts beyond those he had already admitted and for which he had sought our forgiveness.

He concluded with elaborate benedictions, wished us health and long life, posterity and plenty, then took his leave and departed, accompanied by his two barefooted companions wrapped in their dark robes. They were soon swallowed up by the wadi[3] that lay outside the kibbutz fence.

Since the police had proved ineffectual—and had indeed abandoned the investigation—some of our young men suggested making an excursion one night to teach the savages a lesson in a language they would really understand.

Etkin rejected their suggestion with disgust and with reasonable arguments. The young men, in turn, applied to Etkin a number of epithets that decency obliges me to pass over in silence. Strangely enough, Etkin ignored their insults and reluctantly agreed to put their suggestion before the kibbutz secretariat. Perhaps he was afraid that they might take matters into their own hands.

Toward evening, Etkin went around from room to room and invited the committee to an urgent meeting at eight-thirty. When he came to Geula, he told her about the young men's ideas and the undemocratic pressure to which he was being subjected, and asked her to bring along to the meeting a pot of black coffee and a lot of good will. Geula responded with an acid smile. Her eyes were bleary because Etkin had awakened her from a troubled sleep. As she changed her clothes, the night fell, damp and hot and close.

III

Damp and close and hot the night fell on the kibbutz, tangled in the dust-laden cypresses, oppressed the lawns and ornamental shrubs. Sprinklers scattered water onto the thirsty lawn, but it was swallowed up at once: perhaps it evaporated even before it touched the grass. An irritable phone rang vainly in the locked office. The walls of the houses gave out a damp vapor. From the kitchen chimney a stiff column of smoke rose like an arrow into the heart of the sky, because there was no breeze. From the greasy sinks came a shout. A dish had been broken and somebody was bleeding. A fat house-cat had killed a lizard or a snake and dragged its prey onto the baking concrete path to toy with it lazily in the dense evening sunlight. An ancient tractor started to rumble in one of the sheds, choked, belched a stench of oil, roared, spluttered, and finally managed to

---

[3]*wadi*　Channel of a river or ravine.

set out to deliver an evening meal to the second shift, who were toiling in an outlying field. Near the Persian lilac Geula saw a bottle dirty with the remains of a greasy liquid. She kicked at it repeatedly, but instead of shattering, the bottle rolled heavily among the rosebushes. She picked up a big stone. She tried to hit the bottle. She longed to smash it. The stone missed. The girl began to whistle a vague tune.

Geula was a short, energetic girl of twenty-nine or so. Although she had not yet found a husband, none of us would deny her good qualities, such as the dedication she lavished on local social and cultural activities. Her face was pale and thin. No one could rival her in brewing strong coffee—coffee to raise the dead, we called it. A pair of bitter lines were etched at the corners of her mouth.

On summer evenings, when the rest of us would lounge in a group on a rug spread on one of the lawns and launch jokes and bursts of cheerful song heavenward, accompanied by clouds of cigarette smoke, Geula would shut herself up in her room and not join us until she had prepared the pot of scalding, strong coffee. She it was, too, who always took pains to ensure that there was no shortage of biscuits.

What had passed between Geula and me is not relevant here, and I shall make do with a hint or two. Long ago we used to stroll together to the orchards in the evening and talk. It was all a long time ago, and it is a long time since it ended. We would exchange unconventional political ideas or argue about the latest books. Geula was a stern and sometimes merciless critic: I was covered in confusion. She did not like my stories, because of the extreme polarity of situations, scenery, and characters, with no intermediate shades between black and white. I would utter an apology or a denial, but Geula always had ready proofs and she was a very methodical thinker. Sometimes I would dare to rest a conciliatory hand on her neck, and wait for her to calm down. But she never relaxed completely. If once or twice she leaned against me, she always blamed her broken sandal or her aching head. And so we drifted apart. To this day she still cuts my stories out of the periodicals, and arranges them in a cardboard box kept in a special drawer devoted to them alone.

I always buy her a new book of poems for her birthday. I creep into her room when she is out and leave the book on her table, without any inscription or dedication. Sometimes we happen to sit together in the dining hall. I avoid her glance, so as not to have to face her mocking sadness. On hot days, when faces are covered in sweat, the acne on her cheeks reddens and she seems to have no hope. When the cool of autumn comes, I sometimes find her pretty and attractive from a distance. On such days Geula likes to walk to the orchards in the early evening. She goes alone and comes back alone. Some of the youngsters come and ask me what she is looking for there, and they have a malicious snicker on their faces. I tell them that I don't know. And I really don't.

IV

Viciously Geula picked up another stone to hurl at the bottle. This time she did not miss but she still failed to hear the shattering sound she craved. The stone grazed the bottle, which tinkled faintly and disappeared under one of the bushes. A third stone, bigger and heavier than the other two, was launched from ridiculously close range: the girl trampled on the loose soil of the flower bed and stood right over the bottle. This time there was a harsh, dry explosion, which brought no relief. Must get out.

Damp and close and hot the night fell, its heat pricking the skin like broken glass. Geula retraced her steps, passed the balcony of her room, tossed her sandals inside, and walked down barefoot onto the dirt path.

The clods of earth tickled the soles of her feet. There was a rough friction, and her nerve endings quivered with flickers of vague excitement. Beyond the rocky hill the shadows were waiting for her: the orchard in the last of the light. With determined hands she widened the gap in the fence and slipped through. At that moment a slight evening breeze began to stir. It was a warmish summer breeze with no definite direction. An old sun rolled westward, trying to be sucked up by the dusty horizon. A last tractor climbed back to the depot, panting along the dirt road from the outlying plots. No doubt it was the tractor that had taken the second-shift workers their supper. It seemed shrouded in smoke or summer haze.

Geula bent down and picked some pebbles out of the dust. Absently she began to throw them back again, one by one. There were lines of poetry on her lips, some by the young poets she was fond of, others her own. By the irrigation pipe she paused, bent down, and drank as though kissing the faucet. But the faucet was rusty, the pipe was still hot, and the water was tepid and foul. Nevertheless she bent her head and let the water pour over her face and neck and into her shirt. A sharp taste of rust and wet dust filled her throat. She closed her eyes and stood in silence. No relief. Perhaps a cup of coffee. But only after the orchard. Must go now.

V

The orchards were heavily laden and fragrant. The branches intertwined, converging above the rows of trunks to form a shadowy dome. Underfoot the irrigated soil retained a hidden dampness. Shadows upon shadows at the foot of those gnarled trunks. Geula picked a plum, sniffed and crushed it. Sticky juice dripped from it. The sight made her feel dizzy. And the smell. She crushed a second plum. She picked another and rubbed it on her cheek till she was spattered with juice. Then, on her knees, she picked up a dry stick and scratched shapes in the dust. Aimless lines and curves. Sharp angles. Domes. A distant bleating invaded the orchard. Dimly she became aware of a sound of bells. She was far away. The nomad stopped behind Geula's back, as silent as a phantom. He dug at the dust with his big toe, and his shadow fell in front of him. But the girl was blinded by a flood of sounds. She saw and heard nothing. For a long time she continued to kneel on the ground and draw shapes in the dust with her twig. The nomad waited patiently in total silence. From time to time he closed his good eye and stared ahead of him with the other, the blind one. Finally he reached out and bestowed a long caress on the air. His obedient shadow moved in the dust. Geula stared, leapt to her feet, and leaned against the nearest tree, letting out a low sound. The nomad let his shoulders drop and put on a faint smile. Geula raised her arm and stabbed the air with her twig. The nomad continued to smile. His gaze dropped to her bare feet. His voice was hushed, and the Hebrew he spoke exuded a rare gentleness:

"What time is it?"

Geula inhaled to her lungs' full capacity. Her features grew sharp, her glance cold. Clearly and dryly she replied:

"It is half past six. Precisely."

The Arab broadened his smile and bowed slightly, as if to acknowledge a great kindness.

"Thank you very much, miss."

His bare toe had dug deep into the damp soil, and the clods of earth crawled at his feet as if there were a startled mole burrowing underneath them.

Geula fastened the top button of her blouse. There were large perspiration stains on her shirt, drawing attention to her armpits. She could smell the sweat on her body, and her nostrils widened. The nomad closed his blind eye and looked up. His good eye blinked. His skin was very dark; it was alive and warm. Creases were etched in his cheeks. He was unlike any man Geula had ever known, and his smell and color and breathing were also strange. His nose was long and narrow, and a shadow of a mustache showed beneath it. His cheeks seemed to be sunk into his mouth cavity. His lips were thin and fine, much finer than her own. But the chin was strong, almost expressing contempt or rebellion.

The man was repulsively handsome, Geula decided to herself. Unconsciously she responded with a mocking half-smile to the nomad's persistent grin. The Bedouin drew two crumpled cigarettes from a hidden pocket in his belt, laid them on his dark, outstretched palm, and held them out to her as though proffering crumbs to a sparrow. Geula dropped her smile, nodded twice, and accepted one. She ran the cigarette through her fingers, slowly, dreamily, ironing out the creases, straightening it, and only then did she put it to her lips. Quick as lightning, before she realized the purpose of the man's sudden movement, a tiny flame was dancing in front of her. Geula shielded the lighter with her hand even though there was no breeze in the orchard, sucked in the flame, closed her eyes. The nomad lit his own cigarette and bowed politely.

"Thank you very much," he said in his velvety voice.

"Thanks," Geula replied. "Thank you."

"You from the kibbutz?"

Geula nodded.

"Goo-d." An elongated syllable escaped from between his gleaming teeth. "That's goo-d."

The girl eyed his desert robe.

"Aren't you hot in that thing?"

The man gave an embarrassed, guilty smile, as if he had been caught red-handed. He took a slight step backward.

"Heaven forbid, it's not hot. Really not. Why? There's air, there's water. . . ." And he fell silent.

The treetops were already growing darker. A first jackal sniffed the oncoming night and let out a tired howl. The orchard filled with a scurry of small, busy feet. All of a sudden Geula became aware of the throngs of black goats intruding in search of their master. They swirled silently in and out of the fruit trees. Geula pursed her lips and let out a short whistle of surprise.

"What are you doing here, anyway? Stealing?"

The nomad cowered as though a stone had been thrown at him. His hand beat a hollow tattoo on his chest.

"No, not stealing, heaven forbid, really not." He added a lengthy oath in his own language and resumed his silent smile. His blind eye winked nervously. Meanwhile an emaciated goat darted forward and rubbed against his leg. He kicked it away and continued to swear with passion:

"Not steal, truly, by Allah not steal. Forbidden to steal."

"Forbidden in the Bible," Geula replied with a dry, cruel smile. "Forbidden to steal, forbidden to kill, forbidden to covet, and forbidden to commit adultery. The righteous are above suspicion."

The Arab cowered before the onslaught of words and looked down at the ground. Shamefaced. Guilty. His foot continued to kick restlessly at the loose earth. He was trying to ingratiate himself. His blind eye narrowed. Geula was momentarily alarmed: surely it was a wink. The smile left his lips. He spoke in a soft, drawn-out whisper, as though uttering a prayer.

"Beautiful girl, truly very beautiful girl. Me, I got no girl yet. Me still young. No girl yet. Yaaa," he concluded with a guttural yell directed at an impudent goat that had rested its forelegs against a tree trunk and was munching hungrily at the foliage. The animal cast a pensive, skeptical glance at its master, shook its beard, and solemnly resumed its munching.

Without warning, and with amazing agility, the shepherd leapt through the air and seized the beast by the hind-quarters, lifted it above his head, let out a terrifying, savage screech, and flung it ruthlessly to the ground. Then he spat and turned to the girl. "Beast," he apologized. "Beast. What to do. No brains. No manners."

The girl let go of the tree trunk against which she had been resting and leaned toward the nomad. A sweet shudder ran down her back. Her voice was still firm and cool. "Another cigarette?" she asked. "Have you got another cigarette?"

The Bedouin replied with a look of anguish, almost of despair. He apologized. He explained at length that he had no more cigarettes, not even one, not even a little one. No more. All gone. What a pity. He would gladly, very gladly, have given her one. None left. All gone.

The beaten goat was getting shakily to its feet. Treading circumspectly, it returned to the tree trunk, disingenuously observing its master out of the corner of its eye. The shepherd watched it without moving. The goat reached up, rested its front hoofs on the tree, and calmly continued munching. The Arab picked up a heavy stone and swung his arm wildly. Geula seized his arm and restrained him.

"Leave it. Why. Let it be. It doesn't understand. It's only a beast. No brains, no manners."

The nomad obeyed. In total submission he let the stone drop. Then Geula let go of his arm. Once again the man drew the lighter out of his belt. With thin, pensive fingers he toyed with it. He accidentally lit a small flame, and hastily blew at it. The flame widened slightly, slanted, and died. Nearby a jackal broke into a loud, piercing wail. The rest of the goats, meanwhile, had followed the example of the first and were absorbed in rapid, almost angry munching.

A vague wail came from the nomad encampment away to the south, the dim drum beating time to its languorous call. The dusky men were sitting around their campfires, sending skyward their single-noted song. The night took up the strain and answered with dismal cricket-chirp. Last glimmers of light were dying away in the far west. The orchard stood in darkness. Sounds gathered all around, the wind's whispering, the goats' sniffing, the rustle of ravished leaves. Geula pursed her lips and whistled an old tune. The nomad listened to her with rapt attention, his head cocked to one side in surprise, his mouth hanging slightly open. She glanced at her watch. The hands winked back at her with a malign, phosphorescent glint, but said nothing. Night.

The Arab turned his back on Geula, dropped to his knees, touched his forehead on the ground, and began mumbling fervently.

"You've got no girl yet," Geula broke into his prayer. "You're still too young." Her voice was loud and strange. Her hands were on her hips, her breathing still even. The man stopped praying, turned his dark face toward her, and muttered a phrase in Arabic. He was still crouched on all fours, but his pose suggested a certain suppressed joy.

"You're still young," Geula repeated, "very young. Perhaps twenty. Perhaps thirty. Young. No girl for you. Too young."

The man replied with a very long and solemn remark in his own language. She laughed nervously, her hands embracing her hips.

"What's the matter with you?" she inquired, laughing still. "Why are you talking to me in Arabic all of a sudden? What do you think I am? What do you want here, anyway?"

Again the nomad replied in his own language. Now a note of terror filled his voice. With soft, silent steps he recoiled and withdrew as though from a dying creature. She was breathing heavily now, panting, trembling. A single wild syllable escaped from the shepherd's mouth: a sign between him and his goats. The goats responded and thronged around him, their feet pattering on the carpet of dead leaves like cloth ripping. The crickets fell silent. The goats huddled in the dark, a terrified, quivering mass, and disappeared into the darkness, the shepherd vanishing in their midst.

Afterward, alone and trembling, she watched an airplane passing in the dark sky above the treetops, rumbling dully, its lights blinking alternately with a rhythm as precise as that of the drums: red, green, red, green, red. The night covered over the traces. There was a smell of bonfires on the air and a smell of dust borne on the breeze. Only a slight breeze among the fruit trees. Then panic struck her and her blood froze. Her mouth opened to scream but she did not scream, she started to run and she ran barefoot with all her strength for home and stumbled and rose and ran as though pursued, but only the sawing of the crickets chased after her.

VI

She returned to her room and made coffee for all the members of the secretariat, because she remembered her promise to Etkin. Outside the cool of evening had set in, but inside her room the walls were hot and her body was also on fire. Her clothes stuck to her body because she had been running, and her armpits disgusted her. The spots on her face were glowing. She stood and counted the number of times the coffee boiled—seven successive boilings, as she had learned to do it from her brother Ehud before he was killed in a reprisal raid in the desert. With pursed lips she counted as the black liquid rose and subsided, rose and subsided, bubbling fiercely as it reached its climax.

That's enough, now. Take clean clothes for the evening. Go to the showers.

What can that Etkin understand about savages. A great socialist. What does he know about Bedouins. A nomad sniffs out weakness from a distance. Give him a kind word, or a smile, and he pounces on you like a wild beast and tries to rape you. It was just as well I ran away from him.

In the showers the drain was clogged and the bench was greasy. Geula put her clean clothes on the stone ledge. I'm not shivering because the water's cold. I'm shivering with disgust. Those black fingers, and how he went straight for my throat. And his teeth. And the goats. Small and skinny like a child, but so strong. It was only by biting and kicking that I managed to escape. Soap my belly and everything, soap it again and again. Yes, let the boys go right away tonight to their camp and smash their black bones because of what they did to me. Now I must get outside.

VII

She left the shower and started back toward her room, to pick up the coffee and take it to the secretariat. But on the way she heard crickets and laughter, and she re-membered him bent down on all fours, and she was alarmed and stood still in the dark. Suddenly she vomited among the flowering shrubs. And she began to cry. Then her knees gave way. She sat down to rest on the dark earth. She stopped crying. But her teeth continued to chatter, from the cold or from pity. Suddenly she was not in a hurry any more, even the coffee no longer seemed important, and she thought to herself: There's still time. There's still time.

Those planes sweeping the sky tonight were probably on a night-bombing exer-cise. Repeatedly they roared among the stars, keeping up a constant flashing, red, green, red, green, red. In counterpoint came the singing of the nomads and their drums, a persistent heartbeat in the distance: One, one, two, One, one, two. And silence.

VIII

From eight-thirty until nearly nine o'clock we waited for Geula. At five to nine Etkin said that he could not imagine what had happened; he could not recall her ever hav-ing missed a meeting or been late before; at all events, we must now begin the meet-ing and turn to the business on the agenda.

He began with a summary of the facts. He gave details of the damage that had ap-parently been caused by the Bedouins, although there was no formal proof, and enu-merated the steps that had been taken on the committee's initiative. The appeal to good will. Calling in the police. Strengthening the guard around the settlement. Tracking dogs. The meeting with the elder of the tribe. He had to admit, Etkin said, that we had now reached an impasse. Nevertheless, he believed that we had to main-tain a sense of balance and not give way to extremism, because hatred always gave rise to further hatred. It was essential to break the vicious circle of hostility. He therefore opposed with all the moral force at his disposal the approach—and par-ticularly the intentions—of certain of the younger members. He wished to remind us, by way of conclusion, that the conflict between herdsmen and tillers of the soil was as old as human civilization, as seemed to be evidenced by the story of Cain, who rose up against Abel, his brother. It was fitting, in view of the social gospel we had adopted, that we should put an end to this ancient feud, too, just as we had put an end to other ugly phenomena. It was up to us, and everything depended on our moral strength.

The room was full of tension, even unpleasantness. Rami twice interrupted Etkin and on one occasion went so far as to use the ugly word "rubbish." Etkin took of-fense, accused the younger members of planning terrorist activities, and said in con-clusion, "We're not going to have that sort of thing here."

Geula had not arrived, and that was why there was no one to cool down the temper of the meeting. And no coffee. A heated exchange broke out between me and Rami. Although in age I belonged with the younger men, I did not agree with their proposals. Like Etkin, I was absolutely opposed to answering the nomads with violence—for two reasons, and when I was given permission to speak I mentioned them both. In the first place, nothing really serious had happened so far. A little stealing perhaps, but even that was not certain: every faucet or pair of pliers that a tractor driver left in a field or lost in the garage or took home with him was immediately blamed on the Bedouins. Secondly, there had been no rape or murder. Hereupon Rami broke in excitedly and asked what I was waiting for. Was I perhaps waiting for some small incident of rape that Geula could write poems about and I could make into a short story? I flushed and cast around in my mind for a telling retort.

But Etkin, upset by our rudeness, immediately deprived us both of the right to speak and began to explain his position all over again. He asked us how it would look if the papers reported that a kibbutz had sent out a lynch mob to settle scores with its Arab neighbors. As Etkin uttered the phrase "lynch mob," Rami made a gesture to his young friends that is commonly used by basketball players. At this signal they rose in a body and walked out in disgust, leaving Etkin to lecture to his heart's content to three elderly women and a long-retired member of Parliament.

After a moment's hesitation I rose and followed them. True, I did not share their views, but I, too, had been deprived of the right to speak in an arbitrary and insulting manner.

IX

If only Geula had come to the meeting and brought her famous coffee with her, it is possible that tempers might have been soothed. Perhaps, too her understanding might have achieved some sort of compromise between the conflicting points of view. But the coffee was standing, cold by now, on the table in her room. And Geula herself was lying among the bushes behind the Memorial Hall, watching the lights of the planes and listening to the sounds of the night. How she longed to make her peace and to forgive. Not to hate him and wish him dead. Perhaps to get up and go to him, to find him among the wadis and forgive him and never come back. Even to sing to him. The sharp slivers piercing her skin and drawing blood were the fragments of the bottle she had smashed here with a big stone at the beginning of the evening. And the living thing slithering among the slivers of glass among the clods of earth was a snake, perhaps a venomous snake, perhaps a viper. It stuck out a forked tongue, and its triangular head was cold and erect. Its eyes were dark glass. It could never close them, because it had no eyelids. A thorn in her flesh, perhaps a sliver of glass. She was very tired. And the pain was vague, almost pleasant. A distant ringing in her ears. To sleep now. Wearily, through the thickening film, she watched the gang of youngsters crossing the lawn on their way to the fields and the wadi to even the score with the nomads. We were carrying short, thick sticks. Excitement was dilating our pupils. And the blood was drumming in our temples.

Far away in the darkened orchards stood somber, dust-laden cypresses, swaying to and fro with a gentle, religious fervor. She felt tired, and that was why she did not come to see us off. But her fingers caressed the dust, and her face was very calm and almost beautiful.

[1963]
Translated by
NICHOLAS DE LANGE
and PHILIP SIMPSON

Questions

1. What is the effect of the variations in the point of view from section to section?
2. How do the narrator and the other men of the settlement view Geula? How does the reader understand her?
3. What happens to Geula in the story? Why are certain events only implied and not described?
4. What does the story's title signify?

Octavio Paz
(1914–1998)
Mexico

Born in Mexico City in 1914, Octavio Paz spent much of his life as a cosmopolite—a citizen of the world. He lived in Spain during the Spanish Civil War; in 1944, he was in the United States as the recipient of a Guggenheim fellowship; the following year he spent in Paris, where he was befriended by André Breton and other surrealists. From 1962 until 1968, he was Mexico's ambassador to India. As a teacher, he held distinguished teaching positions in both the United States and England: at Cambridge, the University of Texas at Austin, and Harvard. He also lived in the Orient. In all of these different places and careers, Paz continued to write, publishing numerous collections of essays and poems.

Paz's influence on contemporary Mexican writing has been extraordinary. The culmination of his artistic career was marked by the Nobel Prize for Literature, which he received in 1990. On that occasion, his poems and essays were specifically praised. Paz himself reflected on his Mexican heritage:

> I discovered that I was Mexican when I was in the United States in my youth, during the war. We began by not speaking English, and wound up having fights with other children. And then when I went back to Mexico I had the same fights, for the same reasons. I was fourteen, and I couldn't understand it. This experience was rather painful, to be a foreigner in your own place. And then I started to ask myself who I am and why I am Mexican.

As you read "The Blue Bouquet," consider the ways in which Paz's international background influenced both the form and the subject of his story.

THE BLUE BOUQUET

When I woke up I was soaked with sweat. The floor of my room had been freshly sprinkled and a warm vapor was rising from the red tiles. A moth flew around and around the naked bulb, dazzled by the light. I got out of the hammock and walked barefoot across the room, being careful not to step on a scorpion if one had come out of its hiding place to enjoy the coolness of the floor. I stood at the window for a few minutes, breathing in the air from the fields and listening to the vast, feminine breathing of the night. Then I walked over to the washstand, poured some water into the enamel basin, and moistened a towel. I rubbed my chest and legs with the damp cloth, dried myself a little, and got dressed, first making sure that no bugs had got into the seams of my clothes. I went leaping down the green-painted staircase and blundered into the hotelkeeper at the door. He was blind in one eye, a glum and reticent man, sitting there in a rush chair, smoking a cigarette, with his eyes half closed.

Now he peered at me with his good eye. "Where are you going, señor?" he asked in a hoarse voice.

"To take a walk. It's too hot to stay in my room."

"But everything's closed up by now. And we don't have any streetlights here. You'd better stay in."

I shrugged my shoulders, mumbled, "I'll be right back," and went out into the darkness. At first I couldn't see anything at all. I groped my way along the stone-paved street. I lit a cigarette. Suddenly the moon came out from behind a black cloud, lighting up a weather-beaten white wall. I stopped in my tracks, blinded by that whiteness. A faint breeze stirred the air and I could smell the fragrance of the tamarind trees. The night was murmurous with the sounds of leaves and insects. The crickets had bivouacked among the tall weeds. I raised my eyes: up there the stars were also camping out. I thought that the whole universe was a grand system of signals, a conversation among enormous beings. My own actions, the creak of a cricket, the blinking of a star, were merely pauses and syllables, odd fragments of that dialogue. I was only one syllable, of only one word. But what was that word? Who was uttering it? And to whom? I tossed my cigarette onto the sidewalk. It fell in a glowing arc, giving off sparks like a miniature comet.

I walked on, slowly, for a long while. I felt safe and free, because those great lips were pronouncing me so clearly, so joyously. The night was a garden of eyes.

Then when I was crossing a street I could tell that someone had come out of a doorway. I turned around but couldn't see anything. I began to walk faster. A moment later I could hear the scuff of huaraches on the warm stones. I didn't want to look back, even though I knew the shadow was catching up with me. I tried to run. I couldn't. Then I stopped short. And before I could defend myself I felt the point of a knife against my back, and a soft voice said, "Don't move, señor, or you're dead."

Without turning my head I asked, "What do you want?"

"Your eyes, señor." His voice was strangely gentle, almost embarrassed.

"My eyes? What are you going to do with my eyes? Look, I've got a little money on me. Not much, but it's something. I'll give you everything I've got if you'll let me go. Don't kill me."

"You shouldn't be scared, señor. I'm not going to kill you. I just want your eyes."

"But what do you want them for?"

"It's my sweetheart's idea. She'd like to have a bouquet of blue eyes. There aren't many people around here that have them."

"Mine won't do you any good. They aren't blue, they're light brown."

"No, señor. Don't try to fool me. I know they're blue."

"But we're both Christians, hombre! You can't just gouge my eyes out. I'll give you everything I've got on me."

"Don't be so squeamish." His voice was harsh now. "Turn around."

I turned around. He was short and slight, with a palm sombrero half covering his face. He had a long machete in his right hand. It glittered in the moonlight.

"Hold a match to your face."

I lit a match and held it up in front of my face. The flame made me close my eyes and he pried up my lids with his fingers. He couldn't see well enough, so he stood on tiptoes and stared at me. The match burned my fingers and I threw it away. He was silent for a moment.

"Aren't you sure now? They aren't blue."

"You're very clever, señor," he said. "Light another match."

I lit another and held it close to my eyes. He tugged at my sleeve. "Kneel down."

I knelt. He grabbed my hair and bent my head back. Then he leaned over me, gazing intently, and the machete came closer and closer till it touched my eyelids. I shut my eyes.

"Open them up," he told me. "Wide."

I opened my eyes again. The match-flame singed my lashes.

Suddenly he let go. "No. They're not blue. Excuse me." And he disappeared.

I huddled against the wall with my hands over my face. Later I got up and ran through the deserted streets for almost an hour. When I finally stumbled into the plaza I saw the hotelkeeper still sitting at the door. I went in without speaking to him. The next day I got out of that village.

[1961]
Translated by
LYSANDER KEMP

Questions

1. What do the blue eyes represent?
2. What aspects of surrealism have influenced Paz's story?
3. Is it possible to interpret the story literally, or is only a figurative interpretation valid?

Cristina Peri Rossi
(b. 1941)
(Uruguay/Spain)

C ristina Peri Rossi was born in Montevideo, Uruguay, November 12, 1941. She began teaching and writing in the early 1960s and subsequently immigrated to Barcelona in 1972. In Spain, she continued to pursue both of her professions; she was also a journalist for several leftist publications.

Although Peri Rossi has published 20 volumes of poetry and prose (both novels and short stories), little of her work has been translated into English. The three novels available in English are The Ship of Fools (La nave de los locos, 1984), Dostoevsky's Last Night (La ultima noche de Dostoievski, 1992), and Solitaire of Love (Una pasion prohibida, 2000). The Dictionary of Literary Biography states of the first: "The novel presents successive stories of outcasts bereft of belongings and companions, symbolic figures in perpetual flight conscious of traveling without a fixed destination and alienated from society." In the second novel, the author is fascinated with gambling, the addiction from which Dostoevsky suffered, though her setting is contemporary and her protagonist, Jorge, is only incidentally related to the great Russian writer.

"Mona Lisa" is from El Museo de los Esfuerzos Inutiles (1983). Harry Morales, the translator, ranks Peri Rossi as one of Latin America's major contemporary writers, based in part on the fact that her work has been translated into a dozen languages. In 1994, Peri Rossi was awarded a Guggenheim for her fiction.

MONA LISA

The first time I saw Gioconda, I fell in love with her. It was a lazy and misty autumn, and in the distance the outline of the trees and still lakes were dissolving, as in some paintings. It was a quick-moving mist that would muddy our faces and make us vaguely unreal. She dressed in black (a fabric which was nevertheless transparent) and I think someone told me she had lost a son. I saw her from a distance, like an apparition, and from that moment on, I became extremely sensitive about everything relating to her. I learned that she lived in another city, and that sometimes, she would take short walks to alleviate her grief. Immediately—and sometimes, very slowly—I learned about the things she preferred; I elicited her pleasures without even knowing what they were and endeavored to surround myself with objects which pleased her, with that rare quality of a lover for noticing small details, like a scrupulous collector. And, for want of her, I became a collector, looking for comfort in adjacent things. For a lover, nothing is superfluous.

I discovered that Giocondo, her husband, was in a dispute with a painter. He was a wealthy and crude businessman, having become rich in the fabric trade and, like all the people of his class, would set out to surround himself with expensive objects, even though he would haggle over their price. I quickly found out the name of the city in which they lived. It was a sonorous and sweet-sounding name; I was surprised, because I should have guessed it. It was a city of water, bridges, and small windows, built many centuries ago by merchants, Giocondo's ancestors, who, in order to compete with the noblemen and the bishops, hired painters and architects to beautify her, like a lady does with her maidens. They lived in an old, rebuilt palace, on whose facade Giocondo had commissioned gold inlays. Nevertheless, my informant made it clear to me that the most beautiful aspect of the palace's facade was a small landscape painting, a watercolor protected by a wooden frame, which represented the countryside, and in the middle of it, a misty lake, where a levitating skiff was barely depicted. "That was surely commissioned by Gioconda," I thought to myself.

I have to confess that since the first day I saw her, I haven't slept very much. My nights are filled with excitement: it's as if I have drunk too much or ingested some debilitating drug, because when I lie down, my imagination unfurls a somewhat orderly and feverish activity. I prepare ingenious designs, cultivate thousands of plans, and my ideas buzz like drunken bees; the excitement is so intense that I sweat and rush to start various tasks which I interrupt, sought after by another, until dawn, at which time I fall asleep, exhausted. My awakenings are confused and I remember very little about what I designed the night before. I feel depressed until the vision of Gioconda— I'm not a completely terrible designer and should confess that I've completed various drawings of her face since the memory of that first day I saw her—returns meaning to my days and cheers me up, like a secret accessory. I've completely neglected my wife. How do I explain to her what has happened, without betraying Gioconda? But I no longer share her bed, and try to spend all of my time outside, lost amongst the woods that are tenuously drawn in the mist of autumn: those sparse woods and lakes that I called to mind the first time I saw Gioconda and that since then accompany all of my drawings of her. One also falls in love with certain places that one unfailingly associates with the object of one's affection and experiences feverish walks through them, in solitude, but intimately accompanied.

I try to obtain information about the city in which she lives because I'm afraid that some unforeseen danger awaits her. I imagine terrible catastrophes—volcanic eruptions, tidal waves, fires, or the craziness of mankind—the cities, in our times, compete in aggressiveness and jealousy. Mentally, I try to control the river waters that cross her path, and I take the opportunity to take a walk with her over the bridges, those delightful, intimate and damp wooden bridges which creak under the soles of our feet. (I must confess that the first time I saw her, I was dazzled by the beauty of her face and didn't notice her feet. Oh, how there are gaps in our observations. Still, it isn't impossible to fill them, despite the perfection of the other areas. I know that this harmony is never achieved by human beings. But what is precisely amazing about her is the peaceful development and harmony of her traits, one by one, through which, after having seen a fragment, it's possible to imagine the whole).

I'm not worried about the passage of time. I know quite well that her beauty will resist it, endowed as she is with an element of transparency, an inner grace that doesn't depend on the succession of the autumns or the passage of months. Only a provoked act of terrible damage, the intervention of a murderous hand could disrupt that harmony. I'm not afraid for Giocondo, busy as he is with his financial transactions, indifferent to any value that couldn't be accumulated in a well-guarded chest, maintaining a relationship with Gioconda, which is as superficial as it is harmless. Which, up to a certain point, exonerates me from jealousy.

I turned into a miser a long time ago. I economize in every way I can in order to save the money that will allow me to go on the trip of my dreams. I've stopped smoking, I no longer go to the bar, I don't buy myself clothes, and I keep close watch over the management of the house, I carry out all the minor repairs that are necessary and enjoy all the things that men who aren't in love and immoral squander, surely because they no longer dream. I have scrupulously studied the ways I can reach that city, and I know that it won't be long before I can set out on the trip—this vision filling my days with intensity. I don't intend to communicate with Gioconda in any way. I'm sure she didn't notice me when I first saw her, nor would she have noticed any man whatsoever. Dominated by grief, her eyes would look without seeing, perhaps contemplating things that were in the past, and would lock themselves in the calm lakes where I keep on calling her to mind. When my wife questions me, I answer her with vague sentences. It's not only about keeping my secret: the most profound things almost never resist their translation into words.

But I know, I'm sure I can find her. Her unmistakable traits will be waiting for me in some location in the city. As for Giocondo, it seems that he's still in a dispute with a painter. Surely, he hasn't wanted to pay for a painting or is pretending to evict the painter from his studio if the man owes him something. Giocondo is insolent like the rich, and the poor painter must live from his work. My informant assures me that the dispute has been going on for almost three years, and that the painter has sworn to get revenge. What would my Gioconda say about all of this? Despite the reputation that the women in this city have for being concerned individuals, I know that she is unfamiliar with her husband's business affairs. The loss of her son is still recent and she can't find any consolation. Giocondo tries to cheer her up by hiring musicians who sing and dance in the garden, but she doesn't seem to hear them. Gioconda is listless, despite her luxurious low-necked gown. Unfortunately, I'm not a musician; otherwise, perhaps I could gain access to your palace. I would play the flute like no one else, calling to mind the lakes and woods where you usually take your walks in the fall, lakes which are seemingly suspended in the air and where, sometimes, a skiff is levitating. I would compose poetry and sonatas until you smiled softly, almost without wanting to, as a small reward for my work. Oh, that smile, Gioconda, would be a slight compromise, the certainty of having heard me.

I've reached the city of bridges, round lakes, and woods filled with mist that get lost in the horizon, among peaceful clouds. I walk along its narrow and winding streets, with its shaggy dogs and its markets filled with golden brown fruits and silk fabrics. Commerce is everywhere: the oranges and fishes recently pulled out of the sea are shining; the merchants' bids are buzzing in the air; and greedy shoppers monitor containers of gold, purchase lavish jewelry meticulously mounted, and argue over valuable pieces. The streets are damp and, in the distance, drifting woods are forming.

Immediately, I look for someone who can give me information about the Giocondo family. It isn't hard: In this city, everyone knows them; however, for some strange reason, when I interview them, they try to avoid the topic. I offer money; the few coins that I have remaining after the trip, but it's a prosperous city, and luckily for me, small. I try talking to merchants who politely offer me fabric and products from India and, afterwards, to the gondoliers who transport travelers from one location in the city to another. I should say that one of the most intense pleasures one can enjoy here is crossing certain areas in those slender and delicate vessels (which they take very good care of, as if they were precious objects, and decorate in good taste) that glide under the wooden bridges, barely disturbing the green waters. Finally, a young man, whom I pick out because of his humble appearance, but intelligent look, offers to give me information. He makes a terrible revelation to me: The painter whom Giocondo hired and has been in a dispute with for years decided to get his revenge. He's painted a thin moustache on Gioconda's lips, which no one can erase.

[1983]
Translated by
HARRY MORALES

Questions

1. What does a knowledge of Leonardo da Vinci and his famous painting reveal about Peri Rossi's short story?
2. What is the husband's significance in "Mona Lisa"?
3. What important facts does the narrator reveal about himself? What does he fail to tell us about himself?

Virgilio Piñera
(1912–1979)
Cuba

Cuban writer Virgilio Piñera explained that he called his short stories Cold Tales because, "as these are heated times, these Cold Tales should, I think, come in handy." Cold—he wanted us to believe—is synonymous with reality, the hard facts of life, and cold they are indeed. Piñera's images of life in modern Cuba—where his work was banned due to his homosexuality—are macabre and grotesque, often bordering on the taboo. The narrator of "A Few Children" confesses that he devours infants but limits himself to no more than four a year. A character in "Meat" can best be described as autocannibalistic. Two amputees (each with one leg) decide to buy a pair of shoes together in "Affairs of Amputees." Piñera's stories combine the fantasy of Latin American magic realism with the absurdity of Samuel Beckett and Eugene Ionesco.

Mark Schafer (Piñera's English translator) expands on Piñera's world in a brief foreword to the Eridanos Library edition of Cold Tales:

> The author maintains that life neither rewards nor punishes, neither condemns nor saves; or, to be more exact, does not distinguish these complicated categories. He can only say that he lives, that he is not obliged to judge his own acts, to give them any significance whatsoever, to expect vindication at the end of his days.

Except for the seven years from 1950 to 1957, Virgilio Piñera lived in Cuba—often at the poverty level and, for most of his life, in obscurity.

INSOMNIA

The man goes to bed early. He can't fall asleep. He tosses and turns in bed, as might be expected. He gets tangled in the sheets. He lights a cigarette. He reads a little. He turns out the light again. But he can't sleep. At three o'clock, he gets out of bed. He wakes his friend next door and confides that he can't sleep. He asks the friend for advice. The friend advises him to take a short walk to tire himself out. And then, right away, to drink a cup of linden blossom tea and turn out the light. He does all that, but is unable to fall asleep. He gets up again. This time he goes to see a doctor. As usual, the doctor talks a lot but the man still doesn't fall asleep. At six in the morning, he loads a revolver and blows his brains out. The man is dead, but hasn't been able to get to sleep. Insomnia is a very persistent thing.

[1956]
Translated by
MARK SCHAFER

Questions

1. In what sense does "Insomnia" defy categorization as a short story?
2. Of the classical unities (character, setting, time, and conflict) that often give short fiction its form, which—if any of these—apply to "Insomnia"?
3. Is insomnia the opposite of sleep or is it, in fact, something quite different?

Edgar Allan Poe
(1809–1849)
United States

E dgar Allan Poe is often called the father of the modern short story—not only as a result of his own unique tales but also as a result of the critical theory he formulated about the genre. In a famous review of Nathaniel Hawthorne's short stories, Poe wrote the following:

> A skillful literary artist has constructed a tale. If wise, he has not fashioned his thoughts to accommodate his incidents; but having conceived, with deliberate care, a certain unique or single effect to be wrought out, he then invents such incidents—he then combines such events as may best aid him in establishing this preconceived effect. If his very initial sentence tends not to be the outbringing of this effect, then he has failed in his first step. In the whole composition there should be no word written, of which the tendency, direct or indirect, is not to the one pre-established design. And by such means, with such care and skill, a picture is at length painted which leaves in the mind of him who contemplates it with a kindred art, a sense of the fullest satisfaction. The idea of the tale has been presented unblemished, because undisturbed; and this is an end unattainable by the novel. Undue brevity is just as exceptionable here as in the poem; but undue length is yet more to be avoided.

Much of Poe's writing career was typified by hardship and unhappiness. His wife, Virginia Clemm, died six years after they were married. Editors were unsympathetic to Poe's writing and often paid him poorly for his work. Even after his death, Poe's first biographer wouldn't let him rest in peace but conjured up an image of the writer as demonic and unbalanced. These psychological distortions of the man himself are not difficult to come by, however, if one looks at Poe's writings—especially many of his tales of terror or even his poems of frustrated love. Nevertheless, Poe's influence on the short story form cannot be denied. Perhaps the entire sense of modern American gothicism grows from Poe's fiction.

Another way to measure a writer's significance is by his later imitators. For that reason, we cannot resist quoting a parody of a Poe opening sentence (for that special effect) that appeared in a New York Magazine competition a number of years ago:

> Three days have passed since my master decreed that his wife, insatiable Lady Anne the Fat, be sent without food or drink to the bare dungeon, her sole companion a ravening crocodile: now, as I stare into Milady's mad yellow eyes, I slowly realize that she is quite alone in her cell.

THE CASK OF AMONTILLADO

The thousand injuries of Fortunato I had borne as I best could; but when he ventured upon insult, I vowed revenge. You, who so well know the nature of my soul, will not suppose, however, that I gave utterance to a threat. At length I would be avenged;

this was a point definitely settled—but the very definitiveness with which it was resolved precluded the idea of risk. I must not only punish, but punish with impunity. A wrong is unredressed when retribution overtakes its redresser. It is equally unredressed when the avenger fails to make himself felt as such to him who has done the wrong.

It must be understood, that neither by word nor deed had I given Fortunato cause to doubt my good-will. I continued, as was my wont, to smile in his face, and he did not perceive that my smile *now* was at the thought of his immolation.

He had a weak point—this Fortunato—although in other regards he was a man to be respected and even feared. He prided himself on his connoisseurship in wine. Few Italians have the true virtuoso spirit. For the most part their enthusiasm is adopted to suit the time and opportunity—to practise imposture upon the British and Austrian *millionnaires*. In painting and gemmary Fortunato, like his countrymen, was a quack—but in the matter of old wines he was sincere. In this respect I did not differ from him materially: I was skillful in the Italian vintages myself, and bought largely whenever I could.

It was about dusk, one evening during the supreme madness of the carnival season, that I encountered my friend. He accosted me with excessive warmth, for he had been drinking much. The man wore motley. He had on a tight-fitting parti-striped dress, and his head was surmounted by the conical cap and bells. I was so pleased to see him, that I thought I should never have done wringing his hand.

I said to him: "My dear Fortunato, you are luckily met. How remarkably well you are looking to-day! But I have received a pipe[1] of what passes for Amontillado, and I have my doubts."

"How?" said he. "Amontillado? A pipe? Impossible! And in the middle of the carnival!"

"I have my doubts," I replied; "and I was silly enough to pay the full Amontillado price without consulting you in the matter. You were not to be found, and I was fearful of losing a bargain."

"Amontillado!"

"I have my doubts."

"Amontillado!"

"And I must satisfy them."

"Amontillado!"

"As you are engaged, I am on my way to Luchesi. If any one has a critical turn, it is he. He will tell me——"

"Luchesi cannot tell Amontillado from Sherry."

"And yet some fools will have it that his taste is a match for your own."

"Come, let us go."

"Whither?"

"To your vaults."

"My friend, no; I will not impose upon your good nature. I perceive you have an engagement. Luchesi——"

"I have no engagement; —come."

"My friend, no. It is not the engagement, but the severe cold with which I perceive you are afflicted. The vaults are insufferably damp. They are encrusted with nitre."

---

[1]*pipe*   A cask or keg.

"Let us go, nevertheless. The cold is merely nothing. Amontillado! You have been imposed upon. And as for Luchesi, he cannot distinguish Sherry from Amontillado."

Thus speaking, Fortunato possessed himself of my arm. Putting on a mask of black silk, and drawing a *roquelaire*[2] closely about my person, I suffered him to hurry me to my palazzo.

There were no attendants at home; they had absconded to make merry in honor of the time. I had told them that I should not return until the morning, and had given them explicit orders not to stir from the house. These orders were sufficient, I well knew, to insure their immediate disappearance, one and all, as soon as my back was turned.

I took from their sconces two flambeaux, and giving one to Fortunato, bowed him through several suites of rooms to the archway that led into the vaults. I passed down a long and winding staircase, requesting him to be cautious as he followed. We came at length to the foot of the descent, and stood together on the damp ground of the catacombs of the Montresors.

The gait of my friend was unsteady, and the bells upon his cap jingled as he strode.

"The pipe?" said he.

"It is farther on," said I; "but observe the white web-work which gleams from these cavern walls."

He turned toward me, and looked into my eyes with two filmy orbs that distilled the rheum of intoxication.

"Nitre?" he asked, at length.

"Nitre," I replied., "How long have you had that cough?"

"Ugh! ugh! ugh!—ugh! ugh! ugh!—ugh! ugh! ugh!—ugh! ugh! ugh!—ugh! ugh! ugh!"

My poor friend found it impossible to reply for many minutes.

"It is nothing," he said, at last.

"Come," I said, with decision, "we will go back; your health is precious. You are rich, respected, admired, beloved; you are happy, as once I was. You are a man to be missed. For me it is no matter. We will go back; you will be ill, and I cannot be responsible. Besides, there is Luchesi——"

"Enough," he said; "the cough is a mere nothing; it will not kill me. I shall not die of a cough."

"True—true," I replied; "and, indeed, I had no intention of alarming you unnecessarily; but you should use all proper caution. A draught of this Medoc will defend us from the damps."

Here I knocked off the neck of a bottle which I drew from a long row of its fellows that lay upon the mould.

"Drink," I said, presenting him the wine.

He raised it to his lips with a leer. He paused and nodded to me familiarly, while his bells jingled.

"I drink," he said, "to the buried that repose around us."

"And I to your long life."

He again took my arm, and we proceeded.

"These vaults," he said, "are extensive."

"The Montresors," I replied. "were a great and numerous family."

"I forget your arms."

---

[2]*roquelaire* French: a short cloak.

"A huge human foot d'or,[3] in a field azure; the foot crushes a serpent rampant whose fangs are imbedded in the heel."

"And the motto?"

"*Nemo me impune lacessit.*"[4]

"Good!" he said.

The wine sparkled in his eyes and the bells jingled. My own fancy grew warm with the Medoc. We had passed through walls of piled bones, with casks and puncheons intermingling into the inmost recesses of the catacombs. I paused again, and this time I made bold to seize Fortunato by an arm above the elbow.

"The nitre!" I said; "see, it increases. It hangs like moss upon the vaults. We are below the river's bed. The drops of moisture trickle among the bones. Come, we will go back ere it is too late. Your cough————"

"It is nothing," he said; "let us go on. But first, another draught of the Medoc."

I broke and reached him a flagon of De Grâve. He emptied it at a breath. His eyes flashed with a fierce light. He laughed and threw the bottle upward with a gesticulation I did not understand.

I looked at him in surprise. He repeated the movement—a grotesque one.

"You do not comprehend?" he said.

"Not I," I replied.

"Then you are not of the brotherhood."

"How?"

"You are not of the masons."

"Yes, yes," I said; "yes, yes."

"You? Impossible! A mason?"

"A mason," I replied.

"A sign," he said.

"It is this," I answered, producing a trowel from beneath the folds of my *roquelaire.*

"You jest," he exclaimed, recoiling a few paces. "But let us proceed to the Amontillado."

"Be it so," I said, replacing the tool beneath the cloak, and again offering him my arm. He leaned upon it heavily. We continued our route in search of the Amontillado. We passed through a range of low arches, descended, passed on, and descending again, arrived at a deep crypt, in which the foulness of the air caused our flambeaux rather to glow than flame.

At the most remote end of the crypt there appeared another less spacious. Its walls had been lined with human remains, piled to the vault overhead, in the fashion of the great catacombs of Paris. Three sides of this interior crypt were still ornamented in this manner. From the fourth the bones had been thrown down, and lay promiscuously upon the earth, forming at one point a mound of some size. Within the wall thus exposed by the displacing of the bones, we perceived a still interior recess, in depth about four feet, in width three, in height six or seven. It seemed to have been constructed for no especial use within itself, but formed merely the interval between two of the colossal supports of the roof of the catacombs, and was backed by one of their circumscribing walls of solid granite.

---

[3]*d'or*   French: of gold.
[4]*Nemo me impune lacessit*   Latin: No one may insult me with impunity.

It was in vain that Fortunato, uplifting his dull torch, endeavored to pry into the depth of the recess. Its termination the feeble light did not enable us to see.

"Proceed," I said; "herein is the Amontillado. As for Luchesi————"

"He is an ignoramus," interrupted my friend, as he stepped unsteadily forward, while I followed immediately at his heels. In an instant he had reached the extremity of the niche, and finding his progress arrested by the rock, stood stupidly bewildered. A moment more and I had fettered him to the granite. In its surface were two iron staples, distant from each other about two feet, horizontally. From one of these depended a short chain, from the other a padlock. Throwing the links about his waist, it was but the work of a few seconds to secure it. He was too much astounded to resist. Withdrawing the key I stepped back from the recess.

"Pass your hand," I said, "over the wall; you cannot help feeling the nitre. Indeed it is *very* damp. Once more let me *implore* you to return. No? Then I must positively leave you. But I must first render you all the little attentions in my power."

"The Amontillado!" ejaculated my friend, not yet recovered from his astonishment.

"True," I replied; "the Amontillado."

As I said these words I busied myself among the pile of bones of which I have before spoken. Throwing them aside, I soon uncovered a quantity of building stone and mortar. With these materials and with the aid of my trowel, I began vigorously to wall up the entrance of the niche.

I had scarcely laid the first tier of the masonry when I discovered that the intoxication of Fortunato had in a great measure worn off. The earliest indication I had of this was a low moaning cry from the depth of the recess. It was *not* the cry of a drunken man. There was then a long and obstinate silence. I laid the second tier, and the third, and the fourth; and then I heard the furious vibrations of the chain. The noise lasted for several minutes, during which, that I might hearken to it with the more satisfaction, I ceased my labors and sat down upon the bones. When at last the clanking subsided, I resumed the trowel, and finished without interruption the fifth, the sixth, and the seventh tier. The wall was now nearly upon a level with my breast. I again paused, and holding the flambeaux over the masonwork, threw a few feeble rays upon the figure within.

A succession of loud and shrill screams, bursting suddenly from the throat of the chained form, seemed to thrust me violently back. For a brief moment I hesitated— I trembled. Unsheathing my rapier, I began to grope with it about the recess; but the thought of an instant reassured me. I placed my hand upon the solid fabric of the catacombs, and felt satisfied. I reapproached the wall. I replied to the yells of him who clamored. I reechoed—I aided—I surpassed them in volume and in strength. I did this, and the clamorer grew still.

It was now midnight, and my task was drawing to a close. I had completed the eighth, the ninth, and the tenth tier. I had finished a portion of the last and the eleventh; there remained but a single stone to be fitted and plastered in. I struggled with its weight; I placed it partially in its destined position. But now there came from out the niche a low laugh that erected the hairs upon my head. It was succeeded by a sad voice, which I had difficulty in recognizing as that of the noble Fortunato. The voice said—

"Ha! ha! ha!—he! he!—a very good joke indeed—an excellent jest. We will have many a rich laugh about it at the palazzo—he! he! he!—over our wine—he! he! he!"

"The Amontillado!" I said.

"He! he! he!—he! he! he!—yes, the Amontillado. But is it not getting late? Will not they be awaiting us at the palazzo, the Lady Fortunato and the rest? Let us be gone."

"Yes," I said, "let us be gone."

"*For the love of God, Montresor!*"

"Yes," I said, "for the love of God!"

But to these words I hearkened in vain for a reply. I grew impatient. I called aloud:

"Fortunato!"

No answer. I called again:

"Fortunato!"

No answer still, I thrust a torch through the remaining aperture and let it fall within. There came forth in return only a jingling of the bells. My heart grew sick—on account of the dampness of the catacombs. I hastened to make an end of my labor. I forced the last stone into its position; I plastered it up. Against the new masonry I re-erected the old rampart of bones. For the half of a century no mortal has disturbed them. *In pace requiescat!*[5]

[1846]

Questions

1. Does Montresor achieve his goal? Is he able to gain his revenge and "punish with impunity"?
2. In what way is the setting of Poe's story symbolic?
3. Is the pun on the masons/masonry of any further significance?
4. Does Fortunato realize what has happened to him by the end of the story? Is he insane? How is insanity used in the story?

---

[5]*In pace requiescat!*   Latin: Rest in peace!

Katherine Anne Porter

(1890–1980)

United States

Katherine Anne Porter is widely acknowledged as one of the twentieth-century masters of the short story form. Her meticulously crafted stories embody her life-long attempt to, as she expressed it, "discover and understand human motives, human feeling, to make a distillation of what human relations and experiences my mind has been able to absorb. I have never known an uninteresting human being, and I have never known two alike."

Born in Texas, Porter moved frequently, writing continuously—although she destroyed most of what she wrote before the age of 30. She was married three times and worked in a variety of jobs to support herself, including writing for a newspaper and performing bit parts in films. In 1918 she contracted influenza and nearly died during the great epidemic that swept the world that year. Her collection of three novellas, Pale Horse, Pale Rider (1939), incorporates her experience of serious illness. In 1921 Porter went to Mexico to study Aztec and Mayan art and became involved with a revolutionary movement. Later she traveled widely in Europe.

Porter published only one novel, Ship of Fools (1962), which was made into a successful Hollywood film that secured her economic independence. In the novel, which took 20 years to write, she explores the relations among passengers on the transatlantic voyage of a German ship, a microcosm of pre-World War II European society. The novel is allegorical, kaleidoscopic, and episodic—in fact, more like a series of short stories. Most critics believe that it betrays Porter working against the grain of her true talent, the short story form. Through stories collected in Flowering Judas (1930), The Leaning Tower (1944), and several other volumes, she wrote precisely controlled narratives that focus less on plot than on their fully realized characters' illuminating perceptions of experience.

ROPE

On the third day after they moved to the country he came walking back from the village carrying a basket of groceries and a twenty-four-yard coil of rope. She came out to meet him, wiping her hands on her green smock. Her hair was tumbled, her nose was scarlet with sunburn; he told her that already she looked like a born country woman. His gray flannel shirt stuck to him, his heavy shoes were dusty. She assured him he looked like a rural character in a play.

Had he brought the coffee? She had been waiting all day long for coffee. They had forgot it when they ordered at the store the first day.

Gosh, no, he hadn't. Lord, now he'd have to go back. Yes, he would if it killed him. He thought, though, he had everything else. She reminded him it was only because he didn't drink coffee himself. If he did he would remember it quick enough. Suppose they ran out of cigarettes? Then she saw the rope. What was that for? Well, he thought it might do to hang clothes on, or something. Naturally she asked him if he thought they were going to run a laundry? They already had a fifty-foot line hanging right before his eyes? Why, hadn't he noticed it, really? It was a blot on the landscape to her.

He thought there were a lot of things a rope might come in handy for. She wanted to know what, for instance. He thought a few seconds, but nothing occurred. They could wait and see, couldn't they? You need all sorts of strange odds and ends around a place in the country. She said, yes, that was so; but she thought just at that time when every penny counted, it seemed funny to buy more rope. That was all. She hadn't meant anything else. She hadn't just seen, not at first, why he felt it was necessary.

Well, thunder, he had bought it because he wanted to, and that was all there was to it. She thought that was reason enough, and couldn't understand why he hadn't said so, at first. Undoubtedly it would be useful, twenty-four yards of rope, there were hundreds of things, she couldn't think of any at the moment, but it would come in. Of course. As he had said, things always did in the country.

But she was a little disappointed about the coffee, and oh, look, look, look at the eggs! Oh, my, they're all running! What had he put on top of them? Hadn't he known eggs mustn't be squeezed? Squeezed, who had squeezed them, he wanted to know. What a silly thing to say. He had simply brought them along in the basket with the other things. If they got broke it was the grocer's fault. He should know better than to put heavy things on top of eggs.

She believed it was the rope. That was the heaviest thing in the pack, she saw him plainly when he came in from the road, the rope was a big package on top of everything. He desired the whole wide world to witness that this was not a fact. He had carried the rope in one hand and the basket in the other, and what was the use of her having eyes if that was the best they could do for her?

Well, anyhow, she could see one thing plain: no eggs for breakfast. They'd have to scramble them now, for supper. It was too damned bad. She had planned to have steak for supper. No ice, meat wouldn't keep. He wanted to know why she couldn't finish breaking the eggs in a bowl and set them in a cool place.

Cool place! If he could find one for her, she'd be glad to set them there. Well, then, it seemed to him they might very well cook the meat at the same time they cooked the eggs and then warm up the meat for tomorrow. The idea simply choked her. Warmed-over meat, when they might as well have had it fresh. Second best and scraps and makeshifts, even to the meat! He rubbed her shoulder a little. It doesn't really matter so much, does it, darling? Sometimes when they were playful, he would rub her shoulder and she would arch and purr. This time she hissed and almost clawed. He was getting ready to say that they could surely manage somehow when she turned on him and said, if he told her they could manage somehow she would certainly slap his face.

He swallowed the words red hot, his face burned. He picked up the rope and started to put it on the top shelf. She would not have it on the top shelf, the jars and tins belonged there; positively she would not have the top shelf cluttered up with a lot of rope. She had borne all the clutter she meant to bear in the flat in town, there was space here at least and she meant to keep things in order.

Well, in that case, he wanted to know what the hammer and nails were doing up there? And why had she put them there when she knew very well he needed that hammer and those nails upstairs to fix the window sashes? She simply slowed down everything and made double work on the place with her insane habit of changing things around and hiding them.

She was sure she begged his pardon, and if she had had any reason to believe he was going to fix the sashes this summer she would have left the hammer and nails right where he put them; in the middle of the bedroom floor where they could step on them in the dark. And now if he didn't clear the whole mess out of there she would throw them down the well.

Oh, all right, all right—could he put them in the closet? Naturally not, there were brooms and mops and dustpans in the closet, and why couldn't he find a place for his rope outside her kitchen? Had he stopped to consider there were seven God-forsaken rooms in the house, and only one kitchen?

He wanted to know what of it? And did she realize she was making a complete fool of herself? And what did she take him for, a three-year-old idiot? The whole trouble with her was she needed something weaker than she was to heckle and tyrannize over. He wished to God now they had a couple of children she could take it out on. Maybe he'd get some rest.

Her face changed at this, she reminded him he had forgot the coffee and had bought a worthless piece of rope. And when she thought of all the things they actually needed to make the place even decently fit to live in, well, she could cry, that was all. She looked so forlorn, so lost and despairing he couldn't believe it was only a piece of rope that was causing all the racket. What *was* the matter, for God's sake?

Oh, would he please hush and go away, and *stay* away, if he could, for five minutes? By all means, yes, he would. He'd stay away indefinitely if she wished. Lord, yes, there was nothing he'd like better than to clear out and never come back. She couldn't for the life of her see what was holding him, then. It was a swell time. Here she was, stuck, miles from a railroad, with a half-empty house on her hands, and not a penny in her pocket, and everything on earth to do; it seemed the God-sent moment for him to get out from under. She was surprised he hadn't stayed in town as it was until she had come out and done the work and got things straightened out. It was his usual trick.

It appeared to him that this was going a little far. Just a touch out of bounds, if she didn't mind his saying so. Why the hell had he stayed in town the summer before? To do a half-dozen extra jobs to get the money he had sent her. That was it. She knew perfectly well they couldn't have done it otherwise. She had agreed with him at the time. And that was the only time so help him he had ever left her to do anything by herself.

Oh, he could tell that to his great-grandmother. She had her notion of what had kept him in town. Considerably more than a notion, if he wanted to know. So, she was going to bring all that up again, was she? Well, she could just think what she pleased. He was tired of explaining. It may have looked funny but he had simply got hooked in, and what could he do? It was impossible to believe that she was going to take it seriously. Yes, yes, she knew how it was with a man: if he was left by himself a minute, some woman was certain to kidnap him. And naturally he couldn't hurt her feelings by refusing!

Well, what was she raving about? Did she forget she had told him those two weeks alone in the country were the happiest she had known for four years? And how long had they been married when she said that? All right, shut up! If she thought that hadn't stuck in his craw.

She hadn't meant she was happy because she was away from him. She meant she was happy getting the devilish house nice and ready for him. That was what she had meant, and now look! Bringing up something she had said a year ago simply to justify himself for forgetting her coffee and breaking the eggs and buying a wretched piece of rope they couldn't afford. She really thought it was time to drop the subject, and now she wanted only two things in the world. She wanted him to get that rope from underfoot, and go back to the village and get her coffee, and if he could remember it, he might bring a metal mitt for the skillets, and two more curtain rods, and if there were any rubber gloves in the village, her hands were simply raw, and a bottle of milk of magnesia from the drugstore.

He looked out at the dark blue afternoon sweltering on the slopes, and mopped his forehead and sighed heavily and said, if only she could wait a minute for *anything*, he was going back. He had said so, hadn't he, the very instant they found he had overlooked it?

Oh, yes, well . . . run along. She was going to wash windows. The country was so beautiful! She doubted they'd have a moment to enjoy it. He meant to go, but he could not until he had said that if she wasn't such a hopeless melancholiac she might see that this was only for a few days. Couldn't she remember anything pleasant about the other summers? Hadn't they ever had any fun? She hadn't time to talk about it, and now would he please not leave that rope lying around for her to trip on? He picked it up, somehow it had toppled off the table, and walked out with it under his arm.

Was he going this minute? He certainly was. She thought so. Sometimes it seemed to her he had second sight about the precisely perfect moment to leave her ditched. She had meant to put the mattresses out to sun, if they put them out this minute they would get at least three hours, he must have heard her say that morning she meant to put them out. So of course he would walk off and leave her to it. She supposed he thought the exercise would do her good.

Well, he was merely going to get her coffee. A four-mile walk for two pounds of coffee was ridiculous, but he was perfectly willing to do it. The habit was making a wreck of her, but if she wanted to wreck herself there was nothing he could so about it. If he thought it was coffee that was making a wreck of her, she congratulated him: he must have a damned easy conscience.

Conscience or no conscience, he didn't see why the mattresses couldn't very well wait until tomorrow. And anyhow, for God's sake, were they living in the house, or were they going to let the house ride them to death? She paled at this, her face grew livid about the mouth, she looked quite dangerous, and reminded him that housekeeping was no more her work than it was his: she had other work to do as well, and when did he think she was going to find time to do it at this rate?

Was she going to start on that again? She knew as well as he did that his work brought in the regular money, hers was only occasional, if they depended on what *she* made—and she might as well get straight on this question once for all!

That was positively not the point. The question was, when both of them were working on their own time, was there going to be a division of the housework, or wasn't there? She merely wanted to know, she had to make her plans. Why, he thought that was all arranged. It was understood that he was to help. Hadn't he always, in summers?

Hadn't he, though? Oh, just hadn't he? And when, and where, and doing what? Lord, what an uproarious joke!

It was such a very uproarious joke that her face turned slightly purple, and she screamed with laughter. She laughed so hard she had to sit down, and finally a rush of tears spurted from her eyes and poured down into the lifted corners of her mouth. He dashed towards her and dragged her up to her feet and tried to pour water on her head. The dipper hung by a string on a nail and he broke it loose. Then he tried to pump water with one hand while she struggled in the other. So he gave it up and shook her instead.

She wrenched away, crying out for him to take his rope and go to hell, she had simply given him up: and ran. He heard her high-heeled bedroom slippers clattering and stumbling on the stairs.

He went out around the house and into the lane; he suddenly realized he had a blister on his heel and his shirt felt as if it were on fire. Things broke so suddenly you didn't know where you were. She could work herself into a fury about simply nothing. She was terrible, damn it: not an ounce of reason. You might as well talk to a sieve as that woman when she got going. Damned if he'd spend his life humoring her. Well, what to do now? He would take back the rope and exchange it for something else. Things accumulated, things were mountainous, you couldn't move them or sort them out or get rid of them. They just lay and rotted around. He'd take it back. Hell, why should he? He wanted it. What was it anyhow? A piece of rope. Imagine anybody caring more about a piece of rope than about a man's feelings. What earthly right had she to say a word about it? He remembered all the useless, meaningless things she bought for herself. Why? Because I wanted it, that's why! He stopped and selected a large stone by the road. He would put the rope behind it. He would put it in the toolbox when he got back. He'd heard enough about it to last him a life-time.

When he came back she was leaning against the post box beside the road waiting. It was pretty late, the smell of broiled steak floated nose high in the cooling air. Her face was young and smooth and freshlooking. Her unmanageable funny black hair was all on end. She waved to him from a distance, and he speeded up. She called out that supper was ready and waiting, was he starved?

You bet he was starved. Here was the coffee. He waved it at her. She looked at his other hand. What was that he had there?

Well, it was the rope again. He stopped short. He had meant to exchange it but forgot. She wanted to know why he should exchange it, if it was something he really wanted. Wasn't the air sweet now, and wasn't it fine to be here?

She walked beside him with one hand hooked into his leather belt. She pulled and jostled him a little as he walked, and leaned against him. He put his arm clear around her and patted her stomach. They exchanged wary smiles. Coffee, coffee for the Ootsum-Wootsums! He felt as if he were bringing her a beautiful present.

He was a love, she firmly believed, and if she had had her coffee in the morning, she wouldn't have behaved so funny. . . . There was a whippoorwill still coming back, imagine, clear out of season, sitting in the crab-apple tree calling all by himself. Maybe his girl stood him up. Maybe she did. She hoped to hear him once more, she loved whippoorwills. . . . He knew how she was, didn't he?

Sure, he knew how she was.

[1930]

Questions

1. What is the central conflict of the story? What are the husband and wife really disagreeing about?

2. What meanings does the rope acquire during the story for the husband and the wife? For the reader?

3. What is the significance of the story's resolution?

Rodrigo Rey Rosa
(b. 1958)
Guatemala

R odrigo Rey Rosa, who was born in Guatemala in 1958, bases many of his stories on legends and myths indigenous to Latin America and North Africa. Three collections of his stories have appeared in English, The Path Doubles Back (1982), The Beggar's Knife (1985), and Dust on Her Tongue (1989), and an experimental novel, The Pelcari Project (1991). In explanation of his fiction for Sudden Fiction, Rey Rosa wrote the following:

> I like to believe that stories want to be written, that they must make an effort in order to be heard. They suggest themselves to me constantly, but I have little patience, I am lazy. Now and then, however, when I'm in the right mood, I stop to listen to one and sit down to record it. I think that by now they know I am not patient, so they make themselves short.

Rey Rosa has lived in Tangier, Morocco, since 1980. There his fiction captured the attention of author Paul Bowles, who began translating his stories into English.

THE PROOF

One night while his parents were still on the highway returning from someone's birthday party, Miguel went into the living room and stopped in front of the canary's cage. He lifted up the cloth covering the cage and opened the tiny door. Fearfully, he slipped his hand inside, and then withdrew it doubled into a fist, with the bird's head protruding between his fingers. It allowed itself to be seized almost without resistance, showing the resignation of a person with a chronic illness, thinking perhaps that it was being taken out so the cage could be cleaned and the seeds replenished. But Miguel was staring at it with the eager eyes of one seeking an omen.

All the lights in the house were turned on. Miguel had gone through all the rooms, hesitating at each corner. God can see you no matter where you are, Miguel told himself, but there are not many places suitable for invoking Him. Finally he decided on the cellar because it was dark there. He crouched in a corner under the high vaulted ceiling, as Indians and savages do, face down, his arms wrapped around his legs, and with the canary in his fist between his knees. Raising his eyes into the darkness, which at that moment looked red, he said in a low voice: "If you exist, God, bring this bird back to life." As he spoke, he tightened his fist little by little, until his fingers felt the snapping of the fragile bones and an unaccustomed stillness in the little body.

Then, without meaning to, he remembered María Luisa the maid, who took care of the canary. A little later, when he finally, opened his hand, it was as if another, larger hand had been placed on his back—the hand of fear. He realized that the bird would not come back to life. If God did not exist, it was absurd to fear His punishment. The image, the concept of God went out of his mind, leaving a blank. Then, for an instant, Miguel thought of the shape of evil, of Satan, but he did not dare ask anything of him.

He heard the sound of the car going into the garage over his head. Now the fear had to do with this world. His parents had arrived; he heard their voices, heard the car doors slam and the sound of a woman's heels on the stone floor. He laid the inert little body on the floor in the corner, groped in the dark for a loose brick, and set it on top of the bird. Then he heard the chiming of the bell at the front door, and ran upstairs to greet his parents.

"All the lights on!" exclaimed his mother as he kissed her.

"What were you doing down there?" his father asked him.

"Nothing. I was afraid. The empty house scares me."

His mother went through the house, turning lights off right and left, secretly astonished by her son's fear.

That night Miguel had his first experience of insomnia. For him not sleeping was a kind of nightmare from which there was no hope of awakening. A static nightmare: the dead bird beneath the brick, and the empty cage.

Hours later Miguel heard the front door open, and the sound of footsteps downstairs. Paralyzed by fear, he fell asleep. María Luisa the maid had finally arrived. It was seven o'clock; the day was still dark. She turned on the kitchen light, set her basket on the table, and, as was her custom, removed her sandals in order not to make any noise. She went into the living room and uncovered the canary's cage. The little door was open and the cage was empty. After a moment of panic, during which her eyes remained fixed on the cage hanging in front of her, she glanced around, covered the cage again and returned to the kitchen. Very carefully she took up her sandals and the basket, and went out. When she was no longer in sight of the house she put the sandals on and started to run in the direction of the market, where she hoped to find another canary. It was necessary to replace the one which she thought had escaped due to her carelessness.

Miguel's father awoke at quarter past seven. He went down to the kitchen and, surprised to see that María Luisa had not yet come, decided to go to the cellar for the oranges and squeeze them himself. Before going back up to the kitchen, he tried to turn off the light, but with his hands and arms laden with oranges, he had to use his shoulders to push the switch. One of the oranges slipped from his arm and rolled across the floor into a corner. He pushed the light on once more. Placing the oranges on a chair, he formed a bag out of the front of his bathrobe, dropped the oranges into it, and went to pick up the one in the corner. And then he noticed the bird's wing sticking out from under the brick. It was not easy for him, but he could guess what had happened. Everyone knows that children are cruel, but how should he react? His wife's footsteps sounded above him in the kitchen. He was ashamed of his son, and at the same time he felt that they were accomplices. He had to hide the shame and the guilt as if they were his own. He picked up the brick, put the bird in his bathrobe pocket, and climbed up to the kitchen. Soon he went on upstairs to his room to wash and dress.

A little later, as he left the house, he met María Luisa returning from the market with the new canary hidden in her basket. She greeted him in an odd fashion, but he did not notice it. He was upset: the hand that he kept in his pocket held the bird in it.

As María Luisa went into the house, she heard the voice of Miguel's mother on the floor above. She put the basket on the floor, took out the canary, and ran to slip it into the cage, which she then uncovered with an air of relief and triumph. But then when she drew back the window curtains and the sun's rays tinted the room pink, she saw with alarm that the bird had one black foot.

It was impossible to awaken Miguel. His mother had to carry him into the bathroom, where she turned on the tap and with her wet hand gave his face a few slaps. Miguel opened his eyes. Then his mother helped him dress and get down the stairs. She seated him at the kitchen table. After he had taken a few swallows of orange juice, he managed to rid himself of his sleepiness. The clock on the wall marked quarter to eight; shortly María Luisa would be coming in to get him and walk with him to the corner where the school bus stopped. When his mother went out of the room, Miguel jumped down from his chair and ran down into the cellar. Without turning on the light he went to look for the brick in the corner. Then he rushed back to the door and switched on the light. With the blood pounding in his head, he returned to the corner, lifted the brick, and saw that the bird was not there.

María Luisa was waiting for him in the kitchen. He avoided her and ran to the living room. She hurried after him. When on entering the room he saw the cage by the window, with the canary hopping from one perch to the other, he stopped short. He would have gone nearer to make certain, but María Luisa seized his hand and pulled him along to the front door.

On his way to the factory, Miguel's father was wondering what he would say to his son when he got home that night. The highway was empty. The weather was unusual: flat clouds like steps barred the sky, and near the horizon there were curtains of fog and light. He lowered the window, and at the moment the car crossed a bridge over a deep gully, he took one hand off the steering wheel and tossed the bird's tiny corpse out.

In the city while they waited on the corner for the bus, María Luisa listened to the account of the proof Miguel had been granted. The bus appeared in the distance, in miniature at the end of the street. María Luisa smiled.

"Perhaps that canary isn't what you think it is," she said to Miguel in a mysterious voice. "You have to look at it very close. If it has a black foot, it was sent by the Devil."

Miguel stared into her eyes, his face tense. She seized him by the shoulders and turned him around. The bus had arrived; its door was open. Miguel stepped onto the platform. "Dirty witch!" he shouted.

The driver started up. Miguel ran to the back of the bus and sat down by the window in the last row of seats. There was the squeal of tires, a horn sounded, and Miguel conjured up the image of his father's car.

At the last stop before the school, the bus took on a plump boy with narrow eyes. Miguel made a place for him at his side.

"How's everything?" the boy asked him as he sat down.

The bus ran between the rows of poplars, while Miguel and his friend spoke of the power of God.

[1987]
Translated by
PAUL BOWLES

Questions

1. Is Miguel's experiment with faith successful? What does he conclude about God?
2. How does the author use humor to explore serious questions concerning religious belief and doubt?
3. Consider the development of the plot, based on each character's limited understanding of circumstances. How does this structure contribute to the story's effectiveness?

Salman Rushdie

(b. 1947)

(India/England)

On Valentine's Day in 1989, when the Ayatollah Khomeini imposed a death sentence, a fatwa, on writer Salman Rushdie, the Western literary/intellectual establishment was shaken to its roots. Here was something frightfully unfathomable. The Ayatollah accused Rushdie of blasphemy in his fourth novel, The Satanic Verses, and a bounty was immediately placed on the author's head. Anyone who could kill him would be awarded $1 million. The novel had been published in September of the previous year, resulting in an almost immediate furor in India and Pakistan. A Muslim member of parliament in India protested that The Satanic Verses was "an indecent vilification of the Holy Prophet," leading to a banning of the book. Throughout the world, copies of the novel were burned; in Islamabad, Pakistan, an enraged mob stormed the American Culture Center and five of the demonstrators were killed. Violence occurred elsewhere, resulting in the Ayatollah's pronouncement on February 14.

Rushdie was immediately placed under protection by the British police and taken into hiding, where his life took him down a pathway few writers could even imagine:

> I feel as if I have been plunged, like Alice, into the world beyond the looking-glass, where nonsense is the only available sense. And I wonder if I'll ever be able to climb back through the mirror.
>
> Do I feel regret? Of course I do: regret that such offence has been taken against my work when it was not intended—when dispute was intended, and dissent, and even, at times, satire, and criticism of intolerance, and the like, but not the thing of which I'm most often accused, not "filth," not "insult," not "abuse." I regret that so many people who might have taken pleasure in finding their reality given pride of place in a novel will now not read it because of what they believe it to be, or will come to it with their minds already made up.
>
> And I feel sad to be so grievously separated from my community, from India, from everyday life, from the world. (The New Yorker, 25 Dec. 1995)

Before the ten-year span of the fatwa, Rushdie had been one of the most talked about and admired post-colonial writers. Schooled in India and subsequently in England, he published his first novel, Grimus, in 1975. With Midnight's Children (1981), fame was almost immediate; the novel was awarded Britain's prestigious Booker Prize. Shame (1983) was equally admired and praised, followed five years later by The Satanic Verses. During the years of hiding, Rushdie nonetheless continued to write, publishing several volumes of non-fiction, a children's book, and a collection of short stories, East, West (1994). But it wasn't until 1995 that he returned to the novel form with The Moor's Last Sigh (1996) and, subsequently, The Ground Beneath Her Feet (1999).

Always a controversial writer—there were bannings of Midnight's Children and Shame before the controversy surrounding The Satanic Verses—Salman Rushdie has perhaps been more admired and vilified than any other contemporary writer. When the Booker Prize was 25 years old, Midnight's Children was again celebrated as *the most significant work on the list of distinguished titles. Taken together, Rushdie's incredible literary output—even under the weight of unbearable adversity—always breaks new ground, fusing politics, myth, history, fantasy, and controversy into a unique and unforgettable blend.*

THE PROPHET'S HAIR

Early in the year 19—, when Srinagar was under the spell of a winter so fierce it could crack men's bones as if they were glass, a young man upon whose cold-pinked skin there lay, like a frost, the unmistakable sheen of wealth was to be seen entering the most wretched and disreputable part of the city, where the houses of wood and corrugated iron seemed perpetually on the verge of losing their balance, and asking in low, grave tones where he might go to engage the services of a dependably professional burglar. The young man's name was Atta, and the rogues in that part of town directed him gleefully into ever darker and less public alleys, until in a yard wet with the blood of a slaughtered chicken he was set upon by two men whose faces he never saw, robbed of the substantial bank-roll which he had insanely brought on his solitary excursion, and beaten within an inch of his life.

Night fell. His body was carried by anonymous hands to the edge of the lake, whence it was transported by shikara across the water and deposited, torn and bleeding, on the deserted embankment of the canal which led to the gardens of Shalimar. At dawn the next morning a flower-vendor was rowing his boat through water to which the cold of the night had given the cloudy consistency of wild honey when he saw the prone form of young Atta, who was just beginning to stir and moan, and on whose now deathly pale skin the sheen of wealth could still be made out dimly beneath an actual layer of frost.

The flower-vendor moored his craft and by stooping over the mouth of the injured man was able to learn the poor fellow's address, which was mumbled through lips that could scarcely move; whereupon, hoping for a large tip, the hawker rowed Atta home to a large house on the shores of the lake, where a beautiful but inexplicably bruised young woman and her distraught, but equally handsome mother, neither of whom, it was clear from their eyes, had slept a wink from worrying, screamed at the sight of their Atta—who was the elder brother of the beautiful young woman—lying motionless amidst the funereally stunted winter blooms of the hopeful florist.

The flower-vendor was indeed paid off handsomely, not least to ensure his silence, and plays no further part in our story. Atta himself, suffering terribly from exposure as well as a broken skull, entered a coma which caused the city's finest doctors to shrug helplessly. It was therefore all the more remarkable that on the very next evening the most wretched and disreputable part of the city received a second unexpected visitor. This was Huma, the sister of the unfortunate young man, and her question was the same as her brother's, and asked in the same low, grave tones: "Where may I hire a thief?"

The story of the rich idiot who had come looking for a burglar was already common knowledge in those insalubrious gullies, but this time the young woman added: 'I should say that I am carrying no money, nor am I wearing any jewellery items. My father has disowned me and will pay no ransom if I am kidnapped; and a letter has been lodged with the Deputy Commissioner of Police, my uncle, to be opened in the event of my not being safe at home by morning. In that letter he will find full details of my journey here, and he will move Heaven and Earth to punish my assailants.'

Her exceptional beauty, which was visible even through the enormous welts and bruises disfiguring her arms and forehead, coupled with the oddity of her inquiries, had attracted a sizable group of curious onlookers, and because her little speech seemed to them to cover just about everything, no one attempted to injure her in any way, although there were some raucous comments to the effect that it was pretty peculiar for someone who was trying to hire a crook to invoke the protection of a high-up policeman uncle.

She was directed into ever darker and less public alleys until finally in a gully as dark as ink an old woman with eyes which stared so piercingly that Huma instantly understood she was blind motioned her through a doorway from which darkness seemed to be pouring like smoke. Clenching her fists, angrily ordering her heart to behave normally, Huma followed the old woman into the gloom-wrapped house.

The faintest conceivable rivulet of candlelight trickled through the darkness; following this unreliable yellow thread (because she could no longer see the old lady), Huma received a sudden sharp blow to the shins and cried out involuntarily, after which she at once bit her lip, angry at having revealed her mounting terror to whoever or whatever waited before her, shrouded in blackness.

She had, in fact, collided with a low table on which a single candle burned and beyond which a mountainous figure could be made out, sitting cross-legged on the floor. "Sit, sit," said a man's calm, deep voice, and her legs, needing no more flowery invitation, buckled beneath her at the terse command. Clutching her left hand in her right, she forced her voice to respond evenly:

"And you, sir, will be the thief I have been requesting?"

Shifting its weight very slightly, the shadow-mountain informed Huma that all criminal activity originating in this zone was well organised and also centrally controlled, so that all requests for what might be termed freelance work had to be channelled through this room.

He demanded comprehensive details of the crime to be committed, including a precise inventory of items to be acquired, also a clear statement of all financial inducements being offered with no gratuities excluded, plus, for filing purposes only, a summary of the motives for the application.

At this, Huma, as though remembering something, stiffened both in body and resolve and replied loudly that her motives were entirely a matter for herself; that she would discuss details with no one but the thief himself; but that the rewards she proposed could only be described as "lavish."

"All I am willing to disclose to you, sir, since it appears that I am on the premises of some sort of employment agency, is that in return for such lavish rewards I must have the most desperate criminal at your disposal, a man for whom life holds no terrors, not even the fear of God.

"The worst of fellows, I tell you—nothing less will do!"

At this a paraffin storm-lantern was lighted, and Huma saw facing her a grey-haired giant down whose left cheek ran the most sinister of scars, a cicatrice in the shape of the letter *sín* in the Nastaliq script. She was gripped by the insupportably nostalgic notion that the bogeyman of her childhood nursery had risen up to confront her, because her ayah had always forestalled any incipient acts of disobedience by threatening Huma and Atta: 'You don't watch out and I'll send that one to steal you away—that Sheikh Sín, the Thief of Thieves!'

Here, grey-haired but unquestionably scarred, was the notorious criminal himself—and was she out of her mind, were her ears playing tricks, or had he truly just announced that, given the stated circumstances, he himself was the only man for the job?

Struggling hard against the newborn goblins of nostalgia, Huma warned the fearsome volunteer that only a matter of extreme urgency and peril would have brought her unescorted into these ferocious streets.

"Because we can afford no last-minute backings-out," she continued, "I am determined to tell you everything, keeping back no secrets whatsoever. If, after hearing me out, you are still prepared to proceed, then we shall do everything in our power to assist you, and to make you rich."

The old thief shrugged, nodded, spat. Huma began her story.

Six days ago, everything in the household of her father, the wealthy moneylender Hashim, had been as it always was. At breakfast her mother had spooned khichri lovingly on to the moneylender's plate; the conversation had been filled with those expressions of courtesy and solicitude on which the family prided itself.

Hashim was fond of pointing out that while he was not a godly man he set great store by "living honourably in the world." In that spacious lakeside residence, all outsiders were greeted with the same formality and respect, even those unfortunates who came to negotiate for small fragments of Hashim's large fortune, and of whom he naturally asked an interest rate of over seventy per cent, partly, as he told his khichri-spooning wife, 'to teach these people the value of money; let them only learn that, and they will be cured of this fever of borrowing borrowing all the time—so you see that if my plans succeed, I shall put myself out of business!'

In their children, Atta and Huma, the moneylender and his wife had successfully sought to inculcate the virtues of thrift, plain dealing and a healthy independence of spirit. On this, too, Hashim was fond of congratulating himself.

Breakfast ended; the family members wished one another a fulfilling day. Within a few hours, however, the glassy contentment of that household, of that life of porcelain delicacy and alabaster sensibilities, was to be shattered beyond all hope of repair.

The moneylender summoned his personal shikara and was on the point of stepping into it when, attracted by a glint of silver, he noticed a small vial floating between the boat and his private quay. On an impulse, he scooped it out of the glutinous water.

It was a cylinder of tinted glass cased in exquisitely wrought silver, and Hashim saw within its walls a silver pendant bearing a single strand of human hair.

Closing his fist around this unique discovery, he muttered to the boatman that he'd changed his plans, and hurried to his sanctum, where, behind closed doors, he feasted his eyes on his find.

There can be no doubt that Hashim the moneylender knew from the first that he was in possession of the famous relic of the Prophet Muhammad, that revered hair whose theft from its shrine at Hazratbal mosque the previous morning had created an unprecedented hue and cry in the valley.

The thieves—no doubt alarmed by the pandemonium, by the procession through the streets of endless ululating crocodiles of lamentation, by the riots, the political ramifications and by the massive police search which was commanded and carried out by men whose entire careers now hung upon the finding of this lost hair—had evidently panicked and hurled the vial into the gelatine bosom of the lake.

Having found it by a stroke of great good fortune, Hashim's duty as a citizen was clear: the hair must be restored to its shrine, and the state to equanimity and peace.

But the moneylender had a different notion.

All around him in his study was the evidence of his collector's mania. There were enormous glass cases full of impaled butterflies from Gulmarg, three dozen scale models in various metals of the legendary cannon Zamzama, innumerable swords, a Naga spear, ninety-four terracotta camels of the sort sold on railway station platforms, many samovars, and a whole zoology of tiny sandalwood animals, which had originally been carved to serve as children's bathtime toys.

"And after all," Hashim told himself, "the Prophet would have disapproved mightily of this relic-worship. He abhorred the idea of being deified! So, by keeping this hair from its distracted devotees, I perform—do I not?—a finer service than I would by returning it! Naturally, I don't want it for its religious value . . . I'm a man of the world, of this world. I see it purely as a secular object of great rarity and blinding beauty. In short, it's the silver vial I desire, more than the hair.

"They say there are American millionaires who purchase stolen art masterpieces and hide them away—they would know how I feel. I must, must have it!"

Every collector must share his treasures with one other human being, and Hashim summoned—and told—his only son Atta, who was deeply perturbed but, having been sworn to secrecy, only spilled the beans when the troubles became too terrible to bear.

The youth excused himself and left his father alone in the crowded solitude of his collections. Hashim was sitting erect in a hard, straight-backed chair, gazing intently at the beautiful vial.

It was well known that the moneylender never ate lunch, so it was not until evening that a servant entered the sanctum to summon his master to the dining-table. He found Hashim as Atta had left him. The same, and not the same—for now the moneylender looked swollen, distended. His eyes bulged even more than they always had, they were red-rimmed, and his knuckles were white.

He seemed to be on the point of bursting! As though, under the influence of the misappropriated relic, he had filled up with some spectral fluid which might at any moment ooze uncontrollably from his every bodily opening.

He had to be helped to the table, and then the explosion did indeed take place.

Seemingly careless of the effect of his words on the carefully constructed and fragile constitution of the family's life, Hashim began to gush, to spume long streams of awful truths. In horrified silence, his children heard their father turn upon his wife, and reveal to her that for many years their marriage had been the worst of his afflictions. "An end to politeness!" he thundered. "An end to hypocrisy!"

Next, and in the same spirit, he revealed to his family the existence of a mistress; he informed them also of his regular visits to paid women. He told his wife that, far from being the principal beneficiary of his will, she would receive no more than the eighth portion which was her due under Islamic law. Then he turned upon his children, screaming at Atta for his lack of academic ability—"A dope! I have been cursed with a dope!"—and accusing his daughter of lasciviousness, because she went around the city barefaced, which was unseemly for any good Muslim girl to do. She should, he commanded, enter purdah forthwith.

Hashim left the table without having eaten and fell into the deep sleep of a man who has got many things off his chest, leaving his children stunned, in tears, and the dinner going cold on the sideboard under the gaze of an anticipatory bearer.

At five o'clock the next morning the moneylender forced his family to rise, wash and say their prayers. From then on, he began to pray five times daily for the first time in his life, and his wife and children were obliged to do likewise.

Before breakfast, Huma saw the servants, under her father's direction, constructing a great heap of books in the garden and setting fire to it. The only volume left untouched was the Qur'an, which Hashim wrapped in a silken cloth and placed on a table in the hall. He ordered each member of his family to read passages from this book for at least two hours per day. Visits to the cinema were forbidden. And if Atta invited male friends to the house, Huma was to retire to her room.

By now, the family had entered a state of shock and dismay; but there was worse to come.

That afternoon, a trembling debtor arrived at the house to confess his inability to pay the latest instalment of interest owed, and made the mistake of reminding Hashim, in somewhat blustering fashion, of the Qur'an's strictures against usury. The moneylender flew into a rage and attacked the fellow with one of his large collection of bullwhips.

By mischance, later the same day a second defaulter came to plead for time, and was seen fleeing Hashim's study with a great gash in his arm, because Huma's father had called him a thief of other men's money and had tried to cut off the wretch's right hand with one of the thirty-eight kukri knives hanging on the study walls.

These breaches of the family's unwritten laws of decorum alarmed Atta and Huma, and when, that evening, their mother attempted to calm Hashim down, he struck her on the face with an open hand. Atta leapt to his mother's defence and he, too, was sent flying.

"From now on," Hashim bellowed, "there's going to be some discipline around here!"

The moneylender's wife began a fit of hysterics which continued throughout that night and the following day, and which so provoked her husband that he threatened her with divorce, at which she fled to her room, locked the door and subsided into a raga of sniffling. Huma now lost her composure, challenged her father openly, and announced (with that same independence of spirit which he had encouraged in her) that she would wear no cloth over her face; apart from anything else, it was bad for the eyes.

On hearing this, her father disowned her on the spot and gave her one week in which to pack her bags and go.

By the fourth day, the fear in the air of the house had become so thick that it was difficult to walk around. Atta told his shock-numbed sister: "We are descending to gutter-level—but I know what must be done."

That afternoon, Hashim left home accompanied by two hired thugs to extract the unpaid dues from his two insolvent clients. Atta went immediately to his father's study. Being the son and heir, he possessed his own key to the moneylender's safe. This he now used, and removing the little vial from its hiding-place, he slipped it into his trouser pocket and re-locked the safe door.

Now he told Huma the secret of what his father had fished out of Lake Dal, and exclaimed: 'Maybe I'm crazy—maybe the awful things that are happening have made me cracked—but I am convinced there will be no peace in our house until this hair is out of it.'

His sister at once agreed that the hair must be returned, and Atta set off in a hired shikara to Hazratbal mosque. Only when the boat had delivered him into the throng of the distraught faithful which was swirling around the desecrated shrine did Atta discover that the relic was no longer in his pocket. There was only a hole, which his mother, usually so attentive to household matters, must have overlooked under the stress of recent events.

Atta's initial surge of chagrin was quickly replaced by a feeling of profound relief.

"Suppose," he imagined, "that I had already announced to the mullahs that the hair was on my person! They would never have believed me now—and this mob would have lynched me! At any rate, it has gone, and that's a load off my mind." Feeling more contented than he had for days, the young man returned home.

Here he found his sister bruised and weeping in the hall; upstairs, in her bedroom, his mother wailed like a brand-new widow. He begged Huma to tell him what had happened, and when she replied that their father, returning from his brutal business trip, had once again noticed a glint of silver between boat and quay, had once again scooped up the errant relic, and was consequently in a rage to end all rages, having beaten the truth out of her—then Atta buried his face in his hands and sobbed out his opinion, which was that the hair was persecuting them, and had come back to finish the job.

It was Huma's turn to think of a way out of their troubles.

While her arms turned black and blue and great stains spread across her forehead, she hugged her brother and whispered to him that she was determined to get rid of the hair *at all costs*—she repeated this last phrase several times.

"The hair," she then declared, "was stolen from the mosque; so it can be stolen from this house. But it must be a genuine robbery, carried out by a bona-fide thief, not by one of us who are under the hair's thrall—by a thief so desperate that he fears neither capture nor curses."

Unfortunately, she added, the theft would be ten times harder to pull off now that their father, knowing that there had already been one attempt on the relic, was certainly on his guard.

"Can you do it?"

Huma, in a room lit by candle and storm-lantern, ended her account with one further question: "What assurances can you give that the job holds no terrors for you still?"

The criminal, spitting, stated that he was not in the habit of providing references, as a cook might, or a gardener, but he was not alarmed so easily, certainly not by any children's djinni of a curse. Huma had to be content with this boast, and proceeded to describe the details of the proposed burglary.

"Since my brother's failure to return the hair to the mosque, my father has taken to sleeping with his precious treasure under his pillow. However, he sleeps alone, and very energetically; only enter his room without waking him, and he will certainly have tossed and turned quite enough to make the theft a simple matter. When you have the vial, come to my room," and here she handed Sheikh Sín a plan of her home, "and I will hand over all the jewellery owned by my mother and myself. You will find . . . it is worth . . . that is, you will be able to get a fortune for it . . ."

It was evident that her self-control was weakening and that she was on the point of physical collapse.

"Tonight," she burst out finally. "You must come tonight!"

No sooner had she left the room that the old criminal's body was convulsed by a fit of coughing: he spat blood into an old vanaspati can. The great Sheikh, the "Thief of Thieves," had become a sick man, and every day the time drew nearer when some young pretender to his power would stick a dagger in his stomach. A lifelong addiction to gambling had left him almost as poor as he had been when, decades ago, he had started out in this line of work as a mere pickpocket's apprentice; so in the extraordinary commission he had accepted from the moneylender's daughter he saw his opportunity of amassing enough wealth at a stroke to leave the valley for ever, and acquire the luxury of a respectable death which would leave his stomach intact.

As for the Prophet's hair, well, neither he nor his blind wife had ever had much to say for prophets—that was one thing they had in common with the moneylender's thunderstruck clan.

It would not do, however, to reveal the nature of this, his last crime, to his four sons. To his consternation, they had all grown up to be hopelessly devout men, who even spoke of making the pilgrimage to Mecca some day. "Absurd!" their father would laugh at them. "Just tell me how you will go?" For, with a parent's absolutist love, he had made sure they were all provided with a lifelong source of high income by crippling them at birth, so that, as they dragged themselves around the city, they earned excellent money in the begging business.

The children, then, could look after themselves.

He and his wife would be off soon with the jewel-boxes of the moneylender's women. It was a timely chance indeed that had brought the beautiful bruised girl into his corner of the town.

That night, the large house on the shore of the lake lay blindly waiting, with silence lapping at its walls. A burglar's night: clouds in the sky and mists on the winter water. Hashim the moneylender was asleep, the only member of his family to whom sleep had come that night. In another room, his son Atta lay deep in the coils of his coma with a blood-clot forming on his brain, watched over by a mother who had let down her long greying hair to show her grief, a mother who placed warm compresses on his head with gestures redolent of impotence. In a third bedroom Huma waited, fully dressed, amidst the jewel-heavy caskets of her desperation.

At last a bulbul sang softly from the garden below her window and, creeping downstairs, she opened a door to the bird, on whose face there was a scar in the shape of the Nastaliq letter *sín*.

Noiselessly, the bird flew up the stairs behind her. At the head of the staircase they parted, moving in opposite directions along the corridor of their conspiracy without a glance at one another.

Entering the moneylender's room with professional ease, the burglar, Sín, discovered that Huma's predictions had been wholly accurate. Hashim lay sprawled diagonally across his bed, the pillow untenanted by his head, the prize easily accessible. Step by padded step, Sín moved towards the goal.

It was at this point that, in the bedroom next door, young Atta sat bolt upright in his bed, giving his mother a great fright, and without any warning—prompted by goodness knows what pressure of the blood-clot upon his brain—began screaming at the top of his voice:

'Thief! Thief! Thief!'

It seems probable that his poor mind had been dwelling, in these last moments, upon his own father; but it is impossible to be certain, because having uttered these three emphatic words the young man fell back upon his pillow and died.

At once his mother set up a screeching and a wailing and a keening and a howling so earsplittingly intense that they completed the work which Atta's cry had begun—that is, her laments penetrated the walls of her husband's bedroom and brought Hashim wide awake.

Sheikh Sín was just deciding whether to dive beneath the bed or brain the moneylender good and proper when Hashim grabbed the tiger-striped swordstick which always stood propped up in a corner beside his bed, and rushed from the room without so much as noticing the burglar who stood on the opposite side of the bed in the darkness. Sín stooped quickly and removed the vial containing the Prophet's hair from its hiding-place.

Meanwhile Hashim had erupted into the corridor, having unsheathed the sword inside his cane. In his right hand he held the weapon and was waving it about dementedly. His left hand was shaking the stick. A shadow came rushing towards him through the midnight darkness of the passageway and, in his somnolent anger, the moneylender thrust his sword fatally through its heart. Turning up the light, he found that he had murdered his daughter, and under the dire influence of this accident he was so overwhelmed by remorse that he turned the sword upon himself, fell upon it and so extinguished his life. His wife, the sole surviving member of the family, was driven mad by the general carnage and had to be committed to an asylum for the insane by her brother, the city's Deputy Commissioner of Police.

Sheikh Sín had quickly understood that the plan had gone awry.

Abandoning the dream of the jewel-boxes when he was but a few yards from its fulfilment, he climbed out of Hashim's window and made his escape during the appalling events described above. Reaching home before dawn, he woke his wife and confessed his failure. It would be necessary, he whispered, for him to vanish for a while. Her blind eyes never opened until he had gone.

The noise in the Hashim household had roused their servants and even managed to awaken the night-watchman, who had been fast asleep as usual on his charpoy by the street-gate. They alerted the police, and the Deputy Commissioner himself was informed. When he heard of Huma's death, the mournful officer opened of and read the sealed letter which his niece had given him, and instantly led a large detachment of armed men into the light-repellent gullies of the most wretched and disreputable part of the city.

The tongue of a malicious cat-burglar named Huma's fellow-conspirator; the finger of an ambitious bank-robber pointed at the house in which he lay concealed; and although Sín managed to crawl through a hatch in the attic and attempt a roof-top escape, a bullet from the Deputy Commissioner's own rifle penetrated his stomach and brought him crashing messily to the ground at the feet of Huma's enraged uncle.

From the dead thief's pocket rolled a vial of tinted glass, cased in filigree silver.

The recovery of the Prophet's hair was announced at once on All-India Radio. One month later, the valley's holiest men assembled at the Hazratbal mosque and formally authenticated the relic. It sits to this day in a closely guarded vault by the shores of the loveliest of lakes in the heart of the valley which was once closer than any other place on earth to Paradise.

But before our story can properly be concluded, it is necessary to record that when the four sons of the dead Sheikh awoke on the morning of his death, having unwittingly spent a few minutes under the same roof as the famous hair, they found that a miracle had occurred, that they were all sound of limb and strong of wind, as whole as they might have been if their father had not thought to smash their legs in the first hours of their lives. They were, all four of them, very properly furious, because the miracle had reduced their earning powers by 75 percent, at the most conservative estimate; so they were ruined men.

Only the Sheikh's widow had some reason for feeling grateful, because although her husband was dead she had regained her sight, so that it was possible for her to spend her last days gazing once more upon the beauties of the valley of Kashmir.

[1994]

Questions

1. What distinctions does the author make between the moneylender and his children? Why must the children pay for the sins of their father?
2. What does the story say about belief? About fundamentalism?
3. Is the relic from the prophet a negative or positive symbol?

Leslie Marmon Silko

(b. 1948)

United States

Leslie Marmon Silko regards as one of the central formative influences in her life and writing her heritage as a Native American of mixed ancestry (Laguna, Mexican, and white). Born in Albuquerque, New Mexico, she grew up at the Laguna Pueblo and attended the University of New Mexico, graduating in 1969. She subsequently attended law school for several semesters and then taught for two years in Arizona and Alaska before she realized that she wanted to write full-time.

Silko's first novel, Ceremony (1977), explores the author's concern with her complex cultural heritage. Focusing on a mixed-ancestry Laguna Indian who struggles to locate himself within his cultural confusion, the narrative is an innovative weave of elements of Pueblo oral storytelling and contemporary moral and social concerns, including conflicting cultural attitudes toward war, power, cultural differences, and the human need for connection to the earth and nature. Silko has published a collection of poems and stories, Storyteller (1981), and two other novels, Almanac of the Dead (1991) and Gardens in the Dunes (1999). Her short stories and poetry have appeared in a number of collections; she is also the recipient of one of the MacArthur Foundation "genius grants" in 1981.

The story "Yellow Woman" is in the tradition of the "abduction tale," but with a significant difference: The narrator is not certain about what is real and what is not. Silko wrote the following introduction to the story especially for Worlds of Fiction:

> When I was a little girl, Aunt Alice used to tell us kids the old-time stories, the "hummahah" stories. Many of the stories were about the animals and birds and insects and reptiles who the old-time people believe are our sisters and brothers, too, because Mother Earth's spirit gave birth to us all. But there were other stories, too, about the Twin Brothers who went around saving people from giant monsters, about Salt Woman who gave her gift to the Parrot People because they invited her to share their food with them.
>
> There is a whole cycle of Kochininako—Yellow Woman—stories which Aunt Alice seemed to enjoy great deal. In most of the stories, Kochininako is a strong, courageous woman, sometimes a hunter bringing home rabbits for her family to eat; other times she faces dangers or hardships and overcomes them. But in some of the stories Kochininako is swept away by forces and circumstances beyond her. All realms of possibility are open to Kochininako, even that of sorcery.
>
> I wrote "Yellow Woman" when I was 20 years old. I think it was the third short story I wrote for a class I took. Back then, I wasn't thinking about being a writer; writing was just something I loved to do. I planned to attend law school, and later I did attend for three semesters.
>
> I did not know, at the time I began writing this story, what the story would be about; all I had was the notion of this sensuous woman who leaves her family responsibilities behind for a handsome stranger. Then, when I was about one-third of the way into the story, suddenly I remembered all the Kochininako-Yellow Woman stories I had heard while I was growing up. In one story a terrible drought has dried up all the nearby springs and so Kochininako must walk a great distance to find fresh water to carry home. At a distant water hole she encounters Buffalo Man, a supernatural being who is sometimes a handsome man and other times a buffalo. Although Kochininako leaves her husband and goes away with Buffalo Man, the outcome for Kochininako's people is life-saving;

since Kochininako has now become their "sister-in-law," the Buffalo People agree to allow their meat to be harvested by Kochininako's starving people.

In another story, Kochininako meets Whirl-Wind Man at the water hole and goes away with him for a while. When Kochininako finally returns home months later, she is pregnant with twins who later grow up to be the Twin Brothers, who help the people in times of great trouble.

A warning has to go along with this story: In 1976, a Navajo woman who had been a student of mine reported that after six years trying and failing, she had become pregnant during the week our literature class had read and discussed "Yellow Woman." (Leslie Marmon Silko, copyright 1991)

YELLOW WOMAN

I

My thigh clung to his with dampness, and I watched the sun rising up through the tamaracks and willows. The small brown water birds came to the river and hopped across the mud, leaving brown scratches in the alkali-white crust. They bathed in the river silently. I could hear the water, almost at our feet where the narrow fast channel bubbled and washed green ragged moss and fern leaves. I looked at him beside me, rolled in the red blanket on the white river sand. I cleaned the sand out of the cracks between my toes, squinting because the sun was above the willow trees. I looked at him for the last time, sleeping on the white river sand.

I felt hungry and followed the river south the way we had come the afternoon before, following our footprints that were already blurred by lizard tracks and bug trails. The horses were still lying down, and the black one whinnied when he saw me but he did not get up—maybe it was because the corral was made out of thick cedar branches and the horses had not yet felt the sun like I had. I tried to look beyond the pale red mesas to the pueblo. I knew it was there, even if I could not see it, on the sandrock hill above the river, the same river that moved past me now and had reflected the moon last night.

The horse felt warm underneath me. He shook his head and pawed the sand. The bay whinnied and leaned against the gate trying to follow, and I remembered him asleep in the red blanket beside the river. I slid off the horse and tied him close to the other horse, I walked north with the river again, and the white sand broke loose in footprints over footprints.

"Wake up."

He moved in the blanket and turned his face to me with his eyes still closed. I knelt down to touch him.

"I'm leaving."

He smiled now, eyes still closed. "You are coming with me, remember?" He sat up now with his bare dark chest and belly in the sun.

"Where?"

"To my place."

"And will I come back?"

He pulled his pants on. I walked away from him, feeling him behind me and smelling the willows.

"Yellow Woman," he said.

I turned to face him. "Who are you?" I asked.

He laughed and knelt on the low, sandy bank, washing his face in the river. "Last night you guessed my name, and you knew why I had come."

I stared past him at the shallow moving water and tried to remember the night, but I could only see the moon in the water and remember his warmth around me.

"But I only said that you were him and that I was Yellow Woman—I'm not really her—I have my own name and I come from the pueblo on the other side of the mesa. Your name is Silva and you are a stranger I met by the river yesterday afternoon."

He laughed softly. "What happened yesterday has nothing to do with what you will do today, Yellow Woman."

"I know—that's what I'm saying—the old stories about the ka'tsina[1] spirit and Yellow Woman can't mean us."

My old grandpa liked to tell those stories best. There is one about Badger and Coyote who went hunting and were gone all day, and when the sun was going down they found a house. There was a girl living there alone, and she had light hair and eyes and she told them that they could sleep with her. Coyote wanted to be with her all night so he sent Badger into a prairie-dog hole, telling him he thought he saw something in it. As soon as Badger crawled in, Coyote blocked up the entrance with rocks and hurried back to Yellow Woman.

"Come here," he said gently.

He touched my neck and I moved close to him to feel his breathing and to hear his heart. I was wondering if Yellow Woman had known who she was—if she knew that she would become part of the stories. Maybe she'd had another name that her husband and relatives called her so that only the ka'tsina from the north and the storytellers would know her as Yellow Woman. But I didn't go on; I felt him all around me, pushing me down into the white river sand.

Yellow Woman went away with the spirit from the north and lived with him and his relatives. She was gone for a long time, but then one day she came back and she brought twin boys.

"Do you know the story?"

"What story?" He smiled and pulled me close to him as he said this. I was afraid crying there on the red blanket. All I could know was the way he felt, warm, damp, his body beside me. This is the way it happens in the stories, I was thinking, with no thought beyond the moment she meets the ka'tsina spirit and they go.

"I don't have to go. What they tell in stories was real only then, back in time immemorial, like they say."

He stood up and pointed at my clothes tangled in the blanket. "Let's go," he said.

I walked beside him, breathing hard because he walked fast, his hand around my wrist. I had stopped trying to pull away from him, because his hand felt cool and the sun was high, drying the river bed into alkali. I will see someone, eventually I will see someone, and then I will be certain that he is only a man—some man from nearby—and I will be sure that I am not Yellow Woman. Because she is from out of time past and I live now and I've been to school and there are highways and pickup trucks that Yellow Woman never saw.

---

[1]*Ka'tsina* Kachina; in Pueblo culture a beneficent spirit.

It was an easy ride north on horseback. I watched the change from the cottonwood trees along the river to the junipers that brushed past us in the foothills, and finally there were only piñons, and when I looked up at the rim of the mountain plateau I could see pine trees growing on the edge. Once I stopped to look down, but the pale sandstone had disappeared and the river was gone and the dark lava hills were all around. He touched my hand, not speaking, but always singing softly a mountain song and looking into my eyes.

I felt hungry and wondered what they were doing at home now—my mother, my grandmother, my husband, and the baby. Cooking breakfast, saying, "Where did she go?—maybe kidnaped." And Al going to the tribal police with the details: "She went walking along the river."

The house was made with black lava rock and red mud. It was high above the spreading miles of arroyos and long mesas. I smelled a mountain smell of pitch and buck brush. I stood there beside the black horse, looking down on the small, dim country we had passed, and I shivered.

"Yellow Woman, come inside where it's warm."

II

He lit a fire in the stove. It was an old stove with a round belly and an enamel coffeepot on top. There was only the stove, some faded Navajo blankets, and a bedroll and cardboard box. The floor was made of smooth adobe plaster, and there was one small window facing east. He pointed at the box.

"There's some potatoes and the frying pan." He sat on the floor with his arms around his knees pulling them close to his chest and he watched me fry the potatoes. I didn't mind him watching me because he was always watching me—he had been watching me since I came upon him sitting on the river bank trimming leaves from a willow twig with his knife. We ate from the pan and he wiped the grease from his fingers on his Levi's.

"Have you brought women here before?" He smiled and kept chewing, so I said, "Do you always use the same tricks?"

"What tricks?" He looked at me like he didn't understand.

"The story about being a ka'tsina from the mountains. The story about Yellow Woman."

Silva was silent; his face was calm.

"I don't believe it. Those stories couldn't happen now," I said.

He shook his head and said softly, "But someday they will talk about us, and they will say, 'Those two lived long ago when things like that happened.'"

He stood up and went out. I ate the rest of the potatoes and thought about things—about the noise the stove was making and the sound of the mountain wind outside. I remembered yesterday and the day before, and then I went outside.

I walked past the corral to the edge where the narrow trail cut through the black rim rock. I was standing in the sky with nothing around me but the wind that came down from the blue mountain peak behind me. I could see faint mountain images in the distance miles across the vast spread of mesas and valleys and plains. I wondered who was over there to feel the mountain wind on those sheer blue edges—who walks on the pine needles in those blue mountains.

"Can you see the pueblo?" Silva was standing behind me.

I shook my head. "We're too far away."

"From here I can see the world." He stepped out on the edge. "The Navajo reservation begins over there." He pointed to the east. "The Pueblo boundaries are over here." He looked below us to the south, where the narrow trail seemed to come from. "The Texans have their ranches over there, starting with that valley, the Concho Valley. The Mexicans run some cattle over there too."

"Do you ever work for them?"

"I steal from them," Silva answered. The sun was dropping behind us and the shadows were filling the land below. I turned away from the edge that dropped forever into the valleys below.

"I'm cold," I said, "I'm going inside." I started wondering about this man who could speak the Pueblo language so well but who lived on a mountain and rustled cattle. I decided that this man Silva must be Navajo, because Pueblo men didn't do things like that.

"You must be a Navajo."

Silva shook his head gently. "Little Yellow Woman," he said, "you never give up, do you? I have told you who I am. The Navajo people know me, too." He knelt down and unrolled the bedroll and spread the extra blankets out on a piece of canvas. The sun was down, and the only light in the house came from outside—the dim orange light from sundown.

I stood there and waited for him to crawl under the blankets.

"What are you waiting for?" he said, and I lay down beside him. He undressed me slowly like the night before beside the river—kissing my face gently and running his hands up and down my belly and legs. He took off my pants and then he laughed.

"Why are you laughing?"

"You are breathing so hard."

I pulled away from him and turned my back to him.

He pulled me around and pinned me down with his arms and chest. "You don't understand, do you, little Yellow Woman? You will do what I want."

And again he was all around me with his skin slippery against mine, and I was afraid because I understood that his strength could hurt me. I lay underneath him and I knew that he could destroy me. But later, while he slept beside me, I touched his face and I had a feeling—the kind of feeling for him that overcame me that morning along the river. I kissed him on the forehead and he reached out for me.

When I woke up in the morning he was gone. It gave me a strange feeling because for a long time I sat there on the blankets and looked around the little house for some object of his—some proof that he had been there or maybe that he was coming back. Only the blankets and the cardboard box remained. The .30–30 that had been leaning in the corner was gone, and so was the knife I had used the night before. He was gone, and I had my chance to go now. But first I had to eat, because I knew it would be a long walk home.

I found some dried apricots in the cardboard box, and I sat down on a rock at the edge of the plateau rim. There was no wind and the sun warmed me. I was surrounded by silence. I drowsed with apricots in my mouth, and I didn't believe that there were highways or railroads or cattle to steal.

When I woke up, I stared down at my feet in the black mountain dirt. Little black ants were swarming over the pine needles around my foot. They must have smelled the apricots. I thought about my family far below me. They would be wondering about me, because this had never happened to me before. The tribal police would file a report. But if old Grandpa weren't dead he would tell them what happened—he would laugh and say, "Stolen by a ka'tsina, a mountain spirit. She'll come home—they usually do." There are enough of them to handle things. My mother and grandmother will raise the baby like they raised me. Al will find someone else, and they will go on like before, except that there will be a story about the day I disappeared while I was walking along the river. Silva had come for me; he said he had. I did not decide to go. I just went. Moonflowers blossom in the sand hills before dawn, just as I followed him. That's what I was thinking as I wandered along the trail through the pine trees.

It was noon when I got back. When I saw the stone house I remembered that I had meant to go home. But that didn't seem important any more, maybe because there were little blue flowers growing in the meadow behind the stone house and the gray squirrels were playing in the pines next to the house. The horses were standing in the corral, and there was a beef carcass hanging on the shady side of a big pine in front of the house. Flies buzzed around the clotted blood that hung from the carcass. Silva was washing his hands in a bucket full of water. He must have heard me coming because he spoke to me without turning to face me.

"I've been waiting for you."

"I went walking in the big pine trees."

I looked into the bucket full of bloody water with brown-and-white animal hairs floating in it. Silva stood there letting his hand drip, examining me intently.

"Are you coming with me?"

"Where?" I asked him.

"To sell the meat in Marquez."

"If you're sure it's O.K."

"I wouldn't ask you if it wasn't," he answered.

He sloshed the water around in the bucket before he dumped it out and set the bucket upside down near the door. I followed him to the corral and watched him saddle the horses. Even beside the horses he looked tall, and I asked him again if he wasn't Navajo. He didn't say anything; he just shook his head and kept cinching up the saddle.

"But Navajos are tall."

"Get on the horse," he said, "and let's go."

The last thing he did before we started down the steep trail was to grab the .30–30 from the corner. He slid the rifle into the scabbard that hung from his saddle.

"Do they ever try to catch you?" I asked.

"They don't know who I am."

"Then why did you bring the rifle?"

"Because we are going to Marquez where the Mexicans live."

III

The trail leveled out on a narrow ridge that was steep on both sides like an animal spine. On one side I could see where the trail went around the rocky gray hills and disappeared into the southeast where the pale sandrock mesas stood in the distance near my home. On the other side was a trail that went west, and as I looked far into the distance I thought I saw the little town. But Silva said no, that I was looking in the wrong place, that I just thought I saw houses. After that I quit looking off into the distance; it was hot and the wildflowers were closing up their deep-yellow petals. Only the waxy cactus flowers bloomed in the bright sun, and I saw every color that a cactus blossom can be; the white ones and the red ones were still buds, but the purple and the yellow were blossoms, open full and the most beautiful of all.

Silva saw him before I did. The white man was riding a big gray horse, coming up the trail towards us. He was traveling fast and the gray horse's feet sent rocks rolling off the trail into the dry tumbleweeds. Silva motioned for me to stop and we watched the white man. He didn't see us right away, but finally his horse whinnied at our horses and he stopped. He looked at us briefly before he loped the gray horse across the three hundred yards that separated us. He stopped his horse in front of Silva, and his young fat face was shadowed by the brim of his hat. He didn't look mad, but his small, pale eyes moved from the blood-soaked gunny sacks hanging from my saddle to Silva's face and then back to my face.

"Where did you get the fresh meat?" the white man asked.

"I've been hunting," Silva said, and when he shifted his weight in the saddle the leather creaked.

"The hell you have, Indian. You've been rustling cattle. We've been looking for the thief for a long time."

The rancher was fat, and sweat began to soak through his white cowboy shirt and the wet cloth stuck to the thick rolls of belly fat. He almost seemed to be panting from the exertion of talking, and he smelled rancid, maybe because Silva scared him.

Silva turned to me and smiled. "Go back up the mountain, Yellow Woman."

The white man got angry when he heard Silva speak in a language he couldn't understand. "Don't try anything, Indian. Just keep riding to Marquez. We'll call the state police from there."

The rancher must have been unarmed because he was very frightened and if he had a gun he would have pulled it out then. I turned my horse around and the rancher yelled, "Stop!" I looked at Silva for an instant and there was something ancient and dark—something I could feel in my stomach—in his eyes, and when I glanced at his hand I saw his finger on the trigger of the .30–30 that was still in the saddle scabbard. I slapped my horse across the flank and the sacks of raw meat swung against my knees as the horse leaped up the trail. It was hard to keep my balance, and once I thought I felt the saddle slipping backward; it was because of this that I could not look back.

I didn't stop until I reached the ridge where the trail forked. The horse was breathing deep gasps and there was a dark film of sweat on its neck. I looked down in the direction I had come from, but I couldn't see the place. I waited. The wind came up and pushed warm air past me. I looked up at the sky, pale blue and full of rain clouds and fading vapor trail left by jets.

I think four shots were fired—I remember hearing four hollow explosions that reminded me of deer hunting. There could have been more shots after that, but I wouldn't have heard them because my horse was running again and the loose rocks were making too much noise as they scattered around his feet.

Horses have a hard time running downhill, but I went that way instead of uphill to the mountain because I thought it was safer. I felt better with the horse running southeast past the round gray hills that were covered with cedar trees and black lava rock. When I got to the plain in the distance I could see the dark green patches of tamaracks that grew along the river; and beyond the river I could see the beginning of the pale sandrock mesas. I stopped the horse and looked back to see if anyone was coming; then I got off the horse and turned the horse around, wondering if it would go back to its corral under the pines on the mountain. It looked back at me for a moment and then plucked a mouthful of green tumbleweeds before it trotted back up the trail with its ears pointed forward, carrying its head daintily to one side to avoid stepping on the dragging reins. When the horse disappeared over the last hill, the gunny sacks full of meat were still swinging and bouncing.

IV

I walked toward the river on a wood-hauler's road that I knew would eventually lead to the paved road. I was thinking about waiting beside the road for someone to drive by, but by the time I got to the pavement I had decided it wasn't very far to walk if I followed the river back the way Silva and I had come.

The river water tasted good, and I sat in the shade under a cluster of silvery willows. I thought about Silva, and I felt sad at leaving him; still, there was something strange about him, and I tried to figure it out all the way back home.

I came back to the place on the river bank where he had been sitting the first time I saw him. The green willow leaves that he had trimmed from the branch were still lying there, wilted in the sand. I saw the leaves and I wanted to go back to him—to kiss him and to touch him—but the mountains were too far away now. And I told myself, because I believe it, he will come back sometime and be waiting again by the river.

I followed the path up from the river into the village. The sun was getting low, and I could smell supper cooking when I got to the screen door of my house. I could hear their voices inside—my mother was telling my grandmother how to fix the Jell-O and my husband, Al, was playing with the baby. I decided to tell them that some Navajo had kidnaped me, but I was sorry that old Grandpa wasn't alive to hear my story because it was the Yellow Woman stories he liked to tell best.

[1974]

Questions

1. How does the first-person-narrative perspective contribute to your understanding of the woman? What aspects of her character emerge through her own telling of the story?
2. Who is Silva? What qualities in him appeal to the narrator? Why does she return to her own family?
3. How does the setting contribute to the story's meaning?
4. Why and how does Silko interweave elements from her cultural tradition with contemporary issues?
5. What is the story's resolution? What is its theme?

Isaac Bashevis Singer

(1904–1991)

Poland/United States

Isaac Bashevis Singer, the world's foremost writer in Yiddish, is a difficult author to categorize because his fiction resists easy labeling within either American or Yiddish literary traditions. Coming from a family of rabbis (his father and both grandfathers), Singer almost became a rabbi himself; he attended a rabbinical school and seminary but decided not to become a rabbi because "I began to doubt, not the power of God, but all the traditions and dogmas."

Instead, when he was 15, he began to write, inspired by the stories he heard from his family: his father's, populated with imps, devils, and miraculous events, and his mother's, recalling her childhood in the shtetl (Jewish ghetto) of Bilgorai, Poland. In 1935, fearing the threat of a Nazi invasion of Poland, Singer followed his older brother (also a writer, I. J. Singer) to the United States. Many of his stories first appeared in the Yiddish newspaper for which he worked in New York City, the Jewish Daily Forward.

Singer wrote first in Hebrew but changed to Yiddish because Hebrew (before its revival as the national language of Israel) was a dead language. Ironically, it is now Yiddish that is in danger of dying. Irving Howe has observed the following:

> [Singer wrote in] a language that no amount of energy or affection seems likely to save from extinction. He [wrote] about a world that is gone, destroyed with a brutality beyond historical comparison. He [wrote] within a culture, the remnant of Yiddish in the Western world, that [was] more than a little dubious about his purpose and stress. . . .
> It strikes one as a kind of inspired madness: here [was] a man living in New York City, a sophisticated and clever writer, who compose[d] stories about places like Frampol, Bilgoray, Kreshev, as if they were still there.

Although he considered writing in English, Singer stayed with Yiddish because he felt that "a writer has to write in his own language or not at all." Inevitably, much is lost in translation; Howe notes that "no translation . . . could possibly suggest the full idiomatic richness and syntactical verve of Singer's Yiddish."

Singer's stories are moral fables or allegories, set in the shtetls and villages of nineteenth- and twentieth-century prewar Poland. Although magical and supernatural events may frequent them, his narratives are about people struggling with the very human emotional and moral challenges of ordinary life: love and lust, sin and responsibility, faith and doubt, madness and sanity, good and evil. As Singer commented in an interview, "I actually believe that there are powers in this world of which we have no inkling but which have an influence on our lives and on our way of thinking."

Although Singer was a prolific writer of stories for both adults and children, many of them have not yet been translated into English, even though the author translated many of his stories himself. "Gimpel the Fool," considered by many critics to be his finest story, brought Singer an audience of English-speaking readers when it was translated by Saul Bellow. When Singer received the Nobel Prize for Literature in 1978, the Nobel Committee praised his "impassioned narrative art which, with roots in a Polish-Jewish cultural tradition, brings universal human conditions to life."

GIMPEL THE FOOL

I

I am Gimpel the fool. I don't think myself a fool. On the contrary. But that's what folks call me. They gave me the name while I was still in school. I had seven names in all: imbecile, donkey, flax-head, dope, glump, ninny, and fool. The last name stuck. What did my foolishness consist of? I was easy to take in. They said, "Gimpel, you know the rabbi's wife has been brought to childbed?" So I skipped school. Well, it turned out to be a lie. How was I supposed to know? She hadn't had a big belly. But I never looked at her belly. Was that really so foolish? The gang laughed and hee-hawed, stomped and danced and chanted a good-night prayer. And instead of the raisins they give when a woman's lying in, they stuffed my hand full of goat turds. I was no weakling. If I slapped someone he'd see all the way to Cracow. But I'm really not a slugger by nature. I think to myself: Let it pass. So they take advantage of me.

I was coming home from school and heard a dog barking. I'm not afraid of dogs, but of course I never want to start up with them. One of them may be mad, and if he bites there's not a Tartar in the world who can help you. So I made tracks. Then I looked around and saw the whole market place wild with laughter. It was no dog at all but Wolf-Leib the thief. How was I supposed to know it was he? It sounded like a howling bitch.

When the pranksters and leg-pullers found that I was easy to fool, every one of them tried his luck with me. "Gimpel, the czar is coming to Frampol; Gimpel, the moon fell down in Turbeen; Gimpel, little Hodel Furpiece found a treasure behind the bathhouse." And I like a golem[1] believed everyone. In the first place, everything is possible, as it is written in *The Wisdom of the Fathers*, I've forgotten just how. Second, I had to believe when the whole town came down on me! If I ever dared to say, "Ah, you're kidding!" there was trouble. People got angry. "What do you mean! You want to call everyone a liar?" What was I to do? I believed them, and I hope at least that did them some good.

I was an orphan. My grandfather who brought me up was already bent toward the grave. So they turned me over to a baker, and what a time they gave me there! Every woman or girl who came to bake a batch of noodles had to fool me at least once. "Gimpel, there's a fair in Heaven; Gimpel, the rabbi gave birth to a calf in the seventh month; Gimpel, a cow flew over the roof and laid brass eggs." A student from the yeshiva came once to buy a roll, and he said, "You, Gimpel, while you stand here scraping with your baker's shovel the Messiah has come. The dead have arisen." "What do you mean?" I said. "I heard no one blowing the ram's horn!" He said, "Are you deaf?" And all began to cry, "We heard it, we heard!" Then in came Rietze the candle-dipper and called out in her hoarse voice, "Gimpel, your father and mother have stood up from the grave, They're looking for you."

To tell the truth, I knew very well that nothing of the sort had happened, but all the same, as folks were talking, I threw on my wool vest and went out. Maybe something had happened. What did I stand to lose by looking? Well, what a cat music

---

[1] *golem*   According to Jewish legend, a man artificially created by cabalistic rites; a robot or automaton.

went up! And then I took a vow to believe nothing more. But that was no go either. They confused me so that I didn't know the big end from the small.

I went to the rabbi to get some advice. He said, "It is written, better to be a fool all your days than for one hour to be evil. You are not a fool. They are the fools. For he who causes his neighbor to feel shame loses Paradise himself." Nevertheless, the rabbi's daughter took me in. As I left the rabbinical court she said, "Have you kissed the wall yet?" I said, "No, what for?" She answered, "It's the law; you've got to do it after every visit." Well, there didn't seem to be any harm in it. And she burst out laughing. It was a fine trick. She put one over on me, all right.

I wanted to go off to another town, but then everyone got busy matchmaking, and they were after me so they nearly tore my coat tails off. They talked at me and talked until I got water on the ear. She was no chaste maiden, but they told me she was virgin pure. She had a limp, and they said it was deliberate, from coyness. She had a bastard, and they told me the child was her little brother. I cried, "You're wasting your time. I'll never marry that whore." But they said indignantly, "What a way to talk! Aren't you ashamed of yourself. We can take you to the rabbi and have you fined for giving her a bad name." I saw then that I wouldn't escape them so easily and I thought: They're set on making me their butt. But when you're married the husband's the master, and if that's all right with her it's agreeable to me too. Besides, you can't pass through life unscathed, nor expect to.

I went to her clay house, which was built on the sand, and the whole gang, hollering and chorusing, came after me. They acted like bear-baiters. When we came to the well they stopped all the same. They were afraid to start anything with Elka. Her mouth would open as if it were on a hinge, and she had a fierce tongue. I entered the house. Lines were strung from wall to wall and clothes were drying. Barefoot she stood by the tub, doing the wash. She was dressed in a worn hand-me-down gown of plush. She had her hair put up in braids and pinned across her head. It took my breath away, almost, the reek of it all.

Evidently she knew who I was. She took a look at me and said, "Look who's here! He's come, the drip. Grab a seat."

I told her all; I denied nothing. "Tell me the truth," I said, "are you really a virgin, and is that mischievous Yechiel actually your little brother? Don't be deceitful with me, for I'm an orphan."

"I'm an orphan myself," she answered, "and whoever tries to twist you up, may the end of his nose take a twist. But don't let them think they can take advantage of me. I want a dowry of fifty guilders, and let them take up a collection besides. Otherwise they can kiss my you-know-what." She was very plainspoken. I said, "It's the bride and not the groom who gives a dowry." Then she said, "Don't bargain with me. Either a flat yes or a flat no. Go back where you came from."

I thought: No bread will ever be baked from this dough. But ours is not a poor town. They consented to everything and proceeded with the wedding. It so happened that there was a dysentery epidemic at the time. The ceremony was held at the cemetery gates, near the little corpse-washing hut. The fellows got drunk. While the marriage contract was being drawn up I heard the most pious high rabbi ask, "Is the bride a widow or a divorced woman?" And the sexton's wife answered for her, "Both a widow and divorced." It was a black moment for me. But what was I to do, run away from under the marriage canopy?

There was singing and dancing. An old granny danced opposite me, hugging a braided white hallah. The master of revels made a "God 'a mercy" in memory of the bride's parents. The schoolboys threw burrs, as on Tishe b'Av[2] fast day. There were a lot of gifts after the sermon: a noodle board, a kneading trough, a bucket, brooms, ladles, household articles galore. Then I took a look and saw two strapping young men carrying a crib. "What do we need this for?" I asked. So they said, "Don't rack your brains about it. It's all right, it'll come in handy." I realized I was going to be rooked. Take it another way though, what did I stand to lose? I reflected: I'll see what comes of it. A whole town can't go altogether crazy.

II

At night I came where my wife lay, but she wouldn't let me in. "Say, look here, is this what they married us for?" I said. And she said, "My monthly has come." "But yesterday they took you to the ritual bath, and that's afterwards, isn't it supposed to be?" "Today isn't yesterday," said she, "and yesterday's not today. You can beat it if you don't like it." In short, I waited.

Not four months later, she was in childbed. The townsfolk hid their laughter with their knuckles. But what could I do? She suffered intolerable pains and clawed at the walls. "Gimpel," she cried, "I'm going. Forgive me!" The house filled with women. They were boiling pans of water. The screams rose to the welkin.

The thing to do was to go to the house of prayer to repeat psalms, and that was what I did.

The townsfolk liked that, all right. I stood in a corner saying psalms and prayers, and they shook their heads at me. "Pray, pray!" they told me. "Prayer never made any woman pregnant." One of the congregation put a straw to my mouth and said, "Hay for the cows." There was something to that too, by God!

She gave birth to a boy. Friday at the synagogue the sexton stood up before the Ark, pounded on the reading table, and announced, "The wealthy Reb Gimpel invites the congregation to a feast in honor of the birth of a son." The whole house of prayer rang with laughter. My face was flaming. But there was nothing I could do. After all, I *was* the one responsible for the circumcision honors and rituals.

Half the town came running. You couldn't wedge another soul in. Women brought peppered chick-peas, and there was a keg of beer from the tavern. I ate and drank as much as anyone, and they all congratulated me. Then there was a circumcision, and I named the boy after my father, may he rest in peace. When all were gone and I was left with my wife alone, she thrust her head through the bed-curtain and called me to her.

"Gimpel," said she, "why are you silent? Has your ship gone and sunk?"

"What shall I say," I answered. "A fine thing you've done to me! If my mother had known of it she'd have died a second time."

She said, "Are you crazy, or what?"

"How can you make such a fool," I said, "of one who should be the lord and master?"

"What's the matter with you?" she said. "What have you taken it into your head to imagine?"

---

[2]*Tishe b'Av* A Jewish fast day commemorating the destruction of the Temple, celebrated on the ninth day of the month of Ab.

I saw that I must speak bluntly and openly. "Do you think this is the way to use an orphan?" I said. "You have borne a bastard."

She answered, "Drive this foolishness out of your head. The child is yours."

"How can he be mine?" I argued. "He was born seventeen weeks after the wedding."

She told me then that he was premature. I said, "Isn't he a little too premature?" She said, she had had a grandmother who carried just as short a time and she resembled this grandmother of hers as one drop of water does another. She swore to it with such oaths that you would have believed a peasant at the fair if he had used them. To tell the plain truth, I didn't believe her; but when I talked it over next day with the schoolmaster, he told me that the very same thing had happened to Adam and Eve. Two they went up to bed, and four they descended.

"There isn't a woman in the world who is not the granddaughter of Eve," he said.

That was how it was; they argued me dumb. But then, who really knows how such things are?

I began to forget my sorrow. I loved the child madly, and he loved me too. As soon as he saw me he'd wave his little hands and want me to pick him up, and when he was colicky I was the only one who could pacify him. I bought him a little bone teething ring and a little gilded cap. He was forever catching the evil eye from someone, and then I had to run to get one of those abracadabras for him that would get him out of it. I worked like an ox. You know how expenses go up when there's an infant in the house. I don't want to lie about it; I didn't dislike Elka either, for that matter. She swore at me and cursed, and I couldn't get enough of her. What strength she had! One of her looks could rob you of the power of speech. And her orations! Pitch and sulphur, that's what they were full of, and yet somehow also full of charm. I adored her every word. She gave me bloody wounds though.

In the evening I brought her a white loaf as well as a dark one, and also poppy-seed rolls I baked myself. I thieved because of her and swiped everything I could lay hands on: macaroons, raisins, almonds, cakes. I hope I may be forgiven for stealing from the Saturday pots the women left to warm in the baker's oven. I would take out scraps of meat, a chunk of pudding, a chicken leg or head, a piece of tripe, whatever I could nip quickly. She ate and became fat and handsome.

I had to sleep away from home all during the week, at the bakery. On Friday nights when I got home she always made an excuse of some sort. Either she had heartburn, or a stitch in the side, or hiccups, or headaches. You know what women's excuses are. I had a bitter time of it. It was rough. To add to it, this little brother of hers, the bastard, was growing bigger. He'd put lumps on me, and when I wanted to hit back she'd open her mouth and curse so powerfully I saw a green haze floating before my eyes. Ten times a day she threatened to divorce me. Another man in my place would have taken French leave and disappeared. But I'm the type that bears it and says nothing. What's one to do? Shoulders are from God, and burdens too.

One night there was a calamity in the bakery; the oven burst, and we almost had a fire. There was nothing to do but go home, so I went home. Let me, I thought, also taste the joy of sleeping in bed in midweek. I didn't want to wake the sleeping mite and tiptoed into the house. Coming in, it seemed to me that I heard not the snoring of one but, as it were, a double snore, one a thin enough snore and the other like the snoring of a slaughtered ox. Oh, I didn't like that! I didn't like it at all. I went up to the bed, and things suddenly turned black. Next to Elka lay a man's form. Another in my place would have made an uproar, and enough noise to rouse the whole town, but the thought occurred to me that I might wake the child. A little thing like that—why frighten a little swallow, I thought. All right then, I went back to the bakery and stretched out on a sack of flour and till morning I never shut an eye. I shivered as if I had had malaria. "Enough of being a donkey," I said to myself. "Gimpel isn't going to be a sucker all his life. There's a limit even to the foolishness of a fool like Gimpel."

In the morning I went to the rabbi to get advice, and it made a great commotion in the town. They sent the beadle for Elka right away. She came, carrying the child. And what do you think she did? She denied it, denied everything, bone and stone! "He's out of his head," she said. "I know nothing of dreams or divinations." They yelled at her, warned her, hammered on the table, but she stuck to her guns: it was a false accusation, she said.

The butchers and the horse-traders took her part. One of the lads from the slaughterhouse came by and said to me, "We've got our eye on you, you're a marked man." Meanwhile, the child started to bear down and soiled itself. In the rabbinical court there was an Ark of the Covenant, and they couldn't allow that, so they sent Elka away.

I said to the rabbi, "What shall I do?"

"You must divorce her at once," said he.

"And what if she refuses?" I asked.

He said, "You must serve the divorce. That's all you'll have to do."

I said, "Well, all right, Rabbi. Let me think about it."

"There's nothing to think about," said he. "You mustn't remain under the same roof with her."

"And if I want to see the child?" I asked.

"Let her go, the harlot," said he, "and her brood of bastards with her."

The verdict he gave was that I mustn't even cross her threshold—never again, as long as I should live.

During the day it didn't bother me so much. I thought: It was bound to happen, the abscess had to burst. But at night when I stretched out upon the sacks I felt it all very bitterly. A longing took me, for her and for the child. I wanted to be angry, but that's my misfortune exactly, I don't have it in me to be really angry. In the first place—this was how my thoughts went—there's bound to be a slip sometimes. You can't live without errors. Probably that lad who was with her led her on and gave her presents and what not, and women are often long on hair and short on sense, and so he got around her. And then since she denies it so, maybe I was only seeing things? Hallucinations do happen. You see a figure or a mannikin or something, but when you come up closer it's nothing, there's not a thing there. And if that's so, I'm doing her an injustice. And when I got so far in my thoughts I started to weep. I sobbed so that I wet the flour where I lay. In the morning I went to the rabbi and told him that I had made a mistake. The rabbi wrote on with his quill, and he said that if that were so he would have to reconsider the whole case. Until he had finished I wasn't to go near my wife, but I might send her bread and money by messenger.

III

Nine months passed before all the rabbis could come to an agreement. Letters went back and forth. I hadn't realized that there could be so much erudition about a matter like this.

Meanwhile, Elka gave birth to still another child, a girl this time. On the Sabbath I went to the synagogue and invoked a blessing on her. They called me up to the Torah, and I named the child for my mother-in-law—may she rest in peace. The louts and loudmouths of the town who came into the bakery gave me a going over. All Frampol refreshed its spirits because of my trouble and grief. However, I resolved that I would always believe what I was told. What's the good of *not* believing? Today it's your wife you don't believe; tomorrow it's God Himself you won't take stock in.

By an apprentice who was her neighbor I sent her daily a corn or a wheat loaf, or a piece of pastry, rolls or bagels, or, when I got the chance, a slab of pudding, a slice of honeycake, or wedding strudel—whatever came my way. The apprentice was a good-hearted lad, and more than once he added something on his own. He had formerly annoyed me a lot, plucking my nose and digging me in the ribs, but when he started to be a visitor to my house he became kind and friendly. "Hey, you, Gimpel," he said to me, "You have a very decent little wife and two fine kids. You don't deserve them."

"But the things people say about her," I said.

"Well, they have long tongues," he said, "and nothing to do with them but babble. Ignore it as you ignore the cold of last winter."

One day the rabbi sent for me and said, "Are you certain, Gimpel, that you were wrong about your wife?"

I said, "I'm certain."

"Why, but look here! You yourself saw it."

"It must have been a shadow," I said.

"The shadow of what?"

"Just of one of the beams, I think."

"You can go home then. You owe things to the Yanover rabbi. He found an obscure reference in Maimonides[3] that favored you."

I seized the rabbi's hand and kissed it.

I wanted to run home immediately. It's no small thing to be separated for so long a time from wife and child. Then I reflected: I'd better go back to work now, and go home in the evening. I said nothing to anyone, although as far as my heart was concerned it was like one of the Holy Days. The women teased and twitted me as they did every day, but my thought was: Go on, with your loose talk. The truth is out, like the oil upon the water. Maimonides says it's right, and therefore it is right!

At night, when I covered the dough to let it rise, I took my share of bread and a little sack of flour and started homeward. The moon was full and the stars were glistening, something to terrify the soul. I hurried onward, and before me darted a long shadow. It was winter, and a fresh snow had fallen. I had a mind to sing, but it was growing late and I didn't want to wake the householders. Then I felt like whistling, but I remembered that you don't whistle at night because it brings the demons out. So I was silent and walked as fast as I could.

Dogs in the Christian yards barked at me when I passed, but I thought: Bark your teeth out! What are you but mere dogs? Whereas I am a man, the husband of a fine wife, the father of promising children.

As I approached the house my heart started to pound as though it were the heart of a criminal. I felt no fear, but my heart went thump! thump! Well, no drawing back. I quietly lifted the latch and went in. Elka was asleep. I looked at the infant's cradle.

---

[3]*Maimonides*   Spanish rabbi, physician, and philosopher (1135–1204).

The shutter was closed, but the moon forced its way through the cracks. I saw the new-born child's face and loved it as soon as I saw it—immediately—each tiny bone.

Then I came nearer to the bed. And what did I see but the apprentice lying there beside Elka. The moon went out all at once. It was utterly black, and I trembled. My teeth chattered. The bread fell from my hands, and my wife waked and said, "Who is that, ah?"

I muttered, "It's me."

"Gimpel?" she asked. "How come you're here? I thought it was forbidden."

"The rabbi said," I answered and shook as with a fever.

"Listen to me, Gimpel," she said, "go out to the shed and see if the goat's all right. It seems she's been sick." I have forgotten to say that we had a goat. When I heard she was unwell I went into the yard. The nannygoat was a good little creature. I had a nearly human feeling for her.

With hesitant steps I went up to the shed and opened the door. The goat stood there on her four feet. I felt her everywhere, drew her by the horns, examined her udders, and found nothing wrong. She had probably eaten too much bark. "Good night, little goat," I said. "Keep well." And the little beast answered with a "Maa" as though to thank me for the good will.

I went back. The apprentice had vanished.

"Where," I asked, "is the lad?"

"What lad?" my wife answered.

"What do you mean?" I said. "The apprentice. You were sleeping with him."

"The things I have dreamed this night and the night before," she said, "may they come true and lay you low, body and soul! An evil spirit has taken root in you and dazzles your sight." She screamed out, "You hateful creature! You moon calf! You spook! You uncouth man! Get out, or I'll scream all Frampol out of bed!"

Before I could move, her brother sprang out from behind the oven and struck me a blow on the back of the head. I thought he had broken my neck. I felt that something about me was deeply wrong, and I said, "Don't make a scandal. All that's needed now is that people should accuse me of raising spooks and dybbuks."[4] For that was what she had meant. "No one will touch bread of my baking."

In short, I somehow calmed her.

"Well," she said, "that's enough. Lie down, and be shattered by wheels."

Next morning I called the apprentice aside. "Listen here, brother!" I said. And so on and so forth. "What do you say?" He stared at me as though I had dropped from the roof or something.

"I swear," he said, "you'd better go to an herb doctor or some healer. I'm afraid you have a screw loose, but I'll hush it up for you." And that's how the thing stood.

To make a long story short, I lived twenty years with my wife. She bore me six children, four daughters and two sons. All kinds of things happened, but I neither saw nor heard. I believed, and that's all. The rabbi recently said to me, "Belief in itself is beneficial. It is written that a good man lives by his faith."

Suddenly my wife took sick. It began with a trifle, a little growth upon the breast. But she evidently was not destined to live long; she had no years. I spent a fortune on her. I have forgotten to say that by this time I had a bakery of my own and in

---

[4]*dybbuks* Demons or souls of the dead who, according to Jewish folklore, take over the body of living persons. A dybbuk can be exorcised only by rabbinical ritual.

Frampol was considered to be something of a rich man. Daily the healer came, and every witch doctor in the neighborhood was brought. They decided to use leeches, and after that to try cupping. They even called a doctor from Lublin, but it was too late. Before she died she called me to her bed and said, "Forgive me, Gimpel."

I said, "What is there to forgive? You have been a good and faithful wife."

"Woe, Gimpel!" she said. "It was ugly how I deceived you all these years. I want to go clean to my Maker, and so I have to tell you that the children are not yours."

If I had been clouted on the head with a piece of wood it couldn't have bewildered me more.

"Whose are they?" I asked.

"I don't know," she said. "There were a lot . . . but they're not yours." And as she spoke she tossed her head to the side, her eyes turned glassy, and it was all up with Elka. On her whitened lips there remained a smile.

I imagined that, dead as she was, she was saying, "I deceived Gimpel. That was the meaning of my brief life."

IV

One night, when the period of mourning was done, as I lay dreaming on the flour sacks, there came the Spirit of Evil himself and said to me, "Gimpel, why do you sleep?"

I said, "What should I be doing? Eating kreplech?"[5]

"The whole world deceives you," he said, "and you ought to deceive the world in your turn."

"How can I deceive all the world?" I asked him.

He answered, "You might accumulate a bucket of urine every day and at night pour it into the dough. Let the sages of Frampol eat filth."

"What about judgment in the world to come?" I said.

"There is no world to come," he said. "They've sold you a bill of goods and talked you into believing you carried a cat in your belly. What nonsense!"

"Well then," I said, "and is there a God?"

He answered, "There is no God either."

"What," I said, "is there, then?"

"A thick mire."

He stood before my eyes with a goatish beard and horn, long-toothed, and with a tail. Hearing such words, I wanted to snatch him by the tail, but I tumbled from the flour sacks and nearly broke a rib. Then it happened that I had to answer the call of nature, and, passing, I saw the risen dough, which seemed to say to me, "Do it!" In brief, I let myself be persuaded.

At dawn the apprentice came. We kneaded the bread, scattered caraway seeds on it, and set it to bake. Then the apprentice went away, and I was left sitting in the little trench by the oven, on a pile of rags. Well, Gimpel, I thought, you've revenged yourself on them for all the shame they've put on you. Outside the frost glittered, but it was warm beside the oven. The flames heated my face. I bent my head and fell into a doze.

_____

[5]_kreplech_ Yiddish: small casings of dough filled with ground meat, boiled, and usually served in soup.

I saw in a dream, at once, Elka in her shroud. She called to me, "What have you done, Gimpel?"

I said to her, "It's all your fault," and started to cry.

"You fool!" she said. "You fool! Because I was false is everything false too? I never deceived anyone but myself. I'm paying for it all, Gimpel. They spare you nothing here."

I looked at her face. It was black; I was startled and waked, and remained sitting dumb. I sensed that everything hung in the balance. A false step now and I'd lose eternal life. But God gave me His help. I seized the long shovel and took out the loaves, carried them into the yard, and started to dig a hole in the frozen earth.

My apprentice came back as I was doing it. "What are you doing boss?" he said, and grew pale as a corpse.

"I know what I'm doing," I said, and I buried it all before his very eyes.

Then I went home, took my hoard from its hiding place, and divided it among the children. "I saw your mother tonight," I said. "She's turning black, poor thing."

They were so astonished they couldn't speak a word.

"Be well," I said, "and forget that such a one as Gimpel ever existed." I put on my short coat, a pair of boots, took the bag that held my prayer shawl in one hand, my stock in the other, and kissed the mezuzah.[6] When people saw me in the street they were greatly surprised.

"Where are you going?" they said.

I answered, "Into the world." And so I departed from Frampol.

I wandered over the land, and good people did not neglect me. After many years I became old and white; I heard a great deal, many lies and falsehoods, but the longer I lived the more I understood that there were really no lies. Whatever doesn't really happen is dreamed at night. It happens to one if it doesn't happen to another, tomorrow if not today, or a century hence if not next year. What difference can it make? Often I heard tales of which I said, "Now this is a thing that cannot happen." But before a year had elapsed I heard that it actually had come to pass somewhere.

Going from place to place, eating at strange tables, it often happens that I spin yarns—improbable things that could never have happened—about devils, magicians, windmills, and the like. The children run after me, calling, "Grandfather, tell us a story." Sometimes they ask for particular stories, and I try to please them. A fat young boy once said to me, "Grandfather, it's the same story you told us before." The little rogue, he was right.

So it is with dreams too. It is many years since I left Frampol, but as soon as I shut my eyes I am there again. And whom do you think I see? Elka. She is standing by the washtub, as at our first encounter, but her face is shining and her eyes are as radiant as the eyes of a saint, and she speaks outlandish words to me, strange things. When I wake I have forgotten it all. But while the dream lasts I am comforted. She answers all my queries, and what comes out is that all is right. I weep and implore, "Let me be with you." And she consoles me and tells me to be patient. The time is nearer than it is far. Sometimes she strokes and kisses me and weeps upon my face. When I awaken I feel her lips and taste the salt of her tears.

No doubt the world is entirely an imaginary world, but it is only once removed from the true world. At the door of the hovel where I lie, there stands the plank on which

---

[6]*mezuzah* Hebrew: a small scroll inscribed with the Shama from Deuteronomy—"Hear, O Israel"— placed in a case and attached to the doorpost of the home by Biblical command.

the dead are taken away. The gravedigger Jew has his spade ready. The grave waits
and the worms are hungry; the shrouds are prepared—I carry them in my beggar's
sack. Another *shnorrer*[7] is waiting to inherit my bed of straw. When the time comes
I will go joyfully. Whatever may be there, it will be real, without complication,
without ridicule, without deception. God be praised: there even Gimpel cannot
be deceived.

[1953]
Translated by
SAUL BELLOW

Questions

1. In what sense is Gimpel a fool? In what sense is he a wise man? How would you describe Gimpel's morality?
2. How is Gimpel's "foolishness" ultimately vindicated? Why does he leave his family and his village?
3. What does the story suggest about true religious faith?
4. What is the theme of the story?

---

[7]*schnorrer*   Yiddish: a person who begs or sponges off others.

María Teresa Solari

Peru

A ccording to the only information available on María Teresa Solari, her story
"Death and Transfiguration of a Teacher" originally appeared in Antologia del
cuento fantastico peruano, *published in Peru in 1977.*

DEATH AND TRANSFIGURATION OF A TEACHER

The teacher was dead; she had been cut up by the girls who, after killing her, can-
nibalistically disposed of her remains. The teacher was a poet endowed with great
sensitivity and a romantic temperament, having started writing at twenty, although
her career was now over at thirty-five. They were going over the scene of the crime.
All the students were presumed guilty. They were interrogating the top student in
the class:
"Now please tell us everything from the start. . . ."
The girl, a young thing with a blank expression on her face, grabbed one foot and
sardonically exclaimed:
"Here."
"What's that supposed to mean? What are you doing with your foot? Get to the
point!"
"I mean, I started on her foot. I took off her sock and bit into the heel."
"You can't be serious!"
The principal was nonplussed. Actually, all that was left were the gnawed-on
bones. They left a little sign on the macabre residue: "Anatomy Lesson," it said.
One of the murdered teacher's poems went:

Oh, bittersweet youth,
object of my abject toil . . .

And nothing else. She had published only one book, entitled *Destiny.* She was
timid in conversation and at times could not seem to express herself. When she got
frustrated during the torture of her classes, she turned red and her mouth trembled.
But she was incapable of raising her voice. And the classroom noise of the students'
uninterrupted chattering seemed to envelop, disorient and paralyze her. She often
talked about poetry. She tried to explain the magical power of poetic utterance. Something like the supreme effort of the poet to rise above the maddening crowd and to
create. Somewhere in the back of the classroom a girl started going meeeeeooow,
smothering the poetry of the impassioned rhapsodist. The laughter sharpened in tone.

The class became a single giant cat, glaring at the teacher with piercing, bloodshot eyes. Four girls in the front row were singing some pop tune that went:

When I love you
from the bottom of my heart
my brains go
suddenly into knots . . .

The teacher left the room, crestfallen. Looking out at the empty schoolyard, she thought about her Calvary, about poets no longer having any place in this world. Why make teachers cover poets and poetry? It was laughable, and cruel to boot. A little bird swooped down and daintily snatched up a crumb from the gutter. The school's dog wagged his tail as she passed by, and without realizing it she glanced at him tenderly. At least he was sincere. The principal had called her to the office. When she went in, she couldn't help staring at a row of stuffed animals neatly lined up in an open cabinet. She remembered how the day before the principal had ordered them taken out into the sun to keep down the moths. The glass-eyed rabbit and the hawk with one wing stretched out got to sun themselves all morning. She felt the school was lifeless, and the principal just another stuffed animal.

"You don't seem to appreciate how serious the situation is. Your class is a madhouse, I've noticed it when I go by. The students don't respect you; you don't know how to make them respect you. You don't understand the principle of authority. You've just got to face them down and use a firm tone of voice—and make them afraid of you. You can manage them only if they fear you. But what do you do? You talk about poetry, sweetness and light, subtleties that they'll never understand and they don't care about! Stick to the program, right to the end! Hammer on those dates, yes, dates! For example: this poet was born in 1506 and died of tuberculosis in 1526! Therefore, he lived twenty years, wrote twenty books and a dictionary of poetry. Never made a red cent, nobody gave a damn about his books! The first was Illusion, the last, Desperation. Women wanted nothing to do with him, but now he's a great poet. That's all, enough for them to learn and then get on with the next writer!"

She left the office and her spirit seemed to mope along behind her, but at least it wasn't stuffed.

The day of the crime started normally enough. As she entered the classroom a student gave her a bouquet of red roses. Totally unheard of. Some others arranged them in a vase and placed them on the lectern. One girl got up and recited one of Bécquer's[1] poems from beginning to end, the one that starts with "The dark swallows will return." And then, you could have heard a pin drop. One of them—the one that had recited the poem—suddenly came forward and plunged the knife into her before she knew what was happening. She died with a beatific smile on her face and then they simply ate her up. Laughter was everywhere and spring was in the air, as befit the month of October. Later they went home and no one was hungry, although some complained about upset stomachs. A few threw up, but they were mostly calm. Sensitive to the deceased's poetic inclinations, they buried the bones next to a rosebush, but the

---

[1]*Gustavo Adolfo Bécquer* (1836–1870)   Spanish poet and author of romantic prose legends.

dog—who was always hungry—dug them up. And when the principal was notified, she did not know what to make of them, since they did not match any of the bones in her collection. When the teacher did not show up the following day—she had never missed a class—the principal began to suspect something was wrong. Her suspicions were confirmed after questioning the class. There was no accounting for it; this had never happened before at her school. She tried to blame it on the noxious influence of television, but the psychologist she brought in felt that there was more to it: perhaps some of the girls in the class had a congenital predisposition to crime. She called an emergency meeting of the P.T.A. to discuss what should be done, whether to go public or adopt an attitude of prudent silence. More than one father during that long session embarked on a rambling disquisition on how damaging it would be to interrupt or perhaps even end his daughter's studies. Other, more draconian parents noted that the girls' sense of right and wrong would suffer if it were not made clear how they had stepped out of line. Around midnight the sterner ones prevailed; they voted and it was decided to call in the authorities. But who would go to the police with the news? This duty fell to the gardener because, after all, he was the one who found the bones (and the dog chewing on them). So off he went. The police seemed more upset than anyone else. The whole thing was blown up in the press and newspapers sold like hotcakes, although after a while things quieted down and it was all conveniently forgotten. Some of the fathers had a lot of pull and reached an understanding with the court. Money changed hands, classes resumed and the girls did very well in their finals, and 99% of the class passed. The jury admitted that they were very bright. The principal decided to screen all prospective teachers for poetic tendencies, so as to avoid a repetition of this disagreeable and most inconvenient event. She found a taxidermist with literary inclinations to fill the recently-vacated position and keep her supplied with a steady stream of new specimens as well. She even felt a twinge of regret, reflecting on the lost opportunity to stuff the slain Lit teacher and label her "Poet," for an example to all the students: a dangerous breed, an egregious flaw in the Lord's creation. Later on, she and the new teacher started a Taxidermy Club which, to her surprise, proved very popular with the student body, including many of those involved in the incident of the previous year. Not only with the girl with the knife—very bright and a lot of personality, by the way—but also with the best student in the class, who—she knew—had nothing to do with it except for the cannibalism part.

[1977]
Translated by
JOHN BENSON

Questions

1. What views of teaching, poetry, and education are satirized in this story? For what reason is the teacher sacrificed?

2. How does the author's use of grotesque and shocking details and events contribute to the story's effectiveness? Are these elements balanced by the tone in which the story is told?

3. What is the significance of taxidermy to the story?

4. What does the word *transfiguration* in the title suggest about the story's meaning?

John Steinbeck

(1902–1968)

United States

W inner of the Nobel Prize for Literature in 1962, John Steinbeck is linked in the minds of many of his readers with the region about which he wrote so movingly: the Salinas Valley in Southern California, the place of his birth. Critic Donald Heiney made the following observation about Steinbeck:

> Steinbeck is a model example of the modern American nostalgia for the primitive, the counter-reaction to the triumphant urbanization of American culture which took place in the first half of the twentieth century. He stands at the opposite extreme from the Horatio Alger myth, for he admires everything that is not a material success: the have-nots, the misfits, the racial minorities unjustly deprived of their civil and economic rights, the simple, the poor, and the oppressed. His rural heroes, illiterate and sometimes weak-minded, are nevertheless essentially noble; far from realistically described, they are actually poeticized rustics in the traditional romantic manner.

Among his many successful novels, the following stand out as the highlights of Steinbeck's long career: Tortilla Flat *(1935)*, Of Mice and Men *(1937)*, The Grapes of Wrath *(1939)*, East of Eden *(1953)*, *and* The Winter of Our Discontent *(1961)*. "The Chrysanthemums" is from The Long Valley *(1938)*.

THE CHRYSANTHEMUMS

The high grey-flannel fog of winter closed off the Salinas Valley from the sky and from all the rest of the world. On every side it sat like a lid on the mountains and made of the great valley a closed pot. On the broad, level land floor the gang plows bit deep and left the black earth shining like metal where the shares had cut. On the foothill ranches across the Salinas River, the yellow stubble fields seemed to be bathed in pale cold sunshine, but there was no sunshine in the valley now in December. The thick willow scrub along the river flamed with sharp and positive yellow leaves.

It was a time of quiet and of waiting. The air was cold and tender. A light wind blew up from the southwest so that the farmers were mildly hopeful of a good rain before long; but fog and rain do not go together.

Across the river, on Henry Allen's foothill ranch there was little work to be done, for the hay was cut and stored and the orchards were plowed up to receive the rain deeply when it should come. The cattle on the higher slopes were becoming shaggy and rough-coated.

Elisa Allen, working in her flower garden, looked down across the yard and saw Henry, her husband, talking to two men in business suits. The three of them stood by the tractor shed, each man with one foot on the side of the little Fordson. They smoked cigarettes and studied the machine as they talked.

Elisa watched them for a moment and then went back to her work. She was thirty-five. Her face was lean and strong and her eyes were as clear as water. Her figure looked blocked and heavy in her gardening costume, a man's black hat pulled low down over her eyes, clod-hopper shoes, a figured print dress almost completely covered by a big corduroy apron with four big pockets to hold the snips, the trowel and scratcher, the seeds, and the knife she worked with. She wore heavy leather gloves to protect her hands while she worked.

She was cutting down the old year's chrysanthemum stalks with a pair of short and powerful scissors. She looked down toward the men by the tractor shed now and then. Her face was eager and mature and handsome; even her work with the scissors was overeager, overpowerful. The chrysanthemum stems seemed too small and easy for her energy.

She brushed a cloud of hair out of her eyes with the back of her glove, and left a smudge of earth on her cheek in doing it. Behind her stood the neat white farm house with red geraniums close-banked around it as high as the windows. It was a hard-swept looking little house with hard-polished windows, and a clean mud-mat on the front steps.

Elisa cast another glance toward the tractor shed. The strangers were getting into their Ford coupe. She took off a glove and put her strong fingers down into the forest of new green chrysanthemum sprouts that were growing around the old roots. She spread the leaves and looked down among the close-growing stems. No aphids were there, no sowbugs or snails or cutworms. Her terrier fingers destroyed such pests before they could get started.

Elisa started at the sound of her husband's voice. He had come near quietly, and he leaned over the wire fence that protected her flower garden from cattle and dogs and chickens.

"At it again," he said. "You've got a strong new crop coming."

Elisa straightened her back and pulled on the gardening glove again. "Yes. They'll be strong this coming year." In her tone and on her face there was a little smugness.

"You've got a gift with things," Henry observed. "Some of those yellow chrysanthemums you had this year were ten inches across. I wish you'd work out in the orchard and raise some apples that big."

Her eyes sharpened. "Maybe I could do it, too. I've a gift with things, all right. My mother had it. She could stick anything in the ground and make it grow. She said it was having planters' hands that knew how to do it."

"Well, it sure works with flowers," he said.

"Henry, who were those men you were talking to?"

"Why, sure, that's what I came to tell you. They were from the Western Meat Company. I sold thirty head of three-year-old steers. Got nearly my own price, too."

"Good," she said. "Good for you."

"And I thought," he continued, "I thought how it's Saturday afternoon, and we might go into Salinas for dinner at a restaurant, and then to a picture show—to celebrate, you see."

"Good, she repeated. "Oh, yes. That will be good."

Henry put on his joking tone. "There's fights tonight. How'd you like to go to the fights?"

"Oh, no," she said breathlessly. "No, I wouldn't like fights."

"Just fooling, Elisa. We'll go to a movie. Let's see. It's two now. I'm going to take Scotty and bring down those steers from the hill. It'll take us maybe two hours. We'll go in town about five and have dinner at the Cominos Hotel. Like that?

"Of course I'll like it. It's good to eat away from home."

"All right, then. I'll go get up a couple of horses."

She said, "I'll have plenty of time to transplant some of these sets, I guess."

She heard her husband calling Scotty down by the barn. And a little later she saw the two men ride up the pale yellow hillside in search of the steers.

There was a little square sandy bed kept for rooting the chrysanthemums. With her trowel she turned the soil over and over, and smoothed it and patted it firm. Then she dug ten parallel trenches to receive the sets. Back at the chrysanthemum bed she pulled out the little crisp shoots, trimmed off the leaves at each one with her scissors, and laid it on a small orderly pile.

A squeak of wheels and plod of hoofs came from the road. Elisa looked up. The country road ran along the dense bank of willows and cottonwoods that bordered the river, and up this road came a curious vehicle, curiously drawn. It was an old spring-wagon, with a round canvas top on it like the corner of a prairie schooner. It was drawn by an old bay horse and a little grey-and-white burro. A big stubble-bearded man sat between the cover flaps and drove the crawling team. Underneath the wagon, between the hind wheels, a lean and rangy mongrel dog walked sedately. Words were painted on the canvas, in clumsy, crooked letters. "Pots, pans, knives, sisors, lawn mores, Fixed." Two rows of articles, and the triumphantly definitive "Fixed" below. The black paint had run down in little sharp points beneath each letter.

Elisa, squatting on the ground, watched to see the crazy, loose-jointed wagon pass by. But it didn't pass. It turned into the farm road in front of her house, crooked old wheels skirting and squeaking. The rangy dog darted from between the wheels and ran ahead. Instantly the two ranch shepherds flew out at him. Then all three stopped, and with stiff and quivering tails, with taut straight legs, with ambassadorial dignity, they slowly circled, sniffing daintily. The caravan pulled up to Elisa's wire fence and stopped. Now the newcomer dog, feeling outnumbered, lowered his tail and retired under the wagon with raised hackles and bared teeth.

The man on the seat called out, "That's a bad dog in a fight when he gets started."

Elisa laughed. "I see he is. How soon does he generally get started?"

The man caught up her laughter and echoed it heartily. "Sometimes not for weeks and weeks," he said. He climbed stiffly down, over the wheel. The horse and the donkey drooped like unwatered flowers.

Elisa saw that he was a very big man. Although his hair and beard were greying, he did not look old. His worn black suit was wrinkled and spotted with grease. The laughter had disappeared from his face and eyes the moment his laughing voice ceased. His eyes were dark, and they were full of the brooding that gets in the eyes of teamsters and of sailors. The calloused hands he rested on the wire fence were cracked, and every crack was a black line. He took off his battered hat.

"I'm off my general road, ma'am," he said. "Does this dirt road cut over across the river to the Los Angeles highway?"

Elisa stood up and shoved the thick scissors in her apron pocket. "Well, yes, it does, but it winds around and then fords the river. I don't think your team could pull through the sand."

He replied with some asperity, "It might surprise you what them beasts can pull through."

"When they get started?" she asked.

He smiled for a second. "Yes. When they get started."

"Well," said Elisa, "I think you'll save time if you go back to the Salinas road and pick up the highway there."

He drew a big finger down the chicken wire and made it sing. "I ain't in any hurry, ma'am. I go from Seattle to San Diego and back every year. Takes all my time. About six months each way. I aim to follow nice weather."

Elisa took off her gloves and stuffed them in the apron pocket with the scissors. She touched the under edge of her man's hat, searching for fugitive hairs. "That sounds like a nice kind of a way to live," she said.

He leaned confidentially over the fence. "Maybe you noticed the writing on my wagon. I mend pots and sharpen knives and scissors. You got any of them things to do?"

"Oh, no," she said, quickly. "Nothing like that." Her eyes hardened with resistance.

"Scissors is the worst thing," he explained. "Most people just ruin scissors trying to sharpen 'em, but I know how. I got a special tool. It's a little bobbit kind of thing, and patented. But it sure does the trick."

"No. My scissors are all sharp."

"All right, then. Take a pot," he continued earnestly, "a bent pot, or a pot with a hole. I can make it like new so you don't have to buy no new ones. That's a savings for you."

"No," she said shortly. "I tell you I have nothing like that for you to do."

His face fell to an exaggerated sadness. His voice took on a whining undertone. "I ain't had a thing to do today. Maybe I won't have no supper tonight. You see I'm off my regular road. I know folks on the highway clear from Seattle to San Diego. They save their things for me to sharpen up because they know I do it so good and save them money."

"I'm sorry," Elisa said irritably. "I haven't anything for you to do."

His eyes left her face and fell to searching the ground. They roamed about until they came to the chrysanthemum bed where she had been working. "What's them plants, ma'am?"

The irritation and resistance melted from Elisa's face. "Oh, those are chrysanthemums, giant whites and yellows. I raise them every year, bigger than anybody around here."

"Kind of a long-stemmed flower? Looks like a quick puff of colored smoke?" he asked.

"That's it. What a nice way to describe them."

"They smell kind of nasty till you get used to them," he said.

"It's a good bitter smell," she retorted, "not nasty at all."

He changed his tone quickly, "I like the smell myself."

"I had ten-inch-blooms this year," she said.

The man leaned farther over the fence. "Look, I know a lady down the road a piece, has got the nicest garden you ever seen. Got nearly every kind of flower but no chrysanthemums. Last time I was mending a copper-bottom washtub for her (that's a hard job but I do it good), she said to me, 'If you ever run acrost some nice chrysanthemums I wish you'd try to get me a few seeds.' That's what she told me."

Elisa's eyes grew alert and eager. "She couldn't have known much about chrysanthemums. You *can* raise them from seed, but it's much easier to root the little sprouts you see there."

"Oh," he said. "I s'pose I can't take none to her, then."

"Why yes you can," Elisa cried. "I can put some in damp sand, and you can carry them right along with you. They'll take root in the pot if you keep them damp. And then she can transplant them."

"She'd sure like to have some, ma'am. You say they're nice ones?"

"Beautiful," she said. "Oh, beautiful." Her eyes shone. She tore off the battered hat and shook out her dark pretty hair. "I'll put them in a flower pot, and you can take them right with you. Come into the yard."

While the man came through the picket gate Elisa ran excitedly along the geranium-bordered path to the back of the house. And she returned carrying a big red flower pot. The gloves were forgotten now. She kneeled on the ground by the starting bed and dug up the sandy soil with her fingers and scooped it into the bright new flower pot. Then she picked up the little pile of shoots she had prepared. With her strong fingers she pressed them into the sand and tamped around them with her knuckles. The man stood over her. "I'll tell you what to do," she said. "You remember so you can tell the lady."

"Yes, I'll try to remember."

"Well, look. These will take root in about a month. Then she must set them out, about a foot apart in good rich earth like this, see?" She lifted a handful of dark soil for him to look at. "They'll grow fast and tall. Now remember this: In July tell her to cut them down, about eight inches from the ground."

"Before they bloom?" he asked.

"Yes, before they bloom." Her face was tight with eagerness. "They'll grow right up again. About the last of September the buds will start."

She stopped and seemed perplexed. "It's the budding that takes the most care," she said hesitantly. "I don't know how to tell you." She looked deep into his eyes, search-ingly. Her mouth opened a little, and she seemed to be listening. "I'll try to tell you," she said. "Did you ever hear of planting hands?"

"Can't say I have, ma'am."

"Well, I can only tell you what it feels like. It's when you're picking off the buds you don't want. Everything goes right down into your fingertips. You watch your fin-gers work. They do it themselves. You can feel how it is. They pick and pick the buds. They never make a mistake. They're with the plant. Do you see? Your fingers and the plant. You can feel that, right up your arm. They know. They never make a mistake. You can feel it. When you're like that you can't do anything wrong. Do you see that? Can you understand that?"

She was kneeling on the ground looking up at him. Her breast swelled passionately.

The man's eyes narrowed. He looked away self-consciously. "Maybe I know," he said. "Sometimes in the night in the wagon there—"

Elisa's voice grew husky. She broke in on him, "I've never lived as you do, but I know what you mean. When the night is dark—why, the stars are sharp-pointed, and there's quiet. Why, you rise up and up! Every pointed star gets driven into your body. It's like that. Hot and sharp and—lovely."

Kneeling there, her hand went out toward his legs in the greasy black trousers. Her hesitant fingers almost touched the cloth. Then her hand dropped to the ground. She crouched low like a fawning dog.

He said, "It's nice, just like you say. Only when you don't have no dinner, it ain't."

She stood up then, very straight, and her face was ashamed. She held the flower pot out to him and placed it gently in his arms. "Here. Put it in your wagon, on the seat, where you can watch it. Maybe I can find something for you to do."

At the back of the house she dug in the can pile and found two old and battered aluminum saucepans. She carried them back and gave them to him. "Here, maybe you can fix these."

His manner changed. He became professional. "Good as new I can fix them." At the back of his wagon he set a little anvil, and out of an oily tool box dug a small machine hammer. Elisa came through the gate to watch him while he pounded out the dents in the kettles. His mouth grew sure and knowing. At a difficult part of the work he sucked his underlip.

"You sleep right in the wagon?" Elisa asked.

"Right in the wagon, ma'am. Rain or shine I'm dry as a cow in there."

"It must be nice," she said. "It must be very nice. I wish women could do such things."

"It ain't the right kind of a life for a woman."

Her upper lip raised a little, showing her teeth. "How do you know? How can you tell?" she said.

"I don't know, ma'am," he protested. "Of course I don't know. Now here's your kettles, done. You don't have to buy no new ones."

"How much?"

"Oh, fifty cents'll do. I keep my prices down and my work good. That's why I have all them satisfied customers up and down the highway."

Elisa brought him a fifty-cent piece from the house and dropped it in his hand. "You might be surprised to have a rival some time. I can sharpen scissors, too. And I can beat the dents out of little pots. I could show you what a woman might do."

He put his hammer back in the oily box and shoved the little anvil out of sight. "It would be a lonely life for a woman, ma'am, and a scarey life, too, with animals creeping under the wagon all night." He climbed over the singletree, steadying himself with a hand on the burro's white rump. He settled himself in the seat, picked up the lines. "Thank you kindly, ma'am," he said. "I'll do like you told me; I'll go back and catch the Salinas road."

"Mind," she called, "if you're long in getting there, keep the sand damp."

"Sand, ma'am? . . . Sand? Oh, sure. You mean around the chrysanthemums. Sure I will." He clucked his tongue. The beasts leaned luxuriously into their collars. The mongrel dog took his place between the back wheels. The wagon turned and crawled out the entrance road and back the way it had come, along the river.

Elisa stood in front of her wire fence watching the slow progress of the caravan. Her shoulders were straight, her head thrown back, her eyes half-closed, so that the scene came vaguely into them. Her lips moved silently, forming the words "Good-bye—goodbye." Then she whispered, "That's a bright direction. There's a glowing there." The sound of her whisper startled her. She shook herself free and looked about to see whether anyone had been listening. Only the dogs had heard. They lifted their heads toward her from their sleeping in the dust, and then stretched out their chins and settled asleep again. Elisa turned and ran hurriedly into the house.

In the kitchen she reached behind the stove and felt the water tank. It was full of hot water from the noonday cooking. In the bathroom she tore off her soiled clothes and flung them into the corner. And then she scrubbed herself with a little block of pumice, legs and thighs, loins and chest and arms, until her skin was scratched and red. When she had dried herself she stood in front of a mirror in her bedroom and looked at her body. She tightened her stomach and threw out her chest. She turned and looked over her shoulder at her back.

After a while she began to dress, slowly. She put on her newest underclothing and her nicest stockings and the dress which was the symbol of her prettiness. She worked carefully on her hair, penciled her eyebrows and rouged her lips.

Before she was finished she heard the little thunder of hoofs and the shouts of Henry and his helper as they drove the red steers into the corral. She heard the gate bang shut and set herself for Henry's arrival.

His step sounded on the porch. He entered the house calling, "Elisa, where are you?"

"In my room, dressing. I'm not ready. There's hot water for your bath. Hurry up. It's getting late."

When she heard him splashing in the tub, Elisa laid his dark suit on the bed, and shirt and socks and tie beside it. She stood his polished shoes on the floor beside the bed. Then she went to the porch and sat primly and stiffly down. She looked toward the river road where the willow-line was still yellow with frosted leaves so that under the high grey fog they seemed a thin band of sunshine. This was the only color in the grey afternoon. She sat unmoving for a long time. Her eyes blinked rarely.

Henry came banging out of the door, shoving his tie inside his vest as he came. Elisa stiffened and her face grew tight. Henry stopped short and looked at her. "Why—why, Elisa. You look so nice!"

"Nice? You think I look nice? What do you mean by 'nice'?"

Henry blundered on. "I don't know. I mean you look different, strong and happy."

"I am strong? Yes, strong. What do you mean 'strong'?"

He looked bewildered. "You're playing some kind of a game," he said helplessly. "It's a kind of a play. You look strong enough to break a calf over your knee, happy enough to eat it like a watermelon."

For a second she lost her rigidity. "Henry! Don't talk like that. You didn't know what you said." She grew complete again. "I'm strong," she boasted, "I never knew before how strong."

Henry looked down toward the tractor shed, and when he brought his eyes back to her, they were his own again. "I'll get out the car. You can put on your coat while I'm starting."

Elisa went into the house. She heard him drive to the gate and idle down his motor, and then she took a long time to put on her hat. She pulled it here and pressed it there. When Henry turned the motor off she slipped into her coat and went out.

The little roadster bounced along on the dirt road by the river, raising the birds and driving the rabbits into the brush. Two cranes flapped heavily over the willow-line and dropped into the river-bed.

Far ahead on the road Elisa saw a dark speck. She knew.

She tried not to look as they passed it, but her eyes would not obey. She whispered to herself sadly, "He might have thrown them off the road. That wouldn't have been much trouble, not very much. But he kept the pot," she explained. "He had to keep the pot. That's why he couldn't get them off the road."

The roadster turned a bend and she saw the caravan ahead. She swung full around toward her husband so she could not see the little covered wagon and the mismatched team as the car passed them.

In a moment it was over. The thing was done. She did not look back.

She said loudly, to be heard above the motor. "It will be good, tonight, a good dinner."

"Now you're changed again," Henry complained. He took one hand from the wheel and patted her knee. "I ought to take you in to dinner oftener. It would be good for both of us. We get so heavy out on the ranch."

"Henry," she asked, "could we have wine at dinner?"

"Sure we could. Say! That will be fine."

She was silent for a while; then she said, "Henry, at those prize fights, do the men hurt each other very much?"

"Sometimes a little, not often. Why?"

"Well, I've read how they break noses, and blood runs down their chests. I've read how the fighting gloves get heavy and soggy with blood."

He looked around at her. "What's the matter, Elisa? I didn't know you read things like that." He brought the car to a stop, then turned to the right over the Salinas River bridge.

"Do any women ever go to the fights?" she asked.

"Oh, sure, some. What's the matter Elisa? Do you want to go? I don't think you'd like it, but I'll take you if you really want to go."

She relaxed limply in the seat. "Oh, no. No. I don't want to go. I'm sure I don't." Her face was turned away from him. "It will be enough if we can have wine. It will be plenty." She turned up her coat collar so he could not see that she was crying weakly—like an old woman.

[1938]

Questions

1. What does Elisa's husband mean when he refers to her as "strong" near the end of the story? Has her incident with the tinker made her stronger and more capable of living the difficult life of a farmer's wife—or has the incident made her weaker, more vulnerable than she was before?

2. When Elisa talks to the tinker and he describes his lonely nights in the wagon, she has to resist the temptation to reach out and touch his trousers. What are the implied sexual dynamics of their relationship? (For a variation on this theme, read D. H. Lawrence's poem, "The Odour of Chrysanthemums," published before Steinbeck's story.)

3. What do the flowers represent to Elisa? What is the state of Elisa and Henry's marriage?

Graham Swift

(b. 1949)
England

Currently one of England's leading novelists, Graham Swift was born in London in 1949. He attended Cambridge University for his undergraduate degree and subsequently continued graduate studies both there and at York University. His first novel, The Sweet-Shop Owner (1980), was followed by Shuttlecock (1981) and Waterland (1983), which was nominated for the Booker Prize, his country's most prestigious literary award. Waterland also won the praise of American critics, who compared it to the work of William Faulkner. The narrative opens with the discovery of a corpse in the waterlands, the Fens, and then works backward to solve the question of who the murderer was.

Praise for Swift's writing has increased with each of his published works. Ever After (1992) was followed by Last Orders (1996), which was awarded the Booker Prize. The story included here is from Learning to Swim and Other Stories (1982).

LEARNING TO SWIM

Mrs. Singleton had three times thought of leaving her husband. The first time was before they were married, on a charter plane coming back from a holiday in Greece. They were students who had just graduated. They had rucksacks and faded jeans. In Greece they had stayed part of the time by a beach on an island. The island was dry and rocky with great grey and vermilion coloured rocks and when you lay on the beach it seemed that you too became a hot, basking rock. Behind the beach there were eucalyptus trees like dry, leafy bones, old men with mules and gold teeth, a fragrance of thyme, and a café with melon seeds on the floor and a jukebox which played bouzouki music and songs by Cliff Richard. All this Mr. Singleton failed to appreciate. He'd only liked the milk-warm, clear blue sea, in which he'd stayed most of the time as if afraid of foreign soil. On the plane she'd thought: He hadn't enjoyed the holiday, hadn't liked Greece at all. All that sunshine. Then she'd thought she ought not to marry him.

Though she had, a year later.

The second time was about a year after Mr. Singleton, who was a civil engineer, had begun his first big job. He became a junior partner in a firm with a growing reputation. She ought to have been pleased by this. It brought money and comfort; it enabled them to move to a house with a large garden, to live well, to think about raising a family. They spent weekends in country hotels. But Mr. Singleton seemed untouched by this. He became withdrawn and incommunicative. He went to his work austere-faced. She thought: He likes his bridges and tunnels better than me.

The third time, which was really a phase, not a single moment, was when she began to calculate how often Mr. Singleton made love to her. When she started this it was about once every fortnight on average. Then it became every three weeks. The interval had been widening for some time. This was not a predicament Mrs. Singleton viewed selfishly. Love-making had been a problem before, in their earliest days together, which, thanks to her patience and initiative, had been overcome. It was Mr. Singleton's unhappiness, not her own, that she saw in their present plight. He was distrustful of happiness as some people fear heights or open spaces. She would reassure him, encourage him again. But the averages seemed to defy her personal effort: once every three weeks, once every month. . . . She thought: Things go back to as they were.

But then, by sheer chance, she became pregnant.

Now she lay on her back, eyes closed, on the coarse sand of the beach in Cornwall. It was hot and, if she opened her eyes, the sky was clear blue. This and the previous summer had been fine enough to make her husband's refusal to go abroad for holidays tolerable. If you kept your eyes closed it could be Greece or Italy or Ibiza. She wore a chocolate-brown bikini, sunglasses, and her skin, which seldom suffered from sunburn, was already beginning to tan. She let her arms trail idly by her side, scooping up little handfuls of sand. If she turned her head to the right and looked towards the sea she could see Mr. Singleton and their son Paul standing in the shallow water. Mr. Singleton was teaching Paul to swim. "Kick!" he was saying. From here, against the gentle waves, they looked like no more than two rippling silhouettes.

"Kick!" said Mr. Singleton, "Kick!" He was like a punisher administering lashes.

She turned her head away to face upwards. If you shut your eyes you could imagine you were the only one on the beach; if you held them shut you could be part of the beach. Mrs. Singleton imagined that in order to acquire a tan you had to let the sun make love to you.

She dug her heels in the sand and smiled involuntarily.

When she was a thin, flat-chested, studious girl in a grey school uniform, Mrs. Singleton had assuaged her fear and desperation about sex with fantasies which took away from men the brute physicality she expected of them. All her lovers would be artists. Poets would write poems to her, composers would dedicate their works to her. She would even pose, naked and immaculate, for painters, who having committed her true, her eternal form to canvas, would make love to her in an impalpable, ethereal way, under the power of which her bodily and temporal self would melt away, perhaps for ever. These fantasies (for she had never entirely renounced them) had crystallized for her in the image of a sculptor, who from a cold intractable piece of stone would fashion her very essence—which would be vibrant and full of sunlight, like the statues they had seen in Greece.

At university she had worked on the assumption that all men lusted uncontrollably and insatiably after women. She had not yet encountered a man who, whilst prone to the usual instincts, possessing moreover a magnificent body with which to fulfil them, yet had scruples about doing so, seemed ashamed of his own capacities. It did not matter that Mr. Singleton was reading engineering, was scarcely artistic at all, or that his powerful physique was unlike the nebulous creatures of her dreams. She found she loved this solid man-flesh. Mrs. Singleton had thought she was the shy, inexperienced, timid girl. Overnight she discovered that she wasn't this at all. He wore tough denim shirts, spoke and smiled very little and had a way of standing very straight and upright as if he didn't need any help from anyone. She had to educate him into moments of passion, of self-forgetfulness which made her glow with her own achievement. She was happy because she had not thought she was happy and she believed she could make someone else happy. At the university girls were starting to wear jeans, record-players played the Rolling Stones and in the hush of the Modern Languages Library she read Leopardi and Verlaine. She seemed to float with confidence in a swirling, buoyant element she had never suspected would be her own.

"Kick!" she heard again from the water.

Mr. Singleton had twice thought of leaving his wife. Once was after a symphony concert they had gone to in London when they had not known each other very long and she still tried to get him to read books, to listen to music, to take an interest in art. She would buy concert or theatre tickets, and he had to seem pleased. At this concert a visiting orchestra was playing some titanic, large-scale work by a late nineteenth-century composer. A note in the programme said it represented the triumph of life over death. He had sat on his plush seat amidst the swirling barrage of sound. He had no idea what he had to do with it or the triumph of life over death. He had thought the same thought about the rapt girl on his left, the future Mrs. Singleton, who now and then bobbed, swayed or rose in her seat as if the music physically lifted her. There were at least seventy musicians on the platform. As the piece worked to its final crescendo the conductor, whose arms were flailing frantically so that his white shirt back appeared under his flying tails, looked so absurd Mr. Singleton thought he would laugh. When the music stopped and was immediately supplanted by wild cheering and clapping he thought the world had gone mad. He had struck his own hands together so as to appear to be sharing the ecstasy. Then, as they filed out, he had almost wept because he felt like an insect. He even thought she had arranged the whole business so as to humiliate him.

He thought he would not marry her.

The second time was after they had been married some years. He was one of a team of engineers working on a suspension bridge over an estuary in Ireland. They took it in turns to stay on the site and to inspect the construction work personally. Once he had to go to the very top of one of the two piers of the bridge to examine work on the bearings and housing for the main overhead cables. A lift ran up between the twin towers of the pier amidst a network of scaffolding and power cables to where a working platform was positioned. The engineer, with the supervisor and the foreman, had only to stay on the platform from where all the main features of construction were visible. The men at work on the upper sections of the towers, specialists in their trade, earning up to two hundred pounds a week—who balanced on precarious cat-walks and walked along exposed reinforcing girders—often jibed at the engineers who never left the platform. He thought he would show them. He walked out on to one of the cat-walks on the outer face of the pier where they were fitting huge grip-bolts. This was quite safe if you held on to the rails but still took some nerve. He wore a check cheesecloth shirt and his white safety helmet. It was a grey, humid August day. The cat-walk hung over greyness. The water of the estuary was the colour of dead fish. A dredger was chugging near the base of the pier. He thought, I could swim the estuary; but there is a bridge. Below him the yellow helmets of workers moved over the girders for the roadway like beetles. He took his hands from the rail. He wasn't at all afraid. He had been away from his wife all week. He thought: She knows nothing of this. If he were to step out now into the grey air he would be quite by himself, no harm would come to him. . . .

Now Mr. Singleton stood in the water, teaching his son to swim. They were doing the water-wings exercise. The boy wore a pair of water-wings, red underneath, yellow on top, which ballooned up under his arms and chin. With this to support him, he would splutter and splash towards his father who stood facing him some feet away. After a while at this they would try the same procedure, his father moving a little nearer, but without the water-wings, and this the boy dreaded. "Kick!" said Mr. Singleton. "Use your legs!" He watched his son draw painfully towards him. The boy had not yet grasped that the body naturally floated and that if you added to this certain mechanical effects, you swam. He thought that in order to swim you had to make as much frantic movement as possible. As he struggled towards Mr. Singleton his head, which was too high out of the water, jerked messily from side to side, and his eyes which were half closed swivelled in every direction but straight ahead. "Towards me!" shouted Mr. Singleton. He held out his arms in front of him for Paul to grasp. As his son was on the point of clutching them he would step back a little, pulling his hands away, in the hope that the last desperate lunge to reach his father might really teach the boy the art of propelling himself in water. But he sometimes wondered if this were his only motive.

"Good boy. Now again."

At school Mr. Singleton had been an excellent swimmer. He had won various school titles, broken numerous records and competed successfully in ASA championships. There was a period between the ages of about thirteen and seventeen which he remembered as the happiest in his life. It wasn't the medals and trophies that made him glad, but the knowledge that he didn't have to bother about anything else. Swimming vindicated him. He would get up every morning at six and train for two hours in the baths, and again before lunch; and when he fell asleep, exhausted, in French and English periods in the afternoon, he didn't have to bother about the indignation of the masters—lank, ill-conditioned creatures—for he had his excuse. He didn't have to bother about the physics teacher who complained to the headmaster that he would never get the exam results he needed if he didn't cut down his swimming, for the headmaster (who was an advocate of sport) came to his aid and told the physics teacher not to interfere with a boy who was a credit to the school. Nor did he have to bother about a host of other things which were supposed to be going on inside him, which made the question of what to do in the evening, at weekends, fraught and tantalizing, which drove other boys to moodiness and recklessness. For once in the cool water of the baths, his arms reaching, his eyes fixed on the blue marker line on the bottom, his ears full so that he could hear nothing around him, he would feel quite by himself, quite sufficient. At the end of races, when for one brief instant he clung panting alone like a survivor to the finishing rail which his rivals had yet to touch, he felt an infinite peace. He went to bed early, slept soundly, kept to his training regimen; and he enjoyed this Spartan purity which disdained pleasure and disorder. Some of his schoolmates mocked him—for not going to dances on Saturdays or to pubs, under age, or the Expresso after school. But he did not mind. He didn't need them. He knew they were weak. None of them could hold out, depend on themselves, spurn comfort if they had to. Some of them would go under in life. And none of them could cleave the water as he did or possessed a hard, stream-lined, perfectly tuned body as he did.

Then, when he was nearly seventeen all this changed. His father, who was an engineer, though proud of his son's trophies, suddenly pressed him to different forms of success. The headmaster no longer shielded him from the physics master. He said: "You can't swim into your future." Out of spite perhaps or an odd consistency of self-denial, he dropped swimming altogether rather than cut it down. For a year and a half he worked at his maths and physics with the same single-mindedness with which he had perfected his sport. He knew about mechanics and engineering because he knew how to make his body move through water. His work was not merely competent but good. He got to university where he might have had the leisure, if he wished, to resume his swimming. But he did not. Two years are a long gap in a swimmer's training; two years when you are near your peak can mean you will never get back to your true form. Sometimes he went for a dip in the university pool and swam slowly up and down amongst practising members of the university team, whom perhaps he could still have beaten, as a kind of relief.

Often, Mr. Singleton dreamt about swimming. He would be moving through vast expanses of water, an ocean. As he moved it did not require any effort at all. Sometimes he would go for long distances under water, but he did not have to bother about breathing. The water would be silvery-grey. And as always it seemed that as he swam he was really trying to get beyond the water, to put it behind him, as if it were a veil he were parting and he would emerge on the other side of it at last, on to some pristine shore, where he would step where no one else had stepped before.

When he made love to his wife her body got in the way; he wanted to swim through her.

Mrs. Singleton raised herself, pushed her sun-glasses up over her dark hair and sat with her arms stretched straight behind her back. A trickle of sweat ran between her breasts. They had developed to a good size since her schoolgirl days. Her skinniness in youth had stood her in good stead against the filling out of middle age, and her body was probably more mellow, more lithe and better proportioned now than it had ever been. She looked at Paul and Mr. Singleton half immersed in the shallows. It seemed to her that her husband was the real boy, standing stubbornly upright with his hands before him, and that Paul was some toy being pulled and swung relentlessly around him and towards him as though on some string. They had seen her sit up. Her husband waved, holding the boy's hand, as though for the two of them. Paul did not wave; he seemed more concerned with the water in his eyes. Mrs. Singleton did not wave back. She would have done if her son had waved. When they had left for their holiday Mr. Singleton had said to Paul, "You'll learn to swim this time. In salt water, you know, it's easier." Mrs. Singleton hoped her son wouldn't swim; so that she could wrap him, still, in the big yellow towel when he came out, rub him dry and warm, and watch her husband stand apart, his hands empty.

She watched Mr. Singleton drop his arm back to his side. "If you wouldn't splash it wouldn't go in your eyes," she just caught him say.

The night before, in their hotel room, they had argued. They always argued about half way through their holidays. It was symbolic, perhaps, of that first trip to Greece, when he had somehow refused to enjoy himself. They had to incur injuries so that they could then appreciate their leisure, like convalescents. For the first four days or so of their holiday Mr. Singleton would tend to be moody, on edge. He would excuse this as "winding down," the not-to-be-hurried process of dispelling the pressures of work. Mrs. Singleton would be patient. On about the fifth day Mrs. Singleton would begin to suspect that the winding down would never end and indeed (which she had known all along) that it was not winding down at all—he was clinging, as to a defence, to his bridges and tunnels; and she would show her resentment. At this point Mr. Singleton would retaliate by an attack upon her indolence.

Last night he had called her "flabby." He could not mean, of course, "flabby-bodied" (she could glance down, now, at her still flat belly), though such a sensual attack would have been simpler, almost heartening, from him. He meant "flabby of attitude." And what he meant by this, or what he wanted to mean, was that *he* was not flabby; that he worked, facing the real world, erecting great solid things on the face of the land, and that, whilst he worked, he disdained work's rewards—money, pleasure, rich food, holidays abroad—that he hadn't "gone soft," as she had done since they graduated eleven years ago, with their credentials for the future and their plane tickets to Greece. She knew this toughness of her husband was only a cover for his own failure to relax and his need to keep his distance. She knew that he found no particular virtue in his bridges and tunnels (it was the last thing he wanted to do really—build); it didn't matter if they were right or wrong, they were there, he could point to them as if it vindicated him—just as when he made his infrequent, if seismic, love to her it was not a case of enjoyment or satisfaction; he just did it.

It was hot in their hotel room. Mr. Singleton stood in his blue pyjama bottoms, feet apart, like a PT instructor.

"Flabby? What do you mean—'flabby'!?" she had said, looking daunted.

But Mrs. Singleton had the advantage whenever Mr. Singleton accused her in this way of complacency, of weakness. She knew he only did it to hurt her, and so to feel guilty, and so to feel the remorse which would release his own affection for her, his vulnerability, his own need to be loved. Mrs. Singleton was used to this process, to the tenderness that was the tenderness of successively opened and reopened wounds. And she was used to being the nurse who took care of the healing scars. For though Mr. Singleton inflicted the first blow he would always make himself more guilty than he made her suffer, and Mrs. Singleton, though in pain herself, could not resist wanting to clasp and cherish her husband, wanting to wrap him up safe when his own weakness and submissiveness showed and his body became liquid and soft against her; could not resist the old spur that her husband was unhappy and it was for her to make him happy. Mr. Singleton was extraordinarily lovable when he was guilty. She would even have yielded indefinitely, foregoing her own grievance, to this extreme of comforting him for the pain he caused her, had she not discovered, in time, that this only pushed the process a stage further. Her forgiveness of him became only another level of comfort, of softness he must reject. His flesh shrank from her restoring touch.

She thought: Men go round in circles, women don't move.

She kept to her side of the hotel bed, he, with his face turned, to his. He lay like a person washed up on a beach. She reached out her hand and stroked the nape of his neck. She felt him tense. All this was a pattern.

"I'm sorry," he said, "I didn't mean—"

"It's all right, it doesn't matter."

"Doesn't it matter?" he said.

When they reached this point they were like miners racing each other for deeper and deeper seams of guilt and recrimination.

But Mrs. Singleton had given up delving to rock bottom. Perhaps it was five years ago when she had thought for the third time of leaving her husband, perhaps long before that. When they were students she'd made allowances for his constraints, his reluctances. An unhappy childhood perhaps, a strict upbringing. She thought his inhibition might be lifted by the sanction of marriage. She'd thought, after all, it would be a good thing if he married her. She had not thought what would be good for her. They stood outside Gatwick Airport, back from Greece, in the grey, wet August light. Their tanned skin had seemed to glow. Yet she'd known this mood of promise would pass. She watched him kick against contentment, against ease, against the long, glittering life-line she threw at him; and, after a while, she ceased to try to haul him in. She began to imagine again her phantom artists. She thought: People slip off the shores of the real world, back into dreams. She hadn't "gone soft," only gone back to herself. Hidden inside her like treasure there were lines of Leopardi, of Verlaine her husband would never appreciate. She thought, he doesn't need me, things run off him, like water. She even thought that her husband's neglect in making love to her was not a problem he had but a deliberate scheme to deny her. When Mrs. Singleton desired her husband she could not help herself. She would stretch back on the bed with the sheets pulled off like a blissful nude in a Modigliani. She thought this ought to gladden a man. Mr. Singleton would stand at the foot of the bed and gaze down at her. He looked like some strong, chaste knight in the legend of the Grail. He would respond to her invitation, but before he did so there would be this expression, half stern, half innocent, in his eyes. It was the sort of expression that good men in books and films are supposed to make to prostitutes. It would ensure that their love-making was marred and that afterward it would seem as if he had performed something out of duty that only she wanted. Her body would feel like stone. It was at such times, when she felt the cold, dead-weight feel of abused happiness, that Mrs. Singleton most thought she was through with Mr. Singleton. She would watch his strong, compact torso already lifting itself off the bed. She would think: He thinks he is tough, contained in himself, but he won't see what I offer him, he doesn't see how it is I who can help him.

Mrs. Singleton lay back on her striped towel on the sand. Once again she became part of the beach. The careless sounds of the seaside, of excited children's voices, of languid grownups', of wooden bats on balls, fluttered over her as she shut her eyes. She thought: It is the sort of day on which someone suddenly shouts, "Someone is drowning."

When Mrs. Singleton became pregnant she felt she had out-manoeuvered her husband. He did not really want a child (it was the last thing he wanted, Mrs. Singleton thought, a child), but he was jealous of her condition, as of some achievement he himself could attain. He was excluded from the little circle of herself and her womb, and, as though to puncture it, he began for the first time to make love to her of a kind where he took the insistent initiative. Mrs. Singleton was not greatly pleased. She seemed buoyed up by her own bigness. She noticed that her husband began to do exercises in the morning, in his underpants, press-ups, squat-jumps, as if he were getting in training for something. He was like a boy. He even became, as the term of her pregnancy drew near its end, resilient and detached again, the virile father waiting to receive the son (Mr. Singleton knew it would be a son, so did Mrs. Singleton) that she, at the appointed time, would deliver him. When the moment arrived he insisted on being present so as to prove he wasn't squeamish and to make sure he wouldn't be tricked in the transaction. Mrs. Singleton was not daunted. When the pains became frequent she wasn't at all afraid. There were big, watery lights clawing down from the ceiling of the delivery room like the lights in dentists' surgeries. She could just see her husband looking down at her. His face was white and clammy. It was his fault for wanting to be there. She had to push, as though away from him. Then she knew it was happening. She stretched back. She was a great surface of warm, splitting rock and Paul was struggling bravely up into the sunlight. She had to coax him with her cries. She felt him emerge like a trapped survivor. The doctor groped with rubber gloves. "There we are," he said. She managed to look at Mr. Singleton. She wanted suddenly to put him back inside for good where Paul had come from. With a fleeting pity she saw that this was what Mr. Singleton wanted too. His eyes were half closed. She kept hers on him. He seemed to wilt under her gaze. All his toughness and control were draining from him and she was glad. She lay back triumphant and glad. The doctor was holding Paul; but she looked, beyond, at Mr. Singleton. He was far away like an insect. She knew he couldn't hold out. He was going to faint. He was looking where her legs were spread. His eyes went out of focus. He was going to faint, keel over, right there on the spot.

Mrs. Singleton grew restless, though she lay unmoving on the beach. Wasps were buzzing close to her head, round their picnic bag. She thought that Mr. Singleton and Paul had been too long at their swimming lesson. They should come out. It never struck her, hot as she was, to get up and join her husband and son in the sea. Whenever Mrs. Singleton wanted a swim she would wait until there was an opportunity to go in by herself; then she would wade out, dip her shoulders under suddenly and paddle about contentedly, keeping her hair dry, as though she were soaking herself in a large bath. They did not bathe as a family; nor did Mrs. Singleton swim with Mr. Singleton—who now and then, too, would get up by himself and enter the sea, swim at once about fifty yards out, then cruise for long stretches, with a powerful crawl or butterfly, back and forth across the bay. When this happened Mrs. Singleton would engage her son in talk so he would not watch his father. Mrs. Singleton did not swim with Paul either. He was too old now to cradle between her knees in the very shallow water, and she was somehow afraid that while Paul splashed and kicked around her he would suddenly learn how to swim. She had this feeling that Paul would only swim while she was in the sea, too. She did not want this to happen, but it reassured her and gave her sufficient confidence to let Mr. Singleton continue his swimming lessons with Paul. These lessons were obsessive, indefatigable. Every Sunday morning at seven, when they were at home, Mr. Singleton would take Paul to the baths for yet another attempt. Part of this, of course, was that Mr. Singleton was determined that his son should swim; but it enabled him also to avoid the Sunday morning languor: extra hours in bed, leisurely love-making.

Once, in a room at college, Mr. Singleton had told Mrs. Singleton about his swimming, about his training sessions, races; about what it felt like when you could swim really well. She had run her fingers over his long, naked back.

Mrs. Singleton sat up and rubbed sun-tan lotion on to her thighs. Down near the water's edge, Mr. Singleton was standing about waist deep, supporting Paul who, gripped by his father's hands, water wings still on, was flailing, face down, at the surface. Mr. Singleton kept saying, "No, keep still." He was trying to get Paul to hold his body straight and relaxed so he would float. But each time as Paul nearly succeeded he would panic, fearing his father would let go, and thrash wildly. When he calmed down and Mr. Singleton held him, Mrs. Singleton could see the water running off his face like tears.

Mrs. Singleton did not alarm herself at this distress of her son. It was a guarantee against Mr. Singleton's influence, an assurance that Paul was not going to swim; nor was he to be imbued with any of his father's sullen hardiness. When Mrs. Singleton saw her son suffer, it pleased her and she felt loving toward him. She felt that an invisible thread ran between her and the boy which commanded him not to swim, and she felt that Mr. Singleton knew that it was because of her that his efforts with Paul were in vain. Even now, as Mr. Singleton prepared for another attempt, the boy was looking at her smoothing the suntan oil on to her legs.

"Come on, Paul," said Mr. Singleton. His wet shoulders shone like metal.

When Paul was born it seemed to Mrs. Singleton that her life with her husband was dissolved, as a mirage dissolves, and that she could return again to what she was before she knew him. She let her staved-off hunger for happiness and her old suppressed dreams revive. But then they were not dreams, because they had a physical object and she knew she needed them in order to live. She did not disguise from herself what she needed. She knew that she wanted the kind of close, even erotic relationship with her son that women who have rejected their husbands have been known to have. The kind of relationship in which the son must hurt the mother, the mother the son. But she willed it, as if there would be no pain. Mrs. Singleton waited for her son to grow. She trembled when she thought of him at eighteen or twenty. When he was grown he would be slim and light and slender, like a boy even though he was a man. He would not need a strong body because all his power would be inside. He would be all fire and life in essence. He would become an artist, a sculptor. She would pose for him naked (she would keep her body trim for this), and he would sculpt her. He would hold the chisel. His hands would guide the cold metal over the stone and its blows would strike sunlight.

Mrs. Singleton thought: All the best statues they had seen in Greece seemed to have been dredged up from the sea.

She finished rubbing the lotion on to her insteps and put the cap back on the tube. As she did so she heard something that made her truly alarmed. It was Mr. Singleton saying, "That's it, that's the way! At last! Now keep it going!" She looked up. Paul was in the same position as before but he had learnt to make slower, regular motions with his limbs and his body no longer sagged in the middle. Though he still wore the water-wings he was moving, somewhat laboriously, forwards so that Mr. Singleton had to walk along with him; and at one point Mr. Singleton removed one of his hands from under the boy's ribs and simultaneously looked at his wife and smiled. His shoulders flashed. It was not a smile meant for her. She could see that. And it was not one of her husband's usual, infrequent rather mechanical smiles. It was the smile a person makes about some joy inside, hidden and incommunicable.

"That's enough," thought Mrs. Singleton, getting to her feet, pretending not to have noticed, behind her sun-glasses, what had happened in the water. It *was* enough: They had been in the water for what seemed like an hour. He was only doing it because of their row last night, to make her feel he was not outmatched by using the reserve weapon of Paul. And, she added with relief to herself, Paul still had the water-wings and one hand to support him.

"That's enough now!" she shouted aloud, as if she were slightly, but not ill-humouredly, peeved at being neglected. "Come on in now!" She had picked up her purse as a quickly conceived ruse as she got up, and as she walked towards the water's edge she waved it above her head. "Who wants an ice-cream?"

Mr. Singleton ignored his wife. "Well done, Paul," he said. "Let's try that again."

Mrs. Singleton knew he would do this. She stood on the little ridge of sand just above where the beach, becoming fine shingle, shelved into the sea. She replaced a loose strap of her bikini over her shoulder and with a finger of each hand pulled the bottom half down over her buttocks. She stood feet apart, slightly on her toes, like a gymnast. She knew other eyes on the beach would be on her. It flattered her that she—and her husband, too—received admiring glances from those around. She thought, with relish for the irony: Perhaps they think we are happy, beautiful people. For all her girlhood diffidence, Mrs. Singleton enjoyed displaying her attractions and she liked to see other people's pleasure. When she lay sunbathing she imagined making love to all the moody, pubescent boys on holiday with their parents, with their slim waists and their quick heels.

"See if you can do it without me holding you," said Mr. Singleton. "I'll help you at first." He stooped over Paul. He looked like a mechanic making final adjustments to some prototype machine.

"Don't you want an ice-cream then, Paul?" said Mrs. Singleton. "They've got those chocolate ones."

Paul looked up. His short wet hair stood up in spikes. He looked like a prisoner offered a chance of escape, but the plastic waterwings, like some absurd pillory, kept him fixed.

Mrs. Singleton thought: He crawled out of me; now I have to lure him back with ice-cream.

"Can't you see he was getting the hang of it?" Mr. Singleton said. "If he comes out now he'll—"

"Hang of it! It was you. You were holding him all the time."

She thought: Perhaps I am hurting my son.

Mr. Singleton glared at Mrs. Singleton. He gripped Paul's shoulders. "You don't want to get out now, do you Paul?" He looked suddenly as if he really might drown Paul rather than let him come out.

Mrs. Singleton's heart raced. She wasn't good at rescues, at resuscitations. She knew this because of her life with her husband.

"Come on, you can go back in later," she said.

Paul was a hostage. She was playing for time, not wanting to harm the innocent.

She stood on the sand like a marooned woman watching for ships. The sea, in the sheltered bay, was almost flat calm. A few, glassy waves idled in but were smoothed out before they could break. On the headlands there were outcrops of scaly rocks like basking lizards. The island in Greece had been where Theseus left Ariadne.[1] Out over the blue water, beyond the heads of bobbing swimmers, seagulls flapped like scraps of paper.

Mr. Singleton looked at Mrs. Singleton. She was a fussy mother daubed with Ambre Solaire, trying to bribe her son with silly ice-creams; though if you forgot this she was a beautiful, tanned girl, like the girls men imagine on desert islands. But then, in Mr. Singleton's dreams, there was no one else on the untouched shore he ceaselessly swam to.

He thought, If Paul could swim, then I could leave her.

Mrs. Singleton looked at her husband. She felt afraid. The water's edge was like a dividing line between them which marked off the territory in which each existed. Perhaps they could never cross over.

"Well, I'm getting the ice-creams: you'd better get out."

She turned and paced up the sand. Behind the beach was an ice-cream van painted like a fairground.

Paul Singleton looked at his mother. He thought: She is deserting me—or I am deserting her. He wanted to get out to follow her. Her feet made puffs of sand which stuck

---

[1]*Theseus left Ariadne*   Greek mythology: Theseus deserted his benefactor and lover after carrying her away.

to her ankles, and you could see all her body as she strode up the beach. But he was
afraid of his father and his gripping hands. And he was afraid of his mother, too. How
she would wrap him, if he came out, in the big yellow towel like egg yolk, how she
would want him to get close to her smooth, sticky body, like a mouth that would
swallow him. He thought: The yellow towel humiliated him, his father's hands humiliated him. The water-wings humiliated him: You put them on and became a puppet. So much of life is humiliation. It was how you won love. His father was taking
off the water-wings like a man unlocking a chastity belt. He said: "Now try the same,
coming towards me." His father stood some feet away from him. He was a huge,
straight man, like the pier of a bridge. "Try." Paul Singleton was six. He was terrified
of water. Every time he entered it he had to fight down fear. His father never realized
this. He thought it was simple; you said: "Only water, no need to be afraid." His father did not know what fear was; the same as he did not know what fun was. Paul Singleton hated water. He hated it in his mouth and in his eyes. He hated the chlorine
smell of the swimming baths, the wet, slippery tiles, the echoing whoops and screams.
He hated it when his father read to him from *The Water Babies*.[2] It was the only story
his father read, because, since he didn't know fear or fun, he was really sentimental.
His mother read lots of stories. "Come on then. I'll catch you." Paul Singleton held
out his arms and raised one leg. This was the worst moment. Perhaps having no help
was most humiliating. If you did not swim you sank like a statue. They would drag him
out, his skin streaming. His father would say: "I didn't mean. . . ." But if he swam his
mother would be forsaken. She would stand on the beach with chocolate ice-cream
running down her arm. There was no way out; there were all these things to be afraid
of and no weapons. But then, perhaps he was not afraid of his mother nor his father,
nor of water, but of something else. He had felt it just now—when he'd struck out with
rhythmic, reaching strokes and his feet had come off the bottom and his father's hand
had slipped from under his chest: as if he had mistaken what his fear was; as if he had
been unconsciously pretending, even to himself, so as to execute some plan. He lowered his chin into the water. "Come on!" said Mr. Singleton. He launched himself forward and felt the sand leave his feet and his legs wriggle like cut ropes. "There," said
his father as he realized. "There!" His father stood like a man waiting to clasp a lover;
there was a gleam on his face. "Towards me! Towards me!" said his father suddenly.
But he kicked and struck, half in panic, half in pride, away from his father, away from
the shore, away, in this strange new element that seemed all his own.

[1982]

Questions

1. Why are the Singletons referred to so formally, as Mrs. and Mr.?
2. Are your loyalties supposed to be with Mrs. Singleton or her husband? What is the
   core of the conflict between them? With the reservations that each had about the
   other, why did they get married? What is the glue that keeps them together?
3. How do you interpret the swimming metaphor?
4. How effective is the use of a shifting point of view?

---

[2]*The Water Babies*   Fairy tale written by Charles Kingsley (1819–1875), an English novelist.

Véronique Tadjo

(b. 1955)

Ivory Coast

A cross the African continent, Véronique Tadjo is as well known for her poetry as for her fiction. Although born in Paris in 1955, she grew up in Abidjan in the Ivory Coast, where she attended local schools. Her B.A. (in English) is from the University of Abidjan. That degree was followed by graduate studies at the Sorbonne in Paris and further research, as a Fulbright scholar, at Howard University in Washington, D.C. In the early 1980s, she taught in Abidjan; in the past decade, she has increasingly concentrated on journalism and her own creative writing while spending extended periods of time in both East Africa and England.

Besides her poetry and her novels, Tadjo has published two collections of short stories, La Chanson de la Vie (1989) and Le Royaume Aveugle (1990), as well as several children's books. "The Betrayal" is from her novel, Au Vol d'oiseau (1992), translated as As the Crow Flies. This unusual volume is composed of roughly 50 short narrative pieces, which can be read individually as short stories or together as an extended narrative. Tadjo, who writes in French, typically translates her own works into English.

Asked about the complications of being an African writer, Tadjo remarked, "It is a difficult business where talent is not enough. You need determination, endurance, and courage. You have highs and lows, victories and failures, but if you are ready to fight for it and if you believe in yourself, I think there is still room for more writers in African publishing." More specifically, regarding her own writing, Tadjo has stated the following:

> I write because I want to understand the world I'm living in, and because I want to communicate with others my experience of what it is to be living in Africa today. I use my eyes like a camera, trying to record everything, from the most personal emotions to the major crises like wars, death, and AIDS. When asked what my novels are about, I usually sigh heavily and say, "About life," because I cannot explain it in any other way. I am interested in life in its entirety, and this is why I have an aversion to giving names to my characters. I want the readers to see them as human beings first of all. And these human beings are faced with challenges and struggles they must overcome if they want to retain their humanity in the unfavourable context of an African society in crisis.

THE BETRAYAL

One day, a woman and a man who loved each other intensely decided to have a child.

"We cannot live this way without sharing some of our blood," said the woman. "I want our love to become flesh."

"This child will be the carrier of hope, I am sure," agreed the man with a nod. "We will teach him everything we know."

The next day, the woman was pregnant. Before the day was over, she had given birth to a son.

Then the man cried: "Love has won! We have created life! Our son will be our messenger."

Father and mother remained close to the child teaching him to love and to have faith. They spoke to him constantly. The child listened.

"You will cross continents and meet many people. Tell them what we taught you. Rebuild the cities destroyed by violence and oppression. Let wild flowers grow freely and do not crush the clouds. Tell them about the water that never dries up. Dip your hands into the earth and breathe its smell and, above all, believe in yourself."

When the child felt ready, he said goodbye to his parents and left without looking back. With each step he took away from them, he was visibly growing up. So much so, that by the time he could see the city in the distance, he was already a man.

Things were not easy for him. Everywhere he went, he saw nothing but despair. Though the city shimmered with lights and pleasures, if you took only one step away from the main road you could find mud and filth. People wore gold, but if you turned your head a little you could see street children and disabled people in rags. The roads were straight and lit by powerful lamps but, if you wanted to go further, you could inhale the dust of abandoned pathways.

But all this was nothing. The worst part was that people had lost faith. They spoke of freedom and of change, but these were empty words. No one believed in them. The northern wind could blow for weeks and dry people's skin, but the heat would return with greater intensity and stronger stench. People were drifting about, totally out of breath.

And him, what was he doing?

He spent his days growing up and watching life go by. His eyes recorded everything. But in reality, he felt extremely cut off from others. Communication was so difficult that it became painful. What he was looking for always seemed to be elsewhere. At times, he wanted to leave the town, to go away in order to discover something else.

What was more, he could sense he had changed. Oh, not that much, but enough to recognize the difference in himself. He had to try hard not to abandon his beliefs and even though, in his dreams, he still saw his parents and heard their soft words, he also had powerful nightmares which left him without breath in the pit of the night. He had the feeling he was falling into space. His head throbbed and he was scared. He knew very well that this was anguish. And it was so thick and heavy, he could have held it in his hand.

Anguish was wrecking his life. It broke his spirit and stripped him of his strength. "This has to stop," he decided. "This must end."

It was around that time he fell in love.

She had eyes shaped like cowries and her skin was the colour of sand. The city was in her gaze.

For her, time was no obstacle since she considered herself genderless. She was an undefined creature who was going through life halfheartedly and who couldn't care less if she wore a skirt and had pointed breasts.

Her life flowed regularly, and she knew how to take advantage of it. She just lived it. Love was a secondary notion, an awkward feeling. She thought she had too many things to do. Her innocence draped her in unparalleled elegance.

Was that why she looked so beautiful? Was that why he wanted to possess her? He did not know. He only felt this great desire. Morning and evening, her scent had a perverting influence on him. It was a constant battle within him: at the same time, a denial and an acceptance of this passion which would not stop plaguing him.

She agreed to let him speak to her. She could sense in him a strange strength which she was lacking entirely. She sat listening to him while she was wrapping and unwrapping around her finger the white handkerchief her parents had given her. She knew that what he said was part of life, but she felt she wasn't ready for it. She still needed time. A lot of time. Possibly years.

One evening, she drank from a glass he handed her. All of a sudden, the brightness of the lights seemed to crush her. She felt heavy. Her eyes closed.

And that was how he possessed her.

In the city, people became petrified. A thick silence laid over the night. Darkness deepened.

When she regained consciousness, she bore a child in her womb.

"I am dying," she whispered. "This child is not mine. He will bring unhappiness."

Finally, he realized the magnitude of his betrayal and started to panic. He wanted to erase what had happened. He wanted to deny it. But her belly was enormous and as round as the earth. He placed his hand on her distended navel to find out if the child was still alive.

All at once, there was a gigantic flash of lightning which jostled the clouds. The sky started to slip away and trees let out screams. At the same time, an unbearable heat descended. Smoke heavy with dust surrounded nature which burst into flames. A violent breath of air burned people and knocked down buildings. Skin pulled away in layers. Eyes dried up. Big tufts of hair fell out. Everyone died violently. Iron melted down and ran along the ground. The blazing horizon was carved into an enormous mushroom cloud.

[1992]

Questions

1. Does Tadjo employ conventional western stereotypes about city life vs. country life, parents and children, love and passion, or are these dualities given a distinctly African flavor?
2. What distinguishes between the two births in Tadjo's story?
3. What constitutes "betrayal" in Tadjo's brief story? Who (or what) is betrayed?

Amy Tan
(b. 1952)
China/United States

Amy Tan was born in Oakland, California, the daughter of Chinese parents. Her mother left China just before the Communist Revolution; her father was trained as an engineer in Beijing. Tan attended high school in Switzerland, where she and her mother lived briefly after her father's death in 1968. After coming to the United States to attend college in Oregon, she worked as a writer of computer manuals for IBM and received a master's degree in linguistics from San Jose State University.

Two events shaped Tan's discovery that she wanted to write fiction: first, her visit to China with her mother in 1984, which led to her realization that she was part of an extended Chinese family and that her cultural roots were in China, and, second, her admiration for Louise Erdrich's Love Medicine (1984), a group of interlocking stories about several Native American families (see Erdrich's story, "Love Medicine," in this volume) that catalyzed Tan's desire to write about her own experiences as a member of a cultural minority in the United States.

Tan's first story, published in a small magazine, was read by a San Diego literary agent who urged her to develop her ideas into a longer narrative that would explore the cultural and generational conflicts she had begun to consider in the story. The resulting book, The Joy Luck Club (1989), a series of self-contained but related narratives told by a group of immigrant Chinese mothers and their Chinese-American daughters, was both a popular and a critical success: a best-seller that was nominated for the National Book Award and the National Book Critics Circle Award.

Struggling with the anxieties of writing a second novel following her initial success, Tan confessed that in order to write The Kitchen God's Wife (1991), which also focuses on a mother-daughter relationship, she "had to fight for every single character, every image, every word. And the story is, in fact, about a woman who does the same thing: she fights to believe in herself. She does battle with myths and superstitions and assumptions—then casts off the fates that accompany them." Tan has since published two more novels, The Hundred Secret Senses (1995) and The Bonesetter's Daughter (2001).

The story "Half and Half," from The Joy Luck Club, demonstrates Tan's original voice and her fresh vision of cultural bifurcation.

HALF AND HALF

As proof of her faith, my mother used to carry a small leatherette Bible when she went to the First Chinese Baptist Church every Sunday. But later, after my mother lost her faith in God, that leatherette Bible wound up wedged under a too-short table leg, a way for her to correct the imbalances of life. It's been there for over twenty years.

My mother pretends that Bible isn't there. Whenever anyone asks her what it's doing there, she says, a little too loudly, "Oh, this? I forgot." But I know she sees it. My mother is not the best housekeeper in the world, and after all these years that Bible is still clean white.

Tonight I'm watching my mother sweep under the same kitchen table, something she does every night after dinner. She gently pokes her broom around the table leg propped up by the Bible. I watch her, sweep after sweep, waiting for the right moment to tell her about Ted and me, that we're getting divorced. When I tell her, I know she's going to say, "This cannot be."

And when I say that it is certainly true, that our marriage is over, I know what else she will say: "Then you must save it."

And even though I know it's hopeless—there's absolutely nothing left to save— I'm afraid if I tell her that, she'll still persuade me to try.

I think it's ironic that my mother wants me to fight the divorce. Seventeen years ago she was chagrined when I started dating Ted. My older sisters had dated only Chinese boys from church before getting married.

Ted and I met in a politics of ecology class when he leaned over and offered to pay me two dollars for the last week's notes. I refused the money and accepted a cup of coffee instead. This was during my second semester at UC Berkeley, where I had enrolled as a liberal arts major and later changed to fine arts. Ted was in his third year in premed, his choice, he told me, ever since he dissected a fetal pig in the sixth grade.

I have to admit that what I initially found attractive in Ted were precisely the things that made him different from my brothers and the Chinese boys I had dated: his brashness; the assuredness in which he asked for things and expected to get them; his opinionated manner; his angular face and lanky body; the thickness of his arms; the fact that his parents immigrated from Tarrytown, New York, not Tientsin, China.

My mother must have noticed these same differences after Ted picked me up one evening at my parents' house. When I returned home, my mother was still up, watching television.

"He is American," warned my mother, as if I had been too blind to notice. "A *waigoren*."[1]

"I'm American too," I said. "And it's not as if I'm going to marry him or something."

Mrs. Jordan also had a few words to say. Ted had casually invited me to a family picnic, the annual clan reunion held by the polo fields in Golden Gate Park. Although we had dated only a few times in the last month—and certainly had never slept together, since both of us lived at home—Ted introduced me to all his relatives as his girlfriend, which, until then, I didn't know I was.

Later, when Ted and his father went off to play volleyball with the others, his mother took my hand, and we started walking along the grass, away from the crowd. She squeezed my palm warmly but never seemed to look at me.

"I'm so glad to meet you *finally*," Mrs. Jordan said. I wanted to tell her I wasn't really Ted's girlfriend, but she went on. "I think it's nice that you and Ted are having such a lot of fun together. So I hope you won't misunderstand what I have to say."

---

[1] *waigoren* Any person who is a foreigner or, more specifically, any person who is not Chinese.

And then she spoke quietly about Ted's future, his need to concentrate on his medical studies, why it would be years before he could even think about marriage. She assured me she had nothing whatsoever against minorities; she and her husband, who owned a chain of office-supply stores, personally knew many fine people who were Oriental, Spanish, and even black. But Ted was going to be in one of those professions where he would be judged by a different standard, by patients and other doctors who might not be as understanding as the Jordans were. She said it was so unfortunate the way the rest of the world was, how unpopular the Vietnam War was.

"Mrs. Jordan, I am not Vietnamese," I said softly, even though I was on the verge of shouting. "And I have no intention of marrying your son."

When Ted drove me home that day, I told him I couldn't see him anymore. When he asked me why, I shrugged. When he pressed me, I told him what his mother had said, verbatim, without comment.

"And you're just going to sit there! Let my mother decide what's right?" he shouted, as if I were a co-conspirator who had turned traitor. I was touched that Ted was so upset.

"What should we do?" I asked, and I had a pained feeling I thought was the beginning of love.

In those early months, we clung to each other with a rather silly desperation, because, in spite of anything my mother or Mrs. Jordan could say, there was nothing that really prevented us from seeing one another. With imagined tragedy hovering over us, we became inseparable, two halves creating the whole: yin and yang. I was victim to his hero. I was always in danger and he was always rescuing me. I would fall and he would lift me up. It was exhilarating and draining. The emotional effect of saving and being saved was addicting to both of us. And that, as much as anything we ever did in bed, was how we made love to each other: conjoined where my weaknesses needed protection.

"What should we do?" I continued to ask him. And within a year of our first meeting we were living together. The month before Ted started medical school at UCSF we were married in the Episcopal church, and Mrs. Jordan sat in the front pew, crying as was expected of the groom's mother. When Ted finished his residency in dermatology, we bought a run-down three-story Victorian with a large garden in Ashbury Heights. Ted helped me set up a studio downstairs so I could take in work as a freelance production assistant for graphic artists.

Over the years, Ted decided where we went on vacation. He decided what new furniture we should buy. He decided we should wait until we moved into a better neighborhood before having children. We used to discuss some of these matters, but we both knew the question would boil down to my saying, "Ted, you decide." After a while, there were no more discussions. Ted simply decided. And I never thought of objecting. I preferred to ignore the world around me, obsessing only over what was in front of me: my T-square, my X-acto knife, my blue pencil.

But last year Ted's feelings about what he called "decision and responsibility" changed. A new patient had come to him asking what she could do about the spidery veins on her cheeks. And when he told her he could suck the red veins out and make her beautiful again, she believed him. But instead, he accidentally sucked a nerve out, and the left side of her smile fell down and she sued him.

After he lost the malpractice lawsuit—his first, and a big shock to him I now realize— he started pushing me to make decisions. Did I think we should buy an American car or a Japanese car? Should we change from whole-life to term insurance? What did I think about that candidate who supported the contras? What about a family?

I thought about things, the pros and the cons. But in the end I would be so confused, because I never believed there was ever any one right answer, yet there were many wrong ones. So whenever I said, "You decide," or "I don't care," or "Either way is fine with me," Ted would say in his impatient voice, "No, *you* decide. You can't have it both ways, none of the responsibility, none of the blame."

I could feel things changing between us. A protective veil had been lifted and Ted now started pushing me about everything. He asked me to decide on the most trivial matters, as if he were baiting me. Italian food or Thai. One appetizer or two. Which appetizer. Credit card or cash. Visa or MasterCard.

Last month, when he was leaving for a two-day dermatology course in Los Angeles, he asked if I wanted to come along and then quickly, before I could say anything, he added, "Never mind, I'd rather go alone."

"More time to study," I agreed.

"No, because you can never make up your mind about anything," he said.

And I protested, "But it's only with things that aren't important."

"Nothing is important to you, then," he said in a tone of disgust.

"Ted, if you want me to go, I'll go."

And it was as if something snapped in him. "How the hell did we ever get married? Did you just say 'I do' because the minister said 'repeat after me'? What would you have done with your life if I had never married you? Did it ever occur to you?"

This was such a big leap in logic, between what I said and what he said, that I thought we were like two people standing apart on separate mountain peaks, recklessly leaning forward to throw stones at one another, unaware of the dangerous chasm that separated us.

But now I realize Ted knew what he was saying all along. He wanted to show me the rift. Because later that evening he called from Los Angeles and said he wanted a divorce.

Ever since Ted's been gone, I've been thinking, Even if I had expected it, even if I had known what I was going to do with my life, it still would have knocked the wind out of me.

When something that violent hits you, you can't help but lose your balance and fall. And after you pick yourself up, you realize you can't trust anybody to save you— not your husband, not your mother, not God. So what can you do to stop yourself from tilting and falling all over again?

My mother believed in God's will for many years. It was as if she had turned on a celestial faucet and goodness kept pouring out. She said it was faith that kept all these good things coming our way, only I thought she said "fate," because she couldn't pronounce that "th" sound in "faith."

And later, I discovered that maybe it was fate all along, that faith was just an illusion that somehow you're in control. I found out the most I could have was hope, and with that I was not denying any possibility, good or bad. I was just saying, If there is a choice, dear God or whatever you are, here's where the odds should be placed.

I remember the day I started thinking this, it was such a revelation to me. It was the day my mother lost her faith in God. She found that things of unquestioned certainty could never be trusted again.

We had gone to the beach, to a secluded spot south of the city near Devil's Slide. My father had read in *Sunset* magazine that this was a good place to catch ocean perch. And although my father was not a fisherman but a pharmacist's assistant who had once been a doctor in China, he believed in his *nengkan*, his ability to do any-thing he put his mind to. My mother believed she had *nengkan* to cook anything my father had a mind to catch. It was this belief in their *nengkan* that had brought my parents to America. It had enabled them to have seven children and buy a house in the Sunset district with very little money. It had given them the confidence to be-lieve their luck would never run out, that God was on their side, that the house gods had only benevolent things to report and our ancestors were pleased, that lifetime war-ranties meant our lucky streak would never break, that all the elements were in bal-ance, the right amount of wind and water.

So there we were, the nine of us: my father, my mother, my two sisters, four broth-ers, and myself, so confident as we walked along our first beach. We marched in sin-gle file across the cool gray sand, from oldest to youngest. I was in the middle, fourteen years old. We would have made quite a sight, if anyone else had been watching, nine pairs of bare feet trudging, nine pairs of shoes in hand, nine black-haired heads turned toward the water to watch the waves tumbling in.

The wind was whipping the cotton trousers around my legs and I looked for some place where the sand wouldn't kick into my eyes. I saw we were standing in the hol-low of a cove. It was like a giant bowl, cracked in half, the other half washed out to sea. My mother walked toward the right, where the beach was clean, and we all fol-lowed. On this side, the wall of the cove curved around and protected the beach from both the rough surf and the wind. And along this wall, in its shadow, was a reef ledge that started at the edge of the beach and continued out past the cove where the wa-ters became rough. It seemed as though a person could walk out to sea on this reef, al-though it looked very rocky and slippery. On the other side of the cove, the wall was more jagged, eaten away by the water. It was pitted with crevices, so when the waves crashed against the wall, the water spewed out of these holes like white gulleys.

Thinking back, I remember that this beach cove was a terrible place, full of wet shadows that chilled us and invisible specks that flew into our eyes and made it hard for us to see the dangers. We were all blind with the newness of this experience: a Chi-nese family trying to act like a typical American family at the beach.

My mother spread out an old striped bedspread, which flapped in the wind until nine pairs of shoes weighed it down. My father assembled his long bamboo fishing pole, a pole he had made with his own two hands, remembering its design from his childhood in China. And we children sat huddled shoulder to shoulder on the blan-ket, reaching into the grocery sack full of bologna sandwiches, which we hungrily ate salted with sand from our fingers.

Then my father stood up and admired his fishing pole, its grace, its strength. Sat-isfied, he picked up his shoes and walked to the edge of the beach and then onto the reef to the point just before it was wet. My two older sisters, Janice and Ruth, jumped up from the blanket and slapped their thighs to get the sand off. Then they slapped each other's back and raced off down the beach shrieking. I was about to get up and chase them, but my mother nodded toward my four brothers and reminded me: "*Dangsying tamende shenti*," which means "Take care of them," or literally, "Watch out for their bodies." These bodies were the anchors of my life: Matthew, Mark, Luke, and Bing. I fell back onto the sand, groaning as my throat grew tight, as I made the same lament: "Why?" Why did I have to care for them?

And she gave me the same answer: "*Yiding*."[2]

---

[2]*Yiding* Must.

I must. Because they were my brothers. My sisters had once taken care of me. How else could I learn responsibility? How else could I appreciate what my parents had done for me?

Matthew, Mark, and Luke were twelve, ten, and nine, old enough to keep themselves loudly amused. They had already buried Luke in a shallow grave of sand so that only his head stuck out. Now they were starting to pat together the outlines of a sand-castle wall on top of him.

But Bing was only four, easily excitable and easily bored and irritable. He didn't want to play with the other brothers because they had pushed him off to the side, admonishing him, "No, Bing, you'll just wreck it."

So Bing wandered down the beach, walking stiffly like an ousted emperor, picking up shards of rock and chunks of driftwood and flinging them with all his might into the surf. I trailed behind, imagining tidal waves and wondering what I would do if one appeared. I called to Bing every now and then, "Don't go too close to the water. You'll get your feet wet." And I thought how much I seemed like my mother, always worried beyond reason inside, but at the same time talking about the danger as if it were less than it really was. The worry surrounded me, like the wall of the cove, and it made me feel everything had been considered and was now safe.

My mother had a superstition, in fact, that children were predisposed to certain dangers on certain days, all depending on their Chinese birthdate. It was explained in a little Chinese book called *The Twenty-Six Malignant Gates*. There, on each page, was an illustration of some terrible danger that awaited young innocent children. In the corners was a description written in Chinese, and since I couldn't read the characters, I could only see what the picture meant.

The same little boy appeared in each picture: climbing a broken tree limb, standing by a falling gate, slipping in a wooden tub, being carried away by a snapping dog, fleeing from a bolt of lightning. And in each of these pictures stood a man who looked as if he were wearing a lizard costume. He had a big crease in his forehead, or maybe it was actually that he had two round horns. In one picture, the lizard man was standing on a curved bridge, laughing as he watched the little boy falling forward over the bridge rail, his slippered feet already in the air.

It would have been enough to think that even one of these dangers could befall a child. And even though the birthdates corresponded to only one danger, my mother worried about them all. This was because she couldn't figure out how the Chinese dates, based on the lunar calendar, translated into American dates. So by taking them all into account, she had absolute faith she could prevent every one of them.

The sun had shifted and moved over the other side of the cove wall. Everything had settled into place. My mother was busy keeping sand from blowing onto the blanket, then shaking sand out of shoes, and tacking corners of blankets back down again with the now clean shoes. My father was still standing at the end of the reef, patiently casting out, waiting for *nengkan* to manifest itself as a fish. I could see small figures farther down on the beach, and I could tell they were my sisters by their two dark heads and yellow pants. My brothers' shrieks were mixed with those of seagulls. Bing had found an empty soda bottle and was using this to dig sand next to the dark cove wall. And I sat on the sand, just where the shadows ended and the sunny part began.

Bing was pounding the soda bottle against the rock, so I called to him, "Don't dig so hard. You'll bust a hole in the wall and fall all the way to China." And I laughed when he looked at me as though he thought what I said was true. He stood up and started walking toward the water. He put one foot tentatively on the reef, and I warned him, "Bing."

"I'm gonna see Daddy," he protested.

"Stay close to the wall, then, away from the water," I said. "Stay away from the mean fish."

And I watched as he inched his way along the reef, his back hugging the bumpy cove wall. I still see him, so clearly that I almost feel I can make him stay there forever.

I see him standing by the wall, safe, calling to my father, who looks over his shoulder toward Bing. How glad I am that my father is going to watch him for a while! Bing starts to walk over and then something tugs on my father's line and he's reeling as fast as he can.

Shouts erupt. Someone has thrown sand in Luke's face and he's jumped out of his sand grave and thrown himself on top of Mark, thrashing and kicking. My mother shouts for me to stop them. And right after I pull Luke off Mark, I look up and see Bing walking alone to the edge of the reef. In the confusion of the fight, nobody notices. I am the only one who sees what Bing is doing.

Bing walks one, two, three steps. His little body is moving so quickly, as if he spotted something wonderful by the water's edge. And I think, *He's going to fall in.* I'm expecting it. And just as I think this, his feet are already in the air, in a moment of balance, before he splashes into the sea and disappears without leaving so much as a ripple in the water.

I sank to my knees watching that spot where he disappeared, not moving, not saying anything. I couldn't make sense of it. I was thinking, Should I run to the water and try to pull him out? Should I shout to my father? Can I rise on my legs fast enough? Can I take it all back and forbid Bing from joining my father on the ledge?

And then my sisters were back, and one of them said, "Where's Bing?" There was silence for a few seconds and then shouts and sand flying as everyone rushed past me toward the water's edge. I stood there unable to move as my sisters looked by the cove wall, as my brothers scrambled to see what lay behind pieces of driftwood. My mother and father were trying to part the waves with their hands.

We were there for many hours. I remember the search boats and the sunset when dusk came. I had never seen a sunset like that: a bright orange flame touching the water's edge and then fanning out, warming the sea. When it became dark, the boats turned their yellow orbs on and bounced up and down on the dark shiny water.

As I look back, it seems unnatural to think about the colors of the sunset and boats at a time like that. But we all had strange thoughts. My father was calculating minutes, estimating the temperature of the water, readjusting his estimate of when Bing fell. My sisters were calling, "Bing! Bing!" as if he were hiding in some bushes high above the beach cliffs. My brothers sat in the car, quietly reading comic books. And when the boats turned off their yellow orbs, my mother went for a swim. She had never swum a stroke in her life, but her faith in her own *nengkan* convinced her that what these Americans couldn't do, she could. She could find Bing.

And when the rescue people finally pulled her out of the water, she still had her *nengkan* intact. Her hair, her clothes, they were all heavy with the cold water, but she stood quietly, calm and regal as a mermaid queen who had just arrived out of the sea. The police called off the search, put us all in our car, and sent us home to grieve.

I had expected to be beaten to death, by my father, by my mother, by my sisters and brothers. I knew it was my fault. I hadn't watched him closely enough, and yet I saw him. But as we sat in the dark living room, I heard them, one by one whispering their regrets.

"I was selfish to want to go fishing," said my father.

"We shouldn't have gone for a walk," said Janice, while Ruth blew her nose yet another time.

"Why'd you have to throw sand in my face?" moaned Luke. "Why'd you have to make me start a fight?"

And my mother quietly admitted to me, "I told you to stop their fight. I told you to take your eyes off him."

If I had had any time at all to feel a sense of relief, it would have quickly evaporated, because my mother also said, "So now I am telling you, we must go and find him, quickly, tomorrow morning." And everybody's eyes looked down. But I saw it as my punishment: to go out with my mother, back to the beach, to help her find Bing's body.

Nothing prepared me for what my mother did the next day. When I woke up, it was still dark and she was already dressed. On the kitchen table was a thermos, a teacup, the white leatherette Bible, and the car keys.

"Is Daddy ready?" I asked.

"Daddy's not coming," she said.

"Then how will we get there? Who will drive us?"

She picked up the keys and I followed her out the door to the car. I wondered the whole time as we drove to the beach how she had learned to drive overnight. She used no map. She drove smoothly ahead, turning down Geary, then the Great Highway, signaling at all the right times, getting on the Coast Highway and easily winding the car around the sharp curves that often led inexperienced drivers off and over the cliffs.

When we arrived at the beach, she walked immediately down the dirt path and over to the end of the reef ledge, where I had seen Bing disappear. She held in her hand the white Bible. And looking out over the water, she called to God, her small voice carried up by the gulls to heaven. It began with "Dear God" and ended with "Amen," and in between she spoke in Chinese.

"I have always believed in your blessings," she praised God in that same tone she used for exaggerated Chinese compliments. "We knew they would come. We did not question them. Your decisions were our decisions. You rewarded us for our faith.

"In return we have always tried to show our deepest respect. We went to your house. We brought you money. We sang your songs. You gave us more blessings. And now we have misplaced one of them. We were careless. This is true. We had so many good things, we couldn't keep them in our mind all the time.

"So maybe you hid him from us to teach us a lesson, to be more careful with your gifts in the future. I have learned this. I have put it in my memory. And now I have come to take Bing back."

I listened quietly as my mother said these words, horrified. And I began to cry when she added, "Forgive us for his bad manners. My daughter, this one standing here, will be sure to teach him better lessons of obedience before he visits you again."

After her prayer, her faith was so great that she, saw him, three times, waving to her from just beyond the first wave. "*Nale!*"—There! And she would stand straight as a sentinel, until three times her eyesight failed her and Bing turned into a dark spot of churning seaweed.

My mother did not let her chin fall down. She walked back to the beach and put the Bible down. She picked up the thermos and teacup and walked to the water's edge. Then she told me that the night before she had reached back into her life, back when she was a girl in China, and this is what she had found.

"I remember a boy who lost his hand in a firecracker accident," she said. "I saw the shreds of this boy's arm, his tears, and then I heard his mother's claim that he would grow back another hand, better than the last. This mother said she would pay back an ancestral debt ten times over. She would use a water treatment to soothe the wrath of Chu Jung, the three-eyed god of fire. And true enough, the next week this boy was riding a bicycle, both hands steering a straight course past my astonished eyes!"

And then my mother became very quiet. She spoke again in a thoughtful, re-spectful manner.

"An ancestor of ours once stole water from a sacred well. Now the water is trying to steal back. We must sweeten the temper of the Coiling Dragon who lives in the sea. And then we must make him loosen his coils from Bing by giving him another treasure he can hide."

My mother poured out tea sweetened with sugar into the teacup, and threw this into the sea. And then she opened her fist. In her palm was a ring of watery blue sap-phire, a gift from her mother, who had died many years before. This ring, she told me, drew coveting stares from women and made them inattentive to the children they guarded so jealously. This would make the Coiling Dragon forgetful of Bing. She threw the ring into the water.

But even with this, Bing did not appear right away. For an hour or so, all we saw was seaweed drifting by. And then I saw her clasp her hands to her chest, and she said in a wondrous voice, "See, it's because we were watching the wrong direction." And I too saw Bing trudging wearily at the far end of the beach, his shoes hanging in his hand, his dark head bent over in exhaustion. I could feel what my mother felt. The hunger in our hearts was instantly filled. And then the two of us, before we could even get to our feet, saw him light a cigarette, grow tall, and become a stranger.

"Ma, let's go," I said as softly as possible.

"He's there," she said firmly. She pointed to the jagged wall across the water. "I see him. He is in a cave, sitting on a little step above the water. He is hungry and a lit-tle cold, but he has learned now not to complain too much."

And then she stood up and started walking across the sandy beach as though it were a solid paved path, and I was trying to follow behind, struggling and stumbling in the soft mounds. She marched up the steep path to where the car was parked, and she wasn't even breathing hard as she pulled a large inner tube from the trunk. To this lifesaver, she tied the fishing line from my father's bamboo pole. She walked back and threw the tube into the sea, holding onto the pole.

"This will go where Bing is. I will bring him back," she said fiercely. I had never heard so much *nengkan* in my mother's voice.

The tube followed her mind. It drifted out, toward the other side of the cove where it was caught by stronger waves. The line became taut and she strained to hold on tight. But the line snapped and then spiraled into the water.

We both climbed toward the end of the reef to watch. The tube had now reached the other side of the cove. A big wave smashed it into the wall. The bloated tube leapt up and then it was sucked in, under the wall and into a cavern. It popped out. Over and over again, it disappeared, emerged, glistening black, faithfully reporting it had seen Bing and was going back to try to pluck him from the cave. Over and over again, it dove and popped back up again, empty but still hopeful. And then, after a dozen or so times, it was sucked into the dark recess, and when it came out, it was torn and lifeless.

At that moment, and not until that moment, did she give up. My mother had a look on her face that I'll never forget. It was one of complete despair and horror, for losing Bing, for being so foolish as to think she could use faith to change fate. And it made me angry—so blindingly angry—that everything had failed us.

I know now that I had never expected to find Bing, just as I know now I will never find a way to save my marriage. My mother tells me, though, that I should still try.

"What's the point?" I say. "There's no hope. There's no reason to keep trying."

"Because you must," she says. "This is not hope. Not reason. This is your fate. This is your life, what you must do."

"So what can I do?"

And my mother says, "You must think for yourself, what you must do. If someone tells you, then you are not trying." And then she walks out of the kitchen to let me think about this.

I think about Bing, how I knew he was in danger, how I let it happen. I think about my marriage, how I had seen the signs, really I had. But I just let it happen. And I think now that fate is shaped half by expectation, half by inattention. But somehow, when you lose something you love, faith takes over. You have to pay attention to what you lost. You have to undo the expectation.

My mother, she still pays attention to it. That Bible under the table, I know she sees it. I remember seeing her write in it before she wedged it under.

I lift the table and slide the Bible out. I put the Bible on the table, flipping quickly through the pages, because I know it's there. On the page before the New Testament begins, there's a section called "Deaths," and that's where she wrote "Bing Hsu" lightly, in erasable pencil.

[1989]

Questions

1. What does the narrator discover in her exploration of the difference between faith and fate?

2. How does the narrator regard her mother? Does that view change during the story?

3. What elements of the narrator's character are revealed in her reconstruction of major events in her life? How does she see the failure of her marriage related to her brother's death years earlier?

4. How is the Chinese quality of *nengkan*—the ability to do whatever one puts one's mind to—important to the meaning of the story?

Haldun Taner

(1915–1986)
Turkey

In an article called "Before the Flood" in The New York Times Magazine (*June 4, 2000*), *author John Noble Wilford begins with the following observation:*

> Each day the dammed waters of the Euphrates River rise another three feet, encroach-ing on the present and the past in southeastern Turkey. While people in the modern vil-lage of Belkis abandon their homes, archaeologists are fighting a rear-guard action to save what they can from the ruins of Zeugma, once a thriving outpost on the eastern fron-tier of the Roman Empire. Theirs is a losing battle.
>
> When Turkey began building a hydroelectric dam near Belkis in 1992, few were aware of any significant ruins that would be endangered. But villagers, digging up their valuable pistachio trees, kept turning up building stones. Archaeologists eventually arrived on the scene and began digging, uncovering two large hillside villas. Despite pleas from scholars for more time to rescue artifacts, Turkish officials have refused to hold back the flood; the country is in desperate need of electric power. In a few days, the main excavation site will be inundated. By September, some 15,000 acres of the ancient city will be submerged.

Though the situation in Haldun Taner's short story, "To All Eternity," does not in-volve a hydroelectric plant, the issue of "progress" vis-à-vis the preservation of the past is central, perhaps even prescient, since the story was written more than 50 years ago. Taner's translator, Geoffrey Lewis, contextualizes the work by stating the following:

> The Unionists referred to in this story . . . were the members of the Party of Union and Progress, which overthrew the tyranny of Sultan Abdulhamid in 1908, replaced it with a new tyranny, and eventually brought the Ottoman Empire into the First World War, on the los-ing side. There were still quite a few of them around in 1948, when this story was written."

Haldun Taner grew up in Istanbul, where he was born in 1915. His father was a successful lawyer, but Taner chose to study political science and economics at Hei-delberg, until it was discovered that he had tuberculosis. In 1942, after a four-year regimen leading to a cure, he continued his studies at Istanbul University, changing his major to German. He joined the university's Faculty of Letters in 1954. He con-tinued teaching while writing for most of his life. Although he became a successful playwright, Taner is best known for his short stories.

TO ALL ETERNITY

What's the old saying? "In the next world, grace; in this world, place." If it weren't for Razi Bey,[1] we'd never have had a place of our own. All these years I've been a schoolmaster. This is the year when I reach retiring age and till now we've never

---

[1]Bey   Turkish: Mister.

owned a house. Then Razi Bey goes and marries my wife's sister. He's a contractor, wide awake, pushful, enterprising. A previously undivided property on the outskirts of Ay-valik was being divided up. He managed to get hold of twelve acres of it at the price of agricultural land and with his two partners he's set up a housing cooperative. They're selling it off in plots to their friends and relations. None of the local worthies has even put in for one; they're the people who sit with their backs to the sea and reck-on that for the wife and kids to go swimming would deprive the place of its virgini-ty. Well, good luck to them; that's how we've managed to get a share. Naturally, the cooperative's houses will be built by Razi Bey and his partners and they'll make a bit on that too. I don't begrudge them. Every shareholder is being asked to put down a hundred thousand in advance, the balance to be paid off over six years at five hun-dred a month. It's a bargain, dirt cheap.

We've scratched around for cash. We've sold my wife's shop and my National Sav-ings. We've got into debt but we've forked out the hundred thousand. The other shareholders haven't had to do that sort of thing; they're all well-off retired people. Razi Bey and his partners have got their site organized and the building material is all stacked. Swarms of workmen have been brought in. They've started digging the foundations. So far, everything's fine. Then one morning the foreman looked in and said, "There are some great big stones turning up in your plot."

"Well, you'd hardly expect gold nuggets, would you? That's normal enough, isn't it?" I replied.

"These aren't just any old stones. Come and have a look."

I did. Rectangular stones, one side flat, the other all knobs and bumps. "Not im-portant," I said. "Put them on one side: they may come in useful for the building."

After he'd gone I thought I'd take an adze and give one of the stones a bit of a scrape. And what do you think I saw? A relief, a masterpiece. A big-bosomed woman clutching a child to her. Well, it's not surprising. Our Aegean coast is full of ancient works of art.

That evening I told my wife about it. "These may be classical antiquities," I said. "We might show them to Shükran Hanim at the museum."

"Oh come on! Don't make life more complicated!"

My wife has got it in for Shükran Hanim at the best of times, the way every woman who hasn't had an education feels about the woman who has, and has made a career for herself. Yet Shükran Tur is an inoffensive bit of a girl: short, skinny, silver-rimmed spectacles, never married nor likely to at this rate, with a degree in archaeology. Hard-ly opens her mouth. Doesn't smile much. Reads English books.

"What harm will it do if she sees them?" I said. "What if they're antiquities?"

"And will you get a reward if they are?"

"I'd just like to do my duty as a civilized human being."

That day I cleaned two more stones. A ceremonial procession: four people with offerings in their hands and sandals on their feet. Each of them more beautiful and full of expression than the last.

Early next morning, Razi Bey dropped in. "I'll have some tea with you kids this morn-ing," he said. Never before had he dropped in like this. Without beating about the bush, he began, "Well, Sunuhi Bey, I hear you've discovered some antiquities on your plot."

I didn't like his mocking look. "I'm just going to show them to Shükran Hanim, the director of the museum."

"Shükran Tur's on leave. She's at Silifke. She'll be back at the end of the summer. Before that, at least let me have a look at them."

I took him there. He saw them and turned them over and round. The mocking look vanished from his face and he frowned. "Leave it," he said. "They're not antiquities. And suppose they were; would that be your business?"

"We'll just let Shükran Hanim see them."

"You've got a fixation about letting Shükran Hanim see them. I mean, what'll happen if she does?"

"Isn't there such a thing as one's duty, one's duty to mankind, to civilization? What if they're the work of some great artist? What if they're a masterpiece, calling out from centuries past to centuries yet to come?"

"You say the weirdest things, Sunuhi Bey. Seeing they've been underground for centuries, where's the harm if they go on staying there?"

"But humanity . . ."

"Now you're starting on your humanity line. I'm not a complete clod, you know. You haven't mentioned this to anyone else, have you?"

"No."

"Well, don't. In particular, that know-all Shükran Tur mustn't hear about it. Tell the labourers it turned out to be the floor of an old latrine. If any word gets out about antiquities, have you any notion of what will happen to us? The State will requisition the land and get excavations going. The property you got so cheap will be lost to you. The cooperative and all that will be over and done with. You and the rest of the shareholders will end up with nothing."

"What you ought to be saying is that we have a choice between self-interest and duty."

"Ah yes, duty. I knew that was coming. I've told you, don't make a thing of it, that's all."

"May I remind you that I have always lived at peace with my conscience? The one thing I am proud of is my honour, Razi Bey."

My wife chimed in. "Have you been excessively rewarded for your honourable service as a schoolmaster?"

Razi Bey added, "We included you in our group because we thought you were a decent chap. Let's give him a stake in this nice little spot, we said. Are you going to make us regret it?"

"Please don't talk like that," I said. "I'm grateful that you've taken me into your group. I'm grateful all right but . . ."

"Come on, that's enough," said Razi Bey. "We all know you are honour incarnate. And the family are all proud of you. But this isn't just between the two of us. The interests of forty-seven shareholders are involved. One for all and all for one. If you don't keep your mouth shut, it's all done for; all the money and all the hope."

When Razi Bey had gone, I said to my wife, "Was it you who put him up to it?"

"What was I to do? I was afraid you'd go and do something crazy."

"Well what do you think of that? This she calls crazy. Family matters ought to stay inside the family."

"And is your brother-in-law an outsider?"

I had a rotten night and woke up in the morning with a headache.

"When a man gets to my age, what has he to live for? He lives to take things easy. Can someone with an uneasy conscience take things easy?"

"You've retired and you're still giving lectures. Stop being a bore!"

"Yes, maybe at first he lives to eat and drink and sleep. But when all that's taken care of, he aspires to other things. He lives to gain immortality. In order to be able to defy death, the poor devil has two possibilities open to him. Either he can have children and perpetuate his line, or he can compose immortal verses, like Sheykh Galib, or leave his mark on the world in some other way. And how is this done? It can be done with some masterpiece that calls out from centuries past to centuries yet to come. Why did the Pharaohs have the Pyramids built? Why was the Tower of Babel reared to the skies? Why did Alexander and Napoleon set out to conquer the world? Why did Michelangelo do his statue of David? Why did Sinan the Architect build the Süleymaniye Mosque?"

"They all had a home to lay their heads in," replied my better half. "Have you ever owned a house till now? Cut out the rhetoric and stick to the facts. I'm in no mood to listen to you binding on, I've got a headache without that. If you're so keen, go and register as a guide and tell these stories to the German tourist women and those ugly brutes of German travellers with cameras."

I could see I had more chance of being struck by lightning than of persuading her of the immortality of art, so I shut up. All night long I kept falling asleep and waking up. I dreamed about Phidias and Alexander the Great and Sinan the Architect. Funny thing was that Sinan didn't look a bit like the pictures of him in the art-history books.

My wife the mole must have been passing on everything that happened in the house, because next day I was accosted by that great hulking Nuri Iskeche and Sirri Erdem, the retired superintendent of police. Nuri Iskeche was breathing heavily through his nose. "There's some daft gossip going round town," he said. "Or have some antiques really been found on the property of our cooperative, or what?"

I don't know if you've noticed, but these chaps just don't know the word "antiquities."

"I haven't said anything to anybody yet," I said.

"Someone has, because people have heard about it." After that he gave a long sigh. He shook his head from side to side perhaps ten times and muttered, "God give me strength!" Then he said, "If anyone mentions antiques again, I'm not kidding, there'll be bloodshed. We've put exactly fifteen million into this business. It's no joke." He then looked me full in the face with his bloodshot eyes and said, "Friend, I'm an old Union and Progress man: Razi may have told you. Yesterday in the café I swore an oath on my pistol." And off he went. That's what's known as blackmail. Intimidation.

It turned out that Razi had been watching us from a distance. He rushed up and took me by the arm. "Pay no attention to Nuri," he said. "He's very hot-tempered. But you should have seen him yesterday in the café! If Sirri and I hadn't grabbed his hand he'd have fired his pistol. Well, after all, he is a former terrorist."

"Who or what was he going to fire at? The reliefs, or their dead-and-gone artist?"

Sirri joined in the conversation. "The important thing isn't Nuri's reaction but the interests of all of us. Don't you agree?"

Gavsi Bey, a retired member of the Council of State was, on the face of it, the most cultured man among them. At least he didn't call antiquities antiques. "Anatolia," he said, "is like a layer-cake. In it there lie civilizations upon civilizations. All of them were built one on top of the other. Every city, every town, is like that. At one time a German Jew made off with the gold coins he'd got from the top layer of Troy and no one said a word. You know Istanbul, don't you? Istanbul. Wherever you put a shovel, Byzantium comes out from under it. You'll never build a house or a block of flats if you mean to go in for archaeological digs. You mustn't take these things so much to heart. What have they got to do with you?"

Razi too was very loquacious today. "Where were you, Sunuhi, all those years when tribes of tourists were plundering these shores? Even the government turned a blind eye and now are you going to be the lone defender of the legacy of the past? Even Sultan Abdülhamid, do you know what he said? 'If stones come out you can have them; if metal comes out it's mine.'"

Now it was Sirri Erdem's turn. "And, you know, people talk about a place being historical and all that, but it's just fables. Throughout history, so many civilizations have been founded, meant to last to all eternity, and then so many rulers emerged and demolished those civilizations, razed them to the ground and turned them into dust so that they in their turn could last to all eternity. The thing you call history is a vicious circle. My dear Sunuhi Bey, are you a shareholder in the cooperative or a conservator of historical monuments?"

They laughed. The odd thing is that I smiled too, not knowing what I was smiling at. Maybe it was just to show that I was still a party to the conversation, that I was not devoid of sophistication.

Three more days passed. Nuri Bey's terrorist pistol kept getting mixed up in my dreams. At the shareholders' meeting, new elections were held and I was chosen— God knows why—to be Treasurer. We heard that Shükran Tur, the museum director, had met an American at Silifke who got her a fellowship or something. She whizzed into town one evening and whizzed out again, then immediately shot off to Ankara to complete the paperwork. Sunk without trace.

Meanwhile it seems we have a visit from Razi Bey. My wife said to me one evening, "Razi Bey wants the stones."

"What does he think he's going to do with them?"

"How do I know? He said he was going to take them off in a lorry."

"Where to?"

"Somewhere where they'd be safe," he said. He had Gavsi Bey and Sirri Bey with him.

About that time I had a serious inflammation of the kidneys and when I'd got over it I looked like Gandhi. Two months later the building work was finished. Thanks to Nuri Iskeche's intimidatory tactics, one didn't hear much talk in town about antiquities. Anyway, we're all going to be neighbours; there's no room for tension and ill feeling. As the saying goes, don't choose a house, choose a neighbour. Peace and harmony, that's the basic thing. All of us, how many days do we have as guests in this world? Recently, Sirri Erdem married off his daughter—may all our friends have the same good fortune. At the wedding there was eating and a great deal of drinking. When everyone was merry, Razi Bey, Nuri Iskeche and Gavsi Bey took me by the arm and we all embraced and kissed.

"We were on the point of falling out over nothing at all," they said. "Anyway, it's all over and forgotten."

"It's true it's all over, but what I said wasn't wrong. What does man live for?"

"To be able to call out from centuries past to centuries yet to come," said my wife, in a fair imitation of my voice and way of speaking.

Razi Bey looked at Nuri Iskeche. Nuri Iskeche looked at my wife. Gavsi Bey said, "Don't worry. Those masterpieces that call out from centuries past to centuries yet to come, we didn't throw them away or sell them or smash them into little bits. They're in a very secure place."

"Where's that?" I asked.

"They're all in a very safe place; they're still looking to the centuries yet to come and calling out to them."

"Where are they?" I asked.

Proudly Gavsi Bey replied, "We used them to line the walls of the cooperative's septic tank."

"What!" I roared. "Shame on you!"

Gavsi Bey retorted, "Now *you* are behaving shamefully. Credit us too with a modicum of respect for art, of intellect and right thinking. It would have been wrong for us to defile the faces of those lovely ancient reliefs with—you'll excuse me—our excreta. We turned them all backwards. Cheer up! Their faces are to the earth, they are still looking into eternity. They've turned their backsides to our septic tank—the backsides which in life they too used for excreting."

"I give up," I said. "I mean . . ."

What else could I say?

Throughout my life, the expression "I give up" has been the one I've used most often. It's only three syllables, it's easy to say and it does help relieve your feelings. Up to a point.

[1948]
Translated by
GEOFFREY LEWIS

Questions

1. On which side of the issue—the preservation of antiquities or their cover-up for progress—does the author stand?
2. What is the role of the Unionists in the story? Of Sunuhi's wife?
3. Does Sunuhi Bey give in too easily? Is there anything he could have done that would have changed the story's outcome?

Amos Tutuola

(1910–1997)
Nigeria

When Amos Tutuola published The Palm-Wine Drinkard in 1952 (from which "The Complete Gentleman" has been extracted), the Welsh poet Dylan Thomas had this to say in his review of the book:

> This is the brief, thronged, grisly and bewitching story, or series of stories, written in young English by a West African, about the journey of an expert and devoted palm-wine drinkard through a nightmare of indescribable adventures, all simply and carefully described in the spirit-bristling bush.

The "young" English that Thomas referred to was nothing more than Tutuola's use of West African English, still startling to readers who come across it for the first time. Tutuola's "bewitching story" (in the form of the drinkard's quest for his dead palm-wine tapster) leads his main character into many strange and unusual encounters and events, concluding with a visit to the Yoruba afterworld. Tutuola, a master story-teller, has incorporated innumerable traditional Yoruba oral stories into the framework of the Western written narrative. As you will see from the episode included here, the drinkard/narrator earns a boon for his labor, although the story is primarily the young girl's instead of his.

Amos Tutuola was born in Abeokuta, in Western Nigeria. He completed six years of primary school education, which were followed by further training as a blacksmith. All of his colorful narratives incorporate Yoruba folktales and, in many instances, tales that are familiar to the peoples of many different West African ethnic groups. Besides The Palm-Wine Drinkard, Tutuola also published My Life in the Bush of Ghosts (1954), Simbi and the Satyr of the Dark Jungle (1956), The Brave African Huntress (1958), The Feather Woman of the Jungle (1962), Ajaiyi and His Inherited Poverty (1967), and Pauper, Brawler and Slanderer (1987).

Tutuola died in poverty and obscurity in 1997.

THE COMPLETE GENTLEMAN

The Description of the Curious Creature—

He was a beautiful "complete" gentleman, he dressed with the finest and most costly clothes, all the parts of his body were completed, he was a tall man but stout. As this gentleman came to the market on that day, if he had been an article or for sale, he would be sold at least for £2000 (two thousand pounds). As this complete gentleman came to the market on that day, and at the same time that this lady saw him in the market, she did nothing more than to ask him where he was living, but this fine gentleman did not answer her or approach her at all. But when she noticed that the fine or complete gentleman did not listen to her, she left her articles and began to watch the movements of the complete gentleman about in the market and left her articles unsold.

By and by the market closed for that day then the whole people in the market were returning to their destinations etc., and the complete gentleman was returning to his own too, but as this lady was following him about in the market all the while, she saw him when he was returning to his destination as others did, then she was following him (complete gentleman) to an unknown place. But as she was following the complete gentleman along the road, he was telling her to go back or not to follow him, but the lady did not listen to what he was telling her, and when the complete gentleman had tired of telling her not to follow him or to go back to her town, he left her to follow him.

Do Not Follow Unknown Man's Beauty

But when they had travelled about twelve miles away from that market, they left the road on which they were travelling and started to travel inside an endless forest in which only the terrible creatures were living.

Return the Parts of Body to the Owners; or Hired Parts of the Complete Gentleman's Body to Be Returned

As they were travelling along in this endless forest then the complete gentleman in the market that the lady was following, began to return the hired parts of his body to the owners and he was paying them the rentage money. When he reached where he hired the left foot, he pulled it out, he gave it to the owner and paid him, and they kept going; when they reached the place where he hired the right foot, he pulled it out and gave it to the owner and paid for the rentage. Now both feet had returned to the owners, so he began to crawl along on the ground, by that time, that lady wanted to go back to her town or her father, but the terrible and curious creature or the complete gentleman did not allow her to return or go back to her town or her father again and the complete gentleman said thus:—"I had told you not to follow me before we branched into this endless forest which belongs to only terrible and curious creatures, but when I become a half-bodied incomplete gentleman you wanted to go back, now that cannot be done, you have failed. Even you have never seen anything yet, just follow me."

When they went furthermore, then they reached where he hired the belly, ribs, chest, etc., then he pulled them out and gave them to the owner and paid for the rentage.

Now to this gentleman or terrible creature remained only the head and both arms with neck, by that time he could not crawl as before but only went jumping on as a bullfrog and now this lady was soon faint for this fearful creature whom she was following. But when the lady saw every part of this complete gentleman in the market was shared or hired and he was returning them to the owners, then she began to try all her efforts to return to her father's town, but she was not allowed by this fearful creature at all.

When they reached where he hired both arms, he pulled them out and gave them to the owner, he paid for them; and they were still going on in this endless forest, they reached the place where he hired the neck, he pulled it out and gave it to the owner and paid for it as well.

A Full-Bodied Gentleman Reduced to Head

Now this complete gentleman was reduced to head and when they reached where he hired the skin and flesh which covered the head, he returned them, and paid to the owner, now the complete gentleman in the market reduced to a "SKULL" and this lady remained with only "Skull." When the lady saw that she remained with only Skull, she began to say that her father had been telling her to marry a man, but she did not listen to or believe him.

When the lady saw that the gentleman became a Skull, she began to faint, but the Skull told her if she would die she would die and she would follow him to his house. But by the time that he was saying so, he was humming with a terrible voice and also grew very wild and even if there was a person two miles away he would not have to listen before hearing him, so this lady began to run away in that forest for her life, but the Skull chased her and within a few yards, he caught her, because he was very clever and smart as he was only Skull and he could jump a mile to the second before coming down. He caught the lady in this way: so when the lady was running away for her life, he hastily ran to her front and stopped her as a log of wood.

By and by, this lady followed the Skull to his house, and the house was a hole which was under the ground. When they reached there both of them entered the hole. But there were only Skulls living in that hole. At the same time that they entered the hole, he tied a single cowrie on the neck of this lady with a kind of rope, after that, he gave her a large frog on which she sat as a stool, then he gave a whistle to a Skull of his kind to keep watch on this lady whenever she wanted to run away. Because the Skull knew already that the lady would attempt to run away from the hole. Then he went to the back yard to where his family were staying in the day time till night.

But one day, the lady attempted to escape from the hole, and at the same time that the Skull who was watching her whistled to the rest of the Skulls that were in the back yard, the whole of them rushed out to the place where the lady sat on the bullfrog, so they caught her, but as all of them were rushing out, they were rolling on the ground as if a thousand petrol drums were pushing along a hard road. After she was caught, then they brought her back to sit on the same frog as usual. If the Skull who was watching her fell asleep, and if the lady wanted to escape, the cowrie that was tied on her neck would raise up the alarm with a terrible noise, so that the Skull who was watching her would wake up at once and then the rest of the Skull's family would rush out from the back in thousands to the lady and ask her what she wanted to do with a curious and terrible voice.

But the lady could not talk at all, because as the cowrie had been tied on her neck, she became dumb at the same moment.

The Father of Gods Should Find Out Whereabouts
the Daughter of the Head of the Town Was

Now as the father of the lady first asked for my name and I told him that my name was "Father of gods who could do anything in this world," then he told me that I could find out where his daughter was and bring her to him, then he would tell me where my palm-wine tapster was. But when he said so, I was jumping up with gladness that he should promise me that he would tell me where my tapster was. I agreed to what he said; the father and parent of this lady never knew whereabouts their daughter was, but they had information that the lady followed a complete gentleman in the market. As I was the "Father of gods who could do anything in this world," when it was at night I sacrificed to my juju[1] with a goat.

And when it was early in the morning, I sent for forty kegs of palm-wine. After I had drunk it all, I started to investigate whereabouts was the lady. As it was the market-day, I started the investigation from the market. But as I was a juju-man, I knew all the kinds of people in that market. When it was exactly 9 o'clock A.M., the very complete gentleman whom the lady followed came to the market again, and at the same time that I saw him, I knew that he was a curious and terrible creature.

The Lady Was Not to Be Blamed
for Following the Skull as a Complete Gentleman

I could not blame the lady for following the Skull as a complete gentleman to his house at all. Because if I were a lady, no doubt I would follow him to wherever he would go, and still as I was a man I would jealous him more than that, because if this gentleman went to the battlefield, surely, enemy would not kill him or capture him and if bombers saw him in a town which was to be bombed, they would not throw bombs on his presence, and if they did throw it, the bomb itself would not explode until this gentleman would leave that town, because of his beauty. At the same time that I saw this gentleman in the market on that day, what I was doing was only to follow him about in the market. After I looked at him for so many hours, then I ran to a corner of the market and I cried for a few minutes because I thought within myself why was I not created that he was only a Skull, then I thanked God that He had created me without beauty, so I went back to him in the market, but I was still attracted by his beauty. So when the market closed for that day, and when everybody was returning to his or her destination, this gentleman was returning to his own too and I followed him to know where he was living.

Investigation to the Skull's Family's House

When I travelled with him a distance of about twelve miles away to that market, the gentleman left the really road on which we were travelling and branched into an endless forest and I was following him, but as I did not want him to see that I

---

[1]*juju*   Witchcraft, but used more generally as "magic" here, that is, with no negative connotation.

was following him, then I used one of my juju which changed me into a lizard and followed him. But after I had travelled with him a distance of about twenty-five miles away in this endless forest, he began to pull out all the parts of his body and return them to the owners, and paid them.

After I had travelled with him for another fifty miles in this forest, then he reached his house and entered it, but I entered it also with him, as I was a lizard. The first thing that he did when he entered the hole (house) he went straight to the place where the lady was, and I saw the lady sat on a bullfrog with a single cowrie tied on her neck and a Skull who was watching her stood behind her. After he (gentleman) had seen that the lady was there, he went to the back yard where all his family were working.

The Investigator's Wonderful Work in the Skull's Family's House

When I saw this lady and when the Skull who brought her to that hole or whom I followed from the market to that hole went to the back yard, then I changed myself to a man as before, then I talked to the lady but she could not answer me at all, she only showed that she was in a serious condition. The Skull who was guarding her with a whistle fell asleep at that time.

To my surprise, when I helped the lady to stand up from the frog on which she sat, the cowrie that was tied on her neck made a curious noise at once, and when the Skull who was watching her heard the noise, he woke up and blew the whistle to the rest, then the whole of them rushed to the place and surrounded the lady and me, but at the same time that they saw me there, one of them ran to a pit which was not so far from that spot, the pit was filled with cowries. He picked one cowrie out of the pit, after that he was running towards me, and the whole crowd wanted to tie the cowrie on my neck too. But before they could do that, I had changed myself into air, they could not trace me out again, but I was looking at them. I believed that the cowries in that pit were their power and to reduce the power of any human being whenever tied on his or her neck and also to make a person dumb.

Over one hour after I had dissolved into air, these Skulls went back to the back yard, but there remained the Skull who was watching her.

After they had returned to the back yard, I changed to a man as usual, then I took the lady from the frog, but at the same time that I touched her, the cowrie which was tied on her neck began to shout; even if a person was four miles away he would not have to listen before hearing, but immediately the Skull who was watching her heard the noise and saw me when I took her from that frog, he blew the whistle to the rest of them who were in the back yard.

Immediately the whole Skull family heard the whistle when blew to them, they were rushing out to the place and before they could reach there, I had left their hole for the forest, but before I could travel about one hundred yards in the forest, they had rushed out from their hole to inside the forest and I was still running away with the lady. As these Skulls were chasing me about in the forest, they were rolling on the ground like large stones and also humming with terrible noise, but when I saw that they had nearly caught me or if I continued to run away like that, no doubt, they would catch me sooner, then I changed the lady to a kitten and put her inside my pocket and changed myself to a very small bird which I could describe as a "sparrow" in English language.

After that I flew away, but as I was flying in the sky, the cowrie which was tied on that lady's neck was still making a noise and I tried all my best to stop the noise, but all were in vain. When I reached home with the lady, I changed her to a lady as she was before and also myself changed to man as well. When her father saw that I brought his daughter back home, he was exceedingly glad and said thus:—"You are the 'Father of gods' as you had told me before."

But as the lady was now at home, the cowrie on her neck did not stop making a terrible noise once, and she could not talk to anybody; she showed only that she was very glad she was at home. Now I had brought the lady but she could not talk, eat or loose away the cowrie on her neck, because the terrible noise of the cowrie did not allow anybody to rest or sleep at all.

There Remain Greater Tasks Ahead

Now I began to cut the rope of the cowrie from her neck and to make her talk and eat, but all my efforts were in vain. At last I tried my best to cut off the rope of the cowrie; it only stopped the noise, but I was unable to loose it away from her neck.

When her father saw all my trouble, he thanked me greatly and repeated again that as I called myself "Father of gods who could do anything in this world" I ought to do the rest of the work. But when he said so, I was very ashamed and thought within myself that if I return to the Skulls' hole or house, they might kill me and the forest was very dangerous travel always, again I could not go directly to the Skulls in their hole and ask them how to loose away the cowrie which was tied on the lady's neck and to make her talk and eat.

Back to the Skull's Family's House

On the third day after I had brought the lady to her father's house, I returned to the endless forest for further investigation. When there remained about one mile to reach the hole of these Skulls, there I saw the very Skull who the lady had followed from the market as a complete gentleman to the hole of Skull's family's house, and at the same time that I saw him like that, I changed into a lizard and climbed a tree which was near him.

He stood before two plants, then he cut a single opposite leaf from the opposite plant; he held the leaf with his right hand and he was saying thus:—"As this lady was taken from me, if this opposite leaf is not given her to eat, she will not talk forever," after that he threw the leaf down on the ground. Then he cut another single compound leaf with his left hand and said that if this single compound is not given to this lady, to eat, the cowrie on her neck could not be loosened away forever and it would be making a terrible noise forever.

After he said so, he threw the leaf down at the same spot, then he jumped away. So after he had jumped very far away (luckily, I was there when he was doing all these things, and I saw the place that he threw both leaves separately), then I changed myself to a man as before, I went to the place that he threw both leaves, then I picked them up and I went home at once.

But at the same time that I reached home, I cooked both leaves separately and gave her to eat; to my surprise the lady began to talk at once. After that, I gave her the compound leaf to eat for the second time and immediately she ate that too, the cowrie which was tied on her neck by the Skull, loosened away by itself, but it disappeared at the same time. So when the father and mother saw the wonderful work which I had done for them, they brought fifty kegs of palm-wine for me, they gave me the lady as wife and two rooms in that house in which to live with them. So, I saved the lady from the complete gentleman in the market who was afterwards reduced to a Skull and the lady became my wife since that day. This was how I got a wife.

[1952]

Questions

1. What specific aspects of oral narrative can be identified in Tutuola's story?
2. When Amos Tutuola published *The Palm-Wine Drinkard* in 1952, Walt Disney Productions purchased the film rights to the book. What do you think would happen to "The Complete Gentleman" if it were filmed by Disney?
3. Compare "The Complete Gentleman" to the opening of "A Meeting in the Dark" by Ngugi wa Thiongo, included in this volume. What connections can be drawn between the two tales?
4. Although the story is African, does it suggest a universal dimension to the age-old theme of appearance versus reality?

Mark Twain

(1835–1910)

United States

As scholars have noted for years, the underside of Mark Twain's humorous writing is almost always darker, bleaker than its surface reality. In Huck Finn's celebrated journey down the Mississippi River with Jim, the Duke, and the King, there is hardly an on-shore incident (in the small-town communities Twain describes so brilliantly) that doesn't smack of mendacity, gullibility, racism, even stupidity—often on the part of the inhabitants of an entire village. Even the tall tale Twain relates in "The Celebrated Jumping Frog of Calavaras County" clearly implies that for someone to win, someone else may get tricked, taken advantage of. It doesn't take long for the astute reader to understand that Twain's general picture of humankind is pessimistic at best and that humor is his vehicle for getting at something much more serious.

By the time Twain wrote "Luck" (1891), his own life was marred by a series of disappointments: His marriage was deeply troubled, his greatest books were already behind him (and had not always been as successful as he had hoped), and his economic ventures were about to close in on him. The rest of his life would be a series of ups and downs, of dramatic reversals of fortune. As you read Twain's "Luck," try to determine where the story shifts—where the innocent goodwill of Lieutenant General Lord Arthur Scoresby begins to show its true colors.

LUCK

[Note—This is not a fancy sketch. I got it from a clergyman who was an instructor at Woolwich forty years ago, and who vouched for its truth.—M. T.]

It was at a banquet in London in honor of one of the two or three conspicuously illustrious English military names of this generation. For reasons which will presently appear, I will withhold his real name and titles, and call him Lieutenant General Lord Arthur Scoresby, V. C., K. C. B., etc., etc., etc. What a fascination there is in a renowned name! There sat the man, in actual flesh, whom I had heard of so many thousands of times since that day, thirty years before, when his name shot suddenly to the zenith from a Crimean battlefield, to remain forever celebrated. It was food and drink to me to look, and look, and look at that demigod; scanning, searching, noting: the quietness, the reserve, the noble gravity of his countenance; the simple honesty, that expressed itself all over him; the sweet unconsciousness of his greatness—unconsciousness of the hundreds of admiring eyes fastened upon him, unconsciousness of the deep, loving, sincere worship welling out of the breasts of those people and flowing toward him.

The clergyman at my left was an old acquaintance of mine—clergyman now, but had spent the first half of his life in the camp and field, and as an instructor in the military school at Woolwich. Just at the moment I have been talking about, a veiled and singular light glimmered in his eyes, and he leaned down and muttered confidentially to me—indicating the hero of the banquet with a gesture:

"Privately—he's an absolute fool."

This verdict was a great surprise to me. If its subject had been Napoleon, or Socrates, or Solomon, my astonishment could not have been greater. Two things I was well aware of: that the Reverend was a man of strict veracity, and that his judgment of men was good. Therefore I knew, beyond doubt or question, that the world was mistaken about this hero: he *was* a fool. So I meant to find out, at a convenient moment, how the Reverend, all solitary and alone, had discovered the secret.

Some days later the opportunity came, and this is what the Reverend told me.

About forty years ago I was an instructor in the military academy at Woolwich. I was present in one of the sections when young Scoresby underwent his preliminary examination. I was touched to the quick with pity; for the rest of the class answered up brightly and handsomely, while he—why, dear me, he didn't know *anything*, so to speak. He was evidently good, and sweet, and lovable, and guileless, and so it was exceedingly painful to see him stand there, as serene as a graven image, and deliver himself of answers which were veritably miraculous for stupidity and ignorance. All the compassion in me was aroused in his behalf. I said to myself, when he comes to be examined again, he will be flung over, of course; so it will be simply a harmless act of charity to ease his fall as much as I can. I took him aside, and found that he knew a little of Caesar's history; and as he didn't know anything else, I went to work and drilled him like a galley slave on a certain line of stock questions concerning Caesar which I knew would be used. If you'll believe me, he went through with flying colors on examination day! He went through on that purely superficial "cram," and got compliments too, while others, who knew a thousand times more than he, got plucked. By some strangely lucky accident—an accident not likely to happen twice in a century—he was asked no question outside of the narrow limits of his drill.

It was stupefying. Well, all through his course I stood by him, with something of the sentiment which a mother feels for a crippled child; and he always saved himself—just by miracle, apparently.

Now of course the thing that would expose him and kill him at last was mathematics. I resolved to make his death as easy as I could; so I drilled him and crammed him, and crammed him and drilled him, just on the line of questions which the examiners would be most likely to use, and then launching him on his fate. Well, sir, try to conceive of the result: to my consternation, he took the first prize! And with it he got a perfect ovation in the way of compliments.

Sleep? There was no more sleep for me for a week. My conscience tortured me day and night. What I had done I had done purely through charity, and only to ease the poor youth's fall—I never had dreamed of any such preposterous result as the thing that had happened. I felt as guilty and miserable as the creator of Frankenstein. Here was a woodenhead whom I had put in the way of glittering promotions and prodigious responsibilities, and but one thing could happen: he and his responsibilities would all go to ruin together at the first opportunity.

The Crimean war had just broken out. Of course there had to be a war, I said to myself: we couldn't have peace and give this donkey a chance to die before he is found out. I waited for the earthquake. It came. And it made me reel when it did come. He was actually gazetted to a captaincy in a marching regiment! Better men grow old and gray in the service before they climb to a sublimity like that. And who could ever have foreseen that they would go and put such a load of responsibility on such green and inadequate shoulders? I could just barely have stood it if they had made him a cornet; but a captain—think of it! I thought my hair would turn white.

Consider what I did—I who so loved repose and inaction. I said to myself, I am responsible to the country for this, and I must go along with him and protect the country against him as far as I can. So I took my poor little capital that I had saved up through years of work and grinding economy, and went with a sigh and bought a cornetcy[1] in his regiment, and away we went to the field.

And there—oh dear, it was awful. Blunders? Why, he never did anything *but* blunder. But, you see, nobody was in the fellow's secret—everybody had him focused wrong, and necessarily misinterpreted his performance every time—consequently they took his idiotic blunders for inspirations of genius; they did, honestly. His mildest blunders were enough to make a man in his right mind cry; and they did make me cry—and rage and rave too, privately. And the thing that kept me always in a sweat of apprehension was the fact that every fresh blunder he made increased the luster of his reputation! I kept saying to myself, he'll get so high, that when discovery does finally come, it will be like the sun falling out of the sky.

He went right along up, from grade to grade, over the dead bodies of his superiors, until at last, in the hottest moment of the battle of———down went our colonel, and my heart jumped into my mouth, for Scoresby was next in rank! Now for it, said I; we'll all land in Sheol in ten minutes, sure.

The battle was awfully hot; the allies were steadily giving way all over the field. Our regiment occupied a position that was vital; a blunder now must be destruction. At this crucial moment, what does this immortal fool do but detach the regiment from its place and order a charge over a neighboring hill where there wasn't a suggestion of an enemy! "There you go!" I said to myself; "this *is* the end at last."

And away we did go, and were over the shoulder of the hill before the insane movement could be discovered and stopped. And what did we find? An entire and unsuspected Russian army in reserve! And what happened? We were eaten up? That is necessarily what would have happened in ninety-nine cases out of a hundred. But no, those Russians argued that no single regiment would come browsing around there at such a time. It must be the entire English army, and that the sly Russian game was detected and blocked; so they turned tail, and away they went, pell-mell, over the hill and down into the field, in wild confusion, and we after them; they themselves broke the solid Russian center in the field, and tore through, and in no time there was the most tremendous rout you ever saw, and the defeat of the allies was turned into a sweeping and splendid victory! Marshal Canrobert looked on, dizzy with astonishment, admiration, and delight; and sent right off for Scoresby, and hugged him, and decorated him on the field, in presence of all the armies!

And what was Scoresby's blunder that time? Merely the mistaking his right hand for his left—that was all. An order had come to him to fall back and support our right; and instead, he fell *forward* and went over the hill to the left. But the name he

---

[1]*cornetcy* The fifth commissioned officer, who carried the colors, in a troop of cavalry (a position or rank of a cornet).

won that day as a marvelous military genius filled the world with his glory, and that glory will never fade while history books last.

He is just as good and sweet and lovable and unpretending as a man can be, but he doesn't know enough to come in when it rains. Now that is absolutely true. He is the supremest ass in the universe; and until half an hour ago nobody knew it but himself and me. He has been pursued, day by day and year by year, by a most phenomenal and astonishing luckiness. He has been a shining soldier in all our wars for a generation; he has littered his whole military life with blunders, and yet has never committed one that didn't make him a knight or a baronet or a lord or something. Look at his breast; why, he is just clothed in domestic and foreign decorations. Well, sir, every one of them is the record of some shouting stupidity or other; and taken together, they are proof that the very best thing in all this world that can befall a man is to be born lucky. I say again, as I said at the banquet, Scoresby's an absolute fool.

[1891]

Questions

1. Wherein does the conflict reside in this story?
2. What is the significance of the story-within-a-story format?
3. If Twain were writing today, would the story concern a military figure or a person of some other profession?
4. What does the story suggest about the relationship between talent, luck, and success?

John Updike
(b. 1932)
United States

O ne of John Updike's ambitions in college was to be a cartoonist and graphic
artist. After graduating from Harvard with a degree in English instead, he and
his wife went to Oxford on a fellowship, where they both pursued further study in
fine arts. Returning to the States and exchanging the precision of the visual sketch for
equally precise verbal sketches, Updike began writing short stories and soon established his reputation through frequent publication in The New Yorker. Updike drew
on his own childhood in rural eastern Pennsylvania and his later experience in urban
and suburban New York and New England to chronicle cultural changes in a cross-
section of American society, as demonstrated in marriage, family life, sexuality, and
religion. He has described his subject as "the American Protestant small town middle class. I like middles. It is in middles that extremes clash, where ambiguity restlessly rules. . . ."

Occasionally invoking myth and philosophy as the backdrop for his realistic fictional documentations of a sterile secular society, Updike has achieved the position of
a contemporary moralist, exploring an impressive range of American preoccupations
and anxieties. Harry "Rabbit" Angstrom, the protagonist of the "Rabbit" novels—
Rabbit Run (1960), Rabbit Redux (1971), Rabbit Is Rich (1981), and Rabbit
at Rest (1990)—is an unforgettable Updike character; his life from adolescence through
marriage, fatherhood, middle age, and death forms the substance of this multidecade
chronicle of an ordinary man moving through the vicissitudes of American life, driven
by his pursuit of an uncertain American dream. Among Updike's 19 novels to date are
The Centaur (1963), Couples (1968), The Coup (1978), The Witches of East-
wick (1984), Toward the End of Time (1997), Bech at Bay: A Quasi-Novel
(1998), and Gertrude and Claudius (2000), his "prequel" to Shakespeare's Hamlet. His short stories are collected in eight volumes, including Pigeon Feathers (1962),
Museums and Women (1972), Trust Me (1987), The Afterlife and Other Stories (1994), and Licks of Love (2000), which includes "Rabbit Remembered." The
recipient of numerous awards for his fiction, including two Pulitzer Prizes and three
National Book Critics Circle Awards, Updike is also an accomplished poet, essayist,
art critic, and author of children's books.

In a Paris Review interview, Updike explained the following:

> [I regard my books] not as sermons or directives in a war of ideas but as objects, with
> different shapes and textures and the mysteriousness of anything that exists. My first
> thought about art, as a child, was that the artist brings something into the world that
> didn't exist before, and that he does it without destroying something else. A kind of
> refutation of the conservation of matter. That still seems to me its central magic, its core
> of joy.

Through a lush and polished prose style perfectly suited to its subjects, Updike explores his characters' moments of experience and discovery with unerring accuracy.

A & P

In walks these three girls in nothing but bathing suits. I'm in the third checkout slot, with my back to the door, so I don't see them until they're over by the bread. The one that caught my eye first was the one in the plaid green two-piece. She was a chunky kid, with a good tan and a sweet broad soft-looking can with those two crescents of white just under it, where the sun never seems to hit, at the top of the backs of her legs. I stood there with my hand on a box of HiHo crackers trying to remember if I rang it up or not. I ring it up again and the customer starts giving me hell. She's one of these cash-register-watchers, a witch about fifty with rouge on her cheekbones and no eyebrows, and I know it made her day to trip me up. She'd been watching cash registers for fifty years and probably never seen a mistake before.

By the time I got her feathers smoothed and her goodies into a bag—she gives me a little snort in passing, if she'd been born at the right time they would have burned her over in Salem—by the time I get her on her way the girls had circled around the bread and were coming back, without a pushcart, back my way along the counters, in the aisle between the checkouts and the Special bins. They didn't even have shoes on. There was this chunky one, with the two-piece—it was bright green and the seams on the bra were still sharp and her belly was still pretty pale so I guessed she just got it (the suit)—there was this one, with one of those chubby berry-faces, the lips all bunched together under her nose, this one, and a tall one, with black hair that hadn't quite frizzed right, and one of these sunburns right across under the eyes, and a chin that was too long—you know, the kind of girl other girls think is very "striking" and "attractive" but never quite makes it, as they very well know, which is why they like her so much—and then the third one, that wasn't quite so tall. She was the queen. She kind of led them, the other two peeking around and making their shoulders round. She didn't look around, not this queen, she just walked straight on slowly, on these long white prima-donna legs. She came down a little hard on her heels, as if she didn't walk in her bare feet that much, putting down her heels and then letting the weight move along to her toes as if she was testing the floor with every step, putting a little deliberate extra action into it. You never know for sure how girls' minds work (do you really think it's a mind in there or just a little buzz like a bee in a glass jar?) but you got the idea she had talked the other two into coming in here with her, and now she was showing them how to do it, walk slow and hold yourself straight.

She had on a kind of dirty-pink—beige maybe, I don't know—bathing suit with a little nubble all over it, and what got me, the straps were down. They were off her shoulders looped loose around the cool tops of her arms, and I guess as a result the suit had slipped a little on her, so all around the top of the cloth there was this shining rim. If it hadn't been there you wouldn't have known there could have been anything whiter than those shoulders. With the straps pushed off, there was nothing between the top of the suit and the top of her head except just *her*, this clean bare plane of the top of her chest down from the shoulder bones like a dented sheet of metal tilted in the light. I mean, it was more than pretty.

She had sort of oaky hair that the sun and salt had bleached, done up in a bun that was unravelling, and a kind of prim face. Walking into the A & P with your straps down, I suppose it's the only kind of face you *can* have. She held her head so high her neck, coming up out of those white shoulders, looked kind of stretched, but I didn't mind. The longer her neck was, the more of her there was.

She must have felt in the corner of her eye me and over my shoulder Stokesie in the second slot watching, but she didn't tip. Not this queen. She kept her eyes moving across the racks, and stopped, and turned so slow it made my stomach rub the inside of my apron, and buzzed to the other two, who kind of huddled against her for relief, and then they all three of them went up the cat-and-dog-food-breakfast-cereal-macaroni-rice-raisins-seasonings-spreads-spaghetti-soft-drinks-crackers-and-cookies aisle. From the third slot I look straight up this aisle to the meat counter, and I watched them all the way. The fat one with the tan sort of fumbled with the cookies, but on second thought she put the package back. The sheep pushing their carts down the aisle—the girls were walking against the usual traffic (not that we have one-way signs or anything)—were pretty hilarious. You could see them, when Queenie's white shoulders dawned on them, kind of jerk, or hop, or hiccup, but their eyes snapped back to their own baskets and on they pushed. I bet you could set off dynamite in an A & P and the people would by and large keep reaching and checking oatmeal off their lists and muttering "Let me see, there was a third thing, began with A, asparagus, no, ah, yes, applesauce!" or whatever it is they do mutter. But there was no doubt, this jiggled them. A few houseslaves in pin curlers even looked around after pushing their carts past to make sure what they had seen was correct.

You know, it's one thing to have a girl in a bathing suit down on the beach, where what with the glare nobody can look at each other much anyway, and another thing in the cool of the A & P, under the fluorescent lights, against all those stacked packages, with her feet paddling along naked over our checkerboard green-and-cream rubber-tile floor.

"Oh Daddy," Stokesie said beside me. "I feel so faint."

"Darling," I said. "Hold me tight." Stokesie's married, with two babies chalked up on his fuselage already, but as far as I can tell that's the only difference. He's twenty-two, and I was nineteen this April.

"Is it done?" he asks, the responsible married man finding his voice. I forgot to say he thinks he's going to be manager some sunny day, maybe in 1990 when it's called the Great Alexandrov and Petrooshki Tea Company or something.

What he meant was, our town is five miles from a beach, with a big summer colony out on the Point, but we're right in the middle of town, and the women generally put on a shirt or shorts or something before they get out of the car into the street. And anyway these are usually women with six children and varicose veins mapping their legs and nobody, including them, could care less. As I say, we're right in the middle of town, and if you stand at our front doors you can see two banks and the Congregational church and the newspaper store and three real-estate offices and about twenty-seven old freeloaders tearing up Central Street because the sewer broke again. It's not as if we're on the Cape; we're north of Boston and there's people in this town haven't seen the ocean for twenty years.

The girls had reached the meat counter and were asking McMahon something. He pointed, they pointed, and they shuffled out of sight behind a pyramid of Diet Delight peaches. All that was left for us to see was old McMahon patting his mouth and looking after them sizing up their joints. Poor kids, I began to feel sorry for them, they couldn't help it.

Now here comes the sad part of the story, at least my family says it's sad, but I don't think it's so sad myself. The store's pretty empty, it being Thursday afternoon, so there was nothing much to do except lean on the register and wait for the girls to show up again. The whole store was like a pinball machine and I didn't know which tunnel they'd come out of. After a while they come around out of the far aisle, around the light bulbs, records at discount of the Caribbean Six or Tony Martin Sings or some such gunk you wonder they waste the wax on, sixpacks of candy bars, and plastic toys done up in cellophane that fall apart when a kid looks at them anyway. Around they come, Queenie still leading the way, and holding a little gray jar in her hand. Slots Three through Seven are unmanned and I could see her wondering between Stokes and me, but Stokesie with his usual luck draws an old party in baggy gray pants who stumbles up with four giant cans of pineapple juice (what do these bums *do* with all that pineapple juice? I've often asked myself) so the girls come to me. Queenie puts down the jar and I take it into my fingers icy cold. Kingfish Fancy Herring Snacks in Pure Sour Cream: 49¢. Now her hands are empty, not a ring or a bracelet, bare as God made them, and I wonder where the money's coming from. Still with that prim look she lifts a folded dollar bill out of the hollow at the center of her nubbled pink top. The jar went heavy in my hand. Really, I thought that was so cute.

Then everybody's luck begins to run out. Lengel comes in from haggling with a truck full of cabbages on the lot and is about to scuttle into that door marked MANAGER behind which he hides all day when the girls touch his eye. Lengel's pretty dreary, teaches Sunday school and the rest, but he doesn't miss that much. He comes over and says, "Girls, this isn't the beach."

Queenie blushes, though maybe it's just a brush of sunburn I was noticing for the first time, now that she was so close. "My mother asked me to pick up a jar of herring snacks." Her voice kind of startled me, the way voices do when you see the people first, coming out so flat and dumb yet kind of tony, too, the way it ticked over "pick up" and "snacks." All of a sudden I slid right down her voice into her living room. Her father and the other men were standing around in ice-cream coats and bow ties and the women were in sandals picking up herring snacks on toothpicks off a big glass plate and they were all holding drinks the color of water with olives and sprigs of mint in them. When my parents have somebody over they get lemonade and if it's a real racy affair Schlitz in tall glasses with "They'll Do It Every Time" cartoons stencilled on.

"That's all right," Lengel said. "But this isn't the beach." His repeating this struck me as funny, as if it had just occurred to him, and he had been thinking all these years the A & P was a great big sand dune and he was the head lifeguard. He didn't like my smiling—as I say he doesn't miss much—but he concentrates on giving the girls that sad Sunday-school-superintendent stare.

Queenie's blush is no sunburn now, and the plump one in plaid, that I liked better from the back—a really sweet can—pipes up, "We weren't doing any shopping. We just came in for the one thing."

"That makes no difference," Lengel tells her, and I could see from the way his eyes went that he hadn't noticed she was wearing a two-piece before. "We want you decently dressed when you come in here."

"We *are* decent," Queenie says suddenly, her lower lip pushing, getting sore now that she remembers her place, a place from which the crowd that runs the A & P must look pretty crummy. Fancy Herring Snacks flashed in her very blue eyes.

"Girls, I don't want to argue with you. After this come in here with your shoulders covered. It's our policy." He turns his back. That's policy for you. Policy is what the kingpins want. What the others want is juvenile delinquency.

All this while, the customers had been showing up with their carts but, you know, sheep, seeing a scene, they had all bunched up on Stokesie, who shook open a paper bag as gently as peeling a peach, not wanting to miss a word. I could feel in the silence everybody getting nervous, most of all Lengel, who asks me, "Sammy, have you rung up their purchase?"

I thought and said "No" but it wasn't about that I was thinking. I go through the punches, 4, 9, GROC, TOT—it's more complicated than you think, and after you do it often enough, it begins to make a little song, that you hear words to, in my case "Hello (*bing*) there, you (*gung*) hap-py *pee*-pul (*splat*)!"—the *splat* being the drawer flying out. I uncreased the bill, tenderly as you may imagine, it just having come from between the two smoothest scoops of vanilla I had ever known were there, and pass a half and a penny into her narrow pink palm, and nestle the herrings in a bag and twist its neck and hand it over, all the time thinking.

The girls, and who'd blame them, are in a hurry to get out, so I say "I quit" to Lengel enough for them to hear, hoping they'll stop and watch me, their unsuspected hero. They keep right on going, into the electric eye; the door flies open and they flicker across the lot to their car, Queenie and Plaid and Big Tall Goony-Goony (not that as raw material she was so bad), leaving me with Lengel and a kink in his eyebrow.

"Did you say something, Sammy?"

"I said I quit."

"I thought you did."

"You didn't have to embarrass them."

"It was they who were embarrassing us."

I started to say something that came out "Fiddle-de-doo." It's a saying of my grandmother's, and I know she would have been pleased.

"I don't think you know what you're saying," Lengel said.

"I know you don't," I said. "But I do." I pull the bow at the back of my apron and start shrugging it off my shoulders. A couple customers that had been heading for my slot begin to knock against each other, like scared pigs in a chute.

Lengel sighs and begins to look very patient and old and gray. He's been a friend of my parents for years. "Sammy, you don't want to do this to your Mom and Dad," he tells me. It's true, I don't. But it seems to me that once you begin a gesture it's fatal not to go through with it. I fold the apron, "Sammy" stitched in red on the pocket, and put it on the counter, and drop the bow tie on top of it. The bow tie is theirs, if you've ever wondered. "You'll feel this for the rest of your life," Lengel says, and I know that's true, too, but remembering how he made that pretty girl blush makes me so scrunchy inside I punch the No Sale tab and the machine whirs "pee-pul" and the drawer splats out. One advantage to this scene taking place in summer, I can follow this up with a clean exit, there's no fumbling around getting your coat and galoshes, I just saunter into the electric eye in my white shirt that my mother ironed the night before, and the door heaves itself open, and outside the sunshine is skating around on the asphalt.

I look around for my girls, but they're gone, of course. There wasn't anybody but some young married screaming with her children about some candy they didn't get by the door of a powder-blue Falcon station wagon. Looking back in the big windows, over the bags of peat moss and aluminum lawn furniture stacked on the pavement, I could see Lengel in my place in the slot, checking the sheep through. His face was dark gray and his back stiff, as if he'd just had an injection of iron, and my stomach kind of fell as I felt how hard the world was going to be to me hereafter.

[1961]

Questions

1. What is the dramatic conflict of the story? What is its climax?
2. Why, exactly, does Sammy quit his job so suddenly? What does he gain—and lose—in doing so? Sammy sees his decision as heroic; do the girls? Do you?
3. What are Sammy's values? How are they revealed during the narrative? How does his first-person perspective shape the story?
4. How does Updike's style contribute to the effectiveness of the story? What elements make it humorous?
5. Consider whether male and female readers might react differently to this story. What elements might influence different responses according to gender?

Luisa Valenzuela
(b. 1938)
Argentina

Luisa Valenzuela was born in Buenos Aires, the daughter of a physician father and a mother who was a popular Argentinian writer, Luisa Mercedes Levinson. Valenzuela's own literary talent developed early; by the age of 15, she had published her first story. While studying at the University of Buenos Aires, she worked with Jorge Luis Borges at the National Library. When she was 20 she went to Paris to write as a foreign correspondent for Argentinian newspapers; she also wrote for French television and radio.

During her three years in France, Valenzuela met a number of writers and critics who were experimenting with narrative forms and philosophical ideas about language and meaning, ideas that strongly influenced her own writing. In 1966 she published her first book, Clara: Thirteen Short Stories and a Novel, in which she explores the themes of violence, politics, and female oppression in Argentina. Several of her later works have been translated into English, including four collections of stories: Strange Things Happen Here (1975), Other Weapons (1985), Open Door (1988), and The Censors (1992). The novel The Lizard's Tale (1983), the fictionalized biography of a despot who is also a sorcerer, could not have been published in her own country, according to Valenzuela, because of its "mythicized and damning version of recent Argentine history." As Valerie Gladstone has observed, Valenzuela's fiction expresses the view that "political absurdity is matched only by the absurdity of human relations."

In her early stories, Valenzuela experimented with the tradition of Latin American writing called magical realism, in which fantastic events occur within real social settings. More recently she has turned away from that narrative mode, remarking, "Magic realism was a beautiful resting place, but things do go forward." Incorporating public political events, Valenzuela examines the intersecting themes of political oppression, cultural repression, and violence in Latin America, especially as those forces affect the lives of women in their more private psychological and erotic experiences.

Valenzuela left Argentina when the country became a military dictatorship following the death of Juan Perón in 1974. During her time in the United States, she has been supported by a Guggenheim grant as well as by a Fulbright fellowship to the International Writers' Program at the University of Iowa; she has been Distinguished Writer-in-Residence at Columbia University and elsewhere.

In "Strange Things Happen Here," Valenzuela captures the quality of the surreal that invades—and challenges—our concept of ordinary reality.

STRANGE THINGS HAPPEN HERE

In the café on the corner—every self-respecting café is on a corner, every meeting place is a crossing of two paths (two lives)—Mario and Pedro each order a cup of black coffee and put lots of sugar in it because sugar is free and provides nourishment.

Mario and Pedro have been flat broke for some time—not that they're complaining, but it's time they got lucky for a change—and suddenly they see the abandoned brief case, and just by looking at each other they tell themselves that maybe the moment has come. Right here, boys, in the café on the corner, no different from a hundred others.

The brief case is there all by itself on a chair leaning against the table, and nobody has come back to look for it. The neighborhood boys come and go, they exchange remarks that Mario and Pedro don't listen to. There are more of them every day and they have a funny accent, they're from the interior. I wonder what they're doing here, why they've come. Mario and Pedro wonder if someone is going to sit down at the table in the back, move the chair, and find the brief case that they almost love, almost caress and smell and lick and kiss. A man finally comes and sits down at the table alone (and to think that the brief case is probably full of money, and that guy's going to latch on to it for the modest price of a vermouth with lemon, which is what he finally asks for after taking a little while to make up his mind). They bring him the vermouth, along with a whole bunch of appetizers. Which olive, which little piece of cheese will he be raising to his mouth when he spots the brief case on the chair next to his? Pedro and Mario don't even want to think about it and yet it's all they *can* think about. When all is said and done the guy has as much or as little right to the brief case as they do. When all is said and done it's only a question of chance, a table more carefully chosen, and that's it. The guy sips his drink indifferently, swallowing one appetizer or another; the two of them can't even order another coffee because they're out of dough as might happen to you or to me, more perhaps to me than to you, but that's beside the point now that Pedro and Mario are being tyrannized by a guy who's picking bits of salami out of his teeth with his fingernail as he finishes his drink, not seeing a thing and not listening to what the boys are saying. You see them on street corners. Even Elba said something about it the other day, can you imagine, she's so nearsighted. Just like science fiction, they've landed from another planet even though they look like guys from the interior but with their hair so well combed, they're nice and neat I tell you, and I asked one of them what time it was but didn't get anywhere—they don't have watches of course. Why would they want a watch anyway, you might ask, if they live in a different time from us? I saw them, too. They come out from under the pavement in the streets and that's where they still are and who knows what they're looking for, though we do know that they leave holes in the streets, those enormous potholes they come out of that can't ever be filled in.

The guy with the vermouth isn't listening to them, and neither are Mario and Pedro, who are worrying about a brief case forgotten on a chair that's bound to contain something of value because otherwise it wouldn't have been forgotten just so they could get it, just the two of them, not the guy with the vermouth. He's finished his drink, picked his teeth, left some of the appetizers almost untouched. He gets up from the table, pays, the waiter takes everything off table, puts tip in pocket, wipes table with damp cloth, goes off and, man, the time has come because there's lots going on at the other end of the café and there's nobody at this end and Mario and Pedro know it's now or never.

Mario comes out first with the brief case under his arm and that's why he's the first to see a man's jacket lying on top of a car next to the sidewalk. That is to say, the car is next to the sidewalk, so the jacket lying on the roof is, too. A splendid jacket, of stupendous quality. Pedro sees it too, his legs shake because it's too much of a coincidence, he could sure use a new jacket, especially one with the pockets stuffed with dough. Mario can't work himself up to grabbing it. Pedro can, though with a cer-tain remorse, which gets worse and practically explodes when he sees two cops com-ing toward them to . . .

"We found this car on a jacket. This jacket on a car. We don't know what to do with it. The jacket, I mean."

"Well, leave it where you found it then. Don't bother us with things like that, we have more important business to attend to."

More crucial business. Like the persecution of man by man if you'll allow me to use that euphemism. And so the famous jacket is now in Pedro's trembling hands which have picked it up with much affection. He sure needed a jacket like this one, a sports jacket, well lined, lined with cash not silk who cares about silk? With the booty in hand they head back home. They don't have the nerve to take out one of the crisp bills that Mario thought he had glimpsed when he opened the brief case just a hair—spare change to take a taxi or a stinking bus.

They keep an eye peeled to see whether the strange things that are going on here, the things they happened to overhear in the café, have something to do with their two finds. The strange characters either haven't appeared in this part of town or have been replaced: two policemen per corner are too many because there are lots of cor-ners. This is not a gray afternoon like any other, and come to think of it maybe it isn't even a lucky afternoon the way it appears to be. These are the blank faces of a week-day, so different from the blank faces on Sunday. Pedro and Mario have a color now, they have a mask and can feel themselves exist because a brief case (ugly words) and a sports jacket blossomed in their path. (A jacket that's not as new as it appeared to be—threadbare but respectable. That's it: a respectable jacket.) As afternoons go, this isn't an easy one. Something is moving in the air with the howl of the sirens and they're beginning to feel fingered. They see police everywhere, police in the dark hall-ways, in pairs on all the corners in the city, police bouncing up and down on their mo-torcycles against traffic as though the proper functioning of the country depended on them, as maybe it does, yes, that's why things are as they are and Mario doesn't dare say that aloud because the brief case has him tongue-tied, not that there's a microphone concealed in it, but what paranoia, when nobody's forcing him to carry it. He could get rid of it in some dark alley—but how can you let go of a fortune that's practical-ly fallen in your lap, even if the fortune's got a load of dynamite inside? He takes a more natural grip on the brief case, holds it affectionately, not as though it were about to explode. At this same moment Pedro decides to put the jacket on and it's a little too big for him but not ridiculous, no not at all. Loose-fitting, yes, but not not ridicu-lous; comfortable, warm, affectionate, just a little bit frayed at the edges, worn. Pedro puts his hands in the pockets of the jacket (*his* pockets) and discovers a few old bus tickets, a dirty handkerchief, several bills, and some coins. He can't bring himself to say anything to Mario and suddenly he turns around to see if they're being followed. Maybe they've fallen into some sort of trap, and Mario must be feeling the same way because he isn't saying a word either. He's whistling between his teeth with the ex-pression of a guy who's been carrying around a ridiculous black brief case like this all his life. The situation doesn't seem quite as bright as it did in the beginning. It looks as though nobody has followed them, but who knows: there are people coming along behind them and maybe somebody left the brief case and the jacket behind for some obscure reason. Mario finally makes up his mind and murmurs to Pedro: Let's not go home, let's go on as if nothing had happened, I want to see if we're being followed. That's okay with Pedro. Mario nostalgically remembers the time (an hour ago) when they could talk out loud and even laugh. The brief case is getting too heavy and he's tempted once again to abandon it to its fate. Abandon it without having had a look at what's inside? Sheer cowardice.

They walk about aimlessly so as to put any possible though improbable tail off the track. It's no longer Pedro and Mario walking, it's a jacket and a brief case that have turned into people. They go on walking and finally the jacket says: "Let's have a drink in a bar. I'm dying of thirst."

"With all this? Without even knowing where it came from?"

"Yeah, sure. There's some money in one pocket." He takes a trembling hand with two bills in it out of the pocket. A thousand nice solid pesos. He's not up to rummaging around in the pockets any more, but he thinks—he smells—that there's more. They could use a couple of sandwiches, they can get them in this café that looks like a nice quiet place.

A guy says and the other girl's name is Saturdays there's no bread; anything, I wonder what kind of brainwashing. . . . In turbulent times there's nothing like turning your ears on, though the bad thing about cafés is the din of voices that drowns out individual voices.

Listen, you're intelligent enough to understand.

They allow themselves to be distracted for a little, they too wonder what kind of brainwashing, and if the guy who was called intelligent believes he is. If it's a question of believing, they're ready to believe the bit about the Saturdays without bread, as though they didn't know that you need bread on Saturday to make the wafers for mass on Sunday, and on Sunday you need some wine to get through the terrible wilderness of workdays.

When a person gets around in the world—the cafés—with the antennae up he can tune in on all sorts of confessions and pick up the most abstruse (most absurd) reasoning processes, absolutely necessary because of the need to be on the alert and through the fault of these two objects that are alien to them and yet possess them, envelop them, especially now when those boys come into the café panting and sit down at a table with a nothing's-been-happening-around-here expression on their faces and take out writing pads, open books, but it's too late: they bring the police in on their heels and of course books don't fool the keen-witted guardians of the law, but instead get them all worked up. They've arrived in the wake of the students to impose law and order and they do, with much pushing and shoving: your identification papers, come on, come on, straight out to the paddy wagon waiting outside with its mouth wide open. Pedro and Mario can't figure out how to get out of there, how to clear a path for themselves through the mass of humanity that's leaving the café to its initial tranquillity. As one of the kids goes out he drops a little package at Mario's feet, and in a reflex motion Mario draws the package over with his foot and hides it behind the famous brief case leaning against the chair. Suddenly he's scared: he thinks he's gotten crazy enough to appropriate anything within reach. Then he's even more scared: he knows he's done it to protect the kid, but what if the cops take it into their head to search *him*? They'd find a brief case with who knows what inside, an inexplicable package (suddenly it strikes him funny, and he hallucinates that the package is a bomb and sees his leg flying through the air accompanied out of sympathy by the brief case, which has burst and is spilling out big counterfeit bills). All this in the split second that it took to hide the little package, and after that nothing. It's better to leave your mind a blank and watch out for telepathic cops and things like that. And what was he saying to himself a thousand years ago when calm reigned?—a brainwashing; a selfservice brainwash so as not to give away what's inside this crazy head of mine. The kids move off, carted off with a kick or two from the bluecoats; the package remains there at the feet of those two respectable-looking gentlemen, gentlemen with a jacket and a brief case (each of them with one of the two). Respectable gentlemen or two guys very much alone in the peaceful café, gentlemen whom even a club sandwich couldn't console now.

They stand up. Mario knows that if he leaves the little package, the waiter is going to call him back and the jig'll be up. He picks it up, thus adding it to the day's booty but only for a short while; with trembling hands he deposits it in a garbage can on a deserted street. Pedro, who's walking next to him, doesn't understand at all what's going on, but can't work up the strength to ask.

At times, when everything is clear, all sorts of questions can be asked, but in moments like this the mere fact of still being alive condenses everything that is askable and diminishes its value. All they can do is to keep walking, that's all they can do, halting now and then to see for example why that man over there is crying. And the man cries so gently that it's almost sacrilege not to stop and see what the trouble is. It's shop-closing time and the salesgirls heading home are trying to find out what's wrong: their maternal instinct is always ready and waiting, and the man is weeping inconsolably. Finally he manages to stammer: I can't stand it any more. A little knot of people has formed around him with understanding looks on their faces, but they don't understand at all. When he shakes the newspaper and says I can't stand it any more, some people think that he's read the news and the weight of the world is too much for him. They are about to go and leave him to his spinelessness. Finally he manages to explain between hiccups that he's been looking for work for months and doesn't have one peso left for the bus home, nor an ounce of strength to keep on looking.

"Work," Pedro says to Mario. "Come on, this scene's not for us."

"Well, we don't have anything to give him anyway. I wish we did."

Work, work, the others chorus and their hearts are touched, because this word is intelligible whereas tears are not. The man's tears keep boring into the asphalt and who knows what they find, but nobody wonders except maybe him, maybe he's saying to himself, my tears are penetrating the ground and may discover oil. If I die right here and now, maybe I can slip through the holes made by my tears in the asphalt, and in a thousand years I'll have turned into oil so that somebody else like me, in the same circumstances. . . . A fine idea, but the chorus doesn't allow him to become lost in his own thoughts, which—it surmises—are thoughts of death (the chorus is afraid: what an assault it is on the peace of mind of the average citizen, for whom death is something you read about in the newspapers). Lack of work, yes, all of them understand being out of a job and are ready to help him. That's much better than death. And the goodhearted salesgirls from the hardware stores open their purses and take out some crumpled bills, a collection is immediately taken up, the most assertive ones take the others' money and urge them to cough up more. Mario is trying to open the brief case—what treasures can there be inside to share with this guy? Pedro thinks he should have fished out the package that Mario tossed in the garbage can. Maybe it was work tools, spray paint, or the perfect equipment for making a bomb, something to give this guy so that inactivity doesn't wipe him out.

The girls are now pressing the guy to accept the money that's been collected. The guy keeps shrieking that he doesn't want charity. One of the girls explains to him that it's a spontaneous contribution to help his family out while he looks for work with better spirits and a full stomach. The crocodile is now weeping with emotion. The salesgirls feel good, redeemed, and Pedro and Mario decide that this is a lucky sign.

Maybe if they keep the guy company Mario will make up his mind to open the brief case, and Pedro can search the jacket pockets to find their secret contents.

So when the guy is alone again they take him by the arm and invite him to eat with them. The guy hangs back at first, he's afraid of the two of them: they might be trying to get the dough he's just received. He no longer knows if it's true or not that he can't find work or if this is his work—pretending to be desperate so that people in the neighborhood feel sorry for him. The thought suddenly crosses his mind: if it's true that I'm a desperate man and everybody was so good to me, there's no reason why these two won't be. If I pretended to be desperate it means that I'm not a bad actor, and I'm going to get something out of these two as well. He decides they have an odd look about them but seem honest, so the three of them go off to a cheap restaurant together to offer themselves the luxury of some good sausages and plenty of wine.

Three, one of them thinks, is a lucky number. We'll see if something good comes of it.

Why have they spent all this time telling one another their life stories, which maybe are true? The three of them discover an identical need to relate their life stories in full detail, from the time when they were little to these fateful days when so many strange things are happening. The restaurant is near the station and at certain moments they dream of leaving or of derailing a train or something, so as to rid themselves of the tensions building up inside. It's the hour for dreaming and none of the three wants to ask for the check. Neither Pedro nor Mario has said a word about their surprising finds. And the guy wouldn't dream of paying for these two bums' dinners, and besides they invited him.

The tension becomes unbearable and all they have to do is make up their minds. Hours have gone by. Around them the waiters are piling the chairs on the tables, like a scaffolding that is closing in little by little, threatening to swallow them up, because the waiters have felt a sudden urge to build and they keep piling chairs on top of chairs, tables on top of tables, and chairs and then more chairs. They are going to be imprisoned in a net of wooden legs, a tomb of chairs and who knows how many tables. A good end for these three cowards who can't make up their minds to ask for the check. Here they lie: they've paid for seven sausage sandwiches and two pitchers of table wine with their lives. A fair price.

Finally Pedro—Pedro the bold—asks for the check and prays that the money in the outside pockets is enough to cover it. The inside pockets are an inscrutable world even here, shielded by the chairs; the inner pockets form too intricate a labyrinth for him. He would have to live other people's lives if he got into the inside pockets of the jacket, get involved with something that doesn't belong to him, lose himself by stepping into madness.

There is enough money. Friends by now, relieved, the three go out of the restaurant. Pretending to be absent-minded, Mario has left the brief case—too heavy, that's it— amid the intricate construction of chairs and tables piled on top of each other, and he is certain it won't be discovered until the next day. A few blocks farther on, they say good-by to the guy and the two of them walk back to the apartment that they share. They are almost there when Pedro realizes that Mario no longer has the brief case. He then takes off the jacket, folds it affectionately, and leaves it on top of a parked car, its original location. Finally they open the door of the apartment without fear, and go to bed without fear, without money, and without illusions. They sleep soundly, until Mario wakes up with a start, unable to tell whether the bang that has awakened him was real or a dream.

[1975]
Translated by
HELEN R. LANE

Questions

1. Is there a connection among the "strange things" that happen in the story? If so, what is it?

2. Through the characters' private thoughts and imaginings, what do you discover about the world that Pedro, Mario, and the crying man inhabit?

3. Is the story entirely realistic or partly fantastic? How do you determine which? How does the style in which the story is told contribute to its effectiveness?

4. Why do Pedro and Mario ultimately abandon their "finds" without even examining the contents of the briefcase?

Mario Vargas Llosa
(b. 1936)
Peru

In 1990, when Mario Vargas Llosa narrowly lost an election for the presidency of Peru, it looked for a time as if literature had made an unlikely marriage with politics. Readers of Vargas Llosa's fiction, however, had long been aware of the author's growing interest in politics, especially as a part of historical patterns. In The War of the End of the World (1981), he had imaginatively blended past, present, and future Latin American events into a utopian fantasy in which he speculated what might have happened to the entire continent if certain historical episodes had turned out differently.

The fantasy world of Vargas Llosa's earlier work, Aunt Julia and the Script Writer (1977), had already established for the author an international reputation. By some accounts, this novel is one of the major works of El Boom ("the explosion") in Latin American writing. The story—which initially appears to be realistic—recounts the life of a prolific writer of radio soap operas, driven insane by the demands of his mushrooming listening audience. Aunt Julia is also Vargas Llosa's own story of how he became a writer and, in fact, married one of his own aunts. By contrast to these later works, the story included here, "Sunday," is from an earlier stage of Vargas Llosa's writing, Los Jefes (1958), a volume of short stories focusing on adolescence. The story is, further, about machismo and, in this variation of what has been called a ubiquitous Latin American theme, male bonding.

SUNDAY

He held his breath for a moment, dug his nails into the palms of his hands, and said in a rush: "I'm in love with you." He saw her blush suddenly, as if someone had slapped her cheeks, which were of a glowing paleness and very soft. Terrified, he felt confusion mounting in him and turning his tongue to stone. He wanted to run away, to be done with it. In the silent winter morning had come this inner weakness that always disheartened him in decisive moments. A few minutes before, in the animated, smiling crowd that circulated through Central Park in Miraflores, Miguel was still repeating to himself: "Now. When I get to Pardo Avenue. I'll risk it. Oh, Rubén, if you only knew how much I hate you!" Still earlier, in church, while he sought out Flora with his eyes, he discovered her at the foot of a column and, elbowing his way through without excusing himself to the ladies he pushed, managed to get close to her and greet her in a low voice. He stubbornly told himself again, as he did that morning sprawled on his bed, watching for the appearance of dawn: "There's nothing else to do. I have to do it today. In the morning. You'll pay for it, Rubén." The night before, he had cried for the first time in many years when he learned of the cheap trap they were preparing for him. People kept going into the Park, and Pardo Avenue was deserted. They walked along the mall, under the fig trees with their tall dense tops. "I'll have to hurry," Miguel thought. "If I don't, I'm out of luck." He looked around out of the corner of his eye: there was nobody, he could try it. Slowly he put out his left hand to touch hers; the contact showed him what was happening. He begged for a miracle to happen, for that humiliation to cease. "What'll I say to her?" he thought. "What'll I tell her?" She had just withdrawn her hand, and he felt he was dismissed, ridiculous. All the radiant phrases that he had feverishly prepared the night before were dissolved like bubbles of foam.

"Flora," he stammered, "I've waited a long time for this moment. Ever since I met you, I've thought only of you. I'm in love for the first time, believe me. I've never known a girl like you."

Once more a compact white blot on his brain, emptiness. He could no longer increase the pressure: his skin yielded like rubber, and his nails were digging into the bone. Nevertheless, he went on talking, with some difficulty, at long intervals, overcoming his shameful stammering, trying to describe a total, unreflecting passion, until he discovered with relief that they were coming to the first oval on Pardo Avenue, and then he fell silent. Between the second and third fig trees beyond the oval stood Flora's house. They stopped, looked at each other. Flora was still excited, and her confusion had filled her eyes with a damp brilliance. Miguel told himself desolately that she had never seemed so beautiful to him: a blue ribbon held her hair, and he could see the beginning of her neck and her ears, two question marks, tiny and perfect.

"Look, Miguel," Flora said. Her voice was soft, full of music, assured. "I can't give you an answer now. But Mama doesn't want me to go with boys until I finish school."

"Every mama says the same thing, Flora," Miguel persisted. "How's she going to find out? We can see each other whenever you say, even if it's only on Sundays."

"I'll give you an answer now, but I must think about it first," Flora said, lowering her eyes. After a few moments she added, "Forgive me, but I have to go now. It's getting late."

Miguel felt a profound lassitude, something that spread all through his body and softened it.

"You're not angry with me, are you, Flora?" he asked humbly.

"Don't be silly," she replied vivaciously. "I'm not angry."

"I'll wait as long as you like," Miguel said. "But we'll go on seeing each other, won't we? We're going to the movies this afternoon, aren't we?"

"I can't this afternoon," she said gently. "Martha asked me over to her house."

A warm, violent looseness in his guts came flooding over him, and he felt wounded, ashamed, in the face of that answer which he had expected and which now seemed like a cruelty to him. What Melanés had murmured grimly in his ear on Saturday afternoon was true. Martha would leave them alone; that was her usual tactic. Afterward, Rubén would tell those Sharpies—his gang—how he and his sister had planned the circumstances, the time, and the place. Martha would have claimed the right to spy from behind the curtain as payment for her services. Anger suddenly made his hands perspire.

"Don't be like that, Flora. Let's go to the matinee as we planned. I won't mention this to you, I promise."

"I can't go, really," Flora replied. "I have to go to Martha's. She came to my house yesterday to invite me. But I'm going with her to Salazar Park later."

Not even in these last words did he see any hope. For some time afterward he contemplated the spot where her fragile little figure in blue had disappeared under the majestic arch of the fig trees on the avenue. He could compete with a simple adversary, not with Rubén. He remembered the names of the girls Martha invited one Sunday afternoon. He could no longer do anything; he was defeated. Then once more arose the image that saved him every time he suffered a frustration: from a distant background of clouds swollen by black smoke, he was marching at the head of a company of cadets from the Naval School toward a grandstand erected in the park. Important men in formal dress, top hats in hand, and ladies with sparkling jewels were applauding him. Massed on the walks, a crowd in which the faces of his friends and enemies stood out was observing him in astonishment, murmuring his name. Dressed in blue, a roomy cape billowing behind him, Miguel marched ahead, looking at the horizon. With his sword raised, its tip described a semicircle in the air. There in the center of the grandstand was Flora, smiling. On one corner he discovered Rubén, ragged and ashamed. He confined himself to throwing him a brief contemptuous glance. He went marching on, disappeared among the victors.

Like breath on a mirror when one rubs it, the image disappeared. He stood in the doorway of his house. He hated everybody; everybody hated him. He entered and went directly up to his room. He threw himself face-down on the bed. In the warm darkness between his eyes and eyelids the girl's face appeared—"I love you, Flora," he said in a loud voice—and then Rubén, with his insolent jaw and his hostile smile. They stood beside each other, came closer; Rubén's eyes twisted round to look mockingly at him, while his mouth moved toward Flora.

He leaped out of bed. The wardrobe mirror showed him a livid face and rings under his eyes. "He shan't see you," he decided. "He won't do that to me. I won't let him pull that dirty trick on me."

Pardo Avenue was still empty. Quickening his pace, without stopping, he walked toward the crossing at Grau Avenue; there he hesitated. He felt cold: he had forgotten his jacket in his room, and his one shirt was not enough to protect him from the wind that came in from the sea and was caught in the thick branches of the fig trees in a soft rustling. His dreaded image of Flora and Rubén together gave him strength, and he went on walking. From the door of the neighborhood bar next to the Montecarlo theater he saw them at their usual table, in possession of the nook formed by the back and left-hand walls. Francisco, Melanés, Tobías, and the Scholar discovered him and, after a moment's surprise, turned toward Rubén, their faces malicious, excited. He recovered his self-possession immediately. He certainly knew how to behave in front of men.

"Hello," he said to them, approaching. "What's new?"

"Sit down." The Scholar held out a chair for him. "What miracle's brought you here?"

"You haven't been here for ages," Francisco remarked.

"I wanted to see you," Miguel said cordially. "I already knew you were here. What's so surprising about that? Or aren't I a Sharpie any more?"

He sat down between Melanés and Tobías. Rubén sat across from him.

"Cuncho!" called the Scholar. "Bring another glass. And it had better be clean."

Cuncho brought the glass, and the Scholar filled it with beer. Miguel said, "To the Sharpies!" and drank.

"You almost drank the glass too," Francisco observed. "How violent you are!"

"I bet you went to one-o'clock mass," said Melanés, one eyelid creased in satis-faction, as always when he was thinking up some mischief. "Or did you?"

"I did," Miguel said imperturbably. "But only to see a young lady, that's all."

He looked at Rubén with challenging eyes, but the latter did not take the hint. He was drumming with his fingers on the table, the tip of his tongue between his teeth, whistling "The Popof Girl" by Pérez Prado.

"Well!" Melanés applauded. "Well, Don Juan. Tell us, which girl?"

"That's a secret."

"There aren't any secrets among Sharpies," Tobías reminded him. "Have you for-gotten already? Come on, who was she?"

"What do you care?" Miguel asked.

"A good deal," Tobías said. "I have to know who you go with so as to know who you are."

"In the meantime, drink up," Melanés told Miguel. "One to zero."

"Why should I guess who she is?" Francisco asked. "Why not you?"

"I already know," Tobías said.

"Me too," said Melanés. He turned to Rubén with innocent eyes and voice. "And you, brother-in-law, can you guess who she is?"

"No," Rubén answered coldly. "Nor do I care."

"I have a little fire in my stomach," the Scholar remarked. "Isn't anyone going to order a beer?"

Melanés passed a pathetic finger across his throat.

"I have no money, darling," he said, in English.

"I'll buy a bottle," Tobías announced with a solemn gesture. "Let's see who fol-lows me. We have to put out this kid's fire."

"Cuncho, take down half a dozen *Cristales*," Miguel ordered.

There were shouts of joy, exclamations.

"You're a real Sharpie," Francisco agreed.

"A dirty, lousy one," added Melanés. "Yes, sir, a real dude-type, Sharpie."

Cuncho brought the beers. They drank. They listened to Melanés tell sexy stories—crude, extravagant, exciting—and a loud argument about football started between Tobías and Francisco. The Scholar recounted an anecdote. He was coming from Lima to Miraflores on a bus. The other passengers got off at Arequipa Avenue. "At the top of Javier Prado, that big blubber of a Tomasso got on, that six-foot al-bino who's still in grade school, lives around the Ravine—you know him now? Pre-tending great interest in the automobile, he began asking the driver questions, leaning over the front seat while he quietly scraped the upholstery on the back with a knife.

"He did it because I was there," the Scholar went on. "He wanted to show off."

"He's mentally deficient," Francisco remarked. "You do those things when you're ten years old. At his age it's not funny."

"What happened afterward is funny." The Scholar laughed. "'Look, driver, don't you see this big blubber's ruining your car?'"

"'What?'" the driver exclaimed, braking suddenly. His ears red, his eyes fright-ened, Tomasso was struggling with the door.

"With his knife," added the Scholar. "Imagine how fast he left the seat.

"The fat kid managed to get out at last. He began to run along Arequipa Avenue. The driver ran after him shouting, 'Grab that wretch!'"

"Did he catch him?" Melanés asked.

"I don't know. I disappeared. I stole the ignition key for a keepsake. I've got it here."

He took a little silver-plated key from his pocket and tossed it on the table. The bottles were empty. Rubén looked at his watch and got to his feet.

"I'm going," he said. "I'll be seeing you."

"Don't go," Miguel said. "I'm rich today. I'm inviting you all to lunch."

A whirlwind of slaps fell on him; the Sharpies were thanking him confusedly, flattering him.

"I can't," Rubén said. "I have to go."

"Go and don't come back, my fine friend," Tobías remarked. "And greet Martha for me."

"We'll think about you a lot, brother-in-law," Melanés said.

"No!" Miguel exclaimed. "I'm inviting everybody or nobody. If Rubén leaves, that's that."

"You heard him, Sharpie Rubén," Francisco said. "You'll have to stay."

"You have to stay," said Melanés. "You have no choice."

"I'm leaving," Rubén said.

"It just so happens you're drunk," Miguel remarked. "You're leaving because you're afraid of making a fool of yourself in front of us, that's what's the matter."

"How many times have I carried *you* home half-dead?" Rubén demanded. "How many times have I helped you climb up the grating so your father wouldn't catch you? I can hold ten times more'n you can."

"You used to be able to," Miguel said. "Now it's harder to. You want to find out?"

"Gladly," Rubén replied. "Shall we meet tonight, right here?"

"No. Now." Miguel turned to the others, extending his arms. "I'm making a challenge, Sharpies."

Happily he proved that the ancient formula had kept its power intact. In the midst of the noisy enthusiasm he had provoked, he saw Rubén sit down, pale.

"Cuncho!" Tobías shouted. "The menu. And two large beers. A Sharpie has just given a challenge."

They ordered steaks and a dozen beers. Tobías put out three bottles for each competitor and the rest for the others. They ate, scarcely speaking. Miguel drank after each mouthful and tried to show some animation, but the fear of not sufficiently holding his own grew as the beer deposited its acid taste in his mouth. When they finished the six bottles, it was some time before Cuncho took away their plates.

"You order," Miguel told Rubén.

"Three more apiece."

After the first glass of the new round, Miguel felt his ears ringing; his head was a slow roulette wheel; everything was going round.

"I have to pee," he said. "I'm going to the bathroom."

The Sharpies laughed.

"Are you giving up?" Rubén asked.

"I'm going to pee," Miguel shouted. "If you want, have 'em bring more."

In the bathroom he vomited. Then he carefully washed his face, trying to erase every tell-tale sign. His watch showed four-thirty. In spite of his dark discomfort he felt happy. Rubén could do nothing now. He went back to the others.

"Your health," said Rubén, raising his glass.

He's furious, Miguel thought. But I've annoyed him now.

"You smell like a corpse," Melanés observed. "Somebody's died around here."

"I just got here," Miguel asserted, trying to conquer his nausea and dizziness.

"Your health!" Rubén repeated.

When they had finished the last beer, his stomach felt like lead, and the voices of the others reached his ears as a confused mixture of sounds. A hand suddenly appeared under his eyes; it was white, with long fingers; it took him by the chin, made him raise his head. Ruben's face had grown larger. He looked funny, so disheveled and angry.

"D'you give up, snotty?"

Miguel got up suddenly and pushed Rubén aside, but before the fight could develop, the Scholar intervened.

"Sharpies don't fight, ever," he said, forcing them to sit down. "They're both drunk. It's all over. Let's vote."

Melanés, Francisco, and Tobías unwillingly agreed to concede that it was a tie.

"I'd already won," Rubén said. "This fella can't even talk. Look at him."

Miguel's eyes were actually glassy, his mouth was open, and a trickle of saliva dripped from his tongue.

"Shut up," the Scholar ordered. "You're no champion, let's say, at drinking beer."

"You're no beer-drinking champion," Melanés said for emphasis. "You're only a swimming champion, the holy terror of the pools."

"You'd better not say anything," Rubén retorted. "Don't you see envy's gnawing at you?"

"Long live the Esther Williams of Miraflores!" said Melanés.

"A tremendous old fella, and he doesn't even know how to swim," Rubén said. "Don't you want me to give you a few lessons?"

"We know how already, you big wonder," said the Scholar. "You won a swimming championship. All the girls're dying for you. You're a little old champion."

"This one here's no champion of anything," Miguel remarked with difficulty. "He's pure affectation."

"You're dying," Rubén retorted. "Shall I take you home, little girl?"

"I'm not drunk," Miguel assured him. "You're pure affectation."

"You're all cut up because I'm going to fall for Flora," Rubén said. "You're dying of jealousy. You think I don't catch on to these things?"

"Pure affectation," Miguel said. "You won because your father's president of the Federation. Everybody knows he cheated, he disqualified Rabbit Villarán, and you only won because of that."

"At least I can swim better'n you," Rubén said. "You don't even know how to race the waves."

"You don't swim any better 'n anybody else," Miguel retorted. "Anybody can leave *you* behind."

"Anybody," Melanés put in. "Even Miguel, who's an old mother."

"Permit me to laugh."

"We'll permit you," said Tobías. "That's all we needed."

"You're better 'n me because it's winter," Rubén went on. "If it weren't, I'd challenge you to go to the beach, to see if you're so exceptional in the water."

"You won the championship because of your father," Miguel said. "You're pure affectation. When you want t' swim with me, just le'me know, informally. At the beach, at the Terraces, wherever y' like."

"At the beach," Rubén said. "Right now."

"You're pure affectation," said Miguel.

Rubén's face suddenly lighted up, and his eyes, in addition to being filled with rancor, turned arrogant.

"I'll bet you to see who reaches the surf first," he said.

"Pure affectation," Miguel repeated.

"If you win," Rubén said, "I promise you I won't go after Flora. And if I win, you can take your music somewhere else."

"What did you think?" stammered Miguel. "Damn it, what'd you think?"

"Sharpies," Rubén said, extending his arms, "I'm making a challenge."

"Miguel's in no shape now," said the Scholar. "Why not just draw straws for Flora?"

"And why're you butting in?" Miguel asked. "I accept. Le's go t' the beach."

"You're crazy" Francisco remarked. "I'm not going down to the beach in this cold. Make some other bet."

"He's accepted," said Rubén. "Let's go."

"When a Sharpie makes a challenge, everybody puts his tongue in his pocket," Melanés remarked. "Let's go to the beach. And if they don't dare go in the water, we'll throw them in ourselves."

"They're both drunk," the Scholar persisted. "The challenge isn't valid."

"Shut up, Scholar," Miguel bellowed. "I'm a big boy now, I don't need you t' take care of me."

"Well," said the Scholar, shrugging his shoulders, "just suit yourself"

They went out. Outside a quiet gray atmosphere awaited them. Miguel breathed deeply; he felt better. Francisco, Melanés, and Rubén walked ahead, Miguel and the Scholar behind. On Grau Avenue there were pedestrians, the majority of them servant girls wearing bright dresses, on their day off. Ashen-gray men with thick straight hair were walking about, looking covetously at them; the girls laughed, showing their gold teeth. The Sharpies paid no attention to them. They went on with long strides, and excitement was building in them little by little.

"You feel better now?" the Scholar asked.

"Yes," Miguel answered. "The air's done me good."

At the corner of Pardo Avenue they turned. They marched spread out like a squad, all in line, under the fig trees on the mall, over paving stones upraised here and there by the enormous tree roots that occasionally burst through the surface like hooks. Going down along Diagonal Avenue, they passed two girls. Rubén bowed ceremoniously.

"Hello, Rubén," they chanted in duet.

Tobías mocked them in a high-pitched voice.

"Hello, Prince Rubén."

Diagonal Avenue ends in a little ravine which forks off: on one side the Malecón winds along, paved and shining; on the other, there is a slope that follows the hill and leads to the sea. They call it "the slope to the baths"; its paving is similar and shines from the passage of automobile tires and the bathers' feet of many summers past.

"Let's warm up, champions," Melanés shouted, starting to run. The others imitated him.

They ran against the wind and the thin mist that rose from the beach, gripped in an emotional whirlwind. The air penetrated their lungs through their ears, mouths, and noses, and a sensation of relief and sobriety spread through their bodies as the slope steepened, and in a moment their feet were now obeying only a mysterious force that came from the deepest part of the earth. Their arms like propellers, a breath of salt on their tongues, the Sharpies ran down the incline at top speed, as far as the circular platform suspended above the bathhouse. The sea vanished some fifty yards from the bank in a thick cloud that seemed about to dash against the cliffs, the tall dark rocks fronting all along the bay.

"Let's go back," Francisco said. "I'm cold."

At the edge of the platform there is a fence discolored here and there by moss. An opening indicates the beginning of the nearly vertical lower steps leading down to the beach. From there, at their feet, the Sharpies contemplated a narrow ribbon of clear water and the unaccustomed surface of foamy waves.

"I'm leaving if this guy'll give up," Rubén said.

"Who's talking about giving up?" retorted Miguel. "What'd you think?"

Rubén went down the steps three at a time, unbuttoning his shirt.

"Rubén!" shouted the Scholar. "Are you crazy? Come back!"

But Miguel and the others went down too, and the Scholar followed them.

In summer, from the veranda of the long narrow building nestled against the hill where the bathers' rooms are located, as far as the curved edge of the sea, there was a slope with gray stones where people would bask in the sun. The little beach swarmed with animation from morning till night. Now water filled the slope, and there were no bright-colored shadows, no elastic girls with sunburned bodies. No children's melo-dramatic cries resounded when a wave managed to splash them before it ebbed, drag-ging noisy stones and pebbles. They could not even see the edge of the beach, for the tide came in as far as the space bounded by the shaded columns that supported the building and, as the undertow went out, they could scarcely see the wooden steps and concrete supports that were ornamented with barnacles and algae.

"You can't see the breakers," Rubén said. "How'll we do it?"

They stood in the gallery on the left, in the women's section. Their faces were serious.

"Wait till tomorrow," the Scholar urged. "By noon it'll be clear. That way we'll be able to check on you."

"Since we've gone this far, let 'em do it now," said Melanés. "They can check on each other."

"Sounds all right to me," Rubén said. "How 'bout you?"

"Me too," Miguel agreed.

When they had undressed, Tobías joked about the blue veins that ran up Miguel's smooth belly. They went down the stairs. The wooden steps, continually lapped by the water for some months, were slippery and very smooth. Grasping the iron handrail in order not to fall, Miguel felt a tremor rising from the soles of his feet to his head. He was thinking that the fog and cold favored him in one way; his success now depended not on his skill, but chiefly on his resistance, and Rubén's skin was also purple, marked with millions of goose-pimples. One step below, Rubén's well-proportioned body was bent: he was waiting tensely for the end of the undertow and the arrival of the next wave, which came quietly, gracefully, thrusting forward its bor-der of foam. When the wave crest was a couple of yards from the stairway, Rubén dived in, his arms lance-stiff, his hair disheveled by the force of his dive. His body cleaved the air cleanly and dropped in without bending. Without lowering his head or flexing his legs, he rebounded in the foam, almost sank, and immediately slipped into it, taking advantage of the tide. His arms appeared and disappeared in a fran-tic bubbling, and his feet began tracing a fast, cautious wake. Miguel in turn went down another stairway and waited for the next wave. He knew that the bottom was shallow there, that he must dive in like a board, hard and rigid, without moving a muscle, or he would strike against the rocks. He closed his eyes and dove, and he did not hit bottom, but his body was flailed from forehead to knees, and a very sharp stinging sensation arose while he struggled with all his strength to recover the warmth in his limbs that the water had suddenly taken out of them. He was on that unfamiliar section of the sea at Miraflores near the bank, where eddies and opposing currents are encountered, and last summer was so long ago that Miguel had forgotten how to get across them easily. He did not remember that he must relax his body and let go, let himself be carried along drifting submissively, swing his arms only when a wave rises and he is on the crest, on that liquid sheet that escorts the foam and floats on the currents. He did not remember that it is important to bear patiently and with a certain malice that first contact with a sea, exasperated by the bank, that pulls at his limbs and blows water in his mouth and eyes; to offer no resistance, to be a cork, to limit himself to gulping air each time a wave rolls in, to submerge himself—barely, if it breaks far off and comes in gently, or to the very bottom if it breaks nearby—to grasp some stone and wait alertly for the subdued thunder of its passage in order to emerge in just one stroke and continue advancing, furtively, with his hands, until he encounters a new obstacle and then to relax, not fighting against the eddies, to revolve freely in their slow, slow spiral and escape suddenly with a single stroke at the opportune moment. Then a calm surface unexpectedly appears, stirred by harmless combers; the water is clear, smooth, and in some places hidden stones are visible below its surface.

After crossing the choppy area Miguel stopped, exhausted, and gulped air. He saw Rubén nearby, looking at him. His hair fell in bangs over his face. His teeth were clenched.

"Shall we?"

"Let's go."

After swimming for a few minutes Miguel felt the cold that had momentarily vanished coming over him again, and he speeded up his strokes because it was in his legs, especially in his calves, that the water had a greater effect, first making them insensitive, then stiffening them. He was swimming with his face in the water, and each time his right arm rose out of it, he turned his head to expel air and breathe in another supply, at which he submerged his face and chin once more, just barely, so as not to hinder his own progress but, on the contrary, to split the water like a prow and make his forward movement easier. With each stroke he glanced at Rubén swimming smoothly, effortlessly on the surface, not splashing now, with the delicacy and ease of a seagull gliding. Miguel tried to forget Rubén and the sea and the breakers, which must still be far off, for the water was clear and calm, and they were swimming only through newly risen surf. He wanted to remember nothing but Flora's face and the down on her arms that sparkled on sunny days like a little forest of golden threads. But he could not prevent another image from succeeding to that of the girl— the image of a mountain of raging water, not necessarily these breakers (to which he had come once two summers ago and whose waves were intensified with greenish-black foam, because in that spot, more or less, the stones ended and the mud began that the waves brought up to the surface and deposited among nests of seaweed and stagnant water, staining the sea), but rather in a real ocean stirred by inner cataclysms in which were thrown up unusual waves that could have swamped an entire ship and upset it with astonishing rapidity, hurling passengers, lifeboats, masts, sails, sailors, porthole covers, and flags into the air.

He stopped swimming; his body sank until it was vertical; he raised his head and saw Rubén, who was getting farther away. He thought of calling to him on some pretext, of saying to him, "Why don't we rest a minute?" But he did not. All the cold in his body seemed to be concentrated in his calves; his muscles felt cramped, his skin taut; his heart was pounding. He thrust feverishly with his feet. He was in the center of a circle of dark water, walled in by the mist. He tried to make out the beach, or at least the shadow of the cliffs, but that dark mist dissolving at his passage was not transparent. He saw only a narrow surface, blackish-green, and a layer of clouds low over the water. Then he felt afraid. The recollection of the beer he had drunk assailed him, and he thought, "I expect it's sapped my strength." At once his arms and legs seemed to disappear. He decided to go back, but after a few strokes in the direction of the beach, he turned and swam as quickly as he could. "I won't go in to the bank alone," he told himself. "It's better to stay close to Rubén. If I get too tired, I'll tell him, 'You beat me, but let's go back.'" Now he was swimming without any style, his head raised, beating the water with stiff arms, his eyes fastened on the imperturbable body ahead of him.

His agitation and the effort took the numbness out of his legs; his body regained a little warmth; the distance that separated him from Rubén had decreased, and that calmed him. Shortly afterward he caught up with him, stretched out his arm and caught one of his feet. The other stopped at once. Rubén's eyes were very red, and his mouth hung open.

"I think we've got off course," Miguel said. "It seems to me we're swimming parallel to the beach."

His teeth were chattering, but his voice was steady. Rubén looked in all directions. Miguel watched him tensely.

"I don't see the beach now," Rubén said.

"I haven't seen it for a long time," Miguel said. "There's a lot of mist."

"We're not off course," Rubén went on. "Look. You can see the foam now."

As a matter of fact, some combers were coming toward them edged with a border of foam that dissolved and suddenly reappeared. They looked at each other in silence.

"We're close to the breakers now, then," Miguel said at last.

"Yes. We swam fast."

"I've never seen so much mist."

"Aren't you pretty tired?" Rubén asked.

"Me? You're crazy. Let's go on."

Immediately he regretted his words, but it was already too late. Rubén had said, "Okay, let's go on."

He managed to count twenty strokes before telling himself that he could not go on. He was making almost no headway; his right leg was half-paralyzed by the cold; his arms felt awkward and heavy. Panting, he shouted, "Rubén!" The latter went on swimming. "Rubén, *Rubén!*" He turned and began swimming—splashing desperately, rather—toward the beach, and suddenly he was praying to God to save him. He would be good in the future, would obey his parents, would not miss mass on Sunday. Then he remembered having confessed to the Sharpies, "I go to church only to see a young lady," and he felt a knife-sharp conviction: God was going to punish him, to drown him in those turbid waters that he was frantically beating, waters below which an awful death, and afterward hell perhaps, were waiting for him. Then in his anxiety there arose, like an echo, a certain phrase Father Alberto once pronounced in religion class about the divine goodness that knows no limits, and while he flailed at the sea with his arms—his legs dangled like crossed sounding leads—moving his lips, he begged God to be good to him who was so young, and he swore he would go to the seminary if he were saved. But a moment later he corrected himself, shocked, and promised that instead of becoming a priest he would make sacrifices and do other penances, would give to charity, and there he perceived that vacillation and haggling at that critical moment might be fatal. Then he was aware of Rubén's crazed shouts close at hand and, turning his head, saw him some ten yards off, his face half-sunk in the water, waving one arm, begging, "Miguel, brother, come here, I'm drowning, don't go away!"

He stopped perplexed, motionless, and it was suddenly as if Rubén's despair were kindling his own. He felt himself recovering his courage; the rigidity in his legs was diminishing.

"I've got a cramp in my stomach!" Rubén shrieked. "I can't go on, Miguel. Save me! For the sake of what you love most, don't leave me, brother!"

He floated toward Rubén, and he was about to reach out to him when he remembered that drowning persons often manage to grab hold of their saviors like pincers and pull them under, and he kept clear, but the screams frightened him, and he had a presentiment that if Rubén drowned, he would not reach the beach either, so he turned back. A couple of yards from Rubén, who looked like something white and shrunken that sank and surfaced again, he cried, "Don't move, Rubén! I'm going to tow you, but don't try to hold onto me. If you hold onto me, we'll drown, Rubén. You're going to keep quiet, brother. I'll tow you by your head. Don't you touch me!"

He stopped at a prudent distance, reached out his arm until he could grasp Rubén's hair. He began to swim with his free arm, making every effort to help himself with his legs. His progress was slow and arduous; it required all his senses; he scarcely heard Rubén complaining monotonously, suddenly uttering terrible cries, "I'm going to die, save me, Miguel!" or being shaken by retching. He was exhausted when he stopped. He supported Rubén with one hand; with the other he traced circles on the surface. He breathed deeply through his mouth. Rubén's face was contorted with pain, his lips pursed in an unusual grimace.

"It's just a little farther, brother," Miguel murmured. "Keep trying. Answer me, Rubén. Yell! Don't be like that!"

He slapped his face sharply, and Rubén opened his eyes; he shook his head feebly.

"Yell, brother," Miguel repeated. "Try to stretch out. I'm going to massage your stomach. It's just a little farther. Don't let yourself give up."

His hand groped under water, found a hard ball beginning at Rubén's navel and occupying a large part of his belly. He rubbed it many times, slowly at first, then harshly, and Rubén cried out, "I don't want to die, Miguel. Save me!"

He began to swim once more, dragging Rubén this time by his chin. Each time a wave overtook them, Rubén choked, and Miguel shouted to him to spit. He went on swimming, not stopping for a moment, closing his eyes at times, encouraged because a sort of confidence, something warm and proud and stimulating that was protecting him against cold and fatigue had sprung up in his heart. A stone scraped one of his feet, but he merely cried out and went on faster. A moment later he stopped and put his arms around Rubén. Holding him pressed against himself, feeling his head supported on one shoulder, he rested for a long time. Then he helped Rubén to turn onto his back and, supporting him on his forearm, forced him to stretch out his legs; he massaged his belly until the hardness began to yield. Rubén was not screaming now; he was making a great effort to stretch out completely, and he rubbed himself with his hands too.

"Feel better?"

"Yes, brother, I'm all right. Let's get out of here."

An inexpressible joy filled them as they came in over the stones, bending forward to face the undertow, insensitive to the spiny sea urchins. In a little while they saw the edge of the cliffs, the bathhouse, and finally, now close to the bank, the Sharpies standing in the women's gallery, watching them.

"Look," Rubén said.

"What?"

"Don't tell them anything. Please don't tell 'em I screamed. We've always been good friends, Miguel. Don't do that to me."

"Do you think I'd be such a stinker?" Miguel said. "I won't say anything, don't worry."

They emerged shivering. They sat on the steps surrounded by excited Sharpies.

"We were about to send condolences to your families," Tobías remarked.

"You were in for more than an hour," the Scholar said. "Tell us, how was it?"

Speaking calmly, while he dried his body with his undershirt, Rubén explained:

"It wasn't anything. We went out to the breakers and back. So, we're Sharpies. Miguel beat me, by just a stroke. Of course, if it'd been in a pool, he'd have made a fool of himself."

Congratulatory slaps rained on the back of Miguel, who had dressed without drying off.

"You're getting to be quite a man," Melanés told him.

Miguel did not answer. Smiling, he was thinking he would go to Salazar Park that very night. All of Miraflores would already know from Melanés' account that he had won that heroic test, and Flora would be waiting for him, her eyes shining. A golden future was opening out in front of him.

[1958]

Translated by

Mary E. Ellsworth

Questions

1. Does the concept of masculinity give Vargas Llosa's story a universal quality? If so, in what way does it expose gender stereotypes? With a few variations of names and places, could the story take place in the United States? Or is the assertion of masculinity distinctly Latin?

2. Why is the story called "Sunday"?

3. Is it possible to argue that both Miguel and Rubén have "won" by the end of the story?

Yvonne Vera

(b. 1964)

Zimbabwe

Yvonne Vera was born in Bulawayo, Rhodesia, in 1964. Her mother was a schoolteacher and the person most responsible for her early reading. More importantly, Vera began writing when she was still a child. She remembers leaving notes and poems she had written for her mother when her mother was ill. In school, other students identified her as "the writer." After graduation from secondary school, she had the benefit of a vacation in Europe, where the galleries in Florence and Venice particularly engaged her. Subsequent trips to the United States and Canada culminated in her matriculation at York University in Toronto, where she initially studied fine arts with an emphasis on film. She stayed at York long enough to earn a Ph.D. in literature.

Her first book, a collection of short stories called Why Don't You Carve Other Animals (1992), was published while Vera was still in Canada. That collection was followed by her first novel, Nehanda, in 1993. Her third book, Without a Name (1994), was the first one she wrote in Zimbabwe, while at home on a holiday. Set against the backdrop of her country's civil war (itself a controversial topic), Without a Name was the first of Vera's books to take a darker turn, shattering convention by focusing on the rape of a young woman who leaves the countryside for the city. Two years later, Vera's next novel, Under the Tongue (1964), won the Commonwealth Writers' Prize (African area). Neely Tucker has described that novel's focus as "incestuous rape, spousal murder, the death of a young child; it's not a happy place." As in Vera's previous work, the country's recent struggle for independence plays a significant part in the shattered psyches of the main characters. Besides winning her country's major literary award—The Zimbabwe Book Publishers' Association Literary Award—the following year, Under the Tongue was awarded the Swedish Voice of Africa Literary Award.

Butterfly Burning (1998)—in many ways Vera's most accomplished novel—also tackles a daring topic, better left unmentioned (or "under the tongue," to use one of the author's own metaphors) in Zimbabwean society: abortion. As is true of the author's earlier works, in this one brutality and pain are inflicted on women as well as men. The setting is not contemporary but a ghetto in Bulawayo in the 1940s, during the colonial era when Africans were often treated as if they were in a penal colony. With this novel and the two earlier ones—which form a kind of unconventional trilogy—Vera also emerged as a strong feminist writer, at clear odds with the masculine hegemony of her country. American readers have noted affinities between her novels and Toni Morrison's.

Yvonne Vera is currently the Director of the National Gallery in Bulawayo, the city of her birth:

> I was born and raised in Bulawayo. It is the second city, so to speak, in Zimbabwe. Each of the inhabitants here feels a certain marginal identity, and therefore an irrational and fierce love for being here. Bulawayo people have always shaped their identities around the notion of being peripheral, of being drought-stricken for example, and at different times, of political secondariness. The landscape is very distinct, flat for distances, the

thorn bushes scattered everywhere in their sparse vegetation, blooming when they can. And anthills. The sky so low you could lick it. Very blue in winter. . . . I have never wanted to be a writer in exile—I hope never to have to make a decision to leave Zimbabwe, for whatever reason. I hope to continue in this small town, with its gentle and unhurried pace.

In Africa There Is a Type of Spider

In Africa there is a type of spider which turns to air, its life a mere gasp. It vanishes, from the inside out, its legs a fossil, an outline in the future. In Africa there is a type of spider which gathers all its kin before an earthquake, sending messages through the air. Together the family gathers into a cubicle of time, a bowl in a peeling rock, a basin where the earth has been eaten by rain; before an earthquake, before the advance of an enemy, and war. Spider after spider piles into a mound, into a self-inflicted ruin, seeking another kind of escape. Then the top of this spider-mound is sealed with spit, thick and embroidered like lace, bright with sun rays, and rainbows arching like memories. A stillness gathers, before an earthquake, before war. There is a stillness such as has not been witnessed before, and a new climate in that trapped air. Turning and turning, again and again till something is free like a kindness. A spider falls like a pendulum stilled. This is not hibernation for a death: the bodies take flight, free as time. The body vanishes, from inside out. The inside pouring like powdered dust, the legs a fossil. This is the end of creation, the beginning of war. Often, there is a cataclysmic innocence which knows nothing but death.

. . . spider legs, he insisted, after the war had ended. I heard of spider rituals from my uncle Sibaso in 1980, after the armed struggle which freed us from British rule. It was to me an astounding truth to hear, no, to witness, how my uncle ate spider legs throughout the war. He said this was because he knew where spiders went off to die. Was this not a great secret to know? he asked me. In the bush, survival is a skill hewn from the harmonies of nature, nature is an elaboration of the disharmonies of war.

My uncle Sibaso returned to Bulawayo with elaborate claims about the delicacy of our humanity—I only listened to him. He said we were a tenuous species, a continent which had succumbed to a violent wind. I listened to him with a shocked understanding. He said he had harvested handfuls of spider-legs during the war. Who was I to contradict him—a mere girl who had never left the confines of Luveve township where I was born. He had an imagination that claimed supremacy over war, somehow. I knew I could harvest wisdom straight from his mouth.

He slept on the cracked floor of our verandah, polished a brilliant red every morning, with the stars falling straight into his mouth as he snored. How had he survived the war with such a glutinous snore? Yet he had lived to tell many illicit versions of the war even when it seemed unlikely he would be believed. The war had provided him a burden of memory. His future seemed always leaning toward an impeccable horizon. I adored his indifferent embrace of the stars. I envied his type of truth which sounded exactly like a well constructed lie.

Our country needed this kind of hero who had a balm for his own wounds, carried between lip and tongue, between thumb and forefinger, between the earth and the soles of his feet. He was in flight toward an immaculate truth and I followed him closely. Together we sat on garbage cans and watched the cars from Lobels, from Downings, from Haefelis. All of these were bakeries located in the city centre. We watched the papaws fall off the trees at the beginning of the rainy season, and caterpillars curl into rings. A man who worked at Downings told us that they mixed the dough with gumboots, the same way we pounded our blankets when we washed them.

One day a van with a loudspeaker drove past and announced a new product for cleaning our teeth. My uncle Sibaso laughed till he fell asleep. I woke him to tell him that free toothpaste was being distributed door to door, by a lady in a wig. He said it was probably poisoned and we would die a slow death. It would take us about ten years to die. Our teeth would be whiter and firmer but our souls would be dead. After all, our bodies had already died with the war. My Uncle Sibaso kept the toothpaste in a secret place. The future remained ominous.

When I close my eyes to sleep, I have the sensation of drowning. I see a multitude of spider legs stretch into the void which leaps above me; that is the other strange fact about spiders, their ability to walk on water, while humans drown.

On the day of the cease-fire, my uncle Sibaso left his unit and walked till he stood next to a railway station at Cement Siding. He rode from Cement Siding to Bulawayo on the goods train while resting on a single coach full of warm glittering coal. He removed his shirt and blended into the coals. He could feel the breeze and the jutting edges of the coals on his back, the humid warmth. He watched the smoke form patterns above his head. He jumped off at Mpopoma Station before the train entered the Main Station in Bulawayo. Before the wheels ground to a stop, he had fallen into the night; his dark skin protecting him against police whistles, sliding with curiosity and abandon into the music of bicycle pumps at Nandi Bazaar with its wide veranda and long wooden benches, along Bambazonke Road, where the men formed semi-circles and raised greased stems of Hercules bicycle pumps to their lips. Thin rubber stems inside the pumps, vacuum filled, rending high notes. I found him in that quaint music wrought from the stems of bicycle pumps. A type of music which pleaded for you to return to the hurt, to flee from joy. That one, Sibaso, he had a story to tell.

I have seen a spider dancing with a wasp, he says. This type of spider hangs from asbestos ceilings in every township home. I am told that most politicians in Africa learnt their tricks from watching the motions of such a spider. Every spider is a politician, every politician envies a spider. Dancing with a wasp.

Sibaso has beautiful fingers. I wonder how he fought the war with fingers which taper into such a firm and determined gentleness, his skin dark like honey, and always, a certain kind of joy clogging his eyes.

When he arrived from the bush, first he was employed by the Zimbabwe Republican Police. It is better known as ZRP. It used to be called the British South African Police. BSAP. That was during the struggle. Sibaso preferred the brown thick uniform of ZRP to the garments of war which the army wears. He wanted no reminders of camouflage though he had been offered a desk and a swivel chair and had toured the officer's mess at Mbizo Barracks with its ornate but torn leather chairs, the alcohol wafting past every dream, clear liquor suspended in tall cylinders which said Rhodesia.

In an army magazine, he saw a photo of himself in the bush holding an AK rifle, and that concluded that. The caption called him an enemy of the people, a terrorist. He wondered how the picture had been taken without him noticing. If someone had pointed a camera at him, they could equally have pointed a gun. He became immediately suspicious about his survival. He tore off the page and brought it home. He pasted it on his bed.

Sibaso became a policeman. High boots. Large brown belt on which he sat and carefully spread Nugget shoe polish on every weekend, let it dry, then polished till it gleamed. The same with his boots. He placed his hat on a hook very high off the ground so that no one could touch it. He liked being back in Luveve and being a policeman. He was the wrong height for a Policeman, but he was permitted to join because he had fought in the bush and deserved to be a policeman more than anyone else. Sibaso made a short and handsome policeman.

However, he was immensely disappointed that the country could no longer provide bicycles to well trained policemen, even those who had an exemplary army record, and instead made them walk, undistinguished, to a crime scene. He would have liked to drive a jeep, for example, in which he had been thrown into as a youth. He wanted evidence of reversal. There were only a few jeeps left. Instead, my uncle Sibaso had to stand on the side of the road and wave down a lift from potential criminals. Being a policeman offered too many moments of humiliation and powerlessness. He started to detest it a little, and to doubt the value of his return.

My uncle Sibaso says in Africa there is a type of spider which changes colour when mating. It devours its own partner and rolls her into a fine paste. With this it courts its next partner. It offers her this round, perfectly prepared sacrifice in exchange for a brief but sweet liaison. This type of spider hangs between trees and can only be viewed in the light of a full moon. Such a spider possesses a valuable secret, the knowledge that love cannot be founded on mercy, but that mercy can be founded on love. It knows the true agony of ecstasy, that violence is part of the play of opposites, and that during war, there are two kinds of lovers, the one located in the past, and dead, the one in the future, living and more desirable. The past a repast, the future a talisman. This kind of truth also belongs to the fantasy of a continent in disarray.

Each evening when my uncle Sibaso was walking home he held a folded newspaper tightly in his armpit. He read about a policeman who had taken a bribe. My Uncle decided to resign immediately from the ZRP, formerly known as BSAP. After he left, he read about another policeman who stole a watch from the distended arm of a dead politician who had been involved in a horrible accident along the Bulawayo-Victoria Falls road. He had hit a donkey and his car swerved. Then he had hit a large truck from a tobacco company and that had crushed him to pieces. His gold watch lay gleaming on the side of the road where his arm lay. Sibaso felt glad to have followed his impulse to resign when he did. At least no one would ask him for an explanation concerning this widely reported police crime. Then another policeman was discovered wearing women's underwear after fainting during the nineteenth independence day celebrations, and Sibaso vowed that he would not read the newspapers again. He is currently considering joining the army, but does not want to be sent to the Democratic Republic of Congo where Zimbabwe is involved in the civilian war.

He is waiting.

Time is as necessary for remembering as for forgetting. Even the smallest embrace of pain needs a time larger than a pause, the greatest pause requires an eternity, the greatest hurt a lifetime. A lifetime is longer than eternity: an eternity can exist without human presence.

Since leaving ZRP, my uncle has been gathering a certain kind of spider and pinning it down between the pages of his King James Bible. This is a tall spider with long, long legs that are terrifyingly thin, ready-to-disappear type of legs. This spider is almost transparent, its legs wisps of a dancing dark light, like pencil strokes. The legs keep it high off the ground, and there is nothing to it really, just a pale body. An apparition. I saw it walk across our oblong mirror one morning. Then it stopped moving. The mirror looked cracked. I could see my own broken face behind it. Sibaso calls this a post-war spider, a post-dream-generation spider, a hunger-starvation spider— a political manifestation of death. It is fragile like the membrane around dreams,

When this spider passes by, it looks as though you could blow it off its legs with a whisper directed at its awkward legs. The joints upon its legs are mere full stops, abbreviations for a death. Its outline a parenthesis. You find this spider in bathtubs in the early hours of the morning, gawky, sliding into corners, its body weaving like thread, shining like muslin, like malice. It has no predators. It lives off starvation, my uncle says.

Whoever would hunt it would have to lick its invisibility off the ground, like spilt salt. It knows how to live on a margin, brittle, like a shard of glass. Who would want to eat such an already dead thing? In the future there will be no trace of it. It dies outside time.

My uncle Sibaso is learning to live without memory, like this spider. He hardly eats. He does not swallow the stars as he used to and takes his rest in the coolness of the house, a pillow held to his belly, a half finished Coca-cola bottle to his side, its mouth sugary, syrupy, black. He keeps a few crumbs in a plate, to feed his ego, he says. An old coat hangs on the edge of the headboard, dangling royally to the floor like a priest's habit. He searches for a new balm for his wounds. A blue Kariba Battery is on the window sill, recharged by the sun. He has a small portable Panasonic radio which he carries with him and increases the volume whenever he hears something about the war in the Congo. When he learns that this war is over, then he will go and join the Zimbabwean army. There are no other jobs available for someone with his sort of sordid past. There are huge gaps in his memory concerning this country. He spent too many years in the bush.

My uncle is feigning death, as he did in the bush when a dangerous looking spider crept over his arm. He would watch it, holding his breath for as long as he could. He would be still as a rock. There was no mistaking a poisonous spider, all the evidence was there, the legs ferocious, hairy pincers. It had a dead weight about it, on your arm. A confident weight. It strolled all over your arm like a deranged dancer. Outrageous in its design and coloration. You could feel it trying to make a decision, wondering if you were human, and—if you were—if you were already dead. A spider never wastes its venom. You could feel its belly graze your skin. Poised. It made an art of inflicting harm and approaching you in daylight. It had a swiftness about it that seemed not to belong to the species. A lithe body.

Often it lingered suspiciously. If it moved off quickly, then it had granted you a reprieve. The encounter, ironic; death, near and far. They have a name for this sort of spider in Africa, *umahambemoyeni*—the swimmer in the air. It is 1999, and my Uncle Sibaso says he thought he had left this sort of spider in the bush where its charm and dismay belongs.

When Ken Saro-Wiwa[1] was hanged seven times before he died, my uncle Sibaso tied his own wrists together and lay back on his bed, placing his hands under the

---

[1]Nigerian writer hanged by his government in 1995 on trumped-up charges. The inexperienced hangman was not successful in killing Saro-Wiwa the first few times.

pillow. He switched off the radio. He felt that he could not survive the day without injury to himself and was ashamed of the entire continent. He was convinced that he himself deserved to die. On the day he finally turned the radio back on, it was reported that a fire in Nigeria had burnt villagers who were collecting oil from a burst pipe. They lay strewn like burnt wood.

My Uncle Sibaso did not want to be part of a war which was fought in the open, which consisted of breaking street lights and luminous balconies, drinking houses and tailor-shops, fish-seller porches and the smell of roasting plantains. He called this sort of war a window shopping war, an unnecessary war. A war which consisted of ordinary citizens looking for a loaf of bread, and dogs, and roof tops, and tower lights. He did not want the blood-on-tar kind of war where bodies were returned home in bags to be buried by perplexed neighbors. The war of reckless hacking limbs, of bodies burning. He did not want the sunset war witnessed by children and women and invalids. He preferred absence.

He wanted a war in which he waited for days before anything precise happened, while he thought and prepared himself. He wanted to risk his mind, somehow, while lying flat on a rock. He wanted that sort of lizard war, in which he had taken a personal resolve against a personal harm. He did not want a Congo war because he had never been there. How could he fight for a place he had never been? The idea was too absurd for him to tolerate, so he waited for the radio to tell him about the rebels who had surrendered. He heard of the revelers in the street, of an Air Zimbabwe flight which was now available to take you to the Congo. It had become some kind of destination, some place where airplanes could land and where tourists and businessmen were encouraged to go. He was already preparing his mind to join the army. He was already in a job. I never listened to the radio directly and only paid attention to what my uncle Sibaso said he had heard.

. . . spider legs, he said, in his new army attire.

[2000]

Questions

1. Why does Vera use an almost universally loathed creature, the spider, as the central metaphor for her story?
2. What has happened to Sibago by the conclusion of the story? Is he also a spider?
3. Contrast Vera's use of the spider in this story with O'Brien's use of objects in "The Things They Carried," another story about war.
4. What examples of oral storytelling are visible in Vera's story?

Alice Walker

(b. 1944)

United States

Alice Walker, the youngest of eight children, was born to sharecroppers in Eaton-
ton, Georgia. Despite the family's poverty, Walker's mother, a strong, caring
woman, gave her children a strong sense of their own capabilities. Walker was educated at Spelman College in Atlanta and Sarah Lawrence College in New York.
During the 1960s she became active in the civil rights movement both as a case-
worker for the New York City Welfare Department and as an activist for voter reg-
istration in Mississippi. During those years she met and married a white civil rights
co-worker and had a daughter; the marriage was later dissolved.

Walker is a versatile writer who began by publishing poetry. She has published five
volumes to date, most of which are collected in Her Blue Body Everything We Know:
Earthling Poems, 1965–1990 Complete (1991). She has also published several collections of short stories and essays as well as six novels: The Third Life of Grange
Copeland (1970); Meridian (1976); The Color Purple (1982), for which she was
awarded a Pulitzer Prize; The Temple of My Familiar (1989); Possessing the Secret of Joy (1992); and By the Light of My Father's Smile (1998). The subjects
of her fiction include the impact of racism and sexism on the relationships between
black men and women and the affirmative powers of love and family. As she phrases
it, "If art doesn't make us better, then what on earth is it for?" In her well-known essay,
"In Search of Our Mothers' Gardens" (1974), Walker identifies the source of that
conviction by celebrating the heritage of black women's creative spirit—particularly the
inspiration of her own mother—despite their historical exclusion from artistic opportunity: "Our mothers and grandmothers have, more often than not anonymously,
handed on the creative spark, the seed of the flower they themselves never hoped to
see: or like a sealed letter they could not plainly read."

EVERYDAY USE

For your grandmama

I will wait for her in the yard that Maggie and I made so clean and wavy yesterday
afternoon. A yard like this is more comfortable than most people know. It is not just
a yard. It is like an extended living room. When the hard clay is swept clean as a
door and the fine sand around the edges lined with tiny, irregular grooves, anyone can
come and sit and look up into the elm tree and wait for the breezes that never come
inside the house.

Maggie will be nervous until after her sister goes: she will stand hopelessly in corners, homely and ashamed of the burn scars down her arms and legs, eyeing her sister

with a mixture of envy and awe. She thinks her sister has held life always in the palm of one hand, that "no" is a word the world never learned to say to her.

You've no doubt seen those TV shows where the child who has "made it" is confronted, as a surprise, by her own mother and father, tottering in weakly from backstage.[1] (A pleasant surprise, of course: What would they do if parent and child came on the show only to curse out and insult each other?) On TV mother and child embrace and smile into each other's faces. Sometimes the mother and father weep, the child wraps them in her arms and leans across the table to tell how she would not have made it without their help. I have seen these programs.

Sometimes I dream a dream in which Dee and I are suddenly brought together on a TV program of this sort. Out of a dark and soft-seated limousine I am ushered into a bright room filled with many people. There I meet a smiling, gray, sporty man like Johnny Carson who shakes my hand and tells me what a fine girl I have. Then we are on the stage and Dee is embracing me with tears in her eyes. She pins on my dress a large orchid, even though she has told me once that she thinks orchids are tacky flowers.

In real life I am a large, bigboned woman with rough, man-working hands. In the winter I wear flannel nightgowns to bed and overalls during the day. I can kill and clean a hog as mercilessly as a man. My fat keeps me hot in zero weather. I can work outside all day, breaking ice to get water for washing; I can eat pork liver cooked over the open fire minutes after it comes steaming from the hog. One winter I knocked a bull calf straight in the brain between the eyes with a sledge hammer and had the meat hung up to chill before nightfall. But of course all this does not show on television. I am the way my daughter would want me to be: a hundred pounds lighter, my skin like an uncooked barley pancake. My hair glistens in the hot bright lights. Johnny Carson has much to do to keep up with my quick and witty tongue.

But that is a mistake. I know even before I wake up. Who ever knew a Johnson with a quick tongue? Who can even imagine me looking a strange white man in the eye? It seems to me I have talked to them always with one foot raised in flight, with my head turned in whichever way is farthest from them. Dee, though. She would always look anyone in the eye. Hesitation was no part of her nature.

"How do I look, Mama?" Maggie says, showing just enough of her thin body enveloped in pink skirt and red blouse for me to know she's there, almost hidden by the door.

"Come out into the yard," I say.

Have you ever seen a lame animal, perhaps a dog run over by some careless person rich enough to own a car, sidle up to someone who is ignorant enough to be kind to him? That is the way my Maggie walks. She has been like this, chin on chest, eyes on ground, feet in shuffle, ever since the fire that burned the other house to the ground.

Dee is lighter than Maggie, with nicer hair and a fuller figure. She's a woman now, though sometimes I forget. How long ago was it that the other house burned? Ten, twelve years? Sometimes I can still hear the flames and feel Maggie's arms sticking to me, her hair smoking and her dress falling off her in little black papery flakes. Her eyes seemed stretched open, blazed open by the flames reflected in them. And Dee. I see

---

[1] A reference to a television program of the 1960s, "This Is Your Life," in which reunions between long-separated family members and friends were televised live from the studio.

her standing off under the sweet gum tree she used to dig gum out of; a look of concentration on her face as she watched the last dingy gray board of the house fall in toward the red-hot brick chimney. Why don't you do a dance around the ashes? I'd wanted to ask her. She had hated the house that much.

I used to think she hated Maggie, too. But that was before we raised the money, the church and me, to send her to Augusta to school. She used to read to us without pity; forcing words, lies, other folks' habits, whole lives upon us two, sitting trapped and ignorant underneath her voice. She washed us in a river of make-believe, burned us with a lot of knowledge we didn't necessarily need to know. Pressed us to her with the serious way she read, to shove us away at just the moment, like dimwits, we seemed about to understand.

Dee wanted nice things. A yellow organdy dress to wear to her graduation from high school; black pumps to match a green suit she'd made from an old suit somebody gave me. She was determined to stare down any disaster in her efforts. Her eyelids would not flicker for minutes at a time. Often I fought off the temptation to shake her. At sixteen she had a style of her own: and knew what style was.

I never had an education myself. After second grade the school was closed down. Don't ask my why: in 1927 colored asked fewer questions than they do now. Sometimes Maggie reads to me. She stumbles along good-naturedly but can't see well. She knows she is not bright. Like good looks and money, quickness passed her by. She will marry John Thomas (who has mossy teeth in an earnest face) and then I'll be free to sit here and I guess just sing church songs to myself. Although I never was a good singer. Never could carry a tune. I was always better at a man's job. I used to love to milk till I was hooked in the side[2] in '49. Cows are soothing and slow and don't bother you, unless you try to milk them the wrong way.

I have deliberately turned my back on the house. It is three rooms, just like the one that burned, except the roof is tin; they don't make shingle roofs any more. There are no real windows, just some holes cut in the sides, like the portholes in a ship, but not round and not square, with rawhide holding the shutters up on the outside. This house is in a pasture, too, like the other one. No doubt when Dee sees it she will want to tear it down. She wrote me once that no matter where we "choose" to live, she will manage to come see us. But she will never bring her friends. Maggie and I thought about this and Maggie asked me, "Mama, when did Dee ever *have* any friends?"

She had a few. Furtive boys in pink shirts hanging about on washday after school. Nervous girls who never laughed. Impressed with her they worshiped the well-turned phrase, the cute shape, the scalding humor that erupted like bubbles in lye. She read to them.

When she was courting Jimmy T she didn't have much time to pay to us, but turned all her faultfinding power on him. He *flew* to marry a cheap city girl from a family of ignorant flashy people. She hardly had time to recompose herself.

When she comes I will meet—but there they are!

Maggie attempts to make a dash for the house, in her shuffling way, but I stay her with my hand. "Come back here," I say. And she stops and tries to dig a well in the sand with her toe.

---

[2]*hooked in the side*   Kicked by a cow.

It is hard to see them clearly through the strong sun. But even the first glimpse of leg out of the car tells me it is Dee. Her feet were always neat-looking, as if God himself had shaped them with a certain style. From the other side of the car comes a short, stocky man. Hair is all over his head a foot long and hanging from his chin like a kinky mule tail. I hear Maggie suck in her breath. "Uhnnnh," is what it sounds like. Like when you see the wriggling end of a snake just in front of your foot on the road. "Uhnnnh."

Dee next. A dress down to the ground, in this hot weather. A dress so loud it hurts my eyes. There are yellows and oranges enough to throw back the light of the sun. I feel my whole face warming from the heat waves it throws out. Earrings gold, too, and hanging down to her shoulders. Bracelets dangling and making noises when she moves her arm up to shake the folds of the dress out of her armpits. The dress is loose and flows, and as she walks closer, I like it. I hear Maggie go "Uhnnnh" again. It is her sister's hair. It stands straight up like the wool on a sheep. It is black as night and around the edges are two long pigtails that rope about like small lizards disappearing behind her ears.

"Wa-su-zo-Tean-o!"[3] she says, coming on in that gliding way the dress makes her move. The short stocky fellow with the hair to his navel is all grinning and he follows up with "Asalamalakim,[4] my mother and sister!" He moves to hug Maggie but she falls back, right up against the back of my chair. I feel her trembling there and when I look up I see the perspiration falling off her chin.

"Don't get up," says Dee. Since I am stout it takes something of a push. You can see me trying to move a second or two before I make it. She turns, showing white heels through her sandals, and goes back to the car. Out she peeks next with a Polaroid. She stoops down quickly and lines up picture after picture of me sitting there in front of the house with Maggie cowering behind me. She never takes a shot without making sure the house is included. When a cow comes nibbling around the edge of the yard she snaps it and me *and* Maggie and the house. Then she puts the Polaroid in the back seat of the car, and comes up and kisses me on the forehead.

Meanwhile Asalamalakim is going through motions with Maggie's hand. Maggie's hand is as limp as a fish, and probably as cold, despite the sweat, and she keeps trying to pull it back. It looks like Asalamalakim wants to shake hands but wants to do it fancy. Or maybe he don't know how people shake hands. Anyhow, he soon gives up on Maggie.

"Well," I say. "Dee."

"No, Mama," she says. "Not 'Dee,' Wangero Leewanika Kemanjo!"

"What happened to 'Dee'?" I wanted to know.

"She's dead," Wangero said. "I couldn't bear it any longer, being named after the people who oppress me."

"You know as well as me you was named after your aunt Dicie," I said. Dicie is my sister. She named Dee. We called her "Big Dee" after Dee was born.

"But who was *she* named after?" asked Wangero.

"I guess after Grandma Dee," I said.

"And who was she named after?" asked Wangero.

---

[3] *Wa-su-zo-Tean-o!*   A greeting in an African dialect, phonetically rendered.
[4] *Asalamalakim*   Muslim salutation.

"Her mother," I said, and saw Wangero was getting tired. "That's about as far back as I can trace it," I said. Though, in fact, I probably could have carried it back beyond the Civil War through the branches.

"Well," said Asalamalakim, "there you are."

"Uhnnnh," I heard Maggie say.

"There I was not," I said, "before 'Dicie' cropped up in our family, so why should I try to trace it that far back?"

He just stood there grinning, looking down on me like somebody inspecting a Model A car. Every once in a while he and Wangero sent eye signals over my head.

"How do you pronounce this name?" I asked.

"You don't have to call me by it if you don't want to," said Wangero.

"Why shouldn't I?" I asked. "If that's what you want us to call you, we'll call you."

"I know it might sound awkward at first," said Wangero.

"I'll get used to it," I said. "Ream it out again."

Well, soon we got the name out of the way. Asalamalakim had a name twice as long and three times as hard. After I tripped over it two or three times he told me to just call him Hakim-a-barber. I wanted to ask him was he a barber, but I didn't really think he was, so I didn't ask.

"You must belong to those beef-cattle peoples down the road," I said. They said "Asalamalakim" when they met you, too, but they didn't shake hands. Always too busy: feeding the cattle, fixing the fences, putting up salt-lick shelters, throwing down hay. When the white folks poisoned some of the herd the men stayed up all night with rifles in their hands. I walked a mile and a half just to see the sight.

Hakim-a-barber said, "I accept some of their doctrines, but farming and raising cattle is not my style." (They didn't tell me, and I didn't ask, whether Wangero (Dee) had really gone and married him.)

We sat down to eat and right away he said he didn't eat collards and pork was unclean. Wangero, though, went on through the chitlins and corn bread, the greens and everything else. She talked a blue streak over the sweet potatoes. Everything delighted her. Even the fact that we still used the benches her daddy made for the table when we couldn't afford to buy chairs.

"Oh, Mama!" she cried. Then turned to Hakim-a-barber. "I never knew how lovely these benches are. You can feel the rump prints," she said, running her hands underneath her and along the bench. Then she gave a sigh and her hand closed over Grandma Dee's butter dish. "That's it!" she said. "I knew there was something I wanted to ask you if I could have." She jumped up from the table and went over in the corner where the churn stood, the milk in it clabber by now. She looked at the churn and looked at it.

"This churn top is what I need," she said. "Didn't Uncle Buddy whittle it out of a tree you all used to have?"

"Yes," I said.

"Uh huh," she said happily. "And I want the dasher, too."

"Uncle Buddy whittle that, too?" asked the barber.

Dee (Wangero) looked up at me.

"Aunt Dee's first husband whittled the dash," said Maggie so low you almost couldn't hear her. "His name was Henry, but they called him Stash."

"Maggie's brain is like an elephant's," Wangero said, laughing. "I can use the churn top as a centerpiece for the alcove table," she said, sliding a plate over the churn, "and I'll think of something artistic to do with the dasher."

When she finished wrapping the dasher the handle stuck out. I took it for a moment in my hands. You didn't even have to look close to see where hands pushing the dasher up and down to make butter had left a kind of sink in the wood. In fact, there were a lot of small sinks; you could see where thumbs and fingers had sunk into the wood. It was beautiful light yellow wood, from a tree that grew in the yard where Big Dee and Stash had lived.

After dinner Dee (Wangero) went to the trunk at the foot of my bed and started rifling through it. Maggie hung back in the kitchen over the dishpan. Out came Wangero with two quilts. They had been pieced by Grandma Dee and then Big Dee and me had hung them on the quilt frames on the front porch and quilted them. One was in the Lone Star pattern. The other was Walk Around the Mountain. In both of them were scraps of dresses Grandma Dee had worn fifty and more years ago. Bits and pieces of Grandpa Jarrell's Paisley shirts. And one teeny faded blue piece, about the size of a penny matchbox, that was from Great Grandpa Ezra's uniform that he wore in the Civil War.

"Mama," Wangero said sweet as a bird. "Can I have these old quilts?"

I heard something fall in the kitchen, and a minute later the kitchen door slammed.

"Why don't you take one or two of the others?" I asked. "These old things was just done by me and Big Dee from some tops your grandma pieced before she died."

"No," said Wangero. "I don't want those. They are stitched around the borders by machine."

"That'll make them last better," I said.

"That's not the point," said Wangero. "These are all pieces of dresses Grandma used to wear. She did all this stitching by hand. Imagine!" She held the quilts securely in her arms, stroking them.

"Some of the pieces, like those lavender ones, come from old clothes her mother handed down to her," I said, moving up to touch the quilts. Dee (Wangero) moved back just enough so that I couldn't reach the quilts. They already belonged to her.

"Imagine!" she breathed again, clutching them closely to her bosom.

"The truth is," I said, "I promised to give them quilts to Maggie, for when she marries John Thomas."

She gasped like a bee had stung her.

"Maggie can't appreciate these quilts!" she said. "She'd probably be backward enough to put them to everyday use."

"I reckon she would," I said. "God knows I been saving 'em for long enough with nobody using 'em. I hope she will!" I didn't want to bring up how I had offered Dee (Wangero) a quilt when she went away to college. Then she had told me they were old-fashioned, out of style.

"But they're *priceless*!" she was saying now, furiously; for she has a temper. "Maggie would put them on the bed and in five years they'd be in rags. Less than that!"

"She can always make some more," I said. "Maggie knows how to quilt."

Dee (Wangero) looked at me with hatred. "You just will not understand. The point is these quilts, *these* quilts!"

"Well," I said, stumped. "What would *you* do with them?"

"Hang them," she said. As if that was the only thing you *could* do with quilts.

Maggie by now was standing in the door. I could almost hear the sound her feet made as they scraped over each other.

"She can have them, Mama," she said, like somebody used to never winning anything, or having anything reserved for her. "I can 'member Grandma Dee without the quilts."

I looked at her hard. She had filled her bottom lip with checkerberry snuff and it gave her face a kind of dopey, hangdog look. It was Grandma Dee and Big Dee who taught her how to quilt herself. She stood there with her scarred hands hidden in the folds of her skirt. She looked at her sister with something like fear but she wasn't mad at her. This was Maggie's portion. This was the way she knew God to work.

When I looked at her like that something hit me in the top of my head and ran down to the soles of my feet. Just like when I'm in church and the spirit of God touches me and I get happy and shout. I did something I never had done before: hugged Maggie to me, then dragged her on into the room, snatched the quilts out of Miss Wangero's hands and dumped them into Maggie's lap. Maggie just sat there on my bed with her mouth open.

"Take one or two of the others," I said to Dee.

But she turned without a word and went out to Hakim-a-barber.

"You just don't understand," she said, as Maggie and I came out to the car.

"What don't I understand?" I wanted to know.

"Your heritage," she said. And then she turned to Maggie, kissed her, and said, "You ought to try to make something of yourself, too, Maggie. It's really a new day for us. But from the way you and Mama still live you'd never know it."

She put on some sunglasses that hid everything above the tip of her nose and her chin.

Maggie smiled; maybe at the sunglasses. But a real smile, not scared. After we watched the car dust settle I asked Maggie to bring me a dip of snuff. And then the two of us sat there just enjoying, until it was time to go in the house and go to bed.

[1973]

Questions

1. How does the mother, who narrates the story, express her own values as she establishes the story's central conflict? How does the mother's point of view shape the story?
2. What symbolic role do the family quilts play in the story?
3. Are both daughters' positions given equal value? What influences the mother to make the choice she makes between the wishes of her two daughters?
4. How are images and objects of popular culture (such as Johnny Carson and Polaroid cameras) used to develop the story's theme?

Eudora Welty

(b. 1909)

United States

One distinguishing mark of many of Eudora Welty's short stories is her unique use of narrative voice. So famous is Welty for her dialogue (often first-person narratives that are actually monologues) that critics have repeatedly asked her to explain her concept of voice. When she was asked specifically about "Why I Live at the P.O." by Bill Ferris in 1975, Welty gave the following reply:

> I think the ability to use dialogue, or the first person, or anything like that, is just as essential as the knowledge of place and other components of a story. But I think it has a special importance, because you can use it in fiction to do very subtle things and very many things at once—like giving a notion of the speaker's background, furthering the plot, giving the sense of give-and-take between characters. Dialogue gives a character's age, background, upbringing, everything, without the author's having to explain it on the side. He's doing it out of his own mouth. And also, other things—like a character may be telling a lie which he will show to the reader, but perhaps not to the person to whom he's talking, and perhaps not even realize himself. Sometimes he's deluded. All these things can come out in dialogue.

Eudora Welty was born in Jackson, Mississippi. After attending several universities, she began a career as a journalist. During the depression, she worked for the Works Progress Administration (WPA). She has won major literary awards and prizes, including the Pulitzer Prize in fiction for The Optimist's Daughter (1973). Her stories, however, began appearing much earlier. The first of many of these volumes, A Curtain of Green, was published in 1941. Other Welty collections and novels include The Robber Bridegroom (1942), Delta Wedding (1946), The Golden Apples (1949), Thirteen Stories (1965), and Losing Battles (1970). Welty's three lectures at Harvard in April of 1983 to inaugurate the William E. Massy lecture series were collected in the critically praised volume, One Writer's Beginnings (1984).

In "Finding a Voice" (the third lecture in the Massy series), Welty made the following comment:

> Writing a story or a novel is one way of discovering sequence in experience, of stumbling upon cause and effect in the happenings of a writer's own life. This has been the case with me. Connections slowly emerge. Like distant landmarks you are approaching, cause and effect begin to align themselves, draw closer together. Experiences too indefinite of outline in themselves to be recognized for themselves connect and are identified as a larger shape. And suddenly a light is thrown back, as when your train makes a curve, showing that there has been a mountain of meaning rising behind you on the way you've come, is rising there still, proven now through retrospect.

WHY I LIVE AT THE P.O.

I was getting along fine with Mama, Papa-Daddy, and Uncle Rondo until my sister Stella-Rondo just separated from her husband and came back home again. Mr. Whitaker! Of course I went with Mr. Whitaker first, when he first appeared here in China Grove, taking "Pose Yourself" photos, and Stella-Rondo broke us up. Told him I was one-sided. Bigger on one side than the other, which is a deliberate, calculated falsehood: I'm the same. Stella-Rondo is exactly twelve months to the day younger than I am and for that reason she's spoiled.

She's always had anything in the world she wanted and then she'd throw it away. Papa-Daddy gave her this gorgeous Add-a-Pearl necklace when she was eight years old and she threw it away playing baseball when she was nine, with only two pearls.

So as soon as she got married and moved away from home the first thing she did was separate! From Mr. Whitaker! This photographer with the popeyes she said she trusted. Came home from one of those towns up in Illinois and to our complete surprise brought this child of two.

Mama said she like to make her drop dead for a second. "Here you had this marvelous blonde child and never so much as wrote your mother a word about it," says Mama. "I'm thoroughly ashamed of you." But of course she wasn't.

Stella-Rondo just calmly takes off this *hat*, I wish you could see it. She says, "Why, Mama, Shirley-T.'s adopted, I can prove it."

"How?" says Mama, but all I says was, "H'm!" There I was over the hot stove, trying to stretch two chickens over five people and a completely unexpected child into the bargain, without one moment's notice.

"What do you mean—'H'm!'?" says Stella-Rondo, and Mama says, "I heard that, Sister."

I said that oh, I didn't mean a thing, only that whoever Shirley-T. was, she was the spit-image of Papa-Daddy if he'd cut off his beard, which of course he'd never do in the world. Papa-Daddy's Mama's papa and sulks.

Stella-Rondo got furious! She said, "Sister, I don't need to tell you you got a lot of nerve and always did have and I'll thank you to make no future reference to my adopted child whatsoever."

"Very well," I said. "Very well, very well. Of course I noticed at once she looks like Mr. Whitaker's side too. That frown. She looks like a cross between Mr. Whitaker and Papa-Daddy."

"Well, all I can say is she isn't."

"She looks exactly like Shirley Temple to me," says Mama, but Shirley-T. just ran away from her.

So the first thing Stella-Rondo did at the table was turn Papa-Daddy against me.

"Papa-Daddy," she says. He was trying to cut up his meat. "Papa-Daddy!" I was taken completely by surprise. Papa-Daddy is about a million years old and's got this long-long beard. "Papa-Daddy, Sister says she fails to understand why you don't cut off your beard."

So Papa-Daddy l-a-y-s down his knife and fork! He's real rich. Mama says he is, he says he isn't. So he says, "Have I heard correctly? You don't understand why I don't cut off my beard?"

"Why," I says, "Papa-Daddy, of course I understand, I did not say any such of a thing, the idea!"

He says, "Hussy!"

I says, "Papa-Daddy, you know I wouldn't any more want you to cut off your beard than the man in the moon. It was the farthest thing from my mind! Stella-Rondo sat there and made that up while she was eating breast of chicken."

But he says, "So the postmistress fails to understand why I don't cut off my beard. Which job I got you through my influence with the government. 'Bird's nest'—is that what you call it?"

Not that it isn't the next to smallest P.O. in the entire state of Mississippi.

I says, "Oh, Papa-Daddy," I says, "I didn't say any such of a thing, I never dreamed it was a bird's nest, I have always been grateful though this is the next to smallest P.O. in the state of Mississippi, and I do not enjoy being referred to as a hussy by my own grandfather."

But Stella-Rondo says, "Yes, you did say it too. Anybody in the world could of heard you, that had ears."

"Stop right there," says Mama, looking at *me*.

So I pulled my napkin straight back through the napkin ring and left the table.

As soon as I was out of the room Mama says, "Call her back, or she'll starve to death," but Papa-Daddy says, "This is the beard I started growing on the Coast when I was fifteen years old." He would of gone on till nightfall if Shirley-T. hadn't lost the Milky Way she ate in Cairo.[1]

So Papa-Daddy says, "I am going out and lie in the hammock, and you can all sit here and remember my words: I'll never cut off my beard as long as I live, even one inch, and I don't appreciate it in you at all." Passed right by me in the hall and went straight out and got in the hammock.

It would be a holiday. It wasn't five minutes before Uncle Rondo suddenly appeared in the hall in one of Stella-Rondo's flesh-colored kimonos, all cut on the bias, like something Mr. Whitaker probably thought was gorgeous.

"Uncle Rondo!" I says. "I didn't know who that was! Where are you going?"

"Sister," he says, "get out of my way, I'm poisoned."

"If you're poisoned stay away from Papa-Daddy," I says. "Keep out of the hammock. Papa-Daddy will certainly beat you on the head if you come within forty miles of him. He thinks I deliberately said he ought to cut off his beard after he got me the P.O., and I've told him and told him, and he acts like he just don't hear me. Papa-Daddy must of gone stone deaf."

"He picked a fine day to do it then," says Uncle Rondo, and before you could say "Jack Robinson" flew out in the yard.

What he'd really done, he'd drunk another bottle of that prescription. He does it every single Fourth of July as sure as shooting, and it's horribly expensive. Then he falls over in the hammock and snores. So he insisted on zigzagging right on out to the hammock, looking like a half-wit.

Papa-Daddy woke up with this horrible yell and right there without moving an inch he tried to turn Uncle Rondo against me. I heard every word he said. Oh, he told Uncle Rondo I didn't learn to read till I was eight years old and he didn't see how in

---

[1]*Cairo* Cairo, Illinois.

the world I ever got the mail put up at the P.O., much less read it all, and he said if Uncle Rondo could only fathom the lengths he had gone to get me that job! And he said on the other hand he thought Stella-Rondo had a brilliant mind and deserved credit for getting out of town. All the time he was just lying there swinging as pretty as you please and looping out his beard, and poor Uncle Rondo was *pleading* with him to slow down the hammock, it was making him as dizzy as a witch to watch it. But that's what Papa-Daddy likes about a hammock. So Uncle Rondo was too dizzy to get turned against me for the time being. He's Mama's only brother and is a good case of a one-track mind. Ask anybody. A certified pharmacist.

Just then I heard Stella-Rondo raising the upstairs window. While she was married she got this peculiar idea that it's cooler with the windows shut and locked. So she has to raise the window before she can make a soul hear her outdoors.

So she raises the window and says, "Oh!" You would have thought she was mortally wounded.

Uncle Rondo and Papa-Daddy didn't even look up, but kept right on with what they were doing. I had to laugh.

I flew up the stairs and threw the door open! I says, "What in the wide world's the matter, Stella-Rondo? You mortally wounded?"

"No," she says, "I am not mortally wounded but I wish you would do me the favor of looking out that window there and telling me what you see."

So I shade my eyes and look out the window.

"I see the front yard," I says.

"Don't you see any human beings?" she says.

"I see Uncle Rondo trying to run Papa-Daddy out of the hammock," I says. "Nothing more. Naturally, it's so suffocating-hot in the house, with all the windows shut and locked, everybody who cares to stay in their right mind will have to go out and get in the hammock before the Fourth of July is over."

"Don't you notice anything different about Uncle Rondo?" asks Stella-Rondo.

"Why, no, except he's got on some terrible-looking flesh-colored contraption I wouldn't be found dead in, is all I can see," I says.

"Never mind, you won't be found dead in it, because it happens to be part of my trousseau, and Mr. Whitaker took several dozen photographs of me in it," says Stella-Rondo. "What on earth could Uncle Rondo *mean* by wearing part of my trousseau out in the broad open daylight without saying so much as 'Kiss my foot,' *knowing* I only got home this morning after my separation and hung my negligee up on the bathroom door, just as nervous as I could be?"

"I'm sure I don't know, and what do you expect me to do about it?" I says. 'Jump out the window?"

"No, I expect nothing of the kind. I simply declare that Uncle Rondo looks like a fool in it, that's all," she says. "It makes me sick to my stomach."

"Well, he looks as good as he can," I says. "As good as anybody in reason could." I stood up for Uncle Rondo, please remember. And I said to Stella-Rondo, "I think I would do well not to criticize so freely if I were you and came home with a two-year-old child I had never said a word about, and no explanation whatever about my separation."

"I asked you the instant I entered this house not to refer one more time to my adopted child, and you gave me your word of honor you would not," was all Stella-Rondo would say, and started pulling out every one of her eyebrows with some cheap Kress tweezers.

So I merely slammed the door behind me and went down and made some green-tomato pickle. Somebody had to do it. Of course Mama had turned both the niggers loose; she always said no earthly power could hold one anyway on the Fourth of July, so she wouldn't even try. It turned out that Jaypan fell in the lake and came within a very narrow limit of drowning.

So Mama trots in. Lifts up the lid and says, "H'm! Not very good for your Uncle Rondo in his precarious condition, I must say. Or poor little adopted Shirley-T. Shame on you!"

That made me tired. I says, "Well, Stella-Rondo had better thank her lucky stars it was her instead of me came trotting in with that very peculiar-looking child. Now if it had been me that trotted in from Illinois and brought a peculiar-looking child of two, I shudder to think of the reception I'd of got, much less controlled the diet of an entire family."

"But you must remember, Sister, that you were never married to Mr. Whitaker in the first place and didn't go up to Illinois to live," says Mama, shaking a spoon in my face. "If you had I would of been just as overjoyed to see you and your little adopted girl as I was to see Stella-Rondo, when you wound up with your separation and came on back home."

"You would not," I says.

"Don't contradict me, I would," says Mama.

But I said she couldn't convince me though she talked till she was blue in the face. Then I said, "Besides, you know as well as I do that that child is not adopted."

"She most certainly is adopted," says Mama, stiff as a poker.

I says, "Why, Mama, Stella-Rondo had her just as sure as anything in this world, and just too stuck up to admit it."

"Why, Sister," said Mama. "Here I thought we were going to have a pleasant Fourth of July, and you start right out not believing a word your own baby sister tells you!"

"Just like Cousin Annie Flo. Went to her grave denying the facts of life," I remind Mama.

"I told you if you ever mentioned Annie Flo's name I'd slap your face," says Mama, and slaps my face.

"All right, you wait and see," I says.

"I," says Mama, "I prefer to take my children's word for anything when it's humanly possible." You ought to see Mama, she weighs two hundred pounds and has real tiny feet.

Just then something perfectly horrible occurred to me.

"Mama," I says, "can that child talk?" I simply had to whisper! "Mama, I wonder if that child can be—you know—in any way? Do you realize," I says, "that she hasn't spoken one single, solitary word to a human being up to this minute? This is the way she looks," I says, and I looked like this.

Well, Mama and I just stood there and stared at each other. It was horrible!

"I remember well that Joe Whitaker frequently drank like a fish," says Mama. "I believed to my soul he drank *chemicals*." And without another word she marches to the foot of the stairs and calls Stella-Rondo.

"Stella-Rondo? O-o-o-o-o! Stella-Rondo!"

"What?" says Stella-Rondo from upstairs. Not even the grace to get up off the bed.

"Can that child of yours talk?" asks Mama.

Stella-Rondo says, "Can she what?"

"Talk! Talk!" says Mama. "Burdyburdyburdyburdy!"

So Stella-Rondo yells back, "Who says she can't talk?"

"Sister says so," says Mama.

"You didn't have to tell me, I know whose word of honor don't mean a thing in this house," says Stella-Rondo.

And in a minute the loudest Yankee voice I ever heard in my life yells out, "OE'm Pop-OE the Sailor-r-r-r Ma-a-an!" and then somebody jumps up and down in the upstairs hall. In another second the house would of fallen down.

"Not only talks, she can tap-dance!" calls Stella-Rondo. "Which is more than some people I won't name can do."

"Why, the little precious darling thing!" Mama says, so surprised. "Just as smart as she can be!" Starts talking baby talk right there. Then she turns on me. "Sister, you ought to be thoroughly ashamed! Run upstairs this instant and apologize to Stella-Rondo and Shirley-T."

"Apologize for what?" I says. "I merely wondered if the child was normal, that's all. Now that she's proved she is, why, I have nothing further to say."

But Mama just turned on her heel and flew out, furious. She ran right upstairs and hugged the baby. She believed it was adopted. Stella-Rondo hadn't done a thing but turn her against me from upstairs while I stood there helpless over the hot stove. So that made Mama, Papa-Daddy, and the baby all on Stella-Rondo's side.

Next, Uncle Rondo.

I must say that Uncle Rondo has been marvelous to me at various times in the past and I was completely unprepared to be made to jump out of my skin, the way it turned out. Once Stella-Rondo did something perfectly horrible to him—broke a chain letter from Flanders Field—and he took the radio back he had given her and gave it to me. Stella-Rondo was furious! For six months we all had to call her Stella instead of Stella-Rondo, or she wouldn't answer. I always thought Uncle Rondo had all the brains of the entire family. Another time he sent me to Mammoth Cave, with all expenses paid.

But this would be the day he was drinking that prescription, the Fourth of July.

So at supper Stella-Rondo speaks up and says she thinks Uncle Rondo ought to try to eat a little something. So finally Uncle Rondo said he would try a little cold biscuits and ketchup, but that was all. So *she* brought it to him.

"Do you think it wise to disport with ketchup in Stella-Rondo's flesh-colored kimono?" I says. Trying to be considerate! If Stella-Rondo couldn't watch out for her trousseau, somebody had to.

"Any objections?" asks Uncle Rondo, just about to pour out all the ketchup.

"Don't mind what she says, Uncle Rondo," says Stella-Rondo. "Sister has been devoting this solid afternoon to sneering out my bedroom window at the way you look."

"What's that?" says Uncle Rondo. Uncle Rondo has got the most terrible temper in the world. Anything is liable to make him tear the house down if it comes at the wrong time.

So Stella-Rondo says, "Sister says, 'Uncle Rondo certainly does look like a fool in that pink kimono!'"

Do you remember who it was really said that?

Uncle Rondo spills out all the ketchup and jumps out of his chair and tears off the kimono and throws it down on the dirty floor and puts his foot on it. It had to be sent all the way to Jackson to the cleaners and repleated.

"So that's your opinion of your Uncle Rondo, is it?" he says. "I look like a fool, do I? Well, that's the last straw. A whole day in this house with nothing to do, and then to hear you come out with a remark like that behind my back!"

"I didn't say any such of a thing, Uncle Rondo," I says, "and I'm not saying who did, either. Why, I think you look all right. Just try to take care of yourself and not talk and eat at the same time," I says. "I think you better go lie down."

"Lie down my foot," says Uncle Rondo. I ought to of known by that he was fixing to do something perfectly horrible.

So he didn't do anything that night in the precarious state he was in—just played Casino with Mama and Stella-Rondo and Shirley-T. and gave Shirley-T. a nickel with a head on both sides. It tickled her nearly to death, and she called him "Papa." But at 6:30 A.M. the next morning, he threw a whole five-cent package of some unsold one-inch firecrackers from the store as hard as he could into my bedroom and they every one went off. Not one bad one in the string. Anybody else, there'd be one that wouldn't go off.

Well, I'm just terribly susceptible to noise of any kind, the doctor has always told me I was the most sensitive person he had ever seen in his whole life, and I was simply prostrated. I couldn't eat! People tell me they heard it as far as the cemetery, and old Aunt Jep Patterson, that had been holding her own so good, thought it was Judgment Day and she was going to meet her whole family. It's usually so quiet here.

And I'll tell you it didn't take me any longer than a minute to make up my mind what to do. There I was with the whole entire house on Stella-Rondo's side and turned against me. If I have anything at all I have pride.

So I just decided I'd go straight down to the P.O. There's plenty of room there in the back, I says to myself.

Well! I made no bones about letting the family catch on to what I was up to. I didn't try to conceal it.

The first thing they knew, I marched in where they were all playing Old Maid and pulled the electric oscillating fan out by the plug, and everything got real hot. Next I snatched the pillow I'd done the needlepoint on right off the davenport from behind Papa-Daddy. He went "Ugh!" I beat Stella-Rondo up the stairs and finally found my charm bracelet in her bureau drawer under a picture of Nelson Eddy.[2]

"So that's the way the land lies," says Uncle Rondo. There he was, piecing on the ham. "Well, Sister, I'll be glad to donate my army cot if you got any place to set it up, providing you'll leave right this minute and let me get some peace." Uncle Rondo was in France.

"Thank you kindly for the cot and 'peace' is hardly the word I would select if I had to resort to firecrackers at 6:30 A.M. in a young girl's bedroom," I says back to him. "And as to where I intend to go, you seem to forget my position as postmistress of China Grove, Mississippi," I says. "I've always got the P.O."

Well, that made them all sit up and take notice.

I went out front and started digging up some four-o'clocks to plant around the P.O.

"Ah-ah-ah!" says Mama, raising the window. "Those happen to be my four-o'-clocks. Everything planted in that star is mine. I've never known you to make anything grow in your life."

"Very well," I says. "But I take the fern. Even you, Mama, can't stand there and deny that I'm the one watered that fern. And I happen to know where I can send in a box top and get a packet of one thousand mixed seeds, no two the same kind, free."

"Oh, where?" Mama wants to know.

---

[2]*Nelson Eddy*   Popular Hollywood musical star in the 1930s.

But I says, "Too late. You 'tend to your house, and I'll 'tend to mine. You hear things like that all the time if you know how to listen to the radio. Perfectly marvelous offers. Get anything you want free."

So I hope to tell you I marched in and got that radio, and they could of all bit a nail in two, especially Stella-Rondo, that it used to belong to, and she well knew she couldn't get it back, I'd sue for it like a shot. And I very politely took the sewing-machine motor I helped pay the most on to give Mama for Christmas back in 1929, and a good big calendar, with the first-aid remedies on it. The thermometer and the Hawaiian ukulele certainly were rightfully mine, and I stood on the step-ladder and got all my watermelon-rind preserves and every fruit and vegetable I'd put up, every jar. Then I began to pull the tacks out of the bluebird wall vases on the archway to the dining room.

"Who told you you could have those, Miss Priss?" says Mama, fanning as hard as she could.

"I bought 'em and I'll keep track of 'em," I says. "I'll tack 'em up one on each side the post-office window, and you can see 'em when you come to ask me for your mail, if you're so dead to see 'em."

"Not I! I'll never darken the door to that post office again if I live to be a hundred," Mama says. "Ungrateful child! After all the money we spent on you at the Normal."

"Me either," says Stella-Rondo. "You can just let my mail lie there and *rot*, for all I care. I'll never come and relieve you of a single, solitary piece."

"I should worry," I says. "And who you think's going to sit down and write you all those big fat letters and postcards, by the way? Mr. Whitaker? Just because he was the only man ever dropped down in China Grove and you got him—unfairly—is he going to sit down and write you a lengthy correspondence after you come home giving no rhyme nor reason whatsoever for your separation and no explanation for the presence of that child? I may not have your brilliant mind, but I fail to see it."

So Mama says, "Sister, I've told you a thousand times that Stella-Rondo simply got homesick, and this child is far too big to be hers," and she says, "Now, why don't you just sit down and play Casino?"

Then Shirley-T. sticks out her tongue at me in this perfectly horrible way. She has no more manners than the man in the moon. I told her she was going to cross her eyes like that some day and they'd stick.

"It's too late to stop me now," I says. "You should have tried that yesterday. I'm going to the P.O. and the only way you can possibly see me is to visit me there."

So Papa-Daddy says, "You'll never catch me setting foot in that post office, even if I should take a notion into my head to write a letter some place." He says, "I won't have you reachin' out of that little old window with a pair of shears and cuttin' off any beard of mine. I'm too smart for you!"

"We all are," says Stella-Rondo.

But I said, "If you're so smart, where's Mr. Whitaker?"

So then Uncle Rondo says, "I'll thank you from now on to stop reading all the orders I get on postcards and telling everybody in China Grove what you think is the matter with them," but I says, "I draw my own conclusions and will continue in the future to draw them." I says, "If people want to write their inmost secrets on penny postcards, there's nothing in the wide world you can do about it, Uncle Rondo."

"And if you think we'll ever *write* another postcard you're sadly mistaken," says Mama.

"Cutting off your nose to spite your face then," I says. "But if you're all determined to have no more to do with the U.S. mail, think of this: What will Stella-Rondo do now, if she wants to tell Mr. Whitaker to come after her?"

"Wah!" says Stella-Rondo. I knew she'd cry. She had a conniption fit right there in the kitchen.

"It will be interesting to see how long she holds out," I says. "And now—I am leaving."

"Good-bye," says Uncle Rondo.

"Oh, I declare," says Mama, "to think that a family of mine should quarrel on the Fourth of July, or the day after, over Stella-Rondo leaving old Mr. Whitaker and having the sweetest little adopted child! It looks like we'd all be glad!"

"Wah!" says Stella-Rondo, and has a fresh conniption fit.

"*He* left *her*—you mark my words," I says. "That's Mr. Whitaker. I know Mr. Whitaker. After all, I knew him first. I said from the beginning he'd up and leave her. I foretold every single thing that's happened."

"Where did he go?" asks Mama.

"Probably to the North Pole, if he knows what's good for him," I says.

But Stella-Rondo just bawled and wouldn't say another word. She flew to her room and slammed the door.

"Now look what you've gone and done, Sister," says Mama. "You go apologize."

"I haven't got time, I'm leaving," I says.

"Well, what are you waiting around for?" asks Uncle Rondo.

So I just picked up the kitchen clock and marched off, without saying "Kiss my foot," or anything, and never did tell Stella-Rondo good-bye.

There was a nigger girl going along on a little wagon right in front.

"Nigger girl," I says, "come help me haul these things down the hill, I'm going to live in the post office."

Took her nine trips in her express wagon. Uncle Rondo came out on the porch and threw her a nickel.

And that's the last I've laid eyes on any of my family or my family laid eyes on me for five solid days and nights. Stella-Rondo may be telling the most horrible tales in the world about Mr. Whitaker, but I haven't heard them. As I tell everybody, I draw my own conclusions.

But oh, I like it here. It's ideal, as I've been saying. You see, I've got everything cater-cornered, the way I like it. Hear the radio? All the war news. Radio, sewing machine, book ends, ironing board and that great big piano lamp—peace, that's what I like. Butter-bean vines planted all along the front where the strings are.

Of course, there's not much mail. My family are naturally the main people in China Grove, and if they prefer to vanish from the face of the earth, for all the mail they get or the mail they write, why, I'm not going to open my mouth. Some of the folks here in town are taking up for me and some turned against me. I know which is which. There are always people who will quit buying stamps just to get on the right side of Papa-Daddy.

But here I am, and here I'll stay. I want the world to know I'm happy.

And if Stella-Rondo should come to me this minute, on bended knees, and *attempt* to explain the incidents of her life with Mr. Whitaker, I'd simply put my fingers in both my ears and refuse to listen.

[1941]

Questions

1. Is the narrator of "Why I Live at the P.O." objective about her situation or is she distorting the events she tells us?
2. What do we specifically know about Welty's narrator in this story? How old is she? What does she value in life? What does she dislike?
3. Are your loyalties with the narrator of the story or with her family? What kind of family has Welty given us in her story?
4. Is the narrator happy at the end of the story—as she says she is?
5. Do you see any similarities between Welty's narrator in "Why I Live at the P.O." and the grandmother in Flannery O'Connor's "A Good Man Is Hard to Find"?

Edith Wharton
(1862–1937)
United States

E dith Jones Wharton acquired the storytelling impulse early—during childhood she frequently "made up" stories—but actually did not become a serious writer until several decades later. Born to wealthy parents who belonged to the aristocratic society of New York, Wharton spent winters in New York and summers in Newport, Rhode Island, and traveled in France and Italy following her social debut at 18. In 1885 she married a Bostonian, Edward ("Teddy") Wharton, who shared her love of travel but few of her other interests, including her literary ambitions. Teddy later developed serious mental illness. Eventually they divorced (in 1912) and Edith moved to Europe; she lived in France for the rest of her life. Wharton developed several significant intellectual friendships, including an important one with Henry James, whose encouragement and influence throughout her career were invaluable to her.

Wharton's background gave her unique insight into the social world of the dying aristocracy in turn-of-the-century America. Wharton was, according to Sandra Gilbert and Susan Gubar, "an observer who dissected what had been her dilemma—the struggle of the captive lady against the bars of her gilded cage." Her early novel, House of Mirth (1905), is a brilliant indictment of the values of the moneyed class, within which the tragic Lily Bart struggles—unsuccessfully—to locate not only a suitable husband but also herself.

A prolific writer, Wharton published a book a year from 1899 until her death in 1937: 16 novels as well as several novellas, travel narratives, and nearly a dozen volumes of short stories, including some of the best ghost stories in literature. Her major novels besides House of Mirth include Ethan Frome (1911), The Custom of the Country (1913), and The Age of Innocence (1920).

THE MUSE'S TRAGEDY

I

Danyers afterwards liked to fancy that he had recognized Mrs. Anerton at once; but that, of course, was absurd, since he had seen no portrait of her—she affected a strict anonymity, refusing even her photograph to the most privileged—and from Mrs. Memorall, whom he revered and cultivated as her friend, he had extracted but the one impressionist phrase: "Oh, well, she's like one of those old prints where the lines have the value of color."

He was almost certain, at all events, that he had been thinking of Mrs. Anerton as he sat over his breakfast in the empty hotel restaurant, and that, looking up on the approach of the lady who seated herself at the table near the window, he had said to himself, "*That might be she.*"

Ever since his Harvard days—he was still young enough to think of them as immensely remote—Danyers had dreamed of Mrs. Anerton, the Silvia of Vincent Rendle's immortal sonnet cycle, the Mrs. A. of the *Life and Letters*. Her name was enshrined in some of the noblest English verse of the nineteenth century—and of all past or future centuries, as Danyers, from the standpoint of a maturer judgment, still believed. The first reading of certain poems—of the *Antinous*, the *Pia Tolomei*, the *Sonnets to Silvia*—had been epochs in Danyers' growth, and the verse seemed to gain in mellowness, in amplitude, in meaning as one brought to its interpretation more experience of life, a finer emotional sense. Where, in his boyhood, he had felt only the perfect, the almost austere beauty of form, the subtle interplay of vowel sounds, the rush and fullness of lyric emotion, he now thrilled to the close-packed significance of each line, the allusiveness of each word—his imagination lured hither and thither on fresh trails of thought, and perpetually spurred by the sense that, beyond what he had already discovered, more marvelous regions lay waiting to be explored. Danyers had written, at college, the prize essay on Rendle's poetry (it chanced to be the moment of the great man's death); he had fashioned the fugitive verse of his own Storm and Stress period on the forms which Rendle had first given to English meter, and when two years later the *Life and Letters* appeared, and the Silvia of the sonnets took substance as Mrs. A., he had included in his worship of Rendle the woman who had inspired not only such divine verse but such playful, tender, incomparable prose.

Danyers never forgot the day when Mrs. Memorall happened to mention that she knew Mrs. Anerton. He had known Mrs. Memorall for a year or more, and had somewhat contemptuously classified her as the kind of woman who runs cheap excursions to celebrities; when one afternoon she remarked, as she put a second lump of sugar in his tea:

"Is it right this time? You're almost as particular as Mary Anerton."

"Mary Anerton?"

"Yes, I never *can* remember how she likes her tea. Either it's lemon *with* sugar, or lemon without sugar or cream without either, and whichever it is must be put into the cup before the tea is poured in; and if one hasn't remembered, one must begin all over again. I suppose it was Vincent Rendle's way of taking his tea and has become a sacred rite."

"Do you *know* Mrs. Anerton?" cried Danyers, disturbed by this careless familiarity with the habits of his divinity.

"'And did I once see Shelley plain?' Mercy, yes! She and I were at school together— she's an American, you know. We were at a *pension*[1] near Tours for nearly a year; then she went back to New York, and I didn't see her again till after her marriage. She and Anerton spent a winter in Rome while my husband was attached to our Legation there, and she used to be with us a great deal." Mrs. Memorall smiled reminiscently. "It was *the* winter."

"The winter they first met?"

"Precisely—but unluckily I left Rome just before the meeting took place. Wasn't it too bad? I might have been in the *Life and Letters*. You know he mentions that stupid Madame Vodki, at whose house he first saw her."

"And did you see much of her after that?"

---

[1]*pension*   French: small hotel or boarding-house.

"Not during Rendle's life. You know she has lived in Europe almost entirely, and though I used to see her off and on when I went abroad, she was always so engrossed, so preoccupied, that one felt one wasn't wanted. The fact is, she cared only about his friends—she separated herself gradually from all her own people. Now, of course, it's different; she's desperately lonely; she's taken to writing to me now and then; and last year, when she heard I was going abroad, she asked me to meet her in Venice, and I spent a week with her there."

"And Rendle?"

Mrs. Memorall smiled and shook her head. "Oh, I never was allowed a peep at *him*; none of her old friends met him, except by accident. Ill-natured people say that was the reason she kept him so long. If one happened in while he was there, he was hustled into Anerton's study, and the husband mounted guard till the inopportune visitor had departed. Anerton, you know, was really much more ridiculous about it than his wife. Mary was too clever to lose her head, or at least to show she'd lost it— but Anerton couldn't conceal his pride in the conquest. I've seen Mary shiver when he spoke of Rendle as *our poet*. Rendle always had to have a certain seat at the dinner table, away from the draft and not too near the fire, and a box of cigars that no one else was allowed to touch, and a writing table of his own in Mary's sitting room— and Anerton was always telling one of the great man's idiosyncrasies: how he never would cut the ends of his cigars, though Anerton himself had given him a gold cutter set with a star sapphire, and how untidy his writing table was, and how the housemaid had orders always to bring the wastepaper basket to her mistress before emptying it, lest some immortal verse should be thrown into the dustbin."

"The Anertons never separated, did they?"

"Separated? Bless you, no. He never would have left Rendle! And besides, he was very fond of his wife."

"And she?"

"Oh, she saw he was the kind of man who was fated to make himself ridiculous, and she never interfered with his natural tendencies."

From Mrs. Memorall, Danyers further learned that Mrs. Anerton, whose husband had died some years before her poet, now divided her life between Rome, where she had a small apartment, and England, where she occasionally went to stay with those of her friends who had been Rendle's. She had been engaged, for some time after his death, in editing some juvenilia which he had bequeathed to her care; but that task being accomplished, she had been left without definite occupation, and Mrs. Memorall, on the occasion of their last meeting, had found her listless and out of spirits.

"She misses him too much—her life is too empty. I told her so—I told her she ought to marry."

"Oh!"

"Why not, pray? She's a young woman still—what many people would call young," Mrs. Memorall interjected, with a parenthetic glance at the mirror. "Why not accept the inevitable and begin over again? All the King's horses and all the King's men won't bring Rendle to life—and besides, she didn't marry *him* when she had the chance."

Danyers winced slightly at this rude fingering of his idol. Was it possible that Mrs. Memorall did not see what an anticlimax such a marriage would have been? Fancy Rendle "making an honest woman" of Silvia; for so society would have viewed it! How such a reparation would have vulgarized their past—it would have been like "restoring" a masterpiece; and how exquisite must have been the perceptions of the woman who, in defiance of appearances, and perhaps of her own secret inclination, chose to go down to posterity as Silvia rather than as Mrs. Vincent Rendle!

Mrs. Memorall, from this day forth, acquired an interest in Danyers' eyes. She was like a volume of unindexed and discursive memoirs, through which he patiently plodded in the hope of finding embedded amid layers of dusty twaddle some precious allusion to the subject of his thought. When, some months later, he brought out his first slim volume, in which the remodeled college essay on Rendle figured among a dozen somewhat overstudied "appreciations," he offered a copy to Mrs. Memorall; who surprised him, the next time they met, with the announcement that she had sent the book to Mrs. Anerton.

Mrs. Anerton in due time wrote to thank her friend. Danyers was privileged to read the few lines in which, in terms that suggested the habit of "acknowledging" similar tributes, she spoke of the author's "feeling and insight," and was "so glad of the opportunity," etc. He went away disappointed, without clearly knowing what else he had expected.

The following spring, when he went abroad, Mrs. Memorall offered him letters to everybody, from the Archbishop of Canterbury to Louise Michel. She did not include Mrs. Anerton, however, and Danyers knew, from a previous conversation, that Silvia objected to people who "brought letters." He knew also that she traveled during the summer, and was unlikely to return to Rome before the term of his holiday should be reached, and the hope of meeting her was not included among his anticipations.

The lady whose entrance broke upon his solitary repast in the restaurant of the Hotel Villa d'Este had seated herself in such a way that her profile was detached against the window; and thus viewed, her domed forehead, small arched nose, and fastidious lip suggested a silhouette of Marie Antoinette. In the lady's dress and movements—in the very turn of her wrist as she poured out her coffee—Danyers thought he detected the same fastidiousness, the same air of tacitly excluding the obvious and unexceptional. Here was a woman who had been much bored and keenly interested. The waiter brought her a *Secolo*, and as she bent above it Danyers noticed that the hair rolled back from her forehead was turning gray; but her figure was straight and slender, and she had the invaluable gift of a girlish back.

The rush of Anglo-Saxon travel had not set toward the lakes, and with the exception of an Italian family or two, and a hump-backed youth with an *abbé*,[2] Danyers and the lady had the marble halls of the Villa d'Este to themselves.

When he returned from his morning ramble among the hills he saw her sitting at one of the little tables at the edge of the lake. She was writing, and a heap of books and newspapers lay on the table at her side. That evening they met again in the garden. He had strolled out to smoke a last cigarette before dinner, and under the black vaulting of ilexes, near the steps leading down to the boat landing, he found her leaning on the parapet above the lake. At the sound of his approach she turned and looked at him. She had thrown a black lace scarf over her head, and in this somber setting her face seemed thin and unhappy. He remembered afterwards that her eyes, as they met his, expressed not so much sorrow as profound discontent.

To his surprise she stepped toward him with a detaining gesture.

"Mr. Lewis Danyers, I believe?"

He bowed.

---

[2]*abbé*   French: abbot, priest.

"I am Mrs. Anerton. I saw your name on the visitors' list and wished to thank you for an essay on Mr. Rendle's poetry—or rather to tell you how much I appreciated it. The book was sent to me last winter by Mrs. Memorall."

She spoke in even melancholy tones, as though the habit of perfunctory utterance had robbed her voice of more spontaneous accents; but her smile was charming.

They sat down on a stone bench under the ilexes, and she told him how much pleasure his essay had given her. She thought it the best in the book—she was sure he had put more of himself into it than into any other; was she not right in conjecturing that he had been very deeply influenced by Mr. Rendle's poetry? *Pour comprendre il faut aimer,*[3] and it seemed to her that, in some ways, he had penetrated the poet's inner meaning more completely than any other critic. There were certain problems, of course, that he had left untouched; certain aspects of that many-sided mind that he had perhaps failed to seize—

"But then you are young," she concluded gently, "and one could not wish you, as yet, the experience that a fuller understanding would imply."

II

She stayed a month at Villa d'Este, and Danyers was with her daily. She showed an unaffected pleasure in his society; a pleasure so obviously founded on their common veneration of Rendle, that the young man could enjoy it without fear of fatuity. At first he was merely one more grain of frankincense on the altar of her insatiable divinity; but gradually a more personal note crept into their intercourse. If she still liked him only because he appreciated Rendle, she at least perceptibly distinguished him from the herd of Rendle's appreciators.

Her attitude toward the great man's memory struck Danyers as perfect. She neither proclaimed nor disavowed her identity. She was frankly Silvia to those who knew and cared; but there was no trace of the Egeria in her pose. She spoke often of Rendle's books, but seldom of himself; there was no posthumous conjugality, no use of the possessive tense, in her abounding reminiscences. Of the master's intellectual life, of his habits of thought and work, she never wearied of talking. She knew the history of each poem; by what scene or episode each image had been evoked; how many times the words in a certain line had been transposed; how long a certain adjective had been sought, and what had at last suggested it; she could even explain that one impenetrable line, the torment of critics, the joy of detractors, the last line of *The Old Odysseus.*

Danyers felt that in talking of these things she was no mere echo of Rendle's thought. If her identity had appeared to be merged in his it was because they thought alike, not because he had thought for her. Posterity is apt to regard the women whom poets have sung as chance pegs on which they hung their garlands; but Mrs. Anerton's mind was like some fertile garden wherein, inevitably, Rendle's imagination had rooted itself and flowered. Danyers began to see how many threads of his complex mental tissue the poet had owed to the blending of her temperament with his; in a certain sense Silvia had herself created the *Sonnets to Silvia.*

---

[3]*Pour comprendre il faut aimer.*   French: To understand one must love.

To be the custodian of Rendle's inner self, the door, as it were, to the sanctuary, had at first seemed to Danyers so comprehensive a privilege that he had the sense, as his friendship with Mrs. Anerton advanced, of forcing his way into a life already crowded. What room was there, among such towering memories, for so small an actuality as his? Quite suddenly, after this, he discovered that Mrs. Memorall knew better: his fortunate friend was bored as well as lonely.

"You have had more than any other woman!" he had exclaimed to her one day: and her smile flashed a derisive light on his blunder. Fool that he was, not to have seen that she had not had enough! That she was young still—do years count?—tender, human, a woman; that the living have need of the living.

After that, when they climbed the alleys of the hanging park, resting in one of the little ruined temples, or watching, through a ripple of foliage, the remote blue flash of the lake, they did not always talk of Rendle or of literature. She encouraged Danyers to speak of himself; to confide his ambitions to her; she asked him the questions which are the wise woman's substitute for advice.

"You must write," she said, administering the most exquisite flattery that human lips could give.

Of course he meant to write—why not to do something great in his turn? His best, at least; with the resolve, at the outset, that his best should be *the* best. Nothing less seemed possible with that mandate in his ears. How she had divined him; lifted and disentangled his groping ambitions; laid the awakening touch on his spirit with her creative *Let there be light!*

It was his last day with her, and he was feeling very hopeless and happy.

"You ought to write a book about *him*," she went on gently.

Danyers started; he was beginning to dislike Rendle's way of walking in unannounced.

"You ought to do it," she insisted. "A complete interpretation—a summing up of his style, his purpose, his theory of life and art. No one else could do it as well."

He sat looking at her perplexedly. Suddenly—dared he guess?

"I couldn't do it without you," he faltered.

"I could help you—I would help you, of course."

They sat silent, both looking at the lake.

It was agreed, when they parted, that he should rejoin her six weeks later in Venice. There they were to talk about the book.

III

Lago d'Iseo, August 14th.

When I said good-bye to you yesterday I promised to come back to Venice in a week: I was to give you your answer then. I was not honest in saying that; I didn't mean to go back to Venice or to see you again. I was running away from you—and I mean to keep on running! If *you* won't, *I* must. Somebody must save you from marrying a disappointed woman of—well, you say years don't count, and why should they, after all, since you are not to marry me?

That is what I dare not go back to say. *You are not to marry me.* We have had our month together in Venice (such a good month, was it not?) and now you are to go home and write a book—any book but the one we—didn't talk of!—and I am to stay here, attitudinizing among my memories like a sort of female Tithonus.[4] The dreariness of this enforced immortality!

But you shall know the truth. I care for you, or at least for your love, enough to owe you that.

You thought it was because Vincent Rendle had loved me that there was so little hope for you. I had had what I wanted to the full; wasn't that what you said? It is just when a man begins to think he understands a woman that he may be sure he doesn't! It is because Vincent Rendle *didn't love me* that there is no hope for you. I never had what I wanted, and never, never, never will I stoop to wanting anything else.

Do you begin to understand? It was all a sham then, you say? No, it was all real as far as it went. You are young—you haven't learned, as you will later, the thousand imperceptible signs by which one gropes one's way through the labyrinth of human nature; but didn't it strike you, sometimes, that I never told you any foolish little anecdotes about him? His trick, for instance, of twirling a paper knife round and round between his thumb and forefinger while he talked; his mania for saving the backs of notes; his greediness for wild strawberries, the little pungent Alpine ones; his childish delight in acrobats and jugglers; his way of always calling me *you—dear you*, every letter began—I never told you a word of all that, did I? Do you suppose I could have helped telling you, if he had loved me? These little things would have been mine, then, a part of my life—of our life—they would have slipped out in spite of me (it's only your unhappy woman who is always reticent and dignified). But there never was any "our life"; it was always "our lives" to the end. . . .

If you knew what a relief it is to tell someone at last, you would bear with me, you would let me hurt you! I shall never be quite so lonely again, now that someone knows.

Let me begin at the beginning. When I first met Vincent Rendle I was not twenty-five. That was twenty years ago. From that time until his death, five years ago, we were fast friends. He gave me fifteen years, perhaps the best fifteen years, of his life. The world, as you know, thinks that his greatest poems were written during those years; I am supposed to have "inspired" them, and in a sense I did. From the first, the intellectual sympathy between us was almost complete; my mind must have been to him (I fancy) like some perfectly tuned instrument on which he was never tired of playing. Someone told me of his once saying of me that I "always understood"; it is the only praise I ever heard of his giving me. I don't even know if he thought me pretty, though I hardly think my appearance could have been disagreeable to him, for he hated to be with ugly people. At all events he fell into the way of spending more and more of his time with me. He liked our house; our ways suited him. He was nervous, irritable; people bored him and yet he disliked solitude. He took sanctuary with us. When we traveled he went with us; in the winter he took rooms near us in Rome. In England or on the continent he was always with us for a good part of the year. In small ways I was able to help him in his work; he grew dependent on me. When we were apart he wrote to me continually—he liked to have me share in all he was doing or thinking; he was impatient for my criticism of every new book that interested him; I was a part of his intellectual life. The pity of it was that I wanted to be something

---

[4]Tithonus   Greek mythology: a mortal who was loved by Aurora, the goddess of dawn. The goddess asked Zeus to make her lover immortal; unfortunately for Tithonus, she neglected to ask that he be made ageless as well.

more. I was a young woman and I was in love with him—not because he was Vincent Rendle, but just because he was himself!

People began to talk, of course—I was Vincent Rendle's Mrs. Anerton; when the *Sonnets to Silvia* appeared, it was whispered that I was Silvia. Wherever he went, I was invited; people made up to me in the hope of getting to know him; when I was in London my doorbell never stopped ringing. Elderly peeresses, aspiring hostesses, lovesick girls and struggling authors overwhelmed me with their assiduities. I hugged my success, for I knew what it meant—they thought that Rendle was in love with me! Do you know, at times, they almost made me think so too? Oh, there was no phase of folly I didn't go through. You can't imagine the excuses a woman will invent for a man's not telling her that he loves her—pitiable arguments that she would see through at a glance if any other woman used them! But all the while, deep down, I knew he had never cared. I should have known it if he had made love to me every day of his life. I could never guess whether he knew what people said about us—he listened so little to what people said; and cared still less, when he heard. He was always quite honest and straightforward with me; he treated me as one man treats another; and yet at times I felt he *must* see that with me it was different. If he did see, he made no sign. Perhaps he never noticed—I am sure he never meant to be cruel. He had never made love to me; it was no fault of his if I wanted more than he could give me. The *Sonnets to Silvia*, you say? But what are they? A cosmic philosophy, not a love poem; addressed to Woman, not to a woman!

But then, the letters? Ah, the letters! Well, I'll make a clean breast of it. You have noticed the breaks in the letters here and there, just as they seem to be on the point of growing a little—warmer? The critics, you may remember, praised the editor for his commendable delicacy and good taste (so rare in these days!) in omitting from the correspondence all personal allusions, all those *détails intimes*[5] which should be kept sacred from the public gaze. They referred, of course, to the asterisks in the letters to Mrs. A. Those letters I myself prepared for publication; that is to say, I copied them out for the editor, and every now and then I put in a line of asterisks to make it appear that something had been left out. You understand? The asterisks were a sham— *there was nothing to leave out.*

No one but a woman could understand what I went through during those years— the moments of revolt, when I felt I must break away from it all, fling the truth in his face and never see him again; the inevitable reaction, when not to see him seemed the one unendurable thing, and I trembled lest a look or word of mine should disturb the poise of our friendship; the silly days when I hugged the delusion that he *must* love me, since everybody thought he did; the long periods of numbness, when I didn't seem to care whether he loved me or not. Between these wretched days came others when our intellectual accord was so perfect that I forgot everything else in the joy of feeling myself lifted up on the wings of his thought. Sometimes, then, the heavens seemed to be opened.

All this time he was so dear a friend! He had the genius of friendship, and he spent it all on me. Yes, you were right when you said that I have had more than any other woman. *Il faut de l'adresse pour aimer,*[6] Pascal says; and I was so quiet, so cheerful, so

---

[5] *détails intimes*   French: intimate details.
[6] *Il faut de l'adresse pour aimer.*   French: One needs skill to love.

frankly affectionate with him, that in all those years I am almost sure I never bored him. Could I have hoped as much if he had loved me?

You mustn't think of him, though, as having been tied to my skirts. He came and went as he pleased, and so did his fancies. There was a girl once (I am telling you everything), a lovely being who called his poetry "deep" and gave him *Lucile* on his birthday. He followed her to Switzerland one summer, and all the time that he was dangling after her (a little too conspicuously, I always thought, for a Great Man), he was writing to *me* about his theory of vowel combinations—or was it his experiments in English hexameter? The letters were dated from the very places where I knew they went and sat by waterfalls together and he thought out adjectives for her hair. He talked to me about it quite frankly afterwards. She was perfectly beautiful and it had been a pure delight to watch her; but she *would* talk, and her mind, he said, was "all elbows." And yet, the next year, when her marriage was announced, he went away alone, quite suddenly . . . and it was just afterwards that he published *Love's Viaticum.* Men are queer!

After my husband died—I am putting things crudely, you see—I had a return of hope. It was because he loved me, I argued, that he had never spoken; because he had always hoped some day to make me his wife; because he wanted to spare me the "reproach." Rubbish! I knew well enough, in my heart of hearts, that my one chance lay in the force of habit. He had grown used to me; he was no longer young; he dreaded new people and new ways; *il avait pris son pli.*[7] Would it not be easier to marry me?

I don't believe he ever thought of it. He wrote me what people call "a beautiful letter"; he was kind, considerate, decently commiserating; then, after a few weeks, he slipped into his old way of coming in every afternoon, and our interminable talks began again just where they had left off. I heard later that people thought I had shown "such good taste" in not marrying him.

So we jogged on for five years longer. Perhaps they were the best years, for I had given up hoping. Then he died.

After his death—this is curious—there came to me a kind of mirage of love. All the books and articles written about him, all the reviews of the *Life,* were full of discreet allusions to Silvia. I became again the Mrs. Anerton of the glorious days. Sentimental girls and dear lads like you turned pink when somebody whispered, "That was Silvia you were talking to." Idiots begged for my autograph—publishers urged me to write my reminiscences of him—critics consulted me about the reading of doubtful lines. And I knew that, to all these people, I was the woman Vincent Rendle had loved.

After a while that fire went out too and I was left alone with my past. Alone—quite alone; for he had never really been with me. The intellectual union counted for nothing now. It had been soul to soul, but never hand in hand, and there were no little things to remember him by.

Then there set in a kind of Arctic winter. I crawled into myself as into a snow hut. I hated my solitude and yet dreaded anyone who disturbed it. That phase, of course, passed like the others. I took up life again, and began to read the papers and consider the cut of my gowns. But here was one question that I could not be rid of, that haunted me night and day. Why had he never loved me? Why had I been so much to him, and no more? Was I so ugly, so essentially unlovable, that though a man

---

[7]*Il avait pris son pli.*   French: His habits were set.

might cherish me as his mind's comrade, he could not care for me as a woman? I can't tell you how that question tortured me. It became an obsession.

My poor friend, do you begin to see? I had to find out what some other man thought of me. Don't be too hard on me! Listen first—consider. When I first met Vincent Rendle I was a young woman, who had married early and led the quietest kind of life; I had had no "experiences." From the hour of our first meeting to the day of his death I never looked at any other man, and never noticed whether any other man looked at me. When he died, five years ago, I knew the extent of my powers no more than a baby. Was it too late to find out? Should I never know *why*?

Forgive me—forgive me. You are so young; it will be an episode, a mere "document," to you so soon! And, besides, it wasn't as deliberate, as cold-blooded as these disjointed lines have made it appear. I didn't plan it, like a woman in a book. Life is so much more complex than any rendering of it can be. I liked you from the first—I was drawn to you (you must have seen that)—I wanted you to like me; it was not a mere psychological experiment. And yet in a sense it was that, too—I must be honest. I had to have an answer to that question; it was a ghost that had to be laid.

At first I was afraid—oh, so much afraid—that you cared for me only because I was Silvia, that you loved me because you thought Rendle had loved me. I began to think there was no escaping my destiny.

How happy I was when I discovered that you were growing jealous of my past; that you actually hated Rendle! My heart beat like a girl's when you told me you meant to follow me to Venice.

After our parting at Villa d'Este my old doubts reasserted themselves. What did I know of your feeling for me, after all? Were you capable of analyzing it yourself? Was it not likely to be two-thirds vanity and curiosity, and one-third literary sentimentality? You might easily fancy that you cared for Mary Anerton when you were really in love with Silvia—the heart is such a hypocrite! Or you might be more calculating than I had supposed. Perhaps it was you who had been flattering *my* vanity in the hope (the pardonable hope!) of turning me, after a decent interval, into a pretty little essay with a margin.

When you arrived in Venice and we met again—do you remember the music on the lagoon, that evening, from my balcony?—I was so afraid you would begin to talk about the book—the book, you remember, was your ostensible reason for coming. You never spoke of it, and I soon saw your one fear was *I* might do so—might remind you of your object in being with me. Then I knew you cared for me! Yes, at that moment really cared! We never mentioned the book once, did we, during that month in Venice?

I have read my letter over; and now I wish that I had said this to you instead of writing it. I could have felt my way then, watching your face and seeing if you understood. But, no, I could not go back to Venice; and I could not tell you (though I tried) while we were there together. I couldn't spoil that month—my one month. It was so good, for once in my life, to get away from literature.

You will be angry with me at first—but, alas! not for long. What I have done would have been cruel if I had been a younger woman; as it is, the experiment will hurt no one but myself. And it will hurt me horribly (as much as, in your first anger, you may perhaps wish), because it has shown me, for the first time, all that I have missed.

[1899]

Questions

1. In what ways are Lewis Danyers's views of Mrs. Anerton and Vincent Rendle altered by the story's end? In what ways do Danyers's youth and scholarly ambitions influence his attitude toward both the poet and the subject of his poetry?

2. How does the shift in narrative perspective from Danyers's to Mrs. Anerton's shape the reader's understanding of the characters and their choices?

3. How accurate is Mrs. Anerton's conviction that her "experiment" with Danyers's feelings will hurt no one but herself?

4. What does the story suggest about the relationship between life and literature? What does the title mean?

Virginia Woolf
(1882–1941)
England

V irginia Woolf is inarguably one of the giants of twentieth-century literature. A central figure of Modernism—the early twentieth-century movement that altered aesthetic conceptions of literature and other art forms—she crafted a distinctive narrative style through poetic language and experimentation with the basic elements of fiction. The daughter of a distinguished British literary critic, Sir Leslie Stephen, the young Virginia was educated at home, where she read voraciously in her father's library and, at the age of eight, produced a newspaper for her family and friends. Her emotional delicacy during childhood was exacerbated by the deaths, within a ten-year period, of both parents, a brother, and a half-sister. What began as periods of mental instability developed into what is now labeled bipolar (manic-depressive) mood disorder. In 1912, she married Leonard Woolf, a civil servant who strongly supported both her writing career and her intermittently precarious mental health; their lifelong partnership stabilized her life. Nonetheless, after a productive literary career interrupted by periods of depression, Virginia Woolf took her own life by drowning at the age of 59.

During her twenties, Woolf began to publish literary reviews and essays, directed not to scholars or academics but to the "common reader"; indeed, along with her fiction, she is known for her exceptionally fine literary and critical essays. Impatient with the constraints of literary convention after having published two traditional novels, she began to experiment with the elements of narrative, including point of view, time, characterization, and plot. The sketch "Kew Gardens" is among her early experimental narratives; minimizing character and plot, it relies on vivid images and impressionistic patterns. Subsequently, Woolf expanded these new approaches into her longer fiction. Mrs. Dalloway (1925) and To the Lighthouse (1927) are both masterpieces of stream-of-consciousness narration, lyrical language, and a radically new approach to the literary representation of "reality."

Although Woolf is perhaps best known for her serious preoccupation with the nature of time, consciousness, and selfhood, she also had a lighter side. Her comic masterpiece, Orlando (1928), is an unconventional biography in which the subject lives more than three centuries and changes sex during the course of his/her life. Woolf playfully satirizes everything from gender roles and romance to the history of English literature and the conventions of biography itself. As Orlando suggests, Woolf was interested in gender issues long before they became mainstream; her influence is central to the development of feminist literary criticism. In her classic essay A Room of One's Own (1929), she explores with both wit and passion the difficulty women have had in pursuing careers as writers.

Woolf's indelible mark on the course of literature derives from her success in shifting the emphasis in fiction from manners, social custom, and plot to the seemingly inconsequential events that compose every person's experiences and endow them with meaning: relationships, feelings, memories, time, and place. Comprehending the fluidity of experience and of personality itself, Woolf uniquely captured those elusive dimensions in the pages of fiction. She made the following memorable comment in her 1919 literary manifesto, "Modern Fiction":

> Life is not a series of gig-lamps symmetrically arranged; life is a luminous halo, a semitransparent envelope surrounding us from the beginning of consciousness to the end. Is it not the task of the novelist to convey this varying, this unknown and uncircumscribed spirit, whatever aberration or complexity it may display, with as little mixture of the alien and external as possible? We are not pleading merely for courage and sincerity; we are suggesting that the proper stuff of fiction is a little other than custom would have us believe it.

KEW GARDENS

From the oval-shaped flower-bed there rose perhaps a hundred stalks spreading into heart-shaped or tongue-shaped leaves half-way up and unfurling at the tip red or blue or yellow petals marked with spots of colour raised upon the surface; and from the red, blue or yellow gloom of the throat emerged a straight bar, rough with gold dust and slightly clubbed at the end. The petals were voluminous enough to be stirred by the summer breeze, and when they moved, the red, blue and yellow lights passed one over the other, staining an inch of the brown earth beneath with a spot of the moist intricate colour. The light fell either upon the smooth, grey back of a pebble, or, the shell of a snail with its brown, circular veins, or falling into a raindrop, it expanded with such intensity of red, blue and yellow the thin walls of water that one expected them to burst and disappear. Instead, the drop was left in a second silver grey once more, and the light now settled upon the flesh of a leaf, revealing the branching thread of fibre beneath the surface, and again it moved on and spread its illumination in the vast green spaces beneath the dome of the heart-shaped and tongue-shaped leaves. Then the breeze stirred rather more briskly overhead and the colour was flashed into the air above, into the eyes of the men and women who walk in Kew Gardens in July.

The figures of these men and women straggled past the flower-bed with a curiously irregular movement not unlike that of the white and blue butterflies who crossed the turf in zig-zag flights from bed to bed. The man was about six inches in front of the woman, strolling carelessly, while she bore on with greater purpose, only turning her head now and then to see that the children were not too far behind. The man kept this distance in front of the woman purposely, though perhaps unconsciously, for he wished to go on with his thoughts.

"Fifteen years ago I came here with Lily," he thought. "We sat somewhere over there by a lake and I begged her to marry me all through the hot afternoon. How the dragonfly kept circling round us: how clearly I see the dragonfly and her shoe with the square silver buckle at the toe. All the time I spoke I saw her shoe and when it moved impatiently I knew without looking up what she was going to say: the whole of her seemed to be in her shoe. And my love, my desire, were in the dragonfly; for some reason I thought that if it settled there, on that leaf, the broad one with the red flower in the middle of it, if the dragonfly settled on the leaf she would say 'Yes' at once. But the dragonfly went round and round: it never settled anywhere—of course not, happily not, or I shouldn't be walking here with Eleanor and the children. Tell me, Eleanor. D'you ever think of the past?"

"Why do you ask, Simon?"

"Because I've been thinking of the past. I've been thinking of Lily, the woman I might have married. . . . Well, why are you silent? Do you mind my thinking of the past?"

"Why should I mind, Simon? Doesn't one always think of the past, in a garden with men and women lying under the trees? Aren't they one's past, all that remains of it, those men and women, those ghosts lying under the trees, . . . one's happiness, one's reality?"

"For me, a square silver shoe buckle and a dragonfly———"

"For me, a kiss. Imagine six little girls sitting before their easels twenty years ago, down by the side of a lake, painting the water-lilies, the first red water-lilies I'd ever seen. And suddenly a kiss, there on the back of my neck. And my hand shook all the afternoon so that I couldn't paint. I took out my watch and marked the hour when I would allow myself to think of the kiss for five minutes only—it was so precious— the kiss of an old grey-haired woman with a wart on her nose, the mother of all my kisses all my life. Come, Caroline, come, Hubert."

They walked on past the flower-bed, now walking four abreast, and soon diminished in size among the trees and looked half transparent as the sunlight and shade swam over their backs in large trembling irregular patches.

In the oval flower bed the snail, whose shell had been stained red, blue and yellow for the space of two minutes or so, now appeared to be moving very slightly in its shell, and next began to labour over the crumbs of loose earth which broke away and rolled down as it passed over them. It appeared to have a definite goal in front of it, differing in this respect from the singular high stepping angular green insect who attempted to cross in front of it, and waited for a second with its antennae trembling as if in deliberation, and then stepped off as rapidly and strangely in the opposite direction. Brown cliffs with deep green lakes in the hollows, flat, blade-like trees that waved from root to tip, round boulders of grey stone, vast crumpled surfaces of a thin crackling texture—all these objects lay across the snail's progress between one stalk and another to his goal. Before he had decided whether to circumvent the arched tent of a dead leaf or to breast it there came past the bed the feet of other human beings.

This time they were both men. The younger of the two wore an expression of perhaps unnatural calm; he raised his eyes and fixed them very steadily in front of him while his companion spoke, and directly his companion had done speaking he looked on the ground again and sometimes opened his lips only after a long pause and sometimes did not open them at all. The elder man had a curiously uneven and shaky method of walking, jerking his hand forward and throwing up his head abruptly, rather in the manner of an impatient carriage horse tired of waiting outside a house; but in the man these gestures were irresolute and pointless. He talked almost incessantly; he smiled to himself and again began to talk, as if the smile had been an answer. He was talking about spirits—the spirits of the dead, who, according to him, were even now telling him all sorts of odd things about their experiences in Heaven.

"Heaven was known to the ancients as Thessaly, William, and now, with this war, the spirit matter is rolling between the hills like thunder." He paused, seemed to listen, smiled, jerked his head and continued:

"You have a small electric battery and a piece of rubber to insulate the wire—isolate?—insulate?—well, we'll skip the details, no good going into details that wouldn't be understood—and in short the little machine stands in any convenient position by the head of the bed, we will say, on a neat mahogany stand. All arrangements being properly fixed by workmen under my direction, the widow applies her ear and summons the spirit by sign as agreed. Women! Widows! Women in black————"

Here he seemed to have caught sight of a woman's dress in the distance, which in the shade looked a purple black. He took off his hat, placed his hand upon his heart, and hurried towards her muttering and gesticulating feverishly. But William caught him by the sleeve and touched a flower with the tip of his walking-stick in order to divert the old man's attention. After looking at it for a moment in some confusion the old man bent his ear to it and seemed to answer a voice speaking from it, for he began talking about the forests of Uruguay which he had visited hundreds of years ago in company with the most beautiful young woman in Europe. He could be heard murmuring about forests of Uruguay blanketed with the wax petals of tropical roses, nightingales, sea beaches, mermaids, and women drowned at sea, as he suffered himself to be moved on by William, upon whose face the look of stoical patience grew slowly deeper and deeper.

Following his steps so closely as to be slightly puzzled by his gestures came two elderly women of the lower middle class, one stout and ponderous, the other rosy cheeked and nimble. Like most people of their station they were frankly fascinated by any signs of eccentricity betokening a disordered brain, especially in the well-to-do; but they were too far off to be certain whether the gestures were merely eccentric or genuinely mad. After they had scrutinized the old man's back in silence for a moment and given each other a queer, sly look, they went on energetically piecing together their very complicated dialogue:

"Nell, Bert, Lot, Cess, Phil, Pa, he says, I says, she says, I says, I says————"

"My Bert, Sis, Bill, Grandad, the old man, sugar,

Sugar, flour, kippers, greens,

Sugar, sugar, sugar."

The ponderous woman looked through the pattern of falling words at the flowers standing cool, firm, and upright in the earth, with a curious expression. She saw them as a sleeper waking from a heavy sleep sees a brass candlestick reflecting the light in an unfamiliar way, and closes his eyes and opens them, and seeing the brass candlestick again, finally starts broad awake and stares at the candlestick with all his powers. So the heavy woman came to a standstill opposite the oval-shaped flower bed, and ceased even to pretend to listen to what the other woman was saying. She stood there letting the words fall over her, swaying the top part of her body slowly backwards and forwards, looking at the flowers. Then she suggested that they should find a seat and have their tea.

The snail had now considered every possible method of reaching his goal without going round the dead leaf or climbing over it. Let alone the effort needed for climbing a leaf, he was doubtful whether the thin texture which vibrated with such an alarming crackle when touched even by the tip of his horns would bear his weight; and this determined him finally to creep beneath it, for there was a point where the leaf curved high enough from the ground to admit him. He had just inserted his head in the opening and was taking stock of the high brown roof and was getting used to the cool brown light when two other people came past outside on the turf. This time they were both young, a young man and a young woman. They were both in the prime of youth, or even in that season which precedes the prime of youth, the season before the smooth pink folds of the flower have burst their gummy case, when the wings of the butterfly, though fully grown, are motionless in the sun.

"Lucky it isn't Friday," he observed.

"Why? D'you believe in luck?"

"They make you pay sixpence on Friday."

"What's sixpence anyway? Isn't it worth sixpence?"

"What's 'it'—what do you mean by 'it'?"

"O, anything—I mean—you know what I mean."

Long pauses came between each of these remarks; they were uttered in toneless and monotonous voices. The couple stood still on the edge of the flower bed, and together pressed the end of her parasol deep down into the soft earth. The action and the fact that his hand rested on the top of hers expressed their feelings in a strange way, as these short insignificant words also expressed something, words with short wings for their heavy body of meaning, inadequate to carry them far and thus alighting awkwardly upon the very common objects that surrounded them, and were to their inexperienced touch so massive; but who knows (so they thought as they pressed the parasol into the earth) what precipices aren't concealed in them, or what slopes of ice don't shine in the sun on the other side? Who knows? Who has ever seen this before? Even when she wondered what sort of tea they gave you at Kew, he felt that something loomed up behind her words, and stood vast and solid behind them; and the mist very slowly rose and uncovered—O, Heavens, what were those shapes?—little white tables, and waitresses who looked first at her and then at him; and there was a bill that he would pay with a real two shilling piece, and it was real, all real, he assured himself, fingering the coin in his pocket, real to everyone except to him and to her; even to him it began to seem real; and then—but it was too exciting to stand and think any longer, and he pulled the parasol out of the earth with a jerk and was impatient to find the place where one had tea with other people, like other people.

"Come along, Trissie; it's time we had our tea."

"Wherever *does* one have one's tea?" she asked with the oddest thrill of excitement in her voice, looking vaguely round and letting herself be drawn on down the grass path, trailing her parasol, turning her head this way and that way forgetting her tea, wishing to go down there and then down there, remembering orchids and cranes among wild flowers, a Chinese pagoda and a crimson crested bird; but he bore her on.

Thus one couple after another with much the same irregular and aimless movement passed the flower-bed and were enveloped in layer after layer of green blue vapour, in which at first their bodies had substance and a dash of colour, but later both substance and colour dissolved in the green-blue atmosphere. How hot it was! So hot that even the thrush chose to hop, like a mechanical bird, in the shadow of the flowers, with long pauses between one movement and the next; instead of rambling vaguely the white butterflies danced one above another, making with their white shifting flakes the outline of a shattered marble column above the tallest flowers; the glass roofs of the palm house shone as if a whole market full of shiny green umbrellas had opened in the sun; and in the drone of the aeroplane the voice of the summer sky murmured its fierce soul. Yellow and black, pink and snow white, shapes of all these colours, men, women, and children were spotted for a second upon the horizon, and then, seeing the breadth of yellow that lay upon the grass, they wavered and sought shade beneath the trees, dissolving like drops of water in the yellow and green atmosphere, staining it faintly with red and blue. It seemed as if all gross and heavy bodies had sunk down in the heat motionless and lay huddled upon the ground, but their voices went wavering from them as if they were flames lolling from the thick waxen bodies of candles. Voices. Yes, voices. Wordless voices, breaking the silence suddenly with such depth of contentment, such passion of desire, or, in the voices of children, such freshness of surprise; breaking the silence? But there was no silence; all the time the motor omnibuses were turning their wheels and changing their gear; like a vast nest of Chinese boxes all of wrought steel turning ceaselessly one within another the city murmured; on the top of which the voices cried aloud and the petals of myriads of flowers flashed their colours into the air.

[1919]

Questions

1. What are the central ideas or concerns of the story?
2. From what perspective and point of view is the story narrated?
3. In the absence of such conventional narrative elements as plot and characterization, what shapes and unifies "Kew Gardens"?
4. How does imagery—particularly references to color and light—contribute to the story's effect?

Niaz Zaman

(b. 1941)

Bangladesh

I n *her introduction to* Selected Short Stories from Bangladesh *(1998), Niaz Zaman contextualizes the work of her compatriots:*

> *The majority of the stories in this anthology have a rural background. This is not surprising as most Bangladeshis have close links to the countryside. Even writers who have dwelt all their lives in the city have chosen to write about life in the country. Thus, the land and the people who work the land, the monsoon rains, the floods, an unseasonal drought—all these have been the subject of much creative work. . . . Most of the writers in Bangladesh are socially and politically conscious and, in their writings, condemn existing class differences, religious and moral hypocrisy, discriminations against women, the absurdity, and sometimes downright cruelty, of communalism.*

Zaman's career as a writer and critic has been cosmopolitan. She was educated in Bangladesh but holds advanced degrees from American universities. She has travelled, lectured, and taught extensively. During 1982 and 1983, she served as Educational Attaché for the Bangladesh Embassy in Washington, D.C. In addition to publishing and editing numerous critical works, she has collected her own short fiction in The Dance and Other Stories *(1996). Most recently, she has served as the Chairperson of the Department of English at the University of Dhaka.*

THE DAILY WOMAN

The thought of the other child would come at odd times. Like when she was picking the rice, or sweeping the floor, or grinding the red chillies that made her hands smart. At the beginning she had thought of it—her, really, but the child had been taken so early from her that she rarely thought of it as her—when the little one who remained strained at her thin breasts. There had been so little milk for even this one, that she had none to spare for the other. This one was a boy. Everyone said, Boys were better. They would look after you in your old age, they said. That is, if the daughters-in-law let them. Also this one had been bigger. More chance of surviving.

Every year for the last five years—she had been married one year before the first one was born—she had given birth. Not one had lived beyond a day or two. And she had thought that she too, like Fatema, was cursed. And then, she had the two together. Together, they were only a little bigger than the little ones who had died. How long would these two live, she had wondered. Would they too die after two days as the other little ones had? But three days passed and they were still there. Only one had seemed smaller and weaker than the other. More like a wrinkled old woman. Then the two white men had come to see her with Abdul. And almost before she realized it, there was only one child left.

She did not pause as she ground the chillies. Ghater ghat, ghater ghat. The heavy stone roller smoothed the dry, red pods into paste. One did not have to think when one ground chillies, so one could think about the other things one had no time for. A few dabs of water, and then off again, ghater ghat, ghater ghat, as the soft, red, paper-thin skins melted into the flat, yellow seeds and merged to form red paste. A pause to stretch her back, and then another dab of water, and the roller started going back and forth on the smooth grindstone. She must tell them to have the stone pricked once more. The pockmarks all over had disappeared. The auspicious fish design on top had also completely faded out. It was really too smooth to grind the chillies. Most people had started buying powdered chillies, but there were some who liked their spices ground fresh every day, so there was still some work for daily women like her who could not work *bandha*.

She washed the grindstone. Put it back in its place under the sink. What was it like to work *bandha*, she wondered. Leave husband and children and remain in other people's houses? At least for people who worked *bandha* there was a dry place to sleep in at night. In the hut, during the rainy months of *Ashar* and *Sraban*, everything got wet. One's clothes, one's floors—everything. The smooth, hard floor, that she smeared with a mixture of cowdung and mud so that it was almost as nice as Khalamma's floor, turned to muddy paste. But people who worked *bandha* slept inside. There were some even luckier. Like Ali, who got a room all to himself, next to the kitchen. It was small, just big enough for a narrow *chowki*, and when there were guests, the drivers would be given food in his room, so he was expected to keep it clean and just as Khalamma wanted it. But Ali could stretch out there after his fourteen- or sixteen-hour duty—not like some others who could not go to sleep until everyone had gone to sleep, because one never knew when the guests would leave or who would want to come into the kitchen for a glass of water or a cup of tea.

The bundle on the ground stirred. Even before the tiny eyes opened and the mouth started its fine wail, she had scooped it up and uncovered her breast—all the time covering it modestly with her sari *anchal*, so that the head of the baby was inside the *anchal* and only the ragged *kantha* she covered its frail limbs with was visible. She had promised Khalamma that the baby would not disturb anyone. Khalamma would never hear it cry. The nursing soothed the baby, and it was hardly a moment or two before it went back to sleep, its hunger satisfied for the moment. She let it hang on a moment longer to make sure it would not wake up and fuss the moment she put it back on the ground. Satisfied that it was asleep, she put it back, smoothening the soft *kantha* round the frail body so that it would think it was still being held to her breast. She was fortunate that she could bring the child to work with her. Not like Fatema who had to leave her baby at home. Fatema had not been able to give up her job with a paralyzed husband who couldn't work. And she hadn't been able to bring the baby with her to work. The baby had to be given a bottle because Fatema could not come back always to feed it. And when the baby died, the health worker had said the milk had killed the baby. And now Fatema's husband too was dead. It was true that in a way Fatema was better off without a paralyzed husband, but what woman would rather work than have a family? And who would marry Fatema now? A woman who had killed her husband and child? A black foreheaded woman? But weren't all women black foreheaded? Well, not all. Not her Khalamma. Every day a fresh sari and shoes the same colour as her sari. And she smelled nice all the time. Sometimes like roses. What Paradise must smell like.

Ali handed her the fish and explained that it had only to be scaled and its insides cleaned out. Not cut. Khalamma wanted it to be made into a *bideshi* dish, so she must be careful with it. And leave the tail whole. Be sure not to nick the tail the slightest bit. After it was cooked it would look like a fish—only its scales would be golden because of the carrots. Occasionally, when she had cleaned the fish, she had slipped a piece of fish or two into her waist knot, but she wouldn't be able to today, she thought. But the insides she could keep. They never had any use for it. Even Ali scoffed at her for eating what she was sure he ate with relish back home. The oil was particularly good to cook with *sag*, made it special. Perhaps Ali would let her have some of the cauliflower leaves which they threw away. These rich people did not know how to cook. They threw away chicken skins as well. One hardly needed anything more than a pinch of salt, a dab of oil and two pinches of *haldi* and chillies to make a tasty meal out of chicken skins. They never ate the feet either. The first day she had come to work, she had cleaned the feet and put them in with the cut and cleaned chicken. Ali had scolded her. Since that day she had kept the feet aside with the skins to take home with her. After removing the feathers carefully, she had enough skin to make into a dish for two meals.

Fridays were bad days, because that was when the weekly bazaar came and everything had to be cut and cleaned and put away in the cold box. Khalamma would be rushing in and out of the kitchen because that was the day Khalu would have lunch, and no matter how late the bazaar came he had to have it by one o'clock. In most houses the men went to the mosque for Friday prayers, but Khalu didn't. On Fridays her back hurt with all the cutting and cleaning and she could rarely make it home before *asr* prayers. But Friday was also a good day for her. Because she could carry home all the *bashi* stuff, like the old vegetables that had been kept in the *freez* and gone a little stale and dry. Fridays were also the days after their parties, and there would be *polao* to be scraped up from the *hari*, in addition to the *khabar* that Khalamma always kept for her. Nice things like chicken *korma*, or beef *kupta*. Once or twice there had been *biryani* and pieces of chicken *musallam* with *badam* and *kishmish*. And of course there were always sweets. Especially *roshgulla* and *shandesh* and *laddoo*. And *halwa*.

The clothes were already soaking in a pail of warm, soapy water. She had learned this new way of washing from Khalamma. When Khalamma had first poured the soap powder into the pail and told her to wash, she had been perplexed. How was she to wash the clothes without rubbing them with soap and then beating them on the *pucca*? Then Khalamma had shown her how the water was full of soap and all she had to do was to rub the clothes against themselves or each other. There was no need to beat the clothes, just go rub, rub, rub, dip once more in the soapy water and keep aside. After the white clothes were all out of the soap water there were a few more clothes—red, yellow, blue—that had to be kept dry and then dipped one by one quickly into the water so that the colours did not run into other clothes. Then she could throw away the discoloured water and fill the bucket with clean water to rinse the clothes. Once, twice, thrice, so that there was no more soap left in the water and the water seemed as clean as fresh water. Then squeeze all dry, all of them, except the lynol ones. Those had to be hung until the water had all dripped and then hung out smoothly so that there were no wrinkles on them. And then she could have her *chapati* and hot tea. It was always a pleasure to have sweet, hot tea. Two spoons of sugar in the tea—though Khalamma herself always had tea without any sugar. How did they drink tea without sugar? She grimaced at the thought of the sugarless tea that Khalamma drank.

Ali explained to her that Khalamma was afraid of getting fat. All *barolok* were afraid of getting fat. That's why she did not have sugar with her tea. Nor rice nor potatoes. Sometimes she would go on what Ali called diet. Then she would have nothing but tea and tosht in the morning and cucumber in the afternoon. At night, however, she would eat with Khalu—a spoon of rice only, however, or one *chapati*, the small *chapati* she had Ali make for the table not the big, fat ones that Ali made for the kitchen help and himself. They were allowed three of the *chapatis* with their tea. One she ate, sitting in the kitchen, but the other two she took home with the left-over *bhaji* or *jhol*. In that way she only needed to cook a pot of rice for him.

Sometimes she wondered whether, if she had this job when the babies were born, she would have given the little one away. But she could not have brought both with her to work. Of that she was sure. And then it was only after the babies were born that she had met Abdul when he came with the *bideshis* and afterwards got her the job at Khalamma's place. Ali was from the same village as Abdul. That is how Abdul had known that Khalamma was looking for a daily woman to help in the kitchen. He had come with her and told Khalamma that he knew her—though he really didn't. But he had to say it otherwise Khalamma would not have given her the job. And after that day she had never seen him again. Rahima had told her that Abdul must have got a lot of money from the *bideshis*. But she could not believe it. Why would they give the money to him and not to her?

She didn't know whether Abdul had got money, all she remembered was that those had been bad days. The days that they had first come to Dhaka from the village because the river had taken away the last bit of their land. She shivered remembering those days. Everyone had told them how easy it was to get work in the *shahar*, and they had believed what they heard. There were always roads to be broken or built, and houses high as the sky, sprouting like frog umbrellas after the rains. And if one didn't get work as a day labourer, there were always rickshaws to pull in the city. Sometimes people said there were as many rickshaws in Dhaka city as there were people. One could keep all the money one earned after deducting what one had to pay to the *mahajan*. People in town didn't walk. So there was a lot of money in pulling rickshaws. But rickshaw pulling hadn't been easy. His legs and arms had ached and she had to heat mustard oil and rub him down. And then he had fever for three days and she had to buy medicine for him. And during the rains no one wanted rickshaws, because everyone stayed home and there was no building either and they starved. Then they had to pay for the *chhapra*—something they had not reckoned with. Two hundred for a place hardly big enough for the two of them to sleep in at night. And always the rain coming down, making everything wet, making the floor into mud. Then the fever had come back, and he had coughed until she thought his eyes would jump out of his head. His body had felt like fire, and she had prayed that he wouldn't die. She had promised that if he lived she would fast seven days so she had fasted and the babies had popped out before the ten months and ten days that babies took to be ready were over.

How hungry she had been, and the two babies crying together were enough to make her go mad. No one she knew had ever had two babies together. No one in the *para* had seen two babies together and everyone had come to see her and the babies. The white men had also come with Abdul to see her. The man with the red beard had explained to her—sometimes himself, but when she could not understand the way he spoke, Abdul had explained that the other white man wanted to take her child, if she would give it up seeing she had two. The man wanted to take a Bangladeshi child because he had stayed many years in Bangladesh as a child. Now that he was grown up, and his wife and he could not have children, they wanted to adopt a Bangladeshi child. Abdul explained to her that the white man would look after the child well. Then too she must realize that she had nothing to eat herself. How could she feed one child, let alone two? So she had said yes. God who gave her two children who lived would give again some other day. The white man who wanted the child said he would bring his wife the next day. He wanted the child to be a surprise to her. That is why he had not brought her. He wanted to see the child first himself. They had been disappointed earlier.

She had looked at the girl child for a long time the next morning. But she had felt nothing in her heart for the child. She did not even feel a sense of relief that the child would have a future. Amrika was too far away for her to know anything about it. All that she knew about it was that these tall, pinkish-white people came from there. She didn't believe it when Rahima told her that black people also came from there. She had seen no black Amrikun. Only these pinkish white people in their big cars, driven by smart drivers like Abdul. Rahima told her that she was doing a bad thing, and God would be angry with her. In Amrika they would make her child pray to Jishu. She would surely go to hell because she let her child go with kristans. But Amrika and kristan did not make much sense to her. All she could remember was how hungry she had been all the time, and if it had not been for the scraps of food that Rahima gave her at that time surely she herself would have starved and the babies too.

The two men had come the next day, and the white woman with them. She looked old enough to be the man's mother. White hair and wrinkles near her eyes. And thin. No breasts. Or behind. Flat as a fried fish. Her arms were like jute stalks, and the big round bangles made them look even thinner. Everyone gathered round their *chhapra* to look at the *bideshini* who had come to take her little one away. The man with the red beard explained that there were some papers to be signed—a *tip shoi* would also be all right, if she couldn't sign her name. Just to show that the baby had been voluntarily given up by the parents, not stolen or kidnapped. Some papers were in English, some in Bengali. The same thing in both. One for the authorities in Bangladesh, one for the Amrikuns.

The *bideshini* held out her arms for the child. As she put the thin wrinkled old woman into the white woman's arms, she had thought how dark her little one looked next to the white woman's skin. The woman saw her looking at her arms and muttered something to her husband. The man took the child from his wife, and stared at it as if he was seeing a baby for the first time. The woman took off her shiny golden bangles and slipped them onto her wrists. She had not wanted to take the bangles. She was not selling her child for gold. But because she could not feed it. The woman bared her gray teeth in a smile and patted her arms back.

After the car drove away, the people continued to crowd around them. She went back inside her *chhapra* where there was only one little figure now, sleeping peacefully, undisturbed by the departure of the sister he would never know. The child stirred and she picked it up, just to feel it was there. One at least. Proof that she was a mother, not like the *bideshini*, who, despite all her gold, could not be a mother. The golden bangles glistened against her dark skin. And, despite herself, she wondered how much they wee worth. Enough to feed them for ten years, surely. How was she to keep the bangles safe so that no one stole them? After all, the whole *para* had seen the *bideshini* giving her the bangles. She would take the bangles off at night and tie them into her waist knot so that no one could steal them without her waking up.

When Rahima came in late that night after her work, she showed her the bangles, somewhat embarrassed, lest Rahima think she had sold her baby. But Rahima had laughed. Those are not gold, she said. They're brass. She drew her arms back from Rahima. No, she had not sold her baby. But she could not believe that a *bideshini* would wear brass, much less give brass to a poor woman whose child she had taken. I have seen gold, said Rahima, if you haven't and I know what is gold and what isn't. Go with me to the goldsmith tomorrow if you don't believe me.

So the next day she went with Rahima to the goldsmith and tried to sell the bangles to him. But the goldsmith had laughed, yes, laughed. Not asked her where she had stolen the bangles from. He didn't buy brass, he told her. She could get maybe twenty takas from the *bikriwala* for the bangles, maybe even twenty-five depending on their weight. But not from him.

She sighed, and drank the last of her tea. So that was what a Bangladeshi girl child was worth. Two brass bangles. She picked up the boy. Would he have been worth four brass bangles?

[1996]

Questions

1. Are children in "The Daily Woman" regarded as positive or negative forces in their parents' lives? To what extent are they considered "commodities"? Are women anything more than "breeders"?

2. Have the Americans in the story tricked the daily woman into departing with her child, or are there other contributing forces?

3. Does the author provide any hope that the daily woman will escape from her lot in life?

Acknowledgments

CHINUA ACHEBE, "Girls at War," from *Girls at War and Other Stories* by Chinua Achebe, copyright © 1972, 1973 by Chinua Achebe. Used by permission of Doubleday, a division of Random House, Inc. and Harold Ober Associates Incorporated.

AMA ATA AIDOO, "Two Sisters" © Ama Ata Aidoo 1970. The story was first broadcast as a short radio play by The Transciption Centre, London. Reprinted by permission of the author.

AKUTAGAWA RYŪNOSUKE, "Within a Grove," translated by James O'Brien from *Akutagawa and Dazai: Instances of Literary Adaptation* by James O'Brien. Reprinted by permission of the Center for Asian Studies, Arizona State University, Tempe, Arizona.

WOODY ALLEN, "The Kugelmass Episode," from *Side Effects* by Woody Allen, copyright © 1977 by Woody Allen. Used by permission of Random House, Inc.

ISABEL ALLENDE, "And of Clay Are We Created" is reprinted with the permission of Scribner, a Division of Simon & Schuster from *The Stories of Eva Luna* by Isabel Allende, translated from the Spanish by Margaret Sayers Peden. Copyright © 1989 Isabel Allende. English translation copyright © 1991 Macmillan Publishing Company.

HANAN AL-SHAYKH MAALAOUF, "The Unseeing Eye" is reprinted with permission of the author.

RUDOLFO A. ANAYA, "B. Traven Is Alive and Well in Cuernavaca." Reprinted by permission of the author.

MARGARET ATWOOD, "Dancing Girls," from *Dancing Girls and Other Stories* by Margaret Atwood. Used by permission, McClelland & Stewart, Ltd. The Canadian Publishers and the author.

ISAAC BABEL, "My First Goose," translated by Walter Morison, from *The Collected Stories of Isaac Babel*, published by S. G. Phillips, Inc., 1955. Reprinted by permission of Writers House, Inc.

BARBARANEELY, "Spilled Salt," from *Breaking Ice*. Reprinted by permission of Marie Brown Associates. Copyright © 1990.

ANN BEATTIE, "The Burning House," from *The Burning House* by Ann Beattie. Copyright © 1979 by Irony & Pity, Inc. Reprinted by permission of Random House, Inc.

HEINRICH BÖLL, "The Laugher," translated by Leila Vennewitz, from *18 Stories* (New York: McGraw-Hill, 1966). Copyright © 1966 by Heinrich Böll. Reprinted here by permission of Verlag Kiepenheuer & Witsch via Joan Daves Agency/Writer's House, Inc., New York, New York, and Leila Vennewitz.

JORGE LUIS BORGES, "The South," from *Ficciones* by Jorge Luis Borges, translated by Anthony Kerrigan. Copyright © 1962 by Grove Press, Inc. Used by permission of Grove/Atlantic, Inc.

DINO BUZZATI, "The Falling Girl," from *Restless Nights*, copyright 1983 by Dino Buzzati. English language translation by Lawrence Venuti. Published by North Point Press. Reprinted by permission of Lawrence Venuti.

ITALO CALVINO, "The Spiral," from *Cosmicomics* by Italo Calvino, copyright © 1965 by Giulio Einaudi editore s.p.a., Torino, English translation by William Weaver copyright © 1968 and renewed 1996 by Harcourt, Inc. and Jonathan Cape Limited, reprinted by permission of Harcourt, Inc. and The Wylie Agency.

ALBERT CAMUS, "The Guest," from *Exile and the Kingdom* by Albert Camus, trans. Justin O'Brien. Copyright © 1957, 1958 by Alfred A. Knopf, Inc. Reprinted by permission of Alfred A. Knopf, a Division of Random House, Inc.

ANGELA CARTER, "The Courtship of Mr. Lyon," from *Burning Your Boats: The Collected Short Stories* by Angela Carter. New York: Henry Holt, 1995, pp. 144–153. Copyright © Angela Carter 1979. Reproduced by permission of the Estate of Angela Carter c/o Rogers, Coleridge & White Ltd., 20 Powis Mews, London W11 1JN.

RAYMOND CARVER, "Where I'm Calling From," from *Cathedral* by Raymond Carver. Copyright © 1983 by Raymond Carver. Reprinted by permission of Alfred A. Knopf, a division of Random House, Inc.

JOHN CHEEVER, "The Swimmer," from *The Stories of John Cheever* by John Cheever. Copyright © 1964 by John Cheever. Reprinted by permission of Alfred A. Knopf, a Division of Random House, Inc.

NAKAHARA CHUYA, "Shame: A Song of Past Days" (second verse only), from *The Poems of Nakahara Chuya*. Reprinted by permission of Gracewing Publishing, England.

GABRIELLE-SIDONIE COLETTE, "The Seamstress," from *The Collected Stories of Colette*, edited by Robert Phelps and translated by Matthew Ward. Translation copyright © 1983 by Farrar, Straus & Giroux, Inc. Reprinted by permission of Farrar, Straus and Giroux, LLC.

BIRAGO DIOP, "Sarzan," translated by Ellen Conroy Kennedy. Reprinted by permission of Ellen Conroy Kennedy.

JOSÉ DONOSO, "Paseo," from *Cuentos* by José Donoso. Copyright 1971. Reprinted by permission of Agencia Literaria Carmen Balcells.

LOUISE ERDRICH, from *Love Medicine: New and Expanded Version* by Louise Erdrich, © 1984, 1993 by Louise Erdrich. Reprinted by permission of Henry Holt and Company, LLC.

WILLIAM FAULKNER, "A Rose for Emily," from *Collected Stories of William Faulkner* by William Faulkner. Copyright © 1930 and renewed 1958 by William Faulkner. Reprinted by permission of Random House, Inc.

FENG JICAI, "The Street-Sweeping Show," from *Chrysanthemums and Other Stories* by Feng Jicai, English translation copyright © 1983 by Susan Wilf Chen, reprinted by permission of Harcourt, Inc.

CARLOS FUENTES, "The Doll Queen," from *Burnt Water* by Carlos Fuentes, translated by Margaret Sayers Peden. Translation copyright © 1980 by Farrar, Straus and Giroux, Inc. Reprinted by permission of Farrar, Straus and Giroux, LLC.

GABRIEL GARCÍA MÁRQUEZ, all pages from "Balthazar's Marvelous Afternoon" from *No One Writes to the Colonel...* by Gabriel García Márquez. Copyright © 1968 in the English translation by HarperCollins Publishers, Inc. Reprinted by permission of HarperCollins Publishers, Inc.

NADINE GORDIMER, "Town and Country Lovers, Two—Country Lovers," copyright © 1975 by Nadine Gordimer, from *Soldier's Embrace* by Nadine Gordimer. Used by permission of Viking Penguin, a division of Penguin Putnam Inc.

JUDY GRAHN, "Boys at the Rodeo" © Judy Grahn, first published in *True to Life Adventure Stories*, Vol. II, The Crossing Press. Reprinted by permission of the author.

ERNEST HEMINGWAY, "Hills Like White Elephants" is reprinted with permission of Scribner, a Division of Simon & Schuster, Inc., from *The Short Stories of Ernest Hemingway*. Copyright 1927 by Charles Scribner's Sons. Copyright renewed 1955 by Ernest Hemingway.

LANGSTON HUGHES, "Thank You, Ma'am," from *Short Stories* by Langston Hughes. Copyright © 1996 by Ramona Bass and Arnold Rampersad. Introduction copyright © 1996 by Arnold Rampersad. Compilation and editorial contribution copyright © 1996 by Akiba Sullivan Harper. Reprinted by permission of Hill and Wang, a division of Farrar, Straus and Giroux, LLC.

ZORA NEALE HURSTON, "The Gilded Six-Bits," as taken from *The Complete Stories* by Zora Neale Hurston. Introduction copyright © 1995 by Henry Louis Gates, Jr. and Sieglinde Lemke. Compilation copyright © 1995 by Vivian Bowden, Lois J. Hurston Gaston, Clifford Hurston, Lucy Ann Hurston, Winifred Hurston Clark, Zora Mack Goins, Edgar Hurston, Sr., and Barbara Hurston Lewis. Afterword and Bibliography copyright © 1995 by Henry Louis Gates. Reprinted by permission of HarperCollins Publishers, Inc. "The Gilded Six-Bits" was originally published in *Story*, August 1933.

SHIRLEY JACKSON, "The Lottery," from *The Lottery* by Shirley Jackson. Copyright © 1948, 1949 by Shirley Jackson. Copyright renewed 1976, 1977 by Laurence Hyman, Barry Hyman, Mrs. Sarah Webster, and Mrs. Joanne Schnurer. Reprinted by permission of Farrar, Straus and Giroux, LLC.

SVAVA JAKOBSDÓTTIR, "A Story for Children," translated by Dennis Auburn Hill. Copyright 1975 by the American Scandinavian Foundation.

ELIZABETH JOLLEY, "Another Holiday for the Prince," from *Stories* by Elizabeth Jolley, copyright © 1976, 1979, 1984 by Elizabeth Jolley. Used by permission of Viking Penguin, a division of Penguin Putnam Inc.

JAMES JOYCE, "Eveline," from *Dubliners* by James Joyce, copyright 1916 by B. W. Huebsch. Definitive text Copyright © 1967 by the Estate of James Joyce. Used by permission of Viking Penguin, a division of Penguin Putnam Inc.

GHASSAN KANAFANI, "A Hand in the Grave" is reprinted from *Men in the Sun and Other Palestinian Stories* by Ghassan Kanafani, translated from Arabic by Hilary Kilpatrick. Copyright © 1999 by Anni Kanafani. Reprinted with permission of Lynne Rienner Publishers, Inc.

JOHN KASAIPWALOVA, "Betel Nut Is Bad Magic for Airplanes," from *The Night Warrior and Other Stories from Papua, New Guinea*, edited by Ulli Beier, reproduced by permission of John Wiley & Sons, Australia.

KHAMSING SRINAWK, "The Gold-Legged Frog" is reprinted from Khamsing Srinawk, *The Politician and Other Stories.* Copyright © 1958 by Khamsing Srinawk; English translation copyright © by Domnern Garden. Used by permission of the publisher, Silkworm Books, 104/5 Chiangmai-Hot Road, Suthep, Chiang Mai 50200, Thailand.

JAMAICA KINCAID, "My Mother," from *At the Bottom of the River* by Jamaica Kincaid. Copyright © 1983 by Jamaica Kincaid. Reprinted by permission of Farrar, Straus and Giroux, LLC.

MARGARET LAURENCE, "A Bird in the House," from *A Bird in the House* by Margaret Laurence. Used by permission, McClelland & Stewart, Ltd. The Canadian Publishers.

URSULA K. LE GUIN, "Sur" copyright © 1982 by Ursula K. Le Guin; first appeared in *The New Yorker*; from *The Compass Rose*; reprinted by permission of the author and the author's agents, the Virginia Kidd Agency, Inc.

DORIS LESSING, "The Old Chief Mshlanga" is reprinted with permission of Simon & Schuster from *African Stories* by Doris Lessing. Copyright © 1951, 1953, 1954, 1957, 1958, 1962, 1963, 1964, 1965, 1972, 1981 by Doris Lessing. Reprinted by kind permission of Jonathan Clowes Ltd., London, on behalf of Doris Lessing.

CATHERINE LIM, "Or Else, the Lightning God," from *Or Else, the Lightning God and Other Stories* by Catherine Lim. Reprinted by permission of the author.

ARNOST LUSTIG, "The Lemon," from *Diamonds in the Night* by Arnost Lustig, translated by Jeanne Němcova. Evanston, Illinois: Northwestern University Press, 1978. Reprinted by permission of the author.

NAGUIB MAHFOUZ, "Half a Day," from *The Time and the Place and Other Stories* by Naguib Mahfouz, copyright © 1991 by the American University in Cairo Press. Used by permission of Doubleday, a division of Random House, Inc.

BERNARD MALAMUD, "The Jewbird," from *Idiots First* by Bernard Malamud. Copyright © 1963 by Bernard Malamud. Copyright renewed 1991 by Ann Malamud. Reprinted by permission of Farrar, Straus and Giroux, LLC.

RENÉ MARQUÉS, "Island of Manhattan," from *Contemporary Latin American Short Stories*, edited by Pat McNees Mancini. Copyright © 1974 by Random House, Inc. Reprinted by permission of Ballantine Books, a division of Random House, Inc.

BOBBIE ANN MASON, "Shiloh," from *Shiloh and Other Stories* by Bobbie Ann Mason. Reprinted by permission of International Creative Management, Inc. Copyright © 1982 by Bobbie Ann Mason.

WILLIAM SOMERSET MAUGHAM, "The Appointment in Samarra," from *Sheppey* by W. Somerset Maugham, copyright 1933 by W. Somerset Maugham. Used by permission of Doubleday, a division of Random House, Inc. and The Random House Group Limited.

RICHARD MCCANN, "My Mother's Clothes: The School of Beauty and Shame." Appeared originally in *The Atlantic Monthly*. Copyright © 1986 by Richard McCann. Reprinted by permission of Brandt & Brandt Literary Agents, Inc.

JOHN MCCLUSKEY, "Lush Life," from *Callaloo* 13:2 (1990), 201–212. © Charles H. Rowell. Reprinted by permission of the Johns Hopkins University Press.

KATHERINE MIN, "The One Who Goes Farthest Away." Reprinted by permission of the author.

SUSAN MINOT, "Lust," from *Lust and Other Stories* by Susan Minot. Copyright © 1989 by Susan Minot. Reprinted by permission of Houghton Mifflin Company Co./Seymour Lawrence. All rights reserved.

MISHIMA YUKIO, "Swaddling Clothes" by Mishima Yukio, translated by Ivan Morris, from *Death in Midsummer*, copyright © 1966 by New Directions Publishing Corp. Reprinted by permission of New Directions Publishing Corp.

LORRIE MOORE, "How to Become a Writer," from *Self-Help* by Lorrie Moore. Copyright © 1985 by M. L. Moore. Reprinted by permission of Alfred A. Knopf, a Division of Random House, Inc.

TONI MORRISON, "Recitatif," from *Confirmation: An Anthology of African American Women*, compiled by Amiri Baraka and Amina Baraka. New York: Quill, 1983. Reprinted by permission of International Creative Management, Inc. Copyright © 1983 by Toni Morrison.

KERMIT MOYER, "Tumbling" first appeared in *The Hudson Review*. Copyright © 1986 by Kermit Moyer. Reprinted by permission of the author.

ES'KIA MPHAHLELE, "Mrs. Plum," from *Renewal Time*. London: Readers International 1990. Reprinted by permission of Readers International.

SLAWOMIR MROŻEK, "The Elephant," from *The Elephant and Other Stories* by Slawomir Mrożek, translated by Konrad Syrop. Copyright © 1962, 1990 by McDonald & Co. Publishers Ltd. Used by permission of Grove/Atlantic, Inc.

BHARATI MUKHERJEE, "A Father," from *Darkness* by Bharati Mukherjee. Copyright © 1985 by Bharati Mukherjee. Reprinted by permission of Penguin Books Canada Limited.

CARMEN NARANJO, "And We Sold the Rain," translated by Jo Anne Engelbert from *And We Sold the Rain: Contemporary Fiction from Central America*, edited by Rosario Santos. Reprinted by permission of Seven Stories Press.

R. K. NARAYAN, "A Horse and Two Goats" by R. K. Narayan. Copyright 1965, 1970, 1985 by R. K. Narayan. From *Under the Banyan Tree and Other Stories*. Viking Penguin, Inc. First appeared in *The New Yorker*. Used by permission of the Wallace Literary Agency, Inc.

NGUGI WA THIONG'O, "A Meeting in the Dark" is reprinted from *Secret Lives and Other Stories* by Ngugi wa Thiong'o. Copyright © 1975 by Ngugi Wa Thiong'o. Published by Heinemann, a division of Reed Elsevier, Inc., Portsmouth, NH. Reprinted by permission of the publisher.

JOYCE CAROL OATES, "Where Are You Going, Where Have You Been?" by Joyce Carol Oates, published in *The Wheel of Love and Other Stories*, 1970. Copyright © 1970 by Joyce Carol Oates. Reprinted by permission of John Hawkins & Associates, Inc.

ŌBA MINAKO, "The Pale Fox," translated by Stephen W. Kohl, from *The Showa Anthology: Modern Japanese Short Stories, Vol. II*, edited by Van C. Gessell and Tomone Matsumoto, published by Kodansha International Ltd., 1980.

TIM O'BRIEN, "The Things They Carried," from *The Things They Carried* by Tim O'Brien. Copyright © 1990 by Tim O'Brien. Reprinted by permission of Houghton Mifflin Co./Seymour Lawrence. All rights reserved.

FLANNERY O'CONNOR, "A Good Man Is Hard to Find," from *A Good Man Is Hard to Find and Other Stories*, copyright 1953 by Flannery O'Connor and renewed 1981 by Regina O'Connor, reprinted by permission of Harcourt, Inc.

ŌE KENZABURO, "Aghwee the Sky Monster" by Kenzaburo Ōe, from *Teach Us to Outgrow Our Madness*, translated by John Nathan. Used by permission of Grove/Atlantic, Inc.

BEN OKRI, "In the Shadow of War," from *Stars of the New Curfew* by Ben Okri, copyright © 1988 by Ben Okri. Used by permission of Viking Penguin, a division of Penguin Putnam Inc.

TILLIE OLSEN, "I Stand Here Ironing," copyright © 1956, 1957, 1960, 1961 by Tillie Olsen, from *Tell Me a Riddle* by Tillie Olsen. Introduction by John Leonard. Used by permission of Dell Publishing, a division of Random House, Inc.

SEMBENE OUSMANE, "Black Girl," translated by Ellen Conroy Kennedy. Reprinted by permission of Ellen Conroy Kennedy.

AMOS OZ, "Nomad and Viper," from *Where the Jackals Howl and Other Stories* by Amos Oz, copyright © 1965 by Amoz Oz and Massade Ltd., copyright © 1980, 1976 by Amos Oz and Am Oved Publishers Ltd., English translation by Nicholas de Lange and Philip Simpson copyright © 1981, 1976, 1973 by Harcourt, Inc., reprinted by permission of Harcourt, Inc.

OCTAVIO PAZ, "The Blue Bouquet," translated by Lysander Kemp. First appeared in *Evergreen Review*, May–June 1961. Copyright © 1961, 1989 by Evergreen Review, Inc. Used by permission of Grove/Atlantic, Inc.

CRISTINA PERI ROSSI, "Mona Lisa," from *El Museo de Los Esfuerzos Inutiles*. Barcelona, Spain: Seix Barral, 1983. © Cristina Peri Rossi. Reprinted by permission of the Laura Dail Literary Agency, Inc. English translation copyright by Harry Morales 2000.

VIRGILIO PIÑERA, "Insomnia" first published in English by Eridanos Press, Boston, in *Cold Tales* by Virgilio Piñera, translated by Mark Schafer. Copyright © 1985 by Marsilio Publishers, NY. Reprinted by permission of Marsilio Publishers.

KATHERINE ANNE PORTER, "Rope," from *Flowering Judas and Other Stories*, copyright 1930 and renewed 1958 by Katherine Anne Porter, reprinted by permission of Harcourt, Inc.

RODRIGO REY ROSA, "The Proof," from *Dust on Her Tongue*. Copyright © 1989 by Rodrigo Rey Rosa. Reprinted by permission of City Lights Books.

SALMAN RUSHDIE, "The Prophet's Hair," from *East, West: Stories* by Salman Rushdie. Copyright © 1994 by Salman Rushdie. Reprinted by permission of Pantheon Books, a division of Random House, Inc.

LESLIE MARMON SILKO, "Yellow Woman" copyright © 1974 by Leslie Marmon Silko. Reprinted with the permission of The Wylie Agency.

ISAAC BASHEVIS SINGER, "Gimpel the Fool" by Isaac Bashevis Singer, translated by Saul Bellow, copyright 1953, 1954 by the Viking Press Inc., renewed © 1981, 1982 by Viking Penguin Inc., from *A Treasury of Yiddish Stories* by Irving Howe and Eliezer Greenberg. Used by permission of Viking Penguin, a division of Penguin Putnam Inc.

MARÍA TERESA SOLARI, "Death and Transfiguration of a Teacher," translated by John Benson, is reprinted with permission from the publisher of *Short Stories by Latin American Women: The Magic and the Real*, edited by Celia Correas de Zapata. Houston: Arte Publico Press, 1990.

JOHN STEINBECK, "The Chrysanthemums," copyright 1937, renewed © 1965 by John Steinbeck, from *The Long Valley* by John Steinbeck. Used by permission of Viking Penguin, a division of Penguin Putnam Inc.

GRAHAM SWIFT, "Learning to Swim," from *Learning to Swim*. Copyright © 1982 by Graham Swift. Reprinted by permission of A.P. Watt Ltd. on behalf of Graham Swift.

VÉRONIQUE TADJO, "The Betrayal," an extract from *As the Crow Flies* to be published by Heinemann, African Writers Series, 2001. Reprinted by permission of the author.

AMY TAN, "Half and Half." Reprinted by permission of The Putnam Publishing Group from *The Joy Luck Club* by Amy Tan. Copyright © 1989 by Amy Tan.

HALDUN TANER, "To All Eternity," from *Thickhead and Other Stories* by Haldun Taner, translated by Geoffrey Lewis. Forest Books/UNESCO, 1988, pp. 1–8. Reprinted by permission of Geoffrey Lewis.

AMOS TUTUOLA, "The Complete Gentleman," from *The Palm-Wine Drinkard* by Amos Tutuola. Used by permission of Grove/Atlantic, Inc. and Faber and Faber.

JOHN UPDIKE, "A & P," from *Pigeon Feathers and Other Stories* by John Updike. Copyright © 1962 by John Updike. Reprinted by permission of Alfred A. Knopf, a Division of Random House, Inc.

LUISA VALENZUELA, "Strange Things Happen Here," from *Strange Things Happen Here: Twenty Six Short Stories and a Novel* by Luisa Valenzuela, copyright © 1975 by Ediciones de la Flor, English translation by Helen Lane copyright © 1979 by Harcourt, Inc., reprinted by permission of Harcourt, Inc.

MARIO VARGAS LLOSA, "Sunday," from *Los Jefes*, is reprinted by permission of the author.

YVONNE VERA, "In Africa There Is a Kind of Spider," 2000. Reprinted by permission of the author.

ALICE WALKER, "Everyday Use," from *In Love & Trouble: Stories of Black Women*, copyright © 1973 by Alice Walker, reprinted by permission of Harcourt, Inc.

EUDORA WELTY, "Why I Live at the P.O.," from *A Curtain of Green and Other Stories*, copyright 1941 and renewed 1969 by Eudora Welty, reprinted by permission of Harcourt, Inc.

NIAZ ZAMAN, "The Daily Woman," from *The Dance and Other Stories*. Reprinted by permission of the author.